Brass Buttons, Blue Coats

"Remembering All Who Served" 1871 to 1971

by

George E. Rutledge Deputy Chief – Ret.

DORRANCE
PUBLISHING CO
EST. 1920
PITTSBURGH, PENNSYLVANIA 15238

Dorrance Publishing Co
585 Alpha Drive
Pittsburgh, PA 15238
Visit our website at *www.dorrancebookstore.com*

ISBN: 978-1-6442-6155-2
eISBN: 978-1-6442-6132-3

BRASS BUTTONS, BLUE COATS

"REMEMBERING ALL WHO SERVED"

1871 TO 1971

A Biographical and Pictorial History of the Yonkers New York Police Department and All Those Who Served During the First 100 Years, 1871 to 1971.

"Remembering their service"

Author

George E. Rutledge Deputy Chief - Ret.

BRASS BUTTONS – BLUE COATS

"REMEMBERING ALL WHO SERVED"

1871 – 1971

BY GEORGE E. RUTLEDGE
Deputy Chief - Retired

ISBN

All research, design, and layout by the author, George E. Rutledge

Printed and bound in the U.S.A

BRASS BUTTONS – BLUE COATS

Dedication

First and foremost, I dedicate this book to my wife Arline who has always been my constant supporter and council throughout my police career and during the countless amount of time that I spent away from family to work on this research project. In addition, I dedicate it to the men and women of the Yonkers Police Department who have served the Y.P.D. Several of them sacrificing their lives in doing so. Their service and sacrifice must be remembered. What follows is my sincere effort to ensure they are not forgotten.

(My sincere thanks to YPD PO Nick Brilis, Det. Linda Surlak & the Yonkers Police Historical Society for their assistance.)

One Hundred Years of Police Service

1871-1971

How it All Began

In the mid-1860's, after the Civil War had ended, the social makeup of the Town and Village of Yonkers was in turmoil. Transients with no home or employment were flooding our streets, bringing with them many problems for our local Town Constables. However, local newspapers of the day described these constables as ineffective tools of politicians. The village residents felt that roughs and rowdies were taking over the town and something had to be done. A special town meeting was held at Flagg's Hall on July 14, 1866 at 5:15 p.m. A pair of resolutions was offered by Supervisor Isaac H. Knox which would allow for the hiring of fourteen (14) Metropolitan Policemen from New York City to come and serve our community in a professional police capacity. If the resolutions were approved, $20,000 would be appropriated through local taxes to pay for the services of the New York Metropolitan police officers. It was hoped that these officers would make an improvement over the conditions that existed at that time. The citizens passed the resolutions by a vote of 76 to 47. The resolutions submitted read as follows;

Resolved: That it is hereby voted and determined by the lawful voters of the Town Of Yonkers, in pursuant of Chapter 403 of the laws of 1864, that regular patrolmen of the Metropolitan Police to the number of fourteen, of whom at least four shall be mounted, shall be appointed by the Board of the Metropolitan Police for the said Town of Yonkers and that the sum of $20,000 be raised by caps in such towns for contributions to the Metropolitan Police Fund, to pay such regular patrolmen.

Resolved: That it shall be the duty of the presiding officer and the clerk of this town to present to the Board of the Metropolitan Police, and to the Board of Supervisors of the County of Westchester, a certified copy of the proceedings of this town meeting, as far as such proceedings relate to the appointment and pay of regular patrolmen of the Metropolitan Police of said town, said copies to be certified under the hand and seal of said presiding officer and clerk.

When these resolutions were presented to the Metropolitan Police Force and acted upon by the Executive Board of that body, a detail of fourteen men from the New York City Metropolitan Police Force arrived in Yonkers on Friday, August 10, 1866, consisting of two Sergeants and Twelve patrolmen, forming a sub-station of the New York 32nd police precinct. Headquarters was set up in a building formerly known as Melah's Hotel at 9 Dock Street. (Today, renamed Manor House Square.)

The years that followed proved to be busy ones for these "rented" policemen. Open intoxication, vagrancy, disorderly persons, etc., were no longer tolerated and as a result the local Lock-Up was filled quite regularly. In 1871, the experiment that began five years earlier had proved successful. And after a long discussion by the city fathers and town citizens, it was decided that the Town of Yonkers should establish and maintain its own local police force.

On March 30, 1871, the act providing for the formation of a local police force was signed by the Governor and the detail of policemen from New York City were all given the opportunity to return to New York City or become part of the new Yonkers Police Department.

On April 10, 1871 the Yonkers Police Force was officially organized consisting of one Captain, two Sergeants, two Roundsmen, eighteen Patrolmen, one Hostler, and one Doorman. The Captain of Police position, in effect the Chief of the department, was given to John Mangin who, as a sergeant and one of the original detail of New York City policemen, had decided to remain in Yonkers. The annual salary for a patrolman in Yonkers in 1871 was $750.

Any man interested in becoming a Yonkers Policeman had to submit an application, gain favorable opinion following an interview with the Board of Police Commissioners and pass a medical examination by the police surgeon. No written examination was required. The appointment was for life, contingent on good behavior, and there was no maximum age limit. The official roster of the Yonkers Police Force on April 10, 1871 consisted of Captain John Mangin; Sergeant James M. King; Sergeant Charles W. Austin; Roundsmen George W. Osborne and James McLaughlin; Patrolmen John Cogans, James P. Embree, Martin Geary, John Hennessy, Edward Lucas, Richard Laurie, Cassius McGregor, James H. Mealing, Michael Muldoon, Patrick Muldoon, James J. Norton, Henry J. Quinn, John Redding, Sherman H. Smith, Louis Sprenger, John H. Woodruff, Fred H. Woodruff, and Samuel L. Whaley; Hostler (Stable Keeper) James McDevitt; and Doorman (Janitor) Michael Foley.

The actual patrolling of the town was accomplished by foot patrol, mounted patrol, and horse and wagon. Mounted patrol was used primarily for more rural outlying areas. In those early years, our police officers put in very long work hours every day. Although there were three to four patrolmen working each shift, at the completion of each tour of duty, every officer was required to remain at headquarters for an additional six-hour tour. This second shift was called Reserve Duty. Routinely they were not required to go on patrol while on Reserve Duty. Beds were kept at Headquarters for sleeping while on reserve duty, but if extra police were needed in a hurry due to an emergency, they were right on hand. This eliminated the time-consuming task of an officer going out by horse and wagon to try to locate and pick up all off duty men for that emergency.

The boundary of the area patrolled by the Yonkers Police in the 1870's was quite different from today. At the time of the organization of the Department, in addition to the Dock Street headquarters there were two sub-stations. One was located in "South Yonkers" which at that time incorporated the section known as Kingsbridge at Spuyten Duyvil. The second substation was located on Bronxville Road in Yonkers and was referred to as the Bronxville Sub-station. In 1874 the Kingsbridge District was annexed to New York City and, therefore, fell under the jurisdiction of the New York Police. However, the Yonkers Police Department continued to patrol the Bronxville area for many years to come.

The Department's size and operation have changed drastically over more than a century. There are now well over six hundred men and women professionally trained to serve the citizens of Yonkers and deal with the many problems of today's complex technology driven society. The police have gone from a foot and horse patrol department, to an almost completely motorized department. At the Department's inception, the only data base available to an officer was his own memory and his notebook. Today, complex computers provide incredible assistance in the police function. Over the last one hundred forty plus years, our Department has progressed far beyond the wildest dreams and expectations of its early members. In an age of rapidly developing technology, one can only wonder what advances will have been made when the Department is two hundred years old. However, no matter what the future technological advances are, the foundation will always be the police officer and the basic purpose of the Yonkers Police Department has and always will remain unchanged - To Serve and Protect.

PATROLMAN JUSTIN N. FOSTER

NEW YORK METROPOLITAN POLICE DEPARTMENT

The purpose of the researched material contained herein is to document some basic information on all the police officers who have served as members of our police department since its inception on April 10, 1871. Regarding Police Officer Justin Foster, he never had the opportunity to officially serve as a "Yonkers" police officer. However, his service to our community is nonetheless noteworthy.

In 1866 Justin Foster was serving as a police officer with the New York Metropolitan Police Department and was assigned to their 17th Precinct. In that year, on August 10, 1866, and acting upon a formal request from the Town of Yonkers, a detail of N.Y. Metropolitan police officers was organized and was sent to the Town & Village of Yonkers to establish a sub station of the New York 32nd police precinct. Patrolman Foster volunteered to be a part of that detail whose job it was to provide "professional" full time police service for the very first time to our small, but problem plagued community. Foster did his job well, patrolling the streets of Yonkers for two years, and earned the respect of our citizens, and his fellow officers.

A few examples of his diligence are as follows: On Aug 20, 1866, just ten days after arriving in Yonkers, Foster made a good arrest. It was about 3 AM while Foster was walking his post in Getty Square when he came upon three suspicious men. Considering the hour, he stopped all three to investigate. He learned that the two that were in the horse drawn wagon had stopped the 3rd male, a Mr. Frank Imhoff, asking for directions to the Town of Sing Sing. Imhoff provided the information but the two men then threatened to kill him if he was not being truthful. Upon learning this officer Foster promptly arrested the two men and walked them to headquarters and the "Lock Up." The next morning at arraignment both prisoners were released when they agreed to leave Yonkers.

On the very next day, Aug 21, 1866, in a police blotter entry officer Foster was referred to as Acting Roundsman. Possibly for just that day. On that tour at 2:45 AM Foster arrested a male for attempting to shoot another with a revolver. The prisoner was held on $1,000. bail.

Officer Foster had been a Civil War veteran who reportedly had been captured during the war by southern troops. While being held a prisoner for eleven months in the notorious southern prison named Andersonville, he had contracted an illness then termed "consumption." Like most prisoners of war, Foster never fully recovered from the effects of the filth, maltreatment, and his contracted illness.

While he was serving as a police officer in the Town and Village of Yonkers, this illness is said to have recurred. As a result, on November 17, 1868, Police Officer Justin N. Foster died. He was only 32 years of age and left a young wife. His funeral was held in Peekskill where his family originated. Considering the distance to be traveled and the limited mode of transportation available, officer Foster's funeral was well represented by his police department and others. In attendance was a delegation of 39 New York Metropolitan police officers, the Union Veterans Organization of Cortlandtown, and the Peekskill Cornet Band.

Although he died without having an opportunity to join our department when it was organized three years later in 1871, as several of his brother officers did, Justin Foster was, in point of fact, the first professional police officer "serving the Town and Village of Yonkers" to die. For this, I respectfully honor his memory.

THE RESEARCH FOR THESE FIRST 100 YEARS

The Yonkers Police Department has had the good fortune of having some of the best police officers serve their community for nearly 150 years. In early 1871, following the organization of the department, those early police officers, then known more often as Patrolmen, served during difficult times and were limited in their capabilities due to a lack of technology yet to be developed. However, they had no such limitations on their work ethic, dedication, loyalty and an ability to get the job done with whatever resources were available to them. Many were veterans of the Civil War, which had only ended six years earlier, and these new officers in a new department experienced strict and often un-yielding discipline. Many were dismissed from their position of police officer over minor rule violations that today would amount to minor infractions.

As the years come and go, time has a way of having the memory of those who served, along with the early formative years of the Y.P.D., fade and be forgotten. Unfortunately, that was the case with the Y.P.D. Time marches on, technological advances are made, and officers retire, die and are replaced by younger officers who carry on with the difficult job of law enforcement. And those officers who served and laid the foundation for the improvements and growth of the police department, sometimes with their very lives, were forgotten. As the department rapidly moved forward in size and technology there apparently was no time or effort put in place to record and maintain the rich history of our department, and more specifically those who served.

What you will find within these pages are photographs (if available) of every police officer who was appointed to the Yonkers Police Dept. during the departments first 100 years, along with a personal/police profile of the individual and his/her service. On those occasions where an actual photograph of the officer was unavailable, a representative image of some kind and of that time period was substituted to fill the void. The information provided is accurate to the best of my knowledge and obtained from a variety of sources. Where stories report difficulties experienced by various officers, my intent is not to embarrass any one, but to report our history as I understand it. Having proudly served nearly 36 years in this great department my sole purpose is to ensure that those who served as a Yonkers Police officer, for whatever length of time, are forever remembered.

No doubt, this book is the result of my imperfect effort to ensure that all those who served as sworn members of the Yonkers Police Department during just the first 100 years, 1871 to 1971, are not forgotten. In order to accomplish this, over many years I researched several sources of potential police information. The Yonkers Police Dept. itself was able to provide very little information on police officers from the earlier years of the department. The department was, however, enormously helpful and cooperative in providing information on those who served during later years.

Over the course of the history of the Yonkers Police Department, and in particular during the earlier years, there have been many persons who have desired to enjoy a career with the Y.P.D. but were unsuccessful. Their numbers were much greater between 1871 and 1900. Many simply changed their minds, resigned and made career changes. Others found difficulty working within the admittedly rigid rules that were enforced and were consequently dismissed from the department. It would be accurate to state that some of the violations of departmental rules and regulations that were grounds for dismissal throughout the early years of our department, would not be considered very serious today. However, that was a different time and all officers were treated equally harsh for infractions of the rules. Society's tolerance regarding violations in the 1800's was significantly different from today. Even today, not everyone can be successful in the police profession.

My research led me to obtain a great deal of information from cemetery records, family members of former officers, etc., and from a great deal of miscellaneous newspaper clippings. Much of my information was obtained either from The Yonkers Herald newspaper, The Yonkers Statesman newspaper, the Yonkers Herald Statesman newspaper, Harpers Weekly newspaper and Leslie's Illustrated, the last two from which I obtained vintage police images. However almost without exception the news clipping did not identify from which newspaper it had originated. Lacking a specific source, I often could not reference a source at all. But I do acknowledge, and am grateful for, all the public information that was obtained from these three newspapers. I realize that despite my most sincere effort, there will surely be mistakes and omissions contained herein. I apologize in advance for any and all incorrect information and hope you find this reference book of some interest and value.

CAPTAIN OF POLICE JOHN MANGIN

APPOINTED: April 10, 1871
RETIRED: March 11, 1897

John Mangin was born in Tipperary Ireland on January 10, 1828. His father, Thomas Mangin, was a land steward on a local estate. The educational opportunities for young Mangin were very limited and were obtained with great difficulty. He was reported to have said he was required to walk 5 miles to a school which was held in a shoemaker's shop, and his father was required to pay the sum of seven shillings and six pence per school quarter. It is perhaps because of this that Capt. Mangin had such a strong admiration for the American system of public schools.

At the age of twenty John Mangin married Mary, daughter of Michael Purdy, and soon after immigrated to the United States. They would later have four children; two boys and two girls. The sons would be Thomas H., who like his father would join the NYC Police Dept. and earn the rank of sergeant. His other son, Michael J. Mangin would find interest in Yonkers politics. John Mangin and his young

Captain of Police John Mangin (cont.)

wife arrived in New York City in August of 1848. His first employment working in his new country was for the Hudson River Railroad which was under construction at the time, and for which he earned a salary of 75 cents a day. His faithful performance of duty attracted attention and when the trains began running he was appointed acting station agent at Manhattanville. Mangin remained in this position for 8 years and was then appointed station agent in the Town and Village of Yonkers. He remained in Yonkers from 1857 until 1860. On October 12, 1860 John Mangin was appointed to the N.Y.C. Metropolitan Police Department and, apparently having subsequently shown his ability and intelligence by making several arrests, at the completion of only 10 months, he was promoted to the supervisory rank of Roundsman. Surprisingly, it was only two months later that he was again promoted, this time to the rank of Sergeant.

Following the outbreak of the Civil War there was great public anger over the "conscripting" of male civilians into the military, against their wishes, to fight in the war. As a result, a state of chaos, rioting, looting, and lynching erupted all over NYC. It was during these infamous "Draft Riots" in 1863 in which hundreds of people died, including many police officers, that Sgt. Mangin reportedly played a prominent part and was said to have been severely injured.

Following the end of the Civil War, in August of 1866 Sgt. Mangin was advised that the Town and Village of Yonkers NY had expressed a desire to have the NYC police open a substation in their community. Apparently, Yonkers' system of constables and "part time" police officers had been deemed to be completely ineffective. For these services Yonkers would pay $20,000 to the City of New York. Mangin, along with a Sgt. James Flandreau and 12 police officers were detailed to Yonkers and did establish a substation of New York's 32nd police precinct. The 32nd precinct and the Yonkers substation were under the command of NYC Captain Alonzo Wilson. The detail of N.Y.C. Metropolitan Police officers arrived in Yonkers on August 10, 1866 and established their police headquarters at 9 Dock Street. (Since renamed Manor House Square.) This location was a 3 story building and was formerly operated under the business name of Melah's Hotel. Mangin and Flandreau began their assignment of setting up a professional police operation within a newly established police station with relatively nothing to start with. However, these men were not amateurs and were determined to carry out the orders that were given them. They fashioned their operation just as a N.Y.C. police precinct would be operated. This included the Metropolitan Police rules and regulations, strict attention to detail and strict, but usually fair discipline.

On August 13, 1866, just three days after their arrival in Yonkers, Sgt Mangin and the entire detail had hardly taken possession of their new headquarters in Yonkers when information was received by telegram from New York that a prize fight was scheduled to take place, possibly within the boundaries of the Town of Yonkers. Sgt's Mangin and Flandreau left the new HQ accompanied by nearly the entire detail of police officers to do whatever they could to prevent the fight. At 11:50 PM a train arrived at the station in Yonkers and by 12:30 AM the officers had arrested 30 men who they believed were going to be part of the boxing match. They charged all 30 with being “suspicious characters.” The next morning in court all were discharged upon condition they leave Yonkers.

Four years later Sgt. Mangin would face serious physical injury. On Sunday January 16, 1870 an altercation, referred to as the “Battle of the Glen,” took place, the start of which began on Cromwell Pl. At about 4 PM while PO Woodruff was patrolling his “beat” on Pond St, he came upon some drunken men

Captain of Police John Mangin (cont.)

arguing and ordered them to disperse. Instead they resisted his orders and with the help of several friends from "The Glen," overpowered and knocked him to the ground and beat him. He was able to send word to the station for help and in a short while PO's Osborne and Boyd, who had responded to what was termed the "battleground," found a crowd of 100 or so infuriated men who, under the influence of liquor, had resolved to resist the officers. The officers being greatly outnumbered were quickly overpowered, knocked to the ground, and beaten with stones and clubs. Word was again dispatched to headquarters for more aid as quick as possible. More help now arrived in the persons of Sgt Mangin, Rdsmn Austin and Weston and the remainder of the police reinforcements that were in reserve at the station house. When Sgt Mangin and his men arrived at the scene they found that the crowd had swelled to even greater numbers and was in fact a full scale riot. The Sgt remained undaunted. He was well experienced in dealing with situations of this type. Before being detailed to Yonkers he had fought and helped quell the NYC Civil War Draft Riots in which he was severely injured, and many people were killed. Sgt Mangin quickly formed up his officers, gave the order, and with nightstick's swinging the men in blue charged into the riotous crowd. Their aggressive approach caused the group to break and start running. After a severe hand to hand fight in which stones, clubs, and mud flew, 11 of the rioters were captured, charged with Riot, and held in the Lock Up on $500 bail for arraignment the next day. All received substantial fines for their actions.

For over a period of five years this group of officers did an admirable job of initially organizing and then maintaining a professional police presence and providing excellent service to the citizens of Yonkers. Due to a marked reduction in crime and disorderly persons, it was decided by Yonkers' city leaders that Yonkers should have its own police force. On March 30, 1871 an act providing and allowing for the formation of a local police force in Yonkers was signed by the Governor of New York State.

On April 10, 1871 the newly established Yonkers Police Department began its operation. All 14 NYC police officers were given the opportunity to either return to the New York police department or, remain and become a Yonkers policeman. Many returned to New York and were replaced by newly hired Yonkers men. Others stayed with the new department. The most important decision that needed to be made was, who to name as the leader of the new Yonkers department. Both Sgt.'s Mangin and Flandreau had elected to remain with Yonkers. Should they choose Sgt Mangin or Sgt Flandreau who was actually senior to Mangin in time in service with the N.Y. Police Department? Speculation was that both men wanted the new position, but it would be John Mangin, who had made many friends in Yonkers years earlier, that would be chosen to serve as "Captain of Police." This position was the equivalent of a Chief of Police. Sgt. Flandreau, who was no doubt disappointed, decided not to remain a sergeant working for Captain Mangin and, upon his own request, subsequently returned to the N.Y. police.

When Sgt Mangin was chosen to be the Captain of Police for the new Yonkers Police Force on April 10, 1871 the Gazette newspaper wrote the following: *"The appointment of Sgt Mangin as Captain of Police gives the utmost satisfaction to almost everyone, and we are certain it could not have been bestowed upon a more affable, courteous, and obliging officer. Capt. Mangin has been known in Yonkers in a public capacity for over 20 years. And during that time his conduct has been such that his present appointment is only a just tribute to him for the unwavering exertion he always made to benefit the public at large. We wish Capt. Mangin a long, secure, and pleasant enjoyment of the emoluments and honors of his new office."*

Captain of Police John Mangin (cont.)

In the ensuing years Captain John Mangin provided the direction, the guidance, and the strict but fair discipline that molded new policemen into experienced and capable officers. Many of the newly hired men found they were not suited to the long hours and military style discipline that Capt. Mangin employed. Many simply resigned, and many others were dismissed from the department for violating departmental rules and regulations. The rules and regulations of the Yonkers Police Department were promulgated and patterned after the NY police. In fact, initially Yonkers followed the same rule book as did NYC. Although Capt. Mangin was the department's leader, he was subject to direction by, and needed approval of most requests by, a Board of Police Commissioners. Capt. Mangin was in command 24 hours a day, 7 days a week and he would personally hold roll calls as often as was possible.

Ultimately the Yonkers Police Dept. became known as the best in the area. Over the years there were many programs initiated by Capt. Mangin that enabled his police officers to better deal with a variety of crime problems in the city. But the most innovative concept initiated by Mangin was the creation and implementation of what is believed to be the very first "Police Telegraph System" in the United States. This invention provided the police desk officer with the ability to be in touch with the police officer out on his post, using a series of designated coded sounds sent to a specific telegraph call box. There was no voice communication. Our very first telegraphic call box was installed in March of 1874 on Ashburton Avenue.

Though innovative, aggressive, feared by the law breaker, tireless in his drive to make his department the best, and respected by all who knew him, John Mangin was still just a man. His human mortality would soon become apparent.

On Sunday evening, February 14, 1897, Capt. Mangin left headquarters and returned to his home at 45 Post Street to retire for the night. On the next morning the captain was found by his family in an unconscious state. He had apparently been overcome by the fumes from the gas stove in his room; most likely carbon monoxide poisoning. After being treated by doctors he seemed to begin to feel better. For the next few days it was reported that Mangin was alert and cheerful and eagerly met with visiting friends at his home. The captain seemed to be recovering from the effects of the fumes, and it was thought that he would be able to resume his duties. However, the captain suffered a relapse, after which his health failed rapidly. He went into a coma and at 10:15 PM on March 11, 1897 Captain of Police John Mangin died at the age of 70 years.

The news that the captain had died spread rapidly throughout the city and everywhere the deepest sympathy was expressed to the bereaved members of the late captain's family. The officers and men who had worked for him were surprised and a general air of gloom pervaded police headquarters. Captain Mangin was one of the most widely known and popular police officials in the country, and his reputation was of the highest. Although well beyond the age limit requiring retirement, so confident were the police commissioners and the public in the executive ability of the captain that, the question of his retiring was never seriously discussed.

The splendid department which he led and which was taken as a model throughout the state, was organized by him and brought to a state of near perfection by his tireless efforts, attention to duty and practical experience. Following his death, the interior and exterior of headquarters was draped in black mourning cloth and flags throughout the city were authorized to be flown at half-mast.

The funeral for Captain John Mangin was held on Monday March 15, 1897. All members of the department were allowed to attend with the exception of two officers. The large funeral procession passed through the streets from the captain's house to St. Peters Church. Crowds of people lined the

Captain of Police John Mangin (cont.)

streets and watched the cortege move slowly by. Two carriages were needed to convey the elegant and costly floral tributes. One was a large police captain's badge of yellow, with violets used to form the words "Yonkers Police Captain." It stood nearly four feet in height and was surmounted by an American eagle formed of yellow roses. The funeral procession contained not only Yonkers officers, but great numbers from the NYC Police Department. During the mass the late captain was laid out in his full dress uniform, with gold striped sleeves, and his gold police shield. During the service the priest commented, "To you, the police force, by his example and guidance, I will say, he has made you a model force and a credit to the city. Now that he has left you, try to emulate his example, and keep his memory fresh".

Around this same time back at headquarters an unknown man entered and asked permission to see the late captain's office as it had been left. His request was willingly granted. Over the door leading into the small office was a life-like portrait of the deceased captain which was shrouded by funeral drapes.

When Captain John Mangin died, he had gained the respect and admiration of the police department and the entire community. He earned this by his strict regard to duty. His well-known integrity and honesty of purpose rendered his example worthy of emulation. Any fair evaluation of the accomplishments of Captain Mangin's 37 year police career, 26 years as the leader of the Yonkers Police Department, and especially the leadership he provided to our newly formed organization, would most conclude that he was truly............

"THE FATHER OF THE YONKERS POLICE DEPARTMENT"

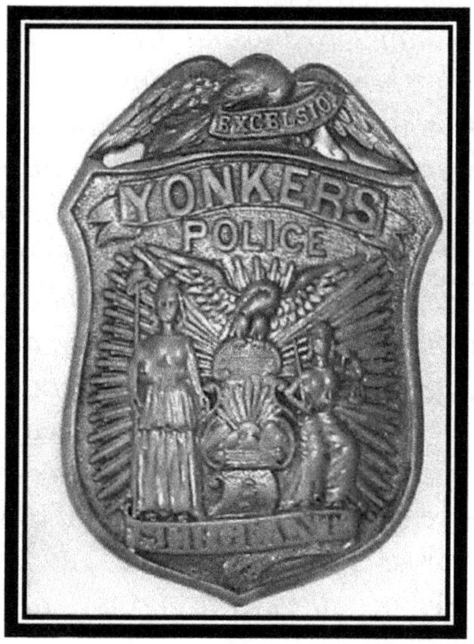

SGT. JAMES M. FLANDREAU

ASSIGNED: August 10, 1866
RESIGNED: April 29, 1871

Little is known of the early years of James Monroe Flandreau other than he was born in New York City in 1820. He was married, became a widower and remarried. Records indicate he was a “Lieutenant of Police” in 1854 under then Capt. Speight, in the Twenty-first Ward in New York City. When Sidney H. Stuart was elected City Judge, Flandreau left the police and was elected a Police Justice to serve the balance of Stuart's term, and presided at the Jefferson Market Police Court during 1857 and 1858. On June 13, 1859 he was reappointed a policeman and assigned to the 32nd precinct. He was subsequently promoted to the rank of Sergeant.

Sgt Flandreau was mentioned prominently in the book by David Barnes: "The draft riots in New York, July 1863." At that time the city was under widespread siege with open rioting, murder and attacking of the police and even having killed a few. In one part the author wrote;

Sergeant Flandreau was left in charge of the station-house, having under his command one officer, two doormen, and two hostlers. On Tuesday, when the force had left for Central Office, a number of ladies and gentlemen residing at Carmansville, Fort Washington, and Tubby Hook, came to the station, and expressed their fears in regard to the destruction of their dwellings, the gentlemen offered their services and Sergeant Flandreau allayed their apprehensions.

"At night he dispatched Patrolman Crosby and Doorman Malone on different reconnoitering duties, which they did most faithfully. Fresh horses were constantly kept on hand, and the few men at his disposal were actively scouting. When not doing this, they made a bold front at the station, demeaning themselves as though the whole force were on hand, and could be brought at once into service. During the night a man living in the neighborhood, one of doubtful character, repeatedly reconnoitered the station, and was inquisitive as to the number of men and the means of defense and offence. He received discreet answers and communicated them to a gang ready for arson and pillage, who thereupon skedaddled.

"On Wednesday, during the morning, the Sergeant was run down with the terrified residents of the vicinity and he endeavored to allay their fears. He told them how thoroughly the precinct had been patrolled, but all in vain so far as a large number were concerned, who packed up their valuables and removed with their families to Westchester County. Confident of his own ability, with his few men and the volunteer force he could raise to preserve order, yet the alarm and absquatulating induced the Sergeant to telegraph for Capt. Wilson and his force. Their return on Wednesday was the signal for a general jubilation. They arrived just in time to check the crowd at Carmansville, above referred to."

In August of 1866, following the end of the Civil War, Sgt. Flandreau was advised that the Town and Village of Yonkers NY had expressed a desire to have the NYC Metropolitan police open a substation in their community. Apparently, Yonkers' system of constables and "part time" police officers had been

Sergeant James Flandreau (cont.)

deemed to be completely ineffective. For these services Yonkers would pay $20,000 to the City of New York. Flandreau, along with a Sgt. John Mangin and 12 police officers, was detailed to Yonkers, which at the time was included in the Metropolitan Police District and did establish a substation of New York's 32nd police precinct. The 32nd precinct and the Yonkers substation were under the command of NYC Captain Alonzo Wilson. The detail of NYC officers arrived in Yonkers on August 10, 1866 and established their police headquarters at 9 Dock Street. (Since renamed Manor House Square.) This location was a 3 story building and was formerly Melah's Hotel. Sgt's Flandreau and Mangin began their assignment of setting up a police headquarters with relatively little to start with.

Although he had been sent along with Sgt Mangin, Sgt Flandreau was the senior sergeant and as such was designated the officer in charge when the 32nd pct. Capt. Wilson was not present. He held that authority for nearly five years. Records indicate these Metropolitan Police Officers, or "Mets" as they came to be known, were well accepted by the citizens and had little trouble organizing a working police station. They operated in Yonkers using the same rules, regulations and procedures that they were required to use in NYC.

Flandreau and the entire detail had hardly taken possession of their new HQ in Yonkers when three days later, on August 13, 1866, information was received by telegram that a prize fight was supposed to take place possibly within the boundaries of the Town of Yonkers. Sgt's Flandreau and Mangin left the new headquarters accompanied by nearly the entire detail of police officers to do whatever they could to prevent the fight. At 11:50 PM a train arrived at the station in Yonkers and by 12:30 AM the officers had arrested 30 men on charges of being "suspicious persons." The next morning in court all were discharged upon condition they leave Yonkers.

On April 10, 1871 the newly established Yonkers Police Department began operating as an independent police agency. All 14 of the N.Y.C. police officers were given the opportunity to either return to the New York police department or remain and become a Yonkers police officer. Many returned to New York and were replaced by newly appointed Yonkers men. Others stayed with the Yonkers department. Initially it appeared that Sgt Flandreau was also remaining. However, the most important decision that needed to be made by the Board of Police Commissioners was who to name as the leader of the new Yonkers department. Both Sgt.'s Flandreau and Mangin had elected to remain with the Yonkers department. Should they choose Sgt Flandreau, who was actually senior to Mangin in time of service with the NYC Police Department? Speculation was that both men wanted the new position, but it would be John Mangin, who had made many friends in Yonkers years earlier, that would be chosen to serve as "Captain of Police." This new position was the equivalent of a Chief of Police.

Sgt. Flandreau, who was the senior sergeant in years of service and who was no doubt disappointed in not being chosen, decided not to remain a sergeant working for Captain Mangin. Upon his request, he was returned to the NYC 32nd precinct effective April 29, 1871.

Police Sergeant James M. Flandreau died on January 29, 1877 at his residence, 100 West 150th Street, after a long illness. He was 56 years of age and had been connected with the New York Police service for upward of 20 years.

SGT. JAMES M. KING

APPOINTED: April 10, 1871
RESIGNED: June 1, 1874

It is believed that James King was appointed to the NY Metropolitan Police Dept. on April 6, 1866 and was assigned to their 3rd patrol Precinct. There came a time in 1866 when the Town & Village of Yonkers, which at that time did not have a full time professional police force, contracted with the New York Metropolitan Police Department to provide 12 police officers and two sergeants to patrol Yonkers. As a result, a substation of the NY 32nd precinct in the Bronx was established and operated from 9 Dock Street, a former hotel in Yonkers. Ptlm. James M. King was one of the officers detailed to Yonkers to patrol our streets beginning on August 10, 1866. On occasion officer King would walk a foot post but he was primarily utilized as a mounted officer patrolling the larger areas of east Yonkers.

The work of these fine officers was so impressive that the town leadership decided to organize our own Yonkers Police Force. Upon the formation of our own Yonkers Police Department on April 10, 1871 all the detailed patrolmen and two sergeants were given the option to return to New York or remain with our new department. Given that choice, Patrolman King chose to remain a member of the new Yonkers Police Force. In addition, one of the detailed NY sergeants was selected to be Yonkers' new Captain of Police.

A sergeant vacancy was now created, and a new sergeant was needed. Apparently, based on reliability, discipline, and the excellent performance of his duties, Ptlm. James M. King was promoted to the rank of Sergeant of Police. This was a substantial achievement since there was no rank of lieutenant at that time and only the Captain of Police was higher in rank. An April 15, 1871 local news article read as follows:

"Ptlm James M. King, who succeeds Capt. John Mangin as Sergeant of Police, is an officer who has earned for himself the respect of all with whom he has come in contact during the time he has held the position of patrolman in Yonkers. He has been on our local force since it was formed, and previously was a patrolman in New York for a little over two years. The Commissioners have made a wise selection. We wish Sgt King every success in his new position."

On one occasion Sgt. King was described, at the time, as "a good officer, very quiet and easy in his manners, but prompt and efficient in cases of emergencies." Two years following his promotion, on August 18, 1873, Sgt King was placed in command of the small Yonkers Police substation in the Town of Kingsbridge, NY responsible for patrolling that location. However, in 1874 the state annexed the Town of Kingsbridge to New York City and at that time the New York police assumed responsibility for policing the Town of Kingsbridge. When they did, Sgt King and his detail of officers were again provided the option to rejoin the NY Police Department or remain with Yonkers. Unfortunately, on June 1, 1874 Sgt James M. King chose to return to the New York police department and Yonkers lost a most valuable officer.

SGT. CHARLES W. AUSTIN

APPOINTED: April 10, 1871
DIED: December 17, 1881

Born in Somers, New York on May 1, 1842, Sgt. Austin, like Sgt. King, was originally a New York City police officer. While assigned to the 22nd precinct he was detailed in August of 1866 to Yonkers to patrol our city on horseback mounted patrol. After proving his skill and dependability to his superiors, Austin was promoted to Roundsman the following year on July 23, 1867. Two years later on September 11, 1869 Roundsman Austin had occasion to arrest a man for incest with the man's own 14 year old daughter. However, after three days of being held at the County Jail without bail, and possibly contemplating his crime, the suspect committed suicide. Case closed. As unusual as that might seem, only two months later, on November 2, 1869, Roundsman Austin arrested a man wanted by the Hackensack N.J. Police Department for murder of his wife and another man. Having been convicted and sentenced by the New Jersey court to death by hanging, rather than wait for the execution the man hung himself in his cell.

On Sunday January 16, 1870 an altercation referred to as the Battle of the Glen took place, the start of which began on Cromwell Place. At about 4 PM while PO Woodruff was patrolling his beat on Pond St, he came upon some drunken men quarreling and he ordered them to disperse. Instead they resisted his orders and with the help of several friends from The Glen, overpowered and knocked him to the ground and beat him. He was able to send word to the station for help and in a short while PO's Osborne and Boyd, who had responded to what was termed the battleground, found a crowd of 100 or so infuriated men who, under the influence of liquor, had resolved to resist the officers. The officers being greatly outnumbered were quickly overpowered, knocked to the ground, and beaten with stones and clubs.

Word was again dispatched to headquarters for more aid as quick as possible. More help now arrived in the persons of Sgt Mangin, Roundsman Austin and Weston and the remainder of the police reinforcements that were in reserve at the station house. When Sgt Mangin and his men arrived at the scene they found that the crowd had swelled to even greater numbers and was in fact a full scale riot. The sergeant remained undaunted. He was well experienced in dealing with situations of this type. Before being detailed to Yonkers he had fought and helped quell the NYC Civil War Draft Riots in which he was severely injured, and many people were killed. Sgt Mangin, after conferring with Roundsman Austin and Weston as to the action to be taken, quickly formed up his officers, gave the order, and with nightsticks swinging, the men in blue charged into the riotous crowd. Their aggressive approach caused the group to break and start running. After a severe hand to hand fight in which stones, clubs, and mud flew, 11 of the rioters were captured, charged with Riot and held in the Lock Up on $500. bail for arraignment the next day. All received substantial fines for their actions.

On April 10, 1871 when our department was organized, Roundsman Austin decided to leave the New York City police department and join the newly established Yonkers Police Department. And when

Sgt. Charles W. Austin (cont.)

Captain John Mangin needed to select a new Sergeant for his department, he knew who to choose. On April 29th at a meeting of the Police Board, and following a recommendation from the captain, Charles Austin was promoted to the rank of Sergeant. A very prestigious position equal to the rank of lieutenant today. At the time a Sergeant was the 2nd highest rank in the department, right beneath Captain of Police. Austin was now of equal rank with his brother who was a sergeant with the NYC Police Department. Although described as a kind hearted and courteous officer, six feet tall and sturdy build, Austin suffered from heart disease, severe back pain and was a chronic insomniac. Based on newspaper accounts of his physical ailments it would seem he was also very depressed. On a number of occasions Austin confided in his longtime friend and superior, Capt. Mangin that he was suffering great pain and could not find relief. The captain was very understanding but was unable to provide any medical help.

On December 17, 1881 at the age of 39 years, Sgt. Charles Austin of 15 Yonkers Ave. took his own life. A large detail of police attended his funeral in a show of deep respect. And over the door to headquarters, in addition to black bunting, a large sign was placed reading, "We mourn our loss."

SERGEANT GEORGE W. OSBORN

APPOINTED: April 10, 1871
RETIRED: March 1, 1905

Sometimes the improbable seems to find a way of surprising us. This seems to be the case of a child born in a small farming hamlet in Westchester County who would later rise to such prominence in law enforcement. George Whitfield Osborn was born around the year 1838 in the village of New Castle, NY. There seems to be no information available about him during his growing up until the year 1865. It was in the early months of this year that Osborn was hired by the New York City Metropolitan Police Department. For him to have accomplished this he must have had someone sponsor him for this position, for politics played a major role in the operation of the police department at that time. He would learn that politics would always maintain influence in police work and toward the end of his career it would have a definite negative impact on him personally.

Having only been a New York police officer for about a year, Osborn was notified that the Town and Village of Yonkers, which had no formal police department, had requested the Metropolitan Police to set up a substation in Yonkers to enforce the law efficiently. He was notified that he would be one of the police officers assigned to this duty. Fourteen officers had already been sent to Yonkers on August 10,

Sgt. George W. Osborn (cont.)

1866 and Osborne would be sent in six days later as a replacement on August 16, 1866.

The detail opened their new headquarters at 9 Dock Street. This fourteen member detail was so effective over the ensuing five years that Yonkers organized their own police department on April 10, 1871. Yonkers offered all the New York officers to remain working for the village as Yonkers police officers and George Osborn was one of those that agreed.

The transition began April 10th and continued throughout the month. Some New York officers remained, and others had to be replaced by newly hired Yonkers men. During this transition a Roundsman position became vacant and due to Osborn's past record of efficiency, dependability, and his dedication to his work, George Osborn was promoted to the rank of Roundsman on April 29, 1871. He had received this first promotion during the first month of the establishment of the new department. He would now perform the duties of a patrol supervisor making the rounds of the various posts checking on the men on duty. In 1872 Yonkers was incorporated as a city whose southern boundaries reached down as far as the areas of Kingsbridge and Spuyten Duyvil.

By 1874 plans were put in place for the annexation of both these sections of the city of Yonkers and for them to be made a part of New York City. Yonkers Sgt. James King, formerly of the New York department, was primarily assigned to the Kingsbridge substation at the time, and when he was notified of the plan he requested, and was granted, permission to join the New York police and remain working at Kingsbridge. The annexation took place in June of 1874 which resulted not only in Yonkers losing the southern part of its city, but also several of its police officers, including Sgt. King, who switched their employment to the New York Police. A sergeant's position was now available. Again, after careful consideration by the leader of the Yonkers Police, Captain John Mangin, Roundsman Osborn's proven diligence and skill in his profession won him the position. On July 15, 1874 George Osborn was promoted to the 2nd highest rank in the department, Sergeant of Police. At that time the rank of Lieutenant did not yet exist.

Sergeant Osborn was said to have had a reputation for being a strict disciplinarian who expected every officer to obey the rules and regulations of the department. Though strict, he was also known to be a fair man who would consider all factors before making any decision. However, his strict adherence to the law did cause him problems. As a sergeant Osborn very often made complaints against businessmen for violating the excise laws, selling liquor on Sundays. As a result, political pressure was brought to bear and the police board issued an order that, effective August 13, 1891, Sgt. George Osborn was transferred from headquarters to the Sub Station at Bronxville, known then as the Fourth Ward. And that the Roundsman there would be moved to headquarters and perform Sgt. Osborn's duties. When questioned by the local newspaper as to why the sergeant was transferred the Police Board members said only that they could assign anyone wherever they wanted for the good of the department. But, clearly, Osborn was being punished and sent to an isolated post with very little to do.

On October 6, 1891 while on duty and driving his horse drawn wagon Osborn was stopped and advise by some citizens that they believed there was a burglary taking place just off Yonkers Avenue. Further that they had knowledge that the house contained several guns belonging to the absent owner. A call to headquarters was made and when several officers arrived as backup, Sgt Osborn and his men

Sgt. George W. Osborn (cont.)

entered the house. In one of the rooms Osborn found the burglar and taking him into custody required the use of his club on the man's head. As a result, the suspect made a complaint against the sergeant for assaulting him. After a review by the Board of Police Commissioners the sergeant was officially censured and reprimanded by the board. This notwithstanding, the burglar whom Osborn arrested was later convicted of his crime.

Because the facilities at the Dock Street headquarters were woefully inadequate, a new police headquarters was built on the corner of Wells Avenue and Woodworth Avenue. On December 20, 1897 at 5:30 PM the entire police department, which included three sergeants, four Roundsman, and thirty police officers, all under the direct command of Sgt. George Osborn, marched in formation from the old Dock Street headquarters to the new police headquarters and Municipal Building.

Though no information is known about his schooling, Osborn must have been an educated man. He was not only a very capable police administrator but because of his academic skills, for some time he was chosen to be placed in charge of the Yonkers Police Pension Fund and was responsible for maintaining all the financial records pertaining to it. For a while he was also responsible for processing the salary accounts for each police officer and ensuring that each received their proper payment. Because of the trust the Police Commissioners had in him it was common practice that whenever the Captain was on vacation or otherwise unavailable, Sgt. Osborn would serve as the Acting Captain of Police.

In 1897 when Captain Mangin died and a replacement was needed, many people considered Sgt. Osborn to be the most qualified officer and the logical choice to become the department's new leader. All that was needed was for him to take the civil service test and, with his intelligence he was sure to receive the position. Even then Osborn must have sensed something negative regarding himself and the politics that permeated the police department because he declined to even take the test. He must have known, even by then, that he had risen in rank as high as he was going to go. But when asked why he did not take the test he would only say, *"I would never get the position no matter."* He was right!

And so it began. On January 9, 1905 the Yonkers Herald Newspaper reported that in a secret order that was marked "Not For The Press," Sgt. George W. Osborn, the oldest member of the department was marked for a severity of treatment not imposed on other members of his rank. The order was said to have directed the sergeant to participate in the newly organized Special Night Detail. Instead of working the long established 6 hour working tour, Sgt. Osborn and a small number of younger officers were required to work 12 consecutive hours from 6 PM until 6 AM in the bitter cold January winter walking foot posts. According to the news account, the reason for this was certain people wanted Osborn to retire and make room for a political promotion. The following day the newspaper reported that the public outcry against forcing certain officers, including Osborn, a man with 40 years police service, to work 12 consecutive hours throughout the night was so strong that the Board of Police Commissioners softened their position somewhat by reducing the hours worked through the night from 12 to 9 hours. The long night patrols during the bitter winter nights, including during a snow blizzard, was also causing some of the officers to become ill. Osborn completed 9 consecutive nine hour night tours before he too fell ill. The newspaper felt that the Police Commission was determined to remove Sgt Osborn and several other senior men from the department through cruel and humiliating treatment.

By January 24th, two weeks after Osborn had been forced to work the Special Night Detail, it was

Sgt. George W. Osborn (cont.)

reported that he intended to submit his resignation and request retirement from the department. It was widely believed that this decision to retire after 40 years of faithful and loyal service was the result of the obvious political pressure being brought to bear regarding his working schedule. As if in evidence of the unfair treatment fostered on Osborn, following his announced plan to retire, the Special Night Patrol was eliminated. Despite what was called the shabby treatment he had been receiving, Sgt. Osborn, as always, maintaining his professional dignity, was steadfast in refusing to make any public comment on his situation other than to confirm his plan to retire.

On February 23, 1905 a meeting of the Police Board, the last in the fiscal year, was held and Sgt. Osborn's request to retire was considered by the board and was unanimously accepted. The sergeant was then summoned before the board and Police Board President Mr. Osterheld said, *"Sergeant, we have received your application and it has been acted favorably upon. We are sorry to lose a good officer. You should be proud of your record, and I wish you success in any undertaking you may begin."* According to the news reporter, the sergeant, with a happy smile upon his face, thanked the board and with a voice trembling with emotion said, *"I have been in the department here and in New York City for forty years, and during that time I have always tried to do my duty faithfully. If I have made any mistakes, I have not done so intentionally"* Further comments were cut short by the commissioners crowding around and wishing the sergeant well.

One must wonder if the circumstances dealing with the treatment of Osborn as outlined are accurate, what must have been going through the sergeant's mind at that moment? The one word that must have entered the sergeant's mind as the commissioners congratulated him must have been, hypocrisy!
Sgt. Osborn's retirement was effective March 1, 1905 and he retired on an annual pension of $800., representing half of his police salary of $1,600. per year. George Osborn left the police department with a record of forty years as a police officer, 31 as a sergeant, which was the rank just beneath the Captain or Chief of Police. And during that entire time he was never found guilty of any performance of duty violation.

George Osborn's retirement, unfortunately, would not be lengthy. On October 3, 1910 he died in his home on Underhill Street at 2:30 AM. He was said to have be in his 67th year of his life. With him were his wife, and his six children. Following the former sergeant's death, the newspapers obituary related that Osborne had been stricken with some form of paralysis three weeks prior, and was unconscious up to a few days before his death. When asked for a comment on the former sergeant's death, retired Captain of Police James McLaughlin paid tribute by stating that Sgt. Osborn was a brave and efficient officer. He did his duty nobly, at all times.

The passing of retired Sgt. George W. Osborn reminded all that the protectors of the early days of Yonkers were leaving them.

PO FRANKLIN BOYD

ASSIGNED: August 10, 1866
RESIGNED: April 24, 1871

On Aug 10, 1866 Patrolman Franklin Boyd was detailed from NY Metropolitan Police 13th precinct to Yonkers. The following month, on September 13, 1866 Boyd was assigned to patrol the Riverfront due to thefts taking place at the waterfront. On that day he arrested two men for stealing a row boat from Staten Island and possessing it in Yonkers.

On September 12, 1867 Boyd was one of the officers involved in quelling a large group of fighting men which was named by the press as the Dudley Grove Riot. Officer Boyd was a mounted patrol officer and on Sunday January 16, 1870 an event referred to as the "Battle of the Glen" took place. At about 4 PM while PO Woodruff was patrolling his "beat" on Pond St, he discovered some drunken men quarreling and he ordered them to disperse. Instead they turned on him and knocked him to the ground and beat him. He was able to send word to the police station for help and in a short while PO's Osborne and Boyd, who had responded, were involved in a tough struggle. Both these officers were also knocked to the ground and beaten with stones and clubs. More help now arrived in the persons of Sgt Mangin, Rdsmn Austin and Weston and the remainder of the force that was in reserve. After a severe hand to hand fight in which stones, clubs, and mud flew, 11 of the rioters were captured and held on $500. bail. Following the establishment of the Yonkers Police Dept. on April 10, 1871 and after two weeks serving as a member of the YPD, on April 24, 1871 his petition to return to NYC police was accepted.

CAPTAIN OF POLICE JAMES McLAUGHLIN

APPOINTED: April 10, 1871
RETIRED: August 17, 1901

Captain McLaughlin was born on August 16, 1843 in Drumshanbo, County Lietrum, Ireland. At the age of seven he came to the America with his parents, and grew up in the town of Norwalk Conn. It was there he received his public education. When he was 18 years old he entered the employ of Fletcher, Harrison & Co., makers of engines and boilers, and whose place of business was at Vestry and West Streets in New York City. On April 1, 1865 following his move to New York, and at the age of 22 years, McLaughlin joined the New York Metropolitan Police Department and was assigned to their 7th patrol Precinct under the command of then Captain Jamieson. The following year on August 10, 1866 he was directed to join a 14 man detail with orders to patrol the Town and Village of Yonkers as part of a substation of the New York 32nd Precinct. The population of Yonkers at the time was 12,756. Although there were several mounted patrol posts, or "routes" in Yonkers, all available records indicate McLaughlin never rode, but always walked a foot post. In the early years his most frequent post was in Getty Square.

As one of the original detail of Metropolitan Police officers detailed to Yonkers, Sgt's Mangin,

Captain of Police James McLaughlin (cont.)

Flandreau and the entire detail had hardly taken possession of their new headquarters in Yonkers when information was received by telegram from New York advising that an illegal "prize fight" was scheduled to take place on a barge on the Hudson River, possibly within the boundaries of the Town of Yonkers. It was believed that many men were on their way to Yonkers to witness the event. Sgt's Flandreau and Mangin left the new headquarters on Dock Street accompanied by nearly the entire detail of police officers; their intent to do whatever they could to prevent the fight. McLaughlin and the other officers in the detail proceeded directly to the Yonkers train station. At 11:50 PM a train arrived in Yonkers and by 12:30 AM the officers had arrested 30 men on being "suspicious characters." McLaughlin arrested five men himself. All were taken and held overnight in the "Lock Up" on James Street. The next morning in court all were discharged upon condition that they leave Yonkers.

In one case of simple intoxication the incident was somewhat out of the ordinary. It was 12 noon on Oct 1, 1866 when Patrolman McLaughlin arrested Daniel Crowley, a Yonkers resident. It was reported that, as he did, the man turned on the officer with savage ferocity and a vicious fight ensued. Although during the wild altercation it was reported that officer McLaughlin's coat had been "torn to shreds," he still maintained control of his prisoner, subdued him, and walked him to headquarters and the "Lock Up" where he was charged with disorderly conduct and assault. The following day at his arraignment the man was found guilty and upon agreeing to compensate the officer $30.00 for the cost of replacing his uniform coat, the magistrate fined the prisoner $2.50 and upon paying the fine he was released.

When Yonkers established its own department on April 10, 1871, McLaughlin and the others were given the choice of remaining and becoming a part of the Yonkers department or returning to New York. McLaughlin, who was a resident of Yonkers at the time, chose to remain in Yonkers. At a meeting of the Board of Police Commissioners on April 29, 1871, following the promotion of Roundsman Charles Austin to Sergeant, James McLaughlin was promoted to Roundsman filling the created vacancy. At a Police Board meeting held on August 4, 1871 the board unanimously adopted a resolution stating... "That the Board express' it's confidence in Roundsman James McLaughlin in the discharge of his duties."

In mid-October of 1871 Roundsman McLaughlin was charged by Capt. Mangin on a citizen's complaint that McLaughlin had clubbed two men he was placing under arrest on September 27, 1871. Six alleged witnesses testified against McLaughlin during a trial before the Police Board, but their testimony contradicted each other. Several civilians and other police officers testified that Roundsman McLaughlin used no more force in making his arrest than was necessary. Following a departmental trial the Police Board ordered that the action taken by Roundsman James McLaughlin was justified and they dismissed the charges against him.

On Nov 25, 1871 the local newspaper reported the following incident. On the Saturday previous a Canal Boat named the American Hero was proceeding down the Hudson to New York City. The "Hero" was lashed together to about a dozen other similar type boats all connected and moving toward New York City. As they were off the shore of Yonkers near the Radford Dock, another boat named the "Miller" was proceeding north toward Poughkeepsie but had accidentally run into the "Hero." Two men aboard the "Hero," Connors and Hill quickly worked to free the boats that had lodged together. After succeeding they were standing on deck discussing the accident when two shots rang out striking both men. When the American Hero boat reached NYC it was learned that Connors had 17 apparent gun pellet wounds to his back, and Hill had 74 similar wounds in his stomach, was in critical condition, and would likely die. The

Captain of Police James McLaughlin (cont.)

shooting was reported to the Yonkers Police and the investigation was assigned to Roundsman McLaughlin and PO Cogans. Initially not even knowing the name of the sloop from which the shots were fired, they proceeded to Poughkeepsie, then to NYC where they located the sloop in question. Following an extensive investigation McLaughlin arrested three men responsible for the shooting. McLaughlin was commended for his diligence in arresting the responsible persons.

The actual details of the incident are not known but, on September 13, 1872, it was reported that Roundsman McLaughlin shot and killed a man while performing his duty. As a result, at a Police Board meeting held September 16, 1872, a motion was made to suspend McLaughlin and bring charges against him. However, a coroner was called in to testify before the board and he stated that based on his inquest investigation McLaughlin was "free from any blame" in the shooting. McLaughlin was immediately returned to full duty.

On May 31, 1873 while on patrol and passing a little store on the corner of Warburton Ave. and Wells Ave., McLaughlin detected a foul odor emitting from the store. Upon investigation, inside he found the dead body of a female who had been deceased for quite some time. The woman's husband became a suspect and following an investigation the man was subsequently arrested, pled guilty to manslaughter, and was sentenced to five years in State Prison.

On March 19, 1874 McLaughlin was detailed from headquarters in Yonkers to the substation located in the Town of Kingsbridge. However, two days later he was reassigned to Yonkers headquarters. He may not have known it at the time, but he was about to continue his rise in the police department. McLaughlin had received his promotion to Roundsman when Charles Austin was promoted, and now on December 22, 1881 he was promoted to Sergeant due to the death of Sgt. Austin. He remained a sergeant for nearly 16 years. Sgt. McLaughlin was a strict disciplinarian, but he recognized the importance of building camaraderie among his men. An example of this was in the summer of 1891 when it as reported that the Y.P.D. had, for the first time, fielded a police uniformed baseball team. The uniforms had no particular P.D. marking but all were, at least, dressed the same. At the time there were several men interested in playing ball but someone needed to organize them in order to compete against other city leagues. That's when then Sgt. McLaughlin, a firm believer in the potential morale building possibilities, volunteered to serve as the team's manager. It is believed the YPD team had a very active and successful year.

Upon the death of Captain of Police John Mangin, McLaughlin was selected to succeed him and on July 30, 1897 he was promoted to the position of "Captain of Police." This position and title was the equivalent of a police chief which made James McLaughlin the commander of the entire Yonkers Police Force.

Following in the footsteps of Yonkers' first police leader, Capt. John Mangin, was a formidable challenge but McLaughlin had worked closely for and with the late Capt. Mangin. Capt. McLaughlin was a stern disciplinarian and did his best to serve the community. However, it was not long before the two politically opposite newspapers argued about the captain's leadership abilities. As a result, on August 17, 1901, the city claimed he had reached the mandatory retirement age of 60 years, and the captain was forced to retire. However, McLaughlin claimed he was not yet of retirement age, and that he was only 58 years of age. As a result, he fought his forced retirement in the courts winning in the State Supreme Court and the Appellate Court but ultimately lost in the Court of Appeals on a filing technicality. He was then

Captain of Police James McLaughlin (cont.)

permanently retired from the police department at half his annual salary of $2,400, that being a pension of $1,200. per year. He then joined his family as a retired gentleman at 205 Warburton Avenue. He and his wife spent the winters in Florida and the summers in Asbury Park, New Jersey. To keep himself busy he entered the real estate and building business constructing several homes along Warburton Avenue near Trevor Park. He worked at this for nearly 20 years before again retiring.

At one point the local newspaper paper, The Yonkers Herald, described Captain McLaughlin as... *"a splendid policeman. He was a man of personal courage, sober, serious and determined - he faced all dangers unflinchingly, asked no quarter and gave none."* It was reported at that time that the retired captain was usually very reluctant to speak about his career in police work. But, on one occasion after retirement he told a story to a reporter of the Yonkers Herald. He related that during a Carpet Shop Strike in 1885 there were many strikers, but one man in particular was a trouble maker and was always agitating the crowd. On many occasions he had been arrogant in his manner with other officers. McLaughlin said he was determined to deal with this man. He saw him on New Main Street in the middle of a large crowd. He started to approach the man with his eyes riveted on him moving straight through the crowd. With night stick in hand he went right up to the man and said, "Get out of my way." The man responded with a curse which was immediately followed by McLaughlin's stick crashing onto the man's head, rendering him unconscious. With that McLaughlin simply stepped over him and walked away. The crowd, having witnessed the swift street justice applied by the officer, quickly dispersed. The retired captain related to the reporter that he never saw the man again.

In another news article in 1908, a debate was being had as to the potential value of using "police dogs" in police work. When retired Capt. McLaughlin was asked his opinion on using these dogs he was reported to have said, "It is an excellent suggestion, one of the best that has been made in years." Of course, it took more than 60 years before this would occur.

Yet again, in February of 1928, the Yonkers Statesman interviewed the long retired McLaughlin, then 85 years old. During this interview they reported that the former captain was the oldest living Yonkers resident who had been in the presence of former President Abraham Lincoln. McLaughlin had apparently told them that as a youth in the winter of 1863 he had an opportunity to drive a New York congressman's team of horses to Washington D.C. On January 1, 1864 McLaughlin said he was fortunate enough to have been allowed to attend the annual public reception at the White House and actually shook hands with President Lincoln. After returning to New York, on April 5, 1865 he was appointed to the N.Y. Metropolitan Police. He stated that he had only been a police officer for about two weeks when, following the president's assassination, McLaughlin was one of the police officers selected to serve as one of the Guard of Honor to watch over the presidents body and direct the mourning crowds as the body lay in state in New York City.

But with age, over the years James McLaughlin developed heart disease and on January 24, 1930 while taking a nap he quietly passed away in his home. He was 87 years old. The funeral for the retired police leader was held from his home and a mass was offered at St. Mary's Church. Nearly 300 people attended the funeral including a police escort of 60 uniformed police officers as well as many prominent city and state officials who came to pay tribute to the former officer. Among the mourners was the

Captain of Police James McLaughlin (cont.)

captain's family including his son John, a retired NYPD sergeant, and his brother Joseph, a retired NYPD lieutenant.

Capt. James McLaughlin, who had served so long and honorably, and along the way raised 12 children, had seen his department grow from 14 men to about 300 prior to his death. With his passing the last remaining link between a modern day police, and the original force of 14 who came here to establish the first real organized policing in the city of Yonkers in 1871, was now broken.

The following was from an interview on August 7, 1926 with a newspaper reporter and written in the Yonkers Herald.....

"I came to Yonkers on August 10, 1866 as one of the fourteen volunteers from the Metropolitan police force. A special order had been issued asking for men to do duty in Yonkers which was to be known as the 32nd sub precinct. I had been on the force about a year and a half and was attached to seven precincts. Only one volunteer was permitted from each precinct, and the quota was not filled until 21 precincts had been canvassed.

The Metropolitan Police covered what is now Brooklyn, Kings, Queens, the Bronx and part of Westchester. The new 32nd sub pct. covered from Spuyten Duyvil to Greenburgh. We were well received by the people of Yonkers when we arrived. There was no time lost. After Captain Wilson established headquarters in the old Melah building on Dock Street, he assigned the men to their posts. I was sent to Getty Square and vicinity.

The force was hardly settled when a call was sent that a gang of rowdies was invading the town. The crowd was rounded up at the New York Central Railroad station and hustled to the lock up on James Street until the next morning when the visitors were told to get out of town. They had come to witness a fight on a barge on the Hudson River.

Before we came to Yonkers we heard that lower breakers were doing pretty much as they pleased. Their actions in some cases where violent, but on the whole the activity was of an annoying nature. It did not take the police long to end the troubles."

Captain McLaughlin humbly told the reporter that he could recall no incident in his career that was worthy of elaboration. He stated that his service ran close to nothing more than ordinary routine duty. It was learned however, that Captain McLaughlin had his coat torn from his back on three different occasions during the performance of his duty and in the breaking up of a gang. He was knocked unconscious on another occasion when attacked by a mob. It was while he was taking a man to the station house who had been disorderly and put up a fight. While crossing the old wooden bridge that spanned the Nepperhan River on North Broadway between Getty Square and Dock Street, a sympathizer of the prisoner hurled a paving block and struck the officer on the side of the head. McLaughlin did not release his hold on the Prisoner, however, and after getting him behind bars, he went in search of the assailant. The stone thrower left town and remained away for some time. When he came back he was arrested for stealing chickens and sentenced to prison.

THE "BLACK MARIA."

PO CASSIUS McGREGOR

APPOINTED: April 24, 1871
RESIGNED: May 20, 1874

Cassius McGregor was among the first few groups of men hired as police officers for the newly formed Yonkers Police Force on April 24, 1871. Prior to his appointment to the "Yonkers Police Force," McGregor reportedly worked for the local "Clipper Factory." On November 1, 1871, just six months after his appointment, McGregor was tried before the Police Board on charges of Neglect of Duty and, following being found guilty, was fined 10 days' pay. Three years later he was again charged with violating police Rules & Regulation #146 on June 3, 1874, found guilty and again fined 10 days pay. And only three months later on September 30, 1874 another Police Board trial was held charging that he violated Rule #34 to wit, "in that he failed to change the sheets and pillow slips" in the headquarters dormitory as directed. He was found guilty and fined 1 days pay. It is not known why but, on December 2, 1874, Cassius McGregor submitted his resignation to the Police Board and same was accepted.

PO SAMUEL L. WHALEY

APPOINTED: April 24, 1871
DISMISSED: September 20, 1871

On April 24, 1871 Samuel Whaley was one among the first few groups of men hired as police officers for the newly formed Yonkers Police Force. Before his appointment he related that he worked as a Clerk for Messrs' Jones & O'Dell in Yonkers. It didn't take long for Whaley to get into trouble with the department. Four months after his appointment, on August 29, 1871, both he and PO Mike Muldoon were tried on charges of Gross Neglect of Duty; both being absent from their assigned posts while patrolling in the Kingsbridge Sub Station area. During the trial while under direct questioning, and to the amazement of the Board of Police Commissioners, officer Muldoon admitted that when he was caught he "was taking a bit of a sleep" while on his post. He further stated that he and officer Sam Whaley had worked out a system between the two of them, each taking turns; one hour working and the other sleeping. Whaley and Muldoon were both found guilty and were Dismissed from the Force effective September 20, 1871.

SERGEANT HENRY J. QUINN

APPOINTED: APRIL 24, 1871
DIED: January 14, 1899

An emigrant to this country, Henry Quinn was born in County Claire Ireland in 1844. A muscular man, seemingly built for hard work, Quinn worked for many years as an iron worker at the Spuyten Duyvil Foundry in lower Westchester Co. A devoted family man with a wife and one child, when not at work, it was said you could always find him at his home on Hawthorne Avenue with his family.

When our department was organized on April 10, 1871, Quinn filed an application for employment as a police officer. It took very little time for the Board of Police Commissioners to act, and he was voted and accepted as a patrolman on April 24, 1871. PO Quinn performed his duties walking foot posts on the west side of the village. On the 18th of March 1874 at a regular weekly meeting of the Board of Police Commissioners the Police Commissioners wanted to recognize what they believed to be excellent police work by two officers. In the last week of December 1873 in the early morning hours of a cold and snowing Sunday morning, officer Henry Quinn, who was patrolling on Detective Patrol in plainclothes,

Sgt. Henry J. Quinn (cont.)

saw suspicious foot prints in the snow at Warburton and Main Streets. Sometime later at the foot of the old railroad depot he saw three men carrying baskets. As Quinn started to run toward them to investigate, they began to run to get away. Rather than yell to them or grab only one man, PO Quinn caught up, passed right by them by 10 feet, then spun around with his revolver in hand and confronted the suspects. He arrested the three men on a charge of suspicion and after walking them, at gun point, to headquarters, it was determined that they possessed the proceeds of a burglary that had just occurred a short time earlier at the home of Mr. Wells on New Main Street. The three men were committed to the White Plains jail pending their trial. The Police Board was so impressed by what they termed a clever capture, that they ordered the following resolutions to be engrossed, framed and presented to Patrolmen Quinn and to officer Lawrence Berrian who discovered the burglary:

WHEREAS; Officer Henry J. Quinn on the morning of December 28, 1873, at the City of Yonkers, did courageously and single handedly capture three burglars while attempting to leave the city, just after committing a burglary, and
WHEREAS; Officer Lawrence Berrian promptly discovered and immediately reported the fact of such burglary having been committed, be it therefore
Resolved, that the zeal, efficiency and courage manifested by the said officers on the occasion aforesaid meets with our warm and hearty approval.
Resolved, that while this board believes and does maintain that discipline must be strictly and to the letter enforced, they at the same time feel equally bound to express approval of acknowledged ability and zeal in the discharge of duty.
Resolved, that the thanks of this board are due and are hereby tendered for the said officers Henry J. Quinn and Lawrence Berrian for their noble discharge of duty.
Resolved, that the foregoing preamble and resolutions be properly engrossed and a copy of same be presented to each of said officers.

These resolutions were later presented to the officers at a roll call with the entire department present.

At one point while the officer was working in plainclothes and performing what was referred to as Detective Duty, the New York Times newspaper recalled an incident that nearly cost Henry Quinn his life. At that time Detective Quinn observed a male standing in an alleyway acting suspiciously. When Quinn tried to approach the male, the suspect pulled out a gun, pointed it at Quinn, and started to back away to escape. Despite having a gun pointed at him the officer made a grab for the suspect who then fired his revolver at Quinn. While the officer ducked, it provided just enough time for the man to make his escape in the darkness. However the male was arrested by Quinn several days later on November 24, 1875 and sentenced to a term in Sing Sing Prison.

The police department was very new and it was important to identify those officers who would be suitable to advance in rank when the need arose. It would appear that Quinn impressed his superiors with his work because on November 21, 1874, he was promoted to the supervisory rank of Roundsman. Seven years following his promotion to Roundsman, as a result of the death of Sgt. Charles Austin,

Sgt. Henry J. Quinn (cont.)

Roundsman Quinn was promoted to the rank of Sergeant on December 22, 1881. Many years later Sgt. Quinn would display quite an act of bravery. On June 17, 1891workers were busy making new sewer connections at # 8 & 10 Dock Street, across from police headquarters, when an accident resulted in the breaking of a gas line. A spark ignited the gas causing a huge explosion knocking two workers on the street to the ground and trapping two others in the hole they were working in. It was reported that the explosion sent a sheet of flame twenty feet into the air threatening the lives of the two dazed workers in the hole. News accounts related that Sergeant Quinn saw the explosion take place and after running to the scene, succeeded in pulling the two men out to safety. Though burned badly, both men survived their injuries.

Throughout his career Henry Quinn was a close confidant of Capt. Mangin and because of his ability to always get the job done, he would be sure to be chosen by Capt. Mangin to work on the most hazardous assignments. Sgt. Quinn was described in news reports as absolutely fearless and as independent a man as ever lived. He had a great sense of humor, great wit, and was a practical joker on occasion. But at the same time he was very blunt and gruff in his demeanor. By his thrift and shrewd business sense he managed to allegedly accumulate considerable money, which he invested in real estate. In the summer of 1898 he was forced to remain out sick for some time due to poor health. But after a lengthy vacation he returned to work, his health thought to be much improved. He resumed his duties with enthusiasm, only to again become ill in November from the strain of police work. Many of his friends recommended that he consider retirement. He was financially very comfortable and did not need to remain with the police department, but stated, "I want to be doing something."

After a short illness, Sgt. Henry Joseph Quinn died on January 14, 1899 at the age of 55 years. The funeral for the late sergeant was attended by large numbers of city officials, residents of the city, and 32 members of the police department including members of the Board of Police Commissioners. The commissioners and police officers were in full dress uniform and were wearing a black crape bow on their left arm. Led by the commissioners in carriages, the police formation proceeded to the home of Sgt. Quinn on Hawthorne Avenue to view the deceased. After a short while the formation followed the casket to St. Mary's Church on South Broadway for the funeral mass. Sgt. Quinn's body was interred in St. Mary's Cemetery.

ROUNDSMAN EDWARD LUCAS

APPOINTED: April 24, 1871
Resigned: June 1, 1874

Prior to police work, Edward Lucas was employed as a coachman in the Village of Yonkers. Shortly after the organization of our police department on April 10, 1871, Ed Lucas applied for, and was accepted as a Yonkers Patrolman on April 24, 1871. He was assigned to patrol the central part of Yonkers for a short while, but by the end of 1871 he was detailed to our southern police substation located in that section of Yonkers then known as Kingsbridge. This rural police detail consisted of a Roundsman and three patrolmen. Lucas' posts usually consisted mostly of patrolling the Riverdale section and Mt St.Vincent area, and at other times further down at Kingsbridge and Spuyten Duyvil.

It is presumed that police officer Lucas displayed substantial initiative and leadership capabilities, because whenever the Roundsman in charge at the sub-station was away or off duty, officer Lucas was given the responsibility of being placed in command of the officers at the sub- station. By the end of 1873 Lucas had been officially promoted to the rank of Roundsman. Following the annexation of the Kingsbridge area of southern Yonkers to New York City in 1874, all the officers at this sub-station were allowed by law, if they chose, to become part of the NYC Police Force. Roundsman Edward Lucas resigned to become a NYC police officer on June 1, 1874.

CAPTAIN OF POLICE
FREDERICK H. WOODRUFF

APPOINTED: April 27, 1871
RETIRED: June 1, 1907

Frederick H. Woodruff was born July 16, 1843 in Bristol England. At the age of five he and his family came to the United States and settled in Auburn New York. Upon his family moving to Yonkers he became employed as a "hatter" at the Waring Hat Factory in Yonkers. He also spent many years serving as a volunteer fireman.

At the outbreak of the Civil War between the states, Woodruff hurried to join the New York State National Guard, Company B, and 15th Infantry Regiment. Additional information concerning his military service is not known. Upon the organization of the Yonkers Police Department, Woodruff quickly filed an application to be hired. On April 27, 1871 he became one of the men that formed the original Yonkers Police Force. It must have been difficult working for a police department that had just been organized. Everyone was required to utilize the NYC police department rules and regulations until Yonkers could draft its own. Ptl. Woodruff worked foot patrol and served under very strict superior officers. His skills

Captain Frederick H. Woodruff (cont.)

and excellent performance being apparently very evident, and likely due to his military experience and discipline, he was promoted to the supervisory rank of Roundsman only two years later on August 18, 1873. In this new position Roundsman Woodruff was required to inspect the patrolmen at roll call prior to their going out on duty, and make his "rounds" checking on the officers while out on their posts. Considering the vast areas to be covered by the various foot posts, locating the officers on their post to check on them must have been a difficult job. However available records indicate he conducted himself with dedication, discipline and dignity.

His next promotion took a great deal longer than the first. In fact, it was over twenty years later, on May 10, 1894, that he received his next promotion to the rank of Sergeant. In the early years attaining this rank was a significant achievement. There were only a few, and the only rank greater was the leader of the department; the Captain of Police. As a sergeant, Woodruff spent a good amount of his time on desk duty, monitoring the activity and efficiency of all the men on each tour and delivering discipline when circumstances required it. After a long, efficient and faithful career, Sgt. Woodruff was destined to be elevated to the head of our department at the misfortune of the current leader, Capt. James McLaughlin. The police board, being very unhappy with Captain McLaughlin's inability to deal with gambling operations in town, was successful in forcing his retirement.

On September 6, 1901 Frederick H. Woodruff was promoted to the position of "Captain of Police" and became the new leader of the Yonkers Police Department, and only the 3rd man to hold that position. The newspapers of the day reported their satisfaction and agreement with Captain Woodruff's appointment. They stated that Captain Woodruff was an honest and efficient officer who was one of the most senior men in the department, and was fully deserving of this position. As the new captain, Woodruff immediately began what was termed a "sensational" campaign against gambling activities in Yonkers, and did so with great success. For several years he was very successful in helping to move our department forward in the new century. Unfortunately, political pressure was growing to have Woodruff retire and allow a new and politically friendly officer to be appointed. To accomplish their goal, Capt. Woodruff was soon to suffer great indignity in an obvious effort by the Board of Police Commissioners, to also force him to retire. It was reported that among other things, even though he was the leader of the department he was forced to "report" all department activities to a subordinate officer.

Apparently, since he had been stripped of his ability to lead effectively, and after 36 years of proud and dedicated service, Capt. Woodruff retired on June 1, 1907. After a comfortable retirement, Ret. Capt. Frederick Woodruff died on March 19, 1926 at the age of 83 years at his home at 46 Hawthorne Avenue. Although Fred Woodruff had been retired for nearly 20 years before he died, the esteem in which his former colleagues and citizens still held him was remarkable. Not only was he a police veteran of 36 years, but he was a Civil War veteran as well. Included in the large overflow crowd of people that came to pay their last respects at his home were members of the Kitching Post # 60 Grand Army of the Republic. Public Safety Commissioner VanKeuren personally supervised the police detail which consisted of a platoon of 40 men who stood at attention. The honorary pall bearers consisted of 3 captains, 1 lieutenant, and two patrolmen. All were former colleagues and friends. A motorcycle escort guided the cortege to the cemetery where a volley of shots was fired and taps was played. One of their finest had passed final inspection.

PO JOHN COGANS

APPOINTED: April 27, 1871
RESIGNED: December 18, 1875

Ptl Cogans was only an officer for 7 months when on Nov. 25, 1871 it was reported that on the Saturday previous a Canal Boat named the American Hero was proceeding down the Hudson to NYC. It was lashed together to about a dozen other similar type boats all moving, connected, toward New York. As they were off the shore of Yonkers near the Radford Dock, another boat named the Miller was proceeding toward Poughkeepsie but accidentally had run into the Hero. Two men aboard the Hero, quickly worked to free the boats that had lodged together. Suddenly two shots rang out striking both men. One man had 17 wounds to his back and the other had 74 shot wounds in his stomach and was in critical condition. The shooting was reported to the Yonkers Police and the investigation assigned to PO John Cogans & Rdsmn. McLaughlin. Following a lengthy investigation an arrest was made. It was good work, however following a number of departmental charges for neglect of duty, and several fines, officer Cogans resigned from the department on December 18, 1875.

PO JOHN T. REDDING # 1

APPOINTED: April 29, 1871
DIED: February 14, 1914

Born June 23, 1846 in County Tipperary, Ireland, John Redding was an Irish immigrant like a number of his coworkers. In 1863, at the age of 17 years and like many young men at the time, he enlisted in the N.Y. State Militia, Co. H, 17th Regiment, hoping to see action in the Civil War. He was disappointed when he didn't participate in any combat. Apparently liking the military life, in 1865 he joined the Navy where he remained until his discharge in 1867. A longtime resident of Hawthorne Avenue, John Redding was a carpenter by trade. When he joined the new Yonkers Police Department on April 29, 1871 at the age of 24 years he was initially assigned to the Kingsbridge substation in Southern Yonkers where, in addition to patrol duty, he built their first "lockup" or jail. It was reported that during his 43 years of service on foot patrol he never received a complaint against him. He was so respected for his dedication to duty that, upon reaching his 40th year, the men presented him with a diamond scarf pin. After 43 years with the Yonkers Police Department, Police Officer John Redding died on February 14, 1914 at the age of 67 years, while still an active member.

PO JAMES H. MEALING

APPOINTED: April 29, 1871
DISMISSED: May 17, 1882

Officer Mealing was one of seven men appointed to the department on the same day. Like his coworker Roundsman Norton, who was appointed to the department that same day, Mealing must have displayed significant leadership potential. After only seven months, on November 8, 1871, Mealing was also promoted to the rank of Roundsman by the Police Board. He was assigned to take command of the substation at Bronxville, NY. Being in an outlying area all patrol was performed by wagon or horseback. Being a good horseman Rdsmn Mealing chose to move about on horseback. It was said Mealing could always be seen on mounted patrol with his pet Newfoundland dog named "Leo" following closely alongside. For reasons that are unknown, on April 16, 1873, and at his own request, Rdsmn Mealing was transferred back to patrolling central Yonkers. The reassignment also resulted in his being returned to the rank of patrolman.

On February 4, 1874 a departmental trial was held charging Mealing with being absent from District while on the sick list and that he attended a "ball night" on Jan 22, 1874. Upon being found guilty he was fined 10 days' pay. On that same day he was charged with violation of rule 172, was found guilty and fined 10 days' pay. On April 18, 1874 Mealing was once again charged with violation of rule 143, found guilty and was fined 3 days' pay. And again, on July 15, 1874 he was charged with Neglect of Duty, found guilty and fined 3 days' pay.

Though Mealing was often found violating the department's rules, at least on one occasion he was able to get some positive notoriety. The following article appeared in the local newspaper, The Yonkers Gazette in 1877:

PO James H. Mealing (cont.)

Any history of the Yonkers Police which omitted mention of Mealing's large Newfoundland dog, Leo, would be incomplete. The dog has gained a high reputation for his many sagacious acts, and has saved his master many steps, and performed work equal almost to another man on the force. Patrolman Mealing is one of the mounted patrol, and the dog would invariably follow him on his rounds. Certain vacant houses the officer was nightly required to walk around and see that all was right. The dog soon learned them all, and upon approaching would scale the fence and dash around the house; and woe to the man who should be caught by this animal. Leo would never allow any familiarity from any person but his master. And it would not be safe for anyone to assault the officer, should the dog be around. When on certain occasions he had been left home, the moment he had his liberty he would start for headquarters and pass through every room looking for his master. If he did not find him there he would go over his rounds and always find the officer before returning. A good story is told of an exploit of this dog in New York City. Patrolman Mealing and Leo were passing along a street in New York one day, when a woman raised a window and cried, "stop thief," after a man who was trying to escape. Mealing took after the man, but seeing that he would not be able to overtake him, told Leo to go for him! The animal understood the command and by running between the man's legs, threw him and he was secured by his master. The man was subsequently convicted as a sneak thief, but would probably have escaped except for Leo's smartness. This dog is at present in retirement in the Town of Sing Sing.

As the years passed it seemed Jim Mealing just couldn't keep out of trouble. On September 17, 1881 he was tried on charges of Neglect of Duty which occurred thirteen days earlier. He was found guilty, fined ten days pay and removed from mounted patrol to foot patrol. Again, on November 2, 1881, he was tried on charges of violating the rules and regulations, was again found guilty, was remanded and sent to the School of Instruction (refresher training) with his pay reduced to $800. per year.

During 1882 there apparently were some hard feelings between PO James Mealing and PO John Edwards, though the cause is unknown. However, it ultimately resulted in both officers being brought up on departmental charges for which a trial was held on May 17, 1882, charging them both with violation of Rule # 10, Conduct Unbecoming an Officer, to wit, a Gross breach of discipline by indulging in a fight. The tempers came to a head one morning a week earlier when, following a verbal argument in the muster room at headquarters they agreed to leave the muster room and go to the police stables to fight, which they did. During the battle it would seem that Edwards got the upper hand because he broke Mealing's nose. Following testimony at their departmental trial by the supervisor who charged the men, both were found guilty and they were dismissed from the force effective May 17, 1882.

ROUNDSMAN JAMES J. NORTON

APPOINTED: April 29, 1871
RESIGNED: June 1, 1874

James Norton was one of the first officers which comprised the Yonkers Police Department when it was first organized. Upon officer Norton's appointment on April 29, 1871, it is presumed that he displayed a great deal of leadership potential in the performance of his duties. For only seven months later, on November 8, 1871, he was elevated to the first line supervisor position, then known as Roundsman. He was promoted by the Police Board, there were no civil service tests, with the specific assignment to take command of the substation located in what was then South Yonkers. (It is now the Kingsbridge section of the Bronx) Working under the direction of Capt. Mangin in the Yonkers headquarters, he performed his duties well and it was reported that he liked the area in which he worked. Shortly after the annexation in 1874 of this southern area of Yonkers into the City of New York, several officers assigned to this substation, including Norton, requested to be allowed to join and become part of the NYC Police Department. Roundsman James J. Norton's request was accepted and he resigned from our department on June 1, 1874 and joined the New York police department.

PO JOHN HENNESSY

APPOINTED: April 29, 1871
RESIGNED: May 20, 1874

On April 29, 1871 Hennessy was one of seven men appointed to the Yonkers Police Department which had been organized only 19 days earlier. Previously John was a Yonkers resident and worked a variety of miscellaneous jobs in town. By all available accounts he was a conscientious officer that could be depended on doing his job. On December 20, 1873 officer Hennessy was assigned to patrol duty from the Kingsbridge substation which was located at that time in the southern most portion of Yonkers. The following year, following the annexation of that section known as Kingsbridge to the City of New York, officer Hennessy submitted a request to the Yonkers Police Board to be allowed to resign and join the NYC police department. His request was approved effective Ma 20, 1874.

PO JOHN H. WOODRUFF

APPOINTED: April 29, 1871
DIED: July 2, 1872

John Woodruff was said to have been born in a small settlement out west approximately 1825 and came to Yonkers around 1845 as a young man. He gained employment with Ackert and Quick and later with Seger and Smith for whom he worked right up to his appointment to the New York City Police in 1860.

Woodruff was a member of the New York Metropolitan Police Departments 20th precinct when, on Oct 16, 1869, he volunteered to be detailed to the 32nd precinct substation that was operating in Yonkers. He was a replacement for another detailed New York officer, Charles McDougall, who was returned to the 20th Pct.

Woodruff was about to face his first brush with death. On this occasion he would win. On January 16, 1870, a cold Sunday afternoon exactly three months after Woodruffs arrival in Yonkers, an altercation later referred to as the "Battle of the Glen" took place; the start of which actually began on Cromwell Place. At about 4 PM while officer Woodruff was patrolling his "beat" on Pond Street, being familiar with the residents, and almost expecting a disturbance in this area, he came upon some intoxicated men quarreling. The officer promptly ordered them to disperse. Instead they defied his orders and he was set upon by the mob that, at each other's call, seemed to spring in numbers right from the earth. Now, with the help of several other intoxicated friends from "The Glen," this large group attacked and overpowered Woodruff, knocked him to the ground and beat him severely. A few sober citizens who observed the dangerous situation the officer was in sent word to the police station for help. In a short while PO's Osborne and Boyd, who had responded to what was later referred to in the newspapers as the "battleground," found an enormous crowd of several hundred or so infuriated men who, under the influence of liquor, had resolved to resist the police. The officers being greatly outnumbered were quickly overpowered. It was later written that...... *" The mob quickly set upon the small relief force and, despite the bluecoats desperate defense, soon trampled them under foot, stamping upon them with their heels, pounding them with their fists, and, thinking these natural weapons of offense insufficient, commenced to batter the unfortunate officers with cobblestones, vulgarly known hereabouts as 'Tipperary Potato's."*

Word was again dispatched by the few sober citizens to headquarters for more aid as quick as possible. More help now arrived in the persons of Sgt Mangin in command, Roundsmen Charles Austin and Cornelius Weston and the entire remainder of the police reinforcements that were in reserve at the station house. (It is worth noting that the entire police detail assigned to Yonkers numbered only twelve. And, it was likely only two thirds, or eight of them were available to respond.) When Sgt Mangin and his men arrived at the scene they found that the crowd had swelled to even greater numbers and was in fact a full scale riot. The sergeant remained undaunted. He was well experienced in dealing with situations of this type. Before being detailed to Yonkers he had fought and helped quell the NYC Civil War Draft Riots in which he was severely injured and during which many people were killed. Sgt Mangin calmly and quickly gathered his officers in a formation, gave the order, and with night sticks swinging the men in blue charged into the riotous crowd.

PO John H. Woodruff (cont.)

Their beleaguered and injured comrades needed to be rescued and they were there to do just that. Heads were struck, faces cut, and scores of rioters fled screaming. Some running one way, some another; some took refuge in the shanties which filled the Glen. But all to no avail. The doors were knocked down and the rioters were dragged out. Officer Osborn, one of the original men overpowered, although covered in mud and scratches, made the first arrest of the day. Following in quick succession was the arrest of ten other prisoners all with torn clothes and *"broken heads."* By seven o'clock that evening the huge disturbance had been quelled. All eleven of the rioters that were captured were charged with Riot, and held in the Lock Up on $500. bail for arraignment the next day. In the morning all received substantial fines from the magistrate for their actions. Surprisingly, despite the wild and violent melee that took place, none of the police officers were seriously hurt. John Woodruff, the officer on his post who was initially attacked, did the best he could under the circumstances and recovered from his injuries.

When the Town and Village of Yonkers organized their own police department on April 10, 1871, Woodruff and all the other New York officers were given until April 29th to decide whether to stay with the new Yonkers "Force" or return to the police in New York City. On April 29th Woodruff had decided to remain with the Yonkers department and was appointed a Yonkers police officer. Based on available blotter entries of the day, Woodruff was assigned primarily to the horseback mounted detail patrolling the Village of Yonkers. He often would be assigned to patrol on horseback in areas then known as "Hog Hill" and "The Glen." But there were occasions when he would be assigned to walk a foot post.

Odds were John Woodruff would have a bright career in the Yonkers Police Department. However, what follows is a chronology of events which evolved in his short life as a Yonkers police officer.

On December 11, 1871 Woodruff was brought up on departmental charges that he was found sitting down resting in the Hudson River Railroad Depot while on duty at 2:25 AM on the morning of Nov 23, 1871. Following a departmental trial, fortunately all charges were dismissed.

In a blotter entry dated March 10, 1872 it indicated that there had been a verbal dispute in headquarters between two officers and that Roundsman James McLaughlin had charged PO John Woodruff and PO Michael Geary with using profane language and Conduct Unbecoming an Officer. The incident occurred while both men were performing reserve duty in the sleeping area of the Headquarters Section Room. As his answer to the Roundsman's charges, John Woodruff then charged PO Mike Geary with assaulting him in the sleeping room without provocation, using rough and profane language against him, and that Geary had said to him, *"I will whip you, you damn Yankee anyway."* The results of the dispute and charges are not known. Again on May 7, 1872 Woodruff was tried on charges of violation of the Rules & Regulations, was found guilty and fined three days' pay.

On Monday July 1, 1872 it was reported that Woodruff had worked the day tour. Following his dinner he began chopping some wood and became ill. Then suddenly the next day at 3 PM, PO John F. Woodruff died leaving behind his wife and one daughter. He was only 47 years old. The local newspaper reported that he had likely died from "congestion of the brain." The paper also wrote that he was considered a respected citizen and a most efficient member of the police department. Further, that he was of a very genial nature, and unassuming in character; two traits that gained for him a wide circle of friends. Upon his death the police station at 9 Dock Street was draped in mourning and the American flag

PO John H. Woodruff (cont.)

was hung at half-mast to show the respect in which he who had answered his last roll call was held by those who did duty with him. Following the funeral an honor guard of approximately 20 police officers escorted his remains to the "Yonkers Cemetery" for internment.

Although John Woodruff had originally been a New York City police officer since 1860, a total of twelve years in uniform, he had been a Yonkers police officer only fourteen months. And he had the dubious distinction of being the very first active duty Yonkers police officer to die.

At a meeting of the Police Board held in March 1874, two years after Woodruff's death, his widow was approved to receive $25.00 a year from the Widows and Orphans fund.

PO LOUIS SPRENGER

APPOINTED: April 29, 1871
DIED: May 22, 1886

Louis Sprenger was one of the initial police officers hired when our department was first organized in 1871. He was born in Kaisers Lauder, Germany on July 25, 1839 and later came to the United States approximately 1855. Prior to his ultimate arrival in Yonkers sometime in 1864, Sprenger had lived in Hartford, Connecticut and was a member of their police department. While there, he and Annie Wagner were married on November 23, 1861. When the Civil War, or as the northerners then called it, the War of The Rebellion, broke out, Sprenger enlisted, and after several battles was promoted to Lieutenant. He served with Company "H," 22nd Regiment of the Connecticut Volunteers. It was reported that because of the high regard in which he was held, the members of the Hartford Police Department presented him with a "fine military sword, suitably inscribed, which he carried throughout the war and which would later become a family heirloom."

Sprenger was said to have come to Yonkers around 1864 and worked his trade as a Brass Founder and Machinist with Osterheld and Eickmeyer. After joining the Yonkers police on April 29, 1871 and working most often in the Kingsbridge section of South Yonkers, and following the annexation of the Kingsbridge section to New York City, on May 20, 1874 Louis Sprenger requested and was transferred to the N.Y.C. Metropolitan Police Department. However, at a meeting of Board of Police Commissioners on July 13, 1874 a petition was received from Sprenger, who was now a NYC officer, requesting that he be allowed to be reinstated to the Yonkers force. Sprenger stated in his request that his resignation from NYC had already been accepted. His petition was approved by the board and he was again appointed a Yonkers officer effective immediately.

On April 28, 1886 Sprenger became ill and was diagnosed as suffering from "Dyspepsia" and was supplemented by "trouble of the brain." On May 22, 1886, after 15 years of efficient service to our department, PO Louis Sprenger died unexpectedly at 11:15 PM in his residence at 5 Jefferson Street. He was 47 years old. He left behind his wife and two children. Lou Sprenger was described as "one of the most popular officers in the police department and that all who knew him had a good word to say for him." His funeral was held at the German Lutheran Church on Hudson Street on June 1, 1886. The funeral cortege was said to have been very large and the church could not contain all who were present. The procession consisted of representatives from the Holsatia Lodge of the Sons of Freedom, a band from the Young Men's Catholic Association, members of the Kitching Post, a Firing Party with members from the Kitching Post of the Grand Army, the hearse with pall bearers, Yonkers police officers as a guard of honor, Yonkers Turn Verein, Yonkers Tutonia, and a long line of carriages. Having been a respected Civil War veteran, military honors were accorded at the Oak Hill Cemetery with three rifle volleys being fired over the grave.

His widow, along with his son Adam 22 years, his daughter Annie 20 years, were approved to receive a police pension of $66.23 a year.

PO MARTIN GEARY

APPOINTED: April 29, 1871
DIED: December 25, 1872

Information indicates that Martin Geary served, either during the Civil War or just following it, in Company "I", 19th U.S. Infantry, in the Union Army. He served in the southern states almost entirely during the term of his enlistment. Following his discharge he came to live with friends in Yonkers and gained employment with the Waring Hat Factory in Yonkers. Upon the organization of the Yonkers Police Department, Martin Geary made application, and along with six others, was accepted as one of our new policemen on April 29, 1871. He had previously worked as a hatter in Yonkers but I'm sure the lure of the uniform and the authority that came with it helped him decide to change jobs. He was 24 years of age, energetic, and had what I'm sure he believed to be, an exciting career ahead of him. But he was soon to learn that the police department was very strict with it's rules and regulations. Only two months later on June 16, 1871 Geary was tried on charges of Neglect of Duty, was found guilty, and received a reprimand. But Geary seemed to be up to the challenge.

In one local newspaper account on August 5, 1871 they reported "James Tracey, from the "Hill," was charged with interfering with Patrolman Geary in the execution of his duty. The officer had apprehended a man for causing a disturbance and was making the best of his way to the police station with the fellow, when Tracey came up behind him and gave the officer "the foot." Both men then started to run from officer Geary. The policeman gave chase and caught the prisoner who resisted and called upon his friend to again try to assist him. Discretion being the better part of valor the 2nd man ran off. Patrolman Geary was then said to have *"tattooed"* the prisoners features in a most artistic manner with his club. The next morning the judge fined the prisoner $25.00, which he did not have, and who was then sentenced to three months in the County Penitentiary for his actions against the policeman.

But fate can be cruel. It was reported in the local news media that one evening in the winter of 1871 at about midnight, while on duty on his foot post and searching for a suspicious person in the neighborhood of the docks along the Hudson River, Geary lost his footing at the rivers edge and fell into the frigid water. Due to the freezing water temperature PO Geary was said to have developed a severe cold and lung problems which resulted in what was then thought to be "consumption," a term later associated with Tuberculosis. The report said he never recovered fully and remained in a weakened state. In fact about ten months later, with Geary still sick from the fall in the water, at a Police Board meeting on Sept 13, 1872 it was resolved that Martin Geary be allowed a leave of absence subject to order and advice of Police Surgeon J. Foster Jenkins, and that said time off be allowed at half pay. His physical health continued to decline and three months later, on Christmas morning of 1872, PO Martin Geary succumbed to his long illness and died in his residence on Riverdale Avenue at the age of only 25 years.

Though he was a police officer for only just over a year, as a sign of respect the police station was draped in black mourning cloth. It was apparent that officer Geary was considered a faithful and efficient officer. When a superior officer was asked to comment he stated that, "Geary was a sober and industrious citizen. And during the short period he was on the police force he exhibited his ability for the position in a

PO Martin Geary (cont.)

most marked manner." As an unusual gesture to their brother officer, the funeral, which was held at St Mary's Church, was paid for by his fellow officers.

Two years following his death, at a meeting of the Police Board held in March of 1874 his widow was approved to receive $25.00 every year from the Widows and Orphans fund.

(The facts surrounding this officers death raise an interesting question for debate; When Geary died it was 1871 and recognized medicine and medical diagnosis were not nearly as good as they are today. As an example, in the late 1800's one coroners inquest report, in explaining the likely death of a baby child from what we now refer to as SIDS, listed the cause of death as "Visitation from God." Not exactly fact specific. And in the case of officer Geary, x-ray's were not available for use until 1895. As such, in the case of officer Geary, x-ray's were not available as a definitive test of lung condition. Furthermore, it is even more interesting that the Police Board made the unusual decision of granting Geary a half pay Leave Of Absence, which seems to clearly imply they believed his illness was incurred from his line of duty accident. As such, given the state of questionable medical diagnostics at that time, it is entirely likely that Officer Geary actually developed pneumonia from his fall into the icy water and, having never recovered, pneumonia was what eventually caused his death. And if that were to be accepted as the likely cause of death, PO Martin Geary would then be the very first Yonkers Police officer to die from injury sustained in the Line of Duty).

PO MICHAEL MULDOON

APPOINTED: April 29, 1871
DISMISSED: September 20, 1871

On April 29, 1871 Mike Muldoon was one of seven new police officers hired by the department. He had previously worked at miscellaneous jobs throughout Yonkers. Patrolling on foot from the 9 Dock Street headquarters, Muldoon seemed to be frequently violating the department rules. On August 4, 1871 he was charged with Neglect of Duty and fined only one day's pay. But at a Police Board meeting on August 29, 1871 he was charged with gross negligence, sleeping on duty. He admitted he routinely took "a bit of a sleep," while on duty; one hour awake, one hour sleeping. He was found guilty and on September 20, 1871, after only 5 months as a police officer, Michael Muldoon was dismissed from the department. Many years later, on March 15, 1897, while eating his breakfast at his home at 140 Voss Avenue, Muldoon choked on his food and died. He was said to be 55 years old. He would never know it but his son, Thomas Muldoon, would later also be appointed a Yonkers police officer.

PO PATRICK MULDOON

APPOINTED: July 11, 1871
DISMISSED: November 21, 1874

The following was written in a local paper: *On July 29 1871 John Savage, a greenhorn, lately imported from the land where the grass grows green, while on Vineyard Ave. got drunk and proclaimed himself an advocate of civil order under mob rule. Ptl. Patrick Muldoon heard his carrying on and took him into custody. John was not content to submit to a cop's dictation and with a view to regain his freedom, he introduced his foot in a circular motion in an attempt to trip the officer. However the officer being perfectly sound on his feet sustained his equilibrium and brought his smiler [club] down on a soft part of John's knowledge box, which brought him down to mother earth. He did not give any more of his ideas of mob rule, but walked away quietly with the officer to the Dock St. H.Q. When brought for arraignment the judge complimented Savage on the spectacle he presented in the upper story. He also complimented the officer the artistic way in which he finished the picture. The prisoner was fined $10.* On September 5, 1873 Muldoon was reassigned to patrol from the Kingsbridge substation. Then on December 10, 1873 he returned to patrol duty from HQ. Following charges in Jan., Feb., March, June and ultimately in November, Muldoon was dismissed from the police department November 21, 1874.

ROUNDSMAN JAMES P. EMBREE

APPOINTED: July 11, 1871
RESIGNED: January 3, 1877

Following his appointment Patrolman Embree was assigned to routine patrol in the central portion of Yonkers until November of 1871 when he was detailed to patrol the southern portion of Yonkers in the section then known as Kingsbridge. On May 19, 1874 Embree was credited with making "a clever arrest" when he took into custody a male who had burglarized a home near Tuckahoe. The suspect was sentenced to one year in the penitentiary. On June 30, 1874 Embree was commended for arresting a suspect for attempted rape. The male was convicted and sentenced to 5 years. On August 19, 1874 Embree was chosen to take charge of our substation in the Bronxville section of east Yonkers and was promoted to Roundsman. He remained in charge of that rural substation until December 27, 1876, when he requested to be returned to patrol duties in the police headquarters area. His request was granted, however it also resulted in Embree being reduced in rank back to patrolman. For reasons that remain unknown, one week later, on January 3, 1877 officer James Embree submitted his resignation from our department.

PO RICHARD LAURIE

APPOINTED: July 11, 1871
DISMISSED: July 10, 1876

Richard Laurie was born in England about 1844 and sometime later immigrated to New York. When Laurie was appointed to our department at the age of 32 years, he was assigned to mounted patrol duty. During one of his tours of duty he was observed to be off his post by the Roundsman, and sitting down resting with his hat off. Charges of Neglect of Duty and Misconduct resulted in conviction and his dismissal from the department on April 30, 1874. However, it wasn't long before Laurie was rehired by the police department, this time as a Police Doorman. His duties were to clean the station house, drive the patrol wagon, and serve as the "Turnkey" or Jailer for prisoners. On March 30, 1876 Laurie received what he really wanted, and was again hired as a police officer. He was assigned to, and lived at, the Bronxville substation in east Yonkers. Despite his being given a second chance, Officer Laurie's frequent violations of departmental rules ultimately led to his permanent dismissal from the department on July 10, 1876.

PO SHERMAN H. SMITH

APPOINTED: July 11, 1871
RESIGNED: May 7, 1873

A Yonkers resident and former hatter, Sherman Smith was, on July 11, 1871, one of four men appointed to the "Yonkers Police Force," which had only been established three months earlier. He performed patrol duty from the Dock Street headquarters. On October 3, 1871 Charles L. Tinnis was arrested by officer Smith for felonious assault on Miss Sarah Carpenter on Nepperhan Avenue near School Street. For his crime Tinnis was sentenced to 5 years imprisonment in Sing Sing. The following month, on November 11, 1871, Smith was detailed to patrol from the Kingsbridge Sub Station in southern Yonkers. On May 7, 1872 Smith was charged and convicted of Neglect of Duty and was fined 3 days pay. Again he was charged, this time with being 7 minutes late for the 6 AM roll call on July 20, 1872 , and was fined 1 days pay. On May 3, 1873 he was charged with being AWOL for 4 hours. He must have said to himself, this is getting expensive. Whatever his thoughts were, before his trial and just four days later on May 7, 1873, PO Sherman Smith submitted his resignation in writing and which was accepted that same day.

RDSMN CORNELIUS WESTON

ASSIGNED: August 10, 1866
RESIGNED: April 24, 1871

Cornelius Weston had been appointed to the NYC Metropolitan Police as a Patrolman on April 5, 1865. Just over a year later, on August 10, 1866, Weston, who had been assigned to the NYC 32nd police precinct, along with several other officers, were detailed to the Village of Yonkers to provide professional police services. Being a trained mounted officer PO Weston continued patrolling on horseback while in Yonkers.

It didn't take long for Weston to prove his courage. On September 27, 1866 a group of children were returning home on the Hudson River from their annual picnic in Hastings on the barge the "Walter Sands." Seven year old John Harrigan accidentally fell overboard. Officer Weston, who was off duty and on the barge at the time, without hesitating jumped overboard to save the boy. Unfortunately, before he could reach him the child sank and drowned. The police blotter entry is said to have read; *"The officer exerted himself nobly to save the child but without effect."* However, he did recover the boy's body.

Apparently having displayed diligence in his police duties Cornelius Weston was promoted to the rank of Roundsman on July 22, 1867. But being a supervisor did not stop Weston from performing regular police duty. On December 24, 1867, Christmas Eve, Roundsman Weston arrested a male for shooting another male in the face below the left eye. The suspect shot the man in a saloon on Main St while in a quarrel over a game. Although the man was not critically injured the suspect was charged with felonious assault with intent to kill. He was convicted and served a year in the County Jail.

On Sunday January 16, 1870, an altercation referred to as the "Battle of the Glen" took place, the start of which began on Cromwell Pl. At about 4 PM while PO Woodruff was patrolling his "beat" on Pond St, he came upon some drunken men quarreling. He ordered them to disperse. Instead they resisted his orders and with the help of several friends from "The Glen," overpowered and knocked him to the ground and beat him. He was able to send word to the station for help and in a short while PO's Osborne & Boyd, who had responded to what was termed the "battleground," found a crowd of 100 or so infuriated men who, under the influence of liquor, had resolved to resist the officers.

The officers being greatly outnumbered were quickly overpowered, knocked to the ground, and beaten with stones and clubs. Word was again dispatched to headquarters for more aid as quick as possible. More help now arrived in the persons of Sgt Mangin, Roundsman Austin, Roundsman Cornelius Weston, and the remainder of the police reinforcements that were in reserve at the station house. When Sgt Mangin and his men arrived at the scene they found that the crowd had swelled to even greater numbers and was in fact a full scale riot. The Sgt remained undaunted. He was well experienced in dealing with situations of this type. Before being detailed to Yonkers he had fought and helped quell the NYC Civil War Draft Riots in which he was severely injured and many people were killed. Sgt Mangin quickly formed up his officers, gave the order, and with nightsticks swinging the men in blue charged into the riotous crowd. Their aggressive approach caused the group to break and start running. After a severe

Roundsman Cornelius Weston (cont.)

hand to hand fight in which stones, clubs, and mud flew, 11 of the rioters were captured, charged with Riot, and held in the Lock Up on $500. bail for arraignment the next day. All received substantial fines for their actions.

On April 10, 1871 the Village of Yonkers officially organized its own "Yonkers Police Force" and all the New York officers were given the opportunity to remain with the new department or return to New York. At a Board of Police Commissioners meeting held on April 24, 1871, Roundsman Cornelius Weston expressed the desire not to join Yonkers' new department, but wished to return to the NYC Municipal Police Dept. from which he had been detailed five years earlier. His request was granted and upon his return to New York he was assigned to the 32nd mounted police precinct.

In 1885 Cornelius Weston was still with the New York police department and had attained the rank of Sergeant.

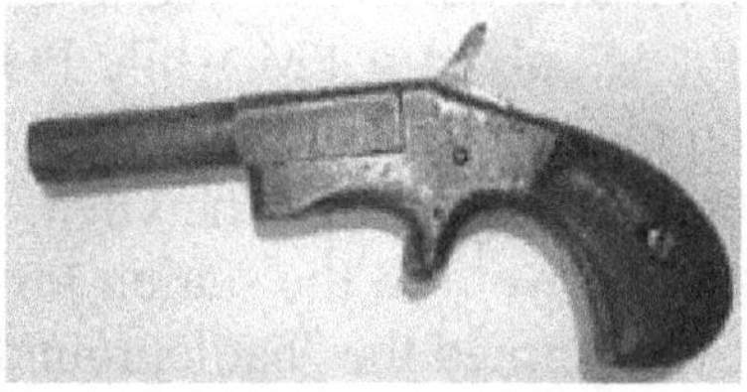

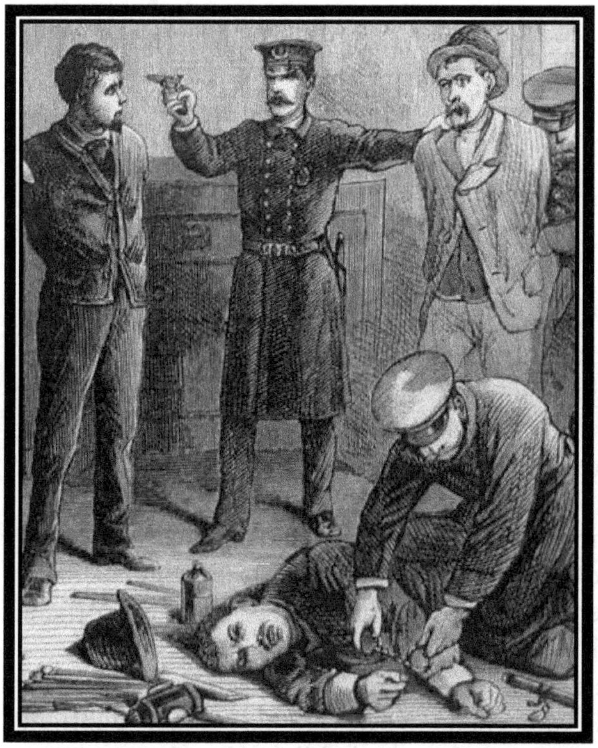

PTL. ALEXANDER STEVENSON

APPOINTED: September 20, 1871
RESIGNED: September 1, 1880

Alex Stevenson was born in Donegal, Ireland and at some point immigrated to the U.S. making his home at 12 Palisade Avenue in Yonkers. His great granddaughter, Margaret Prior, a resident of England in 2003, advised that he married and had five children. The 1870 Census report indicated that Alex, who lived at that time in NYC, was 30 years old, having been born in Ireland about 1840, he was a Printer, was married to Marjorie, also 30 years of age at the time, and at that point had one son, Thomas, who was 3 years old in 1870. A short time later Stevenson moved his family to Yonkers.

He was appointed to the Yonkers Police Department on September 20, 1871, just a few months following the department's organization, which took place on April 10th. Due to his skill as a good horseman he was usually assigned to mounted patrol duty. On one evening on August 8, 1874 Officer Stevenson arrested Mr. Charles Stevens after watching the man taking an impression of a lock on the hat store on North Broadway. The man was convicted and served two years in prison.

Though he was an efficient police officer there were strict rules and tough discipline to contend with. One case in point was on September 30, 1874 when a trial was held by the Board of Police Commissioners to hear charges filed against Stevenson for violation of Rule #34, in that on one occasion he had "Failed to Change The Sheets and Pillow Slips" in the police Reserve Quarters as directed. He was found guilty and fined one day's pay. Nonetheless, the record seems to imply that he was a dependable officer.

On one particular tour Officer Alexander Stevenson was walking his post along "The Flats" (Riverdale Avenue) in South Yonkers and actually enjoying his change of assignment. He usually worked mounted patrol but, on this only slightly warm night, he was enjoying the solitude. It was about 2:30 a.m. on the late tour, July 27, 1875. At this same moment, the home of Mr. Thomas Ludlow (yes, they named the street after him) was being burglarized as he slept. Mr. Ludlow heard a noise, awakened, saw a man in his bedroom and, thinking it was his nephew, said, "Tom, is that you?" At this the man in the room jumped out of the window. Realizing what had happened, Mr. Ludlow sent his gardener and his coachman to notify the police. On their way, they met Officer Mealing on horseback and explained to him what had just happened. Mealing blew his police whistle to attract the attention of any other officers who might be in the area. Roundsman Fred Woodruff and Officer Alex Stevenson, who were reasonably close enough to hear the alarm, responded. The Roundsman sent Mealing toward Mt. St. Vincent and Stevenson down toward the Hudson River Railroad to conduct a search for the suspect. Roundsman Woodruff proceeded to headquarters to call out all of the "reserve" police officers to assist in the search.

Hoping he would be lucky enough to locate the suspect, Officer Stevenson began his search in earnest. Around 3 a.m. he located three men, one of which was carrying a small suitcase, walking on the railroad tracks just below Vark Street. He took them into custody on "Suspicion" and ordered them to

PO Alexander Stevenson (cont.)

accompany him to the station house on Dock Street. Stevenson must have felt a sense of satisfaction as he grabbed the man with the bag by the collar and directed the other two to walk in front. (In these early years, not all police officers were issued or carried handguns, and most of those who did, carried their own. It is not known for sure, but it is likely that Stevenson was not armed.) As they were walking, Stevenson discovered that the male he was holding had a revolver and he took it from him and held it in his hand.

Officer Stevenson's lapse in judgment in not searching his prisoners was about to turn his "satisfaction" into stark fear. However, it should be made known that it was fairly routine to escort prisoners to headquarters without handcuffs because, generally, even criminals respected police officers and obeyed their orders. As the group approached Hawthorne Avenue, the two men who were walking in front abruptly turned and opened fire at the officer with their revolvers. Startled, but reacting instinctively, Stevenson returned fire with the confiscated weapon he held in his hand. However, this sudden "gunfight" caused him to drop the bag and loose his grip on the one prisoner he was holding. The three men ran toward the railroad tracks, covering their escape by continuing to fire at the officer while, at the same time, officer Stevenson returned fire at the three men in the deep pitch darkness of the night. All three escaped; fortunately no one was injured. Stevenson, no doubt soaked in perspiration from the warm summer air and his near brush with death, brought the revolver and the suspect's bag, which contained burglar tools, and extra revolver shell casings into H.Q. to make his report.

When Capt. of Police John Mangin heard what had happened he became extremely angry and ordered out the reserve officers on standby in headquarters and also all those who were off duty at home to report for duty and help search for the suspects by wagon or horseback and cover all probable means of exit from the city. Sometime between 5:00 a.m. and 6:00 a.m., P.O.s James McLaughlin and Patrick Whalen of the reserve platoon who had been out searching for suspects, located a male on the tracks of the Harlem Railroad near the Williamsbridge train station in the southern portion of Yonkers. Appearing suspicious due to the late hour the man was stopped and, having found him to be in possession of a revolver, he was arrested and returned to police H.Q. utilizing the police patrol wagon. During the investigation at HQ he was identified by officer Stevenson as one of the men who had shot at him earlier. In fact the shell casings recovered by PO Stevenson were said to have been of a very unusual pin head type configuration which matched the revolver found on the suspect by PO's McLaughlin and Whalen. At least they had one in custody. The next morning the suspect was taken to a local photography studio where his picture was taken and added to the ever growing Police Rogues Gallery of criminals.

Still angry that one of his officers was shot at and made good their escape, Capt. Mangin reportedly took personal charge of the interrogation of the prisoner. But despite his best efforts, aside from learning that the man's name was George Poxley a.k.a. Chris Pinto, the captain could learn nothing more of value regarding his accomplices. After several days of intense but fruitless "interviews" the prisoner was placed in the County Jail to await action by the Grand Jury. However the captain was not going to give up. He recruited a civilian to work undercover and pretend to be a prisoner. The man was placed in the county cell with Poxley and when he was leaving volunteered to carry a message from Poxley to his friends. Mangin's plan worked. Poxley gave the man a pair of sleeve buttons and directed him to go to a

PO Alexander Stevenson (cont.)

location at the corner of Houston and Wooster Streets in NYC and tell them he is a friend.

When the undercover arrived, at first he was rebuffed, but when they saw the sleeve buttons he was welcomed with open arms. They were eager to hear about Poxley's misfortune. During their talk the man learned that one of the accomplices in the Yonkers burglary was William J. Conroy, of Cold Spring, NY. After the shootout with PO Stevenson, Conroy made his escape by secreting himself on a Canal Boat at Lawrence's Dock. Another accomplice known only as "The Kid" escaped on a passing freight train. They all were a part of a notorious band of burglars and thieves known as the "Highland Brigands" the leader of which was a man named George Ellis.

When Ellis arrived at the gang's location, Captain Mangin and a sergeant were waiting, arrested him and brought him to Yonkers. Following an investigation it was learned that Ellis was wanted in Utica NY for a robbery. While Capt. Mangin was escorting Ellis to Utica handcuffed, and passing through the Highlands, Ellis feigned sickness and jumped from the train while traveling about 40 miles per hour. The captain had the train stopped and upon going back to where Ellis had jumped he found him with his head jammed through a picket fence. He was subsequently delivered to the authorities in Utica without further problem.

Upon the captains return to Yonkers and piecing all available information together it was learned that another member of the "Highland Brigands," Tom Scott, was under arrest in Charleston. The results of the arrest of George Poxley was as follows; The gang leader, George Ellis was sentence to 18 years; Tom Scott for 18 years; George Poxley, convicted of the Ludlow burglary, was sentenced to 15 years; William Conroy, cooperated with authorities and was not prosecuted. However, he was arrested a few months later for attempting to blow up a house in Kingston, NY, received a life sentence, and died in prison.

And thus, by the initial stop of three suspects by PO Stevenson, followed by the arrest of one of the burglars by Sgt. McLaughlin and PO Pat Whalen, and followed up by the skillful strategy of Capt. Mangin, one of the worst gangs that ever infested New York was broken up and most of its members sentenced to state prison.

Alex Stevenson's great granddaughter related that Officer Stevenson continued to serve the department efficiently for several more years when, unfortunately, an influenza virus struck the community and, tragically, his wife and two of his five children died as a result. Stevenson was devastated. With the long hours required by police service in those early years, similar to military life, he had spent very little time with his children. Without a mother for his children it is not unreasonable to assume that he wanted, in fact needed, to rectify that situation. It is believed that it was for this reason that he resigned his position with the YPD on September 1, 1880 and gained other employment which allowed greater time with his children. However, he did not remain a resident of Yonkers for very long. Upon examination of available Yonkers public records the name Alexander Stevenson last appeared in 1880 and never appeared again in future years. His great granddaughter related he moved, exact year unknown, back to Donegal, Ireland with his three children, Alexander Jr. the oldest, Scott, born in Yonkers October 31, 1878 (grandfather of Margaret Prior) and his daughter Marjorie (her married name would later be Reid) who was about 3 months old when they left the U.S. about 1881. It was there he purchased a farm where he would raise his children in the clean Irish air.

PO MICHAEL GEARY

APPOINTED: September 20, 1871
RESIGNED: July 21, 1873

If anyone ever seemed destined to be in a uniform, Mike Geary was that man. Born in Ireland about 1844, he came to the U.S. at the age of 7 years. Upon the outbreak of the Civil War Geary eagerly enlisted in the Army's "Meaghers Irish Brigade." He served in the Union Army for four years, and was wounded twice in action. Upon his discharge he must have found it difficult to find work or to adjust to civilian life for he soon joined the Navy. Then, upon completing his enlistment and receiving his Honorable Discharge, he then quickly joined the Marine Corps. from which he later was also honorably discharged. Upon his return to his home at 38 Jefferson St, he applied for and was appointed to our police dept., which had recently been organized. For two years he patrolled both the central business section of Yonkers and down in the Kingsbridge section. In anticipation of the annexation of Kingsbridge to NYC in 1874, Geary opted to transfer to the NYC Police Department where he remained until he reached retirement age. After retiring from the NYC Police Dept. he died while living in Yonkers on July 3, 1921 at the age of 77 years.

PO ALFRED NODINE

APPOINTED: November 29, 1872
RESIGNED: June 1874

Al Nodine no doubt started his career with the YPD with all good intentions. But he just couldn't keep out of trouble. He was frequently violating department rules. On Oct 22, 1873 he was fined 3 days pay. On November 22, 1873 he violated a rule and was fined 5 days pay. A second charge on that day cost him another 3 days. On Feb 20, 1874 he was again found guilty of a violation and fined 8 days pay. And on April 29, 1874 he was fined 4 days pay for neglect of duty. I'm sure he was thinking that his actions were getting very expensive. Around June of 1874 the Kingsbridge section of Yonkers was annexed to NYC and it believed that Nodine opted to switch to the New York department and resigned from the YPD.

PTL. JOHN HOULAHAN

APPOINTED: January 29, 1873
RESIGNED: September 5, 1880

John Houlahan was first appointed a Police Hostler (stable keeper) with the relatively new Yonkers Police Department on May 3, 1872. However, the following year, on January 29, 1873, due to the untimely death of Ptl. Martin Geary, John got his wish and was appointed a police officer with a yearly starting salary of $750. His apparent skill at horseback riding made him a good choice for mounted patrol duty, which is where he was assigned. He performed his duty with great reliability and several years passed without much notoriety.

Then on December 4, 1879, no doubt a cold and blustery night to be assigned to mounted patrol duty, at about 2:30 in the morning, officer Houlahan was patrolling what was then the very rural, yet exclusive, area of North Broadway near the lower gate leading into "Greystone," Samuel J. Tilden's estate. (Many years later this would become the property of Samuel Untermeyer, which included a large mansion and huge elaborate floral gardens.) As Houlahan approached the gate he saw a man, by his appearance apparently a tramp, sitting on a large bundle. Due to the late hour Houlahan became suspicious. As his horse came abreast of the man the officer asked him where he was from and what he had in the bundle. Not being satisfied with the man's answer PO Houlahan placed him under arrest for "Suspicion" and told him, "I want you to follow me to the station house."

As they both began to walk along North Broadway the suspect started walking faster, apparently hoping to put distance between him and the officer. Anticipating what might happen next Houlahan drew his revolver, displayed it to the man, and told him to be very careful and not to try to escape. Despite the warning the man dropped his bundle and ran in the darkness through the gate of another estate. The officer fired at the man, missing him, but fortunately the male ran straight into a stone wall in the dark, knocking him to the ground and leaving him slightly dazed. Houlahan dismounted, ran over to the suspect and as he attempted to restrain him, a struggle ensued. Houlahan, who was reportedly a stout, muscular man thought he could overcome his prisoner without resorting to violent measures, so he did not use his club or revolver. Just as the officer felt he was gaining control he felt a knife pierce his upper leg. At that point he realized he was in a deadly struggle and quickly clubbed the suspect several times with his revolver allowing himself to roll away and separate from the man. But in an instant the man lunged at the officer in the dark and slashed his face below the right eye. Once again they wrestled to the ground and in a desperate effort to disarm the man Houlahan grabbed the knife and was cut on his right palm.
Houlahan later reported that the suspect put up quite a struggle and they continued to fight out through the gate and onto North Broadway. It was there that officer Houlahan used his club to strike the man on his forehead, right above his eyes. Though he was stunned, the officer struck him several more times, breaking his club in the process.

His prisoner now pretty much under control, but with his leg, face, and hand bleeding and his uniform slashed in several places, officer Houlahan still had to get his prisoner to headquarters at 9 Dock Street. Fortunately he was able to wake a resident and have their hired man harness a horse and wagon and transport him and his prisoner to a cell at headquarters. Upon arrival at the station house the man was recognized by the desk sergeant as a tramp named Daniel Breen, 45 years, homeless and a frequent

PTL. John Houlahan (cont.)

resident of the Yonkers “Lock up.” The police surgeon, J. Foster Jenkins, was called and treated the officers wounds which turned out to be not life threatening. However, the prisoner was not so fortunate and required hospitalization for the multiple wounds to his head.

The weapon used by the prisoner was a large jack-knife and was stained all over with officer Houlahan’s blood. The bundle carried by the “tramp” was found to contain, 3 women’s dresses, 1 overcoat and 1 dress coat, a pair of pants, a skirt, a razor and brush, and a box half full of cigars. Later that morning it was learned that the property recovered had been stolen earlier that same morning from a lager beer-saloon and lodging-house in Hastings on Hudson. The prisoner was charged with burglary and grand larceny. His arraignment on the charges had to be delayed until the prisoner was well enough to be released from the hospital. (There was no mention of a charge of assaulting a police officer.)

It appears apparent that officer Houlahan was a very alert and conscientious officer as he had made two other burglary arrests earlier that same week. In fact on December 3, 1879 at a meeting of the Police Board Houlahan was commended for his fine work in the arrest of two burglars on Nov 27, 1879 in South Yonkers “where his life was in danger.” The circumstances of this arrest were as follows; On Nov 27, 1879 at 2:15 AM while on foot patrol in south Yonkers, officer Houlahan saw two suspicious men in a wagon exit rapidly from a side street. Jumping out in front of them he stopped them and questioned them as to their purpose at that hour. However, they provided no satisfactory answers. A quick search of the wagon produced a hatchet and a large crowbar. Houlahan arrested both men on "Suspicion" and brought them to headquarters and placed them in the “Lock Up.” Following up with an investigation the next morning, he discovered a burglary had occurred right where the two prisoners had left the scene the night before and he also found a loaded revolver which, fortunately for Houlahan, the two men had apparently dropped when they saw the officer approaching them.

The local newspaper was impressed and reported that, due to his bravery and attention to duty, PO Houlahan was entitled to special consideration and honor for his courage and faithfulness. This was an excellent idea. However an award system was not to be instituted in the police department for many years to come. However, in recognition of his alert actions the Police Board raised Houlahan’s salary to $1,000. per year. At the very next Board meeting held on Dec 8, 1879 Houlahan was again commended by the Police Board for another arrest he made only days earlier on Dec 4, 1879. On this occasion Houlahan arrested another burglar by whom the Board reported “his life was imperiled, exhibiting great courage and commendable self-control.” Again in recognition of the officer’s fine work the Police Board once again voted to raise the officer’s salary, this time to the rate of $1,200. per annum effective December 1, 1879.

One might think that officer Houlahan was on his way to an exceptional career. And yet, the following year, on September 15, 1980, police officer John Houlahan was charged with Neglect of Duty which occurred on September 5, 1880. The particulars of the charges are unknown but, as was procedure, Houlahan was required to sign and acknowledge service and notification of the complaint. Apparently extremely indignant over having charges brought against him that he no doubt felt were completely unfounded, he refused to sign the acknowledgment form. And, apparently having no intention of being brought to trial by the Board of Police Commissioners he reportedly walked into headquarters, placed his shield upon the front desk in front of the desk sergeant, and walked out of the door and never returned. Because he did not submit a formal letter of resignation he was deemed dismissed from the Yonkers Police Department effective September 15, 1880.

PO GIDEON C. REYNOLDS # 1

APPOINTED: July 21, 1873
RETIRED: December 1, 1901

Patrolman Gideon Cogswell Reynolds, known to all of his friends as "Gid," was born in New Rochelle on September 29, 1836. He was appointed to the Yonkers Police Department on July 21, 1873 during the time when plans were being made to annex the south Yonkers areas of Kingsbridge and Spuyten Duyvil to NYC. The following month, on August 18, 1873, officer Reynolds and four other officers were detailed to patrol duty in the Kingsbridge substation area. However, upon the annexation of that portion of Yonkers to NYC around June of 1874, and giving those officers the option to remain with the NYC Metropolitan Police, Reynolds decided to continue as a Yonkers officer and returned to duty at the Yonkers headquarters.

A resident of 91 Palisade Ave, Reynolds was assigned to mounted patrol in the rural areas of east Yonkers as well as down to the new Town of Kingsbridge. It was reported that he often worked the steady night patrol. In his early years it was said that he was quite a baseball player with the Yonkers police team. In the mid 1890's while making an arrest, Reynolds was stabbed in the groin. Even so, it was said he never let go of his prisoner and beat the man unconscious with his stick. Reynolds worked out of the 9 Dock St. headquarters for 25 years. In 1898 when the new Wells Avenue H.Q. was built, he spent only three years there, and then retired in 1901. After retiring he worked as a "special policeman" watching over various parks in the city. Gideon C. Reynolds died May 11, 1909 at age 72 years.

DET. WILLIAM B. CARROLL

APPOINTED: July 21, 1873
RETIRED: December 31, 1906

The record clearly indicates that Bill Carroll was one of those people who made a mark in history that is worthy of reflection. He distinguished himself as an outstanding Yonkers police officer who, no doubt, relied on his military experience and background of discipline to be as successful as he was as a police officer.

Born October 23, 1844 in Haverstraw NY, as a teenager Carroll moved to West Farms, N.Y. (Now part of the Bronx) He gained employment there as a laborer. While still a resident of West Farms, Bill Carroll was quick to enlist when the Civil War began. He joined Company "C" of the NY 135th Volunteer Infantry Regiment known as the "Anthony Wayne Guards," as a private and later transferred to the 6th Regiment, Heavy Artillery. Records indicate that this regiment served in several large battles. In 1907 in an article written by the New York Evening Telegram it was reported that, "In this regiment Carroll repeatedly distinguished himself by his intrepid conduct. He was again and again commended for conspicuous gallantry in action." The official record indicated that they lost 130 enlisted men killed in action and 275 enlisted men died of disease.

Years later as the local newspaper was recounting Carroll's career, they reported that he had participated in the campaigns in, Fredericksburg, Chancellorsville, Gettysburg, The Wilderness, Spotsylvania Court House, North Annbold Harbor, Petersburg, Five Forks, and several other engagements. On February 26, 1864 Carroll was promoted to Corporal, and on March 11, 1865 he was promoted to Sergeant. Carroll's grandson, Tom, related that his grandfather, who stood only 5' 8" tall with bright blue eyes, was really a "tough" individual. That, on many occasions in the Army, in order to maintain control and obedience from his men, he had to fight the toughest man in the platoon.

Sgt. Carroll was discharged from the Union Army on June 28, 1865 and mustered out at St. Petersburg, Virginia. Along with his discharge, Carroll carried with him several medals awarded him for his actions during the war. Carroll secured a horse and it took him 30 days to return to West Farms, NY. Though unconfirmed, his family claims that it was then that he joined the NYC Metropolitan Police Dept. However, what we do know is that upon his discharge he returned and lived in West Farms from 1865 to 1869. While there he served as a volunteer fireman as an Assistant Foreman with Volunteer Company "Alert #2."

In 1869 he moved to Yonkers and originally lived at 34 Ingram Street, and later at #18. Once again, having a desire to help people, he served as a volunteer fireman in Yonkers with Protection Engine Co. #1. Carroll joined the Yonkers Police Dept. on July 21, 1873 and quickly gained a reputation as being a hard and tough, no nonsense cop. The daily newspaper of the day reported that one of the arrests that first marked Carroll as a policeman of exceptional efficiency was his arrest of James Downey, alias "Fat Legs," whose bold burglaries had terrorized the city. Shortly after Downey had burglarized the home

Det. William B. Carroll (cont.)

of John Spawn of Hastings on Hudson information was developed that Downey was the prime suspect and while in Yonkers he was located and arrested by PO Bill Carroll. Following his investigation officer Carroll had collected information tending to implicate "Fat Legs" in the burglaries of seven homes in Yonkers. Downey was convicted and sent to Sing Sing Prison for several years.

In another high profile arrest Officer Carroll arrested a man described in the newspapers of the day as the "one of the most notorious desperadoes in the annals of crime in this country." Rumors had it that the man had killed at least one man and wounded several others. The incident occurred in 1885 and the suspect, "Bill" Mason, was wanted in connection with a daring burglary of a home in Dobbs Ferry. A search was began for Mason in most of the cities and towns along the Hudson River. Then, early one Sunday morning, Mason reportedly appeared in Yonkers. The local press reported that, "The terror which this criminal inspired was so great that it was said that more than one policeman who saw him here did not dare to molest him. While yet another who ventured to effect a capture was frightened off when Mason drew his revolver." But when "Bill" Carroll learned that Mason was in town, Carroll went looking for him. It didn't take long. At the intersection of Warburton Avenue and Dock Street the two men met. When Carroll stopped him and asked, "Where are you going?" Mason ignored the question and unknowingly had met his match. Backing down to no man, the officer reached out, grabbed Mason and placed him under arrest. As he did, the man, whose right hand was in his coat pocket holding a gun, fired right through his pocket at the officer. Fortunately the bullet missed Carroll and just passed through the officer's coat. Without even using his stick or revolver, the burly officer grabbed Mason before he could fire again and disarmed and arrested him. The fearsome Bill Mason received 14 years in prison for the Dobbs Ferry burglary, but was never charged for attempting to kill the officer.

Lest one think "Bill" Carroll took life too serious it should be pointed out that in the spring of 1891then Sergeant McLaughlin formed the very first Yonkers Police Baseball Team. And, of course, where ever action was to be, so was Carroll. He tried out for the team and was quickly picked as a starter because of his aggressiveness on the field and his ability to regularly hit the ball over the fence. Along with being noted for being a power hitter, Carroll handled center field while defending and performed equally well.

On August 23, 1891 Carroll came very close to being killed by a burglar. It was about 8:30 PM that Sunday evening, which was a rainy and stormy night, and two gentlemen were standing on the northeast corner of Warburton Ave and Wells Ave in conversation. It was then that one of the men, P.J. Mitchell, who owned the saloon across the street on the south east corner of Wells and Warburton Avenue, noticed that the light he had left on in his establishment suddenly went out. Upon investigation he was confronted by a known burglar named John Faulds trying to leave by the rear door. When he stopped the thief a struggle ensued and the suspect quickly gave up. However, as they started their journey to police headquarters the suspect pulled out a revolver and yelled at Mitchell, "If you don't let me go I'll blow your brains out." Of course, Mitchell let go, the man broke free and he made his escape through the property of Philipse Manor Hall across the street. When Mr. Mitchell reported the incident to Capt. Mangin, the captain sent out a few officers to look for Faulds.

Det. William B. Carroll (cont.)

One officer, Bill Carroll, went to the suspect's home on Elm Street near Nepperhan Avenue to await the suspect's probable return. He didn't have to wait long. As the officer hid in the hall, the suspect entered and PO Carroll stopped him and said, "Is that you, John?" When the man said yes, Carroll said, "I want you," took hold of Faulds and started walking toward headquarters. It is not known why but, for some reason, officer Carroll did not search or handcuff his prisoner. A possible explanation was, in those early years most prisoners submitted to an officers orders without question. In any event, as they approached the Carpet Shop factory at Elm and Palisade Avenue, the suspect stopped, spun around and pointed his revolver at the officer, and with a curse shouted, "Let me go." At that same time he fired two shots at point blank range at officer Carroll. The first round passed through the officer's hat and grazed Carroll's scalp. The second passed directly under the officer's arm. Though this happened in an instant, before another shot could be fired, PO Bill Carroll's nightstick whizzed through the air with lightning speed, striking the man's head and stunning the man momentarily. But as the officer tried to disarm the man a violent struggle began in an attempt to retrieve the weapon. Officer Carroll was ultimately successful in disarming the man and bringing him to the Dock Street headquarters where he was booked on charges of burglary and attempted murder of the police officer.

Of course, these are just a few incidents in an enviable police career filled with arrests and both efficient and excellent police work, performed by a no nonsense street wise cop. In fact, considering the large number of arrests and crimes solved by him throughout his career, it is no surprise that Bill Carroll is believed to be the very first Yonkers police officer to be designated a "Detective." This was a very highly prestigious position coveted by many, but given to few. However, no increase in salary was provided with this new position.

By 1899 PO Bill Carroll had 26 years with the department and was assigned to the Hudson River Railroad. It was during the month of February of this year that PO Carroll made an arrest up in Ulster County for a murder which took place in the Village of Tarrytown, NY on February 18, 1899. According to reports, Carroll, whose outstanding reputation as an excellent detective was known throughout the county, was requested by the Tarrytown police to be detailed to assist in locating a Mr. Harrison Howard who was wanted for killing a man in a saloon brawl in that village. Det. Carroll quickly tracked the man to a brickyard in Kingston N.Y. and made the arrest. The suspect was subsequently sentenced to seven years for manslaughter.

On May 15, 1899, while appearing as a witness in county court in the trial of this prisoner, the officer was approached by officials from the Village of Tarrytown. In an effort to pay tribute and express their appreciation for his assistance, they presented PO Carroll with a neatly engrossed set of resolutions bearing the seal of the village, which thanked him for the aid rendered to their chief.

By 1906 rheumatism was reportedly causing the now 225 pound officer great discomfort. He decided he would retire on the last day of the year. On December 31, 1906 PO "Bill" Carroll completed his tour of duty and returned to the station house. As he entered the front door he was greeted by the Police Commissioners and every member of the police department. When the welcoming commotion quieted down, Captain Of Police Frederick Woodruff stood behind the desk and, calling out the retiring officer's name, made the following remarks:

Det. William B. Carroll (cont.)

"Your comrades, associates and friends in this department, and everyone present here tonight is your friend, and sincerely regret that they are about to lose your companionship and assistance as a member of this force. When a young man, you became a member of this department, after having previously served your country, with courage and faithfulness, and you have devoted your entire younger days to a faithful, efficient and honest discharge of your public duty, and now near the close of an honorable career, we are gathered here tonight to greet you and give evidence of our good will and friendship.
"Your side partners remember, as no others can, the valuable aid and assistance you have given them many times in cases of importance and danger.
"The activity of your life in the public defense is well exemplified in your honorable discharge from the army for services rendered during the darker days of the Great Rebellion, and in you active and honorable service as a volunteer fireman in this city, which, coupled with your praiseworthy record as a police officer, indicate a strenuous life spent in support of your country and state, for which you may justly feel proud.
"You leave us tonight as an active member of this department with the regret of your superiors, the Board of Police Commissioners of the City of Yonkers, and with the regard and regrets of all of your associates and comrades, and with honor to yourself and to the police department of the city.
"As a further expression of our esteem and respect, I now present you with this set of resolutions and with this bouquet of thirty-three carnations, each of which represents a year you have spent in the service of this department."

After a few moments of shaking hands with fellow officers and other well-wishers, Bill Carroll quietly turned in his police equipment; shield, hat wreath, revolver, etc., and simply walked home.

The large framed print that Carroll received containing those special resolutions was 3 ½' x 2' in size and was beautifully designed and placed in a wood gilt frame. It also contained the names of every member of the police department, sworn and civilian, written in script. (This large certificate is now on display, on loan, to the Yonkers Police Museum.) During his retirement years his grandson, Tom Carroll, related that his grandfather carried a cane as he walked around the city. The cane was completely enclosed in leather rings from top to bottom. What was not so apparent was that beneath the leather rings the cane was made from solid lead, top to bottom. One can only speculate as to its purpose. (This, too, is on display in the museum.) In 1908 his son in law, James Garahan, was appointed a Yonkers police officer.

Now referred to affectionately as "Old Bill" Carroll, he was only able to enjoy his retirement for five years. For on December 6, 1911 this well respected gentleman of the community, and a police legend during his time in the police department, died at the age of 67 in his home at 18 Ingram Street after a lengthy illness. But men like him should never be forgotten.

ROUNDSMAN JOSEPH JOHNSTONE

APPOINTED: August 18, 1873
DIED: March 3, 1894

Joseph E. Johnstone was born on April 9, 1846 in that area of the Town and Village of "south" Yonkers, at that time identified as the area of Kingsbridge. His family moved to Yonkers proper when he was two years old and he received his formal education in the public school system.

As a young man Joseph worked a variety of different jobs to help support his wife and children. After giving long thought to the field of police work he submitted the appropriate "blanks," (applications) to the board of police commissioners. At a meeting of the board on August 18, 1873 Johnstone was voted as accepted and given the oath of office. He was directed to immediately report to headquarters for duty that same night. As one might guess, since the police department was only two years old there was little structure or training. However, the police commissioners had previously voted to adopt and have all officers abide by the rules and regulations of the Metropolitan Police Dept. which had patrolled Yonkers from 1866 to 1871.

News reports of the day described Johnstone as *"physically wiry and muscular, quick of observation and prompt in action. He could soon give an obstreperous prisoner a practical demonstration that resistance is useless."* But in addition to his physical prowess Joseph was an intelligent and educated man. He was reported to be "an expert at telegraphing and understood thoroughly the intricate operation of the police telegraph system." Johnstone was also said to be a fine penman and accountant which enabled him to do much of the clerical work at headquarters when needed.

Three years following his appointment he had proven himself to his superiors and was promoted to the rank of Roundsman on December 27, 1876. He was then assigned to, and placed in charge of, the police substation in the section of Yonkers known as Bronxville, located on 'Swain Street' near the Croton Aqueduct. He lived with his wife and 3 children right in the substation. He was a mounted officer who patrolled the eastern portion of Yonkers on horseback. He would later return to duty from the Dock Street headquarters. He was a Free Mason and he was a brother to Yonkers PO Richard M. Johnstone.

At one point Johnstone began complaining of stomach pain and cramps. Police surgeon Dr. Benedict examined him and prescribed a potion for gas. That night, on March 3, 1894 at 3 AM, Johnstone again had severe pain but before any action could be taken he died right in his home at 258 New Main Street. Following an inquest and post mortem it was determined that Roundsman Johnstone had died as a result of a blood clot in his heart. He was only 47 years old.

Because he was always so friendly, civil and obliging, he had many friends within and outside the police department that were shocked by his sudden and unexpected death and which caused great sadness. His funeral was attended in great numbers by civilians and police alike and the police department sent a floral arrangement of roses and carnations in the shape of a Roundsman's shield which was 4' high. Who knows what his future might have held for him!

PO LAWRENCE R. BERRIAN

APPOINTED: August 18, 1873
RESIGNED: April 1, 1881

Believed to have been a Civil War veteran, Berrian was born about 1845. From the day he was appointed in 1873, Lawrence "Claude" Berrian was viewed as a hardworking, conscientious and respected member of our department. He was proud to be a police officer and was always neat in appearance while on patrol duty. On one occasion, he and officer Henry Quinn made a courageous burglary arrest of three suspects. The Board of Police Commissioners were so impressed, they presented both officers with embossed and framed resolutions of commendation at a roll call where the entire department was ordered to be present. Unfortunately, for unknown reasons, Berrian's health began to fail. On March 31, 1881 the local news papers reported that *"due to illness, 'Claude Berrian,' a mounted policeman for eight years, thinks it prudent to resign."* The esteem in which Berrian was held was such that, upon his resignation the Police Board presented Berrian with yet another very flattering embossed resolution, commending him on his valuable contributions and honorable service to our department.

PO CHARLES L. ANDERSON

APPOINTED: July 29, 1874
DISMISSED: January 31, 1885

Charles Lewis Anderson was born in July of 1842. Following his appointment he was assigned to foot patrol on various posts. But according to news accounts he seemed to have trouble getting along with a number of his fellow officers. In particular, there was bad blood between him and PO Henry Cooley. Over several years each filed complaints against the other. In one incident it was reported that Anderson approached a news reporter and related a story about Cooley, that proved to be untrue, that seriously reflected on officer Cooley's character. Though Anderson claimed it to be fact, the reporter had doubts and didn't print it. When Henry Cooley discovered what Anderson tried to do, he filed a complaint with Capt. John Mangin. The charge was taken very seriously and Anderson was brought up on departmental charges by the Police Board. Following a hearing Anderson was found guilty and with eleven years service, was dismissed from the department on January 31, 1885. In May of 1986 Anderson filed an appeal to be reinstated to the department and his case was heard before the State Supreme Court in Poughkeepsie. His appeal was denied. A resident of 101 Palisade Avenue, Charles Anderson returned to his former occupation as a carpenter and died in Yonkers in 1918 at 76.

PO PATRICK P. WHALEN

APPOINTED: July 1, 1874
DISMISSED: January 5, 1876

Patrick Whalen was appointed to the department on July 1, 1874, completed his oath of office, and was directed to report for duty that same night. Later that year on September 30, 1874 PO Stevenson arrested two men for committing a burglary. While walking them to headquarters they broke away and fired at the officer from a gun they had hidden and made their escape.

When Capt. of Police John Mangin heard what had happened he became extremely angry and ordered out the reserve officers on standby in headquarters and also all those who were off duty at home to report for duty and help search for the suspects. They were to search by wagon or horseback and cover all probable means of exit from the city. Sometime between 5:00 a.m. and 6:00 a.m., officers Patrick Whalen and Jim McLaughlin of the reserve platoon, who had both been out searching for suspects, located a male on the tracks of the Harlem Railroad near the Williamsbridge train station in the southern portion of Yonkers. Appearing suspicious due to the late hour the man was stopped and, having found him to be in possession of a revolver, the suspect was arrested and returned to police H.Q. utilizing the police patrol wagon. During the investigation at HQ he was identified by officer Stevenson as one of the men who had tried to kill him by shooting at him earlier. In fact the shell casings recovered at the scene by PO Stevenson were said to have been of a very unusual type firing pin configuration which matched the revolver found on the suspect by PO's Whalen and McLaughlin. At least they had arrested one of the men who was ultimately convicted and sentenced to prison.

Yet, only two months later, on November 21, 1874, Patrolman Whalen was charged with violation of rule #146, found guilty and fined 5 days pay. On May 5, 1875 Whalen was again charged with violation of rule # 146, found guilty and fined 7 days pay.

On December 19, 1875 officer Whalen was assigned to mounted patrol duty. During the tour when the Roundsman checked on officer Whalen he found him making himself comfortable in the kitchen of a house on his patrol route. When the Roundsman went to the front door, he reported that Whalen jumped out a rear window and ran off. Officer Whalen no doubt knew that if he was caught neglecting his duty, the penalty would be severe. But his attempt to keep from being detected failed. He was subsequently charged with being absent from his post. During his departmental trial on December 29th, and 30th, 1875, and while under oath, Whalen lied about his actions while on post, but then confessed; thereby admitting to perjury. He was found guilty and dismissed from the police department effective January 5, 1876.

SGT. RICHARD E. WILCOX

APPOINTED: November 21, 1874
RETIRED: August 17, 1901

Richard Ebitts Wilcox was born in New York City in the year believed to have been 1838. In 1847 he was brought by his parents to Yonkers to live when he was 9 years of age. At that time Yonkers was only a very small unincorporated village consisting mostly of farm land. Wilcox grew up along with Yonkers, watching it grow into a city a great deal larger than when he arrived. He attended local schools but his father died at an early age so Wilcox stopped his schooling at age 14 in order to work and help support the family.

As a young man Wilcox learned the grocery business and was employed by the old "Clipper Works" in the Ludlow section of Yonkers. Apparently an energetic and public spirited man, he joined the Exempt Fireman's Benevolent Association and served as a volunteer fireman with the Lady Washington Hose Company and then helped organize the Hudson Hose Company. In the early 1860's during the Civil War it was reported that Wilcox had enlisted in the Army but for some unknown reason served for only a few months. At the age of 38 he applied for, and was appointed to, the police department on November 21, 1874. When the department discovered he was an excellent horseman he was immediately assigned to mounted patrol duty. Though he was kept very busy working long hours as a police officer, PO Wilcox continued to serve as a volunteer fireman and was even authorized to run with the Hose Cart to all reported fires. In fact he would remain a volunteer fireman throughout his police career. Yet, with all this, he still found time to be an active member of the Yonkers Police baseball team, often competing with the Yonkers fireman and other local teams.

It seems rather clear that officer Wilcox was an efficient policeman. The record indicates that at a Board of Police Commissioners meeting held on January 19, 1881, a resolution was adopted which read as follows: *"Resolved - That the vigilance of Patrolman Richard Wilcox in apprehending and arresting the burglar James Johnson on the morning of January 12th, is earnestly commended by this board. That in recognition of officer Wilcox's action, an action exhibiting praiseworthy fidelity to duty, as well as efficiency and bravery in execution, it is ordered that this resolution be promulgated at the several roll calls next ensuing."*

It is apparent that he displayed a keen ability to get the job done, and as a result he was promoted to Roundsman on July 13, 1892. Again, this time as a patrol supervisor, he must have proved to his superiors to be very effective. As a result, on February 12, 1898 he was then promoted to the rank of Sergeant, one of only four and the second highest rank in the department. Having served with distinction for nearly 27 years, on August 17, 1901 the Board of Police Commissioners officially retired Sgt. Richard Wilcox due to his age having exceeded 60 years.

In his retirement Wilcox worked for many years as a guard for the Westchester Trust Company Bank in Yonkers. While at work at the bank on October 15, 1912 Wilcox was stricken, collapsed, and died before an ambulance could respond. A resident of 178 Warburton Avenue, he was 74 years of age.

PO SAMUEL L. HANLEY

APPOINTED: December 16, 1874
DISMISSED: January 29, 1876

Little is known about Samuel Hanley until he received his appointment to the "police force" on December 16, 1874. He had earlier submitted his application and was called to appear before the police board that day. On that afternoon during the board meeting he was administered the oath of office as "police officer" and ordered to report for duty that same night at the 6 PM roll call. On January 25, 1876 officer Hanley was suspended from duty and brought up on charges for allegedly being intoxicated on duty on his foot Post on Dock Street; the same street headquarters was located. Four days later, on January 29, 1876, the Board of Police met and was prepared to begin the trial against Hanley when they acknowledged receipt of his resignation in writing from the Police Force. Apparently Hanley knew he would be found guilty and would rather have resigned than face dismissal. However the police board chose to ignore his attempted resignation, held the trial without him, found him guilty and dismissed him from the Force that same day.

PO WILLIAM BANKS

APPOINTED: February 18, 1875
DISMISSED: November 25, 1876

Little or no background is known of Bill Banks, but his application to the Yonkers Police Board was approved and he was appointed to the police department on February 18, 1875. Bill walked various foot posts on the west side of the city and the first few months were good However, on June 2, 1875 Banks was convicted of violating departmental rules and fined 6 days pay. On September 2nd of that same year he was again fined, this time 10 days pay. On October 19, 1875 Banks arrested a male as a "suspicious person" and it was later learned that the male was a thief who had burglarized a Yonkers home some time earlier stealing jewelry. He was convicted and served four years in the Albany prison. Throughout 1876 Banks was charged with violating the rules at least four times and fined each time. Finally, on October 25, 1876 Banks was charged with Neglect of Duty by being missing from his post without explanation, and for deportment towards his superior altogether unbecoming a police officer. He was immediately suspended until further notice. The following month, following a departmental trial, Patrolman William Banks was found guilty of all charges and the Board of Police Commissioners dismissed him from the department that day, November 25, 1876.

PO JAMES J. McGOWAN # 10

APPOINTED: March 30, 1876
DISMISSED: December 8, 1897

Born in 1844, McGowan was one of our earlier mounted police officers. From available records he appeared to be an efficient police officer and, in the 1890's, was active in playing on the police baseball team. He was in his 21st year with the department when his wife died in March of 1897 leaving him a widower with six children and all the problems inherent in raising them alone. It was later that year on December 4, 1897 that his sergeant reported that he had seen McGowan returning from duty in an intoxicated condition. Further, that when McGowan entered H.Q. he failed to salute the desk sergeant. After charges and a trial, and having served faithfully for 21 years, McGowan was found guilty and dismissed from the force December 8, 1897. McGowan always claimed he was innocent and, in fact, 14 years later, in June of 1911, after successfully pleading his case, the Yonkers Common Council sent a request to Albany to allow James McGowan to have his case re-heard in an attempt to secure pension payments for him. The results of those efforts are unknown. McGowan died April 17, 1917 at the age of 73 years.

PO THEODORE F. MULLER

APPOINTED: July 10, 1876
DIED: August 5, 1883

Born in NYC about 1853 and after spending his youth on Long Island, Theodore F. Muller came to Yonkers about 1873, moved into an apartment on Prospect Street, and opened up his own butcher shop. Apparently an energetic young man determined to make a good living for himself Muller also opened a grocery store. But then he began to think about the police department. On July 10, 1876 he was hired by the Y.P.D. at the age of 23 years with a salary of $800. per year. Following his probation period, on January 13, 1877 his salary was raised to $1,200. per year. After serving honorably for seven years, on August 1, 1883 Muller became ill and took 5 days leave to rest and gain his health back. Rest would do him no good. On August 5, 1883, Theodore Muller died, reportedly from typhoid fever at the age of 31 years and leaving behind a wife and two children. Muller was described by his captain as, *"a good officer, loyal to the trusts and faithful to the duties imposed upon him by his superiors, and a true type of that material out of which good policemen are made."*

PO WILLIAM M. HATFIELD

APPOINTED: December 1, 1876
RESIGNED: January 3, 1877

William M. Hatfield was born in the United States around 1850, was single, and around the age of 26 years he was accepted for appointment to the Yonkers Police Department on December 1, 1876. Records indicated that his starting salary was $800 a year, which was a bit higher than the usual $750. There are no available records about his service, and one explanation might be is that it was so brief. About a month after his appointment officer Hatfield, for unknown reasons, submitted his resignation effective January 3, 1877. It is not known what he did following his police service however it is believed he was reasonably successful. For, in September of 1886 he was serving as a member of the Yonkers Police Board of Police Commissioners.

PO HENRY L. HILLMAN

APPOINTED: January 13, 1877
RESIGNED: August 24, 1878

Not much is known of the early years of Henry Hillman but it is known that he is believed to have been born in the U.S. about 1847. At the age of 29 years he was approved and appointed a Patrolman in the Yonkers Police Department on January 13, 1877. But Hillman ran into trouble quickly. On May 16, 1877 he was convicted of violating departmental rules and fined 2 days pay. The following month on June 27th he was again fined 2 days pay. He also violated the rules in July and September of 1877. On July 18, 1878 Hillman was again convicted of rule violations and prior to his trial was required to attended the School of Instruction, re-training, with a reduction in pay from $1,000 to $800. During his trial, which was held on August 24, 1878, Patrolman Hillman likely knew the outcome and abruptly submitted his resignation as a police officer effective that same day.

PO JAMES T. NOLAN #4

APPOINTED: January 13, 1877
RETIRED: October 31, 1913

James Nolan was born in County Kerry Ireland in 1850, and arrived in the United States with his parents when he was 8 years old. Upon joining the still very young Yonkers Police Department he was assigned to work foot patrol from the original Dock Street headquarters. He would remain there until the new headquarters was built on Wells Avenue and opened in 1898. Still later, when a substation #2 was opened on Central Avenue in 1901, as a senior man with over 20 years service, he was reassigned there to patrol the more rural east side of the city. And he was still there when this station became the 2nd precinct in May of 1908, and remained until his retirement on October 31, 1913. Nolan served honorably for 36 years and at his last roll call the men of the 2nd precinct presented him with a "Meerscham" smoking pipe along with plenty of tobacco. Seven years later, on September 12, 1920, retired PO James Nolan died in his home at 174 Palisade Avenue at age 70 years.

PO JOSEPH W. ARCHER

APPOINTED: August 28, 1873
RESIGNED: July 15, 1882

Joseph Warren Archer was born in Yonkers on July 7, 1853. Having applied to be a policeman Archer received his appointment on August 28, 1878, at the age of 23 years, and began horseback mounted patrol duties from the 9 Dock Street station house. But, less than four months later he was charged with violation of a departmental rule, convicted and fined one days pay. He apparently was careful after that, for two years. Then on July 21, 1880 he was charged with Neglect of Duty, found guilty and fined five days pay and removed from mounted duty and reduced to walking a foot post. He was fined another days pay on October 19, 1881, suspended for a month and ordered back to duty November 3, 1881. And in a news article on January 5, 1882 it was reported that he had broken a leg without mentioning the circumstances. The extent of his leg injury nor his feelings about the department at that time are unknown. However, it wasn't very long before he submitted his resignation to the police board which was accepted effective July 15, 1882. Joseph Archer died February 23, 1939 in Hackensack, NJ.

PO JAMES G. TICE #4

APPOINTED: July 2, 1879
RETIRED: June 1, 1900

Born August 20, 1846 in Ulster County, NY, James Tice was a veteran and member of the Grand Army of the Republic (G.A.R)., Co. H, 95th Regiment, NY Infantry, having served in several important campaigns of the Civil War under Gen. Grant. After taking up residence in Yonkers he was 33 years old when he was hired on July 2, 1879 by the relatively new Yonkers Police Department. From all available information, he was an efficient, conscientious and capable officer. But, on May 10, 1893, the police surgeon reported to the police board that for some time officer Tice had been reporting sick and exhibiting signs of poor emotional and physical health. Following a complete medical exam the police surgeon recommended Tice be retired on disability pension. However, no action was taken at that time. It wasn't until seven years later that PO James Tice retired on that disability pension on June 1, 1900. After retirement, he worked as a Special Police Officer (Guard) for Oakland and St. John's Cemeteries. He also operated a real estate business for many years out of his home at 16 Ingram Street. Later he moved to Orchard La. in New Paltz, N.Y. where, following a brief illness, he would die on April 26, 1931 at the age of 84 years.

LIEUTENANT PETER McGOWAN

APPOINTED: August 7, 1880
RETIRED: September 5, 1930

Throughout the history of the police department many officers have served for lengthy periods of time; often up to forty years. But Peter McGowan set the record, which has yet to be broken, by serving as an active member of the department for a half century. Fifty years! He was born in the Town of Haverstraw, Rockland Co., on June 25, 1858. His early education was received at the Haverstraw Parochial School, followed by the Wilson Academy. Before joining the police department McGowan worked as a lineman in the employ of the American District Telegraph Company in New York City.

While still residing in Haverstraw when he was appointed a police officer on August 7, 1880, he was the first non-Yonkers resident allowed to be hired by our department. "Handsome Pete" McGowan, as he would later be known to many of his friends and colleagues, was just 22 years old when he received his appointment. During the historic snow blizzard of 1888, Pete McGowan walked his foot post in Getty Square. Throughout his career he would enjoy telling stories about him staying on post during this blizzard and record snow fall. By all accounts he worked hard, paid strict attention to duty, and was

Lt. Peter McGowan (cont.)

rewarded for his honorable service when he was appointed to the rank of Roundsman on May 8, 1899. Three years later, on April 29, 1902, he was promoted to the rank of Sergeant; at the time the second highest rank in the department. By this time McGowan had made an enviable impression on his superiors and as a result was placed in command of the relatively new Detective Bureau. For many years Sgt. McGowan would serve with distinction as a Detective Sergeant.

It was due to his skills, integrity, and the high regard in which he was held by most members of the police profession that he was frequently detailed to the Secret Service for special assignments. Among his special duties he was assigned to the security details for the inauguration of every president up to Warren G. Harding. On April 25, 1908, Det. Sgt. Peter McGowan was promoted to the newly established rank of Lieutenant where he would spend the remainder of his career working as a precinct desk lieutenant. A progressive thinker and a student of police methods, it was about 1908 that Sgt. McGowan was said to have traveled to England and France, to broaden his knowledge of his profession. It was in France that he met M. Bertillion, the originator of the French identification system. It was very often reported that it was McGowan who organized and established the procedures for the use of fingerprints in the Yonkers Police Department as a means of identification to replace the former, and by and large unreliable, Bertillion method of body measurements.

Lt. Peter McGowan retired from the 4th precinct on September 5, 1930 with over 50 years of active service with the police department. This remains a record, in terms of length of active service, that has never been surpassed. A bachelor who never married, Pete McGowan was considered a connoisseur of the arts and was a collector of paintings and various weapons. He was described as "a striking figure with military bearing," who was known for his dignity, impeccable manners, and the prestige he brought to his position. He was a member of the LaRabida Council of the Knights of Columbus, a life member of the New York Lodge #1 Elks, the Royal Arcanum, and the Woodmen of America.

A resident of 274 Warburton Avenue McGowan became ill in the last two years of his life and was first a patient at Yonkers Professional Hospital on Ludlow Street, and for the last year was at the Stamford Hall Sanitarium in Stanford, Connecticut. On January 23, 1935, retired Lt. Peter McGowan died of a cerebral hemorrhage at the age of 76 years. In life McGowan remained loyal to two fundamental virtues which are of the utmost importance in a police officer's performance - courtesy and honesty. It was said that his death dissolved another link to an earlier time when Yonkers was a rural Hudson River village, and our department was in its infancy.

PO HENRY COOLEY # 1

APPOINTED: August 12, 1880
DIED: December 15, 1929

Henry Cooley was born August 4, 1855 in Ireland, but was raised in Ossining N.Y. Prior to becoming a Yonkers police officer, Cooley worked as a coachman. He received his official appointment as a Yonkers Patrolman on August 12, 1880. Like all in the police department at that time he worked out of the only police building, that being headquarters located at 9 Dock Street; later to be renamed 9 Manor House Square. He was a foot patrol officer and would remain such for nearly his entire career. The cornerstone for a new police headquarters located at 20 Wells Avenue was laid in 1898 and when completed the entire department was relocated to their new home.

Henry and his brother George Cooley, (George would later rise to captain,) both were appointed police officers in the then Yonkers Police Bureau, albeit on different dates, and would serve faithfully throughout their careers. Henry Cooley had nineteen years with the department when he had a very interesting arrest for those early years. On November 14, 1899, at about 2:00 AM officer Henry Cooley was walking his post when he was advised by a railroad worker that there were three suspicious men in the area. Cooley met PO John Cahill on the adjoining foot post and after a short time located the men. After confronting the trio, one of the suspects pulled a gun on officer Cahill however following a brief struggle was ultimately arrested by Cahill after a foot chase. A second male was immediately grabbed around the collar and placed under arrest by officer Henry Cooley. When he was grabbed by the officer the male resisted and swung at PO Cooley with an ice pick. Following a brief struggle, officer Cooley fired his weapon striking the suspect in the hand. Cooley then proceeded to march his wounded prisoner from Warburton Avenue and Ashburton Avenue down to Police Headquarters located at 20 Wells Avenue.

Years later in 1925, upon completing 45 years service, the entire time working swing shifts, with an unblemished record, Henry Cooley was presented with, and given the honor of being allowed to wear, a patrolman's gold plated shield and hat wreath. He was the only patrolman ever known to receive such an honor, and at the age of 70 years, was the oldest active duty officer in the department.

Cooley spent his entire career working from the headquarters/ 1st precinct building; first at 9 Dock Street, then at 20 Wells Avenue. Toward the end of his career, due to his advancing age, he was given the privilege of working steady days on a foot post patrolling the area of the waterfront, the Recreation (City) Pier and the New York Central Railroad station. During his long career he had served under 20 mayors, numerous boards of police commissioners, 9 Public Safety Commissioners, and 7 uniformed leaders of the police department.

Although healthy and having just worked patrol the day before, on December 15, 1929, just 8 months short of completing 50 years of active patrol service to the Yonkers Police Department, PO Henry Cooley, a lifelong bachelor, suffered a cerebral hemorrhage in his home at 189 North Broadway, and later died at St. John's Hospital at the age of 73 years.

A large formation of motorcycles and uniformed police lined the street at his funeral along with civilians and politicians in great numbers to display the esteem in which officer Henry Cooley was held.

PO WILLIAM CONKLIN

APPOINTED: October 13, 1880
DISMISSED: May 18, 1887

When Bill Conklin applied to be a Yonkers police officer on Oct 6, 1880, on his application to the Police Board Conklin indicated he was 24 years old, having been born in the United States. He indicated he was married and was working locally as a groom. Bill received his appointment as a police officer on October 13, 1880 but it wasn't long before Conklin began having problems. He was first charged with violating the rules on Sept. 17, 1881 and fined 7 days pay. On February 7, 1883 he was tried on departmental charges of violating the rules and fined 10 days pay. And again, Dec. 5, 1883 and April 21, 1884. On July 16, 1884 again he was tried on charges of Neglect of Duty and was remanded to the School of Instruction with pay reduced to $750. Again he was charged on Sept. 17, and October 15, 1884 and fined. Three years later on May 13, 1887 he was again tried on charges of Neglect of Duty, was suspended and the decision was reserved. On May 18, 1887 the trial reconvened, evidence was reviewed and William Conklin was found guilty and dismissed from the Force May 18, 1887.

PO JOHN RILEY

APPOINTED: October 13, 1880
DISMISSED: March 17, 1881

Similar to his fellow police recruit Bill Conklin, when Riley submitted his application to be hired as a police officer on Oct 6, 1880, Riley indicated he was 29 years old, having been born in the United States. He indicated he was married and worked as a Laborer. John Riley received his police appointment on October 13, 1880, but just like his fellow appointee, Bill Conklin, trouble was in his future. At a meeting of Police Board on March 16, 1881, it was charged that Riley was absent without leave from March 2nd to March 11, 1881. During that time Riley had sent a telegram to the Police Board from a NYC hospital stating he was unable to report as he was sick in a NYC Hospital. After having Sgt Quinn look into the matter and report back, the board decided to find him guilty as charged and John Riley was dismissed from the Police Force effective March 17, 1881.

CAPTAIN OF POLICE WILLIAM H. LENT

Appointed: November 19, 1880
Retired: June 1, 1920

Captain William Lent held the distinction of being the last leader of the police department to hold the title of Captain of Police, this being the equivalent of being the Chief of the Yonkers Police Department. He was born in Dobbs Ferry on June 18, 1856, the son of Samuel H. And Sarah Acker Lent. Young Lent was educated at Dobbs Ferry and in the Twentieth Street School in N.Y.C. After leaving school he entered the wholesale and retail house of D.A. Van Horn, of Park Place, NY; importers of French and plate glass. After spending a year in this clerical position in this establishment, he returned to Dobbs Ferry and engaged in farming. After coming to Yonkers, Lent took up residence at 199 North Broadway.

The Police Board in Yonkers, to which he made application for appointment, consisted of the following gentleman; George R. Dusenburry, president; George W. Cobb, secretary and treasurer; Peter U. Fowler and Col. William Heermance. Upon being hired by the department at the age of 23 years, young

Captain William H. Lent (cont.)

Lent was responsible for the arrests of several persons for committing burglaries and other crimes. He quickly earned a reputation for being very capable and following through on all his assignments. Starting from the early days following his appointment, he displayed that diligence to duty that remained throughout his entire career in the department, and which won for him the promotions which made him the highest ranking officer in the Yonkers Police Department.

Lent received his first promotion to Roundsman on June 23, 1897. For a time, Yonkers was plagued by a large nuisance problem where New York City residents would come to Yonkers in large numbers to gamble on dog fights in the city. Lent was ordered to put a stop to it. In addition, New York City gamblers were coming up the Hudson River by the hundreds on barges, to continue gambling on the dog fights right off the Yonkers shore on the barges. Roundsman Lent hand-picked several officers and set up a number of surveillance's which led to the arrests of many individuals. This type of gambling activity was virtually eliminated.

However, it is worthy of note that Lent was also very athletic. In the late 1800's he was urged by many people in the community to try to form a Yonkers Police baseball team which, while competing with other local teams, would enable them to raise money for a new city ambulance. Roundsman Lent was said to have been one of the most popular men in the department. He was well liked by both officers and patrolmen and readily agreed to make inquiries as to who in the department might be interested in playing baseball for a good cause. He found plenty of enthusiasm and the team was established.

On May 8, 1899, following his passing of the civil service test, William Lent was promoted to the rank of Sergeant, and consequently took on much greater responsibilities. While being a naturally reserved individual by nature, he rigidly enforced the rules of the department with firmness and fairness. When the leader of the department, Capt. Frederick Woodruff, retired, Sgt. Lent competed for the vacant captains position along with sergeants Hugh Brady and Peter McGowan. All three were required to undergo an examination by the police surgeon, Dr. Albert Benedict. Upon completing his exams the surgeon found all three fit for the new position and recommended each equally. When the Board of Police Commissioners met on June 29, 1907 to decide on the new appointment, they decided that although all three sergeants were fine candidates, Sgt. Lent was the senior sergeant in the department and, as a result, a unanimous vote was cast by the board in his favor. The new Captain of Police was then summoned and informed. that he had been chosen to be the new leader of the police department effective July 1, 1907. Commissioner Ewing said that he wanted Lent to know that his appointment was strictly non-political and the board hoped that the captain would assume a non-political attitude in the discharge of his duty. It was reported that Lent said, *"I hope that I will never give you reason to believe that your confidence in me has been misplaced."* The new appointee then took the oath of office and Police Board President Bell pinned the new captain's shield on his coat.

In speaking of police work, Capt. Lent said, I consider the need of more policemen the greatest need of the department today. We require just as many more officers as we can get - fifty, if possible.

The next day the Yonkers Herald newspaper wrote an article in which they attempted to high-lite the new captain's career. They wrote that as a patrolman in 1884 he had at least two exciting incidents with crooks in which he narrowly escaped being shot. The first occurred about 1:30 AM while he was on mounted

Captain William H. Lent (cont.)

patrol in North Yonkers. He had observed a light in the home of a Moresmere Avenue resident. As he approached to check further he observed three men through the window moving about in the shadows. As he dismounted at the front door he saw three men, who had jumped from a side window, run from the side of the house. The officer immediately gave chase, emptying his revolver at them as he ran. He was convinced he hit one but they made good their escaped.

A few weeks later Officer Lent exchanged shots with another burglar. This one occurred about 3 AM. Once again he saw a candle light in the window of a home on Palisade Avenue. He cautiously walked along the side of the house to the rear with his revolver in his hand. Just then a suspect ran out of the rear door. Hold on, or I'll shoot, yelled Lent. But the burglar also had a gun and he quickly turned toward the officer and fired point blank at him. Lent fired back almost simultaneously. Both weapons missed their mark. However, the burglar's bullet was said to have struck officer Lent's coat before smashing through a window. Once again this burglar also made his escape, leaving behind his .45 caliber pistol.

Upon attaining the leadership of our department, Captain of Police William Lent began a vigorous campaign to convince the Board of Police Commissioners that all policemen should be proficient in the use of the firearm they carried. He pointed out that, when a man is appointed a police officer, he is immediately sent out on patrol, usually with a gun in his pocket, with no firearms training at all. This, he believed, was not only dangerous for the public but to the officer's safety as well. Although his recommendation was very logical by even modest standards, his idea was not warmly received by the administration. Their objection being, it would be difficult to convince the men to come in for training on their own time, and if the officers were trained during on duty time, the department would experience a shortage of officers on patrol. (Obviously overtime pay was unheard of to this point.) No firearms training program was instituted. A decision which would likely be the cause of the death of PO Wilfred Matthews from an accidental discharge of his revolver in 1913.

Having led the department for a year, Lent would learn that the city was going to create the position of Chief of Police. Widespread opinion was that he would, of course, get that job. He was wrong. It was given to Mr. Daniel Wolff, a man who had never even been a police officer. Lent remained a police captain in command of the 1st precinct, but never again led the entire police department.

Upon his retirement on June 1, 1920, it was said that in addition to having won recognition for himself, he inspired the men under his command, and won for him their respect and wholehearted support. As long as they did their job, the police officers could find no better friend than Captain William Lent.

After only a little more than a year in retirement, Captain William H. Lent died November 20, 1921 at the age of 65 years.

CAPTAIN GEORGE W. COOLEY

APPOINTED: April 20, 1881
RETIRED: August 6, 1916

Born in Ireland on May 28, 1859, George Washington Cooley came to the United States with his family when he was just 2 years old. His family settled in the Town of Ossining, and when he was able, Cooley took a job as a blacksmith. Although his strength was suited to the work of a blacksmith, he may have concluded that "the nightstick is more powerful than the anvil," because at the age of 21 years he followed in his brother Ptl. Henry Cooley's footsteps and was appointed to the Yonkers Police Department on April 20, 1881.

According to available reports, George Cooley was a hardworking and tough cop. He served as a detective in the 1890's with Det. Bill Carroll as his partner. It was said that Capt. Mangin often remarked, *"..give me Cooley and Carroll and I'll tackle an army."* It seemed clear from the beginning that George

Captain George W. Cooley (cont.)

Cooley was a man of great ambition.

On May 8, 1899, George Cooley was promoted to the rank of Roundsman. During this period of time, news accounts often complained that gambling parlors and pool halls were openly operating illegally. The reports suggested that the Captain of Police, James McLaughlin, was ineffective in dealing with the problem. Roundsman Cooley had several friends on the Board of Police Commissioners and in City Hall, and he used them to good personal advantage. Since the Police Board had apparently lost confidence in the captain's commitment to eradicate gambling, etc., the aggressive and extremely confident George Cooley convinced them he was the man for the job. The problem?......., Cooley was only a Roundsman.

On June 1, 1901, the Police Board created our first Detective Bureau. George Cooley was about to get the chance to deliver on his boasting. Even though he was not certified by Civil Service for a promotion, Roundsman Cooley was placed in command of the detectives, and given the title of "Detective Sergeant." The directive establishing the Detective Bureau required all arrests by uniformed officers, and any criminal information received by the police department, to first be channeled through the "Bureau," which had complete authority to do whatever Cooley deemed best. This obvious circumvention of the Captain of Police made clear to all, just how powerful George Cooley was and earned him the nickname "Big Chief." As a Roundsman, and having more authority than the captain, was unprecedented, but it didn't seem to bother the "Big Chief" at all. He believed he was right and would back down to no man.
On November 13, 1901 George Cooley was officially and properly promoted to the rank of Sergeant. Although completely dedicated to police work, Cooley also invested in real estate. He spent most of his vacations at his summer home, a farm in Pound Ridge N.Y.

In 1904 Det. Sgt. Cooley was still a power to be reckoned with. However some news reports, albeit his political party foes, were continuously criticizing the Detective Bureau under Cooley's command. They pointed out that Cooley's supporters on the Police Board had again gone too far by directing that the "telegraph apparatus" and the station house desk, be placed under the control of Sgt. Cooley. Reports of important cases were no longer read over the station house desk to the uniformed men. Critics felt that Cooley and his men were trying to have all important arrests made by them so they would gain the notoriety. The "Big Chief," no doubt, felt that if the job was ever going to be done right, he would have to see to it himself.

George Cooley was a man with a mission, and he waged a relentless war against criminals in general, and in particular those who crossed the N.Y.C. line in the hopes of finding easy prey in Yonkers. To this end, he would try anything he could think of that might aid in his effort. Some of the reported tactics occasionally utilized by Cooley and his men to induce a confession were, according to reports, "harsh and inhumane." It was once reported that a man suspected of being a horse thief was put in a cell, denied the right to exercise in the jail corridor, not allowed any communications with friends, was not arraigned or charged, and was held for three weeks before being released.

In his effort to enforce the law Sgt Cooley's methods may have seemed harsh at times, but he was also innovative. He was the first to institute a new detail called the "Bum Squad," whereby for the first time officers worked undercover in old ragged clothes dressed as vagrants trying to mingle with suspicious individuals.

Captain George W. Cooley (cont.)

To say that George Cooley was outspoken and opinionated would be an understatement. In July of 1907 the Police Board was considering increasing the numerical strength of the department. The local Newspaper's interviewed several ranking officers in the department regarding their feelings on how many more policemen should be hired. When asked, Cooley gave a characteristic answer. He said, *To put on less than 100 more men would be to throw the money away. And rather than see that happen, it would be better for the city to turn the money over to me to invest in additional farmland in Pound Ridge. One hundred more, or none at all, I repeat."*

Sgt. Cooley's desire to be a police captain was certainly no secret. His ambition was always clear and he would let no one he felt was less competent than he, stand in his way. He had the power and the authority, but he wanted the title. His goal was finally realized when a new 3rd precinct was established. George Cooley was promoted to Captain on November 1, 1909, and was placed in command of the new 3rd precinct at 27 Radford Street. After the ceremony opening the precinct, Capt. Cooley addressed his men and simply said, *"I assure you I will do my best to serve the people and the police department,"* and he meant it.

In 1916 Yonkers was struggling with a troubling trolley car strike. There was picketing and demonstrations throughout the city with the threat of violence being ever present. Captain Cooley worked tirelessly and without taking days off to provide the necessary police protection to avert an outbreak of violence. In a conversation with a newspaper reporter, Cooley talked of meeting with Corporation Council Thomas Curran. After telling Curran that he felt he had malaria, Curran said Cooley should take some time off and get well. Capt. Cooley reportedly answered, *" Tom, with the trolley strike on and its possibilities in mind, I'd rather be carried out on a stretcher than be known as a quitter."* A few days later he became ill but attributed it to the summer heat, and continued his duties. What he didn't know was that he had heart disease. Within 48 hours of his conversation with the reporter, on August 6, 1916, Captain George Washington Cooley died at the age of 57 years.

A rugged, energetic, and powerful man, George Cooley could never be described as being easy going. He was a strict disciplinarian and very religious; keeping a bible at the precinct desk which he encouraged his men to read instead of the newspapers. His stern methods were not welcome by the men, but he was respected for being able to get the job done. He was a loyal friend, but an uncompromising foe who knew no fear.

It was said that there never was a time when the "Big Chief," Captain George Cooley, was not a policeman!

PO GEORGE FRAZIER JR.

APPOINTED: July 20, 1881
RESIGNED: October 19, 1884

George Frazier was born in the City of Yonkers, was single, 24 years old, and was employed as a machinist by trade. He became interested in the police department, and on July 6, 1881 he appeared before the police board for consideration to be appointed a policeman. A meeting of the board was held on July 20, 1881, and George received their approval to be appointed and was sworn in as a police officer that night. He was told to report for duty at 6 PM two days later. It appears that George was unable to obey orders because he was always being brought up on charges. Some of them were, November 30, 1881 for neglect of duty, received a reprimand; March 10, 1883, a complaint by a citizen and fined one Day's pay; on January 17, 1883 he was again charged and received a reprimand; on April 18, 1883 he was fined 10 days pay; on January 23, 1884 he was reprimanded and sent back to the school of instruction with a reduction in salary to $800 a year. Actually it was surprising that he had not been dismissed, but apparently he had enough. He voluntarily resigned from the police department on October 19, 1884.

PO JOHN W. EDWARDS

APPOINTED: January 4, 1882
DISMISSED: May 17, 1882

John Eswards applied to be a police officer at the age of 22, was single and made a living as a painter. He was sworn in as a police officer on January 4, 1882 and was directed to report for duty that very same day at the 6 PM roll call. During that same year there was apparently some hard feelings between Edwards and PO James Mealing, although the cause is unknown. The tempers came to a head one morning when following a verbal argument in the muster room at headquarters, they both agreed to leave and go to the police stables to have a fight, which they did. During the flight it would seem that Edwards got the upper hand because he broke Mealing's nose. Ultimately, it resulted in both offices being brought up on departmental charges for which a trial was held on May 17, 1882, charging them with gross breach of discipline in indulging in a fight. Following testimony by the supervisor who charged both men, both officers were found guilty and dismissed from the police department effective May 17, 1882.

PO ANDREW J. HEALY # 2

APPOINTED: June 7, 1882
DISMISSED: November 22, 1894

A resident of 161 North Broadway, Andrew Healy must have been pleased when he was notified to appear before the Board of Police Commissioners on June 7, 1882 to be considered for the position of police officer. His interview must have been satisfactory and, based on a vote of the Board, he was appointed and duly sworn to this position. For nearly ten years it would appear, with a lack of information to the contrary, that officer Healy was performing his police duties to his superiors satisfaction. In fact he seemed to enjoy the job and even joined the police baseball team in 1891. His position was to play 2nd base; a job he had acquired much experience in playing with the Oak Hills team. He was described as being quick on his feet and was a good hitter as well. He would remain with the team up through 1894 still playing 2nd base. In fact, he was usually put up at bat first because he seldom failed to get a hit.

Unfortunately, shortly after joining the team Andy Healy began to have problems within the department. In June of 1891 Healy, along with most of the department, was assigned to the ceremonies for the laying of the cornerstone for St Joseph's Seminary on May 17, 1891. While on his post Healy observed a man sneak into a designated area without a ticket. He approached the man and unceremoniously removed him from the grounds. Based on the man's complaint, officer Healy was charged with violating departmental rules by roughly treating a citizen at that assembly. The complainant later dropped the charge and officer Healy was only given a reprimand to be more professional in his police conduct.

Later that same month on June 29, 1891 Healy was charged by Sgt. McLaughlin with being absent from duty for 27 minutes while patrolling Post 1 on May 31st. At his trial Healy admitted that he had been necessarily absent from his post, but for only 10 minutes. (Presumably he required a personal). Initially the commissioners reserved decision but, on July 8, 1891 they found him guilty of the charges and fined him one days pay. But he seemed to redeem himself on December 26, 1891when while executing a warrant against a wife beater Healy was attacked by the man and a lengthy struggle ensued. However Healy managed to affect the arrest without any undue force used against his prisoner. This, even though the man was known to be very violent.

Three years later the police board met again to consider two charges of neglect of duty against officer Andrew Healy. First, that on the eve of November 9, 1894 he had failed to report from any police call box on his post after 6:45 PM and was not heard from until he returned from duty at about midnight. At this hearing PO Healy admitted this first charge. The second complaint was that on November 11, 1894, Healy again failed to report from any police box at 7, 8, 9, 9:30, 10, 10:30 PM, and could not be found by the Roundsman on post until 10:40 PM. When Healy was located the Roundsman reported that Healy was in an intoxicated condition and was unfit for duty. Officer Healy again admitted not calling in from his post but denied being intoxicated even though an examination by the police surgeon concluded that he was. A private citizen speaking on Healy's behalf asked the commissioners to take into account the officers past record which he believed was a good one. The man further said that he did not believe there was a better officer on the force for all around police work. The board did not agree. The decision by the police commissioners was that PO Andrew Healy is hereby dismissed from the police department.

LT. GEORGE DINSMORE

APPOINTED: June 7, 1882
DIED: July 28, 1914

George Dinsmore was born in the City of Yonkers, date unknown, and following his formal education, part of which was at PS# 2, he worked a variety of jobs before giving a thought to the police department. But he was pleased when he was called by the police board to be appointed a Patrolman on June 7, 1882. A resident of 6 Willow Place, all indications are that he was a diligent and dependable police officer. George Dinsmore would spend a major portion of his entire career assigned either to the original 9 Dock Street headquarters or later to the 1st precinct at 20 Wells Avenue when construction was completed and it was opened in 1898.

Having apparently proved he was worthy, on May 8, 1899, George received his first promotion to the rank of Roundsman. At that time the first line supervisory rank was that of Roundsman and Dinsmore was very diligent about checking on the men out on patrol.

Six years later, on April 21, 1905, upon the retirement of Sgt George Osborn, Dinsmore was promoted to the very prestigious rank of Sergeant, with only the Captain of Police holding a higher rank. However there was a lot of grumbling throughout the department following his promotion. Just prior, a lot of unfair pressure and burden was placed upon a Sgt Osborn who was senior in rank. News accounts of the day suggested that Sgt Osborn was pressured and ultimately forced to retire just to create an open position for Dinsmore who was said to have been aligned with the right political party.

In 1908 the rank structure in the police department was changed to abolish the rank of Roundsman and add that of Lieutenant and police Chief. It was on April 25, 1908 that Sgt. Dinsmore was then promoted to the newly created rank of Police Lieutenant. Shortly thereafter, upon the establishing of a 3rd precinct at 57 Radford Street in December of 1909, Dinsmore was assigned as a desk lieutenant in the 3rd pct. However, it wasn't long after that he was assigned to the Detective Bureau as a close assistant to then Captain of Detectives, Capt. George Cooley, to find ways to reduce the number of burglaries in the city. Lt Dinsmore remained in the Detective Bureau until May 1, 1914 when a 4th precinct was established on Palisade Avenue and he was assigned there on desk duty.

Throughout his career Lt Dinsmore is said to have never had a negative mark against his record. Unfortunately he began to experience pain in his stomach and on July 28, 1914, following appendectomy surgery, Lt George Dinsmore died from complications. A veteran of 32 years with the police force, and being a widower, he left behind 4 children.

The entire police department was shocked by his death and his funeral was attended by a large uniformed formation in a show of respect. The station house entrance was also draped in black mourning cloth.

Dinsmore had been a member of the Rising Star Lodge of Free Masons, the Terrace City Lodge, Modern Woodmen of America, and he was the secretary to the Yonkers Police Pension Fund.

PO AUGUST DIETZEL #18

APPOINTED: October 3, 1883
RETIRED: December 1, 1913

It is believed that Dietzel was born around 1856 and when August, also known as Gus or Augie, was appointed a patrolman on October 3, 1983 he spent the first eighteen years on foot patrol, working first out of the Dock Street headquarters and then the 1st pct. on Wells Ave. Records indicate he was a conscientious officer with very few complaints made against him. In 1901, when Yonkers opened a substation on Central Avenue, officer Dietzel was one of the officers assigned to that Sub Station #2 to patrol the east side of Yonkers. In 1904 it was reported that he assisted Capt. Lent in preparing the 1903 Annual Report. In 1908, when that substation was established as the 2nd precinct, Dietzel remained at that assignment. In 1913 he endured a difficult family situation when his 17 year old daughter charged him with cruelty, a charge which resulted in his suspension and arrest. However, after an investigation he was exonerated and re- instated with back pay. Several months later, on December 1, 1913 with 30 year's service, PO August Dietzel retired on December 1, 1913 at the age of 58 years. Retired Patrolman August Dietzel died on March 8, 1929 at the age of 73.

PO EDWARD J. MURRAY

APPOINTED: February 11, 1885
RESIGNED: February 14, 1889

Edward Joseph Murray was born in the city of Yonkers in 1863. He received his education, and graduated from St Mary's parochial school. As an adult Ed Murray lived and raised his family at 85 South Broadway in Yonkers. He completed his application, passed a physical exam by the police surgeon, and was appointed a Yonkers police officer on February 11, 1885. Like most other young officers he was assigned to work foot patrol duty from the Police Headquarters building on Wells Avenue. During his tenure Murray's time with the Yonkers Police was not without conflict. Throughout his four year stay Murray was brought up on charges no less than 11 times for a variety of violations of the rules and regulations. On what was to be the last time, on January 19, 1889, police officer Murray was charged with neglect of duty. As a result, he sent a hand written communication to the Board of Police Commissioners stating that he was resigning from the Yonkers Police Department.

The Police Board took the position that since the letter was not delivered by him in person, and since he had not appeared for roll call at the scheduled time, they would not accept his resignation, and instead dismissed him from the police department effective February 14, 1889. According to reports, in 1894 the Village of Hastings hired Edward Murray to be their Chief of Police. Initially he was a one man police force. Later two patrolmen were hired to assist him. As the Chief of Police in Hastings Murray was a highly respected officer. He was noted in the Hastings local newspaper for breaking up what was then known as "The Hotchkiss Gang," which had long terrified those handling railroad freight with robberies.

PO Edward Joseph Murray (cont.)

Chief Murray also broke up another nefarious faction known as the waterfront gang. Unfortunately Murray took ill with a cold which developed into pneumonia. He was treated at Dobbs Ferry Hospital where, despite their best efforts, he died on May 19, 1906 at the young age of 43 years. During his funeral, when the cortège moved through Hastings, all shades in the homes along Warburton Avenue (then named Constant Street) which was where he had lived at the time, were drawn closed in respect and in his honor until the procession had passed. The pallbearers at his funeral included the two other Hastings policemen, 2 Dobbs Ferry officers, and Patrolmen John Scheibel and Henry Miller of the Yonkers Police. Among family and friends attending the funeral was a delegation of 20 Yonkers police officers under the direction of Captain Frederick Woodruff and Sergeant William Lent. Among the floral tributes was a large cross from the Yonkers Police Department.

Chief Murray was survived by his wife and four children. The Chief would never know, but the tradition of policing was to continue in his family. One of his sons, George Murray, was appointed to the Hastings Police Department in 1922 and died in 1966 with the rank of sergeant with 44 years active service. Sgt. George Murray's son, the Chiefs grandson, Edward J. Murray served with the Bronxville Police Department from August 3, 1959 until his retirement as a sergeant on August 4, 1979. The Chiefs granddaughter even married a Hastings police officer.

The chief's grandson, former Sgt. Edward Murray related that Chief Edward Murray, during his tenure, had a brother in law named John George Welch, who was also a policeman, but he did not know in which department. However, it is coincidental that during the same time Chief Murray was a Yonkers police officer, our department had a police officer named John Welch. It is unknown if they were the same person.

The story of Edward Joseph Murray is an unusual one in that the record reflects two stories. One of an officer who apparently had trouble taking orders from others, possibly feeling he knew best. The other of a successful Chief of Police who ran his department with distinction and earned the respect of the entire village.

PO RICHARD M. JOHNSTONE # 23

APPOINTED: May 1, 1885
RETIRED: December 1, 1901

Richard Meeks Johnstone was born on the Shonnard Estate in north Yonkers May 30, 1848. Richard served in the Navy during the Civil War from Oct 26, 1864 to Apr. 17, 1869 as an Apprentice 3rd class. On June 3, 1874, Dick, (as he was known) Johnstone was hired by the police department as a hostler. He performed his duties efficiently, and as a result was appointed a police officer on May 1, 1885. Prior to his employment with the police department, Johnstone made his living as an electrician. After joining the department, this special knowledge resulted in him being placed in charge of maintaining the Police Telegraph System. This was, of course, in addition to his regular patrol duties. Richard Johnstone's brother was Yonkers Roundsman Joseph Johnstone. His nephew, James Thomas, would also later be appointed a Yonkers policeman. In 1901 PO Richard Johnstone retired with 27 years of honorable and efficient service. Just three years later retired PO Johnstone died February 19, 1904 at the age of 55 years.

PO MICHAEL GREGORY # 25

APPOINTED: January 31, 1887
DIED: December 16, 1893

Michael Gregory was born September 30, 1857, in Dunlear, County Lowth, Ireland. He came to Yonkers in 1873, as a young man stood 6' 1" at 180 Lbs, worked as a "Coachman" for Charles Mercer, and lived at 136 Nepperhan Ave. Following his appointment to the police department his duties mainly consisted of foot patrol. Gregory was reported to have been a well-liked and popular member of the police force who could be counted on to perform his duty efficiently. Upon completion of a midnight tour of duty, Gregory was relieved, went home and suddenly became seriously ill. The police surgeon was called and treated him at his house for stomach cramps and vomiting. Unfortunately, later that same evening, December 16, 1893, the officer's condition became critical, and PO Michael Gregory died. Following an inquest, the police surgeon reported the cause of Gregory's death as "shock and internal rupture." Having served only seven years with the department, PO Gregory left behind a young wife. The flag at Headquarters was placed at half mast, and the station house was draped in black mourning cloth. PO Michael Gregory was only 36 years old.

PO JAMES ROBINSON # 30

APPOINTED: June 1, 1887
RETIRED: October 1, 1918

James Robinson was born August 16, 1856 in Manhattan, where he also received his formal education. He was a boiler maker by trade and moved to Yonkers around 1882, taking up residence at 18 Locust Hill Avenue. He was first appointed to the police force on June 1, 1887. However, for reasons unknown, one month later on July 1, 1887 he resigned. Two years later on February 8, 1889, he was again appointed a patrolman. When the YPD organized it's first baseball team, Jim reportedly performed well at first base. When a new Detective Bureau was organized on June 1, 1901, Robinson was one of the first four officers detailed as detectives. That detail lasted only three months and he was transferred back to patrol at substation #2. An assignment, it was said, "more in keeping with his desires as a policeman." Later he was assigned to the telegraph desk at H.Q. In 1918, after nearly 30 years, Jim Robinson retired on October 1, 1918 on a disability pension. Twelve years later, on March 12, 1930, Ret Ptl James Robinson died at age 73 years.

PO GEORGE CARRIGAN # 3

APPOINTED: August 1, 1887
DISMISSED: January 30, 1889

George Carrigan was hired as a Yonkers police officer with the starting salary of $750. per year. By December of that same year, the police board had decided that he had passed his trial or probation period, and they raised his salary to $1,000 per year. However, it would not be very long before Carrigan faced serious charges. On December 12, 1888, Carrigan was charged by a civilian with blackmail. Fortunately for him following his trial, all the charges were dismissed. However, on January 30, 1889, Capt. Mangin suspended Carrigan for missing a roll call in December of 1888. During his trial he claimed he told his doctor to notify headquarters, which the doctor did not do. Carrigan was told that it was his responsibility to notify the police surgeon of his illness along with headquarters. He was found guilty on this charge, along with displaying, "an inability to perform patrol dut due to venereal disease." Upon being found guilty by the Boa Police Commissioners he was dismissed from the force on Januar sued the city claiming he was unfairly treated. In February of 1889, he was awarded $1,076.71 in monetary compensation, but not his job back as a policeman.

PO LEONARD K. DOTY #26

APPOINTED: December 14, 1887
DISMISSED: July 22, 1891

Leonard Kipp Doty is believed to have been born about 1865. Upon his appointment to the Yonkers Police Department on December 14, 1887, and living at 73 N. Broadway, one could assume that Doty expected to have a long and satisfying affiliation with police work. However, this was not to be. He was assigned and walked a foot post just like most other officers and nothing in the early years indicated any problems. But, after only four years on the Yonkers Police Force, PO Leonard K. Doty was reportedly indicted by the Westchester County Grand Jury on May 11, 1891. Doty, a resident of 177 Woodworth Avenue, was charged by a 17 year old girl with felonious assault. The particulars involving this case are not available, but being unable to supply the $5,000. bail that was set in court, he was arrested and placed in confinement. His previous record with the department was relatively good, and during his public service he had made many friends in the business community. In addition to the criminal charges the Board of Police Commissioners had officially charged him with, "immoral conduct, conduct injurious to public welfare, conduct unbecoming an officer, and violation of the law." On July 22, 1891, PO Leonard K. Doty was found guilty of all departmental charges by the police board, and he was dismissed from the police department. The disposition of the criminal charges are unknown. Doty is believed to have moved upstate to the Albany area.

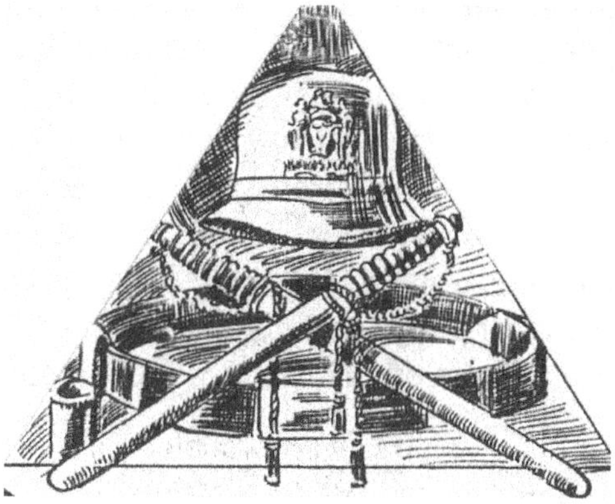

LIEUTENANT DANIEL J. SHEA

APPOINTED: February 8, 1889
DIED: April 6, 1926

Daniel Joseph Shea was born in the City of Yonkers to Daniel and Ellen Shea on December 31, 1864 and received his formal education in the public school system. As a young man he worked as a bricklayer mason. He soon became interested in police work and when he completed his application for appointment to the police department he stated he was 24 years old, married with no children, was a "Journeyman Bricklayer," and lived at 63 Riverdale Avenue.

Daniel J. Shea was appointed to the police department on February 8, 1889 and, along with the entire police department, worked out of headquarters located at 9 Dock Street. His main assignment was walking various foot posts throughout the west side of the city. He was a tough, strong, barrel chested man who loved his work but, being very athletic, was also considered an excellent baseball player. In fact he was one of the original members of the YPD baseball team when it was first organized in 1891. He was best known for his skill as a pitcher but on occasion covered third base. Being a fiercely competitive man his team mates knew that most disputes on the field were best handled by the less than timid Dan Shea.

It is believed Shea first faced gunfire on October 6, 1891. In the early morning hours of that day a citizen call headquarters reporting that he had seen a burglar enter a home on North Broadway. Officer Shea and several other officers were sent by wagon to investigate the burglary report. As they arrived the suspect in the house fired a number of shots at the police officers to give him time to escape. However, following a search the suspect was arrested with the use of Billy clubs instead if firearms.

On June 1, 1901 the Board of Police Commissioners established Police Sub Station # 2 which they located on the corner of Central Avenue at Jerome Avenue. The facility was in direct response to the community's demand for more police presence than an occasional mounted officer. PO Daniel Shea was one of just three of the original officers assigned to provide additional police service. Their service was so well received and appreciated that the residents of the seventh ward had a small silver cup made and had it engraved with words expressing their appreciation to the officers of Sub Station # 2. Officer Dan Shea was one of the officers authorized to accept this beautiful tribute to efficient police work.

Shea must have continued to display significant potential, because on November 13, 1901 he was promoted to the rank of Roundsman. Several years later in 1907 there was a news report that Roundsman Shea and officers Willard Mance and Hall Cougle attempted to effect an arrest of a man named McAvoy who was described as a notorious character. As the officers approached him McAvoy pulled out a gun and started to point it at the officers. Shea and the others, in turn, drew their weapons, fired point blank at the man causing wounds resulting in his death. Lacking ballistic comparison Roundsman Shea never would know if it was his bullet that killed the man.

Later that year on December 31, 1907, Roundsman Shea was promoted to the prestigious rank of Police Sergeant, the second highest rank in the department at the time. However, on May 15, 1908, following the creation of the new rank of Lieutenant and the establishment of a 2nd police precinct, Sgt. Shea was again promoted, this time to Lieutenant. He was then assigned to the new 2nd precinct as a desk officer. Lt Shea was a seasoned officer but he was about to face the challenge of his life.

Lt. Daniel J. Shea (cont.)

It was about two o'clock in the afternoon and off duty Lt Daniel Shea was at his home at 58 Hawthorne Avenue doing some miscellaneous gardening around his house. It was a warm summer day, the 9th of July in 1913, and Shea enjoyed working around the house. It was about that time that a neighbor called over to Shea and advised him that she had seen two suspicious men enter the property right across their street at # 63. Despite his being aware that the residents of that house were vacationing in Europe he dismissed the information outright, reasoning that it was in the middle of the afternoon and it was extremely unlikely anything untoward was taking place. However at the urging of his 18 year old niece Anna Shea, who also saw the men enter the property across the street, the lieutenant walked over to check the house. He found all the windows secure but when he reached the rear door he found that it had been pried open. Quietly he returned to his house across the street and immediately called the 1st precinct requesting assistance. (Remember, there was no radio room to call because there was no communications system as yet.)

Just as he hung up the telephone he heard his niece call out to him that the men were coming out. Shea quickly started for the front door grabbing his Billy club off a table and placed it in his back pocket as he went. He didn't take his revolver. As Shea crossed the street one of the men jumped over the neighbor's fence and began walking away. The lieutenant quickly approached the man, call to him, and just as he was about to grab him, the man pulled a revolver from his pocket and fired it point blank at the lieutenant. The suspect immediately ran north and then toward Hudson Street with Lt. Shea in foot pursuit. However, Shea did not get far. Though he heard the shot, saw the flash, and smelled the gunpowder, he did not realize that he had been shot in the chest. And by a .38 caliber round no less. He later claimed he only became aware of his wound do to the amount of blood he felt dripping from his shirt and trousers. When interviewed later Shea admitted it was then that he, *"felt a little squeamish and pale around the gills as I said to myself, 'you're a goner old sport this time for sure."* At this he walked back to his home and was helped inside by his son-in-law, off duty Lt. Dennis Cooper who called for an ambulance.

It was the "Police Patrol" (Paddy Wagon) not the ambulance that arrived first due to Shea's initial call to the 1st precinct for assistance. PO Andy Thompson placed him into the rear of the "patrol" and took him to St Joseph's Hospital for emergency treatment. At this same time, following the shooting, one suspect ran off, never to be located. The second one which shot the lieutenant ran off and was chased by the lieutenant's niece and several neighborhood residents yelling for someone to stop him. As the man turned off Riverdale, ran down Main Street and approached Market Street he found himself facing motorcycle PO Jim Madden; an intimidating figure on the best of days. The shooter, later identified as John Cassidy, 25 years of NYC, was immediately "restrained" and arrested by officer Madden. Originally brought directly to headquarters by Madden, he was quickly transported to St Joseph's Hospital so that Lt Shea might be able to identify Cassidy as the shooter. The prisoner was brought into the emergency room just as Shea was being prepared for surgery. One look and Shea reportedly stated, *"Yes, that's the guy, and I'll tell you young fellow, if I could get off this table I'd take you in hand myself."* The suspect was booked and arraigned on burglary and assault charges. During several hours of surgery the wounded lieutenant had the .38 caliber slug removed from his chest and he began a surprising recovery.

Lt. Daniel J. Shea (cont.)

Only eleven days later, following a guilty plea by Cassidy to both charges, he was sentenced to 27 years in Dannemora prison. After a lengthy recovery period 48 year old Lt Dan Shea returned to duty as a desk officer. In recognition of Shea's disregard for his own safety and for his off duty actions in attempting to thwart a burglary, which resulted in his being shot, Lt Daniel Shea received.............nothing. He would remain assigned to the 2nd precinct until about 1922 when Public Safety Commissioner Thomas Tobin was sworn in and Lt. Shea was transferred to the 4th precinct on desk duty.

On April 3, 1926, nearly 13 years after the shooting, the local newspaper reported that Lt Shea had been admitted to the hospital. It was reported that the artery in the lieutenant's chest that was struck by the burglar's bullet years earlier was causing Shea his current medical problem and the doctors were trying to determine the best course of medical treatment. It would be of no help. On April 6, 1926 Lt. Daniel Shea died in St Joseph's Hospital at the age of 61 years. The article stated that "he died as a result of a wound suffered 13 years ago when he was shot by John Cassidy, a burglar. " Further that, "Lt. Shea's death was caused by an aneurism of the aorta, the large artery leading from the heart." It was said that the old wound caused a distention of the artery and this brought about the trouble which resulted in the officer's death.

Upon learning of the death of Lt Shea, Public Safety Commissioner VanKeuren issued GO# 62 reading in part,....."The Commissioner of Public Safety has just been informed that Lt. Daniel J. Shea of the 4th precinct died at 1 PM, and further that his death was largely resulting from an injury sustained in performing splendid police work many years ago. The Police Bureau particularly and the City of Yonkers loses the services of a splendidly willing servant, and all that may be done by the corporation of the City of Yonkers should be pressed forward." The commissioner went on to write,..."The commissioner has made careful search of the records within the Bureau of Police and does not find any mention of recognition for the heroic act performed by Lt. Shea at the time of his being shot. He would like to draw attention of the citizenry of Yonkers the fact that we have a glaring example of the lack of appreciation evinced by no meritorious recognition being awarded a member of the Police Bureau who, although off duty, was willing to sacrifice his life, and 13 years thereafter did pay the penalty of splendid police service."

The funeral for the deceased lieutenant was held at his residence at 590 Palisade Avenue. An Honor Guard consisting of Capt. Willard Mance, Capt. Edward Connolly, Act. Capt. William Crough, Act Capt. George Ford, Lt's Peter McGowan and John Scheibel, and Sgt Patrick Flood formed up at the late officer's residence. The entire Traffic Divisions motorcycle unit arrived for the escort. Fifty Five selected police officers representing all four precincts were in formation under the command of Capt. Edward Quirk and all stood at attention and saluted as the body was taken from the home on its way to Sacred Heart Church. Following mass the procession moved to Oakland Cemetery for internment.

Following Shea's funeral the "Yonkers Herald" wrote an editorial which began as follows: "Lieutenant Daniel J. Shea died from the effect of a bullet wound inflicted upon him by a fleeing thief 13 years before. This brave officer passes as a martyr to duty just as though he had fallen on the field of battle, and should be immortalized in the records of the department."

Two years later on March 26, 1928 the Yonkers Police Association held their very first Memorial Service to honor all 30 members of the police department who had died since the Police Association had

Lt. Daniel J. Shea (cont.)

been organized in 1916. As they read the names of the officers, they singled out four whom they categorized as having died in the performance of their duty. Interestingly enough, but certainly no surprise, they listed Lt. Daniel Shea in that category. Clearly, even though thirteen years had passed between Shea being shot and his death, the YPA, the police department, and even the news media considered his gunshot wound to be the ultimate cause of his death, and thus the special honor.

In 2003, following a review of the circumstances of Lt. Shea's death, which was requested by Deputy Chief George E. Rutledge (Ret), Police Commissioner Charles Cola authorized that Lt Shea's name be included on our list of Line of Duty Deaths and be recognized for his sacrifice for the citizens of Yonkers.

PO WILLIAM H. KANE # 3

APPOINTED: February 13, 1889
DISMISSED: July 20, 1891

William H. Kane lived at 14 Jefferson Street and had worked for several years for the Thompson and Fowler Grocer on North Broadway. But Kane wanted more. He took and passed the relatively new instituted Civil Service exam for police officer and was also examined by the police surgeon. Everything seemed fine. Bill Kane was notified to present himself before the Board of Police Commissioners on February 13, 1889 to be considered for the position of police officer. The commissioners voted and Kane was duly elected to the department, along with Charles Waldron, and was given his oath of office and signed the "new stipulation." (Probably an agreement to abide by all the rules and regulations of the department.) He was directed to report to the School of Instruction where he would be on probation, with his pay being set at the rate of $750. per annum as fixed by law. He was also directed to report for patrol duty at 6 PM that same day.

On January 14, 1891 at a regular scheduled meeting of the police commissioners, charges of neglect of duty by officer Kane were considered. It was alleged that officer Kane arrested a woman on Main Street on the night of December 6, 1890 for Intoxication and Disorderly Conduct. At that time Kane sent a message to headquarters for a horse and wagon and assistance. During this arrest it is alleged that Kane allowed his prisoner to escape. After a discussion the commissioner's decision was reserved.

Available information seems to indicate that shortly after his police appointment, Kane's health seemed to deteriorate and aside from work, he seldom left his house. At a Police Board meeting held on February 25, 1891 Police Surgeon Swift sent a communication to the board re: the serious illness of police officer Kane on February 23, 1891. The surgeon advised that he was looking into how to determine the mental condition of PO Kane who was at that time on the sick list. However, the following month on March 21st, Surgeon Swift certified officer Kane fit for duty and he returned to work. But Bill Kane's troubles were not over.

On June 29, 1891 the police board again heard charges placed against officer Kane, this time by a citizen, who alleged that while she was in the city court room the week earlier on the 24th, officer Kane kicked her and called her a dirty bitch. Three independent witnesses testified that they saw no such action by the officer. The police commissioners again reserved decision.

Once more, one month later on July 15, 1891, police officer William Kane was charged with clubbing and shooting at a citizen on July 11, 1891 on North Broadway at Dock Street, without just cause, and just a few doors from headquarters. This time when the Board of Police Commissioners met on July 20, 1891 they found PO Kane guilty of the charges and he was dismissed from the Force.

Considering his poor health record and his unusually erratic, and often inexplicable record of openly violating departmental rules, it is unfortunate that someone did not look closer and consider the officers mental condition which the board had been advised was, at one time, in a serious state. The Police Board apparently did not. Only one year later his behavior may have been explained when, on August 20, 1892, former PO William Kane died at his Jefferson Street home of what was later diagnosed as a tumor on the brain. Though no longer a member of the police department, of his six pall bearers at his funeral, five were current members of the department who obviously wanted to show their respect for a former fellow officer who, possibly should have been retired on a disability instead of being dismissed.

PO CHARLES WALDRON

APPOINTED: February 13, 1889
RETIRED: August 17, 1914

Charles Waldron was born on February 9, 1858 in Haverstraw N.Y. He was a 29 year old miner when he was appointed to the police department. Unlike most police officers, he must have been an experienced horseman because upon appointment he was assigned to mounted patrol duty in the more rural areas of Yonkers, which basically meant anywhere outside the Getty Square area. On one occasion while mounted at North Broadway and High Street, he chased an unattended runaway horse and wagon all the way to Getty Square before he could stop it from running over a pedestrian causing serious injury. He was commended by the police board for his quick action. While residing at 278 New Main Street, in 1906, he was assigned to desk duty in the police telegraph room at headquarters. PO Charles Waldron retired on August 17, 1914 on a pension of $650. a year. Upon his retirement, the position of a patrolman in the telegraph room was discontinued. Charles Waldron died of pneumonia in Yonkers on January 24, 1933. He was 74.

PO HENRY E. HOLT

APPOINTED: May 27, 1889
DISMISSED: September 27, 1990

Henry Holt was born around 1953 in that area known as southern Westchester County, and later named West Farms. His family moved and brought him to Yonkers at the age of one year. As a young man Henry worked as a Coachman and resided at 39 Chestnut Street in Yonkers. When he was appointed a police officer from a civil service list on May 27, 1889 he was 26 years old and was married with two children. But he just couldn't keep out of trouble. He was charged with violating departmental rules on August 14, September 11, November 27, all in 1889, and on February 19, 1890. He was found guilty and fined for each offense. Then, on September 18, 1890 he was charged with violation of rule #10, Neglect of Duty. Though the particulars are unknown, a trial by the police board was held and Holt was found guilty and was dismissed from the police department effective September 27, 1890.

PO EDGAR F. WOOD #12

APPOINTED: May 29, 1889
RETIRED: June 1, 1919

Edgar Wood was born in Yonkers on February 16, 1864. He was a 25 year old teamster at the time of his appointment to the police department and lived at 103 Webster Avenue. Earlier, he had served 6 years in the Navy and upon his discharge then joined the 4th Separate Co. of the NY National Guard. Wood spent many years as an efficient mounted officer, and being quite athletic, was a member of the department's baseball team. In fact, following a contest by the Yonkers Herald newspaper, the citizens of Yonkers voted PO Wood the most popular officer in the department. His prize was a silver mounted revolver of his choosing.

In 1906, due to a variety of problems occurring along the river, officer Wood was placed in charge of the Hudson River "Boat Patrol." It is believed his craft was simply a row boat. He worked this detail each day from 9am to 5pm along the river front, from the north to the south city line, in this police boat. After 30 years of service, all in the 1st Pct, Wood retired on June 1, 1919. He moved to New Rochelle where he worked as a night watchman. On July 5, 1921, while making his rounds, he discovered a multi family residence on fire and quickly ran into the burning building and alerted the residents and moved them to safety. Just moments later he fell dead of a heart attack; only two years after his retirement from the Yonkers Police Dept. He was 57 years of age.

CAPTAIN HUGH D. BRADY

APPOINTED: August 19, 1891
RETIRED: November 30, 1922

Born in Liverpool England in the early 1860's, Hugh Brady reportedly came to the United States at the age of eight months and spent his boyhood years in Holyoke, Massachusetts. In 1889, Brady moved to the City of Yonkers. For a time, Brady worked for the old Yonkers Herald newspaper, and later he entered the painting business working for a Painter. He was working as a painter when he was appointed a policeman on August 19, 1891. He was also president of the Young Men's Catholic Association and a member of the Columbia Hook and Ladder Volunteer Fire Company.

But young Brady also loved the activity involving sports; baseball in particular. In fact when the Yonkers Police baseball team was organized it wasn't very long before this husky built officer named Brady was recognized as being and outstanding pitcher. He not only possessed speed, but a good curve ball as well. It was reported once that Brady seemed alone in his glory as the team's star pitcher.
Working as a foot patrol officer, Brady must have displayed leadership abilities, for on May 8, 1899, Hugh Brady was promoted to the rank of Roundsman. Hugh Brady was married, had five children, and

Captain Hugh D. Brady (cont.)

lived at 13 Randolph Street. A large and burly man, Roundsman Brady took the civil service test for police sergeant. He appeared before the Board of Police Commissioners with his competitors for an oral interview, and shortly after, on September 6, 1901, Hugh Brady was promoted to Sergeant. This rank was the 2nd highest position in the department, right behind the leader, the Captain of Police. Sgt Brady handled his new responsibilities with competence.

On April 25, 1908, an order was issued by the Public Safety Commissioner, establishing the "new" rank of police Lieutenant. All sergeants, including Sgt. Hugh Brady, were automatically promoted to the position of Lieutenant. Lt Brady was destined to be a lieutenant for only one month. Earlier in February of this same year, the common council had voted to divide the city into two patrol precincts, and had created an additional Captain position. It was said that they needed to open a 2nd precinct due to the work being done on the east side constructing the Catskill Aqueduct and Hillview Reservoir and the large work force that would be in Yonkers for several years.

The result of these actions was the promotion of Hugh Brady to the position of Captain, on May 1, 1908. Plans were completed and on May 28, 1908, a 2nd police precinct was opened with Captain Hugh Brady in command. Previously, the new precinct location had been operated as a substation since June 1, 1901. At the opening ceremony, Det. Sgt. Peter McGowan presented Capt. Brady with a gold pin inscribed, "From the Detective Bureau to Capt. Brady, May 1, 1908."

Captain Brady served for several years with distinction at the 2nd precinct. In 1919 he was transferred to command of the 1st Pct. on Wells Ave. Having served the police department for 33 years, Capt. Brady retired on November 30, 1922.

On July 4, 1936, retired Capt. Hugh D. Brady died at the age of 71 years.

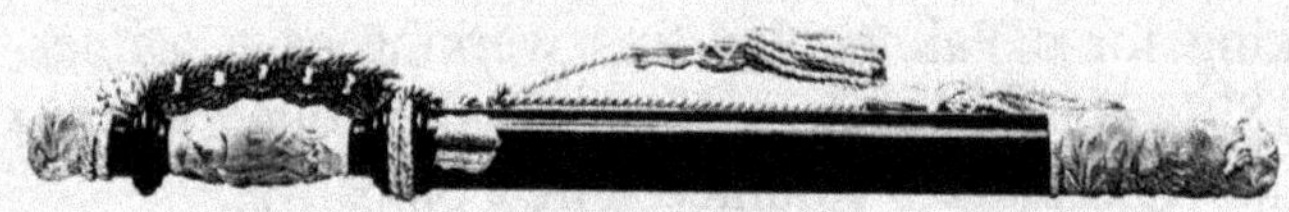

ACT. SGT. WILLIAM M. LAWRENCE

APPOINTED: August 19, 1891
RETIRED: August 31, 1916

Upon his appointment on August 19, 1891, Bill Lawrence patrolled the west and central part of Yonkers. In 1894 Lawrence was offered the post at the Bronxville substation in east Yonkers. Upon acceptance he was promoted to Acting Roundsman effective September 26, 1894. This rural outpost was a small house located on the corner of Bronxville Road and Clark Place and consisted of an office, 2 prisoner cells, a stable, horse and living quarters for Lawrence and his family. He would spend the better part of 17 years at this isolated station. This was a one officer post and a great deal of the time he was on his own. On April 25, 1908, when the rank of Roundsman was abolished, Bill Lawrence was made Acting Sergeant. In May of 1908 when the 2nd precinct opened he was assigned to that precinct where he would remain until his retirement on August 31, 1916. With his health failing, Lawrence moved his family to a farm in Hyde Park NY, where, on April 23, 1929 he died. Having been born in Yonkers about 1863, he was about 66 years old.

PO THOMAS J. MAY # 5

APPOINTED: September 4, 1891
RETIRED: September 15, 1918

Tom May was born October 20, 1869. Prior to being hired by the police department on September 4, 1891 he was gainfully employed as a bricklayer. Officer May spent most of his career working in the original Dock St. headquarters and later the Wells Avenue 1st precinct. However, in 1901 when substation #2 was opened on Central Avenue, Tom May was one of three patrolmen to be assigned there. For a number of years Tom May even played on the police baseball team. Later, for a short while, Tom May served as a detective. In fact, in January of 1905 while still a detective, he arrested a man in a Clinton Street saloon, who was wanted for murdering a man in Pennsylvania. As his seniority increased he would spend his later years assigned to the City Court and in the Mayor's office. His general gruff and confrontational disposition earned him the term "the man with the chesty disposition." When Tom May retired he was the only member of the entire police department who was not a member of the Police Association; by choice. Retired PO Thomas May died April 2, 1961, 43 years after retiring, at 91 years of age.

PO PATRICK J. WELCH # 27

APPOINTED: September 4, 1891
DISMISSED: February 10, 1897

A resident of 32 Prospect Street, Pat Welch was appointed a police officer on September 4, 1891 and assigned to foot patrol. During his early years he was most likely an efficient officer. He involved himself in department activities and in 1894 was a member of the police baseball team. He was described as a robust athlete who was a catcher and did a fine job on the team for two seasons. On May 5, 1894 while arresting a man at 1:30 AM, four of the man's friends proceeded to furiously attack and assault the officer with a chair and sticks. Fortunately two citizens assisted Welch in arresting the five, but leaving Welch's coat with a sleeve ripped off. When arraigned the prisoners were fined $27.00 to replace the officers coat. The Police Board even complimented Welch on his bravery in making the arrest. However, in 1897 Welch was charged with intoxication in uniform on duty. At his trial he promised the Commissioners, *"If it's not too late I'll turn over a new leaf and never drink another drop."* But it was too late. The police commissioners were not interested in promises and Patrick Welch was dismissed from the department effective February 10, 1897.

PO WILLIAM S. GRANGER # 25

APPOINTED: January 13, 1894
RESIGNED: December 4, 1895

Bill Granger was appointed to the department on January 13, 1894 while living at 39 Beech Street. Within that first year, on November 21, 1894, he was charged with leaving his post shortly after midnight without being relieved. Granger admitted the charge and was fined 3 days pay. Two weeks later, on December 9, 1894, following a rash of seven burglaries in a week, PO Granger observed two men on the railroad tracks at 5 AM. Ignoring his order to halt, the two men ran from him down the train tracks. As Granger ran after them he again ordered them to stop and fired his revolver three times without effect. The men escaped in the darkness but the officer was able to recover proceeds from a new burglary. On November 30, 1895 Granger was found leaving a "saloon" on duty at 11:30 PM in an intoxicated condition and when ordered into HQ he became abusive to the sergeant. Deemed unfit for duty it was then his "club, shield, and pistol" were taken from him. On December 4, 1895 a hearing was held, however Granger failed to appear. Instead he sent in his resignation from the police department effective December 4, 1895, which was accepted.

LT. JEREMIAH P. LYONS

APPOINTED: January 17, 1894
DIED: December 16, 1930

"Jere" Lyons, as he was known to his friends, was born in Ireland on June 6, 1865. Following his appointment to the police department January 17, 1894 he was assigned to the Wells Avenue headquarters station. In his early years he was a member of the department's baseball team, and was always considered one of the most popular men in the department. After serving for seven years he was reassigned to Sub Station # 2 at 569 Central Avenue. Always an efficient officer, Lyons was promoted to Sergeant on July 15, 1908, and when a 4th precinct was established on May 1, 1914 he was promoted to the rank of Lieutenant. As a lieutenant he was assigned to desk duty in that precinct. It was said that during his career he had a splendid record for honesty and hard work. In 1930 he had just finished his last day tour, and was due back in for late tour at midnight the following night. It was then that he developed pneumonia, and 5 days later he died on December 16, 1930. Lt Lyons was 65 years old with 37 years service. He received full departmental honors.

SGT. MICHAEL J. HORAN

APPOINTED: March 16, 1894
DIED: November 25, 1917

Born in Middletown N.Y. in 1860, Mike Horan moved to Yonkers and lived at 67 Cliff Avenue with his wife and son. Following his appointment to the police department on March 16, 1894 he performed his patrol duties from the Wells Avenue headquarters station. When Yonkers opened police substation # 2 on Central Avenue on June 1, 1901, Horan was one of three officers assigned there. Having earned a commendable reputation, six months later on December 1, 1901, officer Horan was promoted to the rank of Roundsman. He was said to be a man of "forceful" personality, and was reportedly the owner of some valuable real estate. On May 8, 1909 Rdsmn. Horan was promoted to Sergeant and when the new 3rd precinct building was opened in 1913 at 36 Radford Street, Sgt Horan was assigned there as a patrol supervisor. Sgt Horan would never live to know that his grandson, PO Francis Horan, and his great grandson Francis Jr. would both also be appointed Yonkers police officers. Sgt Michael Horan died suddenly on November 25, 1917 at 57 years of age.

SGT. WILLIAM F. CUNNINGHAM

Appointed: May 11, 1894
Retired: December 16, 1932

Sgt Bill Cunningham spent nearly four decades as a member of this department and played a prominent role in one portion of our police history; "Mounted Patrol".

Bill Cunningham was born in Little Meadows, PA., on December 16, 1868, which is where he received his early education. He came to Yonkers as a young man and worked as a trainman on the New York Central Railroad up until his appointment to the police department on May 11, 1894. Apparently because of his skills as a "horseman," Cunningham was assigned to patrol duties on horseback on a regular basis. He patrolled various rural routes throughout the city until April 27, 1908, when he was promoted to the rank of Sergeant. He continued to perform his new duties on horseback. In May of 1908, Sgt Cunningham was assigned to the newly established 2nd precinct.

A military looking figure with a distinguished appearance, Sgt Cunningham always wore a becoming handlebar mustache. Because of his position as a sergeant, and his past experience with

Sgt. William F. Cunningham (cont.)

mounted patrol, Sgt Cunningham was placed in charge of all mounted officers on patrol. As the leader of the mounted squad, the sergeant led all parades astride his horse "Blackie," along with other members of his mounted unit. Many youngsters reportedly used to go to the 2nd precinct on a daily basis, to watch Sgt Cunningham prepare the mounted patrol for duty. His orders, "Prepare to mount," and then, "Mount," were snapped out in military precision. When motor vehicles took over all patrol and the police horses were sold, Sgt Cunningham remained assigned to the 2nd Pct. However, for the sergeant, it just wasn't the same without his horse Blackie.

On December 16, 1932, after 38 years of service, Bill Cunningham retired from the police department. Because of his popularity, his co-workers at the 2nd Precinct gave him a surprise testimonial dinner. He was brought to the party by his son, Detective Tom Cunningham, and was presented with a watch and chain, suitably inscribed. During the dinner it was pointed out that for most of his career, retired Sgt Cunningham was in charge of the mounted squad. He trained all new officers to ride at the Empire City Racetrack, later renamed the Yonkers Raceway. He was described as being one of the few remaining links to the "old department." A Deputy Public Safety Commissioner who was in attendance cited the former sergeant for his unblemished record, character, and ability. A special illuminated sign over the speakers table bore the inscription, "Faithful Services- Bill & Blackie - 1894 – 1932."
In expressing his thanks Bill Cunningham said, "*This gathering is a gift I will cherish as long as I live. To you younger men I would say just one thing. I urge you to carry on and follow the instructions I gave you. Give the best that is in you, 24 hours a day, for the city you serve and the citizens who look to you for protection. If you do that you will never go wrong.*"

A resident of 438 Park Hill Avenue, Bill Cunningham was on his way to church on February 3, 1946, when he was struck by an automobile and killed. He was 77 years of age. The police emergency officers who responded notified detectives to respond. Detective Cunningham arrived at the scene of what he believed was just another fatality and was shocked to see that it was his father.

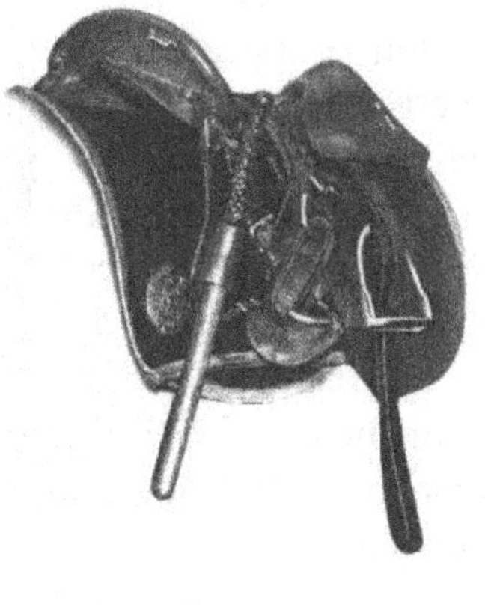

PO JOHN HEALY # 34

APPOINTED: May 15, 1894
DISMISSED: April 12, 1906

John Healy, of 135 Hawthorne Avenue, seemed to have the opportunity for a good career in police work. Not so! He was appointed to the YPD on May 15, 1894 and walked a foot post. In 1902 it appeared he was well liked and was a member of the Yonkers Police Band. (Which was short lived.) And by 1904 he had been assigned as a detective in the Detective Bureau. For some unknown reason the records indicate he was reassigned back to patrol duty on January 19, 1906. And in April of that year he was charged with being intoxicated on duty. At his trial it was pointed out that during his 12 year career, he had various charges preferred against him by supervisors 10 times for violating departmental rules. This last time, although he promised never to drink on duty again, PO John Healy was found guilty and dismissed from the police department on April 12, 1906. In 1925, while Healy was employed with the Post Office in NYC, a rumor was circulated that the police department was considering re-hiring him. The rumor proved to be false.

SGT. JOSEPH M. SCHEIBEL

APPOINTED: May 15, 1894
RETIRED: June 1, 1919

Joseph Scheibel was born around 1867 in Austria and later his family brought him to the United States when he was three years old. He and his brother John, who would later be a Yonkers police lieutenant, both received their education in local public schools. Joe was appointed to the police department on May 15, 1894 and walked a foot post. His superiors must have been pleased with his work because ten years later, on March 8, 1904, he was assigned to the Detective Bureau where, by all accounts, he performed his investigative duties with skill and diligence. Following the establishing of the new 4th precinct on Palisade Avenue, on May 1, 1914 Joe was promoted to the rank of Sergeant and was assigned to the 2nd precinct as a patrol supervisor. Upon completion of 25 years of faithful and honorable service Sgt. Scheibel retired on June 1, 1919. Following his retirement and after working for 15 years for the Yonkers Savings Bank in Getty Square as a security guard, retired Sgt. Joseph Scheibel died on December 5, 1935 at 67 years of age.

CAPTAIN EDWARD T. CONNOLLY

APPOINTED: May 15, 1894
RETIRED: May 10, 1927

Captain Edward Connolly served effectively and efficiently for many years in the Yonkers Police Dept., but this service was not without controversy. Born April 10, 1872 in Massachusetts, Connolly came to Yonkers as a young boy and attended and graduated from PS#6. He was described as always being a student, with self-improvement being his aim. In his early years, Connolly pursued the trade of a bricklayer and plasterer for six years, and served as vice president of the local union. He left this trade when he was 22 years old to be appointed a Yonkers policeman on May 15, 1894.

Shortly after joining the police department, Connolly devoted his spare time in taking a course in the Butler Business School. His main object was to improve his handwriting skills. To this aim, his efforts were successful, as his penmanship was said to be the best in the police department. When a bicycle patrol was initiated in the late 1800's, Ptl. Edward Connolly was one of the first police officers assigned to this duty.

Early in his career Ptl Connolly was involved in a potentially deadly confrontation, but fortunately

Captain Edward T. Connolly (cont.)

he survived. On May 23, 1901 while on foot patrol, Ptl Connolly came upon a man firing a revolver at another man. The patrolman tried to arrest the suspect only to have the man put his gun to the officer's head. Before the man could fire, Ptl Connolly drew and fired his own weapon striking the man in the head. Receiving only minor injuries, the man survived and was ultimately sent to prison. During his career it was said that Connolly made several important arrests. He was also said to be one of the best revolver marksman in the department.

On November 13, 1901 Ptl Connolly was promoted to Roundsman. Six years later, on July 10, 1907, he was promoted to the rank of Sergeant. Upon his promotion to Sergeant at 35 years of age, he was one of the youngest men to attain this rank at that time. In 1908 when the new rank of Lieutenant was established, Edward Connolly was elevated to that rank. It was in that same year that Lt Connolly was one of several officers assigned to the newly opened 2nd precinct.

As a result of the sudden death of Capt. George Cooley, Edward Connolly was promoted to captain on March 21, 1917, at the salary of $2,750 a year. His new assignment was to take command of the 4th precinct. A resident of 119 Convent Avenue, Capt. Connolly was known as a kindly man. His being six feet tall, and of great strength and athletic ability, enabled him to be an effective disciplinarian. Capt. Connolly would, in later years, be gratified that his son Fred Connolly would also join the Yonkers Police Dept. and become a sergeant.

On July 9, 1921, it was announced that Capt. Edward Connolly, the Commanding Officer of the 2nd Pct, had been tried on a variety of charges by the city administration, was found guilty, and was dismissed from the police department. One of the charges was failure to stop gambling in his precinct. He had been suspended on these charges since February of 1921, and had worked during that time as a detective with the N.Y. Central Railroad. Connolly's appeal of his dismissal before the Appellate Division of the Supreme Court failed.

Although few believed the captain was completely innocent of the charges, most believed the punishment of dismissal was too severe. In fact, a petition was circulated that collected 15,000 signatures requesting that Connolly be reinstated as a police captain so that he could then retire and collect his pension. Public opinion worked. On April 22, 1922, nearly a year since his dismissal, Connolly was fully reinstated to the rank of Captain. Most people thought he would now file for retirement and collect his pension. He didn't. He remained with the department for 5 more years. Then, very abruptly, and when he thought the time was right, on May 10, 1927, Capt. Edward Connolly requested that he be retired immediately. His request was granted that same day. But, a few months prior to retiring in 1927, the captain had one more chance to have his name printed in the local paper in a positive way.

In early 1927 the Yonkers Statesman newspaper began a series of interviews with Yonkers Police captains in an effort to gain some personal insight into the men who ran the police force at that time and their thoughts about the department. The interview that follows was held with then Captain Edward Connolly, commander of the 4th precinct, and reflected his personal recollections.

BY: CAPTAIN EDWARD CONNOLLY, in his own words.

Captain Edward T. Connolly (cont.)

"When I first went on post as a Patrolman in Yonkers, the old Central Station (HQ) was in Dock Street and Captain John Mangin was in charge. We worked the two platoon system and I patrolled my beat in the Flats along Riverdale Avenue, south of Prospect Street, with now, Capt. Bill Crough as my side kick. There was just one precinct and the department consisted of 30 men. I was on this post about 15 months when I was sent down with Patrolman Henry Cooley on old Post 3, now the 3rd precinct. I was there about a year and then was put on the Bicycle Squad doing about the same duty as the motorcycle cops do today. While on Bike duty I had my run in with two Italians in a shooting affray that taught me the value of being a good shot and able to handle my gun quickly and well.

One of the greatest assets,in my opinion, for a police officer is to be a good shot and be thoroughly familiar with his gun. My father and brother were both excellent shots with the rifle and I took naturally to shooting. When I took a slant towards police work I picked up the revolver and began practicing with that weapon until I was rated a good shot. I am glad to know that the range shooting for policemen in Yonkers will be revived in connection with the Police School that is to be reopened by Commissioner Cameron. Every cop ought to be able to shoot and shoot well. It's part of his protection and his ability to protect others.

<u>*Prevents a Murder*</u>

It was while riding down Main Street on Bicycle Patrol when I saw two men, one brandishing a revolver and threatening the other. Then he shot at him. I ran toward them and told the armed one to throw up his hands. Instead he drew his gun down on me and fired. But I beat him to the shot and his bullet went wide. I wasn't shooting to kill the man, but to disable him. My shot creased his head by the left ear and he dropped. As I ran toward him he again tried to shoot at me and I hit his hand with my nightstick. He quit then and I took him in.

The point I make is that I was a good and quick enough shot to beat the would be killer to it. Otherwise you'd be looking at a headstone with me under it today instead of talking with me. I've kept up the revolver practice and think it's a good thing for a policeman. The officer does not often have occasion to use his gun, but when he does he ought to be able to shoot straight and quick and that only comes from practice.

I was promoted to sergeant and transferred to the 3rd precinct under Captain Hugh D. Brady. It was while in this precinct that the now Captain Charles O'Mara and I were sent by Capt. Brady about 1 AM on a call to the old tailor store of B. Trager at 110 Riverdale Avenue on a burglar alarm. We found nothing in the storeroom and came out. Then we saw two heads peering from a doorway nearby and after a chase nabbed two men. They proved to be the burglars. O'Mara took from the pocket of one of them what the Yonkers Statesman (newspaper) described as a rapid fire repeating gun; a peculiar specimen of firearm frequently used by professional burglars to kill policemen. These two were well dressed and proved to be professional burglars

Captain Edward T. Connolly (cont.)

Promoted to Lieutenant.

I remained in the Third Precinct until I was made Lieutenant and then I remained there in that capacity until I was made Captain in 1917. Then I was transferred in command of the old Fourth Precinct with the station house at 734 Palisade Avenue. I relieved Capt. George Cougle who was transferred to command of the Third Precinct. About a year later I was transferred back to the Third Precinct, again relieving Capt. Cougle who was transferred to duty at the City Hall under Chief Wolff. After a year I was transferred to the Second and after a year there I was transferred back to the Third. When they abolished the Third and Fourth Precincts under the administration of former Mayor William J. Wallin, I went to the Second.

While on duty here I left the department for a short time and became a special investigator for Chief Edward E. Miles of the New York Central Railway police. (Actually Capt. Connolly was convicted of departmental charges and was dismissed from the Yonkers Police Department. He would later be reinstated following an appeal.) When I returned to the department I was assigned to duty as a special investigator in the First Precinct, remaining there until April 13, 1923. At that time the Fourth Precinct was re-established by Commissioner Thomas M. Tobin with the station house located in the No. 5 Firehouse on Shonnard Place, with Capt. Edward Quirk, now Chief, in command. I relieved Capt. Quirk. The Fourth Precinct includes territory bounded on the south by Ashburton Avenue, on the north by Hastings and the Town of Greenburgh, on the west by the Hudson River and on the east by the Nepperhan River. The precinct was originally established in 1914 under the command of Capt. George Cougle.

Wealthy Residents in the Fourth

The Fourth is peculiar in that it is peopled by the residents of private homes and owners of large estates and wealthy persons. For instance, the Fourth contains the homes of Samuel Untermeyer, William Boyce Thompson, the Thomas Ewing estate, and the residence of John E. Andrus. Most of the river front along the Hudson in the Fourth Precinct is privately owned and does not require the police attention that other sections of the city need. The residents are orderly and permanent for the most part and we have little or no trouble with sneak thieves.

The police personnel of the Fourth Precinct include 41 men as follows; Captain, 4 Lieutenants, 4 Sergeants, and 32 Patrolmen. There are 10 posts with 29 patrol call boxes with the men reporting hourly while on duty. Three men are maintained as Call Officers at the station house. They serve in 8 hour shifts so that one is always on duty to respond to a call by police automobile. Police functions in this precinct are largely preventative and protective. We watch all strangers in this precinct and we ask for an accounting from all of them.

Captain Edward T. Connolly (cont.)

The largest single institution in the Fourth is the plant of the Smith Carpet works, which occupies the site on Nepperhan Avenue, between Lake and Ashburton Avenues. There is very little trouble with these people as they are settled and employed constantly. We have one bank and six schools in the precinct. The schools include the Holy Rosary, St. Joseph's parochial schools and public schools 6, 9, 16, 22, and Gorton High School. These each require policing three times a day due to traffic.

Handsome Pete McGowan

The Fourth Precinct is unique in that it has a desk officer, lieutenant Peter J. McGowan, known as Handsome Pete. He is one of the oldest men in the department. In his younger days he was the Beau Brummel (Cassanova) of the police department. Because of his handsomeness and his smart dress he was always called on for special duty that required a fine looking cop on duty at weddings and similar events. He's still a handsome chap and quite the Brummel, as well as a mighty capable police officer.

The men of the Yonkers Police Department are a fine lot of chaps. I think the personnel of today is the best we have ever had. Policemen today are more keen and alert and up to date than they used to be. They have to be. Modern conditions have brought such changes and complexities in police work that the modern officer has to be more alert to cope with his job.

The Yonkers Police Dept. today is functioning with efficiency under the leadership of Chief Quirk who knows police work from A to Z and who is a natural cop. Wise crooks and criminals will give Yonkers a wide berth as they know that if they pull a job here, we'll land them, and they're bound to get the works. Preventative police work is one of the most effective means of keeping a city well protected and preventing thieves and robbers from preying on the citizenry.

Opening the Police School will be a help to the men who are all keen on their work and ready to make the most of all opportunities to advance themselves in their jobs in protecting the city against disorder and more serious crimes."

After serving 33 years with the police department, and being retired for 24 years, retired Capt. Edward Connolly died on July 8, 1951 at 79 years of age.

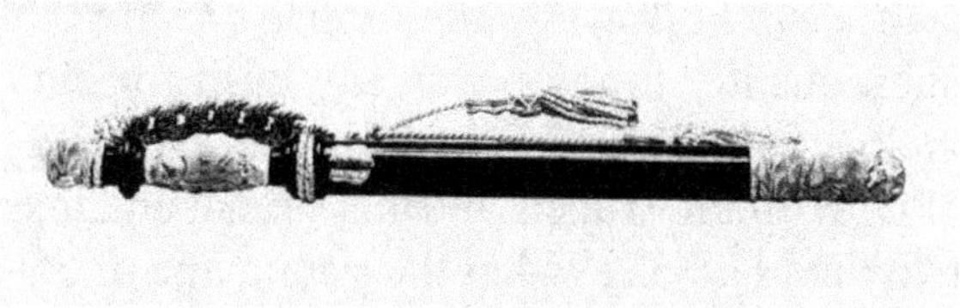

PO LEWIS C. WRIGHT # 35

APPOINTED: May 15, 1894
DIED: July 4, 1898

Lewis C. Wright was appointed to the Yonkers Police Department on May 15, 1894. After a few years on foot patrol, Ptl. Wright was assigned to police Bicycle Patrol duty. A resident of 124 Hawthorne Avenue, and seemingly a very healthy individual, Ptl. Wright suddenly experienced difficulty breathing and developed pneumonia. The doctors tried all remedies available at the time but, within only a few days, on the 4th of July 1898, Ptl Wright died in St. John's Hospital. Although he had only worked as a police officer for just over four years, it was reported that he had earned a first class reputation. He was related to Ptl John J. McCarthy -1 and left behind a wife and three small children. Attending his funeral were 31 uniformed officers, including the Captain of Police James McLaughlin. It was reported that each officer at the funeral detail wore black bows and white gloves. The uniformed pall bearers wore black gloves. And, as was the tradition, the police station was draped in black mourning cloth in memory and in respect for the deceased.

PO THOMAS BEAIRSTO # 40

APPOINTED: May 19, 1894
RETIRED: March 26, 1909

Thomas Beairsto was born in Yonkers Sept. 21, 1868, shortly after the Civil War. Prior to being appointed a policeman, Tom made his living as a carpenter. After being hired by the police department on May 19, 1894 Beairsto worked foot patrol his entire career. First, from the original H.Q. building at 9 Dock Street, and later from the 20 Wells Avenue station house. His record was a fairly good one with only a few violations of the rules. For example: on Feb 7, 1908, he was found guilty of neglect of duty, to wit, reporting late for roll call. He was fined three days pay. Beairsto's health was not very good and following his being out on sick leave for some time, he applied for a disability retirement at half pay. Following the Police Surgeons review, Beairsto was subsequently found physically unfit for duty and his request for disability retirement was granted on March 26, 1909 after 15 years' service. His daughter Irene would later become the daughter-in-law to Yonkers PO William Walsh, and his grandson, Joseph Beairsto would later be a Yonkers sergeant. Thomas Beairsto died Feb 5, 1924 at the young age of 55 years.

CAPTAIN WILLIAM H. CROUGH

Appointed: May 19, 1894
Retired: December 7, 1935

When retired Captain William H. Crough died at the age of 92 years, it brought to an end the life of a man who experienced police work in the horse and buggy days, and yet watched our department move into the computer age.

William Crough was born December 7, 1871 in Marlborough N.Y. in Ulster Co., where he received his education. He came to Yonkers with his family at the age of 16 years. At the time he applied to be a policeman, he worked as a bricklayer, and resided at 127 Clinton Street. Upon his appointment to the department he worked under the leadership of the first Yonkers Captain of Police, John Mangin. One of his earlier assignments was with the bicycle patrol. He must have handled all of his assignments with credit, because after only 5 years of patrol duty, he was assigned to the Detective Bureau on August 17, 1901. This was followed very soon by his promotion to Roundsman on May 14, 1902.

Throughout these years he worked from the original Dock St HQ, and later from the 1st Pct. station on Wells Avenue. Evidently Bill Crough was a very effective officer, because on December 31, 1907, he was promoted to sergeant.

Capt. William H. Crough (cont.)

At that time there was no rank of Lieutenant. However in April of 1908, this position was officially established. One month later on May 15, 1908, Bill Crough was promoted to Lieutenant. His assignment was desk officer at the 1st precinct. He continued to provide excellent service to the department, but his next promotion would not come again for some time. About this time in a special story to the N.Y. Evening Telegram newspaper, Lt. Crough was apparently making a study of Yonkers local "derelicts." Crough, who in the article was reported as being one of the most polite officers in the department, reportedly liked to bring out the latent good qualities in defeated men. He stated that the golden rule had been impressed upon him in his youth, and now guides his conduct.

Lt Crough was assigned from time to time to either desk or general switchboard duty. On June 21, 1918, he was transferred from the 1st pct. to the 3rd pct. as a desk lieutenant. On February 21, 1919, when the 3rd Pct. captain was suspended from duty, Lt Crough was made Acting Captain in charge of that precinct. Later he was returned to duty at the 1st Pct. On December 2, 1925, Lt Crough was transferred to desk duty at the 2nd Pct., but it would last only a month. On January 21, 1926, he was transferred to H.Q. and placed in command of the Traffic Bureau.

Lt Crough was not only a physically strong man, but he also had strong opinions on what was right. For example; Due to his status as the commanding officer of the Traffic Bureau, and his having placed high on the civil service eligible list for promotion to captain, on February 11, 1926 the Public Safety Commissioner advanced him to Acting Captain and ordered him to wear the insignia (shield and bars) of a captain, on his uniform. Lt Crough apparently did not mind the extra responsibility, or not receiving a salary increase. However he did feel it was wrong to be compelled to wear the insignia he had not "officially" earned. He made these feelings known to the Commissioner, who responded by commending Lt Crough for his beliefs, and rescinded the order directing him to wear the insignia of a higher rank.

On June 4, 1926, Lt Crough was transferred to command of the Detective Bureau at H.Q. It was 3 months later on Sept. 1, 1926, with 18 years as a lieutenant, that Lt Crough was promoted to Captain. At his last Detective Bureau roll call all the detectives gathered and presented the captain with a handsome Royal Arcanum ring. In 1931 Capt. Crough was interviewed by a reporter on how it was in the "old days." Having a photographic memory, the captain loved to recall the past, and told of a time when the media rarely used cameras, but instead had artists draw pictures of suspects. Also, fingerprinting was not yet known; police wagons and ambulances were horse drawn; good penmanship was a must, for the typewriter was not yet being used by the dept.

After 42 years' service and having reached the maximum age of 64, Capt. Crough retired on Dec. 7, 1935. On that day more than 100 officers from various precincts attended the captain's last 4 PM roll call. On behalf of the department, Comm. Morrissey presented the captain with an expensive and engraved watch and a gold retirement shield. Capt. Crough was praised highly by Chief Quirk and others, for his dedicated years of efficient service.

Straining to maintain his composure, Captain Crough turned toward his men, stood erect, and with his face scarlet red said, "*Men, I thank you my brothers for these testimonials and your presence here this afternoon. I am sorry to leave here, but I assure you I have only the kindliest feelings for everyone. My*

Capt. William H. Crough (cont.)

greatest pleasure in life was my work here, and my association with you men. As I leave here men, my fervent hope is that each of you is blessed with long life, good health, and good luck." When the captain stopped speaking there was an outburst of applause lasting for several minutes.

Said to be a handsome rugged man, Capt. William Crough had seen the city population grow by 100,000 people, and the police dept. grow from 43 men to 307 during his career. He also witnessed the addition of the 2nd, 3rd, and 4th Pct.'s, the addition of motorcycles and automobiles, the modern radio system, and the Bureau of Criminal Identification. A tough and truly interesting man, William Crough lived and experienced a fascinating police career.

After 28 years in retirement, former Capt. Crough of 15 Overhill Place, who had raised three sons, one of which was a NYC policeman for a short time, fell fracturing his hip, which ultimately led to his death on September 7, 1963 at the age of 92 years. Had he lived only one year longer he would have been proud to see his two grandsons, James and Gerald Curtis, sworn in as Yonkers police officers.

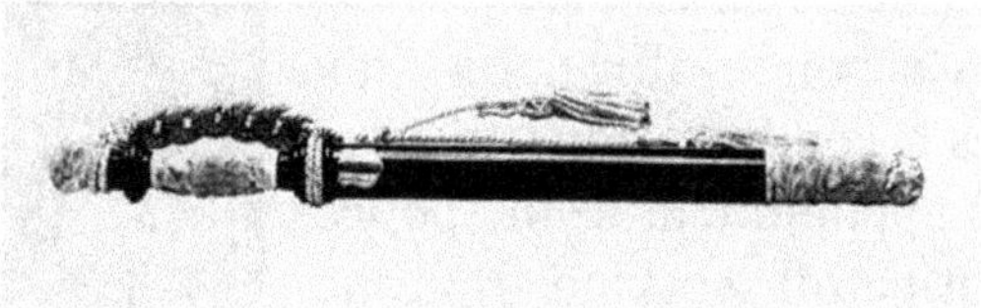

PO JOHN G. WELCH # 22

APPOINTED: May 19, 1894
DISMISSED: November 28, 1906

John George Welch was born on the 30th of March, 1861. According to his granddaughter he was a big man with black hair and blue eyes and was born in Butlers Bridge, County Cavan, Ireland. He would later come to the USA. at the age of 18 years. Prior to becoming a police officer on May 19, 1894 he worked as a laborer and lived at 69 Riverdale Avenue. As a police officer it is believed he performed his duties efficiently; at least most of the time. On November 27, 1906 Welch was tried on charges of being intoxicated on duty 11 days earlier, and being off post in a "saloon" on Dock Street. During his trial even the Captain of Police testified on his behalf attesting to Welch's excellent past record. However the Police Board would not be swayed and found Welch guilty and after 12 years service as a police officer he was dismissed from the department on November 28, 1906. In 1907 Welch unsuccessfully appealed his dismissal in the Brooklyn Supreme Court. He then gained employment as a grounds keeper in Washington Park until he became ill in 1923. On May 13, 1929 John Welch died at age 68.

PO EVERETT C. ARCHER

APPOINTED: May 29, 1894
RESIGNED: October 2, 1901

Prior to his appointment as a police officer on May 29, 1894 Everett Archer worked as a conductor and lived at 104 Linden Street. Upon Archer's appointment to the police department he was assigned to foot patrol working from the original Dock Street H.Q., and later from the 20 Wells Avenue headquarters building. I guess one could presume that he was probably well liked as he was an active member of the police baseball team. However, on September 26, 1901 Archer was tried on charges of leaving his post at the end of his tour without waiting for his relief. At his trial he pled guilty but explained that, in fact, he had waited for his relief, saw his relief a block away, gestured by waving his nightstick at the officer, and only then did he return to H.Q. He believed he had been properly relieved. Nevertheless, the Police Board gave him a formal reprimand for neglect of duty. Quite possibly upset by this decision, the following month PO Everett Archer submitted his letter of resignation, effective October 2, 1901, which was accepted by the police commissioners.

CAPTAIN JOHN A. CAHILL

APPOINTED: January 10, 1895
RETIRED: October 15, 1924

On April 8, 1870, John Cahill was born in a little frame house at the top of Elm Street in the Nodine Hill section of Yonkers. Known as "Jack" to all his friends, Cahill was the oldest of 4 sons. He received his education at St.Mary's School and later at PS # 2. He was given a shotgun by his parents at the age of 10 years. It was not uncommon for youths to head to the woods after school and shoot at targets. This would be the beginning of his athletic interests.

After leaving school he went to work for the Alexander Smith Carpet Mills. Feeling closed in he then became a builders apprentice. There he learned the trade, and became quite proficient, as a bricklayer. In the meantime "Jack" Cahill became interested in sports and his first accomplishment was the game of baseball. Jack became a member of the "Viewvilles," a baseball organization that flourished for many years and produced many fine athletes. He also played ball on the "Adonis" team as well, up on the old Eagle grounds. He was not only good with a bat but was also a fine infielder. At the age of 17 Cahill also became interested in "track" sports and could often be seen practicing the shot-put on the old "buckwheat" track.

Captain John A. Cahill (cont.)

After submitting his application for employment as a police officer, and being certified as being physically qualified by the police surgeon, John Cahill was appointed a Yonkers policeman in 1895. Cahill had begun a career that would blend his police professionalism with his natural talents as a rugged sportsman. Following his appointment Cahill performed foot patrol for a few years, but after a while he was assigned as one of the first bicycle patrol officers in the city. Late in the evening on July 4, 1899 there was an altercation between two men in Coyle's Saloon at 39 Dock Street. Within minutes one man had been shot three times and would die a few days later, and the suspect ran from the scene. Having nothing but a description, within one hour officer Cahill, who was on foot patrol, caught the suspect at gun point trying to leave Yonkers on a freight train at the foot of Main Street. Later that same year on November 14, 1899, officers Cahill and Henry Cooley stopped three suspicious men at 3 am at Ashburton and Warburton Avenue. When Cahill grabbed one man by the arm to question him, the man quickly pressed a gun against Cahill's nose and said, "Release me or I'll blow your head off." Cahill immediately drew his revolver causing the suspect to run. The officer fired a shot but, surprisingly, missed its mark. However after a chase of several blocks he arrested the suspect.

Notwithstanding the shot that missed the suspect, even prior to his appointment to the department Jack Cahill was always a good shot with his rifle. He never lost that skill. In 1899 the owner of a sporting goods store offered a gold medal for the winner of a revolver tournament championship. Cahill hit the bull's-eye 69 times out of a possible 72, which was enough to have him win the medal.

The idea of whether the department should have a full time Detective Bureau was always a political issue. But even though there was no formally organized Detective Bureau as yet, Cahill must have impressed his supervisors enough for them to assign him as a detective by 1900. After long debate, on June 1, 1901 a Detective Bureau was formed, and Det. Cahill and a few other men were assigned under the direction of Det. Sgt. Peter McGowan. Detective Cahill was so efficient, that on September 26, 1901, he was presented with a resolution from the Board of Police Commissioners commending him and other detectives for their arrest of two Mt Vernon men for murdering a Yonkers man. Det. Cahill was publicly commended and his name was placed on the departments "Roll of Honor."

It would seem that Patrolman John Cahill's service and reputation within the police department was also known to many others. In 1904 the New York Daily Tribune wrote an article about officer Cahill, which included a photograph of him in uniform alongside his police bicycle, with the caption, *Champion Automobile Catcher. Bicycle Policeman Cahill of Yonkers, has earned that title.* In the article they wrote that the title was given to Cahill because, for the month ending May 10, 1904 he had arrested or assisted in the arrest of twenty- six speeding drivers, from his bicycle. All twenty-six were later convicted and fined $25.00 each. The news account further related that, *for the last two years Cahill has been a terror to speeding automobiles, but this year he has eclipsed all previous records.*

On July 10, 1907, having scored high on the civil service test, and after 12 years of faithful service, Cahill was promoted to Roundsman. In the following year, in April of 1908 he was promoted to the rank of Sergeant. It was during that year that then Public Safety Commissioner Edgar Hermance offered a "special shield" to be awarded to the best marksman in the department, using their own revolver

Captain John A. Cahill (cont.)

at a 30 foot range. (At this point all members of the department did not have department issued revolvers.) This was a challenge that Sgt. Cahill couldn't pass up. Using his own .32 caliber revolver Cahill easily walked away with the "shield." (Badge) Six months later a similar competition was held for the "shield" but this time Cahill lost it to PO Ed King. The third time around Jack Cahill won it back, earning him the reputation as the best marksman in the department.

John Cahill also had a strong belief that the key to success was plenty of exercise. When he was first appointed and assigned to the bicycle patrol he enjoyed it because of the exercise. Not surprisingly, when motorcycles were introduced, he was not interested in ever riding one. He preferred pedaling. In fact he would often take vacations and pedal about 80 miles a day along with his buddies, PO's Pat Flood and Joe Scheibel. Whenever he had the time Cahill would also swim. He was a strong swimmer and would regard it as almost nothing to swim across the Hudson River, tap the shore on the opposite side and then swim right back. It was simple exercise to him.

Cahill's rapid rise up the ranks continued. On November 1, 1909, John Cahill was again promoted, this time to the newly created rank of Lieutenant. Cahill had spent all of this time working from the 1st Precinct on Wells Avenue. On May 5, 1917 a Riot Squad was formed as a precautionary measure against any disturbance that might occur as a result of the war in Europe. Three squads, consisting of 24 men, were placed under the direction of Lt. Cahill, who was known by all to be in excellent physical condition, and was an excellent shot with a revolver. Lt. Cahill trained all of his men at the Yonkers Armory.

In January of 1918 Lt. Cahill was sent to the NYC Police School of Instruction for four months. His assignment was to learn how to be an instructor in physical training for new police recruits. At the age of 48 years, Lt. Cahill had no trouble keeping up with others half his age. With this new knowledge he would now be able to teach his police officers more effectively. Special emphasis was placed on physical conditioning. In January 1919 Lt. Cahill was detailed to teach in our own "Police Instruction Service." He would do this in addition to his regular duties as a desk lieutenant. Cahill taught our police officers, on his and their own time; classes in physical fitness, self-defense, first aid, swimming, emergency rescue work, and firearms training. He held most of his classes in the Hollywood Inn gymnasium.

On March 31, 1919 Lt. Cahill was transferred from the 1st precinct, to the 2nd precinct, as acting captain, due to the dismissal from the department of Capt. George Cougle. However Lt. Cahill still continued his training of the men. In August of 1919 when Police Clerk Ivers died, Lt. Cahill was made acting clerk against his strong objection. He followed his orders and served in this capacity throughout 1920. But because he was pressured into an assignment he did not want, and it appeared he could not get out of, Lt. John Cahill, who said he was a cop not a clerk, submitted his resignation from the police department. The issue was immediately reconsidered and on January 3, 1921 Lt. John Cahill was reassigned to the 1st precinct as a desk officer. Cahill agreed not to retire.

On December 22, 1921 Lt. John Cahill was promoted to the rank of Captain at the salary of $3,000 per year, and was assigned as the commanding officer of the 2nd precinct. Still he continued as the trainer of the Riot Squad. All throughout his career Capt. Cahill had been an extremely active, dedicated and loyal police officer. He was always liked by his subordinates and peers alike, even though

Captain John A. Cahill (cont.)

he was a strict disciplinarian.

On October 15, 1924 Captain John Cahill retired from active service in the police department. He and his family moved from Yonkers and purchased a 170 acre orange grove in Orlando Florida. While there he continued to maintain his own physical conditioning. In addition, he was reported to have often invited his good friend, Gene Tunney, then a pro boxing champion contender, to come to his farm and train for his future title fights. Cahill was said to be proud of the fact that Tunney would allow Cahill to spar with him and Cahill, even at age 55, reportedly held his own. His good friend Gene Tunney would go on to become the World Heavyweight Boxing Champion for the years 1926 through 1928. After 18 months in Florida Cahill bought a fruit and poultry farm in Brookfield Connecticut and moved there with his family. In later years he would give up his farm and move in with his son.

While living with his son John Jr. in Rome N.Y., retired Captain John A. Cahill died on February 27, 1950, just short of 80 years of age.

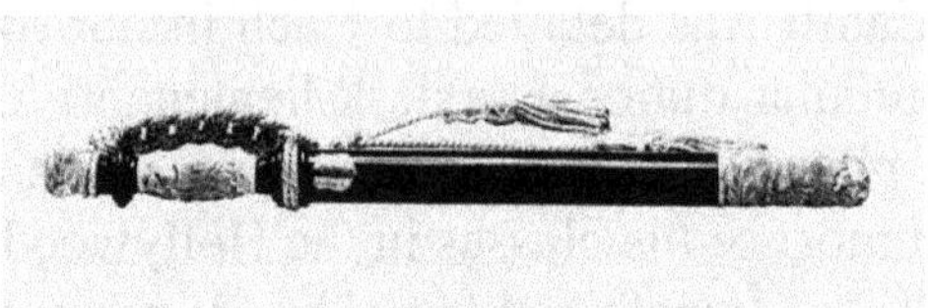

PO EDWARD O'CONNOR #58

APPOINTED: January 22, 1896
DISMISSED: March 24, 1897

Police Officer Edward O'Connor seems to have been one example of just how difficult it was to be a policeman during his time. He was appointed to the police department on January 22, 1896 and with no information to the contrary, during his first year he presumably performed his patrol duties satisfactorily. However, in February and again in March of 1897, he reported himself sick and unable to work. The Police Surgeon was notified, and gave him a thorough examination. The surgeons report indicated that O'Connor's temperature was normal, heart rate normal, tongue not coated, and he had no trouble in his lungs and as such he was judged fit for duty and directed to return to work. But again, while in bed during reserve duty, he told another officer he was too sick to get up. Again he was examined by the police surgeon and found fit for duty. When patrolman O'Connor said he was still too sick to report for duty and would see his own doctor, and failed to appear for roll call, departmental charges were filed against him for disobeying a direct order. At a meeting of the police board O'Connor was found guilty and dismissed from the force effective March 24, 1897.

LT. ALBERT SMALLEY

APPOINTED: April 23, 1897
RETIRED: November 7, 1932

Albert Smalley was born in Uniondale, New York on November 7, 1867. It was reported that he arrived in Yonkers to make his living when he was 19 years old. Following his appointment on April 23, 1897 and his recruit training, Smalley was assigned to foot patrol working from the 9 Dock Street headquarters. (The new Wells Avenue headquarters would not be finished being built for another year.) After 12 years working foot posts, in early 1909 he was assigned to the Mounted Squad where he named his horse King. But before the year was out, on November 30, 1909, Smalley was promoted to sergeant and had to leave his horse behind. Smalley had been working in the 1st precinct, but when a 3rd precinct was established in December of 1909, he was transferred there as a patrol sergeant. He would spend the next 13 years working from the 3rd precinct at 36 Radford Street. On December 1, 1922 Al Smalley was promoted to Lieutenant and assigned as a desk officer in the 4th precinct and following his retirement on November 7, 1932, Ret Lt Albert Smalley died May 3, 1943 at the age of 76 years.

LT. JOHN C. SCHEIBEL

APPOINTED: April 23, 1897
RETIRED: October 8, 1932

Born in Yonkers on October 31, 1873, Scheibel resided at 26 Warburton Avenue. When he was appointed a Patrolman on April 23, 1897, he was a single, 25 year old machinist. Over his years of police service John worked in the 1st, 3rd, and 4th precincts on foot patrol. He was promoted to Sergeant on October 11, 1908, and to Lieutenant on December 23, 1921. Like a number of others, Scheibel began his career as part of the bicycle patrol. Later, as a lieutenant, he was elected president of the Captains, Lieutenants and Sergeants Assoc. in 1927 & 1928. Records indicate that he was a war veteran, dates unknown, and as such had served as president of the Yonkers Police War Veterans Association. His brother Joseph was a Yonkers Sergeant. On October 1, 1928 when the "Lock Up," or City Jail opened on Alexander St., Lt. Scheibel was placed in charge as the Acting Warden until February 1, 1930 when a civilian was appointed. After retiring on October 8, 1932 and being retired for 6 years, John Scheibel died January 12, 1939 at 65 years of age.

LT. WILLIAM F. WELSH

APPOINTED: February 8, 1898
RETIRED: April 19, 1926

William Welsh was born in Yonkers on March 1, 1867. Prior to his appointment to the police department on February 8, 1898 he worked for the Yonkers D.P.W. Following his appointment as a police officer, and only 3 years on patrol duty, on June 1, 1901 Welsh was chosen to be one of the first detectives in the newly established Detective Bureau. This was a prestigious assignment but he received no additional pay. He also spent a short time assigned to substation # 2 on Central Avenue but in 1904 he returned to patrol the west side of the city. On December 20, 1907, Welsh was appointed a Roundsman, and in April of 1908 he was elevated to Sergeant. In 1911 he served for a few years as a detective sergeant but was promoted to Lieutenant on May 1, 1914 and worked as a desk officer in the precincts. He spent most of his years in the 1st, 4th, or 3rd precincts, where he was assigned when he became ill and decided to retire on April 19, 1926. A little more than a year later, retired Lt. William F. Welsh died on December 19, 1927 at his home at 147 Morningside Place at the age of 60 years.

PO PATRICK GORMAN # 46

APPOINTED: February 12, 1898
DISMISSED: November 28, 1906

Patrick Gorman was appointed a Patrolman on February 12, 1898. During the first several years that he worked patrol he appears to have done his job satisfactorily. However, on November 12, 1906 upon reporting for the late tour roll call officer Patrick Gorman advised the desk officer, Sgt Cooley, that he was ill and had pain in his left side. The sergeant sent he home and had the police surgeon respond to Gorman's house to examine him. The surgeon later testified that Gorman was unable to give a coherent answer and it was believed he was intoxicated. Gorman was charged with being intoxicated and at his trial other witnesses gave testimony that he was, and also, was not intoxicated. Capt. Woodruff testified that Gorman's conduct in the past had always been what it should have been with the exception that he "persisted too much in drinking rum." After considering all the evidence, including the fact that he had 8 years satisfactory service, the Police Board voted and dismissed officer Gorman from the police department effective November 28, 1906. In a news article dated April 26, 1907 it was reported that Pat Gorman was appealing his dismissal to the Brooklyn Supreme Court. The disposition particulars are unknown but he was never re-instated.

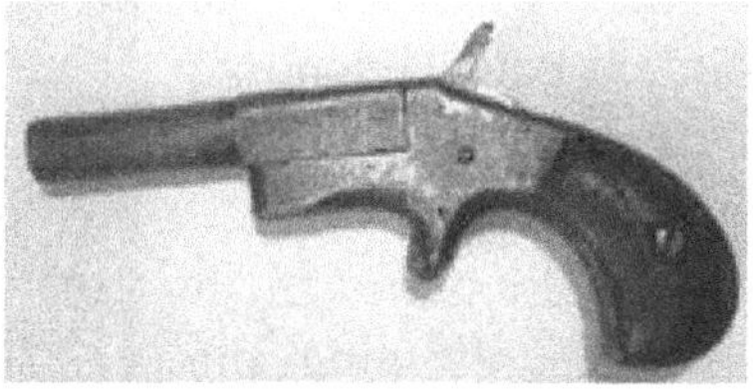

SGT. JOHN W. R. BELL

APPOINTED: March 14, 1898
RETIRED: December 8, 1938

John Bell was born in Yonkers on December 9, 1874, and attended local public schools. Upon his appointment to the Police Department on March 14, 1898 he was assigned to mounted patrol duty on the east side of the city. This duty was very desirable and he must have performed his duty exceptionally well because he served as a mounted officer for over 25 years. Most of his service was performed working from the 2nd Precinct on Central Ave. At one point, for a short period of time around 1912, John Bell was detailed as an acting Sergeant. But later, on October 16, 1929, John Bell was officially promoted to the rank of police Sergeant. After completing more than 40 years of dedicated active service, Sgt. Bell retired on December 8, 1938. The following year, on May 2, 1939, his son, Yonkers police officer William Bell, would come home to discover that his father, retired Sgt John W. R. Bell had died unexpectedly at the age of 64 years.

SGT. JOHN J. HERLIHY

APPOINTED: March 14, 1899
DIED: January 29, 1913

John Joseph Herlihy was born in Yonkers on June 24, 1869 and would later attend Cooper Union School in NYC studying art. When he was appointed to our department on March 14, 1899 he worked out of the Wells Avenue headquarters building as part of the mounted patrol. Known to his friends and fellow officers by the nickname "Crock," Herlihy was apparently a well-liked officer. On May 15, 1909, following his passing of the promotional exam, officer Herlihy was promoted to the rank of Sergeant. Following the opening of a 2nd precinct on Central Avenue in May of 1908, Sgt Herlihy was reassigned to that precinct still on mounted patrol. At one point Sgt. Herlihy became ill and took several days off to recover. Unfortunately, he was more ill than he realized. Sgt Herlihy died in his home at 41 Hawthorne Avenue on January 29, 1913. The cause of death was reported to be pneumonia. At his funeral, 80 members of the department marched as a show of respect and the entrance to the 2nd precinct was draped in black mourning cloth. A member of the local Fraternal Order of Eagles, the 38 year old sergeant left behind a wife and three children.

LT EDGAR W. BUCKOUT

APPOINTED: March 14, 1899
RETIRED: August 1, 1924

Born January 22, 1865 in Brooklyn, Buckout came to Yonkers and eventually worked as a bricklayer. Appointed to the YPD on March 14, 1899 rookie Ptl. Buckout patrolled that part of Riverdale Ave. known as "the flats." He was so popular that he became known as "the mayor of the flats." Buckout always did well on civil service tests and as a result was promoted rapidly. He was appointed Roundsman on December 11, 1907, to Sergeant in April of 1908, and Lieutenant on November 1, 1909. His promotion to Lieutenant was the result of the opening of a new 3rd Pct. on December 1, 1909 where he was then assigned. He would remain there for the rest of his career. In 1916, when the precinct captain died, Lt. Buckout served as acting captain for 8 months. When Lt Buckout retired on August 1, 1924 his nephew Henry Hallam was also a Yonkers policeman. He would never know but Buckout's great grandnephew, Richard DeNike, would later be the Irvington N.Y. Police Chief. Ret. Lt. Edgar Buckout died December 22, 1927.

SGT HENRY J. MILLER

APPOINTED: March 14, 1899
RETIRED: September 1, 1916

"Hen," as Henry Miller was known to his friends, was born in the U.S. on May 23, 1865. His early employment was as a motorman. Upon his police appointment on March 14, 1899 he worked from the Wells Ave. station until he was reassigned to the new 3rd Precinct when it opened Dec. 1, 1909. Miller was said to have been a very religious man who readily admitted that, while he patrolled the streets on duty at night, his only companion was his Rosary Beads. Miller's courage was put to the test on July 12, 1910 when, while on post at the city pier a woman jumped in the river to commit suicide. As the officer attempted to pull her out, he was pulled into the water. Though the woman violently resisted his help, officer Miller was able to rescue her and save her life. On May 1, 1914 Miller was promoted to Sergeant. Unfortunately his last two years of life were very painful. Sgt Miller suffered a stroke which caused him to retire on a disability on September 1, 1916. During this last year he was blind and would not live to see his young son Francis become a Yonkers policeman. Ret. Sgt. Henry Miller died on March 28, 1917.

PO AUBREY N. ATTWELL

APPOINTED: March 15, 1899
DISMISSED: July 7, 1904

Born June 16, 1876, Aubrey Neville Attwell was appointed a police officer on March 15, 1899. And it would appear that officer Attwell was an efficient and brave officer. In fact, on one night in January 1904 he discovered a house fire while on foot patrol, warned the family and saved their lives. However problems were around the corner. In May of 1904 Attwell was charged with failing to arrest three suspected burglars, even though a Police Board member told him not to. When officially charged, Attwell felt this was retribution for his not supporting the new mayor during the recent campaign. The charges were weak and were dropped. However he was then charged with immorality for visiting the home of a single woman while off duty. Attwell felt he was being set up and volunteered to resign rather than face the disgrace of dismissal. His resignation was not accepted and instead he was found guilty and dismissed from the force. He later worked locally as a gardener and registered for the draft in 1917. Aubrey Attwell died March 7, 1926. He was 49 years old.

SGT PATRICK CONDON

APPOINTED: March 15, 1899
DIED: June 23, 1924

Patrick Condon was born in 1871 in Tipperary, Ireland. He came to the United States with one brother while the other remained in Ireland. Like many Irish immigrants before him, Condon first earned his living as a railroad man. He was appointed a Patrolman in the Yonkers Police Department on March 15, 1899 while living at 2 Highland Avenue. For nearly his first 10 years, officer Condon worked from the Wells Avenue station, the only police building in operation. When the newly established 3rd precinct was opened, Condon was promoted to sergeant on Dec. 1, 1909, and was assigned to that precinct. On June 23, 1924 Pat Condon was at home putting on his uniform to prepare for work when, without warning, he unexpectedly dropped dead. Sgt. Patrick Condon was provided with full departmental honors. The 3rd precinct entrance was draped in black mourning cloth and over 125 uniformed officers attended and march in his funeral procession. He was 53 years old.

PO THOMAS F. BURKE

APPOINTED: March 15, 1899
DIED: February 11, 1902

Tom Burke was appointed to the YPD on March 15, 1899. Unmarried and residing with his mother and two sisters on Nepperhan Avenue, Tom Burke was a popular police officer and was reportedly well liked by his peers. It was also reported that he had a spotless record with no violations of department rules. One day while on duty and moving a heavy file cabinet in headquarters he strained himself severely. He was a young man and had been in good health, but in a few days he became delirious. On Feb 11, 1902, while on sick leave and in bed, Tom Burke was visited by two fellow officers. While they were there it was reported that Burke rose to his feet and said, "Well boys, it's time to report." He then suddenly fell to the floor dead. The 33 year old deceased officer's family felt they were entitled to some form of pension benefit. However, the city declined saying, to qualify, an officer must be in service for over ten years, or be injured in the discharge of his duties, which they determined he was not. However, a large police escort was assigned to his funeral.

SGT PATRICK C. FLOOD

APPOINTED: March 15, 1899
RETIRED: August 1, 1927

Born in 1876 in Dublin Ireland, Pat Flood was brought to the U.S. as a baby by his parents. He graduated from St. Mary's School, then DeLaSalle Institute, and later Cooper Union College in NYC where he studied Pharmacology. In fact, prior to his appointment to the police department on March 15, 1899 he worked in a pharmacy. As a young cop Pat Flood served in the Bicycle Patrol and in the early 1900's he was appointed and served as a detective. He was also a member of the short lived YPD Police Band around 1902. On Jan. 19, 1906 he was reassigned from the Detective Bureau back to patrol. A popular officer, "Paddy," as his friends knew him, was an amateur entertainer and singer who sang at many departmental social functions. After several years in the 2nd Pct., Flood was again appointed a detective on June 10, 1918. Seven years later, on June 30, 1925, Flood was promoted to the rank of Sergeant. Following retirement on August 1, 1927, eleven years later on July 29, 1938 Patrick C. Flood died at the age of 62.

PO WILLIAM P. O'MARA #39

APPOINTED: March 15, 1899
RESIGNED: Approximately 1907-1908

Born William Patrick O'Mara March 10, 1876 in Beacon N.Y., O'Mara came to Yonkers as an infant with his parents. A resident of 17 Bayley Avenue, Bill loved to sing Irish songs. After being appointed a police officer on March 15, 1899 he continued to sing at any opportunity; be it a social event or sitting in the police muster room. Records indicate that he was a fine officer and, in 1904, after it was decided a Detective Bureau was to be re-instituted, O'Mara was chosen as one of five men to be detailed there. However, later that same year, some reports claimed that due to politics, he was transferred back to patrol on "mounted" duty. Weighing over 200 lbs., it was said neither he nor his horse were very happy. PO William O'Mara decided on his own to change employment and resigned from the department. Much later, from 1920 to 1923, Bill O'Mara was elected and served two terms as alderman in the 1st ward, being elected in 1919 and again in 1921 and was dubbed the songbird of the Common Council. He was a member of the Yonkers Lodge of Elks, LaRabida Council Knights of Columbus, and the "13 Club." Before his death he was employed as an Inspector on Construction work being done by the New Rochelle Water Supply Co. Bill became ill and died on August 16, 1928 at the age of 52 years. Bill's brother was police captain Charles O'Mara.

SGT. WILLIAM J. HEALEY

APPOINTED: March 15, 1899
RETIRED: February 16, 1928

William Healey was born November 3, 1870 in England and came to the United States with his family at the age of 4 years. A resident of 18 Parker Street, he worked as a grocer prior to joining the police department on March 15, 1899. Healey's police abilities were apparently quickly recognized and within just a few years he was advanced to Detective in the Central Bureau, where he earned an excellent reputation. Bill Healey was also one of the original members of the Police Department Band a few years after joining the department. He served several years as a detective in the 1st and 2nd precincts and, on May 14, 1914, he was promoted to sergeant and assigned to the newly established 4th precinct then on Palisade Avenue. After retirement on Feb 16, 1928 he remained active, and because of his good voice he was active in amateur theatricals. His nephew was Yonkers PO Thomas McCaul. Having been retired only two years, on August 8, 1930, retired Sergeant William Healey died suddenly at the age of 60 years.

PO MICHAEL F. McGRATH #36

APPOINTED: March 15, 1899
DIED: December 25, 1930

A proud native of Ireland, having been born in that country on January 8, 1867, Michael McGrath came to the United States as a young man. Before joining the police department on March 15, 1899, McGrath worked as a bricklayer and lived at 70 St. Joseph's Avenue. Following his police appointment officer McGrath was assigned to the 1st precinct at Wells Avenue on foot patrol duty. He would ultimately spend his entire career of over 30 years working various foot posts out of the 1st precinct, or as it was known, the Wells Avenue station. The first seven of those 30 years were spent working the steady night shift.

Early in his career in 1901 McGrath had an incident where he lost his service revolver. In these early years there were no holsters allowed, only your coat or trouser pocket. McGrath was able to have the departmental charges placed against him dismissed by purchasing a replacement revolver.
Five years later this revolver would come in handy. On June 28, 1906 while preparing for roll call, McGrath had a conversation with another officer in the muster room about a recent murder that had taken place in the south-east section of the city. The other officer jokingly said to McGrath, "Mike, you had better be careful out there tonight. You never know who you might come up against." McGrath assured his fellow officer in his cocky Irish way that if he did, he would make quick work of whoever. Later that night while on his post at Central Avenue and McLean Avenue, McGrath came upon a suspicious man late in the evening walking alone on his post. As he approached the man he called for him to stop. At this point the man turned and fired his gun at McGrath and then ran. Mike returned fire and a running gun battle in the night followed. Neither man was struck and the suspect escaped into the night.

After 30 years of loyal and dedicated service, without warning PO Michael McGrath became suddenly ill and died on Christmas day, December 25, 1930. But before his death PO Michael McGrath was able to see his son George McGrath also be sworn in as a Yonkers policeman.

CAPTAIN MICHAEL O'HARA

APPOINTED: March 15, 1899
RETIRED: December 1, 1925

Michael O'Hara was born September 24, 1868 in County Monaghan, Ireland, and came to Yonkers at the age of 18 years, no doubt with a distinctive Irish brogue. Prior to joining the Yonkers Police Department he spent several years in the insurance business, rising to District Superintendent with the Prudential Insurance Company. Following his appointment to the police department on March 15, 1899, O'Hara was assigned to foot patrol duty in the new constructed headquarters/1st precinct building at 20 Wells Avenue.

Although records are not available, O'Hara must have made a very positive impression with his superiors. Because, on June 1, 1901, with less than two years with the police department, O'Hara was assigned to the newly established Detective Bureau as a Detective. Very unusual to say the least. But,

Captain Michael O'Hara (cont.)

three years later, on March 8, 1904, after being abolished for a short time, a Detective Bureau was re-established. When it came time for staffing the Bureau they replaced three of the original five detectives but once again, one of the men to be reassigned to the Detective Bureau was Patrolman Michael O'Hara. It may be of interest to note that, at that time, being designated a Detective did not result in any increase in salary. The primary reasons one might hope to be a Detective was that you were able to work in what the department referred to as citizen clothes, and you usually worked the day or evening tours; thus allowing a person more time with his family.

As a result of the alleged politically pressured retirement of Sgt. George Osborn one month earlier, promotional tests were held, including a test for Roundsman, on April 18, 1905. All patrolmen who had been at top pay for a full year were eligible to take this exam. Patrolman Michael O'Hara scored the highest score and was certified #1 on the promotional list for Roundsman. At a meeting of the Board of Police Commissioners O'Hara was appointed a Roundsman effective May 1, 1905. No sooner had he assumed his new position, when two days later he was detailed back to the Detective Bureau as an Acting Detective Sergeant. However the following year, on January 1, 1906, changes were again made in the "Bureau" reducing its size by one half. As part of those changes, Roundsman O'Hara was transferred back to uniformed patrol duty.

O'Hara was promoted rapidly, attaining sergeant's rank on May 28, 1908, and the following month on June 1, 1908 he was promoted to newly established rank of Lieutenant. It is important to note that on this date of June 1, 1908, when the rank of Lieutenant was first created, all Roundsmen were automatically promoted to Sergeant and all Sergeants automatically promoted to this new rank of Lieutenant. Following his promotion Lt. O'Hara was then assigned as a desk lieutenant in the newly established 2nd precinct on Central Avenue. And following the opening of the new 3rd. precinct on Radford Street, in December 1909, Lt O'Hara was transferred there as a desk lieutenant.

On August 17, 1914, in a move that didn't last very long, Police Headquarters was moved from 20 Wells Avenue to City Hall, leaving the 1st precinct to remain. Lt. O'Hara was one of three lieutenants assigned to desk duty with a new switchboard to receive calls and then forward them to the appropriate precinct.

On July 3, 1925 Lt. Michael O'Hara was promoted to the rank of Captain, and was placed in command of the 2nd precinct. But only four months later, on November 18, 1925, Capt. O'Hara sent a letter to Public Safety Commissioner Alfred Iles requesting retirement. His letter stated, "Having completed 27 years in the Police Department of the City of Yonkers NY, I respectfully request for retirement as provided by law, same to take effect December 1, 1925." His request for retirement was approved.

After nearly 20 years in retirement, retired Capt. Michael O'Hara died January 23, 1944 at his home at 77 Allison Avenue at the age of 79 years.

PATROLMAN EDWARD BURNS # 42

Appointed: June 20, 1900
Died: September 5, 1904

DIED IN LINE OF DUTY

Patrolman Edward Burns was born in 1872 on Prescott Street, in the Nodine Hill section of Yonkers to his parents William Burns and Annie Bowler Burns. He received his education at Public School #2. Upon completion he took up the trade of a blacksmith with Isaac S. Lawrence, where he remained employed until his appointment to the police department several years later. On January 29, 1896 he married Miss Sarah Nellie Rothing in the home of the bride's parents at 200 Elm Street. The ceremony was performed by Rev. George Cutting, pastor of Yonkers Westminster Presbyterian Church. The new couple made their home at 78 Ash Street.

Ed Burns first applied for employment as a police officer in Yonkers on March 11, 1897. However, he would not be hired for another three years. When Burns was hired as a police officer on June 20, 1900, he was 28 years of age. At the time he was hired he was in fine physical condition having been working as a blacksmith, and he weighed 175 lbs. Police work seemed to agree with him, for it was reported that he rapidly gained weight and strength.

Ptl. Edward Burns (cont.)

Burns was an expert horseman and was physically one of the most powerful men on the force. He stood over 6 foot tall and within a short time he weighed about 220 lbs. Because of his riding skills, soon after his appointment he was assigned to the mounted squad where he primarily patrolled the west side of the city. Interestingly enough, although he was reportedly a skilled horseman, on September 8, 1900 an article appeared in the Yonkers Statesman which related the following:

'On Friday October 7, 1900, Mounted policeman Edward Burns was patrolling the Saw Mill River Road near O'Dell Avenue last evening when the young mare he rode shied at an electric light that had been burning dimly, and that with suddenness flashed brilliantly. Burns was thrown to the ground and sustained injuries to the left hip and back. He managed to get up and secure the mare and telephoned from George Fisher's Saloon at 463 Saw Mill River Road, to the station house at 8:46 PM. Doorman Nolan was sent with the police wagon and he took Burns and the mare to the station." Although an accident of this nature was not uncommon, Ed Burns had no way of knowing how the significance of being thrown from a horse would, in the not too distant future, impact his very life.

On Labor Day, September 5, 1904, Ptl. Burns reported for duty just as he had for the past four years. He was a member of the 3rd section, 2nd platoon. While waiting in the "sitting room" for roll call, Burns, along with fellow officers Dennis Cooper, Tom Beairsto, and Jim Madden began singing. Whenever a song was to be sung, it was said that Ed Burns was sure to join in the chorus. The song chosen by the quartet on this day was the melancholy hymn, "Nearer My God To Thee." No sooner had they finished singing when the bell rang, and the men filed in front of the desk for roll call and to receive their assignments. Within minutes officer Burns would mount his horse and begin the ride that would end in eternity.

At about 1:40 PM Ptl. Burns was riding his horse up Elm Street. It was at this moment that a tragic chain of events were set in motion that would ultimately result in the officer's death. News accounts reported that the conductor of trolley # 501 was proceeding west down Elm St. from Nepperhan Avenue and was approximately in front of the "Turn Verein Hall" at 93-95 Elm St, when he stated he saw a mounted officer sitting on his horse on the south side of the street near the curb. As the trolley approached, the horse suddenly, and with a bound, plunged forward toward the front of the trolley. The officer tried to control the fear struck horse without success. The horse fell to the ground, rolling over onto Burns and the tracks, directly in front of the trolley, colliding with it. The horse immediately jumped to its feet and ran down Elm Street. However in its struggle to stand, the animal bent up the fender of the trolley, and with Burns pinned down, the officer was crushed to death beneath the Life Guard Rail.

News descriptions of the officer's injuries were not very delicate. They said, "The skull of the unfortunate policeman was crushed, every rib in his body shattered, his heart and abdomen walls were ruptured, and he was otherwise injured." Both the motorman and conductor were subsequently placed under arrest by Det. O'Hara, but were later released.

The following day an inquest was held regarding officer Burns' death, and the results of the coroner's investigation were announced as follows: "Ptl. Edward Burns came to his death from injuries received from a fall and by being struck by a trolley car; said injuries being due to an unavoidable accident. The motorman and conductor of the car beneath which Burns was crushed are exonerated from all blame."

It was also reported that, although the horse involved had only been purchased six weeks earlier, it was said to be an excellent horse. In fact, because it was considered gentle, of good disposition, and

Ptl. Edward Burns (cont.)

not afraid of anything, officer Burns had, himself, chosen this new horse to be his mount. At H.Q. a strange coincidence was immediately recalled regarding a premonition Sgt. Brady had the night before the accident. Sgt. Brady recalled that the night before, he continually dreamed of death. He even mentioned this to several officers that morning, stating he felt something of a dreadful nature was going to occur before the day was over. He was right! Following the tragic death of Ptl. Edward Burns, a deep feeling of depression and gloom pervaded police headquarters. Words of sorrow and deepest regret were expressed by all the officers. The leader of the department, Captain of Police Frederick Woodruff said, "*Ptl. Burns was one of the most honest and reliable officers in the department. He was ever ready to do his duty; the embodiment of civility and good nature; always to be depended upon; in the presence of danger he was most courageous*."

Det. Sgt. George Cooley said that he had known Burns since boyhood and had always found him to be an honest and industrious young man. He said he was a good officer, and a kind and indulgent husband and father. Sgt. Brady said, "*Since Burns has been a member of the force, I have found him to be one of the most honest and efficient officers. He was always willing to do his duty and more, if called upon.*" The funeral of Ptl. Edward Burns shield 42, took place on September 8, 1904 at Christ Episcopal Church at the corner of Nepperhan Avenue and Elm Street. Only a few yards from where he died.

At 1 pm the police escort formed in front of police headquarters. Mounted officers Gorman, Smalley, McCarthy, and Bill O'Mara, headed by Police Commissioner Medina, were first in the line of march. Then came the squads of foot patrolmen headed by Capt. Woodruff, and consisting of; Sgt's Osborn, Lent, and McGowan; Roundsman Shea, Connolly Crough, and Horan; Patrolmen Miller, VanMetter, Cooper, Blatzheim, Steuart, J.C. Scheibel, J. Welsh, Kennedy, Nolan, Redding, C. O'Mara, Robinson, H. Cooley, Buckout, Higgins, W.J. Healey, Kiley, Waldron, Cougle, and J. Scheibel; Detective Sergeants Cooley and Dinsmore, and Det's May, Flood, O'Hara, Wood, Mance and King were in plainclothes. All the police patrol officers were in uniform and represented more than one half the numerical strength of our department at that time. This formation was followed in the line of march by 60 uniformed Railroad Co. trolley employees.

The entire escort marched to the home of the deceased officer at 108 Oak Street, and then to the church. It was estimated that approximately three thousand people lined the sidewalk in front of the church. During the service officer William P. O'Mara sang "Calvary." In addition, six fellow officers of Burns sang "Nearer My God To Thee"; The same hymn sung by the deceased officer shortly before he

Ptl. Edward Burns (cont.)

was killed. Burial was at Oakland Cemetery.

It would seem that even at the solemn ceremonial formation for our first officer killed in the line of duty, a petty show of power and authority was displayed. News accounts of the day reported that, upon the mounted men leading the formation from the church, instead of Capt. Woodruff and his uniformed contingent following next, Det. Sgt. Cooley and his six detectives rushed from the rear and wedged themselves in front of the captain and his uniformed men. This seeming to be only one of many displays of who had the most political clout. Even at a policeman's funeral. The fact that petty rivalries for a show of power at such a solemn occasion should have been put aside, was ignored.

Later that same month his fellow officers organized and held a benefit fund-raising baseball game between the "blue coats and red shirts," (police & firemen). The game was held with everyone enjoying themselves, even though the police department lost to the fire department. But most important, over $2,500 was raised for officer Burns' family. On the 14th of the month the Police Board received a letter from Burns' widow which read as follows: "*Words cannot express my thanks to you for your kindness and sympathy shown me in my sad bereavement. No one knows my loss, but it is comforting to think I have so many kind friends, and I wish I knew how to show my appreciation to you all. Hoping you will always cherish sweet memories of those not lost, but gone before. Sincerely.*"

"Nellie" Burns, as his wife was known, would later be hired on January 23, 1911 by the police department as a "Matron" in the police jail.

The tragic death of this 32 year old officer was certainly a tragic loss to his family. He left behind his wife "Nellie," two sons- Lawrence 6 years, and Charles Edward 2 years of age; three brothers and a sister. Ed Burns would never know that his family would continue a tradition of police work. His grandson Robert Burns retired as a Town of Chappaqua, NY police officer. In addition, Roberts's son Lawrence Burns was a detective with the Mt Pleasant NY Police Department.

Police Officer Edward Burns had the unfortunate distinction of being the first Yonkers police officer in our department's history, to die in The Line of Duty!

CAPTAIN GEORGE W. COUGLE

Appointed: June 20, 1900
Dismissed: March 31, 1919

George Wilder Cougle was born on December 4, 1875 in Blumsweet, Kins County, New Brunswick, a dominion of Canada. He spent his boyhood years there where he attended local schools. In 1889 Cougle and his family moved to Forge Village, Massachusetts, where he remained until 1893. It was then that this 18 year old moved to Yonkers and took up residence at 38 William Street. Upon his arrival, he sought out work and found it as a "spinner" in the local carpet mills.

After passing the Civil Service police test, George W. Cougle was appointed a patrolman in the Yonkers Police Dept. on June 20, 1900. George was known to have two brothers who followed him in police work. His brother William Hall Cougle would be appointed a patrolman in 1907 and retire with the rank of lieutenant. His other brother, whose name is not known, would be appointed a policeman in the Providence R.I. Police Dept. in 1913.

When questioned in 1995, the daughter of William H. Cougle stated that her father was a very responsible and disciplined person. However she stated that her uncle, George Cougle, "was a bit

Captain George W. Cougle (cont.)

of a hell raiser." This trait would eventually be his undoing. However, at the turn of the century, George Cougle was a young and energetic man. He was a member of the Y.P.D. baseball team which regularly competed with the Yonkers Fire Dept., and around 1901 he joined with several other officers to organize a "Police Band." Unfortunately it was disbanded after only a few years.

After having been previously abolished for a time, on March 8, 1904 a police Detective Bureau was again established by the Police Board. Ptl. George Cougle was chosen as one of the five officers assigned to this bureau. Det. Cougle either performed his job well or was in political favor, because in 1906 when the Detective Bureau was reduced in size, Cougle remained for a while longer.

It was reported that in the summer of 1906 Ptl. George Cougle was on night foot patrol when he attempted to confront a suspicious man. Before the officer could stop him, the suspect fired a shot at Cougle and ran. It was said that fortunately the bullet only passed through his uniform coat. A foot chase followed but the suspect escaped.

Presumably displaying a keen attention to duty, Ptl. George Cougle was promoted to Roundsman on December 11, 1907. On May 15, 1908, when the rank of Roundsman was abolished, Cougle was automatically promoted to Sergeant. He continued his rapid rise through the ranks by being promoted to Lieutenant on October 11, 1909. His assignment was desk officer in the 1st Pct. In anticipation of the opening of a 4th police precinct, George Cougle received his promotion to the rank of Captain on December 31, 1913.

After much political debate, it was decided that a 4th Pct. would be established. Capt. Cougle, the new commanding officer, was placed in charge of setting up new precinct boundary lines, foot posts, etc. On May 1, 1914 the new 4th precinct was officially opened at 764 Palisade Avenue, with a rental charge of $60.00 a month for the entire building. A compliment of 39 officers and men were placed under Capt. Cougle's charge. At the opening ceremony Capt. Cougle addressed his men and reportedly said, "*I feel I know you share my feeling that we will give them the best that is in us. I will do it myself, and I am sure each of you will do the same. I am likewise positive that there will be no fault to find, for we will do good and clean police work. Our aim will be to win the good will of the people and our superior officers.*"

On March 31, 1919 Public Safety Commissioner O'Keefe announced that he had dismissed Capt. George Cougle from the police department. The action taken was the result of numerous actions brought against the captain on February 21, 1919. At that time Cougle was accused of checking into the Square Hotel in an intoxicated condition, remaining there for several days, and then failing to report for duty. Cougle was officially charged and convicted after trial of: Conduct unbecoming an officer; Entering a place where liquor is sold while not on official business; Neglect of duty; Absent without leave; Failure to report; and Dereliction of Duty. Capt. Cougle also had been charged 9 months earlier on June 10, 1918, with conduct unbecoming an officer. At that time he pled guilty and received the maximum penalty short of dismissal, a fine of 30 days pay.

After being dismissed, Cougle worked for a time as a private detective. Then in the fall of 1925 the former captain became ill, and on December 16, 1925 George W. Cougle died of what is believed to have been a stroke. He was only 50 years old and he would not live to see his son George Cougle Jr. become a Yonkers police officer in 1935.

Captain George W. Cougle (cont.)

Even though he had been dismissed from the department in disgrace 6 years earlier without a pension, George Cougle was accorded high honors at his funeral by the police department. The esteem in which former Capt. Cougle was held was evident by those officials who attended his funeral. The department provided pall bearers consisting of 1-Capt, 2-Lieut's, 2-Sgt's, and 2-Ptlm. Fifty uniformed men consisting of sergeants and patrolmen from various precincts came to pay their respects by marching in uniform from the 1st Pct. to the former captains house.

There is little doubt that former Captain George Cougle made some serious errors in judgment during his career, and he paid a heavy price for them. However it seems clear that he made his mark as a man, a police officer, and a good friend to many.

Photo 1909

CAPTAIN DENNIS A. COOPER

Appointed: June 20, 1900
Retired: October 6, 1939

Dennis A. Cooper was born in Yonkers on November 11, 1875, and received his education at St. Mary's school from which he graduated. Before being appointed as a policeman, Cooper held a clerical position with the local American Express Company. When he applied for appointment to the police department he lived at 50 1/2 Hudson Street and was single. He would later marry the daughter of Lt. Daniel Shea.

After his appointment to the department, on June 20, 1900, Cooper worked predominately on foot patrol. However, on occasion he was assigned to bicycle patrol. In 1902 while the police still worked under the two platoon system, whereby the officers were required to do reserve duty in the station house, there was ample idle time. On one occasion during reserve duty, Cooper brought in his flute to entertain his coworkers. Others started doing the same with other instruments, and very quickly the Yonkers Police Band was formed. This band, which Ptl. Cooper originated, only lasted until 1907 when it was disbanded. Later in 1902 Cooper was already working plainclothes assignments, and was elevated to detective.

Captain Dennis A Cooper (cont.)

Effective January 19, 1906 the Detective Bureau, which was formed in 1901, was reduced in size, with some of the men returning to patrol. However at that same time Dennis Cooper was transferred into the bureau. As reports of the day indicated, Cooper was not new to the "sleuthing business." From 1902 through 1904, Cooper had been in the Detective Bureau, or the "Central Office" as it was also referred. News accounts of that time period reported that during those years, Det. Cooper displayed a truly brilliant record in that he "affected dozens of captures and evidenced ingenuity in detective work that was admirable."

On December 31, 1907 Det. Dennis Cooper began his rise through the ranks and on to notoriety, by being promoted to the rank of Roundsman. Less than a year later on May 15, 1908, after the new police rank of lieutenant was created, Roundsman Cooper was promoted to Sergeant.

In late 1909, plans were being formulated to open a 3rd police precinct for southwest Yonkers. By October 1909 these plans had been approved, and on October 11, 1909 several promotions were made, effective November 1, 1909, to staff the new precinct. Dennis Cooper was one of those men promoted to Lieutenant. By 1912 Lt. Cooper would be working in the 2nd Precinct as a desk officer where he would remain for several years.

By September of 1916 it was clear to the patrolmen of our department that they wanted an organization that could speak for, and work on their behalf, on problems of mutual concern. It was then that the "Police Association of The City of Yonkers" was officially organized and incorporated. Given the level of interest and involvement with his men, it was no surprise that Lt. Cooper was one of eight policemen who signed the Certificate of Incorporation as a witness.

On May 25, 1918, it was announced that the department would soon establish a school to instruct those men who were to be assigned to a new Traffic Squad. From January to May of that year Lt. Cooper had been attending the NYC Police School of Instruction on how to properly handle the flow of vehicular traffic. Upon the lieutenant's return, he was assigned as the commanding officer of this new traffic squad and was directed to set up a traffic school. He was to instruct 18 patrolmen who would be assigned to this new program.

Less than a month later on June 10, 1918, the department abolished it's plainclothes precinct operations, and again organized a Detective Bureau. Lt. Cooper was also chosen to take command of this new bureau, in addition to being the commanding officer and training instructor for the new traffic squad. Fortunately, after two years, on April 2, 1920, Lt. Cooper was relieved of the duties of commanding the traffic unit, and was able to devote full time as the C.O. of the Detective Bureau.

After serving effectively as the C.O. of detectives for several years, on May 21, 1921 Lt. Cooper was suddenly transferred to the 1st Pct. on desk duty. This move shocked the department. It was said that this unwelcome change was reflected in "a gloom that was cast over the members of the Detective Bureau." It was rumored at the time that his testimony at a trial against Capt. Edward Connolly was deemed unsatisfactory and not helpful to the administrations case. This, the men believed, resulted in his transfer. However on June 21st, Lt. Cooper was again put in command of the Detective Bureau. At that time with 22 years of service, Lt. Cooper had served about 17 years as a detective, and was believed to be well qualified to lead them.

Captain Dennis Cooper (cont.)

After returning to the detectives in June of 1922, on December 1st of that year, Det. Lt. Dennis Cooper was promoted to the rank of Captain as a result of the retirement of Capt. Hugh Brady. Upon his promotion, Capt. Cooper was allowed to remain in command of the Detective Bureau. His new salary was $3,000 per year. Reports credited him with having aided in solving a series of murders in 1924 during hostilities between the Hip Sing and the On Leong Chinese Tong gangs. Capt. Cooper caught Lon Chow, one of 37 prisoners arrested, in a raid at their hideout on Herriot Street. Chow was identified as the hatchet man in a series of murders which had occurred throughout the county. During the ensuing years he would leave the detectives and again command the Traffic Bureau.

On October 6, 1939, after 39 years of faithful service, Capt. Cooper retired. He had no plans, however, on sitting home and resting. The following month Cooper campaigned and was elected to the first Common Council under the new City Manager form of government in Yonkers. He was promptly voted Vice Mayor by his peers on the council. He served one term and would not be re-elected in 1941. Cooper later worked through the World War 2 years as head of plant security for the North American Philips Co. of N.Y. in Dobbs Ferry. During the war he worked closely with the FBI and other agencies in anti-sabotage efforts.

Retired Captain Dennis A. Cooper died on May 10, 1948 at his home at 590 Palisade Avenue. Having suffered a heart attack, he had been ill for a week. He was 72 years of age. With his passing, the police department and the city lost a very popular and energetic man who was always involved in police and city activities. Being a devout catholic, Capt. Cooper organized the Holy Name Society in the Police Department and served as its first president. He was a charter member of the Police Association, and in 1925 Cooper organized the Captains, Lieutenants, & Sergeants Association. He also served as its first president in 1925 and 1926. Later, he would again be elected their president in 1932. He was a member of the Knights of Columbus, the Yonkers Elks and the Clinton Athletic Club.

Although he was a capable and tough officer, he also enjoyed a good time. He always observed St Patrick's Day by entertaining the men at H.Q. with Irish tunes on his fife. He was said to get "a kick" out of leading the men out to roll call, on this day, playing the "Wearing of the Green" on his fife.

Captain Dennis A. Cooper was truly one of a kind.

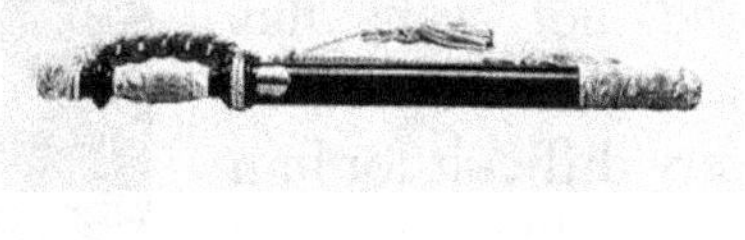

PO JOHN J. EGAN # 44

APPOINTED: November 28, 1901
RESIGNED: September 5, 1904

Very little information is available about patrolman John J. Egan. However, he probably was a likable and social individual because, soon after his police appointment on November 28, 1901, he was one of several men who formed and played an instrument in the Yonkers Police Band. He was a foot patrolman who had his share of complaints made against him by irate citizens, however he was apparently conducting himself according to the rules because, following an investigation these complaints were always dismissed. During the nearly three years Egan was a police officer, politics played a large role in an officer's duty assignment. Everyone seemed surprised when John Egan submitted his letter of resignation. When asked for a reason he was reported to have said, "This is no place for a man anymore, unless he has pull," meaning a friend in high places to look out for you. It appeared that he decided not to work where politics was so prevalent.

SGT. THOMAS KILEY

APPOINTED: November 28, 1901
RETIRED: April 15, 1919

Tom Kiley was born July 18, 1877 in Stamford, Conn. His parents moved to Yonkers when he was an infant and took up residence at 186 Palisade Ave. Upon joining the police department on November 28, 1901 he was assigned to foot patrol in the downtown area. He was also one of the organizers of, and participants in, the Yonkers Police Band around 1902. At this point in time, politics played a substantial role in the operation of the police department. On July 14, 1904 patrolman Kiley was abruptly reassigned to mounted duty. It was thought to be a form of political punishment. He did not want this assignment. Nor, I suspect, did his horse. For Kiley weighed well over 200 lbs. and it was very difficult for him to mount and dismount his horse. Even so, the very next day, while on mounted duty, he made a burglary arrest. On November 1, 1909 Kiley was promoted to sergeant. Due to poor healthy Sgt Kiley retired on a disability pension on April 15, 1919. After a long illness, he died on June 16, 1930 at the age of 52 years.

LT. DANIEL F. MURRAY

APPOINTED: November 30, 1901
RETIRED: March 15, 1934

Daniel Murray was born in New York City August 17, 1870. He came with his family to Yonkers as a small boy and attended and graduated from St. Mary's school. Upon being appointed to the police department on November 30, 1901, Murray first worked foot patrol out of the Wells Avenue station house. He passed the Sgt's exam and was waiting to be promoted. In order to staff a new 3rd Pct., which would soon open, several appointments and promotions were made. On October 11, 1909, Murray was appointed to the rank of Sergeant and assigned to the new 3rd Pct. as a foot patrol supervisor. On May 1, 1914, Murray was promoted to Lieutenant in preparation for the newly established 4th precinct on Palisade Ave. Lt. Murray had an excellent reputation and held several commendations from the police Honor Board. He retired on March 15, 1934 and moved to New Jersey. On July 12, 1950, Lt. Daniel Murray died, one month short of his 80th birthday.

LT. THOMAS F. KENNEDY

APPOINTED: November 30, 1901
RETIRED: December 31, 1936

Tom Kennedy was born January 1, 1874 in County Waterford, Ireland, and a short time later came to Yonkers as a young boy along with his family. He attended school in Ireland and Yonkers. Before his appointment to the police department on November 30, 1901 he worked as a conductor and motorman for the Yonkers Railroad Company. A volunteer fireman before they were a paid department, in 1893 Kennedy joined the "Dutch Five," a nickname for the Irving Hose Co. After being appointed a policeman, Kennedy worked for several years in the 1st precinct. On January 29, 1910, he was appointed a detective, where he served for a time. Several years later on December 22, 1921, Kennedy was elevated to the rank of Sergeant, and on August 1, 1933, he was promoted to Lieutenant. Lt Kennedy was proud that one of his six sons, Det Sgt John Kennedy, was also a Yonkers police officer who would, years later, be a captain. Following his retirement on Dec 31, 1936 and even though he was in excellent health, Ret Lt Kennedy died unexpectedly on March 1, 1945 following an emergency appendectomy.

CAPTAIN WILLARD L. MANCE

APPOINTED: November 30, 1901
RETIRED: December 1, 1927

The story of Willard Mance is that of a farm boy who would rise to prominence in his community. He was born November 1, 1873 on a farm in Cape Vincent, Jefferson County New York. He attended and graduated from Cape Vincent Grammar school. It was then that Willard Mance became a carpenter's helper under the instruction of his father who had his own business. Mance moved to Yonkers in 1895 where he met and married his wife, Miss Josephine Otis, on February 12, 1900.

After passing a civil service test and a physical exam, Willard Mance was appointed a Yonkers police officer. Working out of the relatively new combination headquarters and 1st precinct station house on Wells Avenue, PO Mance worked foot patrol in the downtown Getty Square area. It was not too long however, before officer Mance was assigned to the prestigious Detective Bureau. After several years working as a detective, in January 1906, Captain of Police Frederick Woodruff began a reorganization and downsizing of the Detective Bureau. Although several men were transferred out, detective Mance was allowed to remain in the Bureau. His remaining there possibly indicated the significant confidence Capt. Woodruff had in detective Mance's investigative abilities. Then again it could have been politicians making the decision. It was therefore surely no surprise when PO Mance was promoted to the rank of Roundsman on December 20, 1907, and incredibly only four months later in April of 1908, he was

Captain Willard L. Mance (cont.)

promoted to the rank of Sergeant.

Sgt. Mance was not only an active patrolman and detective, but he was apparently just as quick to get involved as a sergeant. An example of this was on April 27, 1908 at 4:30 AM. Getty Square foot patrol officer Ahearn, who was checking the rear of St. Johns Church, came upon a male carrying a suitcase. When ordered to stop, the man began running. The officer fired several shots at the suspect but missed him and a foot pursuit followed. Sgt Mance was in Getty Square at the time, heard the shots, and quickly joined in the chase, firing his revolver twice at the fleeing male. Sgt Mance and PO Ahearn chased the man up New Main Street, into Ann Street, into the Nepperhan Creek where the man had jumped, and finally arrested the burglar up on Elm Street.

On December 1, 1909, the recently established 3rd precinct was officially opened on Radford Street in a converted two family house. As part of the preparations to staff the new precinct, several men were promoted effective on the opening date of the new precinct. Willard Mance was one of those promoted to the rank of Lieutenant at that time. He was assigned to that precinct as a desk Lieutenant. Lt Mance worked for several years in the 3rd precinct, but eventually he would be assigned to desk duty in the 1st and 2nd precincts as well. Lt Mance's service was apparently, for the most part, efficient. However, it was not without problems. For example, on March 22, 1913, the lieutenant was convicted of violating a number of departmental rules and regulations, and as a result was fined 30 days pay.

Years later in February of 1919, Lt Mance became involved in an investigation of Captain George Cougle, who would ultimately be dismissed from the department. Apparently, the Board of Police Commissioners not only wanted Lt. Mance to testify against Capt. Cougle, but they ordered him to give testimony that would certainly be self-incriminating. Lt Mance refused both orders. He was suspended from duty and ultimately charged with insubordination and disobedience of orders. On April 4, 1919, Lt Mance was found guilty and was again fined 30 days pay.

Lt Mance would not receive his coveted captain's bars until December 1, 1925, sixteen years after his last promotion. Upon being promoted to the rank of Captain, he was assigned as the commanding officer of the 2nd precinct.

Upon his retirement in 1927, Willard Mance began a new career in the real estate and insurance business. In 1929 he decided to enter politics and sought the Republican nomination for Alderman in the 10th Ward but was defeated in the primary election.

On July 6, 1939 Willard Mance left his home at 32 Tuckahoe Road to take a walk. While crossing the Saw Mill River Parkway at Lockwood Avenue, he was struck by an automobile and critically injured. After being taken to Yonkers General Hospital, Retired Captain Willard L. Mance died the next day from his injuries. He was sixty five years of age at his death.

LT. EDWARD KING

APPOINTED: November 30, 1901
RETIRED: June 1, 1933

Born August 9, 1874 in Yonkers, Edward King as a young man was very athletic and played for several years with the N.Y. National Guard championship basketball team, called the "Fourth Separate Co. Five." Prior to becoming a policeman, King worked as a machinist. When he was hired by the police department on November 30, 1901, he was quickly assigned to bicycle patrol duty. By 1907, he and officer Joe VanSteenburgh, were the only two men assigned to motorcycle patrol duty. On October 11, 1909, Ed King was promoted to Sergeant and was returned to precinct patrol duties. Several years later, on December 1, 1925, Sgt King was promoted to Lieutenant, and was assigned as the commanding officer of the Traffic Bureau. In later years, Lt. King would complete his career working from the 3rd precinct as a desk lieutenant until his retirement on June 1, 1933. On April 18, 1944, at the age of 66 years, retired Lieutenant Edward King died unexpectedly at his home in Merrick L.I.

PO JAMES T. MADDEN # 5

APPOINTED: November 30, 1901
RETIRED: January 23, 1940

Jim Madden was born January 23, 1876 in Carmel N.Y., and was brought to Yonkers at age 9 years. He attended St. Mary's school, and later worked as a "hatter" in the Waring Hat Manufacturing Co. Upon his appointment as a policeman on November 30, 1901, Madden was assigned to bicycle patrol. When motorcycles were put into use around 1906, he was one of our first men to be assigned and would earn a reputation throughout the city as being one tough cop. As a young man, Madden was known as a star of the National Guard championship basketball team called, the "Fourth Separate Company Five." In 1913 when Lt. Daniel Shea was shot by a burglar, it was PO Madden who arrested the shooter after a brief foot pursuit. Due to age limitations, Madden was forced to retire on January 23, 1940 at age 64, which was his birthday. Jim's brother was PO Mike Madden; his nephew was Lt Bob Philp; his grandnephew was Sgt Joe Madden; and his grandson was former NYC PO Jim Rice. On July 14, 1950, retired PO James T. Madden died. He was 74 years old.

PO JOHN J. McCARTHY # 4

APPOINTED: December 1, 1901
RETIRED: January 31, 1930

Born in Ireland on August 25, 1873, John Joseph McCarthy came to the U.S. and directly to Yonkers in 1895. Prior to his appointment to the police department on December 1, 1901, he worked as a trolley conductor with the Yonkers Railroad Co. McCarthy served on horseback with the police mounted unit in his early years, and much later would be assigned to Getty Square on foot as security for the various banks. Known as "Brud," a greeting he would call all his friends, McCarthy was the first of five policemen, including his son, who would have the exact same name, requiring the department to identify them all by numbers, 1 through 5. He was McCarthy # 1. His son was # 4. PO Arthur Day was his brother-in-law. After retiring from the police department on January 31, 1930 McCarthy worked as Captain of the Guard at the Habirshaw Cable & Wire Corp. during World War 2. John J. McCarthy-1 died on October 3, 1950 at his 1 Convent Avenue home at the age of 70 years.

LT JOSEPH VanSTEENBURGH

APPOINTED: December 1, 1901
RETIRED: February 16, 1922

Joe VanSteenburgh was born in Yonkers on January 4, 1880. When he applied for appointment to the P.D. in 1901, he was single, 21 years old, and lived at 51 Van Cortlandt Park Ave. After his appointment on December 1, 1901 he worked foot patrol for a while and then was assigned to bicycle patrol. In July 1906 the city purchased its very first Indian motorcycle for $215. and Joe was designated the YPD's very first motorcycle officer. And he was feared by all who might dare to exceed the speed limit. He advanced through the ranks rapidly; Roundsman on December 20, 1907, Sergeant in April of 1908, and Lieutenant on May 15, 1909. Over the years other men were assigned to ride motorcycle duty with Joe, but he remained on the motorcycle the longest. Even after his appointment to Lieutenant. A fact that news accounts attributed to his political friends. After retiring on February 16, 1922 due to a physical disability, Joe VanSteenburgh went into the contracting business. On August 24, 1964, he died at age 84 years.

PO TIMOTHY P. LINEHAN # 45

APPOINTED: December 1, 1901
DISMISSED: July 21, 1903

Timothy Linehan was born in the City of Yonkers and as a young man lived at 88 Maple Street. Little else is known of Linehan other than he was accepted for appointment as a Patrolman in the police department on December 1, 1901. He was hired by the Police Board which was led, at the time, by Comm. Henry Osterheld. Records reflect that he was a member of the short lived Yonkers Police Band and was very likely a very personable man. However, he found himself in serious violations of the rules by the police board. As a result of his record of violations the police board voted to dismiss him from the police department effective July 21, 1903.

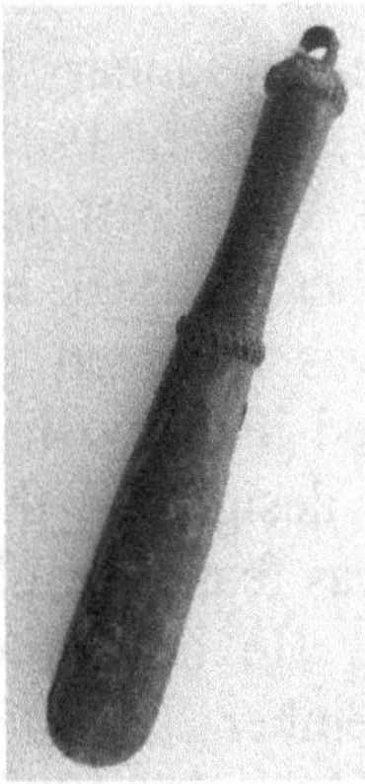

PO MICHAEL MADDEN # 7

APPOINTED: May 14, 1902
RETIRED: September 30, 1933

Born in Carmel NY on May 17, 1871, Mike Madden was employed as a painter before joining the Yonkers Police Department on May 14, 1902. Upon his police appointment, and over a period of time, he would work in both the 1st and 3rd precincts on foot patrol. At one point he was also assigned to the armored motorcycle detail, and as the patrol wagon driver. Being a very big man, Madden was active in police department sports early in his career. Because of his size, he was known as the "strong man." His family was a family of policemen. His brother James T. Madden was assigned to motorcycle duty, as was his nephew, Lt Robert Philp, a department Medal of Honor winner. Mike Madden would not live to see it but his grandson would be Sgt. Joseph Madden. After 31 years of honorable service he retired on September 30, 1933 and only eight years after retiring, Michael Madden died on July 28, 1941 at his home on Broadway in the Bronx. He was 70 years of age.

SGT. WALTER VanMETTER # 6

APPOINTED: May 19, 1902
RETIRED: November 30, 1939

Walter VanMetter was born in Tarrytown, NY on March 26, 1876 where he received his formal education. Several years later he would move to Yonkers and be appointed a policeman on May 19, 1902. He worked foot patrol duty primarily in the 1st and 3rd precincts. However for several years he was assigned to plainclothes duty and also served for a while as a detective. In the early part of his career Walt was well known in sports circles as a star pitcher for the Hollywood Inn baseball team, and the Yonkers Athletic Club. For some unclear reason it was reported that they always called him Walt "Neary," because of a family connection to Sgt Augustus Neary. Walt even organized a police baseball team, but it would ultimately be disbanded. On June 1, 1914, Walter was promoted to the rank of Sergeant. His brother John was also a police officer, as was his cousin, Sgt Augustus Neary. Retired Sgt. Walter VanMetter died on February 15, 1941 at his home at 42 Seminary Avenue. He was 64 years of age.

CAPTAIN CHARLES A. O'MARA

APPOINTED: May 19, 1902
RETIRED: May 10, 1936

Charles O'Mara was born in Beacon New York on May 11, 1872. He received his early education in Beacon and came to Yonkers while still a youth. As a young man O'Mara was employed as a hatter with the old Belknap Factory in Yonkers, and later in the Moquette Mill of the Alexander Smith and Sons Carpet Company. On November 16, 1901, while a resident of 110 Hawthorne Avenue, O'Mara submitted the required two application blanks for employment as a police officer. However, the Police Commissioners took no action on his request. But six months later, on May 19, 1902, the Commissioners approved his application and Charles A. O'Mara was appointed a police officer. He was single, had no military experience, and resided at 115 Palisade Avenue.

After a brief period of being detailed to what was then known as the "School of Instruction" O'Mara was assigned to foot patrol duties working out of the 1st precinct in the Wells Avenue headquarters building. Soon after his appointment he would be assigned to the "bicycle patrol" for a period of two years. When he joined the department, his brother Patrolman William P. O'Mara had already been a Yonkers police officer for a number of years. O'Mara not only worked foot patrol for

Captain Charles A. O'Mara (cont.)

several years but for a while he served as a detective.

On November 16, 1910 O'Mara was promoted to the rank of Sergeant with an annual salary of $1,300. and was assigned to the 2nd precinct. However it didn't take long before he returned to the Detective Bureau and was assigned as a supervisor of a detective squad. On February 8, 1911 while serving as a detective sergeant, O'Mara and his detectives arrested a man wanted for murdering an individual two days earlier at the Hillview Reservoir. After committing the murder the suspect fled the city. Det. Sgt. O'Mara and three detectives traced the suspect to a "saloon" on Canal Street in NYC and within 48 hours had arrested him. Only 10 days later on February 18, 1911 Det. Sgt. O'Mara and his men made another excellent arrest. This time the suspect, who was charged with blackmailing a local businessman, was described as a member of the feared "Black Hand."

On April 27, 1914 Det. Sgt. O'Mara was promoted to the rank of Lieutenant and was returned to uniformed duty at the 2nd precinct as a desk Lieutenant. Later in May of 1920 he would be reassigned to desk duty in the 1st precinct.

On December 22, 1921 Charles O'Mara was elevated to the rank of Captain at a salary of $ 3,000 a year. At the time he lived a 329 Riverdale Avenue. Sometime earlier due to budgetary constraints the 3rd precinct had been closed. On March 15, 1922 the 3rd precinct was reopened and Captain O'Mara was placed in command.

In March of 1926 Captain O'Mara was charged with several violations of the departments rules and regulations including, disobeying orders, neglect of duty, and conduct that is prejudicial to the good order, efficiency, and discipline of the department. The complaint was made by the Public Safety Commissioner and involved the captain assigning two officers to plainclothes duties after allegedly being directed not to do so. Further that he failed to document this detail of personnel in his daily report to the Commissioner. It was pointed out during the captain's trial that the omission in the daily report was merely an oversight by the desk lieutenants. Nevertheless Capt. O'Mara was found guilty and was fined 30 days pay.

The captain was always interested in the activities within the department and tried to motivate his officers with activities of interest. In January of 1928 while serving as the commanding officer of the 3rd precinct, O'Mara, who was an expert shot with a revolver, volunteered to serve as the team captain of the Yonkers Police Pistol Team. The members of the team, who all practiced with a .22 caliber revolver in the state armory on North Broadway at Quincy Place, were preparing for target competition with other departments throughout the county.

When Captain O'Mara was required to retire in 1936 due to having reached his 64th birthday, he had spent the previous 15 years as commanding officer of the 3rd precinct at 36 Radford Street. Due to his popularity with so many people, a retirement testimonial dinner was held for him on May 11, 1936. The affair was attended by Mayor Joseph Loehr and many other city officials, civic and fraternal leaders, South Yonkers businessmen and residents. Nearly 200 people attended the testimonial dinner held at the 8th ward democratic club on South Broadway. Lt. Tom Kennedy, toastmaster for the evening presented Captain O'Mara with a leather wallet and a "purse" of money to go in it. Police Association president Det. Thomas Cunningham presented the guest of honor with a retired captains shield.

Retired Captain O'Mara moved to West Palm Beach Florida after his retirement. It was there at the age of 77 years, while undergoing an operation that he died on February 5, 1948.

PO ARTHUR L. DOTY # 39

APPOINTED: November 25, 1903
RETIRED: November 30, 1933

Arthur Lorraine Doty was born in his family house on Post St. on May 16, 1873. Prior to his police career, Doty worked for his father in the moving and trucking business. Upon entering the police department on November 25, 1903 he was assigned to the main station on Wells Avenue on mounted patrol duty. When the 2nd precinct opened on May 26, 1908 he was assigned there and remained for many years patrolling the east side of the city on horseback. Later, when the use of horses was discontinued, he worked traffic duty, and for his last 14 years, he was assigned to the 3rd precinct located at 36 Radford Street. Prior to retiring on November 30, 1933 and moving to the Bronx, Doty lived with his family at 18 Pelton Street. His brother Frank Doty was also a Yonkers policeman during most of the same years. On October 30, 1949 retired police officer Arthur Doty died at the age of 75 years.

SGT MICHAEL HIGGINS # 7

APPOINTED: November 27, 1903
RETIRED: November 30, 1928

Michael Francis Higgins was born December 11, 1873 in County Cork Ireland, where he lived until 1880 when he moved to Yonkers. He attended St Joseph's Parochial School for his formal education and he became a US citizen in 1896. Before being appointed to the police department on November 27, 1903 Mike was a printer and lived at 237 Vineyard Ave. Upon joining the police department, officer Higgins worked out of the 1st Precinct on Wells Ave. On January 29, 1910 he was elevated to Detective where he remained for several years. When the 4th Precinct was established in 1914 at 764 Palisade Avenue it resulted in Higgins being promoted to Sergeant on May 1, 1914. Sgt Higgins later retired on November 30, 1928 while assigned to the 2nd precinct. A good family man, Higgins had 7 sons and 2 daughters. One of his brothers, Patrick Higgins, was also a Yonkers policeman. On August 5, 1932 retired Sgt. Michael Higgins died of heart disease at age 58.

LT. HENRY BLATZHEIM

APPOINTED: July 15, 1904
RETIRED: February 10, 1923

A former Steam fitter and known as "Blatzie" to his friends, Henry J. Blatzheim, born August 15, 1880, did very well in his early years with the police department. Having been appointed on July 15, 1904 his rise in the ranks was even called "meteoric" by the newspapers. He was promoted to Roundsman December 31, 1907, to Sergeant in April of 1908, and to Lieutenant on May 15, 1909. The media called his promotions a first, noting that at only 28 years of age and with less than 5 years of service, he never wore a service stripe and never would since lieutenants didn't wear them. Blatzheim may have been financially well off as well. During an interview in 1907 with the press, then Lt. George "Big Chief" Cooley referred to Lt. Blatzheim as the "millionaire cop." After 19 years service Lt. Blatzheim retired on February 10, 1923 on a disability pension and moved to Fishkill, NY. In 1928 his son, Francis X. Blatzheim, was a NYPD police officer. Henry Blatzheim died in Fishkill on July 23, 1954 at the age of 73 years.

SGT. JOHN STEUART # 8

APPOINTED: July 19, 1904
RETIRED: October 10, 1942

Prior to his appointment as a policeman, John Pentland Steuart, who was born in NYC on July 9, 1880, was a machinist with the Otis Elevator Company. After his appointment to the police department on July 19, 1904, Steuart worked foot patrol on the west side of Yonkers until 1908 when he and a few others constituted the newly formed first motorcycle squad. They all worked the day and early tour. On November 1, 1909 Steuart was promoted to the rank of Sergeant. In May of 1924 when the newly established Riot Squad was formed, Sgt Steuart was trained and designated as a member. On June 16, 1926 he was assigned to the Detective Bureau where, due to his leadership and investigative skills, he would hold this position for 18 years, right up to his retirement on October 10, 1942. Unfortunately, less than two years later on July 3, 1944 retired Det. Sgt. John P. Steuart died just six days short of his 64th birthday.

PO NELSON H. YOUNG # 47

APPOINTED: September 28, 1904
DIED: December 8, 1913

Nelson Young was born in Ossining, N.Y. on June 5, 1876. His family brought him to Yonkers at age two years. After graduating from PS# 3 Young worked as a foreman with Yerks & Co. in Yonkers. Upon his appointment to the police department on September 28, 1904 he worked foot patrol out of the Wells Avenue station. Later, in May of 1908 when the new 2nd precinct was established on Central Avenue, Young was assigned to that station house. He would again be moved and spend his remaining years in the 3rd precinct at 36 Radford Street. "Nels," as he was known to friends and who was single, became unexpectedly ill and on December 8, 1913, at the age of 37, died of what was then diagnosed as "acute indigestion." Since he had served less than ten years with our department his mother was not entitled to a benefit from the police pension fund. Young was the 4th policeman to die that year. One hundred police officers attended his funeral and marched from his home at 43 McLean Avenue to St. Andrews Church. The procession was led by Chief Daniel Wolf.

LT. ANDREW THOMPSON

APPOINTED: January 11, 1905
DIED: February 18, 1936

Andrew J. Thompson was born October 20, 1876 in Yonkers. Prior to his employment with the police department he was employed as a steam fitter. He was active in the community with a Masonic Lodge, and when he was appointed on January 11, 1905 he worked out of the Wells Avenue station walking various foot posts. On October 11, 1909 Thompson was promoted to the rank of Sergeant. Then, on August 4, 1914, he was elevated to Lieutenant and worked in the newly established 4th precinct as a desk lieutenant. On March 23, 1920, the same day the 4th Precinct was closed and merged with the 1st Precinct, he was placed in command of the Traffic Division. This unit consisted of 22 police officers and 2 sergeants. After attending a traffic school in NYC, Lt. Thompson was responsible for recommending that side cars be used on our motorcycles. On December 2, 1925 Thompson was reassigned to the 2nd precinct on desk duty where he remained for several years. Then suddenly, on February 18, 1936, Lt. Andrew J. Thompson died of a heart attack at the age of 59 years.

CHIEF OF POLICE EDWARD J. QUIRK

APPOINTED: November 25, 1905
DIED: October 28, 1940

Edward J. Quirk was born May 5, 1878 in Killarney, Ireland. In 1898 Quirk emigrated to the U.S. without any family to begin a new life. He became a naturalized citizen in White Plains on May 24, 1904. This husky young man with a heavy Irish brogue first found employment with the Waring Hat Factory. Later he became an iron worker in the foundry of Otis Elevator Co. When Quirk was hired by the police department in 1905 he was 27 years old and lived at 102 Ashburton Ave. After being appointed, young Quirk worked foot patrol on the west side of the city. Reports indicate that within a few weeks of his appointment, he made an excellent arrest. While on his post in North Yonkers, he came upon a burglary in progress. He entered the home alone, disarmed the burglar, and placed him under arrest. Two months later he found the same home being burglarized. The burglar escaped but Quirk recovered the owners property. Because of his aggressiveness and attention to duty, Quirk was often assigned to work in "citizen clothes," or plain clothes duty.

Before the newly established 3rd Pct. opened its doors and its police desk blotter at 6 PM on December 1, 1909, additional supervisory positions were needed to manage the 12 patrolmen that were

Chief of Police Edward J. Quirk (cont.)

to be assigned. On November 30, 1909 Ptl. Quirk was promoted to the rank of Sergeant and was assigned to the new precinct at 36 Radford Street.

On February 12, 1912 Sgt. Quirk made a very unusual arrest of a horse thief. The thief had entered a stable on Hawthorne Avenue and stole some horses. Sgt. Quirk received word of the theft, commandeered a civilian automobile and pursued the thief to 190th Street in NYC. He over took the thief and brought him and the stolen team of horses back to Yonkers.

While assigned to the 1st Pct. for a time, Capt. Lent placed Sgt. Quirk in plain clothes handling gambling investigations. He allowed Quirk to pick his own "strong arm squad" to work throughout the city. In preparation for the opening of a 4th Pct. on May 1, 1914, again promotions were necessary. On April 27, 1914 Sgt. Edward Quirk was promoted to Lieutenant. Upon his promotion, Quirk was assigned to desk duty in the new 4th Pct. He remained in this assignment until the Precinct was closed on March 23, 1920 and merged with the 1st Pct., in an economy move. He was then assigned to desk duty in the 1st Pct.

On May 16, 1921 Public Safety Commissioner Maurice O'Keefe issued an order removing Lt. Cooper as the head of the Detective Bureau and in his place he assigned Lt. Quirk as the new Detective Commander. His Lieutenants salary of $2,650 per year was then increased by $300.
Det. Lt. Quirk remained in command of the Detective Bureau throughout 1921 into 1922. Under Quirks leadership the Detective Bureau was reported to have had remarkable success in ridding the city of several hold up gangs and burglars, all of whom received long sentences at Sing Sing prison upon their conviction.

During this same time, both the 1st and 4th Pct.'s had been closed in an economy measure. However, a new incoming administration promised to re-open the closed Pct's. To do so there was a need for new captains. As a result, on December 21, 1921, Det. Lt. Edward Quirk was promoted to the rank of captain. Following his promotion he was allowed to remain in command of the Det. Bureau.
As the day grew near for the re-opening of the 4th Pct, Capt. Quirk was notified he was slated to be the new 4th Pct. Captain. On June 21, 1922 that order was issued, and at the 4 PM roll call, he was relieved of his Det. Bureau responsibilities. Quirk immediately began to determine the foot post to be manned, their boundaries, and the total number of police officers needed to man the 4th Pct. On June 27, 1922, beginning with the 4 PM roll call, the Pct. opened for business in a completely unsuitable small building behind the fire house at 53 Shonnard Place. The 4th Precincts total complement was 32 officers and men.

Several years earlier in 1919, Chief of Police Daniel Wolff retired, and for the following 7 years there would be no chief of police. The department was led by the Public Safety Commissioner, who was responsible for operating both the police and fire departments. This all changed on September 1, 1926 when Captain Edward J. Quirk was elevated to the position of Chief of Police by Public Safety Commissioner William Cameron. His new salary was $4,000 per year. The appointment was reported to have come as a surprise to him. At 48 years of age he was said to be one of the youngest captains in the department and was certainly not the most senior in time of service. However, apparently all throughout his career Quirk had displayed a tenacity in fighting crime. He was as tough as iron, but everyone knew he was equally as fair.

Chief of Police Edward J. Quirk (cont.)

In 1926 the position of Chief of Police was one which required a civil service test. Commissioner Cameron was so determined to have Quirk be chief, that in order to take no chances, he had the chief's position changed to a noncompetitive one, making it one of appointment of choice. Chief Quirk was directed to report to Commissioner Cameron's office at 3:30 PM at City Hall. From there, both went directly to the 1st Pct. and Headquarters building on Wells Ave. to address the 4 PM roll call. Upon completion of the regular roll call of early tour officers, 50 additional off duty officers left the squad room, joined the men in front of the desk, and stood stiffly at attention. Commissioner Cameron took charge of the ceremony calling the Chief behind the desk. Among his comments Cameron said, "*Of all the acts I have done since I took office, this single act alone received more favorable comment than all others. There was no unfavorable comment to be heard. The people of the city know the long, faithful, honest, and efficient service which has been done by Chief Quirk. You men know better than I do what kind of man he is.*"

The men of the 1st Pct., Det. Bureau, and Traffic Bureau presented their new chief with a gold pen and pencil set and gold cuff links. In addition, the men had bought the chief his new shield which was gold and much more ornate than the city had planned on giving him. Chief Quirk then addressed the large group of police officers before him. He asked, in his distinct Irish brogue, "*What have I done for you in the past that would call for this from you? If anything, I have tried to get the most work out of you that was possible. If that is to bring about such things as this, I will keep on trying.*" He thanked them for the gifts and then said, "*I have gone a step higher in the department, but in spirit I am still on a level with you men.*" The large front room of the Wells Ave. Station was nearly filled with floral tributes of every kind from well-wishers of Chief Quirk. The former Irish immigrant and iron worker had risen to the highest uniformed position in our department. There was no doubt in any one's mind that Quirk was equal to the task. His tough approach earned him the nickname, "The Iron Man."

The uniform of the new chief was the regulation uniform worn by subordinate ranks with the following insignia thereon:

On the cuffs of the chiefs blouse was a 1 1/4" black mohair braid. A second lustrous black mohair braid 1/2" wide was placed just above the lower braid. Three gilt metal stars 3/4 inch wide between points, to be worn on coat collars; and on the center of the wide braid on the outside of each sleeve of the overcoat and office coat.

Chief Quirk was the driving force behind one of the most dramatic and important changes in the Yonkers Police Department's history. Up until 1934, our department had several patrol cars cruising the city. The major shortcoming of this was there were no communication radios of any kind in these police vehicles. On May 1, 1934 Chief Quirk ordered Ptl. Peter Dankovic to visit New York and study the NYC police radio system with a view toward setting up a modern system of Police communications in Yonkers. On August 13, 1934 Ptl. Dankovic received his 1st class radio operators license from the F.C.C. which made it possible to establish our own radio system. On October 13, 1934 our first radio system, with the designated call letters "WPFY," and which cost $11,000, went into service providing one way

Chief of Police Edward J. Quirk (cont.)

communication to 25 police cars. Chief Quirk set the formal and official dedication of the system for October 30, 1934, and invited police dignitaries from NYC and throughout Westchester. Called the most modern radio system in operation, the chief's public education campaign was simply, "Don't delay-telephone."

Depending on the individual, it may at times be difficult to gauge the degree of respect that is felt for a leader. This apparently was not the case with Chief Quirk. As an example; On April 22, 1935 Quirk set sail from NYC on the Ocean Liner Georgic on a visit to his place of birth in Killarney, Ireland. His departure that day was in marked contrast to his arrival in this country. Back then he was alone and friendless. On this day, Mayor Loehr, many local and county officials, and over 100 members of our department assembled to wish him a good trip. Yonkers and NYC motorcycles escorted a caravan of 28 cars which accompanied the chief and his family to the pier. Throughout the trip the motorcycles flanked the chief's vehicle with their lights and sirens wailing all the way to the ship. Upon reaching the pier Chief Quirk observed uniformed police officers from both departments lining both sides of the "gang way."

As he boarded the ship the officers all rendered a "snappy" salute. For 2 hours a bon voyage party was held for the chief and all the throngs of well-wishers, including a delegation of the NYC Police Honor Legion. Until the ship had reached a far distance and was headed out to sea, police siren and horns sounded to provide a real send off for their chief. Customs officials and shipping veterans all agreed that the tribute paid to Chief Quirk had never been surpassed by anyone else in public life. While on deck listening to Irish music for his pleasure, the chief waived smiling and appreciating his spectacular send off. Upon his return to the U.S. the chief was asked his impressions of the police in France, England, and Ireland. He replied, "*They are all well organized and efficient, but Yonkers is second to none. The men who comprise the personnel of our Yonkers force don't have to take a back seat to anybody.*"

Later that year in November 1935 Chief Quick and Lt. Schall completed 30 years of service to the Yonkers Police Department. During an interview with a reporter the chief reminisced and made several comments including the following: *"Policemen today have it much easier than we did in those days,"* he remarked. *Today, unless a man has to do extra duty, he works 8 hours and goes home. But when we first joined the department we were lucky if we got a day off every 30 days.*

'We were given a day off only if the captain had nothing for us to do on that day, and saw fit to let us take off. If not, under the two platoon system, we kept right on working, until the captain decided to give us leave. In those days we were on duty 24 hours a day. We worked two shifts of six hours each and, from 6 to 8 AM, we did the dog watch, as reserve duty was called. We had beds in a dormitory at Headquarters, and even after we went home, if a small fire, accident, disorder or any other thing happened, we could be called back to do extra duty after our regular tours were finished. Now the men work the 3 platoon system with regular time off. I remember a roll call when, with all other patrolmen on different assignments, only two men were assigned to cover the entire city. Herman Schall was given all territory south of Main Street, and I all that north of Main Street to patrol. That was a common occurrence in those days, and I'd say it was some beat." The chief said that snow gave him the worst detail he ever had.

Chief of Police Edward J. Quirk (cont.)

He recalled, *"When it snowed so hard the mounted men could not ride their horses in safety, the captain would assign two men to patrol Nepera Park, and other mounted outlying posts, in an open horse drawn wagon. We could not keep warm no matter how hard we tried. We had blankets, but they were useless on real winter nights. We had to heat bricks to warm our feet, but it didn't help much. That detail was the toughest part of police work. We never minded action. In fact we welcomed it. A good fight was all in a days work then and we always brought in our man or men as the case frequently was."* When asked what was the most important case he had worked on the chief replied, *"Every case is important. A petit larceny theft merits the same careful investigation that a hold up or murder gets."*

During prohibition Chief Quirk worked tirelessly along with federal agents in breaking up several bootleg operations. Following the repeal of prohibition Chief Quirk continued his efforts. In 1936 he directed his detectives to organize an undercover operation which identified dozen of illegal bootlegging operations. Under the chief direction, warrants were obtained for 19 locations, and on February 13, 1936 the chief's men conducted simultaneous raids making arrests and seizures. This was the second such raid since the repeal of prohibition. Nineteen men were arrested. It was reported that these locations were selling liquor "unfit for human consumption".

On April 16, 1936 the Honor Board of the Police Department held their meeting and dinner at the Astor Hotel in NYC. Thirteen police officers were approved to receive awards for their actions. The surprise of the evening occurred when the honor Board voted to give Chief Quirk the highest award within the Public Safety Bureau's Authority. The award which had never before been given, and would be in recognition of his service, was to be specially created to honor Chief Quirk with either a special badge or medal. Although it was planned to have a ceremony for this presentation, for some reason it never took place. The chief had previously been cited by the Honor Legion of the NYC Police Department in 1934 for his work in Yonkers, and they had made him an honorary member of their Honor Legion.

On October 23, 1940 the "Iron Man" was taken to Ossining Hospital paralyzed and in a semi-conscious condition. He apparently was driving through the town when he took ill and stopped at a diner. It was then an ambulance was summoned. Apparently having suffered a stroke, Chief Edward J. Quirk was in very critical condition and was given the last rites of the Catholic Church. During this time police operations were in the hands of the Precinct Captain's, each temporarily in command of his own area and personally responsible to the City Manager. After three days with no change in Chief Quirk's condition, Captain William Kruppenbacher was named Acting Chief on October 26, 1940. On October 28, 1940 Chief Quirk died in Ossining Hospital. Newspaper headlines read, "City Mourns Chief Quirk." It was ironic that to this point, the maximum age for police personnel was 64 years. At 62 years old, the chief was quickly reaching the date when he would have to retire. However, the chief was so well respected that earlier in the year that he died the city requested and achieved a law change exempting the chief's position from the 64 year rule and allowing the chief to remain until age 70.

More than 500 uniformed policemen turned out to honor their chief along with thousands of others who filled Sacred Heart Church and the streets. The funeral procession from the chiefs home at 37 Amackassin Terrace was led by 75 motorcycles from Yonkers, Westchester County Parkway Police, and

Chief of Police Edward J. Quirk (cont.)

Greenwich Connecticut. There were representatives from almost every police department in Westchester County. Six honorary pallbearers from our department flanked the hearse along with six motorcycles as a special guard of honor.

The Herald Statesman editorial headline read, "Edward J. Quirk, Hero of the Storybook Kind." They expressed some of their feelings; *"He was admired for his powerful personality, his dependable sincerity, his vigorous leadership of a body of well-trained men, his vociferous insistence upon law enforcement and upon fair play to the men working under him. As in the case of the truly great, thousands of Yonkers men and women will remember the CHIEF for what they personally knew him to be."*

DETECTIVE CAPTAIN HERMAN G. SCHALL

APPOINTED: November 25, 1905
RETIRED: March 19, 1946

Born March 20, 1881 in Yonkers, Schall was named Herman Garfield Schall. His granddaughter stated that he was given his middle name in honor of President Garfield. Schall received his formal education in Public School # 6. As a young boy he lived at the foot of Main Street where the former Trolley Barn is located. Every morning throughout the year he would get up to meet the 4 AM train at the main station. He would pick up bundles of newspaper from the train, bring them to Thompson's Store in Getty Square where he would fold them and then deliver them on his paper route. He would finish his route just in time not to be late for school. He was always proud of his work ethic. As a young man Schall worked as a shipping clerk for the American Express Company and spoke the German language fluently.

Herman Schall, who was single and had no military experience, applied for employment as a police officer and was appointed on November 25, 1905 as a probationary patrolman. Probation at that time lasted for three years. His assignments were citywide working on foot patrol out of the H.Q. building on Wells Avenue. He seemed to frequently be assigned to the area known as "McLean Heights."

Detective Captain Herman Schall (cont.)

In 1907 Schall was commended by the Police Board for his actions in diving into the "McLean Pond," attempting to rescue a drowning boy. On another occasion at about 6 AM while walking his foot post in "The Heights," PO Schall was at the corner of McLean Avenue and Martha Avenue when he heard a commotion. Upon investigating he discovered that a saloon keeper opening up his business had found a bomb right outside the building. Finding a lit fuse burning toward the dynamite, Schall grabbed the dynamite and pinched out the fuse with his fingers. He was again recognized by the Police Board for his quick action and courage.

On May 26, 1908 the police department organized and opened a 2nd precinct on Central Avenue near Yonkers Avenue. Ptl. Schall was among the men assigned there that day. This precinct was established to deal with the increase in problems that were occurring due to the large influx of construction workers who were building the Catskill Aqueduct. It was during his time as a patrolman in this precinct that officer Schall assisted the fire department in a number of spectacular rescues of several persons who were caught in a fire on Glover Avenue during a winter blizzard. The rescues were accomplished by forming a human chain after the fire ladder had burned away. For his actions, Schall and a firefighter were awarded the Gold Star sleeve insignia, the highest award in the department. However, being of a modest nature, Schall never wore the star on his sleeve cuff, and few even knew that it had been awarded to him.

Officer Schall continued to work in the 2nd precinct for eleven years, until March 21, 1919 when he was transferred to the traffic squad directing traffic. Two months later on May 16, 1919 Ptl. Schall was promoted to the rank of Sergeant at a salary of $1,650. per year. In May of 1924 the department established a riot squad. All members were required to be over six feet tall, were trained in the use of rifles and various other weapons, and in drill and riot formations. Sgt. Schall was among those trained and designated as a member of this squad.

On July 1, 1925 Sgt. Schall, who was # 2 on the civil service promotion list, was promoted to Lieutenant. Sgt. Cunningham, a mounted sergeant with an excellent reputation and more seniority in the department, was passed over without a reason given. Lt. Schall gratefully accepted his new rank at the salary of $3,000. per year and was assigned to desk duty in the 1st precinct.

Lt. Schall, along with Chief Quirk, completed 25 years of service with the department on November 25, 1930. Both he and the chief were appointed on the same day. In recognition of the occasion the officers and men of the 1st precinct honored Lt. Schall upon reaching this milestone. At the 4 PM roll call, 1st precinct commander Capt. Crough presented Lt. Schall with a handsome set of cuff links and a fountain pen.

Schall had been a lieutenant for 17 years simply because he refused to take the exam for the position of Captain. Finally, after pressure from family and friends, he took the test and rated # 1 on the list. Recommendations were received from several members of the Common Council at City Hall to create two new captains positions. The first would be for Schall, and the 2nd for Patrick Sullivan. Sullivan's brother was a city councilman. On February 1, 1942 Herman Schall and Pat Sullivan were promoted to the rank of Captain at the salary of $3,937 per year. Later that same year on October 16, 1942, Captain Schall was placed in command of the Detective Bureau.

Detective Captain Herman Schall (cont.)

In late 1944 a person from out of town made a complaint that he had come to Yonkers, and during a "crap" game he had lost $1,500. His complaint caused quite a stir in the administration regarding how gambling was being dealt with by our police department. As a result of the furor, on October 20, 1944 Detective Captain Herman Schall was removed as the commander of the Detective Bureau, and was replaced by Lt. William Comey. Schall was reassigned to command the 1st precinct. Upon learning of Shall's removal the local newspaper wrote a scathing editorial against the administration, calling the transfer a mistake and an outrage. They went on to describe Capt. Schall as one of the most honest and conscientious public servants in our city. It was not very long before Capt. Schall was again the Detective Bureau commander.

On March 19, 1946, having reached the compulsory age limit of 65 years for police service, Capt. Herman Schall was retired from active duty with an annual pension benefit of $2,350. Public Safety Commissioner Francis Duffy wrote in Shall's retirement order, *I' have by observation perceived in his performance of his police duties, the highest regard for the obligations of his position, the fair treatment of his subordinates, unfailing courtesy to the general public, and a never ceasing campaign against criminal offenders."* On his last day of work Det. Capt. Schall was asked to come into the courtroom alongside his office for just a moment. When he entered the courtroom he found a large gathering of judges, court personnel, ranking police officials, and many friends who proceeded to offer very flattering tributes to the captain. Leaving our police department was a man who set a personal example of good police work, who was proud that in over 40 years he was never late for duty, and who was highly honored for heroism and dependable law enforcement efforts. His career spanned a period of extraordinary evolution of policing.

From horse drawn patrols, to high powered motorization and criminal science. After having been retired only seven months, Herman Schall suffered a stroke at his home at 180 Douglas Avenue. Two days later, on November 3, 1946, Ret. Det. Capt. Herman Schall died. It was unfortunate that having served in the police department for over 40 years, and having reached the point of pension and retirement, that Capt. Schall was to enjoy only seven months of the reward and rest he had earned.

PO DAVID J. DAVIS # 9

APPOINTED: November 25, 1905
RETIRED: October 31, 1933

PO David Davis was born in Ireland on January 22, 1872. He came to the United States at the age of 17 years and was naturalized a citizen in White Plains in 1897. His early employment was working as a coachman. Upon his appointment to the police department on November 25, 1905 Davis was 33 years old and lived at 140 Palisade Avenue. Officer Davis spent most of his career working foot patrol in the 1st and 4th precincts. In 1916 when the Yonkers Police Association was first organized, Davis was one of the original members of the Board of Directors. Being an expert shot with his revolver he became very active with the Yonkers Police Pistol Team which competed all over the county with other departments. Upon his retirement on October 31, 1933 he maintained his residence at 79 Douglas Avenue. On April 28, 1943 retired PO David Davis died at the age of 71 years.

PO OLE A. ANDERSON # 44

APPOINTED: April 14, 1906
DIED: March 24, 1919

Ole Anderson was born on July 1, 1879 in Norway. After arriving in the US and coming to this city Anderson became a naturalized citizen and worked for a while as a steam fitter. Upon being appointed to the police department on April 14, 1906 he was described as being highly recommended by some as being a "calvary man" and excellent horseman. Due to this background, PO Anderson served most of his career assigned to the mounted unit in the 1st and 4th precincts. On one occasion while attempting to arrest a man with a gun, Anderson was forced to shoot the escaping man in the arm in order to protect himself and ultimately take the man into custody. His captain called Anderson a man of high character and an able and efficient officer. A resident of 362 Upland Avenue, Anderson was required to enter St. Johns Hospital for an operation for appendicitis. Unfortunately, following complications from the surgery, PO Ole Anderson died unexpectedly on March 24, 1919. The 4th precinct was draped in black bunting as a sign of respect and most of the department attended his funeral. Ole Anderson was only 40 years old.

PO WILLIAM S. ROTHE # 6

APPOINTED: April 13, 1906
RETIRED: November 26, 1926

Bill Roth was born in Canton, Ohio on December 10, 1868. It is not known where he received his education but in his younger years he worked as a teamster and butcher. He was first employed by the police department as a Hostler on November 30, 1901. However, he was very pleased when on April 13, 1906 he was appointed a regular police officer. He was first assigned to foot patrol in the 1st precinct on Wells Avenue. In March of 1908 he was commended by the Police Board for excellent police work and, as a result, shortly thereafter was appointed a detective. He served in the Detective Bureau for a short time, but on January 29, 1910 was reassigned back to uniform patrol. He remained on regular patrol until May 25, 1918 when he was assigned to a newly organized traffic squad which worked day and early tours directing traffic. But in 1920 he was once again returned to regular patrol duty. Years later in 1939 he legally had the spelling of his last name changed to Rothe and he would never know that his grandnephew, Thomas Wyatt, would be the Chief of the Canton Ohio Police Department in 1997. A resident of Florida after having retired on November 26, 1926, William Rothe died in St. Petersburg Florida on Feb 5, 1951. He was 82.

LT. WILLIAM X. HIGGINS

APPOINTED: January 25, 1907
DIED: March 4, 1938

Born in Yonkers on March 31, 1881, Bill Higgins worked several years as a brakeman for the railroad. Following his appointment as a police officer on January 25, 1907 earning a salary of $750. per year, Higgins was assigned to the Wells Avenue station on foot patrol. He quickly impressed his superiors with his police work and was assigned to the Detective Bureau, or as it was referred to then, the Central Office. He quickly became a trusted confidant of then Police Chief Daniel Wolff. On April 27, 1914 Higgins was promoted to the rank of Sergeant and reassigned to the 1st precinct as a patrol supervisor. He received his promotion to the rank of Lieutenant on July 4, 1925 at the salary of $3,000. and was assigned to the 4th precinct as a desk lieutenant. Still a very trusted employee while Chief Quirk led the department, Lt. Higgins was often placed on special assignment for the chief. When Lt. Higgins died of a heart attack on March 4,1938 his funeral was attended by many public officials and over 100 uniformed officers from the department. He died at the age of 56 years, long before his son, who would later become Captain John "slugs" Higgins, even joined the department.

DET. CAPTAIN GEORGE A. FORD

APPOINTED: January 23, 1907
RETIRED: July 18, 1939

George A. Ford, a man who years later would rise through the ranks of the police department to become one of its most respected officers, was born in New York City on September 5, 1882. He moved to Yonkers with his family while he was still a young boy. He attended St. Mary's Parochial School and later Yonkers High School on South Broadway. At the outbreak of the Spanish American War, Ford abandoned any further thoughts of school and just as soon as he was old enough he enlisted in the U.S. Army. He saw service in the Philippine Islands during that insurrection, and also later in China.

Prior to his appointment to the police department Ford worked as a Pullman conductor with the railroad. George Ford was a very intelligent individual with the ability to speak both Spanish and Philippino. He also was reported to be a good clerk typist and musician. Upon joining the department and working for a short time out of the Wells Avenue station on foot patrol, on March 30, 1908 he was assigned along with PO's James T. Madden, John Steuart, and Jerome Linehan to the newly organized Motorcycle Squad. This squad was led by Roundsman Joseph Van Steenburgh. On May 26, 1908, Ford was transferred to the newly established 2nd precinct on Central Avenue along with his motorcycle. After

Detective Captain George A. Ford (cont.)

a number of years in the motorcycle squad, Ford was teamed up with officer Joe Drohan to work plainclothes duty in the 2nd precinct. On February 8, 1911, Ford and his partner Drohan made a notable arrest for murder by tracking the suspect all the way down to Canal Street in NYC, where the suspect was arrested. Only a week later plainclothes officer Ford, along with his partner Drohan and Det Sgt O'Mara, arrested another man for extortion. The man had been identified as a member of the infamous "Black Hand" organization. No doubt because of his proven investigative abilities, in 1912 officer Ford was elevated to the position of detective.

Being a very active and involved member of the department, and while assigned to the 1st precinct, in September of 1916 Det. Ford assisted in the formation of the "Police Association of the City of Yonkers Inc." In fact he was named one of the directors of the organization and one of the signers of the certificate of incorporation.

On July 16, 1917 officer Ford was promoted to the rank of Sergeant at a salary of $1,650 per year. At that time he was assigned to police headquarters where, in addition to clerical work, he monitored our fingerprint system. The operation of which, he had become somewhat of an expert. In May of 1918 Police Headquarters, which had been located in City Hall for several years, was relocated to the 1st precinct building at 20 Wells Avenue. On June 10th a new "Detective Bureau," which had been abolished several years earlier, was again established. Det. Sgt. Ford was assigned to this bureau in charge of the fingerprint and old Bertillon Identification System of body measurements. In fact, after completing a course in the New York police school, Det. Sgt. Ford inaugurated the Bureau of Criminal Identification (BCI) in our department where he continued as the departments fingerprint expert.

On February 17, 1922 Det. Sgt. Ford was promoted to the rank of Lieutenant at the salary of $2,650 per year. He was allowed to remain in the Detective Bureau because of his many specialized skills. However two years later on October 29, 1924, Lt. Ford was transferred to the 2nd precinct to perform desk officer duties. Earlier in that same year, on April 11, 1924, this very active officer found time to volunteer to serve as the leader of the recently created YPD Glea Club. The following year the city scheduled a large Police and Fire Parade to be held on May 9, 1925 to honor their service. In an effort to prepare the police personnel for the marching that would be required, two months prior to the parade, Lt. Ford was instructed to conduct marching and drill training at the State Armory. Named as "Drillmaster" for this purpose the former military man helped to make the parade a large success.

On January 1, 1926 Lt. Ford was transferred from the 2nd precinct to the office of the newly appointed Public Safety Commissioner as his aide. On February 11, 1926 Ford, who was on the captains promotion list, was appointed Acting Captain with no salary increase and was directed to wear the insignia of a captain on his uniform. On May 17, 1926 Ford requested he not be forced to wear the insignia of a rank he had not yet been promoted to. On November 7, 1927 Lt. (Acting Captain) Ford was returned to the Detective Bureau. It was on December 1, 1931 that George Ford was promoted to the rank of Captain and was allowed to remain as detective commander. His salary was $4,500 per year. For many years he was affectionately known as "The Skipper" to his men.

Considered very popular with his fellow policemen, Capt. Ford organized and was elected to office in the Police War Veteran's Association. He also was elected in 1935 and 1936 as president of the Captain's, Lieutenant's, and Sergeant's Association. A handsome, well-dressed man, careful in his

Detective Captain George A. Ford (cont.)

appearance and professional in manner, Capt. Ford had little resemblance to the traditional derby hatted Detective. He was said to look more like a lawyer.

Det. Capt. Ford retired from the department on July 18, 1939 on a pension of $2,350 per year. A retirement party was given for him by the Police War Veterans Legion of Yonkers. Over 600 people attended the testimonial dinner dance for the retiring captain. At the dinner Det. Capt. Ford was presented with a diamond ring by the members of the department as a token of the respect in which he was held. After leaving the department Ford worked as a chief investigator with Hearst Newspaper and Magazine Publications.

A short while after joining the police department, Captain Ford married one of Captain John Beary's sisters, as did Detective Sergeant Henry Murphy. All three were brothers in law.

On October 1, 1951 retired Detective Captain George A. Ford, a veteran of over 32 years of police service and one of its outstanding leaders, died at the age of 70 years. Captain George Ford would always be remembered by those who knew him not only for his competence, but also his meticulous appearance which enabled him to generate a certain "command presence." In fact it was because of his military bearing that he was usually designated as commanding officer of events such as parades, funeral services, marches by the Police Holy Name Society, etc. He knew how to project, and have his police officers project, an appearance of professionalism. Once again the Yonkers Police Department had lost a talented, energetic, and well respected member of our police community.

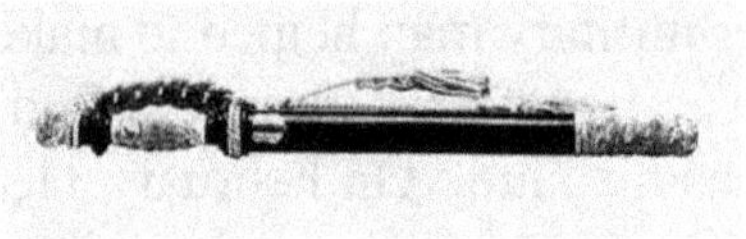

PO MICHAEL E. OTIS # 10

APPOINTED: February 14, 1907
RETIRED: February 29, 1936

Michael Otis was born May 29, 1873 in Wells, NY. He came to Yonkers at the age of 20 years and worked as a printer. He later worked for the Alexander Smith & Sons Carpet Co. He began his police career on February 14, 1907 working foot patrol from the 1st precinct. However, after only a few years he was assigned to the 3rd precinct in 1910. In 1914, when a 4th precinct was established on Palisade Avenue, he was assigned to that precinct for a short time. In June of 1918 he was assigned as a telephone operator at the general switchboard in headquarters. When officer Otis retired on February 29, 1936 he had been assigned to the Radio and Telegraph Division. This division was instituted in 1934 when our first radio communications system, albeit one way transmissions, was put in place. Otis was a charter member of the PBA and the Holy Name Society, where he served as a trustee for both. His son Capt. Edward Otis was appointed to the Yonkers Police Department in 1929. PO Michael Otis died on April 14, 1946 at 72 years of age.

SGT. AUGUSTUS NEARY # 11

APPOINTED: March 6, 1907
RETIRED: August 28, 1941

"Gus" Neary was born in Tarrytown on August 29, 1876. He came to Yonkers at the age of six and received his education in St. Mary's School. In his youth Gus Neary was considered an active and all-around athlete. He was said to have been an excellent boxer and played baseball with what was known as the old "Clinton Team." Prior to joining the police department Gus Neary worked as a hatter. Following his appointment as a police officer, he worked for a time from the 1st precinct, but served nearly all of his 35 years in the 3rd precinct on Radford Street. He was promoted to the rank of Sergeant on May 1, 1914 and remained on patrol duty. Neary retired on his 65th birthday in 1941 as an acting lieutenant. His sons Thomas and Robert also were Yonkers police officers and his brother in law was former Mayor Thomas Larkin. On October 25, 1947, retired Sgt. Augustus Neary died of a heart attack in his home at 179 Valentine Lane at the age of 71.

PO JAMES E. THOMAS # 11

APPOINTED: July 10, 1907
RETIRED: January 31, 1935

James Thomas was born on City Island in the Bronx on June 2, 1878. After moving to Yonkers as a young man he worked as a machinist with the Otis Elevator Co. He also was skilled as a radio mechanic. Upon his appointment to the department on July 10, 1907 he was assigned to foot patrol in the 1st precinct. On December 9, 1912, PO Thomas, who preferred to be called Ed or Edward, was assigned to the new "Automobile Patrol" which was established in the 1st precinct on Wells Avenue. The make of this new "paddy wagon" style motor vehicle was a new 1912 "White." It was the very first motor vehicle utilized by the Yonkers Police Department. Thomas was commended for saving a man's life on Jan. 16, 1927 when the man had become unconscious from illuminating gas and had to be resuscitated. Both of Thomas' uncles, Roundsman Joseph Johnstone and PO Richard Johnstone, had preceded him in the Y.P.D. And his nephew, PO Raymond Thomas, would join the department years later. Upon disability retirement on January 31, 1935 Thomas moved to Cold Springs where, after only seven months, he died on August 31, 1935.

PO AUSTIN BALL # 17

APPOINTED: August 17, 1907
RETIRED: February 29, 1940

A native of Warren, Ohio, Austin Ball was born on March 13, 1879. Prior to his appointment to the department on August 17, 1907, Ball worked as a janitor and chauffeur. As a police officer he worked his first year out of the station house on Wells Avenue. However, in May of 1908 when a 2nd police precinct opened on Central Avenue he was transferred there. In fact, he would spend the rest of his career there. Ball was considered to be an all-around athlete. He was a muscular man, barrel chested, a strong swimmer, a football player, good with the "shot put," and a fine horseman. In his early years he was assigned to mounted duty in the 2nd precinct. It was said he was honored by the department three times for rescues from a swimming area now part of Tibbetts Brook Park. Austin Ball retired on February 29, 1940. His son in law was PO Cecil Cooper, and his grandson was Sgt. Richard Ball. On July 24, 1948 retired PO Ball, of 54 Summit Street, died at age 68.

LT JOHN J. BOYLAN

APPOINTED: August 19, 1907
DIED: July 17, 1934

Born in Ireland on January 15, 1876, John Boylan came to the United States with his parents and sister on May 10, 1897 and worked for a time as a teamster. When he was appointed August 19, 1907, there was only one precinct, so he began his career working from headquarters at 20 Wells Avenue. On December 1, 1909 the new 3rd precinct was established and PO John Boylan was assigned to patrol south west Yonkers. In 1916 Boylan was among the organizers of the PBA, and was one of the signers of the certificate of incorporation. Apparently having earned the respect of his fellow workers, he was elected President of the Yonkers P.B.A. in 1921 and in 1922. On February 17, 1923 Boylan was promoted to the rank of Sergeant at $2,500 per year. His promotion to Lieutenant on May 1, 1927 earned him $4,000 per year as a 4th precinct desk officer. With 27 years service, and while on vacation in the Catskills, Lt. John Boylan died unexpectedly on July 17, 1934. A large honor guard of officers attended his funeral. John Boylan was only 58 years old.

PO JOSEPH J. FOX # 12

APPOINTED: August 19, 1907
RETIRED: January 31, 1934

Although Joseph Fox was born in NYC on November 16, 1883, he received his formal education in Yonkers. In his early years Joe worked as an electrician. At the outbreak of the Spanish American War, Fox joined the Navy where he served 4 years, and was promoted three times. He was a member of Post 27, Spanish American War Veterans. Joe Fox was appointed to the police department on August 19, 1907 and was said to have a great disposition. He worked for many years assigned to a traffic detail at South Broadway and McLean Avenue and it was said his nickname was "the courteous cop." In May of 1924 Joe Fox was assigned to the "Riot Squad" where he received specialized training. He was a member of the PBA, the Police War Veterans Association, and the Police Holy Name Society. On special occasions you could always find him carrying the standard in a color guard. After retiring on a disability, Joe Fox died on May 9, 1934 at his home at 80 Cowles Avenue.

PO WILLIAM S. DECKER #54

APPOINTED: August 19, 1907
RESIGNED: October 20, 1911

Bill Decker must have thought he would have a good career with the police department. But it was anything but. Though little is known about Decker it is known he was appointed on August 19, 1907 and assigned to foot patrol duty. Sometime prior to July of 1909, date unknown, officer Decker was found guilty of violating departmental rules and was dismissed from the department. He appealed his dismissal to the state Supreme Court and on July 7, 1909 it was reported that, although the court felt that the public safety commissioner made statements that were inappropriate, Decker's dismissal was upheld.

Yet, at one point he must have been re-appointed because when the new 3rd precinct was opened on December 1, 1909, PO William Decker was listed as being on the roster. On September 19, 1911 it was reported that the driver of a horse drawn wagon had lost control of the frightened horse which was running wild in the street. Bill Decker, who was off duty and on his way home, observed the danger and grabbed hold of the horse by its bridle. Rearing wildly it broke free but once again Decker grabbed the horse and brought it to a halt, much to the relief of passers by. However, only a month later, on October 20, 1911, PO Bill Decker resigned from the police department.

PO GEORGE F. MONKS # 19

APPOINTED: September 8, 1907
RETIRED: November 1, 1939

George F. Monks was born in Glenham, N.Y. on June 17, 1878 where he attended school. Arriving in Yonkers as a young man his early trade was that of a machinist. Upon his appointment to the police department on September 8, 1907 he was assigned to the 1st precinct where he would spend his entire career. On December 9, 1912, when the first "Automobile Patrol" was instituted, PO Monks was one of two officers assigned as Patrol Wagon Drivers. In his earlier years as a young officer, Monks was quite active. On one occasion on June 6, 1909 while attempting to take a prisoner into custody, he was struck on the head by a beer bottle from behind. He fired his revolver in the air to call for help and ultimately did make the arrest. Another time on December 6, 1912, Monks came upon a burglar inside 107 New Main Street late at night. The burglar pointed a gun at him, but Monks fired first. He missed the suspect, but still made the arrest. Following an eventful career and retiring on November 1, 1939, retired PO George F. Monks died on August 6, 1952 at the age of 74 years.

PO THOMAS F. DOWNEY # 15

APPOINTED: September 11, 1907
RETIRED: September 5, 1939

Tom Downey was born in Ireland on April 1, 1880 and was educated there. After arriving in the U.S., he obtained employment as a railroad conductor. Upon his appointment as a patrolman on September 11, 1907, he worked foot patrol in the 1st precinct on the west side of the city for about two years. However, on December 1, 1909, when the new 3rd precinct was established at 36 Radford Street, Downey was reassigned there for a short time before returning back to the 1st precinct. In 1911 he was assigned to the two wheel motorcycle squad where he remained for only a few years and was returned to foot patrol. In 1916, he was one of the organizers of the PBA and was very active in that organization. On January 7, 1926 he was detailed to the Mayor's office at City Hall on Security Detail. Tom Downey, whose nephews were PO Ed Henebry and PO John J. Wall, retired after 32 years of active police service on September 5, 1939. He moved to Beachwood, N.J. where he died on March 6, 1943 at the age of 62 years.

DET. ABRAHAM BECK # 11

APPOINTED: September 12, 1907
RETIRED: November 30, 1933

Abraham Beck was born in NYC on November 18, 1882. After coming to Yonkers, Beck worked as a salesman. When he was appointed to the police department on September 12, 1907 he was our first Jewish police officer and he was assigned to the 1st precinct. When the 3rd precinct opened in 1909, Beck was assigned there on foot patrol. At one point Beck was also a longtime motorcycle officer in the Traffic Division. Over his career he also worked plainclothes and was first assigned as a detective in 1910. Toward the end of his career, and after his motorcycle duty, Beck was again promoted to detective on October 16, 1930, at the salary of $3,200 per year. Although Beck was of the Jewish faith, it was reported that he had attended every annual Holy Name Society Communion Breakfast since its inception. Beck retired on November 30, 1933 and in 1942 he was designated an honorary life member of the Police H.N.S. In retirement Abe worked as a private investigator in NYC. Ret. Det. Abe Beck died in Baltimore, Maryland on Sept. 24, 1964 at the age of 81.

LT. JEROME M. LINEHAN

APPOINTED: September 12, 1907
RETIRED: December 31, 1941

Jerome Linehan was born in Yonkers on December 22, 1879. He attended local schools, and later made his living working as a machinist. He joined the local National Guard, and because of his interest in sports, he played on their championship basketball team known as the "4th Separates." Jerry, as he was known, was appointed to the YPD on September 12, 1907 and assigned to the 1st precinct on foot patrol. However, on March 30, 1908, only 6 months after his appointment, Linehan and 3 others were detailed to the newly formed "Motorcycle Squad." Throughout most of his career, Linehan would spend many years assigned to the Traffic Division on motorcycle duty. On May 1, 1914, Linehan was promoted to the rank of Sergeant at $2,500 per year and remained assigned to Traffic. As a sergeant he was very active in the Police Association serving as its Financial Secretary. On October 1, 1930, Sgt Linehan was promoted to Lieutenant earning $4,000 per year. He retired from the YPD on December 31, 1941. Lt. Linehan's cousin was PO Francis X. Linehan. On March 12, 1962, Ret. Lt. Jerome Linehan died at the age of 82 years.

PO ALEXANDER REID # 14

APPOINTED: September 12, 1907
RETIRED: October 31, 1934

Born in Ireland on March 6, 1881, Reid came to the U.S. and worked as a truck driver. Upon his appointment to the department on September 12, 1907, Reid was assigned to mounted duty at substation #1 located in Bronxville. On August 9, 1918 he was reassigned to motorcycle duty in the 2nd precinct. But, in October of 1920, he was reassigned to city wide motorcycle patrol. On August 23, 1924 Reid had a bad accident on his police motorcycle while chasing a speeder on Central Avenue, which resulted in the amputation of his lower leg. He was scheduled for disability retirement but declined it, instead requesting he be allowed to remain a police officer. His request was approved, and on December 2, 1925 he was assigned as a clerk in the Traffic Bureau with an artificial leg and continued to work for nine more years. During the 1927 annual Capt.'s, Lt.'s, & Sgt.'s Assoc. dinner, Reid was honored for his courage, determination, and loyalty to the police department. Following his retirement on October 31, 1934 he lived with his son in Tarrytown where he died on October 25, 1947 at the age of 66 years.

LT. MYLES SCULLY

APPOINTED: September 18, 1907
RETIRED: June 11, 1944

Myles Scully was born in Tullow, County Carlow, Ireland, on January 14, 1880. He emigrated to the U.S. at age 18, and worked for the Alexander Smith & Sons Carpet Co. Later he would also work as a motorman in Yonkers. Upon being appointed a police officer on September 18, 1907 he worked foot patrol for several years in the 1st precinct. On June 27, 1922 Scully was appointed a Detective. Five years later, on January 16, 1927 he was promoted to Sergeant and assigned to the 4th precinct on patrol. On June 1, 1942 he was promoted to Lieutenant and served for a time as a precinct desk officer. Two years later, on June 11, 1944, Lt Scully retired and was cited for outstanding service during his entire career. Lt. Scully had served as president of the Police Holy Name Society and would later serve as president of the Police and Fire Retiree's Association. As a young cop he worked hard, off duty, helping other Irish immigrants enter the U.S. He joined the Ancient Order of Hibernians in 1908 and was a past president. Retired Lt. Myles Scully died December 6, 1958 in a motor vehicle accident.

PO WILLIAM FOX O'BRIEN

APPOINTED: September 18, 1907
DISMISSED: January 4, 1909

A native of County Limerick, Ireland, having been born there on July 8, 1879, William F. O'Brien came to America to begin a new life. After applying, and passing a medical exam by the Police Surgeon, he was hired as a Yonkers police officer on September 18, 1907 from 1 Dock Street. Following his training in the School of Instruction he was assigned to foot patrol duties in the central part of town. However, his career would be a relatively short one. On October 28, 1908 charges were filed against him for drinking alcohol on duty. Following a departmental trial he was found guilty and fined 5 days pay. On January 4, 1909 he was again charged with being intoxicated on duty. Knowing the severe penalty he faced he pled not guilty, but despite his best arguments the charges were sustained. Due to his past record of being intoxicated on duty on two different occasions, PO William F. O'Brien was dismissed from the police department. On July 7, 1909 an appeal to the State Supreme Court failed to reverse O'Brien's dismissal.

LT. JOHN J. WILLNER

APPOINTED: September 20, 1907
DIED: September 19, 1930

John Willner was born in Irvington N.Y. on June 26, 1875. He later moved to Yonkers and worked as a hatter at the Waring Hat Factory. Upon his appointment to the police force on September 20, 1907 Willner worked foot patrol in the 1st precinct. On August 4, 1914 he was promoted to the rank of Sergeant. Seven years later, on December 22, 1921, he was promoted to Lieutenant. During his service as a patrolman, a sergeant and as a lieutenant, he remained assigned to the 1st precinct. It is likely that due to his excellent record and capabilities, on September 1, 1926 Lt. Willner was placed in command of the Detective Division, where he remained for a year. One week following gall bladder surgery, Lt. Willner died unexpectedly on September 19, 1930. Known to many as "George," he was described as one of the most popular officers in the department. His funeral was attended by over 100 brother officers and the PBA passed a resolution expressing their sorrow "at losing such a fine man, who had reached near perfection in his dealings with his fellow policemen." Lt. Willner was 55 years old.

LT. JOSEPH D. DROHAN

APPOINTED: September 20, 1907
RETIRED: November 30, 1939

Joe Drohan was born in County Waterford, Ireland on January 28, 1879. After emigrating to the U.S. he gained employment as a hatter. It was said that Drohan was a good athlete and excellent amateur boxer. Shortly after his police appointment on September 20, 1907 he gained praise by making an arrest of a male with a stolen horse and wagon and a loaded handgun. On April 7, 1910 he was assigned to motorcycle duty, but by 1911 he was working plainclothes assignments from the 2nd precinct. On February 8, 1911, along with other detectives, Drohan tracked a murder suspect to NYC and arrested him. Then, just ten days later, he arrested a member of the "Black Hand" for extortion. In May of 1924 Drohan was trained and designated a member of the new Riot Squad. On Jan. 16, 1926 he was promoted to detective, on May 17, 1926 to Sergeant, and to Lieutenant on Jan. 1, 1933. Lt. Joseph Drohan, who retired on Nov. 30, 1939, died on May 26, 1964 at the age of 85 years.

LT. WILLIAM H. COUGLE

APPOINTED: September 20, 1907
RETIRED: March 8, 1939

Born William Hallett Cougle on March 9, 1875 in New Brunswick, Canada, Cougle came to America, became a naturalized citizen and worked as a carpet foreman and chauffeur. When appointed a policeman on September 20, 1907 he was assigned to the 1st precinct, where he would spend most of his career. Throughout the years he was known as "Hall" Cougle to everyone. On April 27, 1914, Cougle was promoted to Sergeant, and on February 17, 1923 to Lieutenant. For both promotions he remained working in the 1st precinct. When he retired to his 4 Alder Street address on March 8, 1939, he kept busy hunting and fishing. When he retired Capt. Beary, his commanding officer, said of Cougle, "No man has ever been more well thought of than Lt. Cougle." During World War 2 he worked as a security officer for the Radio Marine Corp. in NYC. His brother was Capt. George Cougle, and his nephew was PO George Cougle. Ret Lt. William "Hall" Cougle died June 26, 1956 at age 81.

SGT JAMES J. BRAZIL # 24

APPOINTED: September 20, 1907
RETIRED: May 15, 1946

Born in Yonkers on September 9, 1883, Brazil's first job was as a machinist. In February of 1911, four years following his appointment on September 20, 1907, Brazil assisted Det Sgt O'Mara in arresting a member of the infamous "Black Hand" for extortion and blackmail. Brazil was also one of the signers of the certificate of incorporation when the Police Association was formed in 1916. He worked in the 2nd precinct up until his promotion to Sergeant on July 1, 1925, at which time he was sent to the 1st precinct. On January 22, 1929 he was shifted from patrol to the post of Assistant Warden at the newly opened City Jail on Alexander Street. Sgt Brazil retired on May 15, 1946 with nearly 40 years of service; most of which was in the 1st and 2nd precincts. He always had a keen interest in the youth of the city and frequently did volunteer work with them. His uncles were Capt. Charles O'Mara and PO William O'Mara. Ret Sgt Brazil died on August 19, 1953.

PO FRANK V. DOTY # 110

APPOINTED: September 25, 1907
RETIRED: September 30, 1933

Frank Vines Doty was born August 1, 1879. As a young man he first gained employment as a bookkeeper and packer of fine arts. Upon his police appointment on September 25, 1907 at the salary of $2,300, he was first sent to Sub Station # 2, which the following year became the 2nd precinct. When the new 3rd precinct opened December 1, 1909, Doty was assigned there, where he remained for many years. On May 18, 1925 he was appointed a Detective. However, within the year he was back in the 3rd precinct on patrol duty. In 1930 a new Emergency Squad was formed and from 1930 to 1933, Doty was assigned there working from the 1st precinct. After 26 years service, Frank Doty retired on September 30, 1933 on a pension of $1,500. He then worked as a "special policeman" in the Town of Ossining. His brother was PO Arthur Doty and his grandson was Lt Fred Doty. Following surgery, Frank Vines Doty died at the age of 68 on June 4, 1945.

PO BERNARD O'NEILL # 21

APPOINTED: September 25, 1907
RETIRED: November 30, 1939

Known as Barney to his friends in the police department, O'Neill was born in Saugerties, N.Y. on August 22, 1876. He came to Yonkers as a young boy with his family and he attended St. Mary's School. As a young man O'Neill worked as a foreman with the Alexander Smith & Sons Carpet Co. When he reached the age of 21 years the Spanish American War had begun and O'Neill quickly joined the Army. Following his discharge and upon his appointment to the police department on September 25, 1907, he was assigned to the 1st precinct. On December 1, 1909 he was reassigned to the new 3rd precinct where he remained for many years on foot patrol. On May 25, 1919 he was assigned to the Traffic Division directing traffic working the Day and Early tour chart. O'Neill was a proud member of the Yonkers Police War Veterans Association. In fact, Barney was so well liked that upon his retirement on Nov 30, 1939 the War Veterans Legion sponsored a testimonial dinner dubbed Barney O'Neill Night, where over 100 police officers attended. Although Barney lived at 30 Kinross Place, he died in the Bronx on December 2, 1957.

PO MICHAEL A. McCUE # 22

APPOINTED: September 25, 1907
RETIRED: December 31, 1941

Mike McCue was born in Haverstraw, N.Y. on October 7, 1879. He came to Yonkers when he was twenty years of age, and upon his appointment to the police department on September 25, 1907, he spent almost his entire career assigned to the 3rd precinct on foot patrol. Though he walked a foot post he was a very active cop having been twice cited for bravery. On one occasion in 1909 he placed himself in grave danger by rescuing a child from being struck by a trolley car. He was also recognized for rescuing several people from a burning building. Following the child rescue in 1909, PO McCue was commended and authorized to wear a gold star on his uniform cuff. This was our first form of departmental recognition to be worn on our uniform and it is believed he was the first to receive it. Mike retired after more than 34 years of faithful service on Dec. 31, 1941. His nephews were Capt. James McCue and Det. Vincent McCue, and his grandnephew was Lt. Terrance McCue. A resident of 271 Hawthorne Avenue, Retired PO Mike McCue died on September 29, 1947 at the age of 67 years.

PO DAVID PARLIAMENT # 85

APPOINTED: September 25, 1907
DIED: August 3, 1914

Dave Parliament had every reason to look forward to a long police career. But it just wasn't to be. Born in Hardyston, N.J. on October 20, 1874, Parliament came to Yonkers at the age of 12 years and as a young man worked as a driver for local stores. Upon his police appointment on September 25, 1907 he worked in the 1st precinct until December 1, 1909 when he was assigned to the newly established 3rd precinct. All indications were that he was an efficient officer. However, in May of 1914 he was forced to take a leave of absence due to illness. Unfortunately the following month he required surgery for stomach cancer. Following his surgery he continued to fail in health until his death on August 3, 1914 at the young age of 39 years. A police detail of 80 men marched in the funeral procession from his house to the church. The 3rd precinct where he worked was draped in mourning cloth for 30 days. PO David Parliament left behind a wife and seven children. His nephew was PO Joseph Hart who was appointed only three months before his death.

LT. FREDERICK KOLB

APPOINTED: September 27, 1907
RETIRED: April 16, 1940

Fred Kolb was born on July 24, 1883 in Chauncey NY. After moving to Yonkers with his family he worked for a while as a railroad mechanic. Upon joining the police department on September 27, 1907 Kolb was initially assigned to foot patrol in the Wells Avenue station until 1908 when the 2nd precinct was placed in service. While serving in this precinct he was assigned to mounted patrol duty on his horse which he named "Jim." On May 1, 1914, the day a 4th precinct was established, Kolb was promoted to Sergeant. His daughter stated he was very athletic and at one time was the manager of the Y.P.D. baseball team. On June 16, 1934 Kolb was promoted to Lieutenant and began duties as a desk officer. Following his retirement on April 16, 1940, and during WW II, Kolb served with the "Westchester County Volunteers for Defense Auxiliary." Fred Kolb, also an avid bowler in his retirement years, had a brother, PO William Kolb and Henry of the YFD. Retired Lt. Frederick Kolb, father of five children, died on March 16, 1977 in Kent Connecticut at the age of 93 years.

CAPTAIN JOHN A. RYER

APPOINTED: September 27, 1907
RETIRED: March 30, 1939

John Ryer was born in the City of Yonkers on March 31, 1875. As a youth he attended Public School # 6 and the Yonkers High School. Ryer served for 5 years in the N.Y. National Guard, 4th Separate Company. During his service he was also very athletic and played basketball with his units team which was named, "The Fourth Separates."

When he was appointed to the Yonkers Police Dept. at the age of 32, he was assigned to work in the Wells Avenue station. From all indications available, he was apparently a very conscientious officer always ready to do his duty. In fact, on one occasion, on his birthday March 31, 1909, while on foot patrol he observed a runaway horse. Without hesitation he immediately ran into the street and attempted to stop the frightened horse. He was knocked to the ground and run over receiving bruises to his body and face, including damage to his teeth. In addition, his entire uniform was ruined. A short time later an attorney representing the owner of the horse contacted the police commissioners and offered $40.00 to Ryer to compensate for the damage to his uniform. The commissioners voted to allow Ryer to keep the money. Officer Ryer was commended by the department for his actions and later that year, on December 1, 1909, he was assigned to the Detective Division. He received this assignment even though his 3 year

Captain John A. Ryer (cont.)

probation would not have ended until later that year. This opportunity coincided with the opening of a 3rd precinct on that same day.

For unknown reasons, Ryer's detective assignment ended on January 29, 1910 when he was assigned to the 3rd precinct. On October 17, 1912 at 3:30 am while Ryer was on foot patrol, he arrested a man for acting suspiciously. While walking his prisoner to the precinct for investigation the man tried to pull a stiletto knife on the officer but his resistance was quickly overcome.

On July 16, 1917 officer John Ryer was promoted, along with PO George Ford, to the rank of Sergeant. Ryer had placed # 2 on the promotional list with a score of 91.5. He remained in the 3rd precinct as a patrol sergeant enjoying his new salary of $1650. per year. On May 31, 1918, as part of a reorganization which included the moving of Police H.Q. from City Hall to the 1st precinct just a few weeks earlier, Sgt Ryer was selected to become part of a new Traffic Squad to aid in the flow of increased motor vehicle traffic throughout the city. At the time, Yonkers had not yet installed traffic lights. This unit was led by a lieutenant and consisted of two sergeants and 17 police officers. Sgt Ryer and his men enjoyed a modified work schedule of ten day tours followed by ten early tours. They worked no late tours.

During the year 1921 Sgt Ryer was detailed to serve as the Acting Police Clerk for the Police Bureau. Later that year on December 22, 1921, Sgt Ryer was promoted to the rank of Lieutenant at a salary of $2,000 per year. He was assigned precinct desk officer duties. It was during this time that the Yonkers Herald newspaper made a request of the department to provide them with a history of our department. Lt Ryer was assigned the task of providing this information. Ryer proceeded to write an extremely informative article which included a wealth of historical police information and several vintage photographs. Over the next few years Lt Ryer worked in the 3rd and 2nd precincts. In May of 1924, in addition to his regular duties, he was placed in charge of the departments Riot Squad. By 1925 Lt Ryer was serving in the capacity of Acting Captain in command of the 2nd precinct. It was during that time that he complained in an official letter that due to federal law, local police agencies were prohibited from enforcing alcohol prohibition laws. He went on to state that federal agents that had that responsibility were not very cooperative with the Yonkers Police in enforcing reported violations. In spite of the reported temptations faced by the police during the prohibition years, it seems apparent that Capt. Ryer was very serious about his oath of office.

On May 12, 1927 Lt Ryer was sworn in as a Police Captain. The promotion took effect June 1, 1927. At 8 am that date Capt. John Ryer took command of the 4th precinct, succeeding the recently retired Capt. Edward Connolly. Upon taking command of the precinct Ryer asked the men under him to give him the same cooperation that they had given to Capt. Connolly.

On August 10, 1931 a pair of daytime burglars broke into the house at 420 Palisade Avenue while the residents were on vacation. Fortunately they were seen entering the house and the person reported it to the 4th precinct. Capt. Ryer was on duty and in the station house at the time and he, along with PO Joseph Hart jumped into a patrol car and responded. As the officers were pulling up to the scene the thieves saw them and began to run. It was reported that, with Capt. Ryer standing on the running board of the patrol car while it was moving, he fired a shot at the two men causing one to surrender immediately. The second continued to run leading Ryer on a lengthy foot pursuit. Though Ryer was an excellent athlete in his youth

Captain John A. Ryer (cont)

I'm sure he decided there was a quicker way to stop the male. He then fired at the fleeing suspect which caused the man to come to a quick stop and be arrested by the captain. Upon arriving at HQ with his prisoners Chief Quirk commended the captain for his quick and effective police work.

Having reached his sixty fourth birthday and having completed 32 years of service, Capt. John Ryer of 80 Linden Street retired effective March 30, 1939. In a ceremony held at the 4 PM roll call on Ryer's last day, Chief Kruppenbacher paid tribute to the captains years of service and presented him with a wrist watch on behalf of the men in the 2nd precinct.

During his retirement years John Ryer pursued his hobby as an amateur painter He even exhibited some of his work in the art galleries in Miami Beach and Hollywood Florida.

On June 11, 1955, retired police captain John A. Ryer, a first cousin to former Lt. Frank Ryer, died at the age of 80 years in Hollywood Florida where he made his home.

PO LAWRENCE AHEARN # 48

APPOINTED: September 27, 1907
RETIRED: December 31, 1933

In the 1930's "Larry" Ahearn was dubbed the most popular police officer in the department. This title was determined by a Yonkers newspaper poll of Yonkers citizens asking them to vote for their most respected and well liked city employee. Larry won hands down. Ahearn was born in Limerick, Ireland on June 25, 1870, immigrated to America at the age of 9, and came to Yonkers in 1890. As a young man he worked for the Yonkers Railroad Co., serving most of his time as president of the Trolleymen's union local. When hired as a police officer on September 27, 1907 he spent nearly his entire career in the 1st precinct on Wells Avenue on foot patrol. He was a very active "cop" throughout his service and, after 26 years, finished his career on Dec. 31, 1933 being assigned to a foot post at the N. Y. Central Railroad Station. Interestingly enough, Larry's brother Mike was a YPD Hostler who attended to the police stables and the horses housed therein, and his brother-in-law was Yonkers PO Charles Hudd. Retired police officer Lawrence Ahearn died on December 18, 1935 at the age of 65 years.

PO JAMES FITZGERALD # 25

APPOINTED: December 11, 1907
RETIRED: November 30, 1942

James Fitzgerald was born in the City of Yonkers July 31, 1879. Prior to his appointment to the police department on December 11, 1907 Fitzgerald worked as a telephone operator. Following his joining the police department he worked almost his entire career in the 1st precinct, on Wells Avenue, on foot patrol. Later in his career he was detailed to security duty in the Health Center Building at 87 Nepperhan Avenue. But in 1942 Fitzgerald was transferred back to foot patrol in the 4th precinct. It could be that he really did not want to return to patrol duty this late in his career because only a few months later, on November 30, 1942, he retired from the police department just six days short of 35 years service. Jim Fitzgerald was a member of the Modern Woodman of America and the Exempt Firemen's Association. His brother was a Yonkers fire captain. On December 15, 1957 retired PO James Fitzgerald died in St John's hospital at the age of 78 years.

PO EDWARD J. CHARLTON # 26

APPOINTED: December 11, 1907
RETIRED: January 15, 1929

Born on April 19, 1880 in Sawkill N.Y., Edward Charlton later moved to Yonkers as a young man. He listed his early employment as a farmer and stonecutter. Ed joined the Army in June of 1898 for service during the Spanish American War, and was discharged in March of 1899. He would again voluntarily serve in the military from 1903 to 1907. Living at 15 Lockwood Ave., Charlton was hired as a policeman on December 11, 1907 at $2,300 per year. When the 2nd precinct was established in 1908, Charlton was assigned to walk foot patrol there. He would remain in this precinct for the remainder of his career. Twenty one years later on January 15, 1929, upon physical examination, PO Charlton was found physically unqualified to perform his duties and was retired on a disability pension effective that date. Retired PO Edward Charlton died on October 10, 1962 at the age of 82 years.

PO JOSEPH F. SULLIVAN # 79

APPOINTED: December 11, 1907
RETIRED: June 12, 1949

Joseph Francis Sullivan was born June 13, 1884 in Tarrytown, NY and would later move to Yonkers around 1900. Prior to being hired as a policeman his trade was a blacksmith and he lived at 74 Ravine Avenue. He was appointed to the police department on December 11, 1907 earning $2,300 a year. On December 1, 1909 PO Sullivan was reassigned to foot patrol in the newly established 3rd precinct at 36 Radford Street. When the PBA was formed in 1916 Sullivan was one of the signers of the certificate of incorporation. In March 1928 Sullivan was promoted to detective where he remained for several years. Later in his career he would also work from the 4th precinct. When Joe Sullivan retired on June 12, 1949 it was at the maximum retirement age of 65 years, and with over 41 years of dedicated service. Approximately 15 of those years as a detective. He was a highly respected member of the police department. Retired PO Joseph Sullivan of 12 Tower Pl. died on September 9, 1950 at the age of 66 years.

CHIEF OF POLICE
WILLIAM A. KRUPPENBACHER

Appointed: December 12, 1907
Retired: March 4, 1947

The story of William Kruppenbacher is one of stark contrasts. It's the story of hard work, success, and ultimate sadness. William Kruppenbacher was born in Yonkers on January 2, 1884. He received his early education in PS #7 and PS #2, and later graduated from Yonkers H.S. on South Broadway and Nepperhan Avenue. He gained employment with the Otis Elevator Co. as a machinist and was active in the American Federation of Labor. He once contemplated a career as a labor union official but decided to become a policeman instead.

When "Will" Kruppenbacher, as his close friends called him, made application to the police department he lived at 22 Cliff Street. At that time he listed previous employment as machinist, chauffeur, telephone operator, musician, and bookkeeper. He had no military experience, but in addition to English, Kruppenbacher also spoke German.

Upon his appointment to the police department in 1907 he was assigned to the 1st precinct on foot

Chief of Police William Kruppenbacher (cont.)

patrol. In October of 1912 plans were approved for the purchase of a new motorized Police Patrol Wagon. It was reported that the purchase of this vehicle would fill a need long believed to be important. Up to that time prisoners, men or women, were conveyed through the streets in an open wagon, exposed to the view of everyone and which generated many complaints. These complaints later resulted in the wagon being covered, but it apparently was still unsatisfactory. A council resolution was passed and a 1912 "PATROL WAGON" was purchased. The manufacturer was a "WHITE." On December 9, 1912 a General Order was issued establishing the new "Automobile Patrol" and naming as drivers of this vehicle to be PO William Kruppenbacher and PO George Monks. This vehicle was stored in the Wells Ave. headquarters building, and in addition to prisoner transports, it was used as an ambulance. When not transporting prisoners or seriously injured persons, it is believed that Kruppenbacher worked inside headquarters assisting the precinct captain or lieutenant with miscellaneous assignments. This was, no doubt, a very desirable assignment in which Kruppenbacher was fortunate enough to remain for approximately 14 years.

PO Kruppenbacher in the new Patrol Wagon in 1912

Chief of Police William Kruppenbacher (cont.)

Prior to, and up through 1916, the members of the police department felt they had no real unified way in which to voice their grievances against the department or the city. As a result, and after a great deal of planning and organizing, the "Yonkers Police Association" (YPA) was organized. William Kruppenbacher was one of those who served on the first board of directors.

On March 27, 1920 PO Kruppenbacher was tried on departmental charges. Following the trial he was found guilty of violating departmental rules and regulations and was fined 20 days pay. The following month on April 5, 1920 during a reassignment of several officers, and probably as a result of his conviction on charges the month before, Kruppenbacher was transferred from being the driver of the Patrol Wagon to duty in the Traffic Division on foot directing vehicular traffic.

In January 1922, and again in 1923, PO Kruppenbacher was elected and served as the president of the Yonkers Police Association. This was the organization he worked so hard, with others, to establish six years earlier. It must have been around this same time that, although assigned to the Traffic Division, he returned to his duty as Patrol Wagon driver.

According to news reports, Kruppenbacher was said to have topped the civil service promotional list for sergeant and as a result, on May 17, 1926 he was promoted to the rank of Sergeant. He was assigned shield # 17. He was then transferred from traffic and patrol wagon driver duties to the 2nd precinct as a patrol sergeant. Although it took him 19 years to achieve his first promotion, his continuing rise through the ranks would be much more rapid. On November 30, 1926 Kruppenbacher was reassigned to the Traffic Division as a sergeant on foot patrol. In 1927 he was moved to the 3rd precinct for a month but was quickly returned to traffic duties.

Sgt Kruppenbacher continued to display an interest in not only police work, but fraternal activities as well. He was an active member of the Police Glee Club and along with several others he sang at many police social functions to the great enjoyment of the audience.

In 1928 the Yonkers City Jail construction was completed on Alexander Street, and on October 9, 1928, Sgt Kruppenbacher was assigned to duty at the new jail as Assistant Warden. He worked under the direction of Lt. John Scheibel who was assigned there as the Jail Warden. The sergeant remained at the jail until January 22, 1929 when he was returned to the 1st precinct. In February of 1929 Kruppenbacher continued to exhibit the desire to always be involved in departmental activities by being elected Vice President of the Captains, Lieutenants, and Sergeants Association.

On September 6, 1930 Sgt Kruppenbacher was promoted to the rank of Lieutenant and was assigned to desk officer duties at the 2nd precinct. Six years later on January 20, 1936 he was promoted to Captain. His new assignment was to take command of the 4th precinct at 53 Shonnard Place. On his first day of duty at his precinct he was presented with a horseshoe of flowers from the men of the 2nd precinct where he had previously served as a lieutenant for several years. The new captain not only assumed his new responsibilities with enthusiasm, but was immediately named chairman of the committee making plans for the annual Police Association dinner dance.

Chief of Police William Kruppenbacher (cont.)

Apparently being a very competent administrator, Captain Kruppenbacher was utilized in a variety of assignments. On June 1, 1938 he was moved from the 4th precinct to take command of the 3rd precinct located at 36 Radford Street. Less than a year later on February 15, 1939 he was again reassigned to take command of the 2nd precinct at 441 Central Park Avenue. While assigned to the 2nd precinct and while off duty, the captain was attempting to investigate a possible burglary of a garage at 2 AM. While in the dark work area of the garage the 55 year old captain fell into a repair pit fracturing several ribs and causing internal injuries. He was hospitalized in serious condition but he recovered quickly.

On October 23, 1940 the totally unexpected occurred. The usually strong and robust Chief of Police Edward J. Quirk suffered a cerebral hemorrhage and was hospitalized in a coma. In order to maintain continuous leadership of the police department, on October 26, 1940 City Manager Raymond Whitney appointed his most senior and capable captain, William Kruppenbacher, to the position of Acting Chief of Police. He was to hold this position until Chief Quirk regained his health. Unfortunately that did not happen. Chief Quirk died on October 28, 1940.

Acting Chief Kruppenbacher stated, "*As Acting Chief, I voice the unanimous sentiments and sorrow of the entire bureau in the loss of their chief, who was loved and respected because of his fairness to everyone. Personally, after many years of close association, I know him so well and intimately that I feel a deep personal loss. It is a sorrowful task that my first official act as the Acting Chief is to arrange departmental honors for him.*"

The following month, on November 19, 1940, William A. Kruppenbacher was appointed to the permanent position of Chief of Police. Like most leaders, the new chief was liked by some of his subordinates, and disliked by others. He was, however, respected by all as a man who rose through the ranks and earned his position. According to PO John "Red" O'Hare, the founder and first president of the PAL, if it had not been for the cooperation and encouragement of Chief Kruppenbacher, the PAL may never have been organized. According to O'Hare, Chief Quirk had no interest in a PAL.

At that time it should be made clear, however, that Chief Kruppenbacher's leadership of the department was not without controversy. A new city administration was now in office and Patrick O'Hara was appointed to the vacant Public Safety Commissioner position. Then, as now, illegal gambling operated in Yonkers and Comm. O'Hara wanted it stopped. He made it perfectly clear that he was dissatisfied with Chief Kruppenbacher's ability to achieve that goal. In a press release on April 22, 1946, the commissioner warned the chief that, in essence, if changes were not forthcoming, ..."*I will take the Detective Division out of your hands entirely and run it myself.*"

The pressure on the chief by Comm. O'Hara continued. Whether it was justified or driven by political considerations is not exactly clear, but on January 2, 1947 O'Hara told the local newspaper that he was urging Chief Kruppenbacher to retire, thereby, he believed, improving the morale of the entire department. It was evident that there were bad feelings between the two men, but the chief refused to be forced out and intended to remain in the department until the end of the year. He would then be eligible to retire due to the maximum age of 64 years.

Chief of Police William Kruppenbacher (cont.)

The allegations against the chief and his ability to lead the department efficiently were very public and, no doubt, humiliating as well. For on March 4, 1947 at midnight, Chief Kruppenbacher retired from the department on the advice of his personal physician, citing severe symptoms caused by chronic stress. In the letter to Commissioner O'Hara from the chief's doctor regarding the chief's notice of retirement, it read in part,....*that the state of his health is such as to necessitate that he be relieved of his responsibilities incident to his position as Chief of Police."*

Less than three days following his retirement, retired Chief Kruppenbacher ended his life with his revolver. Full departmental honors were accorded the former chief who was buried in his full dress uniform. Over 500 policemen, including all off duty Yonkers men, delegations from other departments in Westchester County, and 100 Yonkers firefighters attended the funeral. Fifty motorcycle police officers from Yonkers and other county departments led the cortege. The police motorcycles included all 13 available in Yonkers, and riders from White Plains, Hastings, Eastchester, Westchester County Parkway Police, Ardsley, Mt. Vernon and Greenberg.

Also joining the procession were 40 retired police officers and 23 retired fire firefighters.
The former chief was a charter member and former president of the Yonkers Police Association, a charter member and former vice president of the Captains, Lieutenants, & Sergeants Association, a charter member and former treasurer of the Police Holy Name Society, member of the N.Y.S. Association of Chiefs of Police, the Honor Legion of the N.Y.P.D., the City Club of Yonkers, the Modern Woodmen of America, Habirshaw Athletic Club, the Yonkers P.A.L., and the First Friday Club.
Reportedly retired Chief Kruppenbacher's wife received an annual police widows pension of $600.

This was truly a sad end to a long and dedicated career in service to the Police Department and the City of Yonkers.

PO JAMES A. KEEHAN # 80

APPOINTED: December 20, 1907
RETIRED: June 15, 1924

Jim Keehan was born on May 20, 1876. Upon his appointment to the police department on December 20, 1907 he was assigned to foot patrol in the 1st precinct on Wells Ave. Available records seem to indicate he was an efficient and dependable police officer. He worked the rotating work schedule until July 7, 1919 when he was assigned to the Traffic Division directing traffic at various intersections. In this assignment he worked only day and early tours. In 1924 Keehan volunteered to work on the committee for the annual PBA Ball which turned out to be a great success. However, even then he was ill and following the police surgeons exam, this illness required him to retire on a physical disability. Unfortunately this illness would ultimately cause his death one year later on January 20, 1925. Before his disability retirement and subsequent death, he was fortunate in one respect that he was able to have seen his son Edward Keehan sworn in as a Yonkers police officer on January 24, 1923.

PO GEORGE F. BRUCE

APPOINTED: December 20, 1907
DIED: January 28, 1924

George Bruce was born in the City of Yonkers on February 8, 1880. He attended local schools and as a young man began working as a painter. With the outbreak of the Spanish American War, Bruce enlisted in the 203rd NY Army Infantry in July of 1898. Following this short and successful conflict he was honorably discharged in January 1899. When Bruce was accepted into the Yonkers Police Department on December 20, 1907 he was assigned to foot patrol in the 1st precinct. After only a few years Bruce was transferred to motorcycle duty in the 2nd precinct. For some unknown reason that assignment did not work out and in 1911 he was reassigned to foot patrol back in the 1st precinct. Although Bruce apparently was a good worker, his health began to fail. On January 28, 1924, after being sick for two years, PO George Bruce died of what was then termed "Brights Disease" which was kidney disease. He was 43 years old and left behind a wife and four sons.

CHIEF OF POLICE DANIEL F. WOLFF

APPOINTED: May 1, 1908
RETIRED: February 15, 1919

Since the organization of the Yonkers Police Department on April 10, 1871, and throughout the ensuing 37 years, the charter of the City of Yonkers had outlined the structure of the police department. An integral part of this structure would be that the police department would be led by a "Captain of Police." There was no position entitled "Chief of Police" authorized, although the duties would have been the same. Upon the retirement of then Captain of Police Frederick Woodruff in 1907, Sgt. William Lent was appointed to that position. Capt. Lent was the most senior ranking officer, rose through the ranks to attain the leadership of the department, and was a highly respected individual.

When rumors began to surface in January of 1908 that Public Safety Commissioner Edgar Hermance wanted to institute the position of Chief of Police, it was expected by almost everyone that the current police leader, William Lent, would receive this appointment. However, this was not to be. In a

Chief of Police Daniel Wolff (cont.)

Yonkers Herald news story on January 16, 1908, it was related that the "Republican political machine" had decided to appoint Mr. Daniel Wolff of 45 Cliff Avenue, and a close friend of former mayor Leslie Sutherland, to be the first Chief of Police. The newspaper stated that an agreement had apparently been reached at city hall allowing the appointment of Wolff, a republican, to be the new chief, and Sgt. Hugh Brady, a democrat, to be given a newly created captains position. This arrangement, no doubt, did not make Captain Lent and his supporters at all happy. First, Capt. Lent was a career police officer, and second, Daniel Wolff had never even been a police officer and had absolutely no law enforcement experience.

Mr. Wolff was said to be a strapping man, 6 feet in height and of Danish decent, who was born August 19, 1865 in what was then known as the West Indies. More specifically he is believed to have been born on the Island of St. Croix in the Caribbean. As a young man he is said to have married a girl named Ester Leigh who had been born on the Island of St. Thomas, and the both of them came to the U.S. together. Wolff was a resident of New York City until 1900 when he then moved to Yonkers. His business was given as a "buyer of goods" in NYC.

Prior to moving to Yonkers and being considered for the Chief of Police position, Wolff was a Captain in the 22 Regiment of Engineers of the New York National Guard. He first entered the National Guard on May 18, 1885. His regiment was originally infantry, but was later changed to engineers. He was honorably discharged in 1890. With the outbreak of the Spanish American War, Wolff re-enlisted, remaining a private for three months, and then was promoted to Corporal. His regiment was stationed at Fort Slocum on Travers Island. They were encamped, ready for a call to the "front" which never came. Wolff advanced from Corporal to Sergeant, to 2nd Lieutenant, 1st Lieutenant and then to Captain. Though in the military during the Spanish American War, Wolff saw no combat. But his keen interest in the military would later leave its mark on the members of the Yonkers Police Department.

On February 5, 1908 the Common Council passed legislation amending the City Charter allowing for the position of a Police Chief and one additional captain. The charter changes provided that the Chief of *Police "shall hold office during good behavior or until permanently incapacitated or unfit to discharge his duties."*

It was on May 1, 1908 that Daniel Wolff was sworn in as the "Chief of Police." It was reported that this news hit the city like a shock wave. Despite the rumors, nearly everyone expected Capt. William Lent, the current leader of the department, to ultimately receive the new chiefs position. They were wrong. On the day of his appointment, at the 6 PM roll call at H.Q., Chief Wolff addressed the men in his newly designed full dress uniform. During his talk he stated that he was grateful for the opportunity to lead this great department. He said his policy would be to rigidly enforce all laws equally and impartially. The chief went on to state that,..... *"I shall conduct the affairs of my office on strictly nonpartisan lines and with absolute impartiality and justice to those under me, thereby hoping to merit the respect, esteem, and affection of the men I have the honor to command. By all who are loyal and faithful in the discharge of their duties, I desire to be looked upon as a sincere friend. I will do all in my power to lessen your hardships, and grant every reasonable request, provided the same does not conflict with the proper discharge of duties."* Even prior to the new chief's appointment it was rumored that he would try to turn

Chief of Police Daniel Wolff (cont.)

the police department into a military organization. In answer to this rumor the chief said,... *"It is not, and never has been, my intention to turn you into a regiment of soldiers."*
Following his address to the men at roll call, Lt. Dinsmore presented the chief with a special new dress baton with white braided tassels.

The chief's new uniform was similar to that worn by an inspector in the NYC Police Department, and differed from the other officers in the Yonkers Police Department in that, the material that comprised his cuffs and collar were made of velvet. On his collar Chief Wolff wore two stars, one on each side, to indicate his rank. His police cap also had a velvet band.

During his talk at a roll call, despite the chiefs denial that he would introduce a military atmosphere into the police department, one only had to consider the chiefs military background, and observe his new military style uniform to expect quite the opposite. And that's just what happened. Just one example was the order to prepare for the very first "Annual Police Parade" which would be incorporated with the annual spring inspection. This was ordered to be held in May of 1909. Eight months prior to the parade the entire department was reportedly drilled in marching and maneuvers on a regular basis at the City Armory or the Empire City Racetrack. All this military style training was conducted during off duty hours with no compensation to the personnel.

On May 15, 1909 the rather flamboyant chief held this historic Annual Police Parade and inspection. With the exception of one man on desk duty in the 1st and 2nd precincts, the entire police

Chief of Police Daniel Wolff (cont)

department participated in the grueling eight mile parade all throughout Yonkers. The temperature that day was in the 80's and the heat was reported to have caused problems with some of the older members of the department. But they kept marching. The parade culminated in Getty Square with a full inspection of all personnel.

The newspaper wrote that the city was left unprotected and the fire department had to do crowd control. They wrote, *"All this for the glory of Chief Wolff."* It was just a few months later, on August 16, 1909, that Chief Wolff requested and received a full and honorable discharge from the National Guard. Apparently his new duties as Police Chief would require all his attention.

In a news article dated October 30, 1909 it was reported that "apparently" Chief Wolf received his appointment illegally by claiming to have taken a non-competitive exam for this position. However, no records could be found of such an exam and, in addition, the listed age limit for such an exam was 35 years.

At the time Chief Wolff was appointed he was 43. As a result of a subsequent investigation, on January 10, 1910 Chief Wolff was ordered dismissed from his position. The order read as follows: *"You are hereby notified that your appointment as Chief of Police of the City of Yonkers, both the provisional appointment under date May 1, 1908, and the subsequent appointment under date of August 25, 1908 were unlawful and irregular and not in conformance with the provisions and requirements of the Civil Service Law, and that you are removed from the position of Chief of Police and your office declared vacant, to take effect immediately."* The chief refused to vacate his office, continued to come to work every day, albeit apparently without any authority, and immediately filed an appeal. On May 24, 1910, by order of the Supreme Court, State of NY. dated May 23, 1910, Public Safety Commissioner James Fleming reinstated Daniel Wolff as Chief of Police. Now back in power and exercising even greater authority, Chief Wolff became the subject of continuous controversy in the media during the ensuing years.

On September 13, 1915, upon Chief Wolff's own application, a special order was issued by State Adjutant General Louis W. Statesbury re-appointing Chief Wolff to the reserve list of commissioned officers with the rank of Captain. When asked why he would want to join the military reserves he stated, "When I learned it was possible under the law to get on the reserve list as a captain, I took advantage of it." On the prospect of becoming involved in a war he said, *"I have no doubt I could be of more service to the country by taking charge of a company as Captain, than by merely entering the service as a private."* Then, on March 12, 1918, Chief Wolff unexpectedly applied for retirement on the grounds of physical disability. His application was granted and he was retired effective February 15, 1919 on a pension of $1650 per year. Once the Chief of Police position became vacant, it remained unfilled until 1926 when Capt. Edward Quirk, a career police officer, received the appointment.

Chief Wolff had remained in office for ten years. This was apparently just long enough to qualify for a pension. After leaving the police department the retired chief established his own private detective agency in NYC.

As time went on he suffered from several heart attacks and on September 15, 1933, retired police chief Daniel Wolff, a longtime resident of 15 Caryl Avenue, died in St. Johns Hospital. He was 68 years of age.

PO JAMES R. BARRY # 31

APPOINTED: July 1, 1908
RETIRED: November 30, 1937

James Richard Barry was born on December 21, 1873. It wasn't until he was 20 that he moved to Yonkers. He began to develop a trade as a butcher, but decided to take the civil service test for police officer for better job security. Upon his police appointment on July 1, 1908 at nearly 35 years of age, he was assigned to the 1st precinct, and later to the 4th walking foot posts. Though in his early years he was assigned to both mounted patrol and bicycle patrol. On June 28, 1928, while assigned to the 4th precinct, Barry was awarded a departmental Honorable Mention for a high profile burglary arrest. Jim Barry retired from the police department on November 30, 1937 after 29 years service. Among his grandchildren were a NY State Trooper, and a Yonkers Assistant Fire Chief. On November 17, 1950, while at his home at 132 Convent Avenue, retired police officer James Barry died at age 76.

LT JOHN F. DAHILL

APPOINTED: July 1, 1908
DIED: April 18, 1927

Born March 13, 1874 in Hartford Conn., Dahill came to Yonkers around 1902. When he was appointed a police officer on July 1, 1908 he worked foot patrol from the 1st precinct. Police discipline was no problem to him. Dahill had served during the Spanish American War from May to October 1898, and also with the National Guard for 7 years. In 1916, following great efforts, the Yonkers Police Association was formed. Due, in part, to Dahill's dedicated effort in accomplishing that goal, he was elected as the YPA's first president, and was dubbed by the press as the "father of the police association." On June 10, 1918 he was assigned to the Detective Bureau serving with distinction. On February 18, 1922, when he was promoted to Sergeant, he remained a Detective Sergeant. He was also the departments fingerprint expert. In January 1926 he was reassigned to 2nd pct. patrol duties. On May 17, 1926 he was promoted to lieutenant working desk duty and serving as the YPD revolver expert, and recruit instructor. Unfortunately illness struck and Lt. Dahill died April 18, 1927.

PO JAMES E. GARAHAN

APPOINTED: July 1, 1908
DIED: September 5, 1913

The future of Jim Garahan's career in the police department was full of potential. But, it was not to be. James Edward Garahan was born in Oswego N.Y. on September 20, 1873. He moved to Yonkers around 1898 and was reported to have worked on the trolley cars for several years. On July 1, 1908 when he was appointed a police officer he worked foot patrol out of the 1st precinct. His father in law, veteran Detective Bill Carroll, had retired only two years earlier. At the start of September 1913 Garahan unexpectedly became ill while walking his post. He subsequently underwent surgery for appendicitis, and as a result of complications died suddenly on September 5, 1913. The officers and men of the 1st precinct were shocked by his death, and as a sign of their respect, the precinct was draped in black bunting for 30 days. A large contingent of police officers, along with an honor guard, attended the funeral at his home at 18 Ingram Street. A member of Division # 14, Ancient Order of the Hibernians, he was only 40 years old.

PO JOHN F. CARSON # 32

APPOINTED: July 1, 1908
RETIRED: December 31, 1933

John Francis Carson was born in Yonkers on May 28, 1883 and attended local public schools. He had indicated on his police application that he had previously worked as a chauffeur and telephone operator. However, up to the time of his appointment as a police officer he had been working as a bricklayer. He must have been an experienced horseman prior to his appointment on July 1, 1908, because upon being hired as a police officer he was immediately assigned to mounted patrol duty in the 1st precinct. Ten years later on August 9, 1918, he was reassigned, this time to motorcycle duty. The following year in April of 1919 his riding days ended and he was sent to the 3rd precinct to do foot patrol. He would remain in a precinct for the remainder of his career. Following his retirement on December 31, 1933, and during World War 2, Carson worked for the Otis Elevator Co. While residing at 22 Dalton Road, retired PO John Carson died on October 21, 1971 at 88 years of age.

PO WILLIAM F. RUSSELL # 30

APPOINTED: July 1, 1908
RETIRED: November 15, 1927

William Russell was born in Yonkers on March 26, 1882. A former mason by trade, Russell was appointed to the police department on July 1, 1908 at the age of 25 years. On one occasion on June 29, 1909 at 9 PM Russell tried to break up a fight. Several men jumped him forcing him to use his "Billy club" on one of them quite effectively. However others continued to fight, one pulling out a revolver, which resulted in PO Russell shooting two of them in the leg before arresting them all. Within a short time he was reassigned to mounted patrol duties in the 2nd precinct. Then on December 1, 1909, when the newly organized 3rd precinct was first opened, Russell was assigned there on motorcycle duty. Despite these assignments he spent most of his career on foot patrol in the 1st precinct. Deemed physically unfit by the police surgeon to perform his duties, Russell was retired on disability pension on November 15, 1927. A resident of 136 Princeton Avenue, Dover, N.J., Bill Russell died there in his home December 11, 1935 at the age of 53 years.

SGT. PASQUALE CILIBERTI # 5

APPOINTED: July 20, 1908
RETIRED: August 23, 1941

Pasquale Ciliberti, the first man of Italian heritage to ever be hired by our police department, was born in Italy on August 24, 1876. His family left Italy and he arrived in America at the age of 11 years. As a young man he worked in a local foundry to earn his living. On his police application he noted he spoke fluent Italian and English. Following his police appointment on July 20, 1908, it didn't take long to realize how valuable his second language would be being able to interpret Italian. It was probably one of the reasons he was promoted to detective where it was said he did an outstanding job. He was described by news reports as "one of the most decorated men in the department's history." In 1926 he was instrumental in capturing 6 truck bandits who robbed a driver on Bronx River Road. For a short time he was returned to regular patrol duties, but on June 10, 1918 he returned to the Detective Bureau. On December 2, 1925 Det. Ciliberti was promoted to the rank of Sergeant. He would retire from patrol duties in the 4th precinct on August 23, 1941. One of his sons was Sgt Frank Ciliberti. While residing at 21 Kettell Avenue, Pat Ciliberti became ill and died on March 1, 1958 at the age of 81 years.

LT. EDWARD F. SHAFFER

APPOINTED: January 15, 1909
DIED: March 31, 1941

Edward Shaffer was born in Tarrytown N.Y. on August 13, 1878. Later, after moving to Yonkers, he gained employment as a carpenter. Having passed the civil service test and physical exam, he was appointed a police officer on Jan. 15, 1909 and assigned to the 1st precinct on foot patrol. After approximately 10 years on patrol PO Shaffer was assigned to H.Q. on the telephone switchboard. On December 23, 1921 Ed Shaffer was promoted to the rank of Sergeant, and then six years later on January 1, 1927 he was again promoted, this time to Lieutenant, and was assigned to the 2nd precinct on desk duty. While hoping to be promoted to the rank of captain, Shaffer's son Arnold was appointed a police officer. Lt. Shaffer was very active in the community affairs. He was a member of the Rising Starr Lodge F.& A.M., and a member of the Yonkers Yacht Club. While in the # 1 position on the captains promotion list, Lt. Shaffer became ill and as a result he died on March 31, 1941 at the age of 62 years.

LT. FRANK E. RYER

APPOINTED: April 15, 1909
RETIRED: January 31, 1942

Born in Yonkers on February 1, 1877, Frank Ryer attended local schools and then worked as a machinist with Otis Elevator Co. and the Alexander Smith Carpet Mills. He served for six years with the old 4th Separate Company of the N.Y. National Guard from 1894 to 1900. Upon joining the police department on April 15, 1909 he was assigned to the 3rd precinct. On July 5, 1924 Ryer was appointed a detective, where he remained for two years, until he was sent back to patrol duty in the 1st precinct. On December 1, 1931 he was promoted to Sergeant, and nine years later, on January 1, 1942, he was promoted to Lieutenant. When he received this promotion to lieutenant he was already preparing to retire the following month due to maximum age limits. Upon retirement on January 31, 1942 he had only been a lieutenant for one month. Lt. Ryer's first cousin was Capt. John Ryer. Ret. Lt. Frank Ryer died in his home on November 23, 1946 at 69 years of age.

LT. JOHN J. McCORMICK

APPOINTED: May 8, 1909
RETIRED: December 31, 1941

Before being appointed a police officer on May 8, 1909 John McCormick worked as a hotel manager in Yonkers. Along with his unmistakable Irish "brogue" he had only been in the US. for about nine years, having been born May 4, 1878 in County West Meath, Ireland. His first police assignment was patrol in the 2nd precinct for nine years when, on June 8, 1918, he was appointed a detective. He was no doubt a well-liked man, evidenced by his winning a popularity contest run by the local merchants association. In early 1921 he arrested a feared gangster for a murder in Yonkers in 1917. On December 23, 1921, he was promoted to Sergeant and, as a tribute to his ability, remained in the Detective Bureau. He was promoted to Lieutenant on May 17, 1926. The respect that the officers had for him was evident when he was elected president of the Captains, Lieutenants, & Sergeants Assoc. in 1933 and 1934. He retired from the YPD on December 31, 1941. A resident of 97 Saratoga Ave. he was a member of the Knights of Columbus. On May 3, 1967 McCormick died 1 day short of 89 years of age.

PO THOMAS F. McCAUL # 33

APPOINTED: May 8, 1909
RETIRED: November 1, 1939

Tom McCaul was born in Yonkers February 7, 1886, attended St. Joseph's Catholic School and later worked in the insurance field. His ability to ride a motorcycle would later be helpful, but not for a while. Upon his appointment to the department he was assigned to the 1st precinct for seven months, and was then sent to the new 3rd precinct which had just opened at 36 Radford Street on December 1,1909. On August 9, 1918 McCaul was "detailed" to motorcycle patrol in the 3rd precinct. Two years later, on April 5, 1920, he was assigned to the citywide Traffic Division on motorcycle duty. Tom, who was best known to his close friends as "Birdie," would remain there right up to his retirement on November 1, 1939. At that time he moved to Florida and was employed by the Florida Racing Commission. Tom McCaul was a member of the Knights of Columbus and the Ancient Order of Hibernians. His uncle was Lt. William Healey. Following a long illness, McCaul died on April 8, 1972 in Miami at the age of 86 years.

PO THOMAS F. HAYES # 37

APPOINTED: October 15, 1909
RETIRED: September 15, 1944

Thomas Hayes was born September 15, 1879 in Yonkers N.Y. Prior to his employment with the Yonkers Police Department he worked as a machinist. When he received his appointment on October 15, 1909 he was assigned to work from the 1st precinct at 20 Wells Avenue. He walked a foot post most of the time but for a while he also was assigned to operate the patrol wagon. Upon the opening of the new 4th precinct in 1914, and a general reorganization, Hayes was reassigned to the 3rd precinct. But within four months, on Aug. 11, 1914, he was returned to patrol duty in the 1st. Tom Hayes probably typified most police officers in that he was never a detective, never assigned to ride a motorcycle, did his job and basically stayed out of trouble. He just walked his post for 35 dedicated years. Almost all of which was in the 1st precinct from which he ultimately retired on September 15, 1944. On March 11, 1950 Tom Hayes died in his home at 30 Locust Hill Ave. following a heart attack at the age of 70 years.

SGT. JOHN F. CAULFIELD # 2

APPOINTED: October 15, 1909
RETIRED: November 30, 1935

Born September 3, 1882 in Yonkers, Caulfield loved motorcycles. On April 7, 1910, only 6 months after his appointment to the police department on October 15, 1909, he was assigned to motorcycle duty in the 3rd precinct. On December 16, 1928 he was promoted to Sergeant and reassigned to the 4th precinct. On August 18, 1929 five "bandits" held up a restaurant in Irvington and shot the owner in the head. As they fled south, the alarm was received in Yonkers. The suspect car was observed at Shonnard Place and North Broadway where Yonkers police began a pursuit and running gun battle. Sgt Caulfield, who was off duty at the time, saw the pursuit and joined in with his own car. At St. Andrews Place and Riverdale Ave. Caulfield cut off the suspect's vehicle and arrested the three men at gun point. He received the departments Honorable Mention, the highest award authorized at that time. On October 1, 1930 he was returned to motorcycle duty and retired November 30, 1935. His brother was PO Frank Caulfield. Sgt. John Caulfield died on May 21, 1940 at the age of 57 years.

PO WILLIAM E. McGRATH # 96

APPOINTED: October 15, 1909
RETIRED: December 31, 1923

Born June 4, 1883 in Yonkers, McGrath was a bricklayer by trade. He attended St Mary's School and later would be hired by the police department on October 15, 1909. Upon his appointment he was initially assigned to the 1st precinct to attend what was then called the School of Instruction. However, following his training he was then assigned to work mounted patrol duty in the 2nd precinct on a horse that was named "Queenie." McGrath remained in this assignment for 14 years when, following a physical exam by the police surgeon, he was found physically unfit to perform his duties and was retired on December 31, 1923 on a disability pension of $87.50 per month. He then returned to his bricklaying trade to earn extra money. During World War 2 McGrath also did security work in NYC. In 1947 he was present to watch his son William McGrath Jr. be appointed a Yonkers police officer. A resident of 183 Yonkers Terrace, retired PO Bill McGrath died in Clearwater Florida on January 19, 1965.

PO HENRY HALLAM # 72

APPOINTED: December 1, 1909
RESIGNED: July 29, 1926

A carpenter by trade, Hallam, who was born April 8, 1888, was appointed to the YPD on December 1, 1909 as a result of the opening of the new 3rd precinct on Radford Street. When it opened, Hallam was instead assigned to the 1st precinct on foot patrol. But he was connected well enough to obtain a good job and keep it. He married Lt VanSteenburgh's sister, and was a grandnephew to Lt Buckout. So it wasn't long before he was assigned to motorcycle duty. In August of 1918 as part of changes in the Traffic unit, Hallam was assigned to motorcycle duty remaining right in Getty Square. Then on May 29, 1922 a series of transfers for Hallam began. First to the 2nd precinct on foot; and a month later back to the Traffic Division. In August 1924 to the 4th precinct on foot; then a year later back to motorcycle duty. On March 25, 1926 he was again sent to the 2nd precinct on foot patrol. Whatever the problem was, Hallam apparently had enough. Three months later, after 17 years service, Hallam resigned from the police department on July 29, 1926.

P.O. EDWARD J. MORRISON # 8

APPOINTED: December 1, 1909
DIED: July 8, 1918

DIED IN LINE OF DUTY

Edward J. Morrison was born to Irish immigrants on April 19, 1879 in the Kingsbridge section of the Bronx, N.Y. After moving to Yonkers Ed Morrison made a living as a painter. In 1998 when his 87 year old daughter Theresa Ahearn was asked if she knew if her father had any hobbies, she answered, *There was no time for hobbies. He was too busy supporting his wife and eight children."* She also said she was proud of the fact that her father was one of the painters that painted St. Patrick's Cathedral.
Though he was able to make a living painting, Ed Morrison wanted the job security of civil service, so he applied for the position of Yonkers Police Officer. At that time he was a resident of 142 Orchard Street.

After passing all the necessary tests he was appointed to the department, along with several other men, on December 1, 1909. Following his training at the School of Instruction, Morrison was assigned to

Police Officer Edward J. Morrison (cont.)

the 1st precinct. Apparently being an excellent horseman, Morrison was quickly assigned to mounted patrol duties. When the city decided to open a 4th police precinct in 1914, which they established on Palisade Avenue, PO Morrison was transferred there and continued on mounted duty..

Police officer Morrison was described as a good family man. Of his eight children, he would ultimately name two of them Edward. The first to be named Edward died very young so he and his wife decided to name the next boy Edward as well. Though it was difficult working the long hours necessary to provide for his family, Morrison, who was frequently assigned to patrol up to the north city line and often near the Samuel Untermeyer Estate, would often be thoughtful enough to bring home some flowers to his wife. Of course he would take them without permission from Untermeyer's gardens, but the flower gardens were so vast they were never missed. His daughter said for recreation her father would, from time to time, take the entire family on the boat ride to "Rockaway." His friend and neighbor, PO Joe Lapchick and his family, would often join them.

Although he was a hardworking man, Morrison was not a strong robust type individual. His daughter described him as tall, very slim build, with red curly hair. Although very well-liked by his fellow policemen, his co- workers had jokingly nicknamed him the "Candy Man" because whenever the weather was very bad or cold, Ed Morrison would call in sick. What no one knew, not even Morrison, was that he was infected with tuberculosis.

On June 7, 1918 PO Morrison was, by mere coincidence, not assigned to mounted duty, but instead was assigned to a foot post. He was on duty at the foot of Ashburton Avenue around 12 noon when he was approached by a boat captain from Long Island who asked PO Morrison to aid him in locating a particular barge in the river that he was to take command of. PO Morrison agreed and they both began checking all the barges tied up at the water's edge. At some point, in an effort to jump from one barge to another, Morrison miscalculated and plunged into the river. His cries for help resulted in a cable being tossed to him. However, he pulled so hard to get out of the water, that he pulled his would be rescuer in the water with him. PO Morrison was in full uniform which included his police choker style blouse coat. When finally pulled from the water, Morrison had nearly drowned and was in serious condition from swallowing a significant amount of water.

An ambulance was summoned from St. Johns Hospital, along with a doctor, and a "Pulmotor" was utilized on officer Morrison to expel quite a bit of water that had been swallowed. Apparently he did not respond very well and was immediately transported to St. Johns Hospital by PO William Kruppenbacher, where Morrison was admitted. Morrison remained hospitalized in serious condition for 13 days. His condition did not improve and on June 20th he was transferred to the Municipal Hospital in Nepera Park. It was there that his health continued to fail. It was reported that Ed Morrison had contracted "pleura pneumonia" from his exposure in the water of the Hudson River.

Despite the doctors best efforts, and due to limited medical technology, PO Edward Morrison died on July 8, 1918 at 5:45 AM. Captain Edward Connolly, for whom the late police officer had worked, expressed his deep regrets upon hearing of the officer's death. He stated, "*He was a good policeman. He always attended to his duties to the best that was in him.*"

The funeral was held from the late officer's home at 12 Orchard Place. Approximately 100 police officers, under the direction of Captain William Lent, formed the funeral escort. As was tradition, the entrance to the 4th precinct was draped in black mourning cloth. Though only 8 years old at the time,

PO Edward J. Morrison (cont.)

Morrison's daughter said she still remembers what seemed like an endless line of blue uniforms that walked from their home all the way to St. Mary's Cemetery. She said her father was waked in his full dress uniform. In 1998, his 87 year old daughter remembered that for several years the Yonkers Police Association would provide shoes and snow suits to all seven children at Christmas. The Salvation Army also helped by supplying the family with a turkey on the holidays for many years.

PO Edward Morrison would never know, but a tradition of policing would continue in his family. His three grandsons, Edward, his namesake, Garrett, and Ronald Morrison, would become sergeants with the Westchester County Department of Public Safety. Edward and Garrett were also both members of the Westchester County Police Emerald Society Pipe and Drum Band. In fact Sgt Edward Morrison would later become the brother in law to Yonkers police Lieutenant John Hurley.

PO AARON H. MARTIN # 44

APPOINTED: December 1, 1909
RETIRED: November 30, 1942

Born December 6, 1880 on a farm in Dobbs Ferry, Aaron Martin moved to Yonkers and gained employment as a steam fitter. From 1901 to 1908 he served in the N.Y. National Guard. When he was appointed a policeman on December 1, 1909 at $2,300 per year, he was assigned to the 2nd precinct to perform mounted patrol duty. His first horse, "Tony," was inadvertently left out in the cold all night instead of being put in the stable, and died. His 2nd horse was named "chubby." PO Martin, who was rarely without his pipe, was later assigned to motorcycle duty in the 2nd precinct on August 9, 1918. In 1920 he was brought up on charges, and as a result he was dismissed from the department on May 21, 1920. Following a court appeal PO Martin was reinstated with back pay on April 9, 1921. On June 25, 1923 he returned to motorcycle duty, but in 1926 was reassigned to foot patrol in the 3rd pct. After 33 years service he retired on November 30, 1942 and became a school crossing guard. Retired PO Aaron Martin died June 11, 1959.

PO PATRICK F. O'DONNELL # 43

APPOINTED: December 1, 1909
RETIRED: July 31, 1938

PO Patrick O'Donnell probably exemplified the typical hard working precinct cop. He was born in Yonkers on July 30, 1875 and graduated from St. Mary's parochial school. On his police application he listed his occupation as a "molder." When he received his appointment to the police department on December 1, 1909 he was assigned to the 2nd precinct on foot patrol. O'Donnell, with his ever present frown on his face, would spend nearly 20 years on foot posts in the 2nd precinct. He was a very active officer who enjoyed an excellent record for arrests and rescues. On one occasion he saved three children walking on railroad tracks from being struck by a train. PO O'Donnell was always on his post, visible and ready to assist the public. His last 10 years, before retiring on July 31, 1938, were spent in the 1st precinct. His brother, PO William O'Donnell, worked in the 3rd precinct. A resident of 764 Warburton Avenue, Retired PO Patrick O'Donnell died May 28, 1955 at age 79 years.

CAPTAIN JOHN J. BYRNES

APPOINTED: December 1, 1909
RETIRED: October 1, 1944

John J. Byrnes was born April 29, 1884 in Glenham N.Y. After taking up residence in Yonkers Byrnes worked as a machinist. While he was living at 26 Garfield Street he filed his application for the police examination. In 1909, while the department prepared to open a new 3rd police precinct, additional personnel were required to staff this new facility. It was on December 1, 1909 that Byrnes became part of a group of sixteen men hired to fill this need.

When the new precinct opened, experienced men from the 1st and 2nd precincts were transferred to the new 3rd precinct. The new men were assigned between the 1st and 2nd precincts. Although it was quite common to be capable of riding a horse, John Byrnes must have displayed exceptional horsemanship skills, as he was assigned to mounted patrol duty in the 1st precinct from his very first day. It wasn't until 1914 that Byrnes would be transferred again. At that time the police department was again preparing to open another precinct. On May 1, 1914 the new 4th precinct was opened which incorporated a reorganization of police personnel. It was at this time that PO John J. Byrnes was reassigned to the new 4th precinct.

On December 1, 1925 PO Byrnes was promoted to the rank of Sergeant. This earned Byrnes an increase in salary to $2,500 per year. Following his promotion he remained assigned to the 4th precinct as a patrol sergeant. In August of 1926 he was reassigned to patrol supervisor duties in the 1st precinct. It

Captain John J. Byrnes (cont.)

would be here that he received his second promotion to Lieutenant on December 1, 1931. He remained working in the 1st precinct but would now perform the duties of the desk officer. His salary was then raised to $4,000 per year.

In December 1939 while assigned to the 2nd precinct and serving as the Acting Captain, Lt. Byrnes was in position number 4 on the civil service list for promotion to captain. Three new captains were appointed on December 15, 1939. Chosen from the list were numbers one, two, and five, skipping two men, including John Byrnes. Prior to these promotions, news accounts at the time made the allegation that only Democrats would be appointed. Numbers one and two were democrats, but number 3, Lt. Edward Shaffer, who was skipped, unfortunately was a Republican. Ironically Lt. Byrnes who was number 4 on the civil service list was in fact a Democrat, but, number 5, Lt. Philip Sheridan, who was also a democrat, had a brother who was the Yonkers City Engineer. Sheridan was chosen over Byrnes.

John Byrnes would have to wait two years before finally receiving his promotion to the rank of Captain. This promotion took place on September 1, 1941. A resident of 50 Locust Hill Avenue, following his promotion, he took command of the 2nd precinct where he had been serving as the Acting Captain. In December of 1943 he was reassigned to command the 1st precinct where he remained until his retirement on October 1, 1944. His annual pension was $2,250. per year.

Having been retired for eleven years, retired Captain John J. Byrnes died on July 6, 1955 in Yonkers General Hospital at the age of 71 years.

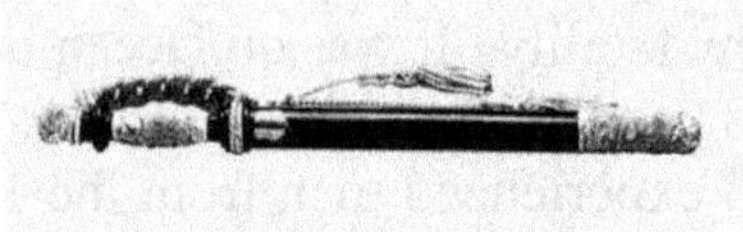

PO TIMOTHY J. REARDON # 16

APPOINTED: December 1, 1909
DIED: January 7, 1922

Born in Westbury L.I. on May 29, 1876, Timothy Reardon attended private schools there and came to Yonkers at an early age. A husky built man, Reardon worked as a motorman with the Yonkers Railroad Company. Following his appointment to the Yonkers Police Department on December 1, 1909 he worked various foot posts in the 1st precinct for about 10 years. On May 16, 1919 he was reassigned to the Traffic Division directing vehicular traffic. Frequently being assigned the same traffic post he became a familiar figure at South Broadway and Hudson Street. A resident of 74 Oak Street, PO Reardon developed a severe cold in the last days of 1921. His illness progressed into pneumonia and he was admitted to the hospital. His condition rapidly worsened and the pneumonia ultimately caused his death on January 7, 1922. PO Timothy Reardon was 45 years old with 12 years police service. He left behind a wife and daughter. He was only 45 years old.

PO HARRY J. WILSON # 134

APPOINTED: December 1, 1909
RETIRED: July 15, 1942

Harry Wilson came to Yonkers when he was 17 years of age. He was born in White Plains on August 3, 1885 and as a young man he gained early employment as a trolley car conductor. When the police department appointed him on December 1, 1909 he was assigned to foot patrol in the 1st precinct. Nine years later, on February 3, 1919, Wilson was appointed a Detective. For several years he participated in the investigations of many serious crimes but in 1926 he was reassigned to the Traffic Division at various intersections. He also spent time in the 3rd precinct before he was ultimately sent to work in the Radio Communications Divisions. It was from here that he retired on July 15, 1942. Following retirement he worked as a security officer for the Radio Marine Corp. in NYC for 10 years. One of his sons, Robert Wilson, later rose to the rank of Inspector with the Westchester County Police Department. Following failing health, Ret. PO Harry Wilson died in St. John's Hospital on November 16, 1958 at age 73.

PO JAMES J. McCORMACK # 45

APPOINTED: December 1, 1909
RETIRED: March 1, 1939

Jim McCormack was a native of Irvington NY, having been born there January 1, 1876. When he took the exam for Yonkers police officer, McCormack had been working for some time in a laundry. Upon his appointment to the department on December 1, 1909 he was assigned to the 1st precinct on foot patrol. He remained there for about 8 years when, around 1917, he clearly won favor with someone and was assigned to administrative duties in the City Court in the Wells Avenue Headquarters building as the Court officer. He apparently proved to be an asset in this position because over the years he worked for several city court judges, and was allowed to remain there right up to his retirement on March 1, 1939. Nearly 22 years "inside." A good detail by any standard. Before he retired on March 1, 1939 he would see his nephew John F. McCormack, who would later become a captain, join the department. A resident of 1 Terrace Place, James McCormack died while visiting his son in Miami Florida on January 11, 1950.

PO PATRICK McCLOUD # 46

APPOINTED: December 1, 1909
RETIRED: July 15, 1935

"Patty" McCloud was born October 15, 1875 in County Sligo, Ireland. Following his move to the United States he would gain employment as a trolley car conductor in Yonkers. When he was appointed to the police department on December 1, 1909 he apparently had the skills of a good horseman. Presumably as a result, he was assigned to the 2nd precinct to perform mounted patrol duties. At that time he lived at 96 Gordon Street. He worked mounted patrol duty for several years and was then reassigned to foot patrol assignments, predominantly in the Lawrence Park section of south east Yonkers. After 25 years service PO McCloud was examined by the police surgeon and it was determined that he was physically unfit for further duty, and was retired on a disability pension effective July 15, 1935. Ret. PO Patrick McCloud, a member of the Modern Woodmen of America, died April 27, 1943 in St. John's Hospital following a brief illness.

CAPTAIN JOHN J. BEARY

APPOINTED: December 1, 1909
DIED: March 12, 1940

John Beary was a local boy having been born in Yonkers on April 29, 1887. After attending and graduating from St. Mary's Parochial School and later, Yonkers High School, he learned a trade as a bricklayer. He completed his apprenticeship and while working, became interested in the police department. Beary, at the time, was over 6 foot tall and 190 pounds, and was living at 177 Stanley Avenue when he filed the police application.

After passing all the required tests John Beary was appointed a policeman at the age of 22 years by Public Safety Commissioner Edgar Hermance. His first assignment was foot patrol duties in the 2nd precinct, which had only opened officially in May of the previous year. It wouldn't be until December 1, 1912 that he would complete his probation period. On May 31, 1918 Ptl Beary was fortunate enough to be accepted into the newly organized Traffic Squad. This new assignment would allow him to work only day and early tours, at various locations and intersections, directing the flow of vehicular traffic. Those assigned to this detail were exempted from having to work the much disliked late tour or "midnight shift."

Several transfers were put into effect April 5, 1920 by then Public Safety Commissioner Maurice O'Keefe. At that time O'Keefe announced plans to experiment with motorcycles with side cars for those

Captain John J. Beary (cont.)

officers who were riding standard motorcycles. He considered this an important safety issue. At that same time many officers were transferred from one assignment to another. Among the men reassigned was Ptl. John Beary who lost his traffic detail and was sent to foot patrol in the 1st precinct.

During this same time frame officer Beary had taken, and passed, the civil service test for sergeant. As a result he was promoted to the rank of Sergeant on December 23, 1921. His sergeant shield number was #18 and his salary was raised to $2,200. Initially he remained in the 1st precinct but one month later, on January 16, 1926, Sgt. Beary was transferred from the 1st precinct to the Detective Bureau. This would last exactly one year.

On January 16, 1927 Beary, who was at the top of the civil service list, was promoted to Lieutenant at the salary of $3,000. a year, and was transferred to desk duty in the 3rd precinct. In October of 1928 he was returned to desk duty in the 2nd precinct. Police work for Lt. Beary was clearly a family affair. Capt. George Ford and Det. Sgt. Henry Murphy each married John Beary's sisters.

Lt. John Beary was promoted to the rank of Captain on May 16, 1936 upon the retirement of Capt. Charles O'Mara. His salary rose to $4,500 a year. One of his brothers in law, Det Sgt Murphy, was promoted to Lieutenant the same day. Capt. Beary received his promotion from Public Safety Commissioner Dennis Morrissey who directed him to take command of the 3rd precinct. On the afternoon of his promotion the men of the 2nd precinct, where Capt. Beary had served as a Lieutenant, assembled there to pay tribute to Beary. The new 2nd precinct commander, Capt. James Cashin, complimented Beary on his promotion and presented him with a traveling bag and an electric razor on behalf of the men in the precinct. Delegations of off duty men from various precincts and divisions assembled at the 3rd precinct station house to welcome Capt. Beary to his new command. Many floral tributes, telegrams and letters of congratulations were received by the new captain.

Only a month later Beary was instrumental in the arrest of armed robbery suspects. Certainly a rare occurrence for a police captain. On June 26, 1936 three "bandits" from Brooklyn held up the A & P store at 636 McLean Avenue. Although his police radio car was only capable of one way transmissions, which caused some confusion as to description and direction of travel, Capt. Beary correctly anticipated their escape route and took up a position on the Saw Mill River Parkway. Though the description of the vehicle was wrong, Beary felt a particular vehicles passengers were acting suspiciously. Because of this he forced the vehicle off the road with his police car. Inside Beary found the wanted thieves, two loaded .38 caliber hand guns, and the $60. that was stolen. Following questioning the men admitted to 25 other holdups in the NYC area. For his actions the Honor Board, following a review of the facts, awarded Captain John Beary an "Honorable Mention" - Class 2 award in recognition of meritorious police work resulting in the apprehension and arrest of armed robbery suspects.

Two years later, on June 1, 1938, Capt. Beary was sent to command the 1st precinct. A month later, on July 9, 1938, the Police Honor Board awarded Beary a Certificate of Excellent Police Work for an arrest he had made of two suspicious men who had recently committed a robbery.

On January 15, 1940, while on patrol, Capt. Beary's patrol car stalled. He would later report that when he pushed the vehicle to start it he experienced angina. Despite this discomfort he remained on duty. Two months later, on March 12, 1940, 1st precinct Capt. John Beary died of a heart attack in his

Captain John J. Beary (cont.)

home at 685 Central Park Avenue. Hundreds of people attended the funeral mass at St. Mary's Church. Twelve motorcycles led the funeral cortege from the deceased captain's house. More than 200 officers and men led the motorcade up South Broadway to St. Mary's Church where hundreds of people attended the mass. Following the mass the marching policemen led the cortege through Getty Square to Palisade Avenue, and onto School Street where all the police officers lined up and saluted as the hearse passed by.

The former captains widow was given a pension of $600. per year. Although Beary had been earning $4,500. a year, with nearly 31 years service, this was the standard pension for a death not related to an on duty incident. Had it been deemed a line of duty connected death she would have been entitled to half her husband's salary as a pension. Mrs. Beary persistently petitioned the City Pension Committee claiming that her husband died as a result of pushing the police car, and that his "death occurred due to service connection to the police department"

On July 12, 1943, following several appeals by Mrs. Beary, the Board of Trustees of the Police Pension Fund, and the Department of Public Safety rendered the following decision; "*That after hearing from all doctors, including the Police Surgeon, all agreed that Capt. Beary died from a heart condition which could have been caused by over exertion on the part of Beary while pushing his police vehicle while on duty. An act which was witnessed by a nearby citizen. We, therefore, find that Capt. John J. Beary met his death from injuries received during the course of his employment as a police officer of the Police Department of the City of Yonkers*".

As a result of this decision Beary's widow was granted a pension of one half her husband's annual salary. Her pension was increased from $600. a year to $2,250. a year.

Notwithstanding the pension committee's ruling in 1943, Capt. Beary's death has not really been considered as being in the category of a "line of duty death" and his name does not appear on any list which memorializes officers in that category. However, it is interesting to note that, in a Herald Statesman news article dated March 25, 1970, it was reported that the Common Council had voted to increase the pensions of widows whose husbands "died in the line of duty." One of those names listed was Capt. John J. Beary!!

PO PATRICK J. O'CONNELL # 42

APPOINTED: December 1, 1909
RETIRED: October 31, 1942

"PJ," as he was known, was a large burly, barrel chested man even when he was first appointed to the department. Before he would retire the cigar smoking cop would weigh over 250 lbs. Patrick O'Connell was born December 27, 1877 in Benoddon, County Waterford, Ireland. He came to America around 1900. Upon his police appointment on December 1, 1909 he was assigned to the 1st precinct where he would remain for the next 31 years. He was a well-known figure to the children near St. Mary's Street and South Broadway where he often helped them crossing the street. After working foot posts and traffic details for 25 years he was detailed to city hall as security in the tax office. Following this he was detailed as the Traffic Division clerk where he was known for his fine penmanship. On Oct. 21, 1942 "PJ" was transferred to the 2nd precinct. If, by this transfer, he was being sent a message, he received it and he immediately retired on October 31, 1942. "PJ" O'Connell died on Feb. 14, 1950 in his 76 Caryl Avenue home at the age of 72 years.

DET. LEANDER SHERMAN # 3

APPOINTED: December 1, 1909
DIED: May 25, 1924

"Lee" Sherman was a well-built man, no doubt from his profession as an iron worker. He was reportedly very athletic in his youth, being an excellent ballplayer with the local champion Viewvilles team. Years later he would also play on the police department's baseball team. Born in Yonkers May 24, 1881 he was 28 years old when he joined the police department on December 1, 1909. He walked a post in the 1st Precinct for 9 years until June 8, 1918 when he was assigned to the Detective Bureau as a detective. Though he was very efficient, around 1922 he requested to return to uniform patrol where he apparently felt the work suited him better. Then, on May 18, 1924 he was again assigned as a detective. Within one week of that date he failed to appear for roll call on May 25, 1924. It was later learned that he had entered the back room of a saloon, sat in a chair, and with his revolver he ended his life. His death shocked his colleagues, and wife and 3 children. A resident of 123 Elm St., with nearly 15 years police service, Detective Sherman's funeral was attended by a large police honor guard.

PO DENNIS McELROY # 38

APPOINTED: December 1, 1909
DIED: October 25, 1916

DIED IN LINE OF DUTY

Dennis McElroy was born in Ireland in 1878 and sometime later would immigrate to the United States to find a better life for himself. He would marry his sweetheart, Margaret, who was born January 8, 1883, and was also a native of Ireland. Although they had several children, unfortunately only their daughter Juel would survive the various illnesses of their time. In 1906 McElroy was listed in the Yonkers City Directory as living at 222 Riverdale Avenue, and with his occupation listed as a "fireman."

He applied for the position of police officer, passed the civil service examination and the required physical examination by the police surgeon. There's no way to tell how long McElroy might have waited on the appointment list for Patrolman but, due to the planned opening of a new 3rd precinct and the need for additional police personnel, McElroy, along with several other men, was hired on December 1, 1909 to coincide with the opening date of the new precinct. He must have been an experienced horseman as a civilian because, instead of being assigned to the new 3rd precinct, he was assigned to mounted patrol

Police Officer Dennis McElroy (cont.)

duty in the 2nd precinct from his first day in the department. Unfortunately, very little is known about officer McElroy's activities as a police officer. However, lacking anything to the contrary, it would appear that he was an efficient and reliable police officer. Although he was most often assigned to mounted duty, he was not always guaranteed to ride. From time to time he would be assigned to walk a foot post.

On October 25, 1916, with seven years of service with the department, officer McElroy stood a late tour roll call for what he believed would be a routine tour of duty. On this tour, instead of his usual mounted assignment, McElroy was assigned to foot patrol and was directed to relieve the early tour officer at bicycle booth # 2 at Tuckahoe Road and Central Avenue. It should be noted that the 2nd police precinct covered the entire east side of the city. And because there were a number of posts which were a long distance from the 2nd precinct, police hostler John Hayes, on this night, prepared to take the men to their distant posts in the police horse drawn wagon, and bring back the relieved men for the "return roll call." As was department safety policy, a kerosene lantern was lit and clearly mounted on the wagons left dashboard.

According to news reports, as the wagon started out, riding in the wagon along with McElroy were PO's Pat Flood and Tom Gleason. As the wagon reached Central Avenue and Yonkers Avenue, another officer was said to have asked to sit in the front seat where McElroy was seated. Apparently being of a congenial nature McElroy was said to have agreed to move to the rear of the wagon. He jumped down from his seat to the roadway and started walking to the rear of the police wagon to climb back on board. It was now 12:15 AM and McElroy had only minutes to live.

One of many styles of patrol wagons used in the U.S. circa 1910

Police Officer Dennis McElroy (cont.)

It is important to understand that all during this same time period the city had been suffering from a very long and disruptive trolley car strike. In the place of the trolleys which were no longer running, independent entrepreneurs began for hire jitney style shuttle services throughout the city with their own automobiles. It is true that these vehicles provided much desired transportation to the public while the trolleys were not available. Unfortunately they were completely unregulated.

As PO Dennis McElroy reached the rear of the police wagon, one of these jitney auto's driving eastbound on Yonkers Avenue on its way to Mt Vernon, struck officer McElroy just before he could climb into the wagon. His body was tossed into the air and it landed on the southeast corner of Yonkers Avenue and Central Avenue near the Empire City Racetrack.

Because the early tour was on its way into the 2nd precinct for relief, in addition to those men going out to their late tour posts, at least six fellow officers witnessed the accident in one way or another. PO Herman Schall, who was standing on the corner of the intersection, did not actually see the accident but saw the vehicle come to a stop about 400 feet from the place of occurrence. Schall approached the vehicle and upon learning what had happened he placed the driver under arrest. PO Pat Flood, who was in the wagon with McElroy only moments before, stated that the speeding vehicle seemed to be headed directly at the wagon but at the last second swerved and just missed it by a foot. He then heard a nightstick rattle to the ground and a voice yell, "one of our men has been struck." A passing vehicle was commandeered by PO Bill Farmer who had just left the police stables on Yonkers Avenue, just west of Central Avenue. Along with another officer, Farmer transported the unconscious McElroy to St. Johns Hospital. As he was being brought into the hospital, and without regaining consciousness, PO Dennis McElroy died.

Following the coroner's inquest it was determined that officer McElroy's injuries reportedly consisted of a fractured skull, a broken neck, arm, and leg, along with extensive internal injuries. Critical testimony was provided by PO John J. Beary at this inquest. Officer Beary testified that earlier in that same day he had obtained a ride to the 2nd precinct in the suspect vehicle, with the same driver that struck McElroy. At that time the driver mentioned to Beary that his vehicle had no brakes. Following the accident an inspection of the vehicle confirmed that fact. McElroy's death certificate listed his place of birth as being in Ireland, his age at 38 years, and his date of birth only as 1878. There was a notation, "Unable to determine month and day."

The funeral for PO McElroy was held on October 27, 1916. The funeral cortege left his residence at 249 Riverdale Avenue and proceeded to St. Peters Church for the mass. Under ordinary circumstances, even if an officer died of natural causes, a police honor guard would have been provided. In addition, most members of the department would have attended the funeral in full dress uniform. However, due to the tensions brought on by the trolley strike and all the police officers being assigned to special strike details to prevent violence, no funeral detail of officers attended this funeral. It is believed, however, that the entrance to the 2nd precinct station house, where McElroy was assigned, was draped in black for 30 days, as was the tradition of the police department.

The operator of the motor vehicle that struck McElroy, James Richardson, 26 years of age, of Mt Vernon, was indicted and later convicted on a charge of 2nd degree manslaughter.

Police Officer Dennis McElroy (cont.)

On February 15, 1917 the Yonkers Police Association held their annual reception and entertainment at Philipsburg Hall located on Hudson Street. According to reports nearly 1200 people attended the event. The printed program that was distributed to the guests contained a memorial to police officer Dennis McElroy.

The officers widow, Mrs. Margaret McElroy, began receiving a line of duty police widows pension equivalent to one half her husband's annual salary. She also received a onetime payment of $400. from the "Police Burial Fund." Three years later on June 1, 1919, Margaret McElroy was hired by the police department to work as a Police Matron in the city jail. She remained working as a police matron for nearly 17 years when she applied for and received a disability pension. Thus she became the first known person employed by the Yonkers Police Department to receive two pensions at the same time. Her husbands and her own. Police officer Dennis McElroy's widow died December 2, 1940.

In 1994 Mr. Jay Simmonds of Peekskill, the only grandson of PO Dennis McElroy, was provided with a photograph of his grandfather by this writer. A picture he had never seen, of a grandfather he never knew.

PO SAMUEL VILLANE # 159

APPOINTED: December 1, 1909
RETIRED: December 1, 1939

Sam Villane was born in Salerno Italy on April 17, 1882. After arriving in America as a young man, Villane was naturalized as a citizen on August 5, 1903. Prior to his employment with the police department Villane worked for a while as a hatter. When he was hired as a policeman on December 1, 1909 he was assigned to the 1st precinct on foot patrol. Because of his ability to speak fluent Italian, Villane was often used by detectives as an interpreter on difficult investigations. In fact on February 8, 1911, while assigned to the 2nd precinct, he assisted Sgt. O'Mara in locating a man wanted for murder in Yonkers. The suspect, who spoke only Italian, was located by both officers on Canal Street in NYC and arrested. On January 16, 1926 PO Villane was assigned as a detective. He would later return to the 4th precinct and after many years he would retire on December 1, 1939. A resident of 28 Cedar Street, Sam Villane died in Yonkers on January 20, 1944, after a short illness, at the age of 61 years.

PO GEORGE T. HINCHCLIFFE # 177

APPOINTED: December 1, 1909
DIED: January 18, 1945

Being very active in sports as a youth, Hinchcliffe played baseball with the old St. Aloysius team and The Blue Bells. A resident of 148 Orchard Street and a molder and pattern maker with Otis Elevator Co., George applied for and was appointed to the police department on December 1, 1909. He was assigned to foot patrol in the 1st precinct until May 25, 1918 when he was assigned to the traffic squad working days and early tours. Hinchcliffe later would serve for nearly 10 years as a Detective. On one occasion as a detective in 1922 he assisted in the arrest of 6 men for multiple armed robberies. He also served as a 4th precinct trustee, was a founding member and organizer of the PAL, and charter member of Div. 4, Ancient Order of the Hibernians. While in the 4th precinct he was regarded by school children as their close friend and confidant. His pockets were always a source of candy. Born September 5, 1883, PO George Hinchcliffe of the 4th precinct died unexpectedly on January 18, 1945 following surgery at age 61 years.

CAPTAIN JAMES F. CASHIN

APPOINTED: December 1, 1909
RETIRED: December 1, 1939

The son of Joseph H. Cashin, a New York City police officer, James Cashin was born in Yonkers on October 7, 1876. He graduated from St. Mary's parochial school in Yonkers, and from St. Joseph's Novitiate in Amawalk N.Y. For a while he worked as a bookkeeper for a prominent contracting firm in Yonkers. Though apparently very capable working with records and books, Jim Cashin had an interest in police work. He filed for and took the civil service examination for police officer. The opening of the new third precinct provided the opportunity he had hoped for.

On December 1, 1909, the official day of opening for the new precinct, James Cashin was appointed a police officer. It was reported that at the time of his appointment, he told a friend that it was like receiving an early Christmas present. Following his initial training at the School of Instruction he was assigned to foot patrol in the first precinct. It is often said that timing is everything. This seemed to have some validity regarding Cashin receiving his first promotion. He had been on foot patrol for nearly 5 years and was number 6 on the promotional list for sergeant. It might have been many years before Cashin might have received this promotion. However the police department decided to open a 4th police

Captain James Cashin (cont.)

precinct which required additional staffing and ranking officers. As a result, effective May 1, 1914, the same day the new precinct opened, Cashin and 10 other patrolmen were promoted to sergeant. His new assignment as a sergeant would be on patrol in the 2nd precinct.

Cashin received his second promotion on April 1, 1917. He was at the top of the list submitted by civil service and was advanced to the rank of Lieutenant. Public Safety Commissioner James Fleming promoted Cashin to fill the vacancy created by Edward Connolly's promotion to captain. Lt. Cashin's new assignment was as desk officer in the 2nd precinct at an annual salary of $3,000 per year.

On August 19, 1926 Lt. Cashin was assigned to desk duty in the 3rd precinct. This would only last for a few months because on January 1, 1927 Lt. Cashin was promoted to the rank of Captain. His salary now increased to $3,400 per year and he was assigned as the commanding officer of the 2nd precinct on Central Park Ave. Once again he had led the civil service list for promotion to captain. He replaced retired Capt. Willard Mance. On his first day in the 2nd precinct he received several floral tributes from some of his many friends. He was the youngest captain in the police department at that time.

Capt. Cashin was placed in command of the 2nd precinct which was located at 569 Central Park Ave. This precinct was first opened as a police substation around 1900, and in May of 1908 it was officially opened as a precinct. Over the years the accommodations became totally inadequate for the increase in personnel. As a result, a new 2nd precinct building was built and later opened on December 16, 1931 at 441 Central Park Avenue. This new combination precinct and fire station cost $187,000 to construct, and it contained ample locker space, a recreation hall, and a hand ball court. At the opening ceremonies Capt. Cashin expressed the thanks of himself and his personnel for the excellent quarters that had been provided for them and pledged their continued efforts in maintaining the protection that residents in that section of the city have a right to expect and demand.

On December 1, 1939, after completing 30 years service with the police department, Captain James Cashin requested, and was granted, retirement from the department. During his career he had earned the respect of his peers and won wide recognition for the brevity and clarity of his official reports. He had won numerous citations for outstanding police work during his long police career. Jim Cashin was a member of the Yonkers Lodge of Elks, the Hudson Boat Club, Lake Avenue Fishing Club, Highland Rod and Gun Club, the Police Holy Name Society, the PBA, and the Captains, Lieutenants, and Sergeants Association. Cashin was a bachelor his entire life. His brothers included Yonkers Police Electrician Gilbert Cashin, and Daniel Cashin, a former corporation council.

On February 21, 1959 retired police captain James Cashin died in his home at 2 Pier Street at the age of 72 years.

CAPTAIN THOMAS P. MORRISSEY

APPOINTED: November 21, 1910
RETIRED: August 12, 1941

Tom Morrissey was always a very athletic individual, particularly as a young man. He especially loved to run. As a youth he often competed in 25 mile marathon runs and in 1906 he competed in the first Yonkers Marathon. In fact news reports indicated that in 1908 he ran and won the Boston Marathon and later was chosen to be a member of the U.S. Olympic Marathon Team.

Morrissey was born in Yonkers on September 2, 1888. Following his attending St. Mary's School, he gained employment as an electrician. It is believed that during this same time period he began to pursue his interest in the sport of running. Though he loved running he couldn't make a living doing it. At the age of 22 years Tom Morrissey was fortunate enough to be appointed to the Yonkers Police Department November 21, 1910. Following completion of his police training at the School of Instruction in headquarters at Wells Avenue, he was assigned to perform patrol duties on foot in the 1st precinct. He remained on foot patrol for just a short time and was then reassigned to motorcycle patrol duties. However for reasons unknown, on April 9, 1913 he was returned to foot patrol in the 1st precinct.

Captain Thomas P. Morrissey (cont.)

As the years passed Morrissey performed his police duties, but he also began to study for promotion. As a result, on December 3, 1917, Tom Morrissey was promoted to the rank of Sergeant with an annual salary of $2,500. During World War 1, and following the United States entry into the war, Sgt Morrissey requested and received a leave of absence so he could enlist in the Navy. He served as a machinist mate, 2nd class, in the Sub-Chaser Division. He served in the Navy from June to December 1918 and received an honorable discharge. Upon returning to the police department he was again assigned to the motorcycle squad. But this time he was a supervisor. Yet, his service was not without difficulties. On June 25, 1921, as a sergeant in the Traffic Division, Morrissey was found guilty of nine violations of the rules and regulations. He was fined 30 days pay and transferred back to foot patrol in the 1st precinct. He could have been dismissed.

A short time later, to the surprise of many, Sgt. Morrissey was once again returned to duty in the Traffic Division om May 29, 1922. It was there on May 8, 1926 that Sgt. Morrissey was awarded a commendation by the police honor board for responding to a call where a child had swallowed Iodine. Morrissey responded with his motorcycle, provide much needed first aid, and was subsequently credited with saving the child's life.

On October 16, 1929 Tom Morrissey was promoted to the rank of Lieutenant at a salary of $3,300. a year and was assigned the standard duty for a lieutenant; that being a desk officer in a precinct. It would be ten years working in this position before Morrissey would be promoted to the rank of Police Captain.

Lieutenant Morrissey received his promotion to Captain on December 16, 1939, and his salary then rose to $4,500. a year. Following his promotion Captain Morrissey assumed command of the 4th precinct on Shonnard Place, filling the vacancy created by the retirement of Capt. James Cashin.

On August 11, 1941, while on vacation, Captain Morrissey wrote a letter to the chief requesting retirement. He explained in his letter that he had been offered an employment position in conjunction with the U.S. Government Defense Act as Chief of Guards at the Wright Aeroplane Factories in Patterson N.J. His request was granted August 12, 1941.

In his new position Tom Morrissey was in charge of 250 guards and special policemen, who guarded the five plants of the Aeroplane Manufacturing Corporation. After several years with this company Morrissey again retired and moved to Florida. In the early 1960's he moved back to Yonkers and, being a widower, lived in the Y.M.C.A.

About this time a large number of retired police officers and firefighters began plans to form a Yonkers Police and Firemen's Retirement Association. In January of 1965 the organization was officially organized and on Jan. 27, 1965 Ret. Capt. Tom Morrissey was elected to be their first president. The retirees held their first meeting in the Exempt Firemen's Hall located at 45 Buena Vista Avenue, and plans were made for an installation of officers dinner to be held that March.

On October 1, 1968 retired police captain Thomas Morrissey, at the time a resident of 190 Palisade Avenue, died at the age of 80 years after an illness of several weeks.

PO HARRY W. SMITH # 54

APPOINTED: March 1, 1913
RETIRED: January 31, 1927

Harry Smith was born in Newburgh N.Y. on December 22, 1881. He was brought to Yonkers by his family when he was 13 years old. When first hired by the police department on March 1, 1013 he was assigned to the 1st precinct. About a year later, when the 4th precinct was opened, Smith was reassigned to work in that station house. On May 31, 1918 he was chosen to work in the newly established traffic squad directing vehicle traffic. His brother was a Mt Vernon police lieutenant. Smith was examined by the police surgeon, found physically unfit to perform his duties, and was retired on a disability pension on January 31, 1927 after 14 years service. Following his retirement he worked for Otis Elevator Co. for a short time. Smith became ill and it was necessary to operate on him for a sinus problem. On February 7, 1932, a short time following surgery complications, Ret PO Harry Smith died at 50 years of age.

PO JOHN J. SPRING # 52

APPOINTED: March 1, 1913
RETIRED: June 1, 1932

Born in Centralia, Pa. on June 20, 1878, John Spring came to Yonkers in 1898 at the age of 20 years. According to his police application, prior to police service Spring worked as a carpet employee. Upon his police appointment on March 1, 1913 Spring was assigned to the 1st precinct on foot patrol. On May 31, 1918 he was assigned to the new traffic squad directing traffic. This was a desirable detail because you worked only day and early tours; no midnight shift. Most of John Spring's career was spent working in the 1st precinct where he spent much of his time as a traffic officer. After 19 years of honorable service PO John Spring was examined by the police surgeon, found physically unfit to perform his police duties, and was retired on a disability pension effective June 1, 1932. A single man who lived at 119 Shonnard Place, Ret. PO John Spring died on June 12, 1953 at the age of 73 years.

PO EDWIN J. STEELE # 53

APPOINTED: March 1, 1913
DIED: January 19, 1931

Edwin Steele was born in New York City on July 23, 1881. Several years later, as an adult, Steele listed his employer as the telephone company. Following his appointment to the police department on March 1, 1913 Ed Steele was assigned to the 2nd precinct on foot patrol. He remained in this precinct until October 22, 1925 when he was reassigned to the 3rd precinct. Little more than a year later, on January 1, 1927, Steele was transferred to duty as a switchboard operator in the 1st precinct. There was no radio system until 1934. On August 16, 1927 he was assigned to a fixed post in the Glen Park working steady days. During the depression, on November 19, 1930 the Yonkers Police Department Relief Committee was formed. At that time members of the department made donations of food and clothing to needy individuals. Ed Steele served on the Needs Review Committee. Steele became ill and while suffering from pneumonia he died of a heart attack on January 19, 1931. An honor guard and 60 department members marched in the funeral procession.

PO LOUIS E. STELZER

APPOINTED: March 1, 1913
RESIGNED: September 20, 1920

Born in Yonkers on July 7, 1890 Lou Stelzer and his family were employed in the fruit business. When he was hired by the police department on March 1, 1913 he worked out of the 2nd precinct on foot patrol duties. His home address at the time was 5 Myrtle Street. Although Stelzer was apparently an efficient officer, after seven years as a police officer he wanted to go into business for himself and resigned on Sept. 20, 1920. Stelzer opened a saloon named the Reviver which was located at 170 Ashburton Ave. not far from his home and would continue to be a good friend of police officers. However, on Aug 26, 1931 his saloon was raided and in accordance with prohibition laws, his liquor was confiscated. Any charges are unknown. According to PO John O'Hare, although of the Jewish faith, Stelzer always led the list of those donating to St Joseph's Church by giving $100 every year. This was a substantial amount of money for the 1920's and no one seems to know why Stelzer made these donations. Records indicate that from 1934 to 1939 Stelzer lived at 18 Locust Hill Avenue, and that in 1939 he was listed as a Yonkers Deputy City Marshall.

PO JOSEPH R. SHEEKY # 49

APPOINTED: March 1, 1913
RETIRED: February 28, 1938

A native of Yonkers, Joe Sheeky was born June 8, 1887 and attended local schools. As a young man he worked hard as a bricklayer. However, he wanted to follow his brother, Harold Sheeky, who was appointed a policeman in 1920. Joe Sheeky was appointed to the YPD on March 1, 1913 and assigned to the 2nd precinct on foot patrol. Later in the early 1920's he worked out of the 3rd precinct. On August 19, 1926 Joe Sheeky was assigned to the Traffic Division directing vehicular traffic. In October of 1934 the police department put into operation its first police radio communications system. It was at this time that several people who had some experience or natural ability in this field were chosen to work in the newly created Radio and Telegraph Division. Sheeky was chosen and named one of the radio operators for the system. He remained there until his retirement on February 28, 1938. A single man, retired PO Joseph Sheeky died of a heart attack on November 16, 1958 at the age of 71 years.

PO JOHN E. SHONTS # 50

APPOINTED: March 1, 1913
RETIRED: April 22, 1939

John Elmer Shonts was born in Yonkers on September 2, 1881. Following his schooling he took up the trade of carpentry. Upon his police appointment to the YPD on March 1, 1913 he was assigned to the 2nd precinct. On May 25, 1918 he was chosen to work in the newly established Traffic Division, working day and early tours from the 1st precinct directing traffic. Due in part to his mechanical skills, for a while in the 1920's he was assigned to the Traffic Division Repair Shop. On July 2, 1929 he was reassigned to foot patrol duties in the 1st precinct. During the time that he was directing traffic he was usually assigned to Warburton Avenue and Main Street and apparently was a well-liked officer. He retired from the department on April 22, 1939. Few people knew him as John. Most referred to him as "Toots" Shonts. PO Shonts' daughter married Detective Andrew Horree. Retired PO John "Toots" Shonts, a resident of 37 Pier Street, died following a long illness on January 25, 1959 at the age of 77 years.

PO WILLIAM PRESCOTT #60

APPOINTED: March 1, 1913
DIED: November 16, 1937

Born in Wales, England on November 16, 1885 Bill Prescott was brought to the United States at the age of 5 years. As a young man Prescott worked as a plumber for 14 years with the George Harper Co. When he was appointed a police officer on March 1, 1913 he was assigned to the 2nd precinct on foot patrol where he would remain. On November 15, 1937 he was feeling well when he reported for duty at the precinct, but later while walking post on McLean Avenue near Webster Avenue he became ill. He called for a radio car which took him home. However, later that day he was rushed to St John's Hospital. The following day, November 16, 1937, on PO Prescott's 52nd birthday, the officer died. The 24 year veteran was married but had no children. A resident of 60 Cook Avenue, Prescott was a member of the Yonkers Lodge of the Elks. An Honor Guard from the police department was provided for the deceased officer and all off duty members of the department attended his funeral. Bill Prescott was only 52.

PO FRANK J. SACKOWICZ # 51

APPOINTED: March 1, 1913
RETIRED: August 5, 1954

A native of Shenandoah, Pa., Frank Sackowicz was born on August 5, 1889. After moving to Yonkers around 1901 he attended PS# 7 and Holy Trinity school where he pitched on the ball team. He worked for some time as a carpet company employee and when he was hired by the police department on March 1, 1913 he was assigned to the 1st precinct. Frank spoke the Polish language which was an asset in our diverse community. He was well liked by his fellow officers and enjoyed singing at various PBA functions. With only two years on the job Sackowicz was called a hero. On July 12, 1915 at 3 AM PO Sackowicz was calling in to the desk lieutenant when he heard screams for help. A three story frame house with multiple families was engulfed in flames. Sackowicz immediately ran into the building through the thick smoke and, kicking in all the doors, woke the sleeping tenants, likely saving their lives. Throughout the rest of his career he rendered loyal and efficient service. PO Sackowicz was retired on August 5, 1954 due to the maximum age limit of 65 years, with over 41 years of service. Frank Sackowicz died on March 9, 1973 at the age of 84.

PO JOSEPH F. TORPEY

APPOINTED: March 1, 1913
DIED: May 5, 1921

Joe Torpey was born in Yonkers on September 28, 1880. He attended Public School # 6 and St Joseph's School for his education. On November 25, 1903 Torpey was appointed a Lineman in the Police Bureau. He apparently had some skill with electricity because part of his duty was to maintain our electronic call box system. Torpey decided to take the test for patrolman. A resident of 37 Moquette Row, he was appointed a police officer on March 1, 1913 and was assigned to the first precinct on foot patrol duty. All available information indicates that for the next eight years he provided efficient service. However, PO Torpey became ill and developed pneumonia. He was in St John's Hospital for three weeks when his condition turned critical and he died on May 5, 1921. The cause was listed as "Water On The Heart." PO Torpey, who was single, served as a lineman and police officer for a combined total of 17 years. PO Joseph Torpey was only 40 years old.

PO MICHAEL J. VAIL

APPOINTED: March 1, 1913
DIED: November 29, 1920

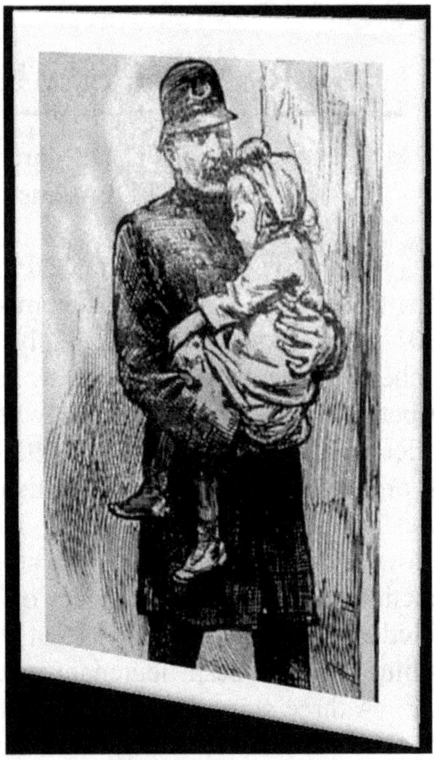

Born in Yonkers approximately 1882, Michael Joseph Vail attended and graduated from St Mary's School. As a young man he worked in the Alexander Smith Carpet Mills. When he was appointed to the department he was assigned to the 3rd precinct where he remained until it temporarily closed due to budget shortages. He was then sent to the 1st precinct. On May 10, 1913, two months after being hired, PO Vail assisted PO Sullivan in arresting several armed and violent strikers. The following month, on June 2, 1913 and while off duty, he was attacked from behind by an intoxicated male resulting in Vail's left leg being broken. Following the healing of his leg he returned to full duty. On July 15, 1915 he was charged with conduct unbecoming an officer for allegedly punching and breaking a citizens nose allegedly for no reason. The disposition is unknown. Around the end of April 1921, PO Vail, who was a member of the Yonkers Lodge of Masons, complained of a cold in his chest. He went off duty on sick leave. Within one week PO Michael J. Vail died on November 29, 1920, in his home at 178 Woodworth Avenue, from acute asthma. PO Vail was single and only 38 years old.

PO WILFRED MATTHEWS

Appointed: March 1, 1913
Died: October 29, 1916

DIED IN LINE OF DUTY

When "Will" Matthews joined the Yonkers Police Department he was already 37 years old. Born in NYC on January 9, 1876, he would go on to move to Yonkers and gain employment as an electrician with the Westinghouse Electric Company. When he was accepted by the police department on March 1, 1913 he was residing on Mile Square Road and was married with a child.

Following his appointment Matthews, along with the 50 other men who were hired with him, remained at the 1st precinct to receive training at the "School of Instruction." On May 14, 1913 PO Matthews was transferred to the 2nd precinct where he was assigned to mounted patrol duties on horseback. No doubt that due to his age he was not immature and was probably very serious about his responsibilities. In fact, one month after his appointment while working the late tour on horseback, he discovered a burglary of an office of the Putnam Railroad line. When he found the broken glass at 5:30 AM he knew that the entry occurred sometime after 2:00 in the morning because at that time, he had

PO Wilfred Matthews (cont.)

checked the doors and glass of this building and several others as per required patrol procedures and found them to be secure. PO Matthews had no way to know that his very life was soon to be in jeopardy.

Possibly adding to the contributing factors leading up to Matthews' fate was, when his group of 51 police officers was hired there were no handguns available to provide to the officers. In fact according to news reports, a majority of the members of the police department were unarmed when they went out on patrol. The city administration had placed money in their budget a number of times to purchase revolvers, however the money was inevitably used for something else. Finally it was reported around September 30, 1916 that 70 new Colt revolvers were issued to most of the men who were working without them. It should also be kept in mind that holsters for their revolvers were not used and most often a police officer kept his revolver in his pocket.

On October 17, 1916 PO Matthews was on duty on official business in the City Court. It was reported that on this day Matthews was sitting on the window sill in the court clerk’s office speaking to him and several other people about some fact of law. The conversation is said to have switched to the new revolvers that had just recently been issued. Officer Matthews then took out his new Colt to show it to the court clerk. He did so with the barrel pointing down and, according to Matthews, without touching the trigger, the weapon accidentally fired. The clerk reportedly said, "Well, it's lucky you didn't shoot yourself." Matthews calmly replied, "But I did." The clerk thought the officer was joking because he seemed so unconcerned, until he saw blood dripping from the officers uniform pant leg. Matthews was then transported to St. John’s Hospital where he was treated and it was learned that the bullet entered the upper calf of his left leg, shattered the bone and exited 8" lower on the opposite side. It didn't seem like a very serious wound but it must have been on Matthews' mind that only the day before PO Dennis McElroy had been struck by a vehicle on Yonkers Avenue and was killed.

Unfortunately reliable antibiotic medication to fight infection was not yet available and it was reported that gangrene set into his leg causing the officer to be in critical condition. Despite the best medical treatment available, PO Wilfred Matthews, just 40 years old, died on October 29, 1916 as a direct result of the leg wound.

Of course the question must be asked, could this injury have been avoided? Keep in mind that Matthews had only had his weapon for less than a month. Also, when he received it, did he receive any firearms safety training? It seems unlikely.

Unconnected but coincidentally, the city was in the middle of a major strike by the trolley car operators. Several violent incidents that had occurred had necessitated posting all available officers in trouble spots throughout the city. As a result, although PO Matthews death would have ordinarily resulted in a large turnout by members of the police department at his funeral, including a police honor guard and escort. Instead, no one from the police department attended. The reason given was that no officers could be spared from working strike duty.

On October 30, 1916 Mrs. Elizabeth Matthews received $400. from the Police Burial Fund of which her husband was a contributor.

PO JAMES J. MADDEN

APPOINTED: March 1, 1913
RETIRED: November 1, 1925

Jim Madden was the brother of former Acting City Court Judge Tracey P. Madden. He was born March 25, 1883 in Yonkers where he grew up, and graduated from St Mary's School. Following his formal education he worked as an apprentice to learn the trade of bricklaying. A strong athletic man, he was single and an excellent swimmer. In fact, as a young man he was awarded a gold watch for swimming across the Hudson River. Upon his police appointment on March 1, 1913 he was assigned to the 2nd precinct on foot patrol. On May 29, 1922, he was transferred to the Traffic Division to perform motorcycle patrol duties. Only a month later, while on duty on June 22, 1922 he fell from the motorcycle, breaking both arms and was in a plaster cast for a year. After his recovery, in June of 1924 he was reassigned to the 1st precinct. Following an exam by the police surgeon he was found physically unfit for duty and was retired November 1, 1925 on a disability pension. Jim Madden died January 21, 1930 at his 22 Stanley Place home. He was only 46.

PO PETER J. McKERNAN # 41

APPOINTED: March 1, 1913
RETIRED: October 15, 1942

Peter James McKernan was born November 26, 1885 in Shenandoah, Pennsylvania. Prior to his police appointment McKernan worked as a machinist and as a telephone operator. Following his police appointment on March 1, 1913 he was assigned to the 1st precinct on foot patrol. On May 31, 1918 he was reassigned to the new Traffic Squad to direct vehicular traffic at various intersections. Presumably due to his excellent police record, on January 5, 1923 McKernan was appointed to the position of Detective. This, however, lasted for only just over a year, and on May 18, 1924 he was reassigned back to the 1st precinct on foot patrol. Pete spent the latter part of his career assigned to the Radio Telegraph Division, which was the communications section within headquarters, and from which he would later retire on October 15, 1942. A resident of 148 Livingston Avenue, McKernan became ill and subsequently was sent to Rosary Hill Hospital where, on October 22, 1963, Peter McKernan died at the age of 78 years.

PO JOHN J. McCARTHY # 65

APPOINTED: March 13, 1913
RETIRED: April 15, 1949

John Joseph McCarthy was one of five policemen serving with the exact same name. Distinguished by number, he was dubbed McCarthy-2. Born in Yonkers on March 28, 1890, he received his education in PS# 3 and Yonkers HS where he excelled in baseball. As a young man he worked in Radcliff's Grocery Store on Riverdale Ave. Following his police appointment on March 1, 1913 he was assigned to the 3rd precinct at 36 Radford Street where he would remain for over 36 years. In November of 1927 PO "Jack" McCarthy made news by arresting a burglar at 5 AM on South Broadway who was wanted in South Africa for murder. "Jack" loved precinct work but on January 16, 1928 someone thought they would do him a favor. He was transferred to the Traffic Division, detailed as inspector of taxi's and buses. McCarthy immediately asked to remain in the 3rd, and the transfer order was canceled. After retirement on April 15, 1949 he became active in local politics in his ward. "Jack" McCarthy died on January 16, 1952 at age 62.

PO THOMAS P. McGURN # 66

APPOINTED: March 1, 1913
RETIRED: December 16, 1933

Thomas Peter McGurn, known to his friends as "Pete," was born on June 15, 1885 in Yonkers. As a young man he worked as an electrician before joining the YPD on March 1, 1913 at the age of 27. One of his children, Thomas Jr., would later also join the Yonkers Police and rise to sergeant. PO McGurn worked his early years in the 3rd precinct. In the 1920's he spent some time in the Traffic Division, but on January 16, 1928 he was assigned to foot patrol in the 2nd precinct. He was a police officer like most, just doing his job without fanfare. McGurn was an avid sportsman. In fact it was reported that he organized the 6th ward Rod and Gun Club on October 6, 1933. He was also an active member of the Maurice O'Brien Association and the Retired Policeman's Association. A year before he retired "Pete" suffered a cerebral hemorrhage resulting in partial paralysis to his left side. A year later, following an exam by the police surgeon, McGurn was retired December 16, 1933 on a disability pension. He died October 3, 1937. He would never see his son join the department or his grandson, Thomas P. McGurn the 3rd, join the Westchester County PD.

PO DANIEL EDWARD QUILTY # 61

Appointed: March 1, 1913
Died: October 15, 1936

DIED IN LINE OF DUTY

Daniel E. Quilty was born in the city of Yonkers on September 11, 1886. His grandparents were immigrants from Ireland. When Dan Quilty was only five years old his father died leaving his mother to raise two boys. Quilty loved sports in general, and in particular he excelled in the game of baseball. He was also a gifted swimmer; a skill he learned the hard way by being thrown into the Hudson River to either sink or swim. He attended and graduated from St Mary's School. While he attended school Quilty spent his weekends earning money by loading fruit and vegetable carts at the Washington Market in New York City.

Following his graduation from school Quilty was hired as an apprentice plumber. Upon completion of his training he was hired as a plumber by the Kern & Carey Co. in Yonkers. Being a very

PO Daniel E. Quilty (cont.)

ambitious person he even attended the Cooper Union School in NYC to learn to read blueprints so that he might be able to earn an increase in salary. Somewhat of a surprise to his family Quilty became interested in the fact that police officers were able to earn a pension after 25 years. A short time later he took the exam for both the Yonkers P.D. and the New York City Police Department, passing both tests.

A resident of 4 Clinton Street at the time, Quilty was notified by the Yonkers P.D. and was appointed a police officer on March 1, 1913. Following his initial rookie year in the 1st precinct, Quilty was then assigned to foot patrol in the 4th precinct when it was first established in 1914. His daughter Margaret would later explain that when her father came home from his first day of work at the 4th precinct, he said that his commanding officer, Captain Edward Quirk, approached him and said in his thick Irish brogue, Quilty, you have a roguish eye. I'm going to have to keep an eye on you. Quirk may have felt that way because Quilty most often had a small smile or smirk on his face which was actually unintentional. Quilty was initially very concerned, but years later he and Quirk would become close friends.

Dan Quilty was married on June 24, 1917 in Brooklyn to Margaret Sheehan while he was assigned to the 4th precinct. Around that time it was said that he was assigned to bicycle patrol in his precinct. According to his daughter he did not like this assignment because there were too many hills in the 4th precinct. Her father apparently preferred walking. In the late 1920's it is said that he was transferred back to the 1st precinct. His daughter remembered a story her father told them about a time when he was on foot patrol checking doors on North Broadway. While he was checking a particular doorway he heard a sound, and before he could react, a large rat jumped on his shoulder. He knocked it off and had to kill it with his night stick. Just another unexpected danger to face on some foot posts at night.

On September 16, 1931 at 2:30 am while working the late tour Dan Quilty was on his foot post in the area of Main Street and Warburton Avenue trying all the store doors on his post. He observed what appeared to be a woman standing on the corner of Main and Mill Street. The woman saw Quilty at the same time and ran back into the darkness of Mill Street. Officer Quilty ran up to and into Mill Street but, in the darkness was unable to locate the suspicious woman. Quilty did hear splashing in the Nepperhan Creek and assumed the suspect was using the shallow creek to escape. A search of the creek failed to accomplish anything but to damage Quilty's uniform.

He notified the station house and within minutes was joined by several other officers. PO Quilty's investigation led him and Sgt. Comey to the rear of 38 North Broadway where a man was found hiding in the bushes. Further investigation revealed that the suspect had committed a burglary at Francis Rogers & Sons at 12 North Broadway and had done so, dressed as a woman. Articles of a woman's clothing along with proceeds from the burglary were also discovered. According to Quilty's daughter he had to buy a new uniform, with no reimbursement, and took a lot of kidding from his fellow officers. She also stated that her father really didn't mind buying a new uniform because Chief Quirk was so pleased with the arrest that he gave officer Quilty four additional days off. It is of interest to note that this same male, who was completely dressed as a woman, was again arrested for burglary in January of 1946. PO Quilty would not be there for that arrest, but Det Lt William Comey, who worked with Quilty on the first arrest, remembered the unusual method of operation of the bogus female.

PO Daniel E. Quilty (cont.)

In April of 1933 Quilty fulfilled his dream. He bought a house at 304 Bellevue Avenue. He didn't know it, but he would not have very many years to enjoy it.Three years later while working the late tour on October 8, 1936 officer Quilty was assigned to Radio Motor Patrol (RMP) duty, patrolling in a radio equipped police car. On this particular night his regular partner, PO Bernard Farrington, was on vacation and his fill in partner was 28 year old PO Charles Brennan. Quilty, who was 50 years of age, was clearly the senior man. At about 2 am the two officers were patrolling along Riverdale Avenue when they observed flames coming out of a 2nd floor window in the Windham Hotel at 5 Hudson Street. After stopping the radio car Brennan jumped out and immediately ran into the burning building. After locating a telephone, Quilty notified headquarters of the alarm of fire and then joined his partner running throughout the building waking and warning all the occupants to immediately evacuate. When the building was empty, PO Quilty could not find his partner Charlie Brennan. He immediately went back into the burning building in search of him. After a short while Quilty found Brennan lying unconscious in a smoke filled hallway. He had apparently been overcome by smoke inhalation.

The 50 year old Quilty, who was about 5' 8" tall and about 150 lbs, quickly reached down and lifted his unconscious partner, who weighed about 220 lbs, up onto his shoulder and carried him out of the building to safety. Brennan was transported to St Joseph's hospital where he was revived and recovered fully. When Quilty carried his partner out of the building he felt a sharp pain in his side but thought no more of it. He never realized how serious this pain would become.

According to reports, shortly following the rescue, Brennan reported that Quilty was complaining of a severe pain on his right side as if something was ruptured. Quilty went on sick leave for a short time but then returned back to work quickly. On October 13th, three days following the incident where he thought he strained himself, Quilty became seriously ill and again went on sick leave. He consulted with a New York City specialist who had him admitted to Mount Sinai Hospital in Manhattan. On October 15, 1936, one week following his partners rescue and the accompanying strain, PO Daniel Edward Quilty died from complications caused by a ruptured appendix.

A special inquiry was conducted by Chief Edward Quirk and his staff to determine if the cause of officer Quilty's death was directly related to Quilty's police action the week prior. It was officially concluded that police officer Dan Quilty ruptured his appendix by the strain of carrying his partner PO Brennan out of the burning building. As a result of the chief's ruling officer Quilty was awarded a full Inspectors Funeral, which is reserved for an officer who died as a result of the performance of his duty. A more practical benefit was that Quilty's widow would receive an annual widow's pension of $1,500 a year instead of the regular widows pension of $600 a year.

On October 19, 1936 full departmental honors were appropriately accorded deceased PO Quilty on the occasion of his funeral. The funeral was attended by nearly 200 uniformed off duty members of the department and large numbers of family and friends. When the funeral procession left the deceased officers home and proceeded to Christ The King Church, they were led by approximately 18 motorcycles from both the Yonkers P.D. and the Westchester County Parkway Police.

PO Dan Quilty was only 50 years old when he died and he left behind his wife and three children, ages 16, 12, and 8 years of age, and his brother John, who was a New York City police officer. He enjoyed fishing, was a member of the Yonkers Lodge of Elks, and was a member of the Royal Arcadum.

PO Daniel E. Quilty (cont.)

In a 1999 interview, Quilty's daughter Margaret said that for many years her father had been active in the PBA and had been the treasurer of the Police Association for 11 years prior to his death. She related that often her father and other police officers would get together on Decoration Day and place flags on the graves of former Yonkers officers who were war veterans. They would also deliver toys to the children of police widows at Christmas time. Margaret Quilty, who is still proud of her father's police service, lamented that their family did not receive the same treatment. She stated that one month following her father's death a sergeant came to pick up her father's police shield and hat wreath. When he left, she said their family never heard from the PBA or the Yonkers Police Department again.

After many years of officer Quilty's sacrifice not being officially recognized, the above report of the circumstances of his death, researched by Ret Deputy Chief George Rutledge, was submitted to the YPD awards committee for consideration for the departments Medal Of Honor, posthumously. On May 19, 2012 PO Daniel Quilty was formally awarded the Medal Of Honor, posthumously, by the Yonkers Police Department. The actual medal was presented to several of officer Quilty's grandchildren who attended the award ceremony.

PO FRANCIS X. LINEHAN

APPOINTED: March 1, 1913
DIED: August 21, 1913

Francis Xavier Linehan was a young man of 29 years when he was appointed a patrolman on March 1, 1913. Along with the 49 other men appointed with him, he had passed the medical exam along with other tests. But Linehan had no idea what the very near future held for him. He was first assigned to the 2nd precinct, but two months later, on May 14, 1913, he was transferred to the 1st precinct on foot patrol. Tragically, on August 21, 1913 police officer Linehan died suddenly and with no warning. Born June 3, 1883 he was only 31 years old when he died and with only five months service as a police officer. The funeral from his home at 54 Caroline Avenue was attended by a large marching contingent of his fellow officers. The 1st precinct entrance was draped in black mourning cloth as a sign of respect. Police officer Linehan was single and left no dependents.

PO JOHN W. LITTLEFAIR # 73

APPOINTED: March 1, 1913
RETIRED: April 16, 1940

A boat builder and auto mechanic by trade, Littlefair was born in South Norwalk Conn. on June 15, 1888. Upon joining the police force on March 1, 1913 he was assigned to the 1st precinct on foot patrol and later to the 4th when it was opened on Palisade Avenue in 1914. Because of his skills as an auto mechanic, in the early 1920's he was assigned as the police department mechanic. On December 29, 1925 he was appointed to the position of detective, an assignment that was short lived. The following month he was reassigned, this time to the Traffic Division where he repaired motorcycles. On July 16, 1930 he was appointed to the position of apparatus mechanic with a salary increase. On serious or fatal accidents he was required to respond, investigate and determine the cause. One could say, he was our first formal "Accident Investigator." On December 1, 1933 he returned to patrol duties in the 4th precinct. After retiring on April 16, 1940 Littlefair's hobby was building cabinets. According to his son he even built a boat in his basement that he could not get out. John Littlefair died on December 28, 1958 at the age of 70 years.

PO HENRY B. KASSIK # 71

APPOINTED: March 1, 1913
RETIRED: October 15, 1939

Henry Benjamin Kassik was a young immigrant from Austria where he was born on June 13, 1879. Arriving in the US at 11 years of age with his family, they settled in Haverstraw NY. Kassik later worked as a Trolley Motorman and with the Alexander Smith Carpet Shop following his move to Yonkers. His brother in law was PO Joseph Lapchick. Upon his appointment to the police department on March 1, 1913 he was assigned to the 1st precinct on foot patrol. Then, on July 7, 1919 he was transferred to the Traffic Division, on traffic posts, where he would remain for the remainder of his career. He could be seen most often in Manor House Square, where he would be stationed directing and controlling the flow of vehicle traffic. Following his retirement on October 15, 1939 he worked for a while as a security guard. His hobbies were making small wood carvings and playing the harmonica. On April 2, 1973 Henry Kassik died at age 93 years.

PO JOSEPH LAPCHICK # 74

APPOINTED: March 1, 1913
RETIRED: July 16, 1933

The brother in law to PO Henry Kassik, Lapchick was also born in Austria, but on February 28, 1876. Joe Lapchick came to Yonkers approximately 1891. He was multi lingual, speaking English, Polish, Russian, and Slovak. Prior to his appointment to the police department on March 1, 1913 he had worked for the Waring Hat Factory and also a Trolley Motorman. When he was appointed a patrolman he worked in the 1st precinct. Later, in 1914 when the new 4th precinct was opened, he was assigned to foot patrol in that precinct where, it is believed, he remained until his retirement on July 16, 1933. After having been examined by the police surgeon and found physically unfit to perform his duties, Joe Lapchick was retired on a disability pension. Although his permanent residence was at 9 Moquette Row, he spent his winters in Miami, Florida. One winter Joe Lapchick suddenly became ill and within two weeks he died, on New Year's Eve, December 31, 1939 at age 63.

PO PATRICK O'KEEFE # 40

APPOINTED: March 1, 1913
RETIRED: November 30, 1939

Patty O'Keefe was a big man standing over 6 feet in height. As a young officer he was slim in build but as the years progressed he filled out in size. He was born January 4, 1884 in Ireland and after arriving in this country he was naturalized as a citizen in June of 1911. He had listed on his police application that his previous employment was as a motorman.

When he received his appointment to the department on March 1, 1913 he was assigned to the 1st precinct on Wells Avenue walking various foot posts. After five years, on May 31, 1918, O'Keefe was assigned to the newly established traffic squad directing vehicular traffic at various street intersections. This new assignment allowed him to avoid working the late tour, and work only day and early tours.

Sometime around 1920 Pat O'Keefe was assigned to the Detective Bureau. On one particular tour on October 7, 1922, while in Getty Square at about 2:45 AM, O'Keefe was advised of a possible burglary in progress in a building on the corner of Prospect Street and Hawthorne Avenue. When he responded, he found an open window. He drew his revolver, climbed through the window, and surprised the burglar. However the burglar didn't surrender and a chase followed resulting in the suspect jumping out a window right into the arms of two uniformed officers.

On January 16, 1926 a shakeup occurred in the Detective Bureau when O'Keefe and eight other detectives, including two sergeants, were reassigned back to patrol duties. Patty O'Keefe was returned to uniformed patrol in the 1st precinct on Wells Avenue.

On December 12, 1928 the First National Bank of Yonkers was transporting $ 104,500. in payroll money to the Alexander Smith Carpet Company. It was 9:10 AM and inside the bank truck, besides the

PO Patrick O'Keefe (cont.)

money, were two security guards and PO Patrick O'Keefe. Officer O'Keefe had been assigned to this detail for the previous three years and it likely had become very routine. The banks "messenger truck," (which was not armored in any way), was on Hudson Street heading east toward South Broadway. As it approached Hawthorne Avenue a male standing in the middle of the roadway pointing a shotgun, blocked the trucks path. Within seconds, three vehicles with eight men, surrounded the truck with guns and held its occupants at gunpoint. PO O'Keefe had his service revolver next to him on the seat but he had neither time nor even thought of reaching for it, since one of the shotguns was placed through the window and up against his chest.

The holdup men demanded and received four bags of money. As they began to leave they all simply opened fire on the messenger truck just before speeding away. Officer O'Keefe fortunately only received minor injuries from the buckshot and broken glass. No one else was injured and the thieves made their escape.

The following day the NYC police department arrested eight suspects in a Bronx "speakeasy," including Vincent "Mad Dog" Cole, the ringleader. When brought to Yonkers all the suspects were identified by witnesses to the robbery in Yonkers and were charged with the crime. Vincent Cole was known to be a "lieutenant" in the Arthur Flegenheimer (a.k.a. Dutch Shultz) gang. Schultz had long been dubbed the "beer baron of the Bronx" as well as in Yonkers. Although the entire gang was charged with the crime, witnesses suddenly changed their minds and said they no longer could identify the gunmen.

All the suspects were released due to lack of evidence and the $104,500. was never recovered.
At the next Honor Board meeting PO Patrick O'Keefe was awarded an Honorable Mention for his bravery during this robbery. This was the highest award provided under departmental rules at that time.
In comparison, the remainder of O'Keefe's career was relatively unremarkable.

Prior to his retirement on November 30, 1939 he was assigned to the 3rd precinct. Following his retirement Pat O'Keefe moved to the town of Stapleton in Staten Island to live with his daughter. He died there on January 21, 1958 at the age of 74 years.

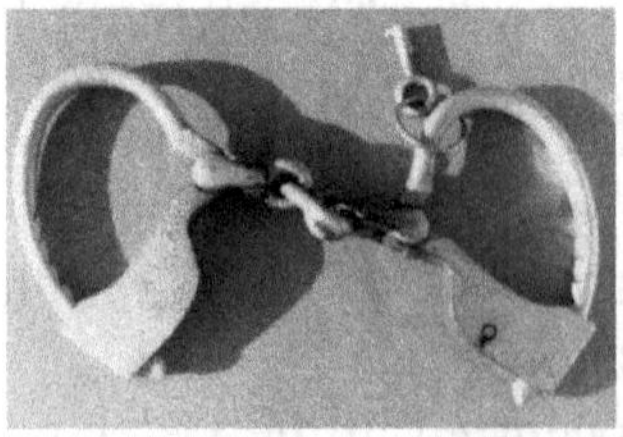

PO FRANK J. WIDMANN # 57

APPOINTED: March 1, 1913
RETIRED: December 2, 1953

Frank Widmann was born in Yonkers on Dec. 2, 1888 and grew up at 87 Maple St. As a young man Frank worked as an electrician. But, being very athletic and nicknamed Honey, his real love was in sports. In fact he never smoked or drank liquor. Prior to his police appointment on March 1, 1913 Widmann was a member of the Mercury's and he was a champion high jumper. Sport enthusiasts of the day worried that if Frank took the police job they would lose their best point scorer in the annual county games. Widmann did take the police appointment and was assigned to the 3rd precinct on foot patrol. On June 23, 1921 he was appointed a detective, but only 2 months later was returned to the 3rd. One exciting day was October 2, 1925 while directing traffic. Widmann tried to stop a speeding car. When he failed he jumped on the running board of a passing vehicle, followed the speeder and shot out the tires while going 50 mph. And in May 1929 Frank was cited for the arrest of a child molester. On December 2, 1953 he retired due to the maximum age of 65 yrs. Widmann died on December 31, 1980 at the age of 92.

PO EDWARD WILCOX # 81

APPOINTED: March 1, 1913
DIED: April 25, 1927

Born in Indiana on Dec. 10, 1877, Wilcox came to Yonkers at the age of 10. He graduated from PS# 2 and was known as an all-around athlete. He later worked for Otis Elevator as a wireman and also for the Yonkers Railroad Co. Upon his police appointment on March 1, 1913 he was assigned to the 4th precinct on foot patrol. After 14 years service and while on school crossing duty at Warburton Ave. and Lamartine Ave., he was struck by a passing car. He recovered, but his family and co-workers reported that from that day on, Wilcox would often act irrational and somewhat unstable. One morning, on April 25, 1927, he dressed for work, ate breakfast with his wife, and then without warning took his own life. The department order on his death read in part...."The death of PO Edward Wilcox marked the end of over 14 years of honest and faithful service." Over 50 members of the department attended his funeral as part of an honor guard for their respected friend. Wilcox was a member of the Rising Star, F & AM Masonic Lodge. He lived at 2 Irving Place and was 49 years old. He left behind a wife.

PO WILLIAM DOWNEY # 76

APPOINTED: March 1, 1913
DIED: June 2, 1927

Bill Downey was born on December 13, 1880 in Danville, Pa. After moving to Yonkers he worked for a time as a clerk. Upon his appointment to the department on March 1, 1913 he was assigned to the 1st precinct. The following year when the newly established 4th precinct was opened on April 30, 1914 Downey was sent there on foot patrol. In May of 1924 he was trained and then designated a member of the new police "Riot Squad." All members of the riot squad were trained for emergencies but remained working in their assigned precinct. On May 30, 1927 at 7:15 am while on foot patrol on Palisade Ave. and Roberts Ave. he became ill and collapsed. He was transferred to the hospital where it was learned he had suffered a stroke. Just a few days later PO Downey died on June 2, 1927 as a result of that stroke. He was accorded a departmental funeral and an honor guard. Approximately 50 fellow officers marched from his home at 145 Morningside Ave. He was 46 years of age.

LT WILLIAM C. FARMER

APPOINTED: March 1, 1913
RETIRED: February 28, 1939

William Farmer was born in the City of Yonkers on August 19, 1886. Upon finishing his schooling he worked for several years as both a painter and a clerk. On March 1, 1913 he was among the large group of 51 men who were appointed to the police department on the same day and his first assignment was in the 2nd precinct. It was because of his experience at riding a horse that he was immediately assigned to the mounted patrol. On December 1, 1922 he was promoted to Sergeant and was assigned to the Traffic Division. On June 1, 1927 he was promoted to Lieutenant and was again assigned to the Traffic Division as 2nd in command. Apparently respected by his peers, in 1929 and 1930 Lt. Farmer was elected president of the Captains, Lieutenants, & Sergeants Association. Soon after his retirement from the 2nd precinct on February 28, 1939 he moved to Florida. It was there in Miami, on December 8, 1946, that Bill Farmer died at the age of 60 years.

PO MARTIN BRODERICK # 68

APPOINTED: March 1, 1913
DIED: May 25, 1938

Martin Broderick was born in Wappingers Falls, NY on March 25, 1878. After arriving in Yonkers and working a variety of jobs, he was appointed to the Yonkers Police Department on March 1, 1913. He was one of a class of 51 new men hired to increase the strength of the department. Following training he was assigned to the 3rd precinct where he would remain for his entire time in the job. A slim built man who wore a mustache in his younger years, Broderick was considered a good, dependable cop. In fact, on January 16, 1925 Broderick was awarded a Commendation for the arrest of a well-known burglar who was just arriving in Yonkers on the trolley car. In 1938 PO Broderick, who lived at 58 Saratoga Avenue, had been with the department for 25 years and was eligible to retire. Unfortunately he had been ill for a long time. Apparently not wishing to prolong his suffering he took his own life on May 25, 1938 at age 60.

PO FRANK CAULFIELD # 83

APPOINTED: March 1, 1913
RETIRED: February 28, 1938

A native of Yonkers, Frank Caulfield was born September 17, 1888. Prior to his employment with the police department he worked as a teamster. Upon his appointment as a police officer on March 1, 1913 he was assigned to foot patrol in the 1st precinct. On May 31, 1918 he was assigned to the newly formed Traffic Squad and would now only have to work the day and early tours directing traffic. But on April 5th 1920 he was reassigned to the 2nd precinct on routine patrol. After he retired on February 28, 1938 Caulfield was designated a "Gold Star Father" following his son being killed in action on Okinawa during World War 2. Franks brother, John, was a motorcycle officer with the Yonkers Police Department. A member of a local Elks Lodge and a resident of 9 Stewart Place, retired PO Frank Caulfield died December 11, 1950 at the age of 62 years.

DET. JOHN J. MULLIGAN # 64

APPOINTED: March 1, 1913
DIED: July 19, 1935

John Mulligan was born in Yonkers on March 28, 1889 and attended local schools. Mulligan made a living as a plumber and occasional chauffeur. Upon his appointment to the department on March 1, 1913 he was assigned to the 2nd precinct on mounted patrol duty. In May of 1914 when a 4th precinct was established Mulligan was reassigned to that location on foot patrol. Possibly due to prior experience riding a motorcycle, on August 9, 1918 he was assigned to the motorcycle squad in the 4th precinct with a special post at Roberts Avenue and North Broadway. On April 5, 1920, following the departments erecting of police booths throughout the city, Mulligan was assigned to the booth at Palisade Ave. and Roberts Avenue. These booths, which were to be manned all three tours seven days a week, had telephones installed in each so that headquarters could contact the detail officer and send him on assignments. There were no police radios. For a while Mulligan was assigned to a motorcycle with a side car which was purchased as part of a safety experiment.

On January 3, 1928 the sister in law of PO Edward Charlton was walking down Midland Avenue with her 22 year old daughter when they were approached by a male who was apparently intent on robbing them. The woman started to scream and the daughter ran. The male walked up to the woman and shot her in the arm and fled the area. When a call for help came into the 2nd precinct, PO Mulligan just happened to be there and responded to the scene on his motorcycle. While searching the area along Mile Square Road he observed a shadow moving on the St. Joseph's Seminary grounds. Mulligan dismounted, ran into the entrance, located the suspect hiding in the bushes with a loaded handgun, and placed him under arrest.

Detective John A Mulligan # 64 (cont.)

During questioning the suspect reportedly admitted the shooting and further stated that he had reloaded his revolver and had decided to shoot any police officer who approached him. He said he saw the motorcycle coming, decided to kill the officer, but then at the last minute changed his mind. It was reported that the 22 year old suspect stated to officer Mulligan, *"If I had shot you, you wouldn't be eating any breakfast tomorrow."* When the next honor board meeting took place PO John Mulligan was awarded an Honorable Mention for this arrest.

On May 13, 1930, in a laundry on Hawthorne Avenue near Prospect Street, two employees became involved in a physical dispute. The result was that one male stabbed the other in the chest puncturing his lung. When the suspect fled, headquarters was notified and a description of the suspect was circulated to the tour working. Again, there was no police radio system. Within one half hour motorcycle officer John Mulligan arrested the suspect on Riverdale Avenue near the city line. Within days the victim of the stabbing died resulting in a charge of murder. On June 10, 1931 the Honor Board again awarded PO Mulligan with an Honorable Mention and in addition advanced him to the position of Detective with a $200. annual raise in salary.

Detective Mulligan's last assignment was a detail to the Public Safety Commissioners office as the inspector of taxi cabs. Officer Mulligan was a detective by merit, but a uniform officer by choice.

In mid-July 1935 PO John Mulligan became ill and was admitted to St. Joseph's Hospital. Following a short illness PO Mulligan died on July 19, 1935. A resident of 49 Amackassin Terrace, John Mulligan was a very popular officer. Also, his brother in law Thomas A. Brogan was a very influential leader in the local Democratic Party.

At officer Mulligan's funeral at Sacred Heart Church, more than 1,000 people crowded into mass, along with 150 uniformed police officers led by Chief Quirk who marched leading the funeral procession. John A. Mulligan was only 46 years old.

PO MAURICE J. O'BRIEN # 59

APPOINTED: March 1, 1913
RETIRED: December 31, 1941

Born July 16, 1879 in Dungarvin, County Waterford, Ireland, Maurice O'Brien was naturalized as a U.S. citizen on February 24, 1907. O'Brien earned his living working as a steamfitter for the railroad in the engineering department. He was also reported to be a good pitcher for local baseball teams. He was a resident of 128 Morningside Avenue when he applied to be a policeman. Upon his appointment on March 1, 1913 O'Brien was sent to the 1st precinct. When the new 4th precinct was established in 1914 he was then assigned there. On May 31, 1918 when the new traffic squad was organized O'Brien was assigned to direct vehicular traffic. Later, working from the 3rd pct., O'Brien received an Honorable Mention for a burglary arrest on Feb. 4, 1936. Throughout the years he raised 8 children and following his retirement on Dec. 31, 1941 he worked as a security guard at the Yonkers Raceway. His grandson was a Pelham NY police officer. Maurice O'Brien died on October 19, 1969. He was 90 years old.

DET. JOHN F. FITZPATRICK # 5

APPOINTED: March 1, 1913
RETIRED: December 15, 1941

Fitzpatrick was born Feb. 1, 1882 in Haverstraw N.Y. where he received his formal education. He moved to Yonkers in 1910 where he married and raised 9 children. Upon his appointment to the police department on March 1, 1913 he was assigned to the 1st precinct on foot patrol. Two years later in 1915 he was transferred to the 4th precinct. Later, on June 23, 1921, he was assigned to the Detective Bureau. In June of 1923 he and his partner, while investigating a burglary, went to Nyack N.Y. to arrest the suspect. The prisoner had a 38 foot boat with him which was impounded. Det Fitzpatrick, who was a licensed boat pilot, sailed the prisoner back to Yonkers in the prisoners own boat. In Sept. 1932, when detectives were decentralized into the precincts, Fitzpatrick went to the 3rd pct. He earned several awards: A certificate of excellent police work 10-21-1933; and two Honorable Mentions 5-23-1936 and 1-24-1937; In December of 1939 he was assigned as court and warrant officer with detective status. After he retired on Dec. 15, 1941 he worked for the Radio Marine Corp. in NYC, and following a short illness John Fitzpatrick died on April 23, 1965 at the age of 83 years.

PO WILLIAM J. KOLB # 72

APPOINTED: March 1, 1913
RETIRED: April 16, 1940

William J. Kolb was born in Yonkers on December 1, 1887. He attended local schools and later gained employment as a hatter. Apparently wanting to follow in his brother Fred's footsteps, who was appointed to the YPD in 1907, Bill took and passed the exam for police officer. Upon his appointment on March 1, 1913 he was assigned to the 1st precinct on foot patrol. And for a while he was assigned to the bicycle patrol. Kolb raised his family from 195 Hayward Street. He remained in the 1st precinct until March 2, 1928 when he was reassigned to the 4th precinct. Following 27 years service Kolb retired April 16, 1940. In 1942 during the war, Kolb worked for the Pinkerton Detective Agency as a guard at the Radio Marine Corp. on Canal Street in NYC, and for a while at the Yonkers Racetrack. Kolb's other brother, Henry, was a Yonkers Fire Captain. Ret. PO William Kolb died on August 3, 1952 at the age of 64 years in his home at 2 Sherwood Terrace.

PO THOMAS MULDOON # 62

APPOINTED: March 1, 1913
RETIRED: September 5, 1939

Born in Yonkers on Dec. 27, 1885, he was the son of former Yonkers police officer Michael Muldoon. He attended local schools and as a young man, worked as a railroad motorman. A resident of 221 Vineyard Avenue, when appointed a policeman on March 1, 1913 he was assigned to the 1st precinct on foot patrol. But when the new 4th precinct was established on Palisade Avenue in 1914 Muldoon was assigned there. Later he was moved to the 2nd precinct. On March 22, 1919 he was detailed to the Traffic Division directing traffic but would later be transferred to the 3rd precinct, back on foot patrol, from which he would ultimately retire on September 5, 1939. A lifelong bachelor who stood over 6 feet tall, Tom Muldoon was said to have been a quiet and reserved man who loved to gamble on the horses, didn't socialize much, and had few friends. In retirement he lived at 221 Somerville Place and according to a neighbor, he lived with only one light bulb and a coal stove. It was said that he liked children but barely tolerated women. His brother in law was PO Patrick Whalen. Tom Muldoon died Aug. 4, 1978 at the age of 92 in the Hudson View Nursing Home.

PO MARTIN F. WHALEN # 55

APPOINTED: March 1, 1913
RETIRED: May 16, 1933

Martin Francis Whalen was born November 11, 1878 in Ireland, and came to the U.S. at the age of 5 years. He attended St. Josephs School. As a youth he was an excellent baseball player. His daughter said he was awarded a gold watch from one of the leagues for being the best ball player in Westchester County. He worked at the Alexander Smith Carpet Mills for several years. Following his police appointment on March 1, 1913 he was sent to the 4th precinct where he spent most of his career on foot patrol. His family said he was a very sensitive and quiet man who regularly opened his home to new Irish immigrants until they found a place to live. Marty Whalen lived at 21 Jones Place where he raised 7 children. After nearly 20 years on patrol he suffered a stroke and as a result was found unfit for duty and was retired on a disability pension on May 16, 1933. His grandnephew was YPD Det Thomas Whalen and his grandson was NYPD Det Sgt Peter Bell. Ret PO Whalen died in his home January 27, 1936.

PO WILLIAM A. WALSH # 2

APPOINTED: March 1, 1913
RETIRED: December 30, 1939

Bill Walsh was born in Newark N.J. on April 1, 1882. He moved to Yonkers at the age of 5 years and attended St.Mary's School. As a youth Walsh played local baseball with a team called the Waverly's and later he even managed the 1906 championship team known as the Valley's. On his application for the police department Walsh listed his employment as a carpet employee. At the age of 30 years Bill Walsh received his appointment to the police department on March 1, 1913 and following the school of instruction he was assigned to the 1st precinct. Later he would be reassigned to the 3rd precinct. In December of 1923, following his arrest of a man who then broke free and attempted to run from the patrol wagon, officer Walsh fired 3 shots and quickly brought the escaping prisoner to a halt. Bill Walsh's daughter in law was the daughter of PO Thomas Beairsto. Having retired on Dec. 30, 1939, Ret PO William Walsh died in Saugerties N.Y. on May 18, 1964 at the age of 82 years.

CAPTAIN CHARLES E. WARD

Appointed: March 1, 1913
Retired: December 23, 1943

Charles Edward Ward was born on October 8, 1882 in the Town of Haverstraw, N.Y. in Rockland County. Haverstraw at that time was not as large a community as was Yonkers and it consisted mostly of farmland. This is where Charles Ward attended public schools. It was reported that he came to Yonkers as a young man around 1901. He made his home at 12 Moquette Row. Following his arrival in Yonkers Ward gained employment as a trolley car conductor and as a clerk with the Alexander Smith & Sons Carpet Mills. At the age of 31 years Charles Ward was appointed to the Yonkers Police Department and was assigned to the 1st precinct on foot patrol.

Absent information to the contrary, it is assumed PO Ward performed his duties with dedication and efficiency. In fact, on June 15, 1921, eight years following his police appointment, PO Ward was assigned to the Detective Bureau, also known as the Central Office, as a detective. He and all the other detectives worked out of the headquarters building on Wells Avenue.

On one occasion he and his partner Det. John Fitzpatrick were assigned to investigate a burglary.

Captain Charles Ward (cont.)

They developed information that their suspect was staying in Nyack N.Y. On June 29, 1923 Det Ward contacted the Interstate Park Police located in Alpine New Jersey, and they borrowed one of their boats. The two detectives took the boat to Nyack where they located the burglary suspect along with his 38 foot boat, and they placed him under arrest. The two detectives, along with their prisoner, sailed back to Yonkers on the impounded 38 foot craft.

Detective Charles Ward was promoted to the rank of Sergeant on June 1, 1927 and was transferred to the 2nd precinct as a patrol sergeant. Shortly after his promotion the members of the Detective Bureau presented their former fellow "sleuth" with a gold signet ring bearing his initials, as a token of their friendship. Not quite a year later Sgt Ward was reassigned from the 2nd to the 4th precinct.

Sgt Ward had taken the civil service test for Lieutenant and had led the list. On January 1, 1931 Ward was elevated to the rank of Lieutenant in order to fill a vacancy created by the death of Lt Jere Lyons. Lt Ward remained in the 4th precinct working as a desk lieutenant.

On December 18, 1939 it was announced that Lt Ward was being promoted to the rank of Captain, and that he was being placed in command of the Detective Bureau. The local newspaper wrote a story that was somewhat cynical. It should be noted that they had no quarrel with Ward being promoted to Detective Captain, but instead they pointed out the fact that the Detective Bureau consisted of 14 detectives and 7 detective supervisors; one supervisor for every 2 detectives. Det Capt. Ward's new assignment earned him $200 more a year than all other captains.

On April 3, 1940, following a meeting of the Honor Board of the Public Safety Department, several members of the police bureau received awards for exemplary police work. Among them was Det. Capt. Charles Ward who, with two other detectives, apprehended a man who had assaulted two women and stole their pocketbooks. Captain Ward was presented with a certificate of Excellent Police Work.

In 1943 Capt. Ward was transferred to command of the 4th precinct. It is likely he was not very happy with his transfer from the Detective Bureau because within several months Capt. Ward retired from the Police Department effective December 23, 1943.

William Walsh, then City Manager and Acting Public Safety Commissioner, stated in the retirement order that he regretted having received Capt. Ward's retirement letter. Walsh wrote, "*I have known him for many years and have always considered him the type of man that deserved the promotions which he received. He retires with the full knowledge that he has served with fidelity and honor the department, his family and himself for the 30 years he has been a member of the police department.*"

Charlie Ward was a tennis enthusiast and he attended nearly all local sporting events; especially at Gorton High School and the college games in which his son played. His hobby was working in his garden at his home. He was a member of the LaRabida Council-Knights of Columbus, and the Police Holy Name Society.

Less than a year after retiring, on October 4, 1944 Ward suffered a heart attack. He had become ill at his home at 146 Morningside Avenue and was rushed to St. John's Hospital. He died within the hour. He would have been 62 years old in 4 days.

PO JOHN J. VanMETTER # 84

APPOINTED: March 1, 1913
RETIRED: August 15, 1945

Although John Joseph VanMetter was born in Tarrytown N.Y. on December 6, 1986, he was raised and received his education in Yonkers public schools. Prior to joining the police department on March 1, 1913 John listed his occupation as a machinist. Following his appointment he was assigned to the 1st precinct on Wells Ave. Five years later, on May 25, 1918, he was assigned to the newly established Traffic Squad. This detail worked only day and early tours and the officers directed vehicular traffic. He worked many years in Getty Square. In 1924 the merchants association recognized him as the year's most popular police officer and rewarded him with a new car. VanMetter's brother Walter and his cousin Augustus Neary were both Yonkers sergeants. And his nephew, Bob Neary, was a Yonkers police officer. Following his retirement on August 15, 1945 VanMetter worked various jobs right up to the mandatory retirement age. John VanMetter died unexpectedly at his home at 32 Purser Place on September 25, 1967. He was 80.

LT THOMAS H. WALSH

APPOINTED: March 1, 1913
RETIRED: November 19, 1943

Thomas Walsh was born on January 19, 1889 in the City of Yonkers. Before becoming a police officer he worked as a plumber but he also had telephone operator skills. Following his appointment to the department on March 1, 1913 he worked for several years in both the 3rd and 4th precincts. Walsh was very popular, well liked and was even known to have sung on various occasions at PBA functions. On January 1, 1927 he was promoted to sergeant at a salary of $2,500. per year. In 1934 when our first police radio communications system was put in operation Sgt Walsh was designated an acting lieutenant in charge of a squad in the new Radio Telegraph Division. On April 16, 1939 Walsh was promoted to the rank of Lieutenant. Following 30 years of service Tom Walsh retired from duty on November 19, 1943 from the 1st precinct. Following his retirement Thomas H. Walsh moved to South Miami Florida where he died in September of 1967.

PO JAMES J. CUMMINGS # 39

APPOINTED: March 1, 1913
DIED: October 12, 1925

Like most men Cummings joined the police department hoping for a better life. Born in Yonkers on June 4, 1884, he had worked for a while as a machinist. Following his police appointment on March 1, 1913 he was assigned to the 1st precinct and walked a foot post for nine years. And from August of 1922 to May of 1924 he served in the Detective Bureau as a Detective. During that time he married his childhood sweetheart which resulted in the birth of his son Pierre in February of 1925. Life seemed good. Then, in October of that year, he became ill. He entered the Port Graduate Hospital in N.Y.C. where, after one month, he died on October 12, 1925 at the age of only 42 years. He was married for two years and his son was only 8 months old. Jim Cummings was very popular and was described by his commander, Captain Quirk, as being one of his most efficient officers. The 1st precinct was draped in mourning and an honor guard and 90 fellow officers stood in formation at his funeral as a sign of respect and a final farewell.

PO ARTHUR DALY # 104

APPOINTED: March 1, 1913
RETIRED: March 3, 1940

Born in County Carey, Kilarney Ireland on the 4th of July in 1880, Arthur Daly came to the United States about 1908. He gained employment as a trolley car conductor and set out to raise a family. He ultimately raised 9 children. Upon his appointment to the police department on March 1, 1913 he worked in the 1st precinct on foot patrol. Seven years later, on July 16, 1920, he was assigned to traffic duty where he remained for most of his career. According to his daughter, her father spoke the Irish Gaelic language, was a pipe smoker, and he loved to do the Irish "Stack of Barley" dance. PO Daly developed severe arthritis and was retired on a disability pension on March 3, 1940. In his retirement he was a big Yankee baseball fan and loved to garden. On December 31, 1965 retired PO Arthur Daly died at the age of 85 years.

PO JOSEPH A. DUFFY # 117

APPOINTED: March 1, 1913
DISMISSED: February 9, 1921

Joe Duffy was born in the Riverdale section of the Bronx on May 1, 1985. He was brought by his parents to live in Yonkers at the age of 9 days. He attended local schools and as a young man gained employment as an electrician. Upon his police appointment on March 1, 1913 he was assigned to the 1st precinct on foot patrol. The following year, on May 20, 1914, he was detailed to plainclothes duty. Sometime later he would be advanced to the position of Detective. In fact, on November 30, 1917 Det. Duffy distinguished himself by chasing and arresting a wanted burglar being pursued by another police officer. Having returned to uniformed patrol, on February 3, 1921 Duffy was charged with storing illegal liquor in his basement during prohibition. He was convicted and dismissed from the department on February 9, 1921. Joe Duffy would later be hired by Con Edison where he worked for nearly 30 years. He retired in 1950 as an inspector. Joseph Duffy died on December 21, 1956 at the age of 71 years.

PO JOHN HATALA

APPOINTED: March 1, 1913
DISMISSED: February 11, 1921

Upon his appointment to the police department on March 1, 1913 John Hatala, who for unknown reasons was known to his friends as "Potato John," was first assigned to the 1st precinct on Wells Avenue and Woodworth Avenue on foot patrol. The following year he was assigned to the 4th precinct when it opened in 1914. On February 2, 1921 the local newspaper reported that PO Hatala was suspended from duty on a charge of stealing several stone steps from in front of school 16. Further, the Public Safety Commissioner was very concerned because Hatala had been charged with committing crimes on two other occasions. A few months earlier he had been charged with assault and robbery but he was later found not guilty. Prior to that he was suspended and charged by another police officer with allegedly stealing roof shingles. Those charges were also later dropped. On this last charge PO Hatala was not so lucky. He was found guilty following a departmental trial and was dismissed from the police department on February 11, 1921.

PO CHARLES M. FOLEY # 180

APPOINTED: March 1, 1913
RETIRED: April 10, 1931

When Charles Foley made application to take the civil service test for Police Officer he listed his date of birth as May 7, 1889 in Yonkers NY, and his occupation as a wireman. Following his police appointment on Mach 1, 1913 it was one month later, on April 9, 1913, that he was assigned to motorcycle duty throughout the 1st precinct. Only one week later, on April 15, 1913, with just over a month on the job, Foley was in Getty Square when he was approached by the caretaker of St. John's Church. The man reported that someone had broken into the church the night before and stole money from the poor box. PO Foley promised to keep a close watch on the church. The following day on April 16, Foley was working the early tour. On this night he was on foot patrol and not with his motorcycle because it was raining heavily. It was nearly midnight and Foley proceeded to go make his 11:55 PM "hit," or report on the call box, to the desk lieutenant. The call box was down in an alley that ran between the north end of St. John's Church and the south end of a row of stores. While standing in the dark at the box, with the rain pouring on him, he heard a prying sound, possibly of a door or window. He started to investigate and turned just in time to see the flash and hear the rapport of a gun pointed right at him. Fortunately the bullet missed him, but only by inches. The round did pass right through his rain coat. Foley drew his colt and returned fire, but the shadowy figure ran off over to Hudson Street and drove away. Not having his motorcycle he was unable to pursue the suspect.

PO Charles M. Foley (cont.)

In August of 1918 PO Foley, along with his motorcycle, was reassigned to patrol the 3rd precinct. On April 5, 1920 he was assigned to booth duty at Palisade Avenue with his motorcycle. On February 3, 1921 both PO's Charles Foley and Joseph Duffy were tried on departmental charges. An anonymous letter had claimed that both men were storing barrels of liquor in the basement of 204 Voss Avenue where they both lived. Of course prohibition was in effect at the time and all alcoholic beverages were illegal. At their trial PO Foley reportedly declined to testify. However, it was reported PO Duffy did testify and he blamed Foley. He tried to place responsibility for the barrels being in the basement on his friend Foley. Duffy testified that when Federal Revenue agents came around it was Foley who paid them to look the other way.

On February 9, 1921 both Foley and Duffy were found guilty of accepting favors and were both dismissed from the police department. Charlie Foley always said he was innocent and was determined to appeal and be re-appointed. After more than two years and following a successful court appeal, Charles Foley was reinstated to the police department on June 25, 1923.

On March 3, 1926 PO Foley was awarded Honorable Mention by the police honor board. The award was the result of Foley discovering a fire in an apartment house while working the late tour. He ran through the building warning all the tenants and likely saving their lives.

Following an exam by the police surgeon officer Foley was found physically unfit to perform his duties and was subsequently retired on a disability pension effective April 10, 1931. Following his retirement Charlie Foley moved to Albany about a year later.

Retired Police Officer Charles Foley died suddenly on January 31, 1943 at the young age of 53 years.

PO CHARLES L. WICHT # 144

APPOINTED: March 1, 1913
DIED: November 15, 1919

Charles Louis Wicht was born in Yonkers on July 1, 1886 in the Nodine Hill section of this city. He attended public school # 7 on Walnut Street and was the 2nd youngest of a family of eight children. As a young man Wicht was gainfully employed as a plumber and was an active member of the Dayspring Presbyterian Church.

Known to all who knew him as Lou, Wicht applied for the job of police officer and received his appointment on March 1, 1913 at the age of 26 years. His first assignment was working out of the 1st precinct on foot and bicycle patrol. It was reported that after approximately 3 years Lou Wicht was transferred to the 4th precinct. It was there he was assigned to motorcycle patrol.

Sometime around the early part of 1919 news reports related that while on duty Wicht was chasing a speeder on his motorcycle when he was thrown from his motorcycle up against a telephone pole. He sustained severe internal injuries which required his confinement to the hospital for three weeks.

At this point it might be of interest to know a little about young Lou Wicht before he became a police officer. Prior to joining the police department, Charles Louis Wicht was recognized as one of the best athletes in the City of Yonkers. He was reportedly a very versatile athlete and starred particularly in track and field events alike. Even though he was very good at sports he was really only interested in the exercise he was getting and not any potential medals. Nevertheless, between the years 1908 and 1912, Wicht won 20 medals. He participated under the colors of the Dayspring Athletic Club, which was one of the city church leagues. It was from this organization that he gained substantial fame and notoriety.

PO Charles L. Wicht (cont.)

In 1908 he began his collection of trophy's by capturing 1st prize in the Dayspring A.C. shot-put meet. He did this despite his slight build, as compared to the typical burly and robust shot-putters. In the same year he won all around honors in the Kings Sons meet. In the two years that followed, his medals increased in number. In 1909 Wicht won medals for the running high jump, relay race, standing broad jump and the 440 yard run. He also captured the point prize for all around prowess in the Yonkers Daily News meet. Seven more medals were won by Lou Wicht in 1910. He took 1st place in the Kuha vs. Opal meet competing in the standing broad jump in September of that year. In the same meet he also won 1st place in the shot-put.

The city's Athletic Carnival was the occasion for more victories on the part of Wicht in 1910. He was a member of the team that won the mile relay race. He won the running high jump, the baseball throw, placed 2nd in the Hop-Step-and jump, and won an individual prize for point scoring. He only went into competition once in 1911, winning 1st place in a city meet in his old specialty, the shot put. Lou Wicht was also very active in baseball and basketball. In baseball he excelled in the position of catcher, and in basketball he could always be counted on to get the tap and hit the basket when on the court. In 1912 Wicht came into prominence once again by winning the shot-put, the 880 yard run, and being a member of the winning Dayspring team in the L.C.A.L. games.

It was shortly after this meet that Charles Louis Wicht joined the police department on March 1, 1913 and basically retired from further athletic competitions. As was mentioned earlier, following Wicht's appointment and later his assignment to ride a motorcycle, he was seriously injured in a motorcycle accident chasing a speeder. He spent several weeks in the hospital. Following the accident, his spirit and determination pulled him through a very painful period; but he had run his last race. Though he seemed to recover from his injuries and returned to work, later that year he would become ill. His family was convinced that the injuries sustained in the motorcycle accident were the cause of his illness. Ultimately PO Charles Lou Wicht died on November 15, 1919 at 8 pm in his home at 23 Van Cortland Park Avenue at the age of 33 years. Less than a year following his accident.

PO Wicht was survived by his wife, 3 daughters, and 5 brothers; two of which were Yonkers firefighters. Wicht was a member of the Dayspring Presbyterian Church and it's athletic club, and he was a member of the Yonkers Lodge of Odd Fellows. His daughter Dorothy, who kept all her father's medals and trophy's in a family display case, was a small child when her father died. However she did have memory of her father's face all scratched and bloody. She also remembered the funeral procession to the church which was accomplished in a horse drawn coach. She also related that when Christmas came that year the PBA delivered gifts to her family. Dorothy received a white sweater she had wanted.

Although Wicht's family believed that he died from injuries sustained in the line of duty, there were no records found indicating any such classification. In fact his death certificate lists his cause of death as diabetic coma. Without a doubt, the community had not only lost a fine young police officer, but one of the best all-around athletes ever produced in Yonkers.

PO PATRICK A. HIGGINS

APPOINTED: March 1, 1913
RETIRED: April 1, 1943

Patrick Higgins was born in Yonkers on June 7, 1884. His education was received in the public school system and as a young man Pat Higgins worked as a grocery clerk. But he wanted more. His brother Michael, who would later become a Sergeant, had already been appointed a policeman in 1903 and he wanted to follow in his brothers footsteps. And so he did. Following Pat Higgins' appointment on March 1, 1913 he was assigned to foot patrol in the 1st precinct. He remained there until 1914 when the new 4th precinct was initially established on Palisade Avenue and he was subsequently assigned to the 4th precinct for the remainder of his career. After 30 years of loyal service he retired on April 1, 1943 on his $1,500 a year pension. During his retirement he lived at 149 Voss Avenue. Unfortunately, within a short time, he became ill and was admitted to St. John's Hospital. Just eight short months after retiring he died on December 7, 1943. He was only 59 years old.

PO JOHN C. FOGARTY

APPOINTED: March 1, 1913
RESIGNED: AUGUST 7, 1923

John Fogarty was appointed to the YPD along with 50 other men on March 1, 1913 at the salary of $2,300 a year and was assigned to foot patrol in the 2nd precinct. On April 5, 1920 he was assigned to the prestigious Traffic Division's Motorcycle Unit. Then on December 14th of that year he was returned to the 1st precinct and later to the 3rd pct. on foot patrol. However he was returned to motorcycle duty on May 29, 1922. It was there on October 19, 1922 that he and his motorcycle were struck by a truck causing relatively minor injuries. After a brief time on the disabled list, on March 1, 1923 he returned to foot patrol duty in the 4th pct, only to resign five months later on August 7, 1923. Although likely, the record is not clear whether his resignation was due to the injury sustained from his motorcycle accident. Several years later in 1929 Fogarty was living at 56 Cricklewood Road and was the proprietor of a tavern at 26 Buena Vista Avenue.

PO PATRICK J. FEENEY #79

APPOINTED: March 1, 1913
RETIRED: November 30, 1939

Patrick Feeney was born on January 7, 1878 in Ballyhaunis, County Mayo, Ireland. Feeney was 21 years old when he came to America in 1899 and would later become a naturalized citizen. One of the jobs he held prior to becoming a police officer was as a foreman with the Westchester Lighting Company. When he was hired by the police department on March 1, 1913 he was issued the standard .38 caliber Colt revolver and his salary was $2,300 per year. Most of his years of service with the department were in the 3rd precinct working on foot patrol where he was well known and liked, among the merchants, residents and school children. Pat Feeney served the department along with his brother, Det. Thomas Feeney. After 26 years service Feeney retired from the police department on November 30, 1939. Nearly 20 years later, on September 6, 1957, Pat Feeney died in a nursing home in Chatham N.Y. at the age of 79 years.

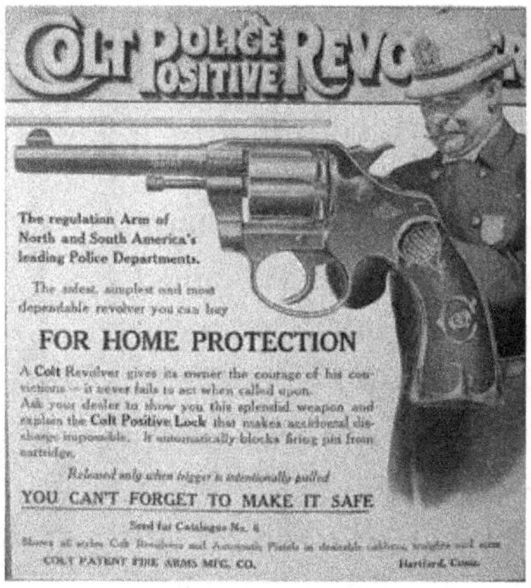

PO THOMAS J. GLEASON #80

APPOINTED: March 11, 1913
RETIRED: October 15, 1945

Thomas J. Gleason was born in Ireland on June 3, 1882 and immigrated to the United States as a young boy along with his family. He received his formal education at St. Joseph's School and developed a keen interest in horseback riding for which he seemed a natural. For several years he worked as a Stream fitter but was appointed to the YPD on March 11, 1913 along with two other new officers. He was hired at the salary of $2,300 from 342 Van Cortlandt Park Avenue and because of his horseback riding ability he was assigned to the Mounted Unit in the 2nd precinct. Later in his career he walked a foot post for many years. Upon the recommendation of the police surgeon Tom retired on a medical disability pension on October 15, 1945 and made his home at 1578 Nepperhan Avenue. Retired PO Tom Gleason died on Nov 7, 1952 at the age of 70 years.

PO CHARLES R. HERRING #69

APPOINTED: March 11, 1913
RETIRED: December 15, 1941

Charles Herring was born August 6, 1888 in Wappingers Falls NY where he also received his education. After arriving in Yonkers he gained employment with the Yonkers Railroad Co. as a Trolley Conductor. Upon his appointment to the police department on March 11, 1913 he was assigned to foot patrol in the 1st precinct. Herrings wife was a local political leader; but not with the party in power. Herring believed that as a result he was targeted and brought up on charges of conduct unbecoming an officer and neglect of duty. Having been found guilty following a trial on December 27, 1927 he was dismissed from the department. His brother in law, later to be Capt. John J. McCarthy-3, was unable to help him. Herring filed suit that he was unfairly treated and, pursuant to a decision by the Appellant Div. of the Supreme Court, on January 22, 1929 he was re-instated and assigned to the 3rd precinct. Following his retirement on December 15, 1941, Charles Herring died on August 27, 1946 at home at 563 South Broadway at age 58 years.

DET. SGT. MICHAEL J. GILMARTIN # 23

Appointed: March 11, 1913
Retired: April 15, 1944

Born in NYC, Mike Gilmartin moved north to Haverstraw NY along with his family. It was there in St. Peters School that Gilmartin received his education as a young boy. He came to Yonkers at the age of 17 years and gained employment with the Alexander Smith & Sons Carpet Co. He apparently was a dependable employee because he was promoted to foreman in the wool department. He left this position to become a motorman with the Yonkers Railroad Company where he was employed for several years.

In 1913 Gilmartin became aware that the police department was preparing to increase the number of police officers in the department. He took the written, physical, and agility exams, passed them all with no problem and was appointed a police officer on March 11, 1913. His salary was $2,300. per year. His initial training took place at the "School of Instruction" in the 1st precinct and he was then assigned to foot patrol in the 2nd precinct. He remained in the 2nd precinct for 13 years when, on March 25, 1926, he was assigned to the Traffic Division on motorcycle duty. Just over a year later, on May 1, 1927, Gilmartin was promoted to the rank of Sergeant at the salary of $2500. per year. He was allowed to remain assigned to the Traffic Division as a patrol supervisor.

Detective Sergeant Michael Gilmartin (cont.)

On January 3, 1931 at about 10:30 PM Sgt. Gilmartin was on patrol with PO William McQuillan when they were advised of a family dispute in an apartment at 22 Warburton Avenue. Unknown to the officers at the time, an emotionally disturbed male, who was armed with two .32 caliber revolvers, was searching for his wife and children who had sought refuge in a friend's apartment at that address. Sgt. Gilmartin and McQuillan responded and approached the rear of 22 Warburton Ave. through Mill Street. Also unknown to them, the suspect had only moments earlier entered the apartment using Mill Street as well. When the suspect forced his way into the apartment he saw his family and several other residents. As they ran to hide from him he fired twice, wounding a male tenant in the arm.

Gilmartin and McQuillan heard the shots, ran up the rear porch stairs and entered the apartment. As they did they saw the suspect jump out from behind a dumbwaiter and fire his gun at a 28 year old female tenant who tried to run away. She was shot in the back and killed. The male ran down the hall and hid. Weapons drawn, the officers slowly moved down the hall searching each room as they went. Suddenly the male jumped out between the officers. Sgt. Gilmartin yelled to his partner "Look out Bill, he's behind you." The suspect turned and opened fire, with two of his rounds striking Sgt. Gilmartin in the head. Though wounded, the sergeant returned fire and then struck the suspect in the head with his gun as he ran by attempting to escape. In doing so he broke his finger. As the suspect attempted to run out of the apartment PO McQuillan fired 5 times. Two rounds struck the man in the head, 2 hit the center of his back, and 1 hit his lower back. He died almost instantly. It was reported that at least 15 shots had been fired by the suspect and the two officers before the brief gun battle ended. Sgt. Gilmartin's wounds were to the side of his head and behind his ear. He would recover but would be left with bullet fragments in his head for many years.

Initially Sgt. Gilmartin was promoted to Detective Sergeant January 16, 1931, just two weeks following the shooting, "for having shown extraordinary heroism under fire on January 3, 1931." Later, following a meeting of the Police Honor Board on June 10, 1931, Det. Sgt. Gilmartin was awarded Honorable Mention for his heroism.

A year later, following a change in administration that started in 1932, Mayor Joseph Loehr felt Det Sgt. Gilmartin deserved greater recognition than had been accorded him thus far. As a result on June 11, 1932, Gilmartin and PO Robert Philp, who earlier had also been involved in a different shooting, were the first Yonkers police officers to ever be awarded the "Medal of Honor."

Det Sgt Mike Gilmartin remained assigned to the Traffic Division, and for some time served as the traffic complaint officer in Special Sessions Court. As 2nd in command of the Traffic Division he frequently served as the acting commanding officer. It was said that his genial disposition, friendly personality and general character earned for him a host of friends, including those who had received summonses.

Following an examination by the police surgeon, Mike Gilmartin was found to be physically unable to perform his duties by reason of a disability arising out of the actual performance of his duties and he was therefore retired on a disability pension on April 15, 1944. It is believed that Mike Gilmartin was the first officer to qualify under the then new three quarters disability pension benefit.

Unfortunately his retirement would not be enjoyed because it lasted only 7 short months. On November 14, 1944 Retired Det Sgt. Michael Gilmartin died at the age of 61 years.

PO ROBERT FENWICK #78

APPOINTED: March 16, 1913
RETIRED: July 31, 1931

Born in Plymouth, Pa. on August 13, 1877, Bob Fenwick eventually made his way to Yonkers and worked as a weaver in the Alexander Smith Carpet Mills. He later applied to the police department, was appointed on March 16, 1913, and was assigned to foot patrol throughout the 1st precinct. After 5 years, on May 25, 1918, PO Fenwick was assigned to the Traffic Division where he was assigned to various intersections directing the flow of traffic. Upon his retirement from the department on July 31, 1931, on a disability pension, he moved to Pine Plains NY. On the morning of April 20, 1941 Fenwick was preparing to visit Yonkers to attend the annual Police Holy Name Society Communion Mass and Breakfast. While sitting reading the obituaries in the newspaper he came upon the obituary of his very good friend, retired Lt. Edward King. It was at that moment that the shock of learning that his old friend had died, that it apparently caused him to suddenly collapse and die from a heart attack at the age of 65 years.

DET THOMAS F. FEENEY #79

APPOINTED: September 25, 1913
RETIRED: November 30, 1939

Tom Feeney was born in County Mayo, Ireland on November 17, 1886. He came to Yonkers around 1905 and a short while later became a naturalized citizen. After attending local schools he gained employment as a chauffeur and as a gas fitter. On March 1, 1913 Feeney's brother Patrick was sworn in as a Yonkers police officer and it was just six months later that Tom Feeney also joined the ranks of Yonkers Finest. Upon his appointment to the department on September 25, 1913 he was assigned to the 1st precinct on foot patrol and only 2 days later he was sent out on patrol. During this first tour of duty Feeney wasted no time and made his first arrest for intoxication. When he called in to desk Lt Steuart, he identified himself, and requested that the lieutenant send the patrol wagon for his prisoner, Lt Steuart responded, Feeney? Who's Feeney? Well, although initially unknown to most of the police department, Tom Feeney would ultimately earn an outstanding reputation.

For a while Feeney had also been assigned to the 2nd precinct. But on September 8, 1919 he was reassigned to the 3rd precinct at 36 Radford Street where he would remain for the rest of his career. The years on foot patrol passed quickly without anything extraordinary occurring that involved PO Feeney

Detective Thomas F. Feeney (cont.)

until the evening of Saturday April 12, 1930. Officer Feeney's son Thomas Jr., who would later become a special agent with the F.B.I., related in 1994 the circumstances as he knew them; Due to a rash of robberies in the city, on April 12, 1930 some officers were assigned to perform stakeout duty. PO Tom Feeney was assigned in uniform to watch the A & P (Atlantic and Pacific Tea Co.) Store at 205 McLean Avenue. At 8:45 pm, while in the rear of the storage room, officer Feeney observed a male with a gun enter the store and announce a holdup. As the employees were forced into the rear store room they had to pass right by PO Feeney. As the suspect entered the room Feeney quickly knocked the gun from his hand, placed his police revolver against the man's back, grabbed him around the neck and told him not to move. Unknown to Feeney at that time was that there were two more suspects involved. At that moment a second suspect entered the store, gun in hand, and saw the police officer holding his accomplice. The male raised his gun and fired at PO Feeney who then began a violent struggle to hold onto his prisoner. The officer was able to return fire but due to the struggle with his prisoner, the bullet missed its mark. However, the prisoner in custody did not escape. Following intensive interrogation, information was elicited which resulted in the other two men being arrested the next day. The very next month, following a meeting of the Police Honor Board, PO Thomas Feeney was awarded the Honorable Mention, which at that time was the highest award that could be received from the police department.

Four years later on April 23, 1934 Feeney was again assigned to stakeout duty in uniform. This detail was the result of what was described in the media as a 6 month reign of terror throughout Westchester, including the City of Yonkers, whereby a particular group of thieves seemed to commit robberies without being caught. On this occasion PO Feeney was surveilling the Summit Garage at 184-192 McLean Avenue and he had concealed himself in an automobile parked across the street from the garage. At about 2:10 am a vehicle pulled up to the front of the garage and 2 men jumped out, spoke to the garage attendant, and then forced him at gun point into the rear store room. PO Feeney saw what took place, exited the vehicle he was in, and started across the street with his revolver in his hand. There was no time to call for backup units and portable radios were not yet available. As he started across the street in the darkness, to his surprise a third male exited the suspect's vehicle. Feeney quickly ran up behind him, put his revolver in the man's back, and ordered him into the garage. As the cash box was being emptied by the other two men, Feeney entered with his prisoner in front of him like a shield. He ordered the surprised men to raise their hands, which fortunately they did without any shots being fired. The officer recovered a loaded .38 caliber revolver from the thieves. While the three were being held at gunpoint the garage attendant called the 3rd precinct and within minutes help arrived to assist PO Feeney with his three prisoners.

The next day the newspaper headlines called Feeney a hero cop and covered the story in grand detail. They also reported that Chief of Police Edward Quirk was so pleased with the arrest that on May 1st he promptly promoted officer Feeney to Detective 1st grade, which included a salary increase of $200. per year. Tom Feeney gratefully accepted the promotion and pay raise, but he requested that he be allowed to remain assigned to the 3rd precinct on uniformed patrol duty. Chief quirk granted his request.

Eighty years later arrests of this kind would prove to be much more commonplace. Though they would still be excellent arrests, and would receive departmental recognition, it would be nothing like the

Detective Thomas F. Feeney (cont.)

fanfare that resulted in 1934. Following Detective Feeney's 2nd arrest, New York City's police commissioner wrote a letter to Chief Quirk stating in part: ".......this police officer displayed the high standard of intelligence, judgement, decisiveness, determination, courage and resourcefulness which every police department values highly, and which, when exemplified, constitute an example for all....." N.Y. Police Commissioner O'Ryan's letter was subsequently printed in their Spring 3100 police magazine.

On May 2nd of that year the officers and men of the 3rd precinct, where Feeney was stationed, gave him a testimonial dinner and presented him with a wrist watch in recognition of his recent accomplishment. A large number of officers attended and the police officers attended en masse. Tom Feeney had received the highest form of praise and recognition; that of his peers.

On May 4th, the South Yonkers Residents Association presented Feeney with a resolution commending him on his recent capture of armed men and his efforts to make south Yonkers a safer place to live. On May 19th the Yonkers Chapter-Irish American Unified Society held their city wide testimonial dinner at the Elks club honoring Det. Tom Feeney. The dinner was attended by 225 men and women including many dignitaries. Many spoke, and each referred to Det. Feeney's act of heroism, his outstanding bravery, high intelligence, courage, etc. However, the shortest speech of all those given that night was by Feeney himself. He simply said, "*I only performed my duty as a policeman. I got the breaks. Any man on the force would have done what I did if he found himself in the same situation.*"

On May 29th the Westchester County Grand Jury also cited Detective Feeney in a lengthy resolution commending him for his outstanding police work.

Following all this notoriety and aclaim, there was no doubt that Tom Feeney became one of the most well known and respected police officers in the city. He received his promotion to detective 1st grade but, took the extremely rare position of preferring to remain in uniform on patrol in the 3rd precinct. He would remain on patrol for another five years, until 1939, when he and his brother Patrick retired together on the same day, November 30, 1939.

In late December 1973 Tom Feeney became ill. Following a short illness the retired detective died in the Yonkers Professional Hospital on New Years Day, January 1, 1974, at the age of 87 years.

PO PATRICK J. McGEORY # 82

APPOINTED: September 25, 1913
RETIRED: March 15, 1934

Patrick McGeory was born in Yonkers on October 17, 1885. As a young man he worked for several years as a chauffeur. When he was hired by the police department on September 25, 1913 he was assigned to the 1st precinct on Wells Avenue. He would ultimately work out of that building for his entire career. When the Police Association was formed in 1916 he became very active as a trustee. Later, in 1919, his popularity enabled him to be elected as the association's President, following John Dahill. Of course he was required to continue to do his patrol work as well. His interest in police association business may have come from his brother who was the president of the Westchester Co. Federation of Labor. However, McGeory served only one year as president of the Yonkers Police Assoc. On January 16, 1926 he had the good fortune to be appointed a detective where he served for several years. After 20 years of honorable police service, Pat McGeory retired on a disability pension on March 15, 1934. On June 25, 1950 Ret PO Patrick McGeory died at the age of 64 years.

PO WILLIAM H. SILINSKI # 122

APPOINTED: December 15, 1913
RESIGNED: March 23, 1920

Bill Silinski was another example of wasted opportunity. Born in Yonkers on July 16, 1882 Silinski attended local public schools. He would later list his employment as a sugar sampler. When he was appointed to the police department on December 15, 1913 he was assigned to the 3rd precinct where he was known to his friends as handsome Bill. On August 10, 1918 he was assigned to motorcycle duty working from the 3rd precinct. On April 14, 1919 Silinski was sent, along with his motorcycle, to work out of the 1st precinct. However, in March of 1920 Silinski and two other officers were charged with conduct unbecoming an officer and failure to report a gambling house. On March 23rd Silinski surprised everyone by submitting his resignation. He stated that he had found work in Brooklyn and could make as much as $45. per week. His police salary at the time was $30. a week. Mr. Silinski died October 9, 1949.

PO HENRY N. SCHADE # 87

APPOINTED: December 25, 1913
RETIRED: August 31, 1939

Henry Nicholas Schade, known to all his friends as Nick, was born in Germany on January 16, 1885. He arrived in the U.S. with his family around 1903 at the age of 18. A big man standing 6' 2" and speaking fluent German, Schade and his brother bill formed the Schade Milk Dairy Co. of Yonkers. When he was later hired by the police department on December 25, 1913 he was first assigned to the 3rd precinct. In time he was then transferred to the 1st precinct where his foot post would usually be in The Hollow section of the 5th ward. He would remain in the 1st precinct for the remainder of his career. Following Nick Schade's retirement on August 31, 1939 he became a real estate broker operating Schade's Real Estate. He also became a builder of private homes. Around 1951 Nick Schade moved to Jacksonville Florida, only to return to Yonkers around 1960. Within one year he would become ill, and after several weeks Ret PO Henry Nicholas Schade died on March 21, 1961 at age 76 years.

PO JAMES F. AHEARN

APPOINTED: May 1, 1914
DIED: October 17, 1921

James Francis Ahearn was born in New York City on April 28, 1884. Following his family's move to Yonkers he attended St Joseph's Parochial School and PS # 6. As a young Man he had worked as a chauffeur but preferred clerical work. In fact he would later organize the Yonkers Retail Clerks Association. Being a proud Irishman and active in the community, Ahearn also served for several years as the president of Division 15 of the Ancient Order of Hibernians. He was also a member of the Modern Woodmen of America, the Chippewa Club, the Holy Name Society, and taught Irish Gaelic dancing in his spare time. Upon his police appointment on May 1, 1914 he initially was assigned to foot patrol in the 3rd precinct but, due to his clerical skills, he would shortly become the clerk to Chief Wolff. A few years later he was transferred and after a short time on patrol in the 2nd precinct Ahearn was reassigned to the Traffic Division as the division's clerk. At one point he developed a medical problem and, four months after undergoing surgery, Patrolman James Ahearn died of surgical complications on October 17, 1921. He was only 37 years old.

PO PATRICK F. WHALEN # 94

APPOINTED: May 1, 1914
KILLED: February 23, 1934

DIED IN LINE OF DUTY

Patrick F. Whalen was born in Yonkers on St. Patrick's Day, March 17, 1885. He was educated in St. Joseph's School and was said to have always been enthusiastic about the police department even as a boy and was eager to join. He had mastered the printing trade and was employed by the Yonkers Statesman newspaper when he made application to join the police and was accepted. This long awaited opportunity came on May 1, 1914, shortly after he reached the age of 29 years, was married and had a child. Whalen's brother-in-law was PO Thomas Muldoon. Paddy had married Tom's sister Rose.

Upon his appointment to the police department Patrick Whalen was assigned to the 2nd precinct. Within a short period of time he was assigned to patrol duties with the precinct mounted unit. On June 20, 1918 PO Whalen was transferred from the 2nd precinct to the 3rd precinct and was assigned to bicycle patrol. On April 16, 1919 he was assigned to motorcycle duty within the 3rd precinct. Effective April 5, 1920 PO Patrick Whalen was transferred from the 3rd precinct to the city wide Motorcycle Squad which

PO Patrick Whalen (cont.)

worked out of the Wells Avenue station. He remained with the Traffic Division, Motorcycle Squad for the next fourteen years, not knowing of the tragic event that awaited him.

On February 23, 1934 officer Whalen, at least according to one eye witness account, was on duty near his parked motorcycle and standing on South Broadway and Prospect Street. At that time Whalen was talking to someone when suddenly a large explosion occurred in front of the RKO Theater Proctor building at # 45 South Broadway. It would later be learned that an electrician was working on a large transformer under the sidewalk area when the explosion happened. A section of the sidewalk 8' wide by 10' long was throw up into the air and landed on the roof of a parked car. The five story theater and office building trembled and glass shattered from many near-by store windows. The lobby of the theater was completely destroyed. Passers-by were thrown to the ground with their clothing on fire. At the moment of the explosion ten year old Gloria D'Addio was walking in front of the theater and was thrown into the gaping hole in the sidewalk. Police later reported that officer Whalen immediately ran to the scene, jumped into the hole created by the blast and rescued the child. Unfortunately, Officer Patrick Whalen lost his own life in doing so.

One story of the heroism that cost PO Whalen his life was related by an eye witness and victim of the explosion, Mr. Frank Nicholas. Mr. Nicholas reported to the local newspaper that he was standing on a ladder up against the marque working when he heard a thunderous noise and he was thrown to the ground. Mr. Nicholas related that amongst all the commotion he had heard the scream of a child. He said, "*….the next thing I saw was Whalen running up the street to where a big hole had been torn in the sidewalk. I looked into the hole and saw the child. Then a huge wall of flame shot up and Whalen jumped into the hole*." Nicholas continued, "*I jumped in the hole also. Officer Whalen's face was all black and charred when I saw him but I heard him yell at me as he held out the child, 'Here, take the kid.' I took the kid and passed her up to someone else up on the sidewalk and then I climbed out*." Apparently when Mr Nicholas entered the hole PO Whalen had already been seriously burned. However, despite this, he thought only of the child's safety, located her amidst the searing heat and passed the child off to be handed up to safety.

Almost immediately after the child was rescued another explosion took place down in the hole resulting in another wall of flame. During the follow up investigation officer Whalen's body was only able to be identified by his revolver and shield that was found with his charred body. He was three months short of completing 20 years police service when he was killed. The following month, on March 17th, St. Patrick's Day, Whalen would have been 49 years old. He left behind a wife and four children. Just as soon as Whalen's body had been positively identified, Chief Quirk and Police Chaplain Father Charles McCarthy went directly to the officer's home at 640 Van Cortlandt Park Avenue to notify his wife and children. Paddy's been hurt...seriously hurt,... said Father McCarthy. Then he and the chief told the story as gently as they could. They told her that her husband, and the children's father, had died a hero. Whalen's wife was grief stricken and inconsolable. It meant little to her at the time to know that due to the circumstances of her husband's death she would receive a widows pension of half of the officers pay, amounting to $1500. a year. The usual widows pension was $50. a month.

Capt. Dennis Cooper, commander of the Traffic Division and officer Whalen's commanding officer, was reported to say, "*No man in the department surpassed Whalen in character and courage. He always played the game fair and square. As a motorcycle policeman he was one of the terrors of the road.*

PO Patrick Whalen (cont.)

He was always a fearless rider. His record was spotless and he was afraid of no man." Mayor Joseph Loehr issued a lengthy statement praising officer Whalen. He said in part..."*This is just another instance of the heroic spirit of members of the Yonkers Police Department and an evidence of their willingness to sacrifice their all in the performance of their duties.*"

The following day, February 24, 1934, Police Chief Edward Quirk issued a General Order which read in part, "*It is my sad duty to report the death of Patrolman Patrick F. Whalen, Motorcycle Squad, Traffic Division, on the morning of February 23, 1934, in the performance of his duty on the occasion of the explosion and fire in the cellar of the Proctor Building. Patrolman Whalen died a hero's death; to save the life of a child he sacrificed his own.....All members of the Police Bureau off duty are ordered to attend the funeral services wearing overcoats and white gloves.......!*"

The funeral took place on February 26, 1934 at St Dennis Church which was completely filled for the service. The day was bitter cold with high winds and a blinding snow storm. Yet the large funeral cortege marched from Whalen's home to the church unflinchingly as the freezing wind and snow whipped at their solemn faces. Led by the entire Yonkers motorcycle squad and 12 New York City motorcycles, 225 members of the Yonkers department marched along with representatives of many adjoining police departments. Even a delegation of 24 members of the Fire Department, for the first time in the city's history, marched in a funeral procession for a police officer. And it was widely believed they only did this because officer Whalen had died in a fire.

On March 16, 1934 at a meeting of the Police Department Honor Board, several awards were approved for a number of police officers. However, despite his heroic act the month earlier, PO Patrick Whalen did not receive an award of any kind. Instead the board voted to ask the city for funds for a bronze plaque to be prepared which would list the names of all the Yonkers police officers who had lost their lives in the performance of their duties. PO Whalen's name would, of course, be among them. This plaque would ultimately be made and hung on the wall entering police headquarters at 20 Wells Avenue where it remained until around 1962. It was then that police headquarters moved to 10 St. Casimir Avenue. The plaque disappeared at that time and has never been recovered. The circumstances surrounding it's loss have never been learned.

Following the discovery of the facts surrounding the death of Whalen by the police departments historian, and after an appeal on the deceased officers behalf, on May 15, 1985, fifty-one years after losing his life while saving a ten year old child, PO Patrick Whalen finally received proper departmental recognition when he was posthumously awarded the police departments Medal of Honor. Unfortunately, at the time, there were no known family members that the award could be presented to.

The search for a living relative of officer Whalen to present the medal to took 14 years. Just by accident Yonkers police officer Thomas Powrie Jr. found a death notice of his great grandfather, who, as it turned out, was the brother to officer Whalen. On May 13, 1999 during Police Week award ceremonies the medal was finally presented to a family member; PO Thomas Powrie Jr. Local newspaper reporters located the former 10 year old, then 76 and living in New Jersey. When she was interviewed she said that she thinks of PO Whalen very, very often. She said at the time of the incident Whalen's wife came to visit her in the hospital. It was very sad, said the woman. I will never forget the strong hands of PO Patrick Whalen who grabbed hold of me after diving into the fire.

PO JOSEPH H. HART # 96

APPOINTED: May 1, 1914
RETIRED: April 30, 1939

Joe Hart was born in Hibernia N.J. on May 5, 1883 where his family were miners. He came to Yonkers with his parents at the age of 12 and attended local schools. When he was appointed to the police department he was assigned to the 3rd pct. for a number of years on foot patrol. He was then moved to the 1st pct. On January 2, 1922 he was detailed to the Corporation Councils office in city hall. On January 13, 1927 two women and a boy were found unconscious in their home from gas. PO Hart, then of the 4th pct., responded and by using the "Schaefer System" of artificial respiration, saved their lives. Only days earlier Hart had revived a seven year old boy using the same method. PO Harts uncle was PO Dave Parliament, his brother in law was PO Ed Feeley Sr., his grandson was Lt Jos. Merrigan, and his great grandson was PO Charles Baker. Following retirement on April 30, 1939 Hart moved to New Jersey where on October 31, 1951 he died at the age of 68 years.

PO JOHN J. McDERMOTT # 89

APPOINTED: May 1, 1914
DIED: February 15, 1944

John McDermott was born in NYC on April 19, 1883. As a young man he was employed as a butcher in the Getty Square area and was active in the Butchers Union activities. When he was appointed a police officer he was sent to work in the 3rd precinct where he remained until May 31, 1918. At that time he was assigned to the newly formed Traffic Squad. Known by all who knew him as "Joe" McDermott, he worked regularly in Getty Square directing traffic along with PO Jim Colgan. Both men were an imposing site, each standing over 6 feet tall. "Joe" McDermott was not only very attentive to his traffic duties, but on March 26, 1931 he assisted detectives in the arrest of two men in Getty Square wanted for murder and arson. After 27 years service he was assigned to clerical duty in the traffic unit. On February 15, 1944, having just started his "early tour" and while seated at his desk, McDermott suddenly fell from his chair and died from cardiac arrest. Being a well-liked and respected officer, all off duty personnel attended his funeral in the form of an honor guard.

PO CORNELIUS F. McINERNEY # 88

APPOINTED: May 1, 1914
RETIRED: November 30, 1942

McInerney was born on August 25, 1885 in Haverstraw N.Y. where he received most of his education. He and his family did not come to Yonkers until he was about 14 years of age. As a young man McInerney initially worked as a bus agent, and later was employed as an electrical lineman for the N.Y. Central Railroad and the N.Y. Telephone Company. In fact he was a delegate and business agent for local 501 IBEW. When he was appointed a policeman he was assigned to the 3rd precinct where he would work his entire career. One example of his diligent service occurred on July 7, 1932 while walking his South Broadway post at 3 am. He observed shadows moving behind # 353 and within minutes McInerney had arrested 2 men at gunpoint for burglary. "Connie" McInerney retired after 28 years of honorable service. His son Tom would later become a NYS Assemblyman. "Con" McInerney died in Yonkers on July 1, 1965, one month short of his 80th birthday.

PO WILLIAM J. O'DONNELL # 90

APPOINTED: May 1, 1914
RETIRED: June 1, 1944

Bill O'Donnell was born in Yonkers on June 25, 1877 where he received his formal education. Prior to his police service O'Donnell worked for Otis Elevator in their foundry. A very robust and outgoing man, O'Donnell was very active in 6th ward politics. One month short of his 37th birthday he was appointed a police officer and assigned to the 3rd precinct. He would remain there until his retirement 30 years later. On September 22, 1928 he was awarded a Certificate of Excellent Police Work for stopping a runaway horse which was endangering the lives of pedestrians. After retiring from the police department on June 1, 1944 O'Donnell worked as a special guard at the J. K. Walding Co. shipyard in Yonkers. O'Donnell's brother Patrick was also a Yonkers police officer, as was his step son PO Steve Ackerman. He was a member of the Yonkers Chippewa Club and the YPD & St Peters Holy Name Scieties. Following a brief illness, and only 4 years after retiring, retired PO Bill O'Donnell died on October 15, 1948 in his home at 243 Riverdale Avenue at the age of 71 years.

PO EDWARD J. RASP # 91

APPOINTED: May 1, 1914
RETIRED: October 31, 1939

A transplanted country boy, Edward Rasp was born December 31, 1876 in Memphis Tenn., and was brought to Yonkers by his parents at the age of three. He was locally educated and graduated from St Mary's School. His early employment was that of a hatter with the Waring Hat Factory in Yonkers. When he was hired by the police department he was paid $2,300 a year and was assigned to work from the 3rd precinct. An efficient and reliable officer, Rasp was also very active in the Police Association. In 1931, during the "great depression," Rasp served on the volunteer "YPD Relief Committee" to help provide food and clothing to the needy. It wasn't until 1935 that he was assigned to directing traffic; most often in Larkin Plaza. Following his retirement on October 31, 1939, around 1941 he became critically ill and required 15 transfusions from his former colleagues to stay alive. Five years later, on December 18, 1946, Ed Rasp died at home at 31 Purser Place following a six week illness.

PO VINCENT SLEDZINSKI # 92

APPOINTED: May 1, 1914
RETIRED: June 20, 1929

Vincent Sledzinski was born April 5, 1879 to Polish immigrants in the then "City of Brooklyn." He and his family would later move to Yonkers where Sledzinski, who spoke fluent polish, would gain employment as a carpet foreman with the Alexander Smith Carpet Co. He would remain employed there for ten years. Following his police appointment on May 1, 1914 he worked foot patrol in the 3rd precinct. On June 10, 1918, after 4 years service, Sledzinski was assigned as a detective. On this date a centralized Detective Bureau, which had been abolished several years earlier, was again organized and Sledzinski was one of six officers assigned. For reasons unknown, on July 15, 1921, just three years later, he was reassigned back to patrol duty where he remained until his retirement from the 2nd precinct on June 20, 1929. His sons-in-law were Capt. Benjamin DeLuccy and PO Stanley Swiechocki. Following a brief illness Sledzinski died in Yonkers General Hospital on July 8, 1944. He was 65 years old.

PO PETER J. SULLIVAN # 93

APPOINTED: May 1, 1914
RETIRED: June 19, 1939

Peter Sullivan was a local boy born in Yonkers on November 4, 1886. He was a product of St Joseph's School where, upon graduation, he earned his wages as a shipping clerk. At the age of 27 he received his police appointment on May 1, 1914 and was assigned to foot patrol in the 3rd precinct. The hiring of Sullivan and his entire recruit class was the biproduct of a 4th precinct being established at 764 Palisade Avenue in 1914. With three years police service Sullivan was drafted into the Army on September 7, 1917 due to the World War, and was sent to France with Co. - B, 302nd Infantry, 77th Div., American Expiditionary Force (A.E.F.), attached to the military police. He was discharged as a Corporal on June 28, 1919. Pete returned to the police department and his old foot post.

Called "Pete" by all the school children on his post, Sullivan would always be seen accompanied by a dog named "Fritz" as he made his rounds. In winter snow or summer heat, "Fritz" waited for, and then followed Pete Sullivan for 10 years. In 1921, during the years of liquor prohibition, PO Sullivan was assigned in plainclothes to the police Vice Squad to assist Federal Prohibition agents in executing search warrants against "still" operators. On September 22, 1928 Sullivan was awarded the highest police award, the Honorable Mention, for arresting a safe burglar, known then as a "Yegg," while in the act at 2:15 am the month earlier. When Pete Sullivan retired on June 19, 1939 he lived at 257 Valentine Lane and was an active member of the P.B.A., Yonkers Police War Veterans Association, and the Police Holy Name Society. Five years later on June 20, 1944, retired PO Peter Sullivan died suddenly in his home at the young age of 53 years.

PO RUDOLPH M. BAUER # 98

APPOINTED: May 1, 1914
RETIRED: July 15, 1939

One of 12 children born to German immigrants, Rudolph Martin Bauer was born in Yonkers on April 7, 1881. Following his local education he would gain work as a caulker. When he was hired by the police department on May 1, 1914, his ability to speak German was clearly an asset. Bauer's initial assignment was in the 3rd precinct. On May 12, 1918, while on traffic duty at Yonkers Ave. and Central Park Ave., Bauer was hit by a car that ran over his leg breaking it in two places. He spent 3 months in the hospital resulting in one leg being 1" shorter than the other. He sued for $25,000 but lost. On December 2, 1925 he was assigned back to traffic duty. On May 5, 1930 Bauer was commended for catching a burglar in a store on Elm St. at 3:30 am. "Rude," as he was known to friends, retired from the 3rd precinct on July 15, 1939 and worked for the Radio Marine Corp. in NYC. His brother Jacob was a NYPD sergeant. A bachelor, Rudy Bauer died September 18, 1974 in the Hudson View Nursing Home at the age of 93 years.

PO JAMES P. FINN # 95

APPOINTED: May 1, 1914
RETIRED: January 1, 1950

James Patrick Finn was born in NYC on December 30, 1884. He was brought to Yonkers as an infant and received his early education in St Joseph's School and PS # 6. His first job as an adult was working as a machinist for the Otis Elevator Company. At the age of 30, Jim Finn was hired as a police officer on May 1, 1914 and was assigned to foot patrol in the 1st precinct on Wells Ave. Four years later, on May 31, 1918, Finn was assigned to the newly established Traffic Unit, directing traffic, working only day and early tours and changing shift every ten days. PO Finn became a very well known figure directing traffic at Warburton Avenue and Manor House Square for the next 25 years. When a traffic light was finally installed, PO Finn was reassigned to the Radio Telegraph Division in headquarters. Forced to retire on January 1, 1950 at the mandatory age of 65, Jim Finn would live only two years, dying on May 16, 1952.

PO JOHN J. RYAN # 117

APPOINTED: May 4, 1914
RETIRED: May 1, 1931

John Ryan was born in Yonkers on February 22, 1890. After attending local schools he gained employment with a local blacksmith as a "horseshoer." At the age of 24 he was hired as a police officer on May 4, 1914 and was assigned to foot patrol in the 1st precinct on Wells Avenue. On May 31, 1918 Ryan was fortunate enough to be assigned to street traffic duty in a newly formed Traffic Division. But just two years later, on July 16, 1920, he was returned to routine patrol duties in the precinct. Following departmental charges, on May 29, 1930 Ryan was found guilty of neglect of duty and was fined 10 days pay. A year later PO Ryan was examined by the police surgeon and was deemed medically unfit to perform his duties and was subsequently retired on a disability pension on May 1, 1931. After living for a while in the Bronx, N.Y., John Ryan moved to Florida. On May 7, 1942 retired PO John J. Ryan died in Miami Florida at the age of 52 years.

PO JOHN A. CUDDIHY

APPOINTED: May 4, 1914
RETIRED: December 1, 1916

Very little is known about John A. Cuddihy. It can, however, be assumed that Cuddihy, who worked as a hatter in a Yonkers hat factory for a time, expected to have a long career with the police department. Lacking information to the contrary we can also assume he was a hard working police officer. Although he was 42 years of age when he was hired, his health must have been satisfactory. Unfortunately with just over a year as a police officer he became ill and on October 30, 1916 the local newspaper reported on the death of another police officer just the day before. In that same news article they briefly reported that......"*John Cudahy (they spelled his name differently) who is assigned to the 1st precinct and who has been ill in St. John's Hospital since September 21st with a kidney condition, is dying!*" It is believed he recovered from his illness but retired on a medical disability that same year on December 1, 1916. John Cuddihy died May 23, 1925, leaving a wife and several children. He would have been about 53 years old.

PO GEORGE J. ILLINGSWORTH

APPOINTED: May 11, 1914
RESIGNED: December 10, 1926

George Illingsworth was born in Yonkers on May 2, 1882. As a young man he worked in the Alexander Smith Carpet Mills as a Weaver. At the age of 32 years he was appointed a police officer on May 11, 1914 at the salary of $2,300. Following a short assignment in the 1st precinct he was transferred to work out of the 2nd precinct on foot patrol. With no records found indicating the contrary, officer Illingsworth seemed to be an efficient police officer. However, on May 22, 1925 he reportedly was suspended from duty following the filing of an assault charge made by his wife. A warrant for his arrest was issued but Illingsworth turned himself in and was released in his own custody. The disposition on this charge is unknown. But on November 30, 1926 he was again suspended without pay. Ten days later he submitted his resignation from the police department effective December 10, 1926. It was reported that he moved out of our city. Records indicate George Illingsworth died October 28, 1943.

PO PATRICK J. McNAMEE # 99

APPOINTED: August 10, 1914
RETIRED: August 19, 1939

Patrick J. McNamee was born on May 11, 1877 in White Plains N.Y. He would later come to Yonkers as a youth and attend St. Joseph's School. One of his earlier jobs was working for the Yonkers Railroad. Following the written and medical exams, Patrick McNamee was appointed to the Yonkers Police Department on August 10, 1914. A resident of 168 Voss Avenue, McNamee worked foot patrol in the 1st and 2nd precincts for a number of years and was a dependable officer. But on September 16, 1926 he was transferred to the 3rd precinct at 36 Radford Street where he would spend the remainder of his career. Thirteen years following his retirement on August 19, 1939 Pat McNamee was just leaving his house when he suffered a heart attack and died on November 3, 1952. Patrick McNamee was seventy five years of age.

PO THOMAS F. COMBS # 100

APPOINTED: August 11, 1914
RETIRED: February 28, 1929

Born July 14, 1889 in Yonkers, Tom Combs attended Yonkers public schools and later, the Cooper Union Trade Institute in New York City. He worked as an apprentice laying brick. When appointed a police officer on August 11, 1914 Combs was assigned to the 3rd precinct for several years. In 1916 when the Yonkers Police Association (YPA) was organized, Combs was instrumental and was a signer of the certificate of incorporation. In 1917 he was elected vice president of the association. When World War I began, PO Combs decided to take a leave of absence and join the Army. He served from August 9, 1918 to February 14, 1919 and upon his discharge was re-instated to the police department.

On the late tour of August 30, 1926 while assigned to the 4th precinct and walking a post, PO Combs came upon an assault and robbery that had just occurred. He began a lengthy foot pursuit during which it was reported that Combs fired his revolver at the fleeing suspect, reportedly emptying and reloading his weapon twice. Fortunately for the thief no bullet found it's mark. He ultimately ran the suspect down and made the arrest.

Following an examination by the police surgeon, PO Combs was found physically unfit to perform his duties and was retired on a disability pension on February 28, 1929. He then began a career as a bricklayer and, later became president of the Bricklayers, Masons, and Plasters Union; local 22. He was a member of the Yonkers Police War Veterans Association and a charter member of the PBA (YPA). A resident of 133 Lake Avenue, Tom Combs died on September 6, 1972 in his home following a brief illness. Retired PO Thomas Combs was 83 years of age.

PO MARTIN J. MAHER # 37

APPOINTED: August 14, 1914
DISMISSED: January 13, 1920

When Martin Maher was appointed on August 14, 1914 he was assigned to the 1st precinct on foot patrol but sometime after 1917 he was reassigned to the 2nd precinct. There is little information available regarding PO Maher's police service record, with the exception of the following; On New Year's Day, January 1, 1920, Maher had worked the late tour but failed to return to the station house in the morning for the return roll call. He was charged with Neglect of Duty and Disobedience of Orders. By January 5th PO Maher had still failed to report for duty or for the hearing on his departmental charges. He was absent without leave. Upon hearing of the charges brought against him it was reported that Maher indicated that he planned on leaving the department. However he never submitted a letter of resignation. Because of his being AWOL, PO Maher was dismissed from the department effective January 13, 1920. Apparently having regained the city's confidence, on January 20, 1932 he was appointed a city jailer. The photo is of Maher in the 1930's in his jailer uniform.

PO PAUL C. BOTH # 102

APPOINTED: November 30, 1916
DIED: September 21, 1941

Paul Both was born in Yonkers on July 23, 1881. He attended Public School # 4 and would later earn a living as a plumber. Following the passing of all the civil service written and medical exams, Paul Both was appointed a police officer on November 30, 1916 and assigned to duty in the 2nd precinct on Central Park Avenue. He worked foot posts in the earlier years and later would work in a radio car. A resident of 35 Dunwoodie Street, PO Both was a member of the newly established St. George Society; a religious organization which consisted of police officers of the Protestant faith. He would never know him but, Both's grandson, Hugh Paul Kelly would be appointed a Yonkers police officer. During most of 1941 PO Both was out on sick leave suffering from cancer. The disease would ultimately take his life September 21, 1941 at the age of 60 years.

PO JOHN J. SHANNON #103

APPOINTED: November 30, 1916
DIED: March 15, 1940

John J. Shannon was born to Irish immigrants in Yonkers on January 3, 1884. However, for reasons that remain unknown, throughout his life Shannon would use the birth dates of March 6, of 1885, 1890, and 1891. He received his early education from St. Joseph's School and as a young man worked as a gas fitter. Following his appointment to the police department, the salary for which was $2,300. a year, he was assigned to the 3rd precinct on foot patrol. Following the involvement of the United States in World War 1, officer Shannon felt compelled to serve his country and took a leave of absence to join the Army on September 28, 1917. He served overseas in combat as a Corporal in Company L, 308th Infantry, 77th Division. The local newspapers reported that Corporal Shannon had an outstanding war record for bravery. He was discharged from the military on May 10, 1919, shortly thereafter was re-instated to the police department, and was returned to duty in the 3rd precinct at 36 Radford Street.

In May of 1924 PO Shannon was one of several men with military experience chosen to be a member of the newly formed Police Riot Squad. Their specialized training was conducted in the Armory on North Broadway.

On December 28, 1929 while walking an early tour foot post, Shannon was assigned to guard the Gristede grocery store at 432 Riverdale Avenue. Upon the store closing at 9 PM officer Shannon observed three men loitering in the shadows nearby. His suspicions aroused, Shannon confronted and questioned the men whose answers were very evasive. The officer drew his revolver and placed the men under arrest for "Suspicion." A quick search of the men found one of them to be carrying a loaded .32 caliber revolver.

Shannon walked them at gun point to a call box on Radford St. to report the incident to the desk lieutenant, and then walked his prisoners into the station house. Following intense questioning the men confessed to stealing the vehicle they had been using from another town, and admitted they were about to holdup the grocery store when they were interrupted by officer Shannon.

On April 23, 1930, following a meeting of the Police Honor Board, which at the time was composed of nine "Special Public Safety Commissioners," PO John Shannon was awarded a police Commendation for his arrest of the three men.

On March 15, 1940, PO Shannon had just finished a late tour working in the communications room which was then designated the Radio and Telegraph Division. He had been assigned there since 1936. Within just a few hours of arriving at his home at 14 Stewart Place, Shannon suddenly suffered a heart attack and died.

A lifelong bachelor, PO Shannon was a former 3rd precinct PBA trustee for many years, a member of the Police Holy Name Society, and a charter member of the Yonkers Police War Veterans Legion. He was 56 years old.

PO GEORGE J. ERLING # 101

APPOINTED: December 1, 1916
DIED: July 1, 1935

DIED IN LINE OF DUTY

George Julius Erling was born in Yonkers on May 12, 1886 and, after receiving his early education in PS # 6, he worked for his father who for many years operated a confectionary (candy) store at Elm Street and Nepperhan Avenue. When his father retired from his business, George Erling found work delivering milk on a route for the Yonkers based Borden Milk Company. Erling left that position when appointed a police officer December 1, 1916. He was a tall thin man standing over 6 feet tall but only weighing 160 lbs. This tall slim appearance gave him somewhat of a gaunt look but his health was fine.

Following his initial training at the School of Instruction at headquarters, PO Erling was assigned to the 2nd precinct. After a short time he was assigned to mounted patrol duty; something he greatly enjoyed. Riding his horse, Erling patrolled the east side of Yonkers on various assigned patrol routes and along with other members of the mounted unit led many of the city's largest parades. His frequent

PO George J. Erling # 101 (cont.)

and enjoyable assignment was patrolling in the Lawrence Park section of the city. When the use of horse patrol was discontinued, PO Erling was assigned to foot patrol in the precinct at his own request. In an interview with his son George F. Erling in February of 2000, his son said his father had a strong dislike for automobiles and did not want to drive one. That in fact, though he did not have a driver's license, he had his wife get one so she could do any required driving. Although he believed cars were dangerous and was reluctant to get a license, in the early 1930's he was ordered by the police department to obtain one and was assigned to a radio car.

Officer Erling was working an Early Tour on Sunday the 30th of July 1935 when a large storm struck the city causing substantial damage. A large tree had uprooted on Central Park Avenue near Heights Drive, falling across the roadway and tearing down power and telephone lines. It was about 11:20 PM and the northeast section of the city was left in darkness. PO Erling, along with other officers arrived, parked their radio cars to block the down tree and stood in the darkened roadway with flashlights diverting traffic around the tree. It was shortly before midnight that a 26 year old driver of a vehicle failed to see officer Erling, and struck him with his car, tossing Erling's body across the roadway and under a nearby power company truck. The vehicle also sideswiped a police car before coming to a stop. The operator of the car was arrested by the other officers at the scene and charged with Reckless Driving.

PO Erling was immediately taken to Lawrence Hospital in Bronxville where it was determined that he suffered a fractured skull, severe internal injuries, and both his legs were broken. He was in an unconscious state throughout his treatment. The injured officer's wife Louise, who had driven him to work for the beginning of his 4-12 shift, was notified and went directly to the hospital. She remained right at his bedside throughout the night. Despite the doctors best efforts PO George Erling never regained consciousness and died shortly before noon the next day, July 1, 1935. He had left behind his wife, his 11 year old son George, and 13 year old son Robert.

Because PO Erling died in the performance of his official duties, for his funeral he received full departmental honors. In the General Order announcing Erling's death, Chief Quirk wrote in part....."*It is my sad duty to report the death of PO George Erling # 101, assigned to the 2nd precinct Radio Division, this morning as a result of an accident in which PO Erling was run over and fatally injured while in the performance of his duty, directing traffic.*" In addition to naming members who would serve as pall bearers, the chief also ordered all off duty officers to attend Erling's funeral mass which was conducted at the Holy Trinity church. Prior to the accident Erling was a lifelong Protestant, while his wife of 15 years and both his sons were Catholic. For some time he had expressed a desire in converting to Catholicism. Because of his expressed plans to convert, Erling's wife had him baptized a Catholic while lying unconscious and just prior to his death. Mrs. Erling received a yearly widow pension of $1,500., which was half of his annual salary. Had he died of natural causes she would have received $600.

In a procession led by Police Chief Edward Quirk, more than 200 members of the department marched from Erling's home at 21 Mitchell Avenue to the church. In February 2000, retired PO John "Red" O'Hare remembered attending the funeral and seeing his deceased brother officer laid out in his full dress uniform. Leading the impressive police procession were all the motorcycles in the Yonkers

PO George J. Erling # 101 (cont.)

Police Department, MT. Vernon, Eastchester, and 11 motorcycles from the Westchester County Parkway Police. As the hearse entered Oakland Cemetery, all 200 uniformed officers lined up and saluted as his casket passed by. On the east side of Yonkers many residents who knew PO Erling from all his years in the 2nd precinct were shocked by his death. In one newspaper report it was written, "*With the sudden death of patrolman George Erling.........a well-known figure in our community passes on. In the days before concrete highways, cars and radios, patrolman Erling rode horseback over our roads on patrol duty. And many will remember with pleasure his tall figure on his chestnut horse.*"

When interviewed in February of 2000, officer Erling's youngest son George, then 76 years of age, stated, "I was only 11 at the time my father died and I remember very little. But I do remember him stopping home now and again with his horse tied up outside. And oddly enough I remember to this day standing outside our house and watching my father go off to work that very last day."

LIEUTENANT ROBERT A. PHILP

APPOINTED: March 3, 1919
RETIRED: March 31, 1958

When Bob Philp was appointed a Yonkers police officer he had no way of knowing how his bravery would be tested and ultimately result in his being awarded the Medal of Honor. Robert Andrew Philp was born in Yonkers on March 24, 1893 and attended local schools. In fact, being a strong and very athletic young man, Bob Philp played ball on the St. Peters Church team. Though he enjoyed sports he earned a living as a plasterer and a bricklayer.

When Robert Philp was appointed to the police department on March 3, 1919 he was immediately assigned to attend the New York City Police School of Instruction. He was instructed in all the physical and academic aspects of police work, remaining there until his graduation on May 9, 1919, whereupon he returned to Yonkers and was assigned to foot patrol in the 1st precinct. Bob Philp was fortunate in that he only remained on routine precinct patrol for about a year when on April 5, 1920 the police department began testing the use of three wheel motorcycles. At this same time a reorganization of the Traffic Division took place and PO Philp was assigned there to motorcycle patrol duty.

On August 30, 1926 officer Philp faced danger and potential injury for the first time. It would not be the last. On this day, during the evening about 10 PM, Philp was patrolling Bronx River Road on his

Lt. Robert A. Philp (cont.)

motorcycle when a speeding vehicle passed him going in the opposite direction. He yelled to the operator to halt; an order that was, of course, ignored. PO Philp turned his motorcycle around and began a pursuit. When he reached speeds of up to 60 mph, and realizing that the vehicle would likely escape, officer Philp drew his revolver and fired two rounds at the fleeing vehicle. At this the car picked up speed. Philp's response was to fire his last four rounds at the car as it sped up a steep, dark, unlit hill in the Town of Bronxville. Unknown to Philp at the time, the two suspects had stopped, turned off their lights, left the emergency brake off, and jumped from the vehicle making their escape. As Philp sped up the dark hill he saw, what would later be determined to be, the stolen vehicle rolling backwards directly at him. Only a sharp turn of his handle bars saved him and his motorcycle from being struck. But it was too close for comfort.

Bob Philp was very comfortable with the use of his revolver and in fact during 1928 he was a valued member of the Yonkers Police Pistol Shooting Team. He was required to be an excellent shot to even make the team. The eleven member Yonkers team was very active in shooting competitions all over Westchester County.

On Sunday, August 18, 1929, Bob Philp had only just begun his day tour on motorcycle duty in northwest Yonkers and had no reason to believe that it would not be a quiet Sunday day tour. Later that day, however, the Yonkers Herald newspaper would issue an "Extra Edition" with the bold headlines reading, "*Four Shot, One Dying; Four Are Arrested*." An episode in which officer Philp would play a prominent role.

In the early morning hours of that day, in a tavern in the Town of Irvington, several men were drinking heavily and became involved in a dispute involving a woman. As a fight erupted, and the proprietor of the tavern approached the men to break up the fight, one of the men pulled out a revolver and shot the tavern keeper in the head. The four suspects fled from the scene in a stolen car they had taken earlier in New York City. Speeding from the scene they wrecked the vehicle and, with the occupant at gun point, quickly hijacked another one and continued on their way. Their direction of travel would ultimately take them into Yonkers. Early morning church parishioners on that Sunday would be startled to see three cars and a police motorcycle speeding through the streets with the occupants of the first car firing a gun at the motorcycle officer, and the officer returning fire.

Following the shooting incident, Irvington had sent out an alarm on the wanted men and a description of the car they were using and advised they may be heading south on North Broadway. PO William "Cy" Tompkins of the 4th precinct, who was about to go out on motor patrol, was given this information and sent out to keep a watch for these suspects. He just reached Shonnard Place and North Broadway when the wanted car sped by. He immediately gave chase in his police vehicle. At that same moment, Sgt. John Caulfield, also of the 4th precinct and on his way home in his private vehicle after working the late tour, observed PO Tompkins begin his pursuit and decided to join him using his speedy "Roadster." At high speeds the three vehicles headed south and turned down Wells Avenue to Warburton Avenue where PO Philp just happened to be sitting on his motorcycle. (Keep in mind that there were no police radios yet). Sensing a serious problem officer Philp joined in the pursuit. As the group sped down Riverdale Avenue PO Philp was gaining on the suspect vehicle when they opened fire on the pursuing officers. Being the closest to the suspects' vehicle and being the most exposed PO Philp was struck almost immediately in the stomach. He had no way of knowing at the time but fortunately the full force of the bullet was deflected by striking the strap of his Sam Browne belt and causing only a flesh wound

Lt. Robert A. Philp (cont.)

to Philp's stomach. Without ever losing control of his "Indian" motorcycle and, not really knowing if his wound was serious, he simply ignored it, unholstered his revolver, and while steering with one hand PO Philp returned fire striking two of the occupants. This was quite an accomplishment when one considers that PO Philp knew he had been shot, the hand gear shift was located on the side of the gas tank (no foot shift) and despite all that was happening, Philp never lost control of his motorcycle.

Meanwhile off duty Sgt Caulfield was able to pull alongside the suspect vehicle at Riverdale Ave. and Valentine Lane and intentionally sideswiped the suspects' car, forcing it to the curb. As the four men jumped from the vehicle they were taken into custody within minutes by PO's Philp, Tompkins, and Sgt Caulfield. The Irvington victim survived his wound resulting in a reduced charge of assault 1st degree.

The following month, on September 26, 1929, the police honor board met and discussed officer Philp's bravery the month before. Based on the recommendation of Public Safety Commissioner Frank Devlin, PO Philp was subsequently elevated to the position of detective. His salary now rose $200. , from $2,500. a year to $2,700. Although he held detective status and received the pay increase, Philp requested that he be allowed to remain in the Traffic Division on motorcycle duty. His request was granted. The official award ceremony for Det. Philp and the other officers involved took place on October 17, 1929 in the mayor's office. At that time Mayor Fogarty presented Philp with the "Insignia of Honorable Mention." The award consisted of a bar with a silver star and was the highest level award that the police department was authorized to give at that time.

Some might think that following that incident a year earlier in which he was shot and slightly wounded chasing suspects on his motorcycle, that officer Philp might be just a little less aggressive. This apparently was not in Bob Philp's nature. On the evening of September 21, 1930 while on motorcycle patrol on Central Park Avenue, Philp was passed by a speeding vehicle which he would later learn was stolen. When he signaled for the 17 year old driver to pull over, the driver swerved his car at the motorcycle attempting to strike Philp with his car. The officer continued his pursuit which took them into the Bronx. When the driver again tried to hit Philp with his car the officer drew his revolver and began firing at the car at regular intervals, ultimately emptying his weapon. The vehicle with its four occupants went out of control and crashed. PO Philp promptly arrested all four.

Having been a motorcycle officer for almost all of his years with the police department, and having held the rank of detective since 1929, on January 1, 1931 motorcycle detective PO Philp was officially transferred from the Traffic Division into the Detective Division as a regular squad investigator. In this new assignment it would only be a short time before, on June 10, 1931, he was awarded two Certificates of Excellent Police Work. One for the arrest of an illegal alien who was deported a short time later, and the second for apprehending four men in a stolen car the previous year on September 21, 1930. During this pursuit on his motorcycle, which was just before leaving the Traffic Division, officer Philp again found it necessary to fire his revolver to stop the fleeing vehicle.

In a local news story it was reported that on June 11, 1932 during the presentation of awards to a number of police officers, Mayor Joseph Loehr, who was then in office, announced that the police department had authorized a new award; the Medal of Honor. He then advised that he was presenting the

Lt. Robert A. Philp (cont.)

Medal of Honor to Detective Robert Philp and Sgt. Michael Gilmartin. Being the highest category of the police awards, this was the first time in the department's history that this medal was ever awarded. The mayor noted that, even though the act of bravery which earned Detective Philp the award and in which he was wounded by a gunshot, had occurred nearly three years earlier on August 18, 1929, and further that, even though Philp had already been awarded the Honorable Mention for that incident, "there was justice in awarding the new medal now."

Detective Robert Philp was promoted to the rank of Sergeant on May 16, 1936 with an annual salary of $3,400. Following his promotion Sgt. Philp, shield # 22, who was reported to have rendered outstanding service while assigned to the Detective Division, working frequently from an office in the 2nd precinct, was reassigned to uniformed patrol supervisory duties in the 4th precinct. During his promotion ceremony Mayor Loehr presented Sgt. Philp with a gold wrist watch which was said to have been suitably engraved.

Bob Philp was without question an exceptional "street cop," but he was even more. He was very concerned about the number of youths that seemed to be getting into trouble for a lack of something better to do. Several police officers began volunteering their time encouraging juveniles to become involved in sporting activities. These officers formed the core of the unofficial Police Athletic League (PAL). After a great deal of planning and organizational recommendations, on the evening of July 14, 1941, PO John J. O'Hare was elected the first president of the newly organized PAL. Among the eight newly elected trustees of the PAL, all of whom worked so hard to see it become a reality, was Bob Philp. He realized that helping the youth of our city would be an important part of reducing juvenile crime.

It was on February 1, 1942 that Sergeant Philp was promoted to the rank of Lieutenant along with a number of others who were promoted as well. His last assignment having been a patrol sergeant in the 1st precinct, Lieutenant Philp was now reassigned to the 4th precinct as a desk officer. He remained in this assignment for the rest of his career.

After having served the police department with honor and distinction for over 39 years, Lt Robert Philp requested and was granted retirement from all active duty on March 31, 1958. Always faced with daunting challenges, Bob Philp met every one head on. Even when his son, Army Lieutenant Robert Philp was killed during World War 2 in the pacific campaign, he never let it affect his aggressive devotion to his duty.

On November 12, 1970 retired Lt. Robert Philp, the nephew of former Yonkers PO Michael Madden and a proud Medal of Honor recipient, died in the Hudson View Nursing Home at the age of 77 years.

DET. WILLIAM J. McQUILLAN # 155

APPOINTED: May 13, 1919
RETIRED: June 15, 1947

Motorcycle officer William McQuillan was one of those officers who, during his career, would have his bravery tested and he would pass with flying colors. Bill McQuillan was born July 15, 1893 in Yonkers and attended PS # 3, and later Yonkers High School. As a young man he worked as an electric meter tester for the Yonkers Electric Light and Power Company. Being an enthusiastic outdoors man he would often join his father, who at the time was a sergeant in the National Guard, on deer hunting and fishing trips up in the Adirondack Mountains. In June of 2000 when his son, William Jr., was asked about his father, he stated his father definitely loved the outdoors but his favorite activity was fishing. "Mac," as McQuillan was known to his friends, and his father were also said to have been excellent basketball players. They both played on the well known National Guard team known as the 4th Separates right in the Armory on North Broadway. Young Bill was also one of the organizers of the original Highland Rod and Gun Club and served as its president in the early 1930's.

Following his appointment to the police department, and after attending the school of instruction for training, McQuillan was assigned to foot patrol in the 1st precinct. Just about a year later, on April 5, 1920, he was reassigned to the Traffic Division on motorcycle duty. For some reason, on July 22, 1922 he

Det. William J. McQuillan (cont.)

was again returned to patrol duty in the 4th precinct. This would last only until August 25, 1924 when he was returned to traffic duty on his Indian motorcycle.

On the evening of January 3, 1931 PO McQuillan was still recovering from appendectomy surgery and was carried as being on light duty status. However this designation did not prevent him from being assigned to patrol duty. He would just use a police vehicle instead of his motorcycle. On this night he and Sgt Mike Gilmartin were sent to a Warburton Avenue address on a violent dispute. Both officers decided to use the rear porches which were in the dead end of Mill Street. Just as they were climbing the stairs they heard gunshots and screaming coming from an upper apartment. At that moment a crazed and jealous husband, who had two handguns, had shot and killed a young woman and wounded a male visitor. The shooters own wife and children ran and hid from him. McQuillan and Gilmartin both ran up the stairs and into the apartment. They had no backup, nor could they call for any. There was no police radio system. The gunman immediately opened fire with several shots, one of which struck the sergeant in the side of the head alongside his ear. Fortunately he would survive. As the man ran through the apartment PO Bill McQuillan returned fire striking the suspect five times, killing him.

For his actions in the face of imminent danger and bravery under fire, on January 16, 1931 McQuillan was honored by being promoted to Detective 1st Grade, with a $200 increase in salary. Although appointed a detective, upon his own request, he was allowed to remain in the Traffic Division on motorcycle patrol. Several months later on June 10, 1931, following a meeting of the Honor Board, Officer McQuillan was awarded the highest medal the department was authorized to present at that time; the "Honorable Mention." Bill McQuillan continued serving in the Traffic Division on motorcycle duty with the rank of detective for another sixteen years.

After serving nearly his entire career in the Traffic Division, Detective William McQuillan applied for and received retirement from the police department on June 15, 1947 after having served honorably for more than 28 years.

Unfortunately less than two years later, on April 1, 1949, Bill "Mac" McQuillan of 214 Buena Vista Avenue, and one of the departments recognized hero's, died of a heart attack at the age of 55 years.

CAPTAIN PHILIP L. SHERIDAN

Appointed: May 17, 1919
Retired: September 4, 1941

Philip L. Sheridan was born in Middletown N.Y. on January 21, 1892. At some point he relocated to the City of Yonkers where, following his formal education, he was able to gain employment as an elevator mechanic. Probably looking for security in his employment, Sheridan applied to take the test for Yonkers Police Officer. At the time he was 27 years old and lived at 266 Burhans Avenue. Phil Sheridan got his wish and, on May 17, 1919, he was appointed to the police department at the salary of $1,250. per year. Following some rudimentary training he was assigned to foot patrol duties in the 1st precinct.

It was only a few months before he was involved in his first challenge to his new authority. The Yonkers Herald newspaper reported that on September 2, 1919, shortly before midnight, four soldiers from Fort Slocum became involved in a wild fight at a local "saloon." PO Sheridan being nearby heard the disturbance and went to investigate. Observing the disorder Sheridan quickly determined which soldier seemed to be the primary trouble maker and proceeded to place him under arrest. The other three soldiers immediately turned on officer Sheridan; but during the ensuing battle the male that was arrested

Captain Philip L. Sheridan (cont.)

did not escape and was "battered badly about the head" by the officer. After Sheridan sounded the alarm, no doubt with his whistle, other police backup officers responded to his aid and all four soldiers were arrested.

On October 1, 1920 PO Sheridan was transferred from the 1st precinct to motorcycle duty in the Traffic Division; an assignment which would represent a significant portion of his career. On December 14th of that year he was assigned as a motorcycle traffic officer in the 3rd precinct at "Police Booth # 2" located at Valentine Lane and Riverdale Avenue. His assignment was to remain in this booth, which was heated with a coal stove, be available to the public, and be prepared to answer any telephone calls by the precinct desk lieutenant who might send him on an investigation. Not being out on active patrol and just sitting in this booth waiting for something to happen was likely very boring. Apparently, because of this inactivity, on July 12, 1921 Sheridan was observed by a supervisor sitting in the booth with his coat and hat off and playing a game of "Checkers" with another police officer from a nearby post. Of course, both men were brought up on departmental charges for neglect of duty, found guilty, and the sentence was to be reprimanded in front of the entire next roll call.

The following year on May 29, 1922 officer Sheridan was returned to citywide routine traffic patrol duties on his Indian motorcycle. Apparently it was about this time that he became very active in Police Association business and, in 1925 was elected Vice President of the Police Association.

There appears to be no doubt that Phil Sheridan had gained the respect and trust of the members of the department while serving as vice president of the YPA because, following a three member race, PO Philip Sheridan of the Traffic Division won the election as President of the Yonkers Police Association for the year 1926. Of course all duties and responsibilities of his office had to be conducted on his off duty time. President or not, he was not excused from his regularly assigned police duties.

By information available, PO Sheridan was very aggressive in the performance of his traffic duties. On one occasion while working the early tour on June 28, 1928 officer Sheridan observed a vehicle being driven on North Broadway at O'Dell Avenue, and "clocked" him speeding at 40 mph. He sped off after the vehicle on his motorcycle and pulling alongside, activated his siren and ordered the driver to pull the vehicle over to the curb. At this, the driver intentionally swerved his vehicle directly at Sheridan in an attempt to knock him off his "bike" and then sped off north towards the Town of Hastings. Regaining control of his motorcycle and before he lost sight of the fleeing car, Sheridan fired three rounds into the escaping automobile. Determined to find this man Sheridan continued to investigate, located the vehicle in Hastings, and placed the driver under arrest.

Having taken and passed the civil service test for Sergeant and ranking # 2 on the promotional list, PO Sheridan, who lived at 273 Parsons Street, was promoted to the rank of Sergeant effective October 16, 1929. He was subsequently reassigned from the Traffic Division to the 1st precinct as a sergeant on foot patrol.

Five years later on October 10, 1934, and following lengthy research, the police department took a progressive and historic step forward. A police radio communication system was placed in operation for the first time. The unit established to operate this new function was named the Radio and Telegraph

Captain Philip L. Sheridan (cont.)

Division (RTD). This new system allowed for the communication between headquarters and police patrol cars; albeit only one way - from H.Q. to the car. The man chosen as commanding officer of the "RTD" (Radio Telegraph Division), was Sgt. Philip Sheridan who was immediately designated an acting lieutenant. Effective January 1, 1937 Acting Lt. Sheridan was promoted to the permanent rank of police lieutenant with a salary of $4,000. a year. He remained the commanding officer of the RTD.

On December 16, 1939 three men were promoted to the rank of Police Captain. Lt. Sheridan had been # 5 on the captains list. On this day numbers 1 & 2 were promoted, but numbers 3 & 4 on the list were skipped in order to reach Lt Sheridan, who was the 3rd captain to be promoted that day. His annual salary was then raised to $4,500. a year. Captain Sheridan was then reassigned as commanding officer of the 3rd precinct.

Over the years Phil Sheridan had long running problems with severe phlebitis in his right leg and chronic gastritis. Upon a physical examination by the police surgeon Sheridan was found to be physically unfit to perform his police duties and consequently he was retired on a disability pension of $2,250. a year effective September 4, 1941.

Retired Capt. Philip Sheridan moved to North Miami Beach, Florida where he later died on March 15, 1963 at the age of 71 years.

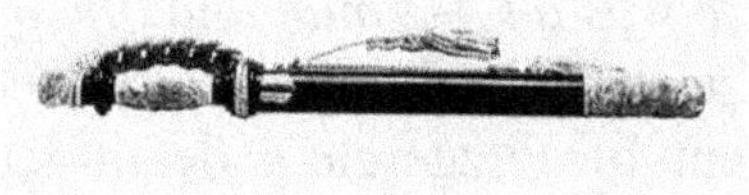

DET. EDWARD F. FITZGERALD # 1

APPOINTED: May 21, 1919
DIED: March 16, 1928

Born Edward Francis Fitzgerald on August 1, 1887 in Yonkers, Ed graduated St Mary's School in 1902. He was employed for 10 years by the New York Central Railroad as a signalman. Following the railroad he worked two years for Otis Elevator Company as a machinist. He even worked as a clerk for a while before joining the Navy on May 29, 1918 during WW 1. He was assigned to the Transport Division and was stationed on supply ships until his discharge on April 26, 1919. Within a month of his discharge he was appointed a police officer on May 21, 1919 at the salary of $2,300. a year, assigned shield # 107, and was assigned foot patrol duty in the 1st precinct on Wells Avenue. Later, for a short while, he was transferred to the Traffic Division but would return to the 1st precinct.

On June 16, 1926 he was promoted to Detective and assigned to the Detective Division with shield # 1. Along with his partner and friend, Det John F. Daly, Fitzgerald gained a reputation of being an excellent detective who made many noteworthy arrests. Because of a natural ability to recognized suspicious persons and activity, he was nicknamed by his coworkers as Eagle Eye. He was said to have been one of the most popular men in the police department and his future held great potential. However, in March of 1928 Fitzgerald became ill with an internal infection and required hospitalization. As his health continued to fail he received a blood transfusion with blood donated by Lt George Ford. As a result his health seemed to improve at least temporarily.

Despite extensive effort by the hospital doctors, on March 16, 1928 Detective Edward Fitzgerald succumbed to Streptococcus poisoning while in St Joseph's hospital and died. It seemed the entire department was shocked by his death. A resolution of regret was even passed by the Police Association and almost every police officer was said to have paid tribute to the detective as being a good cop. Chief Edward Quirk was quoted as saying, "*He was an A-1 man and one of the best detectives ever on the force. I don't know where we will find a man possessing the same excellent qualifications to fill his place*." The General Order notifying the department of Fitzgerald's death read in part,......"his record had been uniformly excellent. He had earned the respect of his associates and the administration of his superiors during his career in the department."

Detective Fitzgerald left behind a wife and a young son, Edward Jr. Many years later during World War 2, his only child Edward Jr. would be killed in 1944 while on a bombing mission over Germany.

The deceased detective had been a member of the LaRabida Council, Knights of Columbus, the Crescent Club, the Yonkers Police War Veterans Legion, and the Police Association . Detective Fitzgerald was laid to rest in the uniform that he wore with such honor and distinction for nearly 10 years. Almost 200 fellow officers in uniform, led by 12 police motorcycles escorted the funeral procession from his home at 10 Hawthorne Avenue. Detective Edward F. Fitzgerald was only 40 years old.

CAPTAIN JOHN J. McCARTHY

APPOINTED: June 2, 1919
DIED: February 19, 1958

According to his family, John Joseph McCarthy was born the son of a New York City police Lieutenant on February 21, 1896 in the City of New York. He came to Yonkers with his family as a youth and attended PS# 10, St. Mary's School, and Yonkers High School. He continued his education by attending the Dwight Institute and then the Woods Business School. It was said of young John that he was an expert stenographer. Following his formal education McCarthy married and had his first child. In May of 1915 he joined the N.Y. National Guard where he served as a Sergeant in Company G, 10th Infantry Regiment until his discharge in June of 1917.

At the age of 23 years McCarthy was working as a house detective at the Waldorf Astoria Hotel in New York City when he was called to be appointed to the Yonkers Police Department. A resident of 90 Radford Street, he was hired on June 2, 1919 with a salary of $2,300 a year, and was issued shield # 108. His first assignment was foot patrol duty in the 1st precinct on Wells Avenue; a relatively typical initial assignment for newly hired rookies.

On January 3, 1921 McCarthy was reassigned to the 2nd precinct with his post being to remain in

Captain John J. McCarthy-3 (cont.)

Police Booth # 1 and be available to citizens in need or to receive direction by phone from the precinct desk lieutenant. Being in the precinct only one month he found himself in trouble by trying to be helpful. On February 24th he had approached a local magistrate regarding a case being prosecuted by another officer. He then proceeded to ask the judge to show leniency to the defendant in that case. Most likely much to officer McCarthy's surprise, his inappropriate request was reported and he was brought up on departmental charges of Conduct Unbecoming an Officer. McCarthy admitted has action, pled guilty, was convicted by the trial commissioner and was fined 5 days pay. A costly lapse in judgment.

The following year, on May 29, 1922, PO McCarthy was transferred from the 2nd precinct to the Traffic Division to serve as their clerk. A move, no doubt, based on his administrative skills learned in school. Two years later he was relieved of his clerk duties and assigned to a traffic post directing vehicular traffic. However in October of 1925 he was returned to patrol duties back in the 2nd precinct.

After placing # 1 on the Sergeant's promotional list, on December 1, 1928 John J. McCarthy was promoted to the rank of Sergeant with shield # 20, and a new salary of $2,800. His new assignment would be as a patrol supervisor in the 3rd precinct.

During this time a very unusual circumstance had existed in the police department. Four police officers had the exact same name, John Joseph McCarthy. The first was hired in 1901, the 2nd in 1913, the 3rd and the subject of this writing in 1919, and seven years later in 1926 the 4th officer with this name was hired. Having four police officers with the same name was causing quite a bit of confusion when General Orders were prepared or when mail for one of them had to be delivered. The solution decided upon to overcome this problem was to identify each McCarthy not only by name but by numbering each of them by seniority from 1 through 4. At that time our subject was identified as McCarthy - 3. But it would not end there. Many years later McCarthy - 3 had a son with the very same name who joined the police department and became McCarthy - 5.

Even though McCarthy had been a sergeant for only a year he became very active in the affairs of the relatively new Captain's, Lieutenant's, & Sergeant's Association, (C.L.S.A.) and at the start of 1929 he was elected the Recording Secretary of the association.

In June of 1932 Sgt McCarthy was reassigned from the 3rd to the 4th precinct. While working that precinct, on January 8, 1934, Sgt McCarthy was instrumental in the arrest of three men wanted in several cities on grand larceny charges utilizing flim flam operations where the victims are duped. At that time Chief Quirk characterized the arrests as one of the best pickups in the history of the department. For his part in this significant arrest Sgt McCarthy was awarded a Certificate of Excellent Police Work by the Police Honor Board.

On April 1, 1936 Sgt McCarthy was promoted again, this time to the rank of Lieutenant at the salary of $4,000. His new area of responsibility would be as a desk lieutenant working in the 3rd precinct. In a local newspaper article announcing his promotion it made mention of the fact that the new lieutenants father, John McCarthy, was an honor lieutenant in the New York City Police Department two decades earlier, and that he was also the nephew of former Yonkers Mayor Michael J. Walsh. During all this time McCarthy continued to maintain his commitment to remain involved in the activities of the C.L.S.A. and in January 1937 he was elected president of this organization. Lt. McCarthy was officially inducted

Captain John J. McCarthy-3 (cont.)

as the C.L.S.A. president at their annual dinner dance which took place in February 1937. More than 600 persons attended the dinner which was held at the Arrowhead Restaurant in Riverdale. It would appear that Lt McCarthy was so effective in his position as president that, in 1940 he was nominated without opposition for a fourth term. Although he was said to have hoped to relinquish the presidency, he agreed to again accept. In fact he continued to be re-elected right up to 1942 when he was promoted to captain. At that time he declined to run for another term and another officer was elected to the presidency of the C.L.S.A. However, despite his years of previous service as the association's president, Captain McCarthy was again elected as it's president for the years 1949 through 1951.

Lt John J. McCarthy, of 121 Elliott Avenue, was promoted to the rank of Captain effective May 1, 1942 with the salary of $ 3,937, and he was assigned as the commanding officer of the 4th precinct. However a few months later in October of 1942 he was placed in command of the 1st precinct. Within one month of his arrival there, possibly to send a message, the captain, with the assistance of his driver made a significant gambling arrest.

In February 1958, Capt. John "Blackjack" or "Lugs" McCarthy, as he was affectionately known, was the commanding officer of the 4th precinct. On February 19, 1958 while at his home at 54 Colgate Avenue sitting watching television, Capt. McCarthy, a veteran of 38 years service, suffered a heart attack and died two days before his 62nd birthday.

Coincidentally, at the beginning of 1958 police employees were given the option to elect to join the Social Security System if they desired. Capt. McCarthy elected to do so. The effective date was March 31, 1958 and contributions would begin then. He never lived to see March and as a consequence his widow was denied Social Security benefits.

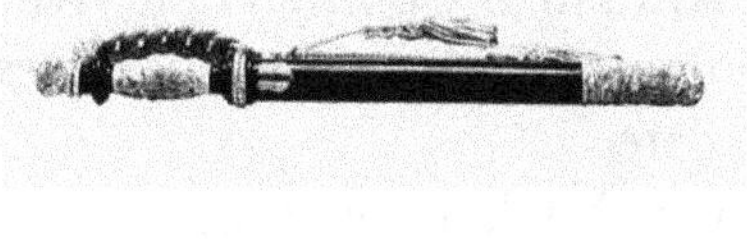

WILLIAM J. COMEY
DEP. PUBLIC SAFETY COMMISSIONER

APPOINTED: May 1, 1920
RETIRED: April 30, 1952

The law enforcement career of William J. Comey is one which most certainly can be categorized as a success story. However, it was also one of the most unusual rises to the leadership of the entire police department that was experienced to that date.

Bill Comey was born in the City of Yonkers on June 16, 1892. He attended and graduated from the St. Joseph's Catholic school system. Not much is known about his early life but it is known that he earned his living as a carpenter. It is fair to assume that like many men at the time, Comey was looking for a decent job that had some degree of security, not to mention a pension. He took the civil service test for police officer, passed and was hired May 1, 1920 at the salary of $1,500. per year. He was then sent for a short time to the NYC Police Department's School of Instruction on law enforcement subjects where he would hopefully learn the basics of police work. When he returned he was assigned to the 1st precinct on Wells Avenue.

Deputy Public Safety Commissioner William J. Comey (cont.)

His precinct stay would be short, for only a little more than two months from his appointment, and with his three month probation period not yet completed, rookie police officer Bill Comey was transferred to the Traffic Division on July 16, 1920. He was assigned to various intersections on foot to direct the flow of vehicular traffic. Like everyone else he worked six days a week, but in the Traffic Division you were only required to work the Day and Early Tour. You were not required to work any late tours. This working schedule by itself was a benefit most officers felt lucky to enjoy. However, on traffic detail you were required to spend nearly your entire tour standing in the street, regardless of weather conditions, directing traffic.

Comey's first taste of notoriety came on January 9, 1922 when then Public Safety Commissioner Tobin publicly commended officer Comey for his heroic action in stopping a runaway horse. Commissioner Tobin had received a letter signed by several citizens relating that while PO Comey was on his traffic post at South Broadway and McLean Avenue, an unattended runaway horse pulling a milk wagon came racing southbound and right toward a trolley. The letter further related that Comey threw his arms around the horses head as it sped by him, and directed it away from the trolley car. However in doing so the horse dragged Comey from McLean Avenue to Ludlow Street before he succeeded in bringing the animal to a stop. Fortunately neither the officer nor any bystanders were injured during the episode.

In 1924 PO Comey was working as a patrol officer in the 3rd precinct and at the time south Yonkers residents were praising the efficiency and dedication to duty of all the men assigned to that station house. In fact on January 16, 1925 it was reported that Comey was again commended, this time by Public Safety Commissioner Alfred Iles, for Comey's keen observation and participation in the arrest of a burglar that had been operating in that precinct.

On January 16, 1926, PO Comey was elevated to the position of Detective in the Detective Bureau. One can only assume that this new assignment was due to the excellent police work performed by the officer. As time passed Det Comey arrested his share of criminals. However there are few things more satisfying to a police officer than when he arrests a person for a sexual assault on a child. And on August 29, 1927, following his investigation, Det Comey located and arrested a 22 year old male for sexually assaulting an 8 year old girl. The child picked the male out of a line up and later though some questioning was necessary, the man confessed.

It was on September 6, 1930 that Det Bill Comey received his first promotion; that being to the position of Sergeant. As was customary he was required to relinquish his detective status and was reassigned to the 1st precinct on Wells Avenue as a patrol supervisor.

It was in this same year that the economy of the country was such that unemployment was extremely high and people in need of basic necessities seemed to be everywhere. In an effort to help those Yonkers citizens who were in need, on November 19, 1930 the Police Association formed the Relief Committee of the Yonkers Police Department consisting of all volunteers. Its purpose was to collect donated items and distribute them to the needy. Sgt. Bill Comey was named Relief Committee Chairman. He was assisted by 34 other police officers on the committee. Following the Christmas holidays, on January 6, 1931 chairman Comey reported to the Police Association that more than two thousand Yonkers

Deputy Public Safety Commissioner William J. Comey (cont.)

individuals who were in need were supplied with food and clothing donated by police officers and local businesses. The programs success was a tribute to Sgt Comey's hard work and organizational skills.
Bill Comey's volunteer work never interfered with his police responsibilities though. In June of 1932 he was awarded a Certificate of Excellent Police Work for tracking a purse snatcher to the NY Central Railroad tracks and making the arrest. Still, new challenges were in store for Sgt Bill Comey.

On October 10, 1934 the police department put in service a state of the art communications system which, for the first time, would allow headquarters to transmit a call from headquarters out to police cars on patrol with new one way radios. To organize and maintain this operation the Radio Telegraph Division (RTD) was established and Sgt Comey was one of the officers transferred to this new Division. Comey was designated an Acting Lieutenant and served as a radio dispatcher.

On January 20, 1936, Bill Comey was officially promoted to the rank of Lieutenant with a salary of $4,000 per year, and he was transferred to the 1st precinct as a Desk Lieutenant. Lt. Comey continued his involvement in a variety of police programs. One example, on April 20, 1936, as the President of the Police Holy Name Society, he led more than 250 police officers and guests in a march into the society's church mass and breakfast. Upon the retirement of the 1st precinct captain, on September 1, 1936 Lt. Comey was designated Acting Captain and commanding officer of the 1st precinct.

Following ongoing complaints about gambling operating openly in Yonkers, on October 20, 1944 Lt Comey was transferred to the Detective Bureau as it's commanding officer. Det Lt. Comey was not unfamiliar with the operations of the Detective Division since he had served as a detective for nearly five years earlier in his career. And he wasted no time in closing down several gambling operations in town, making Public Safety Commissioner Patrick O'Hara very pleased that he had chosen Comey to head the Bureau. On March 5, 1947, directly after Chief William Kruppenbacher retired, Comey was designated by Commissioner O'Hara in an order he issued as his aide with full authority to represent him in the operations of all business in the police chief's office. Det Lt. Comey moved into the former chief's office to take command of the department as he was ordered to do. All orders prepared by Comey were initially signed, Officer in Charge – Chief's Office. Although almost everyone in the police department expected one of the department's captains to be named as the next Chief of Police, it was not to be. Commissioner O'Hara felt that Bill Comey was preeminently qualified, as he put it, to run the department based on his past experience, even though he wasn't a captain. This was certainly not the opinion of some of the current police captains. But, in fact, had it not been for the Veterans Preference Law which went into effect in January of that same year, a bill whereby veterans had absolute preference in promotions and were hired ahead of non-veterans regardless of position of the civil service list, Det Lt Comey, who was # 1 on the Police Captains promotion list, would have been promoted to captain. Instead he was repeatedly skipped over due to the new law and his non veteran status.

Holding the rank of captain or not it was clear that Bill Comey was considered by Commissioner O'Hara as extremely trustworthy, competent, possessing integrity beyond reproach, and in his mind, the only man for the job. The commissioner's opinion was solidified by the Common Council when on July 1, 1947 they voted to create the new position of Deputy Public Safety Commissioner and officially designated Bill Comey to fill that position as the official leader of the police department with a salary of

Deputy Public Safety Commissioner William J. Comey (cont.)

$6,000. per year. Comey was allowed to retain his civil service rank of Detective Lieutenant and was given an immediate leave of absence to begin his new assignment. Each year while he was on vacation an order was issued reverting Comey back to Detective Lieutenant. When his vacation ended, another order was issued granting Comey another leave of absence to fill the Deputy Commissioners job. This was done so that Bill Comey would not lose his civil service status. There were no plans at that time to fill the position of Chief of Police.

Commissioner Comey's duties were outlined in writing as follows; The Deputy Commissioner shall have the authority to take oaths and administer evidence, affidavits and acknowledgements in all matters and proceedings pertaining to the department. He shall have general supervision over the records of the department and it's officers, and shall perform such other duties as may be prescribed by the Commissioner or by law, or by ordinance of the Common Council. It was further stated that until a Chief of Police was appointed, Dep. Comm. Comey would assume all those duties and responsibilities. Fortunately Comey's appointment was warmly received by the news media who had a great deal of respect for him.

After taking the oath of office Commissioner Comey announced several recommended changes in the department. Two of many were, to establish a police Property Clerk Unit for the storage and cataloging of all evidence and property and, to have every police officer photographed for their personnel files. An old practice that, for some reason, had not been followed for some time.

Bill Comey remained the Deputy Public Safety Commissioner under Commissioner Patrick O'Hara until January of 1952. It was then that a Democratic administration came into power and it was reported that Commissioner O'Hara would be replaced. Dep. Comm. Comey let it be known that when that happened he would submit his request for retirement.

On April 30, 1952, Deputy Public Safety Commissioner William Comey, leader of the Police Department, retired from all police service. Following his retirement he held several jobs in private business including managing a Boy's Home and working for an advertising firm in New York City.

After moving to New Jersey, William J. Comey died on May 28, 1976 in a Montvale N.J. nursing home. He was 83 years of age. Although he certainly would have been very proud, he would never know that in 2013, his grandson James Comey would be appointed the Director of the Federal Bureau of Investigation.

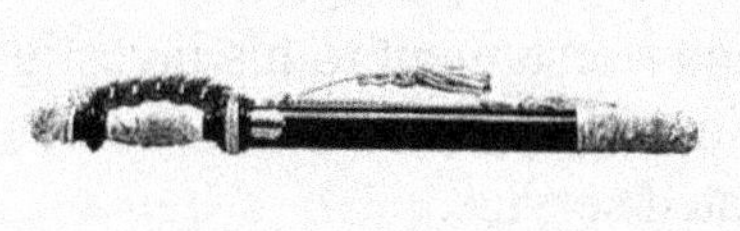

DET. JOHN F. DALY # 9

APPOINTED: May 1, 1920
RETIRED: June 1, 1951

John Francis Daly was born in the City of Yonkers on August 29, 1889. While attending St Mary's School one of his classmates was a boy named Ed Fitzgerald. Prior to joining the police department Daly listed his employment as that of a "Clerk." Upon his appointment to the department he was assigned shield # 109 and to foot patrol duty in the 1st precinct on Wells Avenue. And while walking his post, who was the officer very often walking the adjoining post? His former classmate and friend, PO Ed Fitzgerald. All indications are that John Daly was an aggressive officer, an example of which occurred on April 2, 1926.

On that night at about 11:40 PM Daly was just leaving his home at 46 Herriot Street to report for duty on the late tour. As he did he noticed two men with their hands in the air on the corner of Herriot and Caroline Avenue who were about to be robbed at gunpoint by three males. Officer Daly vaulted over a low fence in his front yard, drew his revolver and ran toward the holdup in progress. As he did, the suspects spotted him running toward them, jumped in their stolen vehicle and sped west on Herriot toward Riverdale Avenue. PO Daly fired one round which shattered the windshield of the car, which was later found abandoned and was recovered. The escape was successful but the robbery was not.

As a result of his actions that evening, on April 26, 1926 PO John F. Daly was awarded the Honorable Mention, the highest police department medal that could be awarded at that time. The award was presented for his bravery in thwarting a holdup. Apparently, based on his past performance along with this recent award, on June 16, 1926 officer Daly was assigned as a Detective in the Detective Bureau with a salary increase of $200. a year. There was only one grade of detective at that time. Ironically, Det Daly was happy to learn that his friend PO Ed Fitzgerald was also elevated to the position of detective on the same day as Daly was. In fact he and Fitzgerald would often work as partners on several high profile cases. It was the beginning of one of the most successful teams of detectives in the police department.

In the beginning of September of 1934 the Detective Bureau received information that a man wanted for the execution style murder of a Philadelphia police officer was hiding in a Yonkers hotel room. On September 6, 1934 Detective Daly, along with several other members of the Detective Bureau, broke into the hotel room, found the suspect and placed him under arrest on the Philadelphia police warrant for murder. It took two years but, on May 23, 1936 Det. Daly was once again awarded the Honorable Mention for his actions in arresting the murder suspect two years earlier. Detective Daly would remain in the Detective Division for 25 consecutive years, despite several changes in political administrations. Quite an accomplishment at that time and a testament to his investigative skills. Over the years he arrested scores of criminals for every type of crime including several murder arrests. He would retire as a detective on June 1, 1951 after 31 years of dedicated service.

Following his retirement John F. Daly moved from his home at 21 Crotty Avenue to Florida. After 31 years of facing danger on a regular basis, on February 5, 1954, John Daly was struck and killed by a car while crossing the street in Hialeah, Florida, the town where he lived. He was 64 years old and retired for only three years.

PO JOSEPH J. CONDON

APPOINTED: May 5, 1920
DISMISSED: July 27, 1925

Despite hopes to make a career with the police department, Condon's tenure would be relatively short. He was born November 28, 1895 in New York City. Following school and miscellaneous jobs he was appointed a police officer on May 5, 1920 and trained at the NYC School of Instruction. Upon graduation he was assigned to the 1st precinct. It wasn't long when, on May 20, 1921, Condon was charged with failing to arrest two intoxicated males. On July 7, 1921 he was found guilty of Neglect of Duty but only reprimanded in front his next roll call. On August 25, 1924 he was reassigned to the Traffic Division, motorcycle duty. But in November of the same year he was returned to patrol in the 4th precinct and resigned in anger but was reinstated a few days later. Then, on July 27, 1925 Condon was charged with being AWOL for 9 straight days. He was notified to appear for a hearing but failed to appear. As per the Rules & Regulations he was automatically deemed dismissed July 27, 1925.

DET. ALEXANDER P. PROGNER # 13

APPOINTED: May 10, 1920
DIED: August 27, 1930

Born in Hungary on February 3, 1886 Al Progner came to America in 1889 and attended local schools. He was naturalized as a citizen in February of 1910. A resident of 41 Ball Avenue, Progner was married with 6 children and worked as a carpenter and foreman with the N.Y. Central Railroad. Al Progner was hired to the police department on May 10, 1920 at the age of 34 years, bringing with him the ability to speak German, Polish, Russian, and of course English. He was originally assigned to foot patrol in the 4th precinct. But after working there for seven years he was elevated to the position of Detective on December 12, 1927. For the next three years Det Progner made a name for himself as being an excellent investigator. However, in the summer of 1930 he was said to have developed an intestinal infection. The problem would not leave and following surgery on August 27, 1930, Det. Alex Progner died from complications. He was accorded full departmental honors including an escort of 8 motorcycles from his 70 Burhans Ave. home. He was only 44 years old.

LIEUTENANT HAROLD A. SHEEKY

APPOINTED: May 18, 1920
RETIRED: May 29, 1958

"Hal" Sheeky, as he was known to his friends, was born and raised in the City of Yonkers. His date of birth was May 30, 1893 and his formal education was provided by St Mary's Parochial School. Sheeky served in the US Army from May of 1918 through April of 1919 as a Master Sergeant in the (AEF) American Expeditionary Force, 302nd Engineers in France. Two of his earlier employers were the Cunard Steamship Company where he worked as a clerk, and he also was a foreman with the Habirshaw Cable Co. in Yonkers. When he was in his youth his favorite pastime was playing baseball.

Appointment to the police department on May 18, 1920 he received his initial training at the 1st precinct and was then assigned to foot patrol in the 3rd precinct. With only a short time on the job Sheeky's life would soon be put in danger and only fate would step in to save him. On April 3, 1922, and while on foot patrol, PO Sheeky attempted to stop and question a suspicious man. As he did, the man drew a revolver and fired point blank at Sheeky. Too close to miss, the bullet fortunately struck Sheeky's nightstick which he held right in front of his body, ricochet off and tore through the officers coat. Incredibly, it was reported that the bullet came to rest in the officers uniform coat pocket. However, the impact of the round against the stick caused it to strike the officer in the stomach, temporarily stunning him. He recovered in only a moment and gave chase, but this short moment gave the shooter the chance to escape capture. In May of 1924 when a large group of men were designated to be part of a new "Riot" squad, Sheeky was one of those named and trained in special tactics.

Lieutenant Harold A. Sheeky (cont.)

It would seem reasonable to assume that Harold Sheeky was a popular and well liked member of the police department since he was elected president of the Police Association in 1924 and again in 1925. Among his many duties and responsibilities, it was reported that Sheeky really enjoyed playing Santa Claus during the yearly Police Association Christmas party for local underprivileged children.

Still with the love of baseball in his heart, in 1928 "Hal" Sheeky was the pitcher for the Police Association's team as they competed with various other baseball leagues. Yet, his sporting interest never stopped him from performing his police duties efficiently. On October 1, 1929 PO Sheeky arrested a man for murder and as a result was awarded the departmental Honorable Mention award.

At one point officer Sheeky was assigned to the Traffic Division on motorcycle patrol; an assignment, it was said, that he thoroughly enjoyed. On January 8, 1936 a local newspaper reported that the Yonkers Police War Veterans' Association had held nominations for a new Commander. Harold Sheeky, who had served as the organizations first Commander since its formation seven (7) years earlier in 1929, had decided not to run for office again and to allow another war veteran to be elected Commander.

After several years in his Traffic Division assignment, he was promoted to the rank of Sergeant on April 1, 1936. His promotion resulted in his reassignment from motorcycle duty to patrol supervisor duties in the 3rd precinct. On February 1, 1942 he was again promoted, this time to the rank of Lieutenant. He remained in the 3rd precinct as a desk lieutenant.

Again displaying a keen interest in the welfare of the police officers, Lt Harold Sheeky was elected to three (3) terms as the president of the Captains, Lieutenants, and Sergeants Association from 1945 to 1947. And throughout most of his career he worked during the same years that his brother Police Officer Joseph Sheeky did.

Following his retirement on May 29, 1958 Lt Harold Sheeky died on July 31, 1967 following a long illness. He was 74 years of age.

PO GEORGE H. McGRATH # 113

APPOINTED: May 10, 1920
RETIRED: March 15, 1949

Born George Henry McGrath on November 9, 1897 in Yonkers, McGrath graduated from St Joseph's parochial school and later PS# 9. At the age of 20 he enlisted in the Naval Reserve during the "Great War" serving briefly from June 8, 1918 to February 18, 1919. Following his discharge he worked with the Yonkers Railroad Co. He was 23 and living on St Joseph's Avenue when he was appointed a police officer on May 10, 1920. And having his father, PO Mike McGrath, also in the department, it was said they were the first father and son to serve at the same time. Immediately upon his appointment he was assigned to the Traffic Division on motorcycle, even though he had to be sent to school to learn how to ride. Sometime later he worked patrol in the 4th precinct and in May 1924 was trained as a member of the Police Riot Squad. McGrath retired March 15, 1949 from the 4th precinct on a pension of $1,650. per year. Married with no children and living at 86 Convent Avenue, George H. McGrath died on February 4, 1954 at the age of 56.

PO THOMAS J. CONDON # 106

APPOINTED: June 15, 1920
RETIRED: December 31, 1923

Thomas Joseph Condon was born in Yonkers on August 27, 1893 and attended St Mary's School and Yonkers H.S. An electrician by trade he was 23 years old when the police department hired him on June 15, 1920. He was assigned to motorcycle patrol in the 1st precinct until August 14, 1921 when he was assigned to the Traffic Division performing citywide motorcycle patrol. On December 7, 1921 Condon was reassigned to foot patrol in the 1st precinct. The next month, on January 14, 1922 he was sent to Traffic, but on foot. Apparently prior to December 1921 Condon had a serious accident on his motorcycle. His daughter in law stated that while on duty he "crashed" into a wall. This would explain his move to foot patrol. On December 28, 1923 two doctors wrote to the department stating he was physically unfit for duty and that due to head and brain injuries he would never be fit for police duty. Condon retired on a disability pension on Dec. 31, 1923. Prior to his death on August 3, 1967 at age 73, Condon worked security at Yonkers Raceway for 12 years. His grandson Patrick would join the NYPD, and Condon's brother was State Senator Condon.

PO EDWARD J. FITZGERALD # 116

APPOINTED: October 7, 1920
RETIRED: March 1, 1949

Edward Joseph Fitzgerald was born in New York City on September 3, 1896. After arriving in Yonkers with his family he gained employment as an electrician "Lineman" with the Westchester Lighting Co. and later the N.Y. Telephone Co. At 18 years of age he joined the Army on July 9, 1918 and served during the war as a Private in the 212th Engineers until his discharge on March 15, 1919. Upon his appointment to the department on October 7, 1920 he was assigned to the 2nd precinct. On January 9, 1922 he was moved to the Traffic Division directing traffic. But on May 18, 1925 he went from foot to motorcycle duty. He returned to the 2nd precinct on March 2, 1928. As a member of the Police War Veterans Legion he would always carry the flag in the color guard. Fitzgerald retired from the 2nd precinct on March 1, 1949 having served 29 years of faithful and loyal service. In 1962 Ed Fitzgerald moved to California. It was in Torrance, Cal. on October 20, 1979 that he died of cardiac arrest.

PO VERNON DUBOIS # 119

APPOINTED: January 16, 1921
RETIRED: August 1, 1930

Vernon DuBois was born in Danville N.Y. on September 22, 1888. Very little is known of his early years but after his arrival in Yonkers he made his living as a Milkman with a horse and wagon. He was also a licensed chauffeur. Residing at 18 Ravine Avenue, Dubois was appointed a police officer on Jan. 16, 1921 at the age of 32 years with a salary of $1,600. per year. Dubois' first, and only, assignment was to the 3rd precinct at 36 Radford Street where he would often direct traffic at McLean Ave. and South Broadway. Little more can be found about PO Dubois' nine year police career, but there is also nothing to indicate that he was anything less than a loyal and dedicated police officer. Following a physical examination by the police surgeon, it was determined that he had Multiple Sclerosis and was retired on a disability pension on Aug. 1, 1930. When he retired he lived at 375 South Broadway, and in 1936 he lived at 4 Cornell Avenue. At one point he lived with one of his two children in Carmel, NY. He died on February 11, 1959 in St. Barnabas Hospital, E. 183rd St., NYC, at 70 years of age.

PO JOHN PATRICK RYAN # 181

APPOINTED: October 8, 1920
DIED: January 18, 1934

John Patrick Ryan was born in the Town of Tarrytown N.Y. on February 3, 1894. He grew up there and as a youth attended Tarrytown's local schools. It is believed that somewhere around his teenage years his family moved to Yonkers. According to police departmental records John joined the US Navy on his birthday, February 3, 1912, and served aboard the battleship USS Georgia. John Ryan's mother, who was confined to a wheelchair, needed her son home to help with the family so, according to his son John P. Ryan Jr. his mother was allowed to "buy" the remainder of his service time from the government so that he could receive an early release. John Ryan Sr. was reportedly discharged from the Navy, again on his birthday, February 3, 1915.

Ryan gained employment with the Sheffield Farms Milk Co. of 80 Woodworth Avenue and was in charge of taking care of the large number of horses maintained by the company to pull the milk wagons. He must have been a natural working with horses and gained a great deal of experience dealing with these animals. At that same time World War 1 was being fought in Europe and the military had a great need for horses for American troops. Another son Thomas related that about that same time the ASPCA was looking for someone who could handle large numbers of horses in preparation for their being shipped off to Europe for the war effort. Apparently it was then that John Ryan left Sheffield Farms and took this job which involved being the "handler" of these large numbers of horses which were gathered in the grassy area then known as "Pechams Lake," a portion of which is now Tibbetts Brook Park. The animals were then removed by train in Dunwoodie to be shipped to the war in Europe.

PO John P. Ryan (cont.)

Like most men at that time Ryan must have been looking for a job with some security so he took the police test, passed it, and at the age of 26 years, was appointed a police officer with the salary of $1500. per year. Following his initial training he was assigned to foot patrol duties in the 1st precinct on Wells Avenue. Because of some unknown reason John Ryan, upon his own request, resigned from the police department on August 31, 1921. However, he was allowed to be reinstated nearly two years later on June 5, 1923. On October 1, 1924 he was transferred from the 1st to horseback mounted patrol duty in the 2nd precinct. With his background with horses this was probably welcome duty. However on September 2, 1925 he was reassigned to routine patrol in the 3rd precinct on Radford Street. On January 7, 1926 PO Ryan was said to have been responsible for saving the lives of a family of 10 who were all nearly overcome when their father attempted suicide by opening up a gas line in his apartment. John Ryan resuscitated the man and by alerting the rest of the family, probably saved their lives. Later he was awarded a departmental Commendation by the Honor Board for his quick action.

Ryan was again moved on February 23, 1926, this time to the Traffic Division, directing traffic. However a great portion of that time he spent detailed to the Police Repair Shop. According to his son Thomas, this was about the time he developed stomach ulcers. Three years later on July 2, 1929 he was transferred to the 4th precinct for patrol duty. Only 3 months later on October 22nd at about 1:45AM officer Ryan was credited with arresting the "Screen Burglar" at gunpoint. The prisoner was found to have a revolver in his pocket. According to his son John Jr, his father also spent some time being assigned to a Police Boat which was maintained at the river at the time. No further information is available on this assignment.

A resident of 23 Gunther Avenue, officer Ryan had 8 children to take care of at the time; 7 boys and 1 girl. But his stomach ulcers became problematic so he entered St John's hospital for surgery to repair the problem. And, according to his son Thomas, he was given the wrong tray of food to eat which developed complications. Three weeks later on January 18, 1934 Police Officer John Patrick Ryan died in the hospital of peritonitis. He was 39 years old. His eldest son John Jr, at about 16 years of age, became the main financial support of the family.

At the funeral at his sister's house at 508 Warburton Avenue, a delegation of over 50 police officers lined the street in a final tribute to their fellow officer and 4th precinct trustee. The Police War Veterans Association, of which he was a member, provided the honor guard and firing squad. Officer Ryan's death was a great loss to the Yonkers Police Department but it was nothing compared to that which his widow and eight children suffered. Unfortunately officer Ryan would never have the satisfaction to know that three of his sons, William, Edward and Thomas would also become Yonkers police officers many years later.

PO JOHN A. DZURENDA # 120

APPOINTED: March 1, 1921
RETIRED: August 31, 1947

John Dzurenda was born to Slovakian immigrants on July 31, 1890 in Ashley, PA. At the age of five years, he and his family returned to Slovakia as his father had to serve in the Slovak military. They returned from Europe and settled in the "Hollow" section of Yonkers at 24 Mulberry Street when John was about 10 years old. It is believed that he attended the Holy Trinity School system and spent a few years at St Andrews University. As a young man John worked as a "Loom Fixer" in the Alexander Smith Carpet Factory up to his appointment to the police department.

Upon being hired as a police officer om March 1, 1921 he was assigned to the 1st precinct on foot patrol and his ability to speak 5 languages was certainly an asset. He spent a few years in the Traffic Division before being assigned to the 4th precinct where he would work for many years. At one point he moved to # 7 Cypress Street where he would remain for a while. PO Dzurenda was commended for bravery by the Public Safety Commissioner when, on November 12, 1925 at 4:30 AM, he ran into a burning smoke filled building and led two trapped women from the 3rd floor to safety. Dzurenda never considered himself a great athlete but was always interested in sports. In October of 1926 he even participated in a citywide sporting competition, competing in the sprint races and the tug of war.

John Dzurenda was an affable and friendly individual, a man of strong religious convictions, and one who was well liked by his peers as well as the public at large. However, physical ailments began to plague him. Following an examination by the police surgeon officer Dzurenda was found to be physically unable to perform his duties, the reasons listed being very ambiguous, and he was retired from the 3rd precinct on August 31, 1947 on a disability pension of $1,500. a year. According to his son Frank, shortly after his father's retirement in 1947, his father consulted a cardiologist and learned that over a period of several years working as a police officer he had suffered seven heart attacks. At that point, the real reason for officer Dzurenda's recurring illnesses and ultimate disability became clear. A short time after the 2nd World War had ended, it was said that John Dzurenda worked in a factory in Yonkers producing parts for the manufacture of Russian tanks. This, despite the cold war tension that arose between the USA and the USSR, following the war.

During his free time Dzurenda liked to busy his hands by threading Rosary Beads and similar small items as well as being excellent at the unusual skill of knitting and crocheting. He was a member of the Police Glee Club, the Police Holy Name Society, Knights of Columbus, the PBA, and he was a devoted member of the "Jednota," an international Slovak Catholic League. Retired officer Dzurenda moved from Yonkers to West Hartford, Connecticut in August of 1957 about the same time as his son Frank. He had two grandsons who were Trumbull Connecticut police officers, and a third who was the Assistant Warden in the Connecticut State Correction System.

On May 9, 1968 while driving to church, as he and his wife did every day, he suffered cardiac arrest, crashed his vehicle and died. John Dzurenda was 77 years of age.

LIEUTENANT HENRY F. MURPHY

APPOINTED: March 1, 1921
RETIRED: March 31, 1950

Henry Murphy was once referred to by the Yonkers Herald Statesman as one of the outstanding police officers in the department. He was born in Baltimore Maryland on June 11, 1892. Following his arrival in Yonkers he gained employment as a chauffeur and funeral director.

He was appointed to the police department on March 1, 1921 at the age of 29 and began his police career by being assigned to foot patrol in the 3rd precinct. In May of 1924 a large number of men were selected from throughout the precincts to be trained and made part of a newly established Riot Squad. These men would only be called to service in times of great emergency. PO Henry Murphy was one of those trained and ready. Murphy remained in the 3rd precinct for 3 years when, on August 21, 1924, he was appointed a Detective in the Detective Bureau. He carried shield # 8. As time went on he apparently proved his value to the leaders of the police department because, on May 19, 1926, he was detailed to work in the Public Safety Commissioners office, retaining his detective status.

On August 1, 1927 Det. Murphy was promoted to Detective Sergeant. He was then assigned to the "Headquarters Division" which enabled then Chief Quirk to utilize Sgt Murphy, his close and trusted subordinate, on special and undercover assignments. It seemed that if the chief wanted an investigation to remain confidential, he would have Henry Murphy handle it and then report directly to him. Later Murphy would again return back to his regular duties in the Detective Division. It was on June 20, 1932 that the sergeant and a few detectives stopped an attempted robbery in progress and recovered a loaded .38 caliber

Lieutenant Henry F. Murphy (cont.)

revolver that the suspect reportedly threatened Murphy with. And in October of 1933 Sgt Murphy was awarded a Certificate of Excellent Police Work for his investigation of a kidnapping case.

On September 6, 1934 it was reported that Det Sgt Henry Murphy, along with some other detectives, arrested a man at the Plaza Hotel, then located at 3 Hawthorne Avenue, who had been wanted for only a few days in the murder of a police officer in Philadelphia, Pennsylvania. The suspect, who while in custody confessed to killing the officer, was found guilty and was later executed by electrocution.

On May 16, 1936 Henry Murphy was promoted to the rank of Lieutenant. At his promotion ceremony the Public Safety Commissioner presented him with a gold watch from the members of the Detective Division as a token of the esteem in which he was held by them. Lt. Murphy, who had been a long time confidential aide to Chief Quirk, was then reassigned to desk duty in the 2nd precinct. Only a few days following his promotion to Lieutenant, the department Honor Board awarded Murphy with the "Honorable Mention" citation for his part in the arrest of the man who killed the Pennsylvania police officer.

Lt Murphy, Capt. George Ford, and Capt. John Beary were all brothers in law. Murphy and Ford had married the sisters of Capt. Beary. What followed was an interesting and ironic turn of events. Murphy had been promoted to lieutenant on the same day that his brother in law Beary was promoted to captain. And now, on July 21, 1939, the day Murphy's other brother in law, Det Capt. Ford retired, Lt Murphy was returned to the Detective Division as an Acting Captain to replace Capt. Ford and he would now be the division's commanding officer. He remained in this assignment until December 16, 1939 when he was returned to Chief Quirks office again.

Events were about to occur that would change Det Lt Henry Murphy's future in the department. Chief Quirk died in 1940 and was replaced by a new chief, William Kruppenbacher, who almost immediately transferred Lt Murphy to the 2nd precinct with a $200. loss of his detective stipend. This was the fate of the man who many prominent citizens recommended to be the new police chief.

On May 16, 1943 Lt Henry Murphy was transferred from the 2nd precinct to the 3rd; the location where his career began and where it would end.

Following his retirement on March 31, 1950 it was noted that Lt Henry Murphy had spent 19 years of his career with the title of detective in various ranks. It was reported that he was cited 4 times by the departments Honor Board for his bravery and excellence in police work. Why had this man not advanced to the rank of Captain? By 1949 he had been passed over twice on the civil service list for Captain due to the "Veteran's Preference" law, whereby veterans were promoted ahead of non-veterans, regardless of their position on the civil service list.

Former police Lieutenant Henry Murphy, 63 years of age, died of cardiac arrest on July 11, 1955 at his home at 426 Park Hill Avenue.

PO WILLIAM CONLIN # 121

APPOINTED: March 1, 1921
DIED: August 23, 1929

Bill Conlin was born July 1, 1893 in Yonkers N.Y. and received his formal education from the Sacred Heart Catholic School. Conlin was working as a salesman when he was appointed to the police department on March 1, 1921. Following some brief training he was assigned to the 3rd precinct for patrol duties until 1928 when he was reassigned to the 4th precinct. Known to his friends as "Stretch," Conlin was very active playing on the Police Association's baseball team. A resident of 23 Jefferson Street, officer Conlin became ill and entered Yonkers General Hospital on May 30, 1929. Unfortunately he was diagnosed with encephalitis of the brain. Although he never lost consciousness his condition worsened. The police association assumed all the expenses for a private room and special nurses but despite the doctors best efforts, police officer Bill "Stretch" Conlin died on August 23, 1929 at the age of 37 years. He left behind a wife, two small children, and his brother, police officer Richard Conlin of the 3rd precinct.

PO WILLIAM O. LaDUE # 36

APPOINTED: June 17, 1921
DIED: February 9, 1942

Born in Beacon New York on June 24, 1895 LaDue came to Yonkers as a child and attended PS # 2. and later worked as a chauffeur. During World War 1 Bill served in the Army's102nd Engineers, A.E.F., from April 17, 1917 to August 26, 1919. Following his police appointment on June 17, 1921 he was assigned to the 3rd precinct. Having been assigned to motorcycle duty in 1924, he was seriously injured on his motorcycle on October 13, 1925. These injuries resulted in him leaving the department on July 14, 1926. However after a lengthy legal fight, LaDue was reinstated December 24, 1929. In January of 1930 officer LaDue was trained and assigned to the newly organized Emergency Squad. On July 9, 1938 PO LaDue was awarded a commendation for rescuing two people who had crashed their vehicle into a gas station causing a fire that burned LaDue's hands. LaDue, who held the Marine pilot's license for all navigable waters was also an ardent deep sea fisherman and swimmer. PO Bill LaDue would became ill and died Feb. 9, 1942 from pneumonia at the age of 46 years.

LT. JOHN R. KILPATRICK

APPOINTED: October 24, 1921
RETIRED: July 31, 1950

Standing 6 feet plus and over 200 lbs., Kilpatrick must have been an imposing figure. Born in Yonkers on August 21, 1898, he attended local schools and earned his living as a clerk. During WW-1 Kilpatrick served in the Navy from June 1918 to February 1919. Following his police appointment on October 24, 1921 he was assigned to work in the 1st pct. on Wells Avenue. However, on May 29, 1922 he was reassigned to traffic duty at various intersections. In May of 1924 he was one of many trained to be part of the Police Riot Squad and on May 18, 1925 he was elevated to detective status working in the Detective Bureau and the Public Safety Commissioners office. During his 8 years as a detective he received no extra compensation. He was promoted to Sergeant on January 1, 1933 and to Lieutenant on April 16, 1939, serving as a desk officer various in patrol precincts. In 1940 Kilpatrick organized the St George Society, a Protestant fraternal group, and in 1949 he was elected president of the Capt's, Lt's, & Sgt's Association. Having retired on July 31, 1950 and after 38 years in retirement, John Kilpatrick died on February 9, 1988. He was 88 years old.

PO THOMAS P. SLATTERY # 124

APPOINTED: October 24, 1921
RESIGNED: June 22, 1926

Having been born in Ireland on April 30, 1899, immigrating to America, and attending local schools, Tom Slattery earned his living as a clerk. During World War 1 he served in the Navy from September 8, 1918 to February 17, 1919. On October 24, 1921 he was appointed a police officer and assigned to precinct patrol duties. Three years later, on August 25, 1924, Tom was reassigned to work the Traffic detail which enabled him to avoid the late tour, which apparently did not agree with him. A year later on May 26, 1925 Slattery was returned to patrol, including on the late tour, in the 4th precinct. It wasn't long before his troubles began. On April 26, 1926, following departmental charges for sleeping on duty, he was fined 15 days pay. Two months later, on June 22, 1926, he was again charged with sleeping on duty. However, when he was notified, he and his wife met with the Safety Commissioner and Slattery requested he be allowed to resign. His resignation was accepted effective June 22, 1926.

CAPTAIN JAMES A. HOLLIS

APPOINTED: December 28, 1921
RETIRED: November 16, 1960

Jim Hollis was born in the city of Yonkers on June 16, 1896 and attended local schools. As he reached the age of 20 years, the war in Europe was raging and when America joined the European allies in their fight against Germany, Hollis wanted to be a part of the action. So, on April 11, 1917 he joined the Army, serving in Europe as a private in the 105th Field Artillery as part of the American Expeditionary Force (AEF). He was honorably discharged on April 3, 1919. After his return home he held a few odd jobs including that of a chauffeur, but his real interest was in becoming a police officer. He took and passed all the required exams for this position and on December 28, 1921 he received a slightly late Christmas present; he was appointed a Yonkers police officer and assigned shield # 127. Following a brief period of some basic police training at the 1st precinct, PO Hollis was assigned to foot patrol duties in the 3rd precinct.

As best as it can be determined, his first few years in the department were relatively routine and unremarkable. That is, until three days before Christmas on December 23, 1924. On this evening it was a cold winter night and patrolman Jim Hollis was walking his post on the early tour. At about 2:30 in the

Captain James A. Hollis (cont.)

morning he was walking up towards the Park Hill Lunch Room at 232 South Broadway. He noticed two males standing outside the restaurant near a car with the engine running. When these men saw officer Hollis they immediately went inside the establishment. His suspicions having been aroused, officer Hollis followed the two men inside and asked them for identification. The two men reached inside their pockets, pulled out handguns and ordered the officer to raise his hands and back up. The officer complied but then abruptly pushed backwards in through the swinging doors into the kitchen. He then immediately drew his revolver, re-entered the restaurant area and opened fire on the two men. The suspects, who were by then, running out through the front door, returned fire at officer Hollis, shattering the front door glass and window. The men discovered their car had stalled and were forced to jump into a taxi to make their escape. As they drove off officer Hollis ran into the street behind them firing his revolver at their vehicle. He then commandeered another auto and pursued the men south down Broadway to Van Cortlandt Park. Once there, the suspects ran into the woods and separated. Officer Hollis eventually caught up with one of the suspects, and another exchange of gunfire occurred. Fortunately for Hollis he was able to physically subdue the male because his police revolver was now empty. Surprisingly, considering the number of shots fired, no one was even injured during this incident. The following month, on January 15, 1925, Public Safety Commissioner Alfred Iles issued an order commending officer Hollis for his bravery under fire during the shootout the month earlier. That order was later determined to have actually awarded Hollis the departments Honorable Mention.

It seems reasonable to assume that officer Hollis continued to prove himself as an outstanding officer, because on October 15, 1927 he was elevated to the position of Detective in the Detective Bureau. This was the beginning of an assignment that would gain Detective Hollis a reputation as an excellent investigator. An example which was typical of his work was, when on January 20, 1928 three men attempted an armed robbery in the Bronx which resulted in a shootout with a New York City police officer. Though the men escaped, it was believed that they lived in Yonkers. As a result Det's Hollis and his partner Det James Tynan were assigned to investigate. Within just days the men were arrested by Det. Hollis and his partner and justice was swift. In less than two months, on March 16, 1928, all three men were convicted and sentenced to 5-10 years in Sing Sing Prison. On another occasion Det. Hollis was awarded a Commendation on April 20, 1929 for his success in locating and arresting a man wanted for murder.

Jim Hollis was not only a good cop but he was a caring person as well. During the Great Depression most people suffered great financial loses, along with the loss of their jobs, which resulted in an inability to provide for their families. It was during this time that the compassion of the members of the police department was exhibited when they formed the Relief Committee of the Yonkers Police Department. Their purpose was to personally donate and solicit additional donations from those citizens of Yonkers who could afford to, any food, clothing and financial assistance they could provide to those in need. According to the January 1931 committee report, the committees efforts were very successful, thanks to police officers like Det James Hollis who had served as the organizations treasurer.

On September 20, 1932 Public Safety Commissioner Morrissey reorganized the Detective Bureau by moving a pair, or team, of detectives from the Central Office at headquarters and have each team work out of one of the four precincts. On this occasion Det's Hollis and Joe Williamson were assigned to work from the 4th precinct.

Det. Hollis had apparently developed an excellent reputation as a very efficient investigator. As such, when Jim Hollis was promoted to the rank of Sergeant on June 16, 1934, coincidentally right on his

Captain James A. Hollis (cont.)

birthday, it was little surprise when he was allowed to remain in the bureau as a detective sergeant. However he would only remain there until October of that year when the department implemented a new division. On October 13, 1934, following a study conducted by the police department, a police radio communications system was put into service. The unit established and made responsible for operating this system was designated the Radio Telegraph Division. However, this new system provided only one way communication; from headquarters out to the 25 police vehicles in service. The patrol cars were unable to answer headquarters. Prior to this date there was no radio communications with patrol cars at all. Although Det. Sgt Hollis was clearly an asset to the Detective Bureau, the chief decided his police skills were needed to help operate this new communication system. As a result, Sgt Hollis was one of only a handful of officers reassigned to operate the Radio Telegraph Division. For his taking on the special duties and responsibilities required, Sgt Hollis was designated an Acting Lieutenant.

Not only was Hollis a reliable officer, but as an active member of the Yonkers Police War Veteran's Association, Act. Lt. Hollis was officially elected as the organizations Commander on February 3, 1937. A proud veteran of World War 1, Hollis succeeded PO John Yascovic as the leader of the police veterans. Act. Lt Hollis remained in the Radio Telegraph Division until December 16, 1939 when he was officially promoted to the rank of Lieutenant at a salary of $4,000. a year. It was at that time that Lt. Hollis was reassigned to precinct desk duty in the 3rd precinct.

On January 1, 1947 James Hollis received his promotion to the rank of police Captain by Public Safety Commissioner Patrick O'Hara, at which time his salary rose to $4,500. Captain Hollis was then named commanding officer of the 2nd precinct. According to one of the officers who worked for him at the time, Capt. Hollis had a very reserved demeanor, but there was no mistaking that he was the boss. He remained in this position until November 16, 1947 when 19 police officers, including four captains, were transferred. When the order was issued, Capt. Hollis was reassigned as the commander of the Detective Bureau. This assignment would last until May 1, 1949 when, in another shakeup, five captains were reassigned. With these transfers Capt. Hollis was sent back to the 2nd precinct to be its commander.

Capt. Hollis had always been very active in fraternal organizations outside and within the police department. In fact, on April 12, 1955, he was installed as the President of the 25 Club of Yonkers. And, two years later in June of 1957, he was again re-elected the President of the Police Captains, Lieutenants, and Sergeants Association. He was first elected their president in 1952 and was, at that time, beginning his 6th elected term in that office.

Nearing the maximum age of 65 years for police service and mandatory retirement, Capt. Hollis voluntarily requested he be retired from all active police service. His request was granted and it took effect on November 16, 1960.

Initially Jim Hollis moved to Yorktown Heights, where he was near to his son, Detective James E. Hollis of the Westchester County Police Department. He later moved to Plantation Florida. Retired Capt. Hollis was a member of the Friendly Son's of St. Patrick, the Yonkers Elks Club, and was a commander of the American Legion Crescent Post # 935.

A widower who remarried, Jim Hollis' health began to fail and on November 28, 1980 he died in New Smyrna Beach, Florida at the age of 84 years.

PO FRANCIS P. HOLLAND # 128

APPOINTED: December 28, 1921
RETIRED: August 1, 1949

One of eight children, Francis Paul Holland was born on July 6, 1899 in Yonkers and was raised at 21 Ludlow Street. As a young man he earned his living working for the Otis Elevator Co. as a machinist. He lived at 118 Elm Street when he was appointed to the police department on Dec. 28, 1921 and was assigned to foot patrol in the 3rd precinct. It was said that whenever PO Holland would arrive on his post he would be met by the same stray dog which would walk along with Holland until the end of his tour. Some years later, on March 24, 1934, officer Holland made one of his more memorable arrests by arresting a husband for killing his wife with a hatchet. He pled guilty and was sentenced to 35 years to life. Holland retired from the 3rd pct on Aug. 1, 1949 after 28 years and moved to 7 acres in Sharon Connecticut. Frank was described by his nephew as very quiet, soft spoken, and loved gardening and carpentry. His brother Albert served 37 years with the NYPD. Married with no children, Frank Holland died on the 4th of July 1985, two days before his 86th birthday.

PO JOHN A. HINKLE # 126

APPOINTED: December 29, 1921
RETIRED: February 14, 1947

John Anthony Hinkle was born in Pineville, Kentucky on April 8, 1893 and is said to have come to Yonkers around 1908. Records indicate that Hinkle was only 15 or 16 years old when he joined the Army on Aug. 31, 1908 and remained for over 13 years until his discharge on Dec. 18, 1921. He was appointed a police officer within two weeks on December 29, 1921 and assigned to the 4th precinct. After reportedly 16 years with an unblemished record, Hinkle reported sick with a heart condition. His doctors and the police surgeon disagreed as to whether Hinkle could perform his police duties any longer, and he was ordered back to duty. He remained home sick. As a result he was subsequently brought up on charges and on July 10, 1937, this man with 8 children, was dismissed from the department. On April 1, 1942, upon Hinkle's appeal, the new Safety Commissioner ruled his earlier punishment too severe and he was re-instated, with no back pay, at the top salary of $2,625. John Hinkle finished his career in the 2nd precinct on Feb. 14, 1947 with 25 years service. On August 23, 1962 retired officer John A. Hinkle died in St Petersburg, Florida at the age of 74.

CAPTAIN EDWARD F. O'CONNOR

APPOINTED: December 29, 1921
DIED: January 28, 1960

Edward Francis O'Connor was born on July 7, 1895 in Beacon New York and came to Yonkers with his parents when he was two years old. He attended and graduated from St. Mary's Catholic Parochial School. Ed O'Connor served as a Corporal in the Army during World War I from June 28, 1916 to April 5, 1919. He served in Battery D, 2nd Field Artillery on the Mexican border, and Battery D, 105th Field Artillery in France with the American Expeditionary Force (AEF). He later was employed by the Yonkers Sugar House as a "sugar sampler." O'Connor was a resident of 85 Buena Vista Avenue and was 26 years old when he was appointment to the police department December 29, 1921. His new police shield was #125. Following some basic police schooling, records indicate rookie officer O'Connor was assigned to the 4th precinct where he worked foot patrol. On November 11, 1926 he was reassigned to the Traffic Division directing traffic at various city intersections.

Being a very sociable and well liked man, it was no surprise when, in 1930, PO O'Connor was elected the new president of the Police Association. It was during this same year that PBA President O'Connor decided something needed to be done about the large numbers of Yonkers citizens who were unemployed due to the Depression and were in need of any assistance they could receive. In response to this need, on Nov.19, 1930 PBA President O'Connor formed the "Yonkers Police Relief Committee"

Captain Edward F. O'Connor (cont.)

consisting of 34 volunteer police officers. It was reported that police personnel donated over $1,500. dollars in cash, in addition to the food and clothing that was donated by them and various civic groups. As a result, president O'Connor's scheduled Christmas party on December 24, 1930 was a large success providing adults and children with clothing, shoes, and other basic necessities.

On March 31, 1931 officer O'Connor was moved from foot post duties in the Traffic Division to citywide motorcycle patrol. It was on June 10, 1931 when O'Connor was awarded a Certificate of Excellent Police Work for making an arrest, while off duty, of a burglar who was breaking into an apartment right next to his. Later that year on December 1, 1931 the very well respected PO O'Connor was elevated to the position of Detective in the Detective Bureau. He received detective shield # 11. On April 5, 1932 Detective O'Connor arrested another burglar who was responsible for attempting to break into the home of Captain George Ford. As a result of this successful investigation, on June 11, 1932 Detective O'Connor was again awarded a Certificate of Excellent Police Work.

On May 23, 1936 Detective O'Connor was once more recognized by the honor board by awarding him the Honorable Mention. He received this citation for his part in the investigation and arrest of several men who were responsible for the gunpoint robbery on October 15, 1935 of the occupants of a home by binding and gagging them.

Detective O'Connor was promoted to the rank of Sergeant on July 16, 1936. Despite his promotion, the usual transfer was waived and Sergeant O'Connor was allowed to remain in the Detective Bureau as a Detective Sergeant. Following his promotion to sergeant, Ed O'Connor relinquished his position as president of the Police Benevolent Association. At that time he not only was lauded by his fellow officers, but by the New York City PBA who honored him with a testimonial dinner.

Detective Sergeant Edward O'Connor was promoted to Lieutenant on December 30, 1939 at the salary of $4,000.00 per year. Following his promotion to Lieutenant, O'Connor was transferred from the Detective Bureau to the 1st Precinct as a desk lieutenant.

On February 4, 1946 it was reported in the news that the Youth Advisory Committee of the Common Council had recommended that a "Juvenile Aid Bureau" be created as a part of the police department. This bureau would be responsible for the handling of all investigations of crimes committed by youths under the age of 16 years. Three months later, on May 1, 1946, Public Safety Commissioner O'Hara announced he would soon establish this Juvenile Aid Bureau within the police bureau and that Lieutenant Edward O'Connor would be placed in charge. Lt O'Connor was directed to make recommendations on how such a bureau should be organized. It was further ordered that all Police Athletic League (PAL) activities would be conducted with Lieutenant O'Connor's authorization and oversight. Effective June 1, 1946 Lieutenant O'Connor was officially transferred to the newly organized Juvenile Aid Bureau as its "Director." The new bureau was located in the Health Center building at 87 Nepperhan Avenue. Lt O'Connor wasted no time. On August 31, 1946 he began a highly publicized membership campaign to obtain 10,000 new juvenile members in the PAL. It was O'Connor's belief that an active PAL could reduce juvenile delinquency significantly. On January 1, 1948 Lieutenant O'Connor was promoted to a newly created captain's position at $4,500. a year, and was officially designated the commanding officer of the Juvenile Aid Bureau.

Captain Edward F. O'Connor (cont.)

As a political move intended to save money, on January 1, 1951 the city closed the 3rd and 4th precincts. As part of a reorganization and consolidation by Public Safety Commissioner O'Hara, the J.A.B. was merged with the Detective Division and Captain O'Connor was designated commanding officer of both functions. His tenure as commanding officer of both of these bureau's was fairly short and he was reassigned to command the first Precinct. As 1960 began, Capt. O'Connor was commanding the 4th precinct and was having severe goal bladder problems. After a stay in Saint Elizabeth's Hospital in New York City he was allowed to return to his home. However, on January 28, 1960 the Captain suffered a stroke and died. He was five months short of the compulsory retirement age of 65 years. At his funeral, more than 500 people, half of which were police officers, attended to pay their respects. Police delegations from throughout the tri-state area attended to bid farewell to their friend and former six term PBA president.

Captain O'Connor, a veteran of over 38 years of police service, was said to be one of the best known and most popular leaders in police circles across the nation. He had been awarded numerous honorariums for his service on behalf of police officers and the youth of this city. It was O'Connor who organized our first Juvenile Aid Bureau, and was president of the Police Athletic League for over a decade, during which time the very popular Halloween Ragamuffin Parade was inaugurated. He was one of the organizers of the New York State Police Conference; President of the former Intercity Police Conference comprised of departments along the Eastern Seaboard; organizer and president of the Westchester County Police conference; member and former president of the Yonkers police Benevolent Association; member of the Yonkers police Captains, Lieutenants, and the Sergeant's Association; the Yonkers Police War Veterans Legion; the Friendly Sons of Saint Patrick; the 105th Field Artillery Association; the Flat Tire Club, and the Eminence Marching Chowder and Hunting Club.

His wife Dorothy was the niece of former Captain Dennis Cooper, and his son Edward Jr. was a former F.B.I. agent. Upon his death the former Herald Statesman wrote an editorial about Captain O'Connor which, in part, read as follows;

"In the death of police Captain Edward O'Connor, Yonkers loses one of its better policeman; a man who had all the choicest qualities for service in the "line of blue" upon which the community leans so heavily for peace of mind and security in the home and business. The mantle that "Ed" O'Connor wore through the years was of no cheap material. Woven through his many years in the police department were superb qualities of good manners, basic courage, intelligence, grit and loyalty. It is our hope that the mantle that falls from captain O'Connor's shoulders will be picked up by a younger member of this department who will set his goals as high, his aim's so worthy, his purposes and methods as constructive as those of "Ed" O'Connor."

Being known as one of the most popular and well liked captain's in the department, if his subordinates were asked about this editorial they would say, no truer words were ever spoken.

PO STEPHEN F. RYAN # 130

APPOINTED: February 18, 1922
RESIGNED: October 26, 1926

Born in Yonkers on October 26, 1894, Steve Ryan attended local schools and would later work as a mechanic and chauffeur. At the age of 23, Ryan joined the Navy on May 16, 1917 and served as a Machinist Mate. Serving nearly 2 years during the World War, Ryan was discharged May 9, 1919. At the age of 28 he was appointed to the police department on Feb. 18, 1922 and assigned to the 3rd precinct. In May of 1924 he was chosen to be part of the new Police Riot Squad and was given extensive special training. Early in 1926 Ryan was called as a defense witness during a department trial against a captain. Ryan believed his future troubles began following his favorable testimony for the captain. He was transferred to the 2nd precinct in August and said, when he reported sick one evening the commissioner ordered him in to work and also took away all his days off for 4 months. It was then he said he decided to resign on Oct. 26, 1926 due to unfair treatment. His new business was 'Ryan's Auto Sales' at 299 South Broadway.

PO JOHN J. JACKSON # 129

APPOINTED: February 18, 1922
DIED: April 1, 1948

John James Jackson was born in Yonkers on January 8, 1898 and would later attend St. Mary's School and Saunders High School. 'Jack,' as he was known, worked several years as a motorman for the Yonkers Railroad Co. Upon his appointment to the police department on February 18, 1922 he was assigned to the 3rd precinct on Radford Street. On March 30, 1935 he was awarded a commendation for chasing three burglars in a blinding snow storm, and arresting them. In 1944 records indicate that he was assigned to the 1st precinct and worked in the Emergency Squad for a while. On March 18, 1948, while at his home at 32 Park Avenue, Jackson fell in his bathtub striking his left side on the side of the tub causing severe pain. He reported sick the next day and was visited by the police surgeon who wrapped his chest in bandages. He was told to just rest. His condition worsened with a 104 fever and he was taken to St. Joseph's Hospital for x-ray's. Within days, on April 1, 1948, he was dead; the result of 3 broken ribs and pneumonia. Officer Jackson was 50 years old.

PO JOHN J. HARDING # 213

APPOINTED: October 7, 1922
RETIRED: July 31, 1954

"Jack" Harding, as he was known, was born on June 28, 1890 in County Kilkenny, Ireland. He came to Yonkers in 1910 and following his formal education he earned a living as a Trolley motorman. As a healthy young man he became a boxing and baseball enthusiast. When hired by the YPD on October 7, 1922 he was assigned to foot patrol in the 2nd pct. and in 1924 was part of the new Riot Squad. Still a sports fan, Jack was an eager participant in the October 11, 1926 Municipal Athletic Games held in the old "Glen Park." Over the years he served in the 2nd & 4th pct's, and the Traffic Div. PO Harding was fortunate to be elevated to Detective on October 10, 1934. On February 15, 1937 he was awarded an Honorable Mention for the arrest of 3 armed robbers. Then, on July 9, 1938 he was awarded a Commendation for a robbery and burglary arrest. But, on October 12, 1942 Harding was reassigned to the 1st pct. from which he retired on July 31, 1954. He was the brother in law to Capt. Patrick Sullivan and Vice Mayor James Sullivan, and uncle to Lt Martin Harding. A resident of 47 Cowles Ave., John Harding died May 6, 1970 at age 79.

PO RAYMOND W. ALLBEE # 131

APPOINTED: October 7, 1922
RETIRED: July 1, 1950

Ray Wadsworth Allbee was born in Yonkers on Mar. 11, 1897. Ray attended PS# 13, Saunders H.S., and from May 27, 1918 to Dec. 27, 1918 he served in the Navy during World War 1 as a Seaman and Cook. Following his discharge he worked as an Airbrake Foreman on the railroad. A relative related that Allbee was very mechanically inclined, loved helping people, and could fix almost anything. The YPD hired him on October 7, 1922 and assigned him to the 1st precinct. But on March 2, 1928 he was moved to the 2nd pct. On April 6, 1931 while off duty on Willow St., Allbee's quick action resulted in the arrest of a male with two revolvers which were to be used against another male. He was commended for his excellent police work. Years later Allbee was returned to the 1st pct. and for several years was assigned to guard the banks in Getty Square. For many years following his retirement on July 1, 1950 he worked with security at the Habirshaw Wire & Cable Corp. A member of the Hawthorne Masonic Lodge, Ray moved to Ocean Grove N.J. where he died on October 5, 1966 at the age of 79 years.

PO JOSEPH W. LUCKEY # 142

APPOINTED: October 7, 1922
RETIRED: March 16, 1962

Joseph William Luckey, born in Yonkers Mar. 17, 1897, reportedly attended the Seton Academy in Yonkers and All Hollows H.S. in the Bronx. While working as a store clerk Luckey was appointed to the YPD on Oct. 7, 1922 and assigned to the 3rd precinct. It quickly became apparent that Luckey was an excellent revolver shot and was recruited to join the YPD Pistol Team. In Jan. 1928 the team competed against the New Rochelle P.D.'s team in the range at the Yonkers North Broadway Armory. On Feb. 24, 1928 PO Luckey was selected to serve on the honor guard as a pall bearer at the funeral of his friend PO John Hudock who was killed on duty. Joe Luckey's foot post usually ran from Riverdale Ave. to the river, and from Herriot St. to the south city line. Upon reaching 65 years of age Luckey was forced to retire on Mar. 16, 1962 and the 3rd pct. held a party for him at Cosgrove's Bar and Restaurant on Riverdale Ave. Joe Luckey died on May 12, 1969 in St. Joseph's Hospital of heart disease and cirrhosis of the liver. He was 72 years of age.

DET. JOSEPH A. CURRAN # 14

APPOINTED: October 7, 1922
RETIRED: January 1, 1940

Joe Curran was born in Yonkers June 18, 1894 and attended St. Joseph's H.S. Curran was said to have been a good athlete while in school and also later playing on the Hollywood Inn team. It was reported that as a young man he was considered Westchester County's premier "shot-putter" and "broad jumper." From August 1918 to February 1919 Curran served as a sergeant in the Army's 35th Field Artillery during World War 1. Previously a plumber, Joe Curran joined the YPD from 19 Ingram St. on Oct. 7, 1922 and was assigned to the 1st pct. In Jan. of 1923 he was reassigned to traffic duty for a short while and then went to the 3rd pct. On Jan. 16, 1926 he was assigned as a Detective in the Bureau of Criminal Identification (BCI). On Sept. 7, 1926 he was sent to the NYPD with Det. J. Baldwin to learn a new records system. In time he would become an expert in crime scene investigations. In addition, he served as PBA president in 1928 and 1929. A member of the Police War Veterans Legion and the Police Holy Name Society, Curran developed heart problems and retired on a physical disability on Jan. 1, 1940 after 18 years and moved to Portland, Oregon. Joe Curran died at age 47 on April 27, 1942.

PO EDWARD F. MESLIN #146

APPOINTED: October 7, 1922
RETIRED: July 16, 1950

Ed Meslin was born in Yonkers on November 13, 1899 and grew up with the ability to speak both English and Polish. Although considered an amateur musician, as a youth he earned a living as an "Armature winder." After being hired by the YPD on Oct. 7, 1922 Ed became a very active officer. He was also active in other police activities, including singing with the police Glee Club. On one occasion on September 27, 1926 while on foot post at 3:55 AM, he investigated a gas leak complaint which resulted in Meslin kicking in a door and preventing a suicide of a woman. Two years later on November 1, 1928 at 1:50 AM, while investigating a domestic dispute, Meslin was nearly run down by the irate husband. After commandeering a car Meslin chased the suspect and made the arrest. After nearly 28 years Ed retired from the 1st precinct on July 16, 1950 and worked as a security guard at the Habirshaw factory. Several years later he moved to Gabriels, NY where, on November 6, 1975, Ed Meslin died at 76 years of age.

PO JOSEPH M. WEBER # 153

APPOINTED: October 7, 1922
RETIRED: September 1, 1951

Born in Spuyten Duyvil, in the Bronx on Dec. 21, 1899 Joseph Martin Weber came to Yonkers and worked as a "machine molder." Following his police appointment on Oct. 7, 1922, during his career he would work in the 1st, 2nd, & 3rd precincts, and the Traffic and Detective Div. He was always known by his peers as a "Good Cop." On the late tour of August 13, 1931 while checking doors on his foot post he found a broken rear door. Hearing noises he entered quietly with revolver drawn, surprised the burglar, and arrested him. At the time Chief Quirk commented, "PO Weber's act was a piece of brilliant police work." On Nov. 16, 1947 Joe was elevated to Detective but decided he preferred uniformed patrol instead. Following his request he was returned to the 3rd precinct on Aug. 1, 1948. A single man, Weber exercised at the YMCA daily to maintain his good physical conditioning. When he announced his retirement on Sept. 1, 1951 PSC O'Hara stated, "He's my ideal policeman. I wish I had an entire department of Joe Weber's." Upon retiring Weber worked as a security guard for Otis Elevator for many years. On Dec. 10, 1972 Joe Weber died at the age of 72 years.

SGT. THOMAS F. FLYNN

APPOINTED: October 7, 1922
RETIRED: September 7, 1962

If a check were made of the police personnel records on Sgt. Flynn, the records would reflect that his name was Francis Thomas Flynn born April 5, 1901. But this was not his name or date of birth. For reasons that had long been forgotten, throughout his career the officer with the name Francis Flynn preferred to be, and was known as, Thomas Flynn. The truth, according to his son, is that when he was preparing to join the police department he was not old enough, being only 19 years of age. But he had a neighbor friend whose name, coincidentally, was Francis Thomas Flynn born April 5, 1901. Wanting desperately to become a police officer, Tom Flynn borrowed his friend's birth certificate, took on the neighbor's name, Francis Thomas Flynn, and with the department thinking he was 21, appointed him to the department. Throughout his entire career no one ever knew the truth or his real name.

In fact, Thomas Francis Flynn was born September 17, 1902 in Dungarvan County, Waterford Ireland. He arrived in the US with his family in 1906 at the age of four. Tom attended St. Joseph's Catholic School, and later as a young man worked in the Alexander Smith Carpet Factory as a machinist. He grew up in the area of St. Joseph's Avenue and Ashburton Avenue and was very athletic in his youth. He ran Track for the Hollywood Inn Track Team as a sprinter and loved to spar with NYC professional boxers also at the Inn. In fact, according to his son, Tom said he always wanted to be a boxer or a policeman. With the police department offering a steady salary the choice was made.

Tom Flynn, known officially as Francis, was appointed on Oct. 7, 1922 at a salary of $2,300. a year and was assigned to the 1st precinct on foot patrol. By 1927 he had been reassigned to the 4th precinct. At 4 AM on the morning of January 15, 1927 while walking his post in the area of Lake and Morningside Avenue, he came upon three men. Not being able to give a reasonable account of themselves

Sgt. Thomas F. Flynn (cont.)

for being in the area, officer Flynn arrested the three for suspicion of committing a robbery an hour earlier. His suspicions turned out to be accurate.

Flynn was not only an active police officer but he still enjoyed sports as well. In 1928 old sports rivalry's between the police and fire departments culminated in a series of baseball games between what was then referred to as the "Red Shirts and the Bluecoats." Of course Tom Flynn was quick to volunteer and it is believed that the police team won two out of three games played.

Shortly after the Police Emergency Squad was established in 1930 Flynn was provided with the available specialized training and was assigned to the Emergency Squad in the 1st precinct on Wells Avenue. On May 6th of that year while still with the Emergency Squad, Flynn and his partners, they worked three at a time on the truck, were involved in a foot pursuit of two men wanted for an attempted felonious assault. The two men were arrested but Flynn suffered a bad laceration to his leg during the chase. Two months later, in July of 1930 during the early morning hours of about 5:30 AM, PO Flynn and his partners were sent on an entry in progress at 440 Park Hill Avenue. The suspect tried to flee but was found hiding in some bushes and was arrested by the officers. The burglar, who called himself the "screen burglar," admitted to committing nearly twenty burglaries in Yonkers and Mt. Vernon.

Officer Tom Flynn had repeatedly exhibited his skill as an effective police officer and it is believed as a result, on September 1, 1930, he was elevated to the position of Detective in the Detective Bureau. Over the years Det. Flynn earned an enviable reputation as an excellent detective and was always prepared to do more. On June 2, 1939, three men whose canoe had capsized on the Hudson River were in the water and in imminent danger of drowning. Det. Flynn, who had responded to the scene, removed his outer clothing and without hesitation, dove into the river with a long rope tied to his waist. With the assistance of Emergency Squad officers, Flynn was able to rescue one of the men in danger. The other men were also rescued. As a result of his heroic action that day, on April 18, 1940, Det. Flynn was awarded the police departments Honorable Mention. With this award Flynn also received three additional percentage points to be added to his score on any future civil service exam. He was also presented with a Certificate of Merit from the U.S. Volunteer Life Saving Corps. at their annual dinner.

Despite Det. Flynn's excellent record, as part of a large personnel "shakeup" in police assignments, Flynn was transferred out of the Detective Bureau on March 1, 1941 and reassigned to the 4th precinct on patrol duty.

Two years later, on November 19, 1943, PO Tom Flynn was promoted to the rank of Sergeant and assigned as a patrol supervisor. He would spend the remainder of his career on uniform patrol. However, his last few years with the department were spent assigned to the Traffic Division as a sergeant, a unit from which he would ultimately retire.

Following his retirement on September 7, 1962, one month short of forty years service, Tom worked as a Sergeant with the security staff at the Yonkers Raceway. He would never live to know it but, many years later his son's nephew Charles Gardner would be appointed Yonkers Police Commissioner.

Eight years after retiring, on September 29, 1970, Ret. PO Tom Flynn died of a heart attack while at work at the Yonkers Racetrack. He was 68 years of age.

PO PIERRE H. LeBAILLEY

APPOINTED: October 7, 1922
DISMISSED: December 20, 1924

"Pete" LeBailley's career seemed in trouble very early on. He was born in Yonkers on Oct. 26, 1893, attended local schools, and later worked as a chauffeur. During World War 1 Pete served as a private in the Army's Aviation section as part of the American Expeditionary Force in Europe. A few years after his discharge he was appointed to the YPD on Oct. 7. 1922 and served in the 1st precinct. For unknown reasons LeBailley resigned on April 18, 1923. But on Dec. 31st he asked for and received reinstatement. While assigned to the Traffic Division he was AWOL for an entire tour, pled guilty and received only a reprimand. However, at that time, he was told that any future infraction would result in dismissal. Unfortunately for Pete, he apparently did not listen. And on December 15, 1924 he was 10 minutes late for roll call and found by the police surgeon to be intoxicated and unfit for duty. Following a trial at which he pled guilty, Pierre LeBailley was dismissed from the department on December 20, 1924. LeBailley died in Yonkers on February 27, 1968.

PO FRANCIS J. SULLIVAN # 152

APPOINTED: October 7, 1922
RETIRED: July 30, 1937

Frank Sullivan is another officer who could not know what life held for him. Born Oct. 11, 1895 in Ansonia, Connecticut, Sullivan would move to Yonkers and work as a steam fitter. He joined the Army August 12, 1916, serving as a Corporal in the Medical Corps. during World War 1, and was discharged August 18, 1920. Upon appointment to the YPD on Oct. 7, 1922 he was assigned to the 2nd pct. on foot patrol. On Mar. 10, 1933 Sullivan was charged with being intoxicated on a school crossing at PS # 15. He had been fined two previous times for being intoxicated on duty, but new charges were never brought as he was admitted to the hospital at that time. Six years later, in 1939, he was still hospitalized with some serious illness, charges were still pending, and he had not been receiving a salary. A civil action was filed and in the settlement it was decided that Frank Sullivan was a police officer up to July 30, 1937, received retroactive pay to that date, and was retired on a disability pension. The pending charges were never addressed and on March 24, 1961 Frank Sullivan died at 65 years of age.

DET. JOHN J. BALDWIN # 6

APPOINTED: October 7, 1922
DIED: August 15, 1951

John Joseph Baldwin, brother of PO Matthew Baldwin, was born June 23, 1893, and graduated from St. Mary's Catholic School. John worked in a factory with his trade being that of a machinist. In February of 1918, during World War 1, John enlisted in the Navy and served as a Machinist Mate as part of a Naval Aviation Group. Due to the Armistice Baldwin was discharged on March 1, 1919.

John Baldwin was appointed a police officer on Oct. 7, 1922 and was assigned to the 1st precinct walking various foot posts. While working a late tour on August 30, 1926, at approximately 2:35 AM an assault and robbery took place on Woodworth Ave., and the suspects had fled on foot to the area of Ashburton Ave. PO Baldwin, who was in the area driving the Patrol Wagon, began chasing the suspects in his vehicle. The pursuit brought P.O. Baldwin to an empty lot on Ashburton Avenue where the two suspects ran and had hidden in the darkness. The newspaper the following day reported that as P.O. Baldwin was searching the lot, he came across a thick clump of bushes. Believing the men may were hiding somewhere in the brush, Baldwin yelled "come out." When there was no reply, Baldwin immediately began firing point blank into the bushes. "Don't shoot! I quit," said one of the men. And as he emerged he was quickly arrested.

The following month PO John Baldwin was detailed to the NYPD School of Criminal Investigation. The skills he learned would permanently and dramatically change the direction of his career and provide new innovative procedures to the Police Department. Following his training in New York, on Nov. 18, 1926, he was reassigned from the 1st precinct to the Detective Division managing the Bureau of Criminal Identification. (BCI) From that point on he would earn the reputation of being one of the best experts in his field. In the beginning of September of 1934 the Detective Bureau received information that a man wanted for the execution style murder of a Philadelphia police officer was hiding in a Yonkers hotel room. On September 6, 1934 Detective Baldwin, along with several other members of the Detective Bureau, broke into the hotel room, found the suspect and placed him under arrest using the Philadelphia police warrant for murder. Certainly this was one of the more satisfying arrests made during his career.

As a war veteran and active member of the Yonkers Police War Veterans Legion, Baldwin held the position of Vice Commander of the Legion for several years. And in the early 1940's he was elected to the prestigious position of Commander of the War Veterans Legion. In addition to his police duties and the Veterans Legion, John Baldwin was also the Financial Secretary for the PBA for several years, member of the Police Holy Name Society, Yonkers Post # 7 American Legion, Yonkers Elks Club, and the Knights of Columbus. Early in his career in 1926, with only four years on patrol duty, when he was first assigned to the BCI with the responsibility for all fingerprinting and crime scene investigations, he had no way of knowing he would spend the rest of his career in that assignment. Nor would he know that his life would be cut short. Det. John Baldwin died Aug. 15, 1951 in Yonkers General Hospital several hours after undergoing an operation. He was 58 years of age. John Baldwin had earned a deep professional respect from the law enforcement community well beyond Yonkers. Following his death all off duty members of the department, along with members from other departments, attended his funeral and presented him with a final salute.

CAPTAIN ANTHONY PRIOR

APPOINTED: October 7, 1922
RETIRED: July 21, 1965

Tony Prior was born to Italian immigrant parents on July 22, 1900 in New York City. When he was just two years old his parents moved their family out of the big city and to the suburbs; to the City of Yonkers. As he was growing up Anthony lived at 57 Claredon Avenue, attended PS# 5, and would later graduate from Saunders Trades and Technical High School. After high school Prior attended the Butler Business School for a while. Following this school Tony Prior worked at a number of jobs including chauffeur and apprentice plumber until the police test was scheduled. When he did take the test he scored number one on the list for Yonkers Police Officer. Upon his appointment as a police officer he was given shield #150 to wear and his salary was $1,600. per year with pay days twice a month. After a few months of basic police training, on January 5, 1923 he was assigned to the 2nd precinct on foot patrol duty. He would learn that his ability to speak Italian would definitely be extremely helpful in conducting investigations involving immigrants from Italy.

It would be less than a year and officer Prior would have his revolver out and at the ready. On July 17, 1923 at about 11:00 PM while he was walking his post he was approached by an off duty officer who

Captain Anthony Prior (cont.)

said he noticed a suspicious vehicle parked on an unlit street and thought it should be checked out. PO Prior accompanied the other officer and found two men sitting in the car. After a brief investigation a fully loaded revolver was found inside the vehicle and a second one on the ground just outside the car. It also was learned that the car had been stolen from Trenton N.J. Both men were arrested and the two revolvers were recovered and held at headquarters.

On March 31, 1926 he was reassigned to the 1st precinct also on foot patrol. Just over a year later on August 24, 1927 officer Prior was elevated to the position of Detective carrying shield # 2. However, for whatever reason, his stay was brief, lasting only 2 months when, on October 14, 1927 he was returned to patrol duties in the 1st precinct on Wells Avenue.

Officer Prior was not only efficient in performing his official duties, but he was also involved in other police activities. Being an exceptional shot with his handgun he joined with several other members of the department on January 5, 1928 to compete in a firearms competition in the Armory on North Broadway in order to form a Yonkers Police Pistol Team. This team later competed all over Westchester County and beyond. Later that same year a suggestion was made that a committee be formed in order that all those members of the department, active or retired, who had died since the inception of the Yonkers Police Association in 1916 be memorialized in some way. PO Tony Prior quickly joined the committee and, following planning and preparations, on March 25, 1928 an event was held at the Knights of Columbus Hall. All the board members of the Police Association attended along with large numbers from the police department and many politicians and business people. A list had been prepared with the names of those officers who had died since 1916 and their names were read out loud, followed by a prayer by the police chaplain. The list, which was to be updated each year, was the beginning of the Lest We Forget list which continued to be maintained and updated each year. (Unfortunately the list only began in 1916 and did not include the names of officers who had died between 1871 and 1916.)

Following the exam for Sergeant, officer Prior scored # 2 on the list and on October 1, 1930 he was promoted to the rank of Sergeant at the annual salary of $3,400. and was assigned as a patrol supervisor in the 4th precinct. Despite the significance of being promoted it did not stop him from participating in a grudge baseball game with the Yonkers Fire Department on the following day. It would seem there had, and would always be, a special friendly competitive spirit between the police and fire departments.

Sgt Prior of the 4th precinct was on routine patrol during the early tour with his driver, PO James McCue on February 2, 1932 when he observed a suspicious male loitering around a home at 1004 Warburton Avenue. The sergeant and his driver attempted to approach the suspect to question him when the man began to run. Following a short foot pursuit he was caught and placed under arrest. Following a search numerous stolen items from previous burglaries were recovered, including a loaded .45 caliber hand gun. In recognition of his alert attention to duty resulting in the removal of a handgun from a known criminal, on April 23, 1931 the Police Honor Board awarded Sgt Anthony Prior a departmental Commendation. Still a sergeant, he would later be moved to the 3rd precinct on June 25, 1932 and then to the 1st precinct on July 29, 1935.

Captain Anthony Prior (cont.)

On April 16, 1939 Sgt Anthony Prior was promoted to the rank of Lieutenant at an annual salary of $4,000. a year. Following his receiving his promotion to Lieutenant, on May 22, 1939, the local newspaper reported that city officials and several of the city's leading organizations were included on a general committee arranging a testimonial dinner for Lt. Anthony Prior to be held at Prior's Casino at 15 Lockwood Avenue. A resident of 26 Roosevelt Street, Lt Prior was reported in the news article to be the first police officer of Italian Heritage to be elevated to the rank of Lieutenant in the Yonkers Police Department.

Over the next 13 years Lt Prior would work in various patrol precincts until June 1, 1952 when he was elevated to the prestigious position of Detective Lieutenant in the Detective Bureau. He remained in the Detective Bureau up until his promotion to the rank of Captain 8 years later, which occurred on March 16, 1960, following the death of Det Capt. Edward O'Connor. His new salary was $7,965. per year. As was expected he was initially transferred from the Bureau to the Communications and Records Division when he was promoted but, after only 3 months, on June 1, 1960 he was returned as the Commanding Officer of the Detective Bureau.

Capt. Prior's last change of assignment occurred on May 1, 1963 when he was transferred from the detective bureau to commanding officer of the 4th precinct.

When Capt. Prior submitted his application to retire and take effect July 21, 1965, he had completed nearly 43 years of police service. At a retirement testimonial dinner given in his honor on October 30, 1965, the retired captain was presented with a city council resolution, signed by Mayor John Flynn, praising Ret. Capt. Prior for his dedication to the police profession. Following his retirement the Public Safety Commissioner, Daniel F. McMahon, sent him a personal letter that stated in part,..."*It is noted that after 42 years of service you are now leaving the active rolls of the police Bureau. The Chief has advised me of your faithful service and I want to take this opportunity to commend you for your fine service. I want you to know it is very much appreciated by all of us. Best wishes for many happy years of retirement*".

Retired Captain Anthony Prior died in his home on November 30, 1973 after a brief illness. He was 73 years old. He had been a member of the Italian American Unity Club, the Holy Name Society of St Bartholomew's Church, the Police Holy Name Society, and the Joseph A. Prior Association, a social and civic club named for his brother. He left behind his wife Margaret and his son, Alphonse Prior, who would later rise to be a Yonkers police lieutenant.

PO WILLIAM F. PARKER # 149

APPOINTED: October 7, 1922
RESIGNED: August 19, 1926

Bill Parker was born in the Town of Haverstraw, NY on August 22, 1898. Little is known about him during his early years, but he did serve in the Army from September 12, 1915 to July 18, 1916, at which time he was honorably discharged. Later while living in Yonkers he took, and passed the test for the police department. On his application he listed his previous employment as that of a chauffeur and that he was able to ride a motorcycle.

Following his appointment to the police department on October 7, 1922 and his assignment to the 2nd precinct, on July 17, 1923, at 11:00 PM, Parker was on his way in to work when he observed two suspicious youths in a parked car. While still off duty, Parker's investigation resulted in the arrest of the two people for possession of a stolen auto and two unlicensed loaded revolvers.

On the following New Year's Eve he was assigned to Mounted horse patrol in Getty Square. Six months later, on July 1, 1924, he was then re-assigned to Motorcycle duty in the Traffic Division. Bill Parker was reportedly a very popular and well liked officer who was very aggressive in his police duties. On May 23, 1925 he again arrested two males at gun point for possession of a stolen auto following a pursuit on his motorcycle. But his aggressiveness nearly cost him his life. It was on November 9, 1925 when, after stopping a speeder, when he approached the vehicle a passenger pushed a gun up against Parkers stomach and said, "Get back on your motorcycle and beat it." After returning to his motorcycle and pretending to begin to leave, Parker swung his "wheel" around and a chase began. When the car came to a stop the man with the gun tried to run away on foot. The officer chased and caught the man, who then tried to pull out his gun once again. But Parker subdued him using his "black-jack," using necessary force and made the arrest.

On March 31, 1926 Officer Parker was returned to mounted patrol in the 2nd precinct. While in the 2nd precinct a complaint was filed against him by a civilian. PO Parker insisted the charge was absolutely false but knew he was sure to face departmental charges and the embarrassment of a trial. After some consideration, Bill Parker decided to submit his resignation from the Yonkers Police Department, effective August 19, 1926.

Years later it was learned that he drove a truck for Borelli Fruits and Vegetables on School Street and Engine Place. Many years later his son Bill Parker Jr., and his grandson Bill Parker, both served in the Yonkers Fire Department. His nephew was retired Yonkers PO John "Jack" O'Brien.

According to his son, PO William F. Parker is believed to have died around 1959 or 1960.

PO RAYMOND CONNOLLY #138

APPOINTED: October 7, 1922
RETIRED: October 1, 1950

Having been born in NYC on April 28, 1897, and later having moved to Yonkers, Ray Connolly received his formal education in his new hometown. He held a number of jobs as a young man including that of a salesman while living at 136 Hawthorne Ave. But on May 2, 1916 he joined the NY National Guard (NYNG), serving with "G" Company, 10th Infantry Div. He first served on the Mexican border and then left Yonkers with his unit for duty during WW 1. He later transferred to the Army Air Corps and served as part of the American Expeditionary Force (AEF) overseas. He was honorably discharged as a sergeant on July 7, 1919.

After holding several odd jobs he was appointed to the YPD on Oct. 7, 1922, and was assigned to foot patrol in the 3rd precinct. Connolly was certainly not afraid to use his revolver. On April 27, 1923, just a few months following his appointment, Connolly tried to pull over a vehicle with two males acting suspiciously. The suspects fled and a pursuit followed with the officer firing several shots at the fleeing car. Though they eluded capture at first, following a brief investigation PO Connolly arrested the men at 259th St. in the Bronx and recovered the stolen auto. He was highly commended for his aggressive police work.

Later that same year on December 9, 1923 once again officer Connolly tried to arrest the occupants of a vehicle, this time for reckless driving. The males attempted to run from the scene and PO Connolly fired three times, striking one of them in the leg. He was able to arrest two of the three.

On October 17, 1925, while walking his post at about 4:30 AM, Connolly saw smoke coming from the windows of a 21 family, 5 story apartment house at 564 South Broadway. He immediately ran and turned in the alarm from the nearest fire alarm box and returned to alert the residents of the danger. Finding the front door locked he smashed the glass with his nightstick, entered and began leading several families out through the heavy smoke to safety. He ran throughout the entire building banging on every

PO Raymond Connolly (cont.)

door to alert any remaining tenants. With the interior stairwell engulfed in flames, nearly 100 people escaped to safety using the fire escape with the assistance of officer Connolly and several other police officers who had arrived at the scene.

The following month on November 2, 1925, officer Connolly was presented with a 14 karat gold medal while at the 4 PM roll call in recognition of his actions and bravery at the fire the month earlier. The medal was the gift of the owner of the apartment house but was presented to the officer by Public Safety Commissioner Alfred H. Iles.

On March 25, 1926 PO Connolly was reassigned from the 3rd precinct to motorcycle duty in the Traffic Division. He would remain there for many years. On May 21, 1927 it was reported that Connolly, who was the secretary of the PBA, was on a committee organizing a group of Yonkers police officers to participate in an "Athletic Meet" to be held in Baltimore, Md., for police officers from all around the country. Being very active in many programs, Connolly was also an excellent shot with his revolver and was a member of the YPD Pistol Team. He was a past commander of the Yonkers Police War Veterans Legion, and served seven terms as president of the Police Holy Name Society beginning in 1944. On November 16, 1947 Connolly was transferred to the Radio and Telegraph Division where he would remain up to his retirement on October 1, 1950.

Following Ray's retirement he worked as the manager of the Tire Department in Sears & Roebuck in Yonkers. In early 1956 he suffered a stroke and required hospitalization. And on April 11, 1956 Ret. PO Ray Connolly died suddenly and unexpectedly. He was about two weeks short of his 59th birthday.

DET. WILLIAM S. DALY # 1

APPOINTED: October 7, 1922
RETIRED: October 17, 1962

Born William Stephen Daly in Yonkers on Oct. 18, 1897, Bill Daly attended local schools here in Yonkers. As a young man he worked a number of different jobs including that of a Clerk and as a Special Private Officer. Following his police appointment he was assigned to foot patrol in the 1st precinct on Wells Avenue. Then in May of 1924 a new unit was organized, designated as the "Riot Squad," and Daly was trained and assigned to it. This, of course, was in addition to his regular patrol duties. However, within a year he would begin a career as a detective that would bring him a great deal of respect and recognition as an excellent investigator.

On July 8, 1926 the 28 year old officer was elevated to the position of Police Detective. However, for reasons unknown, on August 24, 1927 he was returned back to uniform patrol in the 1st precinct. He would spend three more years on patrol before he was again assigned as a detective on February 21, 1930. Upon reassignment as a detective he noticed a wanted poster from the Newark, NJ P.D. advising of two men wanted by them for a murder committed in 1928. It wasn't long before Det Daly learned that the two men wanted in New Jersey might be in Yonkers. After three weeks of investigation and surveillance, on March 26, 1931 Det. Daly, along with a uniformed officer, arrested both men in Yonkers at gunpoint and had them returned to Newark N.J. to face murder charges.

Later that same year on September 8, 1931 at 5 AM a male was shot and killed in his apartment by two armed robbers. As the two men ran from the scene they came upon PO Matthew Baldwin on patrol and an exchange of gunfire ensued. However the men succeeded in escaping. But following a persistent and methodical investigation by Det Bill Daly and his partner, they arrested both suspects on November 13, 1932.

As a result of his excellent arrest record in the Detective Division Daly received many citations. Just to list a few examples; On June 23, 1938 Det Daly was awarded a departmental Commendation for arresting the members of a gang responsible for a burglary, an armed robbery, and for stealing a car. Then on April 12, 1939 Det Daly was awarded two Commendations by the Police Honor Board. One award was for Daly's work which led to the arrest of a male wanted for robbery. The second award was for his work in the ultimate capture and arrest of a male wanted for murder. Due to his being awarded this double tribute, Det Daly was granted the very unusual benefit of being allowed a full one point advantage on Civil Service promotion tests. However he never did received a promotion to sergeant. These awards were followed on April 18, 1940 when he received another Certificate of Excellent Police Work for another Robbery arrest. His ability to solve a crime and make the arrest was quite simply amazing.

While living at 36 Prospect Street Det. Daly reached the age of 65 years, the maximum age allowed for a police officer, and was mandatorily retired from the department on October 17, 1962. He did not want to retire and if the law would have allowed it, he would have remained a "detective" for the rest of his life. Retired Det William S. Daly, later of 40 Park Avenue, a man who had served the police department for 40 years, died from cardiac arrest on February 15, 1968 at the age of 70 years.

PO FRANK J. BUSSARD # 133

APPOINTED: October 7, 1922
DIED: July 7, 1930

Frank Bussard was born in the City of Yonkers on Christmas day, December 25, 1893. He graduated from PS# 6 and after his schooling, for a time, was employed as an inspector with the Yonkers Railroad Co.

Following his appointment to the Yonkers Poice Department he was assigned to foot patrol in the 4th precinct at a salary of $2,300. per year. Bussard was apparently an efficient officer who had a reputation for doing his job effeciently. On one occasion, on February 26, 1928, officer Bussard was off duty and heard the screams of his next door neighbor whose clothes had become engulfed in flames from a gasoline explosion in her apartment. She had been using gasoline as a cleaning fluid when it ignited. Bussard ran to her aid and, picking up a blanket, wrapped it around her and beat out the flames. Though he sustained minimal burns to his hands, the woman's life was saved.

Later that year, on September 22, 1928, the Honor Board awarded him a Commendation for his actions in saving the womans life.

Unfortunately PO Bussard's health began to fail and after a long illness he died in St. Joseph's Hospital on July 7, 1930. The funeral, with included a police escort, was held at his 86 Hamilton Avenue home address.

PO MATTHEW S. LESNICK # 144

APPOINTED: October 7, 1922
RETIRED: August 31, 1945

Matthew Lesnick was born in the city of Yonkers on December 26, 1895. He attended St. Joseph's parochial School and Saunders H.S. On March 15, 1918 Matt joined the Navy serving during WW-1 as a Machinist Mate. He was Honorably Discharged March 15, 1919. During the next few years he worked various jobs including that of a chauffeur and an auto mechanic.

Upon his appointment to the Yonkers Police Department he was assigned to foot patrol in the 2nd precinct. He remained there until August 29, 1930 when he was reassigned to motorcycle patrol duty.

Three years later, on June 17, 1933, he was returned to routine patrol duties in the 3rd precinct. Apparently due to his previous experience as an auto mechanic, on March 1, 1941 he was placed in charge of the Police Repair shop. However, in October of 1942 he was returned to patrol in the 4th precinct.

In a letter from the police surgeon in 1945 it was related that Lesnick suffered from heart disease, asthma and had been out sick since September 26, 1944. As a result PO Lesnick was retired from the YPD on a disability pension on August 31, 1945. His younger brother was Lt Edward Lesnick.

Only three years later, on June 7, 1956, retired PO Matthew Lesnick died. He was 60 years old.

SGT. EMMETT J. JACKMAN # 16

APPOINTED: October 7, 1922
RETIRED: January 1, 1951

Emmett was born in Yonkers on August 22, 1898, attended St. Joseph's School and graduated from the Butler Business School. He joined the Army on May 7, 1917 and served overseas during WW-1 in France with the 58th Artillery Corps. Three years following his military discharge on May 10, 1919 he would receive his appointment to the Yonkers Police Dept. on Oct. 7, 1922 while living at 171 Buena Vista Avenue.

Following Jackman's recruit training he was assigned to the 4th precinct on foot patrol duty. Apparently having proved his abilities as a police officer, on October 16, 1931, he was elevated to the position of Detective. On August 14, 1933 an extortion letter was received by a Yonkers family threatening to kidnap a family member or "blow up" their house if they did not pay a $10,000 extortion demand. The FBI was called in to assist Yonkers detectives in the investigation. Several letters and phone calls were received by the family and following an agreed location to "drop" the money, Det Jackman and his partner arrested one of the extortionists. The next day the 2nd suspect was picked up and charged. As a result of the extortion and threatened kidnaping arrest he had made, in October 1933 the Police Honor Board awarded Det Jackman a Police Commendation.

After having served as a squad detective for a time he was chosen by then Chief Quirk to be the chief's secretary and aide. In this position he worked right in the chief's office and was a trusted confidant. But Jackman was not only trusted by the police department. On April 7, 1936 he was elected Commander of the Veterans of Battery B, 58th Coast artillery Corps. of the U.S. American Expeditionary Force (AEF). As commander he organized the annual May veterans reunion at Fort Trotten. He also served as Commander of the Yonkers Police War Veterans Association. Following his term in this office a testimonial dinner was organized by the war veterans to honor Det Jackman's service to war veteran organizations. It was reported that over 500 people attended the event at Schmidt's Farm in the Town of Greenburgh.

On December 16, 1939 Det. Jackman was promoted to the rank of Sergeant. Due to the trust he enjoyed, he was allowed to maintain his Detective status and remain working as the aide to Chief Quirk. His continued involvement in department activities was again highlighted when on July 15, 1941, following the establishment of the departments first Police Athletic League, Jackman was elected the organizations first "Vice President." All PAL activities and scheduling were conducted by off duty officers on their own time and without any form of compensation.

Although Chief Quirk died in 1940 Det Sgt Jackman remained assigned as Chief Kruppenbacher's aide for nearly two more years. However, on January 31, 1942, Jackman was reassigned to patrol duties in the 3rd precinct which resulted in the loss of his detective status and accompanying detective stipend. He would remain on patrol in the 3rd precinct up to his retirement on January 1, 1951. Sometime after, he and his wife moved to Tucson, Arizona. Twelve years later, on October 6, 1963, Ret. Sgt. Emmett Jackman died in Kingsbridge Veterans Hospital in Bronx N.Y.

PO JOHN E. J. McKEON # 187

APPOINTED: October 7, 1922
DISMISSED: June 15, 1926

Born in Norwalk, Ct. on July 7, 1894 McKeon came to Yonkers and worked as a Steam fitter. After his appointment to the YPD and a short time on patrol, McKeon was assigned to the Traffic Div. directing vehicular traffic. However, on May 22, 1923 he resigned to earn more money as a Steam fitter but was re-instated to the YPD on Dec. 21, 1923. Very little is known about McKeon but, on June 7th, 8th, and 9th of 1926 he was AWOL from duty. He was brought up on charges with a trial date set for the 15th of June. It was reported that in a telephone conversation with Lt George Ford he said he had been visiting friends in Suffern, NY and became intoxicated, and returned three days later. Having secured new employment again as a Steam fitter, where he said he could earn more money, McKeon declined to make a plea or even attend his trial. At the scheduled hearing, to no one's surprise, McKeon was dismissed from the police department effective June 15, 1926. He was last known living at 110 Waring Place and working as a Gardner.

PO GEORGE H. MULLINS # 147

APPOINTED: October 7, 1922
RETIRED: April 1, 1950

Mullins was born at 49 Garden St. in Yonkers on July 4, 1898. He attended St Joseph's School, Yonkers HS, and worked as a machinist at a local factory. Upon his YPD appointment on Oct. 7, 1922 he patrolled the 4th pct. On March 20, 1925 Mullins escaped serious injury while attempting to move 3 intoxicated men from Grant Park. The men attacked Mullins, taking his nightstick from him and causing injury to his head. However, one shot from the officer's revolver ended the struggle and two men were arrested and were, themselves, treated for head injuries. On May 26, 1925 he was assigned to directing vehicular traffic, but later would be re-assigned to the 3rd pct. where he would spend the rest of his career on patrol. While in the 3rd pct. he was often the driver for Capt. Dominico. Mullins was a soft spoken man, a devout Catholic, and a member of the Knights of Columbus. After his retirement on April 1, 1950 he worked as a security guard for Habirshaw Wire & Cable Co. On February 13, 1963 Ret PO George Mullins died of a heart attack. He was 64 years old.

PO JOHN P. CLANCY # 137

APPOINTED: October 7, 1922
RETIRED: August 1, 1949

John Patrick Clancy was born in Tompkins Cove in Rockland County NY on May 30, 1900. He and his family moved to Yonkers in 1910 where he finished his education. He joined the Army on June 25, 1918, serving in France during the war. Upon his discharged on September 25, 1919 he worked as a trolley conductor. When he was appointed to the YPD on Oct. 7, 1922 he was assigned to the 1st pct. on Wells Avenue on foot patrol. On September 3, 1926, while off duty along with two other off duty officers, he was he was charged with Disorderly Conduct by the Tuckahoe P.D. The YPD suspended Clancy, brought him up on departmental charges, found him guilty, and he was dismissed from the police department. However, following an appeal to the courts he was re-instated with back pay on September 2, 1927. Though frequently in violation of the R & R he did rescue a woman from a fire on February 14, 1935. Clancy retired Aug. 1, 1949 and moved to Dobbs Ferry where he died on February 27, 1987 at the age of 86.

PO FRANK E. KESICKE # 154

APPOINTED: October 7, 1922
RETIRED: March 1, 1950

Born in Yonkers on March 8, 1896, Kesicke attended local schools and later worked as an Iron Molder and Gas Engineer. A resident of 96 Lockwood Ave., Kesicke was 26 years old upon his police appointment, stated he spoke Polish, and that he could ride a motorcycle. As such, he was assigned to the 2nd pct. on motorcycle patrol duty. On one occasion while at the police booth on CPA with his motorcycle, there was a robbery at gunpoint just past midnight. Within minutes Kesicke had arrested the three males responsible. And on June 4, 1936 he saved the life of a woman overcome by gas fumes. Unknown to the police department, and while off duty, Kesicke ran his own contracting company building homes. He kept the business in his son Franks name. Kesicke raised his family living on Greenvale Ave. His daughter said he was a tough and gruff man, but loved his family. He bought a 130 acre fully functioning farm in Rhinebeck, NY. He called it "Kesicke's Farm." For enjoyment Kesicke loved deep sea fishing but due to circulation problems he had one of his legs amputated. Following his retirement on Mar. 1, 1950 he lived full time on his farm for 19 years and died on Mar 30, 1969 at age 73.

PO FRANCIS S. O'BRIEN # 148

APPOINTED: October 7, 1922
RETIRED: March 12, 1960

Known as "Mickey" to most everyone due to his early years as a boxer, Mickey was born March 13, 1895 in Yonkers, attended St Joseph's School, and as a young man worked as a Steam fitter and on the NY Central Railroad. He served in the Army from May 13, 1917 to July 19, 1919 during the Mexican Border War with Co. K, 64th US Infantry Regiment, 7th Div. He was said to have carried a wounded Lt. on his back to US lines. The brother-in-law to Capt. John McCormack, "Mick" was appointed to the YPD on Oct. 7, 1922 and while serving in the 4th precinct, on January 13, 1927 he saved 3 people overcome by gas fumes. In 1934 when the first police radio communication system was instituted, O'Brien and others were assigned to the new "RTD," Radio Telegraph Div., as a licensed radio operator. He would remain in this assignment for the rest of his career. Following mandatory retirement on March 12, 1960 due to age, he enjoyed bowling on several championship teams. On June 19, 1969 Ret PO Francis "Mickey" O'Brien died at age 74 years.

PO JAMES J. SKOWRONSKI # 151

APPOINTED: October 7, 1922
RETIRED: January 16, 1933

Born James Joseph Skowronski in Yonkers on March 11, 1900, James would attend local schools and for a short time worked as a mechanic. In August of 1920 he joined the Navy and was discharged in February of 1922. Later that year on Oct. 7, 1922 he was appointed to the YPD and assigned to the 2nd pct. No doubt Jim's ability to speak Polish and Slavic besides English was very helpful to the dept. But starting about 1926 Skowronski began finding himself being brought up on departmental charges for violating rules. In fact over the next six years he was charged numerous times, one nearly causing his dismissal. And yet, on October 19, 1928 he made an important arrest of a male still with the child he had kidnaped, and whose hands were still tied up. Then around 1931 Jim became ill. In 1933 the Police Surgeon advised the chief that due to a chronic incurable nerve disorder Jim had lost months on sick leave. He therefore deemed him unfit for duty and recommended disability retirement, which was granted Jan. 16, 1933. Jim's brother was PO Frank Skowronski. A resident of 19 Manning Ave., James Skowronski died on August 29, 1955 at the age of 55 years.

PO JOHN P. YASCOVIC #169

APPOINTED: October 9, 1922
RETIRED: April 30, 1944

John Yascovic, who as police officer would weigh over 200 lbs. and be known to his friends as "Ox," was born on June 24, 1900 in Hastings, NY. He was born a Yascovic but that was not the original family name. When his grandfather immigrated to the US from Austria the family name was actually "Jaskowitz." However during the immigration process the name was written phonetically and the result was Yascovic.

Following his formal education he served in the Army during WW one as a Corporal in the Tank Corps of the 15th Division. He served from September 1, 1917, and following the wars end was discharged on March 19, 1919. After the war he took up residence in California and worked in the ship yards. At some point he moved to Yonkers and upon receiving his appointment to the YPD on October 9, 1922 he was assigned to foot patrol in the 2nd precinct, but often worked as the Patrol Wagon driver.

Three years later on May 18, 1925 he was re-assigned to the Traffic Division on motorcycle patrol. There seems no doubt that Yascovic took his police duty seriously as evidenced by his action on May 6, 1930. On that date at 3:00 AM and while home off duty and sleeping, he heard a woman screaming for help outside his home at 36 Chestnut Street. Upon looking out the window he saw two men running down the street. He quickly grabbed his revolver and, from his window, fired it in an attempt to stop them, unfortunately without success. But the woman was unharmed. On another occasion only four days later, he was on motorcycle patrol near the Racetrack when he began to chase a speeder. As he pulled alongside the vehicle, three times the driver tried to force his motorcycle off the road. On the third try Yascovic did

PO John P. Yascovic #169 (cont.)

lose control and crash his motorcycle. Though injured he again mounted the machine and continued the pursuit. This time he fired several times striking the windows of the vehicle bringing it to a halt. Of course the driver was arrested and no doubt provided with a severe attitude adjustment. Later Yascovic had his injuries treated at St John's Hospital.

On April 23, 1931 Yascovic was awarded a certificate of Excellent Police Work for his action on three occasions. The first was for locating three males wanted for a robbery on October 2, 1930. The second for arresting suspects on October 3, 1930, who were wanted for stealing a car in Poughkeepsie, NY; and third for arresting other subjects on January 17, 1931 for possession of a stolen car. And again on March 3, 1932 the Honor Board awarded John Yascovic a Commendation for his heroic actions on December 15, 1931. On that date at the scene of a fire PO Yascovic repeatedly ran into a burning building to save women and children by helping them to safety. It seemed that Yascovic just could not escape notoriety. On September 18, 1932 motorcycle officer Yascovic reportedly chased a 7 ton truck, whose driver had fallen asleep going south on North Broadway. Acting quickly Yascovic left his motorcycle, ran and jumped onto the running board, then into the truck cab, and pulled on the emergency brake. There seemed no doubt that his actions saved lives and once again earned the praise of his superiors..

In addition to his traffic duty responsibilities, in August of 1935 Yascovic was named the departments Taxi and bus inspector, working out of city hall. In point of fact he was the police departments first "Hack Inspector," responsible for routine monthly inspections of all automotive public carriers in Yonkers. All bus and taxi's had their brakes, steering, tires, fire extinguishers, and doors inspected and issued a sticker if they passed, and a summons if they failed.

On one occasion while on motorcycle patrol it was reported that, due to a coughing spell, Yascovic lost control of his motorcycle and had an accident. Following an exam by the police surgeon it was confirmed that the officer suffered from asthma. As a result of this diagnosis, on January 16, 1944 he was transferred, for his own safety, from motorcycle duty to foot patrol in the 1st precinct. During a follow-up examination by the police surgeon a determination was made that John Yascovic was no longer physically fit for duty and, after nearly 22 years service, was ordered retired on a physical disability effective April 30, 1944.

Being a veteran of WW 1 John was a member of the Yonkers Police Dept. War Veterans Legion and was very active in the organization. In fact at one time he was elected their president. But following retirement John moved to Richmond, Cal. and worked for the Kaizer shipyards. Ret PO John "The Ox" Yascovic died on January 5, 1967 at the age of 66 years.

PO ROBERT P. MAIER # 164

APPOINTED: October 9, 1922
RETIRED: December 16, 1942

Bob Maier was born in the city of Yonkers on Jan. 10, 1899. As a young man he listed his employment as that of a "Spot Welder." Following the outbreak of World War 1 Maier, who spoke German fluently, enlisted in the Army on Dec. 11, 1917 serving in the Army Air Corps 498th Aero Squad, part of the A.E.F. He was honorably discharged on Jan. 20, 1919. On appointment to the YPD on Oct. 9, 1922 he was assigned to the 3rd precinct on foot patrol. However on April 28, 1923 he was transferred to the Traffic Division directing traffic for a year and then, returned to the 3rd precinct. Later Maier was assigned to the Emergency Squad where he would handle many rescues and saved many lives. On Jan 14, 1928 Maier was commended for rescuing several lives in a fire on January 3, 1928. On Jan. 30, 1942 PO Maier was returned to the 3rd pct. Following an exam by the police surgeon Maier was deemed physically unfit for duty and was retired on a disability pension on Dec. 16, 1942. After living for a while in Madeira Beach, Florida, Bob Maier died on June 23, 1979 in Troy, NY at the age of 80.

PO JAMES J. COLGAN # 157

APPOINTED: October 9, 1922
RETIRED: January 31, 1952

Though Jim Colgan was born in the Riverdale section of the Bronx, on Aug 8, 1896 his family moved to Yonkers. At the start of World War 1, Colgan joined the Army on May 4, 1917 serving overseas with the 58th Artillery. He received a Purple Heart for wounds received and poison gas exposure. He was honorably discharged on May 7, 1919. Jim worked for the Federal Sugar Refinery up to his appointment to the YPD on Oct. 9, 1922. At that time he was assigned to the Traffic Division directing Traffic in Getty Square. Colgan was among those chosen and trained to be part of the new Riot Squad. In 1934 he was awarded a commendation for the arrest of a robbery suspect Dec. 15, 1933. After directing traffic in Getty Square for 25 years, on June 4, 1947 he was re-assigned to the 1st pct. Armored Squad Detail. Five years later, on Jan 31, 1952, he would retire to work as a guard at the Otis Elevator Company. "Big Jim" Colgan, as he was known, would not live to see his daughter Jane become a Yonkers "Policewoman." A resident of 250 North Broadway, Jim Colgan would die unexpectedly in St. John's Hospital on November 27, 1956 at the age of 60 years.

PO HAROLD V. TYNAN # 168

APPOINTED: October 9, 1922
DISMISSED: May 1, 1944

Tynan was born in the city of Yonkers on May 29, 1901, attended local schools, and as a young man worked as a Steam fitter. After joining the YPD on Oct. 9, 1922 he was assigned to the 4th pct. on foot patrol. Four years later, on Sept. 1, 1926, he was re-assigned to the Traffic Div. directing traffic. On Aug. 29, 1927 Tynan was responsible for arresting a male for the sexual assault of an 8 year old female child. Following the installation of traffic lights, on June 29, 1928 Tynan returned to the 4th pct. Over the years Tynan was brought up on charges many times and had been penalized several days pay. On Dec 12, 1942, while working in the 3rd pct., he was determined to be a chronic alcoholic by the Police Surgeon. Again he was charged and again fined. Following his last trial on May 1, 1944 Tynan was found guilty of being intoxicated while off duty and using profanity against a superior officer and was dismissed from the department on May 1, 1944. Harold Tynan died off a heart attack in Haverstraw, NY on Dec. 20, 1951. He was 50 years old.

PO HAROLD J. COLE # 158

APPOINTED: October 9, 1922
RETIRED: November 16, 1950

Cole was born in Yonkers on Aug. 19, 1899, attended local schools, and worked as a "Packer." He joined the National Guard on Sept. 25, 1918 serving up to May 19, 1920. He was hired to the YPD on Oct. 9, 1922 from 144 Linden St. at $2,300 per year and assigned to the 1st pct. On Jan 5, 1923 he was assigned to directing vehicular traffic. After a few years he worked in the 3rd pct. and then was assigned to the Emergency Squad. It was here that on July 30, 1930 he was credited with making the arrest of a long sought after screen burglar. On Jan 13, 1931 a team of armed bandits began a robbery spree by committing 8 holdups in Yonkers and Mt Vernon. In one robbery the victim was shot. Following the last robbery in Yonkers, PO Cole and his partner tracked them to the Bronx where they made the arrest at gun point. He was awarded the "Honorable Mention" and elevated to Detective. He would, however, by choice, remain on patrol. Harold Coles's last police assignment was in the Radio Telegraph Div., from which he would later retire on Nov 16, 1950. A resident of 88 Saratoga Avenue, Ret PO Harold Cole died on December 7, 1964.

LT JOHN E. SACKETT

APPOINTED: October 9, 1922
RETIRED: May 1, 1955

John was one of those very athletic boys. He played baseball with "The Ravens" and other local teams as a pitcher and shortstop, ran track and was a cross country runner. At one time he was also considered the light weight boxing champ of Westchester County. He was born July 29, 1894 and as a young man worked for Otis Elevator Co. Upon his police appointment on Oct. 9, 1922 he was assigned to the 2nd precinct. On June 13, 1928 he was reassigned to motorcycle duty for several years and he remained active in sports by playing on the PBA baseball team. In 1929 PO Sackett was credited with saving the life of a baby in convulsions. Sackett was promoted to Sergeant on Jan. 1, 1933 and returned to the 2nd pct. Ten years later, on Nov 19, 1943, he was promoted to Lieutenant. When he retired on May 1, 1955 he moved to No. Miami Beach, Florida where his son David was a police officer, and where, following a brief illness he died on August 22, 1968. He was 74 years old.

PO TIMOTHY A. MOYNIHAN # 163

APPOINTED: October 9, 1922
RETIRED: February 28, 1950

Born in Yonkers on March 6, 1899 Moynihan graduated from Saunders HS and worked as a chauffeur. He served in the Army during WW 1 from Sept of 1918 up to his discharge on May 1, 1922. He was appointed a police officer on Oct. 9, 1922 and assigned to the 1st pct. Then in May of 1924 he was trained for the newly established Riot Squad. Following his assignment to the Traffic Unit on motorcycle on May 1, 1927, he was credited with saving a life of a man whose clothes had caught fire on June 8, 1927. For his actions Moynihan was awarded the Honorable Mention. Being an expert shot, in Jan. 1928 Moynihan was accepted into the YPD pistol team to compete with other dept.'s. On March 6, 1929 he was moved from Traffic to the 4th pct. Being an auto mechanic, in April of 1934 he was placed in charge of the Police Repair Shop and to also investigate the cause of serious accidents. On Feb. 25, 1941 he returned to the 3rd pct. until August of 1946 when he returned to motorcycle duty from which he would later retire on Feb. 28, 1950. Following retirement he operated his own auto repair shop in Yonkers until his death on Sept 27, 1980 at age 81 years.

PO EDWARD L. McCORMACK # 161

APPOINTED: October 9, 1922
DISMISSED: September 20, 1926

Ed McCormack was born in Manitou, NY on August 26, 1896. Following his formal education he gained employment which he later listed as a Motorman. Ed was a WW-1 veteran having served in the Army from Sept 1917 to January 1918. He was a private in the 7th Field Artillery. Upon his appointment to the YPD October 9, 1922 he was assigned to foot patrol in the 2nd precinct and lived at 142 Morningside Place. It didn't take long for problems to surface. He was charged with Neglect of duty on January 14, 1926 and was fined one day's pay. And again charged with Neglect of Duty on March 15, 1926 and fined five days pay. Then on September 3, 1926, while off duty with two other off duty officers, he became involved in an incident in Tuckahoe involving women and boisterous conduct. Criminal charges for Disorderly Conduct and Criminal Mischief were later dismissed. However his captain brought charges against him, he was found guilty and was dismissed from the police department on September 20, 1926.

PO STEPHEN T. DANKOVIC # 23

APPOINTED: October 9, 1922
DISMISSED: February 6, 1935

Steve, one of 3 brothers who would also join the YPD, was born Aug. 1, 1893 in Brooklyn, NY. He graduated from St Vincent DePaul, Salesian Parochial school in Brooklyn. His family moved to Yonkers and Steve, who stood 6" 4," worked for a butcher delivering meat by horse & wagon and later as a railroad conductor. He was an Army veteran of WW-1 serving in France as a corporal. Though his MOS was Military Intelligence his daughter said he suffered from effects of the enemy poison gas. Upon his appointment to the YPD he was assigned to the 1st pct. and later the 2nd. While in the 2nd pct. he worked mounted patrol on a horse he named "Major." On July 13, 1923 while on mounted patrol Dankovic was thrown from his horse striking his head causing hospitalization. He returned to work in the 1st pct. and on June 16, 1926 he was appointed a Detective up to Dec. 1927 and was moved to the 4th pct. Following charges of neglect of duty on a number of occasions Dankovic pled guilty and was dismissed from the YPD on Feb. 6, 1935. His two brothers, John & Peter remained in the dept. Following many years working security for Con Edison Stephen Dankovic died on October 26, 1969. He was 76.

LIEUTENANT LAWRENCE P. SHEA

APPOINTED: October 9, 1922
RETIRED: November 14, 1960

Lawrence Philip Shea was born in Yonkers on November 16, 1895 the eldest son of recently arrived Irish immigrants. One of six children, Larry attended St. Mary's grade school, as a boy sold newspapers after school in Getty Square and at about age twelve went to work in the shipping department at the Alexander Smith carpet factory. On February 25, 1915 he enlisted in the 10th Regiment, New York Infantry (Yonkers unit of the National Guard) and participated in the punitive expedition (1916-17) against the Mexican bandit, Pancho Villa. Already a sergeant and drill instructor when war was declared against Germany during World War 1, he helped train troops who would later fight in France. He participated in most of the major battles in which the American forces were engaged during World War I. In fact his grandson reported that he was wounded and gassed in France while serving with Company G, 51st Pioneer Regiment of the 42nd Rainbow Division.

Sergeant Shea was also boxing champion of the 28,000 man Rainbow Division and given the name "Kid Decker." He also played amateur baseball and won many awards in regional track and field competitions. Shea studied accounting while with the US Army of occupation in the Rhine Valley in Germany and was honorably discharged on July 5, 1919. Upon his return to the United States, he worked for the U.S. Post Office and the Remington Rand Corporation in Bridgeport, Ct. In June 1922 he married Mary Walder, the Yonkers-born daughter of Swiss and Irish immigrants, and they had three daughters, Dorothy, Mary, and Laurie. The Shea family would live at 582 Van Cortlandt Park Avenue for almost fifty years.

Lt. Lawrence P. Shea (cont.)

Larry Shea was appointed to the Yonkers Police Department on October 9, 1922 with an annual salary of $2,300. As a rookie patrolman he was assigned to the 1st precinct on foot patrol working from the Wells Avenue station house. One of his early assignments was special liquor violation duty. Disguised as laborers, Shea and another patrolman from the 2nd precinct mingled with Empire City Race Track workers in a Yonkers Avenue restaurant and arrested the waiter for violating a prohibition ordinance banning the sale of alcoholic beverages. As a young patrolman he believed firmly in walking his beat so that he could familiarize himself with everyone in the neighborhood and so that they would know who he was. In May of 1924 the police department organized a "Riot Squad." This unit consisted of hand-picked men who were given specialized training in large disorders and crowd control. PO Larry Shea was one of those chosen and trained.

Shea's supervisors must have seen some potential in him because on June 16, 1926 he was assigned to the Detective Bureau as a Detective. However for reasons unknown, on October 14, 1927 he was reassigned to patrol duties in the 1st precinct. Despite this change in assignment he never lost his enthusiasm for the police department and various activities associated with it. In fact, in October of 1930 the local newspaper reported that a baseball game would be held to..."decide the supremacy between the Yonkers Police and the Yonkers Firemen." Of course Larry Shea eagerly joined the police team and participated in the competition. Unfortunately the result of the game is not known.

On December 1, 1931 Shea was again elevated to the position of detective where he would prove to be an excellent criminal investigator. Due to the trust his supervisors had in him, in November 1936, Detective Shea and his partner, Detective John Daly, were assigned to protect Cardinal Pacelli, soon to be elected Pope Pius XII, when he visited the Bronxville home of Joseph P. Kennedy, U.S. Ambassador to Great Britain.

Shea was promoted to the rank of Sergeant on December 16, 1939 after placing second on the civil service promotional exam with a score of 93.75 and was assigned to the 4th precinct. By 1940 he reportedly had received three citations for special police performance. Sgt. Shea had the unique privilege and honor to be the very first Yonkers Police officer selected to attend the three-month FBI National Police Academy in the Spring of 1941 (17th Session). He was detailed to this training on April 7, 1941 where, among many other topics, he learned fingerprinting, criminal forensics, and the investigation of sabotage and espionage cases. He later received additional advanced training from the FBI in counterespionage. Shea impressed the FBI to such a degree that he was invited to join the FBI, but decided to remain with the Yonkers Police. (He would later give a letter of congratulations signed by FBI Director J. Edgar Hoover to his grandson, Larry, forty years later when he was moving to Washington to join the Federal Government. "If you ever have a problem," he told his grandson, "this may help."). Right after his return from the FBI Academy Shea learned that several volunteer members of the department had received permission to form a Police Athletic League in Yonkers. With his background and skill in sports, he was quick to join the volunteers. On July 15, 1941 a meeting was held where the new organizations first president was elected along with his board. Sgt. Shea was elected a trustee in the new PAL.

Sergeant Shea's training at the FBI and additional training at the U.S. Army Chemical Warfare School at Edgewood Arsenal, Maryland, quickly led to his appointment after the outbreak of World War 2 on December 7, 1941, as Director (later Coordinator) of the Yonkers Auxiliary Police Force. Also known

Lt. Lawrence P. Shea (cont.)

as Yonkers Civil Defense. He was one of three Yonkers officers who attended a special Air Wardens' Defense School in White Plains and then trained a bomb squad of 150 men which would have gone into action in the event of air raids on the city. Throughout the war he gave lectures on civil defense, sabotage, air raid protection procedures and related subjects to area schools and civic associations. Having been a war veteran and a charter member of the Yonkers Police War Veterans Legion, Sgt Shea had been serving as Vice Commander of the Yonkers Police War Veterans Legion. However, on October 15, 1942 the organization elected him "Commander" by acclamation.

On December 31, 1945 Shea was promoted to Lieutenant, given a $100. increase in pay, which raised his salary to $3,500., and was assigned to desk duty in the 4th precinct. On June 1, 1946 Lt Shea was again reassigned, this time to the Traffic Bureau. In October of that same year Lt Shea was put in charge of the Motor Transport Maintenance Bureau, which was the police repair shop. This was short lived also, for on November 16, 1947 he was transferred to the 3rd precinct as a desk lieutenant. In 1951, Lieutenant Shea was appointed commander of the newly established Training and Records Division at the Wells Avenue Police Headquarters. According to an article in The Herald Statesman newspaper, this made Lt. Shea the supervisor of the first women (civilian) assigned to work in police headquarters. His daughter, Laurie, related that her father also initiated the school crossing guards program in Yonkers. Then on January 12, 1953 Lt Shea was again reassigned to desk duty in the 3rd precinct.

For many years Larry Shea served as head of the American Legion's Crescent Post No. 935, in Yonkers. He received national citations from the American Legion in 1928 for community service and for increasing the membership of the Crescent Post. He was also a past Commander of the Police War Veteran's Legion and Vice President of the PBA, a post he resigned in 1939 when he was promoted to sergeant. For many years he was also active in the Holy Name Society of St. Denis Catholic Parish.

Larry Shea had a well-deserved reputation as an outstanding Irish tenor and was frequently asked to sing "The Star Spangled Banner," "My Buddy," "Danny Boy" and other songs at parish, community events and at funerals for deceased police officers. It should be no surprise that he was also a member of the police departments singing Glea Club. Throughout his long life he was a devoted family man with a passion for both amateur and professional sports, especially baseball, football and boxing. He knew by heart the records of every professional team and player. In commenting about "Police Personalities," a Herald Statesman reporter singled out Lt. Shea, writing he was one, "*...who can wax hotly about fighters from Jack Johnson to Joe Lewis...Shea's opinions are vivified by personal demonstrations of uppercuts and left hooks...He is handy with the dukes.*" Lt. Shea supervised the 3rd precinct on Radford Street throughout most of the 1950's and personally knew many of the residents of the precinct. He reached the age of 65 years, the maximum allowed for a police officer, and as such was mandatorily retired on November 14, 1960 after serving the people of Yonkers for thirty-eight years.

Lt. Shea and his wife, Mary, moved to the mid-Hudson Valley and later to Port St. Lucie, Florida in the 1970s to live near their daughter, Laurie, and he died in Florida on February 12,1987 of heart failure at the age of 91 years. At that time his daughter Laurie related her feelings in part ending her comments by saying...."*He walked with honor.*" Former Lt Larry Shea's cousin, Captain Bernard McGinn, also served for many years with the Y.P.D. His oldest grandson, Larry Travers (named after his grandfather), works in national security for the federal government in Washington. Larry's youngest grandchild, Patrick Hart, Jr., graduated from the Florida Police Academy and is a detective with the Ft. Lauderdale Police Department.

PO EDWARD C. NEWBRAND # 165

APPOINTED: October 9, 1922
DIED: March 25, 1938

Newbrand wasn't the spelling of Ed's birth name. Being of German ancestry he was actually born Edward Charles "Neubrandt" in NYC on December 10, 1894. But according to his daughter, during WW-2 he changed his name to "Newbrand" due to the disdain by many against those of German heritage.

While still a young boy he and his family moved from NYC to Yonkers N.Y. in 1906. He attended local public schools after which he would, while still being fairly young, gain employment with Otis Elevator Co. During World War 1 he remained working with Otis as a machinist foreman.

It was while living at 230 No. Trenchard Street, and at the age of 28, that he was called for appointment to the police department on October 9, 1922. Following his initial police recruit training he was assigned to patrol duty in the 2nd precinct on Central Avenue. In 1934, the year our first police radio system was inaugurated, Newbrand would be transferred to the 1st precinct both on foot patrol and radio motor patrol.

Eddie Newbrand was reportedly an extremely athletic individual who, prior to the YPD, had gained wide achievements as an outstanding athlete. During his younger years he had earned a large collection of medals for his athletic abilities. In 1913, as a member of the old Crestwood Athletic Club, he won a silver cup from the league as the best 2nd basement of the season. He also won awards for his pitching ability. In 1914 he won a gold medal for the highest fielding averages. That season he was also presented with a silver medal for sprinting. At the height of his amateur baseball career in 1916, it was reported that Newbrand was offered a position on a New York professional team, but declined the offer. Even while working for Otis Elevator he pitched while playing on their baseball team receiving widespread recognition. Even after his police appointment he couldn't resist playing on the police association team.

Newbrand became one of the most well liked men in the 1st precinct following his assignment there in 1934. He was described as a very quiet and soft spoken man who didn't smoke or drink, and loved running and working in his garden. However, despite his athletic conditioning, in the early part of 1938 he became ill and required surgery for a gall bladder problem. Only a few days following his surgery in St. John's Hospital, Edward Newbrand died on March 25, 1938. He was 43 years old.

At the time of his death the rules of the City Pension System provided for a widow's Pension of $600. a year. However, if an officer died as the result of injuries sustained in the line of duty, the widow's pension would be one half of her husband's salary, which in this case would have been $1,500. a year. Newbrand's widow appealed to the City Pension System requesting a line of duty death certification, which would allow for that $1,500. annual pension. She pointed out that her husband had been struck by a car while on duty on June 8, 1926, injuring him seriously and damaging his gall bladder. It took several years, but on March 9, 1943, following appeals to the NYS Supreme Court, the trustees of the police city pension fund officially determined that officer Ed Newbrand had died as a result of injuries sustained in the line of duty and awarded Newbrand's widow the increase in pension she had sought. A very unusual determination indeed, considering he died 12 years after the accident.

PO JOHN J. HIDOCK Jr # 160

APPOINTED: October 9, 1922
RETIRED: August 1, 1950

John was born Oct. 8, 1898 in Yonkers at his home at the corner of Washington St & Riverdale Ave. He attended Holy Trinity School, spoke Polish, Slavish, Russian, and as a young man worked as a chauffeur. John enjoyed golf and in fact he had been a past president of the Westchester County Golf Assoc. Upon his police appointment on Oct. 9, 1922 he was assigned to the 2nd pct. and stationed at the Police Booth at CPA & Tuckahoe Rd with a three wheel motorcycle to answer calls. On Mar. 25, 1926 he was assigned to motorcycle duty in the Traffic Div. and rode for 14 years until April 5, 1940 when he was assigned as a Special Investigator in the Corporation Council's Office. On April 8, 1943 he was returned to motorcycle duty in Traffic up to about 1950 when he was detailed to the Court of Special Sessions. He was often described as the YPD's "good will ambassador" and a great public relations man. When he retired on Aug. 1, 1950 from the Traffic Div. he worked security at Yonkers Raceway. Following a heart attack John Hidock died Dec. 11, 1960 at the age of 62 years.

PO FRANK W. MACKEY # 162

APPOINTED: October 9, 1922
RETIRED: March 16, 1950

Frank Mackey was born in Garnerville, NY on February 16, 1894 and as a young man would work as a chauffeur. When hired by the YPD on Oct. 9, 1922 he was assigned to foot patrol in the 4th pct. Then on May 17, 1929 he was re-assigned to the newly established Armored Motorcycle Squad along with PO Mike Walsh, who would later be killed on duty on his motorcycle. Their duty was to provide security escorts to payroll deliveries and bank money escorts. In 1933 he was re-assigned to using one of the newly purchased armored police cars, doing the same type escorts. On July 17, 1941 the department began the "Dispatch Rider" program and Mackey was assigned there as part of the Traffic Division to patrol on a three wheel motorcycle and enforce parking violations city wide. He remained there up to his retirement on March 16, 1950. Frank's son, Frank Jr was a Westchester Co. police officer and his grandson William was a Westchester Co. police detective. Three years after retirement Frank Mackey died on May 4, 1953. He was 57 years old.

PO JAMES S. BOLAN # 156

APPOINTED: October 9, 1922
RETIRED: September 16, 1951

James Sylvester Bolan was born in Yonkers on August 10, 1893. His father had suffered an injury in his forties and subsequently developed a blood disease which resulted in his death. At that time young Jim Bolan was about 15 and was forced to end his schooling and begin to work to support his mother and siblings. He worked for several years on the tunnels, as a Ford automobile mechanic, and in his early twenties went to work in Yonkers as a Trolley Car conductor.

On October 9, 1922 Bolan, who was 30 years old and stood 6' with a slim build, was appointed a police officer with a starting salary of $2,300. a year. Following a brief time in what was then known as the School of Instruction, and working for a brief period providing security for the mail-cars on the local trains, officer Bolan was assigned to foot patrol duties in the 2nd precinct on Central Avenue. As such he would often be seen working at the school crossing at Central Avenue and Yonkers Avenue seeing to it that school children going and coming from school would be crossed safely. Jim Bolan was reportedly named after his father's brother, James S. Bolan, who would later rise to the rank of New York City Police Commissioner, serving as such from April 15, 1933 to December 31, 1933. On many occasions his uncle tried to encourage him to leave Yonkers to join the NYPD. But young Jim, who by the way was known as "Big Jim" or "Smokey" because of his ever present pipe, preferred to remain in Yonkers. Officer Bolan also had two first cousins, James and William Ward, who were also police officers in New York.

In January of 1928 when the YPD was starting a "Pistol Competition Team" elimination trials were held to determine who was good enough to be on the team and participate in county wide tournaments. An expert shot with his revolver "Big Jim" had no trouble making the team. Many years later, in August of 1948 a well-known Yonkers physician reported that his wife had been shot and killed in their Heights Drive home. As one of the first officers to respond PO Bolan questioned the doctor and within a short time arrested the man for the murder of his wife.

On September 16, 1951, after nearly 29 years service, Bolan retired from the police department, while still assigned to the 2nd precinct. Although Bolan was a true outdoors man, loving fishing, hunting, camping, and boating, he went back to work as a guard for the First National Bank at Central Park Avenue and Tuckahoe Road. His granddaughter Catherine Bolan described her grandfather as follows; "*This is a man who loved all things, wanted to experience everything, and never met anyone he considered a stranger. My grandfather was a good man.*"

Jim Bolan moved to Lake Carmel, NY, and still later to St. Petersburg, Florida. He remarried at the age of 93 years and lived with his new wife in Athens, Alabama. He died there on October 14, 1988 at the age of 95 years.

PO MATTHEW P. BALDWIN # 107

APPOINTED: October 9, 1922
RETIRED: November 7, 1961

It seems that a common thread that runs through most who become police officers is that most are active in sports in their early years. And this applies to Matthew Baldwin who, as a teenager, loved to play baseball and his position was catcher. Matt was born August 6, 1897 and grew up on Clinton Street attending St. Mary's School. As a young man he listed his employment as a clerk and plumber.

During World War 1, in 1918 he reportedly served as a Private overseas with Co. 9, 79th Division of the Army. And I guess that would be no surprise either since his grandfather was a Civil War veteran. Following his discharge he worked as a machinist until his appointment to the Yonkers Police Dept. on Oct. 9, 1922. Following police recruit instruction, Baldwin was assigned to the 1st precinct on Wells Avenue. In May of 1924 Baldwin, along with many others, was chosen and trained in special tactics in case they were called upon to be utilized as part of the new Riot Squad.

As part of transfers effecting dozens of officers, on January 16, 1926, Baldwin was assigned as a detective in the Detective Bureau. Unfortunately for him this assignment would only last five months and then he was returned to patrol duty in the 1st precinct. As an active member of the Police Association Baldwin served on the committee which organized the 1st annual "Memorial Service of the Police Dept." On March 25, 1928 the organization honored the 27 Yonkers police officers who had died to that date, since the association was formed in 1916.

An aggressive officer, Baldwin was quick to take the initiative, conduct an investigation alone if need be, and make the arrest. Bravery was another trait of his, evidenced by his actions at a two alarm fire in a four story building at 128 Main Street on May 12, 1930. While on his post at 6:30 AM and alerted about the fire, Baldwin turned in the alarm and then ran through the building several times alerting and rescuing tenants inside. But it wouldn't be long before he had another brush with danger.

On January 8, 1931 he was on his post at about 5 AM when, unknown to him at the time, two men had broken into an apartment and shot and killed the occupant. As the two men exited the building they came out in front of PO Baldwin who did not hear the earlier shots and was stunned when the men opened fire at him. The officer returned fire which turned into a running gun fight. Despite all the shots fired, luckily Baldwin was not hit and unfortunately the two men escaped. He received no recognition for that job but, he was awarded a departmental commendation on June 11, 1932 for the arrest of a female charged with attempted murder, which he physically prevented.

It was sometime in the mid 1930's that Baldwin was assigned to the Police Emergency Squad. One of his rescues which received much notoriety occurred on July 14, 1939. PO Matthew Baldwin and his partner, PO John Buecherl, of the Emergency Squad were just a few hours into their early tour when they received the call on their one way radio reporting someone hanging from an electrical cable tower near Trevor Park. The officers sped to the nearest call box, as required, notified the desk Lieutenant that they had received the call, and then sped to the scene of the incident. When they arrived Baldwin and his partner found a 13 year-old boy hanging 30 feet in the air from electrical wires in an unconscious condition. Apparently, a short time earlier, the boy planned on fishing the next day but wanted to hide his

PO Matthew P. Baldwin #107 (cont.)

special bait. He chose to hide it on top of a 40 foot electrical cable tower located between the railroad tracks and the Hudson River. As he approached the top, the boy fell, striking high voltage wires. He was severely shocked and scorched by 11,000 volts of electricity, but luckily, he didn't fall to the ground. He was caught 10 feet from the top when his belt buckle became tangled in some wires. As the boy hung there unconscious, PO Baldwin grabbed a pair of rubber gloves and cutting pliers. He climbed the steel tower as quickly and carefully as possible, weaving in and out among the high tension wires. As he approached the boy, it was clear that the boy's clothing was smoldering, and in fact his pant leg was starting to burn. PO Buecherl enlisted the aid of a boater who had a canvass tarpaulin. The tarpaulin was transformed into a make-shift net. From thirty feet up, Baldwin grabbed the boy and cut his belt. The boy fell safely into the tarp being held by Buecherl and others. The boy was taken to Yonkers General Hospital where he recovered. For his action that day officer Baldwin received the department Honorable Mention.

Despite his outstanding record, on April 16, 1946, Baldwin was transferred from the Emergency Squad to the 3rd precinct on routine patrol. The following year he was re-assigned to the Traffic Division, on foot, directing vehicular traffic at various street intersections. He would also spend some time detailed to the Police Repair Shop but would ultimately retire from the Traffic Division on November 7, 1961.

During these later years Baldwin suffered a loss of hearing and eventually became deaf. A resident of 50 Riverdale Avenue, Ret PO Matthew Baldwin developed pneumonia and died on May 2, 1970 at age 73 years.

PO MICHAEL J. REAGAN # 170

APPOINTED: October 9, 1922
RETIRED: November 15, 1948

Michael Joseph Reagan was born Dec 23, 1898 in Yonkers and attended St. Joseph's school. As a young man he worked for the Westchester Lighting Co., and later worked as a Pipe fitter. Reagan was hired to the YPD on Oct. 9, 1922 at $2,300 a year and assigned to the 3rd pct. In Jan 1939 he was commended for refusing a bribe to release prisoners arrested for operating an illegal alcohol "still." Well-liked by his fellow officers, Reagan was elected as a Y.P.A. trustee for the 3rd pct. He was also a charter member of the Protestant St. George Society of the YPD. In 1942 Reagan campaigned to be elected president of the Police Assoc., but lost by a small margin. In late 1948 he was examined by the police surgeon and deemed physically unfit for duty and granted disability retirement on Nov. 15, 1948. In retirement he worked as a guard at the local Herald Statesman newspaper. Mike Reagan's nephews are Deputy Chief Frank and Det. Peter Intervallo. Following a brief illness Mike Reagan died Dec 4, 1972 at age 73 years.

PO THOMAS W. BURROWS # 171

APPOINTED: October 17, 1922
RETIRED: November 1, 1946

A big Irishman, standing 6' 2", Burrows was born in NYC on Mar 28, 1900. He was appointed to the YPD on October 17, 1922 and was assigned to foot patrol. After being assigned to the Traffic Div. on Jan 5, 1923, he was moved to the 2nd pct. on June 29, 1928. On Sept. 6, 1945, with 23 years service, it was reported that while on duty he was kicked in the face by a horse, causing severe face and head injury. When questioned his daughter said he was protecting a child when he was kicked. He never recovered completely. Following a recommendation by the police surgeon Burrows was retired on a physical disability pension on Nov 1, 1946. In fact his daughter said her father was blinded in one eye requiring a glass eye due to the injury. Tom moved to Tampa, Fl. where he worked as a security guard. However he continued to petition the trustees of the Pension Board to grant him a three quarters salary pension due to his injury sustained on duty. His petition was granted in Feb 1947 and the increase in pension dollars was paid retroactively to his date of retirement. While living in Florida Burrows loved fishing to pass time. On April 10, 1964, Tom Burrows died following a short illness. He was 64 years old.

PO EDWARD J. KEEHAN # 172

APPOINTED: January 24, 1923
RETIRED: March 16, 1951

Born October 19, 1897 in Yonkers, Ed Keehan attended local schools and later would obtain employment as a steam fitter. While living at 112 Oliver Avenue he was appointed to the YPD and assigned to the 1st precinct on Wells Avenue. Keehan would serve many years in the 1st precinct earning a reputation of being able to "handle himself." It was said that on more than one occasion when a prisoner attempted to assault him, the prisoner would sincerely regret the attempt. A friendly outgoing officer Ed Keehan was always ready to help a cause. Toward the end of 1930, around the holidays, the YPD formed the "Relief Committee of the Yonkers Police Dept." They were extremely successful in obtaining donations from businesses to give to the needy, and Keehan worked hard as a member to help. In Dec of 1931 he was the Chairman of the annual "Police Association Ball." Following his retirement on Mar. 16, 1951 Keehan, the son of PO James Keehan, died on March 6, 1971 at the age of 73 years.

PO JOSEPH F. FAHEY # 173

APPOINTED: January 24, 1923
RETIRED: October 31, 1947

Joseph Francis Fahey was born in Yonkers on May 26, 1895 and received his education in St. Mary's School. On Sept. 8, 1917 he joined the Army and fought during WW-1 with Battery "D", 106th Field Artillery in the battles of St. Mihiel, France & Chatacourt, Flanders, Belgium. He was discharged April 4, 1919 and worked as a chauffeur. Appointed January 24, 1923 and after a short time on patrol in the precincts, he was assigned to the Traffic Div. on motorcycle patrol where he would spend the majority of his career. On Feb. 28, 1928 Fahey was credited with saving the life of a 16 year old girl who accidentally drank poison. On Jan. 28, 1930 when the "Special Service Squad" (ESU) was put in service, Fahey was an original member of the unit. Fahey also displayed his athletic interest in 1930 playing on the PBA baseball team. In mid-1930 Fahey was returned to motorcycle duty and in Oct 1942 he returned to precinct patrol. Joe Fahey was found to be physically unfit for duty and was retired on a disability Oct 31, 1947. A member of the YPD Police War Veterans Legion his health failed quickly and he died Feb 14, 1948, four months after retiring. He was 52 years old.

SGT JOHN J. BALINT # 7

APPOINTED: January 24, 1923
RETIRED: February 16, 1955

John Balint was born in Czechoslovakia on Jan. 1, 1901 and immigrated to the US with his family at age 1 year. He attended Holy Trinity School, spoke 3 languages, and worked as a chauffeur. Upon his YPD appointment he was assigned to the Traffic Div., and on July 1, 1924 he was moved to the mounted horseback patrol in Getty Square but later was detailed to bicycle patrol. In Sept. 1924 Balint was credited with saving a woman trapped in a building fire who was overcome by smoke. In October of 1926 when the mounted unit was disbanded and the horses were auctioned and sold, Balint was the last to lose his Getty Square mounted duty. He would trade his horse for a motor cycle until April 16, 1939 when he was promoted to Sgt. and sent to the 3rd pct. On Aug. 21, 1942 Balint was inducted into the Army serving during WW-2 in the Military Police Motorcycle Traffic Section in Miami until his discharge on Aug. 8, 1945. Rejoining the YPD he went back on his motorcycle. Following his retirement Feb 16, 1955 he moved to Brewster, NY where he died on May 5, 1964 at age 63.

LT CARL HAFFNER

APPOINTED: January 24, 1923
RETIRED: January 29, 1963

Born Karl Hauffner (he later changed spelling) on January 19, 1899 in the "Flats" area of Yonkers, Carl lived at 126 Riverdale Ave, attended local schools, and worked as a machinist for Otis Elevator Co. He was a member of the Yonkers Teutonia, and the local Masons lodge. Upon his appointment to the PD Jan 24, 1923 he worked the 2nd precinct for a few years until May 18, 1925 when he was appointed a detective. But on Jan 16, 1926 he returned to patrol in the 1st pct. On Aug 26, 1926 while on his post near Getty Square he approached several suspicious men. As he did they all ran with officer Haffner in pursuit, firing his revolver at them. As a result he did arrest one man. Then on Oct 24, 1927 Haffner received notoriety again for his arrest of a man who fired a shot at another. When promotions were made in Jan. 1933, although he was # 2 on the promotion list, he was skipped because he was not a veteran. But 8 months later, on Aug 1, 1933, he was promoted to sergeant at $3,400 a year. Then on April 1, 1938 he was promoted to lieutenant at $4,000. a year. Known affectionately as "Uncle Carl," in Oct. of 1961 he suffered a heart attack and remained on sick leave until his retirement on Jan 29, 1963 on a disability pension. A bachelor, Ret Lt Carl Haffner died April 2, 1966 at age 67 years.

PO EDWARD J. HENEBRY # 176

APPOINTED: January 24, 1923
RETIRED: February 14, 1947

Edward James Henebry was born in Yonkers on May 1, 1901, attended St. Joseph's Catholic School, and years later worked for the Yonkers Electric Light & Power Co. After his police appointment he worked in the 4th pct., Traffic Div., and the Emergency Squad before going to the 1st pct. "Hucks," as he was known, was commended on 4-14-1926 for making a significant arrest. And the next year, on 3-21-1927, he made another burglary arrest after a foot pursuit. Being an excellent shot with a revolver, in 1928 when the YPD Pistol Team was organized, Henebry joined the team. It was about April 1946 after a transfer to the 3rd pct. that he began receiving treatment for a variety of physical illnesses. The following year the police surgeon found him physically unfit for duty and on 2-14-1947 he was retired on a disability. He worked for the Interstate Industrial Protection Co. in NYC. Ed, a nephew of PO Tom Downey, died in his home at 73 Hamilton Avenue on October 28, 1959. He was 58 years old.

PO FRANK McMAHON # 179

APPOINTED: January 24, 1923
DIED: February 17, 1943

Franks career as a police officer would be difficult, including two dismissals. But he would fight his way back. Born Nov 27, 1893 in Newburgh, NY & following schooling and a move to Yonkers, WW-1 broke out and on July 27, 1917 he joined the Army serving overseas in the 105th Machine Gun Battalion until his honorable discharge on Apr 1, 1919. He worked as an electrician prior to his police appointment to the 3rd pct. On Apr 5, 1927 he was charged and convicted of Conduct Unbecoming, to wit, firing his revolver at trees, which resulted in his dismissal on Apr 14, 1927. Though conditionally re-instated, following a series of appeals the city's decision to dismiss was upheld on Nov 30, 1930. This despite an excellent arrest by McMahon on Oct 18, 1930 for burglary and possession of a firearm. On July 1, 1941 a local law was passed allowing for McMahon's re-instatement if the Safety Commissioner agreed, which he did stating, the original punishment was too severe. So on Apr 1, 1942 McMahon was re-instated, with no back pay, after a nearly 14 year absence. On Feb 17, 1943 while at home at 60 Sterling Ave. preparing to leave for duty Frank McMahon suffered a heart attack and died. As a WW-1 veteran he was accorded military & departmental honors. He was 49 years old.

PO STEPHEN RUSNACK # 27

APPOINTED: January 24, 1923
RETIRED: August 1, 1949

Steve was born in Yonkers on August 17, 1901 and attended local schools. As a youth Steve was reported to be an outstanding athlete and considered an all-around champion while playing in the city Industrial League. He worked as a "Hatter" in a local factory until his police appointment. While living at 55 Clinton Street and after being sworn in to the YPD Jan 24, 1923 he was assigned to the Traffic Division directing vehicular traffic. In May of 1924 while still assigned to Traffic Rusnack was trained for potential service in the newly formed Riot Squad. On January 18, 1926 he was assigned as a detective. The next month he arrested 3 men for burglary and sex crimes against children, and was awarded a commendation. But, on May 18, 1926 Rusnack was returned to traffic duty. Rusnack continued in sports on behalf of the YPD and in July of 1927 Rusnack participated in the International Police Games in Baltimore, Md. In Nov. of 1947 Steve returned to patrol duty in the 4th pct. Having spent 24 years in Traffic and then being moved into a pct., he decided to retire on Aug 1, 1949 and move to No. Miami Beach, Fl. where, on November 23, 1972, he died at age 71 years. His nephew was Lt George Rusnack.

PO MICHAEL JACOBS Jr. # 183

APPOINTED: June 25, 1923
DISMISSED: October 27, 1926

Michael Joseph Jacobs was born in the Town of Haverstraw, in Rockland County, NY on September 17, 1897. He and his family moved to Yonkers when he was six years of age. He was educated in Sacred Heart School and PS# 9. Mike enlisted in the NY National Guard in 1916 and later when his company was "Federalized" to active duty for WW-1, he served with Company G, 51st Pioneer Infantry. He participated in several major offenses among which were, Meuse-Argonne, Toul sector, and Saint Mihiel. When the war ended he was serving in Germany as a Corporal. Following his police appointment on June 25, 1923 little is known of his brief service. He was originally assigned to the 2nd precinct and for a short time, in May of 1925, he was detailed to mounted horse patrol. On October 27, 1926 he was charged with being intoxicated on duty and following a departmental trial he was convicted and dismissed from the YPD. Later he worked for several years with the Sheffield Farms Co. A resident of 44 Loring Avenue, Jacobs died on March 4, 1938 in the Professional Hospital in Yonkers following appendectomy surgery. He was 40 years old.

PO JOHN J. DANKOVIC # 182

APPOINTED: June 25, 1923
RETIRED: August 1, 1949

Born John Joseph Dankovic in Brooklyn, NY on December 25, 1895, Christmas day, as a youth he moved to Yonkers with his family, and attended local schools. In 1917 Dankovic joined the Navy to participate in the war in Europe. He served as a Fireman 1st Class aboard a receiving ship. He was honorably discharged two years later and earned a living as a painter. Following his appointment to the YPD he was assigned to the 2nd precinct. It was there that on August 25, 1929 he participated in the arrest of two men for armed robbery. The theft took place in Tarrytown, NY only two hours earlier and the suspects were arrested on a train coming through Yonkers. Dankovic, whose brothers Peter and Stephen were also Yonkers policemen, also worked in the 1st pct. before being returned to the 2nd. He married, had no children and later separated from his wife. He applied to retire on July 1, 1948 but, even though he had completed 25 years, records indicate that his request was denied for unknown reasons. However the following year his retirement request was granted on Aug. 1, 1949 and he began working in the Yonkers Raceway accounting office. Besides his brothers Dankovic's niece was PO Madeline O'Toole. Living alone at 541 Bronx River Rd. in Yonkers, Dankovic died on October 3, 1985 at 89 years of age.

PO RICHARD J. BARRY # 76

APPOINTED: October 13, 1923
DIED: August 2, 1939

Born Dec 16, 1893 in Yonkers, Barry attended St Mary's School and PS # 2. He worked as an Iceman until he joined the Navy on April 6, 1917 to fight in WW-1. He served on the USS Charleston on convoy duty and was discharged Feb. 21, 1919. Upon his appointment to the YPD on October 13, 1923 at $2,300. a year, Rich was assigned to patrol the 2nd pct. Barry was an efficient officer who was also a member of the Yonkers Police War Veterans Legion. On April 23, 1937 while on patrol he observed a vehicle whose occupants they believed were wanted in NYC for assault and intimidating a witness in an organized crime prosecution. Barry arrested them and turned them over to the NYPD 47 precinct. Following a two months illness Richard Barry died on Aug. 2, 1939 at the young age of 45 years. A resident of 235 Nepperhan Avenue Barry left behind a wife and seven (7) children. Barry would never know, but many years later two of his great grandchildren, Ryan Winn and Charles Baker would also be appointed Yonkers police officers.

PO ROBERT O. BUSCH #185

APPOINTED: October 13, 1923
RETIRED: August 15, 1945

Bob Busch was born on May 23, 1893 in Brooklyn, New York and attended local public schools up to the 8th grade. As a young man he reportedly worked in a hat factory in Bridgeport, Ct. Bob entered the Army serving during WW-1 in Europe with the 117th Engineers as a bugler. It was said that he suffered from the effects of poison gas received during one of the battles. As a result he was classified as a disabled war veteran.

Following his appointment to the YPD on Oct. 13, 1923 it wasn't very long before he was assigned to the Traffic Division. It was there that on Nov. 30, 1927 that he saved lives by risking his own. On that day he ran into a burning building and saved two women who were both overcome from smoke inhalation. Returning into the building to continue searching for people who were trapped, he fell through a trap door into the basement. Fortunately he was not seriously injured and he was rescued by members of the fire department. For his actions that day he was awarded the departments Honorable Mention citation. The following year, in June of 1928, PO Busch was re-assigned to patrol duties in the 2nd precinct and after a few years, to the 1st precinct.

On one occasion Police Officer Robert Busch of the First Precinct was working the late tour and was assigned the foot post in Getty Square. Busch was no rookie, was a World War 1 veteran and had 16 years on the department. It was 2:05 a.m. on May 24, 1939 and he had just finished his second "hit" on the call box. As he was continuing to "check his glass" and "try his doors," he spotted two men lurking in the rear of 137 New Main Street in Chicken Island, attempting to break in. He had to act on his own since there was no quick way to call for back up, and he placed the two men under arrest for attempted burglary. The police officer would later explain in his report that he led his two prisoners into Ann Street to call for a car from the nearest call box. Suddenly, one of the suspects pulled a small steel crow-bar from his sleeve and swung at P.O. Busch with the weapon. Busch dodged the blow and grabbed the suspect's wrist as the male continued to attempt to strike him in the head. Busch quickly drew his revolver and fired twice, striking the suspect both times in the stomach. At the same time, the second suspect broke free and fled into Getty Square. Busch fired several shots at the fleeing suspect without effect, but it did attract the attention of P.O. Fred Franz on an adjoining post. Franz caught up to the suspect and placed him under arrest. The first suspect, suffering from gunshot wounds, was transported to St Joseph's Hospital emergency room where he died at 3:05 a.m.

Police Chief Edward Quirk praised the work of Officer Busch for his alertness and attention to duty in discovering an attempted burglary in progress. For his actions that night, on April 18, 1940 he was awarded with departmental recognition in the form of a Commendation. And at the time this award granted him an additional 1 & a half percentage points for his next civil service promotion exam. The shooting brought no public outcry! It was just a case of a police officer, alone, doing his best to do his duty and stay alive. It was clear, under the circumstances, he did what was necessary.

Bob Busch began to develop several medical problems which ultimately resulted in him being retired on a disability pension on Aug. 15, 1945. In retirement Busch enjoyed tennis, stamp collecting, and singing in minstrel shows. He moved to Miami Florida where he worked as a security guard at local race tracks. He also owned and operated a radio and television store. In 1971 he moved to Middletown, Ct. where he would live for 11 years. This former honor police officer who loved dancing and painting pictures, died July 17, 1982.

PO JOSEPH KOSTIK # 186

APPOINTED: December 31, 1923
KILLED: April 17, 1938

Joe Kostik was born July 30, 1896 in his parents Clinton Street apartment in Yonkers. The family later moved to Parsons Street and young Kostik attended local public schools and graduated from Saunders Trades and Technical HS. According to his family he was a good ball player and enjoyed other sports as well. As a young man he worked several different jobs including that of a Motorman on a Trolley car and later as a carpet inspector for the Alexander Smith carpet mills in Yonkers. Following his marriage to his wife they moved to 55 Colin Street where he would raise four boys. He would often take them to the Hudson River where they all enjoyed "crabbing."

Following his appointment to the police department on Dec. 31, 1923, and very minimal police training, Patrolman Kostik was assigned to the 2nd precinct on Central Avenue. Available records indicate he would most often be assigned a foot post or he would work out of a "Police Booth" located at the intersection of Central Avenue and Tuckahoe Road. At the time the 2nd precinct boundaries covered the entire east side of the city; from the north city line to the south city line, and east to west from the towns of Bronxville and Tuckahoe over to approximately the Saw Mill River. Like all the other officers in the

PO Joseph Kostik #186 (cont.)

2nd pct. he handled a variety of crimes, investigations, and accidents; but he was about to receive a life altering change in his assignment.

About 1935 and with approximately 12 years service on the job, officer Kostik was re-assigned to the 1st precinct located at 20 Wells Avenue at the south east corner of Woodworth Avenue. The population on the west side of Yonkers was not only larger, but the number and types of calls for service were, to some degree, more serious in nature. On one evening a news report related that while walking foot patrol PO Kostik observed smoke coming from an apartment at 247 Main Street. He directed a pedestrian to go to the fire alarm box and turn in the alarm while he entered the building. Upon entering the smoking apartment he found Emma Vincent and her 9 month old daughter overcome by the smoke. He led them outside into the yard and proceeded to reenter the apartment. He noticed that there was a box of linens that had been ignited by a cigarette burning and decided to get rid of the smoldering box. After smashing a window overlooking Main Street he tossed the burning box and the burning curtains outside and stopped the spread of the fire. The fire department responded to the scene and sprayed the apartment with water and the building was saved. The news article said the apartment was damaged but the building had been saved by officer Kostik's actions along with his saving the lives of a 9 month old and her mother.

While in the 1st precinct officer Kostik had seniority and as a result often rode in a radio equipped patrol car. This opportunity to ride in a radio patrol car, turned out to have disastrous results several years later.

While working the day tour on April 17, 1938, Easter Sunday, and knowing what time mass would be over, Kostik, the operator of the patrol car, and his partner Albert Liptak stopped by church to say hello to his family as they left church. He nor his family knew of the tragedy that was soon to take place.

While on patrol that day at about 1:15 PM they received a call from headquarters sending them to the Vark Street playground to break up what was described as a very large and unruly dice game. As they responded to the location, some say with a degree of haste, they drove west along Nepperhan Avenue. As they attempted to cross over New Main Street they struck an uneven section in the road which bounced the car and caused Kostik to lose control of the vehicle. The radio car careened into an electric light pole at 102 Nepperhan Avenue, breaking the pole off at its base. The radio car overturned and the light pole fell on top of the vehicle.

Trapped in the badly damaged patrol car, someone called headquarters and the Emergency Squad responded immediately and extricated both officers from the overturned vehicle. Both officers were taken directly to St. Joseph's Hospital on South Broadway for emergency treatment. However officer Kostik, who was only 41 years old, was pronounced dead within ten minutes of arrival. He had suffered a fractured skull, a fractured jaw, and multiple internal injuries. His partner Albert Liptak, who was also critically injured, died the following day.

Public Safety Commissioner Morrissey and Chief Edward Quirk notified the department and the news media that Kostik and his partner would both receive the highest departmental honors due to the losing of one's life while on duty. Officer Kostik's wake was held at his home at 55 Colin Street and the funeral mass was held at St. Nicholas of Myra Church on Ash Street. All off duty officers were directed to attend the funeral in full dress uniform to show their respect to a fallen brother. Column after column

PO Joseph Kostik #186 (cont.)

of blue uniforms, along with many public figures followed the funeral procession and were led by the departments Motorcycle Unit of the Traffic Division.

None of officer Kostik's four boys joined the police department, but one son did join the Yonkers Fire Department. However, Kostik's grandson and name sake, Joseph S. Kostik did join the YPD and retired as a Deputy Chief. His other grandson, Richard Kostik also joined the department and retired as a Detective Sergeant. And finally, officer Kostik's great grandson, once again with the same first and last name, "Joseph M. Kostik," also joined the YPD in 2002 .

While speaking with one of Kostik's son's he related that he still remembers that the last time he saw his father alive was in front of church on Easter Sunday in 1938. He also related that following his father's elaborate funeral, although his mother did receive a pension, they said they never heard from the PBA again.

PO WILLIAM J. DALY # 109

APPOINTED: February 1, 1924
DISMISSED: January 22, 1947

Bill Daly was born in Yonkers on June 1, 1899 and attended local schools. Later he would earn a living as a chauffeur and a salesman. Upon his appointment to the YPD on Feb. 1, 1924 he was assigned to the 1st pct. on foot patrol. Only two years later he was elevated to Detective, and as a result of an arrest on April 20, 1926 and the conviction of a child molester, Daly was awarded a commendation. But, by 1929 Daly had been returned to patrol duties back in the 1st precinct. In 1931 Daly was assigned to the Emergency Squad where he remained for 8 years. Then, on July 1, 1939, he was again assigned to the Detective Bureau. On April 18, 1940 Daly was awarded a Cert. of Exc. Police Work for the arrest of a robbery suspect. However on Oct. 12, 1942 he was reassigned to the 3rd pct. Unfortunately, after more than 22 years service, on November 26, 1945 Daly was criminally charged in connection with a gambling operation by the District Attorney. Following his trial he was convicted and dismissed from the YPD on January 22, 1947.

PO JOSEPH Q. REICHENBACH # 191

APPOINTED: February 1, 1925
RETIRED: April 1, 1950

Joe was a local boy born March 5, 1902 and attended local schools. Following his employment as a "special officer" Joe was appointed to the YPD on Feb. 1, 1925 and on May 18, 1925 he was assigned to the 3rd pct. Before the year was over he would face his first serious test. On Oct 17, 1925 at 4:30 AM a fire had engulfed an apartment building at 564 So. Broadway. With the front stairway destroyed, Joe entered the building using the fire escape, rescued several families, and exited the same way. On Mar 18, 1930 he was assigned to duty with the new armored motorcycle with a side car. He and his partner provided bank escorts for business payroll money. In the fall of 1934 when armored patrol cars replaced the 2 armored motorcycles, Reichenbach patrolled in this new car. In January 1935, while off duty, PO Reichenbach chased 3 men 6 blocks in a snow storm after a theft from a local store. He was awarded a Commendation for the arrest of the thieves. On April 23, 1942 he was again recognized for his quick action in the arrest of 3 men wanted for a robbery which occurred on Sept. 16, 1941. A resident of 61 Putnam Avenue, and having retired on April 1, 1950, Ret PO Joe Reichenbach died April 23, 1983 at age 81.

PO DAVID J. WHELAN # 190

APPOINTED: February 1, 1925
RETIRED: September 10, 1963

David Joseph Whelan was born September 5, 1901 in Yonkers. He attended St Mary's catholic school and as a young man would later work both as a chauffeur, auto mechanic, and for the Alexander Smith Carpet Mills in Yonkers. Dave was a hard worker but his real passion was sports where he became well known throughout the area and was said to have played semi-professional basketball for a number of teams in the metropolitan area.

Dave was a resident of 140 Beech Street when he was appointed a Yonkers police officer on February 1, 1925, attended a school of recruit training, and on May 18, 1925 was assigned to the 1st precinct on foot patrol. However, it wasn't long before he managed to get himself assigned to the motorcycle unit of the Traffic Division.

As a "motorcycle cop" he performed his duty of issuing moving traffic summonses when violators were observed. However Whelan also displayed his alertness to duty when, while off duty on February 19, 1929, he noticed a male driving a car that Dave had been advised at a previous roll call had been reported stolen. After approaching the male, questioning him and a lengthy foot pursuit, officer Whelan made the arrest and charged him appropriately.

The following year on September 18, 1930 a robbery occurred down at the Yonkers Ferry on Alexander Street. Once again officer Whelan was off duty and happened to be in the vicinity during the robbery but not being aware of it, when he observed three men who seemed to switch vehicles for no apparent reason, and it made him suspicious. He made some mental notes and went on his way. It was sometime later after learning of the robbery he requested and was allowed to investigate the crime. Armed with what he remembered at the crime scene the day of the robbery he located and arrested all three men.

For his intelligent police work on these occasions he was awarded a departmental Commendation. Dave Whelan would spend the majority of his career in the Traffic Division assigned to two wheel motorcycle patrol, and he was very happy doing so. He also served several years as the PBA Trustee for the Traffic Division. However, in 1956, possibly due to him getting older, he was transferred to the Traffic Engineering Bureau. His last assignment prior to retirement was collecting coins from parking meters around the city.

Following his retirement on September 10, 1963, and being an avid fisherman, Dave would spend six months a year in Florida fishing. When the annual Old Timers Picnic began in 1978 you could be sure to find Dave there every year enjoying the company of his old time buddies from years earlier. A resident of 60 Cross Hill Avenue Ret PO David Whelan died on December 23, 1997 at the age of 96 years.

PO SALVATORE J. IANNUCCI # 134

APPOINTED: February 1, 1925
RETIRED: June 16, 1950

Salvatore Iannucci was a man who seemed to have more energy than any of his contemporaries. He was born on October 19, 1900 in Naples, Italy. He came to the U.S. at the age of four years and would later become a naturalized citizen. He received his education attending PS# 18. As stated, as a youth Sal was always a high energy young man and was very active playing baseball in the Mount Carmel church league. Iannucci's daughter, Nina, said he was always very active and he joined the Navy on September 1, 1919 during World War I, and was honorably discharged on February 19, 1920, serving only six months. Returning to Yonkers he would gain employment performing various jobs including that of a chauffeur, mechanic, and a sign painter.

Upon Iannucci's appointment to the police department on February 1, 1925 at $1,900 per year he was assigned to patrol in the 3rd precinct and within three years would be part of a tragic accident. On February 17, 1928, at 1:00 AM in the morning, he and officer John Hudock were transporting a female prisoner down to the jail on Alexander Street. They had to commandeer a private vehicle which had only a front seat; being a coupe vehicle it had no rear seat. The prisoner sat next to the driver and officers Iannucci and Hudock had to stand outside on the running boards on each side of the car holding on as best as they could. As they approached South Broadway and Radford St., officer Hudock lost his grip and fell to the pavement striking his head. Though quickly transported, hospitalized and treated, Hudock died on Feb. 21, 1928.

Sal Iannucci was always a good shot with his revolver and as a result he was chosen to compete on the Yonkers Police pistol team in April of 1928. It was a sport he enjoyed and participated in for many years. Through much of his career Sal worked in the 3rd, 2nd, and 4th precincts, and by 1941 he was working in the 1st precinct.

On March 1, 1941 Iannucci was one of five police officers elevated to Detective status. His thorough knowledge of the Italian language had gained him additional respect in the department and had been an asset to police investigations. In fact he was quick to prove his worth. On September 30, 1941 Detective Iannucci and his partner saved a man who was intent on committing suicide by jumping from the roof of a five-story building. Then, on October 14, 1941, a 75-year-old male was the victim of a forcible robbery which caused his death. It was later ruled a murder. Detective Iannucci, along with several other detectives, worked four days tirelessly until Iannucci and his partner made the arrest. His persistent investigative work brought praise to himself and the entire police department. For his excellent police work in locating and arresting the murderer, Detective Iannucci was awarded a departmental Commendation. It took a few years but he also received a commendation for saving the man from attempting suicide as well.

Despite his excellent record, when large numbers of police officers and detectives were reassigned

PO Salvatore Iannucci # 134 (cont.)

as part of a department wide re-organization, Detective Iannucci was transferred back to uniform patrol duty in the 2nd precinct. Though back on patrol duty officer Iannucci never lost his energy or enthusiasm. He continued to be involved with the police pistol team earning several medals and took a special interest in the newly organized Police Athletic League. According to his daughter, Sal Iannucci set up a small gym in his home basement, at his own cost and would bring teens to his home to learn the sport of boxing. He was amember of the department singing Glea club, the Police Holy Name Society, and the Yonkers Police War Veterans Legion.

Following his retirement from the department on June 16, 1950 and moving to Lakewood Ohio, Iannucci owned and operated several different businesses. For the last 25 years of his life he organized and was the leader of a band. He was the lead singer and played the violin, mandolin, and the drums. He and his band played for senior citizens in the Cleveland Ohio area for 25 years which earned him a mayoral proclamation for his service to the community. And in his spare time he sang in the church choir and read poetry to senior citizens and children groups. When he was 90 years of age he was even still ice skating.

He returned to New York while in his early 90s to attend the annual police Old-Timers Picnic I watched him jog down the 50 yard driveway. The man seemed unstoppable with his energy and youthful slim body. At the age of 95 he bought himself a Lincoln town car to enjoy the trips he was planning. But within six months time ran out, and the former honor police officer and detective, the man who had made it seem he would go on forever, died on December 2, 1995. He was 95 years of age.

PO HARRY W. EHRICH # 196

APPOINTED: February 1, 1925
RETIRED: August 1, 1950

Harry Ehrich was born in Yonkers on September 15, 1901 and attended PS # 5. Years later when Ehrich applied for appointment to the YPD he listed his occupation as that of a chauffeur. He was appointed a Patrolman on February 1, 1925 and assigned to duty in the 2nd pct. on Central Avenue which then covered the entire east side of the city. Officer Ehrich was a tall man, and apparently a strong one as well. For on October 9, 1928 he participated in a police – fire sporting competition and was chosen to join the tug-of-war team, the result of which favored the Police Department. In August of 1937 Ehrich was commended for making a burglary arrest of a male with a long criminal record at 4:30 AM. Officer Ehrich spent his entire career in the second precinct and retired on August 1, 1950. A resident of 1537 Central Park Ave., and following a short illness retired police officer Harry Ehrich died in Roosevelt Hospital in NYC on September 21, 1957. He was 56 years old.

DET. MARTIN L. LUNDY # 195

APPOINTED: February 1, 1925
DIED: September 8, 1933

Martin Lundy was born on April 12, 1893 in Lake Waccubuc, NY. At some point he and his family moved Brewster, N. Y. where he received his early education and would later move to Yonkers around 1913. As a young man Marty was employed by the Putnam Division of the New York Central Railroad working as a Tower man at the Van Cortland Park station. He also worked briefly as a telegraph operator. Following his appointment to the police department on February 1, 1925 he was assigned to the Traffic Division directing traffic at South Broadway and McLean Avenue. He was reported to have been cited for bravery in 1928 for rescuing several people in a fire. Two years later he arrested a male wanted for running down a New York City police officer and received another award. Once again, on June 11, 1932, he was awarded a commendation for discovering a fire on March 9, 1932. He turned in the alarm, went into the building, and saved nine persons by carrying them out to the street. On September 20, 1932 he was elevated to Detective 2nd grade with no increase in salary. He was assigned as the driver and partner of Detective Sgt. Henry Murphy and participated in a number of important investigations. Detective Lundy was stricken with an attack of appendicitis and underwent surgery for the problem. Following complications, Detective Martin Lundy died on September 8, 1933. He was only 39 years old.

LT. ARTHUR K. ROWLAND

APPOINTED: February 1, 1925
RETIRED: July 16, 1950

Arthur Rowland was born on November 30, 1896 in NYC. However, as a young boy he moved with his family to Texas where he attended local Texas schools and later worked as an auto mechanic. He joined the Texas National Guard and when the US entered World War I his unit was activated and he served two years overseas in the Army's Rainbow Division. After the war and having received an honorable discharge, he moved to Yonkers. Upon his police appointment on Feb. 1, 1925 he was assigned to patrol duty and reportedly served as a mounted officer for a short time. On February 1, 1942 he was promoted to the rank of sergeant at $2,975 a year and was assigned to the 2nd pct. Three years later on Dec. 29, 1945 he was promoted to lieutenant and served as a desk officer in the 2nd pct. During his career Arthur was always active in PBA activities and the Police War Veterans Legion, of which he was said to have been the past commander in 1946. Upon his retirement on July 16, 1950 he moved his family to live in Austin, Texas. Retired Lt. Arthur Rowland died on January 22, 1958 at the age of 62 years.

PO THOMAS KOLLAR # 194

APPOINTED: February 1, 1925
RETIRED: October 16, 1945

Thomas Kollar was born in the City of Yonkers on December 24, 1902 where he was raised and received his formal education. As a young man Tom worked as a foreman in a local manufacturing plant. On February 1, 1925, at the age of 22 years, Kollar received his police appointment to the YPD and was assigned to the second precinct. In addition to English, Tom reportedly was able to speak Russian, Polish, and Slavic; an ability which could prove to be an asset in police work. Following a year on patrol in the 2nd precinct, on March 25, 1926 Kollar was assigned to horseback mounted patrol in that precinct, but a short time later he would return to foot patrol. Tom apparently had a good singing voice as he was a very active member of the police singing Glea Club and was often detailed to sing in church during the funeral of a deceased police officer. Following an exam by the police surgeon officer Kollar was found physically unfit for duty and was retired on a disability pension on October 16, 1945. Retired police officer Thomas Kollar died on April 23, 1990. He was 87 years old.

SGT. LESLIE L. LINSENBARTH # 15

APPOINTED: February 1, 1925
DIED: July 4, 1963

Leslie Leo Linsenbarth was born in Yonkers on October 24, 1902 and attended PS# 6 and then only up to the 8th grade; which at the time was actually very common. Males were needed to go to work to bring home money for the family. And he did this when he gained work with the telephone company as a "cable splicer."

After passing all the requirements, "Les" was hired by the Yonkers Police Department on February 1, 1925 while living at 82 Warburton Avenue and was assigned to patrol duty in the 1st precinct. But just over two years later he was fortunate enough to be assigned as a Detective in the Detective Bureau on October 14, 1927. Within a month, on November 4, 1927, Det Linsenbarth was commended for what was referred to as "clever detective work" for the arrest of a burglar responsible for an earlier burglary in Leake & Watts. Les was not only aggressive in this police work but he was eager to participate in a baseball game between the police and fire department in June of 1928. Les was always involved in sports, going back to his days in school when he played basketball for the "Yonkers Bantams" city league.

While in the police department Det Linsenbarth earned a Certificate of Excellent Police Work on October 21, 1933 for the arrest of two burglary suspects wanted since December of 1932. Then on October 15, 1935 the family members of a home at 88 Fanshaw Avenue were the victims of a push in robbery where all were tied up, gagged, and robbed of their money and valuables. Following a lengthy investigation Det Linsenbarth and others located and arrested those responsible. This time, on May 23, 1936 he was awarded the departments Honorable Mention.

Regularly exhibiting his investigative skills, on July 9, 1938, Det Linsenbarth was awarded two citations. The first being a Commendation for rounding up a group of youths wanted for burglary, robbery and assault. The second, a Certificate of Excellent Police Work was for a burglary arrest which occurred in early 1937. And again on May 6, 1939 he received another Commendation for the arrest of a murder suspect. He continued to receive numerous other citations as time went on. It is worth noting that departmental awards were not awarded that often during these years but Linsenbarth's work seemed to always stand out and his record was a testament to his investigative skills as a detective.

On May 1, 1942, Det Linsenbarth was promoted to Sergeant and was allowed to remain in the Detective Bureau as a Detective Sergeant. He then spent several month's detailed as the administrative assistant in Chief Kruppenbacher's office until October 12, 1942 when he was transferred to the 2nd precinct as a patrol sergeant.

Due to his regular volunteer work with the Police Athletic League (PAL), on March 18, 1947 Les was placed in charge of the Juvenile Aid Bureau (JAB) and PAL during the absence of the captain. Eventually Linsenbarth was returned to patrol in the 2nd precinct. Unfortunately, after more than 38 years of outstanding and remarkable service, Les became ill with cancer and died on July 4, 1963 at the age of 63 years.

For those who knew him Sgt Leslie Linsenbarth reportedly was a consummate professional; compassionate, devoted to "the job" and always willing to teach young officers their jobs.

PO PERCY N. PHILLIPS #200

APPOINTED: March 16, 1925
RETIRED: April 16, 1951

Percy Phillips was born in the City of Yonkers on Sept. 6, 1902 and attended local public schools. He was appointed to the YPD on March 16, 1925 with a starting salary of $1,940 a year. His first patrol assignment was in the 3rd pct. where he remained for many years. On Jan. 14, 1928 he was commended by the police honor board for rescuing several people from a fire that occurred on January 3, 1928. On January 12, 1934 he was transferred from the 3rd precinct to the Traffic Division on motorcycle duty. Philips remained in the Traffic Division until October 21, 1942 when for a short time he was reassigned to the 4th precinct. However, 6 months later, on April 10, 1943 he was returned to motorcycle duty where he remained right up to his retirement on April 16, 1951. Phillips was a charter member of the Yonkers Police St. George Society, a Protestant religious and fraternal group which was organized in 1941. Following his retirement he worked as a security guard at the Habirshaw Cable and Wire Co. in Yonkers. A resident of 100 DeHaven Dr., Percy Phillips died on March 16, 1969 in Huntington L.I. at the age of 66 years.

DET. THOMAS J. CUNNINGHAM #21

APPOINTED: March 16, 1925
RETIRED: August 1, 1951

Tom was born in Yonkers on July 23, 1893, the son of Sgt. William Cunningham. He attended local public schools including PS# 6. As a young man Tom worked both as a chauffeur and a mechanic. He was appointed to the YPD on March 16, 1925 and assigned to the 3rd pct. However, on April 28, 1925 he was moved to the 2nd pct. on mounted duty under the supervision of his father. On March 30, 1927 he rescued 3 people from a burning building. For his bravery he was awarded the department's highest recognition at that time, the Honorable Mention. Cunningham was always active in PBA affairs and by 1932 he was serving as 1st V.P. His contributions to the police association must have been appreciated because in Jan. of 1936 he was elected President of the association. He would continue to be reelected through 1941. During 1936, his first term as president, a police officer's salary was $3,000 a year, minus an 8% voluntary pay reduction agreed to in order to assist the city in budgetary problems. On Dec. 16, 1939 Cunningham was elevated to Detective and was assigned to the Bureau of Criminal Identification, photographing and investigating crime scenes. He remained in this assignment right up to his retirement on Aug. 1, 1951. One of his children, Edward, was a corrections officer sergeant in Attica prison. Unfortunately his son was killed in the Attica prison riot in 1971. Ret. Det. Tom Cunningham died on Feb. 17, 1976 at the age of 82 years.

PO MICHAEL J. WALSH # 127

APPOINTED: March 16, 1925
KILLED: December 23, 1929

Officer Walsh was a native of Yonkers, having been born there on June 17, 1902. His father Michael Walsh Sr. died leaving his widow and young son residing at 41 Radford St. Of course there was no way to know that this unfortunate circumstance would repeat itself years later. Young Mike Walsh Jr. was raised in southwest Yonkers and was a graduate of our Lady of the Holy Rosary parochial school. Later he would also attend Fordham Preparatory School for a short time. One of Mike Walsh's favorite pastimes was riding his motorcycle.

Following his passing the exam for police officer in Yonkers, Mike Walsh was appointed to the Police Department on March 16, 1925 and began his journey toward a meeting with destiny.

Upon his appointment he was assigned to patrol in the 3rd precinct. The following year, on April 27, 1926, while on foot post at the foot of Ludlow Street he observed two youths carrying large bags. As he approached them they ran resulting in officer Walsh firing and nearly emptying his revolver at them. He was able to arrest one of them for possession of stolen property. Interestingly, no complaint was made and the suspect was later released.

Later that year on September 3, 1926 a career altering incident occurred. In the early morning

PO Michael J. Walsh (cont.)

hours of the day Walsh and two other Yonkers officers, all off duty, became involved in an altercation at 3:30 AM resulting in Walsh and one other officer being arrested by the Tuckahoe Police Department for malicious mischief. That same day, officer Walsh and the other two officers were suspended by Chief Quirk. Following a hearing on departmental charges lodged against him, Walsh pled guilty on September 20 to reduced charges and was fined 30 days pay and in addition his working schedule was arranged in such a way that he would work without having a day off for the following 9 months. It was a severe penalty but he was happy to be able to hold onto his job. The other two officers involved in the Tuckahoe incident were dismissed from the department.

Walsh returned to the 3rd precinct to complete his new nine-month probation when on April 1, 1927 he was called to the Public Safety Commissioner's office. He was advised that one of the men brought up on charges the previous September and who was dismissed, had appealed and won a new trial. To prepare for a new trial officer Walsh was directed to prepare a written statement regarding the facts of the case which would be used against the dismissed officer. Walsh reportedly refused to give information to be used against a former fellow officer. When safety Commissioner Cameron advised him his refusal would be deemed as insubordination, officer Walsh submitted his resignation in writing and it was accepted effective immediately.

On December 27, 1927 Commissioner Cameron concluded a trial against another officer by dismissing him and, surprisingly, filled the new vacancy by reappointing police officer Michael J. Walsh to the Police Department. The reason for Walsh's reinstatement was not made clear and he was returned to patrol duties in the 3rd precinct.

Being a motorcycle enthusiast Walsh must have been very pleased when he was transferred from precinct patrol duties to Armored Motorcycle duty on May 17, 1929. It was about that time that the city purchased armored vehicles and Walsh was assigned to escort payroll and other money shipments traveling throughout the city. By December 23, 1929 Walsh had been in his new assignment for 7 months and, being married three years with a 6-month-old daughter, he was preparing for his baby's 1st Christmas. But fate was about to step in. On this day at about 10 AM Walsh was the lead motorcycle escorting a "money truck" from R. H. Macy & Co. taking money to a local bank. As he rode up eastbound on St. Mary Street he entered the middle of the intersection of St. Mary Street and Jefferson Street, another truck heading southbound, struck Walsh and his motorcycle throwing him 30 feet up against a building wall, breaking his neck. He was immediately taken to St. Joseph's Hospital by the other officers in the escort. However, unfortunately PO Michael Walsh died from his injuries within minutes. One New York City newspaper headline read, "Baby's Santa Claus is dead."

Ironically, Walsh's widow worked as a nurse in a clinic for poor families with babies which was known as the "milk station" and was located right at that same corner of St. Mary Street and Jefferson Street. But on this morning she was not at work yet and was notified of the accident by Chief Quirk. By the time she reached the hospital it was too late and her husband Michael Walsh was dead; Dec 23, 1929.

The funeral for police officer Walsh began at his home at 432 Riverdale Ave. and was attended by more than 100 of his former fellow officers in full dress uniform. Following his death Police officer Michael Walsh's widow received $300. a year from the police pension fund for herself and her newborn baby. Police Officer Michael J. Walsh was only 27 years old.

PO EMIL YACKO # 231

APPOINTED: March 16, 1925
RETIRED: September 1, 1962

Born in Yonkers on Nov. 8, 1902 Emil grew up in the hollow section of Yonkers and is believed to have attended Holy Trinity School along with his cousin Andrew Yacko who also would later join the YPD. When he was appointed a police officer on March 16, 1925 he was assigned to the 4th pct. for a short time and then to the Traffic Division in Getty Square. Yacko was said to be a friendly well liked officer who seemed always to be in a good mood. His wife Anna said his nickname was, "whistling Pete" because his happy personality was evidenced by his frequent whistling. On Sept. 7, 1926 Yacko made a murder arrest while on duty in Getty Square. Three years later on Oct. 1, 1929, following another murder, officer Yacko, found the suspect and made the arrest. For his diligence etc. he was awarded the department's highest medal at that time, the Honorable Mention. Yacko remained in the Traffic Division retiring on September 1, 1962. Retired PO Emil Yacko died May 29, 1977. He was 74 years old.

PO EDWARD H. FEELEY # 100

APPOINTED: March 16, 1925
RETIRED: December 1, 1933

Ed Feeley was born in the town of Oxford NY on Feb. 26, 1896. His family brought him to Yonkers at the age of six and he attended St. Joseph's school. As a young man Feeley joined the Navy on July 16, 1917 serving during World War I and was honorably discharged on Oct. 3, 1919. Returning to NY he worked as a chauffeur. While living at 74 Chestnut St. the YPD hired him on March 16, 1925 and he was assigned to the 2nd pct. In Feb. of 1929 he was reassigned to the 3rd pct. where he would remain for some time. Ed Feeley apparently was a no-nonsense type individual. On February 26, 1929 he arrested a man for public intoxication and criminal mischief. However the man made the mistake of trying to fight officer Feeley. The man was later admitted to the hospital with severe injuries to his left eye following his battle with the officer. Beginning in January of 1933 Feeley became unable to work due to hip and back pain and remained out sick for nine months. Following an examination by the police surgeon he was found physically unfit for duty and retired on a disability pension on Dec 1, 1933. The following year he requested reinstatement, but was denied. He began working for the Alexander Smith carpet factory until they closed in 1954. Ed Feeley would later have the satisfaction of seeing his son Edward Feeley Jr. join the Yonkers Police Department. Following a long illness retired police officer Edward Feeley died on October 20, 1964. He was 68 years old.

DET. JAMES J. MORRISSEY #204

APPOINTED: March 16, 1925
DIED: September 7, 1961

Jim Morrissey was born in the City of Yonkers on November 1, 1897 and attended St. Mary's parochial school. He gained employment, like most men at that time, as a chauffeur. Jim was appointed to the Police Department on March 16, 1925 from 92 Elm St. He was raised there along with his brother Tom Morrissey who at the time was a Yonkers police officer and who would later rise to the rank of captain. Following Jim's appointment to the YPD he was assigned to 1st precinct on foot patrol. Officer Morrissey gained notoriety in April of 1926 when he was instrumental in the arrest of 6 young men for committing a robbery. He continued to enhance his reputation by making another arrest four months later, this time for burglary and which required him to fire his revolver. Interested in all activities in the YPD, in May of 1928 Morrissey was named to an athletic committee to form a Yonkers Police baseball team. The following year in November of 1929 PO Morrissey was named chairman of the executive committee in charge of the annual Police Ball. On October 16, 1952 Morrissey was appointed a Detective in the detective Bureau and would remain there until an illness caused his death on September 7, 1961. He was 63 years old.

PO CECIL R. COOPER # 236

APPOINTED: March 16, 1925
RETIRED: March 1, 1951

Cecil Cooper was born in Yonkers on July 25, 1901 and attended local public schools. As a young man he gained employment as a steam fitter. Cecil was appointed to the Police Department on March 16, 1925 and following his recruit training was assigned to the Traffic Division on foot directing vehicular traffic. The following year, on March 25, 1926, he was allowed to join the motorcycle squad. On April 18, 1927 while chasing a speeder on Warburton Ave. he collided head-on with a truck which threw him off his motorcycle causing severe injuries to his hip and legs. He was lucky to have survived. This was his 3rd motorcycle accident in one year and was injured on each occasion. Once again, he was thrown from his motorcycle on August 14, 1928 on Central Ave. when he ran over oil in the roadway and was once again badly injured. After his recovery, on March 6, 1929 he was reassigned to the 3rd precinct on foot patrol. But, the following month on April 5, 1929, he was reassigned "on paper" back to the traffic division, but actually detailed to the repair shop. PO Cooper would retire from the Traffic Division on March 1, 1951 and died on March 30, 1977. He was 75 years old.

DET. CAPTAIN JOSEPH A. DOMINICO

APPOINTED: March 16, 1925
RETIRED: March 16, 1963

The person described below was one of the more interesting personalities that rose through the ranks of the Yonkers Police Department. Born Joseph Anthony Domonico on October 14, 1903 in New York City, young Joe was brought by his family to Yonkers in 1909 and attended local public schools. He had no military experience but as a young man worked as a chauffeur.

A resident of 38 Lockwood Ave., Joe was appointed to the Yonkers Police Department on March 16, 1925 earning a starting salary of $1,900 a year, and was assigned to the 2nd precinct on foot patrol. It is said that while in that precinct a clerical error was made in the spelling of his last name and from that time forward his last name was spelled as, DOMINICO. That spelling remained with him throughout his entire career.

It is likely that Joe had some type of auto mechanic skills because on December 29, 1925 he was reassigned from the 2nd precinct to the 1st precinct, detailed to duty at the municipal auto Police and Fire Department repair shop as a mechanic. An assignment which was traditionally assigned to a police officer. However, on March 27, 1926 he found himself in an unusual situation when, while driving off-duty, he illegally passed a trolley car on the left side. He was stopped by traffic officer John Buecherl

Det Capt. Joseph Dominico (cont.)

who, coincidentally also had only a year with the department. When Dominico identified himself, Buecherl reportedly replied, "I don't care who you are," and wrote Dominico a summons for reckless driving.

The incident got the attention of the local newspaper which then made the situation even worse. Dominico pled guilty in special sessions court and received a verbal reprimand from the judge. This was quickly followed by his transfer back to patrol in the 2nd precinct. However due to the spotlight brought to bear by the media, acting Capt. Crough preferred charges against Dominico for conduct unbecoming an officer. Young police officer Joe Dominico pled guilty to these charges as well and on April 26, 1926 he was fined three days pay. All this for a simple traffic violation.

Although it was not a good way to bring attention to himself as a relatively new officer, Patrolman Dominico probably redeemed himself when later that year, on September 22, 1926, and while on foot patrol in the 2nd precinct, he observed four suspicious males near their vehicle. Following his investigating the situation, officer Dominico ultimately arrested all four men and recovered two loaded illegally possessed firearms.

Several years later on June 16, 1930 officer Dominico had the rare satisfaction of saving a child's life. While on his post he was advised that a 4-year-old boy had swallowed a poisonous liquid. He immediately entered the home, prepared a mixture of various ingredients and had the child drink it. After vomiting a number of times the boy recovered without complications.

Once again Joe Dominico faced problems, this time serious, when on August 14, 1931 he was arrested and charged with "Abortion," a felony and was released on $500 bail. He apparently had been seeing a female for some time when she learned that she was pregnant. The authorities later learned that an abortion had occurred and ordered Dominico's arrest. That same day he was suspended without pay and on October 7, 1931 he was formally indicted on the charge. However, on April 25, 1932 officer Dominico married the woman involved which prompted the district attorney to dismiss all charges on April 29, 1932. Joe Dominico was reinstated to the police department on June 1, 1932 with the agreement that he would waive almost a years back pay, and he was assigned to the 4th precinct on patrol. Coincidently, Joe and his wife would remain married for 60 years, at which time his wife died. They never had any children.

While working as a 4th precinct patrol officer Dominico had taken and passed the examination for promotion to Sergeant. On January 20, 1936 Joe received his 1st promotion by being elevated to the rank of Police Sergeant at a salary of $3,400 a year. Although fairly unusual, Sgt. Dominico was allowed to remain in the 4th precinct as a patrol supervisor.

Sgt. Dominico continued his efforts to advance in his career by passing the civil service test for promotion to Police Lieutenant. As such, on December 16, 1939, Joseph Dominico was officially promoted to the rank of Police Lieutenant with a salary of $4,000 a year. And, which was most unusual, Lt. Dominico was permitted to again remain in the 4th precinct, this time as a desk officer. On February 1, 1942 Joe Dominico was reassigned to desk duty in the 2nd precinct where he would remain for over a year. It wasn't until Capt. Charles Ward retired that Dominico received the opportunity for another promotion. On December 24, 1943 Lt. Dominico was promoted to the rank of captain earning a salary of

Det Capt. Joseph Dominico (cont.)

$3,937 a year and was placed in command of the 2nd precinct on Central Avenue. Joe had the distinction of being the first Italian-American to achieve the rank of captain in the Yonkers Police Department.

(Young Patrolman Dominico)

Two months following his promotion to captain a testimonial dinner honoring Capt. Dominico was held in February of 1944 at the Vesuvio Restaurant. On behalf of the officers and men of the 2nd precinct Capt. Dominico was presented with a pen and pencil set and a wallet as a token of their esteem. Following his transfer to the 3rd precinct on January 1, 1947 he remained the precinct commander until May 1, 1949 when he was elevated to the position of Detective Captain in command of the Detective Bureau. Further, on May 27, 1952 he was also placed in command of the Juvenile Aid Bureau as well.

Detective Capt. Dominico, a lifelong Yonkers resident and easily recognized by his full head of snow white hair, retired from the police department on March 16, 1963 after completing 38 years of service. A very healthy and active man, he then worked as a sales consultant for the Lockwood Lumber Company from 1963 to 1975. According to family members Joe had a gift for inventing various devices. He was said to have designed heat thermostats, electrical timers, and butterfly anchors used in construction. Joe's nephew was Benjamin DeLuccy, who also rose to the rank of Yonkers Police Captain.

Retired Detective Capt. Joseph Dominico died in St. Joseph's medical Center in Yonkers on April 1, 1998 at the age of 94 years.

PO THOMAS F. BOYLE #212

APPOINTED: March 16, 1925
RETIRED: September 15, 1950

Thomas Francis Boyle was born in Dobbs Ferry, NY on Sept. 23, 1896. At the time his father was a Dobbs Ferry police officer. Several years later his father was killed in the line of duty by touching a live electric wire that had fallen. Young Tom Boyle moved to Yonkers with his mother at the age of four years and attended local public schools. He joined the Navy on Dec. 27, 1917 serving as a Seaman during World War I and was honorably discharged on Feb. 13, 1919. Tom earned his living as an assistant cameraman in the silent film days at the Whitman Bennettt Studios near the city line. Boyle was appointed to the YPD on March 16, 1925 and after only three months, on May 18, 1925, he was transferred to the Traffic Division on foot, directing vehicular traffic. After 17 years, on October 21, 1942 Boyle was reassigned to foot patrol in the 1st precinct. In Sept. of 1947 he was moved to the 4th pct. from which he would later retire on Sept. 15, 1950. Boyle was a member of the VFW, YPD Police War Veterans Legion, Knights of Columbus, and the police Holy Name Society. On June 15, 1955 retired PO Thomas Boyle died from a heart attack in his home at 18 Ellison Avenue. He was 58 years old.

PO ALEXANDER YOUNG #211

APPOINTED: March 16, 1925
RETIRED: March 16, 1949

Alexander Young was born in the City of Yonkers on September 1, 1893 and attended local public schools. He joined the Army on July 9, 1917 and served in France during World War I as a Lieutenant and was honorably discharged on April 12, 1919. At the age of 32 years Young was appointed to the YPD on March 16, 1925 and assigned to the 1st pct. On September 6, 1926 Young was commended for rescuing a woman from a smoke-filled building. Two years later, on March 19, 1928, Young was responsible for the arrest of a burglar wanted for several burglaries. Then, on January 26, 1929, he shot out the windows of a stolen vehicle when the suspect tried to run him down. Young was assigned for a while to traffic duty on foot and later to the Armored Car Patrol. It was while there on June 2, 1939 that he removed his uniform and swam out into the Hudson River with a rope to rescue a man in danger of drowning. Alex was later deemed physically unfit for duty and was retired on a disability on March 16, 1949. Retired police officer Alexander Young died unexpectedly in St. John's Hospital on October 26, 1950 at the age of 57 years.

PO CHARLES CALESE # 177

APPOINTED: March 16, 1925
DIED: January 25, 1930

Charles Calese was born in the City of Yonkers on July 13, 1903. Charlie's parents were Italian immigrants so he spoke Italian fluently as a second language. He attended and graduated from local public schools and gained employment as an electrician and auto mechanic. He was appointed to the YPD on March 16, 1925 from 158 Willow St. with a starting salary of $1,900 a year. Following some basic recruit training, on May 18, 1925, he was assigned to the Traffic Division on foot directing traffic. Later that year on December 2, 1925 he was appointed a Detective in the Detective Bureau. However, for unknown reasons the following month he was returned to traffic duties and then to patrol in the 2nd precinct. Officer Calese would return as a detective in June of 1926, but not for long. This time he was reassigned to patrol in the 3rd precinct at 36 Radford St. In January of 1930 Calese was admitted to St. John's Hospital reportedly suffering from gallstone problems. Within a week officer Charles Calese would die in that hospital on January 25, 1930. Officer Calese was a police officer for less than five years, was married with a three year-old son, and was only 26 years old.

PO JAMES O. PORTER # 231

APPOINTED: March 16, 1925
RESIGNED: September 6, 1933

Jim Porter was born in NYC on April 25, 1899. Following his formal education he enlisted in the Army on Aug. 12, 1916 and served during World War I as a Corporal in Company F., 22nd Infantry Regiment. He was honorably discharged on June 19, 1919. Following his discharge Jim worked as a chauffeur right up to his appointment to the YPD on March 16, 1925. Following recruit training he was assigned to foot patrol in the 1st pct. On Mar. 10, 1927 Porter distinguished himself while on duty at a fire at the foot of Main Street. He and another officer entered the burning smoke filled building and rescued trapped residents. He returned inside a second time, again rescuing additional residents. On his third rescue effort police officer Porter was overcome by smoke and had to be rescued by firefighters. On Dec. 30, 1927 Porter was awarded the department's highest award at that time, the Honorable Mention for conspicuous bravery in the line of duty. In late July 1933 it was alleged that while off duty at the City Pier officer Porter witnessed an assault but took no action. As a result he was brought up on departmental charges and after a 45 day suspension without pay, Porter, who lived at 189 Roberts Ave. decided not to be put through a departmental trial and submitted his resignation effective September 6, 1933.

PO GEORGE S. MILNE # 202

APPOINTED: March 16, 1925
DISMISSED: June 16, 1931

George Milne was born in NYC on Jan. 1, 1899. Records indicate he listed his former employment as a chauffeur. He joined the Army Air Corps during World War I serving from 1918 to 1919. He was hired by the YPD on March 16, 1925 at $1,900 a year and assigned to patrol duty in the 2nd pct. It seemed that Milne was never suited for discipline. On August 17, 1928 he was convicted of neglect of duty and fined 3 days pay. Then on March 13, 1929 he was again charged with neglect and this time fined 10 days pay. On April 4, 1929 while off-duty and intoxicated he was charged with harassing a local saloon owner and insulting his Polish ancestry. Once again Milne was convicted of departmental charges and this time fined 30 days pay. On May 31, 1930 Milne was assigned to a traffic post at Central Park Avenue and Palmer Road. He was charged by the 2nd precinct captain with leaving his post without permission and going to sleep in a parked automobile. He was found guilty of all charges and was dismissed from the YPD effective June 16, 1931.

PO CHARLES W. HUDD # 210

APPOINTED: March 16, 1925
RETIRED: Junc 1, 1955

Charles Waite Hudd was born in Yonkers on May 20, 1897, attended Sacred Heart school, and graduated from Saunders HS. He joined the Army on Sept. 9, 1918 serving during World War I in the 305th Field Artillery in North Carolina. He was honorably discharged on Dec. 30, 1918 having served just over three months. In 1922 he married police officer Lawrence Ahearn's daughter. Three years later, on March 16, 1925, he was appointed to the YPD and after a short time on patrol duty he was assigned to the Traffic Div. directing traffic in Getty Square. Hudd was always interested in firearms and was an avid student of ballistics. When he joined the police pistol and revolver team it was no surprise. He was an excellent marksman and made his own cartridge reloads. He even designed a new handgrip for more stability and modified the barrel and sights on his target weapon. Because of his knowledge of weapons he became the YPD's firearms instructor for annual re-qualifications. Along with serving as the firearms officer and member of the revolver team, officer Hudd continued to direct traffic in Getty Square until July of 1943 when he was reassigned to the third precinct. It was from there that he would retire on June 1, 1955. In 1956 he began working in security for the Phelps Dodge Wire Corp. in Yonkers and retired from there in 1963. Retired police officer Charles Hudd died on August 14, 1970 in Montefiore Hospital in the Bronx New York. He was 73 years old.

SGT. MICHAEL W. GIRASCH #23

APPOINTED: March 16, 1925
RETIRED: March 16, 1956

Mike was born April 28, 1902 in the City of Yonkers, attended and graduated from local public schools and gained employment as a printer and chauffeur. In addition to English Mike spoke three other languages; Slavish, Polish, and Russian. Mike joined the Army National Guard on March 12, 1919 and was discharged four years later in April of 1923.

He received his appointment to the Yonkers Police Department on March 16, 1925 while residing at 220 Somerville Place earning a starting salary of $1,900 a year. He was assigned to the 2nd precinct and said he remembered that at the time he was paid twice a month, the amount being $73.50. He was known to his friends as Mickey, or "Garbage Mike." In 1928 he was a member the YPD Police Glea Club. In 1932 Girasek stated he was assigned for several years to the Emergency Squad in the 1st precinct and later in the 4th. In February of 1942 Mike legally changed the spelling of his last name from Girasek to Girasch. It was in the 4th precinct, on November 9, 1942, that he enlisted in the Navy reserve during World War II, received an indefinite leave of absence from the YPD, and served until he was discharged on May 10, 1945. He was reinstated to the YPD on July 16, 1945 and returned to the 4th precinct. Two years later on September 1, 1947 he, and eight other war veterans received promotions to the rank of Sergeant earning a salary of $3,400 and Mike was transferred to the 2nd precinct as a patrol supervisor. He remained in the 2nd precinct right up to his retirement on March 16, 1956, at which time he purchased a liquor store on Ashburton Avenue which he operated for about 13 years.

He was the organizer and first Commander of the St Casimir's Post of Catholic War Veterans. He was also a member of the Yonkers Police Holy Name Society, the Yonkers Police War Veterans Legion and an uncle to PO's Thomas and Michael Syso but never had children of his own. Mike retired to the house he built at 24 Gavin St. where, on July 18, 1994, he died at the age of 92 years.

PO RAYMOND CAROZZA #215

APPOINTED: March 16, 1925
RETIRED: March 16, 1950

Raymond J. Carozza was born in Yonkers on September 1, 1901 and attended local public schools. Following his graduation, on September 25, 1918 he joined the Navy during World War I, serving with the naval engineers. He received his honorable discharge on July 1, 1921. Ray would later work for many years being employed as a salesman.

On March 16, 1925 he was appointed to the Yonkers Police Department while residing at 150 School St. and earning a salary of $1,900 a year. Following recruit training his first assignment was foot patrol in the 3rd precinct. Carozza, who stood over 6 foot tall, was fluid in the Italian language and was very active in sports and was an eager participant in baseball competitions between the police and fire departments.

On May 18, 1925, with only 2 months on the job, Carozza was assigned to the Traffic Division on foot directing vehicular traffic. On February 23, 1934 Carozza was off duty in the Getty Square area when a massive underground explosion occurred in front of the Proctor Building at South Broadway and Prospect Street (right in front of what was the Proctor movie theater.) A large hole was blown open in the sidewalk and was filled with flames. As a result of the blast a young girl was blown into the pit and was rescued by PO Carozza and another officer who had jumped down in the hole. Following another explosion, that officer, Patrick Whalen, was killed. For his actions that day Carozza was awarded a departmental Commendation.

The following year, on January 24, 1935, Carozza and two other officers chased 3 robbers through snow drifts during a blinding snowstorm and arrested all three. For his determined efforts on that date he was again awarded another departmental Commendation. Being a veteran of the World War 1, the war to end all wars, Carozza was an active member of the Yonkers Police War Veterans Legion. In fact he was elected vice commander for the year 1940. It was about this time that he was assigned to the motorcycle squad.

Officer Carozza had faced dangerous situations in the past, but on December 1, 1947 danger came too close. On that evening while off duty and playing cards at a social club, three armed men entered and during the holdup shot and killed an off-duty Yonkers firefighter and also shot Ray Carozza in the arm. All three suspects were arrested within minutes by another on duty officer, Tom Brooks.

PO Carozza remained on motorcycle duty for nearly his entire career except for his last few years with the department when he served as a complaint officer in Traffic Court. Following his retirement on March 16, 1950 Ray moved to Hastings New York and worked as a salesman for DeFeo Cadillac in Yonkers until 1965. Ray's nephews were detectives Paul and Francis Carozza.

On December 19, 1985 retired police officer Ray Carozza died in the Kingsbridge veterans Hospital in the Bronx New York after a brief illness. He was 84 years old.

PO HERBERT W. SCHANCK #235

APPOINTED: March 16, 1925
RETIRED: June 16, 1950

Police Officer Herbert Schanck was born in New York City on August 6, 1897. He moved with his family to Yonkers as a youth and attended local schools. On August 7, 1914 Herb joined the Navy, serving during World War-1, and was discharged 8 years later in September of 1922. His duty at the time was Quartermaster.

Herb was appointed to the Yonkers Police Department on March 16, 1925 and was assigned to the 3rd precinct on foot patrol. On September 2, 1925 he was reassigned to mounted patrol duty in the 2nd precinct on Central Avenue. He named the horse that was assigned to him "Little Prince." Reportedly the mounted unit was abolished the following year, but on March 31, 1931 Schanck was assigned to the Traffic Division on motorcycle duty. Four years later, in December of 1935, he was transferred to the 1st precinct and was assigned to Armored Car patrol duty where he remained for many years. During this time Herb Schanck was also an active member of the police baseball and basketball teams. He was also an expert shot with his revolver and as a result was named captain of the Police Pistol Team which competed in many competitions throughout the tri-state area. On February 20, 1947 officer Schanck was directed to develop a program of target practice for the entire Police Department. The training took place at the firing range in the old Hudson Tire Corporation on Nepperhan Avenue and Schanck was designated as the official firearms instructor.

In his last few years with the department Schanck served as the Bus and Taxi Inspector in the Traffic Division. Officer Herb Schanck, whose uncle was said to be former Yonkers police officer Louis Wicht, retired from the Traffic Division on June 16, 1950 and moved to Van Nuys, California. Retired officer Herbert Schanck, a former member of the Yonkers Police War Veterans Legion, died in that city on October 12, 1967. He was 70 years old.

PO RICHARD A. HURLEY # 238

APPOINTED: March 16, 1925
RETIRED: March 16, 1954

Richard Hurley was born on April 1, 1896 in Pawtucket, Rhode Island and brought to Yonkers as a child by his family. He attended and graduated from St. Mary's parochial school. On May 29, 1917 Hurley joined the Navy and served overseas during World War I as a seaman aboard the USS President Lincoln, a transport ship, which was torpedoed and sunk in the Atlantic on May 31, 1918. After assisting others into lifeboats Hurley ended up in the water but was later rescued. He was honorably discharged on December 16, 1918. While working as a mail carrier and living at 18 Locust Hill Ave., Dick Hurley was appointed a police officer on March 16, 1925. On March 6, 1929 he was transferred from the 4th precinct to motorcycle patrol in the Traffic Division. However, on August 16, 1930 Hurley was appointed a Detective in the Detective Bureau, but several years later he would return to patrol duties. Following his retirement on March 16, 1954 Richard Hurley moved to Reseda, California where, following a lengthy illness, he died on April 2, 1971. He was 75.

PO CHARLES H. NOLAN # 227

APPOINTED: March 16, 1925
RETIRED: April 16, 1950

Born March 12, 1901 in New York City Nolan moved with his family to Yonkers when he was a boy and attended public schools. As a young man he listed his employment as a chauffeur. Following his appointment to the YPD on March 16, 1925 he was immediately assigned to the mounted patrol unit in the 2nd precinct. But by May of 1926 he was returned to foot patrol due to the abolishment of the mounted unit in the Police Department. On September 7, 1927 and while on foot patrol he saw an unattended runaway horse drawn wagon racing dangerously down the street. He commandeered a delivery truck and had the driver race up to the rear of the milk wagon and with some difficulty pulling on the reins, was able to stop the two horses with no injury. That December he was awarded the department's Honorable Mention for his actions that day. On two other occasions, March of 1928 and April of 1929, Nolan chased stolen vehicles firing shots each time and made arrests in 1929. A very active member in the PBA, Nolan spent his entire career in the 2nd precinct from which he retired on April 16, 1950. Around 1960 he moved to Garden Grove, Cal. where he died on March 1, 1967. He was 65 years old.

PO THOMAS S. BALDASARRE #209

APPOINTED: March 21, 1925
RETIRED: April 15, 1947

An Italian immigrant, the below subject would in years to come, prove himself as an active and aggressive police office, fearless and yet full of compassion. A man well respected by his peers.

Tom Baldasarre was born on January 8, 1901 in St. Valentine, Italy. He was brought to America by his family, raised in Yonkers, and attended PS# 18. Following his education he earned his living driving a truck for a New York City department store. A resident of 201 South Broadway Tom was appointed to the YPD on March 21, 1925, and following his recruit training, on May 18, 1925 he was given his first assignment; patrol in the 3rd precinct. A year later on March 25, 1926 he was reassigned from the 3rd pct. into the Traffic Division on motorcycle duty.

While off duty on August 11, 1926 and enjoying a day at Rockaway Beach Long Island, Baldasarre saw a woman in the water who was about to drown. He quickly swam to her aid and was credited with saving her life. Two months later on October 28, 1926 and while on duty PO Baldasarre, on his police Indian motorcycle, pulled over the driver of a car for drunk driving. One of the men resisted arrest, punched the officer, and then ran off. Baldasarre gave chase firing two shots which stopped the man and the arrest was made.

On June 13, 1928 Tom was transferred from the Traffic Division to the 2nd precinct on foot patrol to make room for another officer who wanted to work in traffic and had a “hook.” On February 8, 1930, Tom was assigned as one of nine officers chosen to serve in the newly organized “Special Service Squadron,” later renamed the Emergency Squad. All the men in this unit were trained in unusual and difficult rescues, etc. utilizing specialized equipment. This new unit operated from the 1st precinct at 20 Wells Ave.

Tom Baldasarre was not only a good cop, but he had a good heart. On January 3, 1935 a story appeared in the local newspapers basically relating the following; on Christmas Eve of 1934 officer Baldasarre was sent to serve a summons on a poor family living on Willow Street. When he saw the conditions they were living in and the near destitute children in the home who seemed to have little or nothing, he left and returned a short while later calling, “Merry Christmas” and carrying a sack full of goodies over his shoulder. The large bag reportedly contained clothing, food, and a modest amount of money, all donated by members of the 1st precinct. On that day Tom Baldasarre was truly Santa Claus.

On April 16, 1946 Tom was transferred from the emergency squad back to patrol duties in the 3rd precinct. He retired the next year on April 15, 1947 on a disability pension following the police surgeon certifying him as being physically unfit for duty. During his career Tom had received several departmental awards, both on and off duty, for excellent police work and for saving lives.

In 1951 Tom purchased a used car business and in 1960 he was a manager of a car dealership on South Broadway.

Ret PO Tom Baldasarre died on April 25, 1961 in the professional hospital on Ludlow Street after a year-long illness. He was 60 years old.

PO THEODORE F. GIZICKY #234

APPOINTED: April 1, 1925
RETIRED: August 16, 1950

Ted was born on May 1, 1899 in Yonkers where he graduated from Yonkers HS. He also attended Cathedral College in the Bronx. Following miscellaneous jobs, Ted was hired as a police officer in the Village of Scarsdale NY. After a short time he left Scarsdale to accept appointment to the YPD on April 1, 1925. His first assignment was directing traffic at various intersections. Having a good singing voice, Gizicky was quickly allowed to join the singing YPD Glea Club. Sadly, on February 24, 1928, they were requested to sing at the funeral services of officer John Hudock who died in the line of duty. PO Gizicky did more than direct traffic. On March 27, 1928 he arrested the driver of the car for illegal possession of a gun. And in April of 1939 he was awarded the departments Honorable Mention for his capture and arrest, the year before, of a man who was trying to escape following a payroll holdup. After 17 years regulating traffic, officer Gizicki was reassigned to patrol in the 2nd precinct. Following his retirement on August 16, 1950 he worked as a district adviser for the Herald Statesman. In 1964 Ted moved to Largo, Florida where, following a long illness, he died on April 2, 1987 at the age of 87 years.

PO JAMES F. HANLEY # 230

APPOINTED: April 1, 1925
RETIRED: May 1, 1950

Born in Yonkers on June 30, 1900 James Hanley attended St. Joseph's parochial school and later worked as a chauffeur. Jim was appointed to the YPD from 21 Vineyard Ave. on April 1, 1925 and was assigned to the 1st precinct on foot patrol. Three years later, on March 2, 1928, he was reassigned to the 2nd precinct. On April 4, 1929 Hanley was alleged to have entered a speakeasy on Walnut Street and threatened the patrons. He pled guilty to conduct unbecoming an officer and was fined 10 days pay. Having been later assigned to the Traffic Division, on October 12, 1942 he was appointed a Detective in the Detective Bureau. Det Hanley was awarded a departmental Commendation on December 21, 1944 for the arrests of 3 armed men in a burglary which occurred on August 3, 1943. However, on November 16, 1845, Det. Hanley was returned to patrol in the 4th precinct. In April of 1947 he injured his right knee and requested retirement on a disability, which was denied. On February 1, 1950 he was assigned to the Radio Telegraph Division from which he would retire three months later on May 1, 1950. James Hanley died from heart failure on February 9, 1990 at the age of 89 years.

PO RALPH COOK #189

APPOINTED: April 1, 1925
RETIRED: September 30, 1949

Ralph Cook was born in Denton, Texas on Aug.16, 1897, and received his education in the public schools in Dallas, Texas. It is believed that as a young man Cook worked as a chauffeur or truck driver. On January 19, 1917, Ralph Cook enlisted in the Navy and served throughout World War 1 aboard the USS Frederick and was honorably discharged on Nov. 25, 1919. Known as "cowboy" to many of his co-workers, Cook was appointed a police officer on April 1, 1925, received about a month of basic recruit instruction, and was assigned to a precinct on foot patrol. PO Cook served in uniform patrol throughout his entire career, working over the years in all four precincts and was also known to many as "Big Cookie." On April 22, 1937 officer Cook was on foot patrol in the Getty Square area about 3:30 PM when he observed a fire in a clothing store at 216 New Main Street. Realizing there were tenants above the store, Cook ran into the store, grabbed a bundle of burning clothes and tossed them from the building. In doing so he burned his hands badly. But before he would allow himself to be relieved from duty to be treated, he directed the firefighters to the upstairs location of a woman who was bedridden, which possibly saved her life. In 1949 he apparently began to have health problems and, following an examination by the police surgeon, PO Cook was deemed physically unable to perform his duties. As a result, on Sept. 30, 1949, he was retired from the department on a disability pension. A resident of 280 McLean Avenue, Ralph Cook then went to work for the Penn Central Railroad freight yard until he again retired in 1962. Former police officer Ralph Cook died on Sept. 7, 1970 in Yonkers at the age of 73 years.

PO CHRISTOPHER CONLAN

APPOINTED: April 1, 1925
DISMISSED: August 31, 1925

Chris Conlan was born June 20, 1894 and while growing up in Yonkers worked as a Teamster truck driver. Following his service in the Army during WW-1 Conlan was hired by the YPD on April 1, 1925 from 555 Nepperhan Avenue and following training was assigned to the 1st pct. Having violated departmental rules Conlan was charged with Conduct Unbecoming a Police Officer and was dismissed from the YPD on August 31, 1925.

PO DARIUS BABA #239

APPOINTED: April 1, 1925
RETIRED: August 1, 1952

Darius Baba was born November 7, 1894 in Urmia, Iran. He came to the US around 1911 and worked for the Alexander Smith Carpet Co. Baba was said to have had skills as a carpenter and spoke four languages in addition to English; Turkish, Assyrian, Armenian, and Persian. On May 25, 1918 he joined the Army serving in Europe during World War I with Company C., 2nd Pioneer Infantry Div. of the AEF. He was honorably discharged on July 9, 1919. Darius was appointed to the YPD on April 1, 1925 and assigned to the 2nd precinct where he worked the majority of his career. In 1926 Baba participated in the Yonkers municipal athletic games. Because of his strength he was on the police tug-of-war team. In the 1940s he became a charter member of the YPD St. George Association. Upon his retirement on August 1, 1952 he worked as a security guard for the First National Bank. A member of the YPD War Veterans Legion and resident of 1 Lawrence Street, Ret PO Darius Baba died on June 12, 1962 in St. John's Hospital at the age of 67 years.

LT. JAMES J. TYNAN

APPOINTED: April 1, 1925
RETIRED: October 16, 1954

James was born in Yonkers on Dec. 10, 1901 and attended local public schools. On Aug. 19, 1918 Jim joined the US Merchant Marine Service during World War I. He was discharged on Feb. 26, 1923. Two years later, on April 1, 1925, he was appointed to the YPD and assigned to the 3rd precinct. On Jan. 16, 1927 while on post he made a good burglary arrest. At some point he must have been detailed to work undercover assignments because in May 1927 he was commended by then Dist. Atty. Rowland for his assistance in making gambling raids in Mount Vernon. Apparently as a result, on June 1, 1927 he was elevated to Detective. Following an attempted holdup in the Bronx, 3 men were arrested on Jan. 21, 1928 by Detective Tynan and charged with the crime. Just two months later, on March 16, 1928, all 3 were convicted and sentenced to 5 to 10 years in prison. On April 20, 1929 Tynan was awarded a Commendation for his part in the arrest of a man wanted for murder. However, on August 29, 1930 he was returned to patrol in the 3rd precinct. Tynan was promoted to sergeant on June 16, 1942 earning $2,975, and was later promoted to lieutenant on January 1, 1948 earning $4,000 a year and assigned to desk duty in the 4th precinct. Lt. Tynan retired from the 2nd precinct on October 16, 1954. He died June 10, 1963 at the age of 61 years.

PO THOMAS BROOKS # 206

APPOINTED: April 1, 1925
DIED: May 24, 1959

Tom Brooks was born March 10, 1900 on North Broadway to Toler and Amanda Brooks. He attended PS # 2 elementary school and studied business courses at Yonkers High School. For six years he held a job as a chauffeur for former mayor, Dr. Nathan A. Warren. When Tom was appointed a policeman along with 23 other men, he was the first African American police officer ever hired by the department. Following his appointment the local newspaper reported, "*He would likely be assigned a beat or post in that section of the city where the Negro population predominates. Some of these areas would be School Street, Waverly Street, Brook Street, New Main Street, and Morgan Street, along with Chicken Island.*"

A big man, standing over 6' and weighing nearly 300 Lbs., with broad shoulders and a sturdy build, he once was asked what led him to seek a job as a police officer. He reportedly answered, "*My size.*" And, "*I wanted to do something permanent with my life's work.*" Tom Brooks also thought the salary was fairly decent. Possessing a cheerful personality, ready smile, snappy wit, and often referred to as Mr. Brooks, he would often politely say, "*Don't call me Mr. Brooks, call me Tom.*" His witty cordiality made him a popular figure on his "old beat" in the 1st precinct.

Patrolman Brooks was a very popular and respected officer. He was very active in the Police Athletic League and was always available to counsel youths who seemed to be headed for trouble. During his career he received several departmental commendations and awards for excellent police work. One award for heroism was received for an incident which occurred on December 1, 1947 when three armed men entered the Calcagno Association clubhouse at 254 New Main Street. The three men were armed, desperate, and while holding the occupants at gunpoint, shot and killed off duty Fireman Anthony Polito and also shot and wounded Polito's brother in law, off duty police officer Ray Carozza. Just at that time Patrolman Tom Brooks, while on foot patrol and calling the precinct from a police call box on Park Hill Avenue, heard the sound of gunshots and, with his revolver in his hand, he entered the club. In an attempt to arrest the robbers a violent struggle began. One suspect escaped but Patrolman Tom Brooks was able to subdue and arrest two of the gunmen.

In the mid 1950's this writer was only a teenager and I lived at 55 Ravine Avenue. "Mr. Brooks" lived at 80 Ravine. In those years my friends and I would often "hang out" on the street corners. That is, until we saw "Mr. Brooks." Even though he did not work in the area where we lived, upon seeing him, along with his reputation for being a no nonsense cop, was enough to make us leave the area; and quickly.

Along with his job as a police officer, Tom Brooks supplemented his income with a second job as a guard at Patricia Murphy's Candlelight Restaurant on Central Park Avenue. His brother Frank was the funeral director at the Brooks Funeral Home at Warburton Avenue and Gold Street. Unfortunately officer Brooks developed a heart condition and on May 24, 1959 he passed away in the Professional Hospital on Ludlow Street at the age of 59 years. At the time he was assigned to the department's Traffic Division. Officer Brooks was a member of the PBA, and was a member and Trustee of Institutional A.M.E. Zion Church.

PO JOSEPH J. KASPERAN #224

APPOINTED: April 1, 1925
RETIRED: June 30, 1950

Joseph Kasperan was born in the City of Yonkers on January 14, 1897 and received his formal education in the public school system. Besides English, Joe spoke Slavic as a second language. As a young man he was employed as a motorman on the local trolley cars in Yonkers. Joe joined the Navy on July 2, 1918 during World War I, but for some reason was discharged 6 months later on December 19, 1918. While living at 57 Belmont Ave., Kasperan was appointed to the Yonkers Police Department on April 1, 1925. Following his basic recruit training his first assignment was patrol in the 3rd precinct. Records are not clear regarding Kasperan but they indicate from 1943 to 1947 he worked in the 2nd precinct and then later was reassigned to the 4th precinct on Shonnard place. Joe was known to his friends as "chew tobacco Joe," because he always had a mouthful of tobacco. Joe Kasperan retired from the YPD on June 30, 1950 and following a short illness he died on January 31, 1971 St. John's Hospital at the age of 74 years.

PO ANDREW S. FISCHER #229

APPOINTED: April 1, 1925
RETIRED: March 1, 1952

Andy Fischer was born December 21, 1901 in the City of Yonkers, grew up on Clinton Street, and attended PS# 10. Following school Andy worked as a furnace stoker for a hotel in New York City. As a youth he was always interested in playing basketball, playing on one of the teams in the City League. He was also a charter member of the Highland Rod and Gun Club of Yonkers. Following his appointment to the YPD on April 1, 1925 it wasn't long before he was assigned to the Traffic Division directing traffic in Getty Square or Manor House Square. On November 6, 1935 while on duty at Manor House Square, Fisher heard yelling. The jewelry store nearby on North Broadway had just had 10 watches stolen and the thieves started to escape. Officer Fischer took up pursuit arresting one of the thieves and recovering all of the watches. For his actions he was awarded a departmental Commendation. On October 21, 1942 Fischer was transferred to the 3rd precinct and often walked a post on South Broadway. Andy Fischer retired on March 1, 1952 and worked as a guard for the Peoples Savings Bank in Getty Square. Fischer's son Andrew Jr, retired from the Eastchester P.D., and his grandson Andrew was also an Eastchester police officer. Another grandson was a White Plains sergeant. Following a long illness retired police officer Andy Fischer died on March 31, 1978 at the age of 76 years.

CAPTAIN JOHN F. McCORMACK

APPOINTED: April 1, 1925
RETIRED: March 1, 1959

John McCormack was born at 38 Vineyard Avenue, Yonkers N.Y. on August 26, 1894 to John and Bridget Manton McCormack. His father was originally from Brooklyn and his mother was born in Dungarvan, County Waterford, Ireland. Unfortunately he never knew his father as he had died prior to John's birth. His widowed mother would then marry Alexander Rohan, also from Ireland, who raised young John as if he were his son. As a youth young John attended St. Joseph's school and later St. Peters School in Haverstraw N.Y. It was approximately 1915 when John McCormack and the Rohan family moved to Yonkers. As a young man McCormack earned a living as an electrician, truck driver and auto mechanic. But when the 1st World War broke out he did not wait to be drafted and on December 5, 1917 he enlisted in the U.S. Army. Following his basic training he served in the 302nd Engineers. Later he was transferred to the Ordinance Corps where he served as an artillery instructor on the French 75 mm artillery weapon. Having completed his enlistment obligation Corporal McCormack was honorably discharged on December 23, 1918.

Apparently still full of an adventurous spirit he would then join the U.S. Merchant Marine and

Capt. John F. McCormack (cont.)

serve a year or two as Electrician 2nd class aboard the SS George Washington and also the S.S. American Legion, making trips to South America and Germany.

Following his passing the civil service test for "Police Patrolman" while living at 1 Jones Place, McCormack was hired by the police department on April 1, 1925 and assigned to the 4th precinct on foot patrol. A year later, on March 25, 1926, he began what some might refer to as a love affair with motorcycles when he was transferred from the 4th precinct to the motorcycle squad of the Traffic Division. He was said to have really enjoyed his assignment riding his Indian motorcycle around town, despite having been cut off by a truck which caused his motorcycle to collide with a fire alarm pole and resulted in a broken leg. But he was also interested in advancement in the police ranks. And after scoring high on the promotional exam, motorcycle officer John McCormack was sworn in to the rank of Sergeant on December 30, 1930, with the elevation in rank to take effect on January 1, 1931. The newspapers of the day thought that this was remarkable in that, in 1930 the police salary scale required a man to serve seven (7) years before he would reach the top of the pay scale. Sgt. McCormack had been with the department for just over five (5) years and was earning a salary of $1,940. per year. When he was promoted, he had not yet even reached top salary, and his salary rose dramatically to $3,400. a year. As a new sergeant his new assignment would be patrol supervisor duties back in the 4th precinct. It is likely that upon his transfer Sgt McCormack believed he would never ride a police motorcycle again. But, on March 31, 1931, only three months later, the sergeant was reassigned back to duties in the motorcycle unit of the Traffic Division.

On June 1, 1932 Sgt. McCormack married Margaret E. O'Brien, daughter of Frank O'Brien, Chief Engineer of the Yonkers Water Department. In 1935 the McCormack's had a son, John.

As Sgt. McCormack continued to serve, riding his motorcycle, in the Traffic Division, he apparently also found time to continue his studies, this time for the Police Lieutenants examination. While residing at 36 Stone Avenue he took the lieutenants exam and scored a 93.06 which placed him # 1 on the promotion list. On July 16, 1935, Sgt. McCormack was promoted to the rank of Lieutenant raising his salary to $4,000. a year, and he was reassigned from Traffic to the 1st precinct as a desk lieutenant. However, as unlikely as it might seem, four months later, on November 22, 1935, he was once again returned to duty as a "riding lieutenant" in his beloved Traffic Division.

In 1936 Lt. McCormack received recognition in a way he could never have imagined. He had made the trip and attended a convention of the American Legion in Los Angeles, California. Being a member of the Yonkers War Veterans Crescent Post # 935 the lieutenant made the trip along with the New York City Police Veterans Legion contingent. The trip was interesting for a number of reasons, but of very particular interest because, while visiting the Glacier National Park in Montana on his way to California, he met, and was formally "adopted" by the Black Feet Indian Tribe. Following an impressive tribal ritual McCormack was given the Indian name, Chief Eagle Fly. He returned home with a feathered war bonnet and a scroll presented by the tribe to certify his acceptance as a member of their tribe.

On November 24, 1939 the Civil Service Commission released the results of the test for Police Captain which had been held some time earlier. Lt. John McCormack, now of 46 Tower Place and serving

Capt. John F. McCormack (cont.)

as the acting commander of the Traffic Division, once again placed # 1 on the promotional list with a score of 90.3. Not only was he about to be promoted to the rank of captain, but on November 30, 1939 he held his first meeting of the Yonkers Police War Veterans Legion in the French Chef Restaurant at 184 South Broadway after having been elected to his first term as the legions commander.

The following month, on December 16, 1939, Lt. John F. McCormack was officially promoted to the rank of police captain and was assigned as the commanding officer of the Traffic Division. He had been serving as the acting captain of this division since the retirement of Capt. Dennis Cooper and had the great pleasure of serving in this division as a police officer, sergeant, lieutenant, and ultimately as a captain. His salary was now raised to $4,500. a year.

Being one of the most respected and well liked officers in the department, it was really no surprise when a large group of friends and members of the police department gathered to honor him on his rise to police captain. The Herald Statesman reported that, on February 11, 1940, seventy-five NYPD motorcycle police officers were among 500 people who attended a testimonial dinner for the captain. The affair, which was sponsored by the Police Golf Association of Westchester, of which Capt. McCormack was a past president, was held at Schmidt's Farm Country Club in Greenburgh. In attendance were large numbers of local, county, state, and federal dignitaries who knew the captain very well. On behalf of the Police Golf Association Capt. McCormack was presented with a new golf bag and clubs. Only the year before, in 1939, the Golf Association had presented "Jack" McCormack, then their president, with an engraved sterling silver platter.

On July14, 1941, following the establishment of the first Yonkers Police Athletic League, it was necessary to elect officers of the league to serve on a volunteer basis as trustees. Considering the involvement in police and civic affairs, it must have been no surprise to anyone when the captain volunteered and was elected as a trustee.

On February 13, 1945 the Yonkers Common Council voted to establish a permanent Yonkers Transit Committee. The committee was set up to ensure more rigid control over the transit companies operating in Yonkers and to also ensure that they live up to their franchise requirements. Due to the complete confidence the Common Council had in Capt. McCormack, he was named to chair the committee. Along with his duties as commanding officer of the Traffic Division, he was named Transportation Administrator. The captain's committee was responsible for recommending the route's and fares of the city's bus and trolley lines, as well as the overseeing of their operations.

According to various newspaper reports, in January of 1947, there was a great deal of dissatisfaction felt by the Public Safety Commissioner as to the competence of then Chief William Kruppenbacher. It was no secret that the commissioner wanted the chief to retire. Though the chief resisted the pressure, word began to circulate that if he did retire Capt. McCormack would be the captain chosen to replace him. In fact, the chief did retire that year but the position would not be filled until January of 1964.

Capt. John F. McCormack (cont.)

Several years later following the establishment of a "Civil Defense" organization, which included the local Auxiliary Police, the city's Common Council determined that they needed a very capable individual to be placed in charge of this new organization. Seemingly without hesitation they chose Capt. McCormack of the Traffic Division to be the "Civil Defense Director" effective January 1, 1953. And, as if to highlight the importance they placed on this new position they authorized $1,000. in additional compensation to Capt. McCormack over and above his police salary. This increase in salary earned McCormack $6,000. a year. He was allowed to keep his civil service police captains rank but was required to take a special leave of absence in order to work full time as the director of Civil Defense. From 1953 through 1956 then City Manager Charles Curran continued to grant annual leaves of absence from the police department. However, in order to maintain his civil service status they set up a process whereby the captain would retain his police position. This was done by officially placing McCormack back to full police duty status, on paper, while he was on vacation each year, and when he returned to work, the leave of absence would be reinstated. On January 24, 1957 McCormack was again granted this type of leave, but this time it was to assume the title and duties of 3rd Deputy Public Safety Commissioner at a salary of $8,250. per year. His duties as director of civil defense remained the same and he continued to contribute to the police pension system.

After serving 34 years with the police department, as well as the Civil Defense, Capt. John F. McCormack retired from all active service in the police department effective March 1, 1959. However, he did continue in his position as Civil Defense Director. Although due to state law he was required to waive receiving his police pension while he remained working for the city, he apparently didn't mind. He enjoyed his job and wanted to continue to work. John McCormack continued with Civil Defense for another five (5) years until June 30, 1964 when he retired from all city employment and was then eligible to begin receiving his police pension.

"Jack" McCormack was a member of the Crescent post of the American Legion, Police Benevolent Association, Police Holy Name Society, Captains, Lieutenants and Sergeant Association, International Association of Chiefs of Police, the Chippewa Club, Irish American Unified Society of Yonkers, past commander of the Yonkers Police War Veterans Legion, and served as chairman of the Traffic Safety Committee of the NYS Association of Chiefs of Police. His uncle was PO James McCormack, his brother in law was PO Frank S. O'Brien, his half-brother was PO Robert Rohan, and his niece was PO Sharon Rohan McMahon.

Following a lengthy illness retired Capt. John F. McCormack died in Yonkers General Hospital on February 7, 1971 at the age of 76 years.

PO FRANK ROWE #222

APPOINTED: April 1, 1925
RETIRED: May 1, 1950

Though seemingly just like all the other men hired by the YPD when he was appointed, Frank Rowe would earn an enviable reputation during his career. Rowe was born on Aug. 4, 1894 in Hastings NY where he received his education. As a young man he moved to Yonkers and gained employment as a chauffeur. In 1916 Frank joined the Army National Guard and was later called up to active duty during World War I and would receive his honorable discharge in 1918.

Frank was appointed to the Police Department on April 1, 1925 and was assigned to the 2nd precinct. It became immediately apparent that he was an expert shot with his revolver so he was recruited to join the YPD pistol team in Jan. of 1928. On July 28, 1931 during the investigation of a motor vehicle accident and while attempting to make an arrest, Rowe was assaulted by several people. News reports related that Rowe was knocked down, nearly unconscious, and had his night stick and revolver taken from him. Someone called headquarters and the Emergency Squad officers arrived, made 3 arrests, and transported Rowe for medical treatment. Fortunately his injuries were not serious.

Following the murder of a man on Feb. 24, 1932 on the corner of Midland Ave. and Murray Avenue, the quick action taken by officer Rowe resulted in the arrest of the suspects responsible. Following his conviction the murderer received 30 years to life in prison. Once again Rowe displayed his diligence when, on June 13, 1932, he was awarded the YPD Honorable Mention award for his capture and arrest of a male, while off duty, for killing his wife and stepchild on March 16, 1932. The suspect was convicted and later executed on January 19, 1933.

Once again Rowe found himself in a dangerous situation when, on January 1, 1941, he was attacked and beaten by a large group of males who were creating problems on New Year's Eve. Despite receiving a fractured nose and a concussion, Rowe was able to hold onto at least one suspect and make the arrest. On October 15, 1945 while investigating a burglary, he set up surveillance and observed a male enter and set fire to an apartment building. Rowe and his partner arrested the man and were also able to quickly extinguish the fire. On another occasion on January 4, 1946, a fire broke out in an apartment house at 118 Woodworth Ave. When the alarm was sent in at 7 PM most of the 18 residents were unaware and were in extreme danger. Officer Rowe and his partner arrived and after several attempts to get past the flames, they were successful at rescuing all the residents.

Frank Rowe, it would seem, wasn't the luckiest person when it came to avoiding injury. In fact, on August 24, 1946, he was nearly killed. He was in the intersection of Palisade Avenue and Ashburton Avenue on a parade detail at 2:49 PM when he was struck by one trolley car, knocking him in front and beneath the body of another passing trolley coming in the opposite direction. He was dragged about 10 feet beneath the trolley before it stopped and he was able to crawl from beneath it. He was taken to St. John's Hospital where he was admitted and treated for multiple contusions to his shoulder and injuries to his head and back. Fortunately, again he recovered from his injuries.

In 1948 Frank Rowe was transferred to the 4th and following an examination by the police surgeon was deemed physically unfit to perform his duties and was retired on a disability pension effective May 1, 1950. Around 1955 Frank moved to Ft. Lauderdale, Florida to live, but five years later in 1960 he moved back up north to east Orange, New Jersey. Following a long illness retired police officer Frank Rowe died in a Veterans Administration hospital on December 10, 1961 at the age of 66 years.

PO ALBERT KILEY #219

APPOINTED: April 1, 1925
RETIRED: January 31, 1949

Albert Kiley was born in the City of Yonkers on January 21, 1893. He received his formal education at St. Joseph's Catholic school and later as a young man worked as a railroad motorman. At the time he lived at 300 Sommerville Place. He was appointed to the Yonkers Police Department on April 1, 1925 and his first assignment was patrol duty in the 1st precinct. But after only one year, on July 3, 1926, he was reassigned to the Traffic Division directing motor vehicle traffic. He was most often assigned to South Broadway and Hudson Street. Having a good singing voice, in 1928 Kiley was a member of the YPD singing Glea Club. After 17 years of directing traffic he was reassigned to the 1st precinct on routine patrol duty. In 1949 while assigned to the 2nd precinct Kiley must have been experiencing medical problems and following an exam by the police surgeon he was found physically unfit to perform his duties. As a result he was retired on a disability pension on January 31, 1949. While living at 42 Mulford Gardens, Al Kiley died in Yonkers General Hospital on May 2, 1952 at the age of 59 years.

PO CHARLES W. HAMM #226

APPOINTED: April 1, 1925
RETIRED: March 31, 1950

Born Charles William Hamm on March 1, 1895 in Hudson NY, he grew up and received his education there. At some point he became a resident of Yonkers residing at 171 Radford St. and worked as a machinist. Charlie enlisted in the Navy on June 7, 1917 and served overseas during WW I aboard the USS Indiana. He received his honorable discharge on Jan. 29, 1919. Hamm was appointed to the YPD on April 1, 1925 and assigned to the 1st precinct on foot patrol. Shortly after midnight on July 24, 1928 while on his post in Getty Square, PO Hamm learned a car had been stolen and saw the vehicle pass by him. Officer Hamm ran after the vehicle firing four shots and he ultimately arrested the thief. On Oct. 9, 1928 he was reassigned to the Traffic Div. directing traffic. Following his retirement on Mar. 31, 1950 he moved to Claverack, NY. A loyal NY Giants baseball fan, Hamm was also a member of the YPD War Veterans Legion, PBA, and the Masons. Having been a widower, he later married the widow of former Lt. Andrew Thompson. Charles Hamm died March 30, 1968 in Claverack, NY at the age of 73 years.

PO DANIEL E. HAGAN #201

APPOINTED: April 1, 1925
RETIRED: November 18, 1931

Dan Hagan was born in County Longford, Ireland on November 19, 1895. After immigrating to the US he would later become a naturalized citizen on March 20, 1919. A resident of 60 Tower Pl., prior to the YPD Hagan worked as an assistant engineer and motorman. He enlisted in the Army on May 17, 1917 during World War I serving as a Corporal in the 33rd Infantry Division. He was honorably discharged on May 21, 1919. He was appointed to the YPD on April 1, 1925 and assigned to the 1st precinct. All indications were that Hagan was going to be a good police officer. On July 10, 1928 at 2:30 AM, while on foot patrol, Hagan came upon a burglary in progress at 22 Washington St. and he arrested two males at the scene. And again on November 30, 1929, officer Hagan's quick action resulted in the arrest of a purse snatcher. However, following an examination by the police surgeon and a neurologist, Hagan was deemed disqualified from performing his police duties and after only 6 years was retired on a disability pension effective November 18, 1931. A resident of 190 Palisade Ave. retired PO Daniel Francis Hagan died on August 29, 1961 at the age of 65 years.

PO THOMAS M. KAZIMIR #233

APPOINTED: April 1, 1925
RETIRED: July 1, 1950

Tom Kazimir was born in Yonkers on Dec. 21, 1903, grew up on Nodine Hill, and attended Holy Trinity Catholic School. Prior to the YPD he owned a grocery store on Webster Ave. in Yonkers. Tom was appointed to the YPD on April 1, 1925 and in a short time was assigned to the Traffic Div. on foot. However, on June 29, 1928, he was reassigned to the 2nd precinct. When it was discovered that Tom was an expert revolver marksman he was immediately made a member of the YPD pistol team. On August 25, 1929 Kazimir and his partner arrested two men on a Yonkers train for a payroll robbery which occurred three hours earlier in Eastview, NY. For this arrest officer Kazimir received a Certificate of Excellent Police Work. Several years later, on January 17, 1937, PO Kazimir arrested three holdup men and was awarded departments Honorable Mention for his work. Tom spent nearly his entire career in the 2nd precinct where he served as a precinct trustee for many years. An avid golfer, Tom retired but went right to work for Anaconda Cable and Wire Co. for 19 more years before he retired permanently. As an elderly gentleman Tom was a quiet, soft-spoken man who loved to golf and smoke cigars. Tom died on October 20, 1997 at the age of 93 years.

PO RICHARD J. CONLIN #208

APPOINTED: April 1, 1925
RETIRED: March 15, 1949

Richard Conlin was born Dec. 2, 1894 in Yonkers and attended Sacred HS. As a young man he gained employment as a mechanic and chauffeur. On June 1, 1918 Rich enlisted in the Army serving in Company E, 49th Engineers, with the American Expeditionary Force (A.E.F.) during World War I. He was honorably discharged on July 22, 1919. He was appointed to the YPD on April 1, 1925 and was assigned to foot patrol in the 3rd precinct. On Jan. 3, 1928 Conlin was commended by the Honor Board for stopping a fire in a ten family building by throwing pails of water and thus saving lives. In Jan. of 1928 Conlin was part of the YPD revolver team competing in local tournaments. While on his post in front of 465 S. Broadway on Oct. 2, 1936, officer Conlin was struck by a car. He received a skull fracture and a broken right arm and leg which resulted in a long hospital stay. In fact he was out disabled 606 days. He ultimately returned to work but suffered recurring medical problems. Following an exam by the police surgeon PO Conlin was retired on a disability pension Mar. 15, 1949. Retired PO Richard Conlin, brother of PO William Conlin, died in his home at 16 Stanley Pl. on May 1, 1966. He was 71 years old.

LT. JOHN J. CURRAN

APPOINTED: April 1, 1925
RETIRED: May 1, 1950

John Curran was born in Yonkers on January 16, 1897 and graduated from St. Joseph's Parochial school. Following school Curran worked as a clerk. John served in the Army from May 3, 1917 as a Corporal with the 37th Infantry Division during World War I and was honorably discharged on February 25, 1918. Curran was appointed to the YPD on April 1, 1925 and following recruit school, on May 18, 1925 was assigned to the 1st precinct on patrol. In 1934 the YPD's first communication system, with call letters WPFY, was instituted. Officer Curran was chosen to be a relief radio operator in that Radio Telegraph Division. On January 1, 1939 John received his promotion to the rank of Sergeant and was assigned to the 2nd precinct as a patrol supervisor. On May 1, 1942 he received his promotion to Lieutenant earning a salary of $3,500 a year and remained in the 2nd precinct as a desk officer. John retired from the 2nd precinct on May 1, 1950. He was a charter member of the St. George Society, the YPD War Veterans Legion, PBA, and Police Holy Name Society. Following a heart attack at his home at 165 Sweetfield Circle, retired Lieutenant John Curran died on December 7, 1966 at the age of 69 years.

PO JOHN HUDOCK # 213

APPOINTED: April 1, 1925
DIED: February 21, 1928

DIED IN LINE OF DUTY

John Hudock was born in Pillar, Austria Hungary on September 16, 1893. When he was a youth of 15 years of age he came to the United States with his family and would later become a naturalized citizen. When the United States became involved in what was then termed "the Mexican border troubles," it was then on April 21, 1914, at the age of 21, John enlisted in the U.S. Army. It was there that John Hudock excelled in his military service. Because of his dedication to duty, his service during World War 1, aka "The Great War," and his ability to serve as an interpreter by speaking five languages, Hudock rose to the rank of "First" or "Top Sergeant" by the time he was discharged six years later on June 4, 1920. He was a veteran of World War 1, having served in the 10th Infantry Regiment, and due to his proficiency with handguns he was certified and assigned for a time as a small-firearms instructor.

On his application for the position of police "Patrolman" John Hudock listed his employment as a

PO John Hudock #213 (Cont.)

machinist. On April 1, 1925, John Hudock was appointed a probationary Yonkers Police Officer at the salary of $1,800 a year, and was assigned to the 3rd Pct.

On February 10, 1927 a news article appeared in the "Yonkers Statesman" newspaper explaining that the members of the police department were to begin revolver practice at the military shooting range in the Armory at 127 North Broadway. It explained that all officers were required to regularly participate in firearms training, and must qualify satisfactorily. Of course this training was accomplished on their own time with no compensation. However, with a new program that was initiated, if an officer could prove he was a near expert shot, he would be excused from any future training. In order to have every police officer fire for qualification, PO John Hudock was assigned as departmental instructor for those in training. Hudock, who was a former "Top" sergeant in the Army, had considerable experience in the use of firearms and in the instruction of recruits. One of the department's most respected war veterans, Lt George Ford, described Hudock as a "Top Kick" of the first order, and a good instructor. To satisfy Hudock and thus be excused from further training, the man had to score 60 hits out of a possible 100 rounds; or, if he hit 6 bulls-eyes within 10 shots at the target he would also be excused. Hudock worked steady days over several weeks in order to test every officer.

In late December 1927 PO Hudock and his partner George Nickels, both of the 3rd pct., were sent to 62 Hawthorne Avenue on a report of a dispute with shots fired. Upon their arrival they found a male who had been shot twice by a .25 caliber revolver, once in each leg. After calling for an ambulance and detectives, Hudock and his partner conducted a search of the building a found an 18 year old male hiding in the basement still in possession of the gun he used to shoot his neighbor during their argument. Although the victim refused to make a formal complaint, PO Hudock immediately placed him under arrest and transported him to the City Jail.

In January 1928 John Hudock was still active in, what appears to have been, his favorite hobby. Target shooting in competition. At that time 25 members of the department were firing elimination rounds at the North Broadway Armory range in order to determine the 12 best shots in the department who would then constitute the Yonkers Police Pistol Team. Once determined the team would compete against members of other teams from various departments around Westchester County. The weapon to be utilized was a specially built, long barrel, .38 caliber frame from which a .22 caliber round would be fired. Of course John Hudock was among that elite group that qualified and comprised the Yonkers Police pistol team.

Less than three years later, on Friday February 17, 1928, P.O. Hudock had just begun working the late tour and had been assigned a foot post in the area of South Broadway and Radford Street. At approximately 1:00 AM PO Sal Iannucci, who had the adjoining foot post with Hudock, came upon a woman standing in the roadway, apparently intoxicated, and trying to flag down passing vehicles. Being intoxicated and disorderly the woman was placed under arrest by PO Iannucci, but the woman resisted being taken into custody. At that point Officer Hudock came upon the pair while walking his post and assisted his brother officer. He commandeered a passing vehicle and placed the female prisoner in the passenger seat. The vehicle being a 2 door coupe with no rear seat, Hudock ordered the operator of the

PO John Hudock #213 (cont.)

vehicle to drive his car to the 3rd precinct so the female could be "booked," and Hudock and Iannucci stood on the running boards on each side of the car, holding onto the vehicle. As the car turned sharply into Radford Street off of South Broadway, Officer Hudock fell from the side of the vehicle striking his head on the pavement.

Another vehicle was commandeered by officer Iannucci and the unconscious and seriously injured officer was picked up and rushed to St. Joseph's Hospital for emergency care. An immediate investigation was begun to determine the possibility that the female prisoner might have pushed the officer off the side of the vehicle. Three days later, on February 20th during those periods of time when Hudock was conscious, his precinct commander, Capt. Charles O'Mara questioned Hudock as to the woman's action, at which time the officer absolved the female from all blame and said he simply lost his grip and fell.

By the 21st Hudock's condition had deteriorated due to his fractured skull and internal injuries and he was given the last rites of the Roman Catholic Church. The PBA paid for a private room and had the best New York City doctors available retained to treat the officer. However, his injuries were too severe and on February 21, 1928 at 11:25 PM John Hudock died; four days after his accident. Officer Hudock was single, only 35 years old, and was one week short of 3 years with the police department.

In General Order # 9 dated February 23, 1928 Public Safety Commissioner Frank B. Devlin announced the death in St. Joseph's Hospital of officer Hudock stating he "*died as a result of injuries received while on duty Friday February 17, 1928 at 12:40 AM.*" He further advised that the funeral would be from the officer's home at 53 Clinton Street on the 24th of February. The funeral mass would be held at Holy Trinity Church on Franklin and Seymour Streets and burial would be in St. Joseph's Cemetery. He requested all off duty officers to attend in dress uniform.

On the day of the funeral the funeral cortege, headed by an escort of 11 motorcycles, marched from the late officers home to the church. It was reported that hundreds of people stood along the line of procession with their hats removed in respect. Immediately behind the motorcycle detail marched more than 100 officers and men of the department headed by the Commissioner of Public Safety and Chief of Police Edward J. Quirk. The large formation was followed by the honor guard consisting of members of the 3rd precinct and co-workers of the deceased. Behind the hearse marched a rifle squad of 8 soldiers sent from Fort Schuyler. Following the mass the formation marched to Ashburton Avenue and Saw Mill River Road where they stopped, stood at attention, and offered a final salute to their brother officer as his remains passed by. At the cemetery a military rifle squad fired three volleys in the air and an army Corporal played taps.

PO Hudock had been considered a good cop and one of the best marksmen with a revolver in the department. He was liked and well known for his ability to speak English, Polish, Russian, Slavic and Hungarian. Chief Quirk was quoted as saying "*It is too bad that a man like John Hudock should be taken away. He was honest, always faithful to his duty, always on the job.*"

PO ROBERT F. TOMPKINS #205

APPOINTED: April 1, 1925
DISMISSED: September 30, 1929

Robert Tompkins was born in the city of Yonkers on December 17, 1897 and attended local schools. He was a veteran of World War I having served in the Navy from April 9, 1917 aboard a ship in the Torpedo Div. He received his honorable discharge on Nov. 16, 1919 and began work as a machinist. Bob was appointed to the YPD on April 1, 1925 earning a starting salary of $1,900 a year and on May 18, 1925, following recruit training, he was assigned to the Traffic Div. directing traffic. He remained there for 3 years and then on June 28, 1928 was transferred to patrol in the 2nd precinct. In mid-Oct. 1928 Tompkins was charged by the Greenburg P.D. with a crime on a complaint from a motorist. The YPD suspended him on Oct. 19, 1928, but following the complainants inability to identify him in a lineup, Tompkins was reinstated to full duty on Oct. 27, 1928 and all charges were dismissed. However the following year on Sept. 24, 1929 Tompkins was charged with conduct unbecoming an officer for trying to obtain a benefit from a citizen for Tompkins to perform his required police duty. He was found guilty and was dismissed from the department on Sept. 30, 1929. Tompkins appealed his dismissal, but his punishment was upheld by the Supreme Court on Feb. 7, 1930.

PO JOHN GLUS #223

APPOINTED: April 1, 1925
RESIGNED: October 20, 1948

John Glus was born February 5, 1901 in Yonkers and attended public schools. Prior to the YPD he listed his occupation as an ironworker. John was appointed to the YPD on April 1, 1925 and following training was assigned to the Traffic Division. In May of 1926 Glus arrested a known "cop fighter" with 31 previous arrests. The male resisted and sustained an injury to his head and then charged Glus with assault. The charges were later dismissed. On Feb. 1, 1933 while assigned to the 3rd precinct John's alertness to duty resulted in the arrest, at gunpoint, of a thief who had just robbed a woman's purse. For his actions on that day, on March 9, 1933 the honor board awarded Glus a Departmental Commendation. While still in the 3rd precinct, on July 10, 1942, Glus filed for a leave of absence due to induction into the Army. However, for reasons unknown, the Army rejected him and he was immediately reinstated to the YPD. From as early as 1928 Glus, known as "Jake," was recognized as an excellent revolver shot and remained a member of the YPD pistol team right up to September of 1948. Then, on October 17, 1948, he was charged with violation of the rules and regulations and was suspended without pay. Three days later, before a hearing took place, John Glus submitted his resignation from the YPD effective October 20, 1948.

PO MICHAEL G. WERTIS #218

APPOINTED: April 1, 1925
RETIRED: May 15, 1950

The below subject is one of those individuals who, without question, was a good cop. And he remained that way throughout his career.

Michael George Wertis was born on June 7, 1900 in Bradock, Pa. where, following his education, he worked as an ironworker and machinist. At one point he moved to Yonkers, took the civil service test for Police Patrolman, and was appointed a Yonkers police officer on April 1, 1925. Following his recruit training, on May 18, 1925 Mike was assigned to patrol duties in the 2nd precinct. Following his transfer to the 1st precinct on March 2, 1928 Mike became very active in PBA activities and was elected trustee in his precinct. In addition to English Mike spoke Polish, Slavish, and Russian.

On March 6, 1929 while on a foot post on the late tour at about 2:25 AM, Mike observed three males standing in a doorway on Nepperhan Avenue and when questioned could give no good explanation for their being there. Upon checking the rear door of the building Wertis found an attempted break-in. He arrested all three who were then charged with attempted burglary. Then, on August 23, 1929, again walking his post at about 8:45 PM, a woman ran out of a Hawthorne Avenue apartment yelling that her husband was attempting to commit suicide. Wertis, with two other officers on adjoining posts, ran in and found the husband unconscious on the bathroom floor due to an open wall gas jet. The man was revived with artificial respiration which saved his life.

On New Year's Eve, December 31, 1929, once again ever alert on his post, while "checking his glass" front and back Mike discovered and open rear door of a restaurant at 69 S. Broadway. Upon entering he found a male suspect hiding in a corner and placed him under arrest for burglary.

On January 28, 1930 Public Safety Commissioner Devlin announced the formation of a "Special Service Squad" to begin patrol at the 4 PM roll call that date. The new squad had nine officers assigned. Three officers working each tour and remaining in readiness at the 1st precinct to respond to any emergency. Considering the reputation Mike Wertis had of being a very active and aggressive officer, it was no surprise when he was assigned to this new squad. Specialized training was provided these officers in first aid and rescue techniques as well as in the use of a specially equipped open back truck. On October 20, 1930 this unit was equipped with a newly purchased 45 caliber Thompson Submachine Gun. Officer Wertis tested the weapon at the State Armory range on North Broadway and was directed to instruct the other squad members on its use. On this same day it was noteworthy that the squad's name was changed from the Special Service Squad to the Police Emergency Squad.

Although Mike was kept very busy in the emergency squad, he remained active in Police Association matters as well. He had been 1st precinct trustee for several years but on May 5, 1939 he was appointed to the position of Secretary of the Yonkers Police Association.

It was a warm day on June 2, 1939, when a call came over the police radio of three men in danger of drowning in the Hudson River. Apparently the three had been in a canoe about 175 feet off shore from the National Sugar Refinery. A problem developed, the canoe capsized, and the men were thrown into the river. One easily swam to shore but the others were floundering.

PO Michael G. Wertis #218 (cont.)

P.O. Mike Wertis of the Emergency Squad and his partner Det. Tom Flynn spotted the men out in the water. They both began removing their outer clothing, and Flynn found a length of rope which he tied around his waist, hoping to leave the other end on shore so that they could be pulled back to safety. Wertis and Flynn dove into the Hudson and started out toward the struggling men. Unknown to them, the distance out to the men was greater than the length of rope they were using, and the rope was gradually being pulled out into the water. P.O. Alexander Young of the Armored Car Patrol, while standing on the shore, observed the problem with the rope. Young located an 85 foot length of rope, took off his uniform, and swam out with the rope to tie it to the end of the shorter one now floating in the water. When Wertis and Flynn reached the two men, one was about to go under. The man was grabbed around his neck under his chin and, using the two connected ropes, all involved were pulled ashore by officers Ed Stosch and Bill Bell, who had waded into four foot deep water. Fortunately, only one of the three men was in serious condition and had to be revived by members of the Emergency Squad who used an "inhalator" and one tank of oxygen.

The whole incident was over in a rather short period of time. Stosch and Bell, who waded into the water with their uniforms on, were ordered to go home to quickly change into dry ones and return to duty. Officers Mike Wertis, Flynn, and Young, all of whom took off their uniforms before entering the water, were directed to remove their wet underclothing, put their uniforms back on, and resume patrol. Which they did.

On April 3, 1948, nine years after the incident, it was announced by the police Honor Board that for his above-mentioned actions, officer Wertis was awarded the departments Honorable Mention.

It was on October 12, 1942 that Mike Wertis was transferred from the Emergency Squad in the 1st precinct and appointed a Detective in the Detective Bureau where he continued to perform his duty with excellence. He did this until he was reassigned to patrol duties in the 1st precinct on April 16, 1946. Later that year in September he was transferred to patrol duties in the 4th precinct on Shonnard Place.

In the late 1940s Mike had earned a break from patrol duties and received it by being detailed as an aid in the office of the Public Safety Commissioner.

All throughout his career Mike was not only an active working cop, but was also very active physically in sports and said to be one of the city's best bowlers, and an enthusiastic tennis player. In fact he was interested in all sports. His brother was Yonkers police officer Joe Wertis.

Mike retired from the police department on May 15, 1950 while living at 24 Emmett Place, Yonkers, and began working as a machinist for the Jacoby Tar Box Co. on Nepperhan Avenue which had a large Navy contract at the time. Sometime later Mike moved to Los Angeles, California where he died unexpectedly on April 27, 1967. He was 66 years old.

PO JOHN SABOL # 220

APPOINTED: April 1, 1925
RETIRED: June 30, 1964

Born in Perth Amboy, NJ on Dec. 25, 1899, John was raised by his aunt and uncle. He came to Yonkers as a young boy and worked as a "special officer" in the security field. He was appointed to the YPD on April 1, 1925 from 354 Ashburton Ave. earning $1,800 a year. After one year that was raised to $1,900. Sabol's first assignment was in the 4th pct. on foot patrol and later in a patrol car. Sabol was a good athlete and often played baseball on the police team. In fact in Oct. of 1930 he and other officers played a series of games against the fire department. It was said to have been a spirited competition. On Feb. 15, 1935 PO Sabol and his partner were sent to the river by the Habirshaw factory on a report of two young boys trapped on floating ice on the river. Sabol and his partner were able to rescue the boys using ropes. On June 30, 1964, after 34 years of service PO John Sabol retired from the YPD to his home at 362 Prescott Street. John was a charter member of the St. George Society, member of the PBA, Modern Woodmen of America, National Slovak Society, and the Nodine Hill Assoc. John Sabol died unexpectedly on May 22, 1972 at the age of 72 years.

PO LEO J. MAGRATTEN # 240

APPOINTED: April 1, 1925
RETIRED: March 1, 1951

Leo Magratten was born on June 5, 1899 on Jefferson St. in Yonkers. He attended and graduated from St. Mary's school. He enlisted in the Navy on Aug. 11, 1918 serving as a "fireman 3rd class" aboard the USS Leviathon during WW-1 and was honorably discharged 9 months later on May 15, 1919. On his application he listed his employment as a "Huckster." Known to all his friends as "Boscoe," Magratten was appointed to the YPD on April 1, 1925 and was initially assigned to Traffic on foot, but in Dec of 1925 was moved to patrol in the 3rd pct. On April 20, 1929 "Boscoe" was commended for saving the lives of two children trapped in a burning building. "Boscoe" was a member of the YPD War Veterans Legion and in 1939 was elected their trustee. In 1947 he was elected the Legion commander. Leo's brother was PO Bill Magratten. Leo, or "Boscoe" was an organizer of the Highland Rod and Gun Club and the west side baseball league. He was an active member of the Hudson Boat Club and the Square Deal Boat Club. He loved hunting, fishing, and handball. Leo Magratten retired from the YPD on March 1, 1951 and worked as a bank guard in Getty Square. "Boscoe" Magratten died on March 25, 1973 at the age of 73 years.

CAPTAIN BERNARD J. McGINN

APPOINTED: April 1, 1925
RETIRED: November 15, 1960

Bernard McGinn was born in the city of Yonkers on December 13, 1900 and would later graduate from St. Mary's elementary school and Yonkers High School. He was very active in sports and a very well-known athlete. As a young man he gained employment as a typist. McGinn was appointed to the Yonkers Police Department on April 1, 1925 and was assigned to the Traffic Division directing traffic; usually at South Broadway and McLean Avenue.

With only two months with the YPD, on May 30, 1925, officer McGinn was off duty when he came upon a motor vehicle accident at Saw Mill River Road and Ashburton Avenue. He stopped his car and went to investigate. As he passed through the large crowd that had gathered he was struck on the head from behind, almost knocking him unconscious. When he reached for his off-duty revolver someone took it away from him. Fortunately, McGinn escaped very serious injury but the assailants were later arrested.

Though very involved in his new career as a police officer, McGinn remained involved with sport competitions. In October of 1926 during the municipal track meet held in the Glen Park, McGinn left his competition in the dust during his sprint race. In an article in the old Yonkers Herald newspaper, it was reported that on July 16, 1927 traffic officer McGinn would compete in the International Police games in

Captain Bernard J. McGinn (cont.)

Baltimore, Maryland, representing the Yonkers Police Department. He was described as a sprinter with quite a few years experience, and that when in the AAU competition he wore the colors of the Hollywood Inn Club. However, while in Baltimore he represented the YPD. And although he didn't take 1st place, it was said he did very well in his competition. Not only was McGinn and excellent runner but he was a good ballplayer as well, playing on the police team in 1928 against the Yonkers Fire Department.

On September 16, 1928 officer McGinn was investigating an incident which appeared to involve a robbery. A pursuit of the two youths took place during which one of the boys, a 12-year-old, was struck by a round from McGinn's revolver. Although the child was critically injured, he did recover. Following an internal investigation by acting chief Capt. Charles O'Mara, it was determined that McGinn's warning shot ricocheted off some object before striking the child. As a result, no departmental charges were lodged against officer McGinn. On June 8, 1929 he was reassigned from the Traffic Division to patrol in the 1st precinct.

McGinn was also very active in Police Association matters and in 1930 was elected Recording Secretary of the PBA. He also served in this capacity in 1931 through 1933. On January 9, 1933 he was returned to the Traffic Division, this time on motorcycle patrol duty.

Officer McGinn was promoted to the rank of Sergeant on April 16, 1939 earning a salary of $3,400 a year. Now, after 6 years of motorcycle patrol, he was assigned to the 1st precinct as a patrol supervisor. As part of a rather large reassignment of personnel, on March 1, 1941, Sgt. McGinn was returned to the traffic division again riding a motorcycle. However, this would last little more than a year; for on October 21, 1942 Sgt. McGinn was transferred to the 2nd precinct on patrol. Three years later, on December 29, 1945, Sgt. McGinn was promoted to the rank of Lieutenant earning $3,500 a year and was assigned to very familiar duties; back in the Traffic Division. But once again this was short-lived. Four months later, on April 16, 1946, Lt. McGinn found himself as a 1st precinct desk officer.

Upon the death of Capt. John J. McCarthy-3, Lt. McGinn was promoted to the rank of Captain on March 1, 1958 with an annual salary of $7,410 a year. Capt. McGinn was then assigned as commanding officer of the Juvenile Aid Bureau (JAB) and was appointed president of the Yonkers Police Athletic League (PAL). At the time the JAB and PAL offices were located in the old Health Center building at 87 Nepperhan Ave., but were moved weeks later to the former city court rooms in police headquarters with a separate entrance at 4 Woodworth Avenue for juveniles.

Sometime later while assigned as the commanding officer of the 4th precinct Capt. McGinn became ill and remained on sick leave for some time. As a result he was examined by the police surgeon and was deemed physically unable to perform his duties and was subsequently retired on a disability pension on November 15, 1960. A cousin to Lt. Larry Shea, McGinn was a member of the LaRabida Council Knights of Columbus, the Crescent Club, PBA, CLSA, the U.S. Volunteer Life-saving Corps, member of the Board of Directors of the Yonkers Family Service Society, and past secretary of the Police and Fire Retirees Association.

While living in retirement with a home at 280 McLean Avenue, and following an extended illness, retired Capt. Bernard McGinn died on May 7, 1969 in the city of Rye New York in a nursing home where he had been for nearly a year. He was 68 years old.

PO GEORGE W. NICKELS #140

APPOINTED: August 16, 1925
RETIRED: October 16, 1952

PO Nickels was born in E. Orange, NJ on Nov 14, 1896. He moved to Yonkers with his parents at the age of 3 years and following his public school education he worked for Otis Elevator as a Foreman. George was appointed to the YPD on August 16, 1925 earning a starting salary of $1,800 a year and was assigned to patrol in the 3rd precinct. Being an expert marksman with his revolver, when the YPD formed a Pistol Team in 1928, George was placed on the team to help in shooting competitions. On Nov. 15, 1941 Nickels was transferred to the Traffic Division on motorcycle duty. However, a year later, on Oct. 21, 1942, he was reassigned to the 1st pct. on foot patrol. On Nov. 16, 1947 he was returned to Traffic, but this time on the three wheel motorcycle on meter summons detail. PO Nickels retired from the YPD's Traffic Unit on Oct. 16, 1952. In retirement George worked for 10 years as a dispatcher for the County Trust Bank. Nickels brother-in-law was PO Joe Fahey and his grandson was PO Bruce Nickels. George was a member of the Odd Fellows, Yonkers Masons, St. George Society, Crescent Club, and the Highland Rod and Gun Club. George W. Nickels died on July 27, 1973 in Lawrence Hospital at age 73 years.

LT . WILLIAM J. TOMPKINS

APPOINTED: August 16, 1925
RETIRED: September 15, 1950

Born May 14, 1899 in Yonkers, Tompkins attended and graduated from Yonkers public schools. Prior to the police department he was employed as a Tinsmith. "Cy," as he was known to all for some unknown reason, was appointed to the YPD on Aug. 16, 1925 and assigned to the 4th pct. On Aug. 18, 1929 a robbery and shooting took place in Irvington and the suspects fled south through Yonkers. Tompkins participated in the pursuit and the arrest of the four suspects involved. For his actions, on Oct. 17, 1929, he was awarded the departments highest award at the time; the Honorable Mention. On Jan 8, 1941 he was assigned to the Traffic Division on motorcycle duty. Having a good singing voice "Cy" was a member of the YPD Glea Club, singing tenor. He was promoted to Sergeant on April 16, 1939 and returned to pct. duty as a patrol supervisor. On Nov 16, 1945 he was again promoted, this time to Lieutenant, earning $3,500 a year. William Tomkins retired from the YPD on Sept. 15, 1950 and moved to Brewster NY where, on May 16, 1974, he died at the age of 75 years.

PO JOHN P. DVOROVY #241

APPOINTED: August 16, 1925
RETIRED: February 28, 1951

John was born in Shamokin, PA on May 1, 1898 where he attended local public schools. He came to Yonkers with his family in 1913 at the age of 15. Prior to joining the YPD he worked as a salesman. He was appointed to the YPD on Aug 16, 1925 and assigned to the 1st pct. Just before election day, a Democratic Party dinner rally was held on November 1, 1925. At that dinner a Democratic candidate for mayor charged that Dvorovy, a former Democrat, was hired as a policeman under the condition that he switch to be a Republican and get 10 other Democrat friends to do the same. Further, that a dinner was held to thank officer Dvorovy and the 10 other men who switched parties. While he and his partner were on patrol in a 2nd pct. patrol car, at 5:25 AM, Dvorovy observed a burglary in progress on McLean Avenue. When they attempted to arrest the suspects a pursuit followed with shots fired into the suspect's vehicle. Following their vehicles crash, the men were arrested in the Bronx. For his actions Dvorovy was awarded a Departmental Commendation. John retired from the YPD and worked for the Herald statesman. John Dvorovy moved from 106 Yonkers Ave. to Poughkeepsie where he died on October 4, 1968 after a short illness. John was 70 years old.

SGT. JOSEPH P. WILLIAMSON #18

APPOINTED: August 16, 1925
RETIRED: August 1, 1952

Williamson was born in Yonkers on March 25, 1902. After attending St. Mary's school Joe worked as a clerk. Williamson, who lived at 211 Buena Vista Avenue, was appointed to the YPD on Aug. 16, 1925 and was assigned to patrol duties in the 1st pct. In Jan. of 1930 Joe was selected to be a member of the newly organized "Flying squad," which would later be renamed the emergency squad (ESU). In July of 1930, while in ESU, Joe made a good arrest of a "screen" burglar who was responsible for multiple burglaries around Yonkers. The following month, on Aug. 28, 1930, he was appointed a Detective in the Detective Bureau. On Dec. 11, 1933 he made a good arrest of a suspect for armed robbery of the Standard Express Co. Joe was promoted to Sergeant on Feb. 1, 1942 and earned $2,975 a year. But as a result, after 12 years, he was reassigned from the DD to the 4th precinct, and later in Jan. of 1948 to the 3rd precinct. Being an expert with his revolver, Joe was a member of the YPD pistol team competing throughout Westchester County. He was also designated a YPD expert on firearms for court testimony. On April 16, 1950 he was assigned to the Radio Telegraph Division, and while living at 140 Voss Avenue, retired on Aug. 1, 1952. It was said that Joe was suffering from a fatal lung disease and was very depressed. On February 18, 1963 Joe was found deceased. He was 60 years old.

PO JOHN J. GILLIS #143

APPOINTED: October 15, 1925
DISMISSED: September 20, 1926

A transplant from the West Coast, John was born in San Francisco, Cal. on March 28, 1895. Later, as a resident of 271 Warburton Ave., John worked as a young man employed as a salesman. He was appointed to the YPD on October 15, 1925, received his recruit training, and then was assigned to the 3rd precinct. On September 10, 1926, 3rd precinct captain O'Mara preferred charges against Gillis. The charges indicated that Gillis had been out with a female around the first of the month. He parked his car, made unwanted advances, and when he was rebuffed he allegedly assaulted the female and fled the scene. Following her complaint Gillis was suspended on September 3, 1926. Then, less than 2 weeks later, on September 15th, Gillis was charged with driving while intoxicated. In addition, reportedly he had lied on his police application not admitting he had been an officer with the St. Paul, Minn. P.D. and had been dismissed. Gillis was found guilty on multiple counts of departmental charges and was dismissed from the Yonkers Police Department on September 20, 1926.

PO SAMUEL J. KELLY #175

APPOINTED: October 15, 1925
RETIRED: November 16, 1950

Samuel Joseph Kelly was born September 9, 1897 in "She Donaghmore," County Tyrone, Ireland. After arriving in the US he was naturalized as a citizen in March of 1924. He listed his employment as a coil winder for Otis Elevator Co. Sam joined the Army on March 16, 1917 during World War I and served in the 71st Regiment of the 21st Infantry Division. Sam was wounded during combat and earned the Purple Heart medal. He was honorably discharged on May 17, 1919. Sam was appointed to the YPD on October 15, 1925 and assigned to the 1st precinct on foot patrol. In 1928 he was listed as member of the YPD revolver shooting team. On April 24, 1929, following an attempted robbery and subsequent pursuit where officer Kelly's partner fired several shots, Kelly arrested the males responsible. On August 18, 1944 he was moved to the 4th precinct. A member of the YPD war veterans Legion, Sam retired on November 16, 1950, moved to Arizona for several years, and in 1981 moved to Newburgh NY. Sam Kelly died on November 23, 1993 at the age of 96 years.

PO FRANK V. SKOWRONSKI #248

APPOINTED: October 15, 1925
RETIRED: September 30, 1945

Frank Skowronski was born in Brooklyn NY on Dec. 23, 1895, came to Yonkers as a child with his family, attended PS #12, and graduated from Yonkers HS. It was said that Frank could speak three languages in addition to English. Frank worked for several years as a bank teller before his appointed to the YPD on Oct. 15, 1925 earning $1,900 a year. His brother James was already a Yonkers patrolman. Initially Frank was assigned to the Traffic Division directing traffic in Getty Square, but on June 29, 1928, as a result of traffic lights being installed, he was moved to the 3rd pct. But, 4 months later, on Oct. 9, 1928, he was returned to the Traffic Division. On Oct. 30, 1943, while walking his post in Getty Square, Frank heard gun shots coming from Engine Pl. Apparently two angry intoxicated men decided to have a duel with shotguns and had already wounded each other a number of times. Skowronski, revolver in hand, ran right between the two armed men and ordered both men to drop their weapons. Both men, wounded and bleeding, complied. The officer retrieved the two shotguns, arrested both men, and had them transported to St Joseph's Hospital. Frank retired on Sept. 30, 1945 on a disability pension, and unfortunately only three months later, on Jan. 8, 1946 died at the age of 50.

PO FRANCIS A. GRADY #207

APPOINTED: October 15, 1925
RETIRED: November 26, 1946

Francis Grady was born in the City of Yonkers on January 9, 1902. As a youth he attended St. Joseph's school and graduated from Yonkers High School. On October 1, 1919, at the age of 17 years, Frank joined the Navy and received his honorable discharge on July 22, 1921. Following his military service he worked as a railroad conductor. He was appointed to the police department on October 15, 1925 earning a salary of $1,900 a year and his first assignment was foot patrol in the 1st pct. Frank was sent on a burglary in progress on Feb. 18, 1928 at 4 AM. He located the suspect, who was armed with a gun, and following a foot pursuit made the arrest. On March 2, 1928 Frank was moved from the 1st to the 4th precinct. Seventeen years later, on November 16, 1945, he was reassigned to the 3rd. Following an examination by the police surgeon, Francis Grady was found disqualified to perform his duties and was retired on a disability pension, effective Nov. 26, 1946. A resident of 207 Riverdale Ave., Frank was suddenly stricken with a heart attack and died on October 31, 1954. He was 52 years old.

PO JOHN A. TIGHE #250

APPOINTED: October 15, 1925
RETIRED: March 16, 1951

John Albert Tighe was born in Yonkers on June 1, 1901. He attended local parochial schools and grew up in the Roberts Ave. area. Prior to the YPD John worked as a carpet weaver at the Alexander Smith Carpet Mills. He was appointed to the YPD on Oct. 15, 1925 and was assigned to direct traffic. In June of 1928 he was reassigned to the 1st pct. where a year later, on March 4, 1929, he made an arrest for possession of a loaded handgun. He worked for many years on foot patrol in the Clinton Street area. On Aug 23, 1929 Tighe assisted in saving the life of a man attempting suicide with open gas jets. Then, on June 11, 1932, he was awarded a Commendation for arresting three burglars two months earlier. He made another good burglary arrest on March 1, 1934 after firing a warning shot. John was very active in the PBA and on January 26, 1944 was elected treasurer. On Sept. 1, 1949 he was reassigned from the 1st pct. to City Court as liaison officer. John retired on Mar. 16, 1951 and moved to No. Miami, Florida and worked as a security guard. John Tighe's son was a retired chief in the town of Pembroke Pines in Hollywood Florida. One grandson was a retired captain from Miami Beach, and the other a retired detective from Plantation Florida. Grandnephews were YPD Lt. Kevin Tighe, Sgt. Bob Tighe, and PO Edward Tighe. Retired PO John Tighe died on July 9, 1986. He was 86 years old.

PO THOMAS C. MAGNER #249

APPOINTED: October 15, 1925
RETIRED: March 1, 1951

Thomas Christopher Magner was born on Christmas Day in the town of Mallow, Co. Cork, Ireland on Dec. 25, 1894. He received his education in Ireland and came to the US when he was 14 years old. Tom enlisted in the Army on August 29, 1918 during World War I and served as a private until his discharge on March 8, 1919. He worked for some time as a trolley motorman until his appointment to the Yonkers Police Department on October 15, 1925. Initially assigned to the 1st pct. he was quickly transferred to the Traffic Division where he would work nearly his entire career directing traffic in Getty Square. He was always spotless and neat in his uniform and never lost his Irish accent. But on December 27, 1943, due to problems with his legs, he was assigned to the 1st precinct and worked the bank detail in Getty Square right up to his retirement on March 1, 1951. He then worked as a guard at the Phelps Dodge cable and wire Corp. up to 1963. His sons were YPD detective Brendan Magner, Westchester County PO Kevin Magner and YFD Capt. Edward Magner. Retired PO Thomas Magner died on October 20, 1970 St. John's Hospital. He was 75 years old.

SGT JOHN G. BUECHERL #11

APPOINTED: October 15, 1925
RETIRED: June 23, 1961

John George Buecherl was born January 1, 1902 in Yonkers, attended PS #10 and Saunders High School, spoke fluent German, and later worked as a machinist. John was appointed To the YPD on October 15, 1925 from 10 Jefferson St. and was assigned to the Traffic Division on foot. In January 1927 he was reassigned to the 2nd pct. On Aug 26, 1929 John made an arrest of 2 men wanted for a payroll robbery in Tarrytown and received departmental recognition for his actions. In January of 1930, when the Emergency Unit was organized, PO Buecherl was chosen to be one of the original nine officers to be trained and assigned there. While in the ESU, on November 5, 1930 he saved a man from drowning in the Hudson River and again received departmental recognition. Once again, on June 8, 1931, he and his partner revived a man from a suicide attempt by gas. John was promoted to Sergeant on February 1, 1942 and was assigned to the 1st pct. Shortly after the formation of the PAL in 1941 Sgt. Buecherl was assigned to the Juvenile Aid Bureau and the PAL. In 1961 it was discovered that PAL money was missing and Sgt. Buecherl was the PAL treasurer. Buecherl abruptly retired on June 23, 1961 following his being indicted for stealing the PAL funds, and admitting his crime. On September 6, 1962 after pleading to a misdemeanor theft, he was sentenced to 60 days in the Westchester County Jail. A resident of 495 Van Cortland Park Ave., John Buecherl died on April 7, 1972 in upstate New York at age 70 years.

PO ARTHUR W. HASLETT #123

APPOINTED: December 1, 1925
RETIRED: March 1, 1951

Arthur was born in the City of Yonkers on January 15, 1902. He attended PS #7, Yonkers High School, and later was employed as a machinist with Otis elevator Co. He was appointed to the YPD on December 1, 1925 and assigned to the 3rd precinct on foot patrol. In his early years he played baseball with the Blue Jay Club and basketball with the Bantams. He was a very big hunting and fishing enthusiast. However, over the next 15 years he would receive charges of conduct unbecoming an officer, neglect of duty, and attempting to resign while intoxicated. Each time he was found guilty and fined 30 days pay and transferred to a different precinct. Arthur was a charter member of the St. George Society in the 1940s. Surprisingly, considering his record of violating the rules, Arthur completed his 25 years and retired on March 1, 1951. He died unexpectedly in his home at 100 Highland Ave. on April 26, 1953. He was 51 years old.

PO STEPHEN J. ACKERMAN #245

APPOINTED: December 1, 1925
RETIRED: May 1, 1951

Stephen Ackerman was born in New York City on November 7, 1903 and later moved to Yonkers along with his family. He received his formal education by attending local public schools. As a young man Steve listed his employment as working as an auto mechanics helper. But Steve wanted more financial security for his family so he took the test for Yonkers police officer. He was successful and was appointed a patrolman on December 1, 1925.

After receiving some very basic instruction on the law and departmental rules and regulations he was assigned to foot patrol in the 3rd precinct. On March 6, 1928 while on foot patrol on McLean Avenue Ackerman observed a man who, while trying to warm himself over a bonfire, inadvertently caught his clothes on fire. The man was screaming and running down the street. Fortunately, officer Ackerman was passing by, ran over to the man and quickly smothered the flames with a coat and saved the man's life. His actions received quite a degree of notoriety in the local newspaper and he was also commended for his lifesaving measures by Chief Quirk.

In January of 1930 when the police Emergency Squad was originally organized, he was one of the original nine police officers chosen, trained, and assigned to work in this new unit. The unit was provided with an open backed truck with bench seats and storage compartments beneath them which contained various types of rescue and first aid equipment. The emergency unit operated out of the headquarters building at 20 Wells Ave.

Over the years Steve Ackerman and the other officers in the Emergency Unit would respond to many calls for help, but on one particular day officer Ackerman would be shocked. In August of 1932, while on one of his rescue calls, he helped recover a deceased man who had drowned in the Hudson River. When they pulled the man from the water he was shocked to discover that the man was his father in law.

After 12 years serving in the Emergency Squad, on January 29, 1942, officer Ackerman was reassigned from the Emergency Unit back to routine patrol in the 3rd precinct and later to the 1st precinct. A resident of 58 Caroline Ave., Steve Ackerman retired from the 1st precinct on May 1, 1951. A member of the Terrace City Bowling club and grandfather to police officer Stephen Kwetchin, Stephen Ackerman died on May 9, 1965. He was 61 years old.

DET SGT PATRICK CHRISTOPHER

APPOINTED: May 20, 1926
RETIRED: July 2, 1963

Patrick F. Christopher was born on March 13, 1901 in the city of Yonkers and attended local schools. As a young man he gained employment with the Otis Elevator Co. working as an Armature Winder. He was a well-liked man and was easy to get along with. He was also a bit of an amateur athlete and displayed his skills playing on the Otis Elevator Athletics basketball and baseball team in an industrial league during the 1925 season.

Pat was appointed to the department on May 19, 1926 and assigned to foot patrol in the 1st precinct on Wells Avenue. Later that year, on November 11, 1926 he was reassigned to patrol in the 2nd precinct. Then on August 24, 1927 he was returned to patrol in the 1st precinct. However on October 13, 1927, he was chosen by then Chief Edward Quirk and was appointed a Detective. His decision proved to be a wise one as within a few days Det. Christopher made a burglary arrest following a brief investigation. His first homicide arrest took place on November 14, 1928 when he arrested two juveniles for randomly shooting and killing a 19 year old male sitting in his vehicle. However, a defining event in his career was about to occur.

In 1929 there was a rash of money receipt holdups of Dugan Bakery trucks in Yonkers. In order to stop this "crime wave" Chief Quirk ordered several of his detectives to each ride in the rear of the bakery trucks on Saturday evenings, the nights the drivers were known to carry considerable amounts of money. The chief gave orders that if anyone attempts to holdup the truck that they're in and brandishes a firearm, shoot to kill. On January 5, 1929 Det. Pat Christopher was riding in the rear of his assigned Dugan Bakery truck. He was sitting in the dark about 6 feet behind the driver Edward McCready. About 6 PM while the truck was heading east on Yonkers Avenue and it approached the intersection of Sweetfield Circle, the detective heard a male yell and ask the driver for a ride. The driver refused and began to continue up Yonkers Avenue on his return trip to Mt Vernon. It was then that this unknown male, later identified as Joseph Scalice 23 years old, jumped onto the running board of the truck, stuck a revolver through the window and pressed the barrel against the driver's head. As he did he yelled, "*Put up your hands you *&%#*@; Hand over the money.*" McCready, the driver, stopped immediately and remained motionless.

Det Christopher had heard the original request for a ride but could not see anyone due to the darkness. But he had drawn his revolver just in case there was a problem. On his second approach when the suspect threatened the driver by putting a gun to his head, Pat Christopher acted instinctively. He raised his revolver, took quick aim and fired one round, striking the suspect in the face just below his left eye. The suspects weapon fell on the front seat and Scalice fell backwards into the street mortally wounded. Though Christopher was certain the man was dead he flagged down a motorist named Rovelli who assisted in transporting the mortally wounded suspect to St Joseph's Hospital where he was pronounced dead. Rovelli was thanked by Det Christopher for his help and after obtaining his identification, Rovelli was sent on his way. However, within only a few hours of investigation it was learned that in fact, Rovelli was Scalice's accomplice in this robbery attempt. Christopher along with other detectives waited for Rovelli to return home, searched his car and found a loaded revolver. After a lengthy and "intense" interrogation Rovelli confessed to being involved and was charged accordingly.

Det Sgt. Patrick F. Christopher (cont.)

The demise of Scalice and the arrest of Rovelli cleared up five other armed robberies in Yonkers.

Det. Christopher was said to be considerably affected by the shooting and was sent home by the chief. He refused to comment at length about the shooting to reporters preferring to treat it as merely part of his duty. Chief Quirk, however, could not have been more pleased. He reportedly stated, "*It was wonderful, wonderful police work. Paddy deserves all the credit in the world for what he did. I am very proud of him...*" The chief stated that he would refer the matter to the departments Honor Board at its next meeting. Following that meeting the Honor Board awarded Det Christopher with the absolute highest award it could confer at the time; the departmental Honorable Mention. In addition to the Yonkers Police Dept., Det Christopher was also recognized for his bravery by the Allan F. Waite American Legion Post by presenting him with a gold medal for his service to his community.

It might be of some interest to note that at the time there was only one grade of detective in the police department. Following the shooting and arrest, then Mayor John Fogarty, who praised the detective's action, expressed regret that the police department did not have two grades of detective so that Christopher could be promoted to the higher grade. The mayor instructed the Public Safety Commissioner to look into establishing two grades, just as NYC had at the time. It cannot be said with complete certainty but it is believed that as a result of Det Christopher's actions on that day, it was not very long after that the Yonkers Police Department established a 1st and 2nd grade detective grading system.

Det Christopher continued to display an enviable record of police excellence in the Detective Bureau. Over his career he had accumulated numerous awards granted by the police honor board for outstanding police work. A few examples are as follows: On April 20, 1929 awarded the Honorable mention for the holdup shooting; On June 11, 1932 a Commendation for the pursuit and capture of three burglary suspects; On May 23, 1936 the Honorable Mention for the arrest of a man wanted for murder of a Philadelphia Pa. police officer; On July 9, 1938 a Certificate of Excellent Police Work for the arrest of two men on burglary charges; On April 23, 1942 a Commendation for the arrest of a murder suspect.

When he was promoted to sergeant on December 16, 1939 he was allowed to remain in the Bureau as a Detective Sergeant. It was said that on one occasion Sgt. Christopher was selected to guard President Harry Truman. Though numerous political administrations of both political parties came and went over the years, Det. Sgt. Patrick Christopher remained assigned to the Detective Bureau right up to his retirement on July 2, 1963 after having completed 37 years service. And most remarkable of all, an incredible unbroken record of nearly 36 years in the Detective Division. An amazing tribute to his knowledge and the esteem in which this man was held.

Ret Det Sgt Christopher was seen in 1980 at the Police Old Timers Picnic. He was described as being distinguished looking, thin build, he stood ramrod straight, was very reserved in demeanor and had with him his ever present cigar in hand. The only thing missing was the old time detectives fedora hat. One could only wonder about the experiences he witnessed spanning the time from the prohibition era right up to 1963. Pat Christopher died Feb. 13, 1983 in St. John's Hospital after a brief illness. He was just short of his 83rd birthday.

Note: Former Police Commissioner Donald Christopher, the sergeant's son, was appointed a police officer in 1960 and they were both on the job at the same time for three years.

PO ALBERT J. PORACH #187

APPOINTED: June 21, 1926
RETIRED: December 15, 1952

Albert John Porach was born in the city of Yonkers on December 22, 1893. He attended local public schools, and in addition to English spoke Polish, Slavic, and Russian. Following school he worked as a carpet weaver and plumbers helper. Al was an Army combat veteran of World War I, having served in the 308th Battalion, 77th Infantry, American Expeditionary Force (A.E.F.). He served from September 1917 up to his honorable discharge as a Corporal in April of 1919. He earned several medals for bravery including the Purple Heart. Following his police appointment on June 21, 1926 he was assigned to foot patrol in the 4th precinct where he served his entire career. In his youth Al Porach played semi pro baseball for the Holy Trinity Church team and later was a proud member of the YPD War Veterans Legion. Al, whose cousin was PO Frank Porach, retired on December 15, 1952 and worked for a while as a security guard. But he most enjoyed light carpentry work and playing pinochle cards. Retired PO Albert Porach died in St. John's Hospital on March 3, 1983 at the age of 93 years.

PO JOSEPH A. NOLAN #124

APPOINTED: July 6, 1926
DIED: April 8, 1936

Joseph Nolan was born in the City of Yonkers on April 18, 1898. He received his education in PS# 12, St. Joseph's School, and graduated from Yonkers High School. For several years he worked as a chauffeur for various local companies and later as a florist. A resident of 62 Summit Ave., Nolan was appointed to the YPD on July 6, 1926 and assigned to the Traffic Division. He was often assigned to Warburton Avenue and Main Street directing vehicular traffic. On July 6, 1934 he was reassigned to patrol duty in the 2nd precinct. On April 3, 1936 Joe became ill suffering from a mastoid infection in his ear and penicillin was not yet available to treat infections. Unfortunately, and very unexpectedly following an operation on his ear, Joseph Nolan died from this condition five days later on April 8, 1936 in the Professional Hospital on Ludlow Street. He left behind a wife and 3 small children. All off-duty officers attended the funeral of their brother officer as a display of respect. Officer Nolan's nephews were Lt. Thomas Kivel and Sgt. Howard Horton. Officer Joseph Nolan died at the young age of 37 years.

PO GEORGE J. TKACH #178

APPOINTED: July 20, 1926
RETIRED: September 1, 1951

George Tkach was born in the City of Yonkers on October 22, 1901 and would later graduate from Holy Trinity Parochial High School. He grew up in the Ashburton Avenue area and the "hollow section" of Yonkers. "Tacky," as his friends knew him, worked as a cement truck driver. He was very athletic and enjoyed fishing, golf, and swimming. He even participated in several competitive foot races. In addition to English George spoke Slavic, Polish, and Russian. He was appointed to the YPD from 52 Clinton St. on July 20, 1926 and assigned to the 1st precinct. He was quickly assigned to the Traffic Unit directing vehicular traffic. Two years later on June 29, 1928 he was reassigned to patrol duty in the 2nd precinct. Upon completing 25 years service he retired from the YPD on September 1, 1951 and worked as a bartender and security guard at the Yonkers racetrack. He was even elected a president of the Retired Police and Fire Retirees Association of Westchester County. George Tkach died on May 28, 1954 in Lawrence Hospital from a heart attack. He was only 51 years old.

CAPTAIN PATRICK J. SULLIVAN

APPOINTED: August 1, 1926
DIED: September 22, 1957

Patrick Sullivan was a native of Yonkers N.Y., having been born there on June 3, 1898. As a youth he attended PS# 7 and graduated from Yonkers High School. As a young man he held a number of jobs, but prior to the police department he worked for the US Post Office as a letter carrier in Mount Vernon, New York. In fact, he was the president of the Letter Carriers Association.

Following his appointment to the Yonkers Police Department on August 1, 1926, with a starting salary of $1,800 a year and very rudimentary recruit training, he was assigned to the 1st precinct on Wells Avenue on foot patrol. The following year, on February 10, 1927, he was reassigned to the Traffic Division at various street intersections directing the vehicular flow of motor vehicle traffic. Officer Sullivan displayed his attention to duty when, on April 5, 1929, he was directing traffic at Warburton Avenue and Ashburton Avenue, and he saw five males sitting in a car that had just been parked. As he approached the car the five males jumped out and began running. When Patrolman Sullivan's order to stop was ignored, he fired his revolver five times at the men without effect. However, after commandeering a car and cutting off the suspects, he arrested two of them and charged them with grand larceny of the

Captain Patrick Sullivan (cont.)

stolen vehicle.

It was possibly that this kind of police work led to officer Sullivan being advanced to Detective on September 20, 1932. Due to budget constraints Detective Sullivan did not receive the standard $200 salary increase provided to detectives. On that date the Detective Bureau's Central Office, located in the HQ building along with the 1st precinct at 20 Wells Avenue, was reorganized so that two detectives would be detailed to work in each of the other three precincts, the 2nd, 3rd, and 4th, in cooperation with the precinct captain, but under direction of the Central Bureau Detective Captain. At that time Detective Sullivan was partnered with Detective John Kilpatrick in the 2nd precinct on Central Park Avenue.

Over the next few years Detective Sullivan established himself as an excellent investigator solving numerous crimes and arresting those responsible. And when Detective Sullivan received his promotion to Sergeant on January 20, 1936, which increased his salary to $3,600, he was allowed to remain in the Detective Bureau as a Detective Sergeant. It is believed this special privilege was allowed due to the respect he enjoyed from his fellow detectives and supervisors. And, four months later, on May 23, 1936, Detective Sgt. Sullivan was awarded the departmental Honorable Mention by the police Honor Board for the arrests of several burglars responsible for numerous entries throughout years 1934 and 1935 and the arrest of a hit and run driver who was later convicted of manslaughter. Both these arrests took place prior to his promotion to sergeant. On July 9, 1938 Sgt. Sullivan's work was once again recognized when he received a departmental Commendation for arresting those responsible for both a burglary and a robbery.

Sgt. Sullivan continued to lead his detectives to achieve an excellent record in clearing unsolved crimes but as he did, he also studied for the civil service examination for police Lieutenant. And as a result, on December 16, 1939, he received his promotion to the rank of Lieutenant. And, breaking with departmental practice and tradition, he was once again allowed to remain in the detective bureau as a detective lieutenant earning an additional $200 over the regular police lieutenant salary. But Det. Lt. Sullivan wasn't finished making his mark on the Yonkers Police Department. On February 1, 1942 he received his promotion to the rank of Captain with the salary of $3,937 a year. Now as Capt. Sullivan, the brother of Councilman James Sullivan, he was initially assigned to command a patrol precinct. However within two weeks of his promotion, on February 15, 1942, Capt. Sullivan was reassigned as a Detective Captain in the Detective Bureau.

However, the captain's incredible record and good fortune by remaining assigned to the Detective Bureau as a captain was short-lived. Eight months later, on October 12, 1942, he was transferred from the Bureau and placed in command of the 4th patrol precinct on Shonnard Place. He had developed an incredible record of accomplishments throughout his years in "the bureau," but he would never again command the Detective Bureau. Over the next 15 years Capt. Sullivan would find himself assigned as the commanding officer of all four precincts for various lengths of time. His last command would be in the 2nd precinct on Central Park Avenue.

Unfortunately Capt. Sullivan would never get to enjoy future retirement. On September 22, 1957 Capt. Sullivan was unexpectedly taken ill and died in St. Joseph's Hospital. He was 59 years of age.

DEP. PUB. SAFETY COMM. JAMES E. McCUE

APPOINTED: September 14, 1926
RETIRED: July 22, 1963

A Yonkers native, James McCue was born in Yonkers on June 18, 1902. He grew up living on Nepperhan Avenue near Moquette Row in a cold water flat. Jim attended Sacred Heart Catholic school and graduated from Yonkers High School. When he became interested in police work he was tall, but was too underweight to pass the medical examination. But he was determined to change that. For weeks before being retested, he ate bananas and drank milk until he gained the weight necessary to pass the test.

As a resident of 13 Parker St. McCue received his appointment to the Yonkers Police Department on September 14, 1926 earning a salary of $1,900 a year. He was initially assigned to the 1st precinct located at 20 Wells Ave. on the corner of Woodworth Avenue. Coincidently the 1st precinct was located in the same building as police headquarters. It was here, for a relatively short period of time, that officer McCue would receive his basic recruit training. But, on November 11, 1926 he was reassigned to the 2nd precinct on Central Park Avenue on routine foot patrol. However, within a year, on December 29, 1927 he

Dep. Public Safety Comm. James E. McCue (cont.)

was reassigned to work in the 4th precinct.

On June 10, 1930 James McCue was awarded a Departmental Commendation for the arrest of an armed man during an attempted burglary. Following the arrest the prisoner admitted that at one point he had his gun pointed at officer McCue and was going to shoot him. But for some unknown reason he decided not to. This incident occurred on February 2, 1931, when officer McCue and Sergeant Anthony Prior, while on routine patrol, saw a suspicious man at 1004 Warburton Ave. When the officers approached him he tried to run but was quickly taken into custody. He had in his possession a loaded 45 caliber semi-automatic pistol and confessed to several other burglaries.

Three years later on October 10, 1934 James McCue was transferred from the 4th precinct to a newly organized Radio and Telegraph Division (RTD) as a radio announcer. He had been certified as a first-class radio telephone operator by the FCC. Three days later the very first police communications system, call letters WPFY, was placed online. And it was officer McCue's historic duty to transmit the very first message sent over a Yonkers Police radio system. The communication system was a resounding success and officer McCue would remain in this assignment for nearly 4 years.

During quiet times in the communications room McCue must have studied for the promotional exam because he passed the civil service test for Sergeant and on April 1, 1938 was promoted to that rank earning a salary of $3,400, and was issued Shield #18. This promotion resulted in his being transferred to patrol supervisory duty in the 3rd precinct located at 36 Radford St. However, his knowledge of the communication system was such that he was more valuable in the communications room than he was on patrol. As a result, two months later, on June 1, 1938 he was reassigned to work back in the Radio Telegraph Division as a dispatcher with the rank of Acting Lieutenant.

Continuing his climb through the ranks, once again Sgt. McCue was promoted, this time to the rank of Police Lieutenant on December 16, 1939 earning a salary of $4,000 a year and he was allowed to remain in the RTD as its commanding officer. He was only one of three men in the department who still held the FCC first-class radio telephone operator's license.

On November 30, 1942 a new position was established entitled Superintendent of Radio; another officer was assigned to this position and was placed in command of the RTD. As a result, Lt. McCue was reassigned and designated to be the fill-in Lieutenant whenever necessary for desk duty in the 2nd and 4th precincts. However he was not to remain in one place for too long. On March 8, 1945 Lt. McCue was designated Acting Captain of the 4th precinct, and when he received his permanent promotion to the rank of captain on November 16, 1945, earning a salary of $3,937, he was transferred to the 3rd precinct as its commanding officer.

Two years later on January 1, 1947 he received the coveted assignment of commanding officer of the Detective Bureau at a salary of $4,700. But, this also would not last. Less than a year later, on November 16, 1947, as part of a so-called reorganization of the Detective Bureau, 19 detectives were transferred, including four captains. McCue was one of those captains. After only 11 months as the detective commander he found himself transferred to the 2nd precinct as their CO.

In 1952 the Police Department had in place the position of Deputy Public Safety Commissioner. This position was the equivalent of the chief of police position which the city had chosen not to fill since

Dep. Public Safety Comm. James E. McCue (cont.)

the death in 1947 of the last chief of police. Instead, they appointed Lieutenant William Comey to that position, with the title of Deputy Public Safety Commissioner, much to the dismay of all the police captains. However, when Bill Comey was retiring due to a change of politics in the city, Capt. Jim McCue was chosen as his successor. The police captains preferred that the position of Police Chief actually be re-instituted, but were pleased that at least a captain received the new assignment.

On May 1, 1952 Jim McCue was officially appointed as the Deputy Commissioner of Public Safety. His responsibility was command of the entire Police Department. However, since it was a non-civil service position, in order to maintain his civil service captain status, McCue was required to take a leave of absence for one year. And in each future year he took another year's leave of absence, returning, on paper, to his rank of captain for two weeks each year during his vacation. This satisfied all civil service requirements to maintain his captain civil-service benefits. As the new leader of the Police Department his salary rose to $6,500 and he was referred to by the rank and file, behind his back, as 52, the number of his city car.

After serving 11 years as the Deputy Public Safety Commissioner, James McCue retired from all active service on July 22, 1963. Jim's uncle was PO Mike McCue, his brother was Detective Vincent McCue, his nephew was Lt. Terrence McCue, and his grandson William Gallagher was a police officer in Indiana.

While living at 26 Woodstock St., Jim McCue became ill and following a long fight with cirrhosis of the liver he died in St. John's Hospital on May 7, 1969 at the age of 66 years.

PO ROBERT J. MULCAHEY #47

APPOINTED: September 17, 1926
RETIRED: November 30, 1939

Bob was born in the City of Yonkers on June 22, 1903 the son of a Yonkers Fire Captain. He received his education from St. Joseph school and graduated from Gorton HS. As a young man he worked throughout Yonkers as a groundskeeper and his family had a tradition working in the Y.F.D. Not only was his father a fire captain, but his uncle, James J. Mulcahey, was a former Fire Chief and organizer of Yonkers' first paid fire department. Yet, Bob decided he wanted to be a police officer. He was appointed to the police dept. on Sept. 17, 1926 earning $1,900 a year and was assigned to the 1st pct. on foot patrol. In June of 1927 he received departmental charges for intoxication while on duty, found guilty, and fined 30 days pay plus loss of two weeks vacation. He was also transferred to the 4th precinct where he would remain. In 1936 he developed respiratory problems causing him to remain out sick right up to 1939. Following a determination by the police surgeon he was retired on a disability pension effective November 30, 1939.

PO EDWARD STOSCH #137

APPOINTED: October 1, 1926
RETIRED: March 31, 1960

Edward Stosch was born July 26, 1901 in Yonkers, NY and was educated in the city's public school system. As a young man he worked for the NY Telephone company as a switchboard repairman. He was also a qualified "Bench Chemist." On October 1, 1926 he received his appointment to the Y.P.D. while residing at 126 Woodworth Ave. Following some basic instruction he was assigned to the 1st precinct on foot patrol. On Sept 6, 1938 PO Ed Stosch and his partner were sent to a burglary in progress at 4 AM inside 193 Elm St. They found a burglar inside and reportedly shouted, "Come out or we'll open fire." The burglar surrendered and they made the arrest at gunpoint. For several years he also worked the Armored Car detail. On Mar 25, 1959 while on traffic duty he was struck by a car, knocked unconscious, and admitted to the hospital. While out on the injured list, on Aug. 22, 1959 he had a heart attack at home at 89 Palmer Rd. Stosch never returned to work. Following determination by the police surgeon, and after more than 33 years service, Edward Stosch retired March 31, 1960 on a disability pension to enjoy hunting and fishing. He moved to Miami Lakes, Florida and died in Hialeah, Fla. on November 8, 1988. He was 87 years old.

CAPTAIN JOHN J. KENNEDY

APPOINTED: October 1, 1926
RETIRED: August 28, 1969

John Joseph Kennedy was born in the City of Yonkers on September 9, 1904 and grew up in the Ashburton Avenue area. He attended local schools, graduated from St Joseph's grade School and later from Yonkers H.S. His parents wanted him to receive his college degree from a Catholic institution and it was during his Catholic education at Cathedral College that he became interested in becoming a priest. He began his studies for the priesthood at St Joseph's Seminary where he remained for about a year. However he would later change his mind and he left the seminary.

"Jack," as he was known, gained employment as a telephone company installer and later as a Foreman for the AT & T Telephone Co. But his licensed trade was as an Electrician. "Jack" was appointed to the Yonkers Police Department on October 1, 1926 at the annual salary of $1,800 while living at 166 Ridge Avenue. He received the privilege of receiving his police recruit training at the NYPD Police Academy, which was quite unusual for Yonkers police recruits.

Upon his graduation from the police academy he was assigned to foot patrol duty in the 1st precinct on Wells Avenue. The New York academy training wasn't very long because he had been working for some time when, on November 11, 1926, he was transferred from the 1st to 2nd precinct.

Captain John J. Kennedy (cont.)

Even in these early years Kennedy's favorite pass time, and passion, was golfing. But after a back injury curtailed his golf game somewhat, instead he would often go on a fishing trip to Canada with several of his friends. And this became an annual event.

On September 17, 1928 the Police Honor Board met and commended Kennedy for his actions on January 3, 1928 while assigned to the 3rd precinct. On this bitter cold night at 10 PM he and officers John Wall, Bob Maier, and Percy Philips rescued 15 trapped people from a hall filled with fire and smoke in a five story building at 480 South Broadway. Kennedy reportedly carried some and led others out to safety on a fire escape or a stairwell.

On October 10, 1934, following the establishment of the department's first police radio communications system, WPFY, Kennedy was appointed a Detective and assigned to the new Radio Telegraph Division. It is likely this assignment was due to his previous experience as a telephone lineman and his electricians license. He was not the only officer reassigned at that time. With this transition to the new communications system, 100 personnel were reassigned throughout the department.

On November 12, 1935 a male was assaulted on South Broadway causing his death. Det Kennedy was assigned the investigation and arrested the suspect several hours later hiding out in a NYC hotel under a fictitious name, and charged him with murder. Det Kennedy was a very active detective. On July 9, 1938 while still a detective he was awarded a commendation for assisting in the arrest of a gang responsible for several burglaries and robberies.

On December 16, 1939 he was promoted to Sergeant at $3,400 a year and assigned as a patrol supervisor in the 4th precinct. Always one to stay involved, in July of 1941 when the Police Athletic League (PAL) was first organized, Sgt Kennedy was one of several volunteers to give their own time to help children to become involved with sports instead of getting into trouble on the streets. As such he was chosen to be on the committee to draft and recommend bi-laws that could properly guide the organization. On November 15, 1941 Sgt. Kennedy was transferred from the 4th precinct to the 2nd and continued his patrol supervisor duties.

On October 12, 1942 Sgt. Kennedy was once again returned to the Detective Bureau as a Detective Sergeant. And as he did when he was only a detective, once again his excellent work was recognized when, on December 21, 1944, the Honor Board awarded him a Commendation for an arrest on August 3, 1943 of three armed men for burglary. Kennedy continued his climb up the ranks when on December 16, 1945 he was promoted to Lieutenant at the salary of $3,500, was transferred out of the Detective Bureau and assigned to desk duty in the 1st precinct. But only for a few months. On April 16, 1946 once again he was returned to the Bureau as a Detective Lieutenant. Loving this assignment as he did it must have seemed too good to be true when, on August 23, 1947 he was assigned as the commanding officer of the Bureau while still a Lieutenant.

June 1, 1952 began the end of "Jack" Kennedy's run in the Detective Bureau when he was transferred to the 1st precinct on desk duty. But he was not finished yet. On March 1, 1959 he was promoted to the rank of Captain at an annual salary of $7,410. His assignment was that of a relief captain rotating throughout the commands to fill in for captains on vacation, etc. For the next several years he was moved around as the C.O. of different commands; November 16, 1960 as C.O. of the 2nd precinct;

Captain John J. Kennedy (cont.)

May 1, 1963 as C.O. of the 1st precinct; August 23, 1965 as C.O. of the 3rd precinct; August 4, 1966 as C.O. of the Traffic Division.

For those who knew him he always had a ready smile. In fact he was known to his friends as "Smiling Jack." His popularity was reflective of the fact that he was elected to ten (10) consecutive terms as the President of the Captains, Lieutenants, and Sergeants Association, serving from 1958 to 1967. In 1969, because he was about to reach the mandatory retirement age of 65 years, he applied for ordinary retirement pension and received standard retirement effective August 28, 1969. However, after having his ordinary pension approved, he applied to receive a 3/4 disability pension from the Yonkers City Pension Fund. He claimed his disability resulted from injury from a motor vehicle accident on duty which occurred on November 18, 1964. His disability pension application was approved by the city. Then on Dec 19, 1969 the trustees of the City Pension system voted to grant him 17/60 th's of his salary to add to his pension. Thereby making his pension higher than his salary was while he was working. His retirement pension was at the time an astronomical $16,393. a year.

Following his retirement Kennedy moved to Boynton Beach, Florida in 1978 where he lived for many years. Captain Kennedy's father was Sgt Thomas Kennedy and his son in law was Det John Bonney.

When his health began to fail Kennedy moved to Vero Beach, Florida in March of 1995. He died there on October 8, 1995 at age 91 years.

PO JOHN J. McCARTHY -4 #143

APPOINTED: October 16, 1926
RETIRED: March 1, 1952

John J. McCarthy Jr. was born in Yonkers on August 27, 1903, the son of Yonkers police officer John J. McCarthy Sr. He attended local schools and obtained employment as a trolley car conductor and later as a caddie master at the Hudson River Golf Club. When he was appointed to the Yonkers Police Department on October 16, 1926 he was assigned to the 1st precinct for his basic recruit training and then was sent to the 3rd precinct on foot patrol. In 1945 McCarthy was moved to the 4th precinct for a year and then returned to the 3rd precinct. During his career there were five men working in the Yonkers Police Department at the same time named John J. McCarthy, which necessitated each been given a number so they could identify one from the other. He was designated McCarthy number 4, while his father was number 1. Following his retirement on March 1, 1952 he moved to 95 Walsh Road. On February 13, 1979, following a brief illness, John J. McCarthy-4 died in Yonkers General Hospital. He was 75 years old.

PO JAMES J. DALTON #130

APPOINTED: November 8, 1926
DIED: January 28, 1942

James Dalton was born in Yonkers on July 30, 1899 and was educated at St. Joseph's Catholic school. He worked as a chauffeur and electrician, and later as a steam engineer. He was single when he was appointed to the YPD on November 8, 1926, and was earning $1,900 a year. He would remain unmarried. Following his basic recruit training he was assigned to the 4th precinct at 53 Shonnard Place. On April 1, 1938 he was reassigned to the Radio Telegraph Division as an announcer, more commonly known as a dispatcher. Being a boat owner he spent his spare time on the Hudson River. He loved sports and when the PAL was organized in 1941, Dalton was named to their Board of Directors. He was also very active in the Yonkers Police Association (YPA) having served as 2nd vice president as well as a trustee. Dalton decided to seek election as the president of the YPA for the year 1942. He campaigned hard, but the night of the election he was required to undergo surgery. That night, January 28, 1942, officer Dalton died unexpectedly of complications from the surgery. Two hours after his death the ballot count determined that he had been elected by 60 votes, posthumously. Jim Dalton was 42 years old.

PO EDWARD W. KRISTAN #183

APPOINTED: November 10, 1926
RETIRED: April 16, 1956

Kristan was born Edward William Kristan on May 22, 1902 in the city of Yonkers. He received his formal education from St. Joseph's H.S. Prior to the YPD he worked as a chauffeur and a clerk in Liggetts Drug Store in Getty Square. He seriously considered being a priest and attended St. Joseph's seminary for a while, however he changed his mind. During World War I had worked as a clerk in the war Department in Washington DC. Around January of 1924 Kristan worked for a short time as an officer with the Scarsdale, P.D. Upon his Y.P.D. appointment on Nov 10, 1926 he was assigned to the 2nd precinct where he would remain for 18 years. In 1944 he was then moved to the Traffic Division directing vehicular traffic. On June 7, 1954 he was working security at City Hall. He later retired on April 16, 1956 from the 1st precinct at 20 Wells Ave. His brother Julius was also Yonkers police officer, his brother Benjamin was a police officer in Pelham New York and his grandnephew was YPD Capt. Fred Hellthaler. A resident of 65 Fowler Ave., retired police officer Edward Kristan died unexpectedly in his home on March 16, 1969. He was 66 years old.

PO PETER F. DANKOVIC #132

APPOINTED: December 1, 1926
DIED: January 27, 1965

Pete's career in the YPD was far from ordinary, as you will see. Born in Brooklyn NY on July 1, 1903, he came to Yonkers as a youth, and graduated from Holy Trinity and Yonkers HS. He lied about his age and at 16 joined the Navy in June of 1919 and was honorably discharged in Jan. 1921. Upon his police appointment on Dec 1, 1926 he was assigned to the 2nd pct. Four years later, in 1930, when the Police Emergency Unit was organized, he was chosen as one of the officers to be trained and assigned. But in Oct of 1934 when the 1st police radio system was established, Dankovic was assigned to the R.T.D. because of his radio communications training in the Navy. He attended the Marconi Radio Institute and RCA Institute in NYC and received a first-class radio operator's license from the FCC. He was placed in charge of all radio equipment and as such was designated an acting sergeant. On Nov 28, 1942 City Mgr. Walsh appointed officer Dankovic to the new position of, Superintendent of Radio System, still as an acting sergeant, and with a salary of $2,975 a year. During World War II Dankovic was also Director of Yonkers War Emergency Radio Service. On January 27, 1965 Superintendent Dankovic died unexpectedly in St. John's Hospital. He was 61 years old.

PO CHARLES L. MOFFAT #97

APPOINTED: December 20, 1926
RETIRED: June 1, 1952

Charles Leo Moffat was born Oct. 4, 1897 at 18 Garden St. in Yonkers, but was raised in an orphanage. He joined the Army on Sept. 6, 1916 serving during World War I in combat with the 108th Infantry Div., A.E.F. During battle he received two purple hearts and was gassed causing temporary blindness. Though in the infantry he often fought on horseback. Moffat was honorable discharge on March 31, 1919. After working as a chauffeur for a time he was appointed to the YPD on December 20, 1926 and assigned to the 2nd precinct. On October 25, 1929, following the armed robbery of a construction company, Moffat arrested the two men responsible onboard a train. On October 17, 1929 he was awarded a departmental Commendation. On September 30, 1929 he was reassigned to the 1st precinct and on January 9, 1933 he was assigned to motorcycle duty where he would remain up to October 21, 1942 when he was returned to the 2nd precinct. Moffat, a member of the YPD War Veterans Legion, retired on June 1, 1952, and moved to Hollywood Florida where he died on January 3, 1983. He was 85 years old.

PO JOSEPH A. MAITRE #28

APPOINTED: January 1, 1927
RETIRED: March 1, 1952

Joe Maitre was born in Yonkers on January 10, 1898 and grew up in the Buena Vista Ave. area. He attended St. Mary's parochial school and then gained employment as a machinist with Otis Elevator Company. On January 1, 1927 Maitre he was appointed to the YPD from 42 Groshon Ave. at the salary of $1,900 a year. He was assigned to the 1st precinct for nearly 20 years walking a post in the Parkhill Avenue area. On April 12, 1941 while on his post near Morgan Street and Nepperhan Avenue, he arrested a male for attempted murder for slashing another male. He was very well liked and respected by all the residents where he worked and he always maintained a well groomed and neat appearance in uniform. When he retired on March 1, 1952 he worked as a guard at the Yonkers Race Track. His nephew was Lt. Robert Maitre Sr. and his grandnephew was Det Robert Maitre Jr. As time went on his health began to fail and he lost sight in one eye. Following a short illness, Joseph Maitre died in St. Joseph's Hospital on April 12, 1974. He was 76.

PO JOHN C. FREY #167

APPOINTED: February 1, 1927
RETIRED: August 1, 1952

Born in Yonkers on Jan. 20, 1899, John received his education in local public schools. Having worked as a concrete worker he joined the Navy on Nov. 2, 1920 and was honorably discharged in Nov. of 1922. On his police application he listed his current employment as a "stationary firemen" and his home address as 4 Convent Ave. Upon his appointment to the YPD on Feb. 1, 1927, earning $1,900 a year, he was assigned to the 2nd pct. where he would work his entire career. On April 12, 1929 at 11:30 PM, and after firing 2 shots from his revolver, officer Frey arrested two men on suspicion of attempted abduction of two young girls. Several years later on Jan. 17, 1937 officer Frey arrested three men responsible for multiple Eastside robberies. For these arrests he was awarded a departmental Honorable Mention. Officer Frey retired on August 1, 1952 after 25 years service and worked as a security guard for the Bank of Canada in NYC. John Frey died on March 19, 1965. He was 66 years old.

PO JOHN J. WALL #54

APPOINTED: February 4, 1927
RETIRED: June 16, 1952

John Joseph Wall was born on Christmas day in 1895. He attended St. Joseph school and as a young man worked as a lineman. At the age of 31 years he was hired to the YPD on Feb 4, 1927 from 182 N. Broadway and assigned to the 3rd pct. On Jan 3, 1928 he was one of 4 policeman credited with saving the lives of 15 people from a fire at 480 S. Bway at 10 PM. Several children were among those carried to safety. His actions were commended by the honor board. On June 17, 1933 he was reassigned to the Traffic Division, armored motorcycle patrol duty. However within weeks, on July 4, 1933, he was transferred back to the 3rd pct. On Dec 29, 1941 at 3 AM while walking his post PO wall came upon three men he believed were attempting a burglary. During his chase Wall fired 3 times but arrested only one suspect. He was awarded a Certificate of Excellence. With the exception of traffic, PO wall served his entire career in the 3rd pct. He would watch his son John be appointed a Yonkers police officer two years before he retired on June 16, 1952. In addition officer Wall's uncle, his mother's brother, was PO Tom Downey, and his cousin was PO Ed Henebry. When John retired on June 16, 1952 he worked as a security guard for the Phelps Dodge Corp. for 10 years. John Wall died Mar 26, 1966 at the age of 70 years.

PO JOHN J. KOMAR #203

APPOINTED: April 16, 1927
RETIRED: July 15, 1944

Born in Austria on Oct 6, 1895, John James Komar immigrated to the US as a boy and was later naturalized as a citizen in White Plains NY. He attended both St. Mary's and St. Joseph's parochial schools and spoke Russian and Polish in addition to English. Komar joined the Army on April 13, 1917 serving as a private with Battery D of the 104th Field Artillery Unit during World War I. He was honorably discharged on Nov. 29, 1918. He worked as a Hatter, bottler, and chauffeur. Following his police appointment on April 16, 1927 he worked his entire career in the 3rd precinct. On March 5, 1934 while on his post he came upon and arrested three men for burglary; and on May 13, 1938 Komar rescued two boys who had fallen into the Hudson River. When he retired on a disability on July 15, 1944, he worked security for a construction company in Yonkers. A member of the YPD War Veterans Legion, and Crescent Post of the American Legion, John Komar died on Feb 23, 1946 in the veterans hospital on Kingsbridge Road in the Bronx. He received full military funeral honors from the American Legion. John was only 50 years old.

PO GEORGE W. FAULKNER #179

APPOINTED: April 20, 1927
RETIRED: September 7, 1960

George Wilson Faulkner was born in West Point, NY on Sept 8, 1895. He attended schools in West Point and, at the young age of 20 years was married. After moving to Yonkers he worked for several years with the NY Central Railroad in NYC as a delivery clerk. A resident of 21 Hildreth Pl., George was appointed to the YPD on April 20, 1927. He was assigned to the 2nd pct. on Central Avenue where he would spend his entire career. George was described by fellow officers as a very quiet and respectful officer who preferred to walk a post rather than ride in a police car, and was never without his pipe. He was still on the job when his son Herbert was appointed to the YPD. George retired on Sept 7, 1960 and worked as a security guard at Wanamaker's department store in the Cross County Shopping Center. George had worked the school crossing at PS# 8 for 30 years. When he retired the Pondfield Road merchants presented him with a gold watch. He was a charter member of the YPD St. George Association and the Cellmates of Westchester County. Following a six-month illness, George Faulkner died in St. John's Hospital on July 18, 1967 at the age of 71 years.

PO FRANK M. STRAUT #221

APPOINTED: May 1, 1927
DIED: January 24, 1950

Frank Straut was born February 5, 1895 in Monsey, New York, in Rockland Co. He came to Yonkers as a small child with his parents and was educated in the Yonkers public schools. After holding a variety of odd jobs, Frank Straut joined the US Marine Corps on June 13, 1917. Frank served as a Sergeant during World War I and was honorably discharged on April 23, 1919. Following the USMC Frank worked as an auto mechanic. He was appointed to the YPD on May 1, 1927 and his first assignment was in the 4th precinct. From 1928 to January of 1934 PO Straut was assigned to the Traffic Division on two wheeled motorcycle duty. On October 26, 1930 Straut arrested a male for public intoxication. However, while attempting to transport the prisoner an attempt was made by the prisoner to grab the officer's revolver. Following a violent struggle the prisoner was subdued. Frank was an expert shot with his revolver and tried out successfully for a spot on the YPD pistol team. On January 24, 1950, while assigned to the 2nd precinct, and living at 70 Radford St., PO Frank Straut died unexpectedly following a short illness. He was a member of the YPD War Veterans Legion and the Hawthorn Lodge of Masons. He was 54 years old.

PO JULIUS E. KRISTAN #34

APPOINTED: May 16, 1927
RETIRED: September 1, 1949

Julius E. Kristan was born in the City of Yonkers on July 1, 1896 and attended Yonkers public schools. As a young man he worked for the New York Central Railroad and the Alexander Smith Carpet Factory. Following his police appointment on May 16, 1927, he was assigned to patrol in the 2nd precinct. Police officer Kristan would remain in the 2nd precinct for his entire career. As a hobby he would spend his off duty time raising chickens in his own chicken coop. Following an examination by the police surgeon, officer Kristan was deemed to be physically unfit to perform his police duties due to a heart condition. As such he was retired on a disability pension on September 1, 1949. Julius' brother, Edward, was also a Yonkers police officer and his brother Benjamin was a police officer with the Pelham Police Department. Kristan was member of LaRabida Knights of Columbus and was active in various Holy Trinity Church organizations. Julius Kristan died unexpectedly in his home at 72 Nichols Ave. on May 21, 1950. He was 53 years old.

PO THOMAS R. FITZGERALD #115

APPOINTED: May 16, 1927
RETIRED: March 31, 1953

Tom Fitzgerald was born in Ireland on September 7, 1902 and was brought to Yonkers by his parents while still a boy. He received his formal education in the Yonkers public school system. Upon his appointment to the YPD on May 16, 1927, earning $1,900 a year, he was assigned to the 4th precinct on patrol. A year later, on July 5, 1928, Fitzgerald received notoriety when, while chasing a stolen car using a commandeered one, he jumped from one car onto the running board of the thief's moving vehicle. At gunpoint, up close and personal, he made the arrest. A big man, Tom was selected to be in the YPD color guard on special occasions and he did so very frequently. He retired from the 1st precinct on March 31, 1953 and worked as a security guard. His brother was Yonkers police officer Edward J. Fitzgerald and his nephew was Det Dominick Gebbia. Tom died unexpectedly on January 12, 1962 at his home at 177 Ashburton Ave. He was 59 years old.

PO JOHN E. SEDLOR #217

APPOINTED: August 1, 1927
RETIRED: September 1, 1953

John Sedlor was born in the city of Yonkers on November 7, 1895 and attended Yonkers public schools. As a young man he made his living working as a steam fitters helper. When he was appointed a police officer in the Yonkers Police Department on August 1, 1927 he lived at 31 Roosevelt St. and earned a starting salary of $1,900 a year. He would spend his entire career in uniform precinct patrol in various precincts. For a time he was teasingly known by his coworkers as "Delaware John." He was given this name after he had stopped what he incorrectly thought was a stolen vehicle from Delaware. John retired on September 1, 1953 and following a lengthy illness John Sedlor died on July 4, 1967 in his home at 139 High St. He was 71 years old.

PO FRANCIS X. MILLER #188

APPOINTED: February 1, 1928
RETIRED: March 1, 1953

Francis Xavier Miller was born in the city of Yonkers on December 27, 1899. Before joining the police department Frank worked as a chauffeur. He was hired by the police department from 42 Carroll St. on February 1, 1928, earning $1,900 a year, and was assigned to the 2nd precinct. On May 23, 1936 Frank was awarded the departments Honorable Mention for a burglary arrest he made on February 4, 1936. On August 28, 1929 he nearly captured a very prolific burglar who had been breaking into homes all over East Yonkers. On this date Miller spotted the burglar running out of a home, fired 5 shots at the thief, but missed and the thief escaped. Then, on October 14, 1935, while on post on South Broadway, he surprised a burglar breaking into a store. He fired once at the man who quickly surrendered. Frank retired on March 1, 1953 and moved to Henderson, NC. Frank's father was YPD Sgt. Henry Miller. Francis Miller died on July 27, 1987 in North Carolina. He was 87 years old.

PO JAMES F. MARTIN #213

APPOINTED: August 16, 1928
DISMISSED: October 9, 1940

PO James F. Martin was born in the Elizabeth City, NC on October 15, 1897. Following his move to Yonkers Jim gained employment with the City of Yonkers working for the Department of public Works. He took the police test in 1924 and received a score of 81.9. A resident of 116 Waverley St. he was hired by the Yonkers Police Department on August 16, 1928 earning a salary of $1,940 a year. He was only the 2nd African-American to be hired by the police department in its history. His first assignment was patrol in the 1st precinct. Jim was charged on October 1, 1940, along with 34 other men, with exhibiting lewd motion pictures in his home. He was found guilty and sentenced to 6 months in the county jail, which was suspended. As a result James, a.k.a. "Cool Breeze," was dismissed from the YPD on October 9, 1940. In 1948 he made an appeal to the mayor for reinstatement, which was denied. Later, Jim worked as a watchman for Yonkers from which he would later retire. James Martin died in Yonkers in July of 1966. He was 68 years old.

PO ALBERT A. WIXSON #105

APPOINTED: August 16, 1928
RETIRED: March 15, 1955

Al Wixson was born in the City of Yonkers on November 14, 1895 and attended local public schools. As a young man he was employed as a designer for Alexander Smith Carpet Mills. When World War I began AL was a member of the Naval Reserve and his unit was activated. He served as a Seaman/Cook from April 23, 1918 to his honorable discharge on July 7, 1919. AL was appointed to the YPD from 107 Ashburton Ave. on August 16, 1928, earning $1,940 a year, and assigned to the 1st precinct. For 3 years, starting Jan. 9, 1933, he served on motorcycle duty, but on April 1, 1936 he was reassigned to the Radio Telegraph Division as a radio repairman. He held the title of Communications Technician. Albert retired from the Communications Division on March 15, 1955 and worked as a driver for the County Trust Bank in Larchmont NY. He was a member of the YPD Police War Veterans Legion and a soft-spoken man who loved fishing during his free time. He died November 9, 1969 at the age of 73.

DET. STEWART L. FREEMAN #12

APPOINTED: December 16, 1928
RETIRED: June 15, 1954

Stewart was born in Charleston, S.C. on October 30, 1896 and came to Yonkers as a child. He attended PS# 2 and graduated from Yonkers HS where he starred on the high school football and baseball teams. A veteran of World War I, Freeman enlisted in the Navy serving on the USS Manchuria and Americana and received his honorable discharge in 1919. Following the military Stew worked as a crane operator. He was appointed to the YPD on Dec. 16, 1928 from 309 Prospect St. and assigned to the 2nd pct. He remained on patrol up to Dec. 22, 1942 when he was appointed as the first African-American Yonkers Detective in YPD history. During his career he made several major arrests and later drove various politicians from City Hall all throughout Yonkers. Upon examination of the police surgeon he was found physically unfit for police duty and retired on a disability pension on June 15, 1954. He then worked as a guard for the United Nations in NYC. A member of the YPD war veterans Legion, Stewart Freeman died on April 12, 1960. He was 63 years old.

PO RAYMOND C. THOMAS #114

APPOINTED: February 1, 1929
RETIRED: March 1, 1954

Thomas was born in Yonkers on June 22, 1902 and attended PS# 2 and Yonkers High School. In 1924, at the age of 22 years, he joined the 27th Military Police Company of the New York National Guard. He was honorably discharged in 1927. Thomas worked driving a truck for Yonkers Building Supply prior to his police appointment. He was hired as a patrolman on February 1, 1929 earning $1,940 a year, and assigned to the 2nd precinct. On June 1, 1947 he was assigned as a Detective in the Detective Bureau and would remain there until October 16, 1952. On that date he returned to patrol in the 3rd precinct. Ray Thomas served for several years as secretary of the Yonkers Police Association and Ray's uncle was PO James Thomas. When he retired on March 1, 1954 Ray lived at 14 Amackassin Terrace where he later became ill. After a two-year illness Thomas died in Rosary Hill Hospice on September 1, 1957. He was 55 years old.

PO EDWARD J. McCREADY #100

APPOINTED: March 1, 1929
RETIRED: August 31, 1955

Ed McCready was born September 17, 1905 in Yonkers and attended St. Joseph's parochial school and Commerce HS. As a young man he worked as a ground hand for the Yonkers Electric Light and Power Company. A resident of 265 Edwards Place, he was appointed to the YPD on March 1, 1929 and was assigned to patrol duty in the 4th precinct. McCready was very athletic as a young man, playing in several baseball competitions between the police and fire departments. By 1931 McCready was working in the Emergency Squad when he was commended by the Honor Board for saving the life of a man who nearly drowned in the Hudson River. And within six months he would save another near drowning victim. On November 15, 1943 he was reassigned from the 3rd pct. to the Radio Telegraph Division in headquarters. On July 1, 1951 he was reassigned from Communications to the Records and Training Division from which he would later retire on August 31, 1955. Ed McCready died February 4, 1968 in St. John's Hospital. He was 62 years old.

LT. STANLEY F. FIGURA

APPOINTED: September 13, 1929
RETIRED: July 31, 1955

Born Stanley Francis Figura on September 22, 1908 in the city of Yonkers, Stan was the son of parents who immigrated to the US from Warsaw Poland in 1885. He reportedly grew up in the Nodine Hill section of Yonkers, possibly on Oliver Avenue. He attended local public schools but left school in the fifth grade.

Figura had earlier been hired by the Yonkers Fire Department, but only remained for a short time. When he was notified that he was eligible for the police department, he accepted appointment to the YPD on September 13, 1929. Figura was described by some of the men who knew him as a great guy and a great boss. He was affectionately known to all his friends as "Razz."

Stan was promoted to the rank of Sergeant on January 1, 1937 and was assigned as a patrol supervisor. Five years later, on February 1, 1942, Sgt. Figura was promoted to the rank of police Lieutenant. Having an excellent singing voice, Stan was accepted as a member of the Yonkers police singing Glee Club in 1943 and was also a member of the Yonkers Chippewa club.

During his career he served in various precincts throughout the city but ultimately retired on July 31, 1955 while working in the 4th precinct as a desk officer. While in retirement he worked in construction for a few years but then moved to Florida and was named an honorary first mate of a small cruise ship line due to his cruising on the ship every single day for several years.

Retired Lt. Stanley Figura died on January 28, 1990 at the age of 81 years.

CAPTAIN EDWARD M. OTIS

APPOINTED: November 1, 1929
RETIRED: May 29, 1969

Edward Michael Otis was born May 30, 1904, the son of Yonkers police officer Michael Edward Otis. He attended local schools, but only to the eighth grade. Rather than further his schooling, like many of his classmates he obtained a job to assist his parents in paying the bills. As a young man Ed Otis worked for several years as a telephone company repairman. A skill that would later serve him well. While living at 278 Mile Square Road, Otis was appointed to the Yonkers Police Department on November 1, 1929 earning a salary of $1,940 a year, and was assigned to patrol duty and the 1st precinct at 20 Wells Ave. Ed quickly earned a reputation of being a cop who could take care of business and was not afraid to use his nightstick.

Seven years later, on April 1, 1936, Otis was reassigned to the 2nd precinct. During the early morning hours, at approximately 2:30 AM on July 6, 1936, police officer Ed Otis was checking his doors along Tuckahoe Road. As he flashed his light into the tavern at 10 Tuckahoe Road he saw a man inside run to the rear. A chase followed that resulted in Otis making the arrest of the burglar.

But two years earlier, in 1934, the police department put in place its very first police radio communications system. And since Ed Otis had telephone repair experience, on January 10, 1938 he was

Captain Edward M. Otis (cont.)

reassigned to the Radio Telegraph Division (RTD) as a police relief communications telephone operator.

On December 30, 1939 police officer Otis was promoted to the rank of Sergeant at the salary of $3,400 a year, and despite his communication skills was transferred from the RTD downstairs to patrol in the 1st precinct on Wells Avenue. However, on November 30, 1942, Sgt. Otis was returned to the Radio Telegraph Division to serve as its commanding officer and was also designated an acting lieutenant.

Acting Lt. Otis received his promotion to the permanent rank of Lieutenant on January 1, 1947 which raised his salary to $4,000 a year. Initially he was reassigned as a relief desk Lieutenant in the first and third precincts, but by November 16, 1947 he was once again returned to the RTD as its commanding officer. Then, April 1, 1950, he was designated commanding officer of not only the RTD, but also the Police Repair Shop, the Painting Bureau, and the Parking Meter Bureau.

On January 16, 1958 he received his promotion to the rank of police Captain earning a salary of $7,410 a year and was reassigned as the commanding officer of the 1st precinct on Wells Avenue. Additional assignments that occurred were as follows; on September 28, 1959 to the Detective Bureau as the CO; on June 1, 1962 the Communications and Records Division as their CO; on November 16, 1960 to the 4th precinct as the CO; on May 1, 1963 to the Traffic Division as the CO; on November 7, 1966 to the 3rd precinct as a CO; on February 8, 1968 to the 4th precinct as CO; and on October 1, 1968 to the 1st precinct as the CO.

Capt. Ed Otis retired, grudgingly, due to having reached the maximum age of 65 years. His retirement date was effective May 29, 1969. He and his wife Margaret lived at 230 Rockne Rd. Ed Otis was characterized by some as being very loud, gruff, and surly. However, most knew his bark was worse than his bite. His nickname was most often simply “EO.”

Retired Capt. Edward Otis died in St. Joseph’s Hospital on January 13, 1979 at the age of 74 years.

PO JOHN CAHILL # 205

APPOINTED: February 1, 1930
DIED: January 23, 1940

John Cahill was born in the City of Yonkers on December 4, 1905 and attended local public schools. It is believed that he lived at 46 Caryl Avenue when he was called for his appointment to the Yonkers Police Department. His appointment date was February 1, 1930 earning a starting salary of $1,940 a year. He was initially assigned to the 2nd precinct on foot patrol but after several years earned a seat in a patrol car with his partner Bill Ferguson. On December 16, 1939 a seemingly routine change in assignment would result in a life altering event. On that date he was transferred from the 2nd precinct to the 4th precinct, and he would be dead in 39 days.

On Sunday, January 21, 1940, Cahill was assigned to a church crossing at St. Joseph's Church at Ashburton Avenue and St. Joseph's Avenue just past noon. While on his post an explosion occurred across the street from him in what he believed to be in 148 Ashburton Ave. Cahill, fearing for the safety of the residents therein, rushed across the street and into # 148 to investigate. He ran into the candy store at that location to a door leading to the basement and to the furnace room. Unfortunately Cahill lost his footing descending the darkened staircase and tumbled down the 11 steps to the concrete floor below. Officer

PO John W. Cahill (cont.)

Cahill sustained a fractured skull in two places. Ironically the explosion actually occurred next door when a frozen water jacket on a coal stove exploded.

When the Yonkers Fire Department responded they found officer Cahill and had him brought to Yonkers General Hospital by ambulance. He was treated for his injuries but remained unconscious in a coma. Despite the doctor's best efforts, officer John Cahill lost his fight for life and died on January 23, 1940. His death came with his wife at his side. The local newspaper wrote, "Patrolman John Cahill paid this morning with his life for the devotion to duty which sent him plunging down an unlighted flight of stairs on Ashburton Avenue........"

Chief quirk ordered that the highest departmental honors, reserved for those who are killed in the line of duty, would be provided to the late police officer John Cahill by his fellow officers. Officer Cahill's family requested an honor guard and to have it consists of Cahill's friends: Lt John McCormick, Sgt William Ferguson, PO's James Dalton, Bernard Farrington, John Forbes, and Henry O'Hare, all under the command of Capt. Thomas Morrissey. Led by Chief Quirk and other high-ranking officers, along with all off-duty members of the department and police Association, they all gathered on January 24th at 8 PM at the 4th precinct. From there the assemblage marched to 37 Tower Pl., the home of officer Cahill's mother-in-law. It was there that the body reposed and there that the members of the Police Department paid their respects.

The following day nearly 200 uniformed officers paid tribute to the deceased young officer by attending his funeral. As a funeral procession of 50 cars led by 10 motorcycle officers passed the police formation and color guard, all stood at attention in the bitter cold and rendered a hand salute. As was tradition the 4th precinct building entrance was draped in black mourning cloth.

PO John W. Cahill, having served only just over 10 years, left behind his wife and a seven-month-old baby daughter. Cahill's wife received a widow's pension of $1,500 a year. John W. Cahill was only 34 years old.

DET. SGT. FRANK CILIBERTI

APPOINTED: February 1, 1930
RETIRED: January 16, 1956

Frank Anthony Ciliberti, or "Chick" as he was known to family and friends, was born in Yonkers New York on May 10, 1907. His father, Pasquale Ciliberti, also a Yonkers police officer, would later retire as a sergeant. Having been born to immigrant parents, Frank spoke fluent Italian.

As a young man Frank worked for Marshall Matheson department store at 5-7 Main Street, and later as a salesman for Beck Shoes in Getty Square. He was known to the local children as Dr. Footsie. When he wasn't selling shoes he was very active in baseball, basketball, handball, and boxing. He was in excellent physical condition and was a man to be taken seriously.

On February 1, 1930 Frank Ciliberti was appointed to the Yonkers Police Department from 136 Willow St. and received an annual salary of $1,940 a year. During his first year as a policeman he continued his sporting interest by playing with the Yonkers Police Association baseball team. But he knew what his police responsibilities were; on August 4, 1935 he captured a burglar following a long foot pursuit. Frank was very smart and understood criminal law very well. As such he was often used as the instructor for new police recruits.

On March 1, 1941 Ciliberti was appointed a Detective and developed an excellent investigative reputation. On June 14, 1944 he was awarded 2 commendations. The first was for his investigation and arrest of a murder suspect and the second for locating and returning a missing teenager. On December 21, 1944 he was awarded a commendation for a murder arrest that took place on March 8, 1943. And at that time, each commendation was accompanied by one percentage point that could be used toward the next promotional exam. In 1944 Frank was also honored by being chosen to attend the specialized training at the prestigious FBI National Academy in Washington, DC. In October of 1946 Frank sent a letter to the Public Safety Commissioner recommending a Yonkers Police School of Instruction (Academy) for recruits and that in-service training be established, and that he be allowed to be assigned as the school instructor. The results of his request are unknown.

Frank was very effective as a detective however, on June 1, 1946, he was transferred out of the Detective Bureau and reassigned to patrol duty in the 2nd precinct; and on September 1, 1947 to patrol in the 3rd precinct. Whatever the reasons may have been for those transfers, things were about to change. On April 16, 1952 Frank returned to the Detective Bureau where, on October 16, 1952, he was promoted to the rank of Sergeant at a salary of $4,200 a year. Frank remained a Detective Sergeant right up to his retirement on January 16, 1956. It was then that he began working as a car salesman for DeFeo Cadillac, where he worked for 10 years.

In 1978 Frank moved with his wife to Boynton Beach, Florida where, on December 25, 1998, Christmas Day, retired Detective Sgt. Frank Ciliberti died. He was 91 years old.

PO HENRY F. O'HARE #106

APPOINTED: February 1, 1930
RESIGNED: July 15, 1944

Henry was born in the City of Yonkers on May 5, 1904, attended PS# 7 and graduated from Saunders high school. As a young man he worked as a timekeeper for the Alexander Smith Carpet Mills and served in the NY National Guard 27th Military Police Co. On Feb 1, 1930 O'Hare was appointed to the YPD earning $1,940 a year. His first assignment was patrol in the 3rd pct. where he would develop an excellent reputation performing his police duties. He was awarded a Commendation on March 30, 1935 for identifying and arresting 3 armed robbery suspects, and a 2nd Commendation on July 9, 1938 for another robbery arrest. On June 1, 1938 O'Hare was reassigned to duty in the 4th pct. And despite his reputation as a good cop, on July 15, 1944 he was found guilty of departmental charges of failing to report from a signal call box for several hours and was fined 30 days pay. That same day, despite having served 14 years as a police officer, he submitted his resignation to the police department. O'Hare moved to Portland Oregon and in 1950 back to New York City. Henry's brother was PO John O'Hare and his nephew was PO Michael O'Hare. Ten years after he resigned, former PO Henry O'Hare died on July 18, 1954 in New York City following a brief illness. He was 50 years old.

PO HAROLD S. CLARK #81

APPOINTED: February 15, 1930
RETIRED: September 16, 1965

During his police career Harold Clark would become one of the most feared police officers in the motorcycle squad. He was born on September 17, 1910 in Brooklyn New York where he received his early formal education and remained until he was fourteen. Following school Clark, who was always of slim build, worked for Chevrolet Motor Co. in Tarrytown and drove a taxi. As a young man he was an accomplished motorcycle rider. On February 15, 1930 he was appointed a police officer with a starting salary of $1,940 a year. His first assignment was foot patrol in the 1st precinct. However, only six months later, on August 29, 1930, and likely due to his motorcycle riding ability, he was transferred to the Traffic Division on motorcycle duty. He was quickly nicknamed "Clarklie," and gained a reputation of giving everyone he stopped a summons. People would say, "He would give his mother a ticket." Thus the fear factor. A charter member of the YPD St. George Society, "Clarkie" served his entire career riding his motorcycle and retired on September 16, 1965. Unfortunately he died just three years later on November 27, 1968 at the age of 58.

PO JOSEPH J. WERTIS #111

APPOINTED: February 15, 1930
RETIRED: October 31, 1955

Joseph John Wertis was born in Yonkers New York on February 2, 1905 and received his early education in local public schools. As a young man he listed his occupation as being a chauffeur and auto mechanic. He also listed languages spoken as Russian and Polish. Joe was appointed to the Yonkers Police Department on February 15, 1930 earning a salary of $1,940 a year and worked uniform patrol in the 1st precinct. On March 30, 1936 while off duty in a NYC subway, he saw an unconscious man lying across the track. He jumped down & lifted the man to safety before the train arrived. On January 7, 1946 he made an arrest of a burglar in Getty Square which made news headlines. The arrest was unusual because the Brooklyn burglar was completely dressed as a woman and actually fooled the officers for brief time. Joe Wertis, whose brother was PO Mike Wertis, retired from the 1st precinct after 25 years service on October 31, 1955. He died 12 years later at home at 27 Rumsey Road on January 1, 1967 at the age of 61 years.

PO ALBERT A. WILL #248

APPOINTED: August 1, 1930
RETIRED: October 1, 1955

A World War I veteran, Albert A. Will was born in Leavenworth, Kansas on March 23, 1900. Little is known of his years as a youth but at the age of 18 he served in the U.S. Navy from April 8, 1918 to his honorable discharge on September 14, 1921. On his application to the Yonkers Police Department he listed his occupation as a Molder, and that he spoke German as a second language. While residing at 56 William St., Al received his appointment to the YPD on August 1, 1930 while living at 117 Oliver Ave. with a starting salary of $1940 a year. His 1st assignment was in the 1st precinct on Wells Avenue on foot patrol. On September 6, 1938 Al Will and his partner PO Ed Stosch were sent to a burglary in progress at 4 AM inside the Tavern at 193 Elm St. They found a burglar inside and shouted "Come out or we'll open fire." The burglar surrendered and they made the arrest at gunpoint. He quickly distinguished himself by making several excellent arrests and as a result, on October 12, 1942, he was appointed a detective. Two years later, on April 16, 1946, he was reassigned back to patrol in the 2nd precinct. Al retired from the YPD on October 1, 1955 and moved to Hollywood Beach Florida to be a manager of a hotel. A longtime member of the YPD War Veterans Legion, Al Will died in Florida on March 29, 1988 at the age of 80 years.

PO JOHN J. O'HARE #29

APPOINTED: August 1, 1930
RETIRED: August 31, 1949

John "Red" O'Hare was born in the City of Yonkers on September 13, 1906. After completing his education and working miscellaneous jobs, O'Hare was appointed to the Yonkers Fire Department in August of 1929. He remained there until his appointment to the Yonkers Police Department on August 1, 1930 along with 6 other men. The starting salary for a police officer at that time was $1,940 a year, payable only once a month, but would increase to $2,500 in three years. In 1931 Mayor Fogarty raised top pay to $3,000 but you were required to work seven years to get there, plus you worked 6 eight hour tours, with only 32 hours off between tours. At the time O'Hare lived at 39 Manning Avenue.

O'Hare's first assignment was uniform patrol in the 2nd precinct on Central Park Avenue. On June 9, 1938 O'Hare was awarded a Certificate of Excellent Police Work for a burglary arrest which occurred on June 2, 1938. On October 30, 1939 O'Hare was on a school crossing at Central Park Avenue and McLean Avenues when he saw a 10-year-old child out in the middle of the road with a truck coming right at the child. O'Hare ran out to save the child but the truck struck them both. O'Hare reportedly was thrown 30 feet along with the boy. The 10-year-old suffered a broken arm while O'Hare's injuries were a fractured spine, along with leg and possible internal injuries.

After being out disabled for some time "Red" returned to duty assigned to the City Court located in headquarters assisting in the arraignment of prisoners. With a keen interest in the youth of the city O'Hare organized a drive to establish a Police Athletic League (PAL). His efforts were successful and on July 14, 1941, during an organizational meeting, John O'Hare was elected the newly created PAL's first president.

Due to his back injury his days on patrol were over, but Red O'Hare kept very involved in the Yonkers Police Association activities. And, on January 25, 1944, he was elected Sergeant-at-Arms of the Association. In the early 1940's "Red" even played on the YPD basketball team and later in 1947 he was the manager of the police softball team.

On August 31, 1949 John "Red" O'Hare retired on a disability pension and moved to Florida. His brother was PO Henry O'Hare, his nephew was PO Michael O'Hare, and his grandson was Lt John Harrigan.

Retired PO John "Red" O'Hare died February 9, 2002 at the age of 95 years.

PO WILLIAM A. MAGRATTEN #24

APPOINTED: August 1, 1930
DIED: May 24, 1952

William A. Magratten was born on April 8 1904 on Jefferson Street In Yonkers. He graduated from St. Mary's Catholic school, and attended Yonkers high school. Before the YPD Bill worked as a milkman for Sheffield Farms Co. With an ability to speak Polish, "Boscoe," as he was known to his friends, was appointed to the YPD on August 1, 1930 while living at 32 Victor St. A sportsman, Bill was very active in fishing, swimming, and handball. His first patrol assignment was to the 2nd precinct on Central Avenue. Ten years later on April 16, 1940 he was transferred to motorcycle duty in the Traffic Division. He was reassigned on November 16, 1947 and returned to patrol duty in the 3rd Pct. Magratten, whose brother was PO Leo Magratten, was a charter member of the YPD St. George Association and was very active in PBA activities and played Santa Claus for many years for the PBA and PAL. While still a police officer Bill became sick and on May 24, 1952 PO William Magratten died at the age of 48 years. Bill had just been elected president of the police Holy Name Society only 3 weeks before his death. On the day of his funeral the city courts were closed in his honor.

PO FRANK P. JORDAN #138

APPOINTED: August 1, 1930
RETIRED: January 15, 1957

Christmas Day in 1906 was the day that Frank Jordan was born in the City of Yonkers. However, unconfirmed reports from a former coworker related that he was actually born Frank Giordano and spoke fluent Italian. After working as a Yonkers city jailer for some time the 23-year-old Jordan was appointed a police officer on August 1, 1930 and assigned to the 2nd Pct. During World War II and at the age of 38 years, Jordan was inducted into the Navy on February 15, 1944 and as such was granted an indefinite leave of absence from the YPD. He served in the shore patrol and was honorably discharged on December 7, 1945 and reinstated to the YPD, returning to the 2nd Pct. Frank, known to his friends as "Zip," was appointed a Detective on April 16, 1946 but his stay was very short. On November 16, 1947 he was returned to the 2nd Pct. While on duty on October 28, 1955 he was struck by a car and severely injured his back. During the exam by the police surgeon it was learned that Frank had Pagets disease of the bones. He remained out injured his last year on the job due to his back injury and was retired on a disability pension on January 15, 1957. A member of the YPD war veterans Legion, Frank Jordan died on July 12, 1969 at the age of 62 years.

DET. CHARLES J. DELLACATO #19

APPOINTED: August 1, 1930
RETIRED: September 1, 1955

Charles J. Dellacato was born in NYC on September 4, 1905. However, he moved to Yonkers with his family while still a child and received his education from PS# 18 and later graduated from Saunders HS. As a young man Charlie worked as a shoe salesman at A & S Beck Shoes in Getty Square and lived at 11 William St. As a young man Charlie really loved sports and was very active in baseball. He was appointed to the Police Department on Aug. 1, 1930 earning a salary of $1,940 a year and was assigned to the 1st Pct. He worked there for 8 years and in 1938 he was reassigned to the 1st Pct. on Wells Ave. On Dec 15, 1939 while walking his post on the late tour, he learned information which resulted in the arrest of a murder suspect. The following year, on Nov. 15, 1941, he was appointed a Detective with a $100 salary increase. But about a year later on October 12, 1942 he was returned to patrol duty in the 1st precinct. Following an arrest he made when he cleared about 17 burglaries along with several other arrests, on September 8, 1950 he was again returned to the Detective Division earning $3,900. Charlie retired from the YPD on September 1, 1955 and worked for Anaconda Cable and Wire Corp. and the Herald Statesman for several years. Later he moved to Kingston New York where he died on May 18, 1982 at the age of 76.

PO ANTHONY J. MILANO #108

APPOINTED: August 1, 1930
RESIGNED: December 14, 1948

Anthony J. Milano was born in New York City on July 6, 1903 and attended local schools in Manhattan. After graduation he gained employment as a chauffeur. A resident of 102 Oak Street he was hired by the Yonkers Police Department on August 1, 1930 earning a starting salary of $1,940 a year and assigned to patrol duty in the 2nd precinct. Milano's career seemed promising, particularly since he had the ability to speak Italian and thought that would be an asset. However, on July 31, 1948 a prominent Yonkers doctor shot and killed his wife in their home in East Yonkers. PO Milano heard the report over the police radio and realized the doctor was a friend of his. He responded to the house and hid the gun in an attempt to help his doctor friend. His actions were discovered and Milano confessed saying he was covering up to protect his friend. On August 2, 1948 he was charged with accessory to murder and immediately suspended without pay. While under indictment, and after 18 years of service, Milano submitted his resignation from the YPD effective December 14, 1948.

PO STANLEY J. SWIECHOCKI #63

APPOINTED: August 1, 1930
RETIRED: August 31, 1962

Stanley Joseph Swiechocki, known to his friends as "Stosch," was born in the City of Yonkers on December 16, 1902. Being the child of immigrants Stanley was able to speak Russian, Slavish, and Polish fluently. After receiving his education in the Yonkers public schools he gained employment as a bookkeeper and later as a salesman.

On August 1, 1930 Stan was hired by the Yonkers Police Department earning a starting salary of $1,940 a year. His residence at the time he was appointed was 20 Palisade Ave. On December 28, 1934 at about 5:30 in the morning while assigned to the 2nd precinct on radio car patrol, Stan and his partner were about to call the precinct from a call box at Kimball Avenue and McLean Avenue. It was then that they saw a suspicious male exit the closed A&P store, join his partner in a car, and start to drive quickly into the Bronx. PO Swiechocki and his partner began the pursuit and Stan fired several shots at the fleeing vehicle blowing out the rear window causing the driver to lose control and the vehicle to crash. Both burglars were quickly arrested and for their actions the officers were awarded a departmental Commendation on March 30, 1935.

Officer Swiechocki retired from the police department on August 31, 1962 and died on April 3, 1982 at the age of 79 years.

PO ALBERT A. LIPTAK # 58

APPOINTED: September 6, 1930
DIED: April 18, 1938

Albert Liptak was born in the City of Yonkers on May 26, 1907. Following his education in local public schools he gained employment as a young man as a chauffeur. Al didn't mind his job but he wanted one with a little more security so he took the test for Yonkers Police Patrolmen. A resident of 136 Hawthorne Ave. at the time, Liptak was notified that he had passed all required tests for the Police Department and was appointed a police officer on September 6, 1930 with a starting salary of $1,940 a year. Following some very brief in-house recruit training Liptak was assigned to foot patrol duty in the 1st precinct at 20 Wells Avenue.

Being a new police officer and not accustomed to the discipline, it didn't take very long before Liptak found himself in violation of the departmental rules and regulations. As such, on January 12, 1931, with only 3 months on the job, he was found guilty of charges of neglect of duty and conduct prejudicial to the efficiency and good order of the police Bureau. Young Liptak pled guilty and, because he was very new and unfamiliar with all the regulations, was only suspended for 3 days without pay.

Subject: PO Albert A. Liptak (cont.)

On April 17, 1938 Al Liptak was assigned to ride in a radio car patrol unit along with police officer Joseph Kostik. Liptak, ordinarily assigned to foot patrol in Larkin Plaza, was substituting for patrolmen Raymond Thomas who had reported sick. Officer Liptak was scheduled to ride with officer Kostik as the message receiver for 4 days. While on patrol that day at about 1:15 PM they received a call from headquarters sending them to the Vark Street playground to break up what was described as a very large and unruly dice game. As they responded to the location, some say with a degree of haste, they drove west along Nepperhan Avenue. As they attempted to cross over New Main Street they struck an uneven section in the road which bounced the car and caused the operator, officer Kostik, to lose control of the vehicle. The radio car careened into an electric light pole at 102 Nepperhan Avenue, breaking the pole off at its base. The radio car overturned and the light pole fell on top of the vehicle.

Trapped in the badly damaged patrol car, someone called headquarters and the Emergency Squad responded immediately and extricated both officers from the overturned vehicle. Both officers were taken directly to St. Joseph's Hospital on South Broadway for emergency treatment, however officer Kostik, who was 41 years old, was pronounced dead within ten minutes of arrival. However his partner Albert Liptak, who was also critically injured, was still alive. It was reported that more than 50 police officers from all 4 precincts went to the hospital to volunteer blood for officer Liptak, in response to an appeal from the police surgeon Dr. Philip S. McCormick. Officer Frank Jordan of the 2nd precinct was selected to provide a transfusion. It was reported in the local newspaper that following x-rays taken of officer Liptak that he had suffered a compound fracture of the jaw, a crushed lung, internal bleeding, and multiple cuts of the head and face and body. Other officers also remained at the hospital throughout the night eager to help save their colleague. However Albert Liptak's condition did not allow for a second transfusion. Police officer Albert Liptak, 31 years old of 19 Van Buren St., who ordinarily would have been walking a foot post but was temporarily filling in for another sick officer, died the following day at 6:20 AM April 18, 1938.

Public Safety Commissioner Morrissey and Chief Edward Quirk notified the department and the news media that Liptak and his partner would both receive the highest departmental honors due to the losing of one's life while on duty. Officer Liptak's wake was held at his home at 19 Van Buren Street and the funeral mass was held at holy Trinity Church on Trinity Street. All off duty officers were directed to attend the funeral in full dress uniform to show their respect to a fallen brother. Column after column of blue uniforms, along with many public figures followed the funeral procession and were led by the departments Motorcycle Unit of the Traffic Division. Police officer Al Liptak had less than 8 years with the Yonkers Police Department.

PO JOHN L. BISHOP #243

APPOINTED: October 1, 1930
RETIRED: April 1, 1956

John Lawrence Bishop was actually born William Edward Chase in the city of Yonkers on Dec. 18, 1906. Both his parents died when he was a child and he was adopted and raised by his grandparents. Following the adoption he changed his name. As a young man he worked as an electrician but wanted something with more steady work. He was appointed police officer Oct. 1, 1930 living at 100 McLean Avenue. His first duty assignment was patrol in the 2nd precinct earning a starting salary of $1,940 a year. On Jan. 11, 1938 he was reassigned to the 3rd precinct, and on Nov. 16, 1947 he was appointed a Detective in the Detective Bureau. Two years later he was back on patrol in the 2nd Pct. During the last few years before retiring John worked a foot post in Getty Square in front of the banks where he was well known by all the merchants. John retired on April 1, 1956 and moved to Stockport, New York. Bishop was a big man and was said to have had a very somber personality. When he first became ill, and believing it to be cancer, he became depressed. His lifeless body was found on June 11, 1957. He was 50 years old.

DET. PAUL ODOMIROK #150

APPOINTED: October 16, 1930
RETIRED: April 1, 1956

Paul Odomirok was born in Yonkers June 29. 1899. He attended public schools # 5 and #9. Paul was raised living at 61 Lockwood Ave. and as a young man worked as a salesman for wholesale barber supplies shipped from France. Paul was appointed to the YPD from 10 Burhans Avenue on October 16, 1930 and assigned to the 1st precinct. Within a short time he was assigned to the then recently established Emergency Squad. Old timers described him as being "one tough Russian." On Jan. 13, 1931 he and his partner responded in the Emergency Truck to the Van Cortlandt Park subway station in search of a holdup team that fled after a robbery. Upon arrival they saw the same suspects holding up a store near the subway station. It was said they stopped the thieves by pointing their sub-machine guns at them, arrested them, and took them back to Yonkers. On June 10, 1931 the Honor Board recognized Odomirok by awarding him the departments highest form of recognition at that time; the Honorable Mention. In addition Odomirok was promoted to detective 2nd grade. Although Odomirok continued to hold that designation until he retired and drew the increased salary, he declined transfer to plain clothes duty in the Detective Division and continued to work in uniform at his request. At one point Det Odomirok was assigned to the Armored Motorcycle. PO Odomirok retired on April 1, 1956 and moved to North Miami, Florida. Ret Det. Paul Odomirok died in Yonkers General Hospital on September 15, 1957. He was 58 years old.

PO CHARLES J. BRENNAN #133

APPOINTED: December 1, 1930
RETIRED: December 31, 1955

Charles J. Brennan was born in Yonkers on January 4, 1907. When he applied to the YPD he stated his occupation was a bricklayer. While residing at 8 Pier St., Brennan was appointed to the YPD on Dec. 1, 1930 earning $1,940 a year. He and his recruit class were fortunate enough to receive their training at the NYC Police Academy. In 1931 Brennan was assigned to the newly formed Emergency Squad for a short period of time. But on Oct. 8, 1936, on patrol at 2 AM with his partner Dan Quilty, they discovered a fire in the Windham Hotel located at 5 Hudson St. Brennan, who was only 28 years old, along with his partner ran into the building to warn the residents to evacuate. The officers became separated in the dark and dense smoke and Brennan became overcome and fell unconscious. Fortunately he was found by his partner PO Quilty who carried him to safety where he could be resuscitated. By 1941 Brennan was assigned to the Traffic Division directing vehicular traffic. On April 1, 1948 he would be transferred to the Radio Telegraph Div. from which he would retire. Upon his retirement on December 31, 1955 Brennan worked as a private investigator in NYC. He later moved to Schoharie, NY where he would die on February 26, 1962. He was 55 years old.

LT WILLIAM F. FERGUSON

APPOINTED: January 1, 1931
RETIRED: March 23, 1966

William F. Ferguson was born in Yonkers on May 2, 1901 and was raised on Orchard Street. He attended local public schools and graduated from Yonkers high school. On his police application Bill listed his employment as a "Caulker" for the Alexander Smith Carpet Mills. While residing at 18 Tower Pl. Ferguson was appointed to the Yonkers Police Department on Jan. 1, 1931 earning a starting salary of $1,940 a year. Following recruit training he was assigned to the 2nd Pct. on April 20, 1931. During his early years his most frequent assigned foot post ran from Central Ave. to the Bronx River Parkway and from Tuckahoe Rd to the north city line. It was reported that whenever possible he sat and rested in a "police booth" located at Central and Tuckahoe Rd. and often studied for promotion. On February 9, 1937 Bill Ferguson was transferred to the 4th precinct. Ferguson was promoted to Sergeant on December 16, 1939, earning $3,400, and he was returned to the 2nd Pct. as a patrol supervisor. He was promoted to Lieutenant on December 16, 1945 and remained in the 2nd precinct as a desk lieutenant. Lt Ferguson retired from the YPD on March 23, 1966. Retired Lt. Bill Ferguson, who was the grandfather of Captain Patrick McMahon, died on April 1, 1981 at the age of 79 years.

PO JOHN P. TERRY #53

APPOINTED: February 1, 1931
DIED: October 28, 1957

John P. Terry was born in the City of Yonkers on November 2, 1904. After receiving his formal education in Yonkers public schools it was reported that Terry worked as an assistant foreman in a local business. After taking and passing the civil service exam for Yonkers Police Patrolmen John Terry received his shield, revolver, and nightstick upon his appointment to the Yonkers Police Department on February 1, 1931. At the time Terry lived at 204 Voss Avenue.

Upon completing some basic Yonkers recruit training in headquarters he was assigned to the 4th precinct earning $1,940 a year. Five months after his appointment, on July 6, 1931, he and six other new officers attended the NYC police department training school located at the time on City Island. He graduated from the school on October 6, 1931 and returned to patrol in the 4th precinct.

In the mid 1930's officer Terry was elected as the 4th precinct PBA trustee and Chairman of the Board of Trustees for the PBA. And in February of 1942, while assigned to the Radio Telegraph Division (Communications Division), he was elected First Vice President of the PBA. But incredibly, while the ballots were still being counted the newly elected president of the PBA, James Dalton, died suddenly and unexpectedly without even serving a day. After much discussion and debate, and PO Terry having been recently elected vice president, Terry was deemed the logical and legal successor and was named PBA president.

The following year in 1943 and again in 1944 PO Terry was re-elected president; this 3rd term being the last one due to PBA term limitations. During the ensuing years he remained assigned to the Radio Telegraph Division for which he held a 3rd class radio operators license. On December 1, 1949, while still in the RTD, Terry was appointed a 2nd grade Detective (there were only 2 grades at that time) earning a salary of $3,400 a year and assigned to the Detective Bureau. And on July 1, 1951 he was granted detective first-grade status raising his salary to $4,000 a year.

Police officer John Terry became ill and, prior to retirement, died on October 28, 1957. He was only 52 years old.

PO FRANK G. CARIELLO #216

APPOINTED: April 6, 1931
DIED: September 21, 1932

Born in Italy on February 13, 1904, Frank Cariello received his early education in Italy. At the age of 8 years he and his parents immigrated to the US, moved to Yonkers and into 85 Oak St. Young Frank finished his education at PS# 18 on Park Hill Avenue. As a young man Frank worked for the County Sand and Gravel company. While living at 55 Alder St., Frank took the police patrolman's test and was said to have topped the list. He was appointed to the Police Department on April 6, 1931.

Upon completing some basic Yonkers recruit training he was assigned to the 3rd precinct earning $1,940 a year. Three months after his appointment, on July 6, 1931, he and six other new officers attended the NYPD training school located at the time on City Island. He graduated from the school on October 6, 1931 and returned to the 3rd precinct on foot patrol. In early September of 1932 he developed a severe sinus infection which, due to a lack of available antibiotics, eventually led to his death on September 21, 1932 in St. Joseph's Hospital. He was only 28 years old and left behind a wife, but no children. He was the great uncle to PO Frank C. Cariello and great great uncle to Capt. Frank C. Cariello Jr.

PO BERNARD J. FARRINGTON #180

APPOINTED: April 16, 1931
RESIGNED: February 23, 1954

Bernard Farrington was born in Yonkers on Dec. 24, 1900, Christmas Eve. Bernie attended local public schools and later worked as a milkman. While residing at 21 Linden St., Farrington was appointed a police officer on April 16, 1931. Following some basic recruit training in Yonkers Bernie was assigned to the 1st Pct. on foot patrol earning $1,940 a year. He and his partner made many arrests, including one on Nov. 21, 1936 when they uncovered a counterfeiting ring and arrested four of those involved. At one point in the late 1930s he was assigned to the Radio Telegraph Division. Years later, on July 8, 1951, he was transferred back to patrol in the 1st Pct. Bernie was very active in the affairs of the PBA and was a member of the YPD singing Glee Club. Farrington found himself in trouble with the department and was suspended without pay on January 21, 1954. The following month Bernard Farrington suddenly resigned from the police department effective February 23, 1954, short of the necessary 25 years to receive a pension. Former PO Farrington, whose nephew would later be deputy chief William Farrington, died in December of 1979. He was 79 years old.

DET ALBERT J. HOFFARTH

APPOINTED: June 1, 1931
DIED: October 30, 1962

Albert Hoffarth was born in NYC on August 6, 1904. Following his formal education Al and his family moved to Yonkers where he gained employment as a house painter. Having his brother Joe, at the time a Yonkers firefighter, working for the city, it was no surprise that Al would also join the police or fire department. And Al chose the police department. Al was appointed to the YPD on June 1, 1931 earning a salary of $1,940 a year. Following some brief training at headquarters he was assigned to patrol duty in the 1st Pct. on Wells Avenue. Within months, on October 30, 1931, he would be reassigned to foot patrol in the 2nd Pct. on Central Avenue. Being well-liked and popular with the men he worked with he was easily elected the precinct trustee on May 5, 1939. It was on October 30, 1942 that he was appointed a Detective; an assignment he would keep for the remainder of his career and where his salary rose to $2,725 a year. Detective Hoffarth developed an excellent reputation as a fine and efficient detective and on December 21, 1944 he was awarded a departmental Commendation for an arrest he made on August 3, 1943 of three armed men for committing a burglary. Hoffarth remained in the Detective Bureau until his untimely death on October 30, 1962 at the age of 58 years.

PO ANDREW YACKO #77

APPOINTED: June 1, 1931
RETIRED: June 30, 1956

Andrew Yacko was born in the City of Yonkers on December 1, 1906 and was raised in the Hollow section of the Yonkers. He attended Holy Trinity grade school and graduated from Saunders high school. Like many in Yonkers at the time Andy worked for the Alexander Smith Carpet factory as a weaver. He married and raised 7 children. When World War II broke out the government tried to draft him but the local newspaper wrote a story about his potential plight having 7 children, and he received a deferment from the draft. Andrew was hired by the Yonkers Police Department on June 1, 1931 while residing at 27 Garfield St. Following some brief recruit training he was assigned to patrol duty in the 2nd precinct earning a starting salary of $1,940 a year. PO Yacko worked his entire career in the 2nd precinct, mostly on a foot post at Yonkers Avenue and Central Park Avenue. When he retired from the police department on June 30, 1956 he worked part-time at the Stewart Stamping Company and while not working enjoyed playing golf and playing the banjo. His first cousin was PO Emil Yacko, their fathers being brothers. Retired PO Andrew Yacko died on February 26, 1976 at the age of 69 years.

PO WILLIAM R. YAMBRA #202

APPOINTED: July 1, 1931
RETIRED: June 15, 1954

William R. Yambra was born in the City of Yonkers on September 7, 1902. Bill attended local public schools and later would serve with the New York National Guard. On his police application he listed his employment as that of a cashier.

Bill Yambra was appointed to the Yonkers Police Department on July 1, 1931 while living at 41 Cowles Ave. Following his basic recruit training Bill was assigned to patrol duty in the 1st precinct earning a starting salary of $1,940 a year. At the time of his examination for the police department, Dr. McCormack, the police surgeon, reportedly indicated that after performing the physical examination, Yambra was the best physical specimen he had ever examined.

In the late 1920s the Police Department had two armored motorcycles which they used for scheduled money escorts. But in 1933 the city purchased one armored coupe patrol car to replace one armored motorcycle. One of the first two officers assigned to patrol in it was PO Bill Yambra. It was estimated that, on average, $1 million a week was provided escort protection service by Yambra and his partner.

On February 19, 1935 Bill was transferred to the 2nd precinct where, while on patrol, he was injured in an automobile accident which caused a severe injury. Despite his injury he continued to work. In the 1940s Yambra was regarded as an excellent shot with his revolver and as such was designated the police departments firearms instructor. He was also on the YPD pistol team participating in competition shooting around the county.

Bill was a fishing and hunting enthusiast but his old patrol car injury returned. Following an examination by the police surgeon PO Yambra was deemed physically unfit to perform his duties and was retired on a disability pension effective June 15, 1954. Ret PO William Yambra died on December 4, 1969 at the age of 67 years

PO FREDERICK J. BAKER #125

APPOINTED: December 16, 1931
RETIRED: March 28, 1945

Frederick Baker was born in the City of Yonkers on Jan. 24, 1904. He attended local public schools and upon graduation he joined the Navy in 1920 and received his honorable discharge in 1923. As a young man Fred worked as a foreman for the Yonkers Electric Light and Power Co. and at one point he served as a New York State trooper. Fred was appointed to the Police Department on Dec. 16, 1931 while residing at 15 Arbor St. Following some basic recruit training Fred was assigned to patrol duty in the 1st precinct earning a salary of $1,940 a year. While in the 1st precinct he worked both foot and radio car patrol. On March 1, 1941 Baker was assigned to work as part of the armored car detail. Though he had always been healthy he began to have trouble with his feet. On April 11, 1945 a local doctor wrote to the chief of police that Fred Baker had developed a progressive deformity of his feet. Actually, Baker had begun to have pain in his feet about 1943 which then forced him to stop working in 1944. It was then that he was placed on sick leave. On April 21, 1945, following an examination by the police surgeon, it was determined that PO Baker could no longer perform his police duties and should be retired on disability pension effective March 28, 1945. Ret PO Frederick Baker died on June 25, 1949 at the young age of 45 years.

PO CONRAD A. FREUND #201

APPOINTED: August 16, 1932
RETIRED: September 15, 1961

Conrad Freund was born in Rotterdam, Holland on April 28, 1905. “Connie” came to the U.S. at one month of age and lived in Hoboken NJ. He would later move to 32 Lewis St. Yonkers and attended PS #16. An entrepreneur, "Connie" worked in the Ice business and was also a self-taught mason. On Aug. 16, 1932 he was appointed to the YPD, and assigned to the 4th pct., but continued working side masonry jobs and started his own business named Connie-Mac Trucking. Freund started building homes on the side. On Dec. 16, 1941 he was reassigned to the 1st precinct. During the time of payless paydays, he was unable to pay property taxes on 4 lots he had on Corbalis Pl and the City took them from him. He later had to buy them back but only could afford two. On Nov. 16, 1945 PO Freund was moved to patrol in the 3rd pct. After retiring on Sept. 15, 1961 he worked for a while painting at Jacoby Tarbox. He loved to play a card game from Holland called "Auction 45." His grand son Cornelius Westbrook was a West Co PO. Freund suffered from an undiagnosed congenital kidney condition which ultimately caused his death on September 19, 1971.

PO ANTHONY A. CURCILLO

APPOINTED: January 1, 1933
RETIRED: March 31, 1948

Curcillo was born June 12, 1899 in Yonkers and attended PS# 18. As a young man, during the years 1919 through 1922, he was an amateur boxer who used the name "Packy Brown" and fought in the light weight ranks. He loved the sport and stayed involved for many years. Over those years he picked up the nickname "Shine" or "Kid Shine." On January 20, 1932 he was hired as a Yonkers City Jailer at $2,700 a year. But later, while living at 200 Willow St. he was hired to the YPD on Jan. 1, 1933 at $1,940 a year and assigned to the 1st pct. On Jan. 30, 1942 he was re-assigned into the Emergency Squad where he would remain for several years. On Mar. 4, 1943 he suffered fractured bones in his neck while rescuing a male stuck in the flooded Nepperhan Creek. He wore a neck brace, off and on, for a long time. On June 2, 1945 Curcillo and his Emergency Squad partner caught armed thieves as they attempted to escape following breaking into the safe in the Yonkers Savings and Loan and stealing over $15,000. On April 16, 1946 Curcillo was transferred from the Emergency Squad in the 1st pct. to patrol duty in the 4th pct. His neck continued to cause him pain and he was placed out on the disabled list. After eleven months the police surgeon examined him and determined he was physically unfit for duty and retired him effective March 31, 1948. After retiring he operated his own taxi business named, "Tony's Taxi." Ret PO Anthony Curcillo died December 10, 1980. He was 81 years old.

PO JOHN R. BELL #216

APPOINTED: January 1, 1933
RETIRED: July 31, 1958

John Ray Bell was born in the City of Yonkers on July 17, 1906. Following his formal public school education “Ray,” as he was known to his friends, worked several different jobs. While living at 4 Orchard Place, and working as a chauffeur he took the examination for appointment to the YPD. While living at 592 Warburton Avenue, “Ray” was officially appointed a police officer on January 1, 1933 and was assigned to routine patrol duties in the 4th precinct. By 1956, with 23 years on routine patrol, "Ray Bell" was assigned to the Communications and Operations Division. He would remain there up to his retirement on July 31, 1958. Ray moved to Coconut Creek, Florida where he enjoyed many years of sunshine. However, nearly forty years after his retirement, John Ray Bell died on July 12, 1996, five days short of his 90th birthday.

PO CLARENCE G. KNAPP #195

APPOINTED: January 1, 1933
RETIRED: May 31, 1951

Clarence G. Knapp was born in the city of Yonkers on April 10, 1901. After his education in the public schools he listed his employment as that of an "Engraver." When eligible he joined the National Guard and it is believed that his unit was activated and he served during WW-1. On January 1, 1933 Clarence was appointed to the Yonkers Police Department at a salary of $1,940 a year, with pay days twice a month. He was assigned to the 2nd pct. on patrol duty. Knapp was a man who grew to about 300 Lbs., reportedly had very bad feet, and very large hands. When the 2nd and 3rd precincts were closed on January 1, 1951, shortly thereafter Knapp was transferred from the 2nd into the old 1st Pct. on Wells Ave He was said to be a nice soft spoken guy but very overweight. When the precincts reopened he was sent back to the 2nd precinct. Officer Knapp was working on Christmas Eve in 1941 with Patrolman Al Rusinko and at the end of their tour they were both charged with missing their "hits." On Jan. 1, 1942 he was fined 10 days pay for the violation. After a physical exam by the police surgeon PO Knapp was found to be unfit to perform his police duties and was retired on a disability pension effective May 31, 1951. A charter member of the short lived YPD St. George Society and resident of 38 Loring Avenue, Ret PO Clarence Knapp died on August 12, 1969. He was 68 years old.

PO JOSEPH H. BARBERI #122

APPOINTED: January 1, 1933
RETIRED: April 21, 1964

Joseph Harvey Barberi was born August 25, 1903 in NYC. Several years later he and his family moved to Yonkers taking up residence at 178 Linden Street. Following his schooling he worked as an electrician and also for the City of Yonkers DPW. It was on January 1, 1933 that Barberi was appointed to the Yonkers Police Dept. and assigned to the 4th pct. Though he had a gruff voice it was said he was a bit of a prankster and had a good sense of humor. In May of 1956 Joe was in the Traffic Division on a three wheel Harley Davidson motorcycle writing summonses for meter violations. In March of 1964 Joe was diagnosed with severe emphysema and heart failure. Following an exam, the police surgeon reported Joe was physically unfit to perform his police duties. As such, and while living at 181 Briggs Avenue, he was retired on a disability pension on April 21, 1964. For a while he tried to work on a few electrical side jobs but his bad health caught up with him. Ret Joseph Barberi died on June 4, 1969. He was 65 years old.

PO MICHAEL T. PERNA #166

APPOINTED: March 1, 1933
DIED: January 18, 1960

Michael Thomas Perna was born March 27, 1905 in New York City. Following his formal public education Mike began a career as an auto mechanic. However, having passed the examination for police Patrolman he was appointed a Patrolman in the YPD on March 1, 1933 and was assigned to the 4th precinct with a salary of $1,940 a year. On July 9, 1938 Perna and his partner Henry O'Hare were awarded a Commendation for the arrest of two youths wanted for 1st degree robbery of a milkman in NYC. And on April 23, 1942 he was awarded a Certificate of Excellent Police Work for another arrest he made. Mike Perna was described as a tough street cop. Following a transfer to the 3rd precinct, on July 11, 1943, he was assigned to Traffic Engineering in the parking meter repair squad. While residing at 115 Brandon Road, officer Perna, reportedly became very quiet and subdued. His lifeless body was found on January 18, 1960. He was 54 years old.

PO ANDREW J. HORREE #225

APPOINTED: July 16, 1935
RETIRED: November 5, 1963

Andrew J. Horree was born in the city of Yonkers on Dec. 1, 1905. He attended local schools and as a young man began a career as a Tool maker. Horree was appointment to the YPD on July 16, 1935 at the salary of $1,940. and was assigned to the 1st pct. On April 14, 1939 it was reported that Horree was awarded a Commendation for actions placing his life at risk or by exhibiting outstanding police work. This award stemmed from early in his career when he assisted an FBI agent, and a NYC Detective in capturing, at gun point, a suspect in a $70,000 5th Avenue jewelry robbery. On August 12, 1940 PO Horree was once again commended for saving the life of a woman who decided to take a swim off the city pier but could not get back out of the water. On January 1, 1951 officer Horree was elevated to the position of Detective at the salary of $3,900. He remained a detective until May 1, 1963 when he was transferred to the 1st precinct on uniform patrol. It was then that he requested retirement from the department which took effect on November 5, 1963. A resident of 37 Pier Street Horree began working as a security guard at the Habirshaw plant in Yonkers. Andy Horree's father in law was former PO Elmer John Shonts. Andy was also a charter member of the Protestant St George Society. Ret. PO Andrew Horree died in May of 1985.

LT. ANDREW J. SUTTON

APPOINTED: July 16, 1935
RETIRED: August 15, 1962

Andrew J. Sutton was born Andrew J. Sukowsky Jr. in Yonkers NY on November 2, 1910. He graduated from PS# 12 and from Gorton HS. While in Gorton Sukowsky starred in basketball, baseball, and football.

Andy was working as both a sales clerk and a truck driver when he took the test for Yonkers Patrolman and placed #1 on the list. While living at 226 Ashburton Avenue he was appointed to the YPD on July 16, 1935 with a starting salary was $1,940. a year. Sukowsky's first assignment was in the 1st precinct in the HQ building on Wells Avenue.

Four years later on December 18, 1939 Sukowsky, who was known by his friends as "Drew," was advanced to the rank of detective in the Detective Bureau. It was here he quickly earned an admirable reputation. On March 6, 1941 he arrested two men responsible for more than a dozen burglaries. And only five days later on March 11, 1941 he and his partner ended a burglary crime wave by identifying and arresting the six men responsible. Then, on Sept. 30, 1941 Andy saved a women who was about to commit suicide by jumping off a roof. On Oct. 17, 1941 he arrested a male wanted for the robbery and murder of a 79 year old man which occurred on Oct. 14th of that month. Det Sutton received a Commendation from the Grand Jury for the way he testified in the case.

On April 24, 1942 the YPD Honor Board awarded Andy with both a departmental Commendation and a Certificate of Excellent Police Work. It is of interest to note that at that time any Commendation awarded carried with it one percentage point toward any promotional exam. The certificate carried with it one half point. Despite this Det Sukowsky, along with 30 other men, were transferred. Det Sukowsky was re-assigned from the D.D. to the 1st precinct. But his dedication continued. One morning at about 2:30 AM while walking his foot post he came across a burning building at 25 Palisade Avenue. Without hesitation he ran through the building waking the residents and helping them to safety.

On Aug. 31, 1943 he was granted an indefinite Leave of Absence due to his induction into the Army during WW-2. Shortly thereafter, on Oct. 4, 1943, Andy officially changed his surname from Sukowsky to Sutton. While in the Army Sutton served in the Pacific Theater of operations with Army Intelligence. He was separated from the military on November 4, 1945 and re-instated to the YPD on Dec. 1, 1945 earning $2,625. On June 1, 1947 officer Sutton was promoted to Sergeant, with a salary of $3,400 by using his disability veteran preference, which at the time allowed veterans to jump to the head of any civil service list regardless of an individuals score.

Sgt. Sutton was transferred to the 2nd pct. as a patrol supervisor. Having received his official discharge, on Sept. 10, 1948 Sutton requested to be allowed to enlist in the Army's Criminal Investigation Division, Reserve Corps, Military Police. His request was approved. In 1948 and 1949 Sgt Sutton served as the 2nd Vice Commander of the YPD Police War Veterans Legion representing the 3rd precinct. On Jan. 22, 1957 Sgt Sutton, topped the promotional list for Lieutenant, using 5 points disabled veterans credit. He was promoted to Lieutenant on June 16, 1957 at a salary of $6,174 a year. On Jan. 1, 1959 Lt Sutton was elevated to Detective Lieutenant in the Detective Division. Det. Lt Sutton retired from the YPD on August 15, 1962. Ret Det Lt Andrew J. Sutton died on February 2, 2000. He was 89 years old.

PO ALEXANDER RUSINKO #38

APPOINTED: July 16, 1935
DIED: October 29, 1962

Alexander Rusinko was born in the City of Yonkers on September 11, 1905. He attended old PS# 20, Yonkers high school, and graduated from Gorton high school. It was reported that in his youth he was very much involved with sports and was described as "a star athlete and basketball star."

Following school Al worked as a Lineman and supervisor for the old Yonkers Electric Power and Light Co, which co-incidentally was located in the old building at Columbus Place and St Casimir's Avenue which years later would be the home of Police Headquarters.

Al was appointed a police officer on July 16, 1935 and assigned to patrol duty in the 2nd precinct located at 441 Central Avenue. Al was not only a very efficient and capable patrol officer but he involved himself in many other police activities. He was selected and completed a state Civil Defense training course held in Albany, NY for instructors in rescue operations. He was also a qualified Red Cross First Aid instructor. In fact in May of 1940 officer Rusinko, at the direction of the Chief of Police, organized and completed a training seminar where he instructed 52 members of the police department in a first aid course. He was not only respected as an excellent instructor but was very well liked by everyone who knew him. And as a gesture of their esteem, the 52 officers he had trained organized and held a testimonial dinner in officer Rusinko's honor to thank him for his efforts. Over 250 people attended the dinner.

Following the original organization of the Police Athletic League (PAL) in 1941, an election was held on July 14, 1941 to elect officers in the PAL. Rusinko was elected one of the first trustees and as such was a charter member of the PAL.

No doubt that due to his medical and rescue training, on October 21, 1942 Al was transferred from the 2nd precinct to the Emergency Squad. Over the years he also served in the Traffic Division and the Traffic Violations Bureau.

On May 1, 1958 Al was assigned to the then Juvenile Aid Bureau (JAB). He was also responsible for training women as School Crossing Guards. Officer Rusinko was very active in all PAL activities with his goal being to help young children stay out of trouble. And it was there in the PAL offices that PO Alexander Rusinko, while at work, was stricken on October 29, 1962 and died at his desk. He was 57 years old.

PO GEORGE J. BAKER Sr. #247

APPOINTED: July 16, 1935
RETIRED: August 15, 1960

George Joseph Baker Sr was born in New York City on August 23, 1906. After his family moved to Yonkers he attended local schools and graduated from Commerce H.S. In fact he was on the committee that designed the Commerce HS graduation school ring. His family related that upon graduation he received and accepted a scholarship from Rutgers University. However, due to the death of his father he felt compelled to drop out of college and go to work. Always interested in sports, during his free time he was either playing football or basketball.

Baker applied to take the police test while living at 85 Buena Vista Avenue and, upon passing same, received his appointment to the YPD on July 16, 1935 and was assigned to the 1st precinct on foot patrol. However, effective October 10, 1942, the City Manager, apparently acting on, what he believed to be, wide open gambling in Yonkers, shook up the department by transferring 30 officers. This actually benefitted officer George Baker, who had been assigned to Traffic duty directing traffic in Getty Square. With the new changes Baker was transferred to the Detective Division as a Detective; which, by the way, raised his detective 2nd grade salary by an additional $100 a year. (There were only two grades of detective at this time.)

On September 1, 1943 Det Baker and his partner Det Louis LiGay arrested one Nick DiCicco for buying and possessing 6 dozen stolen pairs of gloves at 30 cents a pair. Years later Nick DiCicco would become a store owner on Ashburton Avenue known for his shoe shines. On May 30, 1945 Det Baker arrested three men for attempting to obtain drugs fraudulently. Federal narcotic investigators assisted in the investigation. During the arraignment of the three men, one of them feigned illness and then tried to run and escape. But Det Baker had him back in custody in minutes.

On September 4, 1945 Det Baker was notified by telephone that he was going to be transferred from the Detective Division and assigned to the Traffic Division directing vehicular traffic. It was reported that when he arrived at work he made it clear to the chief, in person, that he felt he was being targeted unfairly for extra work for some time. Further, that he was being forced to work specifically on gambling arrests. It was reported that Baker allegedly was disrespectful in making his complaint to the chief. As such, on October 31, 1945 charges were preferred against officer Baker for what was termed "insolent" behavior to a superior. Prior to the transfer or the departmental trial, Det Baker had apparently had enough. He requested, by his own hand, to be transferred from the D.D. to the Traffic Division. The transfer came quickly and the charges were dismissed.

On July 25, 1946, while directing traffic in Getty Square Baker, received information regarding a purse snatch and a description of the subject wanted. Within a short time Baker spotted a man fitting the description and took him into custody and following an investigation the man confessed his crime.

By the end of 1948 the rank and file of the Police Association was very upset about how the department was being run and the Police Associations response to these problems. It was then that George Baker decided to run for president of the Yonkers Police Association. (Y.P.A.) On January 25, 1949, following the counting of all ballots, it was announced that George Baker had defeated the incumbent president, Det Joe Flynn by 19 votes and as such was elected president of the Y.P.A. for 1949.

PO George J. Baker #247 (cont.)

PO George Baker had previously been a detective, was a former star athlete in his younger years, and was a baritone soloist in the Yonkers Police Glee Club. But George was a no nonsense guy. He was a big man, 6' 2" with an imposing figure. His size alone would no doubt keep most people from attempting to become physical with him. If he felt strongly about something you were sure to hear about it; no matter who you were and he didn't sugar coat his words. And by the end of 1949 he, and the majority of the Y.P.A. membership, believed the city was not treating his membership fairly and he wasn't afraid to say so. In fact on January 16, 1951, he took the unprecedented step of having the Y.P.A. attorney, Mr. Sol Friedman, draft an open letter to the Herald Statesman outlining a list of grievances that he felt were valid, but carefully avoided mentioning anyone by name. Nevertheless the publication of this critical analysis caused a tremendous stir in city hall.

The letter was lengthy but in essence there were three points he wanted made. 1 - That the police department was dangerously low on manpower causing a potential danger to the public. And that it didn't seem that the administration was all that interested. 2 - That the police department administration was, in the Y.P.A.'s opinion, running the department in an unfair and prejudiced way. That discipline was not handed out evenly and promotions were politically motivated. In fact, Baker pointed out that four years earlier, in 1947, when a chief's vacancy occurred, instead of appointing someone to the chief's position from the rank of captain, the Public Safety Commissioner, Patrick O'Hara, previously a manager from Otis Elevator, promoted then Lt William Comey to the position of Deputy Public Safety Commissioner; a position which was in fact the same job as the chief of police but now with a different title. Such an appointment was a slight to all the qualified police captains in the department. And 3 - The recent closing of both the 3rd and 4th police precincts; Pres. Baker contended that what was needed to adequately protect the public was to decentralize using four precincts, and not centralize by condensing the troops into two buildings. He contended that, "one would think that we had learned our lesson about centralization when we parked nearly our entire fleet together at Pearl Harbor." The reaction from city hall was swift and City Manager Whitney was definitely not happy. He wrote a strong response to the newspaper and the tensions continued for some time.

On January 6, 1954 it was reported that PO George J. Baker, who had been a fixture directing traffic in Getty Square for many years and was very popular with the business community, was transferred to Parking Meter Maintenance in the Engineering Unit of the YPD Traffic Division. The newspaper indicated that the transfer was purportedly at his own request. In April of 1956 PO George Baker was re-assigned to the Communications Division, which apparently is where he retired from on August 15, 1960. In retirement he worked several years as a clerk at Phelps Dodge Copper Products Corp. in Yonkers. George Baker was followed into law enforcement by his four sons; PO George Jr, Det Reynold, and Capt. Robert, who all joined the Yonkers Police Department, and Trooper William who was appointed a New York State Trooper. Unfortunately Trooper William Baker was killed on duty in a motor vehicle accident.

A resident of 39 Lindsey Street, Ret PO George J. Baker died on March 29, 1970 in Bronx Lebanon Hospital after a lengthy illness. He was 63 years old.

PO JAMES J. LYNN Sr. #151

APPOINTED: July 16, 1935
RETIRED: April 15, 1957

James J Lynn Sr was born in Croton on Hudson on March 22, 1909. He came to Yonkers as a young boy, residing at 112 Oliver Avenue, and attended local schools. He listed his occupation as that of a Lineman and Chauffeur. Upon his appointment to the YPD on July 16, 1935 he was assigned to foot patrol. Lynn quickly became involved in Y.P.A. activities, and on Dec. 11, 1941 it was announced that PO Jim Lynn would serve as the Chairman of the silver anniversary entertainment and dance for the Y.P.A. to be held at the County Center in White Plains. At one point Lynn was appointed a detective, but on Oct. 12, 1942 he was re-assigned to the 2nd pct. During the Yonkers Police Association (Y.P.A.) elections in late 1942 Jim Lynn was elected 1st Vice President of the Y.P.A. Then, in Jan. 1944 Lynn was once again elected 1st Vice President of the Y.P.A. On May 22, 1944 Lynn was transferred to the Traffic Division motorcycle unit where he would remain up to his retirement. He would later see his son James Jr and daughter Grace, both join the YPD. Due to various ailments Lynn was out sick his last year on the job. He was retired on a disability pension on April 15, 1957. Ret PO James J. Lynn Sr. died May 17, 2000 at the age of 91.

PO GEORGE W. COUGLE #48

APPOINTED: September 16, 1935
DIED: April 11, 1937

George W. Cougle Jr. # 48 was born in Yonkers on November 25, 1907 to George Cougle Sr who would later rise to Captain in the Yonkers Police Department. Young George attended PS# 7 and Yonkers H.S. He never married and he remained living with his mother at 38 William Street after his father died. As a young man he worked for the Yonkers branch of the Personal Finance Co. He was appointed to the YPD on September 16, 1935 and assigned to the 2nd precinct. However a short time later he was re-assigned to the 1st precinct working in the Getty Square area where he became very friendly with the local business men. Cougle had a good future to look forward to but at one point he developed an ear infection which reportedly developed into a form of meningitis. He was hospitalized in the Professional Hospital for eight days and he became severely ill and died on April 11, 1937 at the young age of 29 years. He had served less than two years. Officer Cougle was so well liked by the taxi drivers that they all chipped in to send a floral arrangement for his funeral. For his funeral all off duty personnel were directed to attend in dress uniform in a sign of respect. Over 150 officers attended and formed an impressive formation. In addition to his father, the deceased was the nephew of Lt William H. Cougle.

PO THOMAS F. NEARY #85

APPOINTED: October 1, 1935
RETIRED: June 15, 1954

Thomas F. Neary was born in Yonkers on Feb. 1, 909. He graduated from Yonkers High School and attended Columbia University. As a resident of 170 Stanley Avenue he was hired by the YPD on Oct. 1, 1935 with a salary of $1,940. a year. Following his recruit training at headquarters he was assigned to patrol in the 3rd precinct. On Nov. 16, 1945 he was re-assigned to the 2nd precinct. Neary reported sick Jan. 9, 1954 with a heart ailment, had several heart attacks and was subsequently hospitalized several times. In May of 1954 he was examined by the police surgeon and found physically unfit to perform his patrol duties and was retired on a disability on June 15, 1954. In August of 1954 he was hired by the First National Bank reportedly as a head teller with the National bank of North America in Yonkers until he again retired in 1974. He was described by co-workers as a quiet loner, a widower, with no children. His father was Sgt Augustus Neary and his brother was PO Robert Neary. On February 1, 1984 Ret PO Thomas Neary died on his birthday in his home at 26 Post Street. He had just turned 75.

PO FREDERICK J. FRANZ #132

APPOINTED: January 20, 1936
DISMISSED: June 27, 1947

PO Frederick J, Franz was born in the city of Yonkers January 26, 1908. Years later at the age of 28 Franz listed on his YPD application that he lived at 383 Warburton Ave. and was employed as an office clerk. He received his appointment to the YPD on January 20, 1936 and was assigned to the 1st precinct. On September 13, 1937 he was re-assigned to patrol in the 2nd pct. But, on June 1, 1938 he was returned to patrol in the 1st pct. On May 6, 1939 Franz received a Commendation for an excellent arrest, and on April 18, 1940 he was awarded a Certificate of Excellent Police Work for assisting in the arrest of burglars on May 24, 1939, one of which was shot and killed by PO Robert Busch. However on May 15, 1947 officer Franz was charged with Neglect of Duty and following a departmental trial he was found guilty as charged. The following month on June 27, 1947 Frederick Franz was dismissed from the Yonkers Police Department.

PO WILLIAM J. BELL #198

APPOINTED: January 20, 1936
RETIRED: February 11, 1971

William J. Bell was born in the City of Yonkers on November 7, 1908, grew up at 361 Bronxville Road and graduated from Roosevelt H.S. He listed on his police application that he worked as a general mechanic and maintenance man. While living at 153 Glenwood Avenue Bill was appointed to the YPD on Jan. 20, 1936 and assigned to patrol in the 1st precinct. Bill loved sports as a youth and even while in the YPD he played basketball for the Police Association team and some Westchester County teams. On January 22, 1943 Bill was inducted from the YPD into the Army during WW-2 serving in the Military Police section of Chemical Warfare service with the rank of Corporal. He was honorably discharged on October 5, 1945 and was re-instated to the YPD. On Sept. 9, 1955 Bill Bell was transferred from the 1st pct. to the Traffic Division Violations Bureau. Bill retired from the YPD on February 11, 1971. Bill's father had been Sgt John W.R. Bell and Bill and his two brothers in law, PO Ed McEnery and DC Ed Murphy all married three sisters. Unfortunately Bill developed cancer and after a long illness he died on July 30, 1984. He was 75 years old.

PO DOMINICK C. CUCCIA #32

APPOINTED: April 1, 1936
RETIRED: June 16, 1966

Dominick C. Cuccia was born in the city of New York on March 15, 1911. He moved to Yonkers, received his formal education and gained employment as a salesman. Cuccia was appointed to the YPD on April 1, 1936 at the salary of $1,940. His career would move him around quite a bit. First assigned to the 1st pct., on Sept 18, 1936 he was moved to the 2nd pct. Two years later, on Oct. 22, 1938, he was transferred to the 4th pct. on patrol. A year later, in July of 1939, Cuccia was moved back to the 1st pct. for a short while until December 30, 1939, when he was assigned to the Traffic Division, on motorcycle duty. Having a good singing voice, in 1943 he was a selected to be a member of the YPD singing Glea Club. Also during the mid 1940's due to his ability as an expert shot with the revolver he was chosen to be a member of YPD Pistol Team which competed throughout the tri-state area with other police pistol teams. On April 16, 1946 officer Cuccia was assigned as a detective in the Detective Division where he would remain until May 1, 1949 when he returned to the 2nd pct. He did return to the D.D. on Feb 1, 1955, but four years later, on Dec 1, 1959, he returned to the 2nd pct. In 1958 and again in 1959 Cuccia was elected VP of the PBA where he was very involved in the association's activities. On May 20, 1960 PO Cuccia was assigned to the City Court in police headquarters where he remained up to his retirement on June 16, 1966. In 1971 he was elected to the Yonkers City Common Council. Ret PO Dominick Cuccia died on February 23, 1981 at the age of 69 years.

PO ALEXANDER HARRILCHAK #16

APPOINTED: April 16, 1936
RETIRED: July 27, 1971

Alexander Harrilchak was born in Yonkers on September 19, 1906 to Theodizia (nee Mickewich) and Ignatius Harrilchak; the youngest son in a family of five brothers and one sister. According to his son, Al reportedly was a very bright child. He attended PS #9 from the first grade to the 8th grade, was allowed to skip the 7th grade, and received a 100 in the Geography regents. That was his favorite subject.

From 1919 to 1921 he attended Saunders Trade School where he learned a trade in Electric House Wiring. Al spoke Russian, Polish, Slavish, and Ukranian. He was a very big and tall male, but very athletic. He played baseball at 3rd base after graduating from trade school. Al was said to be a .300 hitter and played in the Glen at field #2. He played 4-5 years and was going to go to New Jersey for the International League but was unable to pay his own way. But young Al was most known for his skill at basketball, which he ultimately played for 17 years. He played on Saturday nights and the winner received free membership at the YMCA. While playing basketball he traveled to Springfield, Mass to play with the Long Island Pros. He received $35 to play three games and they won all three games. In 1921 he went to work in the carpet shop as a rug weaver and in 1926 he was given the job of rug counting. In 1927 he quit the shop for an outside job with Standard Oil. At the same time he went to school at nights in New York City to learn to be a plasterer. At Standard Oil he repaired pumps and tanks. After Standard Oil he went to work for Fisher Body in Tarrytown. At that time he was paid $70-80 per week.

Following his job at Fisher body he started taking civil service tests. That's when he was hired by the City of Yonkers as a City Jailer on August 16, 1934 at $2,100 per year. However on April 16, 1936 he was hired as a Patrolman in the YPD from 168 Voss Avenue at $1,940 per year. He spent the majority of his career working patrol in the 2nd precinct with the exception of a short time in the late 1930's when he was assigned to Traffic directing vehicular traffic in Getty Square.

During his early years with the YPD he continued his interest in basketball and played on the Yonkers Police basketball team competing against various leagues. In 1972 Al Harrilchak lived at 168 Voss Ave. Late in his career while on patrol in the 2nd pct. he developed a convulsive seizure disorder which caused him to pass out suddenly for no reason; often while driving the police car. As a result, following an exam by the police surgeon, he was prohibited from driving a radio car. On March 3, 1967 he was officially placed on light duty status as a result of these seizures. For the next several years he worked the foot post around Yonkers and Central Avenue and on occasion as the desk lieutenant's desk aide. "Big Al" retired on July 27, 1971 and after a brief illness died on March 10, 2000 in Maricopa, AZ, at the age of 93 years.

PO JOSEPH S. PODESWA #82

APPOINTED: May 16, 1936
RETIRED: August 8, 1968

Joseph Podeswa was born October 5, 1905 in the Bronx, NY and came to Yonkers with his family at the age of two years. At that time he lived on a farm at 165 Winifred Avenue. He attended PS# 4 and graduated from Yonkers High School. Joe worked as a carpenter as a young man until he became interested in the job security that the police profession provided.

Joe took the examination for police Patrolman, passed it, and was appointed a Patrolman in the Yonkers Police Department on May 16, 1936. Following his appointment and some basic recruit training at headquarters, Probationary Patrolman Joseph Podeswa was assigned to the 2nd precinct on patrol, and earned a starting salary of $1,940 per year.

While assigned to the 4th precinct on November 16, 1941 Joe was appointed a Detective and was assigned to the Detective Division. There was never a doubt that Joe was a good detective but apparently he preferred uniform patrol duty. As a result and at his own request, a year later on October 12, 1942, Joe was returned to uniform patrol in the 2nd precinct. Throughout his career Joe worked in the 2nd, 3rd, and 4th precincts on uniform patrol. But he didn't care much for radio car patrol and preferred walking a foot post and getting to know the store owners on his posts.

Joe Podeswa had two brothers; Albert, a YFD Asst. Chief, and his other brother, YFD firefighter Leo Podeswa who was killed in the line of duty in a fire in the 1940's. In fact Joe's family related that Joe had the mis-fortune to be working that night and was assigned to that very fire where he would learn about his brother Leo.

Joe Podeswa retired from the 2nd precinct on August 8, 1968. Thirty eight years later, Ret PO Joseph Podeswa died on September 6, 1996 at the age of 90 years.

DEPUTY CHIEF JAMES F. TOBIN

APPOINTED: January 1, 1937
RETIRED: January 1, 1977

James Francis Tobin was born in the City of Yonkers on April 14, 1912. He attended St. Joseph's Catholic School and graduated from Commerce H.S. He also attended Columbia University with majors in accounting and finance. There was no question that police officer Tobin was smart, but he was also very athletic playing both baseball and basketball. As a young man James Tobin, who was actually known by just about everyone as "Bob" Tobin, earned a living as a bookkeeper/typist/accountant.

In the late 1930's he applied for the position of Yonkers Police Patrolman while residing at 44 Park Avenue. He passed all the required tests and was appointed a "Patrolman" on January 1, 1937 with the salary of $1,940 per year. Following about five weeks recruit training conducted in police headquarters, on February 9, 1937 Tobin was assigned to patrol duty in the 2nd precinct. However, on September 12, 1939 he was transferred to the Traffic Division working in the office, no doubt due to his clerical skills. A few years into his career Ptl Tobin rescued Ptl. Frank Jordan, who was trapped inside a burning radio car following an accident. It may have been because of that rescue that Tobin was promoted to detective on March 1, 1941.

A few months later, on May 30, 1941, Detective Tobin was off-duty and driving with his family north on Riverdale Avenue. At 7:45 p.m. he heard screams and saw a male running along the street

Deputy Chief James F. Tobin (cont.)

carrying a knife with a large blade. Lying on the ground a short distance away was another male who had just been stabbed. The off-duty officer jumped from his vehicle and began to chase the suspect. Tobin identified himself and took out his revolver. He chased the man into 149 Riverdale Avenue where the suspect lived. When the suspect reached the second story landing, he turned on Tobin and reportedly shouted, "If you come up one step I'll cut your head off." Without hesitation, Det. Tobin started up the stairs telling the suspect to give up the weapon. The male lunged at Tobin with the knife. Tobin sidestepped and fired a shot which struck the suspect in the right thigh, shattering the bone. The confrontation was over and the arrest was made. Tobin received high praise from his superiors for his handling of a dangerous suspect. For his bravery and police action while off duty Det Tobin was awarded the departmental Commendation.

On October 12, 1942 "Bob" Tobin was reassigned from the Detective Bureau to patrol in the 4th precinct. But within a month, on Nov. 19, 1942, he was granted, an indefinite leave of absence due to his enlistment into the Navy. World War 2 was raging for nearly a year with US participation and Tobin wanted in. He served throughout the war with the Naval Intelligence branch of the Navy.

Following the wars end Tobin was honorably discharged on March 2, 1946 with the rank of Chief Petty Officer. He was officially re-instated to the YPD on March 16, 1946 at the salary of $3,000 per year and assigned as an aide to the Chief of Police. On June 1, 1947 Tobin was again assigned as a detective to the Detective Bureau but continued to work as an administrative aide to the Chief.

On Sept 1, 1947 officer Tobin was promoted to the rank of Sergeant with an increase in salary up to $3,400 per year. His assignment of record was the 1st precinct but he was detailed to work in the Public Safety Commissioners office in City Hall. On January 1, 1951 Sgt Tobin was assigned to the Traffic Violations section of the Traffic Division. Nearly two years later, on October 16, 1952, Tobin was promoted to the rank of Lieutenant with the salary of $4,800 per year. Two precincts having been closed since Jan. 1, 1951, it was about this same time that they reopened and Lt Tobin was assigned as a desk officer in the 3rd precinct.

Tobin's ever changing assignments continued. On January 9, 1953 Lt. Tobin was appointed C.O. of the Training and Records Division. And on January 1, 1958 Lt Tobin was promoted to Captain and designated C.O. of the Communications and Records Division with the salary of $7,310 per year and shortly thereafter was commended for designing the very first shoulder patch, triangular in shape, that the YPD ever had. On Dec 15, 1958 he was designated C.O. of the Traffic Div; on May 1, 1963 he was designated commanding officer of the Detective Division; on July 23, 1963 Det Capt. Tobin was designated Acting Deputy Commissioner of Public Safety in command of the entire Police Bureau; In August of 1965 he was assigned as the Planning and Training officer; on February 7, 1969 assigned to the D.D. but served as liaison to Public Safety Commissioners office; on Dec 29, 1970 to the Planning & Research of the Detective Division.

On Jan. 10, 1974 Capt. Tobin was appointed a Deputy Chief by City Manager Dr Seymore Scher and placed in charge of all Staff Services in the YPD with a salary of $24,500 per year. He filled the vacancy created by the retirement of Deputy Chief Edward J. Murphy. After having reached the maximum age allowed by civil service law Deputy Chief James "Bob" Tobin retired on January 1, 1977 after having completed 40 years of service.

Ret. Chief James F. Tobin died on Oct. 28, 1983 in St. John's Hospital at the age of 71 years.

PO ROBERT F. SCHLEGEL #121

APPOINTED: January 1, 1937
RETIRED: May 19, 1964

Bob Schlegel was born in Mt Vernon NY on April 24, 1908 and moved to Yonkers with his family at the age of 6 months. He attended PS # 6 but then his father advised him that it was time to work and earn some money. Young Bob worked for the Armor Meat Packing Co. in Yonkers for 15 years.

It was then he applied for and took the examination for police Patrolman. Having passed the exam Bob was hired by the Yonkers Police Department as a Patrolman on January 1, 1937 at the salary of $1,940 per year. He received six weeks recruit training by various officers at the 20 Wells Avenue Headquarters building and was then assigned to the 2nd precinct on radio car patrol.

For the next five years Schlegel rode with his partner and friend PO John "Red" O'Hare. On October 12, 1942 Bob was appointed a Detective which included a $100. salary increase. But Schlegel said due to politics it wasn't long before he was removed from the Detective Bureau and re-assigned to the Juvenile Aid Bureau. (JAB), minus the $100 stipend. On July 1, 1951 Schlegel was once again assigned as a Detective and it is believed he remained there up to February 25, 1964 when he was again returned to uniform patrol. Retired Capt. John Potanovic described Bob Schlegel, who by the way spoke fluent German, as a "dogged detective" who was very persistent and very dedicated. He would arrive early and leave late so as to be on top of investigations.

Bob's brother was Yonkers Jailer Rudy Schlegel, and his sister Margaret Maxwell was a Yonkers City Jail Matron. On May 7, 1956 he earned a Certificate of Excellent Police Work for a felony assault arrest on June 28, 1954 on the Dunwoodie Golf Club grounds. He received a second one for a burglary arrest on May 1, 1954 on 70 Boulder Trail; He earned two Gannett West Newspaper Macy - Honorable Mention Awards on February 25, 1958 and again on February 2, 1962.

Three months after his return to patrol Bob Schlegel retired from the YPD on May 19, 1964. When he retired he worked nine years for Phelps Dodge in security, and then after moving to Florida he worked 13 more years as security guard in a large Condo Unit. He was 89 years old when he retired from there and then only because his legs caused him great pain. Retired PO Robert Schlegel died in Ft. Lauderdale Florida on September 4, 2003 at age 95 years.

DET. JOSEPH P. FLYNN #61

APPOINTED: January 1, 1937
DIED: January 25, 1964

Joseph Patrick Flynn was born in Yonkers on June 14, 1908, one of 9 children. He attended St. Mary's School and graduated from Yonkers High School. As a young man Joe worked for the City of Yonkers as a Chauffeur in the Water Bureau. Following his appointment to the YPD on Jan. 1, 1937 at the salary of $1,940, Joe was assigned to the 2nd pct. Before long he was assigned to the Traffic Division directing vehicle traffic at the corner of South Broadway and Hudson Street. During his free time Joe was an avid baseball fan and played golf whenever he could. On March 1, 1941 he was appointed a Detective in the D.D. In Oct. of 1942 he was returned to the 2nd pct. and in 1945 was elected President of the Yonkers Police Assoc; (YPA). He would hold that office for four terms. On April 16, 1946 he was again appointed a detective. Det Flynn was widely praised by the Herald Statesman editorial board when he was elected president of the Westchester Co. Police Conference. However in January 1949 Joe Flynn lost re-election to the Y.P.A. presidency. Joe Flynn continued working as a detective throughout his career as well as serving in many fraternal organizations. Unfortunately he never got to retire. Det Joseph P. Flynn died after a short illness on January 25, 1964. He was 55 years old.

PO WILLIAM E. K. SAVAGE #10

APPOINTED: September 1, 1937
RETIRED: September 1, 1962

Bill Savage was born in Yonkers on July 19, 1905 and received his education in local public schools. As a young man Bill worked as an auto worker on the assembly line in Tarrytown. Looking for greater job security Bill decided to join the YPD and was appointed a patrolman on September 1, 1937 at $1,940 a year. At that time he lived at 40 Randolph Street. His first assignment was to the 2nd precinct on patrol duty. On February 16, 1953 he was reassigned from the 2nd to the 3rd precinct where he would remain right up to his retirement on September 1, 1962. According to a YPD old timer who knew Bill Savage, he related that Savage was a good cop who did his job well. But he was described as being a very solemn and quiet individual. Bill Savage's son James was a Yonkers firefighter. A resident of 148 Caryl Avenue, Ret PO William E. K. Savage died the day after Christmas on December 26, 1986.

SGT. EDWARD E. McENERY #4

APPOINTED: September 1, 1937
DIED: October 10, 1965

Edward Earl McEnery was born in Yonkers on September 13, 1908 and received his education from Holy Rosary school and later graduated from Gorton H.S. It was reported that while attending high school he was a very good basketball player. As a young man Ed earned a living as a truck helper. He was appointed to the YPD on September 1, 1937 from 21 Portland Place with a salary of $1,940 a year. He was initially sent to the 1st precinct, but on January 11, 1938 he was re-assigned to the 2nd precinct. Ed continued his interest in sports by playing baseball on the YPD team. Then, on October 12, 1942 officer McEnery was appointed a Detective in the Detective Division.

On December 21, 1944 he was awarded a department Commendation for the arrest of the murderer of a woman on March 8, 1943. Known to everyone as "Mac," McEnery was an avid reader and member of the Chippewa Club. His brothers-in-law were DC Edward Murphy and PO Bill Bell. Three sisters married the three men. Some of his other assignments were, June 1946 from the DD to the 4th pct.; January 1951 to the 1st precinct; October 1952 to the 4th pct.; July 2, 1954 to the Juvenile Aid Bureau (JAB); February 1, 1955 back to the DD; July 16, 1956 to Traffic Violations. On February 15, 1960 Ed became ill while at work and received the last rites of the Catholic Church. But somehow he recovered and returned to work.

On November 16, 1960 PO McEnery was promoted to Sergeant at $6,475 a year and was allowed to remain in the JAB. Sgt McEnery was moved to the 3rd precinct on patrol January 2, 1964, and five days later was sent back to Traffic Violations Bureau. In addition to his two police brothers-in-law his brother Charles was also a YPD police officer, and his son Edward was a Yonkers firefighter. A resident of 38 Morningside Avenue and not yet retired, Sgt Edward McEnery died on October 10, 1965. He was 57 years old.

PO PETER C. DiFIORE #124

APPOINTED: January 1, 1938
RETIRED: February 28, 1963

Peter DiFiore was born in New York City on February 2, 1911. As a youth he received his formal education in NYC and would later move to Yonkers, with his family living at 1 Horatio Street. Growing up he worked several jobs, but prior to the YPD he worked as a chauffeur. Pete was appointed to the Y.P.D. on January 1, 1938 while living at 1 Horatio Street. Following his basic police recruit training he was assigned to patrol duty in the 2nd precinct, earning a starting salary of $1,940 a year. Peter was described by fellow officers as very clean, fastidious, very personable, and yet different from most other officers. However all agreed that while on patrol he was a good street cop.

Pete spent his entire career in the 2nd precinct, and for a good part of that time he served as an administrative aide to the lieutenant. When he wasn't on patrol, he would be in the precinct kitchen cooking for the desk lieutenant and other police officers; he loved cooking and would always be the cook at all police functions. It was said that Pete was a private type person and that he never took his shield off his uniform. He left it at work and never carried an off duty firearm either. He worked off duty as a Maitre D' in a NYC restaurant and often served as a chaperone for the rich and famous women of NYC.

Peter DiFiore retired from the police department on February 28, 1963, earning a pension of $3,375 a year. Pete moved to the Greenwich Village area of New York City; a place where he really seemed to fit in. Pete's brother Edward was a Yonkers Fire Department Lieutenant and his sister-in-law was Yonkers police dispatcher Anita DiFiore.

Although he lived all of his 41 years of retirement in Manhattan, Ret PO Peter DiFiore died in St. John's Hospital in Yonkers on January 8, 2004 at the age of 93 years.

SGT. EDWARD E. O'NEILL # 4

APPOINTED: January 1, 1938
DIED: July 7, 1959

Edward O'Neill, who was known to all his friends as "Emmett," was born October 17, 1911 in Yonkers NY. He attended St. Mary's Catholic parochial school and graduated from Commerce high school. Ed listed on his police application that his previous occupation was that of a plumbers helper.

He was appointed to the Yonkers Police Department on January 1, 1938 from 74 Glenwood Avenue at the salary of $1,940. a year. Following his recruit training he was assigned to patrol duty in the 1st precinct at 20 Wells Avenue. He was still in the 1st precinct when, on December 7, 1941, the Japanese attacked Pearl Harbor and the United States entered World War 2. Eight days later while walking his post "Emmett" O'Neill walked into the Army recruiting office in the Yonkers Post Office and enlisted in the Army on December 15, 1941. In doing so officer O'Neill became the very first YPD police officer to enlist in the military after the US joined WW-2 by declaring war on Japan. Ed was granted an indefinite leave of absence from the department on December 19, 1941 and served in the Italian and African campaigns in Europe. He was honorably discharged as a wounded and decorated veteran on October 15, 1945, and re-instated to the YPD on Nov 16, 1945. Initially O'Neill was assigned back to the 1st precinct, but on April 3, 1946 he was transferred to the Traffic Division directing vehicle traffic.

On August 1, 1947 O'Neill was then moved from Traffic to the 3rd precinct. But it was on Jan 1, 1948 that "Emmett" O'Neill was promoted to the rank of Sergeant, raising his salary at that time to $3,400. Following his promotion he was once again assigned to the 1st precinct, but this time as a patrol supervisor. However, several years later he would be returned to duty in the 3rd pct.

It was there on June 26, 1959, after finishing his tour of duty, that he collapsed at South Broadway and Morris Street. During the fall he suffered a fractured skull and a severe brain injury. Despite the efforts of St. Joseph's Hospital, Sgt Edward Emmett O'Neill died 11 days later on July 7, 1959. He was only 46 years old. He left behind a wife, who died a year later, and three small children; 8 years, 7 years, and 5 years of age. They would be raised by his wife's parents.

SGT. BARTHOLOMEW MURPHY #45

APPOINTED: February 18, 1938
RETIRED: July 31, 1973

Bartholomew J. Murphy is believed to have been born on Morningside Place, in Yonkers on March 13, 1911. Bart's father, a Merchant Marine Seaman, and his mother were both born in Dungarvin, Ireland, County Waterford and later immigrated to the U.S. For many years young Bart and his family lived in Mulford Gardens and he would graduate from St. Joseph's grade School and Sacred Heart H.S. During his school years he was somewhat of an athlete, playing baseball for Sacred Heart and swimming in the Hudson River, which he really enjoyed. As a young man he worked with one of his uncles in NYC running an elevator. And prior to his police appointment he worked on the Tarrytown NY Chevrolet plant assembly line.

On February 18, 1938 Bart Murphy was appointed to the YPD at $1,940 a year, was assigned to patrol in the 1st precinct, and was eligible for the old Yonkers police department City Pension Plan. He was one of the last placed in this plan before all future new hires were entered in the new NYS Police & Fire Retirement System. Bart's daughter said when America joined WW-2 in late 1941 her father always lamented the fact that he could not serve in the military. According to her, Bart said at the time there were three groups by which military service by an active police officer was acceptable. She believes they were, some could be drafted, some could join, and some had to remain to protect the citizens of Yonkers.

On April 1, 1948 Bart was transferred from the 1st to the Radio & Telegraph Division (RTD- later to be renamed the Communications Division) to serve as a telephone operator. While there, in 1958 he was elected Treasurer of the PBA. The following year, on February 4, 1959, Bart was re-assigned to work in the Juvenile Aid Bureau investigating crimes committed by juveniles. While there he was also very active in participating in helping the Police Athletic League operate their youth programs.

Officer Murphy was promoted to the rank of Sergeant on March 13, 1963 at the salary of $7,400 a year and was assigned as a patrol sergeant in the 3rd precinct. However, two months later he was moved to the 1st precinct. On January 24, 1966 Sgt Murphy was transferred to the Communications & Records Division as an administrative supervisor. Two years later, in February of 1968, he was designated as a Communications Division supervisor. In December 1969 he went to the 2nd pct., and in May of 1970 to the Traffic Division for 7 months. On January 1, 1971, when the North and South Commands were established, Sgt Murphy was moved to the South Command.

Sgt Murphy retired from the YPD on July 31, 1973. Following his retirement Bart never worked for pay again; but instead, every day he reported to the U.S. Volunteer Life Saving Corps, located at the foot of Main Street on the Hudson River, to assist in any problems occurring on the river. And many people were rescued by the "Volley's" from drowning over the years. Bart was a tall lean man who had a rugged appearance which signaled he could handle himself in any situation. The truth was that he was a gentleman who enjoyed discovering and sharing stories of the history of the Yonkers Police Department. Ret Sgt Bart Murphy, a resident of 25 Randolph Street, died on February 1, 1991. He was 79 years old.

LT. ARNOLD W. SHAFFER

APPOINTED: February 18, 1938
RETIRED: February 26, 1963

Born in the City of Yonkers on May 12, 1905 and after completing his education, Arnold gained employment as a shipping clerk. He was appointed to the YPD on Feb. 18, 1938 at the salary of $1,940 a year, and was assigned to the 2nd precinct. Four years later, on Oct. 12, 1942, Shaffer was appointed a Detective in the Detective Bureau. However, it was short lived. A month later, on Nov. 10, 1942, he was inducted into the Army to serve during WW-2. Shaffer received an honorable discharge on Aug. 11, 1946 and was re-instated to the YPD on Aug. 16, 1946. He also decided to join the NY National Guard's 107th Infantry Div. Having a good singing voice, in late 1943 he was a member of the YPD singing Glea Club. On Sept. 1, 1947 Ptl Shaffer was promoted to Sergeant and assigned to the 4th pct. He received his promotion to Lieutenant on Jan 16, 1958 at the salary of $6,680 and served as a desk lieutenant. Some officers reportedly said he was a good guy but took things too serious. Shaffer, the son of YPD Lt Edward Shaffer, retired on February 26, 1963, moved to Sarasota, Florida where he died on Dec 18, 1985 at age 80 years.

SGT. BERNARD R. WAGNER #14

APPOINTED: February 18, 1938
RETIRED: March 12, 1963

Bernard R. Wagner, better known to all his friends as "Huntsy," was born in Cleveland, Ohio on March 29, 1907. Following his move to Yonkers Wagner worked as an elevator operator. He was appointed to the YPD on February 18, 1938 and his first assignment was patrol in the 2nd pct. on Central Avenue. Having previously been certified as a Red Cross First Aid instructor, on Oct. 30, 1942 he was assigned to the Emergency Squad in the 2nd pct. On July 16, 1943, during WW-2, Wagner was inducted into the Army and was honorably discharged on Oct. 6, 1945, re-instated to the YPD on Nov 1, 1945 and assigned to the Traffic Div. Upon his military discharge Wagner opted to join the Army Reserve where he was reportedly a member of the 404th Military Police Criminal Investigation Division. It was said he attained the rank of Master Sergeant. Officer Wagner was re-assigned to the Juvenile Aid Bureau (JAB) as a youth investigator on July 6, 1946. On Oct. 16, 1952 he was promoted to police Sergeant earning $4,200. and assigned to a patrol precinct. Wagner was said to have been friendly, outgoing, and well respected by his men as being a "good street boss." Bernie "Huntsy" Wagner retired on Mar 12, 1963. A member of the YPD War Veterans Legion, Wagner died on Dec 19, 1968 at the age of 61 years.

DET. CHARLES L. GORMAN # 2

APPOINTED: February 18, 1938
RETIRED: October 31, 1960

Charlie Gorman was born in Yonkers on August 11, 1910, attended St. Mary's grade school, and graduated from Saunders Trade School where he played varsity football and basketball. After high school he made his living working as a gas station manager. On Feb. 18, 1938 Charlie was appointed to the YPD and assigned to the 1st pct. A year later, on July 1, 1939, he was transferred to the Traffic Division on motorcycle duty; but only for five months. On Dec. 16, 1939 PO Gorman was appointed a Detective. He spent the remainder of his career as a detective developing an impressive reputation. In 1947 when Lt William Comey became Deputy Public Safety Commissioner, Comey had Gorman transferred to his office as his administrative aide. Charlie retired on a disability pension on October 31, 1960. Ret Det Charles Gorman died April 27, 1980 at age 69 years.

LT. WALTER T. DUFFY

APPOINTED: February 19, 1938
DIED: December 9, 1963

Walter Teasdale Duffy was born in Yonkers NY on July 9, 1906. Walter was living at 38 Laurel Place and working as a Bricklayer when he received his appointment to the Yonkers Police Dept. on February 19, 1938. Following recruit training he was assigned to the 4th precinct on patrol and his first shield was #112. Nearly five years later, on November 20, 1943, Duffy was appointed a detective in the Detective Bureau. He remained there until November 16, 1947 when he was re-assigned back to patrol in the 4th pct. In 1948 PO Duffy, a non-veteran, obtained a score of 95%, the highest mark on the sergeant's exam. However at that time there was a law that gave veterans absolute preference for appointments over non veterans on all eligibility lists. As a result Walter Duffy, a non-vet, was passed over for promotion to sergeant 14 times by men who were veterans and claimed their preference. Duffy was finally promoted to sergeant on January 2, 1951 at $4,200 and sent to the 2nd pct. On Oct 16, 1952 Sgt Duffy was placed in command of the Communications and Operations Div. However on Jan 6, 1954 he was returned to patrol in the 3rd pct. In early 1955 Sgt Duffy topped the lieutenant's promotional list with a mark of 86.38%. But he still placed 2nd after a veteran used his veterans preference. But Sgt Duffy was promoted to Lieutenant on June 16, 1955 and assigned as a desk lieutenant in the 2nd precinct. Unfortunately Lt Duffy would never reach retirement. He died unexpectedly on December 9, 1963. He was 57 years old.

PO CHARLES F. STOFKO #229

APPOINTED: February 19, 1938
RETIRED: March 12, 1965

Charles F. Stofko was born in the City of Yonkers on February 25, 1907. He attended local schools, graduated, and as a young man worked hard as a laborer. A resident of 35 Cliff Street Stofko served his country with the 258th Field Artillery of the NY National Guard. Charlie was hired by the YPD on February 19, 1938 at $1,940 a year and was assigned to patrol duty in the 2nd precinct. On November 16, 1947 Stofko was appointed a Detective in the Detective Bureau. He was said to often talk about a day on August 14, 1951 when he and his partner Det Nevin interrupted a robbery in progress and pursued the suspects for 11 miles into NYC. After both detectives fired their weapons at the fleeing auto, their car crashed and the arrest was made. A year later on May 26, 1952 Det Stofko was re-assigned back to patrol in the 1st precinct. Charlie retired on March 12, 1965 and in 1979 he moved to Yorktown. Ret PO Charles Stofko died on March 12, 1985 at the age of 78 years.

PO GEORGE F. McMAHON #11

APPOINTED: February 19, 1938
RETIRED: August 1, 1968

George F. McMahon was born in Yonkers on May 16, 1911. Following his education in St Joseph's parochial school George would gain employment as a "newspaper pressman." While living at 26 Robbins Place George was appointed to the YPD on February 19, 1938 at the salary of $1,940 per year and following some local recruit training he was assigned to foot, and on occasion radio car, patrol in the 2nd precinct. He remained in the 2nd for 17 years until June 13, 1955 when he was re-assigned to the Communications and Operations Division in headquarters serving as a radio room call taker and certified radio operator/dispatcher. Nine years later, on April 27, 1964, he was transferred to Traffic Engineering in the Traffic Division. George retired from the department on August 1, 1968. He was described by his co-workers as "very personable and a quiet guy." He was a member of the PBA and the YPD St George Society. His daughter married YPD PO George Baker Jr, and his other daughter is the mother of YPD Sgt John Viviano. Ret PO George F. McMahon died on August 23, 1973. He was 62.

PO ALLISON HOPPER # 127

APPOINTED: February 19, 1938
RETIRED: March 26, 1963

Allison Hopper was born Leslie Allison Hopper in Yonkers on January 26, 1912. He attended PS# 23 on Van Cortland Park Ave and graduated from Yonkers HS. A resident of 234 Elm Street he played football on the Yonkers HS team for two years. As a strong young man he worked as a General Contractor, was a stonemason by trade and was in business for himself. He did walks, patios, etc. Hopper was never in the military but he listed himself as a veteran in the "C.M.T.C," which stood for Civilian Military Training Corps; a semi-military version of the National Guard which was instituted during the big depression in the early 1930's to provide three square meals a day and a few dollars to the guys who joined. Its purpose was similar to the Civilian Conservation Corps.

Hopper took the test for police officer during the Depression along with 1200 other applicants in need of work and because the list was extended he waited five years for his appointment. When hired on February 19, 1938 he only had a few training classes given by the instructor, Det Frank Ciliberti.

Hopper was assigned to the 1st pct. on Wells Avenue where he would remain for 12 years. He was on foot post for two years and the first time he was assigned in a radio car was after PO's Joe Kostik and Al Liptak's accident in April of 1938 that killed them both. Hopper stated, "The captain knew I didn't drink so he put me in the car for a while." "Al," as he was known, said there was only one car in the 1st pct. in 1938 and the WPFY radio system was only one way transmissions out to the cars. The communications room called a message out to cars. (they only had 3 radio signals; Signal 20 was a Felony in Progress; Signal 21 was a Felony committed or bad accident, and a Signal 22 was all purpose, similar to the current 10-9, "see complainant") The cars then had 10 minutes to find a telephone and call HQ confirming they had received the call and then they would proceed to handle the complaint.

While in the 1st pct. Al was needed as a radio room fill in so he was sent to a government sponsored training school at the NYPD Communications Center to become certified with a class 3 Radio Operators License. Al worked in Communications for about two years as a dispatcher. A typical call was, "HQ to 101 car, a signal 20, a robbery in progress at Riverdale and Pier St, wanted two white males, no further description, 8:45 PM, WPFY, #65." Hopper said even after the two way radio system was instituted around 1940, they still only had 3 radio signals.

In the late 1930's and early 1940's the YPD purchased Ford and Chevrolet coupes, with no back seat and painted solid dark green. During the WW-2, due to a shortage of vehicles, the city would purchase whatever vehicles they could get. By that time the cars were now painted dark green, black, and white just like the NYPD. The siren was of a bullet shape mounted on the roof above the windshield with a green glass front light. To operate the siren the officer would push a button in the center of the dashboard to electronically operate the siren and light up the green light. No flashing, just lit solid green. It is assumed that with the roof of the car being painted white in color, that was the reason it became common for children to yell as the police car passed by, "There goes Snow White and the two dopes."

PO Allison Hopper #127 (cont.)

During the 1940's he filled in from time to time in the Emergency Truck. He stated the Emergency Truck was a special order Chrysler open back truck with heavy duty springs. The cab was extra wide to hold three officers if necessary. The vehicle, a solid dark green color, had a step up arrangement in the rear to get into the back which was wide open and had bench seating and equipment compartments on each side of the rear of the truck. The compartments were under the bench seats and ran from over the wheel wells right up to the cab back. Inside were stored a variety of rescue and first aid equipment including lengths of rope, two oxygen tanks, and various other tools. The Thompson Sub Machine guns were not carried on the trucks but were left stored in the 1st pct., where theoretically you could retrieve them when needed.

On August 27, 1949 Hopper and his partner PO Frank Porach were sent to the Columbia Tavern at 232 New Main Street on a large fight in progress. When they entered they tried to break up the large fight however one of the combatants grabbed officer Porach's night stick from him and began to club him over the head numerous times beating him to the floor. When ordered to drop the stick by Hopper the male ignored the order and PO Al Hopper fired his revolver killing the assailant where he stood. Following an investigation PO Hopper was exonerated of all wrong doing and his actions deemed justifiable homicide.

After 12 years Al Hopper was transferred to the 2nd pct. where he would remain for 13 years. While on the job Hopper developed an interest in bees and became a "Bee Keeper" with three hives at his home which could produce 30-40 lbs. of honey a year, and which was harvested in the fall. This was never a problem because Al lived on one acre on Bryn Mawr Drive. Because of his expertise the YPD called him whenever there was a problem somewhere with bees. He did this even though he was off duty and never got paid for his work. But when the department wouldn't buy him a new protective head netting, he refused any further calls.

Allison Hopper retired on March 26, 1963 after 25 years at age 52 and worked as stone mason again for a few more years. It was about 1965 that he moved to Florida where he worked for the Young Oil Co. Distributors in Pompano Beach, Florida for about 11 years as a warehouse man, and then retired again when he turned 65. Al Hopper lived in a full service retirement community for seniors in Boca Raton, Fla.

Retired PO Allison Hopper died in the hospital from congestive heart failure, in his sleep, on May 6, 2003. He was 91 years old.

PO CHARLES J. ZEKUS #3

APPOINTED: February 19, 1938
RETIRED: July 23, 1963

Charles J. Zekus was born in NYC on January 7, 1909. As a young boy his family moved to Tarrytown, NY where Charlie completed his schooling by graduating from Tarrytown HS. He and his family moved to Yonkers in 1927 and lived at 35 Eastview Avenue. As a young man Charlie worked as a Clerk for General Motors Corp. He was appointed to the YPD on February 19, 1938 at $1,940 a year and was assigned to the 2nd precinct. Charlie was an ardent golfing and swimming enthusiast which occupied most of his off duty time. He was built like a large fire hydrant, very husky but not fat. And always with Charlie was his ever present cigar. He reportedly was a tough cop who took care of problems his own way rarely relying on arresting anyone. Officer Zekus, along with his cigar, spent his entire career on patrol in uniform and when he completed 25 years he retired on July 23, 1963. Unfortunately less than two years later Ret PO Charles Zekus died on March 23, 1963. He was only 56 years old.

DET. ALEXANDER J. FORBES #25

APPOINTED: February 19, 1938
RETIRED: April 23, 1963

Alexander James Forbes was born of Scottish decent on October 5, 1910 in the Nodine Hill section of Yonkers. Living at 4 Chestnut Street he attended public schools and graduated from Saunders H.S. After working several years as a salesman Forbes was hired by the YPD from 4 Chestnut Street on February 19, 1938 and assigned to the 3rd precinct on patrol. On February 1, 1942 Forbes was transferred from the 3rd into the Radio Telegraph Division (RTD), the department's communications center. Al remained there as a Radio Operator until March 16, 1952 when he was appointed a Detective at the salary of $3,900. A former partner, Det Harry O'Neill, said Al was a good detective with a very excellent, but dry, sense of humor. For a time Al served as the administrative aide to Public Safety Commissioner James McCue. On and off he also worked in BCI and was a good fingerprint man. Det Forbes retired as a detective on April 23, 1963 and worked for the next 12 years as a machine operator at the Stewart Stamping Co. in Yonkers. Following a lengthy illness Ret Det Alexander Forbes died on November 18, 1987. He was 77 years of age.

PO AUSTIN MILLEN #118

APPOINTED: February 19, 1938
RETIRED: September 8, 1969

Austin "Ace" Millen was born on August 28, 1910 in the City of Yonkers. He attended St Joseph's grade school and graduated from Gorton H.S. He listed his early employment as being a "Lineman." He was hired by the YPD on February 19, 1938 and was assigned to the 2nd pct. Four years later "Ace" was inducted into the Army for WW-2 on April 13, 1942. He received an indefinite leave of absence on April 15, 1942 and served with the 1st Army Engineers and received a purple heart for serious wounds he received during the African campaign. He was honorably discharged early on July 7, 1943, was re-instated to the YPD on Feb. 15, 1944 and returned to the 2nd pct. Ace, who loved to play cards so much he could play 7 days a week, spent his entire career on patrol in the 2nd precinct. On February 15, 1969 the police surgeon submitted a report to the Chief advising that officer Millen, who had been out sick for the previous year because he had lost his entire left eye to a malignancy, would never return to full duty. This condition resulted in his disability retirement on September 8, 1969. His nephew was PO Thomas Millen. A resident of 98 Lake Avenue retired PO Austin Millen died following a lengthy illness on April 13, 1972. He was 61 years old.

PO FRANK KAMPA #60

APPOINTED: February 19, 1938
RETIRED: March 31, 1950

Frank Albert Kampa was born in New York City on August 24, 1907. His early employment consisted of being a chauffeur and a salesman. He also drove a Good Humor ice cream truck. After passing all required tests Frank Kampa, a resident of 61 Palmer Road, was appointed to the Yonkers Police Department on February 19, 1938 at the age of 30 years. His annual salary was $1,940 a year payable twice a month. Frank was assigned to uniformed patrol for 12 years; first to the 3rd pct. and then on June 1, 1938 to the 2nd pct. He reportedly walked a foot post most often in the Bronxville Road area. Years later upon examination by the police surgeon he was diagnosed with multiple sclerosis, found to be physically unfit to perform his duties and was retired on March 31, 1950 on a disability pension of $1,900, which was half of his then salary of $3,800 a year. On Sept 11, 1951 his request to receive a 3/4 pension benefit was denied. Kampa had a son-in-law, Dave Davies, who was a retired Deputy Sheriff from San Diego County in California. On April 13, 1963 Ret PO Frank Kampa died at the age of 55 years.

PO FRANCIS X. FARRELL #101

APPOINTED: February 19, 1938
DIED: July 12, 1963

Francis Xavier Farrell was born in Yonkers NY on November 10, 1910 and was raised living at 198 Seminary Ave. He attended St Mary's Parochial School, and graduated from Yonkers High School. As a young man he worked as an electrician with a local business. On February 19, 1938 Francis was appointed to the YPD at the salary of $1,940 a year and was assigned to patrol in the 1st precinct on Wells Ave on post 1 and 4, that being from Getty Square to the river and north to Ashburton Ave. After receiving an indefinite leave of absence he enlisted in the Navy during WW 2 on October 2, 1942 and served as an Electricians Mate 2nd class with the Atlantic Fleet. For reasons unknown, after only 5 months, he received an early Honorable Discharge (possibly medical) on March 16, 1943 and was re-instated to the YPD.

Having a good singing voice, in 1943 he was a member of the YPD singing Glea Club. In 1951 Farrell was assigned to the Juvenile Aid Bureau (JAB) where he would remain for the rest of his career working predominately in the PAL and helping children. The PAL was then located on the first floor of 87 Nepperhan Ave. While living in the Glenwood Gardens apartments on Ravine Ave. he retired in March of 1963 but asked for and was granted reinstatement on June 1st. To everyone's surprise, on July 12, 1963 PO Francis Farrell was found dead in a hotel room in Albany NY. Farrell, 52 years old, had been a member and past president of the Police Holy Name Society, member of the Police Athletic League, PBA, YPD War Veterans Legion, Elks Club, Knights of Columbus, and the Friendly Sons of St Patrick.

DET. CHARLES W. GERLOFF #64

APPOINTED: February 19, 1938
RETIRED: August 23, 1969

Charles W. Gerloff was born in New York City February 25, 1907. He came to Yonkers with his family as a youth in 1920, attended public schools and graduated from Commerce H.S. in 1925. As a young man he worked as the manager of Rex Roofing Co. in Yonkers. On February 19, 1938 Gerloff was appointed to the YPD at $1,940 a year and assigned to the 3rd precinct on foot patrol. A resident of 1 Alder Street officer Gerloff was commended several times for arresting people in stolen cars. After a short stay in the 3rd, on October 22, 1938, he was reassigned to the 4th precinct. Gerloff was very active in PBA business and activities, including serving as a trustee, and during the early 1940's he played on the PBA basketball team. He was reportedly a very neat and intelligent officer who did his job well. But trouble was around the corner.

On February 22, 1942 while in the radio car Gerloff spotted a stolen car and gave chase. He fired two warning shots toward the speeding car causing it to crash on Cross Hill Avenue. Though told to stop, the thief exited the vehicle and began to run. Gerloff fired twice, striking and killing the youth. To make matters even worse, the 17 year old youth, Edward Mullins Jr., was the son of Gerloff's best friend. The medical examiners investigation determined that the incident was justifiable homicide under the law, as it existed at that time. But Gerloff was devastated emotionally and never was the same again.

From that point on officer Gerloff preferred not to work in a radio car where he would be busier, but preferred to walk a foot post almost exclusively on Riverdale Avenue. On January 1, 1951 he was transferred to the 1st pct. and on November 9, 1966 to the 3rd pct. On March 7, 1969 he was advanced to the rank of Detective and five months later, on August 23, 1969, he retired. In 1980 he moved to Lady Lakes Florida where he could golf nearly every day. Detective Charles Gerloff died on February 2, 1992 in Leesburg, Florida at age 84.

DET. LEO J. NEVIN #5

APPOINTED: February 19, 1938
DIED: November 16, 1961

The son of a Yonkers Fire Dept. Captain, Det Nevin was born November 20, 1909 in Yonkers, N.Y. He attended PS# 7, graduated from Yonkers High School and attended Manhattan Prep School. A bright young man Leo gained employment working as a Draftsman. However he found his life's work when he was appointed to the YPD on February 19, 1938. Following his recruit training he was assigned to the 3rd precinct at 36 Radford Street. However, less than two years later on December 16, 1939, officer Nevin was advanced to Detective at the salary of $2,300 a year. But, on Oct. 16, 1942 he was returned to patrol in the 2nd precinct on Central Avenue. Then on April 16, 1946 he was again returned to the Detective Bureau, and this time he would stay there. Co-incidentally his brother-in-law was the Asst. Corporation Council in Yonkers. On one occasion on August 14, 1941 Nevin and his partner interrupted a robbery, chased the suspects by car for 11 miles into NYC. Det Nevin fired two shots at the fleeing vehicle which then crashed and the arrest was made. Unfortunately Det Nevin would never retire. He died on November 16, 1961. He was 51 years old.

PO JOHN H. FORBES #75

APPOINTED: February 19, 1938
DIED: August 21, 1949

John H. Forbes was born in Yonkers on June 13, 1910. He received his education at PS# 11 and later graduated from Saunders Trades School. As a young man "Jack" Forbes worked for the Walter B. Cooke Inc. Funeral Home in NYC. Jack was hired to the YPD on February 19, 1938 and assigned to the 4th precinct on patrol. On March 1, 1941 Forbes was assigned to the Traffic Division on foot. But on October 21, 1942 he was transferred from traffic duty in Getty Square to the 3rd precinct. Forbes achieved his goal on April 3, 1946 when he was re-assigned to the motorcycle unit of the Traffic Division. In 1949, while living at 8 Kingman Terrace, he suddenly became ill and, unfortunately, eleven days later on August 21, 1949 PO John Forbes died in Yonkers General Hospital. John H. Forbes was only 39 years old. At the time of his death he was a member of the Yonkers Lodge of Masons, the YPD St. George Society, the YPD Square Club, and the PBA.

PO WILLIAM N. HARDING #74

APPOINTED: February 19, 1938
RETIRED: April 2, 1963

Bill Harding was born in Yonkers NY on March 8, 1907. He attended local public schools, graduated, and as a young man worked as an insurance agent and for Gristede's Restaurant. A resident of 109 Garden Street, later renamed Walsh Road, Bill was appointed to the Yonkers Police Department on February 19, 1938 with a starting salary of $1,940 a year. His first assignment was to the 2nd precinct on patrol. Four years later, on December 22, 1942, Harding was appointed a Detective in the Detective Bureau. However, on April 16, 1946 he was returned to uniform patrol in the 2nd precinct. Bill preferred walking a foot post to riding in a patrol car and for his last five years he worked steady day tours on the post at Central Avenue and Tuckahoe Road. Bill Harding retired on April 2, 1963 and worked as a Yonkers Raceway security guard up to 1977. Ret PO William Harding, known to his co-workers as "The Clutch," and a resident of Hawthorne Avenue, died June 29, 1998. He was 91 years of age.

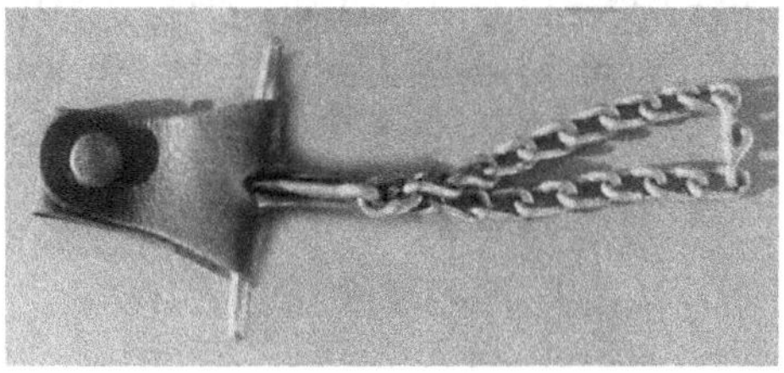

PO MICHAEL NOVOTNY #237

APPOINTED: February 19, 1938
RETIRED: July 2, 1963

Michael Novotny Sr was born in the "Hollow" section of Yonkers on December 16, 1911, and not long after his family moved to 12 Ingram Street. Young Mike attended PS# 12 on Ashburton and later graduated from Saunders HS. While in Saunders he was active in sports but his primary interest was basketball. Following his graduation Mike obtained a job as an "iron worker" in NYC and was one of the men who worked on the George Washington Bridge. In fact it was due to this job that he picked up the nickname, "Iron Mike." When he received his appointment to the YPD on February 19, 1938 he was assigned to the 1st precinct, and while at the 1st, for a short time, he was assigned to the Emergency Squad. On June 1, 1938 he was transferred to the 3rd precinct where he would remain for the rest of his career.

Mike was never really interested in patrolling in a radio car. He much preferred the close and personal interactions with the public while walking a foot post. And that's what he did. Only on occasion he would fill in on patrol in the radio car. But basically, for over 20 years he walked the foot post on South Broadway watching over the merchants and public in general and gaining their respect. To them he was affectionately known as "Mike The Cop."

At the time of his retirement on July 2, 1963 Mike lived at 41 Highland Avenue and began a new career as an Accident Investigator for the J.J. Cassale Trucking Co. located in NYC. He really didn't like the work very much so he took a job as a security guard with the Yonkers Savings Bank where he worked for about 10 years. He also worked part time at the Yonkers Raceway in the money room right up to 1975. It was about then that Mike and his wife moved to Sunrise, Florida.

It was there, in May of 1981 that Ret PO Mike "Iron Mike" Novotny died at the age of 69 years. Mike Novotny lived to see both his sons be appointed police officers. Ret YPD Det Lt Michael Novotny, and PO Robert Novotny, formerly of the Westchester County Parkway Police. Also his nephew Gerry Novotny of the NY State Police.

PO EDWARD J. NUGENT #66

APPOINTED: February 19, 1938
RESIGNED: April 26, 1954

Edward J. Nugent was born December 7, 1905 in the City of Yonkers. On his application to the YPD he listed his residence as 11 Portland Place and his employment as a Housing Technician. Ed was appointed to the department on February 19, 1938 at the annual salary of $1,940. and was assigned to the 1st precinct. After a brief stint in the Traffic Division he was returned to the 1st where, on December 19, 1941, just days after the attack on Pearl Harbor, Ed enlisted in the Army. It is said that Chief Kruppenbacher was not very happy but granted him an indefinite leave of absence.

Following the wars end, Ed received his honorable discharge, was re-instated to the YPD, and assigned to the Traffic Division. While in Traffic and having received the "Kemper Foundation Scholarship," Nugent was granted a leave of absence from September 1, 1946 to January 31, 1947 to attend The Northwestern University Traffic Institute, in Evanston, Ill. On December 9, 1948, while still in Traffic and under the direct supervision of the Public Safety Commissioner, officer Nugent was directed to conduct an engineering analysis of motor vehicle accidents that occurred in Yonkers, and to devise remedial measures. Additionally he was directed to conduct an engineering investigation of traffic conditions and complaints and to develop ways and means to improve traffic conditions in Yonkers.

On Jan 9, 1952 officer Nugent was granted a leave of absence from the YPD to accept a provisional appointment by the city manager, to the position of Superintendent of Traffic, pending adoption of the specifications for the position. As a patrolman his salary was $2,800 a year, and with this new position it was raised to $4,200. a year. On Jan 21, 1952 the Traffic Engineering Division was created and located in headquarters on Wells Avenue, and put under the supervision of "Superintendent" Nugent. As such he was responsible for the installation and maintenance of all traffic control devices and the analysis of all motor vehicle accidents. Nugent reported directly to the Commissioner of Public Safety. On October 1, 1953 this position was made permanent and Supt. Nugent's salary was $4,400. (Ed's brother Mike Nugent was a 3rd Ward Yonkers Councilman.)

Accordingly Nugent was granted a special leave of absence from the police department from December 1, 1953 to November 15, 1954. However, five months into his leave, Nugent submitted his letter of resignation to the Yonkers Police Department to be effective April 26, 1954. He had been with the police department for just short of 16 years; far short of the time necessary to receive a police pension. His name was removed from the rolls of sworn members of the police department.

It is unknown how long Ed Nugent remained in this non civil service position or where he spent the rest of his working years. However it is believed that Edward J. Nugent died in May of 1987. He would have been 81 years old.

CHIEF OF POLICE WILLIAM F. POLSEN

APPOINTED: July 16, 1939
RETIRED: March 31, 1979

Bill Polsen had no way of knowing what the future would hold for him in the police department, but he certainly seemed well suited for the success he would attain. In fact Bill Polsen's way of speaking was one with a delivery style of an intellectual and with the airy, seemingly preoccupied manner of a college literature professor. His physical appearance, standing over 6' with an erect posture, accompanied by his reserved and dignified bearing, along with his uncanny ability to remain calm regardless of the circumstances around him, could have served him just as well were he a high ranking politician; just as well as it actually did serve him as a Police Chief.

William Francis Polsen was born "William Francis Polsenski Jr" on February 21, 1915 at 38 Morningside Avenue, to William F. Polsen Sr, a chief engineer at Con Edison, and Matilda Claus Polsen. As a boy he attended PS# 9 on Fairview Street and later would graduate from Gorton High School. Bill was always full of energy and his first job was selling newspapers. He was in excellent physical condition, as he would remain throughout his career, and when he wasn't in school or working, he was swimming. He had said many times that he always had full intention of attending college. However, although he was an intelligent man with great ambition, in the depression years of early 1930's, financing proved to be in short supply and civil service professions had great appeal.

Chief William F. Polsen (cont.)

As a young man Bill Polsen worked for the Metropolitan Tobacco Co. in Yonkers, and later for a plumbing company in New York City. His daughter related that her father had taken the civil service test for both the Police and Fire departments. She further claims that her father was initially hired by the Yonkers Fire Department, but approximately two weeks later when called for appointment to the police "force" he resigned from the YFD and was appointed a Yonkers police officer on July 16, 1939. His group of four recruits was sworn in by Public Safety Commissioner Denis Morrissey. His first shield was # 50 and his starting salary was $1,940 a year. Co-incidentally, his brother Charles was also hired as a police officer in Yonkers that same day. Prior to the civil service list that Polsenski was on all appointees to the Yonkers Police Department were placed in what was then referred to as the "City Pension Fund," funded and managed by the city. Beginning with Bill and along with all others on his list, from that day forward all hired police officers were placed in the newly established New York State Pension System. A resident of 86 Frederick Street at that time officer Polsenski was assigned to foot patrol in the 1st precinct on Wells Avenue and Woodworth Avenue.

When he first reported for duty he was assigned to walk with a regular uniformed officer and Polsenski wore civilian clothes until he had the money to buy his uniforms down in New York City. Years later he would say that when he was appointed there was still one mounted police officer on patrol in Getty Square, (actually untrue. They were stopped in 1926), that there was only one radio car in the 1st precinct and all other assignments were to foot posts. Further that all city traffic lights were turned off during the late tour. The late tour officer would turn them off and the day tour man would turn then back on. Having an excellent singing voice Polsen was selected to join the police departments singing Glea Club which vocalized at various functions throughout the city.

When the United States entered WW-2 many police officers wanted to enlist in the military. However, then Chief Kruppenbacher issued an order directing no one to join for fear of depleting the police ranks. Bill Polsenski said he tried to join all branches of the service but they turned him down unless he could provide a release from the YPD. That is with the exception of the US Coast Guard. And so, Bill enlisted in the Coast Guard September 11, 1942 and received an indefinite leave of absence from the YPD dated September 12, 1942.

As a Seaman and with previous police experience Bill was placed in charge of a Guard Detail of ten other sailors. Due to having a commercial pilot's license Polsenski was sent to Floyd Bennett Air Base as an apprentice in flight mechanics. He was unable to qualify for flight training due to age limitations. Instead he was transferred to the Massachusetts Institute of Technology for advanced electronics training. He then was sent overseas as a Petty Officer serving in Newfoundland, Iceland, and to the Loran Base Supply Depot in the North Atlantic. Upon his acceptance into the US Coast Guard officer candidate training academy in New London, Ct., and upon graduation, Polsenski advanced to the rank of Chief Petty Officer with a rating as Chief Electronics Technician.

On May 10, 1946 Bill Polsenski was honorably discharged from the Coast Guard and was re-instated to the police department on June 16, 1946. Upon his return he was assigned to the Traffic Division on parking meter enforcement. Having taken and passed the police Sergeant's exam Bill Polsenski was promoted to the rank of Sergeant on June 1, 1947, with the salary of $3,400, and assigned to the 1st precinct as a patrol sergeant. Even so, his new rank didn't stop him from playing on the PBA

Chief William F. Polsen (cont.)

softball team. It was on January 1, 1948 by court order that Bill Polsenski and his brother Charles both changed their surname to Polsen. Also on that same day Sgt Polsen was reassigned to duty in the Traffic Division, motorcycle unit, as a motorcycle sergeant.

Sgt Polsen could not have known at the time but he was about to experience several promotions and many varied assignments. His next move came on May 1, 1949 when he was transferred from motorcycle duty to the 4th precinct as a patrol supervisor. Being a war veteran Bill Polsen was a member of the YPD War Veterans Legion and on November 2, 1949 Polsen was elevated in that organization to Finance Officer. And on November 11, 1950 Sgt Polsen was honored by being installed as 3rd Vice Commander of the legion during their annual Armistice Night Dinner Dance. This organization of war veterans was said to have been formed around 1924, a number of years following WW-1, "The Great War."

On October 16, 1952 having ranked # 1 on the promotion list, Polsen was again promoted, this time to the rank of Lieutenant and the new salary of $4,800 a year. He was to remain in the 4th precinct, but this time as a desk lieutenant. Then on June 13, 1955 Lt Polsen was transferred to the 2nd precinct as a desk officer. But a year later, on June 26, 1956, he was returned to the Traffic Division as the Executive Officer.

Later that year, following a nationwide competition, Lt Polsen was selected and received a fellowship to attend a nine month course of study in the "management" of traffic issues at The Traffic Institute of Northwestern University, in Evanston, Illinois. After being permitted a leave of absence, he and 50 other attendees were selected from all over the United States. The course ran from September 20, 1956 to June 24, 1957 whereupon he graduated along with his classmates.

Lt Polsen returned to his duties in the Traffic Division, but only for a short time. Before taking his nine month leave, Polsen had taken the police captain's test and when the results were made public Lt Bill Polsen ranked # 1 on that list. So, while living at 1 Shonnard Terrace, and only four months after his return, the death of Capt. Patrick Sullivan created the opening in the captain's ranks which allowed Polsen to be promoted to Captain on October 17, 1957. His salary was raised to $6,725.25 and he was assigned as the commanding officer of the 4th precinct at 53 Shonnard Place. In celebration of this achievement his friends held a testimonial dinner dance in his honor at the Polish Community Center.

As mentioned earlier, Polsen moved around very often. Only two months after his taking command of the 4th precinct Capt. Polsen was once again re-assigned to command Traffic Division on January 17, 1958. Although Capt. Polsen was moved to the 3rd pct. on December 15, 1958, he was again returned to command Traffic on May 1, 1963.

Beginning in 1909 both the police and fire departments were managed and controlled by a civilian appointed Commissioner of Public Safety working from City Hall. Both the police and fire chief reported to, and took direction from, this non civil service appointee. During Capt. Polsen's early years in the department he served under a chief of police until that chief's death in 1947. At that time the city decided not to replace the chief through a civil service exam, as had always been the case, but instead changed the local laws to allow for a new position; that of a "Deputy Public Safety Commissioner" who would serve in that capacity once held by a Chief. Like the former chiefs this deputy would run the daily operation of the police department. This, despite the fact that the city charter called for a civil service Chief of Police.

Chief William F. Polsen (cont.)

In the elections of 1963 a new political party came into power. The former Commissioner and Deputy Commissioner of Public Safety were allowed to resign, and a new Public Safety Commissioner, Daniel F. McMahon was appointed on January 2, 1964. The year before, following a law suit, the New York Supreme Court had ruled Yonkers must have a test for chief of police. A civil service test was held in November 1963 and was taken by five of the ten police captains. However, only one captain passed the test achieving a score of 91 percent. And that captain was 48 year old William F. Polsen.

Comm. McMahon was in complete agreement that it was time to return to having a civil service Chief of Police who came up through the ranks. Civil Service certified the list even though there was only one name on it and although Safety Commissioner McMahon had the right to discard the list, he accepted it. On January 24, 1964, after much consideration, he appointed Capt. William F. Polsen, the senior captain in point of service, to be the new Chief of Police in the Yonkers Police Department. Chief Polsen was now the first chief the department had since 1947. His new salary was $12,900 a year. After taking his oath of office Chief Polsen said, "*I am highly honored and deeply touched by this public expression of confidence; and I say to you that this trust will not be betrayed in any extent.*"

Chief Polsen continued working under various Public Safety Commissioners (PSC) until 1973 when then PSC William Sickley retired. And for the first time since 1909 the city decided not to continue funding this office and it was officially abolished. Local law #20-1961 was amended giving the Chief of Police those management, administrative, and jurisdictional responsibilities formerly relegated to the Commissioner of Public Safety. As a result on November 27, 1973 Chief Polsen, for the first time, became the primary and only leader of the Yonkers Police Department; with the exception of having to report to the mayor.

During an interview by a local newspaper reporter Chief Polsen spoke of how proud he was of the men and women in the department and the fine job they were doing, despite not having received a salary increase in two years. He also said there was talk of building a new headquarters across from city hall which he felt would be a great asset and sorely needed. He would never see that happen during his tenure in the department. But the constructing of a police headquarters building across from City Hall actually did occur and opened in 1990.

After much political debate by the city fathers they decided that, with the pending retirement of Chief Polsen on March 31, 1979 due to compulsory age limitations that, the days of a police chief had passed. Instead they approved the hiring of an appointed "Police Commissioner" to replace the position of Chief of Police. Even though the general public was in favor of a police chief, the position was abolished and on October 30, 1978 Daniel P. Guido was appointed the YPD's first Police Commissioner. Between 1978 and 1979 there was a five month period where both the Chief and the Police Commissioner both reported for duty. But PC Guido made it clear from his first day that he was now in command of the department and not the out-going chief. With basically no responsibilities during these five months, the chief could have just made a token appearance at headquarters now and again right up to his retirement. No one would have made note; except Chief Polsen. He reported for work every day up to his last day as Chief.

Following his retirement "the chief" was interviewed by the Herald Statesman and reflected on his career. He related that when he was appointed there was no sophisticated training for recruits. They were given a book of rules and regulations, a manual of procedures, a gun, a badge, and a nightstick. You went

Chief William F. Polsen (cont.)

out on patrol in civilian clothes with an experienced officer until you purchased your own uniforms. Polsen also mentioned how he took over the top spot in the YPD during one of the most tumultuous times in our nation's history. It was a time of campus unrest, youthful rebellion, and of a nation divided by the Vietnam War. It was a time when drugs became the sacrament of many of the nations young. The chief considered his performance during the 1960's among his greatest accomplishments because, considering the size and the geographical location of the city, it did not have a major confrontation during the riotous period of the 1960's. He did regret that he never completed college and obtained a law degree and that a Cadet Program that he initiated was not continued.

Friends and members of the department held a testimonial dinner for the retired chief on June 15, 1979 at the Polish Community Center which was filled to capacity in a show of respect for their last Yonkers Police Chief.

During his retirement years "Chief" Polsen worked in Albany ten years as an assistant to then NYS Assemblyman Gordon Burrows. And later he worked a few years assisting Congresswoman Cecile Singer. He also kept busy during his free time continuing to play golf, tennis, skating, flying, and his ballroom style dancing, at which he was excellent.

While residing at 65 Rockledge Road in Yonkers Ret. Police Chief William F. Polsen died on October 12, 2001 at the age of 86. During his funeral he was accorded full departmental honors including a motorcycle escort representing departments throughout the tri state area. The chief was a member of the Westchester County Chief's of Police Association, NYS Association of Chiefs of Police, the Rotary Club of Yonkers, the Yonkers Elks Club, the Amackassin Club, the Police Benevolent Association, the Capt.'s, Lt's, & Sgt's Association, the Police Holy Name Society, and the former Yonkers Police War Veterans Legion.

Reflecting back to when he retired, the chief's retirement order read in part,..."*The dedication, skills, and integrity he has displayed during his service to the police department shall long be remembered and shall continue to influence policing in Yonkers for many years to come.*"

DET. CHARLES G. POLSEN #11

APPOINTED: July 16, 1939
DIED: September 7, 1964

Charles Gordon Polsenski was born at 38 Morningside Avenue in Yonkers on January 11, 1917. He attended PS# 9 and graduated from Gorton HS. Although not a heavy man, from his childhood the nickname of "Chubby" remained with him throughout his life. And "Chubby" was very athletic, loving golf, hunting, fishing, and swimming. As a young man he worked as a machine operator. Charles was appointed to the YPD on July 16, 1939 and was assigned patrol duty in the precincts. He was said to be very friendly and fun loving, unlike his brother Bill who was more serious. He and his brother officially changed their name from Polsenski to Polsen on January 1, 1948. After working patrol in the 2nd pct. for several years, on Sept 16, 1955 he was re-assigned from the 2nd to the Juvenile Aid Bureau (JAB) and in March of 1956 he was working in the Detective Bureau. Polsen was very active in PBA business and activities. In 1957 he was vice president of the PBA, and in 1958 and again in 1959 he was elected President of the PBA. He also served in the 1st pct. many years. Detective Polsen, a resident of 13 Orient Street, had a heart condition which ultimately caused his death on September 7, 1964. He was a member of the Crescent Club and the Knights of Columbus. Polsen was only 47 years old.

PO STEPHEN SPIAK

APPOINTED: July 16, 1939
RESIGNED: August 21, 1947

Steve Spiak took the civil service test for police officer and topped the list. He was appointed on July 16, 1939 while residing at 39 Madison Avenue. His salary was $1,940 a year. Spiak and those hired from his list were the first to be required to join the newly established New York State Police & Fire Pension System. All prior appointees were in "The City Pension." Assigned to patrol duties he was apparently fairly efficient. In fact he was awarded a Certificate of Excellent Police Work on April 3, 1940 for arresting a burglar in the act several months earlier. In fact it wasn't long before he was appointed a Detective. But on October 12, 1942 Spiak was re-assigned from the Detective Bureau to the 2nd precinct. Spiak was active in PBA and PAL activities and was a charter member of the police St George Society. However, on April 23, 1947 he was charged with a violation and convicted. Steve Spiak resigned from the police department on August 21, 1947.

PO GEORGE B. PHILLIPS #174

APPOINTED: July 16, 1939
RESIGNED: July 16, 1948

George Boydell Phillips Jr. was born in the city of Yonkers NY on April 9, 1914 to George B. Phillips Sr. and Grace Elder Frazier Phillips of 280 Woodworth Ave., Yonkers. After his local schooling he attended the University of Alabama, and gained employment working as a civil engineer for the Bureau of Lands and Mines and the US Army Corps of Engineers.

Sending both himself and his sister to school, he needed to supplement income with dependable employment. He tested for, passed, and was appointed to the Yonkers Police Department on July 16, 1939. He was appointed along with Bill (later the chief of police) and Charles Polsen and Steve Spiak by Public Safety Commissioner Denis Morrissey. They were the first group of police officers appointed that were no longer eligible to participate in the old "City Pension Fund," and instead were required to join the new NYS Employees Retirement System, later to be the N.Y.S. Police & Fire Pension System.

Following some basic police recruit training, Phillips was assigned to uniform patrol in the 1st precinct. However, on January 23, 1942, following the attack on Pearl Harbor and America's entry into WW-2, Phillips enlisted in the Army and his active duty service began on March 15, 1943. Due to his enlistment he received an indefinite leave of absence from the police department. Following the wars end George Phillips Jr. was Honorably Discharged from the Army holding the rank of Captain. While serving during WW-2, he was stationed near Salisbury, England and LeHarve, France, to which he had first arrived on July 19, 1944, and returned to the U.S. in 1946. His final separation from the military was effective April 15, 1948. Upon his return stateside, he submitted his letter of resignation to the Yonkers Police Department, which was accepted and made effective on July 16, 1948. He remained serving as a Reserve Officer until 1953.

George Phillips Jr. was hired, first with the Bureau of Land and Mines, then the Army Corps of Engineers, his final career. His work included inspecting ICBM missile sites, requiring travel, through the Middle East as in Iran, Iraq and Turkey, the Pacific as in Taiwan and for his family to have homes in Okinawa, Japan, Livorno, Italy, Hawaii and finally California. George Phillips retired as a civil servant and opened an antique shop with his wife pursing his lifelong interest in history and fine arts/furnishings.

George B. Phillips Jr. died in 2006 at age 92 years in Redlands, Cal. in San Bernardino, Co. Surviving were his wife of 62 years, Eugenia Carson Phillips, his four children; Susan Hope, Deborah Faith (Ringsmuth), Michael Carson, and Thomas Miles Phillips.

DET. WILLIAM G. RUSHBY #20

APPOINTED: November 11, 1939
DIED: July 17, 1951

William George Rushby was born on September 23, 1910 in Keeseville, NY. He received his education in the schools in Port Henry NY before coming to Yonkers with his family in 1928. His early employment was with Herman Eggars Sr. Co. in Yonkers as a chauffeur.

Bill was appointed to the YPD on November 11, 1939 and assigned to the 4th precinct. Even before America's entry into WW-2, on February 3, 1941 Rushby had the distinction of being the first police officer to be inducted into the Army under the Selective Service Act. However, only 8 months later he was honorably discharged under a law for early release of draftees over 28 years of age and was returned to the 4th precinct. However, shortly after the attack on Pearl Harbor, Rushby was recalled to duty on January 16, 1942 and served as a sergeant with the 716th Military Police Regiment. Following the war he received his honorable discharge on September 15, 1945 and once again returned to patrol in the 4th precinct.

On April 16, 1946 Rushby was appointed a Detective in the Detective Bureau. On Dec 3, 1947 he luckily escaped injury while playing cards off duty as two men robbed the game, shot and killed an off duty fireman and shot and wounded another off duty police officer. Rushby was an ardent sportsman and made annual hunting and fishing trips to Canada. He was noted for his dry sense of humor and ready smile. He was a member of the Crescent Post, American Legion, Police Square Club, PBA, Police War Veterans Legion and the Police St George Association.

Rushby remained a detective right up to his untimely death on July 17, 1951 at the young age of 40 years.

PO FRANK J. ADAMSKI #19

APPOINTED: November 16, 1939
RETIRED: February 24, 1972

Frank Joseph Adamski was born in the Bronx, N Y on October 2, 1910 and would later move with his family to Yonkers. As a youth Frank attended Yonkers elementary schools and graduated from Saunders High School. As a young man he listed his employment as a "Designer."

He was hired by the Yonkers Police Department from 53 Oak St. on November 16, 1939 with a starting salary of $1,940 and was assigned to patrol duties in the 2nd precinct. When Pearl Harbor was attacked and the US entered WW-2, Frank enlisted in the Army and was granted a leave of absence from the department on June 1, 1942. He served as a PFC in the 77th Infantry Division, commonly referred to as the "Statue of Liberty Division." This division participated in the battles in the Pacific for Okinawa, Guam, and the Philippines. His last billet was with the occupational forces in Japan. During his military service he was awarded many citations, including the Purple Heart. Frank was honorably discharged on December 1, 1945 and reinstated to the Police Department two weeks later on December 16, 1945.

Frank spent 27 years in the 2nd precinct but, on November 7, 1966 he was transferred to the 1st precinct. Frank was an easy going guy who was well-liked by his coworkers and had a good singing voice. He was often used for singing at funerals held for members who had passed away or as a soloist at the Holy Name Society Masses. And because of his good voice in the late 1940s he was also member of the YPD singing Glee Club. Frank had been a member of the Yonkers Police PBA, the Police Holy Name Society, the Fraternal Order of Police, and the NYS Federation of police. One of his sons was an ordained priest.

Frank retired from the police department on February 24, 1972, and died on April 6, 1996. He was 85 years old.

DET. VICTOR W. GEIGER # 659

APPOINTED: November 16, 1939
RETIRED: April 30, 1972

Victor Geiger was born February 19, 1911 in Yonkers, attended PS# 7 and graduated from Commerce & Yonkers HS. He worked for 10 years for John Hancock Insurance Co as an assistant cashier but said he couldn't wait to get out of the office so he took the police test. On his application it listed his home address as 47 Claredon Avenue.

Geiger received his appointment to the Yonkers Police Department on November 16, 1939 at the annual salary of $1,940 a year. Paydays came twice a month. He said he was sworn in along with 12 other men at City Hall at 8 AM, sent over to HQ where he met Chief Quirk. He was given a revolver, 6 bullets, his shield and hat wreath and the book of Rules & Regulations. And Quirk told him, "I make the rules here." When he shook Quirks hand he said it was like a vise.

That same day he began working on foot patrol in the 3rd precinct at 4:00 PM, in civilian clothes, walking with a senior officer. His captain was John J. McCarthy -3. "Vic" said he worked four early tours and was then told he was being put into a spot on the chart. When he asked when do I begin he was told tomorrow, on your first early tour, working 6 straight tours with only a 32 hour swing. So, he did what he was told and worked 10 days in a row with no day off when he first started with the department.

He received virtually no recruit training at all; although a few times Lt Harold Sheeky brought his recruit group to the Armory to practice marching. They received revolver qualification at the firing range at the old Hudson Tire Building on Nepperhan Avenue. Within months, on January 12, 1940 he was transferred to the 4th precinct where Capt. Tom Morrissey was the CO. "Vic" said the captain was very gruff person and didn't allow you to stop on post and talk to people. He used to say, "I don't want any "bagging" out there. Just walk your post." (Bagging meaning talking.) "Vic" said in those days the captain had to stand all roll calls, including the late tour. He said maybe that's why they were so grumpy.

Having a love of basketball from his high school days and still being in good physical condition, during the early 1940's officer Geiger played on the PBA basketball team. He was also a very proficient golfer. And he was always willing to help out the Police Athletic League, following its formation, by volunteering his time for their programs, including working in uniform at the Ragamuffin Parade on Halloween. All uniform personnel who worked were not paid but simply volunteered their time. When they learned Victor could type they used him as a "houseman" on occasion. He admitted he was very good at record keeping and office work.

On Oct 12, 1942 he was called off patrol into the 4th by Lt Philp and told there was an order making him a detective and assigning him to Chief Kruppenbacher's office. "Vic" said it must have been his clerk typist background that resulted in the new assignment. However, the chief didn't seem too pleased when he first reported for duty asking him, "What the hell are you doing here? I didn't ask for you!" Geiger was surprised at the chief's anger because as a youth Geiger lived in a seven family building on William Street that Chief Kruppenbacher owned and he often would play with the chief's children.

Now as a detective, Geiger said after a few months things got a little better as far as working conditions, etc. But on April 16, 1946, for whatever reason, he was transferred to the 1st precinct on paper, losing his detective status, but remained detailed to the chief's office. When Chief Kruppenbacher

Det. Victor W. Geiger #659 (cont.)

retired in 1947 and committed suicide, at his funeral all the captains formed up as pallbearers and he, PO Geiger, was directed to stand with them as part of the honor detail. The rest of the department formed up out in the street.

A decision was made at City Hall not to replace the chief with another civil service appointed chief. Instead, Lt William Comey was appointed Deputy Public Safety Commissioner in command of the entire police department, in effect taking the former chief's job. Comey told Geiger, "You know, a new broom sweeps clean," and on Aug 30, 1947 Geiger was transferred out of the old chief's office to the 2nd precinct on patrol. During the previous few years "Vic" had been active in the PBA serving as a trustee, and after this transfer he was elected the PBA Treasurer. Geiger remained in the 2nd precinct for about 11 years both on patrol and often used as the houseman. On May 7, 1956 PO Geiger was awarded a Certificate of Excellent Police Work for a robbery arrest on December 21, 1951 at 315 Saw Mill River Road, and a 2nd certificate for a grand larceny arrest on July 2, 1951 at 7 Burbank St.

On May 1, 1958 he was assigned to the Detective Division where he worked in General Assignment for about five years and then was offered to be the DD desk officer, working a day - early chart with four on and two off. He took it and remained at that job up to his retirement on April 30, 1972.

When he retired he lived at 269 Palmer Road and he took a part time job with the Yonkers Raceway working as an "Observer" looking for professional gamblers, most of whom he knew well. He stayed for two years and left, never to work again. In 1976 he moved with his wife to Mahopac.

Retired Detective Victor Geiger died on July 20, 2006 at the age of 95 years.

PO EDWARD L. SOHR #73

APPOINTED: November 16, 1939
RETIRED: July 15, 1971

Born Edward Lawrence Sohr on September 27, 1914 in Yonkers, Ed graduated from Commerce High School in 1932. He was appointed to the police department from 121 Ludlow Street on November 16, 1939 at $1,940. His first assignment was to the 4th pct. On September 23, 1942 PO Sohr was re-assigned to the 1st precinct on Wells Avenue. Ed was granted an indefinite leave of absence after enlisting in the Navy Reserve on Oct. 28, 1942 during WW 2, serving with the Shore Patrol in Hawaii with the rating of Petty Officer 1st Class. He remained on active duty until his honorable discharge on Jan. 6, 1946. He was re-instated to the YPD on Feb. 1, 1946 In Oct. of 1956 Ed was a patrol wagon driver-desk aide in 1st pct. on Wells Ave, and then on Nov. 9, 1966 he was returned to the 4th pct. to do the same job right up to his retirement. Sohr had a thing where he would never wear short sleeve shirts. He was a very quiet and thin man and was likely self-conscious about his thin arms. He didn't mingle much and brought his lunch in every day. A single man who never married, he was very low profile in the job, but off duty he owned a Mercedes Benz. A resident of 2 Sunnyside Drive, Ed Sohr retired on July 15, 1971 and died on September 16, 1996 in Bel Air, Md, where he had lived for 18 years. He was 81 years old.

PO DAVID LYNCH #71

APPOINTED: November 16, 1939
RESIGNED: May 17, 1948

Police Officer David Lynch was born in the City of Yonkers on January 1, 1915. He attended local schools and as a young man he worked as a "threading helper" at the Alexander Smith Carpet Mills in Yonkers. He was hired to the YPD from 324 Sommerville Place on November 16, 1939 and, following very basic instruction, he was assigned to the 3rd precinct. His starting salary was $1,940 a year. On June 1, 1946 he was re-assigned to the 4th precinct, once again on patrol. In 1947 PO Lynch was reportedly assigned to the Meter Squad with John Baldwin and Mike Perna. On August 18, 1947 Lynch was brought up on charges of assault, abusive language, and conduct unbecoming an officer. Meanwhile, on August 30, 1947 Lynch was transferred from the 4th precinct to the 2nd. On December 6, 1947 his delayed departmental trial was rescheduled, but once again delayed. However, in February of 1948 the trial was concluded and Lynch was exonerated and all charges were dismissed. Living on Morningside Avenue at the time it is not known if the lengthy trial had any bearing, but on May 17, 1948 PO David Lynch, a charter member of the police St. George Association, submitted his resignation effective May 17, 1948. David Lynch died in Yonkers in April of 1973. He was 58.

SGT. JOHN HAVRISH

APPOINTED: November 16, 1939
RETIRED: March 30, 1972

"Big John" Havrish, as he would later be known, was born in the city of Yonkers on February 7, 1917. He attended local elementary schools and later graduated from Gorton High School. As a young man. He worked for the City of Yonkers in the Parks and Forestry Department as a laborer. Havrish was appointed to the Yonkers Police Department on November 16, 1939 from 4 Mulberry St. and was assigned to the 4th precinct. In February of 1942 he was assigned to the 1st precinct, and later moved to the 3rd precinct.

On March 17, 1942 officer Havrish discovered a fire at 25 Palisade Ave. at 2:30 in the morning. He rushed into the building, waking the sleeping tenants and evacuated all of them, as well as those in the connecting buildings. He was later commended for his quick action. On April 11, 1945, following his being drafted into the military, Havrish received an indefinite leave of absence from the Police Department. He served in the Navy, assigned to shore patrol duty during World War II, and was honorably discharged on April 1, 1946. He was reinstated to the police department on April 16, 1946. In addition to English, John spoke Russian. Being very athletic, in the late 1940s John played on the Yonkers police basketball and softball teams.

On January 1, 1951. John was reassigned to the Juvenile Aid Bureau, investigating crimes by juveniles and assisting with Police Athletic League programs. On October 16, 1952 he was promoted to the rank of sergeant with the salary of $4,200 at which time he was assigned to the 1st precinct on patrol as a supervisor. He remained on patrol duties in various precincts right up to his retirement on March 30, 1972. Retired Sgt. John Havrish died on April 5, 1983, at the age of 66 years.

DET. LT. WESLEY D. MARTIN

APPOINTED: November 16, 1939
DIED: December 10, 1975

Wes Martin was born in Yonkers on July 4, 1917. He attended PS # 23, Ben Franklin Jr HS, and graduated from Yonkers HS. As a young man Wes worked as a clerk in the office of the Alexander Smith Carpet factory, along with his brother Bob. He was very good at playing Tennis and also liked Golf. Wesley Martin was appointed to the YPD on November 16, 1939 from 70 Spruce Street and assigned to patrol in the 3rd pct. On April 11, 1944 he was granted an indefinite leave of absence due to induction into the Navy toward the end of WW-2. He was honorably discharged on Feb. 23, 1946 and returned to the YPD on Mar. 1, 1946. The following year, on June 1, 1947 PO Martin, who played on the police softball team, was appointed a detective but was re-assigned to the 2nd pct. on May 1, 1949. Wes was promoted to Sergeant on Oct. 16, 1952 and sent to the 3rd pct. On July 1, 1956 he was promoted to Lieutenant at $5,880 a year and designated a city wide fill in Lt. He was then returned to the DD as a Det Lt. on Feb. 23, 1964. When Capt. Vescio was designated C.O. of the DD, Martin was assigned as his executive officer due to his administrative skills. In 1968 he served as aide to the Chief Polsen for several years right up to his illness and subsequent death from cancer on Dec. 10, 1975. Wesley's brother Bob was also a YPD Lt

PO CHARLES E. McENERY #91

APPOINTED: November 16, 1939
RESIGNED: April 22, 1948

Charles McEnery was born in the City of Yonkers on November 17, 1913, and attended local schools while living at 38 Morningside Ave. McEnery listed his former occupation as an Expressman and painter. While living at 51 Linden Street McEnery was appointed to the Yonkers Police Department on November 16, 1939 with a salary of $1,940. He was initially assigned to the 3rd pct. but at one point was re-assigned to the 2nd pct. on patrol duty. "Buddy" McEnery, as he was known, was appointed a Detective on Oct. 10, 1942. The dates are unavailable, but he was later returned to patrol duties in the 2nd pct. His brother was Sgt. Edward McEnery. On July 22, 1947 McEnery was charged by the department with threatening a civilian with his revolver, insubordination, threatening to assault the 1st precinct lieutenant, and conduct unbecoming a police officer. The following month, on August 30, 1947, while the charges were still pending McEnery was transferred from the 2nd to the 1st precinct. On February 20, 1948 he was found guilty and fined 25 days pay. Two months later, on April 22, 1948, Charles McEnery submitted his resignation to the police department. It is said that Charles McEnery returned to being a painter and then moved to California where he died at a young age.

DEPUTY CHIEF EDWARD J. MURPHY

APPOINTED: November 16, 1939
RETIRED: June 29, 1973

Edward Joseph Murphy was born on March 28, 1912, at Sloan Maternity hospital in New York City to Anna and John Murphy. He was the younger of two boys, born to the couple. Ed was raised in Yonkers, where he attended grammar school until the 8th grade. Ed later continued his education by attending Butler Business School where he completed a course in stenography on June 27, 1929. Having never obtained a high school diploma, Ed went on to obtain his General Educational Development High School diploma in February of 1956.

Ed was employed by John Wanamaker Department Stores from June 1930 to September 1936 in the shipping department. When the United Parcel Service took over the shipping department of Wanamaker's, Ed was transferred to their employ as a stenographer in the delivery department from September 1936 to November 1939. Ed was promoted to the billing department as assistant manager but left the company seeking benefits and job security.

On August 21, 1938, Ed married Loretta Manton and in February 1940, the couple gave birth to a daughter, Loretta. It would be 11 years before the couple gave birth to their second child, a son, Edward.

In preparation for his law enforcement career, Ed Murphy attended an adult education course October 1938 through January 1939, at Commerce High School, sponsored by the Board of Education.

Deputy Chief Edward J. Murphy (cont.)

The course consisted of Yonkers City Government, geographic conditions and city boundaries, requirements for police candidate examination and basic fundamentals of police work.

Ed Murphy was appointed as a Patrolman to the Yonkers Police Department on November 16, 1939 with the starting salary of $1,940. Under the supervision of the police bureau, he was trained in the basic skills, duties and responsibilities of a patrolman. These responsibilities included the handling/firing of a department issued revolver, United States Infantry Drill, physical training, a course in bombs, poison gases, city evacuation, and firefighting. As a patrolman candidate, Ed completed all the courses listed above and was accepted as a full-fledged Patrolman.

Following his training Officer Murphy was assigned to the 3rd precinct at 36 Radford Street on foot and radio car patrol. While there Ed conducted routine police investigations including burglaries, larceny, assaults etc. and served as a precinct clerk, assisting in filing reports, completing orders, and written and verbal precinct communications to personnel.

In 1941 the Yonkers Police Bureau installed two-way radios in their patrol cars. In order to be assigned to a "radio patrol car," sending and receiving these communications, the Federal Communications Commission required all radio operators be licensed. Ed was trained in the federal rules and regulation regarding radio communication and in September of 1941, passed his examination and received his license from the FCC via the Radio Telegraph Division (RTD), as a restricted radio telephone operator.

In March 1941, Ed attended Consolidated Police training School in White Plains, NY. The course ran through June of 1941 and was conducted under the direction of the National Police Academy. The course consisted of police practices and procedures, Judo, the proper handling of firearms and police science. Lectures were given by Special Agents of the Federal Bureau of Investigation. And on June 9th, 1941, Ed received his course completion certificate.

On October 30, 1942, Ed was transferred by City Manager William A. Walsh to Police Headquarters on Wells Avenue to work in the Emergency Squad. Following this assignment Ed received training through the Red Cross in injury first aid, drowning, and respiratory/pulmonary resuscitation. He was further instructed by the Consolidated Edison Company in the use of protective equipment in case of gas emergencies. The police bureau firearms instructor educated Ed in the use of the Thompson sub-machine gun, flare gun, tear gas gun and grenades. This knowledge was applied while responding to all emergency calls throughout the City of Yonkers, regardless of their nature. During this time police officer Murphy also served as a clerk to the Desk Lieutenant and Captain of the 1st Precinct.

During WWII the Auxiliary Police Corp. was formed by a group of patriotic Yonkers citizens. This civic organization requested police department cooperation in instructing its members. In addition to his regular duties with the Emergency Squad, Ed taught courses in Standard Red Cross First Aid including traumatic injury, burns, shock, and resuscitation. On April 16, 1946, Ed Murphy was transferred from the Emergency Squad to the Detective Division as a General Assignment Detective. As a Detective First Grade, Ed was responsible for investigating homicides, serious assaults, burglaries, robberies, rape, arson and all other serious crime investigations. He possessed a comprehensive knowledge of the city and all

Deputy Chief Edward J. Murphy (cont.)

surrounding geographic sub-divisions and worked closely with local, state and federal agencies. On various occasions Det Murphy acted as the Desk Officer for the Detective Division assigning cases, keeping records, filing reports and unofficially acted as a division typist for superior officers. But, on May 1, 1949 Murphy was reassigned from being a detective and transferred to the 4th precinct, and two years later to the 2nd precinct, on uniformed patrol.

In May of 1952, PO Murphy was assigned to the Office of the Deputy Commissioner, Capt. James McCue, in Police Headquarters, as Secretary to the Deputy Commissioner. In this capacity, he performed secretarial duties, transmitting verbal and written orders and directives throughout the bureau, answered communications received by the bureau from citizens of the city, as well as coordinate communication with local state and federal agencies. In addition, Ed was responsible for supplying all precincts and divisions with administrative supplies, managing the files of the Deputy Commissioner's Office, tracking all phases of special orders/directives and disbursements of reports to all precincts and divisions. During this time, he also attended various meetings of the Chiefs of Police of the 39 police departments throughout Westchester County, sponsored by the Sheriff of the County of Westchester at White Plains, NY. While in attendance, Ed recorded the meeting minutes which pertained to problems facing Police Departments throughout the county. The issues debated/discussed were juvenile delinquency, Alcohol Beverage Control (ABC) board violators etc. These minutes were later transcribed by Ed and distributed to the Deputy Commissioner and the Commissioner for reference and guidance.

August 16, 1955, while still assigned to the Deputy Commissioners office, officer Murphy was promoted to Sergeant with an increase in salary to $5,000 a year, and was assigned to the 3rd Precinct. Sgt Murphy was now responsible for the supervision of all radio and foot patrolman in the 3rd precinct in the City of Yonkers. He instructed, assigned and advised patrolmen in his charge, followed up on assigned duties and ensured that assignments were carried out in an efficient and proper manner. Sgt Murphy assumed the role of Acting Lieutenant on several occasions, assigning members of the command to patrol, booking prisoners and directing their confinement to the city jail to await trial, preparing daily reports, reviewing/accepting/receiving patrolman's reports for completeness and accuracy.

Ed took advantage of special training and furthering education opportunities offer by the police bureau. From September 1950 through 1954, Ed took several courses sponsored by the Department of Civil Service. These courses covered Basic Penal Law Fundamentals, Advanced Penal Law and its Relationship to Arrest Procedure, Code of Criminal Procedure and Police Administration.

On March 1, 1958 Sgt Murphy was promoted to the rank of Police Lieutenant with the new salary of $6,680, and was re-assigned to the 2nd precinct on Central Avenue to serve as a precinct desk officer. He later would be re-assigned to the 3rd precinct as a desk officer on February 28, 1963. Due to his administrative skills, on November 30, 1964, Lt. Murphy was assigned to the chief's office as the chief's administrative aide. He remained there just over three years when on February 14, 1968 he was re-assigned back to the Detective Division to supervise their plainclothes unit.

On December 19, 1969, Lt. Murphy was promoted to Captain and his salary rose to $14,625. Captain Edward Murphy was now sent to the 2nd precinct, but this time as it's commanding officer. A year later, on December 1, 1970, Captain Murphy was "detailed" to work in Chief William Polsen's office assisting the chief. However, by the end of the month, December 29th, Capt. Murphy was transferred and

Deputy Chief Edward J. Murphy (cont.)

assigned as the commanding officer of Headquarters Command Division.

On January 8, 1972 it was reported in the local newspaper that it had been decided by City Manager Walsh and Chief Polsen that a new, non-civil service, appointed rank was to be established within the police department. This organizational change was the result of a recommendation by the International Association of Chiefs Of Police (I.A.C.P.) following their study of the Yonkers Police Department. As part of this change there were two new positions created entitled Deputy Chief, and it was decided that Capt. Edward Murphy was to be promoted to one of those positions. On January 10, 1972, Captain Murphy was appointed Deputy Chief of the Police Bureau by acting Commissioner of Public Safety, William H. Sickley. A General Order by the City Manager, Seymour Scher, confirmed the appointment and Chief Murphy was sworn in by the Mayor of the City of Yonkers, Alfred B. Del Bello. Chief Murphy was placed in command of the Administrative and Technical Services Bureau with a salary of $18,750. The units under his command were Headquarters Command, Community Relations, Records and Planning Divisions.

However, in order for Chief Murphy to maintain his civil service status and benefits as a captain he was required to obtain a one year leave of absence. And so Chief Murphy was granted this leave from his civil service captain's rank effective January 10, 1972 through January 9, 1973. On June 29, 1973, after 34 years of dedicated service to the public and to the City of Yonkers, Edward Murphy retired as Deputy Chief of Police.

In retirement Ed remained involved in police related activities. He and fellow retiree Frank Panessa worked to re-establish an old organization, The New York Police and Fire Retiree Association, which was created to help benefit retired police and firefighters. After a great deal of planning, work, and unavoidable delays, the first meeting took place at the 1st precinct at 35 E Grassy Sprain Rd on June 21, 1978. Nineteen retired police officer's attended. Elections were held and Ed Murphy was elected President of this new organization on November 27, 1978. At that meeting Yonkers retired firefighters were also invited and were elected to positions as well. The first group of newsletters was prepared and was hand typed by Ed. He was called a guiding spirit and a keystone in the organization that began with just a few retired members but grew to over 300 members in a short time. In addition to his work with the New York Police and Fire Retiree Association, Ed was a past secretary in the Police Benevolent Association, the Capt's, Lt's, and Sgt's Association, the Policeman's Holy Name Society, the Emerald Society, a member of the Police Athletic League and the Amackassin Club.

Ed Murphy enjoyed boating, swimming, squash, and tennis. He was an avid tennis player winning many awards and competitions. Retirement was spent gardening, working on his car, going out on his boat, taking long car rides with his wife and tinkering around the house.

Edward Murphy died suddenly on November 25, 1979 of a massive heart attack on his way back from church services. He was 67 years old.

PO EDWIN R. ROBERTS #93

APPOINTED: November 16, 1939
RESIGNED: June 16, 1946

Edwin R, Roberts was born in the City of Yonkers on July 17, 1915. After completing his local education he gained employment as an Accounting Clerk. Ed was appointed to the Yonkers Police Dept. from 3 Alder Street on November 16, 1939 and assigned to patrol in the 3rd precinct. On March 20, 1942 PO Roberts was awarded a Certificate of Excellent Police Work for the capture, at gun point, of a burglar on Sept. 13, 1940. Following the outbreak of WW-2 Roberts joined the Navy and received an indefinite leave of absence on April 15, 1942. He received his Honorable discharge on Jan. 21, 1946 and was re-instated to the YPD on Feb. 1, 1946. A charter member of the police St George Society, Roberts played on the PBA basketball team after his military discharge. However on June 16, 1946, only four months after his return, PO Edwin Roberts resigned from the YPD to accept another job offer.

PO EDWARD F. SMITH #251

APPOINTED: November 16, 1939
RETIRED: January 13, 1966

Ed Smith was actually born "Edward Francis Napurski" on January 2, 1911 in Yonkers. He attended local schools, graduating from Yonkers H.S. and later gained employment as a "Splicer's Helper" with the NY Telephone Co. He was multi lingual in that he spoke French and Italian, as well as English. "Smitty," as he was known, was appointed to the Yonkers P.D. on November 16, 1939 from 217 So. Waverly St, and assigned to patrol in the 4th precinct at 53 Shonnard Place. He used to tell the story how on October 4, 1940, after commandeering a passing auto and while standing on the running board, he chased a reckless driver. Only after Smith fired a "warning" shot did the speeding auto stop and the arrest was made. On June 16, 1942 Smitty was granted an indefinite leave of absence due to induction into the Army for service during WW-2. He served as a Technical Sergeant in the Criminal Investigation Division. He received an honorable discharge on November 5, 1945 and was re-instated to the YPD on Dec. 1, 1945 at $2,416 a year. In the late 1940's he played on the PBA basketball team. On Nov 2, 1949 he was elected 4th pct. trustee for the YPD War Veteran's Legion for 1950 and again in 1951. On Jan 1, 1951, while living at 71 Maple Street, Smith was transferred to the 1st pct. But in Oct 1952 he was returned to the 4th precinct where in July 1954 he was detailed to training for bomb defusing. Ed Smith retired from the YPD on Jan 13, 1966 and died on Jan 7, 1974. Ed was 62 years old.

PO JOSEPH F. TUTONI #99

APPOINTED: November 16, 1939
DIED: May 19, 1964

Joseph R. Tutoni was born on April 1, 1911 in New York City. While still very young his family moved to Yonkers and Joe attended Yonkers local public schools. As a young man Joe worked in Beck Shoe Store as shoe salesman. However, after taking and passing the test for police Patrolman Joe was appointed to the police department on November 16, 1939. He was living at 26 Warburton Avenue at the time and his police starting salary was $1,940 a year.

Joe's first assignment was patrol duty in the 3rd precinct. On April 14, 1959 while working the late tour in the 3rd precinct at about 1:15 AM while he was checking the doors on commercial business establishments, he heard glass breaking across the street. He observed a youth running from a liquor store at 553 South Broadway. During a foot chase Tutoni ordered the youth to stop, but he kept running. At this Joe fired twice over the youth's head as a warning but the youth ran even faster and was lost between buildings. When a search was conducted by responding sector cars PO's Joe Yarina & Rocco DelBene found the male and took him into custody.

When Tutoni worked as a detective for a few years he was known by the men as "The Undertaker" because he always wore a black suit, coat, and hat. Joe was transferred back to patrol on May 1, 1963. A resident of 257 Valentine Lane PO Joe Tutoni died suddenly on May 19, 1964 at the age of 53 years.

PUBLIC SAFETY COMMISSIONER FRANK E. VESCIO

APPOINTED: November 16, 1939
RETIRED: January 14, 1972

Born Frank Ernest Vescio on September 23, 1915 in the City of Yonkers, Frank attended PS # 18 elementary school, Benjamin Franklin Jr HS, and graduated from Commerce High School. Frank was bilingual in that he spoke English and Italian fluently. He had a brother Pasquale who, many years later, would be an Assistant Chief in the Yonkers Fire Department. On earlier employment applications Frank indicated he worked as a salesman and as a machinist.

Frank Vescio was appointed to the Yonkers Police Department on November 16, 1939 from 13 Cedar Street at the starting salary of $1,940 and was assigned to the 3rd precinct on foot patrol. On March 20, 1942 officer Vescio was awarded a Certificate of Excellent Police Work for saving a man's life. There had been a motor vehicle accident on McLean Ave. at Radford Street and a man's leg had been crushed and was bleeding profusely. Officer Vescio provided first aid by immediately applying a tourniquet to stop the bleeding. The recognition he received was nice, but the important part was, back then Yonkers Civil Service granted you a half point toward your next promotional exam with every Certificate of Excellent Police Work.

Following the US entry into World War II, officer Vescio enlisted in the Naval Reserve on October 22, 1942 and was granted and indefinite leave of absence from the police department. Soon after his

P.S.C. Frank E. Vescio (cont.)

enlistment he was immediately activated to active duty and served in the regular Navy beginning on November 3, 1942. He received his recruit training at the Marine Corps base at Parris Island, South Carolina. With a rating of 1st class Petty Officer he performed duty in police functions, security, investigations, and worked with military intelligence. Petty Officer Vescio served in the Asiatic Pacific Theater of operations during World War II aboard the USS Wasp and various other ships including a destroyer and an aircraft carrier. While he was serving in the Navy he requested, and was allowed to continue to make contributions to his police pension fund. Vescio was honorably discharged from the Navy on February 7, 1946 and was reinstated to the YPD on March 1, 1946.

On September 1, 1947 officer Vescio received his first promotion, that being to the rank of Sergeant. He was promoted to that rank along with eight other war veterans earning $3,400 a year, and he was assigned as a patrol supervisor in the 4th precinct. On January 1, 1951 Sgt. Vescio was reassigned to the 2nd precinct as a patrol sergeant.

Sgt. Vescio was promoted to the rank of lieutenant on October 16, 1952 with an increase in salary to $4,800 a year. As a lieutenant he would no longer be on patrol, but instead he was now assigned as a desk lieutenant and remained assigned to the 2nd precinct. In those years when lieutenants performed desk duty in the precincts they were the officers who handled the day to day hands-on operations conducted by the police officers on patrol. The booking of prisoners was just one of the responsibilities of the desk lieutenants. Of course the precinct captain was in command, but for all intents and purposes a desk lieutenant was the most visible officer in control of the precinct operation.

On April 3, 1957 Lt Vescio received a certificate of training from the Department of the Army for completing a course of training in explosive ordinance which was conducted in Mt. Vernon New York.

Historically it was unusual for any officer to receive a promotion and remain assigned to the same precinct he worked in with the previous rank. But Vescio did just that when he was promoted from sergeant to lieutenant and remained in the 2nd precinct. It was even more surprising that he again remained in the 2nd precinct when he was promoted to the rank of captain on January 16, 1958. With a new salary of $7,310 a year Capt. Vescio had served continuously in the 2nd precinct as a sergeant, a lieutenant, and now as the precinct commanding officer. However he remained there for only one year and was reassigned as commanding officer of the Communications and Records Division on December 15, 1958. Then, on March 16, 1960 Capt. Vescio was placed in charge of the Juvenile Aide Bureau (JAB) with the responsibility of dealing with crimes by juveniles.

All during his early years he had built a reputation as being a very serious worker who operated strictly by the rules and expected his subordinates to do the same. This attitude made him much different than some other captains. In 1963 the NY State Investigation Commission held hearings on charges that gambling was wide open in Yonkers and the police department was basically corrupt in this area of enforcement. In fact it was alleged that Capt. Vescio had made accusations to then Public Safety Commissioner Milton Goldman that the department was generally incompetent and corrupt when it came to gambling enforcement. Of course this didn't make Vescio very popular within the police department, but he was a man who said what he believed. Vescio's charges hit like a bombshell just before the fall election and, quite possibly, were in part responsible for the Democrats losing the election to the Republicans in November 1963. As a result Public Safety Commissioner Goldman was removed from office by the new administration and on January 2, 1964 replaced by Republican Daniel F. McMahon as

P.S.C. Frank E. Vescio (cont.)

the new commissioner.

One of McMahon's first changes was on January 29, 1964 when he appointed Vescio as a Detective Captain and as the commanding officer of the Detective Division at the salary of $10,400, which included an extra stipend of $400. Years later McMahon would be quoted as saying of Vescio's new assignment, "*Because he was considered a 'whistle blower' he wasn't the most popular man in the department, but he did prove to be hardworking, eager, and resourceful*." McMahon's next change was to replace Capt. Henry Stampur, who had been serving as an aide to Commissioner Goldman, with Lt. George Rusnack who came highly recommended and was a Columbia College graduate.

Even before Commissioner McMahon came into office the Yonkers Police Department's Chief of Police position had been vacant since 1947 following the death of then Chief William Kruppenbacher. This, even though there was a position of Chief of Police called for in the city charter. The previous commissioner, Milton Goldman, had refused to even call for a test. The result was a successful lawsuit which required the appointment of a Chief of Police. Following a civil service exam, Capt. Polsen was the only one to pass. It was at that time McMahon, a Republican, appointed William F. Polsen, a democrat, as the new Police Chief. When asked why he chose Bill Polsen McMahon simply replied, "He was the best man for the job."

Nevertheless, Vescio was outraged and claimed that the test was "rigged" by the democratic city leader Tom Brogan. As previously pointed out, Frank Vescio was no "shrinking violet" when it came to saying what was on his mind. Regardless of the resulting turmoil.

On Nov 19, 1964 then Det Capt. Vescio submitted a request in writing to be allowed to attend the 75th session of the FBI National Academy. In his request he outlined his previous training along with the fact that, at that time he was an instructor, one evening a week, at the Mt Vernon NY Adult Education Program, and had lectured at the Chrysler Training Corp. for FBI conducted schools. Despite his efforts, his request was never acted upon.

In an example of Vescio's determination to be nonpolitical, no matter the cost, in early 1965 he was nominated and awarded the "Citizen of The Year" award from the Yonkers Citizen Union. However he later reconsidered accepting the award because he felt it might appear that as a Detective Captain his law enforcement efforts might be compromised. As a result, on April 9, 1965 he sent a letter to the Citizen Union explaining his position and concluded saying, "I reluctantly must refuse to accept your award."

When Public Safety Commissioner McMahon left office at the end of 1967 to take the position of Westchester County Sheriff, a search was conducted to identify a competent replacement. It was later reported that Capt. Vescio was to be the man that would replace McMahon. On January 16, 1968 Frank Vescio, a civil service captain of police, took a one-year leave of absence from the police department and was appointed to the position of Commissioner of Public Safety, placing him in command of not only the police department, but the Fire Dept. as well. As Commissioner his annual salary jumped to $18,550 from his detective captains pay of $14,500. After taking the oath of office Vescio pledged himself to his office and to the effective work of his predecessor, Sheriff McMahon. Vescio was described as an honest, hard hitting, effective cop by then District Attorney Carl Vergari.

On December 11, 1969, by GO# 196, Comm. Vescio, after having completed two, one year leaves

P.S.C. Frank E. Vescio (cont.)

of absence, and in order not to lose his police pension benefit, returned "on paper only" to the rank of captain and submitted his request to retire as a police captain. At that same time he changed from enrollment in the NYS Police and Fire Pension system to the NYS Civil Service Employees Pension System. However, he remained in the civilian position of Public Safety Commissioner. Politics being what it is, there was a constant political fight to determine whether Commissioner Vescio should continue in this position or be replaced by someone else. It was alleged by a few that the pressure to replace Vescio was the result of his tireless efforts against gambling and other organized criminal activity in the city. To his credit Vescio was successful in retaining his position through the end of 1971.

After 33 years in public life, Comm. Vescio submitted his letter of resignation to City Manager Seymore Scher on Jan. 14, 1972 and he began his retirement.

Det. Steve Kogan was assigned to assist Commissioner Vescio in clearing out his office and then drove him home. Kogan reportedly said, "*He was a gentleman during the whole ordeal. He had nothing unkind to say about anyone. He was a professional. I also worked for him as a detective for several years and he was a respected boss. Under his command, we got the job done. He served well!*"

Frank Vescio loved Golfing. In fact from 1946 to 1950 he was the Captain of the Yonkers Police Golfing Team and Industrial Golf League. In 1947 and 1948 was the Westchester County Police Champion of the Westchester Police Golf Assoc; In 1953 he was the Yonkers City Amateur Champion with the Amateur Golf Assoc; and was past President of the Sprain Valley Golf Association.

Frank Vescio was a member of the Italian City Club, a charter member of the Enrico Fermi Educational Fund, and a member of the Exchange Club of Yonkers. He was also a member of the Yonkers Community Planning Council. In 1965 he was awarded the Policeman of The Year award from the Exchange Club, and in October of 1967 was awarded National Police Officer of the Month by "Master Detective Magazine." That same month he was awarded the Policeman of the Year award by the Yonkers Fire Officers Association. In 1967 he co-authored a book entitled "Community Cooperation Conquers Crime" for the Exchange Club. For his work on this project he was awarded a Commendation by then Gov. Nelson Rockefeller and the NY State Assembly.

After retirement Frank worked at his son William's construction business and in 1977 he made an unsuccessful run for the Westchester County Board of Legislators. Lt Gov. Alfred DelBello, who was mayor during Vescio's tenure was quoted as saying, "*He did his job, and he did his job well. But from time to time he got involved with politics with the city council. And the city council would love him or hate him, depending on what week it was.*"

Frank Vescio was very mechanically inclined, and according to his children he patented a road "Line Marking Machine" in the 1950's and also made several types of burglar alarms systems. Though a strict police disciplinarian, his children said he was a great family man. He played the harmonica to his children when they were young, a tradition he continued with his 11 grandchildren. His favorite way of passing time was to play golf, drive golf balls at the driving range, or walk around the lake at Bear Mountain Park.

Former Detective Captain and Public Safety Commissioner Frank E. Vescio died on August 28, 2003 after a long illness. He was 87 years old.

DET. JOHN M. HEENAN# 644

APPOINTED: November 16, 1939
RETIRED: April 1, 1976

A recognized fingerprint expert later in his career, John Heenan was born in the City of New York on June 12, 1913. He attended St. Jerome's Elementary School in the Bronx, and graduated from All Hallows High School in NYC. He also later listed that he was a graduate of the Institute of Applied Science. As a young man John gained employment as a gas and electric meter reader.

After taking and passing the exam for police officer, John Heenan was appointed to the Yonkers Police Department, from 911 McLean Avenue, on November 16, 1939 at the annual salary of $1,940. Following his recruit training his first assignment was patrol duty in the 4th precinct. During his first year on patrol John worked in an undercover capacity investigating illegal slot machines and conducting investigations of illegal liquor use along with the Detective Bureau personnel. John must have impressed his superiors because in just over a year he was advanced to the position of Detective on March 1, 1941, with an increase in salary of $200. It was at this time that he was assigned to the Bureau of Criminal Identification. (BCI)

On March 7, 1947 it was announced by Deputy Public Safety Commissioner, Detective Lieut. William Comey, that the BCI was going to adopt a 16 hour a day work schedule. And that detective Heenan would be one of three men assigned to this working chart and be on call for the late tour if needed. Over the next few years Detective Heenan would work both in BCI and the general assignment chart in the Detective Bureau. On April 4, 1949 after taking an examination conducted by the Federal Communications Commission, Heenan received a radio telephone, 2nd class operator's license. From this time forward, although assigned to the BC I, he was ordered to substitute for the radio superintendent during his absence for all repairs and adjustments to the radio communication system. However, as the years passed John Heenan became recognized as an expert in crime scene fingerprint identification throughout the metropolitan area. He was also a crime scene investigator taking photographs and searching for evidence at crime scenes.

In 1974, although detective Heenan preferred working in the radio repair section he was named supervising detective in the Bureau of Criminal Identification due to his years of experience in fingerprinting, photography, etc. Detective Heenan remained in BCI right up to his retirement on April 1, 1976.

Retired Detective John Heenan, a resident of 67 Borcher Ave., died on January 17, 1997. He was 83 years old.

PO BERNARD LIPINSKI #68

APPOINTED: December 1, 1939
RESIGNED: January 31, 1946

Bernard Lipinski was born on August 26, 1911 in the city of Yonkers. He attended local schools graduating from Commerce High School and later was employed as a superintendent of construction for a local contractor. Bernie Lipinsky was appointed to the YPD from 124 Park Ave. on Dec. 1, 1939 and was assigned to patrol in the 3rd pct. On Aug. 11, 1940, with only 9 months as a police officer, Lipinski arrested a career burglar at gunpoint in the rear of 157 Richie Drive at 12:30 in the morning. An attempt to escape by the suspect was ended when Lipinsky fired a warning shot. Chief Quirk complemented the officer on a fine job and Lipinski was later awarded a Certificate of Excellent Police Work. On February 19, 1941, Lipinski was granted a leave of absence from the YPD due to his induction into the US Army, under provisions of the US Selective Service Act. About that time, the government apparently made the decision that men 28 years or older should not be drafted and as such on October 15, 1941, Lipinski was honorably discharged and was reinstated as a Yonkers police officer on October 16, 1941. Following his honorable discharge from the Army, after only 8 months, on January 5, 1942 officer Lipinski was authorized to begin writing a series of articles for the Herald Statesman newspaper on the life of a soldier from Lipinsky's perspective; even if only experienced for 8 months. An ardent photographer and a member of the Yonkers Camera Club, he took most of the pictures that appeared with his articles. However on January 23, 1942 Lipinski was recalled into the Army and again received an indefinite leave of absence from the YPD. While in the Army, Lipinski continued to submit stories to the Herald statesman, on his experiences during the war. Following the end of WW-II, there is no police record indicating Lipinski received an honorable discharge, or was reinstated to the Police Department. It is possible that he decided to remain in the military, because on January 31, 1946 it is known that Lipinski submitted his letter of resignation to the Yonkers Police Department. Bernard Lipinski died on February 13, 2001 in Venice, Florida where he lived.

PO GILBERT J. WINN #98

APPOINTED: December 16, 1939
RESIGNED: September 30, 1953

Gilbert J. Winn Jr. was born in Yonkers on March 4, 1910. After a few short term jobs, Winn was hired by the Yonkers Police Department to the temporary position of Police Hostler on July 16, 1933. One year later, on August 16, 1934, Winn was appointed a Jailer in the Yonkers City Jail. With a desire to be a policeman Winn took the civil service test, passed it, and on December 16, 1939 was appointed a police patrolman and was assigned to the 4th precinct. Eight years later, on September 1, 1947 he was reassigned to the 3rd precinct. Then, with no reason given and with nearly 14 years seniority as a police officer, and a total of 20 years service, officer Gilbert Winn Jr. submitted his resignation to the Yonkers Police Department on September 30, 1953. He moved his family to Florida where, on May 15, 1964 Gilbert Winn reportedly died. He was 54.

PO ROBERT E. ROHAN Sr #76

APPOINTED: December 16, 1939
RETIRED: April 2, 1975

Robert E. Rohan was born in the town of Haverstraw, NY on Oct. 5, 1914. When young Bob was only four years old the family moved to Yonkers to 1 Jones Pl. Bob attended St. Joseph's school and graduated from Saunders H.S. As a young man he reportedly gained employment as a tunnel worker. On Dec. 16, 1939 Bob Rohan was appointed to the YPD with a salary of $1,940 and was assigned to patrol duties in the 3rd pct. It was nearly 3 years later when, on Sept. 24, 1942, Rohan was transferred to duty in the 1st pct. Bob was very active with fraternal activities in the YPD. In the early 1940s he was a member of the YPD singing Glea Club, a member of the PBA basketball team, and he often served in the YPD color guard. He also was a member of the PBA, the Police Holy Name Society, and the International Police Association. On Jan. 1, 1951 Rohan was reassigned to duty in the 2nd pct. Bob received a break from patrol duty when on June 13, 1955 he was transferred to the Communications Division as a switchboard and telephone operator. But once again he was returned to the 2nd precinct on May 16, 1960. The father of 9 children, Bob always worked two jobs throughout his career. Officer Rohan retired from the YPD on April 2, 1975 while living at 129 Convent Pl. He would later move to Morningside Avenue. Of his nine children, his daughter Sharon also served and retired as a YPD police officer. A son, Bob Jr, was appointed a YPD police cadet briefly in 1967 but left 4 months later to seek employment elsewhere. Bob's half-brother was former retired Capt. John McCormack, and his son-in-law, husband to his daughter Sharon, was retired Deputy Chief John F. McMahon. After many years in retirement Bob moved to the town of Pine Beach in Toms River NJ, near his son Bob Jr. It was here, on February 14, 1993, that retired police officer Robert Rohan died. He was 78 years old.

SGT. ROBERT E. FOODY #6

APPOINTED: December 16, 1939
RETIRED: September 3, 1968

Bob Foody, whose family reportedly emigrated from County Sligo, Ireland, was born June 29, 1914 in the Bronx, New York. As a youth he moved with his family to Yonkers and attended PS# 16, Gorton and Saunders high schools. Many years later on January 18, 1964 he would obtain his high school equivalency diploma. As a young man Bob listed his employment as a "Color Chemist." On December 16, 1939 Bob was hired by the Yonkers Police Department with a salary of $1,940 a year and was assigned to the 3rd precinct. Having earlier been trained as a certified first-aid instructor, Bob was transferred from the 3rd precinct to the 1st precinct to work in the Emergency Services Unit. On November 20, 1942, due to his enlistment in the Army Air Corps, Bob received an indefinite leave of absence from the Police Department. During World War II he served as a Lieutenant flight leader in the 101st Screaming Eagles Glider Squadron. It was said by friends that he was one of the Glider troops that landed during the invasion of Normandy during the war. Foody was honorably discharged from the Army on November 28, 1945 and returned to the YPD in the 1st precinct on December 1, 1945. On September 1, 1947 Bob was promoted to the rank of Sergeant along with 8 other war veterans and he was assigned to the 4th precinct with the new salary of $3,400. Two years later he would receive his dream assignment. On May 1, 1949 he was reassigned to the Traffic Division's Motorcycle Unit. This was a perfect fit for Bob since he had been riding motorcycles since he was 14 years old and loved riding. Sgt. Foody was a certified motorcycle operator and instructor, had a commercial pilot's license, gliders pilots license, and was an aircraft engine ground instructor. Sgt. Bob Foody remained in the Traffic Division for 19 years and retired on September 3, 1968. Following his retirement he moved to St. Petersburg Florida where he continued to ride his personal motorcycle right up to a short time before his death on May 24, 1993. He was 78 years old.

SGT. JOSEPH V. DOOLITTY #62

APPOINTED: December 16, 1939
RETIRED: July 24, 1969

Joseph V. Doolitty was born in the City of Yonkers on October 31, 1912. He attended St. Mary's elementary school and graduated from Yonkers High School. While in school he was known as "Duke." After graduation Joe worked on the auto assembly line for General Motors in Tarrytown New York. However, wanting more job security, Joe was appointed to the Yonkers Police Department on December 16, 1939 with a starting salary of $1,940. At the time he was living at 82 Hamilton Ave. and was assigned to the 2nd precinct. Over the years Joe was moved several times; on November 16, 1945 to the 3rd precinct, January 1, 1951 to the 1st precinct, and October 16, 1952 to the 3rd precinct. Then on June 3, 1958 police officer Joe Doolitty was promoted to the rank of sergeant with the new salary of $5,935 a year. He was assigned as a patrol supervisor in the 1st precinct. On July 17, 1961 Sgt Doolitty was assigned to the Juvenile Aid Bureau, but on December 15, 1962 he was reassigned back to the 2nd precinct. A resident of 29 Morris St., Sgt. Joe Doolitty retired from the police department on July 24, 1969. Thirty one years later retired Sgt. Joseph Doolitty died on May 28, 2000. He was 87 years old.

SGT. FREDERICK CONNOLLY #13

APPOINTED: December 16, 1939
RETIRED: August 23, 1973

Fred Connolly was born in the city of Yonkers on March 22, 1913 to Yonkers police Captain Edward Connolly, who was a lieutenant at that time. A graduate of Gorton H.S. Fred went on to work as an auto mechanic and later as a "special patrolman." Fred was hired to the Yonkers Police Dept. on December 16, 1939 with a salary of $1,940 a year, and was assigned patrol duty in the 1st precinct on Wells Avenue. Fred's appearance was a stark contrast to his father. His dad was a husky, larger than life man, and Fred's build was very thin and wiry. On November 2, 1944 the Public Safety Commissioner brought him up on charges, along with several other officers and the Chief of Police, for allegedly covering up a gambling operation. The charges were all dismissed. Fred was appointed a Detective on January 1, 1951 and worked with his partner, Det. Al Hoffarth. However, on October 16, 1952 Connolly was transferred back to patrol in the 4th precinct. He was promoted to Sergeant on August 28, 1963 and remained in the 4th precinct. On October 6, 1972 Fred, better known behind his back as "scratch," was detailed as supervisor of the Police Repair Shop and it's mechanic's. Sgt. Fred Connolly retired on August 23, 1973 and died September 26, 1978. He was 65 years old.

DET. CAPTAIN ALEXANDER REID

APPOINTED: December 16, 1939
RETIRED: April 26, 1974

Alexander Reid was born in the City of Yonkers on August 3, 1915, and attended public school # 23, Ben Franklin Jr. H.S., and graduated from Commerce High School. As a young man he worked at several miscellaneous jobs, including that of a mail clerk, until he took the civil service test for police officer in the City of Yonkers New York. He was appointed to the Yonkers Police Dept. on December 16, 1939 with a salary of $1,940 a year. His first assignment following recruit training was patrol in the 3rd precinct located at 36 Radford Street. Being a very athletic young man, during the early part of the 1940's he played on the PBA basketball team.

On November 3, 1942, while still assigned to the 3rd precinct, officer Reid enlisted in the Naval Reserve. He was granted an indefinite leave of absence by the police department and served throughout World War II with the Naval Shore Patrol. Reid received his honorable discharge on March 9, 1946 and was reinstated to the YPD on March 16, 1946 at the salary of $2,875. He was returned to patrol duty in the 3rd precinct.

One can only assume that officer Reid impressed his supervisors with his work because on November 16, 1947 he was transferred from the 3rd precinct to the Detective Division earning the new

Det. Capt. Alexander Reid (cont.)

Salary of $3,100 a year. On May 1, 1948 Detective Reid and his partner investigated the shooting death of a woman at 57 Manhattan Ave. The woman's husband claimed the shooting was an accident. However, following his investigation Detective Reid subsequently arrested the husband and charged him with murder. Despite having an excellent record as a detective, as often is the case, Alex Reid was reassigned back to the 3rd precinct once again on May 1, 1949.

Having ranked # 1 on the civil service test for police Sergeant, on August 1, 1952 officer Reid, a resident of 78 Hamilton Ave., was promoted to the rank of Sergeant by being sworn in at City Hall by Public Safety Commissioner Milton Goldman and was assigned as a patrol supervisor in the 3rd precinct. His new salary was $4,200 per year.

Once again Sgt. Reid was successful when he took the civil service test for police Lieutenant and on August 17, 1955 he was promoted to the rank of Lieutenant and was reassigned from the 3rd precinct to the 4th precinct serving as a desk officer. The salary for a police lieutenant at that time was $5,600 a year. Lt. Reid was moved to desk duty in the 2nd precinct on January 17, 1958, but two years later on March 16, 1960 he was once again returned to the Detective Division as a Detective Lieutenant earning $7,690 a year.

On November 20, 1963 Lt. Reid received his promotion to the rank of Captain of police, receiving a salary of $9,250 a year, and was assigned to the 1st precinct as the commanding officer. However despite his assignment to the 1st precinct, he was detailed as commanding officer of the Detective Division. On November 7, 1966 he was moved to command the 2nd precinct for two years but, on January 18, 1968, Reid was again designated Detective Captain of the Bureau, replacing then Det. Captain Frank Vescio who took a leave of absence to take the job of Public Safety Commissioner. By now Reid's salary had climbed to $13,750.

Beginning on February 3, 1969 through 1971 Capt. Reid commanded the 3rd, 4th, 1st, and again the 4th precinct. Then on October 19, 1971 he was placed in command of the Special Operations Division (SOD), consisting of the Traffic Division, for eight months, and on June 30, 1972 was again placed in command of the Detective Division.

On April 26, 1974 Det. Captain Alexander Reid, known more commonly as "Alec," of "Addie" retired from the Yonkers Police Department. Alex Reid died on October 22, 1993. He was 78.

PO PAUL H. LANE #26

APPOINTED: December 16, 1939
RESIGNED: April 10, 1951

Paul Lane was born Oct 29, 1912 in McAdoo, Pa., his birth name being Paul H. Sokolowsky. Many years later, after moving to Yonkers, he attended local Grammar school and would legally change his surname to LANE. Paul worked as a Textile Weaver with the Alexander Smith Carpet Factory. On December 16, 1939, while residing at 28 Livingston Avenue, Lane was appointed to the YPD and assigned to the 3rd precinct. On April 1, 1941 he was granted an indefinite leave of absence from the YPD due to induction into the Army. He served as a Sergeant in the Pacific during WW-2 and was honorably discharged on Oct. 24, 1945 and re-instated to the YPD on Nov. 16, 1945. On Nov. 2, 1949 PO Lane was elected PBA Trustee of the 3rd precinct by his fellow officers and in 1951 he was elected as the 1st pct. trustee where he was then assigned. Following the police surgeon's recommendation officer Lane received a six months leave of absence without pay and two months into this leave, on April 10, 1951, for unknown reasons PO Paul Lane submitted his resignation from the YPD. A resident of 185 Bretton Road, Paul H. Lane died in August of 1966 leaving a wife, two daughters, and two grandsons. He was only 53.

LT. ROBERT C. MARTIN

APPOINTED: December 16, 1939
RETIRED: January 9, 1976

Bob Martin was born in Yonkers on Colgate Avenue on August 20, 1913. He attended Public Schools # 7 and # 23, and graduated from Yonkers H.S. where he was an excellent softball player. Bob attended Northwestern University for six months but missed his family and returned home. He then attended Pace College in NYC where he received a degree in Accounting. He worked a short while for Esso Oil Co and before the YPD he worked in the Alexander Smith Carpet Shop in the Accounting Dept., along with his brother Wesley. Bob was hired to the YPD on December 16, 1939 with a salary of $1,940 and was assigned to the 1st pct. On April 16, 1946 he was assigned to motorcycle duty in the Traffic Division. Having a good singing voice Bob served in the YPD Glea Club in these early years. Following the reopening of a few precincts that had been previously closed in a cost saving move, on October 16, 1952 Martin was promoted to Sergeant and sent to the 4th precinct. However, on June 16, 1955 he was returned to the Traffic Division. Sgt Martin was promoted to Lieutenant on July 1, 1956 and assigned as a desk officer in the 1st pct. Lt Martin returned to Traffic as the executive officer on July 1, 1958 and was designated it's commanding officer on October 19, 1971. Robert Martin, whose brother was Det Lt Wesley Martin, retired from the YPD on January 9, 1976 and died on October 20, 1982. He was 69.

DEPUTY CHIEF HENRY L. STAMPUR

APPOINTED: December 16, 1939
RETIRED: January 19, 1979

Henry Louis Stampur was born on August 7, 1917 in a house on Parker Street; a house where Mulford Gardens would later be built. He graduated from St. Casimir's school and from Gorton H.S. where, being very athletic and standing 6' 2" tall, he was a member and captain of the All City Basketball Team. After holding down a few miscellaneous jobs including as a letter carrier with the Post Office, Henry applied to the Yonkers Police Department from 29 Cedar St. and was appointed a patrolman on December 16, 1939 with a starting salary of $1,940 a year. His first assignment was foot patrol in the 2nd precinct in East Yonkers. During this time he also played on the PBA basketball team. Just over 2 years following his police appointment Henry was drafted into the US Army on May 16, 1942 following America's entry into World War II. Like many others like him the Police Department granted him an indefinite leave of absence so that he could serve his country. It was reported that he served with distinction in the infantry; first as an enlisted man and later, after attending Officer Candidate school, as an officer. It was said that he served in Germany and France with the 112th Infantry Regiment. Stampur was said to have seen a great deal of combat and was said to have participated in the Battle of the Bulge. Among the several medals that he received during his war years were the Purple Heart, Bronze Star and Silver Star.

Deputy Chief Henry L. Stampur (cont.)

Henry didn't speak much about the war after he returned but he told his wife on one occasion about an incident that changed his outlook on life. He told her he was in combat in a foxhole and asked another soldier to take his post while he took a break away for a cigarette. Right after he took the break the soldier that replaced him was killed by an exploding shell in that foxhole. It could have been Stampur. Stampur was honorably discharged from the Army with the rank of Captain on October 2, 1945 and returned to the 2nd precinct in the Yonkers Police Department on October 16, 1945. On November 11, 1945, Armistice Day, the YPD War Veterans Legion, of which Stampur was a member, held an installation of officer's dinner dance to install newly elected officers. Stampur was installed as a trustee on that date.

On May 20, 1947 the Yonkers Civil Service Commission certified the names of twelve veterans for promotion to sergeant. Eight were disabled veterans and four were regular veterans. Henry Stampur was designated a disabled war veteran. Following the veterans preference law, PO Stampur, along with the eight other veterans, was promoted to the rank of sergeant on September 1, 1947 with a salary of $3,400 a year and he was assigned as a patrol supervisor in the 3rd precinct at 36 Radford Street. On May 1, 1949 he was transferred from the 3rd precinct to the 1st precinct.

Following the re-opening of all 4 police precincts, two of which had been closed since January 1951, Sgt. Stampur was promoted to the rank of police Lieutenant on October 16, 1952 with a new annual salary of $4,800 a year. As a new Lieutenant he was assigned as a desk officer in the 1st precinct on Wells Avenue. Being a well-liked and soft-spoken man, Lieutenant Stampur was honored when a large number of members within the department organized a testimonial dinner at Alex and Henry's restaurant in Eastchester on November 29, 1952 in recognition of his promotion to lieutenant. Beginning on February 19, 1956 through April 2, 1956 Lt. Stampur was detailed for special training at the New York State Police school in Troy New York. When the Traffic Division's commanding officer, Bill Polsen, was on a leave of absence to attend specialized training, Lt. Stamper was detailed to the Traffic Division to serve as their temporary commanding officer. This detail ran from September 8, 1956 to June 24, 1957. On January 16, 1958 Lt. Stamper was appointed a Detective Lieutenant and was detailed to the Public Safety Commissioner's office. He remained there until January 1, 1959 when he was promoted to the rank of captain with a salary of $7,310 a year and was named commanding officer of the 1st precinct.

Whenever the need arose Lt. Stamper served as an instructor for newly hired police recruits who, after their appointment, were trained at the Naval reserve building on Alexander Street. In 1956 Lt. Stamper was appointed assistant director of in-service training for the New York State Police training program. And he was a graduate of the joint FBI/Sheriff's Department school of police administration in 1964.

By 1963 Lt. Stampur had again been serving as the aide to Public Safety Commissioner Milton Goldman in City Hall. However, following the city elections and the change of administration, Stampur was removed from that position in January of 1964 by the new Public Safety Commissioner Daniel F. McMahon, who chose his own aide.

On December 16, 1964 he and several other members of YPD were honored by receiving a plaque from the PBA in recognition of 25 years service. Over the next few years Capt. Stampur was reassigned to several different commands as the commanding officer, i.e. August 23, 1965 1st precinct, November 7, 1966 4th the precinct, February 8, 1968 3rd precinct, October 1, 1968 2nd precinct, February 7, 1969

Deputy Chief Henry L. Stampur (cont.)

Records Division, February 2, 1970 3rd precinct, and May 14, 1970 4th precinct.

On December 1, 1970 the Public Safety Commissioner decided that it would be more efficient and economical to centralize the entire police department by closing 3 of the 4 police precincts. Only the 4th precinct would remain open and all operations would be coordinated through that one building and its command officer. Capt. Stampur was chosen to be that officer. Within a month, it has been reported, the control of the men and the overwhelming flow of paperwork through one central location made that new plan unworkable. It was then that effective January 1, 1971, a month later, that they opened a second police building. The former 4th precinct was renamed the North patrol command and the former 2nd precinct was renamed the South patrol command. The 1st precinct, now located at 730 E. Grassy Sprain Rd., remained open but only as a muster location. The 3rd precinct operated in the same way as the 1st precinct under this revised plan.

On June 30, 1972 Capt. Stampur was placed in command of the Special Operations Division. And then on April 24, 1974 Capt. Stampur was assigned to the Detective Division as a Detective Captain in command.

July 1, 1977 was the date that Capt. Stampur reached the pinnacle of his career. It was then that he was appointed a Deputy Chief of Police earning a new salary of $27,000 a year. Chief Stampur was placed in command of the Field Services Bureau in charge of all patrol operations and all the patrol command's in the city.

Upon his retirement, on January 19, 1979 Chief Stampur was given a testimonial dinner, which drew a large attendance, where he was presented with a City of Yonkers Proclamation of merit from Mayor Angelo Martinelli; a large plaque with all his police shields that he had worn were attached, and an artist's drawing, done by then Lt Ben Ermini, depicting Chief Stampur in some flamboyant uniform and standing in front of a castle named, "YPD." The drawing was entitled the "Polish Prince."

During his long career he had commanded all Divisions of the YPD except the Youth Services Division. His personnel folder reflected numerous citations from the Department and from various Civic groups for outstanding performance during his long career. He and Lt Bob Martin were brothers-in-law. Stampur's sister Cecelia married Lt. Bob Martin

On February 14, 1983 Retired Chief Stampur, of 128 Van Cortland Park Avenue, was taking a walk on Valentine's day to pick up a card for his wife when he suffered a heart attack and died. He was 65 years old.

LT. EUGENE A. REYNOLDS

APPOINTED: December 16, 1939
RETIRED: March 23, 1972

Eugene A. Reynolds was born in the city of Yonkers on August 23, 1911. "Gene," as he was known, attended both Sacred Heart parochial elementary, and high school, from which he graduated. On an early employment application he listed his previous occupation as an "information clerk." After passing all required civil service examinations for police Patrolman, Gene Reynolds was appointed to the Yonkers Police Department on December 16, 1939 at $1,940 a year and was assigned to patrol duty in the 2nd precinct. On November 15, 1941 officer Reynolds was transferred to the Traffic Division on foot directing vehicular traffic at various intersections. However, due to his previous clerical experience he was actually detailed to the police chief's office for a short while as an administrative aide. A year later on October 21, 1942 he was reassigned to patrol duty in the 3rd precinct. Five years later, on August 1, 1947, Reynolds was again assigned to the Traffic Division but served only as the division's clerk. Police officer Reynolds was assigned to the Training and Records Division in headquarters on July 1, 1951 performing administrative duties. He remained working in headquarters even when he was promoted to Sergeant on November 16, 1960, and still remained there when promoted to Lieutenant on July 2, 1965. Gene was still assigned in headquarters when he retired on March 23, 1972. Retired Lieutenant Eugene Reynolds moved to Elizaville, NY where, on December 17, 1975, he died in a Rhinebeck NY hospital. He was 64 years old.

PO AMBROSE VANTASSEL #141

APPOINTED: December 30, 1939
RETIRED: May 3, 1973

Ambrose VanTassel was born at 54 Linden St. in the City of Yonkers on July 15, 1911. A few years later the family moved to 94 Linden St. where Ambrose began attending Benjamin Franklin Jr. H.S. and graduated from Yonkers High School. As a young man he worked as a truck driver in the tri-state area and also worked on the docks in NYC for several years. Another job he held was as a special patrolman on a local golf course. He then started a new job driving the trolley cars in Yonkers. His regular route was from the south city line to the northern most part of Nepperhan Avenue. According to his son Paul, his Dad said it was an okay job at the time but working the night shift was very boring. As a young man Ambrose would spend his spare time in the State armory on No. Broadway where his father was the Armorer and cook in the Army Reserves.

While living at 100 McLean Avenue VanTassel was appointed to the Yonkers Police Department on December 30, 1939 with an annual salary of $1,940 a year. Following his recruit training officer VanTassel was assigned to the 1st patrol precinct on Wells Avenue. Having a good singing voice, in 1943 he was a member of the Yonkers P.D. singing Glea Club. And he continued working down at the docks after he finished working midnights on the police department. VanTassel worked a combination of foot and radio car patrol for 8 years in the 1st precinct and on September 1, 1947 he was transferred to patrol duty in the 2nd precinct at 441 Central Park Ave. Every summer his dad would take the entire family to a rented cabin on Lake Saint Catherine in Vermont. When Ambrose wasn't working and had a little time he would enjoy bowling with friends. He was an avid bowler and spent many hours at the CYO bowling.

Three years after being assigned to the 2nd precinct Ambrose was once again returned to patrol duty in the 1st precinct on January 1, 1951. However, it was just two years before he was again returned to the 2nd precinct on February 16, 1953. This time officer VanTassel would spend seven years in a radio car in the 2nd precinct before he was reassigned to patrol duty in the 3rd precinct on February 3, 1960. "Ambie," as he was known to friends, was assigned to the Headquarters Command Division on January 1, 1971 and his duties were listed as Community Relations. This assignment didn't last very long, because on August 24th of that same year he was transferred back to patrol duty in what was now the South patrol command at 441 Central Park Ave. This transfer back to patrol duty was no doubt the result of VanTassel's own request to go back on patrol. Anyone who knew or worked with him knew that he was not a desk type person. In fact he was one tough cop who took no nonsense from the criminal element.

But, once again officer VanTassel was returned to headquarters on December 20, 1971 assigned to the Records, Service and Maintenance Division. He would remain there right up to his retirement on May 3, 1973. Retired police officer Ambrose VanTassel, father of two Yonkers police officers, Paul and Kenneth, and a charter member of the former Yonkers Police St. George Society, died on December 1, 1982. He was 71 years old.

CAPTAIN JOHN J. McCARTHY -5

APPOINTED: December 30, 1939
DIED: November 14, 1969

John Joseph McCarthy was born in the City of Yonkers on January 22, 1917. His father John J. McCarthy Sr. would later rise to the rank of Yonkers police Captain, and his grandfather, John McCarthy was a retired NYPD Lieutenant. Young John McCarthy attended St. Mary's parochial elementary school, Manhattan preparatory school in New York City, and Manhattan College in New York City from 1931 to 1935.

Having a father and grandfather in law enforcement, there was never a doubt that John would follow in their footsteps with a police career. And so it was that on December 30, 1939 John Joseph McCarthy, a resident of 121 Elliott Ave., was appointed a Yonkers police officer with a salary of $1,940 a year and was assigned to foot patrol in the 4th precinct at 53 Shonnard Pl. When he was appointed he was one of five members of the department with the exact same name. In order to avoid confusion in written orders and mail, each had a number attached after their name. Number one going to the most senior McCarthy; #3 was given to his father, and he was designated McCarthy #5

Just prior to the United States entry into World War II McCarthy was inducted into the Army and received an indefinite leave of absence from the police department on November 6, 1941. Upon his entry into the Army Private McCarthy was sent for training first to Camp Upton, then to Fort Bragg, N.C.

Capt. John J. McCarthy-5 (cont.)

where he was attached to the Field artillery. After completing a course in the operation of the machine gun he was eventually promoted to Corporal and later to Sergeant. Sgt McCarthy was then moved to the Military Police at Fort Bragg and was selected to attend Officer Candidate School (OCS) at Ft. Oglethorpe, Ga. On October 14, 1942 it was reported that McCarthy had graduated from OCS as a 2nd Lieutenant and was reportedly the first Yonkers police officer to obtain a Commission while in the military. McCarthy would eventually attain the rank of Major serving as an Intelligence Officer in the U.S., Australia, Alaska, and New Guinea. He was said to hold a Top Secret Clearance.

McCarthy was honorably discharged from the Army and re-instated to the police department on December 1, 1945 and returned to duty in the 4th precinct. But he remained a reserve officer in the Army Reserve. On December 22, 1946 at 1:52 AM at a fire at 3 Dudley Place, McCarthy suffered smoke inhalation when he entered a burning building by crawling on his knees and rescued several residents who were trapped in the building. He was later commended for his actions. On February 1, 1950 McCarthy was transferred to the Traffic Division on traffic duty. However on March 16, 1951while still in the Traffic Division and still an Army Reserve officer, McCarthy was activated to active duty to serve in Korea during that conflict.

On October 16, 1952 McCarthy was promoted to the rank of police Sergeant at $4,500 a year, even though he was still on active duty in the Army. He was released from active duty and reinstated to the YPD on February 1, 1954 and was assigned to the 2nd precinct as a patrol supervisor.

A resident of 68 Livingston Avenue Sgt McCarthy received his promotion to the rank of Lieutenant on September 1, 1955 with the salary of $5,600 a year and, although assigned to the 1st pct. was utilized as a "floating" lieutenant in whatever precinct needed a desk officer. On May 22, 1963 McCarthy was promoted to the rank of Captain at $9,450 a year and was placed in command of the Communications & Records Division in headquarters. Then, on November 7, 1966 Captain McCarthy, often referred to as "Junior McCarthy," was placed in command of the 1st precinct. On June 14, 1968 Capt. McCarthy was placed in command of the Records Service & Maintenance Division in headquarters at 10 St. Casimir Avenue. It was during this time that the department instituted a police River Patrol with and old obsolete boat. The captain was also in charge of that new project which lasted only a few months and the boat became unsafe and the entire program was scuttled.

Four months later, on November 16, 1968 he was placed in command of the 4th precinct, and on February 7, 1969 re-assigned to the 1st precinct located in the headquarters building.

A resident of 21 Boxwood Drive, on November 14, 1969 Capt. McCarthy was off duty in his car at 3:22 AM at the intersection of Central Park Avenue and Balint Drive, when he lost control of his vehicle, crashed into another vehicle, and was killed instantly. Captain John J. McCarthy -5 was only 52 years old.

LT. WILLIAM T. WARNOCK

APPOINTED: December 30, 1939
RETIRED: March 26, 1965

William Thomas Warnock was born in the City of Yonkers on April 20, 1916. He attended local public schools and graduated from Yonkers H.S. in 1933. Following his schooling Bill worked for several years in the Alexander Smith factory in Yonkers as a clerk. As a resident of 500 Van Cortland Park Ave., Bill was appointed to the Yonkers Police Department on December 30, 1939 with the annual salary of $1,940 a year. His first assignment was patrol duty in the 1st precinct located at Wells and Woodworth Avenues. Having a good singing voice it wasn't long before Bill joined the Police Department's singing Glea club.

Just prior to the United States entry into World War 2 Bill Warnock was inducted into the Army on August 8, 1941 and was granted an indefinite leave of absence from the Police Department. Bill served in the Army's Criminal Investigation Branch during the war on the Mexican border and in New Guinea. He received his honorable discharge on November 5, 1945 holding the rank of staff sergeant, and was reinstated to the YPD in the 1st precinct on December 1, 1945 at the salary of $2,406. While residing at 28 Wolfe St., on June 1, 1947, officer Warnock was promoted to the rank of Sergeant by utilizing his disabled veterans preference and with his salary rising to $3,400 a year. This special preference, which no longer exists in civil service law, allowed all disabled veterans to move right to the top of the promotional list ahead of all non-veterans. As a new patrol sergeant he was transferred from the 1st precinct to duty in the 2nd precinct at 441 Central Park Ave. During 1947 Bill played on the Yonkers police softball team in a police league which competed against other police departments throughout Westchester County.

Being a war veteran Warnock was a member of the fraternal YPD War Veterans Legion, as was most other war veterans in the department. On November 11, 1949 at the organization's annual meeting Sgt. Warnock was elected, by acclamation, as their new commander. After several years as a patrol supervisor Sgt. Warnock was transferred on October 16, 1952 to duty in the 3rd precinct located at 36 Radford St. On October 17, 1957 Sgt. Warnock received another promotion, this time to the rank of police Lieutenant with a new salary of $6,174 a year. Though unusual at the time, Lt. Warnock was allowed to remain in the 3rd precinct serving as a desk officer. However, on February 28, 1963 Lt. Warnock was reassigned to desk duty in the 2nd precinct. During his career his family related that he had delivered four babies and he told them he was scared every time.

Lt. Warnock retired on March 26, 1965 and was hired as Director of Security at the Gestetner Corp. on Nepperhan Avenue. During his time with the Police Department his friends used to consider him somewhat of a ladies man. He loved being in the limelight and actually was an amateur actor in many church productions. And it was said that he actually did appear in a few commercials and two movies by actor Woody Allen; those being, "Crimes and Misdemeanors," and "Stardust Memories." He was also very active with an acting group in the old Racket Club on Park Hill Avenue which is where he picked up his nickname, the "Thespian." Bill had one relative in the YPD, that being an uncle who was a former police officer named Edward Keehan. His father's sister married Keehan.

Ret Lieutenant William Warnock died on April 25, 2005. He was 89 years old.

PO STEPHEN KANTOR #199

APPOINTED: December 30, 1939
RETIRED: September 7, 1972

Steve Kantor was born in Yonkers on October 6, 1917, attended and graduated from local schools. As a young man Steve worked as a sash worker for the Alexander Smith Carpet Factory in Yonkers. As a second language Steve spoke fluent Russian. Steve, or as all friends knew him, "Pip," lived at 17 Colin Street when he was appointed to the Yonkers Police Dept. on December 30, 1939. Starting salary was $1,940 a year and his first assignment was patrol duty in the 2nd precinct. Being very athletic, during the early 1940s Steve played basketball on the PBA basketball team. He also played softball for the PBA during 1947. On November 16, 1947 officer Kantor was appointed a detective in the Detective Bureau now earning $3,100. This assignment lasted only four years and on January 1, 1951 he was returned to duty in the 2nd precinct where he would remain for the rest of his career. Steve, who served in the National Guard, had two brothers who were also Yonkers police officers; police officer Theodore Kantor and Lt. Russell Kantor. A charter member of the former YPD St. George Society, PO Steven Kantor retired from the Yonkers Police Dept. on September 7, 1972 and died on December 12, 1988. He was 71 years old.

PO CARMINE J. APADULA #219

APPOINTED: December 30, 1939
RETIRED: May 1, 1974

Carmine Apadula was born in Yonkers on April 17, 1912. He attended and graduated from local public schools. As a second language Carmine spoke fluent Italian and worked at a variety of different jobs including that of a laborer before taking the exam for Yonkers Police Patrolmen. Carmine was appointed to the YPD on December 30, 1939 while living at 169 Oak St. His first assignment was patrol duty in the 4th pct. Part of the duty performed there was as the captains administrative aide. He remained in the 4th pct. until November 16, 1947 when he was appointed a detective in the Detective Bureau. Receiving this designation increased his salary by $100. On January 1, 1951 Detective Apadula was reassigned back to patrol duty, this time in the 1st precinct. He remained there until November 7, 1966 when he was returned to the 4th precinct and again served as the captain's aide. In 1967 Carmine completed courses from Manhattan College and earned a BA degree. Carmine's nephew was YPD Detective Charles Apadula. Carmine Apadula retired from the police department on May 1, 1974 while living at 35 Bryant Rd. However, in the mid-1990s he developed Alzheimer's disease and moved in with a daughter in the South Nyack, New York where he later died on June 19, 2003. He was 91 years old.

LT. LOUIS J. LIGAY

APPOINTED: December 30, 1939
DIED: October 31, 1961

Louis Joseph Ligay was born in Allentown, Pa. on August 11, 1913. He moved to Yonkers with his family as a young boy and grew up on Jefferson Street. He attended St. Casimir's Parochial School where he became fluent in speaking Polish, and graduated from Commerce H.S. In his youth he was very athletic and was a member of YMCA swimming and wrestling teams. As a young man he worked as a bank teller in a NYC bank. A resident of 110 Morris Street, Ligay was appointed to the YPD on December 30, 1939 and assigned to the 2nd pct. on foot patrol. On March 27, 1941 and again on February 13, 1946 he was certified and issued a Restricted Radio Telephone Operator Permit by the FCC presumably to work as a dispatcher in the Communications Division. He was designated "Operator 91."

On Dec. 1, 1942 officer Ligay was appointed a detective and "partnered" with Det George Baker. On May 30, 1945 a large narcotics operation was ended when Ligay and Baker teamed up with the Federal Bureau of Narcotics and arrested three men. However on Nov. 16, 1947 Ligay was returned to duty in the 3rd pct. For a week in April 1955 Ligay was detailed to a Police Traffic Training Course in Utica NY. While living at 29 Knowles St. PO Ligay received a promotion to the rank of Sergeant on Sept. 1, 1955 earning $5,000 a year and was assigned to the Traffic Division. In 1956 Sgt Ligay served occasionally as an instructor for new recruits trained at the Naval Reserve Center on Alexander St. On June 16, 1958 Sgt Ligay was promoted to the rank of Lieutenant and was assigned as a precinct desk officer. On Halloween night, Oct. 31, 1961, Lt Ligay was off duty and on his way in to work the Halloween parade detail when he had a sudden heart attack and died right in Larkin Plaza. He was 47 years old. Lt Ligay's grandson, Craig Martin, was a Connecticut State Trooper.

PO ROBERT A. NEARY #84

APPOINTED: December 30, 1939
RETIRED: February 24, 1972

Bob Neary, whose father at the time was Sgt. Augustus Neary, was born on September 3, 1912 in the City of Yonkers. He attended local schools and graduated from Commerce H.S. in 1931. He worked for several years as a truck driver before taking the civil service test for police patrolmen. But on December 30, 1939, while residing at 170 Stanley Ave., Bob Neary was appointed a Yonkers police officer with a salary of $1,940 a year, and was assigned to patrol duty and the 1st precinct at Wells Avenue. Months before America's entry into World War II officer Neary was inducted into the Army on April 16, 1941. He subsequently received an indefinite leave of absence from the YPD. Bob served his country during the war as a PFC in the Field Artillery and with the 8th Division Military Police. He was honorably discharged on September 6, 1945 and reinstated to the YPD on October 16, 1945.

In the mid 1940's Bob served as the PBA recording secretary and often part of the Color Guard of the YPD Holy Name Society. He remained assigned to the 1st precinct until November 9, 1966 when he was transferred to duty in the 4th precinct on Shonnard Place where he remained right up to his retirement. During his last years working in the 4th precinct he served as the desk lieutenant's aide and as the patrol wagon driver. He retired from the police department on February 24, 1972 and died at the age of 68 on February 8, 1981.

Bob was extremely well liked by his co-workers. So much so that when he died they established an annual basketball tournament at Christ the King Church named the "Bob Neary Memorial Tournament." Along with his father, who was a Yonkers police sergeant, his brother Tom was a Yonkers police officer. A son Robert was a Westchester County Judge, and another son Joseph was retired from the LAPD.

CAPTAIN STEPHEN A. KAPUTA

APPOINTED: December 30, 1939
RETIRED: June 30, 1972

Stephen A. Kaputa was born in Yonkers on April 12, 1910. He attended local schools graduating from PS# 5 and Saunders Trade & Technical HS. Due to his keen interest in music, for a short while he attended the NYC College of Music, but later dropped out. As a young man he worked as a Machinist and Truck driver and was driving a truck right up to his police appointment. But that appointment became very difficult to accomplish.

On December 14, 1939 the Herald Statesman reported that the outgoing Democratic organization was reportedly going to make as many appointments and promotions as possible in the Police Department on Dec. 16, 1939. In doing so they would skip all Republicans whenever possible in order to promote Democrats. And they did. Steve Kaputa had been on the civil service list for patrolman for some time and had already been skipped twice, reportedly due to political affiliation. With the upcoming appointments Kaputa thought he had solved his political problems and would be appointed. He was wrong and would be skipped once again.

A resident of 70 Fairmont Avenue, Kaputa was finally hired by the Yonkers Police Department on December 30, 1939. Although he was originally # 5 on the civil service Police Officer list, he was

Capt. Stephen A. Kaputa (cont.)

skipped over for appointment three times. The reason for his being passed over in not known, however, according to the local newspaper, "failure to get the approval from his district ward leader" was the reason. Upon his police appointment he earned $1,940. a year and was assigned to the 1st precinct on Wells Avenue. On January 12, 1940 he was reassigned to the 4th precinct on patrol.

During the early months of 1941 there was a rash of burglaries in the N/W section of Yonkers that was making the residents very concerned and upset. But the problem was resolved when, on March 10, 1941, six burglars were arrested by PO Kaputa and several other officers in his precinct. For his actions he was commended by Chief William Kruppenbacher. The following year, on March 20, 1942, Officer Kaputa was awarded two commendations for his excellent police work on various assignments. The first award was for arresting a male on March 9, 1941 and obtaining a confession for several burglaries in the 4th precinct, and the 2nd was for the apprehension of a burglar on May 22, 1941.

Following December 7th 1941, and the United States' entry into WW 2, officer Kaputa felt very strongly and wanted to serve his country in the military. However at that time the Yonkers draft board had in place an exemption from service for married men and for police officers. He tried to join the Army, Navy, Marine Corps, and Coast Guard, but was turned down by all due to his draft board classification. But Kaputa was determined to, as he put it, "get into the action." In early 1942 he filed an appeal with the Selective Service Board in Yonkers to be re-classified 1-A so he could serve his country. In June 1943 he was notified that his appeal was granted and he was re-classified as 1-A. And, as he had hoped, he was inducted into, not the Army, but the Marine Corps on July 17, 1943 and was granted an indefinite leave of absence from the YPD. He couldn't have been happier. He served in the South Pacific Theater of operations as a mechanic in a Fighter Plane Squadron, Marine Air Wing I, serving in various locations overseas. He was honorably discharged as a sergeant on October 19, 1945 and reinstated to YPD on November 1, 1945 at a new salary of $2,406.

Officer Steve Kaputa once again received notoriety when, on Jan 4, 1946 about 7 PM, he and his partner PO Frank Rowe, while on routine patrol, came upon the six family wood frame house at 116 Woodworth Avenue engulfed in flames. After turning in the alarm, Kaputa and his partner tried unsuccessfully to enter the front of the building to assist the tenants. Having been forced back they then ran up the back porch steps and found 18 people huddled together in the smoke. He and his partner guided them all to safety. The news reports that cover the story at the time related the Kaputa had only recently returned to duty after 28 months service overseas as a sergeant in the Marine Corps and who was decorated for bravery.

What follows is a list of his assignments and promotions as they occurred throughout Steve Kaputa's career. On April 16, 1946 he was appointed a detective in the Detective Bureau. However, using his disabled veteran's preference which was allowed at that time, just over a year later, on June 1, 1947, he was promoted to the rank of sergeant at the new salary of $3,400 and was assigned to the 1st precinct as a patrol supervisor. Two years later on May 1, 1949 Kaputa was reassigned to the 4th precinct as patrol Sergeant. On January 1, 1951, following the closing of two precincts, Sgt. Kaputa was moved again, this time to the 1st precinct.

Capt. Stephen A. Kaputa (cont.)

Sgt. Kaputa may have been moved around quite a bit but it never prevented him from continuing his studies for police promotion. He was determined to continue moving up the ranks. And he was successful. On October 16, 1952 Sgt. Kaputa was promoted to the rank of Lieutenant at the annual salary of $4,800. and remained assigned to the 1st precinct as a desk lieutenant. Never letting up on his desire to move forward up the ranks, on November 16, 1960 Lieutenant Kaputa was promoted to the rank of Captain with the salary of $7,965 a year. As a new captain he was assigned to headquarters as the commanding officer of Communications and Records Division.

Three years later on May 16, 1963 he was reassigned to the 2nd precinct as a relief captain and utilized to fill vacancies created by captains being on vacation, etc. On January 29, 1964 he was transferred back to headquarters once again as commanding officer of the Communications and Records Division. On February 8, 1968 Capt. Kaputa was assigned to the 1st precinct, now located at 730 East Grassy Sprain Road, as the commanding officer. But before he could even finish one year in the 1st precinct, on October 1, 1968 he was transferred to the 4th precinct as their commanding officer.

By now even a casual observer might conclude that Capt. Kaputa was not being looked upon favorably by the chief, his superior in the police department. Although the reason is not known, one quick look at the number of transfers he had received, and that conclusion was plausible. And the moves continued. On November 16, 1968 he was transferred to headquarters as commanding officer of Service and Maintenance Division, and on October 1, 1969 to commanding officer of Records Service and Maintenance Division. The transfers kept coming. On February 2, 1970 he was designated as commanding officer of the Traffic Division, and on December 1, 1970 as commanding officer of the 4th precinct. He remained in the 4th precinct and was there when, on January 1, 1971, it's designation was changed to the North Patrol Command.

Capt. Steve Kaputa retired from the North patrol command on June 30, 1972 while living at 13 Fenimore Avenue. Captain Steve Kaputa, a tough no nonsense kind of guy who, in his day, had a reputation of being a good take charge street boss, died on February 26, 2007. He was 96 years old.

LT. LESTER B. BRENT

APPOINTED: February 1, 1942
RETIRED: September 14, 1969

Lester Brent was born in the Bronx NY on Dec. 15, 1913. However, his actual surname was believed to be Bianchi, a name he later changed to Brent. After moving to Yonkers he attended local elementary schools and graduated from Roosevelt H.S. where he played basketball. As a young man Brent worked for several years as a cashier clerk for the Chrysler Corp. in the Bronx, NY. On February 1, 1942 Les Brent was appointed to the YPD earning $1,500 and was assigned to duty in the 1st precinct. During WW-2 officer Brent was inducted into the Army on May 11, 1943, receiving an indefinite leave of absence from the YPD, and was honorably discharged on February 7, 1946. He was re-instated to the YPD on March 1, 1946. All his service time counted toward his seniority in the YPD. On Sept. 1, 1947 Les Brent was promoted to the rank of Sergeant at $3,400 a year and assigned to the 2nd pct. In 1951 he was moved back to the 1st pct. and in 1952 to the 4th. On June 16, 1955 Sgt Brent received a promotion to Lieutenant at $5,600 and was assigned as desk officer in the 4th pct. On Nov. 9, 1966 he was transferred to the 1st pct. where he remained up to his retirement on Sept. 14, 1969. Brent retired and moved to Florida where he was hired as the Chief of Police in a small town. Ret Lt Lester Brent, a former member of Yonkers Police War Veterans Legion, died on Oct. 1, 1990. He was 76 years old.

LT. JOHN F. FLYNN

APPOINTED: February 1, 1942
RETIRED: January 30, 1973

John Francis Flynn was born in Yonkers on May 4, 1914. He attended local public schools, Sacred Heart high school, and graduated from high school in Garrison NY in 1932. Prior to the YPD John worked as a steam fitter and also with the NYC transit system. He was appointed to the YPD on Feb. 1, 1942 and was assigned to the 1st precinct. John was a big man standing 6 ‘ 4". “Big John” Flynn was assigned to the police repair shop for a short time in 1947, but on July 16, 1956 was appointed a Detective in the Detective Bureau. His first promotion was to Sergeant on April 16, 1958 and he was assigned to the 2nd precinct as a patrol supervisor. On Mar. 16, 1962 he was promoted to Lieutenant and reassigned to the 1st precinct as a relief desk lieutenant for all the four precincts. Big John Flynn, as he was most often referred to, was also nicknamed “Whispering Smith,” for calling you to the side and speaking to you very softly. Lt. Flynn was detailed as City Court liaison on March 3, 1969 to August of 1971 when he was placed in charge of the newly established Community Relations Unit with the designation of Detective Lteutenant. John Flynn retired on January 30, 1973 and died in Florida on August 22, 1991. He was 77 years old.

PO ROLAND W. WILDEY #197

APPOINTED: February 1, 1942
RETIRED: November 3, 1972

Roland Wildey was born on June 25, 1913 in the City of Yonkers. He attended public school #7, public school # 5, then graduated from Roosevelt High School. Following his graduation he enlisted in the New York National Guard and was assigned to the 27th Military Police Company, Special Troops, 27th Division, National Guard. He received an honorable discharge several years later. As a young man Roland worked for Con Edison Co. and the Yonkers Herald Statesman newspaper. He also did carpentry work on the side.

"Red," as he was known, was appointed to the YPD on February 1, 1942 and assigned to the 1st precinct. About a year later he was reassigned to the 3rd precinct and on May 22, 1944 was assigned to the Traffic Division on motorcycle duty. Roland loved shooting his revolver at the range and was an expert shot. He was a member of the Yonkers Pistol and Revolver Club on Nepperhan Avenue which used a range in the Hudson Tire Company. On January 23, 1947, though still in traffic, he was designated the YPD firearms expert and placed in charge of inspections of departmental weapons and firearms training. On February 20, 1947 he and police officer Herb Schanck were directed to arrange for, and schedule, firearms target practice for the entire police department. On May 7, 1956 officer Wildey was awarded a certificate of excellent police work for rescuing several people from a fire at 18 Jefferson St. on February 14, 1954. Following a serious motorcycle accident on May 31, 1963 Roland Wildey never road again, but was assigned as the clerk in Traffic Court and later worked in the Traffic Violations Bureau. His last duty was as Service Manager in the police repair shop where he remained right up to his retirement on November 3, 1972. Roland was a member of the Police Square Club of Westchester County and a 1st degree Mason in the Yonkers Lodge # 1040. He was also a member of the Sons of the American Revolution. A resident of Mahopac New York, retired police officer Roland Wildey died on August 29, 1995. He was 82 years old.

PO JOHN J. GREVERT #86

APPOINTED: February 2, 1942
RETIRED: October 25, 1969

John J. Grevert, better known to all who knew him as "Jack, was born in the City of Yonkers on March 26, 1911. He attended PS # 9 and graduated from Commerce High School. He gained a trade as an electrician and worked for Otis Elevator for 14 years as an "elevator tester."

Jack was appointed a Patrolman in the Yonkers Police Dept. on February 1, 1942 while residing at 9 Spruce Street, His starting salary was set at $1,500 a year; for unknown reasons, less than men hired two years earlier. His first assignment was to patrol in the 1st precinct. On Jan. 1, 1947 Jack was re-assigned to the Juvenile Aide Bureau (JAB) where, along with investigating crimes by juveniles he became very active in sports. That year he was the manager of the Yonkers Police softball team.

PO Grevert ran for, and was elected as President of the PBA from 1952 through 1956. On November 26, 1954 PBA Pres. Grevert was assigned to the office of Capt. John F. McCormack, Director of Civil Defense, to assist the captain in CD matters. When his term as PBA president expired in 1956 he announced on Jan. 11, 1956 that he declined to accept his unanimous re-election for a 5th term. At the time he was also the president of the N.Y.S. Police Conference. However Grevert did decide to run again in 1960 and won election as PBA president up to 1965. On Aug. 27, 1965 he was re-assigned to the J.A.B. and on Feb. 8, 1968 to the Traffic Division on foot. However he actually was placed in charge of the school crossing guards.

"Jack" Grevert retired on October 25, 1969 and moved to Mahopac where he died on December 26, 2002. He was 91 years old.

PUBLIC SAFETY COMMISSIONER
WILLIAM H. SICKLEY

APPOINTED: March 1, 1942
RETIRED: May 4, 1973

Bill Sickley was born in the City of Yonkers on September 17, 1912 and completed his formal education in local schools. Bill had a natural talent for repairing automobiles and subsequently worked many years as an auto mechanic and garage operator. He was one of those unusual men who it seemed could fix anything and was just naturally gifted in the technical operation of a variety of things. In fact, throughout his adult life he was an enthusiastic amateur "ham" radio operator.

On March 1, 1942 Sickley was appointed a Yonkers police officer while residing at 1 Phillipse Place earning an annual starting salary of $1,500 a year and was assigned to foot patrol in the 1st precinct located at 20 Wells Avenue. At that time, once you had completed three years with the department your salary rose to $1,800. One year after the entry of America into WW-2, and at the age of 30 years, Sickley enlisted in the US Coast Guard on October 10, 1942. As such he received an indefinite leave of absence from the department to serve in the military. When the war ended Bill received his honorable discharge on November 1, 1945 and was returned to duty in the Yonkers Police Department on November 16, 1945, at the salary of $2,200 a year. He was assigned to patrol out of the 1st precinct..

On April 3, 1946 officer Sickley was transferred from the first precinct to the Traffic Division

P.S.C. William H. Sickley (cont.)

motorcycle unit. On July 28, 1946, while still in the Traffic Division, he was officially designated "apparatus mechanic" for the repair and maintenance of the police motorcycles. On November 17, 1947 he was technically reassigned from the Traffic Division to the Motor Transport Maintenance Division, which was part of the Radio Telegraph Division (RTD), but continued to work as a mechanic. On January 5, 1948 when vacation orders were issued, the order specifically instructed that Sickley was to be designated a "master mechanic" with 22 days of vacation with pay. This was two days more vacation than all other police officers.

Being a veteran and member of the Yonkers Police War Veterans Legion, in November of 1948 Bill Sickley was elected and installed as Commander of the War Veterans Legion at a dinner dance at a restaurant at 20 Pelton Street. He was the first World War II veteran to be designated as commander. He replaced outgoing Commander, Leo Magratten.

Having spent relatively little time on uniform patrol in a precinct since his appointment, on April 7, 1949 Sickley was transferred from the Radio Telegraph Division to the 3rd precinct on patrol duty. About two years later, on January 1, 1951, following the closing of two precincts, he was moved to the 1st precinct. When those two precincts were reopened, on October 16, 1952 Bill was reassigned to patrol in the 3rd precinct. Sickley would remain on patrol in the 3rd pct. for about 8 years with various partners until April 1, 1960 when he was promoted to the rank of Sergeant, earning the salary of $6,275. and was assigned as a patrol supervisor in the 2nd precinct at 441 Central Park Avenue.

Later, after a year in the 1st precinct, on February 26, 1964 Sgt Sickley was appointed a Detective Sergeant at $8,200 and assigned to the Detective Division. It was there that he was directed to organize a Narcotics Unit within the DD to address an increased level of use and sale of heroin. He was very successful in forming and supervising this unit and, given his natural technical skills, became an expert in installing eavesdropping devices (wiretaps) when authorized by a court order. In May of 1965 "Sam," as Detective Sergeant Sickley was affectionately known by his co-worker friends, was once again instructed to organize another new unit to be named the Intelligence Unit (IU). This unit would be responsible for gathering strategic intelligence on all forms of organized criminal activities and those persons involved, and activities and organizations, including the Communist Party USA, Black Panther Party, etc., that might be deemed subversive or disruptive within Yonkers or the country in general. He was given two patrolmen, Tom Powrie, his old 3rd precinct partner, and George Rutledge, to get the unit up and running.

Two months later on July 2, 1965 Sgt Sickley was promoted to Lieutenant at $9,160, reassigned "on paper" to the Communications & Records Division, but remained in Command of the Intelligence Unit. Over the years the unit increased its personnel and was extremely successful in accomplishing its mission. On January 26, 1968 Sickley was advanced to Detective Lieutenant at $13,150. and remained the commanding officer of the IU. Then, while still serving as commanding officer of the Intelligence Unit, the city manager also assigned him to work as a special assistant to the manager for investigations involving the corruption of city employees other than police officers. For this additional second assignment he reported directly to city manager Seymour Scher and by-passed the chief of police.

Because of the trust and confidence the city manager had gained in Lt. Sickley, during the temporary absence of then Public Safety Commissioner Frank Vescio, on November 5, 1971 the manager appointed Sickley to be Acting Public Safety Commissioner at $26,500., in command of both police and

P.S.C. William H. Sickley (cont.)

fire bureaus. Purposely overlooking anyone of the rank of Captain. Comm. Vescio was scheduled to return to duty on January 14, 1972. However, on that date Vescio announced he was retiring. It was then that City Manager Seymore Scher asked Bill Sickley to remain in that temporary position until further notice. Apparently the City Manager was pleased with Sickley's performance in that position because on February 24, 1972 Scher appointed Sickley to the full time position of Public Safety Commissioner. Of course Sickley had to take a year's leave of absence from his civil service police lieutenant's position in order for him to maintain his civil service status as a police lieutenant and accompanying pension benefits. However, before each year was completed he would have to return to the police Bureau as a police lieutenant for about two weeks before returning to his position as public safety Commissioner. Generally this two week period took place during his vacation.

During Comm. Sickley's administration the police bureau was reorganized into three separate bureaus; Field Services Bureaus, Administration Services Bureau, and Inspectional Services Bureau, each commanded by a deputy chief. Other changes made under Comm. Sickley's administration included; Establishment of the Getty Square patrol detail; return of the vehicle repair shop to the police Bureau from the Department of Public Works; the assignment of a special Task Force to work high crime areas from 6 PM to 2 AM; the start of the police departments own training school for rookie patrolman and in-service training; centralization of the Detective Division back to headquarters; the establishment of a central booking desk for prisoners at headquarters; the position of desk Lieutenants was discontinued and replaced with Sergeants; Lieutenants were assigned as executive officers to captains; the purchase of new radio cars, including 10 with anti-speeding detectors; and the planned computerization of police records.

On April 6, 1973 Commissioner Sickley announced his plan to retire effective May 4, 1973. In a letter to Sickley the city manager commended him on the excellent job that he had done and conveyed his sincere appreciation. In part he wrote, "*...most of all, from your personal example, you have conveyed throughout the Police Department the unblemished integrity which you sustained throughout your career. You have personally contributed to the improved performance and professionalization of the Yonkers police Bureau, contributing directly to the dramatic reduction in the Yonkers crime rate*."

Following his retirement Bill Sickley planned on traveling across the country and spending any additional time in his summer home in Hopatcong, New Jersey. He was able to do this for nearly 6 years. However, on February 10, 1979, William H. Sickley died in the Dover General Hospital in Dover New Jersey after a short illness. He was 66 years old. Bill was a member of the opera's Lodge of Masons, the Police Square club of Westchester County, the Lowerre Post, the Veterans of Foreign Wars, Yonkers Elk's Lodge, the National Campers and Hikers Association of Buffalo New York, and the International Fan Trailer Club.

PO EUGENE J. DOBSON #55

APPOINTED: December 16, 1942
RETIRED: July 20, 1971

Born Eugene Dobrosky on June 23, 1913 in White Plains New York, "Gene" attended local public schools. Over the years he worked a number of jobs as a young man and then took the examinations for Yonkers Police Patrolman and Fireman. He passed both and was appointed a Yonkers Fireman on April 1, 1942. Later that year he was called by the YPD for appointment and decided to accept. Eugene was appointed to the Yonkers Police Department on December 16, 1942 and assigned to the 3rd precinct on patrol. He was inducted into the Army Air Corps on April 16, 1943, received an indefinite leave of absence, and served in England as a technician 4th class. He was honorably discharged December 1, 1945 and returned to the police department's 3rd precinct on January 16, 1946. On April 3, 1946 he was transferred from the 3rd precinct to the Traffic Division motorcycle unit where he would remain for the rest of his career. He was one of the first officers to be trained with the very first Radar equipment used by the YPD against speeders. In the 1940's Dobson was an excellent shot with his revolver and on September 18, 1948 the local newspaper reported that he was a member of the police department's pistol team which was competing in the annual police pistol tournament. It was on April 10, 1951 that Eugene Dobrosky legally changed his name to Eugene Dobson. Gene and his wife both loved to ride motorcycles and continued to do so after he retired on July 20, 1971. An avid golfer, Ret PO Eugene Dobson died on February 22, 1998. He was 84 years of age.

PO STEPHEN MOROCH #41

APPOINTED: December 16, 1942
RESIGNED: June 8, 1944

Steve Moroch was born in the City of Yonkers on February 26, 1913 and attended local public schools. On his application to the YPD he listed his employment as a "car loader." Steve Moroch was appointed to the Yonkers Police Department on December 16, 1942 while living at 28 Palmer Avenue. Following some basic police training Patrolman Steve Moroch was assigned to patrol duty in the 2nd precinct. Very little is known about Steve or his time in the 2nd precinct but, for unknown reasons he submitted his resignation from the Yonkers Police Department, effective on June 8, 1944.

LT. WILLIAM MALCOLM

APPOINTED: December 16, 1942
RETIRED: January 25, 1973

William Malcolm was born in the City of Yonkers on July 27, 1910 and attended Gorton and Roosevelt high schools up to the 10th grade. As a young man he gained a trade as a plumber and also worked as a guard in Sing Sing prison. Bill was appointed to the Yonkers Police Department on December 16, 1942 from 147 Ridge Avenue at the salary of $1,500 a year. His first assignment was patrol duty in the 4th precinct. However, less than a year later on, September 17, 1943, Bill was granted an indefinite leave of absence to serve in the Navy during World War II in the Pacific Theater of operations. Following the war he was honorably discharged as a Petty Officer 1st Class on October 6, 1945 and reinstated to the Police Departments 1st precinct on January 16, 1946. Between 1951 and 1952 he served in both the 1st and 4th precincts.

On April 16, 1958 Bill Malcolm was promoted to Sergeant earning the salary of $5,935 and was assigned to the 3rd precinct as a patrol supervisor. Five years later, on February 28, 1963, he was promoted to the rank of Lieutenant earning $8,300 and was returned to the 1st precinct, this time as a desk officer. He would later be moved to the 2nd precinct on March 16, 1964 where he would serve for many years. During a number of years in the 2nd he was in charge of the traffic detail provided to the Yonkers Raceway to safely expedite the exiting of over 30,000 people when the races ended. On April 24, 1972 he was transferred to the Inspectional Services Division where he remained up to his retirement on January 25, 1973. Bill Malcolm was of the more soft spoken "bosses" and was well liked and respected by everyone. Following his retirement he continued playing golf, skiing, playing tennis, and doing small plumbing jobs, which he did throughout his career. In fact, years earlier, in 1953-1954 he was designated the Yonkers city tennis champion. Bill, who was always of slim build, even enjoyed long distance running and even ran a marathon just for fun.

A longtime member of the Amackassin Club, retired Lt. Bill Malcolm died on May 20, 1997. He was 86.

LT. VITO CAMPERLENGO

APPOINTED: December 16, 1942
RETIRED: August 3, 1972

Vito Camperlengo was born the 2nd of four children on August 29, 1915 in a house at 138 Linden Street in Yonkers. As a youth he attended PS# 2, located on School Street, Benjamin Franklin Jr HS, and he graduated from Yonkers H.S. and was fluent in both English and Italian. He also attended Westchester Community College earning several credits. It was the 1930's, the depression, and at the time he had been working as a "Railway" mail clerk and was familiar with the routes of the trains. So one day he simply rode the freight car all the way to Oklahoma and enrolled in Medical school. He reportedly spent two years in Oklahoma Medical School studying to be a doctor. However, on one of his summers in Yonkers he had a serious accident injuring his leg and leaving him with a permanent limp. Unfortunately he lost too much time recovering which resulted in him dropping out of Medical School.

Vito returned to Yonkers and he joined the Civilian Conservation Corps that FDR started during the depression and as a member helped create the parks that are still along the Seven Lakes Drive located in upper New York State. Later he began working for the US Post Office where he remained up to being called by the YPD. All this time Vito was somewhat of an outdoors-man. He loved camping, fishing, and hunting.

Vito received his appointment to the YPD on December 16, 1942 while living at 604 Bellevue Avenue and with an annual salary of $1,500 per year, payable twice a month. Following his recruit training he was assigned to the 4th precinct on foot patrol. In the 1940's while a still a patrolman Vito served as the Treasurer of the YPD Holy Name Society. On New Year’s day, January 1, 1951, he was reassigned to the 1st precinct to perform his patrol duties. However on October 16, 1952 he was returned to work in the 4th pct.

Vito's first promotion came on February 1, 1956 when he was promoted to Sergeant with the new salary of $5,250 per year. He remained in the 4th precinct as a patrol supervisor. As intelligent as Sgt Camperlengo was it was no surprise when he was promoted to the rank of Lieutenant on April 2, 1959 with the salary of $6,680 a year. Following this promotion he was assigned as a desk lieutenant in the 1st precinct on Wells Avenue. But, once again the 4th precinct got him back as a desk officer on March 16, 1960. Lt Camperlengo served as the president of the Capt's, Lt's, & Sgt's Assoc, for three terms; 1968 through 1970. And still interested in sports he used to play softball with the PBA at Tibbetts Park. He was also very active in PBA business and activities.

Then, after nearly 30 years in the precincts, on April 7, 1971 Lt Camperlengo was elevated to Detective Lieutenant and assigned to the Detective Bureau. One of the most respected and well liked "bosses" on the job, he remained in the DD right up to his retirement from the department on August 3, 1972. In 1959 Vito, who was known by close friends as Bill, had built a summer home in Southampton, LI. with the help of his police buddies. After retiring he moved there permanently. Vito’s grandson is YPD PO William Camperlengo.

Ret Lt. Vito Camperlengo died on August 13, 2010, two weeks short of his 95th birthday.

PO DOMINICK A. SARUBBI #193

APPOINTED: December 16, 1942
RETIRED: April 1, 1968

Dominick A. Sarubbi was born in the City of Yonkers on March 18, 1913. When he completed his education he worked as a "material checker" for a local manufacturing plant. Dominick was appointed to the Yonkers Police Department on December 16, 1942 from 53 Kettell Avenue at the salary of $1,500 a year and was assigned to the 2nd precinct at 441 Central Park Avenue. Sarubbi, who spoke Italian as a second language, remained on patrol duty in the 2nd precinct for 16 years until September 29, 1958 when he was transferred to the Communications and Records Division as a Radio-Telephone Operator in the Communications room. His primary job was to dispatch police radio cars to calls for service. He remained there for ten years until February 14, 1968 when he was re-assigned to the Property Clerk Room in headquarters. Dominick continued working in the Property Clerk Room right up to his retirement on April 1, 1968. Retired PO Dominick Sarubbi, who had suffered from heart problems for many years, died September 7, 1981. He was 68 years old.

PO BERNARD H. MURPHY #88

APPOINTED: December 16, 1942
RETIRED: January 11, 1973

"Bernie" Murphy was born in Yonkers on Sept. 26, 1911 and attended Gorton high school up through the 10th grade. As a young man he worked as a Bricklayer and as a security guard for Otis Elevator. Bernie was appointed to the YPD on Dec. 16, 1942 from 60 Warburton Ave. and was assigned to the 3rd pct. at the starting salary of $1,500 a year. And only four months later, on April 15, 1943, Murphy received an indefinite leave of absence from the YPD to join the Army during the war. He held the rank of Technical Sergeant and was assigned to the intelligence and security section. He was honorably discharged on Dec. 10, 1945, returned to the police department on Jan. 16, 1946, and was assigned to the 3rd pct. On Aug. 1, 1947 Murphy was assigned to the Traffic Division for meter enforcement duty. As a member of the Yonkers Police War Veterans Legion, on Nov. 1, 1949 he was elected 3rd vice commander. On January 1, 1951 he was reassigned to the 1st pct. and on Oct. 16, 1952 was returned back to the 3rd. On June 16, 1957 Murphy was appointed a detective but was returned to patrol three years later on June 1, 1960. But, once again he was assigned to the DD on March 16, 1961, but moved out again to the first precinct on May 1, 1963. On November 9, 1966 Murphy was reassigned to the 4th precinct and on February 14, 1968 Murphy was assigned to the H.Q. PO Bernard Murphy retired on Jan. 11, 1973 and died on Jan 8, 1988. He was 76 years old.

PO STEPHEN SZECSY # 36

APPOINTED: December 16, 1942
RESIGNED: March 11, 1946

Steve Szecsy was born in Yonkers NY on December 14, 1911. Following school Steve worked as a manager for Western Union. Steve was appointed to the Yonkers Police Department on December 16, 1942 while living at 601 Warburton Ave. His first assignment was the 1st pct. On April 16, 1943 he was inducted into the Army and was granted an indefinite leave of absence. He never returned to the YPD and while still in the Army he tendered his resignation from the police department effective March 11, 1946.

PO MORRIS LAIBOWITZ #121

APPOINTED: January 16, 1943
RETIRED: March 23, 1972

Morris Laibowitz, known to only close friends as "Mush," was born April 23, 1910 in Yonkers N. Y. where he attended local schools and graduated from Saunders Trades and Technical High School. Prior to the YPD Laibowitz worked as a plumber, carpenter, and did painting for military contractors at a US army base in Rome, New York. He also worked as an iron worker building bridges in the tri state area. Though having a slim wiry build, he had hands like a bear and was known for his strength. He was a very athletic individual and enjoyed boxing and basketball in the early years, particularly in the 1920s and 1930s. Morris, who spoke Hebrew as a second language, was appointed to the Yonkers Police Department on January 16, 1943 with a starting salary of $1,500 a year and was assigned to the 3rd precinct. On April 3, 1946, he was transferred from the 3rd to motorcycle duty in the Traffic Division. He worked nearly his entire career on motorcycle patrol except for two years in the late 1960s when he inspected taxicabs and buses in the YPD Hack Unit. He was very professional in his duties but it would be an understatement to say that he was not a soft-spoken individual. He was your stereo-typical tough cop. "Mush" retired on March 23, 1972 and kept busy fishing, cooking and working around the house. Later in life he joined the US Volunteer Life-Saving Corps, a rescue team that patrolled the Hudson River. Ret PO Morris Laibowitz died November 17, 1992 in St. John's Riverside Hospital he was 82 years old.

SGT. THOMAS P. McGURN

APPOINTED: January 16, 1943
RETIRED: July 8, 1971

Tom McGurn was one of those people that were part of an extended police family. He was born in Yonkers on February 14, 1912 to Yonkers police officer Thomas McGurn and attended Commerce High School and as a young man earned his living as a truck driver. An active sportsman, McGurn loved to hunt, fish, golf, and go hiking. On January 16, 1943 Tom was appointed to the Yonkers Police Department, earning $1,500 a year and was assigned to patrol in the 4th precinct. In the 1940's he served as the vice president of the YPD Holy Name Society. On January 1, 1951 he was moved to the 1st precinct, but in October of 1952 was returned to the 4th. On July 1, 1956 Tom was assigned to the 1st pct., but was detailed to the Court of Special Sessions. During these years he was very active in PBA business and activities and in January of 1957 was elected PBA President. That same year he was also elected president of the NYS Police Conference. McGurn was appointed a Detective on June 16, 1957 and although promoted to Sergeant on July 3, 1963 with the salary of $7,150, he remained working in the Detective Division (D.D.) as a Detective Sergeant.

On February 26, 1964 Sgt McGurn was transferred from the D.D. to the 1st pct., and two years later to the 4th. In 1969 he was working in the Traffic Violations Bureau and then in 1971 was placed in charge of the city's school crossing guards. On Jan. 1, 1971 he was assigned as a desk officer in the South Command up to his retirement on July 8, 1971. Not only was Tom's father a Yonkers police officer, but his son, Tom McGurn was a sergeant with the Westchester Co. P.D. and his son-in-law, Andy Biro, was a former Yonkers police officer.

Unfortunately Tom McGurn would live for only 9 months in retirement in Copake, NY. He would die of cancer in Yonkers on April 3, 1972 at age 60 years.

LT. EDWARD C. LESNICK

APPOINTED: February 15, 1943
RETIRED: June 25, 1976

Born Edward Charles Lesnick in Yonkers on June 24, 1913, Ed attended local schools and graduated from Commerce High School. Before the Y.P.D. Ed was hired by the Y.F.D. on January 16, 1943 and would switch to the police dept. when called a month later. He listed his military training as the "Citizen Military Camp" during the early part of World War II. Ed was hired by the Yonkers Police Department on February 15, 1943 with a salary of $1,500 a year and assigned to the 3rd precinct. On January 1, 1951 he was reassigned to the 1st precinct at 20 Wells Avenue. However, the following year, on October 16, 1952, he was returned to the 3rd precinct. Ed was a real talker. His nickname behind his back was "The Bloop" but he really was a nice guy.

On March 16, 1962, officer Lesnick was promoted to the rank of Sergeant, earning $7,000 a year, and was re-assigned to duty in the 4th precinct at 53 Shonnard Place. In March of 1964 Sgt. Lesnick was once again returned to duty in the 3rd and in November of 1966 he was reassigned to the 1st precinct as a patrol supervisor. On December 15, 1967 Sgt. Lesnick was promoted to the rank of Lieutenant and assigned to the 3rd precinct as a desk officer earning $10,645 a year. When the precinct designations were changed from numbers to being called commands on January 1, 1971, and reduced down to only two, the North command and South command, Lt Lesnick was assigned to desk duty in the South command. On March 12, 1972 Lt. Lesnick was reassigned as a supervisor in the Communications Division in headquarters where he would remain right up to his retirement on June 25, 1976. Ed Lesnick was the younger brother of former Yonkers police officer Matthew Lesnick. And Ed's nephew was Yonkers firefighter Matthew Lesnick.

Following his retirement Ed Lesnick moved to Payson, Arizona where on June 6, 1984 he died at the age of 70 years.

PO FRANCIS S. PORACH #75

APPOINTED: February 15, 1943
RETIRED: March 23, 1972

Francis Porach was born in Yonkers on Nov. 2, 1910. He attended Holy Trinity School and graduated from Gorton HS. Frank was hired by the Yonkers Water Department on Feb. 17, 1936. When he was hired by the YPD on Feb. 15, 1943 he lived at 430 Walnut St. and his salary was $1,500 a year. His first assignment was patrol in the 2nd pct. Four years later, on September 1, 1947 he was reassigned to duty in the 1st pct. at 20 Wells Avenue. While working the late tour on Aug. 27, 1949 Frank and his partner were sent to break up a fight at a bar at 232 New Main St. During the altercation someone took Frank's nightstick away from him and started to beat him over the head severely. Fortunately, his partner, Al Hopper shot and killed the assailant before the man killed officer Porach. Frank was later moved to the 2nd pct. on Jan. 1, 1951. He was reassigned to the Communications and Records Division in H.Q. on Jan. 24, 1966 performing clerical duties. It is believed he was assigned to this desk duty due to having had a permanent colostomy implanted. He remained in this assignment right up to his retirement on March 23, 1972. Eleven years after he retired, in 1983 he and his wife moved to St. Petersburg Florida. One of Frank's favorite pastimes was fishing whenever he had the opportunity. Ret. PO Frank Porach died on October 4, 1991 from pneumonia in Pinellas Park, Fla. He was 80 years old.

PO FRANK P. PANESSA #18

APPOINTED: March 1, 1943
RETIRED: May 17, 1973

Francis A. Panessa was born in Yonkers on May 13, 1916. On his application for appointment to the YPD Frank listed his previous employment as that of a "time keeper" and "office clerk." Frank received his appointment to the police department on March 1, 1943 with a starting salary of $1,600 a year while living at 55 Alder Street. His first assignment was in the 1st pct. Frank spoke Italian as a second language which was no doubt helpful as a police officer. On May 7, 1956 he was awarded a Certificate of Excellent Police Work for a grand larceny arrest he made on Aug. 13, 1952 at 15 Main St. On Jan. 17, 1958 he was reassigned to the Traffic Division for Parking Meter Repair duty and on March 21, 1963 he was moved to 2nd pct. patrol duty. However, after only one month, on April 8, 1963 he was assigned to the Communications Div. dispatching radio cars to calls for service. Frank was assigned to his last duty assignment on February 14, 1968 when he was transferred to HQ in the Property Clerk Office. He retired on May 17, 1973 while living at 42 Tower Place. On June 21, 1978 Frank was the co-founder, along with Deputy Chief Edward Murphy, of the organization now named the New York Police & Fire Retirees Assoc. Ret PO Frank Panessa died on August 22, 2006. He was 90 years old.

DET. VINCENT P. McCUE #14

APPOINTED: March 16, 1943
DIED: June 28, 1967

Born Vincent Paul McCue in Yonkers on July 25, 1912, he attended PS# 9 and graduated from Yonkers high school. He would later also graduate from Manhattan College majoring in business administration. Following his schooling he would gain employment as an engineer. He reportedly served in the military from May 13, 1939 to March 16, 1943 when he was appointed a police officer. In fact, on March 27, 1944, he requested full service pension credit toward his retirement starting on May 13, 1939 when he was actually certified for his police appointment but he was unable to accept because he was in the military at the time. His request was granted. When Vincent was appointed to the Yonkers Police Department his starting salary was $1,600 a year and his first assignment was patrol duty in the first precinct. In 1944 he was assigned to work in the emergency squad for a short time, however for most of the time spent in the 1st precinct he served as the Patrol Wagon driver. (Paddy Wagon-and precinct captain's aide) During the 1940's "Vince" served as the Financial Secretary of the YPD Holy Name Society. On March 16, 1952 he was appointed a Detective in the Detective Bureau at $3,900 a year. By 1956 he was assigned to the Bureau of Criminal Identification (BCI) where he would remain for over 12 years. Vince McCue's brother was Capt. James McCue, his uncle PO Mike McCue, and his nephew Lt Terrence McCue. Vincent McCue died from cancer on June 28, 1967 in St John's Hospital. He was only 54 years old.

PO ERNEST V. NIZZICO #184

APPOINTED: January 16, 1944
RETIRED: December 9, 1971

Ernest Nizzico was born in Tagliacozza, Italy on March 24, 1916. Ernie came to the U.S. with his family and settled in Bridgeport, Ct. The family then moved to Yonkers where Nizzico attended local public schools including Benjamin Franklin Jr H.S. Ernie spoke Italian fluently as a second language and worked as a machinist. He served in the US Army Air Corps from May 22, 1942 to his discharge on November 1, 1943. Following his military service Ernie worked for the Blair shipyards in Yonkers. On Jan. 16, 1944 Nizzico was appointed to the YPD and following recruit training was assigned to patrol duty in the 1st pct. Ernie was a very soft-spoken individual who pretty much kept to himself. For the most part Ernie either walked a foot post or remained in the precinct as the desk aide. He was very meticulous and liked to read books on philosophy. Some of PO Nizzico's assignments are as follows; On Sept. 1, 1947 Ernie was transferred to the 2nd pct., on June 1, 1953 to the 4th pct., on Aug. 6, 1953 to the 3rd pct., on Dec. 14, 1970 transferred to the Records Div. Ernie's nephew was Lt. Bob Day. PO Nizzico retired on December 9, 1971 and died on November 11, 2000. He was 84 years old.

DET. HELEN J. O'LEAR # 4

APPOINTED: July 1, 1944
POSITION ABOLISHED: September 30, 1952

Toward the end of World War 2, on June 21, 1944, Mrs. Helen J. O'Lear of 72 Buena Vista Avenue, was one of two of the city's first women ever to be sworn in as a Policewoman in the Yonkers Police Dept. Mrs. Helen C. Murray was appointed at the same time. Their positions were termed "temporary war appointments" and were scheduled to last only for the duration of the war. These positions, which took effect July 1, 1944, were only provisional as no test had been taken by either of the women.

Policewoman O'Lear, whose annual salary was set at $1,600. was issued the standard issue police shield #260. She was also issued a .32 cal. 2 inch barrel revolver. Her uniform was simply to wear a navy blue 2 piece suit with a white blouse. Her revolver was carried in her purse. O'Lear and Murray were both assigned to attend a course of instruction at the NYPD Policewomen's Bureau. In addition, in January 1945 both women were enrolled in a police training school at Syracuse University. This was said to be the first of its kind to be held at a University in the country.

Upon returning from school O'Lear was assigned to the Detective Bureau without holding the rank of detective. A short time later Plwn O'Lear would be assigned to the Juvenile Aid Bureau where she would work closely with the PAL. At some point she was allowed to carry detective shield #4, even though it is not clear whether she was ever "officially" appointed a detective. During her 8 years of service there was never a Civil Service test scheduled for the position of Policewoman, nor was there in existence a certified civil service list to appoint a "permanent" policewoman from. In 1952 such a list was established. However, by that time she was too old to qualify to take the test. By law, once a civil service list existed for Policewoman, a provisional appointee who was not on that list, such as Plwn O'Lear, could no longer continue to hold her position. On September 30, 1952 her provisional position was abolished and her employment with the Yonkers Police Department was terminated. And no other woman was ever appointed from the established list.

POLICEWOMAN HELEN C. MURRAY #257

APPOINTED: July 1, 1944
RESIGNED: January 15, 1946

Born Helen Constance Murray in Newport Rhode Island on December 12, 1911, Helen attended local schools and also graduated from Nursing School. Following her training she obtained employment as a Nurse Technician. During WW-2 there was a shortage of available men who were able to pass the tests to become police officers. Up to that point there had never been a female police officer in the Yonkers P.D.; but some were suggesting that it should be tried. The idea was given the go ahead but no civil service test was given. Two women were simply chosen.

Helen Murray was hired by the YPD on July 1, 1944 on a provisional temporary basis as a temporary war appointment with a salary of $1,600 a year. At the time she lived at 255 Sprain Road, Yonkers. She and another woman, Helen O'Lear, were appointed at the same time. They were both given the title of "Policewoman." Murray was assigned shield #257 and was issued a .32 caliber 2" barrel revolver. She only worked in plainclothes and was never even required to obtain a uniform. However, she was required to attend special courses in the NYPD police academy for policewomen. During her employment she was utilized as an investigator in the Juvenile Aide Bureau checking for underage drinking in licensed premises.

However, by General order #6 dated January 15, 1946, Miss Murray had tendered her resignation and same was accepted effective that date. She said she was leaving due to personal reasons however it was learned she married a Mr. William Smith who was serving in the military at the time. Now married her name was changed to Helen Smith and she reportedly moved to England to be with her husband. After returning to the states, in 1960 her and her husband moved to Richmond, Va. Helen C. Smith, 93, of Richmond, Va., died on November 19, 2005.

LT. WILLIAM D. CAIRNS

APPOINTED: March 28, 1945
RETIRED: April 21, 1977

William Cairns was born in the City of Yonkers on August 21, 1915. He attended and graduated from Commerce High School and Pace University in New York City, majoring in accounting and business administration. Following his schooling he gained employment as an accountant. Bill served in the Army prior to and during World War II as a sergeant beginning on October 15, 1940 and receiving his honorable discharge on September 1, 1942. Why he was discharged prior to the end of the war is not known.

He applied for appointment to the Yonkers Police Dept. while residing at 180 Palisade Ave. and received that appointment on March 28, 1945 earning a starting salary of $1,600 a year. His first assignment was to the 1st precinct on patrol. An old story was passed around that on July 25, 1949 while he and his partner were on patrol they saw a horse bolt and start to run into traffic. With his partner driving, it is said that Cairns jumped from the police vehicle onto the horse, bringing it to a stop, and preventing an accident.

As a war veteran and a member of the Police War Veterans Legion, on November 11, 1950 Bill was elected Quartermaster for the organization. On July 1, 1951 officer Cairns was transferred to the Communications and Operations Division as a telephone operator. Bill was promoted to Sergeant on June 16, 1955 earning $5,000 a year and was assigned to the 4th precinct as a patrol supervisor. "Cairnsie," as he was nicknamed, was promoted to the rank of Lieutenant on May 31, 1958 earning $6,580 a year and reassigned to desk duty remaining in the 4th precinct.

Shortly after the new 1st precinct was built at 730 E. Grassy Sprain Rd., on November 7, 1966, Lt Cairns was assigned there as a desk officer. Bill was always an excellent shot with his revolver and as such on February 14, 1968 the chief assigned him to Headquarters Command Division designated as the Department Range Officer. As Range officer Lt. Cairns provided all required firearms training for all personnel within the police department. On January 1, 1971 when centralization of the 4 Precincts took place, Lt Cairns was assigned to desk duty in the South Patrol Command. Two years later on March 12, 1973 Lt. Cairns was reassigned to the Central booking section. He retired from the police department on April 21, 1977.

Retired Lt. William Cairns died September 23, 1990 at the age of 75.

PO WILLIAM W. BECKMEYER #112

APPOINTED: October 1, 1945
RESIGNED: July 1, 1948

Bill Beckmeyer was born in the City of Yonkers on October 25, 1916. He attended local schools and gained employment as a sign painter. Records indicate that Bill served in the military during WW-2 and was honorably discharged from the Army on September 15, 1945.

Beckmeyer was appointed to the Yonkers Police Department the following month on October 1, 1945 while living at 40 Van Cortlandt Park Avenue earning a salary of $1,600 a year. On August 13, 1946 Beckmeyer was transferred from the 1st precinct to the newly established Motor Maintenance Transport Division, which actually would not officially be established until October 1, 1946. This division would be a part of the Traffic Division. It basically was a police repair shop for police cars. However on October 24, 1946 Bill was transferred from this Transport Division back to the 1st precinct on patrol.

On June 21, 1947 PO Beckmeyer requested and was granted a one-year leave of absence. On July 1, 1948 he sent a letter to the police chief stating that he had re-enlisted in the Air Force in June for a three year enlistment. After conferring with civil service the YPD determined that he had effectively resigned on the date of his letter.

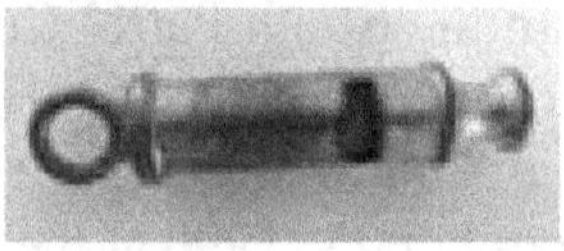

LT. ARTHUR MOYNIHAN

APPOINTED: October 1, 1945
RETIRED: November 16, 1971

Artie Moynihan was born August 17, 1914 in Wyckhoff, NJ where he received his formal education. As a young man, on his police application he listed his occupation as a carpenter and auto mechanic. Moynihan's build was wiry, rugged and tough. He had red hair, always smoked a pipe, and was actually very quiet and an introvert as well as being very moody.

About 1939 Arthur joined the Army and found himself in the middle of WW-2 for the duration. He served in the China, Burma, and India campaign during World War II as a Master Sergeant for six years, was wounded, and was honorably discharged a disabled veteran.

Arthur was appointed to the Yonkers police department on October 1, 1945 with a starting salary of $1,600 a year and assigned to the first precinct. However, due to his skills as an auto mechanic on October 24, 1946, he was assigned directly to the Motor Transport Division (police repair shop) at the foot of Main Street just past the Rail Road bridge on the right just before the City Pier. Moynihan took and passed the police sergeants exam and, being designated a disabled veteran, regardless of his score and position on the list, he went right to the top of the Sergeants list due to a veterans preference law that was in effect at the time.

Arthur was promoted right out of the repair shop to the rank of sergeant on September 1, 1947 with a salary of $3,400 a year and was assigned as a patrol supervisor in the 3rd precinct. He was now a sergeant, but he had never been on patrol duty because of his Repair Shop detail. Arthur Moynihan was a Sergeant on foot patrol when, in September of 1947, he was attacked and severely beaten by the Pass brothers; - Ossie, Lassie, and Mossie Pass, after Moynihan found them in a stolen car. They left him beaten and even took his gun. They were later arrested by PO's John Havrish and John J. McCarthy-5, two very big men, and were taught a lesson about assaulting a police officer.

At one point Sgt Moynihan violated some serious departmental regulations and was suspended without pay on January 7, 1950. He was later found guilty of the charges and dismissed from the police department effective May 18, 1950. However, Moynihan filed a court appeal that his punishment was too severe, was successful, and was reinstated to the police department on March 1, 1958.

Sgt Moynihan, who lived at Salisbury Road, was promoted to the rank of Lieutenant on December 31, 1963 and was assigned to the 3rd precinct as a desk officer. He later took the Captains test and came out # 1 on the promotion list but for unknown reasons he went to the Civil Service Commission and had his name permanently removed from the list. He apparently did not ever want the responsibility of the position of captain.

Lt Moynihan, the father of eight children, retired from the YPD on November 16, 1971 and died on April 17, 1983. He was 68 years old.

CAPTAIN MICHAEL OSTROWSKI

APPOINTED: October 1, 1945
RETIRED: January 20, 1972

Michael "Whitey" Ostrowski was born in Hastings NY on April 18, 1916. At some point his family moved to Yonkers and Michael grew up on Riverdale Avenue. Young Michael attended PS# 10, Benjamin Franklin Jr HS, and graduated from Gorton HS. He reportedly was an excellent athlete in high school and played with the locally famous Clinton Athletic Club from Riverdale Avenue, excelling in baseball and basketball. Known to all his friends as Whitey, due to his blonde hair, as a young man he worked as a chauffeur for a time.

Prior to the U.S. entry into WW-2 Mike Joined the Army on March 4, 1941 and served in Europe as a Technical Sergeant in a rifle platoon. He landed in the first wave of the 1944 D-Day invasion of Normandy, France and five days later was captured by German soldiers and held prisoner in a German POW camp for eight months until he was liberated by Russian troops. Retired Captain John Potanovic related that "Whitey" Ostrowski was a prisoner of war with another man from Yonkers who used to imitate and ridicule the Nazi guards causing the American prisoners to be afraid that they were going to be shot by a firing squad. Ostrowski was honorably discharged from the Army September 15, 1945.

It's not clear when Whitey might have taken the Yonkers Police exam but, the following month following his discharge, on October 1, 1945, he was appointed to the police department. At that time he

Capt. Michael Ostrowski (cont.)

was a resident of 46 Riverdale Avenue, his starting salary was $1,600 a year, and he was assigned to foot patrol in the 1st precinct. Although he was appointed in October of 1945, he was certified to be appointed on March 28, 1945 while still in the Army and, as such, his police seniority began on that date. Ostrowski spoke Russian fluently as a second language which came in handy on a number of occasions. Being very athletic Whitey played on the Police Department PBA softball team in the late 1940's along with PO's Stampur, Sohr, Harrilchak, Rohan, Havrish and others.

On May 21, 1947 Yonkers Civil Service certified Patrolman Ostrowski as being a disabled veteran and as such he had absolute veterans preference for promotion over non veterans; regardless of how he scored on the promotional examination as long as he passed. "Whitey" Ostrowski, as a veteran, scored a 75 on the Sergeant's exam and with his veteran's preference went to the top of the list. As such he was promoted to the rank of Sergeant on September 1, 1947, along with eight other patrolmen certified as disabled veterans, with a salary of $3,400 a year. Following his promotion he was assigned as a patrol supervisor in the 3rd precinct. Four years later, on January 1, 1951, he was reassigned to the 1st precinct on patrol.

Sgt Ostrowski was promoted to Lieutenant on October 16, 1952 earning $4,800 a year and was sent to the 4th pct. as a desk officer. The way the police organization was structured at the time, the captain may have been in overall command of the precinct but it was the desk lieutenant who controlled the daily activities of the precinct personnel; including booking and bailing prisoners under appropriate circumstances.

On November 16, 1960 Lt. Ostrowski received his promotion to Captain with a raise in salary to $7,865 and for a few years served as a relief captain in the 2nd pct. However, on May 1, 1963 he was given his own command; that of commanding officer of the 3rd precinct.

Over the next several years he served as commanding officer of the following commands; November 7, 1966 to 2nd precinct, October 1, 1968 to 3rd precinct, February 7, 1969 to the 2nd precinct, and on January 1, 1971, when centralization of the precincts took place combining them into two commands, Capt. Ostrowski was designated commanding officer of the South Command.

A resident of 89 Amackassin Terrace and member of the VFW Post #1666, Capt. Ostrowski retired from the YPD on January 20, 1972. He died February 17, 1983 at age 66 years.

PO FRANK VASIL #230

APPOINTED: January 1, 1947
RETIRED: June 25, 1976

Born in Yonkers on Feb. 16, 1914, Frank's last name at birth was said to be "VASILISYN." It was many years later that he changed his name to Vasil. Frank attended local public schools and graduated from Commerce HS. At the age of 28 Frank entered the Army during WW-2 on Nov. 19, 1942 serving in the Army's Battery B, 228th Field Artillery Battalion. He served in Central Europe, Normandy, and later Germany as a truck driver. He was honorably discharged on Oct. 31, 1945 as a Private First Class. Frank spoke Russian as a second language and worked for a while as a machine operator. Frank was appointed to the YPD on Jan. 1, 1947 earning a starting salary of $1,940. On February 5, 1947 he attended the NYC Police Academy recruit training school and upon graduation was assigned to the 4th precinct on foot patrol. On January 1, 1951 he was reassigned to the first precinct but on October 16, 1952 he was returned to the 4th. Frank was moved to the 2nd pct. on March 19, 1956, remaining there for seven years when, on August 1, 1963 he was transferred to the 1st pct. On Nov. 9, 1963 he was returned to the 4th pct. where he remained assigned to the City Hall Security detail right up to his retirement on June 25, 1976. Ret PO Frank Vasil died in St John's Hospital on October 31, 1978. Frank was 64 years old.

PO RICHARD F. DOHENY #90

APPOINTED: January 1, 1947
RESIGNED: January 15, 1947

Richard Doheny was born in New York City on January 25, 1913. Following his formal education he worked various jobs until America's entry into WW-2. It was then, on March 12, 1942, only three months after the attack on Pearl Harbor, that Doheny joined the Army. He received his honorable discharge on October 1, 1945. While residing at 133 Shonnard Place and working for the Yonkers DPW, Doheny received his appointment to the Yonkers Police Dept. on Jan. 1, 1947 along with several other recruits. He and the other recruits began their basic recruit instruction however, after only two weeks, on January 15, 1947, Richard Doheny apparently decided for reasons unknown, to resign from the YPD and return to his previous employment with the Yonkers DPW. Former PO Richard F. Doheny, father of Lt. Richard Doheny, died in August of 1979 at the age of 66 years.

PO DANIEL G. RANELLONE #36

APPOINTED: January 1, 1947
RETIRED: June 1, 1973

Dan Ranellone was born in Italy on March 15, 1916 and immigrated to the U.S. with his family as a child. He attended local Yonkers schools and graduated from Commerce H.S. Dan joined the Army and served during WW-2 in US Army Air Corps beginning on January 15, 1942. He served as a Corporal with the specialty of Radio Repairman. He was honorably discharged on Dec. 30, 1945. On his application to the YPD he listed his employment as a "card stripper." When Dan received his appointment on January 1, 1947 his starting salary was listed as $2,625. He attended the NYC Police Academy for his recruit training. His first assignment was dated February 5, 1947 and he went to the 1st pct. on Wells Ave. His post covered the Park Hill section of the 1st pct. Although he was appointed in January of 1947 he was given war seniority back to Nov. 16, 1942. because he was certified by civil service for appointment but was in the Army when called. On March 25, 1958 he underwent spinal fusion surgery and, after a great deal of therapy, he returned to duty. On Nov. 9, 1966 he was reassigned to the 4th pct., and on Feb. 21, 1969 to headquarters in the Property Clerk Unit. Dan's last duty assignment began on Dec. 29, 1970 when he was assigned to the Records Division where he remained up to his retirement on June 1, 1973. A resident of 41 Virginia Pl., Ret. PO Dan Ranellone died on August 20, 2004. He was 88 years old.

PO CASIMIR J. MORRIS #240

APPOINTED: January 1, 1947
DIED: October 12, 1972

Born Casimir Mroz in Yonkers on February 21, 1917, he attended local public schools, and graduated from Gorton H.S. At one point he changed his name to Morris and listed his previous occupation as a Laborer and Weaver at the Alexander Smith Carpet Factory. Casimir served in Army during WW-2 from August 2, 1941 and was honorably discharged as a sergeant in October of 1945. Morris was appointed to the Yonkers Police Department on January 1, 1947 with a starting salary of $1,940. On February 5, 1947 he attended the New York City police academy recruit training school and upon graduation was assigned to the 4th pct. on patrol. On January 1, 1951 he was reassigned to the 1st precinct. But, on October 16, 1952 he was returned to the 4th where he worked for 20 years, most often as the patrol wagon driver. Casimir Morris loved to cook the chowder at all police clambakes and was affectionately known as "Cas." Unfortunately PO Casimir Morris died unexpectedly on October 12, 1972. He was 55 years old.

CAPTAIN ROMAN P. FEDIRKA

APPOINTED: January 1, 1947
RETIRED: January 21, 1977

Roman P. Fedirka was born in Falls River, Mass on April 22, 1916. He and his family moved to Yonkers where Roman attended local schools and graduated from Saunders High School. Following his formal education Roman worked as a statistical clerk. Right from the start he was very good at dealing with very detailed clerical or paperwork issues.

During WW-2 Fedirka served in the US Coast Guard as a Seaman from August 8, 1942 up to his honorable discharge on September 26, 1945. He was appointed to the Yonkers Police Department on January 1, 1947 and received his recruit training at the New York City police academy recruit school where he trained for 10 weeks. Upon his graduation he was assigned to the 3rd precinct on Radford Street on foot patrol. Four years later, on January 1, 1951 he was re-assigned to the Traffic Division as a clerk in Traffic Violations Unit. He was very comfortable there and during his off-duty time studied as much as possible for promotional examinations.

Consequently on September 1, 1955 officer Fedirka received his first promotion; that being a promotion to the rank of Sergeant earning $5,000 a year and he was reassigned to the 4th precinct as patrol supervisor. The following year, on February 1, 1956, he was transferred to the 2nd precinct, again as a patrol supervisor.

Sgt Fedirka was a very serious man who was determined to rise in the ranks of the police

Capt. Roman P. Fedirka (cont.)

department. And, as a result of those many long hours of studying, he took and passed the test for police Lieutenant. It was on April 16, 1958 that he received his promotion to police Lieutenant and having his salary raised to $6,580 a year. His new assignment was to the 3rd precinct as a desk officer. Lt Fedirka was very good at dealing with the administrative aspects of police work and, as such, on November 21, 1961 he was reassigned to Criminal Court as Court Liaison Officer coordinating the appearances of those police officers reporting to court for arraignments or trials.

On October 6, 1972 Lt Fedirka received his promotion to the rank of Captain, raising his salary to $18,150 and he was placed in command of the Youth Services and Community Relations Division. His responsibilities also included the operation and supervision of personnel in the PAL. On August 24, 1973 Capt. Fedirka was once again transferred, this time to commanding officer of the Headquarters Command Division. And being a man who was comfortable in administrative duties this assignment was a perfect fit. Over the next few years he received a number of different assignments; First, on October 25, 1973 he was assigned as commanding officer of the Inspectional Services Division. Then on August 20, 1974 he was reassigned to the communications division as its commanding officer. And on May 10, 1976 he was transferred to the Field Services Bureau on citywide uniformed patrol.

At this point in his career it is very likely that he was not interested in returning to the uniformed patrol duties because only seven months later, on January 21, 1977, after having lived in Yonkers most of his life, Capt. Roman Fedirka retired. Prior to retirement the captain bought three years military time for pension purposes. He was a member and past president of the Yonkers American Legion and a member of the Catholic War Veterans Association.

In November of 1999 Ret Capt Fedirka moved to Lombard, Ill where, on March 12, 2000, only four months after he arrived, he died at the age of 83 years.

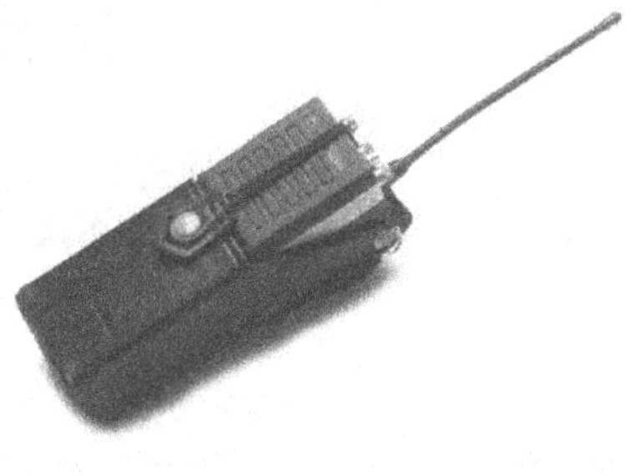

PO EDWARD G. LEAVY #181

APPOINTED: January 1, 1947
RETIRED: February 10, 1972

Born Edward George Leavy on Feb. 22, 1910 in Ireland he attended schools in both Ireland and later in Gorton HS and Commerce HS. Ed joined the National Guard in 1931 at age 21 as an MP. He served for 6 years but did not re-enlist. He then worked 5 years as a truck driver for Macy's Dept. Store. But during WW-2 he joined the Army on Nov 7, 1942 serving as a Staff Sergeant in France, Belgium, and Germany with 9th Armored Div. assigned as a traffic control officer with the MP's. He was honorably discharged on Nov 17, 1945. Ed was appointed to the YPD on January 1, 1947 and assigned to the 3rd pct. Although his appointment date was in 1947, his civil service longevity began on Mar 28, 1945 when he was certified for appointment but was still in the Army. On August 1, 1947 he was transferred from the 3rd pct. to the Traffic Division on foot directing traffic. He was known to local shoppers and residents affectionately as "The Sheikh," "Hands," "Fingers," or the "Sentinel of Getty Square." Leavy was given these nicknames because of the sharp and military style that he directed vehicle traffic in Getty Square while wearing his white gloves and displaying his trademark quick snap of the wrist. In Jan 1959 he was re-elected to his 10th term as Treasure of the West Co Police Conference. On January 1, 1971 Getty Square was honorarily renamed "Edward Leavy Square" in honor of officer Leavy's 25 years service, most of which were spent directing traffic in the "Square." He retired less than two months later on Feb 10, 1972. Ed and his wife moved to Toms River, NJ where he died on Mar 10, 1986 at age 76.

SGT. LOUIS J. CACACE #32

APPOINTED: January 1, 1947
RETIRED: June 25, 1976

Born Louis Joseph Cacace on January 26, 1915 in Yonkers, young Louis attended local public schools and graduated from Saunders High School. He was a very athletic young man and while in high school was a boxer in the Golden Gloves. On February 23, 1943 he was certified for appointment to the Yonkers Fire Department however following an examination he was found physically unqualified for the position. At the time he lived at 55 School St. His previous employment was that of a metal worker and movie projector operator. Lou served in the Marine Corps during World War II from February 21, 1944 up to his honorable discharge on November 27, 1945.

Louis was officially appointed to the Yonkers Police Department on January 1, 1947. However, his civil service longevity began on March 28, 1945 when his name was certified for his Yonkers Police appointment but he was still serving in the Marines Corps. On February 1, 1947 he attended the NYC Police Academy recruit training school and upon graduation his first assignment was patrol duty in the 3rd precinct located at 36 Radford Street. On January 13, 1949, while on his foot post, officer Cacace found an open door at 251 South Broadway. With gun in hand he entered and found two men breaking into a safe and arrested both of them. For his actions, three days later on January 16, 1949, he was transferred from the 3rd precinct to the Detective Division as a Detective. Lou was known by his family as Gigi, and by his police friends as "Louie Cacotch."

Being an excellent shot with his revolver, in the late 1940s he was a member of the YPD pistol team competing in annual police pistol tournaments in the metropolitan area. On May 7, 1956 Louis received a Certificate of Excellent Police Work for a robbery arrest which occurred nearly 6 years earlier on November 13, 1950 at Summit St. And, on April 16, 1958, while still a detective, Cacace was promoted to the rank of Sergeant earning a salary of $5,835 a year and was reassigned to the 2nd precinct as a patrol supervisor. On January 10, 1962 Sergeant case was reassigned to the 1st precinct and a year later to the 4th precinct.

Over the years Sgt Cacace was assigned to a number of different precincts and ultimately was assigned to the North Command at 53 Shonnard Place on January 1, 1971 when the numbered precinct concept was discontinued and replaced by centralized commands. While there, he was awarded a Certificate of Excellent Performance of duty by the Westchester Rockland newspaper chain during the second quarter of 1973.

Sgt. Cacace retired on June 25, 1976 while residing at 271 Hyatt Ave. Cacace's uncle was Yonkers City Court Judge Bob Cacace, his grandson was PO Dan Cacace of the Newtown, Ct. P.D., his cousin was Det Dominick Gebbia, his son was a Yonkers Fire Department Lieutenant, and his brother-in-law was Yonkers PO Roland Hall who married Cacace's sister.

Retired Sgt. Louis Cacace died on December 17, 1987. He was 72 years old.

PO WILLIAM E. McGRATH Jr. #94

APPOINTED: January 1, 1947
RETIRED: February 20, 1976

Bill McGrath Jr. was born in the city of Mt Vernon, NY on April 27, 1913, the son of Yonkers police officer Bill McGrath Sr. McGrath lived in Yonkers where he attended local schools and upon graduation gained employment as an insurance inspector and taxi driver. Bill joined the Army on April 29, 1941, prior to the US being attacked, trained and served over four years as a combat medic in the European Theater. He saw action tending the wounded in the Ardennes, Normandy, and the Rhineland. He was honorably discharged on Sept. 26, 1945. William McGrath was appointed to the Yonkers Police Department on January 1, 1947 with a salary of $1,940. However, due to being in the Army when first called for appointment, his police seniority began on March 28, 1945. On February 5, 1947 he attended the NYC Police Academy recruit training school for 10 weeks and upon graduation was assigned to foot patrol in the 2nd pct. On January 1, 1951 Bill was reassigned to Communications & Records Division as a switchboard operator/dispatcher. He remained in "the Radio Room" for 25 years until January 9, 1976 when he was re-assigned to patrol in the then North Command. PO Bill McGrath retired on February 20, 1976. Ret. PO Bill McGrath Jr died on December 7, 1998. He was 85.

PO DANIEL L. SCHIAVONE #92

APPOINTED: January 1, 1947
RETIRED: March 1, 1973

Born Daniel Louis Schiavone on Jan. 11, 1915 in Yonkers NY, he attended local public schools, and following graduation worked as a Weaver for the Alexander Smith Carpet Mills. During WW-2 Schiavone joined the Army on May 20, 1942 and served in the Army's Signal Corps up to his honorable discharge on Sept. 25, 1945. Dan was appointed to the Y.P.D. from 160 Oak St. on Jan. 1, 1947 with a starting salary of $2,625. Though appointed in 1947, his seniority actually began on January 16, 1943 when his name was called to be hired, but he was serving in the Army. On February 5, 1947 Schiavone attended the NYC Police Academy recruit training for 10 weeks. Upon graduation, he was assigned to the 2nd pct. However, before the end of the year, on Sept. 1, 1947, he was transferred from the 2nd to the 1st pct. In 1958 officer Schiavone made a burglary arrest which won for him a Citation of Excellence from the Macy Westchester newspaper chain. Again in 1960 he earned departmental recognition for another burglary arrest while on his foot post. On June 18, 1965 officer Schiavone was reassigned to the 3rd pct. Nearly four years later, on Jan. 1, 1969 he was transferred to the Traffic Div. in the Traffic Violations Unit from which he later retired on March 1, 1973. His son Daniel was a retired Harrison NY police officer. Ret. PO Daniel Schiavone died in his home on July 23, 1996 at the age of 81 years.

PO ANDREW MAYBO #68

APPOINTED: January 1, 1947
RETIRED: June 1, 1969

Andy Maybo was born on March 15, 1914 in Yonkers and graduated from Saunders HS where he was recognized as an excellent basketball player. Following school he worked as an auto mechanic. Andy served in the Army Air Corps as a staff sergeant in the Transportation Section during World War II from May 21, 1942, up to his honorable discharge on Jan. 10, 1946. Following his discharge he was officially appointed to the YPD on January 1, 1947 earning $2,625 a year. However his civil service seniority actually began in Dec. of 1942 when he was first certified for appointment but was in the Army. Maybo attended the NYC Police Academy for recruit training for 10 weeks. Upon graduation he was assigned to the 1st pct. on foot patrol. Over the next few years he changed assignments quite often. For example; Nov. 16, 1947 he was assigned to the Traffic Division on foot patrol; April 11, 1949 from traffic to the 4th pct.; Jan. 1, 1951 to the 1st pct.; Oct. 16, 1952 to the 4th pct.; June 20, 1956 to the 1st pct.; Jan. 23, 1962 to the Traffic Division for parking meter enforcement; March 21, 1963 to the 3rd pct.; April 27, 1964 to the 1st detailed to City Hall security; Nov. 9, 1966 to the 4th pct. still detailed to City Hall security. Andy retired on June 1, 1969 living at 233 Gailmore Drive but he later moved to Salisbury, NY. Andy died on May 3, 1986 in Daytona Beach Florida where he was visiting. He was 72.

PO ANTHONY MAGALETTA #37

APPOINTED: January 1, 1947
RETIRED: February 7, 1975

Anthony was born on Feb. 11, 1913 in Yonkers, attended local schools, and graduated from Commerce HS. As a young man he worked as a clerk in the Yonkers Post Office. He had been a member of the 27th Military Police Co. in the National Guard when he joined the regular army on October 14, 1940. During WW-2 Tony served in England as an Army MP and received his honorable discharge as a First Sergeant on Oct. 12, 1945. Magaletta was appointed to the YPD on Jan. 1, 1947 earning $2,625 a year. However, his longevity began on Dec. 16, 1942 when he was first certified for appointment, but was still in the Army. PO Magaletta attended the NYC Police Academy for recruit training and upon completion he was assigned to patrol in the 1st pct. However, the following year he was reassigned to the 2nd pct. On Dec. 21, 1953 he was granted a temporary leave of absence to accept appointment as Temporary Superintendent of Traffic earning $4,400 a year. The following year, on June 1, 1954, he was officially designated the permanent Superintendent of Traffic at $4,600 a year. On Jan. 1, 1975 he was given the title of Traffic Coordinator at $18,043. He retired a month later on Feb. 7, 1975. An avid golfer, Ret PO/Superintendent of Traffic Anthony Magaletta died July 25, 1991 at 78 years of age.

PO EDWARD V. BALUN #203

APPOINTED: January 1, 1947
RETIRED: June 30, 1973

Born Edward Vincent Balun on January 15, 1916 in Yonkers NY, Ed attended local schools and graduated from Saunders HS. Ed held a few different jobs until he joined the Army Air Corps on August 19, 1941. During World War II he served as a Quartermaster in the Motor Transport Unit with the rank of Technical Sergeant. He was honorably discharged on November 27, 1945. He worked for a while as a chauffeur but was appointed to the Yonkers Police Department on January 1, 1947 earning $1,940, and on February 5, 1947 attended the NYC Police Academy for 10 weeks. Upon graduation he was assigned to patrol in the 4th precinct. Only a few short months later on November 16, 1947 officer Balun was transferred from the 4th precinct to the Traffic Division on motorcycle duty where he would remain for the remainder of his entire career. Ed retired June 30, 1973 and moved to Greenville, SC where he seemed to enjoy playing golf. However, to everyone's shock, Ret PO Edward Balun died on September 26, 1991. He was 75 years old.

PO JOHN P. McMAHON #106

APPOINTED: August 1, 1947
RESIGNED: December 5, 1947

John Philip McMahon was born August 23, 1921 in the city of Yonkers and graduated from Sacred Heart High School in 1938. Following graduation McMahon joined the Army, and during World War II, served with the US Raider Battalion in the Philippine Islands. Jack, as he was known, received several decorations including a Purple Heart for injuries on Okinawa. Following his discharge he returned to Yonkers and while living at 104 Amackassin Terrace joined the Yonkers Police Department on August 1, 1947. He had only just completed his recruit training when on December 5, 1947 Jack submitted his resignation to the Yonkers Police Department. It was then that he joined the Westchester County Parkway police. For several years McMahon rode a motorcycle on Parkway patrol. But, eventually he would be promoted to Chief of Detectives and retired in 1969 after 20 years of service with the rank of Lieutenant. Following retirement Jack worked for the State Department (CIA) in Vietnam as a police adviser from 1969 to 1973. After returning to the states he worked for several years as a teacher and then retired in 1976 to West Harwich, MA. His brother-in-law was Yonkers police officer Albert Higgins.

John Philip McMahon Jr died on July 18, 1999 in West Harwich, MA at the age of 77 years.

PO DOMINICK J. MARSH #8

APPOINTED: August 1, 1947
RETIRED: October 4, 1963

Dominick Marsh was born in Yonkers NY on March 9, 1915. Being of Italian heritage it was thought that he shortened his name at one point. Dom served during WW 2 in the Army from Dec. 13, 1938 up to his honorable discharge as a disabled veteran on Oct. 5, 1945. Dom worked as a correction officer in Sing Sing State Prison and his father was a Yonkers firefighter. When he took the YPD police test he lived at 8 Dunston Ave. in Yonkers. However, because he was a disabled war vet, civil service law at that time, allowed him to be moved to the top of the list. He was appointed to the YPD on Aug. 1, 1947. As a rookie he attended the NYC Police Academy and after graduation was assigned to the 4th pct. He was considered an enigma by his co- workers. He was strong as a bull but very withdrawn. He wouldn't speak unless spoken to, and yet was a good piano player. He was affectionately known as "The Wooden Indian" because he would stand so still and quiet on his post in Getty Square or in an Ashburton Ave doorway, just staring for hours like a wooden Indian. Dom worked in all four precincts during his career. Records indicate that following an examination by the police surgeon Dominic Marsh was retired on a medical disability effective July 31, 1962. However the records also indicate that this disability retirement was rescinded and he was listed as having retired from the YPD on October 4, 1963. Retired PO Dominic Marsh died in his city of residence, Shasta, Cal. on August 29, 2003.

PO JAMES J. BRODERICK #7

APPOINTED: August 1, 1947
RESIGNED: January 31, 1951

Jim Broderick was born in Yonkers on April 24, 1917 the son of a Yonkers City Court judge. Jim was apparently a very academic student type and prior to the YPD was attending college. Jim served in Army during WW-2 from February 6, 1941 up to his honorable discharge on December 8, 1945. He was appointed to the Yonkers Police Department on August 1, 1947 with a salary of $1,940. His first assignment was in the 2nd precinct on uniform patrol. Pursuant to the GI Bill Broderick was granted a one year leave of absence without pay from July 1, 1948 to July 1, 1949 to continue his college education. Following his leave of absence he was reinstated to the YPD back to the 2nd precinct at $2,500. a year. He had two brothers; Harry, who was a Yonkers police officer, and Thomas a local doctor. James Broderick resigned from the YPD on January 31, 1951 and died in February of 1972 at the age of 54 years.

LT. HAROLD J. POWERS

APPOINTED: August 1, 1947
RETIRED: April 1, 1988

Harold Powers was born in Yonkers on August 29, 1924 on the Street formally named Garden Street; now Walsh Road. He attended St. Joseph's grade school and graduated from Gorton high school and the Pace Business Institute. As a young man Harold was very athletic all throughout school and was an avid ballplayer. Following school he gained employment as an oiler in the Habirshaw Cable & Wire Corporation. Harold served in the Army during World War II from March 15, 1943, including 13 months on Iwo Jima, right up to his honorable discharge as a sergeant on February 27, 1945.

When he came home he decided to take some time off collecting unemployment payments of $20. a week for 52 weeks. He liked to say he was in the 52 - 20 club. He applied to the Yonkers Police Department while residing at 743 Palisades Ave. and was appointed a Patrolman on August 1, 1947 earning $1,940 a year. His first assignment following ten weeks of recruit training at the NYC Police Academy was patrol in the 4th precinct. While assigned there he played on their precinct softball team. On January 1, 1951 he was moved to the 1st precinct for short time, until October 16, 1952, when he was returned to the 4th precinct.

In the 1950s Powers was a member of the Yonkers Pacoy Club of 171 N. Broadway and played on their club softball team competing with various teams and traveling along the Atlantic seaboard. Harold had a good personality and was very friendly but he always seemed to have a scowl on his face. He rarely smiled. If you didn't know him you would think that he was very grouchy. As a result he gained the nickname of "Happy" Powers. Officer Powers was promoted to Sergeant on April 15, 1958 earning $5,835 a year and was assigned as a patrol supervisor in the 1st precinct. Two months later, on June 3, 1958, he was once again returned to his familiar 4th precinct.

"Happy" was promoted to the rank of Lieutenant on November 16, 1961 earning a salary of $7,360 a year and was reassigned as a desk officer in the 3rd precinct. The following year, on June 13, 1962, he was moved to desk duty in the 2nd precinct at 441 Central Park Avenue. Over the next several years he was transferred several times to various precincts performing desk duty. But on March 12, 1973 he was reassigned as the booking lieutenant in Central Booking. He remained there right up to his retirement on April 1, 1988 and continued living at 331 Sommerville Place. "Happy" Powers raised eight children including a daughter, who was a NYPD detective, and a son who was a Yonkers firefighter.

Retired Lt. Harold Powers died on January 3, 1999 at the age of 74 years.

PO JEROME V. McGILLICUDDY #90

APPOINTED: August 1, 1947
RESIGNED: January 31, 1959

Jerry was born in Brooklyn, NY on April 17, 1921, was raised in the Riverdale section of Bronx, and received his education there. He was a WW 2 veteran having served in the Army Air Corps. He joined on January 3, 1943, and saw combat in North Africa. He was honorably discharged on February 6, 1946.

Having moved to Yonkers, Jerry was appointed to the Yonkers Police Department on August 1, 1947 earning $1,940. He attended the NYC Police Academy for ten weeks and following graduation was assigned to the 4th precinct. He had part of one finger missing and was almost disqualified by the police surgeon from being appointed. On July 24, 1948, about 2 AM, while voluntarily working steady late tours, a male attempted suicide by jumping into the Hudson River off the Pier. Officer McGillicuddy jumped in water and rescued the man and, for which, he received a departmental Commendation on December 13, 1950. On April 11, 1949 he was reassigned from the 4th pct. to the Traffic Division on foot directing traffic. PO McGillicuddy was very active in PBA and PAL activities and was a past president of the YPD Holy Name Society. In the 1940's he even served in the YPD Holy Name Society Color Guard.

After a short stay in the Juvenile Aide Bureau, on July 1, 1951 he was appointed a Detective. Jerry always had a special interest in the law. While in the D.D. he voluntarily worked steady late tours and attended law school during the day. However, in 1952 he was moved to the 1st pct. on patrol but continued in law school. In late June of 1956 McGillicuddy graduated and received his law degree from the New York Law School and was admitted to the bar.

On July 1, 1956 Jerry was detailed to work in the Public Safety Commissioners office in City Hall and later that month was detailed to the NYPD Police Academy for special training in their legal bureau. When he returned, on August 20, 1956 he was assigned to the Traffic Division but detailed to the Court of Special Sessions as the YPD legal Officer. In June of 1958 he was offered the job of "Clerk of the Court" if he could obtain a leave of absence for three months for special training, which he did receive.

Officer McGillicuddy resigned from the police department on January 31, 1959 and worked as the Yonkers Chief Court Clerk. Several years later Jerry retired and moved to Florida where he died on November 14, 1981, reportedly in an automobile accident. He was 60 years old.

LT. PATRICK J. CURRAN

APPOINTED: August 1, 1947
RETIRED: August 11, 1972

Pat Curran was an imposing figure of a man standing well over 6' tall and over 200 Lbs. He was born Dec 3, 1920 in Yonkers where he attended St. Joseph's elementary school and graduated from Roosevelt HS. As a young man he was an excellent basketball player. Prior to the YPD Pat worked as a waiter. Curran served in Army Air Corps during WW-2 from August 12, 1942, with his military specialty being an Armorer, and received his honorable discharge on Nov. 6, 1945. Patrick was appointed to the YPD on August 1, 1947 with a salary of $1,940 a year. He received his recruit training at the NYPD Police Academy and was assigned to the 3rd pct. A sports enthusiast, Pat played on the 1947 Police Softball team and in the late 1940's served in the YPD Holy Name Society Color Guard. On Nov. 16, 1947 he was transferred to the Traffic Division directing traffic. As a member of the YPD War Veterans Legion, on Nov. 2, 1949 he was elected Quartermaster for the organization. The following transfers occurred; On June 1, 1953 to the 4th pct.; on Feb. 7, 1955 to the Juvenile Aide Bureau; on Dec 16, 1958 to the DD but out on May 31, 1960 and back to the Traffic Division. On July 1, 1961 PO Curran was promoted to Sergeant at $6,525 a year and assigned to the 3rd pct. as a patrol supervisor. On Jan 10, 1962 he was moved to the 2nd pct. On Jan 14, 1966 Curran was promoted to Lieutenant at $9,090 a year and went to the 1st pct. as a desk officer. But on Nov 7, 1966 he was moved to the 4th on desk duty. On Aug 13, 1971 he was reassigned to HQ Command, detailed as the YPD Court Liaison officer. Pat Curran retired from the YPD on Aug 11, 1972 and died on June 24, 1989 at age of 68 years.

PO JOHN T. DOLAN #21

APPOINTED: August 1, 1947
RESIGNED: October 31, 1953

John Dolan was born in the Bronx NY where he received his education. After moving to Yonkers and working at several miscellaneous jobs, including that of a bookkeeper, John served in Army during WW-2 from October 15, 1940 up to his honorable discharge on September 9, 1945. John was appointed to the Yonkers Police Dept. on August 1, 1947 along with 13 other recruits. Dolan and his entire recruit class were sent to the NYPD Police Academy for recruit training. Upon his graduation Dolan was assigned to the 2nd precinct on routine patrol. His starting salary at that time was $1,940 a year. According to GO# 82 John Dolan resigned from the YPD on October 31, 1953 reportedly to join NY State Police. John Dolan died on July 14, 1989.

DEPUTY CHIEF JOHN F. McMAHON Jr.

APPOINTED: August 1, 1947
RETIRED: September 30, 1989

The subject of this writing is one of those individuals who most people would hope they could have an opportunity to work for. He was a big man, but even on those rare occasions when he had cause to be angry, he still always spoke with a soft controlled voice. When he became a supervisor, if you were a police officer working for him and had a problem, he always found a way to resolve the issue to everyone's satisfaction. He rose through the ranks to Deputy Chief but was always affectionately referred to as "Captain Jack." And it would not be an exaggeration to say that he was extremely well-liked and respected, particularly by the rank-and-file police officer.

John F. McMahon Jr. was born on August 12, 1925 in the City of Yonkers, along with his twin brother Joseph. He attended PS# 23, Benjamin Franklin Jr. HS, and graduated from Gorton H.S. As a young boy Jack was a great swimmer. In fact he entered and won several local swimming competitions as a youth. And while in high school he played on the school football team.

Following his formal education "Jack" McMahon was employed as a truck driver, despite the fact that he did have some training as a Surveyor and Architectural Draftsman. McMahon served in Army Air

Deputy Chief John F. McMahon (cont.)

Corps during the last year of World War 2 beginning on January 26, 1945 and following the wars end he was honorably discharged on November 28, 1945. After the war Jack, and many other men looking for a secure job, took the civil service test for Yonkers Police "Patrolman." His patrolman's list was the first list to be established after WW-2 and he placed # 15 on that list.

John F. McMahon was appointed to the Yonkers Police Department on August 1, 1947 while residing at 171 Elm St. The salary of a new police officer at that time was $1,940 per year, and they were only paid twice a month, not every two weeks. "Jack," as he was known, received his recruit training, along with all the other recruits hired with him, at the New York City Police Academy which at the time was located in an old six story warehouse on Huber St in lower Manhattan. Yonkers Public Safety Commissioner Patrick O'Hara was a friend of then NYC Police Comm. Wallender and received permission to send down the Yonkers recruit class. Jack said they had different instructors for the Yonkers class because of the difference in laws for a 1st class city like New York and for a 2nd class city like Yonkers. The new men were said to have all bought their uniforms at "Palmieri's" Clothing on 3rd Ave. near Fordham Road for about $300.

Upon his recruit class graduating from the police academy, Jack was assigned to the 1st precinct, located at 20 Wells Ave. on routine foot patrol. When he began working in the 1st precinct, police officers were required to work 6 eight hour tours, with a 32 hour "swing" off in between each set of tours. There was no compensatory time and time off for extra hours worked was granted at the captains discretion. In 1947 a police officer basically needed about 15 years on the job before being eligible to even be considered for a summer vacation. Jack, and all the other new men, were required to work all parades, special events, Election Day, Spring and Fall Inspection days, all without pay or time back. And at that time the state only provided for a 28 year retirement plan.

On August 28, 1949 officer McMahon was commended by Deputy Public Safety Commissioner Comey for assisting in crowd control, etc., while off duty, at the scene where officer Frank Porach was beaten to the ground with his own nightstick. However, in order to stop the assault the suspect was shot and killed by officer Porach's partner, PO Al Hopper.

On February 19, 1953, while walking his post, McMahon observed moving shadows inside the Gotham Jewelry store at 15 Main St. He confronted the thief, but the man refused to submit to arrest. With the suspect trying to escape officer McMahon chased him up a building ladder to the roof, and made the arrest. For his actions, officer McMahon was commended by Public Safety Commissioner Patrick O'Hara for his keen observation, aggressive pursuit of the suspect, and ultimate arrest.

Young officer McMahon was a very intelligent individual who was determined to make his mark in the Yonkers Police Department. As such he put his mind to studying all the laws that the civil service test might base exam questions on. His long hours of studying paid off and on June 16, 1955 PO John F. McMahon was promoted to the rank of Sergeant earning a salary of $5,000 a year. His first assignment as a patrol supervisor was in the 3rd precinct located at 36 Radford St.

During an award ceremony held by the police department Honor Board on May 7, 1956, Sgt. McMahon was awarded 3 certificates of excellent police work; the first for a robbery arrest that he made

Deputy Chief John F. McMahon (cont.)

on April 27, 1952 at 15 Yonkers Ave. The second award was for locating and capturing an escaped prisoner on February 24, 1954 on the corner of Elm Street and Oak Street. The third award was for taking into custody for observation an emotionally disturbed male on May 24, 1955 at 78 Warburton Ave. On September 3, 1956 Sgt. McMahon was transferred from the 3rd precinct to the 2nd precinct at 441 Central Park Ave.

Sgt. McMahon received his second promotion, this time to the rank of Lieutenant, on January 16, 1958 earning a salary of $6,580 a year and he remained in the 2nd precinct, but was assigned as a Desk Officer. Over the next nearly 10 year period Lt. McMahon was transferred several times. They were as follows; On December 15, 1958 to the 3rd precinct as a desk officer; on December 22, 1958 he was returned back to the 2nd precinct on desk duty; on June 13, 1962 he was returned back to 3rd precinct once again on desk duty; on March 16, 1964 transferred to the 1st pct. on desk duty; on November 7, 1966 once again back to the 3rd on the desk; and on December 15, 1967 transferred to the 2nd precinct on desk duty.

Lt. McMahon continued his rise in the police department when, on November 14, 1969 he was promoted to the rank of Captain earning $14,625 a year. Captain McMahon's first assignment as a captain was as commanding officer of the 1st precinct on E. Grassy Sprain Road. Even though Capt. McMahon was now at a command level, the transfers and reassignments seemed to keep coming. On May 14, 1970 he was moved to the 4th pct. as an Early Tour Captain on patrol. On December 1, 1970 he was designated Operations Officer at the 4th precinct as part of what would be an unworkable and therefore failed initial attempt at the centralization of the patrol precincts into one command. On January 1, 1971 a new and modified centralization plan was put in effect where the 4 precincts were changed to a two command concept consisting of a North Command and a South Command.

On August 11, 1971 "Capt. Jack" was reassigned to the newly organized Community Relations Unit as its commanding officer. The initial complement consisted of Capt. McMahon, Lt John Flynn, and police officers Lorenzo Paul, Nicholas Rossi, Rita Gross Nelson and Samuel Belton. The unit began operating in the old 3rd precinct at 36 Radford Street but was soon moved to a storefront location on Warburton Avenue. Seventy five percent of the cost of operating the unit came from securing a federal grant. While still assigned to that unit, on August 13, 1971, he and all the police officers assigned to the unit received appointments as detectives. However, less than a year later, very likely due to the end of federal funding, the captain and all his personnel were all returned to their original ranks and assignments on June 30, 1972, and Capt. McMahon was reassigned to the North Command as the commanding officer.

Once again the string of transfers began. On October 26, 1973 to HQ Command Division as commanding officer; On November 12, 1973 to the Communications Division as commanding officer. On August 20, 1974 to HQ in the Records Division as the commanding officer. On January 6, 1975 to the Special Operations Division (SOD) as the commanding officer. On September 3, 1979 back to the North Command as the CO. On April 1, 1980 to the Courts and Detention services division as the CO. On February 9, 1981 to Administrative Services Division as the CO. On September 13, 1982 to the Inspections Unit as a Patrol Captain. On July 1, 1983 to the N/E Patrol Command located at 730 E. Grassy Sprain Rd. as the CO. Capt. McMahon was later assigned to the Field Services Bureau as a Patrol

Deputy Chief John F. McMahon (cont.)

Captain almost up to his retirement.

Throughout his career Capt. McMahon had proven himself many times over as an extremely capable and intelligent supervisor and administrator. It had always been his desire to retire as a deputy chief but, it seemed unattainable. One likely reason was that it was believed that the perception by those above him in rank, was that he was too close and friendly to the rank and file men and women. Further it is believed he was considered somewhat of a rebel by never hesitating to question his superiors regarding those department policies that he was convinced were unsound and counterproductive. It was clear to any objective observer that the many transfers he received throughout his career and, although being the senior captain, was skipped over for a promotion to deputy chief several times, was a form of retribution for McMahon being very independent and outspoken.

It is of interest to note that Capt. John F. McMahon Jr.'s father, John F. McMahon Sr., was also appointed a Yonkers police officer on March 3, 1919. However, less than two years later he decided to make a career change due to financial considerations and resigned from the YPD, at his own request, effective September 6, 1920. He would then work as a plumber and trucker.

Capt. McMahon married police officer Sharon Rohan which made her father, retired police officer Bob Rohan, McMahon's father-in-law. Capt. McMahon's brother-in-law was YPD Capt. John Higgins, and his nephew was retired captain Patrick McMahon.

"Capt. Jack," as he was known universally throughout the department, was preparing to retire when he was notified that he was finally going to be promoted to the rank of Deputy Chief. In fact, on September 30, 1989, he did receive his long deserved promotion to Deputy Chief but, following the official swearing-in ceremony he notified the police department that he was retiring effective that very same day.

Retired Deputy Chief John F. "Jack" McMahon still resides in northern Westchester along with his retired police officer wife, Sharon.

LT. JAMES A. BALONE

APPOINTED: August 1, 1947
RETIRED: March 9, 1972

James A Balone was born in Yonkers NY on Nov 26, 1921. He graduated from Commerce HS and gained employment as a clerk. Jim served in the Army Air Corps during WW-2 from Aug. 12, 1942 as an NCO in charge of Flight Control, and was honorably discharged on Nov 17, 1945 as a Corporal. He was appointed to the YPD on Aug. 1, 1947 earning $1,940 a year and received his recruit training at the NYC Police Academy. Upon graduation he was assigned to the 2nd pct. Jim was appointed a Detective on January 1, 1951 earning $3,500. On Oct. 7, 1951 Det. Balone investigated a stabbing incident and ultimately arrested the suspect for murder and was commended for his action. He was transferred out of the DD on May 27, 1952 and moved to patrol in the 1st pct. On April 16, 1958 Balone was promoted to Sergeant with the salary of $5,835 and was reassigned to the 2nd pct. On Jan. 10, 1962 Sgt Balone was moved to the 3rd pct. On Feb. 28, 1963 Sgt Balone was promoted to Lieutenant at $8,400 a year and was assigned to desk duty in the 1st pct. Following the reorganization of all four pct's into two patrol commands, on January 1, 1971, Lt Balone was assigned to desk officer in the North Command. Lt Balone retired from the YPD on March 9, 1972. It was reported that in Sept. of 1974 Jim Balone changed his last name to "Malone." Ret Lt James Balone (Malone) died a month later on October 17, 1974. He was only 52 years old.

PO MICHAEL J. SYSO #5

APPOINTED: August 1, 1947
DIED: February 23, 1980

Mike Syso was born in Yonkers on April 26, 1920 and was a graduate of Roosevelt high school and the Butler Business School for bookkeeping. Mike was a veteran of WW 2 enlisting in the Army on July 17, 1941 serving as a captain and automatic weapons platoon commander. He was honorably discharged on November 6, 1946. Mike worked as a weaver in the Alexander Smith carpet Mills. A resident of 75 Lockwood Ave. he was appointed to the YPD on August 1, 1947 and was assigned to patrol in the 4th precinct. On January 1, 1951 he was reassigned to the 1st precinct for a year and in Oct. of 1952 was moved into the Juvenile Aid Bureau. On May 18, 1962 Syso and a number of other officers were credited with arresting burglars who had been terrorizing residents all over the county. A number of assignments were as follows; June 14, 1968 to the Traffic Engineering Department, January 1, 1974 to the Records Division, August 27, 1974 to Special Operations as the desk aide, June 20, 1979 to the N/E patrol command as the precinct desk aide. Mike was very active in the PBA and the PAL. His brother was Detective Thomas Syso and his uncle was Sgt. Michael Girasek. Mike became ill before he could retire and died on February 23, 1980 at the age of 59 years.

LT. GEORGE F. RUSNACK

APPOINTED: August 1, 1947
RETIRED: January 10, 1986

George was born in the city of Yonkers on December 29, 1921. He attended St. Peter's school, Sacred Heart high school, and graduated from Columbia University in New York City. He also attended nine months at Radio Mechanic School. On personnel records he listed his early employment as a student and stock recorder. And for a while George worked in New York City for the RCA Corporation. It was said that he grew up in the area of Riverdale Avenue and Downing Street. Records indicate he served during World War II in the Army Air Corps as part of the ground crew. He served in Africa for about three years from March 4, 1943 to January 20, 1946 as a cryptographer in North Africa. He was honorably discharged from the Army Airways Communications Systems Squadron with the rank of Sergeant. Upon his discharge he joined the Army reserve where he remained for about 10 years. It was there on September 13, 1950 that Sgt. Rusnack received his commission as an Army 2nd Lieutenant. He would eventually attain the rank of Army reserve Captain.

George was appointed to the Yonkers Police Department on August 1, 1947 while living at 17 Stanley Ave. Starting salaries for new recruits at that time was $1,940 a year. He attended the New York City police Academy along with others hired with him and upon graduation was assigned to the 3rd precinct walking foot posts on South Broadway. Like many others in the police department George was very athletic and played on the 1947 police softball team. On January 1, 1951 officer Rusnack was transferred to patrol duty in the 1st precinct on Wells Avenue. Eleven years later, as part of a citywide departmental reorganization, on October 16, 1962, officer Rusnack was reassigned to the Traffic Division. However he worked as a clerk, not on patrol.

On July 1, 1956 George Rusnack was promoted to the rank of Sergeant earning $5,250 a year and was transferred to the 3rd precinct. Two years later, on July 1, 1958, he was assigned to clerical duties in the Traffic Violations unit. George was very good at taking civil service exams and as a result on November 16, 1960 he was promoted to the rank of Lieutenant earning $7,175 a year and this time was

Lt. George F. Rusnack (cont.)

assigned as a desk officer in the 3rd precinct.

Following the appointment of the new Public Safety Commissioner, Daniel F. McMahon in January of 1964, Lt Rusnack was chosen by him to be his administrative aide in City Hall and was so assigned on February 3, 1964. On the 26th of that month he was elevated to Detective Lieutenant, assigned to the Detective Bureau, but detailed working in Comm. McMahon's office. Det Lt Rusnack remained in that position assisting Comm. McMahon, and later his successors, Comm. Frank Vescio, and lastly Comm. William Sickley, who was the last to hold that position. When Sickley retired in 1973 the Public Safety Commissioner position was abolished as was George Rusnack's assignment and complete control of the YPD was restored to Chief Polsen. As a result, on July 2, 1973, Rusnack was stripped of his detective status and reassigned as the executive officer in the South Patrol Command at 441 Central Park Avenue.

From this point on Lt. Rusnack received several different assignments. On October 1, 1975 to Headquarters Command Division in charge of Central Records; on October 9, 1981 to the Northeast Patrol Command as their executive officer; on July 1, 1983 to command of the Administrative Services Division, and on April 1, 1985 to executive officer of the Communications Division.

Having reached the maximum age allowed by law, with nearly 40 years service, and having health issues with his heart, Lt George Rusnack retired on January 10, 1986 and moved to Brick town, NJ where he organized a Neighborhood Watch for their community. Throughout his career as a supervisor Rusnack was very active in the Capt's, Lt's, & Sgt's Association business serving as Secretary for many years. Most of his life he loved fishing and while in Sacred Heart school and Colombia University, he was an aggressive basketball player.

His uncle was PO Stephen Rusnack. (His father's brother) and his brother in law was PO Ray Bartko. (They married sisters) Also, Rusnack's wife's uncle was PO Frank McMahon.

Ret Lt George Rusnack died on April 13, 2002 in Ocean County, Bricktown, NJ. He was 80 years old.

LT. HAROLD J. O'NEILL

APPOINTED: August 1, 1947
RETIRED: June 18, 1975

Harold O'Neill was born in Yonkers on June 1, 1922. He grew up on the west side of Yonkers, attended local public schools, and graduated from Saunders H.S. While a student at Saunders Harry was already a powerful and aggressive teen who played on the Saunders football team and was also the catcher for their baseball team. And his strength wasn't by chance. He worked out with heavy weights to develop the strength he later had. As a young man he listed his employment as that of a machine operator.

During WW-2 young Harry O'Neill decided to join the Navy to serve his country. He served aboard an LSM, a medium Transport Ship # 262. Harry served from March 9, 1943 to January 6, 1946. He said he and his shipmates endured several Japanese Kamikaze attacks on his ship in the Pacific, but luckily they were never struck. He was known to his friends as "Harry O," and behind his back as, "Harry the Horse" due to his amazing strength.

While residing at 120 Woodworth Avenue Harry joined the YPD on August 1, 1947 with an annual salary of $1,940., and received his recruit training at the NYC Police Academy. Following recruit graduation his first assignment was patrol in the 4th precinct on Shonnard Place. Still a lover of sports Harry played on the police Softball team as their catcher in 1947. A few years later he was reassigned to the 1st precinct on Wells Avenue on January 1, 1951, once again on patrol. Years later, on January 1, 1957 he moved to 66 Pembrook Drive in Yonkers.

Good fortune came Harry's way when, on May 27, 1952, he was appointed a Detective in the D.D. The detective shields carried by detectives back then were the same basic design as they were in 2013, with the exception that in 1952 there was no blue enamel on the shield.

Harry faced a real test under fire early in his career. On September 8, 1954 at 8:15 p.m. a holdup team robbed the delicatessen at 148 McLean Avenue at gunpoint and escaped with $448. This same team was also believed to be responsible for several other holdups in the Bronx and Manhattan. As a result they had been dubbed the Delicatessen Bandits. Firearms were always displayed and sooner or later someone was going to get hurt.

It was about 9:45 p.m. on September 12, 1954 and Detectives Harry O'Neill and Bob Maitre Sr., were on patrol in unmarked radio car # 286 with O'Neill as the "operator" and Maitre as the "message receiver." What an unlikely pair they were. Although both were excellent police officers, Bob Maitre was always quiet, unassuming, and soft spoken. Harry O'Neill was very outgoing, gregarious, and not the least bit afraid to speak his mind. And yet the two actually made good partners and worked well together.

On this evening while driving south on South Broadway, Det. O'Neill attempted to turn around at 261st Street in the Bronx when, according to Bob Maitre, Harry spotted a plate that he knew right away was on their wanted list for the robberies. When interviewed, Harry actually still remembered the plate number. He said he would never forget it; NY3638. Expecting that the two suspects in the stolen vehicle were armed, Maitre drew his revolver as O'Neill pulled alongside the car. As Det. Maitre got out, the suspects sped off, followed closely behind by the two detectives. The pursuit wound its way through residential side streets in the Riverdale section of the Bronx at high speeds with Det. Maitre firing his

Lt. Harold J. O'Neill (cont.)

revolver at the fleeing vehicle. (A perfectly legal and accepted practice back then.)

As Harry O'Neill told the story he said, they immediately tried to call for backup units but had trouble with the radio system, which he said actually consisted of two separate systems. The old one and a new one not yet fully functional, but both on line together. Between the screeching of tires, multiple shots being fired from the radio car, and adrenaline, they had great difficulty getting through to Headquarters. But the chase continued and Maitre kept firing his revolver at the bandits.

At one point as the suspect vehicle took a sharp turn, the passenger door swung open and the passenger fell out on his back and began to roll. It was not clear whether the door just popped open or if one of Det. Maitre's rounds found its mark. As the driver of the suspect vehicle continued to speed away, O'Neill and Maitre brought their unit to a stop. With the intention of scraping up their soon to be prisoner, they climbed out of their car with their revolvers at the ready. To their surprise (maybe shock is a better word), as they walked toward the male on the ground he jumped up like nothing had happened and began firing at the two detectives. Bob Maitre was a step or two ahead of O'Neill and only about 20 feet from the shooter when the near point-blank firing started. Maitre explained, "*I was really stunned when he fired at us and I raised my gun and tried to return fire, and that's when I found out that my gun was empty.*"

Without hesitation Maitre reported that Harry O'Neill ran forward toward the suspect and began firing his revolver in what was later termed by the media as a running gun battle. Harry recently told me, "*The guy was shooting, and I was shooting, and pretty soon I just heard my gun making a clicking noise. I was empty.*" In that short moment it must have seemed like time stood still, and then in seconds it was over and the suspect disappeared into the darkness of the side yards. Incredibly, neither the officers nor the suspect were hit. What remained were two police officers standing in the street probably somewhat dazed at what had just transpired. Bob Maitre said he'll never forget the look on Harry O'Neill's face as Harry walked over to him and calmly but seriously asked, "*Would you look and see if I was hit.*" It sounds funny now, but Harry said it wasn't at the time.

Though they couldn't believe it, neither one of them had a scratch. Of course there were no protective vests back then and they only carried the six rounds that were in their revolvers. Throughout his career Harry O'Neill remained angry that the suspects made good their escape. But both former detectives readily admitted that they were very lucky that day in 1954 and still don't know why they weren't at the very least wounded. Though their Sunday early tour began quietly, it ended much differently than they ever could have imagined.

Four years later on March 15, 1956 Det O'Neill was promoted to Sergeant with the salary of $5,250. and temporarily placed in command of the Traffic Division during the temporary absence of Lt Henry Stampur. On March 25, 1959 he was still in Traffic but as a Traffic Patrol supervisor. Also during that year, due to his knowledge of the law, Harry was used as an instructor at HQ for training new recruits.

On November 16, 1960 Sgt O'Neill was promoted to the rank of Lieutenant with the salary of $7,175. and was moved to the 4th pct. as a desk lieutenant. On Nov. 7, 1966 he went to the 2nd pct. as desk lieutenant, on April 17, 1970 to Detective Lieutenant in the DD, April 6, 1971 to the North Command as a desk officer, July 10, 1972 to Planning & Records Division, and March 12, 1973 to the Communications Division.

Lt Harold O'Neill retired from the YPD on June 18, 1975. After retiring he then worked as head of security for Consumer Reports on Nepperhan Ave. in Yonkers. He later retired from that job as well.

Lt Harold J. O'Neill (cont.)

Harry loved Civil War History and read many books on the subject. His uncle Edward O'Neill was a NYPD Captain in Homicide during the 1920's and '30's, his son in law was YPD PO Anthony Dellacamera and one of his daughters, Rona Dellacamera, was a School Crossing Guard supervisor with the YPD. Harry had a brother in law named Al Polowicz who was a Hastings sergeant but he died young. And Harry had a brother Eddie who was a top reporter with the NY Daily News.

As he became older and suffered from health problems he lived in Connecticut with his daughter Melanie DiCaprio. He had two other daughters; Tara Duda and Alicia Bellantoni. His only son and namesake, Harold Jr died in a drowning accident in June 1968.

Following a long illness Ret Lt Harold O'Neill died in Danbury, Ct. on October 24, 2009. He was 87 years old.

PO CHARLES F. FOWLER #22

APPOINTED: August 1, 1947
RESIGNED: October 31, 1952

Charles Francis Fowler was born on Oct 11, 1917 in Yonkers. He attended Longfellow Jr HS and graduated from Gorton HS. He joined the Army Air Corps on April 29, 1941 serving as a B-29 pilot and flying instructor attaining the rank of Captain. He received his honorable discharge on Dec 20, 1945. He was appointed to the YPD on Jan 1, 1947 from 257 Warburton Ave earning $1,940 a year and was assigned to the 2nd pct. In the Police Academy he was named Company Commander of the Yonkers group by his fellow recruits as he had held the highest rank among them in the military. Being a very athletic guy Fowler played on the 1947 Police Softball team. Fowler resigned on Oct 31, 1952 reportedly to work as an investigator for the Yonkers Corporation Council office. For six years he served on the former County Board of Supervisors and in 1963 he retired as the Yonkers Assistant Assessor after nine years in that position. Charles Fowler died on Dec 4, 1981. He was 64.

CAPTAIN JOHN T. HIGGINS

APPOINTED: August 1, 1947
RETIRED: January 30, 1976

John T. Higgins was born in the City of Yonkers April 6, 1916. He attended Sacred Heart Elementary School, graduated from Gorton high school, and attended Roanoke College in Salem, Virginia. His major in college was business administration and police science from which he graduated earning his Bachelor's degree. Following school he worked for a while as a railway postal clerk and lived at 34 Fairview St.

John served in the Army infantry during World War II, as a sergeant with the 169th Infantry Division. He enlisted prior to the attack on Pearl Harbor on January 7, 1941 and was honorably discharged on October 21, 1945. He applied to the Yonkers Police Dept., took the test, and came out # 7 on the list. His Patrolmen's test was the first list to be established after WW 2. John was appointed to the police department on August 1, 1947. His salary was $1,940 per year, with pay days twice a month. He bought his uniforms at "Palmieri's" on 3rd Ave. near Fordham Road in the Bronx for about $300.

John attended the NYC Police Academy which at the time was located in an old 6 story warehouse on Huber St in Lower Manhattan. Yonkers P.S.C. Patrick O'Hara was a friend of then NYC Police Comm

Captain John T. Higgins (cont.)

Wallender and received permission to send down our recruit class. John said they had different instructors because of the difference in laws for a 2nd class city. Following graduation, when he began working in the precinct they worked 6 tours, with 32 hours off between the change in set of tours. There was no compensatory time and time off was granted at the captains discretion. An officer needed about 15 years seniority before being eligible for a summer vacation. All officers worked all parades, special events, Election Day, Spring and Fall Inspection days, all without pay or compensation. And at that time it was a 28 year retirement plan.

Following his graduation from the NYC Police Academy he was assigned to the 1st precinct on patrol duty. He remained in the 1st precinct until June 16, 1955 when he was promoted to the rank of Sergeant with the annual salary of $5,000 a year. His new assignment as a sergeant was to the 4th precinct as a patrol supervisor. He remained in the 4th precinct for nearly three years when, on January 16, 1958, Sgt Higgins was promoted to the rank of Lieutenant. His new salary was $6,580 a year and he was reassigned as a desk lieutenant in the 2nd precinct. Then came a series of various desk duty assignment as follows; June 3, 1958 to the 4th, March 16, 1954 to the 3rd, and on July 5, 1965 to the 1st precinct.

While residing at 171 Elm Street, John Higgins attained the top civil service rank when he was promoted to Captain on August 29, 1969 and assigned as the commanding officer of the Records Division in headquarters. A captain's salary at that time was $14,625. From that time forward Capt. Higgins was moved very frequently. Two months after arriving at headquarters he was reassigned as the patrol captain; and two months later was placed in command of the 4th precinct. Then, five months later on May 14, 1970, he was sent back to command the Records Division. From there he commanded the South Patrol Command, HQ Command, detailed to the office of Deputy Chief, command of the Inspectional Services Division, back to C.O. of the South Command, and on August 19, 1975 as C.O. of the Youth Services and Community Relations Division. That would be his last assignment.

On January 30, 1976 Capt. John Higgins, or "Slugs" as he was affectionately known, would retire from the Yonkers Police Department. Capt. Higgins will always be remembered by all who worked for him as an easy going, soft spoken, gentleman, but a man who expected his officers to do their job. Captain John Higgins' father was YPD Lt William Higgins and his brother-in-law was Deputy Chief John F. McMahon. Ret Capt. John T. Higgins died on August 3, 1990. He was 74 years old.

DEPUTY CHIEF WILLIAM J. FARRINGTON

APPOINTED: August 1, 1947
RETIRED: October 31, 1985

Born William Joseph Farrington in Yonkers NY, Bill attended local schools and graduated from Gorton HS. He attended the New York University School of Communications and Washington Square College for Business and Journalism completing his studies in August of 1947. Bill served on active duty in the Naval Reserve during WW 2 from July 14, 1942 up to December 15, 1945 when he was honorably discharged as a Quartermaster First-Class.

Farrington's grandfather was an Assistant Chief in Yonkers Fire Dept., but he didn't follow in his career choice. Instead, Bill applied for employment with the Yonkers Police Department while residing at 6 Lafayette Place. His previous employment was that of a special delivery messenger for the US Post Office and as an Oiler for Habirshaw Corp. His Patrolmen's test was the first list to be established after WW 2 and he placed # 17 on the list. Bill Farrington was appointed a Yonkers Patrolman on August 1, 1947 and was assigned to the 3rd precinct. His salary at the time was $1,940. per year, with pay days twice a month. He bought his uniforms at "Palmieri's" on 3rd Ave. near Fordham Road in the Bronx for about $300. His recruit class was said to be the first to attend the NYC Police Academy in several years.

When he began working in the 3rd precinct they all worked six tours with 32 hours off between change of tours. There was no compensatory time and time off was granted at the captain's discretion. An officer needed about 15 years on the job before being eligible for a summer vacation. Men were required to work all parades, special events, Election Day, Spring and Fall Inspection days, etc. all without pay or

Deputy Chief William J. Farrington (cont.)

time back. And at that time it was a 28 year minimum retirement plan.

Bill was reassigned from the 3rd precinct on January 1, 1951 and sent to the 1st precinct on routine patrol duty. The following year, on May 27, 1952, Bill was appointed a detective in the Detective Bureau where he earned a reputation as an excellent investigator. He received his first promotion on July 1, 1956 to the rank of Sergeant earning a salary of $5,250 a year and was reassigned as a patrol supervisor back in the 1st precinct.

Once again Sgt. Farrington received a promotion. This time he was promoted to the rank of Lieutenant on March 16, 1960 and had his salary raised to $7,175 a year. And Lt. Farrington remained assigned to the 1st precinct as a desk officer. He had a reputation as a no-nonsense boss and was a strict disciplinarian. Six years later, in November of 1966, Bill was reassigned as a desk officer in the 4th precinct.

Bill was very determined to rise in the ranks of the police department and put a great deal of time into studying for promotion. So it was no great surprise when, on December 19, 1969, Lt. Farrington was promoted to the rank of Captain earning a salary of $14,625 a year and was designated the commanding officer of the 3rd precinct at 36 Radford St.

Toward the end of 1970 the Yonkers city manager was determined to centralize and consolidate the four precincts concept, possibly into only one command. On December 1, 1970 Farrington was detailed to Chief Polsen's office to assist in the plans to implement the centralization. The final plan called for the closing of two precincts, the first and the third, and renaming the other two precincts as the North and South patrol commands. Those two were previously known as the fourth and second precincts respectively. On January 1, 1971 the centralization plan was put in effect and Capt. Farrington was designated the commanding officer of the North patrol command. He was chosen for this assignment over three senior captains who worked under his command. And yet, they all got along so well that there was never a problem with personality conflicts.

A year later, on January 28, 1972, Farrington was placed in command of the Inspectional Services Division. Having previously proved his administrative capabilities, it seems likely that this was the reason that, on October 27, 1972, Capt. Farrington was promoted to the rank of Deputy Chief with a new salary of $22,500 a year. For a short time he remained in command of the Inspectional Services Division, but on May 6, 1974 he was designated the commanding officer of the Internal Affairs Division holding the rank of Deputy Chief.

It would appear that chief Farrington ran into some difficulties in the job, because for reasons unknown, on January 19, 1979, Chief Farrington was reduced back to the rank of captain and reassigned as the CO of the Inspectional Services Division. And that began a string of transfers. Later that year in October of 1979, Capt. Farrington was first transferred to the Field Services Bureau as a patrol Captain and then on November 2, 1979 he was assigned as the CO of the Administrative Services Division. In February of 1971 to CO of the Courts and Detention Services Division, and on September 13, 1982 back as a patrol captain.

Apparently Bill Farrington's problems, be they political or otherwise, were resolved. For on May 31, 1985 Farrington was reappointed a Deputy Chief in charge of the Support Services Bureau.

DC Farrington retired from the Yonkers Police Department on October 31, 1985. He died on May 20, 2002 at the age of 80 years.

CAPTAIN JOHN F. POTANOVIC

APPOINTED: August 1, 1947
RETIRED: January 6, 1975

Born John Francis Potanovic on March 21, 1925 in Yonkers, John grew up at 3 Allen Ave. in the Dunwoodie section of Yonkers. (It was said that the Cross County Shopping Center was just a large pond back then and Central Ave was one lane each direction). John attended PS# 4 to the 4th grade and then moved to 37 St Joseph's Ave. and attended St Joseph's grade School. He graduated in 1939 along with Bill Nugent and Frank Bruno, both of whom would also join the YPD. John attended Gorton HS but left in his junior year in March of 1942 to join the Navy. He was only 16 years old so he forged his birth certificate to join but was caught and he had to wait until he was 17 years old, and then joined the regular Navy.

He enlisted August 11, 1942 and received his boot camp training in Newport R.I. Following graduation he was sent to Iowa State College in Ames, Iowa and his was the first class that was sent there from the U.S.N. The reason the Navy sent him and others to Electrical and Diesel Engineering School at Iowa State College was, due to the high influx of new recruits after Pearl Harbor the existing Naval Training Schools couldn't handle them and numerous colleges like Purdue and Northwestern built new modern dorms and took them in on their campuses. They were the first class sent to Ames. While there he studied Naval Engineering. Just before graduation he volunteered for the Submarine Service and was sent

Captain John F. Potanovic (cont.)

to New London, Ct. for training. Upon graduation he was assigned to the submarine USS R-6, an old WW 1 boat patrolling the Atlantic. Later he was assigned to the newly constructed USS Archerfish SS311. After a shakedown cruise they were sent to patrol in the Pacific theater of operations. He started off as an "oiler" in the engine room and later was promoted to the auxiliary gang which maintained hydraulics, refrigeration, pumps, air compressors, plumbing, etc. John made 7 war patrols and rose to Petty Officer 1st class, Motor Machinist Mate. On his 5th patrol near Tokyo they followed the Japanese 69,000 ton Aircraft Carrier "Shinano" for 6 hours and sank her with 6 torpedoes. It was reportedly the largest ship ever sunk by a submarine. For that, he and his shipmates received the Presidential Unit Citation.

Following his 7th patrol the Atomic bomb was dropped and the Japanese surrendered. He said he had the privilege of being present in Tokyo Bay for the Japanese surrender signing aboard the USS Missouri. Petty Office Potanovic was discharged on April 6, 1946 and worked as an Assistant Engineer aboard a tug boat with the Maritime Commission.

After taking the Yonkers Police Patrolman test he placed # 11 on the list. He was appointed to the YPD on August 1, 1947 and was issued shield # 9, which was later changed to # 218. His Patrolmen's test was the first list to be established after WW 2. The salary was $1,940 a year, and he was assigned to the 4th precinct where they had to buy their own uniforms. It took 7 years to achieve top pay of $3,000 and it was a 28 year retirement plan. All officers were required to work 6 tours on and 32 hours off. His salary was $1,940. per year, with pay days twice a month, not every two weeks. They bought their uniforms at "Palmieri's" on 3rd Ave. near Fordham Rd for about $300. His recruit class was said by him to be the first in many years to attend the NYC Police Academy. At the time it was located in an old 6 story warehouse on Huber St in Lower Manhattan. PSC Patrick O'Hara was a friend of then NYC Police Comm Wallender and received permission to send down the Yonkers recruit class.

John said Yonkers men had different instructors because of the difference in laws for a 2nd class city. Recruit training consisted of 3 days in the Academy and 2 in Yonkers precincts. There was no compensatory time and time off was granted at the precinct captains discretion. Police officers needed 15 years on the job before being eligible for a summer vacation. They worked all parades, special events, Election Day, Spring and Fall Inspection days, all without pay or time back.

Following graduation from the police academy Patrolman John Potanovic was assigned to the 4th precinct on foot patrol. Then four years later on Jan. 1, 1951 he was reassigned to the 1st, then located at 20 Wells Avenue until October 16, 1952 when he was once again returned to the 4th.

When only on the job a few months he was sent with his partner to Trevor Park on a report of dead body. They found a nude body of a female near the baseball field. While waiting for detectives Potanovic noticed drag marks that came from a bench a distance away. There he found a wallet with the ID of a man. Further investigation resulted in Potanovic having solved the murder of a prostitute. The killer was convicted and served a lengthy term in Sing Sing Prison.

On one cold winter day tour "Potsey," as Potanovic was known to his friends, was sent to a report of several youths stranded on an ice flow on the Hudson River off Trevor Park. The youths were jumping on the ice when a piece broke off and the section they were standing on got caught in the tide carrying them away. Potanovic and his partner couldn't reach them. They raced south to the Con Ed Dock at Glenwood Ave and as the youths were passing by on the ice Potanovic was able to toss a rope to them,

Captain John F. Potanovic (cont.)

rescuing them all. One of the youths, a Richard McConville, would grow up and join the YPD.

John was an original member of the 4th pct. Softball Team with the logo on the t-shirt of a full mug of beer and the words "4th Pct. Police." They used to play in an old field off North Broadway by the Andrus Home competing with other league teams. In the 1950's John was also a member of the Pacoy Club at 171 North Broadway and played on their club softball team competing with other teams while traveling along the Atlantic Seaboard to play. At one point PSC Goldman had surgery on his leg and required a driver. John, as a PO, was offered the job of driver and accepted the job so he could study for promotion. It worked. Patrolman Potanovic was promoted to the rank of Sergeant on April 16, 1958 with a new salary of $5,835 a year and was allowed to remain in the 4th precinct as a patrol supervisor.

In the next few years Sgt Potanovic moved around quite a bit. On Nov 16, 1960 he was sent to the 1st pct.; on Jan 10, 1962 to the 2nd pct.; on Mar 16, 1962 back to the 1st pct.; and on May 1st 1963 to the 3rd pct. On Dec 31, 1963, New Year's Eve, Sgt Potanovic was promoted to Lieutenant with a salary of $8,400 a year and was assigned as a desk lieutenant in the 2nd precinct.

Lt Potanovic was promoted to the much coveted rank of Captain on November 28, 1969 with the salary of $15,125 a year. His new assignment was in Headquarters Command covering any precinct in need of a captain on a temporary basis. On Dec 20, 1969 Capt. Potanovic was assigned as commanding officer of the 1st precinct. As a captain John also moved around over the next few years. On Dec 1, 1970 to commanding officer of the Records Division; On Jan 1, 1971, when the North and South Command concept was initiated he was assigned as CO of the South Command. When the South Command was established he was named commanding officer over 3 senior captains who worked patrol under his command. Fortunately they all got along well so there were no hard feelings. On Jan 28, 1972 designated CO of HQ Command Div; on June 30, 1972 to Records Service & Maintenance Division as CO; On Oct 6, 1972 to the office of Deputy Chief for Field Operations; On March 8, 1973 as CO of Communications Division; On Nov 12, 1973 to Headquarters Command Division as CO; and on April 26, 1974 to the Special Operations Division as CO.

Captain Potanovic retired from the YPD on January 6, 1975. In retirement he moved to Florida and was head of a security company called "Internal Affairs' for the Broward County school system in Florida where he lived. He administered a security detail of about 60 people covering 130 schools. And John was good at his job. In February 1975 he received a letter of thanks and appreciation from the Broward County School Board for his "excellent investigative work you performed in helping to solve the bombing which occurred in the McArthur HS on Feb 7, 1975." Though local and federal authorities were involved, John developed an informant which led to an arrest of the bomber.

After about 13 years with the school district he retired again. His sister in law Alice was PO Dorothy Yasinski's sister. One of his daughters, Teri of Boca Raton Florida is a retired Deputy Sheriff from Broward County. Nephews are Lt. Edward Potanovic and PO Scott Harsany, husband of Sgt Meredith McLaughlin. John was one of those individuals who was liked and respected by all who worked with and for him because he was a "boss" who was fair, friendly, and could relate very well with the police officers.

Ret Capt. John "Potsey" Potanovic still lives in Yorktown, Heights, NY.

PO JOSEPH A. VERGARI #2

APPOINTED: August 1, 1947
RESIGNED: August 31, 1948

Joseph Vergari was born in Yonkers on November 29, 1924. He lived at 110 Waverly St. and listed his occupation as a student. On March 11, 1943 Joe joined the United States Marine Corps during World War II and was honorably discharged on March 17, 1946. He was appointed to the Yonkers Police Department on August 1, 1947 earning a salary of $1,940 a year. He attended the New York City police academy recruit school and upon graduation was assigned to the 3rd precinct. Vergari received a special leave of absence without pay for a year. However, having an engineering degree he decided to pursue that line of work and submitted his resignation from the police department effective August 31, 1948. Joe Vergari died March 6, 2001 in New London, Connecticut.

PO HARRY R. BRODERICK #130

APPOINTED: November 1, 1947
RETIRED: February 20, 1980

Born Harry Regis Broderick in Yonkers NY on June 4, 1919 he attended local elementary schools, and graduated from Gorton high school. Due to his scholastic grades he was accepted into the national honor Society and was awarded a New York State College veteran scholarship. He attended Manhattan College, Fordham University, and New York Law School. His majors were liberal arts and law. He graduated with a BA degree. Harry joined the Army during World War II on Feb. 26, 1942, attaining the rank of Technical Sergeant and was trained in military intelligence. Harry saw a great deal of combat and among his medals he earned a combat medal with three battle stars, including one for participating in the Battle of the Bulge. He received his honorable discharge on Jan. 7, 1946. Broderick was appointed to the YPD on Nov. 1, 1947 with a starting salary of $1,940 a year. Following his recruit training he was assigned to patrol duty in the 1st precinct. On Nov. 1, 1949 Harry was detailed to the Juvenile Aid Bureau where he remained until Nov. 1, 1952 when he was returned to patrol in the 1st pct. While assigned to the first pct., Broderick would earn several departmental awards for excellent police work. He was reassigned to the 4th pct. on Nov. 9, 1966 and after a while was assigned the steady post in Getty Square where he was known by everyone. He would remain there right up to his retirement on Feb. 20, 1980. Harry's brothers were former Yonkers PO James Broderick and Dr. Thomas Broderick. His father was Judge Broderick.

A resident of 18 Arthur Street, Harry Broderick died on March 3, 1992. He was 73 years old.

DEPUTY CHIEF EDWARD A. JONES

APPOINTED: April 16, 1948
RETIRED: April 19, 1985

Edward A. Jones was born in Brooklyn, NY on May 6, 1922 and attended Annunciation Jr. high school in NYC in 1936. He graduated from Regis high school in New York City in 1940 with four years of Latin, three years of Greek, and two years of German, algebra and geometry. As a young man he would gain employment as a Grocery warehouseman in Long Island City, New York.

Jones joined the Navy during WW 2 on April 14, 1942 serving in the Atlantic, Caribbean, Pacific, and China Sea. He also served with great distinction in the Pacific Theater as a Medic and Chief Petty Officer on the LSM-3, an amphibious assault ship, participating in numerous military engagements. He was discharged as a Chief Petty Officer Pharmacists' Mate on February 13, 1948. He was appointed to the Yonkers PD two months later on April 16, 1948 while living with the family of (Lt) Joe Huerstel at 1039 Central Park Avenue. However, he received war time seniority in the police department dating back to August 1, 1947 because he was called by civil service for appointment, but was still on active duty in the Navy.

His Patrolmen's test was said to be the first list to be established after WW 2. and he rated # 9 on the list. His salary was $1940. per year, with pay days twice a month. He bought his uniforms at

Deputy Chief Edward A. Jones (cont.)

"Palmieri's" on 3rd Ave. near Fordham for about $300. Jones received his recruit training at the New York City police Academy. At the time it was located in an old 6 story warehouse on Huber St in Lower Manhattan. When he began working in the pct. they worked 6 tours rotating with 32 hours off between sets of tours. There was no compensatory time and time off was granted at the captains discretion. And you needed 15 years seniority before being eligible for a summer vacation. You were required to work all parades, special events, Election Day, Spring and Fall Inspection days, all without pay or time back. And at that time it was a 28 year retirement plan. Following his appointment and recruit class graduation he was assigned to 1st precinct on patrol. On January 1, 1951, when two patrol precincts were closed, he was transferred to the 2nd precinct on patrol. However, four months later on May 5, 1952, he was returned to the 1st precinct once again.

Effective October 16, 1952 city manager Charles Curran appointed Jones, of 10 Cottage Place., Gardens, "*...........a substitute Sergeant in the Police Bureau, during the leave of absence of John J. McCarthy-5 who, after his promotion to sergeant, was granted that leave for military service*." Though only a temporary Sergeant, Jones had all the authority of a permanent sergeant and was assigned as a patrol supervisor in the 4th precinct. Nine months later, on July 27, 1953 Jones was appointed to the permanent position of Sergeant at a salary of $4,300. a year and remained in the 4th precinct.

On June 16, 1957 Sgt Jones was promoted to Lieutenant at the salary of $6,174 and, once again, he remained in the 4th precinct as a desk lieutenant. On July 2, 1965 he was promoted to Captain at a salary of $9,620 and was designated the "relief captain" working out of the 1st precinct. On August 23, 1965 Capt. Jones was reassigned from patrol and designated the commanding officer of the Juvenile Aid Bureau. Three years later, on February 14, 1968 Capt. Jones was transferred to the Detective Division in charge of the plainclothes unit. But just one year later on February 3, 1969 Capt. Jones was designated commanding officer of the entire Detective Division.

On June 30, 1972 Capt. Jones was reassigned from the Detective Division to commanding officer of the 2nd precinct located at 441 Central Park Ave. But, once again Capt. Jones had his assignment changed. On October 26, 1973 he was moved from the 2nd precinct and placed in command of the North Patrol Command (former 4th precinct) located at 53 Shonnard Pl. Two years later, on August 22, 1975, Jones was designated the commanding officer of the Training Unit. On July 1, 1977 Jones was once again designated the commanding officer of the Detective Division earning a salary of $25,026 a year. However two years later on January 19, 1979 Jones was appointed to the position of Deputy Chief of Police in charge of the Field Services Bureau which comprised all patrol operations.

DC Jones retired on April 19, 1985 and remained living at his home at 105 Amackassin Terrace. Edward Jones had developed an accomplished record within the Department, earning numerous commendations for his police work, including a special commendation from the Mayors of the Cities of New York and Yonkers for his critical role in the investigative task force that led to the arrest and conviction in the infamous Son of Sam case. Chief Jones was a proud member of the Yonkers PAL, the Police Emerald Society and the Captains, Lieutenants and Sergeants Association. An avid Notre Dame, Mets and Giants fan, Chief Jones was said to be a great cook with a keen sense of humor who loved his off season trips with his wife to Cape May, New Jersey.

Chief Jones died in Jacobi Hospital, on January 22, 2007, due to severe burns he received in a fire in his home on January 12, 2007. He was 84 years old.

SGT. WALTER CHRYSTONE #56

APPOINTED: July 1, 1948
RETIRED: July 1, 1983

For those who knew and worked with him in the police department, Walter Chrystone was a friendly soft spoken gentleman with a personality which seemed to border on being shy. His low key demeanor seemed to hide the man he truly was. He was simply a humble man.

He was born Wladyslaw Krzytoforski in Bayonne NJ on February 9, 1920. However, even when he was a child he always used the name Walter Chrystone and did so throughout his life. Walter attended PS# 7 and graduated from Commerce high school. On an early police employment application he listed his occupation as a toll booth collector.

Following the outbreak of WW-2 Walter joined the Army Air Corps on August 6, 1943 and served as a Flight Gunner on B-17s with the rank of Technical Sergeant. Walter was a top turret gunner in a B-17 (Flying Fortress) bomber plane throughout his service. He participated in several extensive bombing raids with the 15th Air Corps, 815 Bombardment Squadron, over Germany while operating out of Foggia, Italy. On his 25th bombing mission his plane was shot down over Ruhland, Germany. His turret canopy had been blown off but he was able to parachute safely. However he fell into enemy hands and became a prisoner of war by the Germans. During that action he received shrapnel wounds to his right wrist and was disabled for 7 months. He was later awarded the Purple Heart. Following his internment in the German prisoner of war camp he was liberated by the US 14th Armored Division at the POW camp in Mussberg, Germany. He flew many of his missions over the Rhineland and Central Europe. Technical Sgt Chrystone was honorably discharged on November 23, 1945. Chrystone was awarded several military medals among them, the Purple Heart, the Africa-Europe Campaign Medal with 3 battle stars, 3 Bronze Stars, and the Air Medal.

Walter was appointed to the Yonkers Police Department on July 1, 1948 from 55 Chestnut Street at $1,940 a year. He was sent to the NYC police academy for recruit training and upon graduation was assigned to the 1st pct. As part of a department wide reorganization, on July 16, 1956, Chrystone was appointed a Detective in the Detective Division. But three years later, on December 1, 1959 he was re-assigned back to patrol in the 1st precinct. On May 20, 1960 he was moved to the "radio room" working as a dispatcher, and on February 14, 1968 he was assigned to the Records Division performing clerical duties.

On Jan 3, 1969 Walter was promoted to Sergeant earning $11,600 a year and was transferred to the 2nd precinct as a patrol supervisor. On March 12, 1973 he was transferred to the North Command as a Station House Supervisor, or desk officer, which until that date had been the duty of a Lieutenant. On June 20, 1979 Sgt Chrystone was moved to the North East Command on East Grassy Sprain Rd where he remained on patrol duty right up to his retirement, which occurred on July 1, 1983. Walter was related through marriage to Sgt Louis Dearstyne.

Ret Sgt Walter Chrystone died on March 29, 1987. He was 67 years old.

PO JOSEPH V. ROSKO #155

APPOINTED: July 1, 1948
RETIRED: September 15, 1977

Joe was born in Yonkers on Jan. 12, 1916. He graduated from Saunders HS and later worked as a checker for Refined Syrups Co. Joe loved pigeons. He raised and raced them as a hobby and belonged to the Westchester Hills Pigeon Racing Club. He was known to his friends as "Pigeon Joe." He joined the Army on June 3, 1941 just prior to Pearl Harbor and served in the field artillery as a Technical Sergeant. He fought in several battles and during the landing at Normandy, on June 7, 1944, was wounded by shrapnel on the left side of his face which earned him the Purple Heart. He also was awarded the Bronze Star on July 15, 1944. Joe was honorably discharged on Oct. 13, 1945 and returned to Yonkers. He was hired by the YPD on July 1, 1948 from 38 Groshon Ave earning $1,940 a year. Following his recruit training he was assigned to the 1st pct. On Dec. 16, 1954 he was reassigned from the 1st pct. to the Traffic Division on three wheel motorcycle patrol issuing summonses for meter violations. He remained in this assignment for 16 years, and on Jan. 1, 1971 he was reassigned to the South patrol command on patrol duty. However that change lasted only 10 months. On October 19, 1971 he was returned to the Traffic Unit, this time enforcing street cleaning ordinances. Joe Rosko retired on September 15, 1977 and would die eight years later on March 28, 1985. He was 69 years old.

PO THEODORE KANTOR #199

APPOINTED: July 1, 1948
RETIRED: July 2, 1973

Theodore Kantor was born in Yonkers on Feb. 4, 1920. He attended local schools and after graduation gained employment as a grocery store manager. Following Pearl Harbor Ted joined the Navy on April 24, 1942. Ted served proudly on the USS Battleship "New Jersey." He was honorably discharged on November 20, 1945. With a desire to have a job with security Ted was appointed a police officer on July 1, 1948 from 17 Colin Street. The starting salary at the time was $1,940 and his first assignment was patrol duty in the 2nd precinct. Teddy, as he was known, was very active in sports and in 1948 played on both the PBA baseball and basketball teams. Though most of his career was spent in the 2nd pct., on Nov. 7, 1966 he was reassigned to the 1st pct., but on February 7, 1969 he was returned to the 2nd. On Oct. 6, 1972 Ted was transferred to the Youth Services and Community Relations unit from which he would later retire. Two of Ted's brothers, PO Steve and Lt. Russell, also were members of the Yonkers Police Department. Ted Kantor retired from the Police Department on July 2, 1973. A resident of Briarcliff Manor, NY, Ted had been retired from the department for 37 years, but unfortunately he developed Parkinson's disease. Retired police officer Ted Kantor died on February 5, 2010, the day after turning 90 years of age.

PO FRANK J. ZAMBORSKY #253

APPOINTED: July 1, 1948
DIED: October 12, 1973

Frank Zamborsky was born in Yonkers on Aug. 13, 1924. He attended both Gorton and Saunders high school's where he learned a trade in Arc Welding. Frank, who spoke Polish as a second language, listed his early employment with the post office. He served in the Navy in the aviation branch as part of the ground crew during World War II with a rating of Metalsmith 2nd class. He served from March 17, 1943 to his honorable discharge on April 4, 1946. Frank was hired to the YPD on July 1, 1948 from 16 Croton Terrace. His first assignment was in the 2nd pct. on Central Avenue. On May 18, 1962 Frank and others trapped a group of professional burglars in the act. As they tried to escape Zamborsky gave chase and made the arrest at gunpoint. On Nov. 7, 1966 Frank was reassigned to the newly opened 1st pct. on E. Grassy Sprain Rd. He was placed in the Community Relations Unit in Jan. of 1971 but on Aug. 24th of that year he was transferred to the North Command. While there he served as a desk lieutenants aide and did so until his health caused him to remain out sick for a lengthy period. Unfortunately his health did not improve and PO Frank Zamborsky died on October 12, 1973. He was only 49 years old.

LT. ROBERT J. MAITRE

APPOINTED: September 1, 1949
RETIRED: August 1, 1989

Born in North Yonkers on June 21, 1925 Bob Maitre moved to Lawrence Street where he was raised, and graduated from St Dennis School and Yonkers High School. Bob joined the Navy in 1942 serving on the Destroyer USS Champlin and participated in the invasion of Sicily and France. They performed mostly convoy duty and at the end of the war they were in Tokyo Bay during the signing of the Japanese surrender. Maitre was honorably discharged in 1945.

Following his honorable discharge Bob attended Pace Business School in NYC for a while, and then was appointed a police officer effective September 1, 1949. He was appointed while living at 106 Valentine Lane and earned a starting salary of $2,300 a year. Following his basic recruit training Bob's first assignment was to the 1st precinct on Wells Avenue, but he would only remain there a short time. One day while on duty he observed a mugging occur at the foot of Main Street, pursued the suspect on foot and made the arrest. As a result he was rewarded by being appointed a Detective on January 1, 1951 and assigned to the Detective Division. He remained in the Detective Bureau for about 13 years and was reassigned back to patrol duty in the 3rd precinct on May 1, 1963 working with PO Bill Youshock. But before he did the following occurred;

On September 8, 1954 at 8:15 p.m. a holdup team robbed the delicatessen at 148 McLean Avenue at gunpoint and escaped with $448. This same team was also believed to be responsible for several other holdups in the Bronx and Manhattan. As a result they had been dubbed the Delicatessen Bandits. Firearms were always displayed and sooner or later someone was going to get hurt.

It was about 9:45 p.m. on September 12, 1954 and Detectives Bob Maitre Sr., and Harry O'Neill were on patrol in unmarked radio car #286 with O'Neill as the operator" and Maitre as the message receiver. What an unlikely pair they were. Although both were excellent police officers, Bob Maitre was always quiet, unassuming, and soft spoken. Harry O'Neill was very outgoing, gregarious, and not the least bit afraid to speak his mind. And yet the two actually made good partners and worked well together.

Bob Maitre related that on this evening, while driving south on South Broadway, Det. O'Neill attempted to turn around at 261st Street when he spotted a plate that he knew right away was on their wanted list for the robberies. Expecting that the two suspects in the stolen vehicle were armed, Maitre drew his revolver as O'Neill pulled alongside the car. As Det. Maitre got out, the suspects sped off, followed closely behind by the two detectives. The pursuit wound its way through residential side streets in the Riverdale section of the Bronx at high speeds with Det. Maitre firing his revolver at the fleeing vehicle. (A perfectly legal and accepted practice in 1954.)

They immediately tried to call for backup units but had trouble with the radio system, which they said actually consisted of two separate systems. The old one and a new one not yet fully functional, but both on line together. Between the screeching of tires, multiple shots being fired from the radio car, and adrenaline, they had great difficulty getting through to Headquarters. But the chase continued and Maitre kept firing his revolver at the bandits.

Lt. Robert J. Maitre (cont.)

At one point as the suspect vehicle took a sharp turn, the passenger door swung open and the passenger fell out on his back and began to roll. As the driver of the suspect vehicle continued to speed away, Maitre and O'Neill brought their unit to a stop. With the intention of scrapping up their soon to be prisoner, they climbed out of their car with their revolvers at the ready. To their surprise, as they walked toward the male on the ground he jumped up and began firing at the two detectives. Bob Maitre was a step or two ahead of O'Neill and only about 20 feet from the shooter when the near point-blank firing started. Maitre explained, "*I was really stunned when he fired at us and I raised my gun and tried to return fire, and that's when I found out that my gun was empty.*"

Without hesitation Maitre reported that Harry O'Neill ran forward toward the suspect and began firing his revolver in what was later termed by the media as a running gun battle. Harry recently told me, "*The guy was shooting, and I was shooting, and pretty soon I just heard my gun making a clicking noise. I was empty.*" In that short moment it must have seemed like time stood still, and then in seconds it was over and the suspect disappeared into the darkness of the side yards. Incredibly, neither the officers nor the shooter were hit. What remained were two police officers standing in the street probably somewhat dazed at what had just transpired. And both the suspects made good their escape.

Bob Maitre was promoted to Sergeant on September 13, 1968 earning $10,575 and was assigned as a patrol supervisor in the 2nd precinct. However, on May 21, 1971, Sgt Maitre was returned to the D.D. as a detective sergeant where he would remain until 1977. He felt his most significant investigation was being a supervisor of the squad of detectives assigned to the investigation of the murder of police officer Harold Woods in September of 1974. Bob was the D.D. supervisor working that night and responded to the scene of the shooting.

Sgt. Maitre was still in the Detective Division when he was promoted to Lieutenant on February 18, 1977. At that time he was reassigned as a city wide patrol Lieutenant where he remained right up to his retirement.

Bob retired from the YPD to his home on Tower Place in Yonkers on August 1, 1989. Throughout his life Bob Maitre loved running for miles just to keep fit. He even ran in several marathons including the NYC marathon in 1979. And he continued to run well into retirement. At the age of 85 he stopped running but continued to play golf and a little tennis.

Bob's son is Ret. Det. Bob Maitre Jr., and his uncle was PO Joseph Maitre.

LT. JOHN L. FAVAREAU

APPOINTED: September 1, 1949
RETIRED: July 4, 1980

John Leo Favareau was born September 3, 1916 in Yonkers NY. He attended St. Mary's elementary school and graduated from Commerce High School. Prior to the YPD he listed his previous employment as a mail carrier for the post office. He also worked for a time for United Distillers of America in Yonkers.

John joined the Army Air Corps during World War II on May 22, 1942. When the war ended Favareau was part of the occupation forces in Japan. He received his honorable discharge as a Staff Sergeant on December 14, 1945. Among many citations Sgt Favareau was awarded were the Asiatic Pacific Campaign medal, a Silver Service star, a Bronze Service Star, a Distinguished Unit Citation and a Philippine Presidential unit citation. Prior to his police appointment he married Cecelia Anne O'Boyle on June 26, 1948, at St. Peter's Church on Riverdale Avenue.

John Favareau was appointed to the Yonkers police department, from 89 Buena Vista Ave., on September 1, 1949 earning an annual salary of $2,300 a year. Following his recruit training he was assigned to patrol duties in the 4th precinct. When two precincts were closed on January 1, 1951 John was reassigned to duty in the 1st Precinct on Wells Avenue. However, on October 16, 1952 when the precincts were re-opened, he was reassigned back to duty in the 4th precinct. John was an original member of 4th precinct Softball Team which had a logo on their t-shirts of a mug of beer and the words "4th Pct. Police." He played first base.

John received his promotion to the rank of Sergeant on July 1, 1958 with a salary of $5,835 a year and was reassigned as a patrol supervisor in the 3rd precinct. He received his second promotion to the rank of lieutenant on February 27, 1963 with a salary of $8,300 and this time was assigned to the 2nd precinct as a desk officer. "The Fav" as he was known, was loud and very outgoing as a desk lieutenant but was a real good boss who was easy to work for and well respected. In November of 1966 Lt. Favareau was transferred to the 4th precinct where he remained until October 6, 1972 when he was reassigned to traffic court as the liaison to the police department.

John remained in Traffic Court right up to his retirement on July 4, 1980 while residing at 292 Sommerville Place. John had been a member and past secretary of the New York Police and Fire Retiree Association, and a member of the Police Emerald Society of Westchester since 1968.

Ret Lt. John Favareau died on May 15, 1997 at the age of 80. years.

DEPUTY CHIEF OWEN J. McCLAIN

APPOINTED: September 1, 1949
RETIRED: August 31, 1989

Owen McClain was born in the Lincoln Park section of the City of Yonkers on July 27, 1925. He grew up living on Palisade Ave near old Garden St, now Walsh Road. He attended PS# 12, PS# 7, Benjamin Franklin Jr. HS, and graduated from Saunders Trades and Technical HS. As a young man he worked as an usher in the Proctors Theater, the Yonkers Hat Factory, and the Alexander Smith Carpet Mills.

He joined United States Marine Corps during World War 2 on June 17, 1943 right after his 18th birthday. During his service young Owen saw action on Okinawa and participated in the beach assault on the Japanese held Pacific island attol of Tarawa. He was also stationed in the Hawaiian Islands and Guam. Pfc. McClain received his honorable discharge on November 29, 1945.

Owen was hired as a police officer on September 1, 1949 while living at 47 Hudson St. earning a starting salary of $2,300 a year. Following his recruit training his first assignment was to patrol duties in the 3rd precinct. Not long after, on January 1, 1951, McClain was moved to the 1st precinct. Then, on August 19, 1952 PO McClain was transferred to the Traffic Division where he was assigned to the three wheel motorcycle on parking meter summons detail. During this time he worked a second job for several

Deputy Chief Owen J. McClain (cont.)

years as a dispatcher for Valentine Taxi on Riverdale Avenue and Valentine Lane. He remained there for little over two years when, on December 16, 1954, he was reassigned back to patrol in the 1st precinct. On May 7, 1956 PO McClain was awarded a Commendation for a felonious assault arrest he made on May 11, 1952 at 22 Croton Terrace. At that time it was reported that he struggled with a suspect and while trying to make the arrest, the suspect pressed a gun against McClain's stomach and pulled the trigger. Fortunately the weapon misfired.

Owen McClain was promoted to the rank of Sergeant on March 16, 1962 earning a salary of $7,000 a year and was returned back to where he first started; in the3rd precinct as a patrol supervisor. While performing his duties as a supervisor he was determined to continue his rise through the ranks by studying faithfully. As a result, on January 14, 1966, Sgt. McClain was promoted to the rank of police Lieutenant earning a salary of $9,090 a year. Following this promotion he was transferred to the 4th precinct performing the duties of a desk officer.

Over the next several years McClain was moved several times. In November of 1966 he was returned to the 3rd precinct. In December of 1969 he was reassigned to 4th pct. And in June of 1970 he was returned to desk duty in the 3rd precinct. Following the implementation of a new centralization plan whereby the first and third precincts were closed, on January 1, 1971 Lt. McClain was transferred to the South Patrol Command as a desk officer.

On March 12, 1973 Lt. McClain was reassigned to the Internal Affairs section of the Inspectional Services Division. In this assignment he worked alongside Lt. Bill Farrington investigating claims of wrongdoing made against police officers. The following year, on May 6, 1974, the Internal Affairs section was renamed the Internal Affairs Unit, separate and aside from any other division and reporting directly to the police chief.

Owen achieved the highest civil service rank in the YPD on July 1, 1975 when he was promoted to the rank of Captain. His new salary was $22,647 a year and he was assigned as the commanding officer of the Headquarters Command Division at 10 St. Casimir Avenue. Nearly four years later, on January 1, 1979, Capt. McClain was reassigned to the Field Services Bureau as a patrol duty captain. He performed his duties patrolling in uniform and more often than not working steady Late Tours. Capt. McClain was a no-nonsense supervisor and required everyone to follow the department's rules and regulations to the letter. He was a firm believer in discipline and was not shy about letting you know how he felt on a particular issue. He was also very strict when it came to an officer's appearance in uniform. Particularly the requirement that you wear your uniform hat. While working the midnight shift, if he felt certain officers were not doing their job appropriately, he would not approach the officers, but instead would summon their supervisor to meet up with him. He would then lay the law down to that supervisor to pass down to the officers. He was a strict believer in the chain of command. Particularly at 4 in the morning. If you were working patrol during those years, the first thing you would want to know upon arriving at work was, whether Captain "Midnight" was working that tour.

On May 14, 1982 Capt. McClain was reassigned to the Northeast Patrol Command, located at 35 E. Grassy Sprain Rd., and designated as their commanding officer. As part of his duties he was also responsible for the Special Operations Unit, a.k.a. the Traffic Unit.

Following Capt. Fernandes' appointment as police commissioner he designated Capt. McClain as

Deputy Chief Owen J. McClain (cont.)

the commanding officer of the Detective Division effective July 1, 1983. McClain was definitely a very hands-on type boss and could be seen almost every night on local television giving press releases and updates on various crimes and other situations. He was the department's de facto press officer.

Two years later, on May 31, 1985, Capt. McClain was elevated to the rank of Deputy Chief in command of the entire Investigative Services Bureau. This Bureau included both the Detective Division and the Youth Division. Three years later, on May 23, 1988, Chief McClain was reassigned as the Chief of Support Services Bureau.

Chief McClain retired on August 31, 1989 to his home at 90 Amackassin Terrace. During his career he had a reputation of being a very strict disciplinary. But once you became friendly with him you would see that he was a decent man trying to do the right thing for his profession. After retirement he tried without success to return as the Yonkers police commissioner.

Owen McClain was very active in Irish Affairs in the city of Yonkers. In fact he was the host of a local Irish TV talk show. He was also a long time member of the St Patrick's Day Parade Committee and was even the parade Grand Marshall in 2007, a member of the Friendly Sons of St Patrick, and the Westchester County Emerald Society. He was also an active member of the Yonkers Police Athletic League Advisory Board.

Ret Chief McClain's brother was Ret Det Walter McClain and his son-in-law was Ret Det Sgt Richard Kostik. Ret. DC Owen McClain died January 17, 2016. He was 90 years old.

LT. JOSEPH T. NADER

APPOINTED: September 1, 1949
RETIRED: July 27, 1977

Joseph T. Nader was born in Yonkers on March 4, 1917 while living at 25 Palisade Ave. He was the son of immigrant parents from Lebanon. He said his grandfather was originally from a small part of Syria that contained primarily Christians, not Muslims. Joe was raised as a Catholic but was fluent in speaking Arabic and Italian. During WW 1 his father, who had immigrated to the US in 1906, was unable to serve, not being a citizen, so from 1917 to 1919 he brought his family to Philadelphia to live and where he could work. When they moved to Yonkers Joe attended and graduated from PS #12, St Joseph's School, and graduated from Saunders HS with a trade in electric wiring. But he was unable to get accepted into the Electrical Union. For the next several years he worked miscellaneous jobs including singing with a band in the Green Hat Bar on Nepperhan Ave.

In 1935 a friend told him if he joined the N.Y.S. National Guard he could earn $1.00 for a two hour drill day and $1.00 a day for two weeks training, plus food, medical, and a roof over his head. So, in 1935 he joined. By 1939 he was a Staff Sergeant in charge of Security at the Yonkers Armory on North Broadway. He was part of the Communications Company of the Infantry Div. The war in Europe was raging and things didn't look good for America staying out of it. At the time the US Army was very undermanned so as a cautionary measure on Oct 15, 1940, prior to America joining the war, Nader's unit, the 27th Infantry Div of the N.Y.S. National Guard was activated and merged into the regular Army. He said the 27th Division was the first to enter into the Pacific Theater of operations when they arrived in Hawaii.

Joe's background in electric wiring enabled him to be utilized in the communications field. In fact, he was designated a Training and Drill Instructor. Nader said he was told he was on his way to being promoted to First Sergeant when he was encouraged to attend OCS School. He did this in 1942 and graduated a 2nd Lieutenant. His military career during WW 2 brought him all over the world and he rose to the rank of Captain but, being a communications expert and instructor, he never saw any combat. At one point while serving in Egypt he was recruited by the British 8th Army to serve as an interpreter for the Arab language; and he laughed saying he was actually paid for it!

His last duty station was in Italy before he returned to Fort Dix, NJ in Sept 1945. At that time he was offered a full discharge or a discharge with a Reserve Commission as a captain. He opted for the reserve commission. He returned to Yonkers and worked for Sears & Roebuck Co. in Yonkers. And later he started a Painting Contracting Business until Sept of 1946 when he was again activated for two more years. His assignment was to eliminate all unnecessary radar stations along the entire east coast. As his two years was ending, in early September of 1948 he took the Yonkers Police officer test while wearing his Army Captains uniform. Do to the poor police salary, only about 25 men took the test. He was discharged from the military on September 22, 1948.

There was a great deal of prejudice at the time. A police Sergeant who was doing the investigation and apparently going to deny his appointment because of his nationality said to him, "You have too many proteins in your system." Joe told me, "can you imagine? Here I am, a WW-2 veteran, tall, lean, and mean. And I'm not good enough?" But Joe Nader was not going to back down. Joe was finally appointed to the YPD from 51 Chestnut Street on September 1, 1949 at $2,300 a year, but only after he threatened

Lt. Joseph T. Nader (cont.)

to sue the city. He was just short of being 32 years of age and used his military time to qualify. When hired he was given a 5" barrel colt positive, shield and hat wreath, nightstick, and a dark blue armband with white letters "YPD" to wear on post over his civilian clothes while he walked a foot post along with a regular officer. He had to buy everything else including the ammunition for his revolver. The long overcoat alone cost $80. A substantial sum in 1949.

He was assigned to the 2nd pct. under Capt. James Hollis. During firearms training he was required to purchase his own cartridges to use on the range. After a short time Capt. Pat Sullivan took command and Joe served as his aide. Against his wishes on Jan. 1, 1951 he was assigned to the Juvenile Aide Bureau. But on Feb. 16, 1951 he was once again activated, this time for the Korean War. He was sent to Ft. Gordon, Ga. n a Basic Training Company as a "Trainer," supposedly for only 9 months. Nine months became 2 years. When two years were up, just before his discharge he was made Battalion Commander. He was discharged in 1953 and returned back to the YPD and the 2nd pct. on March 6, 1953.

Again he served both as the captains aid and rode a sector car with PO Victor Geiger. On Dec. 1, 1956 he was appointed a Detective in the D.D. and as a detective received an additional $100. a year. Upon taking the Sgt's exam he placed 5th on the list. He was passed over several times until he visited Democratic City Leader Tom Brogan and he was promoted within two weeks, on May 16, 1957, at salary of $5,512. and went to the 2nd pct. On Jan 17, 1958 he was appointed a Det. Sgt and assigned to the D.D. as a supervisor. On May 9, 1962 Det Sgt Joe Nader was awarded the 1st place Macy Newspaper Award for his part in the investigation and arrest of a murder suspect. He also received the 2nd class award for the capture of five men in connection with the armed hold-up of a jewelry store the previous October. He was the first man ever cited for the high awards twice in the same quarter.

He remained in the D.D. until he was promoted to Lieutenant on Feb. 28, 1963 at $8,300 and was sent to the 2nd pct. as a desk lieutenant. On Mar. 16, 1964 he was reassigned to the 1st pct. as the desk Lt. Then, on Nov. 7, 1966 he was reassigned to the 4th pct. on desk duty. A year later on February 14, 1968 he was assigned to the Communications Division as a tour supervisor. On Dec. 29, 1970 he was assigned to HQ Command for training duties. On Sept. 11, 1973 he was moved to the Crime Prevention Unit where he remained up to retirement. Lt Nader retired from YPD on July 27, 1977 and worked full time as a private investigator. He also retired from the Army Reserve with the rank of Lt Colonel. He had served as the president of the Police and Fire Retirees Assoc. from 1983 to 1989 and then as Honorary Legislative Chairman of the association. He also worked several years as a legislative assistant to NY Congresswoman Nita Lowey.

Although a Christian by faith, Joe was indeed of Middle East heritage. As such the Yonkers Arabic community, admiring him for attaining the rank of a police lieutenant, considered Joe a leader and spokesman for their community. As such, whenever there was a "family" feud, Joe could always resolve the issue because of the esteem in which the Arabic community held him.

Joe Nader was, throughout his life, a military man. If ever there was a person born to be a soldier, it was Joe Nader. He had a military bearing which set an example for young officers, and as such earned their respect. During and after his retirement he was very active in working to improve the lives of military veterans.

Retired Lt Joseph T. Nader died after a long illness on July 15, 2010. He was 93 years old.

PO ROBERT SAKOWITZ #112

APPOINTED: September 1, 1949
RESIGNED: May 5, 1951

Bob was born in Yonkers on June 12, 1918 the son of Yonkers PO Frank Sakowicz, (he spelled name different). Bob spoke Polish as a second language and was employed as a truck driver. Personnel records indicate that Bob served 6 years in the Army during World War II but no further information is available. He was appointed to the YPD on Sept. 1, 1949 from 24 Locust Hill Ave earning a salary of $2,300 a year. Following his recruit training he was assigned to the 2nd pct. On Aug. 17, 1950 he borrowed a new car from a show room for a test run, kept it for 5 hours and had a head on collision with a trolley car. He suffered severe head injuries, a broken nose, ribs, left leg, and multiple lacerations. A complaint was made and he was brought up on departmental charges. When the precincts were closed on January 1, 1951 Sakowitz was reassigned to the 1st pct. Bob Sakowitz resigned from the YPD on May 5, 1951. He died in August of 1975 at the age of 57 years.

SGT. JOHN K. O'CONNELL #23

APPOINTED: September 1, 1949
RETIRED: June 29, 1972

John "Jack" O'Connell was born in Yonkers on April 6, 1921 and attended and graduated from Gorton H.S. As WW-2 was raging "Jack" joined and attended the US Merchant Marine Academy at Kings Point, LI from 1942 to 1943 at which time he graduated from same. He served on active duty in the Navy from June 15, 1944 to July 19, 1946 when he received an honorable discharge. But O'Connell loved the Naval Service so much, he joined the Naval Reserve, working his way up through the ranks to full Commander. While in the Reserves "Jack" was appointed to the Yonkers Police Dept. on Sept 1, 1949 at $2,300 a year and assigned to precinct patrol duty. He was appointed a Detective on Oct 16, 1952 serving in the D.D. A member of the Y.P.D. H.N.S. and having a great singing voice, he often served as a soloist at the HNS masses. Oct 16, 1962 Det O'Connell was promoted to the rank of Sergeant at the salary of $6,900 a year and returned to patrol duty as a patrol supervisor. However, on June 14, 1968 he was again returned to the DD as a Det Sergeant up to Feb. 3, 1969. It was then he was reassigned to the Youth Division. "Jack," a proud Irishman, had pure white hair later in his career. And as result of this and his Naval service he was nicknamed by his friends "Commander Whitehead."

Sgt John O'Connell retired from the YPD on June 29, 1972 and died on January 23, 2009. He was 87 years old.

PO STANLEY B. KUCMIEROWSKI #256

APPOINTED: June 1, 1950
RETIRED: June 29, 1973

Born Stanley Robert Kucmierowski in Yonkers NY on April 7, 1922, "Smitty" as he was known, attended local public schools and served in the Army during WW 2 from April of 1940 up to his honorable discharge in June of 1945. His sister said that he was at Pearl Harbor when the Japanese attacked on Dec 7, 1941 but was unharmed. Stanley, who spoke Polish as a second language, was said to have been an amateur boxer while serving in the military winning several championships. As a young man he worked as a clerk for the IRS. Stan was appointed to the YPD on June 1, 1950 with a starting salary of $2,800 a year. He lived at 35 Oak St. and was assigned to the 3rd precinct. Sometime later he was moved to the 2nd pct., and on June 20, 1956 he was reassigned to patrol in the 4th pct. He also served for a while in Traffic directing vehicular traffic. He married his wife, Lorraine nee Poloso, on Oct 12, 1952. His son Stanley followed him in law enforcement and is retired from the NYPD. Stanley Kucmierowski retired on June 29, 1973 and moved to Brewster, NY where he died on April 10, 1993. He was 71 years old.

PO WILLIAM H. PECKNE #136

APPOINTED: June 1, 1950
RETIRED: September 15, 1980

Born William Harris Peckne in Yonkers on Nov. 9, 1925, Bill graduated from Gorton HS and was known as “Harris” Peckne. While in Gorton HS he was an excellent Football player. He joined Navy during WW-2 on Sept. 29, 1943 serving in the Asian-Pacific Campaign and was honorably discharged on April 8, 1946. After the war he attended Champlain College for business in Plattsburg, Bill’s former occupation was listed as a mechanic and for fun he rode a motorcycle. Bill was appointed to the YPD on June 1, 1950 from 163 Villa Avenue. His salary was $2,800 a year and he was assigned to the 2nd pct. On Oct, 16, 1952 he was moved to the 3rd Pct., on Nov. 9, 1966 to the 4th pct., and on Dec. 29, 1967 back to the 2nd pct. In 1976 he lived at 93 King Avenue. You could always here Bill coming because he always wore taps on his shoes.

He retired on Sept 15, 1980 and for a while lived in San Diego, Cal. A member of Police Holy Name Society, in 1991 Bill was living in Sarasota, Fla where he died on April 26, 2002. He was 76 years old.

DET. LT. NORMAN P. FITZGERALD

APPOINTED: June 1, 1950
RETIRED: January 11, 1974

Born Norman Peter Fitzgerald in Yonkers on Jan. 21, 1926, Norm was raised in the Nodine Hill section of Yonkers. He attended St. Joseph's elementary school, graduated from Gorton HS and attended the Community College of NY (Baruch University). As a young man he listed his employment with the NY Railroad.

Norm joined the Navy on June 8, 1943 during WW 2 serving as a "belly gunner" on a Navy "P.V. Ventura" aircraft, part of a bomber squadron. He received his honorable discharge on April 8, 1945.

Norman “Red” Fitzgerald was appointed to the YPD on June 1, 1950 from 63 Oak St. His starting salary was $2,800 a year and following recruit training was assigned to the 1st pct. On May 7, 1956, during award ceremonies, Fitzgerald received a Certificate of Excellent Police Work for a robbery arrest he made on April 20, 1952 at 14 Caryl Avenue. He received a second Certificate for a robbery arrest he made on April 27, 1952 at 15 Yonkers Avenue; a 3rd certificate for capturing an escaped prisoner on Feb. 24, 1952, and a 4th certificate for subduing an emotionally disturbed person on May 24, 1955 at 78 Warburton Ave. On June 16, 1957, he was elevated to Detective in Detective Division. However, a year later, on April 16, 1958 he was reassigned back to patrol in the 2nd pct.

“Red” Fitzgerald received his promotion to the rank of Sergeant on Feb. 27, 1963 and had his salary raised to $7,400 a year. As a sergeant he was assigned as a patrol supervisor in the 3rd pct. for three months, and on May 1, 1963 was moved to the 4th precinct. On Nov. 7, 1963 “Red” was again moved, this time to the 1st pct. at 20 Wells Avenue. It was about that time that 20 Wells Avenue was closed and the 1st pct. and headquarters were moved to 10 St. Casimir Avenue.

At that time Sgt. Fitzgerald was sent to the 4th precinct where he was assigned by the captain to work in plainclothes investigating illegal gambling operations within the precinct boundaries. He was assigned PO William Grogan to assist him. Sgt Fitzgerald was an amateur photographer and utilized his skills taking pictures to obtain evidence of gambling on film.

Due to his skills investigating gambling and his unquestioned integrity, Sgt Fitzgerald was detailed from the 4th precinct to the Intelligence Unit on December 29, 1967. On February 14, 1968 Sgt Fitzgerald, along with all members of the Intelligence Unit, was assigned to Detective Division “on paper,” but remained detailed to the plainclothes Intelligence Unit. "Red" or "Fitzy," as he was known, was a big heavy set man who loved black and white photography and processed and printed his own photographic evidence. No one in the unit was a detective at that time. On January 1, 1971 he was reassigned to the D.D. as a Gambling Unit sergeant, but was not elevated to Detective Sergeant until July 1, 1971. And three months later, on October 22, 1971, Det. Sgt. Fitzgerald was transferred back to the Intelligence Division.

Two months later, on December 1, 1971, Det Sgt Fitzgerald was promoted to the rank of Lieutenant earning $15, 698, was designated a Detective Lieutenant, and was named commanding officer of the Intelligence Division. Lt. Fitzgerald’s wife Alma worked for the YPD in the Communications Division as a civilian telephone operator. His son was Det Lt. Patrick Fitzgerald and his daughter was Det Ann Fitzgerald. He was also related through marriage to former YPD police Lineman (electrician) Thomas Fitzgerald.

Det Lt Norman Fitzgerald retired from the Yonkers Police Dept. on January 11, 1974 and moved with his wife to Florida. He died there on July 20, 2004 at the age of 78 years.

PO WILLIAM F. GRAY #147

APPOINTED: June 1, 1950
RETIRED: April 12, 1972

Born William Francis Gray on April 27, 1921 in Yonkers in the Nodine Hill section, Bill attended local public schools. While in school he was active in the YMCA basketball leagues playing around the county. During WW-2 Bill joined the Coast Guard on June 3, 1942 serving on several troop transport ships including the USS William Black transporting troops to England and to Guadalcanal. Gray was honorably discharge on Feb 15, 1946. After the war he worked for Otis Elevator Co for a few years as a Time Keeper. On June 1, 1950 he was appointed to the YPD and went to 3rd pct. He worked 6 days a week and received no O.T. for anything; Inspections, parades, and court. After a few years he was moved to the 2nd pct. Bill served as a Detective for several years and during 1964 received Honorable mention and letters of commendation from the Sheriff's office on his excellent investigative skills. He returned to patrol in the new 1st pct. in 1966. When he retired in 1972 he worked as a chauffeur for the European American Bank for over 10 years. Bill always loved golf, while on job and after he retired on April 12, 1972.

PO JOHN SABOLYK #243

APPOINTED: June 1, 1950
RETIRED: October 1, 1983

"Jack" Sabolyk was born in the city of Yonkers on September 4, 1919. He attended Holy Trinity parochial school and graduated from Roosevelt HS where he was said to be a star football player and very active in all sports. Jack joined the Navy on February 14, 1942 during WW 2, and served aboard the USS Fitch-DD 462, as a petty officer first class. He participated in the Asiatic Pacific campaign, European, African, and the Normandy invasion. He said his ship was reportedly the first to fire on the beaches and was directly involved in the rescue of sailors and officers of the USS Cory which was hit and badly damaged. He was discharged on November 10, 1945. Jack was appointed to the YPD on June 1, 1950 from 274 Hayward St. with a starting salary of $2,800 a year. His first assignment was in the 2nd pct. On Oct. 16, 1952 he was reassigned to the 1st pct., but on Oct. 1, 1953 he was returned to patrol in the 2nd pct. He would remain there for the rest of his career, serving as the precinct trustee for many of those years. His last few years he served as the captain's administrative aide and retired on October 1, 1983. Being an avid golfer, Jack always said he wanted to have his ashes spread around the 18th golf hole at the Dunwoodie Golf course. Jack died on May 26, 2002 at the age of 82 years.

PO JOHN T. WALL #215

APPOINTED: June 1, 1950
RESIGNED: October 31, 1956

John Thomas Wall was born in the City of Yonkers on July 6, 1925, two years before his father John J. was appointed to the YPD. Young John was a graduate of Yonkers HS. He reportedly served in the Army toward the end of WW 2 working in the Motor Pool. John was appointed to the YPD on June 1, 1950. His starting salary was of $2,800 a year, was known as "Junior," and was assigned to the 1st pct. He was also known by co-workers as "Winky" because he fell asleep so easily on the late tour. On June 10, 1953 he was transferred to the Traffic Division motorcycle unit. But on Feb. 15, 1955 he was moved to the 4th precinct on patrol. A year later, on Mar. 1, 1956, he was transferred to the Communications Division as a dispatcher. John resigned from the YPD on Oct. 31, 1956, and moved to Wooster, Mass. working for a trucking company.

LT. LAWRENCE T. KELLY

APPOINTED: June 1, 1950
DIED: March 3, 1979

Born Lawrence Thomas Kelly in Yonkers on Dec. 2, 1922, Larry attended Manhattan prep school and Manhattan College and worked as a postal clerk in NYC. Kelly served in Navy from Aug. 2, 1942 up to his honorable discharge on Feb. 11, 1946. Kelly was appointed to the YPD from 133 Webster Ave. on June 1, 1950 with a starting salary of $2,800 a year. Following his recruit training he was assigned to the 3rd pct. On Jan. 1, 1951 he was reassigned to duty in the 1st pct. on Wells Avenue. Then, on Oct. 16, 1952 he was moved to the 3rd pct. on patrol. On Aug. 16, 1955 he was reassigned to the Training and Records Div. On Mar. 16, 1962 "Lonnie" Kelly, as he was known, was promoted to the rank of Sergeant with an annual salary of $7,000, and sent to the 2nd pct. On May 1, 1963 he was reassigned to the 4th pct. On Nov. 7, 1966 he was moved to the 3rd pct. On May 19, 1967 Kelly was promoted to Lieutenant earning $10,654 and was assigned to the 1st pct. as a desk officer. On January 1, 1971 Lt Kelly was reassigned to the North Command, but on March 12, 1973 he was transferred to Central Booking in the City Jail on Alexander Street. Unfortunately, "Lonnie" Kelly, who was said to have been DC Bill Farrington's brother-in-law, never reached retirement. He died suddenly on March 3, 1979. He was 56 years old.

PO RAYMOND G. JAMISON #31

APPOINTED: June 1, 1950
RETIRED: June 30, 1984

Ray was born Raymond Gerald Jamison on May 29, 1920 on Wells Avenue in Yonkers. As a youth he moved to Bartholdi Place, off Ravine Ave, where he was raised. He attended Holy Rosary school and Yonkers HS. As a young man he enjoyed baseball and played on the Yonkers "City League" as an outfielder.

Records indicate he served in the Army infantry from Mar 25, 1942 to Nov 28, 1945 (nearly 4 yrs.) in the Pacific Theater of operations, and was honorably discharged a Corporal. His nephew, Joe Jamison, said his uncle earned about 14 medals but he, Ray, was reluctant to discuss them. His nephew Joe Jamison believed he also earned the Silver Star and thinks that he also fought on Saipan. He said his uncle told him that he was about 100 feet from war correspondent Ernie Pyle when he was killed in April of 1945 on a small island named IeShima, a part of the Okinawa islands.

This writer interviewed Ray Jamison about his military service on August 5, 2005. At first he did not want to discuss it but, since I had known him from when I was a teenager, and with a great deal of encouragement he related the following to me, grudgingly:

Ray joined the Army and was assigned to the 77th Infantry Division. He said he was, at 21, the youngest in the Division. He spent two years training in places like Louisiana, Virginia, and various deserts, but eventually was shipped overseas to Hawaii. He, and his Army Division, along with the 1st Marine Division, all participated in the attack on the Japanese held Island of Guam. During heavy fighting he was wounded in the arm, but remained in combat. He said he spent two months there.

After a brief rest they participated in the assault on the Japanese held island of Leyte in the Philippines where he spent another two months in heavy combat. Then, on Feb 18, 1944 he participated in the assault on Eniwetok Atoll. This was a joint Marine and Army operation on an island which was located on the N/W edge of the Marshall Islands nearest Japan.

After another short break he participated in the attack on Okinawa itself, where there were massive casualties. Before the Okinawa campaign was finished, Ray said there was over 12,000 U.S. killed in action, and 38,000 U.S. wounded. In one particular action the American front line had been cut off by Japanese infantry and the American front line had no communications support from the rear. A communications wire had to be dragged nearly a mile through enemy lines and through heavy fire up to the US front lines to reconnect communications. Ray Jamison volunteered, succeeded, and by sheer luck, survived. For his action he was awarded the Bronze Star.

Sometime later during heavy shelling he was struck in the forehead with shrapnel and received a Purple Heart for this wound. He didn't know why but, he never received the Purple Heart medal for his shoulder wound. He also confirmed that he was close to war correspondent Ernie Pyle when he was killed in April of 1945.

When they left Okinawa his Division began to prepare to invade Japan. He jokingly said he probably spent more time aboard ship than some sailors. Along with the Bronze Star and the Purple Heart he accumulated about a dozen other medals and campaign ribbons. All this from the most reserved, quiet, soft spoken and unassuming man you could ever meet. I've known the man since I was 12 years old,

PO Raymond G. Jamison #31 (cont.)

having lived in the same building as Ray. And during all these many years I've never heard him use profanity or become angry. An absolute gentleman. Upon learning of his military background in 2005, and knowing this quiet gentleman, I was simply amazed.

After Ray's discharge he worked for the NYC Street Lighting Bureau. As a resident of 55 Ravine Ave and upon joining the YPD on June 1, 1950 he was assigned to the 1st precinct on Wells Avenue on foot patrol. After a few years, on Oct 15, 1953, he was assigned to the Traffic Division on foot directing vehicular traffic, for about 12 years, most of which was in Getty Square. According to Ray, at that time there were no traffic lights in Getty Square. Ray worked five tours, days and early tours, 7 hours a tour, 9am to 4pm, then 4pm to 11pm. There were always two men in Getty Square directing traffic. When traffic lights were installed he was reassigned onto 3 wheel motorcycle duty on the Street Cleaning Detail working the day tour. Around 1980 he had an accident in a radio car sustaining injuries to his head and was reassigned to headquarters to handle the pistol permit section.

When he retired on June 30, 1984 he lived on Arthur Place in Yonkers for several more years, but on January 1, 1990 he moved to Hudson, Florida.

Ray's brother Joseph was a retired police officer in the NYPD, and his nephew, Joe Jr, was an Inspector in the NYPD Narcotics Task Force. His niece (his brother Joe's daughter) married YPD PO Carmine Cavallo.

While in retirement in 2005 Ray was dealing with skin cancer, loss of a kidney, diabetes, prostate cancer, and heart disease. But, when I talked to him, you wouldn't know it. He was as jovial and friendly as ever. Two years later Ray died on August 5, 2007. He was 87.

CAPTAIN VINCENT J. ANDERSON

APPOINTED: June 1, 1950
RETIRED: June 15, 1975

Upon meeting Vincent Anderson it was evident that he was very friendly, outgoing, and self-confident. It was also obvious that he was intelligent and you could tell he was likely to be a rising star in the Yonkers Police Department. Yet, fate would have its way.

Born Vincent Joseph Anderson in Yonkers September 13, 1926, he was educated in Yonkers at Sacred Heart Elementary and High School, graduating in 1944. Upon graduating he was said to have been accorded every regents degree grant available but opted, instead, to join the US Navy during WW-2. Anderson served in Navy during from September 28, 1944, entering at the age of 18 years, and served up to his honorable discharge on July 3, 1946. It was reported he served in the Pacific Theater as an Electricians Mate until the war ended. After the war he was accepted to enter the US Air Force Academy, which he ultimately declined. He then joined the 101st Signal Battalion of the NY National Guard. Following his military service he was allowed to join the Metallic Wire Lathers Union Local #46 in NYC where he worked for several years.

"Skippy," as he was known to family and friends, was appointed to the YPD June 1, 1950 from 739 Palisades Ave. with a starting salary of $2,800 a year and was assigned to the 4th precinct. Two months later on August 19, 1950 the 101st Signal Battalion was activated and was merged into the regular Army's 1st Division for service during the Korean War. Anderson received an indefinite leave of

Capt. Vincent J. Anderson (cont.)

absence from the YPD and served as a Technical Sergeant in Supply. He was discharged on October 11, 1951 and was reinstated to the YPD on December 1, 1951 earning $3,000 and was assigned to the 1st precinct.

On October 16, 1952 he was reassigned to the 4th precinct. While there he was a member of 4th pct. Softball Team with a logo on the t-shirt of a mug of beer and words "4th Pct." As a young cop he was determined to make rank so he attended any promotional course he could, including the well-known Delahanty Institute for police promotion which was held in NYC.

A smart and aggressive officer, it was no surprise when he was appointed a Detective on December 1, 1956, receiving a $100 stipend for this assignment. However, this would be short-lived because PO Anderson was promoted to the rank of Sergeant on June 16, 1957 and had his salary raised to $5,512 a year. But the promotion resulted in his transfer from the D.D. to patrol supervisor duties in the 3rd precinct. He remained assigned there until April 2, 1959 when he was promoted to the rank of Lieutenant earning $6,580 per annum and was then transferred to the 1st precinct at 20 Wells Avenue as a desk officer.

In 1965 he was selected and did attend the renowned FBI National Academy's 76th session studying police management in Quantico, Va. beginning on September 3, 1965 and graduated on November 23, 1965. He was the first police officer from the Yonkers P.D. to ever be invited and accepted to attend this prestigious academy. And he graduated with the distinction of being the first police officer from Westchester County to be elected by his peers as the class president of the 76th session. This was a first for Westchester County. But to those who knew “Skippy,” this was no surprise. When he returned he was assigned to the 4th precinct on November 7, 1966 but detailed to Planning and Training Division.

A resident of 9 Jody Lane, Yonkers, Lt. Anderson was appointed a Captain on May 19, 1967 earning $11,850 a year and was allowed to remain assigned to the 4th precinct, but was assigned as the Liaison Officer for Yonkers Civil Defense.

In the ensuing years Capt. Anderson was moved around several times, i.e.; February 2, 1968 Records Service and Maintenance Division as the CO; on Feb. 7, 1969 to the 3rd precinct as the CO; on Feb. 2, 1970 to the Records Division as the CO; on May 14, 1970 back to the 3rd as the CO; on Jan. 1, 1971 to the North Command as the Operations Officer; on Jan. 28, 1972 to the Training Division as the CO; and on Jan. 6, 1975 to HQ Command Division assigned to the Records section.

Apparently Capt. Anderson had a problem just before reaching his 20 years which would enable him to retire. He had earlier been found guilty of some departmental rule and fined 30 days. When notified, he decided to retire. However, he was short 22 days. But after appealing to the mayor, the city allowed him to credit 22 days owed to him by the city and which he used to reach the 20 year mark and did retire on June 15, 1975.

In retirement “Skippy” traveled the world and claimed to be friendly with "Eva Perron," first lady of Argentina. As a result he claimed he was given ownership of a silver mine there. At one point he owned and operated a bus company in Elmsford and was the part owner of the Windham Hotel in Yonkers along with former PO Charles Fowler. He also worked as a consultant and estimator for the Walter Bale Construction Co in Elmsford for the last 16 years of his life.

A resident of Ossining for 20 years after moving from Jody Lane in Yonkers, Ret Capt. Vincent Anderson died in Rosary Hill on February 27, 1999. He was 72 years old.

DET. THOMAS S. POWRIE #661

APPOINTED: June 1, 1950
RETIRED: July 12, 1985

Thomas Shaw Powrie was born in the city of Yonkers at 5 Maple St. and would remain living there for the rest of his life. He attended PS#2 on Waverly Street, which was later renamed Benjamin Franklin Jr. HS, and graduated from Gorton HS. He attended Grove City College, in Grove City, PA. for a short time majoring in electrical engineering. He enjoyed playing baseball and did so on a local team named the "Nepperhan Tigers." Tom joined the Marine Corps during WW-2 on Aug. 27, 1942 and served aboard various aircraft as a radar technician and navigator. Holding the rank of Technical Sergeant, Powrie served in the Asiatic Pacific Theater of operations participating in action in the north Solomon Islands and Guadalcanal. He was honorably discharged on Nov. 11, 1945. Following the war he was a bank teller and then a wirelather. He was often referred to by his middle name, Shaw. Tom was appointed to the YPD on June 1, 1950 earning $2,800 a year and was assigned to the 3rd pct. in May of 1965 he was detailed to the newly established Intelligence Unit. While there he was appointed a detective on July 1, 1971. On Nov 15, 1974, he was reassigned as a desk officer in the Det. Div. from which he retired on July 12, 1985. Being a bowling enthusiast, Tom was a member of the YPD bowling team and a founding member of the Polish Community Club's Athletic Center. Tom's son is Ret Det Thomas Powrie Jr, his daughter-in-law is Ret PO Viola Powrie, and his wife's grandfather was PO Patrick Whalen who was killed in the Proctor Building explosion. Retired Det Thomas Powrie died on June 6, 1995. He was 71 years old.

PO RUDOLPH G. FRICCHIONE #162

APPOINTED: August 1, 1950
RESIGNED: August 31, 1952

Subject was born Rudolph George Fricchione on April 17, 1925. Records indicate that Fricchione served in the U.S. Navy during World War II. Following his discharge he worked for a time as a "checker." He was appointed to the Yonkers Police Department on August 1, 1950 from 104 Alexander Pl. with a starting salary of $2,800 a year and was assigned to patrol duties in the 2nd precinct. While there he was granted a leave of absence without pay on June 1, 1952 up to June 30, 1952. On July 1, 1952 he was reinstated to the Yonkers Police Department now earning $3,000 a year. However, only two months later, on August 31, 1952, Rudolph George Fricchione tendered his resignation from the YPD and same was accepted.

DET. FREDERICK J. BENJAMIN #630

APPOINTED: August 1, 1950
RETIRED: June 8, 1979

Born Frederick Joseph Benjamin on September 8, 1924 in the City of Yonkers, Fred graduated from Saunders HS. He also attended the Eastern School for Physicians aids in New York City and the Manhattan College for printing. He served in the Army during WW 2 from March 15, 1943 to January 26, 1946 when he was honorably discharged. He worked for a time as a clerk but was appointed to the YPD on August 1, 1950 from 110 Morris St. with a starting salary of $2,800 a year. His first assignment was in the 1st pct. On October 16, 1952 Fred was reassigned to the 3rd precinct at 36 Radford St. It was on January 6, 1959 that Fred was detailed to the Deputy Commissioner's office as an administrative aide. Following the appointment of police Chief William Polsen, Fred was assigned as his administrative aide. While there, on January 28, 1966 Fred was appointed a Detective but remained the chiefs administrative aide. On January 29, 1971, Det. Benjamin was transferred to the Criminal Identification Unit detailed to process all pistol permit applications. He retired on June 8, 1979, moved to Tamarac, Florida, and died on May 4, 2002. He was 77 years old.

SGT. JOSEPH J. AUGUSTINE #29

APPOINTED: August 1, 1950
RETIRED: January 6, 1978

Joe was born Joseph Jacob Augustine in Yonkers on Oct. 21, 1921. He attended and graduated from Commerce HS. As a young man he worked as an ice and coal dealer and later was hired by the Westchester Co. P.D. as a Special Parkway officer. Joe enlisted in the Army on Oct. 15, 1940 where he served as a Lieutenant during WW 2 in the Pacific Theater of operations with the MP's in the 27th Division of the National Guard. Later he was assigned to the 162nd Military Police Prisoner of War Processing section. Upon his honorable discharge on Dec. 7, 1945 as a 1st Lieutenant, he obtained work as a bartender in the Polish Community Center. Joe was appointed to the YPD from 63 Croton Terrace on Aug. 1, 1950 with a starting salary of $2,800 a year and was assigned to the 2nd pct. On Nov. 15, 1961 Joe was promoted to Sergeant earning $6,525 and was reassigned to the 4th pct. as a patrol supervisor. He was returned to the 2nd pct. for a few years but on Nov. 7, 1966 he was assigned to the Traffic Division. Four years later he was again moved, this time to the Communications Division. His last transfer was on March 12, 1973 to the South Command as a desk Sergeant, a job from which he would retire on Jan. 6, 1978. He moved to St Petersburg Fla. where he was a member of the 55 and Alive Bowling Club. Joe Augustine died there on April 25, 1999. He was 77 years old.

SGT. ROBERT E. LINSCOTT #49

APPOINTED: August 1, 1950
RETIRED: August 31, 1970

Robert Edward Linscott was born on November 21, 1924 in Thompsonville, Connecticut. After he and his family moved to Yonkers Bob attended and graduated from Yonkers HS and was a 1943 graduate of the US Merchant Marine Academy. He served in the Navy from July 1, 1946 to June 16, 1947 as a Lieutenant senior grade. He was said to have served on destroyers in the Atlantic Ocean and remained in the Naval Reserve for several years.

Bob was appointed to the Yonkers Police Department on August 1, 1950 from 640 O'Dell Ave., earning a starting salary of $2,800 a year. Bob's first assignment was patrol duty and the 2nd precinct. On January 21, 1952 he was reassigned from the 2nd precinct to the Traffic Division in the newly established Traffic Engineering Division. He also rode the two wheel motorcycle for several years.

Bob was apparently an adventurous individual by nature. While assigned to the Traffic Engineering Division, he teamed up with Sgt. Bob Foody of the Traffic Division, and officer Richard Swerdlove to purchase an Aeronca Chief, a two passenger plane, which they kept at the Westchester County Airport. PO Linscott, a naval officer right after World War II and at the time a lieutenant in the Naval reserve, received instruction to obtain his pilot's license. Still a member of the Naval reserve, he was granted a leave of absence from November through December of 1955 to attend the US Naval Command Administration and Training school at the Naval Shipyard in Brooklyn New York.

On June 25, 1961 police officer Linscott was working an off-duty security detail at Patricia Murphy's Candlelight Restaurant on Central Park Avenue. At about 2 AM while making his rounds he encountered three males attempting to break into the main office. He confronted the thieves and shots were fired by both Linscott and the suspects, all without effect, and the men escaped by jumping from a rear window.

On April 15, 1964 Bob was appointed a Detective and transferred from the Traffic Division to the Detective Division in the Bureau of Criminal Identification. In the police department Linscott was designated the ballistic and small arms expert for the YPD. He remained in this assignment until January 14, 1966 when he was promoted to the rank of sergeant earning $8,165 a year. No longer a detective, he was assigned as a patrol supervisor in the 2nd precinct.

The following year, on July 17, 1967, Sgt. Linscott was reassigned to the Communications and Records Division but detailed to the Forensic Laboratory which was under the Detective Divisions control. He was elevated to Detective Sergeant on February 23, 1968 and placed in charge of the Bureau of Criminal Identification and the Forensic Laboratory. He remained in this assignment up to April 17, 1970 when he was reassigned back to patrol duties in the 3rd precinct. It was here that Sgt. Linscott retired from the police department on August 31, 1970.

Following his retirement from the Yonkers Police Department Bob operated a security business in upstate New York for a few years and then moved to Maine in 1975 where he was appointed Chief of Police of the Wells, Ma. police department. While serving as the chief of police Bob developed a hobby building cannons. He actually built a three quarters scale model of an 1857 Civil War cannon which weighed around 800 pounds. The wheels, taken from a hay wagon, weighed 75 pounds each, and the

Sgt. Robert E. Linscott #49 (cont.)

carriage was made from solid oak. He was a regular participant in local Civil War re-enactments. In 1986 Chief Robert Linscott retired from the Wells, Maine Police Department.

Following his retirement Bob suffered a heart attack in 1986 and later moved to Flagler, Beach Florida in 1992. Due to his heart condition he could not hold a pilot's license so, while in Florida, he turned to experimental aircraft, actually building a "Gyroplane," a helicopter like craft with an open cabin. He didn't need a license to fly them.

Bob was a member of the law enforcement Blue Knights Motorcycle Club, the Palm Coast Rod and gun club, a life member of the NRA, the experimental aircraft Association and the aircraft owners and pilots Association. He was also a past master and life member of the Diamond Thistle Masonic Lodge, in Yonkers New York.

At one point Bob moved to Daytona Beach Florida and on March 11, 1997, while flying one of his experimental helicopter style aircraft, the aircraft crashed and burned, killing him. Bob Linscott was 72 years old.

DET. JAMES T. WALDRON #657

APPOINTED: October 16, 1950
RETIRED: November 1, 1984

Jim was born in Yonkers on Aug. 1, 1925. He graduated from Sacred Heart Grammar school and Gorton HS. He enlisted in the Navy during WW 2 on Dec 12, 1942 and was honorably discharged on Nov 5, 1946, having served on a Destroyer manning depth charges. Jim worked for a short while at Otis Elevator Co. until called by the YPD. He was appointed to the YPD from 6 Fowler Avenue on Oct. 16, 1950 earning $2,800 a year and was assigned to 1st pct. A few years later he worked in the 3rd pct. for many years in a radio car. In the late 1960's Jim was detailed and later assigned as an investigator in the Intelligence Unit where he later was appointed a detective on July 1, 1971. Jim Waldron retired from the YPD as a detective on Nov. 1, 1984 and remained retired. Jim was a sportsman who loved hunting, fishing, bowling, baseball and football. He was a very easy going, friendly guy willing to help anyone. He was a member of the Yonkers Elks Lodge and the VFW Post 3083. After retiring he moved to his summer home in Berne, NY for five years and then to Wappingers Falls, NY. He was there only one year when, having suffered from Alzheimer's disease and later leukemia, Jim Waldron died on Sept 28, 1990. He was 65 years old.

SGT. JAMES O. POTTER #10

APPOINTED: March 26, 1951
DIED: June 14, 1969

Born October 17, 1923 in Yonkers Jim graduated from Saunders HS. He served in the Army from July 2, 1943 to October 23, 1945 in the US Army Air Corps as a Staff Sergeant with the 763rd bomber squadron as an aerial gunner. Jim was appointed to the YPD from 27 Spruce Street on March 26, 1951 earning $2,800 a year. He previously worked as a State Trooper in Monroe, NY. Following recruit school Jim was assigned to the 2nd precinct. The following year on October 15, 1952 Potter was transferred to the 4th pct. and on December 16, 1954 he was moved to the 2nd pct. In 1958 Potter was elected Financial Secretary of the PBA. On April 1, 1960 he was promoted to Sergeant with a salary increase to $6,275 and was reassigned to the 4th pct. as a patrol supervisor. On May 1, 1963 Sgt Potter was moved to the 1st pct. and on March 16, 1964 to the 4th pct. Unfortunately Jim developed kidney cancer and as a result, on February 8, 1968, he was assigned to the Traffic Division detailed to the Traffic Violations Unit in a light duty capacity. Due to complications from his disease, Sgt James Potter died on June 14, 1969. He was only 36 years old.

LT. RUSSELL KANTOR

APPOINTED: March 26, 1951
RETIRED: April 1, 1988

Russell Kantor was born in the City of Yonkers on October 21, 1925. Russ attended local schools and graduated from Roosevelt High School where, having played basketball, he was named captain of their team. Being of the Russian Orthodox religion Kantor spoke Russian fluently as a second language. Shortly after graduating from high school Russ joined the Navy on March 22, 1944. He was stationed in the South Pacific serving as a Radioman 3rd class during the closing years of WW-2. He received the American Theater Medal, the Asiatic Pacific Medal and the World War II Victory Medal. He was honorably discharged as a Petty Officer 3rd class on May 8, 1946.

Russ worked a few different jobs after the war including that of a bartender but, while living at 17 Colin Street, he was eventually hired by the YPD on March 26, 1951 from 17 Colin Street and assigned to the 2nd precinct. Fifteen years later, on November 7, 1966, PO Kantor was transferred to the newly opened 1st precinct located on East Grassy Sprain Road.

On May 20, 1967 officer Kantor was promoted to the rank of Sergeant at the new salary of $8,855 a year and was assigned as a patrol supervisor in the 4th precinct. But on December 1, 1970 he was re-assigned to the Communications Division (Radio Room) as a tour supervisor.

When the police department was re-organized into a two command centralized operation on Jan. 1, 1971, Sgt Kantor was assigned to the newly named North Patrol Command, which was a combination of the old 4th and 1st precincts. The first few years he worked as a patrol sergeant but later, when the long tradition of lieutenants serving as desk officers was discontinued, sergeants replaced them performing that duty. Consequently on March 12, 1973 Sgt Kantor was designated a 4th precinct "Desk Sergeant."

It was on April 9, 1976 that Sgt Kantor received his promotion to Lieutenant and was assigned to the Headquarters Command Division. However the following month, on May 10, 1976, he was moved to the "Radio Room" as the communications supervisor. Lt Russell Kantor retired from the YPD on April 1, 1988 after thirty seven years service.

He was a member of the Police and Fire Retirees Association, a longtime parishioner of Holy Trinity Russian Orthodox Church where he was a senior warden for many years and was a trustee of the church, a member of their Legacy Society and he sang tenor in the church choir. He was also a member of the Scarsdale Elks Lodge where he was Exalted Ruler for four terms. He was also named Elk of the Year from 1997 to 1998. Ted Kantor was an avid golfer, and after his retirement, he joined the Dunwoodie Senior Golf League where he had a hole in one three times. He enjoyed music, singing and dancing. Russ had five brothers, John, Stephen, George, Alexander and Theodore Kantor and two sisters, Anne Walsh and Rose Arthurs. Stephen and Theodore were also Yonkers police officers.

Ret Lt Russell Kantor died on March 23, 2010 in his residence on Rockne Road in Yonkers, NY. He was 84 years old.

SGT. DONALD E. GIVLER #31

APPOINTED: March 26, 1951
RETIRED: June 2, 1983

Born Donald Eugene Givler on November 7, 1927 in Buffalo NY, Don attended local public schools. As a young man he was employed as a Dental Mechanic. During WW 2 Don joined the US Navy on Nov 1, 1943 and served in the Pacific. He was honorably discharged on June 13, 1946 as a Pharmacist Mate, 2nd class. Don was appointed to the YPD on March 26, 1951 from 21 Maple Place earning $2,800. His first assignment was to the 2nd pct. Eight years later on Nov. 9, 1959 he was transferred to the Communications Division as a “dispatcher” of radio cars, and on Mar. 13, 1963 he was reassigned to the 2nd pct. Upon his promotion to Sergeant on Dec. 31, 1963 he was then assigned to the 3rd pct. as a patrol sergeant. The following transfers then followed; on Nov 7, 1966 to the 1st pct. as a patrol Sgt. On Oct 22, 1969 back to the Communications Div. On Mar 12, 1973 to the South Command as the newly established Desk Sergeant or as it was designated, "Station House Supervisor." On July 1, 1980 once again back to the Communications Division, this time in the Tele Serve Unit from which he retired on June 2, 1983. Don Givler was a unique guy with a great personality. You could identify him from far off. He walked with his head cocked to one side and he claimed to be part American Indian. As result he was affectionately nicknamed "Chief." He was a real gentleman and a good boss to work for. Following retirement he moved to Berkeley Township, NJ where he died on December 7, 2004. He was 77 years old.

PO JOHN E. RICH #235

APPOINTED: March 26, 1951
RESIGNED: June 16, 1953

John E. Rich was born in Yonkers on July 25, 1925 and attended local public schools. Records indicate that he served in the Navy during WW-2 from December 20, 1943 up to his honorable discharge on January 28, 1946. Following his military service John was employed as a Wire Twister at the Habirshaw Cable and Wire Corp. Rich was appointed to the YPD on March 26, 1951 earning a starting salary of $2,800 a year. At the time he lived at 43 Hart Avenue. Following his recruit training he was assigned to the 1st precinct. However, John Rich submitted his resignation from the YPD effective June 16, 1953 in order to be appointed to the State Police.

LT. WILLIAM J. NUGENT

APPOINTED: March 26, 1951
RETIRED: April 1, 1988

Bill Nugent was born in Yonkers on December 22, 1925. He grew up living on Palisade Ave. and graduated from Gorton H.S. in June 1943 at age 17 years. Wanting to serve during WW 2, it was just a few short months later that he joined US Marine Corps on Nov 9, 1943, completed boot camp at Parris Island, SC, and advanced infantry training at Camp LeJeune, NC. He was then moved to Norfolk Va. and shipped out for the Pacific Theater of Operations by way of Panama, Hawaii, and in June of 1944 participated in the landing and battle on the island of Guam.

For his service on Guam he earned a battle star. On February 19, 1945 the landing and assault on the island of Iwo Jima took place. Nugent and his outfit was scheduled to land on day 2, Feb 20th, but due to rough seas and landing vehicle problems, he hit the beach on day 3, Feb 21st. Nugent was a PFC and was designated a "Scout Sniper." His weapon, the M-1 Garand. The fighting was fierce and casualties were heavy. As a result of this and his leadership skills he was given a field promotion to Corporal and made Squad Leader. For his service on Iwo Jima he received another battle star and the Bronze Star for Valor. He remained on the island until April 1, 1945 and was relieved. Throughout Guam and Iwo Jima, as Bill put it, "I never received a scratch." Throughout the remainder of 1945 he and his regiment trained for the invasion of Japan which was said to have been scheduled for Nov 1, 1945. During this time Nugent served as an Acting Sergeant. Fortunately the war ended. He was honorably discharged a Corporal on Christmas Eve, December 24, 1945.

Bill worked for Western Electric as an Installer for a time and then for the National Biscuit Co. as a "Checker." At the time of his appointment to the YPD, on March 26, 1951, he lived at 18 Eastman Place and earned a starting salary of $2,800 annually. Following police recruit training his first assignment was to the 1st pct. on Wells Ave. Then on October 16, 1952 he was sent to 4th pct. and on June 18, 1954 from the 4th to 3rd. He served there on patrol for several years but at one point was given the opportunity to work in the captain's office as the C.O.'s aide. He accepted and worked there for a number of years, right up to his promotion to Sergeant on December 19, 1969, which increased his salary to $11,600 a year. Following his promotion he was reassigned as a patrol supervisor in the 2nd precinct.

Because of his military experience Bill was utilized quite often whenever they needed to provide a color guard. Nugent was also a member of the original YPD bowling team when he was the captain's aide in the 3rd precinct.

Sgt Nugent received his promotion to Lieutenant on April 24, 1972 earning $15,698 annually, and was transferred to the Inspectional Services Division as a city wide patrol lieutenant. On March 12, 1973 Lt Nugent was moved to the South Patrol Command on Central Park Avenue as the Executive Officer. His last assignment was on July 26, 1974 to the North Command at 53 Shonnard Place as the Executive Officer where he remained right up to his retirement on April 1, 1988.

Bill Nugent, who was well liked and respected by all, lived at 12 Kenilworth Rd, Yonkers and during his retirement he loved to walk long distances. In 2005 he moved to Jefferson Village in Yorktown Heights. He died on July 6, 2013. Bill was 87 years old.

DET. RICHARD H. SWERDLOVE #638

APPOINTED: March 26, 1951
DIED: August 23, 1980

Born Richard Haskell Swerdlove in the Bronx, NY on March 30, 1925, Rich attended and graduated from local schools. Following high school Rich joined the Navy serving during WW 2 from July 23, 1943 to his honorable discharge on December 21, 1945. His rating was a Signalman 2nd class and he served in the Asiatic Pacific Theater. It was said that Richard had flown planes during his service in World War II but it is unconfirmed. After the war he had a private pilot's license for his own use only. In 1950 he attended and graduated from the University of Miami with a BA degree and spoke Spanish fluently as a second language. Following college he worked briefly as a salesman at Strauss Stores.

He was appointed to the YPD at $2,800 from 54 First Street on March 26, 1951 and assigned to the 1st precinct. On October 16, 1952 he was moved to the 3rd precinct on patrol. The following year, on March 7, 1953, he was transferred from the 3rd to the 2nd precinct. On December 1, 1956 he was reassigned to the Communications and Operations Division, and on June 23, 1964 to Detective in the Detective Division. On February 3, 1969 he was moved from the DD to the 3rd precinct. On June 30, 1969 PO Swerdlove received a special commendation from the Westchester County District Attorney's office which commended him on his excellent testimony during the trial of several defendants for serious crimes including manslaughter. On December 29, 1972 he was reassigned to Headquarters Command Division detailed to the Communications Division dispatching radio cars. A short time later he was assigned to the Bureau of Criminal Identification (BCI), then renamed Criminal Identification Unit, where he was a crime scene photographer and evidence collector.

A resident of Croton Falls, NY, and having a Bachelor's Degree, Rich taught part-time in the high school system in northern Westchester where he lived.

A 29 year veteran of the Yonkers police department Richard Swerdlove was killed one early Saturday morning, on August 23, 1980, when his car went off the road and plunged into the Nepperhan Creek near Ashburton Avenue and Saw Mill River Road. He was on his way home after working the early tour when the accident occurred about 2 AM. He was 55 years old.

SGT. JOSEPH M. FITZPATRICK #50

APPOINTED: March 26, 1951
RETIRED: July 28, 1972

"Joe Fitz" was born in Yonkers on June 28, 1923 and graduated from Gorton HS. Joe served in the Army during WW 2 from May 21, 1942 to Oct 10, 1945 as a Corporal in the Signal Corps with special training as an Aviation Cadet. He gained early employment with Western Electric Co. as installation technician. He was appointed to the YPD on March 26, 1951 from 40 Locust Hill Ave earning $2,800 a year and assigned to the 1st precinct. On Aug. 27, 1952 he was reassigned to the Traffic Division. Four years later, on July 16, 1956, he was moved to the 4th pct. on patrol. Then, on Dec. 1, 1956, he was appointed a Detective in the DD, receiving a $100 raise, increasing his salary to $4,930. He remained for four years and was returned to the 4th on Nov. 16, 1960. On May 18, 1962 it was reported that officer Fitzpatrick and other officers arrested a number of suspects responsible for numerous burglaries in Yonkers and throughout Westchester Co. On Dec. 31, 1963 Fitzpatrick was promoted to Sergeant and assigned as a patrol supervisor in the 3rd pct. After a short stint in the Communications Div., on Jan. 1, 1971 he was transferred to the North Command from which he retired on July 28, 1972. After retiring he opened an Auto Body Shop on Alexander Street. His brothers were YPD Lt Ray Fitzpatrick, YFD Asst Chief Tom Fitzpatrick. Retired Sgt Joseph Fitzpatrick died on May 2, 1989. He was 65 years old.

PO HARRY R. TOOP #192

APPOINTED: March 26, 1951
RESIGNED: September 15, 1952

Harry Toop was born in the Bronx, NY on March 13, 1928. On his police application he listed his occupation as a student. Harry served in the Navy from May 14, 1945 and received his honorable discharge on December 23, 1946. Harry Toop was appointed to the police department on March 26, 1951 while living at 10 Halstead Avenue and had a starting salary of $2,800 a year. Following training he was assigned to the 1st precinct at 20 Wells Avenue. After 18 months service Harry Toop submitted his resignation while in the 2nd precinct effective September 15, 1952.

CAPTAIN LAWRENCE W. CONLEY

APPOINTED: March 26, 1951
DIED: October 22, 1982

Born Lawrence William Conley in Yonkers NY on May 31, 1924, Larry attended Gorton High School but graduated from Halstead High School on North Broadway. Soon after graduation and just 18 years old, Larry Conley wanted to serve during WW 2 and as such joined the Navy Reserve Coast Guard on September 24, 1942. He was stationed in Florida and Alaska as a 1st class Quartermaster/Signalman up to his honorable discharge on December 5, 1945. After his discharge he remained in the Naval Reserve until March 31, 1947.

Larry worked a number of miscellaneous jobs including the Yonkers Tree Service and that of a Salesman at Sears and Roebuck Department Store. And when he applied for the Yonkers P.D. Patrolman's test he listed on his application his address as being 127 New Main Street. He was still living there when he received his appointment to the Yonkers Police Department on March 26, 1951. His starting salary was $2,800 a year and after some rudimentary recruit training he was assigned to patrol duty in the 1st precinct located at 20 Wells Avenue. The following year, on October 16, 1952, he was reassigned to patrol in the 3rd precinct.

Captain Lawrence W. Conley (cont.)

On November 15, 1955 the local newspaper reported that the October session of the Grand Jury in White Plains had commended officer Conley for his work in solving a burglary which took place the previous month on October 4th at a gas station located at 414 McLean Avenue. He was also commended by the Grand Jury for his "splendid conduct and intelligent testimony in this burglary case."

On August 7, 1955 a seven year old boy fell into the Saw Mill River near Ashburton Avenue striking his head. PO Larry Conley and his partner Joe Yarina shed their uniforms and jumped into the water to save the child. Unfortunately, despite their effort the child died.

On December 1, 1956 Patrolman Conley was transferred from the 3rd precinct to Detective Division and appointed a Detective. This assignment earned him an additional $100 pay increase. Det. Conley remained in this position until June 16, 1957 when he was promoted to the rank of Sergeant. As a sergeant his salary rose to $5,512 a year and he was reassigned as a patrol supervisor in the 1st precinct at 20 Wells Avenue.

On November 16, 1962 Sgt Conley continued on his determined effort to rise up in the ranks by being promoted to Police Lieutenant. Following his promotion to Lieutenant his salary rose to $7,175 and he was allowed to remain in the 1st precinct, but this time performing the duty of a desk lieutenant. On July 5, 1965 Lieutenant Conley was reassigned to the 3rd precinct at 36 Radford Street "on the desk." However, two years later, on April 1, 1967, he was again moved, this time back to the 1st precinct on the desk. It would be nearly four years later before he would again be reassigned on January 1, 1971 to the North Command on the desk. On this date a new centralization plan became operational and the 1st and the 3rd precincts stopped operating as precincts. The 4th and the 2nd were re-named the North and South Commands. Lt. Conley was moved, yet again, on October 6, 1972 to the Headquarters Command Division detailed to the Court of Special Sessions as the YPD liaison officer facilitating the criminal cases to be heard and the supervision of the officers called to testify.

On February 11, 1976 Lt. Conley achieved the prize that all aspiring officers seek; he was promoted to captain earning $11,970. His promotion was the result of the retirement of Capt. John Higgins and now "Captain" Conley was designated commanding officer of the Headquarters Command Division.

Nearly four years later, on November 2, 1979, Capt. Conley was transferred to the Field Services Bureau as a city-wide patrol duty captain. Unfortunately, on May 14, 1982 Larry became ill with cancer and was moved to the Inspector General Services Unit as the temporary commanding officer. Actually, he remained out on sick leave right up to his death on October 22, 1982. He was 58 years old.

Following his death Police Commissioner Charles Connolly was quoted as saying, "Larry Conley was a good man who cared deeply about his family, his religion, his country, and the Yonkers Police Department. In the four years that I have been here I got to enjoy his wit and sense of caring; and I particularly got to know what made Larry Conley tick. The man had a sense of character and personal courage, and I will certainly miss him."

If you met and got to know Larry Conley, you immediately liked him. He was that type of man; A very outgoing friendly person who always looked out for his men. If someone under his command developed a problem in the job, he would work to help the officer. And when nothing could be done, it was not unusual that he would, and actually did, take responsibility for the officers' actions and accept the

Captain Lawrence W. Conley (cont.)

punishment on their behalf. He was a special man.

Although he was a very happy go lucky guy who loved to talk, blessed with a quick Irish wit, and who loved a party, he was very serious about his job and was reportedly not one to back down to anyone. If he had something that bothered him he would let you know.

There came a time during the summer of 1978 when there was word that a large demonstration would take place at the Indian Point Power Station up county. A large contingent of Yonkers officers were requested and supplied, with Capt. Conley in command. They arrived stood their posts, all without incident. It turned out to be a very uneventful, very quiet, and a very, very hot day. Rumors spread that cold beer had somehow been delivered to help mitigate the oppressive heat. True or not, an investigation was started by Yonkers Comm. Daniel Guido to identify those officers involved and to bring charges against them. To prevent any such embarrassing investigation going public Capt. Conley advised PC Guido that any inappropriate activity that may have occurred was his responsibility and he made an agreement with the commissioner that he, and only he, was responsible and would accept any punishment. He was penalized 30 days and he accepted it willingly to protect his men and the good name and reputation of the police department.

Being the man that he was with that incredible wit, he used it with great success on a particular night. In February of 1979 Bob Taggart had been promoted to Sergeant and he related how Capt. Conley once again used his wit to make the entire room roar with laughter. Bob Taggart tells the story this way;

"Both Commissioner Dan Guido and Capt. Conley were at my promotion party. There came a point during the festivities when Larry Conley stood up and demanded some silence whereupon he said, 'I'd like to ask Commissioner Guido to come up and join me in offering a toast to our new sergeant.' "Guido stood up next to Larry and held up his glass. (I do not know what Guido had in his glass but I suspect it was a soft drink.) Larry held up a glass of beer and had everyone else in the room stand. Then he said. 'I'd like to congratulate Bob Taggart on his promotion to sergeant. I believe we should all wish him good health and much success in the future.' Then he said 'hear hear,' everyone else joined in and Larry drank his beer, as all of the other guests drank whatever they had handy. At the conclusion of the toast he remained standing with his glass held high and while he continued to hold the attention of the crowd he said, 'I want everyone to take notice that I offered this toast not with the customary glass of Champagne, but with a simple glass of beer. But I want you all to know that it was good beer ... It was not as good as the beer we had at Indian Point, but then again it was not nearly as expensive.' (Referring to his 30 day fine.) The room erupted in laughter. Even the usually stern Comm. Guido couldn't hold back a smile. That was classic Larry Conley. He had an incredible sense of humor, great wit, and definitely class.

Larry was a charter member of the Westchester County Police Emerald Society Pipes & Drums Band, and played the drums. He was also a past president of the Yonkers Police Holy Name Society, a member of the Friendly Sons of St. Patrick of Westchester, the Ancient Order of Hibernians, the Yonkers City Fife and Drum Corps., the NYC Police Emerald Society, the Yonkers Elks Club Lodge 707, and the Knights of Columbus LaRabida Council. He was also an assistant scout master, secretary of the Tower Ridge Yacht Club, a former trustee of both the PBA and the Capt's, Lt's, and Sgt's Association, the Amackassin Club, the American Legion, and the US Coast Guard Academy Alumni Association.

LT. FREDERICK E. DOTY

APPOINTED: March 26, 1951
RETIRED: April 17, 1971

Fred Doty was born in Yonkers on August 30, 1927, attended PS# 22, Longfellow Jr H.S. and graduated from Saunders HS. He was educated in engineering. Fred then joined Army, serving from 1946 to his honorable discharge in 1949. Because of his skills in engineering he was assigned to be part of the Manhattan Project, an operation dealing with Atomic energy, in Los Alamos, New Mexico. As history tells us, this is where the first atomic bomb was developed.

Upon his discharge as a Sergeant he was hired by the NY Telephone Co. where he worked for about two years. It was then that he took the test for Yonkers Police Patrolman, along with 140 others and yet only 12 passed. All 12 were eventually appointed from the list. Doty was appointed to the YPD on March 26, 1951 and was assigned to the 3rd pct. There was virtually no serious police recruit training at that time. Only a few basic class room lectures by other ranking officers. He just reported for duty and went on patrol in a gray work type "uniform" along with a senior officer.

About that time the Korean war was just beginning. Believing he might be re-called up to serve and have to start over as a private, he had earlier joined the Army Reserves on December 20, 1950. He was right; his unit, the 332nd Engineers Aviation Battalion of the Army Air Corps, was activated on June 1, 1951. Fortunately he remained in Texas and ultimately rose to the rank of First Sergeant. He was recommended to attend Officer Candidate School but declined.

Following the war and his honorable discharge on December 17, 1952, he was reinstated to the YPD on January 16, 1953 where he had only been on patrol for two months in his recruit gray uniform before being activated. He went right back to the 3rd pct. again in grays, but now earning $3,100. He worked the foot post on South Broadway as a steady assignment. During his leave of absence from the YPD when activated into the military, he had to continue contributing to the State Pension System in order to keep credit for years of service. On December 1, 1956 he and several others passed the Sergeants exam and all on the list were assigned to the D.D. as part of a training program. When each man was called to get promoted to sergeant, he would be transferred out of the D.D. When Doty was promoted to sergeant on June 16, 1957 he was reassigned from the Detective Division to the 4th pct. as a patrol supervisor.

While there he was approached by a captain and asked if he wanted to go to the Traffic Division. He certainly did, since he already knew how to ride a motorcycle. He was assigned to Traffic on November 16, 1960 and would later say that Traffic was the very best job he ever had and should have stayed right there.

Sometime later he was asked to go to the Detective Division as a Det. Sergeant and of course he said yes. He was transferred into the D.D. on May 1, 1963 and because of his knowledge from the telephone Co. he worked predominantly on gambling investigations installing the wiretaps, etc. He was promoted to Lieutenant on December 31, 1963 and effective the same day, was appointed a Detective Lieutenant and remained in the D.D.

Lt Doty was very serious about his job but he said, it became obvious to him that a few were not,

Lt. Frederick E. Doty (cont.)

so he asked for a transfer and was sent to the 2nd pct. on June 14, 1968. He remained there right up to his retirement on April 17, 1971. Lt Doty planned the date he would retire, but not what would happen on his last tour the night that he retired. He was working an early tour as the 2nd pct. desk lieutenant and about 9 PM two officers brought in a prisoner. During processing in front of the desk and Lt Doty, somehow the man was able to grab and rip the gun out of the arresting officer's holster. He quickly lifted the gun up and pointed it right at Lt Doty's head as he yelled incoherently. Doty would later say at first he thought it was a "goodbye" type joke but the gun was so close he could see the lead slugs in the revolvers cylinder. Fortunately after some very tense minutes the man was convinced into putting down the gun and the stand-off ended. That was it. Lt Doty stood up, said I'm finished, and walked out the door and went home into retirement.

During this time for about 15 years he worked for Tarricone Oil Co. as a Truck Mechanic. Because he could never completely get the oil out of his hands he was teased and nicknamed "Gloves." Many years earlier he had bought a summer home in Westerly RI so when he retired he moved there and bought an Exxon service Station. Several years later Fred Doty moved to Mahopac NY.

Fred's grandfather was PO Frank Doty, his great uncle was PO Arthur Doty, his Son is former PO Edward Doty who joined YFD and rose to Assistant Chief, another son James is with the YFD, and a third son Robert is a sergeant with the Westchester County Dept. of Corrections.

Retired Lt. Fred Doty died November 27, 2011. He was 84 years old.

DET. ROCCO A. DELBENE #649

APPOINTED: November 1, 1951

RETIRED: February 21, 1986

"Rocky" DelBene was born in Yonkers on December 29, 1924. He attended PS#2 and graduated from Commerce HS. He was very athletic and loved softball, bowling, hunting, and fishing. Rocky served in the Army during WW 2 in Europe from August 4, 1943 to March 1, 1946, and was honorably discharged as a Master Sergeant and company clerk. He listed his previous occupation as a Bookkeeper in General Contracting. He was hired to the YPD from 85 St Andrews Place on Nov. 1, 1951 at $2,800. a year and following training was assigned to the 2nd pct. on patrol duty. The following year on Oct 16, 1952 he was reassigned to patrol in the 3rd pct. It was on Jan. 30, 1963 that Rocco was appointed a Detective and assigned to the D.D. working General Assignment. He would remain in the DD for 23 years, right up to retirement. In his last years in the job he served as the D.D. desk officer. He was a member of the Lowerre VFW Post and enjoyed golfing. Rocco's brother was the late PO Alfred DelBene who died in 1958. Following retirement on February 21, 1986 Rocky moved to Gulf Port, Florida. In early June 2006 he was diagnosed with inoperable cancer of the kidney and died there in the hospital on June 28, 2006. He was 81 years old.

PO JULIUS DEMKOWSKI #146

APPOINTED: November 1, 1951

RESIGNED: November 23, 1954

Julius Demkowski was born in Yonkers on April 12, 1920 and attended local schools. Julius served in the Navy during WW 2 from January 23, 1941, working as an aircraft mechanic, up to his honorable discharge on February 7, 1947. He received his appointment to the Yonkers Police Dept. on November 1, 1951 while living at 10 Stewart Place. Following a short time on patrol he was assigned to the Traffic Division on motorcycle patrol on Aug. 20, 1952. Demkowski became involved in an internal investigation which he wanted no part of. As a result officer Demkowski resigned the next day on November 23, 1954. On April 27, 1955 he requested reinstatement but was denied. He tried again in Oct of 1955 but was again denied. When he first resigned he worked as a car salesman. Later Demkowski later worked for many years as a guard at the Yonkers Raceway. A resident of Yorktown, NY, former PO Julius Demkowski died in Yonkers on September 5, 2008. He was 88 years old.

DET. LT. JAMES A. BARRIER

APPOINTED: November 1, 1951
RETIRED: November 4, 1971

Jim Barrier was born November 18, 1919 in Barber, North Carolina. He attended local elementary schools, moved to Yonkers and graduated from Gorton high school in 1939. He also attended Johnson Smith University in Charlotte, North Carolina from 1940 to 1942.

Jim entered the U.S. Army Air Corps on June 17, 1942 serving with the military police. While in the Army his highest rank held was as a 2nd lieutenant. He received his honorable discharge on January 9, 1946. With a keen sense of the importance of education, Jim Barrier reentered Smith University and earned his bachelor's degree. In 1948 to 1950 Jim worked as a teacher of American history in a high school in Columbia, South Carolina. He returned to Yonkers and from 1950 to 1951 he worked as a recreation supervisor in Parks Dept. in the city of Yonkers.

Making use of his years of military police service, Jim Barrier applied for and was appointed to the Yonkers Police Department on November 1, 1951 from 28 Horatio Street, earning a starting salary of $2,800 a year. His first assignment following recruit training was to the 2nd precinct. Continuing his education officer Barrier received his Master's degree from Columbia University in June of 1952 and he spoke French as a second language.

Having left the department on an unpaid leave of absence to continue his formal education, Jim returned and was reinstated to the YPD on June 16, 1953. On April 1, 1960 Jim Barrier made Yonkers police history when he was promoted to the rank of Sergeant; the very first black Yonkers police officer to be promoted to higher rank. He was assigned as a patrol supervisor in the 1st precinct located at 20 Wells Avenue. His new salary was $6,380 a year.

Jim Barrier was one of the founders of, and was the first president of, the Yonkers Police Guardians organization which was organized in April of 1963 and the members met in his basement at 67 Bushy Ave. When the Westchester County Guardians Association was first organized, Sgt. Jim Barrier was elected as its president for the first two years.

On November 7, 1966 Sgt. Barrier was reassigned to the 4th precinct at 53 Shonnard Place. On May 19, 1967 he was promoted to Lieutenant and remained in the 4th precinct as a desk officer. As a lieutenant his salary was $10,645 a year. On February 14, 1968 Lt Barrier was assigned to the Headquarters Command Division as a community relations officer working closely with the minority community. On July 12, 1968 Lt Barrier was appointed a Detective Lieutenant assigned to the Detective Division, but remained detailed working in the Community Relations Unit.

Jim Barrier retired from the YPD on November 4, 1971. For fun he loved to play a card game called Gin Rummy. He and his wife never had children. A tall imposing figure, he was known by many as "Big Jim."

Ret Lt. James A. Barrier died on February 4, 1988 at the age of 68 years.

PO WILLIAM J. RYAN #233

APPOINTED: November 1, 1951
RETIRED: May 4, 1984

Bill Ryan was born in the City of Yonkers March 28, 1925. He attended local public schools and graduated from Saunders HS. Following school Bill joined the Navy during WW 2 on August 23, 1943 serving in the Pacific as a Fleet Oiler. He received his honorable discharge on March 11, 1946. Following the Navy Bill worked as a labor foreman. He was appointed to the YPD on Nov. 1, 1951 from Martin Ray Place with a salary of $8,210 a year. His first assignment was patrol in the 2nd pct. A year later, on Oct. 9, 1952, Ryan resigned from the YPD for personal reasons but requested, and was granted, reinstatement on July 1, 1953. Upon his return he was assigned to patrol in the 1st pct. Thirteen years later, on Nov. 9, 1966, he was reassigned to the 4th pct. where he remained working as a desk lieutenant's aid right up to his retirement on May 4, 1984. Ryan was a member of the PBA, YPD Holy Name Society, and the Cellmates Association of Yonkers. His father was Yonkers PO John P. Ryan and his brothers were YPD PO's Thomas and Edward Ryan. Bill's son David was also appointed to the YPD in October of 1972 but resigned in June of 1973. A month later, in July of 1973, he died in a drowning accident at the age of 26 years. Ret PO William Ryan died on February 2, 1993 in Charleston, NC. where he had moved in 1986. He was 67.

PO RAYMOND D. CAMPANARO #71

APPOINTED: November 1, 1951
DISMISSED: January 29, 1963

Ray Campanaro was born in the City of Yonkers on April 14, 1921. Following his schooling he worked as a stock clerk for a local company. Ray joined the Army Air Corps during WW 2 on March 26, 1943 and received an honorable discharge on March 1, 1946. Ray was appointed to the YPD from 11 Woodruff Ave. on Nov. 1, 1951 earning $2,800 a year and was assigned to the 2nd precinct. On May 7, 1956 Ray was awarded a Certificate of Excellent Police Work for a robbery arrest he made on Dec. 21, 1951. Ray had a steady sector he patrolled with his regular partner, Vincent Romagnoli. In Feb. of 1962 he and his partner became involved in activity that resulted in their dismissal from the department on January 29, 1963.

LT. JOSEPH P. HUERSTEL

APPOINTED: November 1, 1951
RETIRED: November 1, 1989

Joe Huerstel was born in NYC on October 26, 1919. After moving to Yonkers with his family Joe attended PS# 7 on Trenchard Street and later graduated from Saunders HS. As a young man Joe worked the trade he had learned in Saunders; that being an auto mechanic. During WW 2 he joined the Army on February 26, 1943 serving as a Radio Dispatch Gunner, and was honorably discharged on March 1, 1946.

Joe took and passed both YPD and the YFD exams, but the Yonkers Police Dept. called him first. He was appointed to the YPD from 27 Palisade Avenue on November 1, 1951 earning a starting salary of $2,800 a year and was assigned to the 1st precinct at 20 Wells Avenue. Being a very hard worker, while in the YPD he always worked a second job with Broadway Wheel Alignment as their radiator repairman almost up to his retirement.

Huerstel was promoted to Sergeant on December 31, 1963 and was assigned as a patrol supervisor. Less than a year later, on July 2, 1965, he was appointed a Detective Sergeant and replaced the outgoing commanding officer of the very new Narcotics Unit. Despite having little knowledge about narcotic investigations in particular, Huerstel was able to mold this new unit into a very effective operation. Part of his success was due to his ability to motivate his detectives by utilizing his great "people" skills" which led to respect by all who knew him. On Aug. 4, 1973 Joe was promoted to Lieutenant and was assigned to city-wide patrol duty.

When Joe was notified he was going to be mandatorily retired on December 1, 1983 due to age 64 years, he decided to institute litigation under the Age Discrimination & Employment Act of 1967. He claimed he not only did not want to retire but was in perfect health and, in fact, had never been out sick during his entire career. While his suit progressed in the courts he was in fact retired against his will on December 1, 1983. On November 14, 1984 a judgment was issued from the US Federal Court, Southern District, that being a healthy employee, Huerstel was in fact, discriminated against and the City of Yonkers was ordered to re-instate Lt. Huerstel to the Yonkers Police Dept. retroactively to November 30, 1983 with all due back salary. This decision did not affect anyone else as his was not a class action suit.

On February 8, 1985 Comm Fernandes issued a Personnel Order reinstating Lt. Huerstel to the YPD as per the court order, and assigned him to the 3rd Pct.; however he was immediately detailed to the Communications Div.

In mid-1989 Lt Huerstel was again notified that when he reached the age of 70 years he would again have to retire effective November 1, 1989. However, two months prior to this second scheduled retirement, in September of 1989, Huerstel again sought an appeal to remain a sworn member of the YPD. However, in February of 1990 the NY State Comptroller dismissed his appeal. Now, having turned age 70 in October, on November 1, 1989 Lt Huerstel was retired, once again, against his wishes, from the 1st pct. where he had been serving on patrol as a Watch Commander. Joe was now officially and permanently retired from the YPD. Not happy about the outcome, Joe busied himself around his house tending to his vegetable and rose garden.

Ret Lt. Joe Huerstel died on May 9, 2003. He was 83 years old.

DET. JOHN H. BONNEY #657

APPOINTED: November 1, 1951
RETIRED: February 10, 1972

John Bonney was born on Nov. 5, 1924 in the town of Irvington N. Y. where he attended St. Theresa's elementary school in North Tarrytown, and later graduated from Irvington high school. He loved golf, softball, swimming, football, and track. While in school he was said to have won several medals in track competitions and was known as "Jack rabbit." John served in the Navy during World War II beginning on Sept. 27, 1943 aboard the USS Augusta which we used to transport Pres. Truman in 1945. He received his honorable discharge on April 6, 1946. Following the military he gained employment as a bookkeeper and he was also a lather in the Wire Lathers union, #46. His first wife was the daughter of Capt. John Kennedy. John was appointed to the YPD from 35 Chase Ave. on Nov. 1, 1951 and was assigned to the 1st precinct. On Oct. 16, 1952 he was reassigned to the 4th precinct. Then, on February 26, 1954 PO Bonney was returned to the 1st precinct. Three years later, on July 1, 1957, John was appointed a Detective in the DD. In 1958 Det. Bonney was elected 2nd vice president of the PBA. He would then spend the next 12 years being transferred in and out of the Detective Division. But finally, on November 28, 1969 he was again appointed a Detective and would remain in the DD up to his retirement on February 10, 1972. John Bonney died September 16, 2001 at the age of 76.

PO STEPHEN K. McKEE #228

APPOINTED: November 1, 1951
RESIGNED: October 31, 1953

Born on Feb. 6, 1928 in the NYC Riverdale section of the Bronx, NY young Steve attended school in the Washington Hts area of the city. For a while he held miscellaneous jobs until Oct. 3, 1949 when he was hired as an officer with the Washington DC Metropolitan P.D. He resigned from that job to accept appointment to the YPD on Nov. 1, 1951. He was appointed from 618 South Broadway and was first assigned to the 1st precinct. He was later reassigned to the 4th precinct but decided to resign from the YPD on Oct. 31, 1953 to join the N.Y.S.P. as a Trooper in Troop K in Hawthorne. McKee rode a motorcycle for about 6 months and remained a trooper until about 1955 and then was appointed to the N.Y.P.D. That same year he was called by the F.D.N.Y. and went with them, remaining for 12 years and retiring on a disability pension. McKee then worked for the United Nations as Fire and Safety officer for15 years. He lived in Riverdale the entire time until 1999 when he moved upstate to Lake George.

DET. JOSEPH G. YARINA #674

APPOINTED: November 1, 1951
RETIRED: January 13, 1972

Joe Yarina was born in Czechoslovakia on September 9, 1919. He came to the USA in June of 1925, became a naturalized citizen and grew up on Porach St. Later he became a member of the "Hollow A.C. Club." He attended Holy Trinity Grammar School and graduated from Yonkers HS. Joe spoke Slovak as a second language. He worked for a while in the Alexander Smith Carpet Factory.

During WW 2 he served in Army beginning on June 30, 1942 with a specialty as a Radar Spotter, serving in the U.S. and in Panama. He received an honorable discharge on January 28, 1946. Following his discharge he worked aboard various ships on the Hudson River and then worked on the assembly line at the General Motors Plant in Tarrytown for several years.

Joe took the test for the Y.P.D. and placed # 10 on the list. On November 1, 1951 he and 12 others were appointed at a salary of $2,800 a year. At the time he lived at 566 Saw Mill River Rd. Following recruit training he was initially assigned to the 2nd precinct, but on October 16, 1952 he was sent to the 3rd pct.

On August 7, 1955 a 7 year old boy fell into the Saw Mill River near Ashburton Ave, striking his head. PO Yarina and his partner, Larry Conley shed their uniforms and jumped into the water to save the child, unfortunately the child died. In October Of 1958 Yarina was awarded the Gannett newspaper Macy award of Honorable Mention for the investigation and arrest of a robbery suspect. Eleven years later on March 13, 1963 he was reassigned to the Juvenile Aid Bureau. (later renamed the Youth Division) at the time located in HQ at 10 St Casimir Ave. Joe was very active in helping with programs run by the PAL for children. He also loved golfing and competed in many local golf tournaments.

On January 1, 1971 Joe was appointed a Detective and worked as a Detective Division desk officer right up to his retirement on January 13, 1972. Joe was tall, about 6' 1" slim build, and very soft spoken and reserved. He always seemed to be in control of his emotions and never spoke loudly in anger. Det Joe Yarina retired, and 3 months later, in April of 1972, took job in the office at the Yonkers Raceway processing applications for harness racing licenses. In 2002 at the age of 83 he was still there after 30 years, but working only 3 days a week. He worked there until about 2005 during major building renovations, and then moved to his son Stephen's house in Chicago, IL. enjoying a few rounds of golf. But time caught up to Joe Yarina and he died on February 10, 2014. He was 94 years old.

PO GEORGE A. LAZAROW #191

APPOINTED: November 1, 1951
RETIRED: February 1, 1985

George was born in Thompsonville, Ct. on December 6, 1920. As a young man he worked as a receiving Clerk at the former Otis Elevator Co. George served in Army, shortly after WW-2 broke out, serving from October 9, 1942 in the 58th Signal Repair Co. as a Technician 4th grade in Central Europe. He was also designated a Physical Education Director and a Supply Sergeant. He received his honorable discharge on Nov. 22, 1945. When he was hired by the YPD on Nov. 1, 1951 he lived at 2 Lafayette Place. His first assignment was to the 1st pct. earning $2,800 a year. On Jan. 30, 1963 he was detailed to security around City Hall. On April 27, 1964 he was moved to the Traffic Division where he worked for several years on meter summons detail. On January 1, 1971 George was reassigned to the North Command, but on Oct. 19, 1971 he was transferred to the Special Operations Division detailed to the Traffic Enforcement Squad in the street cleaning unit. When George retired on February 1, 1985 it is said that he worked for Richards Taxi for 10 years here in Yonkers. George died December 7, 2006 after having just turned 86 the day before.

PO ROBERT A. MOORE #195

APPOINTED: November 1, 1951
RETIRED: July 31, 1955

Robert A. Moore was born on June 1, 1926 in NYC where he received his formal education. He served in the Army during WW 2 from October 1, 1943, assigned to the Military Police, and was honorably discharged on August 3, 1946. After the military he worked miscellaneous jobs including that of a chauffeur. Bob was appointed to the YPD on November 1, 1951 from 20 Mildred Street and earned a starting salary of $2,800 a year. He was initially assigned to the 2nd pct. on patrol and later moved to the 1st pct. On June 10, 1953 he was transferred into the Traffic Division on 2 wheel motorcycle duty. While on motorcycle patrol on February 22, 1954 Moore had an accident in which he sustained a serious injury. Moore sued the City of Yonkers charging insufficiently street lighting resulting in Moore and his motorcycle falling into a hole which fractured his skull. He was subsequently awarded a disability retirement pension on July 31, 1955. On Dec. 9, 1958 former police officer Robert Moore was awarded $37,500 in a settlement against the city of Yonkers. After working as an armored car driver in the 1990's, Bob Moore and his wife moved to Jensen Beach, Florida where he died on July 27, 1999. He was 73 years old.

DET. STANLEY J. STYPULKOWSKI #626

APPOINTED: November 1, 1951
RETIRED: February 12, 1981

"Stosch," as he was known by his friends, was born in Yonkers on Nov. 22, 1922. He related that his parents died when he was just eleven years old and was raised by an aunt. He attended public school, but quit, lied about his age, and joined the Army at age 16, on Nov. 9, 1939. Of course once WW 2 broke out he was in for the duration which resulted in him serving 6 years, two of which were in combat, and being honorably discharged on June 19, 1945.

Yes, Stan served in the Army but rarely spoke of it. However the following was learned about some of his military experiences:

During his service he had been designated a Truck Driver in the Army's 1st Div, "The Big Red One." Assigned to the European Theater of Operations he had fought in the battle for Anzio, in Italy, and at the bloody massacre at the Kasserrine Pass in North Africa where the Americans were reportedly slaughtered, and yet, he said, he never received a scratch. Many years later, after Stan had died, in a letter to Stan's widow from a fellow war squad member, the man related to her that on one occasion in combat while riding in the truck they were strafed by German aircraft. He said everyone jumped out to take cover but not Stan. Instead he stood up in the driver's seat, and pulled a John Wayne. He grabbed the mounted .50 cal. machine gun and kept firing at the planes which were very low. He was twisting and turning around as he did until his ammo belt was empty.

After a long wait in England he participated in the Invasion of Normandy on June 6, 1944 by landing on Omaha Beach with his halftrack vehicle at 0900 hrs. In his vehicle were 7 soldiers and two pieces of artillery pieces. During an interview with the Herald statesman in 1994 Stan was quoted as

Det. Stanley J. Stypulkowski #626 (cont.)

telling the reporter, "*I had a feeling I wasn't going to make it. You could see guys dropping all over the place, floating bodies, burning ships, it was a mess. I remember guys yelling at us about where not to go because certain areas had not been cleared of mines*." Within a very short time his truck received a direct hit by German Artillery shell. He woke in the sand with a shrapnel hole in his chest the size of a silver dollar. Luckily for Stan the shrapnel that punctured his chest did not hit any vital organs. He was evacuated and had 3 operations in England. He never returned to combat again and was then assigned to the Military Police in Paris, France. He was awarded the Purple Heart, the Combat Infantryman's Medal, three Campaign Medals with Battle stars for North Africa, Italy, and Normandy. He was honorably discharged as a Private First Class.

Following his discharge Stan worked for a while as a mailman but was appointed to the Yonkers Police Department on November 1, 1951 from 34 Rose Hill Terrace with a starting salary of $2,800. His first assignment was patrol duty in the 1st precinct. His first partner after earning a "seat" in a radio car was PO Tom Giannico. On October 16, 1952 he was reassigned to the 4th precinct. However, he would return to the 1st precinct on October 1, 1953 where he would remain for nearly 12 years.

It was on February 26, 1965 that Stan was appointed a Detective in the DD. Unfortunately, after only six months as a detective, and as part of a department wide shakeup, on August 27, 1965 Stan was returned to uniform patrol in the 3rd precinct. He was moved a few more times; Nov. 16, 1965 to the 1st, Nov. 9, 1966 to the 4th, and then on January 26, 1968 he was returned to the DD once again as a detective.

Det Stypulkowski was a hardworking and a highly self-motivated detective, but liked working by himself. So for most of his time in the DD he never had a partner, by choice. And yet his crime clearance rate was as good as any team of detectives. He was the recipient of multiple police commendations, Macy awards, and departmental Honorable Mentions which he earned throughout his term serving as a detective.

Stanley retired from the YPD as a detective 1st grade on February 12, 1981. He was proud of his career and of his son William who was an FBI agent.

After a long illness Ret Det. Stanley Stypulkowski died on March 28, 1998 at the age of 75.

DET. SGT. CHARLES R. TAYLOR #74

APPOINTED: November 1, 1951
RETIRED: November 6, 1981

Charles Taylor was born in the City of Yonkers on March 11, 1922. He attended PS# 6 and later graduated from Gorton High School. In 1950 he graduated from St. Paul's Poly Technical Institute in Lawrenceville, Virginia with a Bachelor of Science degree. In later years he continued his education by attending New York Columbia University where he had accumulated 32 of 36 credits toward a Master's degree.

Charlie was always interested in helping children so it was no surprise when he took a job as a playground supervisor for the Yonkers recreation Department. Following the outbreak of WW 2 Charlie served in the U.S. Army from December 9, 1942 in the Army Quartermaster Corps in supply, right up to his honorable discharge as a staff sergeant on February 2, 1947.

A resident of 128 Woodworth Ave., Taylor received his appointment to the Yonkers Police Department on November 1, 1951. His starting salary at the time was $2,800 a year and following recruit training he was assigned to the 1st precinct on patrol duty. Three years later, on July 1, 1954, police officer Taylor was transferred from the 1st precinct and was appointed a Detective in the Detective Division. This assignment was significant in that he was only the 2nd black police officer to ever be appointed a detective in the Yonkers Police Department. The first was Det. Stewart Freeman appointed to the department in 1928.

Detective Taylor was designated Detective 1st grade on August 1, 1955 and remained in the D.D. working in general assignment until 1964 when he was assigned to the newly formed Narcotics Unit.

Det Sgt Charles R. Taylor #74 (cont.)

During the January 1964 term of the Westchester County Grand Jury, they issued a special commendation to Det. Taylor for a murder arrest he made along with the expert testimony that he provided which resulted in a conviction.

He remained in the D.D. for many years, until March 6, 1972, when he was assigned to the Intelligence Division as a Detective. Detective Taylor was honored when he was selected and attended the FBI's prestigious National Academy in Quantico Virginia from September 25, 1972 to December 15, 1972, the date of his graduation.

He remained in the Detective Division right up to his promotion to Sergeant on September 17, 1976. Actually, there was no vacant sergeant's position available for Detective Taylor so his promotion to sergeant on that date was in a temporary and acting capacity. It wasn't until five months later, on February 18, 1977, that a vacancy became available through a retirement and Charles Taylor attained the permanent rank of sergeant. Following his promotion to sergeant he was assigned to the Youth Services and Community Relations Division as an investigative supervisor.

Sgt. Taylor was elevated to Detective Sergeant status on July 1, 1981 and once again assigned to the Detective Division. However, only a few months later, on November 6, 1981, Detective Sgt. Charles Taylor retired from the Yonkers Police Department.

Taylor was one of those men whose knowledge about our community seemed boundless and he was sought out by younger detectives for his wealth of information. He was known by most of his friends as "old folks." He was a true gentleman who was well-liked and respected by everyone who knew him within the department as well as members of outside agencies.

Sergeant Taylor was one of the original organizers and founders of the Police Departments Guardians Association which was formed in April of 1963 and he was named Man of The Year by the YMCA. In 1962 he received a first-place Macy award. In 1963 he was awarded the Macy's Honorable Mention citation and in 1964 he received the Macy 2nd place award. In 1966 he received the Westchester Rockland Newspaper honorable Mention award and in February of 1968 he was awarded a YPD commendation for a murder arrest he made. And in 1969 he was awarded the Westchester Rockland Newspaper Honorable Mention.

Retired detective Charles Taylor, one of our most respected and admired men, died on June 6, 1999 at the age of 77.

PO GEORGE E. WHITING #75

APPOINTED: March 16, 1952
RESIGNED: August 31, 1953

George Whiting was born in Yonkers on May 21, 1925. Following his formal education George joined the Navy during WW 2 on July 21, 1942 and received his honorable discharge on May 26, 1946. Following his military service Whiting worked as a laborer for Mt. Hope Cemetery. He received his appointment to the YPD on March 16, 1952 while living at 46 Griffith Avenue and earned a starting salary of $2,800 a year. During recruit training he received instruction in HQ by Lt. Larry Shea, wore grays, and walked post with a senior officer. Following training he was assigned to the 1st precinct and later to the 4th. However, this would not last very long. George had also taken the NY State Police examination and when they called, he accepted the appointment. He resigned from the YPD on August 31, 1953. On May 30, 1956 George's brother was shot and killed during a bar room dispute. Following his retirement from the State Police George Whiting died on March 22, 2004 in Tioga, NY. He was 78.

PO JOSEPH A. GRECO #32

APPOINTED: March 16, 1952
RETIRED: April 27, 1989

Joe Greco was born Giuseppe Greco in NYC on April 21, 1927. As a baby his family moved to Yonkers and Joe attended PS# 2, Ben Franklyn Jr. HS, and graduated from Commerce HS. Right out of school and only 18 years old Joe joined the Army on July 11, 1945 serving as company clerk typist with Co. A, 350th Infantry Battalion. Following his honorable discharge on May 11, 1947 he worked as a chauffeur for his family owned business, the Waverly Bleach Co. on Waverly Street in Yonkers. Joe was appointed to the YPD on March 16, 1952 while residing at 153 Waverly Street. His starting salary was $2,800 a year, he paid for all his uniforms, and his first assignment was patrol in the 1st precinct. While basically still considered a rookie, with only seven months as a police officer, on Oct. 16, 1952 Greco was assigned to the Traffic Division on two wheel motorcycle patrol. He remained on patrol as a "motorcycle cop" for seventeen years and on March 3, 1969, while still assigned to the Traffic Division, he was detailed to Traffic Court as the Traffic Court liaison officer. Joe remained there up to his retirement on April 27, 1989. Joe was an active member of the Rauso AMVETS veterans post on Waverly Street and enjoyed playing golf in his retirement years.

DET. THOMAS R. GIANNICO #672

APPOINTED: March 16, 1952
RETIRED: May 3, 1984

Tom Giannico was born in Yonkers on Aug. 3, 1923, attended local schools and graduated from Saunders HS. After graduation he joined the Navy during WW 2 on Mar. 17, 1943 as a Seaman 1st class serving aboard the aircraft carrier USS Langley. He was honorably discharged on Nov. 14, 1945. Tom worked both as a Toll Collector on the Saw Mill River Parkway and for General Motors in Tarrytown, NY. Tom Giannico was appointed to the YPD on March 16, 1952 from 562 Van Cortlandt Park Avenue earning $2,800 a year and was assigned to the 1st pct. on patrol. On Nov. 9, 1966 Giannico was transferred to the 4th pct and on June 12, 1967 he was reassigned to the Youth Division as a youth crime investigator. On June 14, 1968 he was reassigned, on paper, to the Detective Division but still serving with the Youth Services Division. On Jan. 1, 1971 Tom was officially appointed a Detective in the DD. But after several years he was assigned as the Detective Division's desk officer. Wanting to earn some overtime pay before he retired, on Oct. 21, 1983, upon his own request, he was transferred out to patrol in the N/E Patrol Division from which he retired a year later on May 3, 1984. In 1992 Tom moved to Bedford Hills, NY. He loved to golf at every opportunity but also enjoyed fixing broken watches. Ret PO Thomas Giannico died in St John's Hospital on May 21, 1998 at the age of 74.

LT. FRANCIS D. DUFF

APPOINTED: March 16, 1952
RETIRED: July 21, 1978

"Frank" Duff was born in Yonkers on Jan. 12, 1927. Frank grew up on Morningside Avenue, attended public schools and graduated from Yonkers HS. He joined the Navy during WW 2 on Jan. 4, 1945 serving on the Pacific Island of Guam. He was honorably discharged on June 29, 1946. Duff worked for several years as a letter carrier for the Post Office but was appointed to the YPD on Mar. 16, 1952 and was assigned to the 1st pct. On Oct. 16, 1952 Frank was reassigned to the 4th pct. and later moved to the 2nd pct. on Dec. 16, 1954. On Dec. 14, 1967 Duff was promoted to Sergeant earning $8,855 a year and was moved to the 1st pct. On Dec. 20, 1969 Sgt. Duff was transferred to the 3rd pct. On Jan. 1, 1971 Sgt Duff was assigned to the South Command and also moved his family to Wappingers Falls, NY. On March 12, 1972 Sgt Duff was sent to the Communications Division. And when, on April 24, 1972, he was promoted to Lieutenant at $15,698 a year he remained in the Communications Division. A friendly man with a quiet personality, Frank Duff retired from the YPD on July 21, 1978 and worked as mail carrier for Poughkeepsie Post Office from which he retired a second time in 1987. Ret Lt Francis Duff died on June 2, 1993 in Poughkeepsie, NY. He was 66 years old.

LT. CHARLES J. CLARK

APPOINTED: June 1, 1952
RETIRED: June 21, 1991

"Joe" Clark, as he was known by all, was born Charles Joseph Clark in Yonkers on December 20, 1927. He attended and graduated from Yonkers and Commerce high schools. Shortly after graduation "Joe" joined the Navy on June 14, 1945 serving as a Seaman 1st Class. He was honorably discharged following the end of WW 2 on August 23, 1946. After the Navy he worked for a while as a bookkeeper but on June 1, 1952 Charles Clark was appointed to the YPD earning $2,800 a year and was assigned to the 1st precinct. His uncle was PO Harold Clark. On October 16, 1952 officer Clark was transferred to the 3rd precinct and one year later, on October 1, 1953, he was reassigned to the 2nd precinct. Joe was placed in plainclothes on April 5, 1965 and moved into the Juvenile Aide Division. The following year, on Feb. 11, 1966, he was promoted to Sergeant and returned to the 1st pct. Sgt Clark was later moved to the 3rd pct. on May 20, 1969. On March 12, 1973 Sgt Clark was reassigned to the South Command serving as the Station House Supervisor. On February 17, 1984 Clark was promoted to Lieutenant and assigned to the Communications Division. On August 16, 1984 Lt Clark was assigned to HQ as the aide to the Commissioner. However, two years later, on March 11, 1986, he was returned to the Communications Division. "Joe" Clark remained in Communications right up to his retirement on June 21, 1991.

DET. MICHAEL E. FEDOR #24

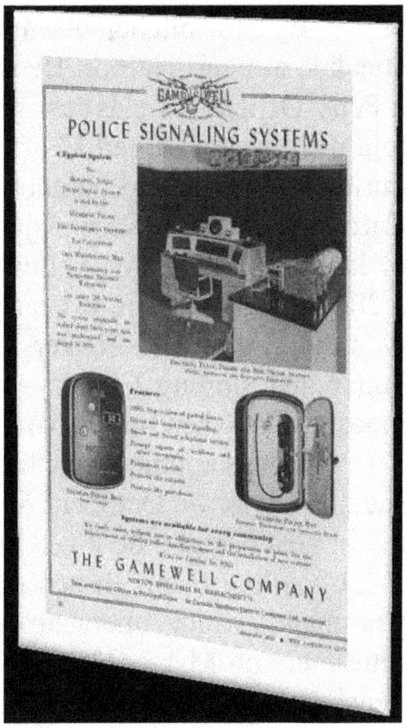

APPOINTED: June 1, 1952
RESIGNED: July 18, 1956

Mike Fedor was born in Yonkers on Feb. 2, 1922. He was said to have been born to Slavic immigrants, spoke Slavic fluently, and likely changed his name to Fedor from his original birth name. He attended local schools and was said to have been a good pitcher on school and city teams and often played in the Glen field. He served in the Army from during WW 2 from Sept. 2, 1942 up to his honorable discharge on Dec. 5, 1945. He reportedly worked as a stock clerk and as a prison guard in Sing Sing prison. Mike Fedor was appointed to the YPD on June 1, 1952 from 30 Rossiter Avenue and assigned to the 2nd precinct. On May 12, 1954 he was assigned to the Traffic Division. The following year on February 1, 1955 officer Fedor was appointed a Detective in the Detective Bureau. Fedor was said to have been a real nice guy, stocky build, always smiling and full of life. Despite this, on July 18, 1956 1st grade Det Fedor, upon his own request, submitted his letter of resignation effective that date. Former Det. Michael Fedor died on December 10, 2010 in Pinellas, Florida. He was 88.

PO ANDREW POLOCHKO #41

APPOINTED: June 1, 1952
RETIRED: March 23, 1972

Andy was born in Yonkers the son of Czechoslovakian immigrants. As a kid he loved baseball and was a sand lot pitcher. As a young man he joined the Navy on Sept 18, 1941, just prior to our being attacked at Pearl Harbor. He served up to October 22, 1945 and was honorably discharged. He served as a Petty Officer 1st class assigned in the boiler room aboard USS North Carolina throughout the war. He told me his ship earned 15 Battle Stars and 54 campaign ribbons. His ship was torpedoed and nearly sunk during one battle and on another occasion it was struck by a Kamikaze plane. Andy said the USS North Carolina served in every major campaign in the Pacific during the war, from Guadalcanal to the surrender of Japan in Tokyo bay. Following his military service Andy worked as a Stock Clerk. He spoke Slovak as a 2nd language and in his early years he was a body builder and weight lifter. In fact on one occasion he won the title of Mr. Yonkers and Mr. Westchester for best physique. He also had a hobby of playing the guitar and singing Country Western Songs with various small bands. For excitement he loved riding motorcycles when he was young.

He was appointed to the YPD on June 1, 1952 at the annual salary of $2,800 and following training, such as it was, on October 16, 1952 he was assigned to the 3rd pct. If given a choice he preferred walking a foot post because he loved meeting a talking with people. In the 1950's he was a charter member of the YPD bowling team. When the South Command was established on January 1, 1971 he reported to that Command, which operated out of the old 2nd pct. at 441 CPA. Andy worked there right up to his retirement on March 23, 1972. He bought one year military time to enable him to retire a little early. His pension was $10,000 and he went to work for Yonkers Raceway as Security Guard where he remained for 23 years.

Andy Polochko died, November 15, 2007 at St. John's Hospital. He suffered a massive heart attack and died quickly with his wife Eileen at his side. He was 83.

PO WILLIAM J. WALL #158

APPOINTED: August 1, 1952
RESIGNED: July 25, 1961

William J. Wall was born on October 7, 1926 in Yonkers, NY. He attended St. Mary's grade school and graduated from Yonkers HS. Bill was a championship roller skater in his youth. Bill enlisted in the Navy reserves in October of 1943 and served on Liberty ships as an armed guard. He later served on the USS Baldwin, DD714, which was in Sasebo, Japan after the Japanese surrender. His rating was a signalman 2nd class in the USNR. Following the Navy Bill worked as a stock Clerk in Otis Elevator Co. "Willie" Wall, as he was known, was appointed to the YPD on August 1, 1952 from 258 Woodworth Avenue earning a starting salary of $2,800 a year. PO Wall was assigned to the 1st precinct following his recruit training. He reportedly worked in the Emergency truck for a short time but most often he walked a foot post; generally in the Getty Square area. Eight years later, on April 4, 1960, he was reassigned to the 2nd precinct. He would later be moved to the 3rd precinct. Bill's brother Jim was a Westchester County motorcycle officer, and years later his nephew, Jim Wall, would be a Sgt with the Ossining PD. Bill Wall was suspended on July 6, 1961 through July 15, 1961 for violating departmental rules and regulations. However, before he could face departmental charges he resigned from the YPD on July 25, 1961. In March of 1962 he requested reinstatement but his request was denied. When he left the YPD he worked for Ciba Geigy until his death from cancer at his home on Abbott Place, Yonkers, on September 16, 1980. He was 53 years old.

PO LEO M. MUSCARI #25

APPOINTED: August 1, 1952
RETIRED: August 1, 1971

Leo Michael Muscari was born in the City of Yonkers on December 3, 1925. He attended local schools and graduated from Saunders HS. Leo served in Army during WW 2 as a Corporal from March 17, 1944 up to his honorable discharge on May 18, 1946. Following the military Leo gained employment working as a butcher. On August 1, 1952 he was appointed to the YPD from 78 Cornell Avenue earning a starting salary of $2,800 a year. His first assignment was patrol in the 1st precinct. Fourteen years later, on November 9, 1966, Muscari was transferred to the 4th precinct and assigned as the "Patrol Wagon driver," a hold over designation from the days of Paddy Wagons. He was actualy the desk lieutenant's aide. His last assignment began on January 1, 1971 when he was assigned to the Community Relations Division. But, after 19 years, and having purchased 1 year of military time from the pension system, officer Leo Muscari retired from the YPD on August 1, 1971. He would live out his retirement at 24 Pier Street.

SGT. ALFRED E. NAPOLIONE #18

APPOINTED: August 1, 1952
RETIRED: January 5, 1989

Alfred Emanuel Napolione was born in the City of Yonkers on November 3, 1926. He attended and graduated from Roosevelt HS. Al served in the Navy during WW 2 beginning on October 31, 1944 aboard the USS Philadelphia as a Seaman 1st class. He was honorably discharged on June 12, 1946. It was reported that Al worked for the General Motors auto plant in Tarrytown.

After taking the test for police Patrolman, Al rated number one on the civil service list and was appointed to the Yonkers Police Department on August 1, 1952 from 44 Griffith Avenue. His starting salary was $2,800 a year and he was assigned to the 1st precinct on Wells Ave. On October 16, 1952 Napolione was reassigned to the 3rd precinct, and on January 4, 1954 he was moved to patrol duty in the 2nd precinct. On January 1, 1971, when the precincts were renamed patrol commands, Al remained in the then renamed South Command.

On April 9, 1976 PO Napolione was promoted to Sergeant earning $9,300. and assigned to the North Patrol Command at 53 Shonnard Place. Three years later on June 20, 1979 Sgt Napolione was moved to the Northeast Patrol Command located at 730 East Grassy Sprain Road. On May 7, 1984 he was reassigned to the Youth Services Division as a supervisor of youth crime investigations and would remain there up to his retirement on January 5, 1989. Al was a football coach for North Yonkers Boys Club and a member of the Yonkers Elks Club. In 1990 Al moved to Lauderdale Lakes in Florida but, Ret. Sgt Alfred Napolione died in Plantation, Florida on October 9, 1993. He was 66 years old.

PO ARTHUR ROTH #112

APPOINTED: October 16, 1952
RETIRED: April 5, 1985

Arthur Roth was born October 29, 1922 in Czechoslovakia. He came with his family to US as a youth and settled in Ossining, NY. Arthur attended Ossining public schools graduating from Ossining HS where he played the Trumpet in the school band. He worked in various bands to earn some money and also worked for Max Braun Meat Packing Co. in Yonkers. He enlisted in the Army during WW 2 on Aug 12, 1943 and served in the 90th Infantry Division in General Patton's 3rd Army and with the 802nd Tank Destroyer Battalion. During one of the battles he was wounded by shrapnel in his leg and was awarded the Purple Heart. During fighting in occupied France he was captured by the Germans and held prisoner for about 6 months until he was able to escape. He was hidden by a French family and lived on potatoes found in the fields and was ultimately reunited with his military outfit.

"Artie" served in the Ardennes in the "Battle of the Bulge," Central Europe, Normandy, and the Rhineland. Among other medals, he earned the Combat Infantryman's Badge and was honorably discharged on December 5, 1945. He later worked miscellaneous jobs including that of a Masseur and was an avid weight lifter and body builder who competed in several body building competitions including down in Madison Square Gardens in NYC.

Artie joined the Yonkers Police Department on October 16, 1952 from 236 Riverdale Ave. at a salary of $2,800 a year and was assigned to the 3rd pct. Later he would also serve in the 2nd pct. On October 16, 1965 he was assigned to the Youth Division as a plainclothes investigator. On July 15, 1977 Arthur Roth was transferred to the South Patrol Command from which he retired on April 5, 1985.

When he retired he busied himself feeding stray cats, which he loved, at the City Pier. He always could be found with a cigar in his hand and was blessed with a very mellow disposition. Ret PO Arthur Roth died on November 20, 1992. He was 80 years old.

LT. WILBERT C.O. SCHULZ

APPOINTED: October 16, 1952
RETIRED: April 13, 1990

Wilbert Charles O. Schulz was born on October 16, 1927 at 84 Kimball Avenue in Yonkers, NY. He attended local public schools and graduated from Saunders HS. "Wilbur," as he was known, was always athletic and particularly loved running. His running was interrupted when he was drafted into the Army Dec. 14, 1945 where he served in the Motor Pool. He also trained as a boxer and had 10 fights in the ring. He was honorably discharged on Oct. 3, 1947 and then fought in the local Golden Gloves for a while. He worked for the US Post Office on 34th St in NYC and also worked as a Mason Tender for Firebrick Construction Co. in Platsburg, NY. Schulz was appointed to the YPD on his birthday, October 16, 1952, from 84 Kimball Ave. earning $2,800 a year. Following training he was assigned to the 1st pct., and on Dec. 4, 1952 he was assigned to patrol in the 2nd pct. In Mar. of 1963 Schulz was detailed to Emergency Service Training with the NYPD at Randall's Island and upon completion was assigned the YPD ESU. On Feb. 26, 1964 Wilbert was appointed a Detective, where he remained up to his promotion to Sergeant on July 2, 1965. His salary rose to $7,260 and he was reassigned to the 3rd pct. On Mar. 28, 1966 he was moved to the 2nd for a while but was returned to the Detective Division on Jan. 13, 1967 as a Det. Sergeant. Schulz was promoted to Lieutenant on Dec. 10, 1971 and elevated to Det Lt. earning $26,411. But on Oct. 6, 1972 he was reassigned to the North Command as a desk officer. He was moved to patrol in the Inspectional Services Division on Mar. 12, 1973 and shortly thereafter assigned as a Central Booking officer up to his retirement on April 13, 1990. Although his legs caused him a great deal of pain from arthritis, after retiring he continued his love of outdoors by walking long distances.

PO FLOYD E. DAUGHERTY #170

APPOINTED: October 16, 1952
RESIGNED: May 4, 1955

Floyd Daugherty was born on Dec. 2, 1925 in Evansville, Indiana. He joined the Navy during WW 2 in June of 1943 and was honorably discharged in January of 1946. Following the military he worked as a butcher. Daugherty was appointed to the YPD on Oct. 16, 1952 from 976 Midland Avenue with a salary of $2,800 a year. His first assignment was to patrol in the 1st precinct. On Dec. 4, 1952, following his recruit training, Floyd was transferred to the 2nd precinct. Six months later, on June 10, 1953, he was reassigned to the Traffic Division on 2 wheel motorcycle patrol. But he didn't last there for long. On December 16, 1954 Floyd was transferred from Traffic out to the 1st precinct. Five months later, on May 4, 1955, for reasons unknown, PO Floyd Daugherty submitted his resignation from the Yonkers Police Department and same was accepted.

DET. FRANK A. BRUNO #641

APPOINTED: October 16, 1952
RETIRED: August 8, 1973

Frank Bruno was born in Yonkers on July 24, 1924. And although he lived on Cook Avenue, he attended St. Joseph's Catholic elementary school on Ashburton Avenue. He later attended Sacred Heart HS and Roosevelt HS. Following school he worked for his father in their shoe repair shop, and drove a bus for Bernaccia Bros. for 8 years.

Frank was appointed to the YPD on Oct. 16, 1952 from 495 Van Cortlandt Park Ave, earning a starting salary of $2,800 a year. He stated that he was sworn in at City Hall with other recruits, was sent to headquarters where he was given a .38 positive S&W revolver, 6 rounds of ammunition, a flashlight, a night stick, and a book of rules and regulations. Lt. Larry Shea told them all to go home and wait for a call. That night Frank was called and told to report for duty the next morning at the 3rd precinct. He was "broke" in by walking various foot posts with senior officers. Earlier recruit classes that were hired attended the NYPD police academy, but he said his class did not. They did, however, receive firearms training in the basement of the Hudson Tire Company on Nepperhan Avenue where there was a shooting range.

Just over a year later, on Jan. 4, 1954 Bruno was transferred from the 3rd to the 2nd pct. on radio car patrol where he remained for just over nine years. On Dec. 9, 1958 Frank and his partner Joe Clark had the job of investigating a fire which ultimately took the life of a fellow 2nd pct. officer, Louis Bruno, who was off duty that night. On March 13, 1963 Frank was reassigned to the Juvenile Aide Bureau (JAB), where he worked as a plainclothes investigator of juvenile crime. All during this time Frank continued to work a second job as a "Lather" in the Wire Lathers Union. Two years later, on August 13, 1965, Frank was appointed a Detective assigned to general assignment in the Detective Division. His first partner was Det Joe Surlak, then Rocco DelBene and John Bonney. At one point he worked in the burglary squad for a while. Det Bruno remained in the D.D. for eight years, earning several awards for his investigative ability, and then retired as a detective on August 8, 1973.

Five years later, in 1978, his son Frank Jr would be appointed a police officer and rise to the rank of captain. And Frank Jr's daughter, Frank Sr's granddaughter, was sworn in as a Yonkers officer in 2007. Three generations of Bruno's serving the YPD.

When Det Frank Bruno retired he owned and operated a tavern in the Yonkers Motor Inn, 300 Yonkers Avenue for about 10 years. When his lease expired he moved his operation to the Parkdale Lounge on Yonkers Avenue opposite the bath house. Two years later, in 1985, Frank was hired by the Jacob Javitz Center in NYC as their Public Safety Supervisor where he remained for 14 years; but he received no pension from them.

It was around 1990 when Frank was accepted into the NYPD Emerald Society Pipes and Drums Honor Guard. In every parade they marched in Frank carried the flag right up front and was still doing so in 2011, after more than 20 years. He also served for many years as the 2nd Vice President of State of New York Police & Fire Retirees Association and still held that position in 2014.

PO BENJAMIN A. DeLUCCI #157

APPOINTED: October 16, 1952
RESIGNED: November 23, 1954

Benjamin Anthony DeLucci was born in the city of Yonkers on Feb. 7, 1929. He was a Navy Veteran having served from Feb. 14, 1946 to his honorable discharge on Dec. 16, 1947. DeLucci was appointed to the YPD on Oct. 16, 1952 from 280 Riverdale Ave. The starting salary was $2,800 a year and his first assignment was patrol in the 3rd precinct. On June 1, 1953 DeLucci was reassigned from the 3rd precinct to the Traffic Division on motorcycle patrol but trouble was on the horizon. Ben was involved in a departmental investigation and rather than face charges he resigned from the YPD on November 23, 1954. On November 15, 1955 he requested reinstatement but his request was denied. Once again he applied for reinstatement on November 17, 1958, but was once again denied. After leaving the YPD he was hired by the Teamsters local 456 in Yonkers and drove a truck for many years. He even worked as a union business agent for a short time and after many years retired from the Teamsters. Later he and his family moved to Ormond Beach, Fl. where he died on March 18, 2005 at the age of 76 years.

PO IRA F. FLEMING #53

APPOINTED: October 16, 1952
RESIGNED: March 30, 1961

Born Ira Francis Fleming on Sept. 25, 1925 in Yonkers, Ira attended local public schools and immediately joined the Marine Corps on June 17, 1943 during WW 2. Following the war's end he was honorably discharged on Mar 2, 1946. After working for several years as a laborer, Ira was appointed to the YPD on Oct. 16, 1952 from 80 Douglas Ave. His starting salary was $2,800 a year and he was assigned to the 4th pct. On Dec. 16, 1954 he was reassigned to the 2nd pct. Then on Sept. 3, 1956 he was returned to patrol in the 4th pct. He was said to have been as neat as a pin in uniform just like a Marine but he violated department rules and was brought up on departmental charges. Prior to a trial Fleming resigned from the YPD effective March 30, 1961. Former PO Ira Fleming would ultimately move to Los Angeles, Cal. where he died on April 24, 2008. He was 82 years old.

PO JOSEPH G. SOKOL #160

APPOINTED: October 16, 1952
RETIRED: April 25, 1991

Joe Sokol was born in the city of Yonkers on April 17, 1929. He attended Gorton and Saunders high schools with a trade as an auto mechanic. After leaving school and at the age of 17 years, Joe joined the Navy on June 27, 1946 serving aboard ship as a Boilerman 3rd class. He was honorably discharged on June 27, 1949. Sokol was appointed to the Yonkers Police Department on October 16, 1952 from 170 Palisades Ave. with an annual salary of $2,800 a year. Following recruit training wearing "grays" and working with a senior officer, Joe was assigned to foot patrol in the 1st precinct at 20 Wells Avenue. However, later that year on December 4, 1952 he was reassigned to the 4th precinct at 53 Shonnard Place. Joe received his dream assignment on October 15, 1953 when he was assigned to the Traffic Division on two wheel motorcycle patrol.

Joe had a very friendly and outgoing personality and adapted well to the high esprit de corps of the motorcycle unit. Still in Traffic, on December 1, 1970, Joe was relieved of routine traffic patrol and designated as the "Taxi and Hack Inspector." As such he was responsible for the safety certification of all taxi's, limousines, tow trucks, school buses, etc. On November 1, 1985 Sokol was appointed a Detective but remained in his assignment. This Detective designation ended when he was returned to the rank of police officer. Joe's brothers-in-law were PO Edward Opaciuch and Deputy Chief Frank Sardo. Sokol, Opaciuch, and Sardo all married three sisters. Joe's daughter Cindy married PO Anthony Gaudio, and his granddaughter, Laura Mulligan was also appointed a Yonkers police officer.

Joe retired from the YPD on April 25, 1991. He died eight years later on September 14, 1999 at the age of 70.

LT. CORNELIUS J. RIORDAN

APPOINTED: October 16, 1952
RETIRED: February 1, 1990

Cornelius John Riordan was born in New York City on January 11, 1930. Connie moved to Yonkers with his family when he was young and attended local public schools. Upon his graduation from high school he gained employment as a receiving clerk for Otis Elevator company. Several years later, after taking the police patrolmen's test, Connie was appointed to the Yonkers Police Department on October 16, 1952. At the time he lived at 56 Herriot St. and his starting salary was $2,800 a year. His first assignment was patrol duty in the 3rd precinct located at 36 Radford St. On August 30, 1957 Connie was awarded a certificate of excellent police work for the actions he took at a fire that occurred at 3 Lawrence St. months earlier.

Having a little clerical experience, on February 27, 1963 he was detailed to the Deputy Commissioner's office as the Commissioners aide and later as the aide to the chief of police. On January 14, 1966 Connie was promoted to the rank of Sergeant earning $8,165 a year and was assigned to the Youth Division as an investigative supervisor. Two years later, on June 14, 1968, he was transferred to the Detective Division and elevated to Detective Sergeant status. Five years later, on March 14, 1973, Connie was promoted to the rank of Lieutenant, earning $17,472 a year, and transferred from the DD to the Inspectional Services Division. It was on August 24, 1973 that he was assigned to the Youth Services and Community Relations Division initially as the executive officer, and then on January 1, 1979 he was designated their commanding officer, still with the rank of lieutenant. But, six years later, on April 1, 1985 he was reassigned to the Administrative Services Division as the executive officer. Once again he was designated commanding officer of this division as a lieutenant on October 19, 1987.

Lt Riordan retired from the YPD on a disability pension on February 1, 1990 and moved to Viera Florida with his wife. It was there that retired Lt Cornelius Riordan died on March 26, 2004. He was 74 years old.

PO VYTAUTIS J. PETUTIS #29

APPOINTED: October 16, 1952
RETIRED: February 18, 1988

"Vic," as he was known by all, was born Vytautis John Petutis in the City of Yonkers on January 6, 1924. He attended local public schools and worked as both a laborer and as a Special Police Officer in Playland Amusement Park with the then Westchester County Parkway Police. "Vic" was a military veteran having served in the Army during WW 2 from July 1, 1943 up to his honorable discharge on January 7, 1946.

Petutis was appointed to the YPD on October 16, 1952 from 131 Riverdale Ave. earning $2,800 a year. Following his training he was assigned to the 3rd precinct at 36 Radford Street. His recruit class consisted of Frank Bruno Sr., Con Riordan, Ben DeLucci, Artie Roth, Ira Fleming, Albert Musone, Wilbert Schulz, Floyd Daugherty, and Joe Sokol. Records indicate that Vic worked in the 3rd precinct his entire career. Although it is believed he may have worked for a short time in the North Command around 1985. "Vic" was an imposing figure to say the least. He stood about 6' 3" and weighed about 250 Lbs. Maybe he couldn't catch you on the run, but if he grabbed you, it was all over.

Petutis retired from the YPD on February 18, 1988. Although he had a great deal of trouble with his legs, he enjoyed 18 years of retirement. "Vic's" grandson John Petutis was appointed a Yonkers police officer. Ret PO Vytautis Petutis died of a heart attack in his house on Wellesley Avenue on August 14, 2006 at the age of 82 years.

DET. JOHN W. BALISCAK #661

APPOINTED: November 1, 1952
RETIRED: May 16, 1986

John Baliscak was born in Yonkers on May 10, 1923, attended local schools and in addition to English, spoke Russian, Slavic, and Polish fluently. John joined Army Air Corps on January 28, 1943 during WW 2 serving most of his hitch in Newfoundland, Greenland, with the purpose being to prevent any potential invasion by the enemy through that area. He was honorably discharged on January 10, 1946 and following his military service he worked for the NY Central Railroad as a railroad detective. John also worked for City of Yonkers as a Motor Equipment Operator in the Street Lighting Bureau from 1951 to October of 1952.

It was on November 1, 1952 that he was appointed to the YPD from 137 Webster Avenue earning $2,800 a year. He related that he walked a post in the 1st precinct for about a month, with a senior man, in civilian clothes with his shield pinned on his jacket. He said he had to buy his uniforms, including the long calf length overcoat, which cost him $101. A lot of money at that time. On December 4, 1952 he was officially assigned to patrol in the 4th precinct.

On June 1, 1953 he was moved to the 2nd pct. up to November 7, 1966 when he was reassigned to the 1st pct. John left patrol when he was transferred to the Youth Division on Dec. 1, 1966. The Y.D. was then located in the HQ building then located at 10 St Casimir Avenue. He was elevated to Detective status on January 26, 1968 and assigned to the Bureau of Criminal Identification (BCI). This unit's name was later changed on Dec. 29, 1970 to the Criminal Identification Unit (CIU). A short time later, following the purchase of the alcohol Breathalyzer machine, John was certified as an operator and said he was only the second Detective in the county to receive a conviction based on the use of same.

John's last assignment was on Oct. 21, 1983 when he was assigned to the Intelligence Unit before he retired on May 16, 1986 and remained living at 949 Palmer Rd. His brother-in-law was PO Anthony Barton; they both married sisters. After retiring John worked as security guard in Yonkers General Hospital until 1999. Ret. Det. John Baliscak died on July 19, 2002 at the age of 79.

SGT. CHARLES J. McCAULEY #61

APPOINTED: November 1, 1952
RETIRED: May 16, 1986

Charles McCauley was born in the Town of Hastings NY on February 19, 1923. Charlie attended local public schools and graduated from Roosevelt HS. Working on cars came naturally to him so he worked for a while as an auto mechanic. He later gained employment as a bus driver for Liberty Lines Bus Co.

It was while residing at 291 Riverdale Avenue that McCauley received his appointment to the Yonkers Police Department on November 1, 1952. His starting salary was $2,800 a year and he was initially assigned to the 1st precinct on Wells Avenue. On one occasion Charlie and his partner received a call for help from a stranded boat operator on the Hudson River. Charlie commandeered a citizens boat from the Habirshaw Club and went out and rescued the stranded boater. He brought him to Alpine, NJ, without permission, because it was closest. Unfortunately the rescued man sent a thank you to the Yonkers Public Safety Commissioner advising of the circumstances about being brought to New Jersey. The commissioner wasn't happy. As Charlie said, "no good deed goes unpunished."

Six years later, on January 1, 1958, McCauley was appointed a detective and was assigned to the Bureau of Criminal Identification (BCI). His primarily job was crime scene photography and evidence collection. But he kept a side job working as an auto mechanic on trucks for Tarricone Oil Co.

Charlie was scheduled for promotion to Sergeant in Nov. of 1969 but suffered a heart attack. His hospitalization delayed his promotion by two months. On January 9, 1970 McCauley received his promotion to the rank of Sergeant, earning $12,495 a year, and was reassigned to the Communications Division. On October 5, 1972 Sgt McCauley was assigned as a patrol supervisor in the North Command. But he would move again.

On Sept. 28, 1973 he was assigned to the police auto Repair Shop as a supervisor of the police mechanics. He was returned to patrol duty in the North Command three years later on Feb. 16, 1976. Sgt McCauley retired from the YPD on May 16, 1986 while living at 108 Grove Street and spent his free time on his boat named "Miss Behave" in City Island.

In retirement Charlie worked occasionally taking photographs at weddings and at one time was also the Exalted Ruler of the Elks Club in Yonkers, of which he was a long time member. He also worked part time for a citizens crime watch program in the 3rd precinct. A good natured man, Charlie would have you believe he was a very serious person. However he was a really nice guy, well-liked and respected by all who knew him. One of his sons, Brian, retired as a Yonkers police Lieutenant, and the other, Charles was a Westchester Co. P.D. police officer.

Ret Sgt. Charles J. McCauley died on January 7, 1994 at the age of 70 years.

PO ANTHONY E. BARTON #102

APPOINTED: December 1, 1952
RETIRED: April 21, 1973

Anthony Edward Barton was born Anthony Barteski in Plymouth, Pa. on August 3, 1925. His name was changed some years later. He grew up in Lynwood, Pa where he attended their public schools up to the 11th grade. His family then moved to Yonkers and he attended and graduated from Saunders HS. Tony joined the Navy during WW 2 on Aug. 1, 1943 and served as an aircraft mechanic with the rank of 1st class Petty Officer. He was honorably discharged in May of 1946. Following the Navy Tony worked as a Ticket Agent at Grand Central Terminal in NYC. He remained there right up to his appointment to the YPD on December 1, 1952. He could have been appointed 6 months earlier if he used his veterans credits but he chose to save them. He was appointed from 27 Lawrence Street earning $2,800 a year and his first assignment was patrol in the 4th precinct. Two years later, on Dec. 16, 1954 Barton was reassigned out to the 2nd pct. Tony left patrol on Feb 6, 1963 when he was transferred to the Juvenile Aide Bureau (JAB) since renamed the Youth Division. Barton was appointed a Detective in the D.D. on July 29, 1968 but was returned to patrol in the 3rd pct. two months later on Oct. 1, 1968. On July 9, 1969 records indicated he was in the Community Relations Unit serving as the School Crossing Guard liaison officer for the YPD. On October 16, 1972 he was assigned to the Youth Division where he remained up to his retirement on April 21, 1973. PO Barton was a very quiet, soft spoken individual whose brother-in-law was Det John Baliscak. He was a member of the Yonkers Elks Club and the Lowerre Veterans Post on McLean Ave. Anthony Barton died on November 25, 2013.

PO VINCENT W. ROMAGNOLI #245

APPOINTED: December 1, 1952
DISMISSED: January 29, 1963

Vincent Romagnoli was born in Yonkers on October 29, 1929. Vinnie graduated from local public schools and joined the Army in October of 1946 following WW 2. He received his honorable discharge in March of 1948. Following the military he obtained a job working as a chauffeur. Romagnoli was appointed to the Yonkers Police Dept. on December 1, 1952 from 46 Stratton Street earning $2,800 a year and was assigned to the 2nd precinct. On August 30, 1957 he was awarded a Certificate of Excellent Police Work for his quick action at a fire at 115 Sedgewick Avenue on May 24, 1956. In February of 1962 he and his partner were both brought up on charges and they were both suspended on Feb. 6, 1962. A trial was scheduled but on January 29, 1963 Romagnoli pled guilty and was dismissed from the YPD effective that date. Vincent Romagnoli died on February 28, 1999 in Schoharie, NY. He was 69 years old.

PO WALTER MORAVSKY #208

APPOINTED: December 1, 1952
RESIGNED: February 27, 1953

Walter Moravsky was born in the City of Yonkers on September 29, 1927. After attending local schools, Walter joined the Navy during WW 2 on October 2, 1942 and was wounded in combat leaving him unable to remain in the military. Walt was honorably discharged on June 25, 1943. He was appointed to the Yonkers Police Dept. on December 1, 1952 from 7 Cottage Place Gardens earning a starting salary of $2,800 a year. Following some basic rudimentary training he was assigned to patrol duty in the 2nd precinct. A few months later, on February 16, 1953, he was reassigned from the 2nd precinct to the 1st precinct at 20 Wells Avenue. Moravsky submitted his resignation from the YPD after only short time, effective February 27, 1953, one day short of completing his three month probation period. He re-applied to the YPD on August 17, 1953 but his request was denied. It's not known when but, at one point, Moravsky changed his name to Moray. He had a large family, all of which had the surname of Moray. One of his son's was Det. Walter Moray and another, Gerard Moray, was a Yonkers City Jailer, and daughter Rosemary who was also a Detention Officer (Jailer.). Former PO Walter (Moravsky) Moray died on August 17, 1985 at the age of 57 years.

PO WILLIAM S. YOUSHOCK #140

APPOINTED: December 1, 1952
RETIRED: April 4, 1986

William Stephen Youshock was born in Russelltown, NY on April 7, 1922. He moved to Yonkers with his family and graduated from Commerce HS. While attending school and being fluent in Ukranian, he was very athletic, was an excellent Softball player and a great hitter. Following school he worked as a laborer. Bill joined the Navy during WW 2 on Aug. 21, 1942 and his specialty was a "Chief Metalsmith." He was honorably discharged on Jan. 10, 1946. But Bill remained in the Naval Reserve, and as a result was called to active duty again for the Korean War serving from May of 1951 to September 1952. Bill was appointed to the YPD on December 1, 1952 from 226 Ashburton Ave earning $2,800 a year, and was assigned to the 4th pct. However his civil service seniority actually began on Mar 16, 1952 when he was called for appointment but was serving in the military on active duty. Two weeks after his appointment he was transferred from the 4th to the 3rd precinct. Fourteen years later, On Nov. 9, 1966, Bill was reassigned to the 2nd precinct and on Mar 18, 1981, was assigned to the North Command. On Mar 22, 1984, and with 32 years seniority, Bill was assigned to HQ serving as building security in the lobby of 10 St Casimir Avenue. After nearly 34 years with the YPD, Bill Youshock retired on April 4, 1986 and busied himself golfing. Bill had two sons who also became police officers; Eugene with the YPD and Warren with the Westchester Co. P.D. On Dec. 10, 1989, Retired PO William Youshock, who had become seriously ill, was found deceased in his home. He was 67 years old.

DET. CHARLES R. JACKSON #626

APPOINTED: December 1, 1952
RESIGNED: January 15, 1970

Charles Richard Jackson was born on June 18, 1929 in Yonkers NY while his family lived at 9 Ludlow Street. They later moved to 20 Culver St in 1938 where he grew up as child. Charlie attended PS #3, Hawthorne Jr. H.S., and graduated from Gorton High School. He also completed four years of college with Pre-Law as a major. Two of those years were in Lincoln University in Oxford, PA. on a basketball scholarship, and then he transferred to Adelphi University in Garden City, L.I. on another scholarship from which he graduated with a BA degree in 1953. He would later complete his graduate studies at CCNY while working in the police department. Jackson was very athletic and while in college played varsity basketball and was semi-pro-on New York City teams.

Charles Jackson was hired by the Yonkers Police Department on December 1, 1952 with a salary of $2,800 a year from 20 Culver Street. His first assignment was to patrol duty in the 3rd precinct at 36 Radford Street. Officer Jackson was granted a short leave of absence, with pay, from August 1, 1953 to August 17, 1953 to attend a seminar at the University of Michigan, in Ann Arbor, Michigan. The trip was sponsored by the National Conference of Christians and Jews.

On January 11, 1954 PO Jackson was granted an indefinite leave of absence due to being inducted into the Army. During his service he was assigned to the Criminal Investigation Division (CID). While in the Army Jackson held the rank of Corporal and also served in the military police in Korea in the investigative section. He was discharged on October 27, 1955 and was reinstated to the YPD on December 16, 1955 and returned to patrol duty in the 3rd pct.

On June 18, 1957 officer Jackson was appointed a Detective in the Detective Bureau by then PSC Milton Goldman. Like all detectives at the time, Jackson was assigned to investigate a variety of serious crimes. But within a short period of time he was also assigned to Investigate narcotics violations and did so with his partner Detective Charles Taylor. During his off duty hours Det Jackson attended Baruch College from 1957 to 1960 and had accumulated 32 of 36 credits toward a Master's Degree. He later was successful in obtaining his Master's Degree from the City College of New York.

In 1960 while investigating narcotic and other crimes in Yonkers, Jackson was detailed to the office of the Westchester County District Attorney. At that time there was a series of hotel robberies throughout the county of Motels that were committed by some black suspects who lived in Harlem New York. One of the suspects was frequently coming up to Westchester with some of his friends and committing these robberies. At one point Det Jackson received a call while he was off duty and was asked to meet with then District Attorney Leonard Rubenfeld. Jackson was advised that the DA was looking for a detective, specifically a black officer, to work under cover in the areas of the Harlem to gather information on this gang that would lead to their arrest. Advance approval had been given by Chief Polsen and the NYPD police Commissioner. At the time choices were limited as there were only about 3 or 4 black officers working in the police departments throughout Westchester County. Detective Jackson accepted the offer. Although he was from Yonkers he was very familiar with the area of Harlem because while in college he often would go there to play basketball with friends. Charlie later said this assignment was the best thing that ever happened to him in his police career because it gave him an opportunity to

Det. Charles R. Jackson #626 (cont.)

learn about undercover work which no one had any experience with in the City of Yonkers.

The investigation he was assigned to, which included infiltrating their gang, lasted for about a year and a half, before they were successful and able to secure indictments and make the arrests, approximately in 1961. He not only cleared the robbery offenses that plagued Westchester County, but personally gained new undercover experience by frequently buying illegal narcotics from the gang. With his assignment successfully completed Det Jackson was returned to working as a squad detective in Yonkers. However he had gained knowledge and experience in the narcotics field that no other detective had at that time.

In the early1960s there was a great deal of illegal narcotics, mostly heroin, being sold and used throughout Yonkers. However, little attention was being paid to the problem by the news media and to some degree, the YPD. It wasn't until some of the narcotic violators, like one of the local "junkie's, started dealing around Roberts and Palisade Avenue, the "north end," that the Monsignor of Christ the King Church complained about the problem to Chief Polsen and PSC Dan McMahon, that something finally was done. It was decided that a special unit, dedicated exclusively to enforcing the illegal drug laws, was required. It was on September 1, 1964 that a special YPD Narcotics Unit was established.

This new unit consisted of then Sgt. William Sickley as its supervisor, and detectives Charles Jackson, chosen due to his previous undercover work that he had done for the West DA, his DD squad partner Charles Taylor, Peter McMahon, and Armando DeBlassis. They established an office in headquarters at 10 St. Casimir Avenue, but kept separate and aside from the detective division. Later, as the number of arrests increased, other officers were added to the unit. The earliest ones were PO Nick DiMase, Leslie Feuer, Joel Parisi, Barbara Gonsalves, and Bonita Faranda. Although Sgt Sickley initially commanded the unit and was trained in the installation of court approved wiretaps, he had very little knowledge about narcotics and within a short time he was reassigned to the newly established Intelligence Unit in May of 1965. Sgt Joseph Huerstel was named as the new commander of the Narcotics Unit.

By this time Jackson had earned an enviable reputation in the YPD, and throughout the county as well, due to his successful undercover operation working with the county DA. As such, it was no great surprise when, at the request of the Special Assistant to the Governor in March of 1966, Det Jackson was detailed from the Detective Division's Narcotics Unit to serve full-time on a committee on urban affairs.

Former Yonkers PSC Daniel McMahon, who had been elected West Co. Sheriff and was familiar with Det Jackson's special narcotic investigation experience, asked Chief Polsen to allow Charlie, once again, to help out with some county wide investigations. The chief and Jackson both agreed and he was granted a leave of absence from the YPD for one-year from January 15, 1968 to January 14, 1969 to serve with the Westchester County Sheriff's office investigating narcotics trafficking throughout the county. Sheriff McMahon was extremely pleased with what Det Jackson was able to accomplish, so when that year was completed, upon McMahon's request, Charlie's leave of absence was extended to run a second year from January 15, 1969 to January April 19, 1970. At that time Jackson was the president of the Westchester Guardians Association.

As the date of January 14, 1970 approached, Yonkers Public Safety Commissioner Frank Vescio advised Det Jackson that due to the rules of the Civil Service Commission Jackson would not be able to obtain another extension to his leave of absence. He would have to either return to the Yonkers Police

Det. Charles R. Jackson #626 (cont.)

Department or resign. This was certainly a dilemma. But, when faced with this decision and after careful consideration, Detective Jackson, an officer with 17 years service with the YPD, a Yonkers resident of 40 Ridgeview Ave., and earning a salary of $10,500 a year, he decided to remain with the Westchester County Sheriff's Office and resign from the Yonkers Police Department effective January 15, 1970. Fortunately, he did maintain credit for his years of service with Yonkers and merged the time with his county service.

During the years serving with the Sheriff's office he would ultimately rise to the position of the Chief Criminal Investigator and head of their Narcotics Bureau. While leading the Sheriff's Narcotic's Bureau there came a time when Jackson was named to be in charge of a Federal Strike Force against narcotic violators throughout all of NY, NJ, and Ct. During his years with the Sheriff's office Charlie served with distinction and raised the level of efficiency throughout his bureau. Det. Jackson retired in 1975 from Sheriff's Dept. as Chief of the Bureau of Criminal Investigation. He was succeeded in this job by former Yonkers Det. Thomas McInerney.

In 1975 he would then be hired by the National Football League as Deputy Director of Security and retire from that position in 1997. Though officially retired, the NFL continued to utilize Jackson, particularly providing assistance to the NFL Commissioner regarding the Superbowl and post season work, occasionally for security details and escorts up to 2008.

Some of the recognition that he earned was, in April of 1966 Certificate or Honorable Mention from the Westchester newspaper award plan; July of 1966 graduated from the Federal Bureau of narcotics training school; September of 1966 was appointed to the faculty of the Westchester community college; September 1966 received a letter of commendation from the Westchester County grand jury; September of 1966 received a departmental commendation; October 1966 a Certificate or Honorable Mention in Westchester newspaper award plan; April of 1966 departmental commendation for the arrest and conviction of two persons for armed robbery; March 1967 received a departmental Commendation with honor bar for the arrest and conviction of two men for murder of an elderly woman.; From March to April of 1967 served as the instructor for eight week seminar on narcotics for 60 students. The seminar was part of the Mount Vernon adult education program.; May of 1967 received a letter of commendation from the Westchester County grand jury where a special commendation was voted by the April term for undercover work of purchases of narcotics.

The story of Yonkers Det. Charles Jackson is one of great personal accomplishment and great benefit to the agencies he worked for. There is absolutely no doubt that the Yonkers Police Department's loss was clearly Westchester County's gain.

DEPUTY CHIEF RUDOLPH M. DeDIVITIS

APPOINTED: January 1, 1953
RETIRED: January 28, 1993

Born in Yonkers Dec 21, 1928, Rudolph Michael DeDivitis attended local public schools and graduated from Saunders Trade School in 1946. This would be the very same building that he would return to many years later when, in 1990, the former Saunders School building would be converted into the Cacace Justice Center, part of which would house Yonkers Police HQ. But that was still in the future. Following school he listed on an employment application that he was working as a Clerk.

Officer DeDivitis joined the Navy during the Korean War on February 27, 1952 and served aboard the Attack Transport A.P.A. 204-USS Sarasota, including 19 months on overseas duty. Rudy was appointed a police officer on January 1, 1953 from 60 Lewis Parkway earning $2,900 a year while he was still on active duty in the Navy. As such he was immediately granted an indefinite leave of absence from the YPD to continue his military service. This leave was to continue right up to his military discharge. He later received his honorable discharge from the Navy on Nov 20, 1953 and on January 1, 1954 he was reinstated to duty in the 3rd precinct. Rudy preferred walking a foot post over riding in a radio car and most often he was regularly assigned to walk South Broadway. As such he made many acquaintances and good friends who trusted him. His good communication skills would later prove to be a career changer.

It was reported that one evening while off duty and at his home he was contacted by a man he vaguely knew from his post. The man told him he had just killed someone and wanted to turn himself in to Rudy. He did and Rudy made the murder arrest which received wide media coverage. Apparently as a

Deputy Chief Rudolph M. DeDivitis (cont.)

result of this arrest, on August 27, 1965, PO DeDivitis was appointed a Detective in the Detective Division. His salary at that time was $7,300.

Detective DeDivitis was promoted to the rank of Sergeant on December 14, 1967 earning $8,855 a year and was transferred to duty in the 2nd precinct. One month later, on January 26, 1968, he was designated a Detective Sergeant and returned to the DD. While there he supervised general assignment detectives but was very knowledgeable involving gambling investigations. About three years later, on October 22, 1971, he was assigned to the Intelligence Unit, still as a detective sergeant, to specifically supervise the investigations of gambling operations throughout Yonkers.

On April 24, 1972 Rudy received his promotion to Lieutenant and on that same day was designated a Detective Lieutenant earning $15,698. He was also allowed to remain in the "IU" in the gambling unit. While serving in this capacity he was selected to attend the 92nd session of the FBI National Academy in Quantico, Va. from January 6th to March 31, 1973. He also completed courses at the University of Virginia and the City College of NY. A few months later, on May 3, 1973, DeDivitis was designated commanding officer of the Intelligence Unit.

In Oct of 1982 Rudy was re-assigned from commander of the IU and designated the Executive Officer in the Detective Division. Less than two years later, on August 16, 1984, DeDivitis was promoted to the rank of Captain earning $44,255 and was assigned to Field Services Bureau as a patrol duty captain. But, this would last for less than a year for on May 31, 1985 he was appointed a Detective Captain and designated the commanding officer of the DD.

But this too would be short lived. Only seven months later Capt. DeDivitis was appointed, by then Comm. Joseph Fernandes, as a Deputy Chief of Police and place in command of the Support Services Bureau. He would later be placed in charge of the Investigative Services Division on May 23, 1988.

On March 9, 1990 the local news media announced that PC Fernandes was retiring and City Manager Neil DeLuca had named the 61 year old DeDivitis, a 37 year veteran at the time, to be the interim or acting police commissioner while a search for a "permanent" commissioner was completed. Rudy DeDivitis willingly assumed the $81,600 a year job effective March 16, 1990. Following his oath of office DeDivitis said, "*I'm going to call upon my 37 years of experience with the YPD to do the best possible job that I can.*" At that time the city manager and Mayor Henry Spallone both gave strong indications that DeDivitis would be the one to be chosen for that assignment. But it was not to be.

Act. PC DeDivitis remained in this position, the leader of the Yonkers Police Dept., for five months but never received the official confirmation by the City Council to become permanent. Much to DeDivitis' disappointment, on August 27, 1990, an "outsider," Robert K. Olson was appointed as the full time Police Commissioner. At that point Rudy returned to his deputy chief position and Comm. Olson, doing what any smart outsider would do, appointed DeDivitis as First Deputy Chief; basically the commissioners right hand man for advice. Rudy held that position right up to his retirement on January 28, 1993.

Upon his retirement in 1993 "Rudy" wrote an open letter to all department members through the YPD "Call Box" Newsletter talking about how police work had changed over the years. He closed by saying, "*I am very proud to have had an opportunity to serve the department and I am grateful to have experienced an interesting and rewarding career in law enforcement. I will continue to maintain interest and support of the men and women of the Yonkers Police Dept. in all their endeavors.*"

DET. LT. MARTIN J. HARDING

APPOINTED: April 16, 1953
RETIRED: June 21, 1991

For anyone who knew Marty Harding it would seem he was destined to be a police officer. His father Patrick spent 6 years in the "Civic Guard" in County Kilkenny, Ireland before immigrating to America and moving to Yonkers. And his father's brother, John Harding, was appointed a Yonkers police officer on October 9, 1922.

Martin Joseph Harding was Born June 3, 1929 in Yonkers in the Dunwoodie section of town and as child moved to 10 Tompkins Ave. in Nepera Park. He attended St Mary's School to the 8th grade and then Gorton HS. While in school he was very active in Track and Field events, particularly running. He graduated from Gorton H.S. and then worked as a Lineman for Westchester Light & Power Co. here in Yonkers (now Con Ed). As a young man he was always interested in riding motorcycles and as an enthusiast he participated in many dirt bike type riding competitions on his Harley Davidson motorcycle.

In 1947 Marty joined the Marine Corps Reserve serving a 21 month term and was discharged in 1948. Despite his previous service in the Marine Corps he was drafted into the Army on January 9, 1952. Having previously taken the YPD "Patrolman's" exam, on April 16, 1953 he was called for appointment to the YPD but was still in the Army. Arrangements were made to allow that, while home on liberty, he was appointed a Patrolman and that same day he was granted a leave of absence by the police department to finish his military obligation.

On Jan 8, 1954 he was honorably discharged and was reinstated to the YPD in April of that year at the salary of $2,900. a year. His first assignment was to the 3rd precinct on foot patrol with virtually no training except for a few classes given by then PO Al Rusinko. Marty walked various posts in the 3rd for five years and rode in a radio car for another six years.

A proud Irishman and always having an interest in the N.Y.P.D. Emerald Society Pipe & Drum Band, Harding joined the N.Y.P.D. band in 1962 and would remain a member for 17 years. On June 14, 1965, following the death of then Hack Inspector PO John Karasinski who was killed in an off duty motor vehicle accident, PO Harding was assigned to the Traffic Division, two wheel motorcycle, as the new Hack Inspector. Upon his appointment to Sergeant on December 14, 1967 at $8,855, Marty was re-assigned back to 3rd as a patrol supervisor. On April 16, 1969 Marty was transferred him back to Traffic as the Hack Inspector once again; but this time as a sergeant.

From November of 1970 to January of 1971 (3 mo's) Marty attended a Traffic Science Training Program at the N.Y.S. Police Academy in Albany. Upon his return, the precincts had been reduced from four to two and the traffic unit was now disbanded, divided and assigned in each command. The North Command and the South Command. Since there was no longer a Traffic "Division," effective January 1, 1971 he was detailed to the Parking Authority located in Larkin Plaza where he was placed in charge of all Meter Maids. However about two weeks later, on January 18, 1971 he was assigned to the North Command leading a Special Enforcement Squad.

Later that year on October 19, 1971 Sgt Harding was assigned to the new Special Operations

Det. Lt. Martin J. Harding (cont.)

Division (S.O.D.) leading the Tactical Patrol Force. A week later on October 27, 1971 he was still in S.O.D. but now was the Traffic Enforcement Patrol Supervisor. In 1971 when President Nixon visited Westchester County and Yonkers, Sgt Harding led the motorcycle escort of the motorcade throughout all of Westchester County for over 54 miles. Days prior to the Presidents arrival Sgt Harding worked closely with the Secret Service on the safety of the route to be utilized. Up to that point, like everyone else, portable radios for motorcycle officers were fastened to their belts making it nearly impossible to hear over the roar of the engine. So, prior to President Nixon arriving, always the problem solver, Sgt Harding bought the necessary parts to mount a speaker on the motorcycle that was connected directly to the portable radio. This was our first motorcycle mounted police radio speaker.

On February 26, 1972 Sgt Harding was installed as President of the Westchester County Police Emerald Society; an organization that he had been a member of for many years and which represented 26 county police departments. On August 24, 1973 Marty Harding was promoted to Lieutenant at the salary of $18,018 and was assigned to HQ as the Executive Officer to DC Frank Sardo. In addition he also served as the aide to Chief William Polsen. While in this assignment, and with his mind always thinking of new ideas, for some time he had been very unhappy with the appearance of the department's original triangle patch. So, in his spare time, he began working on new design. The original "department" patch was in a triangle shape with a very bland grayish blue color. Marty designed a new patch; dark blue with Gold letters in center and outside trim. And then he convinced Chief Polsen to authorize the new patch. It went into effect January 1, 1975 and within a short time all the old patches had been replaced on all uniforms.

During this same time period Lt Harding became aware that the Yonkers Police Department did not have a department flag. He immediately began work to have a Yonkers Police Dept. flag designed. It would be our very first Y.P.D. flag. He succeeded in receiving approval for the design and the funds and ordered the flag at a cost of $395. During this same two year period while he worked for the Chief and Deputy Chief he also recommended and established our first Hostage Negotiating Team in the Y.P.D. and was trained for this work in the N.Y.P.D.

In September of 1974 when PO Harold Woods was killed on duty and awarded our departments Medal of Honor, Harding learned that we had no such actual "medal," only an honor bar. As usual, if it needed doing Marty was right there volunteering. He contacted the N.Y.P.D. for the necessary information and we had the first ever Medals of Honor made. The medals were fine but they didn't include ribbons to hang the medal around a recipients neck. So Marty's wife bought ribbon and made several of them for presentation purposes.

Still a member of the N.Y.P.D. Pipe band, Lt Harding decided that we should have our own band here in Westchester. He and a few others had been practicing playing the bag pipes in his basement since 1972, but in 1974 the Westchester County Emerald Society Pipe Band, with Lt Harding as their founder and "Bandmaster," made its debut in March in the St Patrick's Day Parade. They wore police dress blue uniforms with green berets with their police hat wreath on same. Marty would remain their Bandmaster up to 1984.

In 1975 plans were in place to form an Anti-Crime Unit in the Yonkers Police Dept. and Lt Harding was assigned to be the commanding officer of the new Anti-Crime Unit, later renamed the Street Crime Unit. On April 7, 1978 he was awarded the first ever "Police Supervisor of the Year Award" by the

Det. Lt. Martin J. Harding (cont.)

Yonkers Exchange Club for the units previous year arrest record.

In 1979 the new Police Commissioner, Daniel Guido, chose Harding to attend the 117th session of the FBI National Academy in Quantico Va. from April 1, 1979 to June 15, 1979. Upon his return he was replaced as head of the Anti-Crime Unit and was placed in charge of a summer Parks Patrol detail. On September 17, 1979 he was transferred to the North Command on Shonnard Place (old 4th pct.) as a patrol "Zone Commander." On February 17, 1981 the new Police Commissioner, Charles Connolly, directed Harding to research and establish an Inspections Unit which he would command. He did this for a year and on January 1, 1982, against his wishes, he was persuaded by Comm Connolly into volunteering to be the Commanding Officer of the Internal Affairs Division. However, it would be a few years before he would be advanced to Detective Lieutenant. But he wasn't the type to sit in an office. When he and his partner, then Sgt Mike Novotny, weren't working an investigation, they were out on patrol responding to jobs and making arrests.

In 1990, with Marty still the C.O. of the I.A.D., a security problem became apparent in the operation of the Special Investigations Unit (SIU) resulting in a number of people being transferred to other assignments and the office location closed. A few S.I.U. detectives were allowed to continue their assignment but their unit was merged within the offices of the Internal Affairs Division. The Medical Control Unit was also merged into the office space of the I.A.B. The result being that Det Lt Martin Harding was in command of all three units. Despite all the administrative responsibility Marty had to be active, preferably on the street. He remained in the I.A.B. assignment for over 10 years before retiring on June 21, 1991.

Continuing in the law enforcement tradition, Marty's daughter Rosemary was a police captain in the Norwalk Ct. P.D. According to Det John Baliscak, a long time expert in the Criminal Identification Unit, Lt Harding, who was one of the first Yonkers officers certified to administer the newly instituted "Breathalyzer," was the first officer to obtain a conviction on its use. Det Lt Martin Harding couldn't help himself from getting involved in anything that needed to be done. I guess he had excess energy and put it to good use for the benefit of the Yonkers Police Department.

After retirement Marty split his time living in Yonkers and in the winter in Florida. But he would eventually return to live permanently with one of his daughters.

A heavy smoker, Marty developed emphysema and struggled with it for many years. At first he would ride around with oxygen hooked up to his nose and a lit cigarette in his hand. He said he just couldn't quit "and at this stage, what's the point?" It was the emphysema which ultimately resulted in his death on July 31, 2009. He was 80 years old.

DET. THOMAS H. SYSO #640

APPOINTED: September 1, 1953
DIED: January 2, 1971

Thomas Henry Syso was born in Yonkers on May 6, 1926, attended PS#24, Longfellow Jr HS, and graduated from Commerce HS. Tom worked a number of different jobs, but just prior to the YPD was employed as a shipping supervisor. Tom served in Army during the Korean War from September 29, 1950 up to his honorable discharge on September 23, 1952. Tom served as a Corporal with the 40th Military Police Co. in both Korea and Japan.

Tom was appointed to the YPD on September 1, 1953 from 24 Locust Hill Avenue at the starting salary of $2,900. a year. His first assignment was patrol in the 1st precinct. On May 1, 1963 Tom was appointed a Detective in the Detective Bureau and in his last several years Det Syso served as the D.D. desk officer. Tom's brother was PO Mike Syso and his uncle was Sgt Mike Girasek. Tom had no children and lived at 25 Summit Street with his wife. Unfortunately, with just over 17 years on the job, Det Thomas Syso died suddenly on January 2, 1971. He was only 44 years old.

PO MICHAEL J. O'HARE #138

APPOINTED: September 1, 1953
RESIGNED: December 11, 1956

Michael John O'Hare was born in Yonkers on May 5, 1929, the son of Yonkers PO John O'Hare. His uncle Henry was also a Yonkers police officer. Mike attended and graduated from the local public school system. Previous to the YPD he worked for the Anaconda Cable and Wire factory. He was appointed to the Yonkers Police Department on September 1, 1953 from 559 Nepperhan Ave. earning $2,900 a year. His first assignment was patrol duty in the 4th pct. Mike was a member of the Chippewa War Veterans Post honor guard. On one Memorial Day, May 30, 1956, following a 6th ward parade, all the participants went to the either Brunkies Tavern on the N/E corner, or to the SOS Club (Son of the Sixth ward) on the N/W corner of Nepperhan Ave for food and liquid refreshments. O'Hare was off duty in the Honor Guard but wore his revolver. A fight broke out with some firefighters and a large fight started. At some point Michael O'Hare reportedly was knocked down, drew his revolver and shot into the crowd and killed a man. The man killed was the brother of a former Yonkers police officer. O'Hare was suspended on May 31, 1956 and was indicted for the shooting. However, following a trial O'Hare was acquitted. It was not too much later that Michael O'Hare resigned from the YPD on December 11, 1956.

DET. DOMINICK J. GEBBIA #645

APPOINTED: September 1, 1953
RETIRED: April 26, 1972

Dominick Joseph Gebbia was born in Yonkers on June 16, 1931. He attended Saunders HS but actually graduated from New Mexico high school in Santa Fe New Mexico in 1950. As a youth of about 17 years Dom joined the Army Signal Corps on July 1, 1948. He served as a Sergeant in Korea for 19 months in the 51st Signal Battalion Corps. His MOS, "military occupational specialty," was Combat Communications in "I" Corps. and he was honorably discharged on April 16, 1952. He served for a short while as a Westchester Co. Parkway Police "Special" until he was called by the YPD.

Dominick was appointed to the Yonkers Police Department on September 1, 1953 from 77 Livingston Ave and was assigned to the 1st precinct on foot patrol. On May 16, 1955 PO Gebbia was reassigned from the 1st pct. to the Traffic Division on a three wheel motorcycle assigned to parking meter enforcement. A while later he was assigned to two wheel motorcycle patrol but it only lasted for short time because while riding northbound on Central Avenue at Tuckahoe Road, a female driver abruptly turned across Central Avenue and ran right into the side of him. As a result he received serious injuries. While he recovered he worked in the Traffic Violations Unit performing clerical duties.

Dominick was appointed a Detective on January 1, 1969 serving in general assignment in the Detective Division. However, when an Auto Theft Unit was established a short time later, Gebbia partnered up with Det's Armando DeBlassis and John Raffa and those three constituted that unit. He had some experience with vehicle identification while working off duty as a car salesman for Lincoln Mercury on South Broadway and Caryl Avenue. They received their auto theft training, including how to locate hidden Vin numbers, at a school in Long Island. Prior to the Auto Theft Unit being established, if law enforcement needed help determining whether a vehicle was stolen they would contact the N.A.T.B., the National Auto Theft Bureau. Though national in size it was a private organization which was funded and operated by groups of insurance companies, not a government agency.

Dominick related that he was related in various ways to Sgt Lawrence Mesler, former Yonkers PO Patrick McElmeel, Sgt Louis Cacace, PO Roland Hall, and PO Thomas Fitzgerald. Det Gebbia retired from the Detective Division on a disability pension effective April 26, 1972. He currently resides in Apollo Beach, Florida.

DET. THOMAS J. McINERNEY #635

APPOINTED: September 1, 1953
RESIGNED: April 8, 1970

Thomas Joseph McInerney was born on August 23, 1931 in the City of White Plains, NY. He attended Eastview Jr. HS and then moved to Yonkers where he attended and graduated from Commerce HS. Tom was very athletic and while at Commerce he was a member of the school's baseball and basketball teams. Upon graduation, and only 17 years of age, Tom joined the US Air Force on March 15, 1949. Within a short period of time the Korean war began but Tom served in the Pacific islands of Guam, Okinawa, etc. Having served nearly four years and attaining the rank of Staff Sergeant, Tom received his honorable discharge on November 2, 1952. He took the Yonkers police exam and then worked driving a truck. He later learned that he passed the police test and on September 1, 1953 was appointed to the YPD while residing in the Cottage Place Gardens complex.

Following some basic recruit training Tom was assigned to the 4th precinct at 53 Shonnard Place and earned a salary of $2,900 a year. He was a very friendly and outgoing type guy whose personality fit right into the 4th pct. which loved to party whenever possible. In fact, Tom was an original member of the 1950's 4th precinct softball team which wore a T-shirt with the logo on it of a mug of beer, with a foaming head, and the words "4th Pct." Tom was also very active in all PBA activities. In fact, in January of 1959 he was elected Financial Secretary of the PBA and in July of 1959 he was even serving as a member of the police Color Guard.

PO McInerney was appointed a Detective on August 16, 1959 and in that year a detective earned $5,475 a year. Tom was assigned to General Assignment investigations and did so efficiently up to May 1, 1963 when he was returned to uniform patrol. It is worth noting that during this time politicians had a great deal of improper control over police assignments. If someone had a better "hook," you were out and they were in. Fortunately for Tom his return to patrol only lasted 9 months and on February 26, 1964 he was returned to the DD and his salary had risen to $7,350.

During the ensuing years Det McInerney was assigned to gambling investigations along with a few other thoroughly trusted detectives. And, as a testament to his popularity, on January 24, 1968 it was announced that he had been elected president of the Westchester County Detectives Association. Following his election it wasn't long before the Yonkers Public Safety Commissioner tried to direct and control the county detectives organization through Tom. Tom refused saying he would do his job, but the county organization was off limits. As a result, less than 6 months later, on June 14, 1968, Tom's integrity paid a price when he was again returned to uniform patrol. There seemed no end to the "games" being played because he was put back in the DD on December 20, 1969 and bounced right out 6 days later on December 26th.

It is very likely Tom McInerney was getting very tired of politics in the YPD. This was all happening right at the time that former Yonkers Public Safety Commissioner Daniel F. McMahon, who was the Westchester Co. Sheriff, was recruiting several members of the YPD to leave Yonkers and join the Sheriff's office as investigators. A number of other Yonkers officers were also asked and did accept that offer. Apparently thinking about it, Tom took a leave of absence to run from January 9, 1970 to April 8, 1970 and worked with the county to see if it suited him. It did, and effective April 8, 1970, Det Thomas

Det. Thomas J. McInerney #635 (cont.)

McInerney, a veteran Yonkers officer with 17 years seniority, resigned to join the Sheriff's Office as a Senior Criminal Investigator. Shortly thereafter he was appointed a Chief Criminal Investigator in charge of organized crime and narcotics investigations. While there, McInerney was selected and did attend the prestigious FBI National Academy in 1972. His class, which coincidentally included a former YPD colleague, Det Charles Taylor, was the first FBI class to be held in Quantico, Virginia. Tom retired from the Sheriff's office in 1974 with a combined 22 years law enforcement experience between Yonkers and the county Sheriff's office.

Following his retirement Tom moved to Florida and was head of a security detail named "Internal Affairs" for the Broward County school system, where he lived at that time. He administered a security detail of about 60 people covering 130 schools. Sometime later Tom was hired by the Broward County Sheriff's Office as an Administrative Commander. While with Broward County Tom furthered his education by receiving a Bachelors and Master's degree in Criminal Justice Administration. As a result he received the prestigious national award of "Who's Who" in Education in 1979. While working full time and continuing his education Tom was an adjunct instructor at the Criminal Justice Institute in Broward and St. Lucie counties. Tom retired from the Broward Co. Sheriff's Office with the rank of Lt. Colonel.

In 1994 he moved to Port St. Lucie and was hired as Director of Law Enforcement in the St Lucie County Sheriff's office. Sadly, his wife Doris died in July of 2006. She died just before Tom's retirement as a major in the St Lucie County Sheriff's department on July 31, 2006. They had purchased a home in Murphy NC for their retirement after Tom's 52 years in law enforcement.

Tom McInerney did retire after 50 years in law enforcement as a Major and Director of Law Enforcement in the St Lucie Co. Sheriff's Office. Throughout all his years in law enforcement Tom McInerney received several awards and commendations in each of the law enforcement agencies he worked.

He recently remarried and today Tom still enjoys living in the sunshine state and has no plans to return to work again. Tom has four children from his 54 year marriage to his first wife Doris, and eleven grandchildren and two great grandchildren. And Tom's love of his chosen profession seems to have been contagious. Something he is very proud of. His son Tom Jr retired as a Lieutenant from the Coral Springs, Fl. P.D. and then joined the Florida Dept. of Law Enforcement (DLE), retiring in 2010 with the rank of Regional Director. His grandson, Tom, is an eight year deputy (2011) with the Broward Co. Sheriff's Office.

His second son Scott served 25 years with the Davie, Fl. P.D. retiring with the rank of Major. And he also joined the Florida Dept. of Law Enforcement and is currently a supervisor in the Corruption Internal Affairs section. And Scott's daughter, Tom's granddaughter, is a crime analyst with the DLE.

A daughter, Sharon, resides in Apex, NC with her family, and another daughter, Melissa, resides with her family in Broward Co. Florida.

In conversations with Tom it was very clear that he felt that his experience working as a detective with the Yonkers P.D. was an important and intricate part of his total half century of law enforcement experience. However, he felt that his most significant accomplishment was being a mentor to young law enforcement officers, many of whom rose to attain command positions.

It is very obvious that, considering Tom McInerney's long and successful career in law enforcement, once again the Yonkers police department's loss was another agencies gain.

PO JOSEPH J. SANTAMARINA #69

APPOINTED: September 1, 1953
RETIRED: January 11, 1974

Joseph John Santamarina was born in the City of Yonkers on September 25, 1930. He attended local public schools and graduated from Yonkers HS. Shortly after finishing school Joe joined the Army on January 3, 1949 and served as a Sergeant in a HQ Company, Artillery Computing Section. He received his honorable discharge on December 5, 1951. For a while Joe worked as a shipping clerk, but was appointed to the YPD on September 1, 1953 from 71 Dunston Avenue earning a starting salary of $2,900 a year. Following his recruit training he was assigned to the 2nd precinct. After a time he was assigned a steady sector along with PO Pete McMahon.

Both men formed a construction company working during their off duty hours. They had the Cross County Center contract for snow removal and anything to do with construction. Joe worked his entire career in the 2nd pct. and was considered a good cop receiving numerous awards.

Patrolmen Joe Santamarina and his partner McMahon won risk of life awards in 1970 in connection with police work during a holdup of the Horn and Hardart Restaurant at the Cross County Center in Yonkers. The men received a call that a holdup was in progress and, being familiar with the layout, entered the restaurant through a cellar and surprised the two gunmen. The patrolmen captured them after a short exchange of gunfire, preventing one of the bandits from shooting the restaurant manager. The following year, in February 1971, the Yonkers Exchange Club named Santamarina and his partner "Policeman of The Year" for their actions on that day. A citation presented to the patrolmen read in part, *"The action taken by Officers Santamarina and McMahon to prevent the threat of imminent physical harm to a citizen and the loss of a large amount of money, at personal risk of their own lives, exemplifies the true meaning of the Policeman's Code of Ethics."* Joe also worked his construction job over the years with Pete McMahon. Because Joe always talked so low and softly he was often nicknamed "mumbles." Joe Santamarina retired from the YPD on January 11, 1974 to his home in Irvington, NY.

DET. WALTER R. McCLAIN #658

APPOINTED: September 1, 1953
RETIRED: June 24, 1988

Born Walter Raymond McClain in Yonkers on August 31, 1926, one of ten children, he grew up living on Palisade Avenue near Garden St, later renamed Walsh Rd. Walt attended and graduated from Yonkers public schools and immediately following school Walter joined the Army during WW 2 on December 11, 1944. He served as a Corporal with the 974th depot repair squadron in the Asiatic Pacific campaign. He was honorably discharged on December 11, 1946.

Prior to working for Yonkers Walter worked as a driving instructor and trolley car conductor. He had taken both the police and fire department exams and was first hired by the Yonkers Fire Dept. However, a short time later Walt was called for appointment to the YPD. He chose to resign from the YFD and accept appointment to the police department on September 1, 1953. He lived at 47 Hudson Street, his salary was $2,900, and his first assignment was foot patrol duty in the 1st precinct on Wells Avenue.

Thirteen years later, on January 28, 1966, Walter was appointed a Detective in the Detective Division but was assigned to work in what was then named the Bureau of Criminal Investigation (BCI). The units name was changed to the Criminal Identification Unit and years later to the Crime Scene Unit. His job was to identify, photograph and collect evidence at serious crime scenes.

On December 1, 1977 Det McClain was reassigned to the Arson Squad and received specialized training to determine the cause of a fire and determine if it was an Arson. His last assignment was on January 29, 1986 when he was reassigned to the Special Investigation Unit, now renamed the Intelligence Unit. Walter was a very big, but friendly man with an easy going personality. His brother was Deputy Chief Owen McClain. Det Walter McClain, a member of the Yonkers PBA, the police Holy Name Society and the Westchester Police Emerald Society, retired from the YPD on June 24, 1988 to his home on Midland Avenue in Yonkers. However, because of his fingerprinting experience he was hired back by the YPD, for a short time, on a part time basis working in CIU with fingerprinting issues.

Ret Det Walter McClain died on March 20, 2012 at the age of 85 years.

PO JOHN J. DiGILIO #239

APPOINTED: September 1, 1953
RETIRED: September 7, 1973

John James DiGilio was born in the City of Yonkers on Dec. 5, 1928. Jack, as he was known, attended local public schools and graduated from Saunders H.S. As a second language Jack was able to speak Italian fluently. DiGilio entered the Army during the Korean War on Dec. 13, 1950 and received his honorable discharge on Nov. 26, 1952. At one point he listed his previous occupation as an installer at the Tarrytown General Motors factory. DiGilio was hired by the YPD on September 1, 1953 from 269 Jessamine Ave. His starting salary at the time was $2,900 a year and his first assignment was patrol in the 1st pct. After gaining a few years seniority Jack's usual assignment would be in the "money escort" car. On Mar 13, 1963 Jack was reassigned to the 2nd pct. on patrol. However, four years later on June 12, 1967 he was reassigned to the Traffic Engineering office. Once again he was moved on Nov. 10, 1970, this time to the Property Clerk Unit. DiGilio's last assignment took place on Jan. 1, 1971 when he was assigned to the Records Division from which he would later retire on Sept. 7, 1973. After he retired Jack worked as a manager for the White Swan Uniform company on St. Casimir Avenue. Several years later he moved to Florida and died on June 6, 2013. Jack's son, John J. DiGilio Jr. is a retired New York City Detective.

PO RICHARD H. BANKS #90

APPOINTED: September 1, 1953
DIED: August 23, 1967

Richard Henry Banks was born in NYC on June 10, 1928. After moving to Yonkers with his family he attended and graduated from local public schools. Following high school Richard joined the Navy on Apr. 12, 1946 and was honorably discharged on March 28, 1949. Following the military Rich worked as a mechanical Inspector. Richard Banks was appointed to the YPD on Sept. 1, 1953 from 4 Potomac Street and following training was assigned to a foot post in the 1st pct. On Feb. 15, 1955 officer Banks was reassigned to the Traffic Division to a three wheel motorcycle on Parking Summons Detail. The following year, on July 16, 1956, he was moved back to patrol in the 4th pct. He was transferred to the 1st pct. on Dec. 1, 1956 and while there, on Aug. 28, 1956, he was assigned to the Emergency Services Unit. Four months later, on Dec. 15, 1958, he was reassigned to the Juvenile Aide Bureau (now Youth Div.). In Feb. of 1963 he was returned to patrol in the 1st pct. but took a leave of absence without pay on Oct. 23, 1963, due to health reasons but returned to duty in the 3rd pct. on April 27, 1964. But it was obvious that he was not well. He was diagnosed with emphysema and tuberculosis, became seriously ill, and died on Aug. 23, 1967 having served just short of 14 years as a police officer. Richard Banks was only 39 years old.

DEPUTY CHIEF FRANK M. SARDO

APPOINTED: September 1, 1953
RETIRED: April 17, 1986

Frank Michael Sardo was born on Ashburton Avenue in Yonkers on December 18, 1926. He attended PS# 12. and completed his schooling in Longfellow Jr H.S. and graduated from Saunders H.S. During his high school years he was on the school's football team.

At the age of 17 years, and while WW-2 raged on, young Frank wanted to be a pilot. So on December 18, 1943 he joined the US Army Air Corps. He reportedly began training in flight school but during a physical it was discovered that he had a "pin" in his wrist from an injury he received years earlier. As a result he was discharged on September 20, 1945 after only 19 months of service, rather than for the duration of the war. Frank was always good with math so it was no surprise that he quickly gained employment as a Clerk Accountant.

Frank Sardo was appointed to the police department on September 1, 1953 from 70 St Joseph's Avenue at a salary of $2,900, and was assigned routine patrol duties in the 4th precinct. A year later on December 16, 1954 he was transferred from the 4th to the Traffic Division on two wheel motorcycle duty. Frank served in Traffic with men like Sgt Bob Foody, PO's Bill Kamp, John Reinberger, Ed Balun, Gene Dobson, Bob Linscott, Ben DeLuccy (not the captain), and others.

On November 16, 1960 he was promoted to the rank of Sergeant and assigned to a precinct as a patrol supervisor. But shortly thereafter he was returned to motorcycle duty as a traffic sergeant. Five years later, on January 14, 1966, he was appointed to Lieutenant and assigned as a desk lieutenant in the

Deputy Chief Frank M. Sardo (cont.)

3rd precinct. During this time Frank's skill with numbers became apparent and he became known to be one of the best officers capable of crafting any variation of working schedule that the department required. He was quite simply excellent with working schedules and duty charts.

On December 20, 1969 he was appointed a Det Lieutenant and assigned to the Detective Division and he remained there until January of 1972 when the City Manager, Dr Seymour Scher, and Police Chief William Polsen implemented a re-organization of the departments hierarchy. They had decided there was a need for a rank between the chief of police and the captains in the department and this rank would be designated "Deputy Chief." It would be an appointed position, and so no civil service test would be given. After due consideration Chief Polsen decided on the two to be promoted to this brand new position of "Deputy Chief." They would be Capt. Edward Murphy and Det Lt Frank Sardo. On January 10, 1972 Lt Frank Sardo and Capt. Murphy assumed their new positions. At the time there was a great deal of heated discussion regarding Chief Sardo's appointment to Deputy Chief from the rank of Lieutenant, having never been a captain. But Chief of Police Bill Polsen had decided Sardo was who he wanted and as a result, eleven days later, on January 21, 1972 Deputy Chief Sardo was officially promoted from the civil service list to the rank of captain, but remained in his appointed position of Deputy Chief.

Deputy Chief Sardo remained in this position up to May 30, 1985 when, at his own request, he was returned to his civil service rank of Captain and assigned as the C.O. of the 3rd precinct. Capt. Sardo retired from the 3rd precinct on April 17, 1986.

DC Sardo, who could speak Italian fluently, lived at 44 Rushby Way for many years and had two Y.PD. brothers in law; Sardo, Det Joe Sokol, and PO Ed Opaciuch each had married one of three sisters. Frank was also very active in the activities of the Capt's, Lt's, and Sgt's Association. In fact he served as the association Vice President for a time. He enjoyed golfing while his health was good but in the last few years enjoyed going to the gambling casino's playing the poker slot machines.

Several years later he and his wife moved to Monroe, NJ where at one point he began what would be a long illness. On June 8, 2009 Ret DC Frank Sardo died at the age of 82 years.

PO PETER J. McMAHON #224

APPOINTED: September 1, 1953
RETIRED: January 11, 1974

Pete was one of those very hard working men who not only did his job as a police officer, but worked another full time job throughout nearly his entire career. Peter Joseph McMahon was born in Yonkers on Nov. 9, 1927. He attended local schools and graduated from Mark Twain Jr. HS. It's believed that Pete left high school at the age of 17 to join the US Naval Air Corps on Feb. 27, 1944 during WW 2. He served as a Seaman 2nd Class and was honorably discharged on July 3, 1946. He worked many years as a security guard and as a union brick layer. He was appointed to the YPD on Sept. 1, 1953 from 821 McLean Ave. and earned a starting salary of $2,900 a year. His first assignment was patrol in the 2nd precinct. On May 16, 1960 Pete was appointed a Detective and served in the Detective Division up to Feb. 26, 1964 when he was returned to patrol in the 2nd pct. where he remained the rest of his career.

On one occasion in the 1970's Pete and his partner, Joe Santamarina, were sent to Gimbels Department Store to meet security who had arrested two shoplifters and were to transport them to Central Booking. With Santamarina remaining in the car, Pete approached the thief who immediately wrestled the officer to the ground and removed his revolver. During the struggle all six rounds were fired striking two guards until one guard fired his weapon and killed the shoplifter. Pete was very lucky that day.

He always worked a second job operating a construction business along with PO Joseph Santamarina, with whom he was appointed. They owned the M. & S. Construction Company together and were also partners in the 2nd pct. for years. They had the Cross County Center contract for snow removal and anything to do with construction, including painting parking lines, blacktopping parking lot areas, cement or brick work, and were in charge of arranging for all police security details. All this and handled his sector as well. Throughout his career Pete earned numerous police Commendations and Macy Honorable Mention awards.

Patrolmen McMahon and his partner Joe Santamarina won risk of life awards in 1970 in connection with police work during a holdup of the Horn and Hardart Restaurant at the Cross County Center in Yonkers. The men received a call that a holdup was in progress and, being familiar with the layout, entered the restaurant through a cellar and surprised the two gunmen. The patrolmen captured them after a short exchange of gunfire, preventing one of the bandits from shooting the restaurant manager. The following year, in February 1971, the Yonkers Exchange Club named McMahon and his partner "Policeman of The Year" for their actions on that day. A citation presented to the patrolmen read in part, "*The action taken by Officers Santamarina and McMahon to prevent the threat of imminent physical harm to a citizen and the loss of a large amount of money, at personal risk of their own lives, exemplifies the true meaning of the Policeman's Code of Ethics*."

Pete loved baseball, softball, football, and fishing and retired from the YPD on Jan. 11, 1974 and continued with his construction business. Ret PO Peter J. McMahon died in April of 1986. He was 58.

PO ALFRED J. DelBENE #40

APPOINTED: September 1, 1953
RESIGNED: April 8, 1965

Al DelBene was born in Yonkers on March 11, 1923. He attended local schools and graduated from Yonkers HS. Al worked as a painter for a few years but after the beginning of WW 2 he joined the Army Air Corps on Jan. 15, 1943. He served as a Drill Sergeant and attended school for the Military Police. He was honorably discharged as a Master Sergeant on Jan. 1, 1946. Al was appointed to the YPD on Sept. 1, 1953 from 130 Elm Street earning $2,900 a year and his first assignment was to the 1st precinct. Al loved music and in 1958 he had a band named the "Country Troubadours." PO DelBene attended the Bolan Academy of Criminology and on Feb. 4, 1959 was assigned to the Juvenile Aide Bureau which incorporated the PAL. While living at 33 Rossiter Ave. Al resigned from the YPD on April 8, 1965 stating in his letter of resignation that he was doing so reluctantly and due to financial considerations. However, on Apr. 8, 1966 he applied for reinstatement but was denied citing his one year limit to be considered had expired by one day. Al's brother was Det Rocco DelBene. Former PO Alfred DelBene died in October of 1985 in Los Angeles, Cal. He was 62 years old.

PO THOMAS J. NOLAN #135

APPOINTED: September 1, 1953
RETIRED: June 15, 1973

Thomas J. Nolan was born in Ireland on July 3, 1925 and came to US with his family at the age of six. They moved to NYC and Tom attended Power Memorial HS. and became a naturalized citizen on Sept. 14, 1933. Joining the Navy during WW 2 Tom Served as a Seaman 1st class from July 31, 1943 to Mar. 21, 1946. He worked for a while as a security guard until Sept. 1, 1953 when he was appointed to the YPD from 200 Ashburton Avenue. His salary was $2,900 a year and he was assigned to the 4th pct. Three months later, on Dec 1, 1954, he was moved to the 2nd pct. at 441 CPA. On Aug. 20, 1958, after the Emergency Service Unit was re-constituted, after having been disbanded since the 1940's, Nolan was trained in NYC at Randall's Island by the NYPD ESU instructors and assigned to our ESU. On April 27, 1966 Nolan saved the life of a man impaled by a chain link fence pole on CPA. Ten years later, on Nov. 7, 1966, Nolan was reassigned to routine patrol in the 1st pct. Then, on Feb. 2, 1970, he was transferred to HQ. Following the centralization of the precincts on Jan. 1, 1971, Tom was assigned back to patrol in the now South Command (old 2nd pct.). Tommy Nolan retired from the YPD on June 15, 1973. Tom was described as an easy going guy with a dry sense of humor and light Irish brogue. Ret PO Thomas J. Nolan died on March 31, 1983 at the age of 57 years.

PO EDWARD J. KOZLOWSKI #221

APPOINTED: September 1, 1953
RETIRED: April 14, 1977

Edward Joseph Kozlowski was born on July 17, 1922 in Amsterdam, NY. He attended local public schools in that city and graduated from Amsterdam vocational high school. Following his schooling he moved to Yonkers and worked miscellaneous jobs for a while. However, following the outbreak of WWII, he joined the Army on October 19, 1942 and served as an MP with the 796th Military Police Battalion. He received his honorable discharge on January 8, 1946. Ed was appointed to the YPD on September 1, 1953 from 100 McLean Avenue and had a starting salary of $2,900 a year. Following his recruit training he was assigned to the 3rd precinct on Radford Street. On January 1, 1971 he was reassigned to patrol in the South Command, but only until the end of the year. On December 20, 1971 he was reassigned to the Records Service and Maintenance Division located in headquarters performing clerical duty. On August 20, 1974 Ed was assigned to the Special Operations Division but his duties were delivering mail throughout the department. Ed suffered a stroke on February 10, 1976 and was partially paralyzed and remained out on the sick list right up to his retirement from the department on April 14, 1977. Ret PO Edward Joseph Kozlowski died on October 11, 1990 at the age of 68 years.

SGT. ROBERT W. BUTLER #59

APPOINTED: September 1, 1953
RETIRED: June 15, 1972

Robert William Butler was born in Yonkers on Jan. 21, 1927. He attended Catholic schools and graduated from Sacred Heart HS. Following school Bob joined the Navy on Feb. 11, 1944 during World War II. He served as an operator of a Landing Ship Transport (LST) bringing combat troops to the beach. He was said to have been a decorated veteran of the Okinawa campaign. Bob received his honorable discharge on June 14, 1946. He was appointed to the YPD on Sept. 1, 1953 while residing at 6 Cottage Place Gardens earning $2,900 a year and his first assignment was patrol in the 4th pct. A few years later, on Oct. 19, 1955, he was reassigned to the 2nd pct. Bob was appointed a Detective on Jan. 30, 1963 but returned to patrol in the 2nd precinct February 25, 1964. Robert Butler was promoted to the rank of Sergeant on Sept. 12, 1969 earning a salary of $11,600 a year and was assigned as a patrol supervisor in the 3rd pct. Over the next few years he was moved to the Communications Division, to the South Command, and on Feb. 10, 1972 to the North Command. It was from here that Sgt. Butler retired on June 15, 1972 after having purchased one year and 3 months of military time credit from the pension system. Bob and his wife moved to Fishkill NY where he began working for IBM. He was a member of the LST Association, NY amphibious service. Retired Sgt. Robert Butler died on June 9, 2001 in Fishkill NY. He was 74 years old.

PO HOYT W. ROGERS #28

APPOINTED: September 1, 1953
RETIRED: January 22, 1976

Hoyt Walter Rogers was born in Concord, North Carolina on February 18, 1921 and is where he also attended the local school system. It was reported that when he was a child his father was a sheriff in one of the small towns in North Carolina. Hoyt was a big man, standing over 6' 2" tall, about 250 lbs., with a distinct southern drawl and was known to everyone as "Buck" Rogers, after an old movie hero of the 1940s.

According to son, Hoyt Jr., his father "Buck" joined the Army Air Corps, just before Pearl Harbor, on September 4, 1941 and was trained as an Aerial Gunner. He later saw action in the North Africa campaign as a waist gunner on a B-17 bomber. In 1943 on his last scheduled mission their plane was shot down over Italy and Rogers bailed out. A German fighter plane strafed Rogers in his parachute striking him several times in the left shoulder and upper body. He survived four days in a raft with three others while bleeding until picked up by a British Destroyer which delivered him to Africa for medical treatment. Rogers resisted a recommendation to have his arm amputated. He underwent three serious spinal back surgeries to help alleviate pain and another 30 miscellaneous surgeries for wound problems, skin grafts, and emerging shrapnel removal. Hoyt Rogers was honorably discharged on January 24, 1945 as a Staff Sgt with 100 % medical disability. For his service Rogers was awarded the Silver Star, Bronze Star, two purple hearts, and various air medals.

Prior to the military Rogers was said to have worked as a jeweler in Hastings New York and also as a private investigator. Hoyt Rogers was appointed to the Yonkers Police Department on September 1, 1953 while residing at 783 Warburton Ave. in Yonkers. His starting salary at the time was $2,900 a year and his first assignment was patrol duty in the 1st precinct on Wells Avenue. Five years later, on January 17, 1958, officer Rodgers was reassigned to patrol in the 2nd precinct located at 441 Central Park Ave. He was moved once again, on August 10, 1961, this time to patrol in the 3rd precinct located at 36 Radford St.

While still assigned to the 3rd precinct, on November 12, 1965 while on duty, he attempted to break up a large disorder and fight that was taking place in a bar and restaurant named the "Upstairs Room" on South Broadway. While attempting to arrest one of the participants in the fight the male resisted and using his fingers gauged both of Rogers eyes nearly blinding him. In an oversight no one in the police chief's office, nor anyone in City Hall, ever notified the pension system of his injuries. A state pension requirement. This oversight would cause him much difficulty years later when attempting to retire on a disability.

After having been out disabled for a year with severe eye damage, Hoyt returned to work on light duty as a desk lieutenant's aide. On Nov. 7, 1966 he returned to work assigned to the 1st precinct at 730 East Grassy Sprain Road and the following year, on June 23, 1967, he was returned to working in the 3rd precinct. Three and half years later, on Jan. 1, 1971, when the centralization plan of the precincts was implemented, Hoyt was transferred to the "South Patrol Command."

It was around this time that officer Rogers was deemed to be legally blind in one eye when in

PO Hoyt W. Rogers #28 (cont.)

sunlight. However, when he requested disability retirement the department was unable to retire him legally on a disability pension because, as mentioned earlier, the pension system was never notified that he had been assaulted and received his permanent eye damage. As a result, his request for disability retirement was denied and he was assigned to work desk duty on steady late tours. PO Rogers complained that, although on light duty and having been denied his retirement request, he shouldn't have to work steady late tours, but requested instead to work three tours of duty like all precinct personnel, but on desk duty. The department denied his request with no reason given.

It was at this point that Rogers reported himself sick and unable to work. When he did not report for duty as ordered by police surgeon Dante Catullo, records indicate he was dismissed from the department. The date of dismissal is not known. Rogers fought back. He sued the city with his own money, because the PBA declined any association attorney assistance, and after a year, Hoyt won his job back as a police officer with back pay. And this time he was assigned to desk duty working three tours. Now, Hoyt Rogers had a son who was also a Yonkers police officer. And coincidentally, following his father's court decision, his son PO Hoyt Rogers Jr, who was working plainclothes duty at the time, was curiously and immediately transferred back to uniform patrol in the 4th pct.

Throughout most of "Buck's" adult life he suffered from his severe war injuries which were plainly visible by large ugly scarring. Then he received his eye injuries. Overall he underwent 33 operations, some serious, including spinal back surgeries to help alleviate pain from his wounds and some to remove emerging pieces of shrapnel. And for most of his life he suffered from nightmares from the ordeal. And then, in 1975, "Buck" suffered a stroke following his last surgery and which left him paralyzed.

Hoyt "Buck" Rogers was ultimately retired on ordinary disability on January 22, 1976.
His last days were spent in Lawrence Hospital as a quadriplegic. War hero and Ret PO Hoyt W. "Buck" Rogers died Oct. 22, 1979 at the age of 58 years.

PO NICHOLAS F. ROSSI #116

APPOINTED: September 1, 1953
RETIRED: July 11, 1972

Nicholas Rossi was born in the city of Yonkers on June 10, 1927 and attended local public schools and had the ability to speak Italian fluently. He gained employment with Teamsters Local 456 as a truck driver. Nick joined the Navy toward the end of WW 2 on May 16, 1945. He received his honorable discharge on August 4, 1946. Nick received his appointment to the Yonkers Police Department on September 1, 1953 while living at 299 New Main Street. His starting salary was $2,800 a year and his first assignment was to patrol in the 1st precinct. On December 16, 1954 Nick was transferred from the 1st to the Traffic Division on two wheel motorcycle patrol. In the mid 1950's Rossi organized and coached a basketball team he named the "Dumontiers" the members of which were predominately from the Park Hill Avenue and School St. area.

On April 21, 1960 Rossi was suspended without pay for a serious infraction of the departmental rules. As a result, on July 2, 1960, he was found guilty and fined an unprecedented 102 days pay. The usual punishment for a very serious infraction is a fine of no more than 30 days or dismissal. He was also transferred from Traffic out to patrol in the 4th precinct. He was one of the original members of the 4th pct. Softball Team with the logo on their t-shirt of mug of beer and words "4th Pct."

On February 19, 1968 PO Rossi was reassigned to the Youth Division as a youth crime investigator. He was appointed a Detective on June 14, 1968 and remained in Youth Division performing Community Affairs duties working with members of the community. However this detective status lasted for only a short time.

After retiring from the YPD on July 11, 1972 he was self-employed driving a limousine and later as a consultant for Teamsters local 456 in Yonkers and was a member of the Yonkers PAL Advisory Board of Directors. He also claimed he was a part owner of the "Bachelors 3" nightclub in Manhattan along with NY Jets Football legend Joe Namath. In later years he worked as director of security at the Westchester Towne House (later renamed the Carvel Inn) on Tuckahoe Road where he also lived alone for many years. Nick was a big, strong, powerful man whose mere physical presence could be very intimidating. He moved in the fast lane as a divorced guy which, as he claimed, led him to work security as a body guard for such celebrities as Frank Sinatra, Dean Martin Sammy Davis Jr., Bob Hope, Willie Mays, Jane Mansfield, and many more. And he had the posed photographs to prove it.

Ret PO Nicholas Rossi, a member of the Police Athletic League Board of Directors, died on April 14, 2004. He was 76 years old.

LT. JOHN J. RENNER

APPOINTED: September 1, 1953
RETIRED: June 29, 1973

John Joseph Renner was born in the City of Yonkers on Dec. 6, 1928. He attended PS#2, Ben Franklin Jr. HS, and graduated from Saunders HS. John was said to have joined the Navy on Jan. 7, 1948 not long after completing H.S. While in the Navy Renner served as an aircraft navigator aboard the aircraft carrier USS Cabot. It was reported that on one occasion his plane had to ditch in the ocean due to mechanical failure. After his honorable discharge from the Navy on Sept. 21, 1949, John joined Army National Guard. He was subsequently drafted into the Army on Nov. 8, 1951 against his objection that he had already served in the Navy.

Renner served during the Korean War with the 7th Infantry Battalion and reportedly took part in the infamous fight for "Pork Chop Hill." On one occasion while in camp in Korea he caught a Korean male servant stealing from his foot locker. A scuffle ensued and during a fight over his rifle, Renner was shot in the leg but later recovered with no lasting disability. Renner was discharged from the Army on Aug. 7, 1953. He was appointed to the YPD from 172 Elm St. on Sept. 1, 1953 at a starting salary of $2,900. a year. He listed his previous occupation as a bookkeeper and he lived at 172 Elm St. Following recruit training he was assigned to patrol in the 1st precinct.

PO Renner was granted a leave of absence without pay from the YPD under the GI Bill to continue his college education at Oswego State Teachers College, Oswego, NY beginning on Sept. 1, 1954 up to June 30, 1955. He returned earlier and on Feb. 15, 1955 was reinstated to the YPD as PO and assigned to the 4th precinct, now earning $3,800. a year. On Sept. 17, 1956 PO Renner was reassigned from the 4th pct. to the Traffic Division, but assigned to the Traffic Engineering Bureau. He remained there for just over six years and on Jan. 30, 1963 was returned back to patrol in 1st precinct. The following month on Feb. 27, 1963 Renner was promoted to the rank of Sergeant and transferred to the 3rd pct. as a patrol supervisor. His new salary was now $7,400 a year.

On his own time Sgt Renner continued his education earning a Bachelor of Civil Engineering from NY University in 1965. In 1967 he applied for, and was awarded, a fellowship for 12 months of graduate study, full time, at the John Jay College of Criminal Justice in NYC. Once again having obtained another leave of absence, Renner attended from Sept. 1, 1967 through Aug. 31, 1968, and earned his Master's degree in Public Administration.

On May 26, 1971 Sgt Renner was returned to patrol as a sergeant in the South Command. Seven months later, on December 10, 1971, John Renner was promoted to Lieutenant and reassigned to the North Command at 53 Shonnard Place as a desk lieutenant, now earning $15,698. His last assignment occurred on March 12, 1973 when he was moved into the Communications Division at H.Q.

After retiring on June 29, 1973, John moved from his home in Monsey NY to Ft Myers Fla. and opened up a Printing Business which he operated for several years, and then a Dairy Queen Ice Cream Store. He also dabbled as a Day Trader in the stock market. When early in his career he was given the option to join the Social Security system, he declined. John lived in Florida for 28 years and suffered a brain aneurysm at home in Fort Myers, Fl. He had surgery to repair the damage and had been on a respirator but he never recovered and died six weeks later on December 27, 2001.

LT. OWEN A. HUNTLEY

APPOINTED: September 1, 1953
RETIRED: April 21, 1972

Owen Archer Huntley was born in the Bronx NY on Sept. 1, 1927. Following his family's move to Yonkers, he attended and graduated from Roosevelt HS. Owen joined the Navy on Sept. 15, 1944 during WW 2. He served as a Navy Fire Controlman 3rd class and was honorable discharge on Sept. 13, 1947. Following his military he worked as a security guard in NYC. He was appointed to the YPD on Sept. 1, 1953 from 97 Caryl Ave. earning $2,900 a year and his first assignment was to the 2rd pct. on foot patrol. Huntley was promoted to Sergeant on April 1, 1960 earning $6,275 and was reassigned to the 3rd pct. as a patrol supervisor. Then on Jan. 10, 1962 he was returned to the 2nd, and on Jan. 2, 1963 to the 4th pct. On March 25, 1966 Sgt Huntley was promoted to the rank of Lieutenant and assigned to desk duty in the 2nd pct. In 1968 he was moved to the 3rd, and in 1969 to the 4th on desk duty. Lt. Owen Huntley, father of former PO Keith Huntley and brother-in-law to Ret PO James McCabe, retired from the YPD on April 21, 1972.

SGT. RICHARD J. BALL #47

APPOINTED: September 1, 1953
RETIRED: December 31, 1991

Richard John Ball was born on Nov. 2, 1929 in Yonkers and graduated from Saunders HS. While in school Dick Ball was on the school track team and ran in cross country races. Following school, "Dick," as he was known to his friends, worked various jobs until he joined the Army during the Korean War as an MP from Jan. 26, 1951 up to his honorable discharge on Dec. 31, 1952. Richard Ball was appointed to the YPD on Sept. 1, 1953 while residing at 38 Gordon Street earning $2,900 a year and he was assigned to the 2nd pct. However, two days later, on Sept. 3, 1953, he was reassigned to the 3rd pct. On Sept. 29, 1958 Ball was transferred to the Communications Division in headquarters as a Radio Dispatcher and Teletype Operator. He remained there right up to his promotion to Sergeant on Mar. 25, 1966 and at that time was reassigned as a patrol supervisor in the 4th pct. On November 7, 1966 Ball was assigned to a new police building at 730 East Grassy Sprain Road designated the new 1st pct. as a patrol sergeant. But, once again he was moved, this time to the 4th precinct on Dec. 9, 1970. About a year later, on Oct. 19, 1971, Sgt Ball was assigned to the Traffic Division. He didn't really care for riding a motorcycle. In fact, on Oct. 25, 1977, while he was riding, he was struck by an uninsured driver receiving serious injuries. In the future he supervised his men from a radio car. Nearly 20 years later Sgt Ball was reassigned to the Field Services Bureau on July 15, 1991 as an aide to a Deputy Chief. "Dick" Ball, whose grandfather was PO Austin Ball, retired from the YPD on December 31, 1991. Ret Sgt Richard "Dick" Ball died on February 13, 2015. He was 85 years old.

CAPTAIN WILLIAM J. KAMP

APPOINTED: September 1, 1953
RETIRED: July 19, 1991

Bill Kamp was born in the City of Yonkers on October 6, 1931. He attended local public schools and later graduated from Saunders HS. Immediately following his schooling Bill was three weeks shy of turning 18 years of age when he joined the Army on October 30, 1949. He was shipped over to Europe and shortly thereafter the Korean War began. However, Bill spent over two years serving in Italy assigned to the 351st Infantry, 88th Division. Despite being assigned to the infantry, he had been trained as a tank mechanic in Fort Knox so he served his time in a Tank Unit Service Company, attached to the Infantry. He would later receive his honorable discharge as a Corporal on December 31, 1952.

Following his discharge from the military Kamp worked for the GM Auto plant in Tarrytown as an assembler for less than a year. Following that job Bill Kamp was appointed to the Yonkers Police Department on September 1, 1953 from 383 Warburton Avenue, earning a starting salary of $2,900 a year. His first assignment was patrol duty in the 4th precinct at 53 Shonnard Place. Three years later, on December 1, 1956, Kamp was reassigned from the 4th to the Traffic Division on two wheel motorcycle patrol duty. His patrol vehicle was a tank shift, kick start, Harley Davidson two wheel motorcycle. As a motorcycle cop he was affectionately known by his co-workers as "Whitey" due to his light color hair. And that nickname stuck with him throughout his entire career.

Captain William J. Kamp (cont.)

In 1958 Bill Kamp was one of only three men recognized in the YPD as an expert marksman with his revolver and who competed regularly in revolver competitions. He really enjoyed target shooting and belonged to several local gun clubs. By September 14, 1967, and at that time still a police officer, Bill Kamp, along with PO Joe Campanaro as his shooting partner, was still winning trophy's for excellence for his shooting skills.

Bill loved motorcycle duty but he was also determined to rise in the ranks of the department. Ten years from his traffic assignment, on January 14, 1966, officer Kamp was promoted to the rank of Sergeant with a salary of $8,165 a year and was given the unusual privilege of remaining in the Traffic Division as a motorcycle patrol sergeant. Sgt Kamp was very well respected by his former co-workers.

Sgt Kamp had not lost his desire to rise in the ranks and toward that end studied whenever possible. His hard work was rewarded when he was promoted to the rank of Lieutenant four years later, on December 12, 1969, earning the salary of $13,300 a year, and was reassigned from the Traffic Division, after thirteen years, to the 2nd precinct as a desk officer. But that assignment lasted only about a week; on December 20, 1969, Lt. Kamp was moved from the 2nd precinct desk duty and reassigned to the 3rd precinct to serve as a desk officer there.

On January 1, 1971 the controversial centralization of the patrol precincts took place, merging the four precincts into two, and renaming the two, Patrol Commands. At that time Lt. Kamp was assigned to what had been renamed the South Patrol Command, previously known as the 2nd precinct. At that time the South Command comprised that area of the entire city considered the south end; from the Hudson River to the Bronx River. He continued his duties there as a desk officer and being the focal point of authority for all police personnel, booking and bailing prisoners, etc. Later that year, on October 19, 1971, Lt. Kamp was transferred to the newly organized Special Operations Division (SOD) which was originally designed for the operation of the Traffic Division. Offices for SOD were located in 10 St Casimir Avenue and the first commanding officer of SOD was Capt. Alexander Reid. Oddly enough, shortly after they established SOD, they incorporated the Emergency Service Unit (ESU) as part of SOD with the idea that when an ESU officer was needed to fill a temporary vacancy in an ESU truck, instead they would use a motorcycle officer rather than hiring. According to Kamp this was an unworkable administrative nightmare that ended quickly. The Public Safety Commissioner also tried assigning the traffic officers to work from the two patrol commands. But that didn't work well either. Ultimately SOD, and all of its traffic officers, was relocated to 730 East Grassy Sprain Road.

Although Lt. Kamp's time as a lieutenant in Traffic was ever changing and unpredictable, it only last six months. On April 24, 1972 Lt. Kamp was transferred from Traffic to the Inspection Services Division as a patrol Lieutenant operating patrol car #358. Among the duties of the Inspections Lieutenant was to provide citywide inspection of the patrol operations overseeing the manner in which officers were following departmental policy and procedures. When violations were observed appropriate disciplinary action was to be taken. When problems with existing procedures were discovered, recommendations were to be made to modify them.

On July 18, 1974 Lt Kamp was assigned to the North patrol command and detailed, against his strong objection, to take command of the newly organized Community Patrol Unit located at 150 Warburton Avenue. When Kamp made known his disappointment with this assignment, Chief Polsen

Captain William J. Kamp (cont.)

reminded him that he was #1 on the Captains promotion list. Enough said. The CPU was a federally funded program to reach out to the residents of the west side of the North Command in order to foster better relations between the police and the community. However, grant rules restricted the officers assigned to always remain within the designated area and not leave, for any reason. Including backing up other officers on dangerous calls that might be nearby. These restrictive rules caused a great amount of frustration and anger among the rank and file assigned.

Fortunately this assignment lasted only 6 months because, on January 27, 1975, Lt Kamp was promoted to the rank of Captain with a salary of $23,984. Bill Kamp would relate that there was a vacancy in the Records Division due to a captain being suspended, and Kamp was sent to take his place. While there, trouble was brewing elsewhere. At that same time the PBA had been meeting with the chief regularly about problems their officers were having with the North Command captain, Edward Jones. Jones was a strict disciplinarian and morale was very low. In an effort to alleviate the controversy Chief Polsen reassigned Capt. Jones and on September 1, 1975 Bill Kamp was designated commanding officer of the North Patrol Command.

The newly hired police commissioner, Dan Guido, wanted to put in place a new computerized Modat communications system. After interviewing all his captains Guido chose Capt. Kamp for that job. On September 3, 1979 Kamp was once again reassigned. This time he was placed in command of the Communications Division in headquarters, which made him responsible for every aspect of our communications systems and all of its complexities. It was about this time that Capt. Kamp was offered the position of Deputy Chief, which he declined.

Capt. Kamp remained in that job for nearly eleven years when, on July 6, 1990, the newly hired Police Commissioner, Robert K. Olson reassigned him as commanding officer of the Policy and Development unit located in headquarters. PC Olson was determined to upgrade and revise our policies and procedures and believed Kamp to be the right man for the job.

According to Bill Kamp, he and Comm. Olson really did not work well together. There was mostly unspoken tension. Until one day when Comm. Olson told Kamp in essence, I'm not giving you any overtime because you are financially comfortable and don't need any extra money. Kamp said he told Comm. Olson, *"my personal finances are none of your business."*

Within three months from being assigned to the Policy and Development Unit, PC Olson changed his mind and said he had a different job for Capt. Kamp. On October 1, 1990 Kamp was again moved, this time to command the Inspectional Services/Special Projects Unit reporting directly to Commissioner Olson. According to Kamp it was a nothing job with no responsibilities. The message was clear. It was while in this assignment that Capt. Bill Kamp submitted his request for retirement after nearly 38 years of service to be effective July 19, 1991. His request was granted.

Bill Kamp was an intelligent man. He took his responsibilities very seriously throughout his career but always had a ready smile and a good sense of humor. He was not only respected by his subordinates, but he was well liked as well. He was a gentleman as well as a boss.

Capt. Kamp was married to former Diane Sullivan who was a YPD Parking Enforcement Officer when they met, and later became a sworn member of the police department on April 5, 1968. Bill Kamp never pursued employment after retirement and is enjoying the fruits of a long career.

SGT. JOSEPH T. ROMANCHUK #27

APPOINTED: October 6, 1953
RETIRED: August 24, 1979

Joseph T. Romanchuk was born in NYC to Ukrainian-Polish parents on Nov. 1, 1926. He attended NYC elementary schools and after moving to Yonkers, graduated from Saunders HS. Following his graduation Joe joined the Navy on Nov. 25, 1944 during WW 2. He served as a Fireman 1st Class up to his honorable discharge on July 12, 1946. Romanchuk later gained employment as a machinist and as a butcher. He was appointed to the YPD on Oct. 6, 1953 from 346 Prescott Street earning $2,900 a year and his first assignment was to the 4th pct. Joe was a certified Red Cross swimmer and was known to his friends as "Joe Rome." On Sept. 29, 1958 Joe was reassigned to the 2nd precinct, and on Feb. 27, 1961 to the 3rd pct. Joe was always “acting the clown" pulling pranks on fellow officers, often to their annoyance, and his hobby was researching WW-1 and the men who flew in the early airplanes during the war. Joe was promoted to sergeant on Dec. 12, 1969 earning a salary of $11,600 a year and assigned as a patrol supervisor in the 1st pct. After that he moved often. On Dec. 1, 1972 to Communications Division, on Jan. 1, 1971 to the North Command, on Oct. 25, 1973 to the South Command on desk duty, and on Mar. 16, 1979 back to the North Command on patrol. Sgt Romanchuk retired from the YPD on Aug 24, 1979 and died April 4, 1994 in Yonkers at the age of 67.

PO HERBERT C. FAULKNER #179

APPOINTED: January 1, 1954
RETIRED: August 30, 1991

Herbert Calvin Faulkner was born to Yonkers police officer George Faulkner on Nov. 9, 1928 in Yonkers NY. He attended local public schools and graduated from Commerce HS. At the age of 19 years Herb joined the Navy on Dec. 8, 1947, served as a Fireman 1st Class, and received his honorable discharge, following the end of the Korean War, on Nov. 5, 1953. He worked about a month as a machine operator and then was appointed to the YPD on Jan. 1, 1954 from 52 Hildreth Place earning $3,100 a year and assigned to patrol in the 2nd pct. On Nov. 7, 1966 he was reassigned to the newly opened 1st pct. at 730 East Grassy Sprain Rd. On July 11, 1969 he was awarded a Commendation for outstanding police work for one of the arrests he made. For a time Herb’s health was not good and on May 14, 1971 he was assigned to the Records Service and Maintenance Division in a clerical position. However, on Aug. 20, 1974, he was returned to patrol in the South Command. Due to health concerns PO Faulkner was returned, on paper, to clerical duties in HQ on July 1, 1991. However, he had actually been out sick for a lengthy time with cirrhosis of the liver. Herb Faulkner retired from the YPD on Aug. 30, 1991. Ret PO Herbert Faulkner died just over five months after retiring on Feb. 4, 1992. He was 63.

PO PATRICK J. McELMEEL #93

APPOINTED: January 1, 1954
RESIGNED: March 24, 1959

Patrick Joseph McElmeel was born on March 4, 1930 in Yonkers and attended local schools. At the age of 17 "Patty," as he was known to friends, joined the Army serving from Jan. 25, 1947 to his honorable discharge on Jan. 27, 1950. After working several years as a carpenter Pat was appointed to the YPD on Jan. 1, 1954 from 159 High Street. He was assigned to the 4th precinct on patrol earning $3,100 a year. On Dec. 1, 1956 Pat was reassigned to the Traffic Division on motorcycle duty. Pat's cousin was Det Dominick Gebbia who, when asked, related the following; Pat was 5th on the Sergeants list when he was about to be brought up on charges for violating departmental rules. Rather than face a hearing McElmeel submitted his resignation effective March 24, 1959. Pat moved to California where he worked as a mailman and then moved to the east coast of Florida, in Ft Lauderdale, with his family where he had an A/C repair business with his son's.

PO JOHN DROSDOWICH #189

APPOINTED: January 1, 1954
DIED: September 7, 1982

John Drosdowich was born in Yonkers on Nov. 22, 1926. He attended local public schools and graduated from Halstead HS on North Broadway. A short time later he joined the Army on Feb. 13, 1945 and served as a Corporal in the Infantry for the remainder of the war in the Philippine Islands. During his service John had been trained in specialized jungle warfare. He received his honorable discharge on December 14, 1946. After working several different jobs, Drosdowich was appointed to the YPD on Jan. 1, 1954 from 54 Mulford Gardens. His starting salary was $3,100 a year and he was assigned to the 3rd pct. On Aug. 20, 1958 when ESU was reestablished, after having been disbanded in the 1940's, John was one of those selected and trained to comprise the personnel of the re-constituted Emergency Services Unit. He received his ESU training from the NYPD ESU at Randall's Island in the city and was assigned to ESU in the 1st pct. On Nov. 9, 1966 he was sent to the 4th pct. in ESU. He remained in ESU in the 4th pct. up to Oct. 26, 1979 when he was reassigned to the N/E Patrol Command, later renamed the new 1st pct., at 730 E Grassy Sprain Road, riding alone in a one officer sector. While on duty on Sept. 7, 1982, during an early tour, officer Drosdowich died while seated in his radio car, apparently of a heart attack. PO John Drosdowich was so well liked and respected by the members of the YPD that a memorial plaque with his picture was hung in the police gymnasium in his memory. John was only 55 years old.

DET. ARMANDO A. DeBLASSIS #626

APPOINTED: January 1, 1954
RETIRED: January 7, 1977

"Mandy," as he was known to all, was born in Italy, Armando Anthony DeBlassis, on September 19, 1927. However, "Mandy" was automatically a US citizen because his father was a US citizen when Armando was born. The family ultimately moved to Yonkers and Armando attended PS# 18, Benjamin Franklyn Jr. HS, and graduated from Saunders HS. While in school he played baseball, enjoyed boxing, and, as one might expect, spoke Italian fluently.

Toward the end of WWII when he was 18 years old, Mandy joined the Navy on April 14, 1945 serving as a Seaman 1st class in the Battalion Post Office. He received his honorable discharge on July 30, 1946. Following the military he worked for several years as an auto mechanic.

It was on January 1, 1954 that Armando DeBlassis was appointed to the Yonkers Police Department while residing at 11 Huber Place, and following recruit training was assigned to the 2nd precinct earning $3,100 a year.

On May 16, 1960 "Mandy" was appointed a Detective in the Detective Division where he would remain for the remainder of his career. He was assigned to General Assignment investigations for a number of years, but on September 1, 1964, Mandy was selected as one of four detectives to form a new investigative unit; the "Narcotics Unit." Being the senior man in the new unit, whenever new officers were assigned DeBlassis was designated their training officer and "handler" as they conducted undercover narcotic purchases. Later DeBlassis was also a trained expert in auto theft Investigations and as such, he and his partner formed the first Auto Theft Unit within the DD.

Det DeBlassis was a very active detective and as a result he received several departmental awards, including five Commendations and four Certificates of Excellent Police Work. In February of 1966 he and his partner, Det John Skelton, were named "Policemen of the Year" by the Yonkers Exchange Club for their excellent police work over the previous two year period.

On September 24, 1974 he was one of several recipients chosen from across the United States to receive a National Award for excellent police work during a ceremony which was held at the White House by President George Ford. He was even fortunate enough to have had his picture taken with President Ford.

Det DeBlassis retired from the police department on January 7, 1977 to his home on Hillside Ave. His wife, Frances, was also a Yonkers Detective and his cousin was PO Joe Campanaro. A veteran and member of American Legion Post# 1508, Ret Det Armando DeBlassis died on April 10, 1991 at the age of 63 years.

PO LOUIS F. BRUNO #176

APPOINTED: January 1, 1954
DIED: December 9, 1958

Lou Bruno was like every other individual appointed to the YPD in that he expected to have a long and interesting career. Unfortunately that was not to be. And as a result, little is known about the man, Louis Frederick Bruno. He was born in Yonkers on July 18, 1930, and it is believed he attended and graduated from local public schools. He was appointed to the Yonkers Police Dept. on January 1, 1954 from 191 Winifred Avenue, Yonkers. As with the others hired with him, his starting salary was $3,100 a year and he was assigned to patrol duty in the 2nd precinct. He had been working in the 2nd pct. for about five years when tragedy struck. It was on December 9, 1958 during the early morning hours when a fire broke out in Bruno's home. He lived there with his mother and sister and he was off duty at the time. One of the responding 2nd pct. officers, Joe Campanaro, related the following;

"I never had the chance to really know Lou. He filled in when the E-unit was short handed a few times. He was a good cop, always wore his uniform with pride. I remember one hot summer's day Lou was assigned to the E-Unit with me and he wore a tie and long sleeved shirt because he felt that the summer issued short sleeve, open collar shirt looked unprofessional. The material was light blue and it looked like it was made from light blue dungaree material. Of course I went back to my locker and changed so we would be the same. Lou was good-looking, single and had a great gift of gab and got along with everyone in the 2nd Precinct. I was working the night Lou's house caught fire. By the time we arrived the house was fully engulfed and his mother told me that Lou believed his sister was still inside the house and that he ran back inside to find her. Lou suffered severe burns that night as a result of his actions and we thought that his sister had escaped the fire. But she did not. I went to St. John's church on Yonkers Ave. and pick up a parish priest."

Another officer who responded and was assigned the "job," PO Frank Bruno, related the following;

"I was working the late tour partnered with Charles (Joe) Clark in the sector north of Midland Ave up to the City Line. It was about 2:15 AM when we were hitting the box at Kimball Ave when I saw a large glow in the distance. We drove to Winifred Ave and saw 191 Winifred Avenue in flames. Immediately I called in a 10-11 (fire). I found off duty PO Louis Bruno wandering around outside the house in a daze condition with his night clothes nearly burnt off and severe burns about his body arms and face. When questioned Lou was basically incoherent but said he was cold. I gave Lou my overcoat and put Lou in the radio car and took him to Lawrence hospital where they treated him as best they could."

However, off duty officer Louis Bruno died that morning, December 9, 1958, as a result of his severe burns. He was 28 years old.

Lou Bruno's sister also died in the fire. PO Frank Bruno said Lou Bruno, no relation, was a great guy, single with a good sense of humor, good looking, which the ladies all liked. He usually worked the west side of the 2nd pct. over to the Saw Mill Parkway and his partner was Ambrose VanTassel. He had another sister who was a Nun, and two brothers, Frank and Peter. One of them was a Yonkers Firefighter.

PO EDWARD J. RUFFALO #223

APPOINTED: January 1, 1954
RESIGNED: March 17, 1964

Edward John Ruffalo was born in the Town of Tuckahoe on July 1, 1928. A year or so after high school Ed joined the Army in 1947 and was honorably discharged in 1948. He must have remained a member of the active reserve because it was said he was called back to active duty to serve during the Korean War from 1950 through 1952 when, once again, he was honorably discharged. Ed was appointed to the Yonkers Police Department on January 1, 1954 from 18 Orchard Street earning a starting salary of $3,100 and was assigned to the 4th precinct. He was married to PO Leonard Cannavo's sister and it was reported that they had marital problems which ended in divorce. On one occasion he received a gunshot wound to his leg which he said was accidentally inflicted. His marriage had ended and he also decided to end his career with the YPD. On March 17, 1964, PO Edward Ruffalo tendered his resignation from the Yonkers Police Dept. and same was immediately accepted effective that date. Ed Ruffalo died April 23, 2015 at the age of 86.

PO LOUIS J. GASPARRO #85

APPOINTED: April 1, 1954
RESIGNED: October 23, 1959

Louis Joseph Gasparro was born in the City of Yonkers on April 28, 1929. Lou attended and graduated from local public schools. Shortly after school and just 19 years old, Louis joined the Marine Corps on June 28, 1948. He was honorably discharged on February 24, 1950. For the next four years Lou worked as a carpenter and then took the YPD police examination. He was appointed a police officer on April 1, 1954 from 18 Vineyard Avenue, and following some basic training was assigned to the 3rd precinct. His starting salary was $3,100 a year. On June 18, 1954 Gasparro was granted a leave of absence from September 16th to the 30th of 1954. But before the date for the leave to start, it was revoked "in all respects" because Louis Gasparro submitted his resignation from the YPD effective August 31, 1954 and same was accepted. Although no explanation is available, records indicate that Lou was "re-instated" five years later on September 1, 1959, only to again resign a month later on October 23, 1959. Lou's brother was PO Nicholas Gasparro. Former PO Louis Gasparro died on Jan. 22, 2006 in Scottsville, Va. He was 76.

PO ALFRED J. PORTANOVA #425

APPOINTED: April 1, 1954
RETIRED: March 2, 1978

Alfred Joseph Portanova was born in Italy on November 10, 1928, the “birthday” of the US Marine Corps. At age of 10 or 11, just before WW 2, Al was conscripted into the Italian dictator Benito Mussolini's youth "Blackshirts." Shortly thereafter he arrived in US with his parents at age 12 yrs. In Italy he had been in the 3rd grade but due to his inability to speak English he was placed down in the 1st grade in PS# 18 on Lockwood Ave. However, being good in math and history and learning the English language fast, he was advanced to the 5th grade in two years. After PS 18 he graduated from Benjamin Franklin Jr HS and later Yonkers HS.

Al would later become a Naturalized citizen under his father’s papers. At the age of 17 Al joined and served in the US Marine Corps from January 18, 1946 to November 21, 1947 at which time he received his honorable discharge. Portanova attended school to be a Dental Technician but had to drop out due to high tuition costs. That’s when he began working as a laborer in construction. He said he even worked building the Tappan Zee Bridge. Just as it was finished he was called for appointment to the YPD.

Alfred Portanova was appointed to the Yonkers Police Department on April 1, 1954 from 90 Ash Street. His starting salary was $3,100 a year and his first assignment was foot patrol in the 3rd precinct. When he finally was assigned a radio car his partner was PO Charles Jackson. Due to a family relationship through marriage to Democratic City leader Tom Brogan Al was appointed a Detective on June 1, 1960. When he worked as a detective he was nicknamed by the men as "The Undertaker" because he always wore a black suit, black overcoat, and black fedora hat. At one point Brogan was having political difficulties and lost a bit of his political clout. As a result, Portanova and five other detectives, known as Brogans boys, were reassigned back to patrol duty. And so, on May 1, 1963, Al was reassigned to the 4th precinct on patrol with partner PO Guildo Fiorile. Like many, Al was unhappy with the treatment of police officers by the department’s leadership, so he campaigned and was elected the 4th precinct trustee. The beginning of his PBA relationship.

Al was a very physically strong, powerful, aggressive and opinionated officer who was universally respected by the rank and file officers as well as Yonkers politicians. The officers in the 4th precinct saw how he stood up for them and as a result, in 1968, he was elected president of the PBA. On February 14, 1968 Al was reassigned (on paper only) to HQ Command Division, but since he had been elected president of the PBA, he functioned full time in that capacity in an office in headquarters provided by the department.

Due to his well-known temper, when it came to politicians and other opponents of benefits for the police officers in the PBA, he was actually feared by many. And with good reason; Al was a well-built physically fit man. And he would not only not hesitate to pound his fist on a desk to make a point, but he might even throw the desk or a chair across the room. Though offered to be promoted to detective, Al refused saying, for the most part, he predominantly represented the uniform patrol officer, and if being a police officer was good enough for them it was good enough for him.

During his presidency, which lasted right up to his retirement in March 2, 1978, he was so successful in his negotiations with the City of Yonkers that he brought the Yonkers P.D. from the lowest paid department in the area to the highest when he retired. He negotiated for police superior officers as

PO Alfred J. Portanova #425 (cont.)

well as police officers, he won pay differential by rank for all superior officers, won overtime pay for officers attending court and other directed details such as Election Day, etc. he won elimination of female Parking Enforcement Officers, known as "Meter Maids," and created more police officer jobs to do that work. When he learned that the 25 year, half pay, bill actually provided a retiree with only 38% of his salary, Portanova lobbied in Albany and won a change in legislation providing for full 50 % retirement pay if chosen.

On one occasion when students in Gorton HS were near rioting on school grounds police were not allowed on the grounds to take action. The school children were throwing things at the police who surrounded the school and were actually being spit on by the students. But the police officers remained calm. PBA Pres. Portanova met with then City Manager Seymour Scher and suggested that a letter from the Manager complimenting the officers on their restraint would be appreciated and help morale. The Manager stated he wouldn't think of it. He reportedly said, "*If they're professional they can take being spit on.*" Al Portanova reportedly replied, "*Oh; and you're a professional, right*?" And with that it was said that he proceeded to spit at the city manager and then asked, how do you like it, and stormed out of the room. He expected to possibly be fired. Instead the next day the city manager invited him for a drink at the Holiday Inn. Amazing.

On another occasion when a Local 456 Teamster official was trying to obtain the same pay raise as the police had received, he was quoted in a newspaper saying the police were no better than garbage men. When Al read that he called the Teamster official and demanded an apology in the newspaper. The official reportedly began yelling saying do you know who I am? I own every truck that moves in Yonkers. Al quickly responded, *That's true, but I own the streets that they drive on. And as of today no trucks will move in Yonkers without being visited by a police officer*. When just about every truck was summonsed or impounded, and for three days there was virtually no commercial traffic in Yonkers. Teamster officials begged the PBA to allow them to move the trucks about Yonkers without a problem. Only after the apology, Al said. And he got it. Another example of the fierce loyalty and protectiveness he had for his members.

Although Al Portanova retired in 1978 he continued to be seriously respected by almost all who knew him. He always did what he thought was right. He was a man of honor. He was the former president of the PBA, Founder and first president of the NY Metropolitan Police Conference, Chairman of the Tri City Police Conference (Yonkers, Mt Vernon, New Rochelle.), and Vice Pres. of the Interstate Police Conference. His cousin was PO Dominick Borrelli.

A resident of 495 O'Dell Avenue, Ret PO Alfred J. Portanova died on Christmas day, December **25, 2005**. He was 77 years old.

DET. LT. ANTHONY D. RAGAZZO

APPOINTED: April 1, 1954
RETIRED: September 27, 1990

Anthony Ragazzo was born in Yonkers on Dec. 7, 1927, attended local schools and graduated from Saunders HS. Not long after school and the end of WW 2, Tony joined the Army on Feb. 14, 1946. He was assigned as an antitank driver in an antitank company, within the 31st Infantry Division. He was honorably discharged on March 29, 1947. On his application to the YPD Tony listed his current employment as a truck driver.

Anthony Ragazzo received his appointment to the police department on April 1, 1954 while living at 808 Bronx River Rd. His first assignment was to the 2nd precinct and his starting salary was $3,100 a year. On August 20, 1958 he was assigned to the recently re-constituted Emergency Services Unit (ESU), which at the time was named the Accident Investigation Emergency unit. (AIE). While assigned to the 2nd precinct Ragazzo received his emergency and rescue training at Randall's Island in New York City by the NYPD ESU. On November 7, 1966 he was reassigned to the newly opened 1st precinct on E. Grassy Sprain Road, still working in the emergency squad. Ragazzo always remembered a job where the roadway gave way and a worker was buried up to his neck in mud, unable to breath. The walls of the soil were crushing him. Ragazzo and other ESU officers freed the man and he survived. However, he returned to routine patrol duties in the 2nd precinct on May 29, 1967.

Ragazzo was promoted to the rank of Sergeant on May 5, 1972 with a salary of $13,685 a year and was assigned as a patrol supervisor in the North command. Five years later, on Feb. 18, 1977, Sgt Ragazzo was appointed a Detective Sergeant in the Detective Division supervising a squad of detectives and directing their investigations of a variety of major violent crimes which resulted in prosecution and conviction. In 1978 he was awarded the Westchester Rockland Police Honor Award. In March of 1979 following one investigation where a father is thought to have paid and had his two sons murdered, arrests and convictions were secured and Det Sgt Ragazzo was named Police Officer of the Year by the Yonkers Exchange Club, received the Macy newspaper award, the Columbian Association award and departmental recognition.

On August 16, 1984 Tony was promoted to the rank of Lieutenant with a salary of $40,475 and remained in the Detective Division as a Detective Lieutenant serving as the Executive officer. The following year, on Feb. 22, 1985, he was chosen by the commissioner to be the commanding officer of the Special Investigation Unit, often known as the Intelligence Unit, and continued to hold the rank of Detective Lieutenant. In this new position he was responsible for some of the most sensitive and high profile investigations including those involving organized crime individuals as well as dignitary protection details. As such he attended the Secret Service School in Washington DC in 1986.

Tony Ragazzo retired as a Detective Lieutenant on September 27, 1990 and moved to Ft Lauderdale, Fla. But he didn't just relax. He served for several years as an HOA board member of his 400 unit condo complex as well as serving on their landscape committee and being their director of security with 20 security guards. All volunteer work. But Tony loves living in Florida and when not golfing frequents the casino gambling tables for entertainment.

DET. BRENDAN D. MAGNER #631

APPOINTED: April 1, 1954
RETIRED: April 3, 1981

Brendan Magner was born in Yonkers on February 13, 1930, attended Halstead school on North Broadway and Lamartine Avenue, and graduated from Gorton HS. Following school and at 17 years of age, Brendan joined the Army on March 18, 1947 serving as a Corporal and was honorably discharged on August 10, 1948. On an early employment application he listed his occupation as an "Inspector." Brendan was appointed to the YPD on April 1, 1954 from 63 Portland Place and was assigned to the 1st precinct earning a starting salary of $3,100 a year. On December 16, 1958 Magner was reassigned to the Emergency Service Unit which had just recently been re-constituted. It should be noted that, at that time, the unit was named the Accident Investigation Emergency (AIE). That name was on their then unit circular shoulder patch. PO Magner received his specialized emergency training at Randall's Island by NYPD ESU instructors.

On June 1, 1960 Brendan was appointed a Detective in the DD. However, on May 1, 1963, as part of a major reorganization, he was transferred back to patrol in 4th pct. He was returned to the DD on Feb. 26, 1964. Det Magner was transferred to the Bureau of Criminal Identification (BCI) as a crime scene fingerprint and photograph detective. "Buddy" as he was known to family and friends, remained a detective but was transferred to the Intelligence Unit on May 15, 1972 assigned to gambling investigations.

Following his retirement on April 3, 1981 Magner worked as a confidential investigator with the NYS Off Track Betting in the Metro area. Brendan, whose uncle was PO Tom Magner, was a member of PBA, Police Holy Name Society, Police & Fire Retirees Association, Friendly Sons of St Patrick, Past Pres. of the Yonkers Amackassin Club, and former coach for the Yonkers Colts Boys Club football and baseball teams. Ret Det. Brendan Magner died on April 8, 2005 at the age of 75.

PO ROLAND E. HALL #62

APPOINTED: April 1, 1954
RETIRED: July 31, 1986

Born Roland Edwin Hall on June 14, 1922 in Marianna, Pa.. he attended and graduated from Bethlehem HS in Marianna, PA. Not long after his schooling he joined the Navy on October 1, 1942 during WW 2 and served as a Seaman 1st Class until his honorable discharge on December 27, 1945. Following his discharge he worked as an auto assembler at the General Motors plant in Tarrytown. Roland was the brother in law of Sgt Louis Cacace, having married Lou's wife's sister. He became interested in police work and was appointed to the YPD on April 1, 1954 from 25 Marion Avenue. His first assignment was to the 3rd precinct and earned $3,100 a year. On July 17, 1961 he was reassigned to the Traffic Division on foot directing traffic, and on March 21, 1963 was returned to patrol in the 1st pct. Other assignments were, on Nov 9, 1966 to the 3rd pct., on Jan 1, 1971 to the South Command, and on June 23, 1972 to Special Operations Division on parking meter enforcement. Roland retired from SOD on July 31, 1986. He moved with his wife to Manchester, NJ where he later died on February 27, 2007 at the age of 84 years.

PO EDWARD T. SEMAN #217

APPOINTED: December 1, 1954
DIED: August 3, 1968

Edward Thomas Seman was born in Yonkers on May 18, 1928. He attended local public schools and graduated from Saunders high school. Ed, who spoke Czechoslovakian as a second language, listed his early employment as that of a "Battery Inspector." Ed joined the Army on August 19, 1950 during the Korean War and served in the Signal Corps as a Sergeant. He received his honorable discharge on May 19, 1952.

Ed Seman was appointed to the YPD on December 1, 1954 from 72 Chestnut Street. Following his recruit training he was assigned to the 4th precinct earning a salary of $3,100 a year. During his early years with the YPD Ed was an excellent bowler on their bowling team. Twelve years after his first assignment, on November 9, 1966, officer Seman was transferred to the Records Division in headquarters performing clerical duty. Ed's brother Joseph was a Westchester County P.D. police officer, and his son was Sgt Matthew Seman of the Westchester Co. P.D. Without warning, off duty police officer Edward Seman died suddenly at his home on August 3, 1968. He was only 40 years old.

DET. JAMES W. DOWNEY #641

APPOINTED: December 1, 1954
RETIRED: January 6, 1978

James Ward Downey was born in Yonkers on Apr. 4, 1931. He attended local public schools and graduated from Yonkers HS and for a few years he worked as a mechanic. During the Korean War "Jack" joined the Marine Corps on April 23, 1951 serving in Motor Transport. He was discharged under Honorable Conditions on May 25, 1952. Following his discharge he joined the wire lathers union in White Plains. It would be a job he would work at occasionally over the years for extra money. Jim was appointed to the YPD on Dec. 1, 1954 from 239 Oak Street. He was assigned to the 4th pct. earning $3,100 a year and was an original member of 4th pct. Softball Team. As a police officer Jim was very active playing softball on the PBA softball team. In fact in 1960 he managed the PBA Softball team. On May 1, 1958 Jim was reassigned to the Juvenile Aide Bureau. He was very outgoing and friendly with a dark complexion. As a result his friends referred to him as "Spanish Jack." He was appointed a Detective on Feb. 26, 1964 but was returned to patrol on Feb 3, 1969. He would again be appointed a Detective on Oct 26, 1973 and he remained there right up to his retirement on Jan 6, 1978. Being an avid golfer Jim moved to Myrtle Beach, S.C. to play golf but also opened a jewelry store. James W. Downey, whose nephew was PO Michael Buono, developed heart problems and died on May 6, 1997 in Myrtle Beach, SC. He was 66 years old.

PO YASKO GREEN #126

APPOINTED: December 1, 1954
RETIRED: May 12, 1978

Yasko Green was born in Yonkers on Aug. 1, 1930, and attended and graduated from local public schools. In high school he was very athletic and ran on the track team. Yasko joined the Army during the Korean War on April 20, 1951 and was honorably discharged on April 19, 1953. He was appointed to the YPD on Dec. 1, 1954 from 121 Palisade Ave. earning a salary of $3,100 a year. His first assignment was foot patrol in the 1st pct. Yasko worked as a youth investigator in the Juvenile Aide Bureau from Feb. 6, 1963 up to April 27, 1964 when he was returned to patrol in the 1st pct. He was moved to the 3rd pct. on Nov 9, 1966 and the new South Command on Jan 1, 1971. His last assignment was on June 19, 1974 when he returned as a youth investigator in the now Youth & Community Relations Division. After retiring on May 12, 1978 Yasko owned and operated a liquor store on Palisade Ave for several years, and then worked for Liberty Bus Lines, County Limousine Service, and the Academy Bus Co. He was a member of the Terrace City Lodge #1499, Samuel Dow Post # 1017, and the Westchester-Rockland Co. Police Guardians Association. Ret. PO Yasko Green died on April 9, 2001. He was 70 years old.

PO JOHN SILINSKY #157

APPOINTED: December 1, 1954
KILLED: September 30, 1982

John Silinsky was born in the City of Yonkers on September 3, 1924, one of ten children. He attended local public schools and graduated from Saunders high school. John served in the Army during World War II from April 16, 1943 up to his honorable discharge on April 25, 1946. During his service in China, Burma and India, he was assigned as an Army cook and Supply Sergeant. He held the rank of Technical Sergeant. Following his military service John worked miscellaneous jobs until June 30, 1954 when he was hired by the Yonkers Department of Public Works as a sanitation man.

He remained in that position for only five months right up to his appointment to the police department on December 1, 1954. John was hired while residing at 125 Elm St., earned a starting salary of $3,100 a year, and his first assignment, following recruit training, was to the 4th precinct. As a rookie patrolman in the 4th precinct John had the ability to type. As such, he was often assigned as the precinct captain's aide and driver. His nickname by his friends in the 4th precinct was "Yocko."

Twelve years later, on November 6, 1966, officer Silinsky was transferred to patrol duty in the 1st precinct on E. Grassy Sprain Rd. But, on January 1, 1971, when a centralization plan for all four precincts was put into effect, John was reassigned to the South Patrol Command, formerly the old 2nd precinct. Upon his arrival, the precinct captain, John Potanovic, again assigned Silinsky as his aide. During this time John was considered by the captain as a definite asset to the operation of the South

PO John Silinsky #157 (cont.)

patrol command.

On June 17, 1973 John was reassigned to the Headquarters Command Division as an aide to the Deputy Chief of Field Service's Bureau. However, on October 7, 1977, he was reassigned to the aide of the Administrative Services Deputy Chief. While in these positions John was very active in PBA business and for many years was in charge of the PBA's Flower Fund.

Like most police officers John Silinsky held a second job to earn extra money. On September 26, 1982 at approximately 12:15 AM, police officer John Silinsky, off duty and in civilian clothes, was working as a motel clerk at the Deegan Motel located at 3600 Bailey Ave in the Bronx, NYC. It was where he had worked off duty for the previous 15 years and had never carried a gun while working off duty. At one point he walked out of the lobby to check the parking lot. He checked some license numbers on autos in the lot, and was returning to the lobby when he apparently observed two suspicious males in the lot. He did not take refuge inside the motel office, but instead slammed the door closed leading from the parking lot to the lobby. As the two males tried to force entrance to the lobby, Silinsky held the door against them by putting his shoulder to it. As he was bending down to activate a slide bolt on the bottom part of the door, one of the males fired a shot through the hollow core door which struck the officer in the back of the head.

While this was taking place, there was a terrified chambermaid locked in the motel office. Her name was Alice Bryant of 2285 Andrews Ave. in the Bronx and she informed the NYPD investigating detectives that she looked through a window which separates the office from the lobby and saw officer Silinsky lying on the floor in a pool of blood and attempting to write something on the wall by using his finger, dipped in his own blood. The markings he made could not be made out clearly but it is believed he was trying to write the license number of the car used by the suspects. Police Officer John Silinsky was treated by doctors at Montefiore Hospital performing surgery to remove the bullet from his brain, while over 100 off duty Yonkers police officers filled the hospital volunteering to give blood. However, despite the surgeon's best efforts PO Silinsky, having been on life support, died four days later on September 30, 1982, the result of a 9 mm gunshot wound to the head.

The PBA offered a $10,000 reward for any information that led to the arrest and conviction of the shooters. The NYPD assigned a 20 detective task force to investigate the murder. After a lengthy investigation two suspects were arrested and convicted of second-degree murder. Officer John Silinsky, who lived at 20 Gordon Street and had completed 27 years and 10 months as a Yonkers police officer, was just 58 years old. Yonkers Police Commissioner Charles Connolly commented that *"John was probably one of the most respected police officers in our department."*

Officer Silinsky's death was classified a line of duty death, and as such he was given full departmental honors at his funeral. The funeral mass was held at St. Casimir's Church on Nepperhan Avenue. Hundreds of uniformed officers, under the command of Sgt. George Rutledge, filled the street in front of the church in formation to bid farewell to their "brother." Escorting the officers remains to and from the church were 25 motorcycle officers along with the Westchester County Emerald Society Pipe Band. As the casket was carried out following mass, a lone piper, PO John Rinciari, played taps.

Slain PO John Silinsky was survived by a wife, two children, five brothers and four sisters. His nephew Anthony Chiarella would be appointed a Yonkers police officer and rise to the rank of Lieutenant.

PO JOSEPH P. CAMPANARO #192

APPOINTED: December 1, 1954
RETIRED: February 10, 1972

Born Joseph Paul Campanaro in Yonkers on January 25, 1923, Joe attended local public schools and graduated from Saunders HS. While there he was very athletic and played on the school football team. Following graduation Joseph gained employment working for the Western Electric Company in Kearney, NJ.

Joe served in the Navy during WWII from Dec 26, 1942 to Nov 20, 1945 and served aboard an Aircraft Carrier, the USS Tripoli CVE 64 (nicknamed Kaiser Coffins). Their ship did submarine patrol in the Atlantic and was part of a task force that made the first capture of a German sub. After Germany surrendered they were sent to the Pacific and operated out of Pearl Harbor until Japan surrendered. Kaiser Coffins, was a term used by the survivors of torpedoed CVE (Converted Vessel Escort) aircraft carriers. These converted liberty ships had no armament and sank within minutes after being hit. Joe's main duty was to keep the ship on an even keel so that the planes had a level deck to land on. He had to keep a daily log of the fuel oil consumed and also run daily water hardness tests of the Boiler Feed Water to prevent scale buildup in the ships boilers. His rate was Water Tender 1st Class."

After his discharge he returned to Western Electric for a short time, then worked as an auto mechanic, and just prior to the YPD worked in the Brooklyn Navy Yard as a machinist.

Joe was appointed to the YPD from 70 Kettell Avenue on December 1, 1954 and was assigned to the 4th precinct earning $3,100 a year. He was an original member of 4th pct. Softball Team with the logo on the t-shirt of a mug of beer and words "4th Pct." He also enjoyed handball and golf with other police officers. On February 15, 1955 Joe was reassigned from the 4th to the 2nd precinct. A short time later plans were being made to re-instate the Emergency Squad which had been disbanded by the Safety Comm. Patrick O'Hara in the 1940's to save money. Joe was one of many selected to be trained in preparation for this new assignment. From March 17 to the 28th of 1958 Joe and many other designated officers were trained by NYPD ESU instructors at Randall's Island on how to handle various types of emergency situations and operate specialized equipment.

On August 20, 1958 the Emergency Unit was once again established and Joseph Campanaro was assigned to that unit, which at the time was named the Accident Investigation Emergency (AIE). But Joe was not only good with emergencies and rescue work, but during 1958 he was one of only three men recognized as expert shooters in the YPD and competed regularly in revolver competitions.

Four years later, on January 10, 1962, "Campy," as he was most often known, was transferred to the Traffic Division on motorcycle patrol. And in September of 1967 while still in Traffic, Joe was still winning trophy's for excellence for his competition shooting skills. Joe had two cousins in the YPD; PO Ray Campanaro and Det Armando DeBlassis. Joe retired from the YPD on February 10, 1972 and moved to Florida where he remained for 10 years. He worked construction for a while and then worked for Fast Chemicals Products where he was responsible for production, maintenance, and hiring.

When he returned to New York he went to work in West Point where he later retired as a supervisor in the power plant.

PO EDWARD F. COOK PO #154

APPOINTED: December 1, 1954
RETIRED: August 30, 1991

Edward Francis Cook was born in the town of Dobbs Ferry on Jan. 29, 1929. After moving to Yonkers with his family Ed attended Gorton HS and graduated from Saunders HS. Ed joined the U.S. Marine Corps on Jan. 29, 1946. He served in the 1st Marine Div. and was stationed in Ting-Sau, China. During his service Ed held the rank of Staff Sergeant and served as a Motor Vehicle Dispatcher. He was honorably discharged on Mar. 31, 1953. Following his discharge he worked for the Federal Reserve Bank of New York. Edward Cook was appointed to the YPD on Dec. 1, 1954 while living at 42 Cedar Place, his starting salary was $3,100 a year, and he was assigned to the 3rd pct. PO Cook remained in the 3rd until Jan. 18, 1960 when he was moved to the Traffic Division on Parking Enforcement. On Jan. 1, 1971 Ed was assigned to the North Command for a short while. But later that year, on Oct. 19, 1971, he was assigned to the Special Operations Division detailed to Street Cleaning Enforcement. On July 9, 1979 Ed was transferred to the Youth Division and in 1984 was assigned as the department's mail courier. On July 1, 1991 he was assigned to Administrative Services Division as the Court Liaison officer. Ed retired the following month on August 30, 1991, after nearly 37 years of honorable service. Ed's nephew was Ret Lt David (Gross) Lavezzoli. Ret PO Edward F. Cook died on December 15, 2010. He was 81 years old.

PO EDWARD R. BROZMAN #228

APPOINTED: December 1, 1954
DIED: September 5, 1961

Edward Robert Brozman was born in the City of Yonkers on April 22, 1927. At the age of 18 and right out of high school Ed joined the US Marine Corps in September of 1945 right at the end of WW 2. His enlistment was shortened due to the war's end and he was honorably discharged in November of 1946. Prior to the YPD Ed, who had a very friendly and outgoing personality, worked for several years as a Good Humor ice cream salesman. He received his appointment to the Yonkers Police Dept. on December 1, 1954 while living at 51 Van Cortlandt Park Avenue. Following a few weeks of recruit training Brozman was assigned to foot patrol in the 1st precinct and was earning a starting salary of $3,100 a year. He later worked from a radio car with his partner, then PO Owen McClain. Ed was known to his friends by the nickname "Breezy." Ed suffered a heart attack on June 29, 1960 which left him with damage to his heart. Unfortunately, Edward Brozman suffered another heart attack on September 5, 1961 which caused his death. He left behind a wife and two very young female children. PO Edward Brozman was only 34 years old and only three weeks short of his third wedding anniversary.

CAPTAIN GEORGE R. POJER

APPOINTED: December 1, 1954
RETIRED: May 1, 1991

George Rudolph Pojer was born in Yonkers on March 24, 1927 and was raised in the Hollow section of the city. He attended local public schools and graduated from Roosevelt HS. Besides English, George could speak both Polish and Czechoslovakian. His family operated Pojer's Bakery on the corner of Walnut St and Porach St. George, who stood 6' 2" tall worked there as a teenager for many years before serving in the Navy during WW 2 from 1943, up to his honorable discharge on August 23, 1946. While in the Navy he worked as a Radio Operator, Seaman 1st Class, and his duties involved supervising the processing and detention of German Afrika Corps prisoners in a clerical capacity. Following the war he returned to the bakery. He was appointed to the Yonkers Police Department on December 1, 1954 from 434 Walnut Street and his starting salary was $3,100 a year.

Pojer's first assignment was patrol in the 1st pct., then located at 20 Wells Avenue. While there he was a member of the YPD bowling team. Nine years later on February 27, 1963 he was promoted to the rank of Sergeant earning $7,400 and was sent to the 3rd pct. at 36 Radford St. for two months, and then out to the 2nd as a patrol supervisor. While in the 2nd precinct Pojer was designated as the Police Recruit Class coordinator and placed in daily charge of the new recruits as they attended the NYPD Academy in the fall of 1964 and also the recruit class in the Spring of 1965. He was also the recruit instructor for the

Captain George R. Pojer (cont.)

Yonkers recruits during that time period.

In April of 1965 Sgt Pojer completed a 16 week Youth Division Training Course at the NYPD Police Academy. And four months later, on August 20, 1965, Sgt. Pojer was advanced to Detective Sergeant and assigned to the Detective Division as a squad sergeant with a new salary of $8,820. His duties were serving as a general assignment detective supervisor. On August 29, 1969 he was promoted to the rank of police Lieutenant and was allowed to remain in the DD as a detective lieutenant assigned as the Executive Officer and earning $14,050. In January of 1972, while in the D.D., Lieutenant Pojer requested and was selected to attend the prestigious FBI National Academy in Quantico, Va. from January to March of 1972. Lt Pojer remained in the D.D. until August 24, 1973 when he was promoted to the rank of Captain earning $19,800 and was reassigned to the Youth Services and Community Relations Division as the commanding officer.

On January 6, 1975 Capt. Pojer was assigned as the commanding officer of the Training Division, but a year later, on February 16, 1976, he was returned as the CO of the Youth Services and Community Relations Division. (Youth Division.) Three years later, on January 19, 1979, George was advanced to the appointed position of Deputy Chief and placed in overall command of the Investigational Services Bureau. He filled a vacancy created by the reduction in rank of Chief Farrington back to Captain. Pojer's salary as a Deputy Chief was $26,536 a year. But in true political fashion brought to bear by the Democratic City Leader, Chief Pojer was returned to the civil service rank of Captain on May 31, 1985, and replaced by a friend of those in political power. Pojer was then assigned to the 1st precinct located at 730 East Grassy Sprain Road. In 1990, while still the CO of the 1st precinct, Capt. Pojer, along with Capt. George Rutledge, organized a city wide Disorder Control Task Force which trained over 100 police personnel in riot control tactics.

The following year, on May 1, 1991, Capt. George Pojer retired from the police department. In retirement you could often see George at Friendly's Rest. on Tuckahoe Rd with his wife. George was a dedicated stamp collector and that occupied much of his retirement years. He was also an avid gin player, a lover of classical music, was an avid model train enthusiast and loved to play bingo and golf. He was truly a gentleman, an all-around nice guy and was what some would call a deep thinker.

I think it would be accurate to say that there would be very few who would have a bad thing to say about George Pojer. Ret. Capt. George Pojer died on Oct. 3, 2006. He was 79 years old.

PO FREDERICK J. GUILFOYLE #50

APPOINTED: December 1, 1954
RETIRED: March 21, 1986

Frederick Guilfoyle was born on January 8, 1924 in Yonkers where he attended public schools and attended Gorton HS and Saunders HS. As a young man he listed his occupation as a grocery clerk and lived at 37 Hawthorne Avenue. Fred joined the US Army Air Corps on June 2, 1942 during the early days of WW-II. He served as a Staff Sergeant in the 329th ARMU Air Force Base. His MOS was Radio Operator/ Mechanic Gunner. Among the locations he saw action was in Sicily and Tunisia. For his service he awarded several medals including two combat stars. He was honorably discharged on June 2, 1945 and was a former member of the Veterans post 1666. Fred was appointed a Yonkers police officer on Dec. 1, 1954 with a salary of $3,100 a year. Following two weeks of training on December 16, 1954, he was assigned to the 4th precinct. On Jan. 24, 1966 he was transferred to the Youth Division as a youth investigator, but two months later he was returned to patrol in the 4th pct. On Nov. 7, 1966 he was re-assigned to the newly opened 1st precinct where he remained until Jan 1, 1971 when the patrol commands were put in effect and he was assigned to the North Command. Fred had an easy going personality and was a real gentleman. On June 17, 1975 he was assigned to the Criminal Identification Unit (CIU), and then to the Warrant Squad, from which he later retired on Mar. 21, 1986. Ret PO Frederick Guilfoyle died April 19, 2009. He was 85 years old.

PO ROBERT F. LENNON #208

APPOINTED: December 1, 1954
RESIGNED: June 3, 1964

Robert Lennon was born in Yonkers on Aug. 9, 1928. He attended local public schools but apparently left on Nov 27, 1945 to join the Army Air Corps of Engineers. On May 26, 1947, Bob Lennon received his honorable discharge. However, he apparently had remained in the active reserve because he was again called to active duty to serve during the Korean War from June 1, 1951 to his discharge on Dec 19, 1952. On Dec 1, 1954 Lennon was appointed to the YPD from 22 Mulford Gardens. His first assignment was in the 4th pct. with a salary of $3,100 a year. After only 7 months Lennon was detailed for a short time to plainclothes duty in the D.D. on gambling investigations. On Dec 1, 1956, he was reassigned from the 1st to the Traffic Division on 3 wheel motorcycle patrol writing meter summonses. As a second job Bob was a self-employed insurance salesman and decided he could make more money doing that full-time. He resigned from the YPD on June 3, 1964. In January 1967 he was appointed a deputy sheriff for Westchester County and was assigned as a corrections officer on October 1, 1969. Bob's nephew was PO William Howell. Former PO Robert Lennon died January 8, 1997 in Beacon NY at the age of 68 years.

CAPTAIN GEORGE MEIKLE

APPOINTED: December 1, 1954
RETIRED: February 1, 1983

George Meikle was born in the City of Yonkers on April 2, 1924. He attended local public schools and graduated from Gorton High School. After working a variety of miscellaneous jobs, on January 15, 1943 Meikle joined the Army Signal Corps during WW 2. As a PFC he was assigned to Company B, 93rd Signal Battalion, serving in Europe in the Ardennes, Central Europe, France, and the Rhineland. Meikle received his honorable discharge on January 1, 1946.

Following his military service George worked at several jobs including as a sworn police officer in Washington, DC. Following his move back to Yonkers he was appointed a Yonkers police officer on December 1, 1954. Following recruit training he was assigned to foot patrol duty in the 4th precinct earning $3,100 a year. George remained in the 4th precinct for twelve years, until March 25, 1966, when he was promoted to the rank of Sergeant and was re-assigned to the 3rd precinct as a patrol supervisor. But he continued his climb up the ranks by being promoted to the rank of Lieutenant three years later on December 19, 1969. His salary rose to $13,300 a year and was allowed to remain in the 3rd precinct but performing the duties of a desk lieutenant.

Effective January 1, 1971 the department centralized the precinct concept by closing the 3rd and

Captain George Meikle (cont.)

1st precinct locations and consolidating them into the remaining two precincts. The 2nd was renamed the South Patrol Command and the 4th was renamed the North Patrol Command. It was then that large scale transfers occurred and Lt Meikle was transferred to the South Command as a desk officer. The following year, on April 24, 1972, Meikle was reassigned to the Inspectional Services Division. His responsibilities in this job were city wide patrol overseeing the discipline and effectiveness of the patrol operation and to report to the chief on a daily basis.

In March of 1973 the traditional position of a desk lieutenant behind the desk was discontinued and the desk officer position was now assigned to "desk sergeants." As such, when Lt Meikle was transferred to the North Command on March 12, 1973, he performed in the newly created position of precinct "Executive Officer." The "Exec" was second in command of the precinct.

Barely becoming comfortable in his new position, just over a year later, Meikle was promoted to the rank of Captain on July 26, 1974. His salary was now $21,588 and he was assigned to work on patrol in uniform as the citywide patrol captain. Up to this point captains never wore a uniform unless it was for ceremonial purposes. A business suit was the dress attire for all other captains.

This uniform duty lasted for only six months, for on January 6, 1975 Captain Meikle was reassigned to the Youth Services Division as its commanding officer. In this capacity he had the responsibility for the operation of youth crime investigations as well as the Police Athletic League and all the activities that unit provided to the youth of the city. On September 13, 1982 Capt. Meikle was once again returned to patrol duty in the Inspections Unit and once again wearing his uniform.

Being sent back on patrol in uniform as a captain may only be coincidental to the fact that five months later Capt. Meikle retired from the police department on February 1, 1983.

PO JOHN P. REINBERGER #227

APPOINTED: December 1, 1954
RETIRED: August 9, 1985

John Philip Reinberger was born in Yonkers on August 14, 1921. He graduated from Holy Eucharist Elementary Catholic School and later graduated from Yonkers High School where he was an excellent ball player and catcher. For a while after school "Jack," as he preferred to be called, worked in the Alexander Smith Carpet Shop. During WW 2 Jack joined the Army on September 25, 1942 and served as a platoon sergeant in Panama and in the Philippines. He was honorably discharged on October 31, 1945 and would never talk about his military service. He then went back to work with the Alexander Smith Carpet Co. as a Mill worker.

Jack was appointed to the Yonkers Police Dept. on December 1, 1954 from 5-73 Schroeder Street, earning a starting salary of $3,100 a year. After two weeks training, on December 16, 1954, he was assigned to the 4th precinct. Two years later, on December 1, 1956, Reinberger was reassigned from the 4th to the Traffic Division on foot directing vehicular traffic. Then, on August 14, 1959, Jack was assigned to two wheel motorcycle patrol throughout the city. He would spend the rest of his career on motorcycle patrol. He was reportedly a legend among other new traffic officers and was an excellent motorcycle cop. However, his personal or people skills were a bit lacking. He was very hardnosed and abrasive when dealing with a motorist he pulled over. But he was the same with everyone. He was not a warm and fuzzy kind of guy. If he knew and respected you, OK. If not, he had no time to waste on those he deemed to be fools.

No question, Jack was a tough cop, but a good cop. He was considered, during his time, to be the best at testifying at traffic trials. It was even said he never lost a traffic trial prosecution. In fact he was frequently used as an instructor in the police academy training recruits on how to prepare a case for traffic court prosecution, which had to be prosecuted by the police officers themselves.

Jack Reinberger was very active in the PBA playing for many years on their softball team, even after he retired. He received a plaque from the PBA for playing ball for 30years. Jack rode his police Harley Davidson motorcycle on patrol right up to his mandatory retirement due to age on August 9, 1985. And he kept playing ball with the PBA until he was 70.

In 1995 Jack received by-pass heart surgery but it didn't slow him down. During his later retirement years he loved to gamble at Atlantic City casinos on slot machines. He was a member of the Westchester County Police Emerald Society and the Yonkers Police Holy Name Society.

A resident of 155 Livingston Avenue, Jack, who was a diabetic, and known by his "real close" friends as "Pappy," suffered a stroke and died on July 4, 2005 at the age of 83 years.

PO THEODORE E. WESTERVELT #22

APPOINTED: December 1, 1954
RETIRED: June 1, 1979

Theodore Edward Westervelt was born on November 26, 1932 in Mt Vernon, NY. At one point his family moved to Yonkers where he attended public schools, including Gorton HS. Right out of school Ted joined the Marine Corps on August 7, 1950 serving during the Korean War with the 2nd Armored Amphibious Battalion in the 3rd Marine Division. He was honorably discharged as a Corporal on February 22, 1952.

For two years he earned his living as a truck driver, but on December 1, 1954 he was appointed to the Yonkers Police Department from 307 Walnut St. His first assignment was to patrol in the 2nd precinct and his starting salary was $3,100 a year. On August 20, 1958 Ted was assigned to the newly reconstituted Emergency Services Unit, known then as the Accident Investigation Emergency, working out of the 2nd precinct at 441 Central Avenue. He received his emergency rescue training at the NYPD police school of instruction at Randall's Island in New York City.

On April 24, 1964 Public Safety Commissioner Daniel F. McMahon publicly commended police officer Westervelt for his efforts in trying to save a young Cub Scout who had drowned in the Saw Mill River several days earlier. He advised that immediately after Westervelt's arrival on the scene, some 75 feet north of the O'Dell Ave. bridge, he took off his gun belt and heavy exterior clothing and entered the river in an attempt to retrieve the body of a 10 year old boy.

Ted was later transferred to the Traffic Division on April 5, 1965 and assigned to two wheel motorcycle patrol duty. It was an assignment that he loved and he would remain there right up to his retirement on June 1, 1979. A resident of Mahopac, NY, after retiring Ted started his own auto parts repair business along with his son. But Ted also spent some time at his winter home in Myrtle Beach, SC along with his wife Elaine, who was also a retired Yonkers police officer.

DET. LT. HAROLD A. NASCE

APPOINTED: December 1, 1954
DIED: January 15, 1984

Harold Andrew Nasce was born in the city of Yonkers on March 12, 1927. It was reported that he grew up in the area of Claredon Avenue and Yonkers Avenue. Harry, as he was known, attended local public schools including Saunders high school. However, World War II was in progress and Harry wanted to get into the action. He quit school after the 10th grade and joined the Army on March 22, 1945 during the tail end of the war. Records indicate he served as a cook with the rank of PFC and was honorably discharged on November 26, 1946.

In his early years he worked for a short time for General Motors plant in Tarrytown on the assembly line. Four years following his discharge from the Army and around the time of the Korean War, Harry joined the Marine Corps on August 20, 1950 serving as part of the occupation and rebuilding of Japan after World War II. His daughter reported that he later achieved the rank of Master Sergeant while serving in Camp Lejeune. He received his second honorable discharge, this time from the Marine Corps., on August 30, 1951. While serving in the military Nasce earned his GED diploma.

Harry never really was involved with sports but he was a bodybuilder as a young man and because of his strength he was nicked named "Harry The Horse." At that time it was said that he had an 18 inch neck and a 33 inch waist. Prior to the YPD Harry listed his occupation as a carpenters helper.

Harry Nasce was appointed to the Yonkers Police Department on December 1, 1954 while residing at 344 Glen Hill Ave. Following recruit training he was assigned to patrol duty in the 1st precinct earning a starting salary of $3100 a year. Twelve years later, on February 26, 1964, Harry was appointed a Detective in the Detective Division. Five years later, on February 3, 1969, Detective Nasce was returned to uniform patrol duty in the 4th precinct due to his high position on the sergeants promotion list.

On August 29, 1969 officer Nasce was promoted to the rank of Sergeant earning a salary of $11,600 a year and he was reassigned to the 1st precinct as a patrol supervisor. But this assignment only lasted 3 months, for on November 28, 1969, Sgt. Nasce was appointed a Detective Sergeant and he was reassigned back to the Detective Division.

Sgt. Nasce was promoted to the rank of Lieutenant on April 24, 1972, earning a new salary of $15,698 a year and because of his experience was allowed to remain in the Detective Division as a Detective Lieutenant. And this would be his last assignment. Detective Lt. Nasce was a tough boss to work for because he insisted on having the job done right, and quite possibly because of his military background. Harry was a very active member of the Yonkers police Holy Name Society. His wife was Angela Nasce who worked as a civilian in the Police Commissioner's office.

On January 15, 1984, and while off duty and walking along Willow Street, Detective Lieutenant Harry Nasce suffered a sudden heart attack and died right where he fell. He was 56 years old.

LT. ARTHUR M. HOLSBORG

APPOINTED: July 16, 1955
RETIRED: January 7, 1977

"Artie" was born Arthur Milton Holsborg on May 5, 1929 in Pittsfield, Mass. His family moved to Yonkers when he was a youth, he attended local public schools and graduated from Yonkers HS. Right out of high school, and only 17 years old, Arthur joined the Army on May 7, 1946, right as WW-2 was ending. He served in Germany with the Military Police with the rank of Corporal. He received his honorable discharge on August 7, 1947.

Arthur attended school for, and was later licensed as, a Dental Technician. He also was trained and certified by the FCC as a licensed Telephone Operator. And yet in his desire to continue his education Artie also attended the City College of NY majoring in Police Science, and the Baruch School of Administration. He also earned his Master's degree from Fordham University. On his police application Arthur Holsborg listed his occupation as a salesman.

Holsborg was appointed to the Yonkers Police Dept. on July 16, 1955 earning a starting salary of $3,600 a year and his first assignment following recruit training was foot patrol in the 1st precinct at 20 Wells Avenue. Three years later, on August 20, 1958, when the previously disbanded Emergency Unit was re-established, Holsborg was assigned to the Emergency Unit working out of the 1st precinct. However, one year later, on August 14, 1959, Arthur was reassigned to the Traffic Division writing meter violation summonses.

On February 27, 1963 Arthur was promoted to the rank of Sergeant while living at 40 Caryl Avenue, and had his salary raised to $7,400 a year. And, he was allowed to remain in the Traffic Division as a patrol supervisor. It was there that he attended a three week course of instruction at the Northwestern Traffic Institute in Evanston, Illinois from March 8th to the 26th of 1965. One of the duties Arthur had while in Traffic was to serve as the police department's safety officer. In this capacity he acted as a liaison to the school children teaching bicycle and other forms of safety. An intelligent and well-spoken man Arthur had no trouble speaking before large groups and was very effective in getting his message across.

Sgt. Holsborg was transferred to the Planning and Training Division on January 24, 1966. The chief of police recognized that Holsborg had excellent administrative skills and wanted to put them to good use by assigning Arthur to working on budget issues, training initiatives, and formulating plans of operation that might better serve the YPD. And he was apparently very good at his assigned duties. For, when he was promoted to the rank of Lieutenant on September 15, 1972, the chief allowed him to remain in his same administrative assignment right up to his retirement on January 7, 1977. Five years later his son Michael was appointed a Yonkers police officer.

PO EDWARD R. BARICKO #115

APPOINTED: December 16, 1954
RETIRED: June 30, 1972

Edward Baricko was born in Yonkers on January 12, 1923. He attended local public schools and graduated from Gorton HS. On December 8, 1942 Ed enlisted in the Army serving overseas four years manning the large artillery guns of the 456th Battalion. Operating as an offensive segment of Gen. Patton's Third Army, Ed's outfit participated in battles in France, Germany and Belgium, and Ed was wounded by enemy fire during the Battle of the Bulge. For the combat operations he participated in Ed earned five battle stars and the Purple Heart, among other campaign medals. He was honorably discharged as a Corporal on October 29, 1945. Before the YPD Ed worked for the Alexander Smith Carpet Mills in Yonkers. He was appointed to the police department on December 16, 1954 from 16 Madison Avenue. His first assignment was foot patrol in the 1st precinct where he earned $3,100 a year. Ed was a quiet guy who always did his job and respected authority. On November 7, 1966 Ed was reassigned to the 4th precinct where he remained right up to his retirement, after 18 years, on June 30, 1972. He was able to retire two years early by purchasing two years and eight months military time, which was applied to his pensionable years of service. After retirement he worked as a Financial Expediter for Chase Manhattan Bank. Formerly a resident of 26 Bennett Avenue, Ed Baricko moved to Hyde Park, NY where he would later die on July 29, 2013.

PO MICHAEL J. CHRISTOPHER #131

APPOINTED: July 16, 1955
RETIRED: May 31, 1974

Michael Joseph Christopher was born in the City of Yonkers on October 21, 1928. He attended local public schools, including Roosevelt HS and Gorton HS. Right after the end of WW 2 and following Mike's 17th birthday, he joined the Army Air Corps. on November 13, 1945. During his enlistment Mike served as a Radio Operator up to his honorable discharge on November 10, 1948. Following his military service Mike worked for several years as a truck driver but decided the police department had much more job security. He received his police appointment on July 16, 1955 while living at 10 Cottage Place Gardens. His starting salary was $3,600 a year and following recruit training his first assignment was to foot patrol in the 1st precinct. Eleven years later, on November 9, 1966, he was reassigned to the 4th precinct where he would remain on patrol duty right up to his retirement on May 31, 1974.

PO JAMES A. FARRAR #91

APPOINTED: July 16, 1955
RESIGNED: March 20, 1962

James Arthur Farrar was born in New York City on December 7, 1923. Following his schooling Farrar joined the Navy during WW 2 on December 7, 1942 and was honorably discharged on March 4, 1946. Little is known about Farrar but it is believed he worked for the Post Office after the military. Prior to his police appointment he worked as a Dog Catcher for the City of Yonkers. His uniform was the same as a police officer except for the shield and hat wreath. He also wore "putties." He was appointed to the Yonkers Police Dept. on July 16, 1955 earning $3,600 a year and was assigned to the 2nd precinct on Central Avenue. When he rode, his partner was PO Norman Fitzgerald and when he walked he had post #1, the area of Yonkers Avenue and Central Avenue or post 14, Tuckahoe Rd. and Central Ave. Although not authorized it was said that on occasion Farrar wore his old putties with his police uniform on duty. Ret Capt. Potanovic said Farrar was a tough cop who was not afraid of anything and was particularly adept at handling wild animals. At one point Farrar was brought up on departmental charges and suspended on March 8, 1962. He never went to trial because he resigned from the department on March 20, 1962. Former PO James A. Farrar died in January of 1992 in Saratoga N.Y. at the age of 68 years.

PO ALBERT E. HIGGINS #204

APPOINTED: July 16, 1955
DIED: February 22, 1983

Albert Edward Higgins was born in Yonkers on April 5, 1928. He attended local public schools and graduated from Sacred Heart high school. After holding a few miscellaneous jobs, "Albie" joined the Army on July 15, 1948 and served as a Corporal right up to his honorable discharge on Feb. 8, 1951. Following his military service Al worked as a letter carrier for the Post Office. Albert Higgins was appointed to the Yonkers Police Department on July 16, 1955 from 216 Voss Ave. His starting salary at the time was $3,600 a year and his first assignment was to the 1st precinct on foot patrol. He worked in the 1st pct. for nearly 11 years when, on Jan. 24, 1966 he was transferred to the Communications Division as a call taker and radio dispatcher. Al was an introvert by nature and kept mostly to himself. He was very quiet, soft-spoken and yet very high strung and a worrier. He seemed always nervous and wherever he worked he would pace back and forth. On June 20, 1979 he was reassigned from Communications to the N/E Patrol Command working as a desk officer. During this time he kept to himself and his moods seemed to grow darker. It should be noted that his work performance was very good. Unfortunately, and suddenly Al Higgins was found deceased on Feb. 22, 1983. He was 54 years old.

PO ARISTEDE V. MASTRODDI #234

APPOINTED: July 16, 1955
RETIRED: May 4, 1973

Born Aristide Vincent Mastroddi on September 10, 1925 in Taglicozzo Italy, “Rip or Rippy,” as he was to be known by everyone, immigrated to Yonkers in 1929 with his family at the age of four. Rip attended local public schools and graduated from Saunders HS. Right out of high school Mastroddi joined the Army Air Corps during WW 2 on July 23, 1943. He served in the Air Corps as a Master Staff Sergeant as a crew member on Bombers as an aerial gunner and photographer. Following the war he was honorably discharged on Dec. 11, 1945. Rip then worked as a laborer in the Hod Carriers Union. But, apparently the military wasn’t finished with him. On Feb. 8, 1949 Mastroddi was back in the Air Force. He served during the Korean War as an aerial gunner and was assigned to the Strategic Air Command from 1949 to 1953. He received his second honorable discharge on Feb. 8, 1953.

On July 16, 1955 Aristide Mastroddi was appointed to the YPD earning a starting salary of $3,600 a year and was assigned to the 1st precinct. On Feb. 1, 1960 he was detailed to Emergency Service Unit training with the NYPD. When he returned he was assigned to ESU, then named Accident Investigation Emergency (AIE) with his partner PO Ben Ermini. While off duty Rip always worked construction jobs for extra money. On April 5, 1965, he was given the opportunity to be assigned to the Traffic Division’s motorcycle unit and said yes.

Mastroddi worked traffic in the motorcycle unit of the Traffic Division for the next eight years, right up to his retirement from the YPD on May 4, 1973. He retired with 18 years’ service because he purchased two years military service time from the pension system. "Rip" always loved motorcycles and when his children were little he taught them all to ride. He also enjoyed boating. When he retired he worked with his son Robert as a special investigator with Material Damage Adjustment Corp. of Somerset, NJ. A member of the PBA, Police Holy Name Society, Police and Fire Retirees Assoc, and the Yonkers VFW, Ret. PO Aristide Mastroddi died on September 16, 1998 at the age of 73.

PO HOWARD R. EVANS #139

APPOINTED: July 16, 1955
RETIRED: April 14, 1988

Howard Ross Evans was born in the City of Yonkers on June 14, 1932. He grew up in southwest Yonkers near Riverdale Avenue and Post Street and even then, as it was later, he was always known as "Howie." Following his high school graduation Howard joined the Naval Reserve in 1950 and was activated during the Korean War in 1951. Howie served as a Seabee in the 7th Mobile Construction Battalion, known as the "MCB Seven." He served on active duty from March 12, 1951 up to his honorable discharge on January 9, 1953. During his military time he served in Rhode Island to open a Seabee Camp which closed after WW 2, to French Morocco, to Guantanamo Bay Cuba, and was then discharged.

Following his military service Evans worked as a union carpenter for the next two years. Evans was appointed to the police department on July 16, 1955 earning $3,600 a year and his first assignment was to foot patrol in the 3rd precinct. At that time there were 3 radio cars in the 3rd precinct. But only one was used for patrol purposes. Of the other two, one was for the sergeant's use and the other was assigned to the precinct captain. On August 20, 1958 Evans was selected and assigned to the newly reorganized Emergency Service Unit. Actually, at that time it was known as the Accident Investigation Emergency Unit. Years later the name would be changed to the Emergency Service Unit. Evans was sent to the NYPD school at Randall's Island for training in emergency rescue and accident investigation. The very first emergency unit patch was light blue and white in color, round, and it had on it the markings "AIE" "Accident Investigation Emergency."

In the early 1960's when the Wells Avenue headquarters was closed and moved to 10 St. Casimir Ave, the entire HQ administrative operation was to be located on the 4th floor. PO Evans along with PO Mike Slattery was detailed to construct all the needed office space, since they were both previously in the building trade. In fact, when the Mini Pct. named the Community Patrol Unit "CPU" was opened on 250 Warburton Avenue in 1974, Evans did all the carpentry work to make the necessary offices. During the 1960's Howie was very active in the PBA and served two terms as their Vice President. But he later lost a run for president to Al Portanova.

PO Evans remained assigned to ESU up to October 25, 1973 when he was reassigned to HQ for a short time and then moved into the Warrant Squad where he remained right up to his retirement on April 14, 1988. Following retirement Evans worked in NYC for the NY Catholic Archdiocese as a Contracting Consultant overseeing and bidding out all jobs over $20,000. He worked there for 12 years. During this time, and sometime in the 1990's while building a deck for a relative, he fell off and shattered his entire pelvis. Pelvic reconstruction was not completely successful and he was never without pain or able to walk again without assistance. Then, in 2001 Evans was diagnosed with Liver cancer. He readily admitted he couldn't stand the pain from his surgical repair and the illness from his liver. Ret PO Howard Evans, a longtime member of the Yonkers Elks Club, was found dead in his home on September 20, 2002. He was 70 years old.

PO ARTHUR E. ENGEL #209

APPOINTED: July 16, 1955
RETIRED: June 24, 1977

Arthur Earl Engel was born in the City of Yonkers on August 5, 1925. He attended local public schools and graduated from Saunders High School. Directly after graduation, and only 18 years of age, Arthur decided to join the Navy during WW 2 on July 8, 1943. During his enlistment he served as a "Coxswain" and aviation mechanic. Artie received his honorable discharge on August 4, 1947. He then obtained employment as a shipping clerk until called by the YPD. Engel was appointed to the police department on July 16, 1955 from 75 Catskill Avenue. His starting salary was $3,600 a year and his first assignment was foot patrol in the 2nd precinct. Eleven years later on November 7, 1966 Engel was reassigned to patrol duty in the brand new 1st precinct at 730 E. Grassy Sprain Road. On January 1, 1971 following the centralization plan which eliminated two precincts and changed the names of the two that remained, Artie was transferred to the old 4th precinct which had been renamed the North Command. He would remain working there on parol right up to his retirement on June 24, 1977. Although he was in the 25 year retirement plan, PO Engel, a very low key personality type, retired after only 22 years because he purchased three years military time from the pension system.

PO PASQUALE G. TRONCONE #213

APPOINTED: October 1, 1955
RETIRED: March 11, 1976

Pasquale George Troncone was born in Mt. Vernon NY on July 5, 1928. After his formal education, and at the age of 17, Patsy, as he was known, joined the Navy on September 10, 1945 right at the end of WW 2. He received his honorable discharge on August 20, 1946 having served less than a year because the war had ended. Troncone earned a living for several years as an auto driving instructor. Pasquale Troncone was appointed to the YPD on October 1, 1955 from 13 Nepperhan Avenue. His salary was $3,600 a year and his first assignment was patrol in the 1st precinct at 20 Wells Avenue. A few years later on December 1, 1958 he was reassigned to duty in the 2nd precinct at 441 Central Park Ave. Patsy was a tough street cop for the beginning of his career but he began having health difficulties. As a result he was assigned to work as a mechanic in the Police Repair Shop on November 9, 1966. He remained there until August 20, 1974 when he was reassigned to the South Patrol Command. But it is believed that he was actually on sick leave most of this time and Troncone retired while on sick leave on March 11, 1976. Following his retirement Patsy worked driving a taxi in NYC and at one point was severely burned in a motor vehicle accident. Ret PO Pasquale Troncone died on February 15, 1993 in the Bronx, NY. He was 64 years old.

PO EUGENE DUGAN #89

APPOINTED: October 1, 1955
DIED: April 24, 1968

"Gene" Dugan was born in Yonkers on June 3, 1925. He attended local public schools and graduated from Saunders HS. World War 2 was raging so when he finished school he joined the Army on April 30, 1943 serving in the Transportation Corps. He received his honorable discharge on Jan. 16, 1946. He worked a number of different jobs up to 1954 when he was appointed to the Yonkers Fire Dept. He had also taken the police test and after one year as a firefighter he was called for appointment to the YPD. He resigned from the YFD and was appointed a police officer on October 1, 1955 while residing at 5 Cottage Place Gardens. Following his recruit training he was assigned to the 3rd pct. on foot patrol earning $3,600 a year. When the department decided to re-establish the previously abolished Emergency Services Unit, Dugan was among those chosen to be trained by the NYPD ESU instructors at Randall's Island in NYC. On August 20, 1958 the Yonkers ESU unit became operational and Dugan was assigned working from the 1st precinct. On November 9, 1966 he remained in ESU but worked out of the 4th precinct. One of Gene's brothers, Tom, was a Detective and another, Joe, was a YFD lieutenant. On April 24, 1968, while off duty at his home, PO Eugene Dugan unexpectedly suffered a massive heart attack and died at the age of 42 years.

PO LEWIS B. SHAPIRO #49

APPOINTED: October 1, 1955
RETIRED: June 10, 1976

Lewis Buddy Shapiro was born in Brooklyn NY on Feb. 27, 1931. Following his schooling "Buddy," as he was always known, joined the Navy on Feb 27, 1947. And if the record is correct he was only 16 years old. He was honorably discharged on October 13, 1950. Buddy worked a number of jobs but primarily was a truck driver. However, he was appointed to the Yonkers Police Dept. on October 1, 1955 while residing at 290 Warburton Avenue. Following recruit training he was assigned to the 1st precinct on foot patrol earning $3,600 a year. In the 1950's good police assignments were decided by politicians, and Buddy likely knew one. About a year after his appointment he was assigned to the Traffic Division on two wheel motorcycle patrol. On August 17, 1960 he was returned to patrol in the 1st and apparently wasn't very happy about it because, three months later, on November 30, 1960 he resigned from the YPD. However, after 8 months he requested reinstatement and it was granted effective July 1, 1961 and he returned to the 1st pct. But, on March 28, 1966 he was returned to motorcycle duty where he remained up to his retirement on June 10, 1976. Ret PO Lewis Buddy Shapiro died on August 3, 2004 at the age of 73 years.

POLICE COMMISSIONER JOSEPH V. FERNANDES

APPOINTED: October 1, 1955
RETIRED: March 15, 1990.

Joseph V. Fernandes was born in the City of Yonkers on April 15, 1932 while his family lived at 112 Ashburton Avenue. But Joe grew up as a youth living at 143 Nepperhan Ave. where he attended St. Casimir's Roman Catholic elementary school and then attended Sacred Heart High School and graduated with honors. During his high school tenure he participated in various sports opportunities but favored basketball. He was even granted a full scholarship to attend the Georgetown University School of Foreign Service in Washington D.C. Unfortunately, during his first year he had to leave the University and return to Yonkers due to a family medical crisis. But Joe went on to graduate from John Jay College of Criminal Justice in New York City with an Associate's and a Bachelor's Degree, both in criminal justice.

Being of Portuguese heritage Joseph quite naturally was able to speak Portuguese but was also able to speak French as well. He was Joe to almost everyone but was called "Buddy" by his family members. Prior to the police department Joe was employed by a Yonkers Electronics firm as a Quality Control Tester. Joe Fernandes joined the NY National Guard in January of 1952 serving as an MP and upon completion of his military obligation, was honorably discharged in 1958.

Joseph V. Fernandes was appointed to the Yonkers Police Department on October 1, 1955 while

Police Commissioner Joseph V. Fernandes (cont.)

residing at 143 Nepperhan Avenue. Upon completion of his basic police recruit training probationary Patrolman Joseph Fernandes was assigned to foot patrol duty in the 1st precinct earning a starting salary of $3,600 a year. Less than nine months later, on July 16, 1956, Fernandes was transferred to the Traffic Division assigned to parking meter enforcement on a three wheel motorcycle.

Eight years later, February 26, 1964, Joe was appointed a Detective assigned to the Detective Division in a general assignment investigation squad. Joe Fernandes was promoted to the rank of Sergeant on February 11, 1966 earning the salary of $8,165 a year and was allowed to remain in the D.D. as a Detective Sergeant supervising a squad of detectives. Although Sgt. Fernandes was transferred out of the D.D. to the 2nd precinct on January 13, 1967, he was returned to the D.D. as a Det. Sergeant on September 26, 1968. However, once again Sgt. Fernandes was transferred out of the D.D. to the 2nd precinct as a patrol supervisor on September 5, 1969.

Sgt. Fernandes was promoted to the rank of Lieutenant on November 28, 1969 earning $13,300 a year and subsequently transferred to the 1st precinct at 10 St. Casimir Ave. assigned as a precinct desk officer. This lasted only one month when, on December 13, 1969, Lt. Fernandes was reassigned as a desk officer in the 2nd precinct.

Lt Fernandes had developed an excellent reputation, not only as an efficient officer, but a man with integrity and who could be trusted with delicate and sensitive investigations. As a result, on March 12, 1973 he was assigned to the Internal Affairs Division; a unit that was responsible for investigating fellow police officers who had been charged by a civilian with some type of improper conduct. Once again, because of his reputation, those investigated were comfortable in the knowledge that they would be treated fairly.

Lt Joseph Fernandes was promoted to the rank of police Captain on January 21, 1977 earning $22, 647 a year and was assigned to the 2nd precinct as their commanding officer. Capt. Fernandes remained there until 1983 when changes were about to take place. From 1980 to 1983 the Police Commissioner was Charles Connolly. On June 6, 1983 Connolly resigned from the police department and effective that same day Capt. Joseph Fernandes was chosen to serve as the "acting" police commissioner. Joe was 51 years old, a 28 year veteran of the department and he had a reputation as being an evenhanded administrator. He assumed this position while the city commenced a search for a permanent commissioner.

After lengthy discussions by the City Council as to who would be best to serve as the regular full time position of police commissioner, it was decided that Joe Fernandes was the best man for the job and appointed him as the Yonkers Police Commissioner on October 18, 1983. At that time the commissioner's salary was $52,005 and Fernandes lived at 80 Kimball Terrace. It was pointed out that Fernandes was the first minority officer, being of Portuguese descent, to be appointed a Yonkers police Commissioner.

At the time of his appointment to Police Commissioner, the city manager explained that Joe received his appointment because of his extensive knowledge of the department's operation, the respect he holds among his peers and his professional record of achievements.

During his career he had served in the department's Traffic Division, Detective Division, Patrol Division and Internal Affairs Division. He was a member of the Police Holy Name Society, Westchester

Police Commissioner Joseph V. Fernandes (cont.)

County Police Association, and the New York State Hispanic Society of Law Enforcement Officers. He lived in southeast Yonkers with his wife, Maria and his brother, Francis, was a Detective Lieutenant in the Yonkers Police Department.

Prior to Commissioner Fernandes' appointment he was preceded by two commissioners from outside police agencies with no previous knowledge about Yonkers and its history. As such, many changes were implemented that were not very popular. Following Comm. Fernandes' promotion to police Commissioner he made a number of decisions and transfers that he believed would be beneficial to the citizens of Yonkers. Following his appointment, and due to severe budget constraints, he closed down the PAL in an effort to put more officers back on street patrol by reassigning the officers who had worked there, but he later re-instated the PAL and its personnel. He transferred the Detective Captain from commander of the D.D. to command of the North Patrol Command. In his first two months as police commissioner, Fernandes had made changes within Internal Affairs, the Inspections Unit, the Detective Division, the Northeast Command, the North Command, the Southwest Command, the Narcotics Unit, Detention Services, Youth Division, Community Services, Records Division, and the Communication Division.

Joe Fernandes was a very energetic individual who seemed to be working, in one way or another, all the time. Not only was he determined to implement policies that he believed would result in a better police department, but he was also very conscious of the public relations aspect of policing. As such he was always eager to shine a spot light on the good that the Y.P.D. accomplished. One of the programs that he instituted was an annual full week of police activities during National Police Week whereby the public was invited to visit and gain better insight into the department.

On March 8, 1990 it was announced in the local newspaper that P.C. Fernandes was stepping down and retiring after seven years as police commissioner effective March 15, 1990. Fernandes was quoted as saying, "*It's time for Commissioner Joe Fernandes to become Joe Fernandes, a citizen of the city.*"

Upon Comm. Fernandes' retirement, Acting Commission DeDivitis issued a retirement order which read in part, "The dedication, skill and integrity he has displayed during his service to the department shall long be remembered, and shall continue to influence policing in Yonkers for many years to come. The profession is losing a fine officer."

Not long after retiring Joe Fernandes made a big personal decision. He moved from Yonkers and is now living in Portugal. He died there on January 1, 2015. He was 82 years old.

PO EDWARD FEELEY Jr. #100

APPOINTED: October 1, 1955
DIED: August 12, 1983

Another example of a police family; Edward Feeley was born in Yonkers to Yonkers police officer Edward Feeley Sr., on July 21, 1928. Ed Jr. attended and graduated from local public schools and, following graduation at the age of 18 years joined the Navy on January 23, 1946, shortly after WW 2 ended. He was honorably discharged on June 3, 1948. Ed was a big man; not only tall but big boned and weighing well over 230 Lbs. His hands seemed to be the size of a catcher's glove and his very ruddy complexion added an intimidation factor when he became angry. His nickname among friends was "Moose," obviously due to his size. Despite his appearance Ed Feeley was a real gentleman.

Young Ed made his living driving a truck. But, on October 1, 1955 Edward Feeley Jr was appointed to the Yonkers Police Department from 296 Nepperhan Avenue. His starting salary was $3,600 a year and following basic recruit training he was assigned to foot patrol in the 4th precinct.

On January 18, 1960 "Moose" was reassigned from the 4th to the 3rd precinct at 36 Radford Street. Ed Feeley was a no nonsense type guy who kept his assigned post clear of problems. And at times he could possibly have been considered a little rough making an arrest. Quite likely from taking advice from his old timer cop father who was appointed in 1925. On August 3, 1966 Feeley was suspended for using excessive force in making an arrest. Pending departmental trial Ed was transferred to the 2nd precinct on November 9, 1966. Seven days later, on November 16, 1966 Feeley was found guilty of those charges, fined 14 days pay, and reinstated to duty.

On March 6, 1968 Feeley was moved to the Communications Division working as a radio car dispatcher. For many years Ed served on the committee for the annual retirees Old Timers Picnic preparing and serving food and was an active member of the police Holy Name Society. After seven years "inside," on September 29, 1975 Feeley was transferred to the North Command, back on patrol. His last assignment occurred as the result of him developing a heart condition. As such, he was reassigned to the Administrative Services Division in headquarters on January 1, 1979 serving as building security at the headquarters entrance at 10 St. Casimir Ave. It was there that he would sit for hours with a calculator attempting to calculate the incomprehensible issues involving the stars and the Universe.

One evening while off duty some youths outside his home in Hastings NY were causing a disturbance. He ran out and chased them down the street, which resulted in a heart attack and his death that night on August 12, 1983. He was 55 years old.

PO GILDO J. FIORILE #202

APPOINTED: October 1, 1955
RETIRED: June 24, 1987

Known to all his friends as Joe, Gildo J. Fiorile was born on June 27, 1923 in Ossining NY. He attended Ossining elementary schools and graduated from Ossining HS. Not long out of high school and during WW 2, "Joe" joined the Army on February 19, 1943. He achieved the rank of Master Sergeant, spoke Italian as a second language, and following the end of the war was honorably discharged on February 7, 1946. He then joined the NY National Guard's 101st Signal Battalion in Yonkers. As a result, when the Korean War broke out Fiorile's outfit was activated and once again he served on active duty from August 19, 1950 to December 5, 1951. And he remained in the reserves.

Gildo was appointed to the YPD on October 1, 1955 while living at 9 Greene Place. He began by earning $3,600 a year and following basic training was assigned to foot patrol in the 2nd precinct. He was reassigned a few more times; on April 4, 1959 to the 4th precinct, on November 7, 1966 to the 1st precinct, and on January 1, 1971 he was assigned to the new North Command at 53 Shonnard Pl. He would remain there the remainder of his career.

During the 1950 it was reported that Deputy Commissioner Comey was tired of guys on Reserve Status going on military leave and leaving the department shorthanded during the Korean War. Comey ordered all new personnel and old timer reservists to quit the Reserves. Gildo refused, as did everyone else, but Fiorile took the City to court and won.

Fiorile was very active in PBA business and served several years as a trustee. He was a nice easy going guy with a very friendly personality. His brother-in-law was Ret PO Dominick Marsh and his son was former PO Richard Fiorile. Gildo retired from the YPD on June 24, 1987 and remained in Yonkers. Ret PO Gildo "Joe" Fiorile died in January of 1995. He was 71 years old.

CAPTAIN BENJAMIN J. DeLUCCY

APPOINTED: October 1, 1955
RETIRED: May 27, 1982

Having been born in the City of Yonkers on October 16, 1930, Ben DeLuccy attended local schools, graduated from Roosevelt HS, and attended Iona College for two years with a major in business administration. Following the outbreak of the Korean War Ben joined the Army on March 12, 1951 and served as a PFC up to his honorable discharge on February 21, 1953. Following the military he worked as a union construction worker, specifically as an "oiler."

Benjamin DeLuccy was appointed to the Yonkers Police Department on October 1, 1955 while residing at 38 Lockwood Avenue. His starting salary was $3,600 a year and following his basic recruit training he was assigned to patrol in the 2nd precinct. Benny was a fun loving, high energy guy with a great sense of humor. But he knew the only way to get ahead and make more money to support his family was to get promoted. So he studied and went to promotional schools. His efforts paid off when he was promoted to the rank of Sergeant on March 15, 1962, raising his salary up to $6,900, and he was reassigned as a patrol supervisor in the 1st precinct.

During the next few years Sgt DeLuccy was moved around a bit. First, on May 1, 1963 he was moved to the 3rd precinct, and on January 2, 1964 he was returned back to the 1st precinct. But he never stopped studying and on December 14, 1967 he was promoted to the rank of Lieutenant earning what was

Captain Benjamin J. DeLuccy (cont.)

thought at the time to be an incredible salary of $9,870 a year. He was now assigned as a desk lieutenant in the 4th precinct. The job of "Lieutenant" was deemed to be the ultimate in authority for a police officer. Although there was always a precinct captain, he rarely had any interaction with the police officer. But the desk lieutenant, he controlled every move you made. Standing roll calls and checking in for return roll calls. And, making your hourly "hits" on the call box to him at your designated time, not early and not late. The lieutenant booked and, when appropriate, bailed crimes less than a felony right from his desk. He took and vouchered the bail money, personal property of a prisoner and the evidence from the crime, along with maintaining the everyday goings and comings of all police personnel in the precinct blotter. All this and much more was now the responsibility of Lt. Benjamin DeLuccy.

Two years later, on May 19, 1969, Lt DeLuccy was transferred to the 2nd precinct performing the same desk officer duties. DeLuccy left the precinct work for a while when he was assigned to the Communications Division on March 8, 1973. He remained there until January 21, 1977 when he was promoted to the rank of police Captain. He remained assigned to Communications but his salary rose to $23,984 a year. As a captain he was moved around a bit once again. On September 19, 1977 to commanding officer of the Training Division, on January 1, 1979 to commanding officer of the Communications Division, and on September 3, 1979 to commanding officer of the North East Patrol Command at 730 East Grassy Sprain Road.

Capt. Benjamin DeLuccy, a well-liked and respected "boss" and friend, whose cousin was Lt Alphonse Prior, retired from the police department on May 27, 1982. He died September 11, 1998 at the age of 67 years.

PO JOHN P. DOWNEY #161

APPOINTED: October 1, 1956
RESIGNED: November 15, 1957

John Patrick Downey was born in the City of Yonkers on Aug. 3, 1929. As a young man John was said to be an excellent auto mechanic. Available records indicate that he served in the US Marine Corps following WW 2 from 1946 to 1948 and was honorably discharged. Following his military service John worked as an Electrical Inspector. John Downey was appointed to the YPD on Oct. 1, 1956 while living at 473 Nepperhan Avenue. Following recruit training John was assigned to foot patrol in the 4th pct. earning a starting salary of $3,780 a year. Although he is said to have been a nice guy and a good cop, he decided to take the Yonkers Fire Dept. test, which he passed. As a result, John resigned from the YPD on November 15, 1957 in order to be appointed to the Fire Department. He remained with the YFD right up to retirement and later moved to Sarasota, Florida. Former PO John Downey developed heart problems and died on October 17, 2010. He was 81 years old.

PO THOMAS S. HARGRAVES #504

APPOINTED: October 1, 1956
RETIRED: January 21, 1977

Tom Hargraves was born in Yonkers and attended St. Dennis School and later graduated from Saunders HS. While in school he was very much into sports and enjoyed swimming, baseball, football, and basketball. He joined the Navy in Mar. 23, 1951 during the Korean War and served aboard the USS Carter Hall. Tom was honorably discharged on Mar. 9, 1955 having served 4 years as a Boatswains Mate 1st class. He worked for while in the A&P and was then called by the YPD. Hargraves was appointed to the YPD on Oct. 1, 1956 while residing at 143 Linden Street. Following his recruit training he was assigned to foot patrol in the 1st pct. earning $3,780 a year. Following training by the NYPD ESU instructors Tom was assigned to the re-established Emergency Service Unit on Aug. 20, 1958. On May 1, 1963 he was appointed a Detective and assigned to work in the Gambling Squad. On Feb. 23, 1968 he was reassigned to patrol in the 2nd pct. and in Feb. of 1969 he was honored as "Policeman of The Year" by the Yonkers Exchange Club. On Apr. 30, 1970 PO Hargraves was transferred to the Communications Division dispatching radio cars and did so right up to his retirement on Jan. 21, 1977. After retirement he was hired as Director of Security in Yonkers General Hospital for several years, and then worked at Ceiba Geigy. During his career he served as a trustee of the DD, was a member of the PBA, HNS, and Knights of Columbus. He had 5 children and 15 grandchildren. Ret PO Thomas Hargraves died on October 30, 1999 at the age of 67.

DEPUTY CHIEF ANTHONY J. TOCCO

APPOINTED: October 1, 1956
RETIRED: November 1, 1989

Of all of the police officers who have served in the Yonkers Police Department, "Tony" Tocco was perhaps one of the more well-known and, at times, controversial figures of his time.

Anthony Joseph Tocco was born in Yonkers on May 2, 1932 and grew up in the Park Hill Avenue section of Yonkers. Tony attended local public schools as well as Westchester Community College and John Jay College.

Following graduation at the age of 18 years, records indicate Tony joined the Army National Guard on August 19, 1950 with the Korean War having begun in June of that year. Anthony served in Korea as a Corporal up to March 29, 1951. It is not clear what occurred in the interim but apparently Anthony Tocco joined the US Air Force on November 2, 1951. He remained there throughout the war years and was honorably discharged as a Staff Sergeant on September 2, 1955. Following his military service Tony worked as a Telephone Installer and Repairman along with general clerical work. He was also a member of the Wood, Wire and Metal Lathers Union Local #46 where he worked when he took the YPD police exam.

Anthony Tocco was appointed to the police department on October 1, 1956 while residing at 495 Van Cortlandt Park Avenue. Following his recruit training he was assigned to uniform patrol in the 3rd precinct earning a starting salary of $3,780 a year. In July of 1959 it is known that he was serving as part

Deputy Chief Anthony J. Tocco (cont.)

of the YPD Color Guard due to his previous military training.

Five years later, on January 30, 1963, officer Tocco was appointed a Detective working general assignment investigations in the Detective Division. And three years later, on March 25, 1966, he began his rise through the ranks when he received his promotion to the rank of Sergeant. As a sergeant, and earning the new salary of $8,165, he was returned to patrol duty in the 1st precinct working as a patrol supervisor. It was around this time that he was detailed to accompany and supervise a class of new police recruits as they made their daily trip to the NYPD police academy for three months by bus. On November 7, 1966 Sgt Tocco resumed his patrol duties but this time in the 2nd precinct. On February 23, 1968 Tocco was briefly returned to the DD as a Det. Sergeant but remained only a year, returning to patrol on February 3, 1969 in the 4th precinct.

Sgt Tocco received his promotion to the rank of Lieutenant on October 6, 1972 and his salary at that time was $16, 516 a year. Following his promotion he was allowed to remain assigned to the North Command (formerly the 4th pct.) but was now designated a "desk lieutenant." It is worth noting that in years past when lieutenants were still on desk duty, which was the case up until early 1973, although sergeants were your immediate supervisor and the precinct captain was in overall command, as a police officer your main concern was to stay in the good graces of the desk lieutenant. He was often referred in an exaggerated way as a "god" as far as you were concerned. You rarely had any interaction with the captain but the lieutenant controlled you and the sergeants. The desk lieutenant was without any question "the boss." Lt Tocco took to this new authority with complete ease. Tocco was a no nonsense guy who knew how to handle himself and having been given the power of a desk lieutenant, it fit like a glove. He had an air about him that left no doubt as to who was the boss and he would often remind you of that fact. He also had a temper that erupted after very little provocation. Behind his back he was nicknamed "TTT," for "Tough Tony Tocco." Having said that, Lt Tocco was a very strong supporter of the cop on the street, in that no cop should take any abuse from anyone and should use any necessary force without hesitation.

In March of 1973 a restructuring of the department occurred. As part of it the assignment of lieutenants on desk duty was discontinued and they were replaced by desk sergeants. It was then that the position of a captain's "Executive Officer" was established and filled by a lieutenant. In addition, an Inspectional Services Division was established whereby lieutenants would be assigned to work a patrol duty working chart. As a result of these changes, on March 12, 1973 Lt Anthony Tocco was reassigned to the Inspectional Services Division on citywide patrol.

Two years later, on October 1, 1975, Lt. Tocco was brought in from patrol and assigned as the Executive Officer in the South Command. He remained in the South Command for six years when, on October 2, 1981, he was transferred to the Detention Services Division which encompassed and was located in the City Jail building on Alexander Street. In this assignment he was responsible for the processing of prisoners, temporary housing, and transport to court. He was also designated as the supervisor of the Warrant Squad. The following year, on September 13, 1982, Tocco was designated as the Warrant Squad commanding officer.

On July 1, 1983 Lt. Tocco was appointed a Detective Lieutenant and was assigned to work in the police commissioner's officer as the commissioner's executive officer. In that capacity he dealt with the everyday administrative responsibilities that were part of running the police commissioner's office. On

Deputy Chief Anthony J. Tocco (cont.)

February 1, 1984 Lt Tocco was awarded a departmental Commendation for single handedly apprehending at gun point two armed robbers, while off duty, during the robbery of a Yonkers jewelry store on September 20, 1983.

On August 16, 1984 Tocco was promoted to the rank of Captain earning a salary of $44,255. and was assigned to the Field Services Bureau working as a citywide duty captain on patrol.

Capt. Tocco achieved the much sought after position of Deputy Chief on May 31, 1985 with a salary of $60,700 a year. He was assigned as the Deputy Chief of Field Services Bureau, that being everything that had to do with patrol operations and all the personnel assigned thereto.

"Chief" Tocco retired from the YPD on November 1, 1989 while living at 49 Rockledge Road in Yonkers and later moved to Vero Beach Florida with his wife Dorothy. Throughout his career Chief Tocco was an avid golfer and enjoyed playing handball. He was a member of the police Holy Name Society, Captains, Lieutenants, and Sergeants Association, the Knights of Columbus and the VFW.

During his career Chief Tocco received the following awards: April 25, 1960 Macy Newspaper Award— August 16, 1963 Commendation from NYPD Police Commissioner-----October 21, 1963 Macy Newspaper award-----March 11, 1965 Commendation from YPD Police Commissioner----On November 30, 1983 Gannet Westchester Newspaper award Category 1, 1st Place— January 31, 1984 YPD Commendation---- -February 16, 1984 received the PBA John Karasinski off duty award------- April 24, 1984 N.Y.S. Governors Certificate of Merit----May 11, 1984 Westchester Co. Colombian Police Association Award for Bravery.

Ret Deputy Chief Anthony J. Tocco died in Florida on April 7, 2004. He was 71 years old.

LT. VICTOR H. LaQUADRA

APPOINTED: October 1, 1956
RETIRED: March 31, 1988

Victor Hugo LaQuadra was born in the Bronx, NY, on April 3, 1926. His father, who was a musician, died when he was about 8 months old. He attended local schools in the Bronx and graduated from Evander Childs HS. World War 2 was in full gear and Vic convinced his mother to allow him to join the Marine Corps, which he did when he was 17. However, they would not accept him until he turned 18 years of age. And they meant it. On his 18th birthday in 1944 Vic was on a train on his way to boot camp in Parris Island, SC. He had earlier volunteered to be part of an elite group known as the Para Marines who were flown into combat areas and parachuted into dangerous areas of the jungle and fight as infantry. When he completed boot camp he was advised the Para Marines had been disbanded due to excessive casualties upon landing into jungle combat. As a result Vic was assigned to the 1st Marine Air Wing as part of the air field ground crew for repair and service.

Vic served throughout the USA and Shanghai, China. Following the end of the war and upon his return to the states he was discharged on August 29, 1946 with the rank of Corporal. Vic studied music for a year then took business courses at the Delahanty Institute in NYC. He began working for the NY Central R.R. System as a train secretary in the Club Car of the 20th Century Limited, a first class line. Vic moved to Ohio for a short time but returned to live at 218 McLean Ave. It was from here he took and passed the YPD test.

Vic was appointed to the YPD on October 1, 1956 earning $3,780 a year and was assigned to the 3rd precinct as a rookie in gray uniforms. He said he bought all his equipment and was only supplied with the revolver, shield and hat wreath. His captain at that time was Capt. John J. McCarthy-3, a.k.a. "blackjack."

With a strong desire to be a success, Vic studied hard for the sergeant's exam. His work was rewarded when he was promoted to Sergeant on July 2, 1965 earning $7,260 and was reassigned to the 2nd precinct. His captain was Capt. Alex Reid. At that time all police salaries were based on the results of what was called the Robinson Survey, which recommended a sliding salary scale for all ranks based on numbers of years of service. It was extremely unpopular. For Sgt LaQuadra it meant as a new sergeant he earned $1,200 a year less than some other sergeants. Fortunately the salary schedule was re-negotiated more equitably.

Sgt Laquadra was promoted to the rank of Lieutenant on December 19, 1969 and had his salary increased to $13,300 a year. His new assignment was to the 3rd precinct as a desk officer. From here he moved several times. On June 12, 1970 to the 4th, on March 12, 1973 to Inspectional Services Division, May 6, 1974 to Field Services Bureau on patrol, July 1, 1975 to Communications Division, and on August 16, 1976 to Central Booking. And on July 21, 1980 Vic finally received a steady day tour assignment as liaison officer to Traffic Court when Lt John Favareau retired.

Lt Vic LaQuadra retired from the YPD on March 31, 1988 and the following year moved to Stormville, NY.

LT. ALPHONSE A. PRIOR

APPOINTED: October 1, 1956
RETIRED: October 4, 1985

Alphonse Anthony Prior was born in Yonkers on January 4, 1931. He was the son of a Yonkers police Sergeant, Anthony Prior, who would later rise to the rank of captain. Young Al attended PS# 24, then PS# 5, and graduated from Commerce High School. The Korean War had been in progress for 6 months when, one day before his 20th birthday, Al joined the US Air Force on Jan. 3, 1951. He served for four years in a clerical capacity, including a year in Greenland, and was honorably discharged on Dec. 7, 1954. Following his discharge Al worked for the N.Y. Central Railroad as a clerk.

Al was appointed to the Yonkers P.D. on Oct. 1, 1956 while residing at 57 Claredon Avenue. Following his recruit training Al was assigned to the 2nd pct. earning a starting salary of $3,780 a year. In 1958, following plans to re-establish the previously abolished Emergency Service Unit (ESU), Al was selected and trained by the NYPD ESU instructors at Randall's Island in the Bronx. On Aug. 20, 1958 PO Prior was officially assigned to the new Accident Investigation Emergency (AIE) which was later renamed ESU. He worked in ESU for 8 years and then on Nov. 9, 1966 he was returned to routine patrol in the 2nd pct.

Al was promoted to the rank of Sergeant on Dec. 14, 1967. His salary rose to $8,855 and he was reassigned to the 1st pct. as a patrol supervisor. On March 6, 1968, he was moved back to the 2nd pct. Al was then promoted to Lieutenant on Nov. 10, 1972 earning $16,516 and was assigned as Executive Officer in Central Records in HQ. In Oct. of 1975 he was placed on patrol in the Field Services Bureau and in Jan. of 1979 moved to patrol in the South Command. His last assignment was on Jan. 1, 1980 when he was transferred to be a Central Booking lieutenant. Not only was his father a captain, but his cousin was Capt. Ben DeLuccy and his step son was Det Sgt Bill Rinaldi. Lt Alphonse Prior retired from the YPD on Oct. 4, 1985 to his home in Yonkers, but later moved to Florida where he still resides.

PO JOSEPH S. SEBECK #177

APPOINTED: October 1, 1956
RETIRED: October 1, 1975

Joseph Louis Sebeck was a police officer. But many believed he had a secret desire to be up on stage entertaining people. He was born in the city of Yonkers on Sept. 30, 1925, attended local public schools, and graduated from Gorton HS. Joe joined the Navy on Dec. 27, 1943 during World War II. He served as a Machinist Mate 3rd class aboard the USS Missouri and was present aboard ship in Tokyo Bay during the surrender signing by the Japanese. He received his honorable discharge on Mar. 1, 1946. .

Following his discharge Joe worked for a short time as both a salesman, and for the Alexander Smith Carpet Shop. He also worked at the General Motors plant in Tarrytown NY. He was appointed to the Y.P.D. on Oct. 1, 1956 while residing at 397 Prescott St. His starting salary was $3,780 a year and following recruit training, his first assignment was foot patrol in the 1st precinct. Joe was assigned to the Detective Division, not as a detective but as a "silver shield" on Feb. 12, 1971 and was assigned as a youth investigator for crimes committed by juveniles. He remained in this assignment right up to his retirement on Oct. 1, 1975.

Joe had the gift of gab and love to entertain people. It was said that while in the Youth Division he and PO Bonita Faranda performed comedy acts at various gatherings. It was said that Joe was the straight man in the act and was even a good tap dancer. He used to M.C. all of the Minstrels at Holy Trinity Church in the Hollow. In 1975 Joe moved to Lake Luzerne, NY and remained retired. Joseph Sebeck died September 2, 2002. He was 76 years old.

PO THOMAS J. HART #171

APPOINTED: October 1, 1956
RESIGNED: June 14, 1957

Thomas John Hart was born in the City of Yonkers; date unavailable. He is said to have attended local public schools and as a young man was employed as a machine operator. Hart joined the Marine Corps. during the Korean War and served from 1951 up to his honorable discharge in 1954. Tom was appointed to the Y.P.D. on October 1, 1956 from 500 Van Cortlandt Park Avenue and following training was assigned to the 1st precinct earning $3,780 a year. For unknown reasons Tom Hart resigned from the police department on June 14, 1957.

PO ALPHONSE C. IMPALLOMENI #211

APPOINTED: October 1, 1956
RETIRED: August 4, 1978

Al was born Alphonse Camille Impallomeni in the city of Yonkers on November 20, 1934. Al grew up in the Nodine Hill section of Yonkers and attended PS# 23 and graduated from Saunders HS. Following school Al worked as a carpenter to earn a living. Not long after the end of the Korean War Alphonse joined the Army on March 8, 1954 and was sent to Korea serving with the 184th Construction Combat Engineers for a year. He received his "release" from active duty in December of 1955; allowed to return home, and was placed in the inactive reserve. After completing three years service he received his honorable discharge in March of 1957.

Al was an avid sportsman who loved the outdoors and hunting and fishing. Upon his release from the military Al worked for Tetrad Co., whose technicians would grind down diamond particles for use on the tip of phonograph needles.

Al received his appointment to the Yonkers Police Department on October 1, 1956 while residing at 6 Van Cortlandt Park Ave. Following recruit training he was initially assigned to patrol in the 1st precinct at 20 Wells Avenue and earned a starting salary of $3,780 a year. Shortly after reporting to the 1st precinct officer Impallomeni was working an early tour in Getty Square when he was confronted by a man with a rifle who mistook the officer for an old adversary. He held the officer at gun point for several minutes and then fired at PO Impallomeni with the intent to kill. He missed, but PO Impallomeni did not. However the suspect recovered from his wound and was sent to prison. Al began installing roofs while off duty and did so for many years as a second job.

Seven years later, after having taken the NY State Police exam, Al was called for appointment. He accepted and resigned from the YPD effective October 1, 1963 and was appointed a "Trooper" on October 7, 1963. Seven months later, due to being assigned to work in upper N.Y.S. far from his home and family, Al requested to be reinstated to the YPD. His request was approved and he was reinstated to work in the 2nd precinct effective May 20, 1964 with the salary of $6,850.

The following year, on April 5, 1965, Al was transferred to the Traffic Division on two wheel motorcycle patrol. He remained in Traffic up to June 23, 1972 when he was transferred back to patrol duty in the North Patrol Command, which then incorporated the old 1st and 4th precincts. Also working in the North Command at the time was his wife's brother, PO William Leavy.

PO Alphonse Impallomeni retired from the YPD on August 4, 1978. Shortly thereafter he moved to the rural town of Washington, Maine living on several acres of land where he could be around the wildlife that he enjoyed. He was even hired as a carpenter for the state of Maine department of transportation and retired again 17 years later.

SGT. ERIC J. BAUER #15

APPOINTED: October 1, 1956
RETIRED: November 25, 1977

Eric Joseph Bauer was born in NYC on May 3, 1931. He attended local NYC public schools and graduated from the Textile high school in 1949. Following a few years of miscellaneous jobs Eric joined the Army during the Korean War on Jan. 30, 1952. He was honorably discharged as a Corporal on Oct. 29, 1953. Eric Bauer was appointed to the Y.P.D. on Oct. 1, 1956 while residing at 10 Stillwell Ave and was assigned to the 2nd precinct earning a salary of $3,780 a year. He was reassigned to the plainclothes Juvenile Aid Bureau on April 5, 1965. On Apr. 13, 1966 at about 3:30 AM, after having finished working an early tour, Bauer was in plainclothes in the lobby of the Dunwoodie hotel bar at 300 Yonkers Ave. He was approached by two intoxicated males who physically assaulted him, displayed a gun and fired 4 shots at the off-duty officer. Bauer returned fire but neither man was hit. The suspect ran to his hotel room locking himself in, but upon forcible entry, he was taken into custody. Officer Bauer was later commended by the detective captain for his restraint and judgment in this matter. Two years later, on June 14, 1968, Eric was reassigned back to patrol duty in the 3rd precinct for only a few days and then assigned to the 2nd precinct. On April 9, 1976 Eric was promoted to the rank of sergeant earning $18,043 and was transferred to the North Command as a patrol supervisor. Sgt Bauer would remain there right up to his retirement on November 25, 1977.

DET. LEON A. WYKA #637

APPOINTED: October 1, 1956
RETIRED: March 2, 1989

Born in Yonkers on Nov. 4, 1926, Leon Alfred Wyka attended local public schools and graduated from Saunders HS. Leon joined the Navy during WW-2 on Oct. 12, 1944. He earned the rating of Machinist Mate 3rd Class and served with the "Seabee's" and the Shore Patrol. He received his honorable discharge on June 29, 1946. Leon worked for Otis Elevator as a "wireman" for elevator controllers. However, on Oct. 1, 1956 Wyka was appointed to the YPD while residing at 48 Oak Street. His first assignment was patrol in the 2nd precinct earning $3,780 a year. Two months later, on December 1, 1956, he was reassigned to the 4th pct. He remained in the 4th for just over 6 years when, on Feb. 6, 1963, he was transferred to the Juvenile Aide Bureau (JAB). Later renamed the Youth Division. He was appointed a Detective in the D.D. on Apr. 9, 1965, but 3 years later, on Oct. 1, 1968 he was reassigned to patrol in the 3rd pct. On April 27, 1970 he was once again appointed a detective working as their desk officer in his later years, right up to his retirement on March 2, 1989. Leon had the pleasure of watching his son Glenn be sworn in as a Yonkers police officer in 1997.

PO CARMINE J. CAVALLO #180

APPOINTED: October 1, 1956
DIED: December 3, 1982

When you talk about nice guys, you must include Carmine Cavallo. He was born Carmine John Cavallo on April 16, 1932 in Yonkers NY. He attended the local school system and graduated from Saunders HS. Following graduation he worked miscellaneous jobs until entering the Army on Nov. 7, 1952 during the Korean War. It was reported that he served in Korea, part of that time in combat, from 1952 through 1954. He held the rank of Sergeant and was said to have been awarded the Korean Service Medal with two bronze stars, the Combat Infantryman's Badge and the National Service Defense Medal. "Sonny," as he was known to his friends, was honorably discharged on Nov. 6, 1954.

Following his discharge Carmine worked on the line as an assembler for the General Motors plant in Tarrytown. On Oct. 1, 1956 Carmine Cavallo was appointed to the Y.P.D. while residing at 84 Ravine Avenue. His starting salary was $3,780 a year and following recruit training he was assigned to foot patrol in the 4th precinct. To be close to work he built his home on Woodycrest Avenue. Eighteen years later, on June 19, 1974, he was transferred to the Youth Services and Community Relations Division at 21 Alexander Street. In this assignment he worked in plainclothes investigating crimes committed by juveniles and worked closely with Family Court. At one point "Sonny" was reassigned back to duty in the 4th precinct and he served as the desk lieutenant's aide. That would be his last assignment. It becomes clear to even the casual observer that Carmine and his family were very much a part of serving the City of Yonkers. Carmine's brother is Ret Det Andrew Cavallo, his wife Ann's uncle was the late PO Raymond Jamison, his sister Edith married the late Det Thomas Dugan, of his three children, including a daughter Donna, his son Robert is a retired YFD Assistant Chief and Thomas was a YFD Captain.

On December 3, 1982 off duty PO Carmine Cavallo was in his vehicle when he suddenly suffered a massive heart attack and died. He was 50 years old.

DET. ALBERT M. CICALO SR. #625

APPOINTED: October 1, 1956
RETIRED: April 1, 1981

Albert Mario Cicalo was born in the City of Yonkers on August 10, 1931. He attended local public schools and graduated from Yonkers HS. On August 15, 1951 Al joined the Air Force during the Korean War, served as a Corporal, and was honorably discharged on March 4, 1952. Following the military Al joined the Teamsters union and worked as a truck driver. However, his wish was granted when he was appointed to the police department on October 1, 1956. A resident of 95 Claredon Avenue, Al's salary was $3,780 a year and his first assignment was patrol in the 2nd precinct. In 1958, following plans to re-establish a previously abolished Emergency Service Unit, Al was selected and trained by the NYPD ESU instructors at Randall's Island in N.Y.C. On August 20, 1958 PO Cicalo was officially assigned to the new Accident Investigation Emergency (AIE) and later renamed E.S.U. He worked in ESU for 8 years and then on November 9, 1966 he was returned to patrol in the 2nd precinct. Once again Al was fortunate when, on February 23, 1968, he was appointed a Detective in the DD. In October of 1975 he was named president of the Italian City Club, and was the General Chairman of the Columbus Day Celebration Committee. Al was also very proud when his son, Al Jr. was appointed a Yonkers police officer and later a detective. Det Albert Cicalo Sr. Retired from the YPD on April 1, 1981 and worked for several years as a car salesman for Lincoln Park Mercury on South Broadway.
Ret Det Albert Cicalo Sr. died September 7, 2015. He was 84.

PO LOUIS J. GIACOMO #105

APPOINTED: October 1, 1956
RESIGNED: December 31, 1960

Louis James Giacomo was born in the City of Yonkers on March 11, 1929. He attended and graduated from local public schools and would later be employed as a laborer and roofer. Lou served in the Army during the Korean War from 1948 up to his honorable discharge in 1952. He was appointed to the Y.P.D. on October 1, 1956 while living at 209 Stone Avenue. Following recruit training he was assigned to foot patrol in the 2nd precinct earning $3,780 a year. It is possible that officer was having health issues. In one new report it indicated that Patrolman Giacomo was placed on forced sick leave from the 2nd precinct without pay, effective October 27, 1960. Yet another report indicated that Giacomo requested and received an unpaid leave of absence from Oct. 16, 1960 to December 31, 1960. In any case, upon the end of his leave PO Louis Giacomo resigned from the YPD effective Dec. 31, 1960.

PO WILLIAM S. VANCE #589

APPOINTED: October 1, 1956
RETIRED: March 19, 1987

Bill Vance was born in Yonkers on January 23, 1930 and grew up in the Glenwood and Ravine Ave area. He attended local public schools, including Saunders HS, but quit in the 11th grade and joined the Naval Reserve in 1947. He and the other reservists attended meetings at the Jewish Community Center or at the Commerce HS because the future Naval Reserve building at 21 Alexander Street had not yet been built. On June 11, 1948 he requested to go on active duty for a four year enlistment. Bill served aboard a Destroyer in "Task Force 77." When the Korean War started in June 1950 Bill served off the coast of North Korea, his ship exchanging fire with shore batteries. Vance was a Gunners Mate 3rd class on Anti-Aircraft Guns, serving as the "Gun Captain" in charge of the detail. He was honorably discharged on June 11, 1952.

Following his discharge he was hired by Otis Elevator Co. in 1952 for a short time as a wire repairman, and then to Habirshaw Co. where he remained for four years. It was then, on October 1, 1956, that William Vance was appointed to the Yonkers Police Dept. from 78 Glenwood Avenue. His recruit class received two weeks of police recruit training in the former Naval Reserve Training Center at 21 Alexander St. Bill's first assignment was foot patrol in the 1st precinct earning $3,780 a year. Upon his appointment his group was the first group that did not have to buy their own uniforms and they were the first group to begin using the new three quarter length, open neck, overcoat for foot men which replaced the former 3/4 length "choker" coat and the long full length, to mid-calf overcoat collared and buttoned at the neck. He remained in the 1st for 4 months and on December 1, 1956 was moved to the 4th precinct. He was an original member of 4th precinct softball team with the logo on the t-shirt of a mug of beer and words "4th Pct." Yes, back then the 4th was definitely a partying precinct.

PO Vance remained in the 4th until May 1, 1963 when he was appointed a Detective. Early on Det Vance gained the nickname "Philo," which was taken from a 1940's radio program with a detective named "Philo Vance." Two of his early partners were Det's Leon Wyka and Al McEvoy. Det Vance received departmental recognition for his part in identifying and arresting two holdup men who beat a 70 year old man on March 15, 1964. "Philo" remained in the D.D. up to October 1, 1968 when he was returned to patrol in the 4th precinct. He would return to the Detective Division on December 11, 1970; but on July 16, 1971 he was returned to patrol back in the 4th, now re-named the North Command. There, he partnered up with PO Charles Storms.

On September 15, 1972 Bill Vance was transferred to the Youth Division at 21 Alexander Street as a youth investigator, investigating crimes committed by juveniles. Coincidentally one of the officers he worked with in the Youth Division was his old precinct partner, Charlie Storms. In 1982 Bill Vance endured the nightmare of learning that his son was the victim in a senseless homicide. With incredible strength and sense of duty, following a period of mourning, Bill Vance returned to duty. Bill was a tall man standing about 6' 2" and was very friendly and outgoing. And he remained that way up to and after his retirement on March 19, 1987.

"Philo" was always a motorcycle rider and a longtime member of the Blue Knights Motorcycle Club. He remained a loyal member upon retirement.

PO GEORGE J. PIERRO #114

APPOINTED: October 1, 1956
RETIRED: January 21, 1977

Born in the City of Yonkers on July 23, 1926, George J. Pierro attended local public schools and graduated from Saunders HS. Right after his 17th birthday George joined the Navy during WW 2 on August 25, 1943 and during his service he served with the 136th Seabee's Battalion. Following the war's end he was honorably discharged on January 10, 1946. Over the next 10 years George worked various jobs but on October 1, 1956 he was appointed to the YPD from 54 Linden Street. Following recruit training he was assigned to the 2nd precinct earning a salary of $3,780 a year. A year later, on January 1, 1958, Pierro was reassigned to foot patrol duty in the 1st precinct on Wells Avenue. In 1963 while on patrol on the late tour Pierro chased a burglar at 4 AM. After a long pursuit Pierro shot and wounded the suspect and made the arrest. After being moved to the 4th pct. for a time, on January 1, 1969 Pierro was appointed a Detective in the DD. He remained a detective for 3 years and on March 9, 1972 was returned to patrol in the South Command. George Pierro retired from the YPD on January 21, 1977. He died 19 years later on December 31, 1996 at age 70.

PO GEORGE W. CIPOLLA #159

APPOINTED: November 1, 1956
RETIRED: December 15, 1972

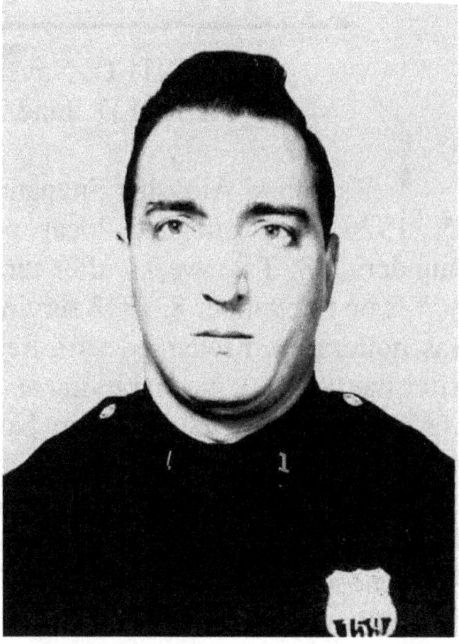

George Cipolla was born in the City of Yonkers on December 14, 1927, and attended and graduated from local public schools. He served in the US Army during the Korean war from August of 1950 up to his honorable discharge on May of 1952. Following his military service George worked on the assembly line for the General Motors plant in Tarrytown. He was appointed to the Yonkers Police Department on November 1, 1956 while living at 442 Walnut Street and following his recruit training his first assignment was in the 1st precinct. On August 15, 1960 George was reassigned to the 2nd precinct and assigned to work in the Emergency Services Unit. Unfortunately, on December 11, 1961, while directing traffic at an accident scene on C.P.A., south of the 2nd precinct, Cipolla was struck by a passing motor vehicle and sustained severe and life changing injuries. As a result officer Cipolla remained out injured for most of the years 1962 through 1969 working only occasionally on light duty. Due to his injuries he required multiple surgeries and at his best walked with cane. Though seriously disabled George came back to work on February 14, 1968 detailed to the Intelligence Unit on light duty/clerical. George Cipolla received his disability retirement on December 15, 1972 and lived with his wife in Peekskill up to his death on January 22, 1994. He was 66 years old.

PO EDWARD REICH #12

APPOINTED: November 1, 1956
RETIRED: January 21, 1977

Edward Reich was born in the City of Yonkers on April 2, 1932 and attended and graduated from local public schools. Shortly after his schooling the Korean War began and Ed joined the US Air Force on December 28, 1950. He was honorably discharged as an Airman 2nd class on July 16, 1954. Following the military Ed worked in paint production, company unknown. He was hired to the Yonkers Police Department on November 1, 1956 while residing at 6 Lockwood Avenue. His first assignment was patrol in the 2nd precinct earning a starting salary of $3,780 a year. After fifteen years of being on radio car patrol, on Dec. 20, 1971, Ed was reassigned to a steady day detail working in the Records Division. However, on Aug. 20, 1974 he was returned to patrol duty in the South Command, formerly the 2nd precinct. Ed Reich, who was a quiet individual who kept to himself, retired on Jan. 21, 1977 while living on Jessamine Avenue. Ret PO Edward Reich died suddenly and unexpectedly in June of 1981. He was only 50 years old.

LT. RAYMOND A. FITZPATRICK

APPOINTED: November 1, 1956
RETIRED: June 23, 1983

Raymond Aloysius Fitzpatrick was born in Yonkers on August 25, 1926. Ray attended local public schools and graduated from Saunders HS. Two weeks after turning 17 Ray joined the Navy during WW 2 on September 8, 1943 serving on a destroyer on burial detail. Ray was honorably discharged as a Seaman 1st Class on March 24, 1946. After the war Ray made a living as an apprentice electrician installer. He was appointed to the YPD on November 1, 1956 from 78 Hamilton Avenue, received a starting salary of $3,780 a year and was assigned to the 3rd precinct. When the department decided to re-establish the previously abolished Emergency Services Unit, Fitzpatrick was among those chosen to be trained by the NYPD ESU instructors at Randall's Island in NYC. On August 20, 1958 the Yonkers ESU unit became operational and Ray was assigned working from the 1st precinct. Ray was promoted to the rank of Sergeant on January 14, 1966 earning a salary increase up to $8,165 and was assigned as a patrol supervisor in the 2nd precinct. By the end of the year, on November 7th he was moved to the 4th pct. On January 1, 1971 Sgt Fitzpatrick was reassigned to the South Command. Ray was promoted to Lieutenant on August 24, 1973 earning $18,018 and assigned to the Inspectional Services Division on citywide patrol. He was moved to the Communications Div on June 19, 1974 and designated the Criminal Court Liaison on February 16, 1976. Ray remained there up to his retirement on June 23, 1983. Ray's brother was Sgt Joseph Fitzpatrick. Ret Lt Raymond Fitzpatrick died on August 18, 1984 at the age of 57 years.

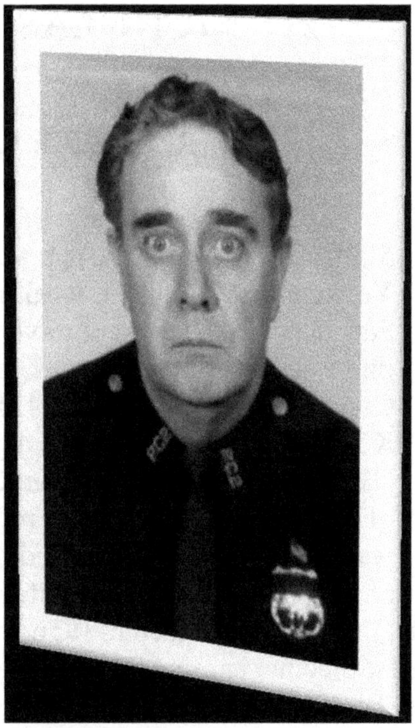

PO RICHARD J. EVANS #17

APPOINTED: November 1, 1956
RETIRED: June 25, 1987

Richard John Evans was born in Yonkers on June 29, 1925, attended PS# 13, Hawthorne Jr, HS, and Commerce HS. Only 9 months into WW 2, Rich, or "Red" as he was known, left school at age 17 to serve his country and joined the Navy on August 22, 1942. During the war he served on a destroyer in the Atlantic participating in the invasion of Sicily, and later while serving on the destroyer USS Hunt in the Pacific, his ship was attacked and struck by Japanese Kamikaze planes with minimal damage. However the plane struck the Captains Bridge and left the enemy pilot's scattered remains throughout the bridge area. Richard was honorably discharged at the end of the war, on August 22, 1945, as Yeoman 3rd class. Rich worked as clerk in Safeway Supermarket for a while and then for Time Warner Inc in NYC in the Mail Room.

He was appointed to the police department on November 1, 1956 from 23 Lawrence Street and earned $3,780 a year. He and the other "rookies" were given recruit gray uniforms to wear and they attended 7 weeks of training by a few ranking police officers in the Naval Reserve Armory building at 21 Alexander St. Upon graduation his first assignment was to the 3rd precinct at 36 Radford Street on foot patrol duty. He remained there until a centralization plan was implemented on January 1, 1971 and he was reassigned to the South Command, which had been the old 2nd pct.

At one point Rich suffered a debilitating nervous condition and after a time out sick returned to duty detailed to the Internal Affairs Division as a desk officer in the early 1980's. Later he was reassigned to the Records Division performing administrative duties, including a time working as the administrative aide to Deputy Chief of Patrol, Anthony Tocco. Rich's nephew was PO Howard Evans. Richard remained assigned to Records Division right up to his retirement on June 25, 1987. After moving to Southbury, Ct in 1998 Ret PO Richard "Red" Evans died on June 1, 2003 at the age of 77 years.

PO NICHOLAS A. GASPARRO #85

APPOINTED: November 1, 1956
RESIGNED: January 15, 1958

Nicholas Anthony Gasparro was born in Yonkers on April 5, 1926 on Oak Street, and was raised in the Park Hill section of Yonkers. He attended local public schools and graduated from Saunders HS. Nick went to work for an aircraft plant in LI, became interested in flying and took lessons. Nick served in the Army Air Corps from 1944 through 1953, serving in both WW 2 and the Korean war. He couldn't be a pilot but served as an Engineer/Right "Blister" waist gunner and emergency pilot on B-29's on the Island of Tinian in the Pacific. He related that he did 15 combat missions, was shot up and crash landed on Iwo Jima, earned two Air Medals, and a Presidential Unit Citation. Nick, whose brother was PO Louis Gasparro, was appointed to the YPD on November 1, 1956 from 18 Vineyard Avenue. Following recruit school he was assigned to the 1st precinct earning $3,780 a year. Nick most often worked in Getty Square directing traffic. Officer Nicholas Gasparro resigned from the YPD on January 15, 1958 in order to be appointed to the Nassau County police Department from which he later retired. After retiring Gasparro lived in Florida for 27 years, and then moved to Fairmont, West Va. Where he still resides today.

PO ANDREW J. ROZA #7

APPOINTED: November 1, 1956
RETIRED: March 25, 1994

Born Andrew Joseph Roza in NYC on Sept. 22, 1935, and attended local Yonkers public schools and graduated from Roosevelt HS. Following high school he gained employment as a District Manager for the Herald Statesman newspaper. He remained there right up to his appointment to the police department on Nov. 1, 1956 while living at 145 First Street. Following recruit school his first assignment was patrol in the 2nd pct. earning $3,780 a year. When the department decided to re-establish the previously abolished Emergency Services Unit, Roza was among those chosen to be trained by the NYPD ESU instructors at Randall's Island in NYC. On Aug. 20, 1958 the Yonkers ESU unit became operational and Roza was assigned working from the 2nd pct. In 1961 Andy was granted an unpaid leave of absence due to joining the Army National Guard. He served as a sergeant in the Signal Corps and in Supply and his leave ran from September 30, 1961 to August 16, 1962, when he was reinstated to the YPD and reassigned back into ESU. Andy continued to serve in the Emergency Service Unit up to December 1, 1971, and was then assigned as the 2nd precinct's captain's aide. In 1990 he began working steady midnights as a desk officer right up to his retirement on March 25, 1994, having completed nearly 38 years of service. Andy lived in Yonkers but enjoyed his summer home at the New Jersey shore.

Unfortunately, Ret PO Andrew J. Roza, whose son William was a member of the Yonkers Fire Dept., died on May 10, 2015. He was 79 years old.

CAPTAIN BENEDETTO ERMINI

APPOINTED: November 1, 1956
RETIRED: January 11, 1985

"Ben" Ermini was born on September 26, 1935 on one of the last remaining farms in the City of Yonkers. The little farmhouse was located at the end of Greenvale Avenue and was known as "Lesko's Farm." Ben was the youngest of three children. It is ironic that 27 years later in 1962 Ben was to build his own family home approximately 200 yards away, at the corner of Hillside Avenue and Meadowbrook Place, in the area known by most residents as "Policeman's Hollow." The area was given this unofficial name because of the many police officer families living in that small community. The residents at the time included Deputy Chief James "Bob" Tobin, Sergeant Jack O'Connell, Sergeant Don Givler, PO Frank Vasil, and Detective's Armando and Fran DeBlassis.

Ben received his elementary and junior high school education at PS# 16 and graduated from Gorton High School in 1953. While attending Gorton High School he was active in sports and in his senior year was captain of the varsity football team. After graduation from high school he worked in the construction field for several years. He became a member of the Union of Operating Engineers and worked as an Oiler on heavy construction equipment. In addition to English Ben spoke Italian as a second

Captain Benedetto Ermini (cont.)

language.

After passing the civil service test Ben was appointed to the Yonkers Police Department on November 1, 1956 with the starting salary of $3,780. and was assigned to foot patrol in the 4th Precinct. On Oct. 26, 1958 Ben received an indefinite leave of absence due to induction into the Army. For reasons not known, two weeks later on November 10, 1958, Ben Ermini was reinstated to the police department. Three years later on Nov. 9, 1959 Ben was transferred to the 1st Precinct and assigned to the Accident Investigation Emergency Squad. He and his partner Aristede "RIP" Mastroddi were known as the "Flying Squad" because of Rip's notorious driving skills and ability to get to the scene of the incident in rapid fashion. Later Ben would be assigned to a 1st precinct sector car on patrol and partnered with his longtime friend John Bonney.

The newly appointed Public Safety Commissioner, Daniel McMahon, learned that Ben had natural artistic drawing skills and on September 23, 1964 transferred him to the Detective Division as a detective and as the department's composite artist. While serving as a detective he and his partner Brendan Magner were assigned to investigate the Jewish Community Center arson fire that took the lives of 12 people including 9 children. As a result of their investigation a 16-year-old worker at the Center was arrested and convicted of the crime. Ben and Brendan spent a year working with the Westchester County District Attorney's Office in preparation of the trial. They were also assigned to investigate a number of serious charges made against the Yonkers Fire Department regarding the actions of Fire Department personnel during the incident. Following a meeting of the police Honor Board Ben and Brendan received a Department Commendation for their work in bringing the case to a successful conclusion. On October 22, 1971 Det. Ermini was reassigned to the police Intelligence Unit conducting gambling investigations.

On May 5, 1972 Ben was promoted to the rank of Sergeant with a salary of $13,685. and on that same day was designated a Detective Sergeant. He was responsible for the supervision of a squad of detectives in the Detective Division handling general assignments. On September 22, 1974 Sgt. Ermini and his squad were assigned to supervise the investigation of the shooting death of Yonkers Patrolman Harold Woods. Under Sgt Ermini's direction the investigative team was able to develop information through an informant that led to the arrest and conviction of the two individuals responsible for the officer's death. Sgt Ermini and investigative team members were required to travel to New Orleans, Louisiana to pick up and return one of the suspects. The suspect refused to waive extradition and an extradition hearing and Governor's warrant process was required to return the suspect to Westchester County for prosecution. The second suspect was arrested in New York City.

Ben Ermini was promoted to Lieutenant on April 9, 1976 at a salary of $20,642. and assigned as Commanding Officer of a new federally funded program designed to work more closely with the community. The "Community Patrol Unit" as it was named, was a store front mini precinct located at 250 Warburton Avenue. He served in that capacity until 1978 when he was designated by then Commissioner Daniel Guido to direct the Integrated Criminal Apprehension Program (ICAP). ICAP was a United States Justice Department program focused on the reorganization of law enforcement objectives to improve efficiency and service delivery. The Yonkers Police Department was selected by the US Justice Department to participate in the program. ICAP resulted in a number of organizational policy and procedural changes that drew the attention of the national law enforcement community.

Lt Ermini was selected and invited to attend the prestigious FBI National Academy in Quantico

Captain Benedetto Ermini (cont)

Virginia in 1980 and was a member of the 121st session graduating class. Upon his return from the Academy he was designated as a Detective Lieutenant on Sept. 29, 1980 serving as the Executive Lieutenant of the Detective Division where he served until 1981 when he was reassigned as the Commanding Officer of the elite Police Intelligence Division. On Oct. 12, 1983 he was transferred from the Intelligence Division to the 3rd Precinct as their executive officer by newly appointed Police Commissioner Joseph Fernandes and replaced by the Commissioner's brother, Lt. Frank Fernandes. Ben was promoted to Captain on August 16, 1984 at the salary of $44,255, assigned as a citywide patrol captain, and five months later retired from the Yonkers Police Department on January 11, 1985.

After retirement Ben was hired as a consultant with Public Administration Service in McLean Virginia where he provided the investigative analysis for the management studies of numerous law enforcement agencies throughout the United States. In 1989 he was asked to become the Director of the Missing Children's Division of the National Center for Missing and Exploited Children in Alexandria Virginia. The National Center was established by the US Congress in 1984 and serves as the nation's clearinghouse for missing and exploited children. Ben has been responsible for the development and implementation of the Center's case management system, Case Analysis Support Division, Forensic Imaging Unit, and the Project ALERT (America's Law Enforcement Retiree Team) Program.

In 2005 Ben and his wife Kathleen lived in Gainesville, Virginia. They have three grown children; a son Edward, an ENT surgeon with a practice in Lumberton, North Carolina, a son David, an architect living and working in Virginia Beach, Virginia, and a daughter Lisa, a senior web designer for an International Consulting Company, living in Leesburg, Virginia./

PO EDWARD J. RYAN #183

APPOINTED: November 1, 1956
RETIRED: January 18, 1980

Ed was born Edward Joseph Ryan in Yonkers N.Y. on February 4, 1930, one of eight children. Ed attended local public schools and Longfellow Jr HS. On his police application Ed indicated that he previously worked as a construction laborer for various contracting companies. Ed's father had been Yonkers PO John P. Ryan and Ed's two brothers were PO Bill Ryan, and PO Tom Ryan.

Edward Ryan was appointed to the Yonkers Police Department from 15 Dunston Avenue on November 1, 1956. His starting salary was $3,780 a year and, following recruit training, his first assignment was to the 2nd precinct at 441 Central Park Avenue. During his first year he walked a foot post and the next seven years he rode in a sector car with then PO Russell Kantor. Starting from the day he was appointed Ed never stopped working construction jobs five days a week during the day, whenever he was working early or late tours. Ed preferred a closer contact with the public so he requested to walk foot post assignments. He walked several including, Post 2 on McLean Avenue, post 1 around the Yonkers Avenue area, and post 14 on Tuckahoe Road. And he had a reputation of being a no nonsense cop on post too.

Ed was always very interested in firearms and at one point even obtained a federal firearms dealers license which allowed him to buy and sell firearms from his home. It was his hobby, but also another source of income. He was also an expert shot with the YPD issued revolver. In 1958 Ryan, along with PO Joe Campanaro and PO Bill Kamp, comprised the members of the YPD Pistol Team which competed throughout the east coast in shooting competition tournaments against other police departments and the FBI. He said they practiced by firing 1000 rounds a week at the Ardsley range. Ed and his team had to provide their own ammunition for each event.

Ed remained in the 2nd precinct for his entire career right up to his retirement on January 18, 1980; coincidentally the same date, January 18th, that his father PO John Ryan died in 1934. Ed was retired from the YPD but didn't stop working construction jobs. While working with Yonkers Contracting Ed was sent to work with Con Edison digging and putting in new gas mains. He was even certified and licensed for use and detonation of dynamite. Ed finally stopped working construction but maintained his interest in firearms as his hobby.

PO JOHN T. BRANDT #78

APPOINTED: November 1, 1956
RESIGNED: September 1, 1964

John Thomas Brandt was born in Yonkers on March 23, 1935, attended local public schools and graduated from Roosevelt high school. Following school he served in the Army as a Corporal from July 9, 1953 to April 16, 1955 in the signal Corps. Records also indicate he graduated from New York University in NYC with a Bachelor of Science degree and attended Cortland State Teachers College from 1955 to 1956 majoring in general education and recreation. John was hired right out of college by the police department on November 1, 1956 from 82 Pomona Avenue. His starting salary was $3,780 and he was initially assigned to the 2nd pct. A month later he was moved to the 4th pct. John's nickname was "Jackie," he had a good personality, was a lot of fun and was also a good ball player. He had the following additional assignments; on May 16, 1960 to the second precinct, on February 4, 1962 the Traffic Division, on April 27, 1964 still in the Traffic Division but working in Traffic Engineering. Brandt resigned from the YPD while assigned to the Traffic Division on September 1, 1964 upon his own request reportedly to work as a State Conservation Officer. Former PO John Brandt died on April 5, 1910 in Montgomery, NY at age 75 years.

PO THOMAS A. FERGUSON #66

APPOINTED: November 1, 1956
RETIRED: July 1, 1977

Born Thomas Alexander Ferguson in Yonkers NY on July 17, 1931, Tom attended and graduated from local public schools. A few years later, while the War as being fought in Korea, Tom Ferguson joined the Marine Corps on March 4, 1951 and was shipped to Korea serving as a Sergeant and participated in combat operations against the enemy from Aug 31, 1951 to Aug 9, 1952. Tom served as a machine gun unit leader. He was honorably discharged on June 1, 1953. For the next three years Tom worked as a union Lather. He was appointed to the police department on Nov. 1, 1956 from 268 Glen Hill Avenue. Following his recruit training he was assigned to the 1st pct. at 20 Wells Avenue earning $3,780 a year. Tom was reassigned to the 3rd pct. on foot patrol on Apr. 27, 1964. A soft spoken man of few words, he preferred walking to riding in a radio car. On Nov. 15, 1969 Ferguson was transferred to the Communications Division, and worked as a dispatcher of radio cars. Tom did this right up to his retirement on July 1, 1977. Sometime later Tom moved to Homosassa Springs, Florida to enjoy his retirement.

PO JOHN J. O'BRIEN #111

APPOINTED: November 1, 1956
RETIRED: January 19, 1982

John Joseph O'Brien, or "Jack," as he was known to all, was born in Yonkers on January 19, 1933. He attended local public schools and graduated from Saunders HS. A resident of 2 Vineyard Avenue, and right out of high school, Jack joined the Air Force during the Korean War on August 13, 1951 serving as an Aircraft Mechanic attached to the 612th F.T.R. Bomber Squadron. He was honorably discharged on July 9, 1954 with the rank of Airman 2nd class. Upon discharge Jack worked as a "Gas Maintenance Man."

Jack was appointed to the YPD on November 1, 1956 from 5 Myrtle Street earning a salary of $3,780 a year. His first assignment was to the 1st precinct for training but a month later, in December of 1956, he was reassigned to the 4th on foot patrol. In 1958, following plans to re-establish the previously abolished Emergency Service Unit, Jack was selected and trained by the NYPD ESU instructors at Randall's Island in the city. On August 20, 1958 PO O'Brien was officially assigned to the new Accident Investigation Emergency (AIE) which was later renamed Emergency Service Unit.

On November 16, 1965 O'Brien was transferred to the Traffic Division Motorcycle Unit, detailed to the Safety Education Unit. At the time the Traffic Division was housed in the garage at Columbus Place, the back entrance to headquarters at 10 St. Casimir Ave. But on December 1, 1970 Jack was assigned to full time traffic enforcement duties with his motorcycle. Jack was well liked and had a friendly out-going personality always with a ready smile. He maintained a youthful look for so many years that his coworkers teased him about using some youth serum. He remained in Traffic right up to his retirement on January 19, 1982 and remained living in his home in Dobbs Ferry. A short while after retirement Ret PO John "Jack" O'Brien moved to Trumbull, Ct. He died there June 22, 2015.

PO JAMES F. CORCORAN #187

APPOINTED: June 16, 1957
RETIRED: June 27, 1985

Jim Corcoran was born in Yonkers on Dec. 20, 1929 and attended local public schools, graduating from Yonkers H.S. He joined the Navy on Mar 11, 1948 and received an Honorable Discharge on Mar 7, 1952. He applied to the Yonkers P.D. while living at 55 Chestnut Street, listing his occupation as a "driver." Upon his appointment to the YPD on June 16, 1957 he was assigned to the 3rd pct. on foot patrol. Later he would earn "a seat" in a radio car and would ride with his steady partner Russ Morvant in an orange and blue Plymouth radio car. Jim was a relatively quiet guy who did his job and would never be described as a party animal. But he was active in many PBA functions and was always willing to help. He was known to all his friends as "Corky." On Jan 1, 1971, when the precincts were closed due to centralization and the North and South Commands were established, Jim was assigned to the South Command. Always working in some uniform assignment, Jim also worked in SOD for a number of years and then returned to the 2nd pct. and retired on June 27, 1985. Jim and his family moved to Bradenton, Fla. where he lived up to his illness and subsequent death on August 20, 2009. He was 79.

PO DENIS F. HOGAN #34

APPOINTED: June 16, 1957
RESIGNED: February 29, 1964

Denis F. Hogan was born in Yonkers on May 23, 1933 and attended and graduated from local public schools. He listed his employment as an Expediter in the foundry department of Otis Elevator. He was appointed to the YPD on June 16, 1957 living at 44 Yonkers Avenue. Following recruit school he was awarded a set of handcuffs for attaining the highest marks in recruit school which was held by Lt Harold O'Neill. His first assignment was patrol in the 4th precinct earning a starting salary of $3,969 a year. His brother-in-law was Sgt Al Napolione who said that Denis had a great personality and a wonderful Irish wit which seemed to get him out of a number of difficulties. On Mar 16, 1961 Denis was transferred to the 2nd pct., but on February 29, 1964 Denis Hogan resigned from the YPD due to what he termed family problems. In February of 1965 he submitted a request for reinstatement but it was denied. At one point he was in his car when it was hit by a train in Brentwood LI. He was seriously injured but lived. Former PO Denis Hogan died on September 1, 1965 at the age of 32 years.

DEPUTY CHIEF JOHN P. DUFFY

APPOINTED: June 16, 1957
RETIRED: June 26, 1997

The subject of this profile was one of the more noteworthy members of the Yonkers Police Department. He was born John Patrick Duffy in Yonkers on May 28, 1933. "Red Duffy," as he would become known to everyone, attended Sacred Heart School and was a graduate of Gorton H.S. Prior to the Yonkers Police Department "Red" was employed as a Maintenance Mechanic for the Yonkers Municipal Housing Authority where he began working on June 16, 1954.

Duffy was appointed to the Yonkers Police Department on June 16, 1957 earning a starting salary of $3,969 a year. At the time of his appointment he lived at 8 Mulford Gardens and he said he was supplied basic uniforms, his shield and a revolver, but had to buy everything else with his own money. At the time he said a Choker coat cost $85.00 and the long winter, calf length coat, cost $105.00.

Following his appointment he received several weeks in house recruit training at Police headquarters on Wells Ave. by then Sgt Harry O'Neill. Firearms instruction was held at a range at the old Hudson Tire Co. on Nepperhan Ave. Upon completion of the recruit schooling he was assigned to 4th pct. patrol.

On February 4, 1959 he was assigned to the Emergency Service Unit in 2nd precinct when Ben DeLuccy, who had only been there a short time, asked for a transfer. To be certified in ESU it required he attend 80 hours of instruction with the NYPD ESU School at Randall's Island, NYC. His partner in the

Deputy Chief John P. Duffy (cont.)

truck was PO Tom Nolan, a good friend with a thick Irish accent.

On April 22, 1964 Duffy was appointed a Detective in the Detective Bureau. During his time as a detective Duffy gained an impressive record. On May 1, 1964 he received a letter of Commendation from then Sheriff John Hoy on his being awarded a Certificate of Honorable Mention by the Westchester Newspaper Police Honor Awards for Distinguished Performance of duty during the 1st quarter of 1964. He received this award again for the 3rd quarter of 1964. And again he received it from Sheriff Hoy for both the 2nd and 3rd quarter of 1966. And in August of 1966 he was commended by the FBI Assistant Director of the NY office for his participation in a joint investigation resulting in a bank robbery arrest. He would remain working as a detective right up to his promotion to Sergeant which took place on November 28, 1969. His salary then rose to $11,600 and he was transferred to the 2nd precinct as a patrol supervisor.

During his more than five years as a detective Duffy clearly made an excellent impression on his commanding officer. It became clear that his investigative skills were not to be wasted because after only two weeks following his promotion, on December 13, 1969, Sgt. Duffy was returned to the Detective Division as a Detective Sergeant. And yet, despite his apparent effectiveness, on December 11, 1970 Sgt. Duffy was returned back to uniform patrol duty as a patrol sergeant. Could politics have been in play here? Apparently so because, on January 28, 1972, Duffy was once again transferred back to the Detective Division as a Detective Sergeant.

It was said that in 1972 Duffy was detailed to the Forensic Lab for 3 or 4 months to supervise the analysis of 6,000 bags of heroin. He was assigned to the lab at that time because D.C. Murphy did not trust the former director of the lab to get the job done in a timely fashion. However Sgt Duffy was very meticulous and kept a very detailed record of who analyzed how many bags of Heroin per day on a lined pad. It was his version of a modern spreadsheet which he would show to DC Murphy weekly.

Sgt. Duffy remained in the D.D. right up to March 14, 1973 when he was promoted to the rank of Lieutenant earning a salary of $17,472 a year and was reassigned to work in the Inspections Unit. Two years later, on July 1, 1975, Lt Duffy was reassigned to work in the Internal Affairs Division as their executive officer. And four years later, on October 3, 1979, Lieut. Duffy was designated the commanding officer of the Internal Affairs Division.

On January 1, 1982 Lt. Duffy was transferred, once again, back to the Detective Division, as a Detective Lieutenant where he remained right up to his promotion to the rank of Captain on February 17, 1984. Upon his promotion to captain his salary rose to $40,601 a year and Capt. Duffy was reassigned to the Field services Bureau as a patrol duty captain or watch commander.

John Duffy's diverse knowledge continued to grow when on March 11, 1985 he was transferred to the Training Unit serving as the commanding officer. However, on January 13, 1986, Capt. Duffy was once again transferred, this time to the 2nd precinct as their commanding officer. And the changes and reassignments kept coming. On April 4, 1988 he was assigned to the Courts and Detention Services Division as their commanding officer. And on October 1, 1990 he was reassigned to the 4th precinct as their commanding officer.

Duffy seemed to have reached the pinnacle of his career went on March 14, 1994 he was appointed to the rank of Deputy Chief by Commissioner Olson. However, on March 20, 1995, Chief Duffy was reduced back to the rank of captain by a new police commissioner and designated commanding

Deputy Chief John P. Duffy (cont.)

officer of 4th precinct again. Following the election of a new mayor and the appointment of a new police commissioner, Duffy was once again appointed a Deputy Chief on April 23, 1996. A longtime resident of Morningside Avenue, Deputy Chief Duffy retired from the Yonkers Police Department after more than 40 years service on June 26, 1997.

Chief Duffy was an avid N.Y. Giants football fan, and attended nearly every Giants home game at the Meadowlands in NJ. He also enjoyed going to N.Y. Ranger hockey games with his grandsons. He was a graduate of the FBI National Academy in 1980, which he said lasted 14 weeks, and where he said he rated number one in his class. During his career Chief Duffy was the recipient of many awards, commendations, and letters of appreciation from the citizens of Yonkers. He was one of the original members of the Westchester County Emerald Society Pipe band as a Tenor Drummer where he enjoyed twirling his padded drum sticks while marching in parades. Duffy was a member of the Police Holy Name Society, Police Emerald Society, FBI National Academy Association, and the Friendly Sons of St Patrick.

Retired Deputy Chief John P. Duffy, a lifelong Yonkers resident, died on Saturday, March 25, 2006 at St. John's Riverside Hospital. He was 72 years old.

PO ADOLPHE J. DePESSEMIER

APPOINTED: June 16, 1957
RETIRED: August 28, 1991

Adolphe John DePessemier was born on November 16, 1928 in Manhattan on 10th St in the Chelsea section of NYC. His father, who was born in Belgium with French ancestry, later moved his family to the Bronx. Young Al attended Bronx elementary and Vocational H.S. from 1943 to 1945, leaving school in 11th grade.

Al joined the Navy on January 12, 1946 serving as a Fireman 1st Class on a Destroyer. He received his honorable discharge on September 23, 1949. Following the military Al worked for the Ward Leonard Co. in Mt Vernon producing electrical components and parts for the military requiring a top secret clearance from the FBI.

"Frenchy," as he was known to all his friends, was appointed to the police department on June 16, 1957 while living at 23 Crescent Place, Yonkers. Following recruit school Al was assigned to the 2nd precinct and his starting salary was $3,969 a year. Six years later, on August 1, 1963, Frenchy was reassigned to patrol in the 1st precinct on Wells Avenue.

Al must have considered himself very fortunate when, on August 13, 1965, he was appointed a Detective in the D.D. However, he was then disappointed when on January 14, 1966, only 5 months serving as a detective, he was transferred back to patrol in the 4th precinct. Later in 1966 a new 1st precinct building was constructed at 730 East Grassy Sprain Road and on November 7, 1966 Al was assigned there.

On January 1, 1971 a precinct centralization plan went into effect. The 1st and 3rd precincts ceased to operate as precincts and the 1st was merged into the 4th and renamed the North Command, and the 3rd likewise was merged into the 2nd precinct which was renamed the South Command. Among those transferred at that time was officer DePessemier who was moved to the North Command, once again on patrol.

PO DePessemier was once again appointed a Detective on May 13, 1981and assigned to the Intelligence Unit investigating organized crime activity in Yonkers. He worked there for about 6 years and then due to budget tightening measures the department had to eliminate one detective position. As a result, a senior detective from the D.D. "bumped" Al from the Intelligence Division and Al was returned back to patrol in the 1st precinct, but mostly on desk duty, and from which he retired on August 28, 1991.

During his career Al earned several awards including; in 1964 Honorable Mention from the Westchester Rockland Newspaper Honor Board for outstanding police work; on May 4, 1966 Honorable Mention from the Westchester Rockland Newspaper Honor Board for distinguished police performance; on July 11, 1969 a YPD Commendation; on August 18, 1969 Honorable Mention from the Westchester Rockland Newspaper Honor Board for distinguished police performance; and on June 6, 1991 a YPD Honorable Mention for a burglary arrest. Unfortunately he began suffering from Dementia causing hospitalization from time to time. Ret PO Adolphe DePessemier died in a nursing home in Queens NY on January 10, 2003. He was 74 years old.

PO JOHN J. HRESKO #104

APPOINTED: December 16, 1957
RETIRED: June 21, 1991

John Joseph Hresko was born in the city of Yonkers on February 18, 1930. He attended local elementary schools and graduated from Yonkers high school. After working several years for the Habirshaw Wire and Cable Co., John joined the Army in March of 1951, during the Korean War. He served in an Artillery Battalion up in Massachusetts and was honorably discharged in March of 1953 with the rank of Corporal. John listed his employment as that of a repairman. Hresko was hired by the police department on December 16, 1957 earning $3,969 a year. He pointed out that at that time all police officers received 28 days vacation. However, those vacation days included your days off as well. Following his initial police training his first assignment was foot patrol duty in the first precinct. Nine years later, on November 9, 1966, he was reassigned to the 4th precinct, which had its name changed in 1971 to the North Command. John had the nickname of, "The Panda," presumably due to his short, stocky physical stature. John was a very personable and talkative individual and as such always preferred walking a foot post where he could interact with the public one on one. His most frequent assignment was a foot post in the Getty Square area where John would remain working right up to his retirement on June 21, 1991.

PO DAVID LEE #228

APPOINTED: December 16, 1957
RETIRED: January 8, 1980

David Gordon Lee was born in Yonkers on Jan. 3, 1934. Dave attended local public schools and graduated from Saunders HS. Following school and at the age of 17 years Dave joined the Marine Corps on Feb. 23, 1951 during the Korean War. He received his honorable discharge holding the rank of Sergeant on Feb. 23, 1954. Following his military service Lee was employed by the City of Yonkers as a laborer and on Dec. 16, 1957 David Lee was appointed to the YPD earning a starting salary of $3,969 a year. Following his recruit training he was assigned to foot patrol in the 1st pct. After nearly four years, PO Lee resigned from the YPD on June 15, 1961 for personal reasons but applied for, and was reinstated to the 1st pct. on Feb. 1, 1962. Dave was transferred to the Juvenile Aide Bureau (Youth Division) on Apr 27, 1964. He returned to patrol in the 1st pct. on Jan. 24, 1966. On Nov. 9, 1966 he was transferred to the 4th pct. where he retired on January 8, 1980. Dave was an active member of the Westchester-Rockland Guardians Association. Ret. PO David G. Lee died in May of 1985 following a long illness. He was only 51 years old.

PO THEODORE MILLER #289

APPOINTED: December 16, 1957
RETIRED: September 5, 1986

Teddy Miller was born in the City of Yonkers on May 14, 1935, attended local public schools and graduated from the high school of Commerce. At the age of 18 Ted joined the Naval Reserve on September 1, 1953, served two years active duty and four years inactive reserve. During his enlistment Ted attained the rank of Petty Officer 3rd Class and received his honorable discharge in 1959.

On his police application Miller listed his employment at the time as a Clerk working in his father's restaurant. Ted was appointed to the police department December 16, 1957 from 260 Woodworth Ave. and following basic recruit training in a room in the Wells Avenue headquarters building was assigned to the 4th precinct earning a starting salary of $3,969 a year.

Right from his initial firearms training Ted realized he was a very good shot with his revolver. So it was no surprise when, in early 1960's, he was designated a member of the YPD Revolver Shooting Team competing throughout the tri state area against other police departments. Ted received a certificate of firearms qualification from the National Police Officers Association of America, and was awarded a Class C. 2nd place award by the Westchester County Police Pistol and Revolver League in September of 1963. During the early 1960s Ted was a certified FBI firearms training school instructor at Camp Smith in Peekskill New York assisting in the firearms training of police officers.

After receiving a federal grant entitled the Law Enforcement Education Program (LEEP), which was offered to all police officers across the country, during his off duty hours Ted attended and graduated Summa Cum Laud from Mercy College with a Bachelor's degree in sociology and psychology.

On March 31, 1972 PO Miller rescued a 5 year old child who had fallen into a swimming pool on Pine Street and was unconscious. Miller administered mouth to mouth resuscitation and revived the child. For his actions he was recognized by the US Congress commending him for his action that day and presented him with a certificate of commendation signed by then President Richard Nixon. And on July 7, 1972 Ted also received the Order of Michael the Archangel Police Legion award for that same earlier rescue.

On July 14, 1972 officer Miller was appointed a Detective in the DD where he remained for over three years, and on December 31, 1975 he was transferred from the Detective Division out to uniform patrol in the South patrol command. On December 4, 1981 Ted Miller was reassigned to the Communications Division where he was assigned to the Tele Serv Unit which took police reports over the telephone at headquarters. He was also a certified NYSPIN operator.

For many years Ted was married to PO Frances McLaughlin Miller, but after many years they divorced.

PO Theodore Miller retired from the YPD on September 5, 1986. After a ten year hard fought battle with cancer Ret PO Ted Miller died on April 2, 2016. He was 80 years old.

PO ANTHONY CENELLI # 216

APPOINTED: December 16, 1957
RETIRED: January 5, 1979

Anthony Joseph Cenelli was born on May 14, 1926 to Nicholas and Frances Giuliani Cenelli in Yonkers NY, but due to family difficulties they moved to Hawthorne where he attended Jr HS. His family returned to Yonkers and Anthony attended and graduated from Saunders Trade and Technical School. It was there that he studied auto mechanics, a trade which he enjoyed all his life.

Tony Joined the Army in June of 1944 at age 18 and served overseas as a Corporal in several countries in Europe, including Belgium and France, with the 159th Artillery Battalion of the 106th Infantry Division. His MOS was in the Motor Pool as a mechanic. He received his honorable discharge following the wars end in July of 1946.

Previous to the YPD he worked as an automobile mechanic for the Ford Dealership in Yonkers for many years as well as a mechanic for the Silver Lining Linen Company in Yonkers. Anthony Cenelli was appointed to the YPD on December 16, 1957 earning a starting salary of $3,969 a year. However, suddenly after only four days, Tony resigned on December 20, 1957 having decided that he wanted to go back to his job as an auto mechanic. Coincidentally his old job sent him to work as a civilian auto mechanic in the old police repair shop. It was there that he became comfortable being around police officers and decided to reapply for reinstatement to the YPD. He was reinstated a year later on December 19, 1958, one day before his eligibility for reinstatement would have expired. Tony was trained and assigned to the 1st precinct on a foot post.

After working patrol for ten years, on February 14, 1968, he was detailed to work as an auto mechanic in the police repair shop working on police cars. He remained in the repair shop for several years until August 20, 1974 when the repair shop was staffed with civilians and Tony was reassigned to the Warrant Squad. In the late 1970's he was transferred to the North Command on radio car patrol with PO Charles Safko. It was from here that Anthony Cenelli retired from the YPD on January 5, 1979. Years later he would watch his son David be appointed to the police department.

Tony was a very soft spoken man who had the ability to reason in difficult situations. His love for his country and for western music led him to playing the guitar, which he did as often as possible at various functions. A member of the Police Holy Name Society, the PBA and the police retirees association, Tony became ill and entered St Johns Hospital on April 26, 2006 with Emphysema. He did come home but, on March 23, 2007, Ret PO Anthony Cenelli died in St. John's Riverside Hospital at age 80 years.

PO HARRY OLEFERUK #151

APPOINTED: December 16, 1957
RESIGNED: April 1, 1966

Harry was born in the City of Yonkers on May 4, 1933. He attended local elementary schools, graduated from Saunders high school and attended Manhattan College in NYC from September of 1950 to March of 1951 where he studied engineering. He worked construction jobs for a while and then on March 11, 1953 he joined the Army serving during the last few months of the Korean War. He was honorably discharged on March 4, 1955. Harry was appointed to the YPD on December 16, 1957 earning $3,969 a year and was assigned to foot patrol in the 3rd precinct. During his off duty hours Harry had his own small business driving a truck to make extra money.

Without mentioning a word to anyone, Harry went on vacation from the 3rd precinct in March of 1966 and while away mailed a letter from a PO Box in Stone Harbor NJ to the police chief, indicating he was submitting his resignation from the YPD. In the letter he stated that his shield, hat wreath, revolver, etc. were all in his locker and he was resigning from the department effective immediately. At the time Harry lived at 1 Elinor Place and his resignation was accepted effective April 1, 1966.

PO BRUNO E. CIPOLLINI # 59

APPOINTED: December 16, 1957
RETIRED: January 20, 1978

Bruno E. Cipollini was born in New York City on February 4, 1932. Following his family moving to Yonkers he attended local Yonkers public schools and graduated from Gorton High School. Shortly after graduation Bruno joined the Air Force on January 1, 1951 during the Korean War. He served as a Flight Engineer and held the rank of Sergeant up to his honorable discharge on December 22, 1954. Bruno worked for a number of years as an auto mechanic until he received his appointment to the police department on December 16, 1957. At the time he was living at 26 Meadowbrook Place in Yonkers. Following his recruit training he was assigned to the 2nd precinct earning a salary of $3,969 a year. On March 16, 1961 officer Cipollini was reassigned to the 4th precinct on Shonnard Place. Five years later, on November 7, 1966, he was transferred to patrol in the 1st precinct at 730 E. Grassy Sprain Rd, which had been built that same year. Though destined to remain on patrol, Bruno was not only a good street cop, but he involved himself in serving as a trustee in the PBA and assisting the organization in many other ways. On January 1, 1971, following the new centralization plan of closing and renaming precincts, Cipollini was transferred to the North Command, which would be his last assignment. He completed seven more years on patrol there and then retired on January 20, 1978. Ret PO Bruno Cipollini died on August 31, 2001 at the age of 69 years.

DET. SOLOMON SPIVEY #666

APPOINTED: December 16, 1957
RETIRED: September 17, 1987

Born "King Solomon Spivey Jr," on August 18, 1928 in Yonkers, even as a youth he was known to everyone as Sol. But to his family he was "Junior." In fact throughout his entire career most people thought his full name was Solomon Spivey. He attended local elementary schools, Benjamin Franklin Jr HS, and graduated from Saunders HS. Shortly after his graduation Sol joined the U.S. Navy on November 26, 1946 and was assigned to the submarine service. He completed his four-year enlistment and was honorably discharged on July 11, 1950, just after the Korean War began.

Spivey was a large built man with an imposing presence, and following his military service he worked as a warehouse man. It was also said that he worked construction and helped build the Tappan Zee Bridge. He lived on Riverdale Avenue and was coaxed into taking the Yonkers police test by PO Charles Gerloff, who was the foot man on Riverdale Avenue at the time. Sol took the test, passed, and was appointed to the Police Department on December 16, 1957 from 119 Riverdale Ave. Following his recruit training Sol was assigned to the 1st precinct on foot patrol with a starting salary of $3,969 a year.

On February 26, 1964 Sol was appointed a Detective in the Detective Division earning $7,050 a year. Being a detective didn't last long because on August 27, 1965 he was returned to patrol back in the 1st precinct. The following year, on November 9, 1966, he was moved to the 4th precinct, and on November 6, 1967 was transferred to the Youth Division as a youth crime investigator. On June 14, 1968 Sol was once again appointed a detective, working general assignment crimes. Det. Spivey remained in the Detective Division right up to his retirement on ordinary disability on September 17, 1987. Sol was a member of the Yonkers Masons, the Westchester Police Guardians Association, and the Yonkers PBA. Even before he retired Sol's health was failing, and only three months later, on December 16, 1987, exactly thirty years from the day of his appointment, Ret Det "Solomon" Spivey died at the age of 58 years.

LT. GEORGE R. KOVALIK

APPOINTED: December 16, 1957
RETIRED: March 27, 1992

George Richard Kovalik was born in Yonkers on Feb. 21, 1930, attended local public schools and graduated from Commerce HS. Soon after the Korean War began George joined the Air Force on Nov. 1, 1950. During his 3+ years George served as an armorer for fighters and bombers. He was honorably discharged on Jan. 8, 1954. He worked for a time as a paymaster for some company but on Dec. 16, 1957 he was appointed to the YPD from 336 Edwards Place. Following recruit training he was assigned to the 4th pct. earning $3,969 a year. Just over 5 years later, on March 13, 1963, he was first reassigned to the 2nd precinct and then on Nov. 7, 1966 to the 1st. Kovalik had been previously trained by the NYPD ESU instructors in April of 1963 for assignment in our AIE, but was not assigned. But finally, on Feb. 2, 1970, George was detailed to the Accident Investigation Emergency. Ten years later on July 7, 1980 Kovalik was promoted to Sergeant and first assigned to the North Command and then on Dec. 14, 1983 to the 2nd. He received his promotion to Lieutenant on May 29, 1987 and was sent to the Communications Division. The following year, on April 11, 1988, Lt Kovalik was assigned to the 1st precinct as a Watch Commander. Throughout his career George was a golf player and for years worked a side job painting and doing wallpaper jobs. Lt George Kovalik retired on March 27, 1992.

PO RICHARD J. SABOL #24

APPOINTED: December 16, 1957
RESIGNED: April 16, 1964

Richard Joseph Sabol was born in Yonkers NY on March 21, 1934 and attended and graduated from the Yonkers public school system. Immediately following school and at the age of 17 years Richard joined the US Marine Corps in 1951, serving during the Korean War. He was honorably discharged in 1954. Following the military Richard worked as a Lineman right up to his police appointment. He was officially appointed to the Yonkers Police Department on December 16, 1957 earning a starting salary of $3,969 a year. Following recruit training he was assigned to patrol in the 2nd precinct. However, after more than six years with the YPD PO Sabol submitted a letter to the department advising that he was resigning from the YPD, effective April 16, 1964, to accept an appointment as a police officer with the New York City Police Department. It was heard that he served a full career with the NYPD and retired from same under honorable conditions.

PO JOSEPH E. GUGLICH #429

APPOINTED: December 16, 1957
RETIRED: January 5, 1979

Joseph Edward Guglich was born in Yonkers on March 19, 1931 and attended and graduated from the Yonkers public school system. As soon as Joe finished school, and at the age of 17 years, he joined the Army in June of 1948. Two years later, on June 25, 1950 the Korean War began and Joe found himself right in the middle of it.

He was sent to Korea from Fort Bragg, N.C. with the 4th Signal Battalion 10th Corps. and landed at Inchon with the 1st Marines and 7th Infantry Division in September of 1950. He remained in Korea serving as a Corporal until August 1951 and then was sent back to the states and was honorably discharged in April of 1952.

Following the military Joe was self-employed until he was appointed to the police department on December 16, 1957 from 31 Orchard Street. His first assignment, following recruit school, was patrol in the 2nd precinct earning $3,969 a year. In February 1962 Joe received two weeks Emergency Service training by the NYPD and was assigned to the Accident Investigation Emergency (AIE) later renamed ESU in the 2nd precinct.

On January 24, 1966 Joe was reassigned to the Juvenile Aide Bureau (JAB), later renamed the Youth Division. He remained there up to May 19, 1967 when he resigned from the YPD for personal reasons. However, he requested and was granted, reinstatement on April 19, 1968 and was assigned to patrol in the 3rd precinct. Joe was appointed a Detective on February 2, 1970 but was returned to patrol in the South Command on July 16, 1971. His last assignment was to the North Command on May 31, 1973 from which he would retire on January 5, 1979.

Ret PO Joe Guglich moved to Florida enjoying the warm weather and was very active in veterans affairs. He is a member of the Korean War Veterans Association Chapter 210 in Brevard County, and also VFW Post 1666 on Yonkers Ave, in Yonkers since 1965. Joe is determined to do his part to make sure the Korean War will not continue to be known as "The Forgotten War." He will tell you it seems to have been forgotten that nearly 45,000 US personnel were killed or missing during this un-declared war that was called a police action. This doesn't include wounded.

Joe participated in serving coffee and donuts on Tuesdays to veterans of all wars who attend the Viera, Fl. VA Clinic, where many of the vets look forward to talking with other vets about their experiences. At one point they were taking donations at various Publix Supermarket stores in order to collect enough money to erect a Korean War Monument to all branches of the military that served from 1950 through 1953. They also include those who are still serving from the day of the 1953 Armistice to the present in Korea. And many of the veterans attend local schools in Brevard County and speak about their experiences to the school children.

PO JOSEPH A. CALBI #65

APPOINTED: December 1, 1957
RETIRED: April 4, 1986

Joseph A. Calbi was born in Yonkers on October 7, 1933 and grew up in 24 William Street near Prescott St in the Nodine Hill section of Yonkers. He attended local elementary schools and while attending Saunders HS he was very athletic in several sports. While there he played football and was a champion handball player. Joe graduated from Saunders on June 24, 1952 and joined the Navy two days later on the 26th during the Korean War. He served in the US Navy from June 26, 1952 up to his honorable discharge in 1956. Joe served 29 months in the Navy's Crash and Rescue Team in Brunswick, Ma. He also served as a parachute rigger for a bombardier squadron. During his four years in the Navy he said he never served aboard any ship; he always flew in various aircraft.

Following the Navy Joe worked for Otis Elevator Co. for a year right up to his appointment to the police department on December 16, 1957 from 24 William St. earning $3,969 a year. He said his training consisted of being given an old .38 cal. positive revolver, a nightstick, shield and wreath, taught a little about the law and how to write a summons and was sent on patrol. His first assignment was in the 1st precinct on foot patrol and later in a radio car.

Following Emergency Service Training by the NYPD, in April of 1963 Joe was assigned to the Emergency Services Unit in the 1st precinct and rode in an ESU truck for 9+ years. Calbi related that the worst job he had was a fire in the Jewish Community Center in Yonkers in July of 1965 where he and PO Evans had to help remove eleven (11) bodies. On November 9, 1966 he was assigned to the fourth precinct ESU and later, on February 2, 1970, he was moved to headquarters working ESU. On December 9, 1972 Calbi was reassigned from ESU to headquarters working in the Communications Division until January 29, 1974 when he was assigned to the Property Clerk Unit. PO Calbi remained there 12 years right up to his retirement on April 4, 1986. Shortly thereafter Joe and his wife moved to Florida.

PO JOHN E. WAGNER #57

APPOINTED: December 16, 1957
RETIRED: August 30, 1991

Known by all his friends throughout his life as "Huntsy," John Wagner was born in Hastings-on-Hudson on December 25, 1927, Christmas Day. John attended local public elementary schools and graduated from Saunders high school with a trade in Auto Mechanics. Even as a young man John was built very sturdy and as such played on the school football team.

Wagner enlisted in the Army on November 12, 1945 following the end of World War II. He served as a Corporal in the infantry in Germany and was honorably discharged on August 9, 1948. Interestingly enough, the very next day John reenlisted in the Army, on August 10, 1948, and was stationed at Fort Knox Kentucky. He was promoted to the rank of Sergeant on November 7, 1951 and was assigned to the 101st Airborne Division. At this same time the Korean War was in progress. Wagner received his honorable discharge on June 23, 1952 and began employment at the Habirshaw Cable & Wire Corp.

On January 25, 1953 John married Rose Lomma, who was a cook at the "Casa Lomma," a restaurant /bar he frequented on Warburton Ave. Soon after, while working at Habirshaw, his leg was crushed in an accident. Doctors told him that he would not walk again. However, he did recover well enough to barely pass the police physical fitness test; in fact, he said he probably would not have been hired had he not scored #1 on the written test.

He was appointed to the police department on December 16, 1957 from 49 Warburton Avenue earning $3,969 a year. His first assignment, following recruit training, was foot patrol in the 4th precinct. He was assigned shield # 57 and often walked a post on Ashburton Avenue spending many tours visiting the firehouse on Vineyard Avenue. He liked to tell the story, or was it a tale, that he actually responded to a fire one night with the fire department because one of the firefighters was out sick. He said he was handed turn out gear and was told "*don't do anything kid, just stay with the truck in case a boss shows up to count helmets.*"

Seven years later, on November 5, 1964, Wagner was transferred to the Communications and Records Division performing clerical duties. On February 14, 1968 his job assignment name was changed to the Records and Service Maintenance Division, but his duties remained the same. He remained there for 22 years until December 17, 1990 when he was reassigned to the Planning Unit in the Administrative Services Division.

Jack, as he was known by family members, loved football, trivia and reading. He especially enjoyed reading history books. He was a walking encyclopedia on World Wars I & II and had a great friendly personality and enjoyed telling stories. His daughter, Elizabeth (Betty) Wagner Kwetchin was appointed a police officer in 1985, following in her Dad's footsteps.

John Wagner retired on August 30, 1991 and passed his shield, #57, to his daughter Betty who wore it until her retirement on February 5, 2009. John's son-in-law was PO Stephen Kwetchin. And, on July 29, 2011, his daughter Betty pinned shield #57 onto her niece (Huntsy's granddaughter), Amy Kielb. Of course the family was very proud and just as sure that she will wear old #57 with the same dignity as her grandfather and Betty had, for the previous 54 years.

Retired PO John Wagner died on February 27, 1999 from esophageal cancer. He died at home with his wife and four daughters at his bedside. He was 72 years old.

PO MICHAEL H. HUDAK #215

APPOINTED: December 16, 1957
RETIRED: January 6, 1978

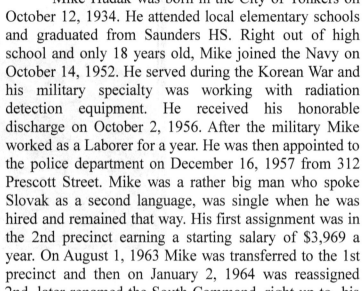

Mike Hudak was born in the City of Yonkers on October 12, 1934. He attended local elementary schools and graduated from Saunders HS. Right out of high school and only 18 years old, Mike joined the Navy on October 14, 1952. He served during the Korean War and his military specialty was working with radiation detection equipment. He received his honorable discharge on October 2, 1956. After the military Mike worked as a Laborer for a year. He was then appointed to the police department on December 16, 1957 from 312 Prescott Street. Mike was a rather big man who spoke Slovak as a second language, was single when he was hired and remained that way. His first assignment was in the 2nd precinct earning a starting salary of $3,969 a year. On August 1, 1963 Mike was transferred to the 1st precinct and then on January 2, 1964 was reassigned back to the 2nd precinct. Mike remained in the 2nd, later renamed the South Command, right up to his retirement on January 6, 1978. Though single, throughout most of his time on job Mike worked a second job carrying caskets at funerals for Duchinski Funeral Home. Even after retiring he continued to work for Duchinski driving the limousine. Mike became ill, entered the hospital and on February 15, 2015 Ret PO Michaek H. Hudak died. He was 80 years old.

PO GEORGE S. BUGOS #21

APPOINTED: December 16, 1957
RESIGNED: June 14, 1959

George Stephen Bugos was born in Yonkers on Dec. 24, 1931. He attended local schools and upon completion joined the Air Force serving from 1952 to his honorable discharge in 1956. On his police application he listed his employment as an "inspector." George was appointed to the police department on December 16, 1957 from 225 Ashburton Avenue. He was assigned to patrol duty in the 3rd precinct earning $3,969 a year. Bugos resigned from the YPD on June 15, 1958 but was reinstated on January 16, 1959. However, five months later, on June 14, 1959, Bugos again submitted his resignation for unknown reasons and same was accepted.

PO ROBERT T. WILSON #2

APPOINTED: December 16, 1957
RETIRED: January 6, 1978

Born Robert Terrence Wilson in Yonkers on Nov 11, 1931, young Bob attended local schools and graduated from Saunders H.S. in 1949. While in high school it was reported that he was somewhat of a star basketball player. After school he was first employed as a Hack Inspector in NYC for a short time and later, in February of 1951, he joined the Marine Corps serving during the Korean War. Bob served as a radio operator and was honorably discharged as a PFC in February of 1954.

About 1956 Bob was appointed to the NYC Transit Police Dept. Following training in the NYC Transit Police Academy, Bob worked as a NYC Transit police officer, but remained for only about a year.

It was then that the YPD called and he was appointed a Yonkers police officer on December 16, 1957. Bob was assigned to the 3rd precinct earning a starting salary of $3,969 a year and he remained there for about seven years. During those seven years Wilson established an enviable record and reputation by his fair, tough, and aggressive enforcement of the law. When he was working there were relatively few problems on his post. As a result of his excellent police work, he was appointed a Detective in the Detective Division on February 26, 1964, but only for only few months. He candidly admitted he didn't like that type of work and on April 16, 1964 he requested a transfer out of the Detective Division and was returned back to the 3rd precinct on foot patrol.

On Feb 2, 1968 Bob was reassigned to the 2nd precinct on patrol. He always preferred walking a foot post but would ride whenever required. He walked his post, usually Riverdale or McLean Ave., being very conscientious and getting to know most everyone on his post. Though he was a no nonsense cop, and the public knew it, he was fair to all and was respected and well-liked by the residents and merchants on his post because they felt safe when he was working. An early and original form of Community Policing.

PO Robert T. Wilson #2 (cont.)

Bob utilized his summons book with great effect, but his "no one gets a pass" style caused him frequent difficulties. In fact, on one occasion he was actually removed from his post and transferred to an "inside" job clearly as a form of punishment that Bob said was because he wrote summonses to people who were friends with high ranking officials. And for a street cop like Bob Wilson, to be taken off the street, that was punishment. By 1969 Bob had been placed on desk duty in the 2nd precinct where he remained for some time. However, his captain, Capt. Ostrowski, allowed him to walk a post and break in a rookie or ride in a radio car from time to time. During his years out of uniform it was said at some point he had also worked for short periods in Communications, Detention Services and the Youth Division.

Some of his awards are as follows: on August 10, 1961 he received a Citation of Commendable Merit from Macy Westchester Newspapers Police Honor Award, 2nd place, covering period of April, May, and June of 1961; on October 27, 1965 he received an Honorable Mention from the Westchester Rockland Newspapers Police Honor Awards, for the 3rd quarter period of 1965 and which was presented by then Westchester Co. Sheriff John Hoy.

On December 25, 1969 a news article announced that a testimonial affair was held at the Bajart veterans Post of the American Legion where Wilson received a certificate of appreciation. On February 13, 1970 he received the Police Officer of the Year award from the Yonkers Exchange Club where he was presented with a special plaque. On that occasion he was described as...... "*an example of what an ideal police officer should be. His police work has won prestige, respect, and admiration of the 2nd precinct personnel and the Yonkers Police Dept.*"

When Wilson thanked the audience, and being a man of few words, he remarked that, "*I'll always cherish this. It proves a point.*" He was clearly referring to his earlier removal from his foot post and put inside because he gave summonses to the "wrong people," as he put it. On January 26, 1972 he received a Certificate of Excellent Police Work; In 1973 the Macy Newspaper chain presented Wilson with the "Outstanding Policeman of the Year" award; and he was awarded the 1975 PBA Policeman of the Year Award while serving as 2nd Vice President of the PBA.

After Bob retired from the YPD on January 6, 1978 he moved from Caryl Avenue to Gainsvoort, NY to live and he became involved in politics. In 1983 Bob actually established the local Conservative Party in the Town of Northumberland and he was elected in 1984 and 1985 to the County Board of Supervisors running solely on the Conservative Party ticket.

Bob's family had a long tradition of service; His brother is YPD Ret Capt. Richard Wilson-(also former USMC); a nephew, YPD Sgt Richard Wilson; his Uncle was former YPD PO Stephen McKee, his grandfather was a Battalion Chief in the F.D.N.Y., and Bob's wife, Ann Marie's grandfather was YPD Sgt Henry Miller (ca 1899) on her mother's side.

Unfortunately Bob started suffering from dementia. Then, due to advancing Alzheimer's disease, Bob was placed in a nursing home in 1996 and Ret PO Robert Wilson died on July 8, 2005 at age 73.

PO NORMAN DOWNES #403

APPOINTED: March 16, 1958
RETIRED: May 26, 1978

Norman Downes Jr. was born in the city of Yonkers on July 15, 1932. He attended local public schools and graduated from Roosevelt HS. While attending Roosevelt HS Norman was very athletic and was a member of the Cross Country Running Team. In 1949 their team was All City and All County Champions. Following high school Norman attended several semesters at Columbia University in NYC.

At the age of 18 years Norman served in the Army beginning on Nov 9, 1950. He served during the Korean War initially as a Corporal and Chief Clerk in the Finance Office, but later volunteered to be part of the 82nd Airborne Division, 1st Ranger Battalion, as a paratrooper. He said that it was some of the toughest training he ever endured coupled with multiple jumps from a plane, but he was determined to prove he was as good as anyone else. And he did. He was honorably discharged from the Army on Nov 8, 1953.

Norman Downes was appointed to the Yonkers Police Department on March 16, 1958 earning a starting salary of $4,165 a year. He was appointed along with Mike D'Ambrosio, Bill Kennedy, Tom Ryan, Charlie Safko and Pete Leinen, and his first assignment was to patrol duty in the 2nd precinct. However, before the year was out, on December 1, 1958 Norman was reassigned to the 1st precinct at 20 Wells Avenue. Other transfers and assignments occurred as follows; on November 9, 1966 to the 4th precinct; on August 8, 1969 to the 3rd precinct; on January 1, 1971, when a precinct centralization plan was implemented and the 4 precincts were reduced to 2 and renamed commands, Norman was assigned to the South Command located at 441 Central Park Avenue. For a short time during his career in the 1970's Downes was selected to serve in the Scooter Squad where certain officers were to perform patrol duty on red police Lambretta motor Scooters.

Officer Downes, known affectionately by his friends as “Stormin Normin,” retired from the Yonkers Police Dept. on May 26, 1978. Following his retirement Norman owned and operated a tavern on Tuckahoe Road named "Upsndowns." Downes sold the tavern in 2001 and was appointed a Yonkers Deputy City Marshall.

Very early in his career he was the organizer of the very first Yonkers Police Guardians association in the late 1960's. Norman was chosen to serve as its first president but he felt that a ranking officer would achieve greater goals for the organization and that Lt James Barrier should be, and was, elected president. Norm cared deeply about his friends in the police department and as such every year he organized a church memorial service honoring those black police officers who had died over the years. And in November of 2001 he was elected President of the Westchester-Rockland Police Guardians Association. On June 15, 2006 the Yonkers Mayor selected Norman Downes to be appointed to the position of Chief City Marshal, City of Yonkers, after having worked for five years as Deputy City Marshall. Despite the heavy responsibilities with the City Marshall position, there was rarely a time when Norm couldn’t be seen with a smile and a warm friendly welcome for all those he knew.

Unfortunately his health took a turn for the worse and Ret PO Norman Downes died March 15, 2011. He was 78 years old.

DET. LT. JOHN F. SKELTON

APPOINTED: December 16, 1957
DIED: October 25, 1987

John Francis Skelton was born in Yonkers NY on Mar. 9, 1929. He attended Holy Rosary Catholic elementary school and graduated from Saunders HS. Skelton was known by everyone throughout his life as Frank Skelton, not John. Frank was a member of local 226 of the Wood, Wire Metal Lathers union where he worked, even while a police officer, for 17 years. "Frank" was appointed to the YPD on Dec. 16, 1957. Following training he was assigned to the 3rd pct. on foot patrol earning $3,969 a year. On May 1, 1963 Frank was appointed a Detective in the DD serving up to Feb. 3, 1969 when he was returned to patrol in the 4th pct. However, after only 6 months he was again designated a Detective on Aug. 8, 1969 and assigned to work in the Burglary Squad. Two years later, on July 16, 1971, Frank was reassigned to the South Command. Skelton was promoted to the rank of Sergeant on Feb. 18, 1977 earning $18,043 and sent to the North Command as a patrol supervisor. He was returned to the S/C on Jan. 1, 1979. While there he often was placed in charge of the Yonkers Race Track traffic detail. In his prime he enjoyed playing softball as well as fishing and hunting. Sgt Skelton was promoted to Lieutenant on Aug. 16, 1984 and assigned as a Communications Division supervisor. On March 11, 1986 Lt Skelton was appointed a Det. Lt. in the DD but shortly thereafter became seriously ill and remained on the sick list until his death on Oct. 25, 1987. Det Lt John Skelton was 58 years old.

PO THOMAS T. RYAN #181

APPOINTED: March 16, 1958
RETIRED: April 10, 1993

Born Thomas Theodore Ryan on Jan. 10, 1932 at 23 Gunther Ave in Yonkers, Ryan was one of 8 children. His father was Yonkers PO John P. Ryan. He had two brothers who also joined the YPD: William and Edward. Tom attended Mark Twain Jr. HS. and left without graduating. After working as a laborer for a while Tom entered the Army on July 10, 1952 and by Dec. 30, 1952 was sent to Korea on a troop ship. Tom served as a supply sergeant, received his GED diploma, and was honorably discharged in May of 1954. He was appointed to the YPD from 23 Gunther Ave on March 16, 1958 earning $4,165 a year and was assigned to the 4th pct. wearing his father's shield, #181. On Mar 13, 1963 he was reassigned to the 2nd pct. On Nov. 7, 1966 Tom was moved to the 1st pct. but the very next year, on Aug 18, 1967, he went back to 2nd. Nearly all of his career was spent on patrol but toward the end of his career Tom served as the 2nd precinct captain's aide. Tom Ryan, a good natured and happy go lucky guy, retired from the YPD on April 10, 1993. In retirement he took up playing golf which he admitted he was not a very good at.

PO PETER J. LEINEN #9

APPOINTED: March 16, 1958
DISMISSED: July 25, 1975

Pete Leinen was born in the city of the Yonkers on May 3, 1935, and attended and graduated from local public schools. Immediately after high school he joined the Navy on October 15, 1952, during the Korean War, and was honorably discharged on April 13, 1956. Pete was a carpenter by trade and worked as such until he was appointed a police officer. He received his appointment to the police department on March 16, 1958 while residing at 123 Oliver Ave. Following his recruit training his first assignment was on patrol in the 1st precinct with a starting salary of $4,165 a year. Pete's brother Ray was also appointed a Yonkers police officer in 1963. On July 10, 1978 Pete was reassigned to the 3rd precinct, and the following year, on January 1, 1971 he was moved to patrol in the South Command. Throughout the years he had a few problems with the department regarding violations of the rules and regulations. And at one point was charged with a serious act which resulted in Leinen being dismissed from the department effective July 25, 1975.

DET. WILLIAM T. KENNEDY #643

APPOINTED: March 16, 1958
RETIRED: February 8, 1980

Bill Kennedy was born in Yonkers on March 27, 1933 and graduated from Sacred Heart High School. Following school Bill had been an electrician's apprentice in New York City local #3. Bill joined the Navy on March 16, 1953, a few months before the Korean War cease fire, and did serve in Korea during the war. He was honorably discharged on March 8, 1955. Bill was appointed to the police department on March 16, 1958 while residing at 4 Purser Place. He was issued shield #74, and following training was assigned to the 1st precinct on foot patrol earning $4,165 a year. Surprisingly, two years later, on May 16, 1960, he was appointed a detective, but six months later, on November 16, 1960 he was returned to patrol in the 3rd precinct. Then came a series of transfers; 3-16-1961 to the 1st, 1-10-1962 to the 2nd, 1-2-1963 to the 1st, 11-9-1966 to the 4th pct. Then, on April 27, 1970 Bill was assigned to the Detective Division, but as a "silver shield," working Youth Bureau Investigations. And he was appointed a Detective once again on September 15, 1972. In 1976 Bill and his partners solved a difficult organized crime murder of a male in front of the Saw Mill Diner. On December 1, 1977 Det Kennedy was assigned to the YPD Arson Squad from which later retired on February 8, 1980. He moved to New Jersey where he continued to work on his golf game.

SGT. MICHAEL A. D'AMBROSIO #51

APPOINTED: March 16, 1958
RETIRED: April 19, 1978

Mike D'Ambrosio was born in Yonkers on September 7, 1933 and attended local public schools. He graduated from Saunders Trade & Technical H.S. (1948 - 1951) having studied chemistry. He attended New Paltz State Teachers College from 1952 to 1953 and the City College of New York in 1960. Mike also attended Iona College from Oct. 5, 1967 to June of 1968 for an Advanced Spanish speaking course. He was fluent in both Italian and Spanish.

On his application to the police department he listed his home as 326 Walnut Street and his occupation as "truck driver." After passing all the requirements he was appointed to the Yonkers Police Department on March 16, 1958 from the Walnut Street address at a salary of $4,165 a year. Following his recruit training his first assignment was to the 1st precinct on Wells Avenue. But after only 3 months, on June 30, 1958, he was re-assigned to the 4th precinct. On January 18, 1960 Mike was transferred to the Traffic Division on two wheel motorcycle patrol and in 1960 then Senator, and future president, John F. Kennedy campaigned in Yonkers and his motorcade was escorted by Yonkers motorcycle officers including PO Mike D'Ambrosio. Four years later, on November 9, 1966, he was returned to patrol in the 2nd precinct.

Mike was promoted to Sergeant on May 19, 1967 at $8,855 a year and was assigned as a patrol supervisor in the 3rd precinct. On one cold winter night while on patrol he responded to a fleeing auto theft suspect who was being chased by PO's John Bocskay and Bob Martin. At one point the suspect had drove his car right off the city pier and into the Hudson River to escape. It was said that Mike was lowered by rope into the freezing river and rescued the suspect. For his actions he received departmental recognition.

On Feb. 19, 1968 he was assigned to the Youth Division as an investigative supervisor but the next month, on March 6, 1968 he was returned to the 3rd pct. Several assignments followed; on December 1, 1970 to HQ in Communications, on December 9, 1970 to 4th pct. patrol, on January 1, 1971 to South Command, and on October 6, 1972 to Youth Services & Community Relations Division.

Sgt. Michael A. D'Ambrosio #51 (cont.)

Mike was the first person holding the rank of Sergeant to be elected as president of the YPD Captains, Lieutenants, & Sergeants Assoc. He served as such from January of 1973 through December of 1977. He was re-elected to that position for eight consecutive years. At the time, even though the CLS Association had their own organization, they could not bargain with the city for benefits or raises. The officers in the department were under the PBA for this purpose and they could not even serve on the PBA board and had no say in negotiating matters with the city. Through a great deal of effort by Mike and the association with the city and state, the officers association received de-certification by the Public Employees Relations Board (PERB) from the PBA and were authorized for the very first time to negotiate with the city for themselves. Mike did not seek re-election for 1978 and retired from the department on April 19, 1978. At the time he was living at 66 Bajart Place, in Yonkers.

Mike retired from the department but never lost his endless energy. He had a way of becoming friends with people in local business, local and state politics, and various unions. It often seemed like he knew everyone. Upon his retirement in 1978, he was appointed to the Yonkers Parking Authority and then became a board member to the Westchester County Parks and Recreation Board. He served for many years as a member of the PAL Board of Directors participating in many committee endeavors. He always chaired the annual PAL Poster Child competition and served on the annual PAL Luncheon committee which raised a great deal of money to keep the PAL programs operational.

Mike was also a semi-professional photographer. He was always ready with a camera at an event and he provided copies of pictures to those who wanted them at no cost to them. He was on salary as a part time reporter for the local weekly newspaper, The Home News & Times, and also worked for Local #456 as their official photographer for anything that they wanted recorded; be it parties or picketing. Mike did freelance work that enabled him to become friends with people such as Frank Sinatra, Dean Martin, Jackie Kennedy Onassis, Jane Mansfield and many others. If that wasn't enough he also worked for Saw Mill Auto Wreckers in Mt Vernon. Mike, or as he was affectionately known to his friends, "Junie" or "Mikey D," also had a condominium in Ft Lauderdale where he could relax; probably for no more than ten minutes, knowing him.

Mike became ill with heart problems and following surgery, complications set in and Ret Sgt Mike D'Ambrosio died on April 30, 2009. He was 75 years old.

PO CHARLES S. SAFKO #51

APPOINTED: March 16, 1958
RETIRED: July 1, 1979

Charles Safko was born in Yonkers NY on August 24, 1927 where he grew up, attended and graduated from the public school system. A short time after graduating high school and following the end of WW 2, Safko joined the Marine Corps on November 3, 1945. He served in the Pacific as a radio operator and, following his honorable discharge as a PFC on August 13, 1948, he was awarded the World War II victory medal and China service medal. During his service in the Pacific he learned to speak limited Japanese.

Charlie Safko gained employment as a construction worker and steel carrier/laborer until March 16, 1958 when he received his appointment as a Patrolman in the Yonkers Police Dept. He was hired from 44 Caroline Avenue earning a starting salary of $4,165 a year. Following recruit training he was assigned to the 1st precinct on Wells Avenue. About eight years later, on November 9, 1966, "Chuck," as he became known, was transferred to the 4th precinct where he would remain for the rest of his career. On February 11, 1967 at 11:30 PM and following an armed robbery, PO Safko, who was off duty, observed the suspects running from the scene. He gave chase, fired two warning shots, and tackled one of the robbers. After a violent struggle he arrested the man without firing another shot. For his outstanding action and bravery that evening PO Charles Safko was awarded the department's Honorable Mention. Chuck was your basic street cop but had a very unusual personality and was an almost nonstop talker.

Charles Safko retired from the YPD on July 1, 1979 and after a time moved from Ossining, NY to Florida's West coast.

PO MATTHEW F. MELVIN #43

APPOINTED: May 1, 1958
RESIGNED: April 12, 1960

Matt was born in Yonkers about 1935, attended local public schools and graduated from Gorton H.S. Matt was very active in sports and was a co-captain of the football team. Prior to the YPD Melvin listed his employment as a White Plains police officer. Matt Melvin was appointed to the YPD on May 1, 1958 from 4 Glenwood Terrace. Following recruit training he was assigned to patrol in the 4th precinct. Melvin submitted his resignation effective April 12, 1960 for personal reasons. Several years later he said he regretted leaving and had worked for the Yonkers DPW from where he retired. Lt. Christopher Melvin said Matthew Melvin was his father's 1st cousin and was now deceased (2003).

PO JOHN J. MAGILTON #248

APPOINTED: May 1, 1958
RETIRED: April 5, 1980

John Magilton was born in the Nodine Hill section of Yonkers on August 8, 1934. He attended public school #23 and later graduated from Saunders high school. As an 18-year-old right out of school John joined the Marine Corps in October of 1952 during the Korean War. He was said to have served as a sergeant in an engineering construction division. He received his honorable discharge in August of 1955. Following his military service John made a living with his trade as being a carpenter. He was appointed to the Police Department on May 1, 1958 from 23 Cedar St. His starting salary at that time was $4,165 a year and his first assignment was to the 4th precinct on foot patrol. Five years later on May 1, 1963 officer Magilton was appointed a detective in the Detective Division. However that assignment lasted less than a year, and on February 26, 1964 he was returned to the 4th precinct on uniform patrol and would remain there right up to his retirement on April 5, 1980. John was soft-spoken, a real gentleman and a very disciplined individual. Due to his personality he was nicknamed "Gentleman John" and while in uniform he preferred to walk a foot post rather than patrol in a radio car. And one of the posts that he was most often assigned was on Lake Avenue. Following his retirement, and being a skilled carpenter and painter, he worked for St. Joseph's Seminary and the Westchester Country Club. Several years later John moved to LaGrange New York where I'm sure he spent his leisure time hunting and fishing.

SGT. ALEXANDER J. SACCAVINO #79

APPOINTED: May 1, 1958
RETIRED: September 16, 1978

Born in New York City on Dec. 4, 1933, Alexander Joseph Saccavino attended and graduated from James Monroe high school in NYC. Shortly after his school graduation Al joined the Marine Corps on Mar. 31, 1953 during the last few months of the Korean War. He served in the infantry as a Sergeant E-4 and was released from active duty on Mar. 30, 1956. He received his honorable discharge on Mar. 30, 1961. Following his military separation in 1956 Al attended Westchester Community College studying construction and he would later work as a bricklayer. Al was appointed to the police department on May 1, 1958 and following training was assigned to the 2nd precinct earning $4,165 a year. Al was teased by his co-workers calling him, "Bag Of Wine," due to a play on his name "Sack of Vino." On September 15, 1972 Al was promoted to Sergeant with a raise to $14,399, and was reassigned as a patrol supervisor in the North Command. On February 16, 1976 Sgt Saccavino was moved to the South Command from which he retired on September 16, 1978. In retirement Al kept busy holding both a real estate license and an insurance salesman license.

PO RAYMOND J. BARTKO #132

APPOINTED: May 1, 1958
RETIRED: March 1, 1980

Born Raymond John Bartko in Yonkers NY on January 21, 1928, Ray attended local public schools and graduated from Yonkers HS. Right out of high school and just 17 years old Ray joined the Navy on June 21, 1945, at the tail end of WW 2, just before Japan surrendered in August of 1945. He was honorably discharged as a Seaman 2nd class on July 23, 1946. Ray worked many years as a truck driver until he was appointed to the police department on May 1, 1958 while living at 110 Morris Street. His starting salary was $4,165 a year and he was assigned to foot patrol in the 4th precinct. His brother in law was Lt George Rusnack. Around 1968 Ray was assigned to the Traffic Division on a three wheel motorcycle issuing parking summonses. He remained there until October 19, 1971 when the three wheel "bikes" were said to have been eliminated and Ray issued street cleaning summonses from a radio car. On April 4, 1979 PO Bartko was reassigned to patrol duty in the South Command where he remained right up to his retirement on March 1, 1980.

DET. LT. DONALD J. BEATTIE

APPOINTED: May 1, 1958
RETIRED: April 30, 1998

Born, Donald James Beattie, in Yonkers on March 15, 1934, Don was raised in Yonkers, attended local schools, and graduated from Yonkers H. S. Two years later in Feb. 1954 Don joined the US Army receiving his basic training at Fort Dix, N.J. He served in an Infantry Battalion in Fort Knox, Kentucky as a Company Administrative Assistant. He was honorably discharged as a Corporal in February 1956. Don then worked for Otis Elevator Co. on Woodworth Avenue for two years as a "Packer." During that time as a resident of 108 Elm Street, he filed and took the Civil Service test for Police Officer. After passing the test he was appointed a Yonkers police officer on May 1, 1958 at an annual salary of $4,165. Following only two weeks of classroom training in the Wells Avenue headquarters, PO Beattie was assigned to patrol duty in the 4th precinct. Though not assigned to the Emergency Services Unit officer Beattie was always eager to be involved as much as possible. As such he volunteered to be detailed to the NYPD ESU training school at Randalls Island in NYC from April 1, 1963 to April 12, 1963 for specialized "rescue training." With this training he could now be used as a "fill in" for assignment in the Yonkers ESU.

A very well liked, friendly and sociable individual, Don Beattie was also very active in the Police Benevolent Association. Following the opening of a new 1st precinct at 730 East Grassy Sprain Road on Nov 9, 1966, Donald was reassigned from the 4th precinct to this new 1st pct. On January 1, 1971, following a precinct centralization and the renaming of the 4th pct. to the "North Patrol Command," officer Beattie was then assigned to that location.

Upon Don Beattie's promotion to the rank of Sergeant on Nov. 24, 1978, at a yearly salary of $21,142., he was assigned to the South Patrol Command as a patrol supervisor. His commanding officer recognized his dedication and skill and recommended PO Beattie for assignment in the Detective Division. And in 1981 Beattie was assigned to the D.D. as a Detective Sergeant in command of the Burglary Unit.

On August 16, 1984 he was once again promoted, this time to the rank of "Lieutenant" at the annual salary of $40,475. Following his promotion he was reassigned as the 3rd precinct executive officer. On November 13, 1987 Donald was once again advanced to "Detective" Lieutenant and, due to his reputation of competence and reliability, he was assigned to the highly sensitive position of "Executive Officer and Aide to the Police Commissioner." Following six years as the commissioners executive officer, in 1993 Det. Lt. Donald Beattie was reassigned to that of "Executive Officer" in the Detective Division. When Lt. Beattie reached the mandatory retirement age of 62 years, as outlined in the section of the pension system to which he belonged, he was simply not ready to retire. He said, "I'm not ready." Determined to remain working, Lt Beattie switched to another section of the police pension system which would allowed him to remain working until age 64 years. When he did reach age 64 he retired from all active service on April 30, 1998 after more than 40 years of honorable and efficient service.

Det. Lt. Donald Beattie is the brother in law to retired Yonkers police captain James Bubbico, and was the recipient of six Certificates of Excellent Police Work, and two Westchester/Rockland Newspaper Honorable Mention awards.

Ret Lt. Donald Beattie died on September 17, 2004 following a short fight against cancer.

DET. FRANCIS J. CAROZZA #650

APPOINTED: May 1, 1958
RETIRED: April 5, 1980

Born in Yonkers on Sept. 5, 1933, Francis J. Carozza attended local public schools and graduated from Yonkers high school. Frank, as he was known, joined the Navy on Mar. 4, 1953 during the last few months of the Korean War, but his Navy enlistment was cut short after boot camp for medical reasons. Frank was later honorably discharged. Frank attended the Pace Business School for typing for a year, and also studied at the American Institute of Banking. Frank then gained work as a teller in a local bank.

He was appointed to the Y.P.D. on May 1, 1958 while residing at 117 Park Hill Ave. His starting salary was $4,165 a year and his first assignment was to the 1st precinct. While serving in the old 1st precinct on Wells Avenue, he also was assigned to the Emergency Service Unit where he served for four years.

Eight years later, on June 10, 1966, Frank was appointed a detective and was sent to the Internal Revenue's school for Special Agents where for 7 weeks he was trained in procedures of financial investigations and served as a liaison to IRS agents. On October 20, 1966 through January 12, 1967 he attended and completed an instructional course in Radiological Monitoring which was offered by Cornell University in conjunction with a Civil Defense program. Initially after being appointed a detective he worked general assignment investigations. But due to his banking background he was later assigned to all fraud investigations involving banks. On November 15, 1974 Det Carozza was reassigned to the Intelligence Division assisting in the investigations involving organized crime.

Frank's cousin was PBA President Paul Carozza and Frank himself served as Treasurer of the PBA for many years. Det Francis Carozza retired from the Intelligence Division on April 5, 1980 to accept employment that encompassed both his passions; police work and banking. After 10 years in that job Frank retired again and moved to Bluffton, S.C. where he continued to work on his golf game and tennis. Frank now volunteers as a patrol guard in the gated community where he now lives, which is Sun City in Hilton Head.

PO LOUIS D. FERRAIOLA #200

APPOINTED: August 16, 1958
RETIRED: January 11, 1984

Born Louis Dominick Ferraiola in Yonkers NY on February 7, 1929, Lou attended local public schools and graduated from Saunders HS. Following the outbreak of the Korean War Ferraiola joined the Army on August, 19, 1950 serving in Korea as a supply driver and communications lineman. He was honorably discharged on May 7, 1952. Following the military Lou worked several years in construction as a laborer. But on July 16, 1957 he was hired by Yonkers to work in the police department as a garage attendant for the 2nd precinct. Enjoying a close up look at the police operation, Lou took the police test, passed, and was appointed a Patrolman on August 16, 1958. At the time he lived at 54 Oak Street, earned a starting salary of $4,165, and following recruit training was assigned to the 2nd precinct. On August 1, 1963 he was moved to the 1st pct. for a short time, but on January 2, 1964 was returned to the 2nd precinct. In 1967 the Westchester County Grand Jury voted a special Commendation to PO Ferraiola for his courageous and resourceful action in the capture and arrest of the person responsible for an armed robbery on April 19, 1967 and the intelligent manner in which he testified before the grand jury. Lou Ferraiola, who spoke Italian fluently, retired from the YPD on January 11, 1984. He moved to northern Westchester to relax.

PO JAMES V. GIORDANO #14

APPOINTED: August 16, 1958
RETIRED: August 21, 1970

Jim Giordano was born in Yonkers NY on July 7, 1933 and graduated from Roosevelt high school. He was appointed to the YPD from 60 Woodruff Avenue on Aug. 16, 1958, received recruit training and was assigned to the 2nd precinct earning $4,165 a year. About 6 years later, on Apr. 27, 1964, Jim was transferred to the Traffic Division assigned to two wheel motorcycle patrol. Only 3 months later, on July 12, 1964, Giordano was involved in an accident with his motorcycle on Central Avenue in which she was severely injured leaving him with a permanent limp and ending his police career on a motorcycle. Jim was reassigned to duty in the 3rd precinct but was retired on a disability pension Aug. 21, 1970. Following his retirement he was a self-employed contractor. On Dec. 22, 1982 at about 11 PM Giordano was struck by a car at CPA and Palmer Road and was transported to Lawrence Hospital where he was pronounced dead. He was 49 years old.

PO TIMOTHY McGRATH #537

APPOINTED: August 16, 1958
RETIRED: August 18, 1978

Tim McGrath was born in the City of Yonkers on December 8, 1931. He was a product of the Yonkers school system from which he graduated. Directly out of school, and just 17 years of age, Tim joined the Army on December 26, 1948. He served as a PFC working as a clerk typist and was honorably discharged on Sept. 12, 1952 during the Korean War.

Tim was appointed a police officer on Aug. 16, 1958 earning a salary of $4,165 and his first assignment was patrol in the 3rd precinct. He was a very sociable individual but was noted for having a quick temper. On Feb. 26, 1965 Tim was appointed a Detective in the DD where he remained up to August 25, 1967 when he was returned to patrol in the 3rd precinct. On June 9, 1968 while on patrol at 6:45 AM Tim McGrath & his partner Bob Lorenz observed 274 Hawthorne Ave. to be on fire. After advising H.Q. they ran into the building to wake tenants. During the rescue they were overcome by smoke inhalation and were hospitalized. For their actions they were both awarded the departmental Honorable Mention. On Jan. 1, 1971, following the centralization of the precincts, Tim was reassigned to work from the South Command at 441 Central Park Ave.

Following specialized training by the NYPD, McGrath was assigned to the Emergency Service Unit on September 28, 1973 working from the North Command. “Timmy” McGrath retired from the YPD on August 18, 1978 and was hired as the Director of Security for Yonkers General Hospital on Ashburton Ave. His nephew, also named Tim McGrath, later joined the YPD.

His former partner, Bob Lorenz, said McGrath was a real cop’s cop who took no nonsense from anyone. He was a hot head at times, but you could always count on him to back you up.

After a long difficult illness Ret PO Timothy McGrath died on December 11, 1991. He was 60 years old.

PO RICHARD R. HENDRICKS #169

APPOINTED: August 16, 1958
RETIRED: February 5, 1987

Richard Robert Hendricks was born on April 13, 1930 in Yonkers NY, attended local public schools, and left Saunders HS without graduating. He was inducted into the Army on March 16, 1951 during the Korean War and served in an artillery unit as a Corporal training and directing personnel in Anti-Aircraft tactics. While in the Army he earned his Government Equivalency Diploma. He was released from active duty on February 21, 1953 and honorably discharged on February 27, 1957. Hendricks worked for several years installing storm windows until he was appointed to the police department on August 16, 1958 from 609 Nepperhan Avenue. His first assignment was to the 4th precinct on foot patrol earning $4,165 a year. On February 10, 1972 Rich was transferred to the Training Unit in the firearms section as the department's firearms instructor. In September of 1977 he attended Instructor Training School in Saratoga Springs. He also attended the FBI Firearms training school from September 10th to the 14th, 1972. Officer Hendricks was responsible for all the in service firearms training for the YPD and was also trained and designated the YPD's Armorer and explosives expert. PO Hendricks retired from the YPD on February 5, 1987 and died on July 29, 1991. He was 61 years old.

PO ROBERT S. LAMANCE #165

APPOINTED: August 16, 1958
RETIRED: August 16, 1982

Robert Stephen Lamance was born in the city of Yonkers on April 3, 1934. He attended and graduated from local public schools and right after graduation, on July 9, 1953, Bob joined the Army. He received his honorable discharge in June of 1955. Following his military service Bob gained employment by working for the Otis elevator Company. However, on August 16, 1958 while living at 16 Cedar St., Bob was appointed a patrolman in the YPD. Following his recruit training his first assignment was patrol in the 3rd precinct earning a starting salary of $4,165 a year. On January 24, 1966 Bob was assigned to work in the Emergency Services Unit operating from the 1st precinct. Known to his good friends as "Hondo," Bob had received his ESU training from the NYPD. However, only 3 months later, on April 13, 1966, Bob requested to be transferred out of the Emergency Unit and was reassigned to the Communications and Records Division working as a dispatcher in the radio room. He remained in this assignment up to January 9, 1976 when he was transferred back out to patrol duty and to the South patrol command. Three years later, to the day, on January 9, 1979 he was returned to the Communications Division again working as a dispatcher. In February of 1980 officer Lamance suffered a heart attack and subsequently retired from the police department on August 16, 1982. Retired PO Robert Lamance died on June 20, 1993 at the age of 59 years.

PO EMANUEL J. STELLA #85

APPOINTED: August 16, 1958
RETIRED: March 8, 1985

Although born in Yonkers NY on October 1, 1926 with the name Emanuel Stella, Manny was known to all as just that, "Manny." He grew up in Yonkers in the area of Palisade Ave. and Schroeder Street and attended and graduated from local schools. At the age of 18 years and just out of school, Manny joined the Navy on October 13, 1944 serving during World War 2. He served aboard the USS John Q. Roberts, a high speed transport ship and he said he and his shipmates were in Tokyo Bay during the official surrender of Japan. Following the end of the war, he received his honorable discharge on June 18, 1946.

Following his military service he worked a variety of jobs but on his application for the police test he listed his employment as a "Toll collector" on the parkway. A resident of 5 Waring Row Manny was appointed to the Yonkers Police Dept. on August 16, 1958 earning a salary of $4,165 a year. Following his basic recruit training he was assigned to patrol duty in the 1st precinct located at 20 Wells Ave.

On December 1, 1964 officers Emanuel "Manny" Stella and Tom Brink, both assigned to the 1st precinct out of 10 St. Casimir Avenue, and assigned as regular partners, were working the Late Tour. At about 0345, hours while driving through the parking lot of the Dunwoodie Motel at 300 Yonkers Avenue, they observed a holdup taking place in the office of the hotel clerk. The suspect saw the police car in the parking lot and ran out of the office in an attempt to escape. As he did he began firing at Stella and his partner with his handgun. A running gun battle followed which resulted in the suspect being wounded but still able to escape limping into the woods. However, within just a short period of time the arrest was made of that shooter and later his accomplice. Both Manny Stella and his partner were highly commended by their superiors and were awarded departmental recognition. As a result of officer Stella receiving the Honorable Mention award, the second highest awarded at that time, he was appointed a Detective effective December 4, 1964. He and his partner both were transferred to the DD but after only a short time, and at their own request, were returned to precinct patrol duty. However, both officers continued to receive 3rd grade detective pay.

By 1966 he was living at 141 Rockne Road and on November 9th of that year was reassigned to patrol in the 4th precinct. On Feb 6, 1970 Manny Stella was again assigned in the Detective Division as a detective. But, as before, just four months later on June 12, 1970, he was reassigned to patrol in the 1st precinct at 730 East Grassy Sprain Rd. He preferred uniform patrol.

On Jan. 1, 1971, when the precinct centralization plan was implemented creating the North and South Commands, Stella was moved to the North Command. However, on Sept. 17, 1971 Manny was transferred to the South Command where he would remain on patrol up to his retirement on March 8, 1985. During retirement Manny kept busy working in a gas station at the top of Lockwood Ave.

Manny Stella was still a resident of 141 Rockne Road when he became ill and moved in with his son Michael, a corrections officer. After a lengthy illness Emanuel "Manny" Stella died on January 19, 2011. He was 84 years old.

PO ANTHONY F. BAIOCCO Sr. #128

APPOINTED: August 16, 1958
RETIRED: October 30, 1963

Anthony Francis Baiocco was born in the city of Yonkers on January 18, 1928. He attended and graduated from local public schools and following his graduation he joined the Marine Corps toward the end of the war in 1945. He served honorably and was discharged in 1948. Following his military he was hired by the Yonkers DPW where he enjoyed his work. Nonetheless, Tony took and passed the Yonkers Patrolman civil-service exam and accepted appointment to the YPD on August 16, 1958. At that time he was living at 128 School St. Following his recruit training he was assigned to the 4th precinct earning a starting salary of $4,165 a year.

As the record indicates, apparently Anthony was very conflicted about where he should be employed. Just short of a year later, on July 31, 1959, he resigned from the YPD to return to the DPW where he could earn more money. Yet, on Jan 18, 1960 he sent a letter to PSC Goldman requesting to be reinstated to the YPD indicating that he was a member of the Hod Carriers Union AFL-CIO of Yonkers and previously working nights in the YPD had caused a family problem. However that issue had been resolved. His request for reinstatement was approved effective March 1, 1960.

Evidently the DPW wanted him back and on Oct 9, 1962 Baiocco was offered the position of Motor Equipment Operator in the DPW at $19.80 a day. He could now operate bull dozers and front end loaders. The temptation was too great. So, on October 15, 1962, Baiocco once again resigned from the YPD while still in the 4th. And, once again just a year later, on Oct 14, 1963, he requested to be reinstated again to the YPD and once again his request was approved effective Oct 23, 1963, and this time he was assigned to the 1st pct. At the time he lived at 37 Caroline Ave.

Then, one last time, only a week later, he again submitted his resignation from the YPD, apologizing and stating that the cause for resigning was due to tremendous amount of pressure from his family. Same was accepted effective Oct 30, 1963. Anthony would live to see two sons, Anthony Jr and Mark appointed to the YPD. Anthony Baiocco Sr retired from the Yonkers DPW and died on July 14, 2006 at the age of 78 years.

DET. JOSEPH E. SURLAK #642

APPOINTED: September 16, 1958
RETIRED: January 13, 1994

Born in Yonkers on March 18, 1936, Joe Surlak attended PS# 4, Mark Twain Jr HS, and graduated from Roosevelt HS. Following his graduation and due to an interest in drafting, Joe attended the Chicago Technical Institute for Architectural Drafting from January to Sept. of 1954. Young Joe was always very athletic and interested in sports. As a youth he was a member of the police PAL's softball team and also played with the team known as the Pioneers. He even experienced playing against the inmates at Sing Sing prison in Ossining. He was later hired as an Expediter for Otis Elevator Co.

Joe joined the Army National Guard's 101st Signal Battalion on North Broadway on February 13, 1958, served six months active duty, and was honorably discharged in 1964. When he took the police test Joe was on active duty in Georgia and had to get military leave to come home, take the test, and return to Georgia.

While living at 14 Huber Place Joe was scheduled to be appointed with the group appointed on August 16, 1958. However he was still on active duty. The following month, while working in Otis he was called over to headquarters, without knowing why, and was sworn in on the spot. He was appointed to the YPD on September 16, 1958.

Joe related that in the late 1950's, early 1960's the police recruit training was not very good. While dressed in a gray shirt and slacks he said training consisted of several weeks of sitting in a room at headquarters ostensibly being instructed in police procedures by then PO Eugene Reynolds and then Sgt Harold O'Neill. Neither of whom were certified instructors. However he said they talked mostly about sports. And, he said, they never received any firearms training during that period. Following recruit training he was assigned to the 1st precinct walking or riding with a senior officer and earning $4,165 a year. In February of 1960 PO Surlak was detailed to the NYPD ESU training school at Randall's Island to prepare him to serve in our Emergency Service Unit whenever needed. Six years following his police appointment Joe was assigned to the plainclothes Juvenile Aid Division investigating crimes by juveniles. But it was a year later, on April 9, 1965, that Joe was appointed a Detective assigned to the Detective Division earning a salary of $7,300 a year. Joe's enthusiasm, natural intuition and street smarts made him a natural for the job. He was a friendly, well-liked and respected detective.

In the late 1960's Joe was assigned to the Narcotics Unit working undercover. His partner was "Jack" Roach and he remained in "Narco" for four years. While there, he and Det Roach arrested the operators of a hi-jacked flatbed trailer full of stolen copper on the thruway. He and Roach both were awarded Policeman of the year in 1969 by the Yonkers Exchange Club. His skill as a detective was obvious but his background in drafting led him to be recognized as the department's expert on detailed crime scene drawings used for court presentations in serious cases, along with his other investigative duties.

In 1977 the infamous "Son of Sam" murderer, David Berkowitz, was arrested by Yonkers and NYC police at his home at 35 Pine Street in Yonkers. From the beginning of Berkowitz's string of murders and throughout them all, Yonkers detectives were closely working with the NYPD on identifying the shooter. Det. Surlak was working the night of Berkowitz's arrest and said when Berkowitz was taken

Det Joseph E. Surlak #642 (cont.)

into the Detective Division smiling he proudly announced, "I'm the Son of Sam." Following his arrest a formal ceremony was held in the NYPD's headquarters honoring all those police officers who assisted in the successful capture of Berkowitz. About a dozen Yonkers officers were invited and attended including Det Joseph Surlak.

In the late 1970's, early '80's Joe was not a new recruit but he, like many like him, believed it was important to remain in good physical condition in order to handle certain situations without getting injured. As a result the idea was born that the YPD should have its own gymnasium for members to use while off duty. However, neither the city nor the police department were able to provide any financing for such a project. But this didn't stop Joe and the other members from forming what was called the Gym Committee. They obtained permission to use space in a basement room in the 1st pct. at 730 E. Grassy Sprain Rd. and accepted donations of used weights and other equipment just to start. Because the interest in a police gym grew so rapidly, Joe and the committee wrote an application for a state grant and $10,000 was awarded to upgrade the "police gym" with state of the art equipment. That grant was renewed every year.

Joe was always very athletic and a very active member of the PBA. He played on their softball and basketball teams for many years. And for more than ten years he served as a Detective Division trustee and later as the Chairman of the Board of Trustees. He was also a very big Ranger hockey fan and loved to play the game himself. In 1992 through 2002 he was a member of the Yonkers Police Hockey Team which competed annually with the Fire Dept. where all proceeds from each game were donated to local charities. And in his spare time he worked a side job installing chain link fences to earn additional money. Joe was very proud to watch his daughter Linda be appointed a YPD police officer in 1988 and later also be appointed a Detective. During the early 1990's, one of Joe's last assignments was that of an Arson investigator where he remained right up to his retirement.

Detective Surlak retired on January 13, 1994 but never really slowed down. In 2011, when he wasn't golfing, he was still playing an occasional hockey game.

CAPTAIN JOSEPH P. MESSINA

APPOINTED: February 1, 1959
RETIRED: August 29, 1991

Capt. Messina was born Joseph Peter Messina on December 14, 1928 in New York City. As a youth Joe's family moved to Yonkers and he attended Mark Twain Jr. High School and later graduated from Yonkers HS. Joe then attended the YMCA Trade and Technical High School in NYC learning a trade in refrigeration, air condition repair and oil burner repair. As a young man he was very athletic and enjoyed bowling, swimming, boating, and Judo. As a second language Joe was fluent in Italian.

In 1950 he joined the Air Force serving during the Korean War as a Staff Sergeant. He worked as a senior Aircraft Mechanic Flight Engineer and received his honorable discharge in 1954. Following his military service Joe worked for the United Parcel Service.

Having taken and passed the civil service exam for Patrolman and by using his military service time for credit, at the age of 30 years Joe was appointed to the police department on February 1, 1959 from 68 Alexander Avenue. Following his basic recruit training his first assignment was to the 2nd precinct earning the starting salary of $4,165 a year.

Officer Messina worked on patrol for four years and then on May 1, 1963 he was appointed a Detective in the Detective Division working general assignment investigations. He remained there less than a year and on February 26, 1964 he was transferred to patrol back in the 2nd precinct.

It would be nearly ten years later when, on October 26, 1973, that Messina would receive his first

Capt. Joseph P. Messina (cont.)

promotion; that being to the rank of Sergeant. Following his promotion he was reassigned as a patrol supervisor in the North Patrol Command at 53 Shonnard Place earning the salary of $15,708. During his stay in the North Command he would work both as a patrol supervisor and at times as the Station House Supervisor; formerly known as the desk officer and which had previously been the duty of lieutenants.

Sgt Messina would receive his second promotion on October 20, 1978 when he was promoted to Lieutenant. As was tradition, following his promotion he was reassigned from his previous assignment to a new one; this time to the Communications Division in headquarters supervising all internal communications and radio car dispatching. With his new rank came the salary of $24,187. The following year on March 16, 1979 Lt Messina was reassigned to the North Command as a patrol lieutenant for a short time, but on September 17, 1979 he was returned to the Communications Division. There were other routine reassignments as well; On December 21, 1982 he was assigned to the Inspectional Services Division on citywide patrol overseeing all patrol operations first hand. And on July 1, 1983 he was designated as the Executive Officer in the North East Command at 731 East Grassy Sprain Road'

As it was with each of his promotions, following a great deal of studying, and on this occasion, an outstanding evaluation and recommendation from then Capt. John McMahon, Lt Messina was promoted to the rank of police Captain on September 30, 1983. The new captain was once again returned to patrol as a city wide patrol duty captain assigned to the Field Services Bureau earning a salary of $38,668 a year.

Two years later, on September 10, 1985, Capt. Messina was assigned as the commanding officer of the Administrative Services Division located in headquarters. Then on April 4, 1988 Captain Messina returned to his original work assignment, the 2nd precinct, but this time as their commanding officer. Two months later the captain watched proudly as his daughter Jill Messina was sworn in as a Yonkers police officer. She would later retire as a lieutenant.

Captain Joseph Messina retired from the Yonkers Police Department on August 29, 1991. He enjoyed his retirement years spending time in both Yonkers and Ft. Lauderdale, Florida.

PO EUGENE R. ABBATIELLO #263

APPOINTED: February 1, 1959
RETIRED: March 19, 1987

Eugene Robert Abbatiello was born on February 7, 1935 in Yonkers and grew up on Maple Street. He attended PS# 23 and graduated from Yonkers HS. "Gino," as he was known by everyone, worked as a painter in an auto body shop in Hastings. He remained there right up to his appointment to the YPD on February 1, 1959 from 26 Yonkers Avenue. While in training he wore a gray shirt and pants along with a gray fedora hat while on patrol with a senior officer. He was provided with a shield, hat wreath, nightstick, flashlight, .38 cal. colt positive revolver, (no holster) and later a set of blue uniforms. Following recruit training his first assignment was to the 4th pct. on foot patrol earning $4,165 a year. Early in his career he received a citation of commendable merit from the Macy newspaper chain in recognition for his work in connection with the arrest of three alleged safe burglars while walking his foot post at 2:15 in the morning. When they tried to escape he fired a warning shot and made the arrest. On April 6, 1968 he was detailed to the Intelligence Unit for less than a year and on February 7, 1969 returned to the 4th. During most of the 1970's Gino served as a desk aide. On May 23, 1981 he was reassigned to the 1st precinct on E. Grassy Sprain Rd as a desk officer where he retired from on March 19, 1987. Gino loved to hunt and fish and had a brother who was a Hartford, Ct. police officer who survived being shot on duty. After retiring, Gino worked for a medical billing consulting company before retiring entirely.

PO EDWIN W. REILLY #83

APPOINTED: September 1, 1959
RETIRED: April 28, 1988

"Footsie" as he was known to everyone on the job was born Edwin William Reilly in Yonkers NY on May 16, 1936. He had previously worked as a Special Officer for the Westchester County Parkway Police, before it changed its name. He served in the Army from Aug. of 1953 and was honorably discharged in Aug. of 1956. He was appointed to the YPD on Sept 1, 1959 from 54 So. Devoe Ave. earning $4,165 a year. Incidentally, he picked up the nickname "Footie" due to his size 14 and half feet. Following recruit training he was assigned to the 2nd precinct. On March 16, 1961 he was moved to the 3rd, and on Aug. 10, 1961 to the 4th. Twelve years later, on Oct. 25, 1973, "Footsie" was transferred to HQ, detailed to the Courts as the YPD liaison officer. When he retired on Apr. 28, 1988 he was presented with a plaque by members of the local D.A.'s office staff. On the plaque was a full size bronzed 14 and a half police shoe. His brother Bob was a retired Westchester County Parkway police officer. After retirement on April 28, 1988 Ed moved to Long Beach Island, NJ. In 2006 Edwin Reilly lived in Beach Haven, NJ, and was suffering from congestive heart failure, kidney failure, and emphysema. Unfortunately Ret PO Edwin "Footsie" Reilly succumbed to his illness and died on Sept 26, 2009. He was 73 years old.

DET. ANDREW A. MARCHIONNI #688

APPOINTED: September 1, 1959
RETIRED: February 11, 1994

Andrew Marchionni was born in Yonkers on June 13, 1934 and graduated from Commerce HS. He joined the Army on April 9, 1954 serving as a sergeant in charge of the officer's mess hall. A veteran of Korea, Andy was honorably discharged on Feb. 14, 1956. Andy worked for the Wall Street Journal for a short time, as a Westchester Co. Special Police officer in Playland, and then for General Motors in Tarrytown. It was on Sept. 1, 1959 that Andy was appointed to the YPD while residing at 136 Yonkers Ave. Following training he was assigned to the 1st pct. at Wells Avenue earning $4,165 a year. On Aug. 15, 1960, Marchionni was assigned to the Traffic Division on two wheel motorcycle duty. Ten years later, after suffering a heart attack, on Dec. 1, 1970 Andy was assigned as the Taxi and bus inspector, a.k.a., Hack Inspector. Andy's brother-in-law was then Councilman Charles Cola Sr. On Oct. 26, 1983 Marchionni was reassigned to the North Command, and then on Mar 22, 1984 to the Records Division. On November 1, 1985 PC Fernandez appointed him a Detective to work in the Pistol Permit section of the Records Div. Andy Marchionni retired from the YPD on February 11, 1994. He was a past president of the Columbia Association, a Charter Member of the Dunwoodie Youth Club, and a member of the St Ann's Men's Club. Ret Det Andrew Marchionni died on August 22, 2000. He was 66 years old.

PO ANTHONY R. LACOPARRA #575

APPOINTED: January 1, 1960
RETIRED: February 14, 1992

Anthony Lacoparra was born in the City of Yonkers on August 3, 1935. He attended local public schools and following graduation Tony joined the Army on July 8, 1954 and was honorably discharged on May 10, 1956. He gained employment as an office clerk but while there took the test for police Patrolman. Tony was appointment to the YPD on Jan. 1, 1960 while living at 21 Wolffe Street. Upon completion of his recruit training he was assigned to the 3rd precinct on foot patrol earning $4,480 a year. He walked a post for three years until Mar 13, 1963 when he was reassigned to patrol in the 2nd precinct in east Yonkers. In this precinct he patrolled in a radio car along with a partner for nearly six years when, on Jan. 7, 1969, he was reassigned to the Records Division performing clerical duty until Jan. 1, 1971 when he was assigned to work in the Property Clerk Unit. Tony Retired on Feb 14, 1992 and moved to Port St. Lucie, Florida. A very soft spoken man, Tony really enjoyed the sun of south Florida.

DET. THOMAS F. DUGAN #629

APPOINTED: January 1, 1960
RETIRED: August 30, 1991

Thomas Francis Dugan was born in the City of Yonkers on November 19, 1928. He spent his very early years attending school in East Yonkers but after moving to the North Yonkers area, graduated from Sacred Heart grade school and later from Gorton High School in 1945. Several years later he earned an Associate's degree from Westchester Community College.

He joined the Army right out of high school on January 23, 1946 at the age of 17 years. He served for two years being trained as a medical corpsman and later in the Military Police. He received his honorable discharge on July 23, 1947.

Following his military discharge Tom worked a variety of jobs; he was in the carpenters union, worked on the line at the Chevrolet plant in Tarrytown, and at a family run gas station. But he received his first public employment job on November 19, 1957 when he was appointed to the Yonkers Fire Department on November 16, 1957 and served in Engine's 9 and 2 in their rescue units. However, Tom's older brother Eugene had been a Yonkers police officer since 1955 and that job apparently aroused Tom's interest. So Tom took the police test, passed it, and was notified of his pending appointment. On December 31, 1959 Firefighter Thomas Dugan, a resident of 26 Fero Street, resigned from the YFD, and on January 1, 1960 was appointed a police officer in the Yonkers Police Department earning $4,480 a year.

His first assignment was to the 4th precinct on uniform patrol. However, six months later on July 1, 1960 he was transferred to the 2nd precinct where he was assigned to the Accident Investigation Emergency (AIE) Unit, later officially renamed the Emergency Service Unit. I'm sure his military training as a Corpsman helped in this assignment. PO Tom Dugan remained in the 2nd precinct Emergency Squad up to May 1, 1963 when he was appointed a Detective in the Detective Bureau working in "General Assignment."

By 1971 Det Dugan had made an enviable reputation for himself as to his capabilities, honesty, and integrity. As a result, on October 22, 1971, he was reassigned to the prestigious Intelligence Unit (IU). It was this unit that conducted highly sensitive investigations in cooperation with other local, county and federal agencies. Tom worked organized crime and gambling investigations while in this unit. On November 15, 1974 Tom returned to the Detective Division working predominantly on Arson and Burglary investigations.

Nine years later on October 21, 1983 Det Dugan was once again returned to the IU, but by then it had been re-named the Special Investigations Unit (SIU). And once again, primarily because of his knowledge and experience, Tom was assigned to the Organized Crime section. But there came a time when Tom was not comfortable with the operation of the SIU and asked out. So, as before, but this time on August 21, 1989, he was returned to the Detective Division and assumed desk officer duty which lasted for about a year.

In 1990 a security problem became apparent in the operation of the SIU resulting in a number of people being transferred to other assignments and the office location closed. A few SIU detectives were allowed to continue their assignment in the SIU, but their Unit was merged within the offices of the Internal Affairs Division. It was then that Det Dugan was once again re-assigned back to the SIU in the IAD office and resumed his duties investigating organized crime. He did this for his last year on the job.

Det. Thomas F. Dugan (cont.)

On August 30, 1991, over 31 years since his appointment and with 28 of those years serving as a detective, First Grade Det Thomas Dugan retired from the Yonkers Police Department. Throughout his career Det Dugan had a way of being involved in and assigned to the most difficult and high profile investigations that occurred. The homicide investigations he worked on over the years are absolutely too numerous to begin to list. However after retiring Tom often referred to the part he played in the investigation of the murder of Yonkers police officer Harold Woods in 1974 and the murder of PO John Silinsky in 1982 when he and Det Souza were detailed to the NYPD's 50 pct squad to assist in working this murder investigation. These homicides were special. These were personal!

But Tom Dugan's service to the City of Yonkers didn't end with his retirement. In 1992 Mayor Terrence Zeleski recruited Tom to serve as an investigator and consultant looking into official corruption as part of the newly created Chief Examiner's Office. Their job was to conduct auditing and look for ties from organized crime to City Hall. This office has since been renamed the office of the Inspector General.

In 1993 Tom was appointed to the board of directors of the Industrial Development Agency and elected its Vice Chairman.

In 1994 he was appointed to the Yonkers Civil Service Commission and was elected as its president. He held this job up to June of 2000. In the year 2000 Tom was appointed Vice President of the Ridge Hill Development Corp.

In 2002 he was appointed to the Yonkers Empowerment Corp and served as its secretary. He was also named president of the N-Valley Technology Center located on Nepperhan Avenue and Axminster Street.

In 2004 Tom was a founding member of the board of directors which researched and ultimately opened a new banking institution in Yonkers named, The Westchester Bank on Central Park Avenue. And among many of the business ventures Tom Dugan involved himself in, many were all during the same time.

It was also in 2004 that Tom became ill and ultimately required, and received, a double kidney transplant. The surgery was a success and after convalescing, Tom went right back to work. Unfortunately in his last year Tom developed an unrelated illness which ultimately took his life. Ret Det Thomas Dugan died December 7, 2009 in the City of Yonkers for whom he worked over 50 combined years. He was 81.

Tom was a founding member of the Westchester County Police Emerald Society, the Yonkers Elks and the Friendly Sons of St Patrick. In the Public Safety area his brother "Gene" Dugan was a Yonkers police officer in ESU until his untimely death; his brother Joe is a retired Yonkers Fire Lt; his grandsons are Sgt John Marello, and PO Thomas Marello of the 4th precinct. Sgt Marello's wife PO Stacey Marello is also assigned to the 4th; his great nephew is PO Raymond Dugan; his brothers in law are Ret Det Andy Cavallo and the late PO Carmine Cavallo; and Tom's 2nd cousin is retired Police Commissioner Charles Cola.

DET. CAPTAIN THOMAS A. KRESSMAN

APPOINTED: January 16, 1960
RETIRED: January 10, 1997

Thomas Anthony Kressman was born on October 31, 1933 in the city of Yonkers. However, he attended and graduated from Cardinal Hayes high school in New York City, attending from 1946 to 1950. Many years later he would also earn an Associate's degree from Westchester Community College earning the top Iona award for his studies in criminal justice. Following his formal education Tom would gain employment working for the New York Central Railroad Company.

Having applied for, and having passed all the required testing, Tom received his appointment to the Yonkers Police Department on January 16, 1960 while residing at 11 Portland Place. Following the mandatory recruit training Tom's first assignment was to the 1st precinct, located at 20 Wells Ave., on foot patrol while earning a starting salary of $4,480 a year. Tom remained on foot patrol in the 1st precinct until November 9, 1966 when he was reassigned to the 4th precinct.

On January 1, 1971 a large centralization plan was put into effect whereby two of the four precincts, the first and the third, were basically closed as an operating precinct. The two remaining precincts, the second and the fourth, were renamed the South command and the North command. All personnel who had been assigned to the first and third precincts were reassigned and merged into the North and South Patrol Commands. Police officer Kressman remained assigned to the new North command designated as the Patrol Wagon Driver, which in reality had been a long abolished position and

Det. Capt. Thomas A. Kressman (cont.)

was actually a position serving as the precinct captains aide.

Tom continued to work as the captain's aide up to May 5, 1972 when he was promoted to the rank of Sergeant and earned a new salary of $13,685 a year. Following his promotion Tom was transferred to the South Patrol Command serving as a patrol supervisor.

Sgt. Kressman was a very friendly, outspoken and high energy individual who put 100% into everything he did. So it was no surprise when, in 1974, he was detailed to headquarters working as the executive officer for the chief of police.

On February 11, 1976, Sgt. Kressman was promoted to the rank of police Lieutenant. With this promotion, instead of being transferred, he was allowed to remain working as the chief's executive officer earning a salary of $20,642. Lt. Kressman was an invaluable aid to then police chief William Polsen and, following the chief's retirement and replacement by a police commissioner, Kressman's value to the office was very apparent and he was allowed to remain as the executive officer for two successive police commissioners. His potential as an administrator was also apparent and as such he was selected to attend the 124th class of the National FBI Academy in Quantico Virginia from January 1981 to March of that year when he graduated and returned to the YPD. In addition, on April 28, 1981, Lt Kressman was designated a Detective Lieutenant. However, on July 1, 1983, following the appointment of a new police commissioner, Tom lost his detective lieutenant status and was reassigned to the North Patrol Command as a patrol Zone Lieutenant.

On May 23, 1986 Lt. Kressman was promoted to the rank of police Captain and assigned to the Field Services Bureau as a citywide duty captain. Capt. Kressman received his first command assignment on January 18, 1988 when he was designated the commanding officer of the 3rd precinct on Riverdale Avenue. No doubt based on his past performance, ability, and integrity, on April 12, 1990 Capt. Kressman was designated a Detective Captain and assigned to the Inspectional Services Division in command of the highly sensitive Internal Affairs Unit.

Two years later, on October 12, 1992, he was reassigned from the Internal Affairs Unit to commanding officer of the prestigious Detective Division. Five years later, on January 10, 1997, Det. Capt. Thomas Kressman retired from the Yonkers Police Department.

As a young man back in 1952, and shortly after graduating from high school, Tom had joined the Naval Reserve. He remained a member of the Naval Reserve for 37 years throughout most of his police career, later retiring from the Navy in 1989 as a Chief Petty Officer. Tom Kressman was also a very active member of the Police Emerald Society of Westchester County, serving several years as a trustee. He also was a past president, secretary, and trustee of the Police Holy Name Society over a ten year period. Tom has several cousins that are or were members of the YPD. They include, Lt Thomas Kivel, Sgt Michael Kivel, PO's William and Keith Kivel, Det William Kennedy, and PO Richard Kressman.

Ret Det Capt. Tom Kressman divided time between Yonkers and Florida where his favorite pass time was golf.

PO THOMAS F. ALLISON #274

APPOINTED: January 16, 1960
DIED: November 10, 1969

Born Thomas Francis Allison in Yonkers NY on January 30, 1929, Tom attended St Joseph's School and Gorton HS. Upon graduation he entered the Army on December 12, 1950, serving during the Korean War, with duty in England. He was honorably discharged on November 28, 1952. Tom worked for a time in Otis Elevator Co. and listed on his police application that his special qualifications were in the field of printing.

He was appointed to the Yonkers Police Department on January 16, 1960 while living at 65 Vineyard Ave. Following basic recruit training he was assigned to patrol in the 4th precinct earning $4,480 a year. Nearly seven years later, on November 9, 1966, Tom was transferred to patrol in the 3rd precinct. Throughout 1968 and 1969 he and PO Anthony Troia were partners working on what was then the Dog License Census and later in the 3rd Precinct Warrant Squad re: Scofflaw violators, etc.

Allison loved to play Golf. Unfortunately on November 10, 1969 Tom suffered a heart attack during a game of golf on the Dunwoodie Golf Course. He was driven to the hospital where he quickly suffered another heart attack which took his life. A member of the Police Holy Name Society and a resident of 263 Palisade Ave, Allison left his widow, Jean, but no children. Allison's widow received a widow's pension of $2,400 a year. PO Tom Allison was only 40 years old.

DET. WILLIAM E. GROGAN #662

APPOINTED: January 16, 1960
RETIRED: March 21, 1981

William Edward Grogan was born November 8, 1935, in Yonkers, NY. About four years later in March of 1939, his mother Celeste Jarolemon Grogan died in St. Joseph's Hospital from a fractured skull as a result of a fall down the stairs of the apartment house at 14 (then Stone Street), now Coyle Place, where they lived.

Bill was raised by his father, Raymond Lewis Grogan. Many times Bill was cared for by the WPA Work Center while his father was out on a road gang during the Depression.

Bill was educated in the Yonkers school system – PS#13-Hawthorne Junior High School and graduated from Gorton High School in June 1953. In January 1953, while still at Gorton High School, Bill enlisted in the Marine Corps Reserve (an infantry rifle company in New Rochelle.) He said his was the first enlistment in the Marine Corps of that year. Bill served six years of active and reserve duty, received Weapons Ordinance School in Little Creek, VA, and was honorably discharged as a Corporal on February 13, 1959. For the remainder of 1959 Bill was employed as a truck driver.

On January 16, 1960, Bill was sworn in as a probationary Patrolman in the Yonkers Police Department from 52 Radford Street and assigned to the 4th Precinct on Shonnard Place. Following the probationary period during which he earned a starting salary of $4,480 a year, he walked a foot post and also worked as a temporary, then later permanent, assignee in a precinct radio car. For a time he was detailed as a Juvenile Aid Officer and also a Police Dispatcher in the Communications Division. While in the 4th Precinct on occasion he worked plainclothes burglary and gambling investigations.

On December 29, 1967 Grogan was detailed to what was then a relatively recently organized Intelligence Unit. However, on February 14, 1968, Bill was officially transferred to the Detective Division as a "silver shield" working from the Intelligence Unit. Grogan's general responsibility was investigating highly sensitive and confidential investigations including operations conducted by organized crime. However, in his early years in the "IU" his area of expertise was investigating and monitoring those individuals involved in civil disobedience and disruptive organizations such as the "Students For a Democratic Society" (SDS), "Black Panther Party," "Black Liberation Army," "Communist Party USA" etc., all of which used violence regularly to show their open hate for America.

Due to the expertise he had developed in these areas, in June of 1969, he was subpoenaed to appear before the then U.S. Senate Committee on Internal Security in Washington D.C. Along with other law enforcement officers from across the country, he gave testimony regarding the actions, financing, and aims of people and groups dedicated to the overthrow of the U.S. government and how these organizations and individuals were connected to the City of Yonkers. Bill Grogan was promoted to Detective on July 1, 1971 and remained assigned to the Intelligence Division.

On Oct 27, 1972, when Det. George Rutledge was promoted to Sergeant and assigned to patrol supervision, Det. Grogan was reassigned to the Organized Crime desk. At the invitation of, but never officially assigned to by the Yonkers Police Department, he became a quasi-member of the Southern District Federal Strike Force whose mission was the investigation of Organized Crime and Official

Det. William E. Grogan #662 (cont.)

Corruption. He attended meetings and worked with them for approximately ten years. On just one case he worked in conjunction with the NYC Police Dept. in apprehending and convicting 13 persons responsible for importation and wholesaling of major quantities of Cocaine from Colombia. He interfaced on a regular basis with members of the New York State Commission of Investigation (SIC), the New York State Police, the Westchester District Attorney's Office, the New York City Police Department, Military Intelligence, Interpol, and many other state and federal law enforcement agencies across the country.

In 1979, he was detailed by then PC Daniel Guido to work with the New York State Senate Crime Committee and conducted an investigation into Organized Crimes' control of the toxic waste industry in the New York Metropolitan area. This investigation was conducted in cooperation with the New Jersey State Police, the Rockland County Sheriffs' Office, and the Southern District Federal Strike Force. The investigation also resulted in the publication of a non-fiction book titled, "Poisoning for Profit," written by two criminologists from the University of Delaware – Alan Block and Frank Scarpitti.

At one point Bill was even requested by the N.Y. State Investigations Commission on (SIC) to assist in the investigations and hearings relative to organized crime's influence within the City of Yonkers government. When Charles Connolly was appointed police commissioner he requested that these organizations reimburse the city for Grogan's salary and pension costs. They agreed for a while but eventually the reimbursement stopped and as a result Det Grogan was returned to regular duty in the IU in December of 1980. In February 1981, he submitted his request for retirement and same was effective March 21, 1981.

Bill had been a member of the Westchester Co. Police Emerald Society, International Association of Chiefs of Police, Westchester Co. Detectives Assoc., Brewster Elks Club, and the Yonkers PBA. He retired as 1st grade detective from the Intelligence Division.

Upon retirement, Bill was hired as Director of Security for Hudson Wire Company which was headquartered in Ossining, NY. Hudson produced a semiconductor product for military and civilian application which included copper and copper alloy wires plated with precious metals of silver, gold and platinum. After approximately 18 months, Bill was promoted to Director of Personnel and Security. In 1988, Hudson purchased its biggest competitor, International Wire Products, and became Hudson International Conductors with plants in Ossining and Walden, NY, Inman, SC, and Trenton, GA. In 1991, Hudson was purchased by Phelps Dodge Corporation headquartered in Phoenix, Arizona.

Bill retired as the Corporate Director of Human Resources and Director of Security due to all northern plants being shut down and their operations being moved to the southern locations. A generous retirement was offered by Phelps Dodge and accepted by Bill.

Ret Det Grogan moved to Virginia where he should be very proud and satisfied with his accomplishments within law enforcement as well as private industry.

POLICE COMMISSIONER
DONALD P. CHRISTOPHER

APPOINTED: April 16, 1960
RETIRED: April 30, 1998

The subject of this profile was justly regarded as one of the most well respected members of the Yonkers Police Department during his tenure.

Donald Patrick Christopher was born in Yonkers on March 14, 1936 to one of the most respected Yonkers Police officers of his time; Det. Sgt. Patrick Christopher. Don attended St. Mary's parochial school and graduated from Sacred Heart H.S. Following his graduation Don joined the Army Reserve on October 8, 1954 and served up to October 7, 1956. He later received his honorable discharge on September 30, 1962. In the late 1950's he was employed as a "Checker" with the Otis Elevator Company.

Christopher was appointed to the police department on April 16, 1960 while residing at 167 Oliver Avenue. Following his recruit training he was assigned to the 2nd precinct earning a starting salary of $4,480 a year. As a young cop Don worked side jobs off duty painting and hanging wallpaper to earn extra money. But his off duty work didn't hinder him from developing a reputation of dedication and hard work toward police work. For instance; on March 25, 1964 Christopher was awarded a departmental Commendation for saving a baby's life. And the following year, on March 23, 1965, he was awarded

Police Comm. Donald P. Christopher (cont.)

another Commendation for his work arresting those responsible for a burglary.

On November 9, 1966, upon the opening of a newly built and dedicated 1st precinct at 730 East Grassy Sprain Rd., officer Christopher was reassigned to this precinct on patrol. On February 2, 1970 he was accepted to serve in the department's Emergency Service Unit and received his tactical and rescue training from the NYPD ESU instructors at Randall's Island in NYC.

Don served in ESU right up to his promotion to Sergeant on December 14, 1973 where his salary rose to $15,708 a year. Upon this promotion he was transferred from ESU to the North Patrol Command at 53 Shonnard Place serving as a patrol supervisor. After only a few months Sgt Christopher was designated the ESU supervisor responsible for those assigned to ESU and their training and equipment acquisition. On September 20, 1974 he was reassigned to the South Command but continued to serve as the Supervisor/Coordinator of the citywide Emergency Services Unit which operated out of the North and South Commands.

On September 5, 1975 Christopher was elevated to Detective Sergeant earning $18,043 and assigned as a detective squad supervisor in the Detective Division. It was here Christopher continued to gain the respect of those who worked for him by his ability to remain calm and calculating and always applying measured decisions.

Although his job was very time consuming he always found time to study. And as a result, on January 19, 1979, Sgt. Christopher was promoted to Lieutenant at $25,927. Standard procedure was, upon receiving a promotion the individual would be transferred to a different assignment. No doubt as a testament to his ability to lead his squad to efficiently investigate and clear nearly all cases they handled, Christopher was allowed to remain in the Detective Division as a Det. Lieutenant and, since at the time the Detective Division was without a captain in command, an extremely unusual decision was made. Det. Lt. Christopher was designated the commanding officer of this most sensitive and important position which historically had been held by a captain.

Despite his many responsibilities Christopher was able to attended Westchester Community College earning several credits and he attended numerous FBI courses and seminars. On May 1, 1981 Det Lt Christopher was promoted to the rank of Captain with his salary rising to $28,963. Once again, despite departmental past practice, Christopher was allowed to remain in the Detective Division still as its CO, but now with the rank of captain.

Two years later, on July 1, 1983, Acting Commissioner Joseph Fernandes transferred him out of the D.D. and reassigned him as the C.O. of the North Patrol Command. But this assignment lasted for only two years. For on December 17, 1985 Capt. Christopher was once again returned to the DD as its commanding officer.

On March 16, 1990 Don Christopher was selected by the police commissioner to be elevated to the rank of Deputy Chief earning a salary of $78,250. His promotion filled a vacancy created when DC DeDivitis was appointed Acting Police Commissioner. Because of his many years of experience DC Christopher was assigned to the Investigational Services Bureau overseeing all investigative units including the Detective Division, Youth Division, Narcotics Unit, Forensic Laboratory, and the Criminal Identification Unit. Upon his elevation to Deputy Chief Mayor Henry Spallone said, "*This is a great day for a great officer.*" Christopher was quoted as saying, "*I was very fortunate in my life to have a police*

Police Comm. Donald P. Christopher (cont.)

officer I could look up to. He was a loyal police officer, a dedicated man, and a cop's cop." referring to his father, former Det Sgt Patrick Christopher.

On December 4, 1993, Christ the King Church in Yonkers, honored Deputy Chief Donald Christopher as Man of the Year with a dinner at the Manor House restaurant in Hastings-on-Hudson. This honor was bestowed upon chief Christopher for his outstanding work with the Yonkers Police Department. They stated that, *"Christopher was a highly respected police officer due to his integrity and dedication to the department and his fairness dealing with individuals. His expertise and his talents have made, and will continue to make, the quality of life better for the city of Yonkers."*

Following the mayoral election in November, on December 17, 1995 it was reported that newly elected Mayor John Spencer had nominated DC Don Christopher to be the next police commissioner replacing Comm. Albert McEvoy who was appointed by the previous mayor, Terrence Zeleski. PC McEvoy was being reduced in rank to Deputy Chief. Spencer said, *"Based on Christopher's career, his performance, and his leadership style, he will be a benefit to the Yonkers Police Department."* Christopher received council confirmation to the $101,000 a year job and was officially sworn into office on January 11, 1996. During his comments Commissioner Christopher relater that, "*although I have spent the last 22 years as a supervisor, I spent the last 35 years as a cop*."

Just over two years later in April of 1996 PC Christopher announced his plans to retire. In his farewell note to the department in the Newsletter on April 16, 1998 the Commissioner wrote;----

"After 38 years of service, I will be retiring from the Yonkers Police Department effective April 30, 1998. My decision to retire was determined for me by the mandatory age requirement of the pension system. I can vividly recall the day I was appointed to the Police Department and how, at that time, retirement seemed to be so far off in the future. The time, however, passed very quickly, especially the last five years.

"Like a book, life is comprised of chapters and phases that commence at birth. Well, I am moving to the next chapter and, frankly, I'm looking forward to it. I intend to spend more time with my family and doing the things I want to do, when I want to do them. That includes, of course, playing golf. The downside to all of this is that I will miss 'the job' and the many wonderful people I have had the good fortune to meet and work with. I firmly believe that the Yonkers Police Department is an excellent law enforcement agency. That excellence has been achieved as a result of the efforts by all of you; your dedication and your talent is extraordinary.

"As your Commissioner, I want to express my gratitude for the support, assistance, and cooperation you afforded me. I am certainly honored and proud to have served as your Commissioner and I thank Mayor John Spencer for providing me the opportunity. May God bless all of you and your families with good luck and good health and may he keep you safe."

Upon his retirement, a party was held in his honor at the Manor House restaurant where, among many honorariums, he received a plaque from the dinner committee which contained his six police shields (PO, Sgt, Lt, Capt., D.C., and Commissioner). On the plaque it read, "In recognition of your 38 years of outstanding and dedicated service to the citizens of Yonkers and your fellow officers. Best wishes in your retirement."

Police Comm. Donald P. Christopher (cont.)

Comm. Christopher had received numerous letters of commendation from civilians, D.A.'s, and a Mayor. He attended many FBI and New York City schools and seminars. He is an active member of Christ the King Church, the Police Holy Name Society, Friendly Sons of Saint Patrick and Captains Lieutenants and Sergeants Association. He is on the Board of Directors for St. Joseph's Medical Center and nursing home. Don served as first vice president for the PBA from 1965 to 1973 and as a vice president for the CLSA from 1984 to 1990. Christopher was one of the originators of the annual Joe Madden Memorial Golf Outing. Joe Madden, a former Yonkers police sergeant, died of cancer at Rosary Hill. All proceeds of the golf outing are donated to Rosary Hill.

Ret. Comm. Don Christopher remained living in Yonkers enjoying golf and spending quality time with his family.

Unfortunately Don became ill and after several years fighting he died on April 8, 2018. He was 82.

LT. EDWARD J. POWERS

APPOINTED: April 16, 1960
RETIRED: June 13, 1991

Ed was born on Dec. 10, 1930 in Williamsburg, Va. Years later his family moved to Yonkers where he graduated from Saunders HS in 1948. Right after graduating Ed joined the Navy serving from June 10, 1948 with the Navy Shore Patrol and holding the rating of Petty Officer 3rd class. Ed received his honorable discharge on May 27, 1952 and his service time qualified him as a Korean War veteran. He later worked for Singer Sewing Machine Co, and then took a job as a Correction Officer in Sing Sing Prison.

Several years later Powers was appointed to the White Plains P.D. as a Patrolman and worked there for 5 years. But since he lived out of town, in Yonkers, he was told he was ineligible to be promoted, so he took the Yonkers police test, passed, and was appointed to the YPD on April 16, 1960. His first assignment, following recruit training, was foot patrol in the 4th precinct earning $4,480 a year. At the time he lived at 317 Warburton Ave. and later 78 Glenwood Ave. During the early 1960's he was the founder and captain of the YPD bowling team playing leagues at the Homefield Bowling Lanes. Four years later, on Sept. 23, 1964, Powers was reassigned to the Records Division performing clerical duty. At one point Powers was directed to research the feasibility of organizing a Harbor Patrol and how best to obtain a boat at no cost. After several months of work PO Powers reported on how such a unit could be formed and had located a boat that was available to Yonkers at no cost; albeit one that was in extremely poor condition. Subsequently, on July 12, 1968, Powers was one of the original men reassigned to the Service & Maintenance Division and detailed to the newly established, and ill fated, YPD Marine Unit.

The Marine Unit lasted less than a year before being disbanded and on Oct. 1, 1969 PO Powers was returned to patrol in the 4th precinct. In the early 1970's he was also an early member of the Westchester County Police Emerald Society Pipes & Drums Band. In Jan. of 1976 Ed Powers, who was very mild mannered and soft spoken, was transferred to the Warrant Squad which operated out of offices on the 2nd floor of the City Jail on Alexander Street. On Sept. 20, 1979 Ed received his promotion to the rank of Sergeant earning $23,086 and was assigned to the Field Services Bureau as a patrol Sergeant working out of the 1st precinct. Sgt Powers was offered the opportunity to work in the Internal Affairs Division, which at the time was a pathway to detective status. He accepted and on June 24, 1987 he was transferred to I.A.D. And as he had hoped, the following year, on July 1, 1988, Powers was designated a Detective Sergeant and remained working in I.A.D.

Det Sgt Powers received his second advance in rank when, on Dec. 2, 1988, he was promoted to the rank of Lieutenant. His new assignment would be as a supervising lieutenant in the Communications Division. But, less than a year later, on Sept. 16, 1989, he was reassigned to the 2nd precinct as a patrol lieutenant. In short time he would be serving as their executive officer.

His last assignment was back to the Communications Division on February 9, 1991 as the executive officer. Lt Edward Powers, whose brother James was a former YPD officer, retired from the YPD on June 13, 1991 and remained retired at his home in Wappingers Falls, NY.

Ret Lt. Edward J. Powers died on June 28, 2008 at the age of 77.

PO ROBERT TIMAN #205

APPOINTED: April 16, 1960
RETIRED: May 21, 1981

Bob Timan was born in Yonkers NY on Sept. 16, 1934, attended local schools and graduated from Saunders HS. Bob joined the Navy on Sept. 22, 1952 and his assignment was Underwater Coastal Locator, a classified operation. He was honorably discharged as a Boatswains Mate 3rd Class on July 22, 1954. Following his military service he listed his occupation as that of a Bartender. Bob was appointed to the YPD on April 16, 1960 while living at 136 Harrison Avenue. Following recruit school his first assignment was to the 2nd precinct earning $4,480 a year. On Aug. 13, 1965 he was reassigned to the Juvenile Aide Division. It was here that Bob Timan, who was rarely without a cigar protruding from his mouth, gained the nickname of "Popeye" due to his barrel chest physique. On June 14, 1968 he was transferred to the 3rd precinct. However, the following month he was detailed to the newly established Marine Unit working at the Hudson River off a boat named the Scoter. Unfortunately the Marine Unit didn't last very long and Bob was returned to the 3rd precinct on Oct. 1, 1969. Just over a year later, on Feb. 12, 1971, he was once again returned to the Youth Division. On Feb. 22, 1979 he was sent to the 2nd precinct, and on July 1, 1980 he was reassigned to the Criminal Investigation Unit (CIU). After being assigned to patrol in the North Command on April 1, 1981, Bob retired from the YPD on May 21, 1981. In 1975 Bob moved to Carmel, NY. It is while living there that he died June 21, 2006 at the age of 71.

PO LAWRENCE BRACEY #70

APPOINTED: April 16, 1960
RETIRED: January 10, 1985

Larry Bracey was born in the Town of Tuckahoe, NY on February 13, 1929. Following his family moving to Yonkers Larry attended local public schools and graduated from Saunders HS. Larry joined the Army during the Korean War on January 23, 1951. He served as an infantry Corporal where he served bravely in combat several times and which earned him several citations. He was honorably discharged from the Army on January 23, 1953. Following his military service Larry married, had six children, and raised his family working as an auto metal finisher with the General Motors Factory in Tarrytown, NY. Bracey was appointed to the YPD on April 16, 1960 while residing at 50 Ravine Avenue. His starting salary was $4,480 a year and his first assignment was to the 2nd precinct at 441 Central Park Avenue. Larry was a very personable individual but maintained a low profile while working. He remained in the 2nd precinct for his entire career, retiring on January 10, 1985. Ret PO Lawrence Bracey died on November 9, 2001 at age 72.

PO RONALD F. O'ROURKE #166

APPOINTED: April 16, 1960
DIED: October 12, 1979

Ronald Francis O'Rourke was born in the City of Yonkers on April 3, 1936 where he attended local public schools. He later graduated from Manhattan Preparatory School in NYC. Directly following his graduation Ron joined the Navy on January 7, 1955 and was honorably discharged as a 3rd Class Petty Officer on December 12, 1956.

With an early interest in being an attorney, Ron attended the Bridgeport University in Connecticut studying pre-law from 1958 through 1959. However, the opportunity presented itself and Ron accepted an appointment with the White Plains Police Department as a patrolman. But, being a Yonkers boy, he took the Yonkers police test, passed, and was appointed a Yonkers police officer on April 16, 1960.

When hired Ron lived at 58 Hudson St., and following his recruit training was assigned to patrol duty in the 2nd precinct earning a starting salary of $4,480 a year. Three years later, on August 1, 1963, he would be reassigned from the 2nd to the 1st precinct and on November 9, 1966 he was moved to the 4th precinct. Officer O'Rourke was reassigned to the Special Operations Division to work in the Tactical Patrol Unit on October 19, 1971.

He remained there just over a year, and on January 29, 1973 he was transferred to work in the Training Division as a police department instructor. Part of his responsibilities was to train new police recruits in the various aspects of police work and to also conduct in-service training for all members of the department. "Ronnie" O'Rourke, as he was known, was one of the friendliest and well-liked members of the Yonkers police department. If you were around him for just a few moments, with his great Irish wit, you would find yourself smiling. He had that impact on people. Ron was a founding member of the Westchester County police Emerald Society Pipes and Drums Band and had also served as the president of the Westchester County Police Emerald Society.

Unfortunately, while off-duty, Ron O'Rourke died suddenly and unexpectedly in the middle of the night on October 12, 1979. And although this was not a line of duty death, during his funeral hundreds of fellow officers showed the depth of their respect for the man by lining the streets in formation and saluting as the hearse passed by. PO Ronald O'Rourke was only 43 years old.

DET. MICHAEL A. LORENZO #636

APPOINTED: December 16, 1960
RETIRED: January 13, 1995

Mike was born Michael Anthony Lorenzo December 13, 1933 in Far Rockaway, Queens NY. After moving to Yonkers he attended St. Joseph Grade School, graduated from Gorton High School and received his Bachelor of Science degree in criminal justice from Iona College.

As a youth Mike joined Marine Corps Reserve, remained for a short time until the Korea War broke out, then switched and joined the regular Navy for 4 years. He served in the Navy from September 17, 1951 to September 20, 1955, and as such he was a Korean War veteran. While in the Navy he was certified for underwater diving, holding the rank of Petty Officer 2nd class. Following his military Mike worked as a salesman.

Michael A. Lorenzo was appointed a Yonkers police officer on December 16, 1960 from 109 Amackassin Terrace at the salary of $4,480. a year. And following basic recruit training his first assignment was patrol duty in the 2nd precinct. Nearly eleven years later, on July 16, 1971, he was advanced to Detective along with Joe Rodriguez, Joe Kostik, Vincent Montemurro, Bill McBride, Rey Baker, and Al Chiaverini. For several years he was partnered up with PO Ted Miller. At that time he lived at 1 Hillbright Terrace. In March of 1979 following one investigation where a father is thought to have paid and had his two sons murdered, arrests and convictions were secured and Det Lorenzo was named Police Officer of the year by the Exchange Club.

Mike was an excellent detective, however, on October 21, 1983 he was reassigned to patrol in the NE Patrol Command. Then, three years later, on July 25, 1986, he was returned to the Detective Division as a detective where he served in a General Assignment squad and often as the desk officer.

On September 20, 1990 Mike was assigned to the Special Investigation Unit where he remained up to his retirement on January 13, 1995.

He was a certified NRA Pistol Instructor and as such was always willing to help anyone with a problem with their weapon. He was a member of the Tower Ridge Yacht Club in Hastings, an avid sportsman who enjoyed hunting, fishing and boating and was a former member of the Columbian Association. Mike was proud to see his son Michael J. be appointed a Yonkers police officer and later a Detective and their service to the department actually overlapped for a number of years.

Anyone who knew Mike knew that he had a great sense of humor and he rarely missed an Old Timers Picnic where he enjoyed the company of fellow retirees. Unfortunately Mike became seriously ill and after a very long fight, Ret Det Michael A. Lorenzo died on April 15, 2008. He was 74 years old.

PO JOSEPH T. DREXEL #247

APPOINTED: December 16, 1960
RETIRED: February 4, 1981

Joseph Thomas Drexel was born in Yonkers on Mar. 8, 1930. He attended local schools and graduated from Saunders HS with a trade in carpentry. Joe entered the Army on Aug. 19, 1950. He served for 21 months during the Korean War as a Sergeant assigned to the Army Signal Corps. He was honorably discharged on May 13, 1952. He liked to tell the story of how, while being separated and lost from his squad, he captured a Chinese Communist soldier and turned him in when Drexel located his base. Joe was appointed to the YPD on December 16, 1960. Following training he was assigned to foot patrol in the 1st precinct earning a salary of $4,480 a year. On June 18, 1965 he was reassigned from the 1st precinct to the 4th. On November 9, 1966 Joe was transferred to the brand new, just built, 1st precinct at 730 East Grassy Sprain Rd. Nearly 5 years later, on January 1, 1971, Joe was returned to the 4th, which had been renamed the North Command on that date. On March 30, 1979 Joe would watch as his son, Thomas, be appointed to the YPD. Joe retired from the YPD on February 4, 1981 and moved to Winterhaven, Florida where he would die on August 6, 2004 at age 74.

PO CHARLES M. SCHRENKEL #279

APPOINTED: December 16, 1960
RESIGNED: August 31, 1962

Charles Michael Schrenkel was born in the city of Yonkers on February 24, 1936. He attended and graduated from local public schools. Right after finishing school Charles join the Army from November 15, 1954 and was honorably discharged on February 3, 1955. For several years prior to the YPD Charlie worked as a bus driver. He was appointed a police officer on December 16, 1960 while residing at 545 mile Square Road. Following his recruit training he was assigned to patrol duty in the 2nd precinct earning a starting salary of $4,480 a year. All available records indicate that he was a satisfactory police officer, and yet for reasons unknown on August 7, 1962 PO Charles Schrenkel submitted his letter of resignation from the YPD effective August 31, 1962.

DET. PAUL D. CAROZZA #647

APPOINTED: December 16, 1960
RETIRED: January 13, 1995

Born Paul Dominick Carozza in the Park Hill section of Yonkers NY on Oct. 15, 1933, Paul attended St Mary's elementary School, and graduated from Yonkers HS. He later attended college in NYC for two years. Paul joined the Navy in 1954 serving on the Aircraft Carrier USS Hornet. He was assigned as a Radar Specialist in the (CIC) Combat Information Center and attained a rating of Petty Officer 1st class. Carozza was honorably discharged on May 7, 1957. Following his military service Paul worked as a heavy equipment operator and Inspector for Anaconda Cable and Wire Co.

On Dec.16, 1960 Paul was appointed a police officer from 210 Oak Street. Following recruit training Paul was assigned to foot patrol in the 1st precinct earning $4,480 a year. He would be reassigned to the 4th precinct on Nov. 9, 1966. However, he was there only two months when, on Jan. 13, 1967, he was assigned as a Detective in the D.D. working General Assignment. He spent 11 years in a detective squad until Jan. 1978 when he was elected president of the PBA. While serving as PBA president he was allowed to keep his detective status and he remained the PBA president for the remainder of his career. In 1981 he also was elected and served as President of the N.Y.S. Metropolitan Police Conference for 14 years, simultaneously, with that of being PBA president. His Metro office was located in Albany.

Paul introduced a new approach to police union leadership by aggressively lobbying in Albany and Washington DC to enact legislation to enhance the quality of life for Yonkers police officers, and police officers throughout N.Y.S. One of his negotiated accomplishments was to obtain from the city a 232 day annual work duty chart of working 4 tours with 72 hours off duty. He also was instrumental in gaining from the pension system a stipend amounting to 1/60 th of one's pay for every year after 20 years, up to 15 years. Also, additional retirement legislation, detective's tenure, a police Bill of Rights, and much more.

Paul served on the committee that erected a police memorial in Albany honoring police officers killed in the line of duty. Also, the Committee for a National Police Monument in Washington DC. He also served on a Congressional committee for law enforcement which secured a $100,000 life insurance policy for officers killed in the line of duty. In the many years that Paul has served as Yonkers PBA president and Metro president, he has met with many heads of state such as; Governors Cuomo, Rockefeller, and Carey. He had also met with presidents Reagan, Bush (41), Carter, and many US senators and congressmen. On his office wall you could see some of the photos of Paul with political dignitaries as well as sports celebrities.

In June of 1994 Detective Paul Carozza, then president of the Metropolitan Police Conference of New York State, and president of the Yonkers PBA, was selected as the 1994 honorary law-enforcement Man of The Year by the Westchester Co. Detectives Association and all law enforcement agencies in New York State. Paul received his award on October 20, 1994.

After retiring on January 13, 1995 Paul organized and was President of the New York Police & Peace Officers Assoc Inc. operating out of his house at 42 Midland Ave, Yonkers.

Paul was married to the former Rose DePalma and had three sons. Mark, a Yonkers police officer, Paul, and Robert who passed away in 1990. His cousin is Det Francis Carozza and his uncle was PO Ray Carozza. Ret Det. Paul Carozza died on February 11, 2016 at the age of 82 years.

PO DONALD P. LYNCH #278

APPOINTED: December 16, 1960
RETIRED: January 3, 1981

Don was born Donald Patrick Lynch in Brooklyn in New York City on August 23, 1936, but attended school at Rice High School/New Paltz Central. Following high school Don joined the US Marine Corps on November 15, 1955. His MOS (Military Occupational Specialty) was Communications/ Radio Operator serving with the 2nd Marine Division out of Camp Lejeune, NC. He was honorably discharged as a Sergeant on November 15, 1958 and began working as a machinist.

Don was appointed to the police department on December 16, 1960 from 402 Riverdale Avenue. He earned a starting salary of $4,480. and was assigned to the 2nd precinct on patrol duty. On November 7, 1966 he was reassigned to patrol in the 1st precinct then located at 10 St Casimir's Ave. “Donnie” was transferred to the 4th precinct on February 7, 1969, but it was on February 2, 1970 that Don was assigned to the "AIE," Accident Investigation Emergency, better known as the Emergency Service Unit (ESU).

All throughout his career Donnie was a tough street cop and very proficient in the skills necessary for working in ESU. He also was known as a first class prankster. He was always pulling some prank on a fellow worker who would inevitably pull one against Don. He had a great sense of humor and you never knew what to expect from him. In the early to mid-1960's police cars did not have air conditioning. It has been said that when Don was first assigned to the Emergency Unit, the trucks had no AC so he had the idea to buy a portable AC unit. He and his partners all chipped in and bought a portable air conditioning unit that had a fan, and you had to fill the box with ice. It plugged into the cigarette lighter. As could be expected other officers teased him about being spoiled for weeks.

Aside from a few different locations from which he worked, he spent the next 11 years in the Emergency Squad working mostly from the 2nd precinct. And that is where he ultimately retired from on January 3, 1981. That same year he moved to Port Orange, Fla with his wife Marge where he lived for 21 years. Don was the Warehouse Manager/Vice President with C.B.M. Building Materials and had retired from Florida Hospital-Ormond, in Environmental Services and was eventually employed by Daytona Auto Auction. He was a life member of the Marine Corps League, member of the Irish American Club, and a member of the New York State Police and Fire Retirees Association.

Unfortunately and unexpectedly Donald Patrick Lynch, of Port Orange, FL, died on Sunday, October 19, 2005 at St. Lukes/ Mayo Clinic, in Jacksonville, FL. He was 69.

PO WILFRED J. NOYE #284

APPOINTED: February 8, 1961
RETIRED: October 16, 1982

Wilfred John Noye was born on Nov. 5, 1931 in the Bronx, NY. His family moved to Pennsylvania and "Willie," as he was to be known, attended and graduated from Pine Grove high school in Pine Grove, PA. On May 3, 1951, during the Korean War, Willie joined the Marine Corps and was honorably discharged as a sergeant on May 2, 1954. Following his military service Noye worked construction as a laborer and truck driver. He received his appointment to the YPD on Feb. 8, 1961 while residing at 25 Hudson View Terrace. Following the recruit training his first assignment was to the 1st pct. while earning a starting salary of $4,620 a year. Five years later, on Nov. 9, 1966, he was reassigned to the 4th precinct for two months and on Jan. 13, 1967 he was appointed a Detective. Willie Noye served as a detective for two years and on March 7, 1969 was transferred out to patrol in the 3rd precinct. In Jan. of 1971 he was assigned to the South Command until Jan. 29, 1973 when he was transferred to the Special Operations Division detailed to the Tactical Patrol Force. On April 4, 1979 he was returned to patrol in the South command and later retired on Oct. 16, 1982. Willie was one of those men with a very outgoing and jovial personality who was also active in the PBA playing on their softball team. Shortly after retiring he suffered a stroke which made it difficult to walk. In June of 1985 retired PO Wilfred Noye died at the age of 53 years.

LT. EDWARD S. A. RUBEO

APPOINTED: February 8, 1961
RETIRED: April 30, 1981

Edward S. A. Rubeo was born in the city of Yonkers on Nov. 3, 1935 and at the time he lived at 126 Saratoga Avenue. He attended local public schools and graduated from Yonkers High School. He joined the National Guard in June of 1953 and served as a Corporal in the 42nd Military Police Company for three years as an instructor. He was honorably discharged in June of 1956. Ed's trade was said to be that of a licensed "blaster," and he was certified by the Yonkers Combustible Dept., as well as the Town of Greenburgh. Ed was appointed to the YPD from 126 Saratoga Ave on Feb. 8, 1961 earning $4,620 and following training was assigned to the 1st pct. on patrol. On Nov. 9, 1966 Rubeo was reassigned to the 4th precinct. He received his promotion to Sergeant on May 5, 1972 earning $13,685 and was transferred to the South Command as a patrol supervisor. He was again promoted, this time to Lieutenant on September 21, 1977 earning $21,407, and assigned to the Field Services Bureau as a city wide patrol lieutenant. In Jan. of 1979 he was returned to the South Command and on Jan. 1, 1980 was transferred to the North Command. When Ed retired on April 30, 1981 he was living in Wappingers Falls.

DET. MURDO F. URQUHART #654

APPOINTED: February 8, 1961
RETIRED: April 1, 1983

Murdo Fyfe Urquhart was born in the City of Yonkers on Dec. 7, 1934. Murdo attended local public schools including Roosevelt high school for a short time but later graduated from Halstead high school in 1952. On Jan. 26, 1953, during the Korean War, Murdo joined the Marine Corps where he served as a Proof Technician for Small Arms. He had served in the DMZ in Korea and later served with the 2nd Marine Division at Camp Lejeune, NC where he would be honorably discharged on Jan. 26, 1956. Following his military service Urquhart worked for a time as a Warehouse-man.

Murdo was appointed to the Y.P.D. on February 8, 1961 while residing at 125 Elm St. His starting salary at the time was $4,620 a year and his first assignment was to patrol in the 1st pct. On April 22, 1964 Murdo was assigned as a Detective with his new partner, Det Paul Carozza, where he would remain for his entire career.

Murdo was a big man, about 6' 2" and 240 lbs. and along with his police duties, Murdo was very active as a volunteer in PBA activities. He played and was the coach on the PBA Basketball team for a number of years, as well as being the Manager and coach of their softball team for over 15 years. He also served many years as the Sgt. at Arms for the Police Association.

Det. Urquhart served with distinction in the Detective Bureau for 19 years. During his tenure he earned three Westchester Macy Honorable Mention Awards, two Commendations, and a Certificate of Excellent Police Work. His brother in law was PO Patsy Bruno.

Det Urquhart retired as a first grade detective after 22 years with the police department on April 1, 1983. After retirement he went to work as head of security at Cypress Gardens in Winterhaven, Fla.

Ret Det. Murdo Urquhart died on July 1, 2002 following surgery for a cancerous tumor. He was 67 years old.

DET. THOMAS F. BRINK #148

APPOINTED: February 8, 1961
RETIRED: February 12, 1981

Thomas Francis Brink was born in the city of the Yonkers on March 31, 1937. He attended local elementary schools and graduated from Gorton high school. Directly following his graduation Tom join the Army on September 4, 1956 and served as a Corporal for 22 months in the 101st Transportation Depot, Central Command, in Japan. Tom received his honorable discharge on September 9, 1958. Tom's father was in the moving business so Tom had been helping him with the moves since he was 15 years old. But that was just a part-time job so Tom took a job as a machine operator.

Thomas Brink was appointed to the Yonkers Police Department on February 8, 1961 while residing at 188 Ashburton Avenue. Upon completion of his recruit training he was assigned to the1st precinct on foot patrol and earned a starting salary of $4,620 a year.

In December of 1964 officer Brink was involved in a shootout with a holdup man at the Tuckahoe Motel where he wounded the suspect. On December 4, 1964 PO Brink was awarded the Medal of Honor for his action that day. He was also promoted meritoriously to Detective 3rd grade. (Below is the story on the day that he earned the Medal of Honor.) On his request he was allowed to remain on uniform patrol. However, on February 6, 1970 he was assigned to the Detective Division. This only lasted two months and again, at his request, on April 22, 1970 he was reassigned back to patrol in the 3rd precinct at 36 Radford St. But only four months later, on September 7, 1970, he was transferred back to the 1st precinct. Then, upon the centralization of the four precincts into two commands on January 1, 1971, he was reassigned to the North Command (old 4th pct.) at 53 Shonnard Place.

On April 19, 1972 and again on July 21, 1972, Brink was awarded certificates of excellent police work by the department's awards committee. Tom stood only 5'8" tall but was a tough, hard-working

Det. Thomas F. Brink #148 (cont.)

Irishman. Following in his father's footsteps, throughout Tom's career he owned and operated his own moving company, "Brinks Moving and Storage," while he was off duty. Despite the difficulties working rotating shifts Tom never stopped working his moving business while off duty.

Detective Brink continued working from the North command right up to his retirement on February 12, 1981. But he only retired from the police department. He still maintained his moving business for many years which he said kept him in good physical condition. And he was still operating loaded moving trucks in 2012. However, an infecton in his foot and amputation ended his moving business and also resulted in his death on June 12, 2014. He was 77.

DET. THOMAS F. BRINK
MEDAL OF HONOR RECIPIENT

December 1, 1964 was a rather cold winter night but, surprisingly, the heater was actually working in radio car 103. Police officers Tom Brink and Emanuel "Manny" Stella, both assigned to the 1st precinct out of 10 St. Casimir Avenue, and assigned as regular partners, were working the Late Tour. They had listened to the desk lieutenant at roll call give out the usual special attentions and miscellaneous complaints, had their revolvers inspected and then began their tour. After filling up the radio car with gas they stopped and picked up containers of coffee and began to check their sector.

The night was relatively quiet. Then at about 3:45 AM the officers drove east on Yonkers Avenue and into the Dunwoodie Motel parking lot at 300 Yonkers Avenue to make a U-turn to return west bound. However, while pulling through the lot PO Brink was able to see through the large glass front window of the motel. For an instant he wasn't sure what he was seeing. But, yes, there was a male with a mask over his head being handed money while holding a gun to the night clerks head. PO Brink immediately jumped out of the radio car and started for the motel entrance. Officer Stella serving as the "recorder" called in a robbery in progress over the radio, "103 car - Dunwoodie Motel - holdup, holdup."

The suspect must have noticed the marked unit pull up and he bolted out the front door. As PO Brink yelled for the bandit to stop, the male turned back to the motel and ran up the exterior stairs to the 3rd floor level walkway. Brink, revolver in hand, ran right up the stairs after him and kept yelling for him to stop. As the suspect ran across the walkway toward the end of the building he suddenly turned, crouched down, and opened fire twice at officer Brink. When interviewed many years later Brink still remembered very clearly; "*When he opened fire I remember thinking to myself, 'This F#%$*#* is trying to kill me.' And I didn't remember hearing the gunfire, just seeing the muzzle flash. I threw myself against the wall as flat as I could get, there was nowhere to hide, as a bullet passed my face and chipped the wall right alongside me causing pieces of the shattered cement to sting my face*."

Though under tremendous pressure PO Brink dropped to one knee and fired twice. One shot missed but the other hit the suspect in the ankle. The man went down for a second but continued to run with a limp. The suspect fired several more times at Brink but missed each time, instead smashing a window alongside the officer and striking a wood casing about a foot away. Brink fired two more rounds on the run and missed with both. As the man reached the end of the walkway he turned and took aim once again at Brink. But Brink fired first with his 5th round. "*I thought I hit him in the lower back/buttock area because he fell and slid about 15 feet, got up and staggered into the railing at the end of the walk and fell*

Det. Thomas F. Brink #148 (cont.)

over it."

The man later identified as John Hutchings, 28 years old of 7 Mooney Place, Yonkers, fell about 40 feet to the ground. That didn't seem to matter because as he looked up at the cop he fired one more time at officer Brink. The officer returned fire with his last round and missed. But Hutchings rose, despite his gunshot wound, scaled a six foot high wall and headed toward the railroad tracks and ultimately toward the toll booth on the Saw Mill River Parkway. The shooting had finally stopped and both men had emptied their weapons. All was quiet now except for the wailing of the responding backup unit sirens.

During the wide and extensive search for the suspect, the toll booth operator on the Saw Mill Parkway called in a suspicious man report to the YPD. One of the units that responded, Det's Brendan Magner and William Vance, who had obtained a description from officer Brink, saw a male limping by the toll booth. They approached the suspect, revolvers drawn, and heard him yell out, "*Don't shoot, I've been shot enough.*"

Within one half hour of the initial robbery report, John Hutchings was in the custody of Det's Magner and Vance and Hutchings was on his way to the hospital for treatment of his wounds. Ret Det Vance related that when Hutchings was lying on the ER treatment Gurney, they noticed that almost unbelievably the bullet that struck him in the ankle, simply fell out of the wound onto the sheet. Sometime later while being treated and questioned by then Det John Roach he reportedly told the detective, "*It would have all been worth it I had only killed that cop.*"

Officer Brink stated that the follow up investigation revealed that Hutchings not only had committed a number of other robberies at gunpoint in Yonkers, but was reportedly wanted in Albuquerque, NM for three other holdups and for killing three people.

Shortly after the arrest and interrogation of Hutchings it was learned that there had been a second suspect involved in the holdup who had slipped away from the motel undetected during the gun battle between Brink and his accomplice. He was identified as Timothy Murphy, 24, of 381 South Broadway. Murphy was a local Yonkers trouble maker and was known to off duty PO John Karasinski from high school. When PO Karasinski, who was off duty at the time, heard the wanted bulletin on his police radio scanner that Murphy was wanted, he located Murphy at Poplar and Willow Streets and arrested him within a few hours of the robbery. Both suspects were convicted and sentenced to long terms in prison.

Public Safety Commissioner Daniel F. McMahon, who had been leading the police department for only a year and who had reportedly re-instated an honor award system in the YPD, acted incredibly swift in recognizing the officers' actions. On December 4, 1964, only three days after the shooting both officers were honored with high department honors. PO Thomas Brink was awarded the departments Medal Of Honor (MOH), and his partner PO Emanuel Stella was awarded the departments Honorable Mention. Officers Magner, Vance, and Karasinski also received departmental recognition. Comm. McMahon stated, "*They pursued their duties under a hail of gunfire and at the very edge of eternity.*" Chief Polsen stated, "*It is not too often that our officers get the opportunity to prove themselves under fire. Patrolmen Brink and Stella had this opportunity and they stood as men. I am deeply proud.*" The Yonkers Herald Statesman wrote in part, "*Officers Brink and Stella have added luster to the Yonkers Police Department and Commissioner McMahon has added some high polish.*"

Det. Thomas F. Brink #148 (cont.)

The awarding of the "The Medal" to PO Brink was particularly rewarding because he was the first to receive this highest police honor in 32 years. The last officer, prior to Brink, to earn the Medal of Honor was motorcycle officer Robert Philp who was wounded while chasing an armed robber along Riverdale Avenue. Philp received his "medal" on June 15, 1932. As is traditional, those awarded the MOH are meritoriously elevated to Detective 3rd grade and received the additional listed contractual allowance; which in 1964 was $250. per year. If they remain on patrol they continue to receive 3rd grade detective status for the remainder of their career. If assigned to the Detective Division they may increase to 1st grade. Both officers accepted assignment to the DD. PO Brink did so reluctantly as he much preferred uniformed patrol duty. Not surprisingly within a few months both officers requested to be returned to patrol duty. Their request was approved.

Reflecting back on this award it is interesting to note that PO Tom Brink never actually received "the medal" at the time it was awarded to him. The police department did not have such a medal and officer Brink was told that even if they had one designed, the medal was too expensive for them to purchase. However he was welcome to purchase one himself. What Brink was presented with was an honor bar of green, white, and blue enamel with a gold star in the center. (This is not even the correct honor bar for this award.)

Although the very first Yonkers Police Department "Medal of Honor" was awarded back in 1931, no one had ever taken the time to design or authorize the making of such a medal. It wasn't until after the murder of PO Harold Woods in September of 1974, and the subsequent awarding of the medal posthumously to his wife, that Lt Martin Harding designed a medal and approval was given for Wayne Silversmith on South Broadway in Yonkers to make several of them. In fact, the first ribbons prepared for the presentation medals were made by Lt Harding's wife.

When the medals were made and were actually delivered to the department, a ceremony was held in City Hall on May 6, 1975 and Det. Thomas Brink, along with other subsequent recipients of the award, including former Det. Kenneth Zajac, Det. Anthony Cerasi, and Dorothy Woods, the widow of PO Harold Woods, were brought together and all were officially presented their Medals of Honor on that same day. Det. Thomas F. Brink had finally received his Medal of Honor nearly eleven years after it was awarded.

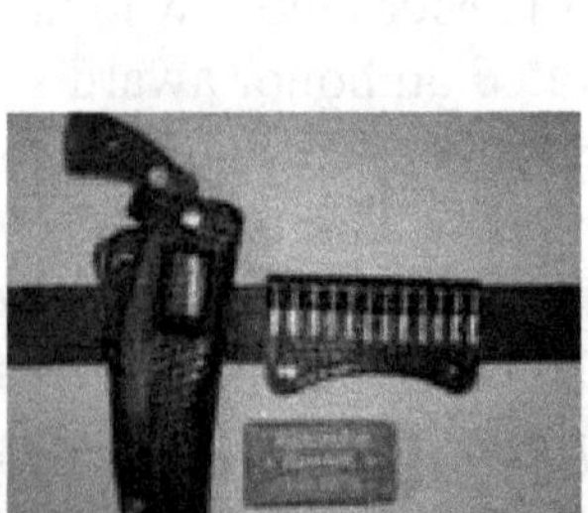

PO JOHN J. DOYLE #107

APPOINTED: February 8, 1961
RETIRED: February 5, 1987

John Joseph Doyle was born in Yonkers on Aug. 22, 1934 and is believed to have grown up in the Riverdale Ave area of Yonkers. He attended Saunders high school and later obtained his high school equivalency Diploma. John listed on his police application that he worked as a salesman. He was appointed to the YPD on Feb. 8, 1961 while residing at 23 Mulford Gardens. His first assignment was patrol duty in the 1st precinct earning a starting salary of $$4,620 a year. On Nov. 9, 1966 John was transferred to the 4th precinct on patrol duty. However, on Jan. 7, 1969, he was reassigned to steady days in the Records Division performing clerical duty. On Jan. 1, 1971 when the 4 precincts were centralized into 2 commands, and at his own request, John was assigned to duty in the South Patrol Command which had previously been the 2nd precinct. And on Sept. 15, 1972 Doyle was reassigned to patrol duty in the North Command on Shonnard Place. A resident of 36th Street in the Bronx, John Doyle retired from the police department on February 5, 1987. Several years following retirement and due to recurring health issues John moved north of Westchester Co. to live with his daughter where he died on Feb 15, 2016.

LT. RALPH P. ALEXANDER

APPOINTED: February 8, 1961
DIED: November 4, 1987

Born Ralph Preston Alexander Jr. on Nov. 12, 1938 in the Bronx NY, Ralph attended Bronx elementary schools and graduated from St. Agnes high school in NYC in 1956. Following high school Ralph joined the Army Reserve on Oct. 6, 1956 and was assigned to a communications platoon. He was honorably discharged in 1962 holding the rank of Sergeant. However, while in the Army reserve Ralph was employed as a security supervisor at the Cross County Shopping Center in Yonkers. He was appointed to the YPD on Feb. 8, 1961 while living at 46 Stratton St. and was assigned to the 1st pct. while earning a salary of $4,620 year. On March 28, 1966, Ralph was reassigned to the Communications Div. as a dispatcher. While there he was promoted to Sergeant on May 5, 1972, now earning a salary of $13,685 a year, and was transferred to the North Command. On February 18, 1977, he was promoted to Lieutenant and was reassigned back to the Communications Div. as a supervisor. In the early 1980s Ralph was assigned as the executive officer for the Records Div. But, on Dec. 21, 1983, he was returned, once again, to Communications as their executive officer. Ralph was a friendly, easy-going man of stocky build who was referred to by all his friends affectionately as "Huggy Bear." Ralph would see his son Richard be appointed to the YPD in Sept. of 1986. Unfortunately, just over a year later on Nov. 4, 1987, Lt Ralph Alexander died suddenly and unexpectedly while off duty in his home. He was only 48 years old.

DET. LT. JOHN M. ROACH

APPOINTED: February 8, 1961
RETIRED: January 5, 1991

John Michael Roach was born in Yonkers NY on October 31, 1936. He attended Yonkers elementary schools and later graduated from Gorton high school. Immediately after graduation "Jack," as he was known, joined the Marine Corps on August 10, 1954. During part of his enlistment he served in Japan where he attended Military Police school and subsequently served with Military Police for two years. He was honorably discharged on August 9, 1957 as a Corporal.

Following his discharge, from Aug 1957 to June 1958 "Jack" attended and graduated from the Institute of Drafting in NYC. However on his YPD application he listed his employment as a truck driver.

"Jack" Roach was appointed to the Yonkers Police Department on February 8, 1961 while living at 373 South Broadway. Following his recruit training he was assigned to foot patrol in the 1st precinct earning a starting salary of $4,620 a year. In less than four years, on September 23, 1964, "Jack" was assigned as a Detective in the Detective Division located in headquarters at 10 St Casimir Avenue. Initially he worked general assignment investigations but in time he was part of a team called the Gambling Squad consisting of then Det Sgt Fred Doty, Jack Roach and Tom Hargraves. They became very proficient in surveillance and the installation of electronic eavesdropping devices; "wire-taps."

On January 13, 1967 Roach was returned to patrol duty in the 3rd precinct. And yet, a year later, on February 23, 1968, he was again assigned as a detective, this time detailed to work in the Narcotics Unit. He proved himself to be an excellent detective and remained in the DD up to September 21, 1977 when he was promoted to the rank of Sergeant. His salary rose to $18,712 but, as was the practice, he was transferred from the DD and assigned to the South Command as a patrol supervisor.

However his past proven value to the department as a detective resulted in his being reassigned once again to the Detective Division as a detective squad supervisor on January 20, 1979. Jack Roach had continued to study and was now very high on the list to be promoted to the rank of Lieutenant. As such it was decided he should be returned to patrol duty to re- familiarize himself with uniform patrol policies, etc, before being promoted. And so, Sgt Roach was transferred out to patrol in the 4th precinct on October 28, 1983. Four months later, on February 17, 1984, Sgt Roach was promoted to Lieutenant earning $37,132 and remained in the 4th precinct as a patrol lieutenant.

When a lieutenant vacancy occurred in the DD there was no real doubt as to who was most qualified to fill the position. On May 4, 1984 Lt Roach was reassigned to the Detective Division as a Det. Lieutenant and due to his vast investigative experience and leadership abilities, as well as his popularity among everyone, he was assigned to the very important, and new, position of Major Case Coordinator. This job was established specifically for him because of his outstanding capabilities in coordinating all the complicated aspects of a difficult investigation which would nearly always result in arrests and convictions. Without question the detective captain was in command of the entire Detective Division. But, basically that was an administrative position. However, the man who held the position of major case lieutenant, in this case Jack Roach, was the tough hard-nosed boss who had to make sure things got done in the office and out on the street. And Jack fit the position perfectly.

Det. Lt. John M. Roach (cont.)

As you might expect from a former Marine, Jack Roach had a take charge attitude and insisted that things be done his way. With an ever ready cigar in his hand he held sway over all that occurred in the Detective Division, and did so with great results.

Throughout his police career Jack was always a very active member of the PBA and for many years played on the PBA softball team. He also served for several years on the annual old-timers retiree picnic committee. Throughout his career, particularly as a detective, he received multiple commendations and awards too numerous to list along with recognition from many law enforcement agencies throughout the metropolitan area.

Det. Lt. John M. Roach retired from the Yonkers Police Department on January 5, 1991. Always a proud former Marine, following his retirement from the YPD, Jack Roach purchased a boat for his family's enjoyment and named it the, "GRUNT."

DET. LOUIS M. FERRARA #690

APPOINTED: January 1, 1962
RETIRED: June 27, 1994

Louis Matthew Ferrara was born on April 15,1932 in Yonkers and raised in the Park Hill section of Yonkers. Lou attended local public schools graduating from Saunders HS in 1952 as class president. Six months later, on Dec. 27, 1950 during the Korean War, Lou joined the Navy. He served as a gunners mate 2nd class on a Destroyer patrolling off the coast of Korea. He received his honorable discharge on Oct. 22, 1954. After his discharge he worked for several contractors as a union operating engineer. Lou was appointed a police officer on Jan. 1, 1962 from 35 Vernon Place. Lou's starting salary was $4,850 a year and his first assignment was to the 2nd precinct. Lou's personality was very outgoing and he could never be accused of being shy. On Nov. 7, 1966 he was reassigned from the 2nd to the 1st precinct. On Feb. 2, 1970, following NYPD ESU training at Randall's Island in NYC, Lou was assigned to the Emergency Service Unit. He remained in that job for 11 years when, on May 13, 1981, he was assigned as a Detective in the Detective Division. He was always an aggressive cop in ESU and his work ethic worked to his advantage in the DD. He also had the privilege of watching his son Stephen be appointed a Yonkers police officer. Lou Ferrara retired from the YPD as a detective on June 27, 1994 and took a job as the head of security for Yonkers General Hospital on Ashburton Avenue. He has since stopped working and is enjoying retirement.

PO WILLIAM R. SCHULTZ #158

APPOINTED: January 1, 1962
RETIRED: October 25, 1983

William Schultz was born in Yonkers on June 22, 1937. He attended PS# 13 and would later graduate from Roosevelt H.S. Bill joined the Army National Guard's 101st Signal Battalion in 1955 and served both active and reserve duty and was later honorably discharged in 1961. Bill was appointed to the Y.P.D. on Jan. 1, 1962 while living at 7 Rossiter Ave. Following his basic recruit training he was assigned to the 2nd pct. earning a salary of $4,850 a year. As a young cop Bill enjoyed sports and for many years played on the PBA softball team. He also related that his grandfather was PO Arthur Doty. Bill remained in the 2nd pct. right up to Feb. 2, 1970 when he was selected to serve in the Emergency Service Unit. He received his ESU training at Randall's Island in NYC by NYPD ESU instructors. Schultz enjoy the high-pressure work that came with ESU and remained working in ESU from the 2nd precinct until the last few years before retiring when he was transferred to the Communications Div. due to health problems. William Schultz retired from the Yonkers Police Department on October 25, 1983 and died 10 years later on September 19, 1993. He was 56 years old.

LT. RICHARD L. VANE

APPOINTED: January 1, 1962
RETIRED: January 2, 1992

Richard Lewis Vane was born in Yonkers, New York on June 21, 1935 in the old St. John's hospital located at the corner of Palisade and Ashburton Avenues. He was raised in North Yonkers, attended Sacred Heart grade school and graduated from Gorton high school. After graduation Rich began working at Refined Syrup and Sugar "the sugar house" located on Vark Street.

He enlisted in the U.S. Army January 18, 1955, and was stationed at Ft. Devens, MA in the Army Security Agency where he attained a top secret and cryptographic clearance. He transferred to Camp Gordon, GA where he attended and graduated the Military Police academy. He was stationed via troop transport ship, on the USS Harry Taylor, to the port of Bremerhaven, Germany. Vane served as a corporal for the 339th Communications Recon Company in Nuernberg. He was stationed throughout Europe over the next three years where the Army Security Agency spied on Russian troop movements. Upon completion of his tour of duty in Europe and his return to the U.S. he was assigned to the 504th Military Police Company in Ft. Eustis, VA. One year later he was honorably discharged on January 16, 1959 and returned to Yonkers speaking fluent German. He returned to work at the "sugar house" as a Transportation Dispatcher.

Rich was appointed to the police department on January 1, 1962 while residing at 8 Portland Place. Following recruit training he was assigned to foot patrol in the old 3rd precinct at 36 Radford Street earning $4,850 a year. He worked eight years in the 3rd earning an enviable reputation along with many police awards for excellent service. Prior to becoming a supervisor he was decorated by the Yonkers Police Department with five Commendations, eight Certificates of Excellent Police work and two Honorable Mention Macy Awards. On November 6, 1970 he was transferred to the 4th pct., and on May 31, 1973 to the South Command at 441 Central Park Ave.

At one point the police department began the process of promoting individuals to the rank of Sergeant even though there was no vacancy in that rank. The individual promoted was designated a "temporary sergeant." On February 17, 1977 Richie Vane was promoted to "Temporary Sergeant" earning $18,712 a year and was assigned to the North Command as a patrol supervisor. Several months later a sergeant vacancy became available and on July 8, 1977 Vane's position was made permanent. He was reassigned to the North East Command on September 16, 1982.

Sgt Vane was promoted to Lieutenant on February 17, 1984 at $37,132 a year and was reassigned to the 4th precinct as a patrol lieutenant. Over four years later, on December 10, 1990, Lt Vane was again moved, this time to the 1st precinct at 730 East Grassy Sprain Rd serving as their Operations Lieutenant. In this job he served as a problem solver for the captain. In mid-1991 Lt Vane was assigned to the Communications Division as a tour supervisor from which he retired on January 2, 1992 after 30 years service.

In 1995 he and his wife moved to their dream home by the water in Punta Gorda, FL where they live today.

LT. LOUIS F. POLIDORE

APPOINTED: January 1, 1962
RETIRED: May 15, 1987

Louis Franklin Polidore was born in Yonkers on Dec. 1, 1937. He graduated from local Yonkers public schools and upon graduation, in Jan. of 1955, he joined the Navy. Lou served on the destroyer escort USS Snowden. He was honorably discharged in Nov. of 1958. Prior to the YPD he had been working as a Larchmont police officer. He was appointed to the YPD on Jan. 1, 1962 while living at 9 Leonard Place. Following training he was assigned to the 2nd pct earning $4,850 a year. He remained on patrol there for 16 years up to Oct. 20, 1978 when he was promoted to Sergeant and began earning $21,142. Upon his promotion he was reassigned to the North Command as a patrol supervisor. On June 20, 1979 he was moved to the N/E Command and three years later on Sept. 16, 1982 he was returned to the North Command. He was promoted to Lieutenant on Sept. 30, 1983 earning $35,384 and was assigned to the Inspections Unit on citywide patrol. His transfers continued; on December 21, 1983 to Detention Services (Central Booking Officer) and on Aug. 16, 1984 to the 1st pct as the Watch Commander. He also served as a Communications Div. supervisor. Lou was a big man standing over 6' and weighing well over 220 Lbs and was always smoking a huge cigar. He had 5 children, one of which, Vincent, was a Scarsdale police officer. Lt Polidore retired from the YPD on a disability pension on May 15, 1987 and shortly thereafter developed a heart condition and later, cancer of the spine. Ret Lt Louis Polidore died on July 30, 2000 at the age of 62 years.

PO EMIL J. NOSCHESE #286

APPOINTED: January 1, 1962
RETIRED: January 9, 1976

Emil Joseph Noschese was born in Yonkers on Sept. 21, 1938. He attended local schools and graduated from Roosevelt H.S. Following school Emil worked both as a truck driver and as a draftsman. He served in the Air National Guard from Mar 20, 1957 and was honorably discharged on Mar 20, 1963. He was appointed a police officer on Jan. 1, 1962 from 39 Manning Avenue. Following training he was assigned to the 1st pct. at 20 Wells Ave. earning $4,850 a year. On Apr 5, 1965 Emil was assigned to the Traffic Division on two wheel motorcycle duty and on Jan. 18, 1971 the Traffic Div. was decentralized and split up among the four precincts. PO Noschese was assigned his motorcycle patrol duties in the North Command. However, only nine months later on Oct 19, 1971 the Traffic Unit was re-established under the Special Operations Division and he and his motorcycle returned to S.O.D. A very active member of the PBA and a longtime member of their Softball Team Emil retired on a disability pension on January 9, 1976 following a motorcycle accident and moved to Florida with his wife.

PO STEPHEN A. FEDOR #44

APPOINTED: January 1, 1962
RETIRED: January 14, 1982

Stephen Arthur Fedor was born in the City of Yonkers on August 25, 1927. Steve attended local elementary schools and later graduated from Commerce HS. Years later he would also earn a Bachelor of Science degree from St. Thomas Aquinas College in Sparkhill, NY. Following high school Steve joined the Army on March 6, 1956 serving as a Corporal in the Medical Corps. He was separated from active duty on January 8, 1958 and honorably discharged on March 6, 1962. Steve was then employed by the Otis Elevator Company in their mailing department.

Fedor was appointed to the Yonkers Police Department on January 1, 1962 while living at 354 Palisade Ave. His first assignment was foot patrol duty in the 1st precinct where he earned a starting salary of $4,850 a year. On November 9, 1966 Steve was moved to the 4th precinct. On February 2, 1970, following specialized training by the NYPD ESU instructors, Steve was assigned to our Emergency Squad working out of headquarters. On January 1, 1971 he was transferred to the North command but remained working in ESU.

He said he will always remember the day that he and his partner were the first to arrive at the scene of the armed robbery and subsequent shooting of PO Harold Woods on September 18, 1974. They did the best they could by administering first aid to the officer and attempting to slow the bleeding. But despite their best efforts, and those of the doctors in the hospital, the PO Harold Woods died four days later on September 22, 1974. A day Steve Fedor will never forget.

A more satisfying assignment occurred two years later. In 1976 a child rapist was terrorizing Yonkers by abducting young girls and assaulting them. Every cop was angry and wanted this man. A great deal of effort was put forth by all officers throughout the city trying to locate and arrest the man. On November 30, 1976 PO Fedor and his partner, while working a fill in spot in a sector car, located the suspect and following a high speed pursuit stopped and arrested the male who was later convicted on all counts. Officer Fedor was awarded a departmental Commendation for his keen observation and actions. During his last three years in the department he was assigned to the Youth Division from which he would later retire.

A former president of the Yonkers Police Holy Name Society, Steve Fedor retired on January 14, 1982 and moved to Florida and later to Virginia where he volunteered as a Eucharistic Minister in their local church. Steve Fedor and his wife now enjoy their retirement years spending time visiting their children and grandchildren.

PO HUGH K. HOGUE #47

APPOINTED: January 1, 1962
RETIRED: January 11, 1995

Born Hugh Kelsey Hogue in the City of Yonkers on May 22, 1933, "Kelsey" as he was known to all, attended local schools and graduated from Commerce HS. Not long after school Kelsey began working as a truck driver and in a shipping and receiving department of a local factory. In February 1953, while the Korean War was still going, Kelsey joined the Army. During his enlistment he served as a Cook and was honorably discharged as a Corporal in February of 1955.

He was appointed to the YPD on January 1, 1962 from 16 Croton Terrace. Following recruit training he was assigned to foot patrol duty in the 1st precinct earning a starting salary of $4,850 a year. Officer Hogue was a tall man standing 6' 3," slim build and recognizable easily because of a prominent stutter when he became excited. On November 9, 1966 Hogue was reassigned to the 4th precinct.

On May 18, 1970 while on foot post at 2:45 AM Hogue discovered a fire at 19 Croton Terr. He ran through building kicking in doors warning people to leave, no doubt saving many lives. For his actions he was awarded a Commendation. Then, on August 1, 1972, while on his foot post he discovered another fire at 19 North Broadway. Hogue entered and located an elderly woman who was reluctant to leave. During his attempted rescue he was overcome by smoke and hospitalized. For this rescue he was awarded a Certificate of Excellent Police Work and the Macy Award in 1973. In 1975 while assigned to the Community Patrol Unit, CPU, he requested to be transferred out of the CPU back to regular patrol in the North Command, which was granted.

On June 20, 1979 PO Hogue was reassigned to duty in the North East Patrol Command at 730 East Grassy Sprain Road. He was assigned to the Special Operations Division on July 17, 1987 working steady days serving as the department's mail courier. Kelsey remained in this assignment right up to his retirement on January 11, 1995. During his career he earned four CEPW, three Commendations, and two Westchester Rockland News Honorable Mention awards.

Ret PO Hugh "Kelsey" Hogue died on October 22, 2012. He was 79 years old.

SGT. RUSSELL L. MORVANT #1

APPOINTED: January 1, 1962
RETIRED: July 15, 1983

Russell Louis Morvant was born in the City of New York on January 11, 1937. After his family moved to Yonkers Russ attended local Yonkers public schools and graduated from Yonkers high school. Years later he would earn a Bachelor of Science degree in Criminal Justice from Mercy College in 1979.

Following high school graduation Russ joined the Navy on August 18, 1954 where he was trained in the 5" gunnery school. He received his honorable discharge on November 8, 1957 as a Petty Officer 2nd class. On his police application Russ listed his previous occupation as a clerk with First National Stores.

Morvant was appointed to the Yonkers Police Department on January 1, 1962 while living at 8 Purser Place. Following his basic recruit training his first assignment was foot patrol in the 3rd precinct earning a starting salary of $4,850 a year. Russ was a very soft spoken individual, low key and hard to rattle. On October 13, 1969 Russell Morvant and his partner James Corcoran responded to a report of an emotionally disturbed person barricaded in his apartment with his two year old son and a rifle. Shots had already been fired at his wife. As soon as the officers arrived at the address three rounds struck the roof of their radio car. But because they knew a child was in the apartment the officers held their fire. When they approached the apartment door the male fired at them through the glass pane in the door. Still they held their fire. After great effort the officers convinced the man to surrender without firing a shot. For their firearms discipline and professional handling of the problem, they were both awarded a departmental Commendation.

On January 1, 1971, when a precinct centralization plan was implemented, Russ was reassigned to the South Command; formerly the 2nd pct. On June 23, 1972 Russ was reassigned to the Special Operations Division (SOD) working steady late tour on street cleaning summons detail. Then on April 4, 1979 he was reassigned back to patrol in the South Command for just three months and was moved to the North East Command on East Grassy Sprain Road.

Officer Russell Morvant was promoted to the rank of Sergeant on May 1, 1981 earning $23,086 and was transferred to the North Command as a patrol supervisor. Russ retired from the YPD two years later on July 15, 1983 and after a time moved to Nevada. During his early years as a police officer Russ was very active in sports and for many years played on the PBA softball team. As he got a little older he didn't play softball anymore but he stayed very active with the local Nevada Senior Olympics and won a Gold and Silver medal. The Gold for the basketball "Free Throw Shots" (28 out of 30), and the Silver for what they called the "Shoot Around." And Russ is proud to know his son Russell T. Morvant is a Sergeant with the Scarsdale P.D.

PO JAMES J. McCABE #43

APPOINTED: January 1, 1962
RETIRED: January 14, 1983

Jim McCabe was born in Yonkers July 22, 1936. He attended local schools and graduated from Sacred Heart H.S. Jim joined the Navy on July 20, 1954 and served up to his honorable discharge on July 12, 1957. Following his military service Jim worked as a machine operator at the Phelps Dodge Corp. He received his appointment to the Y.P.D. on Jan. 1, 1962 while residing at 54 Waring Pl. Following his recruit training he was assigned to a foot post in the 1st pct. earning a starting salary of $4,850 a year. Nearly 5 years later, on Nov. 9, 1966, PO McCabe was transferred to the 4th pct. where he was assigned to a radio car and partnered with PO John Doyle. Jim was also very athletic and was an active member of the PBA softball team. He was also very active on the PBA board and in 1978 was the PBA's vice president. On June 20, 1979 Jim McCabe was reassigned to the North East command located on E. Grassy Sprain Rd. During the 1970's the YPD formed a counseling unit where those dealing with alcoholism could seek confidential help. Jim McCabe was designated as one of those volunteer counselors. Even after Jim retired from the YPD on Jan. 14, 1983 he gained a full time job with the city's Employees Assistance Program as a substance abuse counselor. Jim was proud to watch his son, James Jr. be appointed to the Y.P.D.

PO GEORGE J. BAKER Jr. #53

APPOINTED: April 1, 1962
RETIRED: January 14, 1983

George Joseph Baker was born in Yonkers on Oct. 30, 1937, attended local schools and graduated from Saunders HS with a trade in carpentry. Following graduation George then attended the Chicago Technical College, Chicago, Ill. studying blue print reading from 1956 to 1958. George was a carpenter by trade and worked as a member of the Carpenters Union. He was appointed to the YPD on Apr 1, 1962 from 14 Richmond Pl. After recruit training he was assigned to the 2nd pct earning a starting salary of $4,850 a year. He would remain on patrol in the 2nd pct his entire career with only the last few years there serving as a desk officer. In Feb. of 1967 his C.O. recommended him for recognition for his having obtained critical information on June 1, 1966 regarding the murder of an elderly woman. His information resulted in the arrest of the murderers. For his part he was awarded a Commendation on Feb. 9, 1967. George was a big man who stood about 6' 3" tall at about 275 Lbs and was known to most friends as “Big George Baker.” George's father was PO George Baker Sr., his brothers were Capt. Robert Baker and Det Reynold Baker. Another brother, NYS Trooper William Baker was killed in an on duty motor vehicle accident. His nephew is PO John Viviano and George's father in law was PO George McMahon. George Baker retired on January 14, 1983 and died suddenly on January 5, 2003. He was 65 years old.

SGT. JOSEPH A. MADDEN #74

APPOINTED: April 1, 1962
DIED: July 22, 1986

Joseph A Madden was born in the City of Yonkers on December 15, 1934. He attended and graduated from local public elementary and high school. Joe served in the Army from 1954 to 1956 and following his honorable discharge gained employment with Consolidated Edison Co. He was working there when he took the Yonkers Patrolman's test. Joe was appointed to the Yonkers Police Department on April 1, 1962 while residing at 271 Hawthorne Avenue. Following his two week recruit training, which ran from October 15th to November 1, 1962 at Iona College, Joe was assigned to patrol duty in the 3rd precinct earning a starting salary of $4,850 a year. Joe quickly became one of those men you enjoyed being around and had great respect for. Joe stood about 6' 3" tall but was not at all intimidating. If you were standing a school crossing in the freezing weather, and Joe came riding by, it was not unusual for him to stop and stand your crossing while you warmed up in the car. Joe quickly earned the respect of the desk lieutenants and by 1969 he was often allowed to "take the desk" for the lieutenant for various periods of time.

Joe's nickname, for reasons unknown, was "Hoxie," and he had a saying he frequently used under appropriate circumstances; "Asalta Balatta" which supposedly translated loosely as, "Jump Ball." At one point auto thefts on Bronx River Road were becoming so common that a two man, plainclothes, auto theft detail was formed around 1977 working a steady midnight tour. Having a reputation for being an aggressive cop, Joe volunteered and was chosen. He worked this detail from about 1979 to early 1983 making large numbers of arrests for attempted auto theft. Often these arrests were preceded by wild pursuits into NYC before being completed.

Joe Madden was appointed a Detective on April 22, 1983. It seemed he knew everyone in the 3rd precinct which was a great asset while conducting investigations. Det Madden was promoted to Sergeant on March 11, 1985 and was assigned as a patrol supervisor in the 3rd precinct. A story has it that, it was his first night as a sergeant when an emotionally disturbed person went wild and was in the act of gouging out his father's eyes. In order to stop the crazed male an officer used his nightstick. Unfortunately the male died. All the officers involved became very anxious until Sgt Madden arrived and in his usual and professional way, directed them to simply write in the report exactly the way it happened and don't worry.

He was a natural at taking charge in a calm manner. In fact, it was not uncommon for Madden to get a call at any and all hours of the day or night, to come into the precinct to give advice on handling a delicate incident. It was jokingly said, Shakespeare could not have written a better UF# 39 report than Joe Madden. During his off duty time Joe golfed at every opportunity. He loved the game. And then Sgt Madden became ill and was diagnosed with a brain tumor. There was very little that could be done and Joe knew it. Despite his illness he continued to work whenever he could until he was overcome by the disease. Sgt Joseph Madden was admitted into Rosary Hill and died a very short time later on July 22, 1986 at the age of 51 years.

Shortly after his death a large number of former co-workers established a fund raiser named the Sgt Joseph Madden Annual Memorial Golf Tournament where all money raised was donated to the Rosary Hill Home in Hawthorne, NY.

PO JAMES R. POWERS #88

APPOINTED: January 1, 1963
DIED: September 13, 1963

James R. Powers was born in New York City on March 19, 1940. After moving to Yonkers he attended local public schools, left high school early and at the age of 16, and on December 28, 1956 he joined the Navy. He earned his GED diploma in the Navy and was honorably discharged on December 22, 1959. Following his military Jim earned living driving a truck. Jim Powers was appointed to the Yonkers P.D. on January 1, 1963 from 78 Glenwood Avenue. He followed his brother PO Edward Powers who had been appointed in 1960. Following recruit training Jim was assigned to foot patrol in the 4th precinct earning $5,200. a year. On September 13, 1963 while off duty, and with just over nine months following his appointment, PO James R. Powers was found, unexpectedly dead near the train tracks at the Greystone Railroad Station. He was only 23 years old.

PO ROBERT D. CORBETT #279

APPOINTED: January 1, 1963
RETIRED: April 8, 1983

Robert Daniel Corbett was born in Yonkers NY on June 8, 1937. He attended local elementary schools and graduated from Sacred Heart HS in 1955. Bob joined the NY National Guard in Dec. of 1956 and served in the Signal Corps as a Sergeant E-5 and was honorably discharged. He worked as a stock clerk/order clerk, but on Jan. 1, 1963 Bob received his appointment to the Y.P.D. while residing at 37 Currans Lane. The starting salary was $5,200 a year and following recruit training he was assigned to foot patrol in the 1st pct. at 20 Wells Ave. Four years later, on Nov. 9, 1966, PO Corbett was transferred to duty in the 4th pct where he would remain for the remainder of his career. Bob was a very friendly and talkative individual with a high energy personality. He was always a bit husky in build and had red-ish blonde hair. So it wasn't long before he was affectionately nicknamed, "Red Round." Bob spent his entire career in uniform but the last few years he served as the 4th pct captain's aide. During the late 1970's the YPD formed a counseling unit where those dealing with alcoholism could seek confidential assistance and Bob Corbett volunteered, was trained and certified by Rutgers University and was designated as one of those counselors. He retired to his home in Yonkers on April 8, 1983 and was then hired as the Security Manager for M.C.I in Rye Brook. He then worked as a security supervisor for 10 years at St. John's Hospital. Ret PO Robert D. Corbett died in Mt Sinai Hospital on August 28, 2011. He was 74 years old.

PO FRANCIS T. THUMAN #4

APPOINTED: January 1, 1963
RETIRED: January 23, 1997

Francis Thomas Thuman was born in the Bronx, NY on New Year's Day January 1, 1935. He attended and graduated from St. Barnabas Elementary School on McLean Avenue bordering the Bronx and completed his education at Roosevelt High School. Following his high school education Frank attended the Bartlett School of Tree Surgery in Westport Ct. He then worked for the Bartlett Tree Co. in White Plains and later Community Tree in Hastings, NY.

Frank passed the Patrolman's civil service exam and was appointed to the Yonkers Police Department on January 1, 1963 from 1531 Central Park Avenue. He explained that from the date of his appointment up to April 1, 1963 he rode in the backseat of a radio car wearing a gray type uniform and learning "on the job" from senior officers. His recruit class of 23 men then received three weeks of classroom training by a few ranking officers in headquarters at 10 St. Casimir's Avenue. After the three weeks they were provided with their regulation blue police uniforms. Following Frank's recruit training he was assigned to patrol duty in the 2nd precinct earning a starting salary of $5,200 a year.

Six years later, on May 20, 1969, he was reassigned to patrol in the 4th precinct. Frank was later transferred on February 22, 1974 to the Communications Division dispatching radio cars. However, just two years later, on May 10, 1976, he was returned to duty in the South Patrol Command. In March of 1977 Frank became acutely aware of a need within the department for alcohol abuse counseling for members of the police department. He took it upon himself to contact NYPD chaplain Monsignor Dunn for guidance on establishing a program similar to what was in place in the NYPD. After meeting with the Yonkers Police chaplains and police surgeons, a meeting was held with Chief Polsen. After being given a detailed briefing on the proposal the chief approved the program which would be based on Alcoholics Anonymous. Frank Thuman was designated one of the official volunteer counselors.

On July 19, 1978 Frank was assigned to the Communications Division working in the NYSPIN (New York State Police Information Network) section which interfaced with all law enforcement agencies nationwide including Interpol. It was here that officer Thuman became exceptionally proficient in that special field. Because he seemed to know every aspect of the operation he was occasionally, and in good humor, referred to as the NYSPIN god. Officer Thuman remained in that assignment right up to his retirement on January 23, 1997 after having served honorably for over 34 years.

Frank was a very religious man who studied the bible scriptures but also enjoyed hunting and competitive Trap shooting at the Bethlehem Rod and Gun Club in Ulster County.

LT. GEORGE C. MacDONALD

APPOINTED: JANUARY 1, 1963
RETIRED: January 9, 1998

George Charles MacDonald was born in Yonkers on Nov. 14, 1936. He attended local public schools and graduated from Saunders HS. George joined the Marine Corps on Jan. 25, 1955. He held the rank of Sergeant and served as a drill instructor as well as doing duty at sea. George received his honorable discharge on Jan. 23, 1959. Following his military service, he worked as an industrial truck mechanic. He was appointed to the Y.P.D. on Jan. 1, 1963 while living at 40 Van Cortlandt Park Ave. Following his recruit training he was assigned to the 4th pct earning a starting salary of $5,200 a year. A bit uncharacteristic for a former Marine, George was very soft-spoken and had an easy-going demeanor which made him very easy to get along with. For many years he was assigned to the Getty Square on steady days primarily for bank security. George was an excellent shot with his revolver, and not surprisingly, was recruited to join the YPD pistol team. He, and a few other officers, competed in various competitions in the tri-state area and won numerous trophies for their marksmanship. George MacDonald was promoted to the rank of Sergeant on Jan. 18, 1982 earning $28,313 a year. With his promotion came a transfer to the South Command as a patrol supervisor. On April 11, 1988 Sgt. MacDonald was promoted to the rank of Lieutenant earning $51,609 a year. As a lieutenant he was designated a watch commander and the 4th pct. Lt. MacDonald was assigned to citywide patrol in the Field Services Bureau in 1996, but on Sept. 9, 1996 he was designated the Executive Officer in the 2nd pct. Lt. George MacDonald retired from all active duty on January 9, 1998 and moved to NJ.

PO WILLIAM F. LEONARD #176

APPOINTED: January 1, 1963
RESIGNED: December 4, 1964

William Francis Leonard was born in New York City on November 11, 1936. He attended local NYC schools and graduated from All Hallows Institute located at 111 E. 164th Street in the Bronx. Bill received an honorable discharge from the Army after serving from April 20, 1959 to March 31, 1961. Prior to his police service Bill worked as an insurance clerk. He received his appointment to the YPD on January 1, 1963 while residing at 418 Park Hill Avenue. Following recruit training he was assigned to patrol duty in the 3rd precinct earning $5,200 a year. As rookie Leonard was described as being very quiet and seldom spoke unless spoken to. PO Leonard found himself in serious trouble on July 13, 1964 and was subsequently suspended. William Leonard resigned from the YPD effective December 4, 1964, three months after his brother Michael was appointed to the YPD.

CAPTAIN JAMES C. BUBBICO

APPOINTED: January 1, 1963
RETIRED: July 5, 1990

James Cosimo Bubbico was born in the City of Yonkers on June 6, 1940. He attended local public schools and graduated from Saunders high school. Shortly after finishing high school Jim joined the Army on August 14, 1958 and was trained in Military Police school. He was honorably discharged as a Specialist 4th class on August 14, 1961. Following his military service Jim gained employment as a truck driver.

Bubbico was appointed to the Yonkers Police Department on January 1, 1963 from 110 Park Hill Avenue. Following his basic recruit training "Butch," as he would be known throughout his career, was assigned to the 3rd precinct at 36 Radford Street earning a starting salary of $5,200 a year. His partner for several years, and good friend, was Vincent Patalano.

Apparently "Butch" not only worked a busy sector but also was determined to find time to study for a promotional exam to police Sergeant. As a result of his effort, on October 22, 1969 he was promoted to the rank of Sergeant, and with this promotion came a raise in salary to $11,600 along with a transfer to the 1st precinct as a patrol supervisor. However, less than five months later, on March 3, 1970, Sgt Bubbico was returned to supervisor duty in the 3rd precinct. On January 1, 1971, the day a precinct centralization plan was implemented, Sgt Bubbico was assigned to the former 2nd precinct, then renamed

Captain James C. Bubbico (cont.)

the South Patrol Command, which also incorporated the boundaries of the old 3rd precinct. Once again this assignment was fairly brief because, before the year ended, on December 10, 1971, Sgt Bubbico was reassigned to the North Patrol Command located at 53 Shonnard Place.

Five years after his promotion to sergeant, on April 12, 1974, "Butch" Bubbico was promoted to the rank of Lieutenant. His new salary at that time was $19,671 and he was reassigned to the Inspectional Services Division as a city wide patrol lieutenant.

In early 1974 the police department applied for and was awarded a $400,000 federal grant to establish a unit that would implement a Community Policing form of patrol in a designated area of the city. That unit was named the Community Patrol Unit and six months into its operation Lt Bubbico was named as its commanding officer. However, upon his own request Lt Bubbico was returned to patrol supervisory duty in the North Command on July 19, 1976.

On July 8, 1977 the department established a new unit within the police department; that being the Crime Prevention Unit. This unit was a one officer unit and the officer assigned to make it operational and effective was Lt Bubbico. Part of his duty was to establish crime patterns and report his findings to the police chief. He also conducted safety surveys of various business establishments and recommended ways to better protect their property. He also was responsible to meet with and give safety talks to any home owner group in the city.

Lt Bubbico was returned to patrol duty on January 1, 1979 in the North Command, at the time designated a Zone lieutenant. But, two months later, on March 16, 1979, Bubbico was reassigned to the Youth and Community Relations as their Executive Officer and, in addition, he was designated the commanding officer of the Crime Prevention and Crime Analysis Unit. While in these assignments he was designated a Detective Lieutenant on October 21, 1983.

On April 11, 1988 Lt Bubbico was promoted to the rank of Captain and designated commanding officer of the Community Affairs Division at 21 Alexander Street. After 29 years of service Capt. James Bubbico retired from the police department on July 5, 1990. Following his retirement from the YPD "Butch" Bubbico moved to Arizona to enjoy his retirement years.

DET. ROBERT J. LORENZ #683

APPOINTED: January 1, 1963
RETIRED: June 17, 1989

Robert John Lorenz was born in the City of Yonkers on December 21, 1936. He attended local public schools and graduated from Saunders High School. In May of 1954 Bob joined the Naval Reserve and served two years active duty. He was later honorably discharged in May of 1962 as a Radio Operator with the rank of Petty Officer 3rd class. Bob always had a keen interest in photography so in 1957 he attended and graduated from a seven month course at the N.Y.S. Institute of Photography. Despite his interest, he would work as a stock clerk.

Bob Lorenz was appointed to the YPD on January 1, 1963 while living at 155 Stanley Avenue. Following recruit training he was assigned to patrol duty in the 3rd precinct earning $5,200 a year. On June 9, 1968 while on patrol at 6:45 AM Lorenz and his partner Tim McGrath observed 274 Hawthorne Ave to be engulfed in flames. After advising the fire department the officers ran into the building to wake tenants. During the rescue of 13 tenants both were overcome by smoke inhalation and were hospitalized. For their actions Lorenz and his partner were both awarded the departmental Honorable Mention.

On April 22, 1970 Bob was reassigned to the Communications Division as a radio dispatcher. He finally was able to utilize his photography skills when on August 30, 1971 he was assigned the Criminal Identification Unit photographing crime scenes, etc. Due to his abilities in photography and dark room photo printing, PO Lorenz was reassigned as a Detective to the Intelligence Unit on March 9, 1973 where his skills could be used for surveillance photography. Bob was later transferred to the Detective Division on October 21, 1983 working on general assignment investigations. Five years later, on July 1, 1988, Det Lorenz, also affectionately known to his friends as "Chico," or "Sundance" was returned to the former Intelligence Unit but since renamed the Special Investigations Unit. Det. Robert Lorenz retired on June 17, 1989.

PO MORRIS A. DeLASHO #107

APPOINTED: January 1, 1963
RETIRED: July 22, 1981

Morris Anthony DeLasho was born in the City of Yonkers on December 2, 1939. "Butch," as he was known even as a youngster, attended local schools graduating from Yonkers High School. He learned to speak and understand Italian from his parents. Butch joined the Army in October of 1957 and was honorably discharged in August of 1959. On his police application DeLasho listed his previous employment as having been appointed on a Patrolman with the Westchester County Parkway Police January 21, 1961. DeLasho was appointed to the YPD on January 1, 1963 from 108 Waverly Street. Following his recruit training he was assigned to patrol duty in the 1st precinct earning $5,200 a year. On August 13, 1965 he was reassigned to plainclothes duty in the then Juvenile Aide Bureau. Three years later, on June 10, 1968, Butch was transferred back to uniform patrol in the 1st precinct. In January of 1971 he was moved to the North Command and in January of 1979 to the South Command most often walking a post rather than being in a radio car. He retired from the YPD on July 22, 1981.

PO WILLIAM M. WIGHTON #129

APPOINTED: January 1, 1963
RESIGNED: July 14, 1964

Bill Wighton was born in Yonkers on August 1, 1938. Following his formal education and just 17 years old, Bill joined the Navy in September of 1955. He was honorably discharged in 1959. Following his military service Bill worked as a photographer and later earned a Bachelor's of Science degree in Criminal Justice. Wighton was appointed to the Yonkers P.D. on January 1, 1963 while living at 5-2B Cottage Place Gardens. Following training he was assigned to the 4th precinct earning $5,200 a year. At one point PO Wighton decided he preferred to live on the West coast and on July 14, 1964 he resigned from the YPD. He then moved to California and was appointed a Los Angeles police officer, retiring after 26 years service. Former Yonkers officer William Wighton died on June 25, 1999 after a long illness while living in Valencia, Cal. He was 60 years old.

SGT. MORGAN H. DILLON #63

APPOINTED: January 1, 1963
RETIRED: May 31, 1985

Morgan Harry Dillon Jr. was born in the city of Yonkers NY on October 24, 1940. Morgan attended local public schools and graduated from high school. He worked for several years as a laborer in the construction field and then took the police Patrolman's exam. He was appointed to the YPD on January 1, 1963 from 10 Cherokee Road. Following his basic recruit training he was assigned to the 2nd precinct earning the starting salary of $5,200 a year. The following year, on November 12, 1964, Dillon was reassigned to the Traffic Division in the Traffic Engineering Dept. About a year later, on March 28, 1966, he was again moved, this time to the Youth Division as a plainclothes youth crime investigator.

On June 14, 1968 Morgan, who actually preferred to be called Bill because he felt Morgan sounded stuffy, was transferred back to patrol duty in the 4th precinct. But that only lasted two years, and on September 9, 1970 he was once again assigned to youth investigations. But, not for long. On March 6, 1972 Dillon was again returned to patrol in the North Command.

The following year Dillon was promoted to Sergeant on December 14, 1973 earning $15,708 and was assigned to the 1st precinct as a patrol supervisor. In 1977 Sgt Dillon was reassigned to the South Command and in late December 1979 while on patrol Sgt Dillon attempted to arrest a suspected car thief. The two men fought over the sergeant's gun and the suspect was shot in the leg.

On February 8, 1980 Sgt Dillon was charged with disobeying a direct order and insubordination. Following a department trial Dillon was dismissed from the YPD by PC Guido effective March 27, 1981. He immediately filed an appeal with the state Supreme Court. He won his appeal and was reinstated to the Northeast Command when a judge ruled the dismissal of Dillon was too harsh a punishment. Later he was assigned to Detention Services in the City Jail. In November of 1984 while Sgt Dillon was on duty, one of the prisoners committed suicide but no responsibility was placed against Sgt Dillon. However it is likely that he decided he was not taking any chances. He retired six months later on May 31, 1985.

Sometime later Dillon moved to Florida to enjoy the sunshine. Twenty six years later, following a lengthy illness, Ret Sgt Morgan Dillon died in Ormond Beach, Florida on August 29, 2011. He was 70 years old.

PO FRANK C. CARIELLO #287

APPOINTED: January 1, 1963
RETIRED: March 7, 1985

Anyone who knew Frank Charles Cariello knew him mostly as “The Fish.” No one remembers why, mostly because he’s been called that since he was a youngster. But Frank was born in Yonkers on July 6, 1934, attended local public schools and graduated from Saunders High School with a trade in Auto Mechanics.

At the age of 18 years Frank joined the Army on November 7, 1952, was sent directly to Fort Dix for training and received orders for overseas duty as part of the "Far East Command." In no time he was on his way to join the Korean War to fight in an infantry unit. After returning to the states he was separated from active duty on September 15, 1954. For his service Frank was awarded seven medals including the Bronze Star, and the Combat Infantry Badge. Following his inactive reserve he was honorably discharged on October 31, 1960. Following his military service Frank worked as an auto mechanic and a truck driver.

He was appointed to the YPD on January 1, 1963 while residing at 152 Waverly Street and following recruit training he was assigned to the 3rd precinct earning $5,200 a year. On January 1, 1971, following the implementation of a precinct centralization plan whereby the 1st and 3rd precincts were closed and patrol commands were established, he was reassigned to the old 2nd precinct, which had been re-designated the South Command. Frank was later reassigned to the Special Operations Division on June 23, 1972 working Parking Meter Enforcement on a three wheel motorcycle. He remained there for nearly seven years and on April 4, 1979 was transferred back to the South Command on patrol. On July 1, 1980 he was moved to the Records Division and on October 10, 1983 to the South West Command on Riverdale Avenue, the former 3rd pct, as the captain’s aide.

PO Frank Cariello retired from the YPD on March 7, 1985 and in 2007 moved to Tennessee to be with his grown children. Frank “The Fish” Cariello is very proud of his family’s history of service in law enforcement. His son Frank is a Yonkers Deputy Chief, his nephew is Ret PO Mark Levito, his father was a Westchester Co. Deputy Sheriff, his uncle was YPD PO Frank Cariello, and his grandfather was a Carabiniere (Police officer) in Italy.

Unfortunately Frank died unexpectedly on April 7, 2012. He was 77 years old.

SGT. JOSEPH F. REAGAN #11

APPOINTED: January 1, 1963
RETIRED: January 5, 2001

Joseph Francis Reagan was born in the City of Yonkers on December 12, 1938. He attended St. Joseph's School on Ashburton Avenue, then Manhattan Prep for high school but ultimately graduated from Archbishop Stepinac high school in White Plains. He also attended Manhattan College for two and a half years. Following his graduation from high school Joe was hired by the US Post Office as a mail carrier.

Following his passing the police test, Joe was appointed to the Yonkers Police Department on January 1, 1963 while living at 30 Locust Hill Avenue. Following recruit training he was assigned to patrol in the 4th precinct earning a starting salary of $5,200 a year. Nearly three years later, on November 16, 1965, he was transferred to the 1st precinct on patrol. On March 28, 1966 Joe was reassigned to the Youth Division assigned to plainclothes juvenile crime investigations.

Reagan's investigative abilities and experience resulted in his being appointed a Detective in the D.D. on July 16, 1971. However just over a year later, on September 15, 1972, he was returned to patrol duty in the North Command. During the ensuing years he worked patrol in one of the busiest patrol sectors in the North Command with his partner Charlie Storms. He received numerous awards and letters of commendation for his police service.

On July 7, 1977 Joe was appointed a "temporary" Sergeant, a position which was taken from a valid civil service promotion list for sergeant, but having no vacancy available. He was assigned as a patrol supervisor in the South Command, and when a sergeant vacancy did occur Reagan was appointed to permanent Sergeant on September 21, 1977 earning $18,712. On September 1, 1999 Sgt Reagan was reassigned to the Courts serving as the YPD court liaison officer.

For many years Joe was very active in the PBA playing on their softball team and was also the coach for the Yonkers Judges softball team in the Yonkers Court League, winning one championship. Joe was very involved in community activities. He was one of the original members of the North Yonkers Boys Club, securing the 99 year lease from Yonkers and assisted in building the clubhouse on Ridge Ave. He was very active in the BPOE Elks #707, rising to the Exalted Ruler of the Yonkers branch and when they combined with Mount Vernon, forming the Mt. Vernon/ Yonkers Elks #707, he rose to be a District Deputy and New York State Vice President, later in his Elk career. Joe was also a member of the Knights of Columbus in Yonkers, rising to a Fourth Degree Knight.

Joe liked to play golf, later teaching his grandson's to play. He also served several years as a trustee in the PBA and later in the Capt's., Lt's., and Sgt's, Association. But everyone probably remembers him as an avid crossword puzzle player spending his down time solving them. His son is Det Joseph Reagan Jr. and his uncle was Yonkers PO Michael Reagan. After serving more than 38 years Sgt Reagan retied on January 5, 2001 and enjoyed watching his grandchildren play travel ice hockey, often going to numerous out of state tournaments with them. But he really did enjoy sitting on the beach with his family in Wildwood Crest, NJ swimming, body surfing and yes, doing his crossword puzzles.

Unfortunately only seven years later Ret Sgt Joseph F. Reagan died on January 22, 2008. He was 69 years old.

PO RONALD F. LAZAROU #206

APPOINTED: March 13, 1963
RETIRED: January 11, 1985

Ronald Lazarou was born in Yonkers on June 13, 1937. He attended local public schools and graduated from Yonkers HS. Shortly after graduating Ron joined the Army on Feb. 7, 1956 and served on active duty until Dec. 18, 1957 when he was honorably discharged. Following his military service he worked as a laborer in the construction field. Ronald Lazarou received his appointment to the Y.P.D. on March 13, 1963 while living at 64 Pomona Ave. Following his basic recruit training he was assigned to patrol duty in the 2nd precinct earning a starting salary of $5,200 a year. Five years later, on June 14, 1968, officer Lazarou was assigned to patrol duty in the 1st precinct. But, a little over two years later, on January 1, 1971, following the implementation of a precinct centralization plan, Ron was reassigned back to the old 2nd precinct, at that time renamed the South Patrol Command. It was there that he was assigned to work in the Emergency Service Unit. On December 4, 1981 Lazarou was transferred to the North Command but still working in the Emergency Unit. It was from there that he retired on January 11, 1985. At that time Ron had stated that he had won $1 million in the state lottery and that was the reason that he chose to retire at that time. Ron's stepbrother was Yonkers police officer George Lazarou.

PO ANTHONY T. CAMPANARO #289

APPOINTED: March 13, 1963
RESIGNED: April 8, 1965

Born Anthony Thomas Campanaro on November 11, 1941 in Yonkers NY, Tony attended local public schools and graduated from Lincoln HS. Shortly after graduating Tony joined the Navy on January 13, 1960 serving as a Petty Officer 3rd Class and was honorably discharged on January 12, 1962. He was very interested in construction and gained employment as a bricklayer. Campanaro received his appointment to the YPD on March 13, 1963 from 128 Murray Avenue. Following his 6 week basic recruit training he was assigned to patrol in the 2nd precinct earning a starting salary of $5,200 a year. On April 6, 1965 Anthony Campanaro submitted a letter of resignation stating it was with deep regret that he was resigning from the police department. That his tenure had been a very positive experience and if conditions warranted, he hoped he would be considered for reinstatement. His resignation was effective April 8, 1965 and he reportedly moved to Connecticut to build homes. He never reapplied for reappointment.

PO SALVATORE J. LAINO #478

APPOINTED: March 13, 1963
RETIRED: April 18, 1986

Sal Laino was born in Yonkers on Mar. 2, 1936. He attended local public schools and later graduated from Saunders H.S. Sal joined the Marine Corps on April 28, 1954 and was honorably discharged as a Corporal on Apr. 28, 1957. Sal worked as a machine operator for several years before applying to the police department.

Sal received his appointment to the YPD on March 13, 1963 from 776 Schroeder Street and was assigned to the 1st pct earning $5,200 a year. In May of 1964 officer Laino received departmental recognition for his part in identifying and arresting two holdup men who beat a 70 year old man in his store on March 15, 1964. In that instance the robbery occurred on an Early Tour while Laino was on foot patrol. The suspects beat the man with a rifle, which Laino later found discarded in a trash can. Sal had stopped the men earlier just on suspicion, and took their names and where they were staying. Later, following the robbery, and along with some detectives, officer Laino arrested them at the old Royal Hotel. On Nov. 9, 1966 Laino was reassigned to patrol in the 4th pct. At an award ceremony held on May 10, 1969 he was awarded the department's second highest award, the Honorable Mention, presented for acts of bravery involving personal risk to life.

PO Laino was appointed a Detective on Jan. 23, 1970 but preferred patrol duty instead and on Dec. 11, 1970 he returned to patrol in the 4th pct. It was then that Sal began a steady foot post in Getty Square giving particular attention to the several banks at that location. He worked that post right up to his retirement on April 18, 1986, at which time he moved to Florida. During his career Sal Laino received the following awards; April 29, 1964 a Macy Award, February 2, 1965 a second Macy Award, July 21, 1966 a third Macy Award, February 28, 1969 a fourth Macy Award, July 11, 1969 a department Commendation, 1982 and 1986 Certificates of Excellent Police Work, May 2, 1969 the department Honorable Mention.

Sal was proud to watch as his son's Dale and Bryan Laino also joined the Yonkers Police Department.

PO JOHN S. KARASINSKI #94

APPOINTED: March 13, 1963
DIED: June 6, 1965

John S. Karasinski was born in Yonkers on July 2, 1940. He attended Sacred Heart HS and graduated from Saunders HS in 1958. It was said that John was able to somehow understand sign language. John was honorably discharged from the Army after serving from February 4, 1959 to Feb. 3, 1961. While in the Army he was very active in sports and was on the Army swimming and football teams. Following his military service John worked as a construction laborer. He was appointed to the YPD on Mar. 13, 1963 from 425 Prescott Street and on Aug. 1, 1963, following recruit training, was assigned to patrol duty in the 1st pct earning $5,200 a year. A year later, on April 27, 1964, John was assigned to the Traffic Division. He worked for a while as the hack inspector but regularly rode the 2 wheel motorcycle. While off duty during the early morning hours of December 1, 1964 Karasinski learned of a holdup that had just occurred involving a shootout and that he knew the suspect. While off duty Karasinski located and arrested him for the robbery. He was awarded a Commendation.

While off duty on June 6, 1965, John and his friends were driving on Rte. 9 in Briarcliff, NY when they lost control, striking a tree and John was killed. He was a police officer for just over two years and was only 24 years old. John was honored by the PBA by having an off duty award named after him; the "John Karasinski Off Duty Award." John's sister was PO Dorothy Yasinski and his niece was Det. Patricia Yasinski.

PO PATSY J. BRUNO #93

APPOINTED: March 13, 1963
RETIRED: March 31, 1983

Patsy John Bruno was born in the City of Mt Vernon on March 22, 1936. He attended local Mt Vernon schools and graduated from Evander Childs High School in New York City. After he graduated from school Patsy joined the Marine Corps on August 19, 1953 and was honorably discharged as a Corporal on October 30, 1956. Prior to the YPD Pat made his living driving a truck. He was appointed to the police department on March 13, 1963 while living at 229 Lockwood Avenue and began earning a starting salary of $5,200 a year. Following recruit training Patsy was assigned to patrol duty in the 1st precinct. On February 2, 1970 he was reassigned to headquarters, trained by the NYPD, and assigned to the YPD Emergency Service Unit. Over the years Patsy worked in both the North and South Patrol Commands but predominantly in the South Command where he remained in the Emergency Unit right up to his retirement on March 31, 1983. Patsy Bruno's brother-in-law was Det Murdo Urquhart.

PO HENRI R. VERNE #193

APPOINTED: March 13, 1963
RETIRED: April 7, 1983

Henri Ricardo Verne was born on March 30, 1939 in Detroit Michigan to parents who had emigrated from the island of Jamaica. Henri attended elementary school in Detroit but his family would later move to New York City where he attended NYC public schools. He graduated from the High School for the Industrial Arts in Manhattan majoring in architecture. Upon graduation he worked for a company in the Bronx that designed government equipment.

Hank, as he was known to all his friends, was appointed to the Yonkers Police Department on March 13, 1963 while residing at 1069 Colgate Ave. in the Bronx. Following his recruit training Hank was assigned to the 3rd precinct earning a starting salary of $5,200 a year.

The following year, on February 26, 1964, Hank was selected to be appointed a detective in the Detective Division which allowed him to not only work in plainclothes, but raised his salary to $6,250 a year. Hank was a natural at this job; very polished, professional, and very much a gentleman. He had the intelligence to do the work, but just as important, he had the skill at conversation which was helpful in eliciting needed information. He was one of those very friendly and quite talkative individuals. During his time in the D.D. he was also detailed for a short time to the Intelligence Unit for special organized crime investigations.

Following more than four years in the D.D., on July 26, 1968, officer Verne was reassigned to patrol duty in the 4th precinct and worked several years with his partner, PO Robert Cannon. On June 20, 1979 Hank was reassigned from the 4th precinct to the Northeast Patrol Command located at 730 E. Grassy Sprain Rd. The area covered by this precinct encompassed the entire North East section of the city of Yonkers. Three years later, on September 13, 1982, PO Verne was transferred to the South Patrol Command located at 441 Central Park Ave. It would later become evident that Hank had a plan for his future following retirement, which he did on April 7, 1983 after completing 20 years of service.

Following his retirement, and apparently with his plan in motion, Henri and his family moved around the country and at one point moved to Hawaii where he lived for several years and invested in real estate. He then moved his family to the Palm Beach Polo and Country Club in Wellington, Florida. This was an upscale area of Palm Beach, Florida where he and his family remained for 12 years. In 2008 they move to the Miromar Lakes Country Club condo's on the west coast of Florida. During all these years Henri was investing heavily in real estate and he and his wife Joyce were obviously very successful business people. He and his wife designed and built a thriving villa resort business. Just prior to his death, he and his wife Joyce were the owners of multiple rental properties in Florida, and several other locations in the Caribbean. He even had a website advertising rentals which he owned in Hawaii, in St. Thomas, Key West Florida, Palm Beach Florida, and Jamaica, which was his favorite island.

Hank loved the tropics and was said to be able to light up the room with his Salsa dancing and was described as the definition of a true gentleman. Having basically never been sick a day in his life, it was a shock when he was diagnosed in May of 2010 with stage four brain cancer.

Despite a hard fought battle, retired police officer Henri R. Verne died in Florida on June 12, 2011. He was 72 years old.

PO FRANCIS C. FLORIO #99

APPOINTED: March 13, 1963
RETIRED: July 23, 1987

Frank, as he was always known, was born in the Bronx NY on Aug. 19, 1940. After his family moved to Yonkers Frank attended local schools and graduated from Saunders HS. Frank joined the Naval Reserve serving on active duty from December 15, 1958 to December 6, 1960 and following his release from active duty he remained in the Reserve up to June 8, 1981 when he retired with the rating of Fireman and received his honorable discharge. However, in the interim, Frank worked for the Anaconda Cable and Wire Corp. He was appointed to the YPD on Mar. 13, 1963 from 42 Herriot St. and was assigned to patrol duty in the 3rd pct earning a starting salary of $5,200 a year. On Nov. 7, 1966 he was reassigned to duty in the new 1st pct at 730 E. Grassy Sprain Rd. On Jan. 1, 1971 Frank was transferred to the old 4th precinct, then renamed the North Command. During most of his time there he walked the foot post 10-East, at Tuckahoe Road and Central Park Avenue. But he was a very active foot cop. In 1975 Frank was honored by being the recipient of the PO Harold Woods on duty award from the PBA. And in 1976 he was honored again by being named Police Officer of the Year by the Yonkers Exchange Club. On June 20, 1979 he was moved to the North East Command, but continued to walk the same foot post. Officer Florio was well known to all the merchants and residents in the area and was well respected. He retired from the YPD on July 23, 1987 and sometime later moved to Florida to enjoy the sunshine.

PO ANDREW W. BIRO #138

APPOINTED: March 13, 1963
DISMISSED: September 25, 1972

Andrew Biro was born in Yonkers on June 6, 1940. Andy attended local public schools and would later graduate from Yonkers HS and would later be employed as a clerk. He was appointed to the Y.P.D. on Mar 13, 1963 while living at 32 Mulford Gardens and was assigned to the 2nd pct. For reasons unknown, on March 18, 1966, Biro was reassigned to the Communications and Records Div. in H.Q., and on Feb. 14, 1968 was assigned to Communications as a Dispatcher. In Jan. of 1969 he was reassigned to patrol in the 3rd pct, but two years later, on Jan. 1, 1971, he was transferred out to the South Command. The following year, on Feb. 12, 1972, he was moved to the North command. It was here that on Aug. 30, 1972 he was suspended on suspicion of committing a serious violation of the rules and regulations. The following month, on September 25, 1972, Andrew Biro, a relative of Sgt. Tom McGurn, was dismissed from the Yonkers Police Department.

PO STEPHEN J. ZACK #251

APPOINTED: March 13, 1963
RESIGNED: February 23, 1965

Stephen Zack was born in Yonkers NY on August 27, 1941. He attended local public schools and graduated from Sacred Heart High School. Following high school Zack joined the Navy in July of 1959 serving as a Medic and was honorably discharged in August 1962. Previous to the police department Zack worked as a Lab Technician. Stephen Zack was appointed to the police department on March 13, 1963 from 47 Portland Place earning $5,200 a year. Following recruit training Zack was assigned to patrol in the 4th precinct. Officer Zack resigned from the YPD on February 23, 1965 to accept appointment to the Yonkers Fire Department.

PO DONALD A. GRONO #241

APPOINTED: March 13, 1963
RETIRED: March 13, 1983

Donald Grono was one of those men whose personality was friendly but low key; very easy going but level headed, and he could definitely be relied on to get the job done. He was born Dec. 24, 1940 in Yonkers NY. He attended local public schools and later graduated from Saunders HS with a trade in carpentry. Don joined the Army on May 8, 1958 and was honorable discharged on Feb. 8, 1960. It was then he put his carpentry skills to use working as a carpenter; a trade he would put to use throughout his police career while off duty. Donald Grono was appointed to the YPD on March 13, 1963 while residing at 145 Beech St. and earned a starting salary of $5,200 a year. Following his recruit training he was assigned to patrol duty in the 1st precinct at 10 St. Casimir Ave. On Nov. 9, 1966 Grono was moved to the 4th precinct. On May 4, 1967 it was reported that officer Grono and his partner, Larry Kunze, were commended by the department for their work in the apprehension of two persons responsible for an armed robbery on March 20, 1967. Following Don's request, on Feb. 2, 1970, he was assigned to the Emergency Service Unit. He worked in ESU for about nine years and, again at his request, was returned to patrol duty in the North Command. On June 20, 1979 he was reassigned to the North East Command on E. Grassy Sprain Road for 10 months. It was then, on April 14, 1980, that Don was transferred to the Youth & Community Services Div. as a juvenile crime investigator where he remained right up to his retirement on March 13, 1983, exactly 20 years after his appointment.

DET. CHARLES E. CRAWFORD #663

APPOINTED: March 13, 1963
RETIRED: March 19, 1983

For those who knew and worked with Det Crawford they would no doubt describe him as standing about 6' 4" tall, and he had the most even tempered and easy going personality you could imagine, despite his size. Charlie Crawford was born on December 13, 1936 in the City of Yonkers. He attended local public schools and would later graduate from Saunders High School. With his height and athletic ability Charlie played on a basketball team in the 1950's called the "Dumontiers." Shortly after high school graduation Charlie joined the Air Force in March of 1955 until his honorable discharge in March of 1959. Upon discharge Crawford gained employment as a truck driver. Charlie was appointed to the YPD on March 13, 1963 from 99 Jefferson Street earning a starting salary of $5,200 a year. Following recruit training his first assignment was patrol in the 1st precinct. Nearly seven years later, on January 1, 1971, he was reassigned to the North Command. However, on October 25, 1973 Crawford was appointed a Detective in the DD and would remain there right up to his retirement on March 19, 1983.

PO PETER J. BIANCHI # 98

APPOINTED: March 13, 1963
RETIRED: July 12, 1984

Peter Bianchi was one of those long serving members of the Yonkers Police Traffic Divisions motorcycle unit who was not only good at his job, but was well liked and respected by his coworkers. He was born in Yonkers on January 2, 1940, attended local public schools, and graduated from Yonkers High School. Following high school Pete joined the Marine Corps on July 31, 1957 and served as a sea going Marine on patrol in the South China Sea. He was honorably discharged with the rank of Corporal on July 30, 1959. Pete worked hard as a gardener for several years until he was appointed to the YPD on March 13, 1963. At the time he lived at 256 New Main Street, earned a starting salary of $5,200 a year and his first assignment was patrol duty in the 1st precinct. Two years later, on November 16, 1965, PO Bianchi was transferred to the Traffic Division on motorcycle duty. On July 11, 1968 he was granted a six month leave of absence and was reinstated on January 30, 1969 and returned to motorcycle duty where he remained right up to his retirement on July 12, 1984.

PO HAROLD L. WOODS #531

APPOINTED: March 13, 1963
Killed: September 22, 1974

Harold Woods was born in the City of Yonkers on March 19, 1940. As a youngster Harry lived in the Martin Ray Place apartments located on Central Park Avenue where the Curran Court apartments are now located. They were originally built for returning military personnel to live after WW 2. Harry attended local schools and graduated from Sacred Heart High School in Yonkers.

Shortly after graduating from high school Harry, as he was known, joined the Navy on July 3, 1958 serving through July 1, 1960 as a Seaman and would later receive his honorable discharge.

When Harry applied to take the Yonkers police test he listed his current occupation as a machine operator. Harold Woods received his appointment to the Yonkers Police Department on March 13, 1963, while residing at 1 Cottage Place Gardens, as part of a recruit class of 13 new officers. Following several weeks of recruit training rookie police officer Harold Woods was assigned to patrol duty in the 3rd precinct earning a starting salary of $5,200 a year.

Harry initially walked foot posts primarily, but on occasion was assigned to radio car patrol. On September 10, 1965, at about 2:10 AM, PO Woods and PO Richard Banks, both of the 3rd precinct, were sent by Communications on an “Entry in Progress” at 205 McLean Avenue. Upon arrival they saw three males in vehicle double parked with lights out. As the approached the vehicle began to flee and officer

PO Harold L. Woods #531 (cont.)

Woods and his partner began pursuit. They pursued at speeds over 90 mph passing lights and stop signs and being forced to a stop at Van Cortlandt Park Avenue and Thurman Street, all three males were arrested at gunpoint. Upon returning to the original location with their prisoners, they found two burglaries; at 203 and 205 McLean Avenue. Proceeds of the burglaries were located in the suspect's vehicle. Their Commanding Officer, Capt. John Kennedy, recommended they both receive departmental Commendations.

A year later, on October 19, 1966 PO Woods received a letter of commendation from the Westchester County Sheriff on behalf of the Board of Judges of the Westchester Newspaper Police Honor Awards. In it he was advised that he had been awarded a certificate of Honorable Mention for his distinguished performance of police duty during the 3rd quarter of 1966.

Thinking there might be greater advancement opportunities in the NYPD, Harry took their exam, passed, and was called for appointment. With some reluctance Harry resigned from the Yonkers Police Dept. on February 28, 1967 to accept appointment in the NYPD. In less than seven months Harry Woods requested and was granted reinstatement to the YPD on September 6, 1967 earning $6,810, and was returned to the 3rd precinct. He reportedly told friends that it was too dangerous in the city.

Officer Woods, also known as "Woodsie" to many, was transferred to the Headquarters Command Division on August 4, 1968 and assigned to work in the Communications Division dispatching radio cars. While there he studied hard for the Sergeants exam and ultimately passed and was number four on the list for promotion. But it was not to be.

On September 18, 1974 at about 10:30 PM Harry was on his way to work the midnight shift. He stopped in the A&P Supermarket at O'Dell Avenue and Nepperhan Avenue to pick up milk for coffee in the communications room. Unknown to him, a robbery was in progress inside as he entered. Everyone was standing still and very quiet and immediately he knew something was wrong. He reportedly demanded to know what was wrong and announced he was a police officer. One of the robbers who was standing very close placed a gun to officer Woods' throat and fired, severing his spinal cord. Harry lay bleeding as they made their escape.

When the police were called the Emergency Unit provided first aid to Harry until an ambulance arrived and transported him to the hospital. Despite the best efforts of the doctors, PO Harold Woods died of his wound four days later on September 22, 1974. He was only 34 years old. He left behind a wife and three small children.

As a line of duty death officer Woods was afforded an Inspectors funeral with full honors. Thousands of police officers from all over the country attended the funeral held at Sacred Heart Church on Shonnard Place. In November of 1974 the American Federation of Police posthumously awarded their Medal of Honor to the late PO Harold Woods. Years later Officer Woods was posthumously awarded the Yonkers Police Department Medal of Honor, which was presented to his widow Dorothy.

PO JESSE W. TAYLOR #508

APPOINTED: November 20, 1963
RETIRED: April 6, 1984

Although born and raised in the south, Jesse Taylor was as New York as they come. He was born in West Virginia on May 25, 1939, attended Virginia local schools, and graduated from Kimball High School in Kimball West Virginia. Following graduation Jesse earned a living as a Welder. At one point, having moved to Yonkers, he was later appointed to the police department on November 20, 1963 from 10 Altamont Place, Yonkers, earning a starting salary of $5,200 a year. Following recruit training Jesse was assigned to patrol duty in the 1st precinct. On November 9, 1966, as part of a large personnel reorganization, Taylor was reassigned to the 4th precinct. Officer Taylor was appointed a Detective on January 13, 1967 and remained in the Detective Division up to December 11, 1970 when he was returned to patrol duty in the 4th precinct. During his service in the DD and the 4th precinct he was a very active officer who earned many awards and commendations. On June 20, 1979 Taylor was transferred to the North East Command on patrol where he would remain up to his retirement on April 6, 1984.

PO STANLEY P. GALUSKA #240

APPOINTED: November 20, 1963
RETIRED: April 18, 1986

Stanley P. "Sonny" Galuska was born in the City of Yonkers on May 19, 1937. He attended Yonkers elementary schools and graduated from Saunders High School. Immediately following graduation "Sonny" joined the Navy in August of 1954, served on active duty as a Signalman until March of 1956 and was honorably discharged. For several years Galuska worked long hard days for his father who operated a blacktop business until he received his appointment to the YPD on November 20, 1963 while living at 318 Edwards Place. Following his recruit training "Sonny" was assigned to patrol duty in the 4th precinct earning a starting salary of $5,200 a year. His radio car partner for many of the ten years on patrol in the 4th precinct was Eugene "Gino" Abbatiello. On July 2, 1973 Galuska requested and was assigned to the plainclothes Youth Division investigating crimes committed by juveniles. "Sonny" Galuska, whose uncle was PO Richard Tocci, and his brother in law was PO Joe Abbondola, enjoyed this work and remained there right up to his retirement on April 18, 1986. He retired to Sloatsburg, NY.

CAPTAIN ROY C. McLAUGHLIN

APPOINTED: November 20, 1963
RETIRED: February 6, 1997

Roy McLaughlin was a man who was very serious about his service in law enforcement and his children apparently felt the same way. Roy was born in the City of Mt Vernon on November 20, 1935. Following his family moving to Yonkers he attended local public schools and later graduated from Saunders High School. Two years later, on April 12, 1955, Roy joined the Army serving as a clerk with the rank of Specialist 3rd Class. He was honorably discharged on February 5, 1957. Roy listed on his police application that he was employed as a factory worker.

McLaughlin was appointed to the Yonkers Police Department on his birthday, November 20, 1963, while living at 107 McLean Avenue. When his recruit class finished their training Roy was assigned to patrol duty in the 1st precinct earning a starting salary of $5,200 a year. On November 9, 1966, as part of a large reorganization, McLaughlin was reassigned to the 4th precinct for patrol duty.

On May 4, 1967 it was reported that officer McLaughlin had been awarded departmental recognition from Public Safety Commissioner Daniel F. McMahon for intelligent police work in the apprehension of an armed robber at the Windham Hotel on Hudson Street at 5:30 a.m. on Feb. 25th of that year. McLaughlin was checking the hotel and walked in during the robbery. He made the arrest at

Captain Roy C. McLaughlin (cont.)

gunpoint.

Roy received his first promotion to the rank of Sergeant on December 10, 1971 earning a raise in salary to $13,685 and was reassigned as a patrol supervisor in the South Patrol Command. Six months later, on May 6, 1972, Sgt McLaughlin was transferred to the North Patrol Command. He continued patrol duty supervision until March 12, 1973. Up to that point, historically police lieutenants were assigned as desk officers in patrol precincts. However, a reorganization of duties in the police department was implemented and effective in March of 1973 sergeants were now designated as "Station House Supervisors," formerly designated desk officers, and McLaughlin was so assigned on that date. After all the station house supervisor assignments were filled, the remainder of the sergeants continued with patrol duties. They were then supplemented on patrol by many former desk lieutenants. It was also at this time that the position of precinct executive officer was instituted. On April 26, 1974 Roy was reassigned to the South Command doing the same job on desk duty.

On January 27, 1975 McLaughlin was again promoted, this time to Lieutenant with a salary of $20,642 and was transferred to Field Services Bureau and assigned as a city wide patrol lieutenant. Four years later, on January 19, 1979 McLaughlin was promoted to the rank of Police Captain. His new salary rose to $26,536 and he was reassigned as the commanding officer of the Internal Affairs Division.

Over the ensuing years Capt. McLaughlin had his assignments changed a number of times, ie; July 9, 1979 to Inspectional Services Division as the CO; September 17, 1979 to Courts and Detention Services as the CO; April 1, 1980 to commanding officer of the North Command; July 1, 1983 back to Courts and Detention Services; April 4, 1988 to CO of the Communications Division; October 18, 1991 designated the Executive officer to the Deputy Chief of Field Services Bureau; and lastly on April 4, 1988 to command of the 4th precinct from which he would later retire on February 6, 1997.

During his career Capt. McLaughlin earned his Associates Degree from Westchester Community College and his BS from Mercy College. He was also privileged to be selected, and did attend, the prestigious National FBI Academy in Quantico, VA. Roy was an early member of the Westchester County Emerald Society Pipes and Drums Band as a piper, which he remained active in even after retirement.

Roy was particularly proud that four of his children, Lt Andrew, Sgt Roy D., Sgt Meredith, and Sgt Mitchell McLaughlin followed his career choice by joining the Yonkers Police Department.

PO RICHARD PRENDERGAST #16

APPOINTED: November 20, 1963
RETIRED: May 19, 1984

"Rich" J. Prendergast, as he was known, was born on Yonkers NY on July 21, 1938. He attended local public schools and later graduated from Saunders High School. Shortly after graduation Rich joined the NY National Guard on January 20, 1957 serving as a Physical Training instructor and Company Sports Sergeant. He completed his reserve obligation and was honorably discharged as a Sergeant on August 5, 1962. Following his initial active duty training Rich gained employment as a trailer driver for the United Parcel Service.

He was appointed to the Yonkers Police Department on November 20, 1963 while residing at 95 Sedgewick Avenue. Following his recruit training he was assigned to patrol in the 3rd precinct earning a starting salary of $5,200 a year. On January 24, 1966 Richard Prendergast was selected to be assigned to the Emergency Service Unit (ESU) and received training in all aspects of medical emergencies, rescue work, and special weapons and tactics situations. Although today's ESU is equipped with the most state of the art equipment and training, in earlier years they were not as fortunate. PO Prendergast and fellow ESU officers had to make do with what little equipment they were provided and yet expected to save lives and peacefully resolve all major situations.

On May 25, 1970 a Class 3 Commendation, retroactive to October 1969, was awarded to Patrolman Richard Prendergast for his first aid efforts to revive a man who later died from stab wounds, on Oct. 7, 1969 at his home. Prendergast quickly gathered preliminary information which several hours later led to the capture of two murder suspects in New Jersey.

In February of 1975, Police officer Richard Prendergast, the Exchange Club's Policeman of the Year, was honored by the club at a luncheon and commended by city and police officials for his having researched, recommended and established an emergency medical response service in May of 1974 "unparalleled in the state." This while there was an emergency within the city due to the discontinuance of private ambulance service. Prendergast, on his own and within 24 hours, had organized a complete ambulance service set up within the Police Department with the help of the Volunteer Ambulance Service. In accepting a plaque from the Exchange Club and a proclamation from Mayor Martinelli, Prendergast said "*Yonkers is the only large city in the country with an emergency squad with all of its members trained as Emergency Medical Technicians*."

Rich would become so proficient in handling medical situations that he was often nicknamed "Doc" by some of his colleagues. Prendergast would remain assigned to the 4th precinct (for a while renamed the North Command) for nearly his entire career, right up to his retirement on May 19, 1984. Following his retirement Rich Prendergast and his wife moved to Arizona where they enjoy the climate.

PO EDWARD A. WISSNER #212

APPOINTED: November 20, 1963
RETIRED: April 13, 1990

Ed Wissner was born in Yonkers NY on August 31, 1941. He attended local public schools and later graduated from Yonkers High School. While in school Ed was very athletic and as such played football and baseball. He also attended New York University for one year and later in his career would earn an Associate's degree. On his police application Ed listed his employment as a machine operator for the Anaconda Corp. in Hastings, NY.

Ed Wissner was appointed to the police department on November 20, 1963 while living at 23 Alder Street and began earning a starting salary of $5,200 a year. Following recruit school for his class of 16, which included his childhood friend, Raymond Leinen, Ed's first assignment was patrol in the 1st precinct located at 10 St. Casimir Avenue.

In 1965 Ed was almost inducted into the Army during the Viet Nam War. Though willing to serve, when Public Safety Commissioner Daniel McMahon was notified, he formally requested of the Yonkers Draft Board to give draft deferments to "all" Yonkers police officers due to police manpower shortages. The board granted his request.

As part of a large patrol reorganization, on November 9, 1966 Wissner was moved to the 4th precinct on patrol. While in the 4th, later renamed the North Command, Ed was very proficient in his ability to execute outstanding warrants along with his regular patrol duties. No doubt because of this ability, PO Wissner was assigned to work in the departments Warrant Squad, with offices located in the city jail building on Alexander Street.

In 1985 while assigned to Courts and Detention Services Division in the Warrant Squad, Wissner and his partner, and childhood friend PO Ray Leinen, were honored as Police Officers of the Year by the Yonkers Exchange Club. They received the award for several investigations, one being the arrest of a Florida fugitive for a double homicide and four attempted murders.

Throughout his career Ed never stopped participating in sports while off duty by playing softball on the PBA softball team and assisted with PAL softball games. Ed was also fortunate to see his son's, Mark and Kevin, also be appointed to the YPD.

After working ten years in the Warrant Squad with his friend and partner Ray Leinen, PO Edward Wissner retired from the YPD on April 13, 1990. After his police retirement, in 1992 Ed then coached varsity baseball and junior varsity basketball at the Hackley School in Tarrytown for 18 years. He retired from that job in 2010.

PO ROBERT A. SASKO #91

APPOINTED: November 20, 1963
RETIRED: July 26, 1985

Bob Sasko love to talk and had a friendly and outgoing personality to match. He was born in Yonkers on Nov. 28, 1936, attended Hawthorne Jr. HS, and graduated from Saunders HS. Bob joined the Army on Jan. 29, 1954 serving in Korea in the 34th Infantry Scout Dog Platoon as a Specialist 3rd Class. He received his honorable discharge on Jan. 19, 1957. Bob later gained employment as a clerk in St. Joseph's Hospital. Bob Sasko received his appointment to the Y.P.D. on Nov. 20, 1963 while living at 541 Schroeder St. Following his training he was assigned to the 1st pct on patrol duty earning a starting salary of $5,200 a year. On Jan. 1, 1971 Bob was assigned to the North Command at 53 Shonnard Place. On June 20, 1979 Sasko was reassigned to the North East Patrol Command on E. Grassy Sprain Rd. Sasko retired on his own application on July 26, 1985 while living in 1853 Central Park Ave. However, he later applied for and was granted an accidental disability pension effective Feb. 19, 1986. Reportedly, at one point he had been working an off-duty detail and was struck by a car. The resulting injuries were considered when granting his disability pension. Following his retirement he and his wife moved to Orlando Florida where on November 14, 2004 retired PO Robert Sasko died. He was 68 years old.

PO FRANCIS X. COYNE #218

APPOINTED: November 20, 1963
RETIRED: February 16, 1984

Francis X. Coyne was born in Yonkers on Feb. 18, 1932 and would later graduate from Commerce HS. Frank entered the Army on August 6, 1952 during the height of the Korean War and served as a Company Clerk and Supply Sergeant. He was honorably discharged as a Master Sergeant on Aug. 5, 1954. Frank worked for many years as a machine operator for the Otis Elevator Co. He received his appointment to the Yonkers Police Dept. on Nov. 20, 1963 while residing at 138 Orchard St. Following his training Frank was assigned to the 4th pct on patrol earning a starting salary of $5,200 a year. On April 24, 1964 Safety Comm. Daniel F. McMahon publicly commended police officer Coyne for his efforts in trying to save a young Cub Scout by jumping into the river. Frank would remain in the 4th precinct for nearly 20 years when, on Sept. 13, 1982, he was reassigned to patrol duty in the South Command. After spending his entire career on patrol Francis Coyne retired on Feb. 16, 1984 while living in Mahopac, NY. In 1988 Frank and his wife moved to Citrus Springs, Florida where he drove a school bus. In his free time Frank enjoyed his computer, golfing, boating, was a motorcycle enthusiast, and enjoyed Elvis memorabilia. His nephew was Yonkers Pubic Safety Dispatcher Milton Craven. Retired PO Francis X. Coyne died on May 10, 2005 in Inverness, Florida at the age of 73 years.

CAPTAIN RONALD J. MARTINO

APPOINTED: November 20, 1963
RETIRED: January 22, 1999

Ronald J. Martino was born in Yonkers NY on July 6, 1937. He attended local public schools and would later graduate from Commerce High School. Three months after his graduation Martino joined the Marine Corps on September 8, 1955. After basic recruit and combat training he served as an administrative clerk with the rank of Sergeant up to his honorable discharge on September 4, 1959. Following his discharge Martino listed his employment as that of a Clerk.

He was appointed to the Yonkers Police Department on November 20, 1963 while residing at 77 William Street. In 1963 there was no Training Division in the YPD and recruit training for "rookie" Patrolman Martino and the rest of his recruit class was held in a room on the 5th floor of police headquarters at 10 St. Casimir Avenue. They received their firearms training at the old Hudson Tire Co. shooting range on Nepperhan Avenue. Following his basic police training officer Martino was assigned to the 1st precinct on patrol duty earning a starting salary of $5,200 a year.

On January 1, 1971, following the implementation of a precinct centralization plan consolidating four precincts into two patrol commands, Ron Martino was reassigned to the newly designated North Patrol Command. He worked patrol there for a little over a year when, on May 6, 1972, he received his

Captain Ronald J. Martino (cont.)

promotion to the rank of Sergeant. His salary was increased at that time to $13,685 and he was transferred to the South Patrol Command working as a patrol supervisor.

Historically, for most of the existence of the YPD, police lieutenants were those officers who were assigned to work as precinct desk officers. However, the prevailing wisdom in city hall in 1973 was that lieutenants on desk duty was a waste of experience and talent for that rank. As such, on March 12, 1973, lieutenants were removed from desk duty, some placed on patrol and some to the newly created position of Executive officer, and replaced with sergeants performing desk duty. It was then that Sgt Martino was removed from patrol and assigned to desk duty, then renamed Station House Supervisors, in the South Command.

The following year, on September 20, 1974, Sgt Martino was moved to desk duty in the North Command. It was while there, on June 10, 1975, that he watched his younger brother Alan be sworn in as a Yonkers police officer. Though recently promoted, Martino was determined to continue to rise in the ranks. And he did. On July 1, 1975 Sgt Martino was promoted to the rank of Lieutenant earning $20,642 a year and was reassigned to the Field Services Bureau working as a citywide patrol lieutenant. On May 10, 1976 Lt Martino was moved from patrol duty to the Communications Division as a "radio room" tour supervisor. Yet, three years later, on March 16, 1979, Martino was returned to patrol duty and utilized as a "fill in" lieutenant in the two patrol commands as an executive officer.

He was returned to the Communications Division once again on October 9, 1981 but this time as the divisions Executive Officer. Lt Martino remained in this assignment for ten years, and on February 9, 1991 was transferred to the 3rd precinct as their Executive Officer. And in 1992 he was moved to the 2nd precinct as their Executive Officer.

Ron Martino was promoted to the rank of Police Captain on September 6, 1996 and was reassigned to the Field Services Bureau as a city wide patrol captain. But, the following year, on November 4, 1997, Capt. Martino was again returned to the Communications Division, this time as the commanding officer. Capt. Martino's last assignment occurred on September 8, 1998 when he was designated the C.O. of the 2nd precinct where he remained for nearly four months and retired from the YPD on January 22, 1999. Ret Capt. Ronald Martino died October 26, 2014.

PO MICHAEL J. DUKE #245

APPOINTED: November 20, 1963
RETIRED: January 12, 1984

Mike Duke was born in of Yonkers on Mar 4, 1936. He attended local schools and graduated from Saunders HS. Toward the end of the Korean War Mike joined the Air Force on April 7, 1953. He served as an airman 1st class and was honorably discharged on April 6, 1957. Following his military Mike worked for several years in a warehouse. Mike took the civil service test for police officer and learned he was number 1 on the list for appointment. He received his appointment to the Y.P.D. on Nov. 20, 1963 while residing at 431 Van Cortland Park Ave. Upon graduation from recruit training Mike was assigned to patrol duty in the 3rd pct located at 36 Radford St., and earned a starting salary of $5,200 a year. Nearly 5 years later, on April 26, 1968, Mike was transferred to H.Q. and assigned to the Communications Div. dispatching radio cars. He remained there for nearly 6 years and on Jan. 29, 1974 was reassigned back to patrol duty in the South Command. On Jan. 1, 1979, due to a heart condition, Mike was reassigned to the Special Operations Division serving as the Police Department's mail courier. He retired from the police department on January 12, 1984 and after a while moved to Beverly Hills, Fl. where he died on Jan 29, 2018 at age 81.

LT. THOMAS J. KIVEL

APPOINTED: November 20, 1963
RETIRED: January 8, 1999

Thomas Kivel was one of those people who were able to keep even-tempered no matter what the situation was. He was born in Yonkers on July 2, 1942, attended local schools and would later graduate from Saunders HS. On his police application he listed his employment at that time as a clerk for the A&P Supermarket. Tom was appointed to the Y.P.D. on Nov. 20, 1963 while living at 27 Corbalis Pl. Following his basic training he was assigned to the 4th pct earning a starting salary of $5,200 a year. On Nov. 7, 1966 he was reassigned to the 1st pct, and on Mar 23, 1970 to patrol in the 4th pct. Tom Kivel was promoted to the rank of Sergeant on Dec. 10, 1971, earning $13,685 and reassigned as a patrol supervisor in the South Command. He was promoted to Lieutenant, on July 12, 1980 earning $24,411 and was moved to the North Command serving as a Watch Commander. Five years later, on Nov. 18, 1985, Lt Kivel was reassigned to the Field Services Bureau to serve as a citywide patrol Lieutenant. On Mar 16, 1990 he was reassigned to the Communications Div. as their supervisor. Lt Thomas Kivel retired from the Police Department on Jan. 8, 1999 after 35 years service. During his career Tom always maintained a low-key presence. As a result his friends would tease him and affectionately nicknamed him "Claude Raines," a character in the old movie, "The Invisible Man." Tom's cousin was Sgt. Howard Horton and nephews Sgt Michael Kivel and PO Keith Kivel.

PO RICHARD J. CAPRARO #124

APPOINTED: November 20, 1963
RETIRED: August 19, 1988

Richard Capraro was born in Yonkers on May 22,1940. He attended local schools where he displayed a keen interest in sports. Following graduation "Dick," as he was sometimes known, worked as a bank teller. While living at 26 Meadowbrook Pl. Rich was appointed to the Y.P.D. on Nov. 20, 1963 earning a starting salary of $5,200 a year and was assigned to the 4th pct. On Nov. 7, 1966 he was reassigned to the newly opened 1st pct at 731 East Grassy Sprain Rd. He remained there until Jan 1, 1971 when he was assigned to the Emergency Service Unit in the South Command. On Sept. 10, 1971 Dick was reassigned to the Radio Room on dispatching duty. On January 9, 1976 he was returned to duty in the South Command. While there Rich served many years as the Desk Officer. Toward the end of his career he would be assigned to the Warrant Squad from which he would retire on August 19, 1988. Dick played softball for the PBA for many years, and also for the Old Timers Softball League. After retiring Dick worked at the Batting Cage on Mostyn St. until it closed. He loved sports and was a huge Giant's and Yankee's fan. His son was PO Richard Capraro. On August 26th Dick Capraro died suddenly while sitting in a chair in his home. He was 67 years old.

PO JOSEPH I. ABBONDOLA #201

APPOINTED: November 20, 1963
RETIRED: May 10, 1995

Joe Abbondola was born in Yonkers on Nov 6, 1939. Following his public school he graduated from Commerce HS. Joe joined the Naval Reserve serving on active duty from July 3, 1958 through July 1, 1960 and received his honorable discharge. Joe worked for several years as a construction laborer up to his appointment to the Y.P.D. on Nov. 20, 1963 while living at 27 Lockwood Ave. Following the graduation of his recruit class Joe was assigned to the 4th pct. By Jan. of 1967 Joe had been transferred to the 1st pct, and sometime later to the Communications Div. In Jan. of 1972 PO Abbondola was reassigned to the North Command and was assigned to a sector riding with PO Richard Tocci, his uncle. Abbondola's mother was Tocci's sister. By 1987 Joe had been transferred to the Youth Division and on Dec 25, 1987 all Youth Officers, including Abbondola, were re-designated with the title "Investigator." However there was no increase in salary. PO Joe Abbondola remained in the Youth Division up to his retirement on May 10, 1995 after more than 31 years service.

SGT. JOSEPH E. GRADY

APPOINTED: November 20, 1963
RETIRED: August 22, 1985

Joseph Grady was born in Yonkers on June 10, 1940. He attended the St. Joseph's Catholic school system up to high school, and graduated from Saunders HS in 1959. On his police application Joe listed his current employment as a wire inspector for the Anaconda Wire and Cable Corp. Joe Grady was appointed to the Y.P.D. on Nov. 20, 1963 while residing at 271 Hawthorne Ave. Following training his first assignment was in the 4th pct. earning a starting salary of $5,200 a year. As part of a department wide reorganization, on Nov. 9, 1966, Joe was reassigned to patrol in the 3rd pct. Following a precinct centralization plan, which went into effect Jan. 1, 1971, officer Grady was reassigned to the South Command located at 441 Central Park Ave. Joe Grady was appointed to Sergeant on Sept. 17, 1976, had his salary was raised to $18,043 a year, and he was reassigned to the North Command as a patrol supervisor. He remained there until he retired on August 22, 1985 and first moved to Myrtle Beach, S.C. and later moved to Las Vegas where he worked for seven years as a security guard in the Hotel Casino Circus Circus. Joe's favorite past time was fishing, hunting, and a good game of cards. Retired Sgt. Joseph Grady died on April 8, 2003. He was 62 years old.

PO LEONARD J. CANNAVO #48

APPOINTED: November 20, 1963
RETIRED: February 23, 1984

"Lenny" Cannavo was born on July 22, 1941 in the City of Mt Vernon. His family subsequently moved to Yonkers and he attended local public schools and would graduate from Commerce High School. One month following graduation Lenny joined the Navy on July 6, 1959 serving aboard the Destroyer, USS Purdy, and later as a Radar Man 3rd class as well as Internal Security and "Brig" guard. He was honorably discharged on August 15, 1962. Cannavo, who spoke Italian as a second language, gained employment with the Post Office. He was appointed to the police department on November 20, 1963 while residing at 18 Orchard Street. Following his recruit training he was assigned to the 1st precinct earning a starting salary of $5,200 a year. On March 28, 1966 Lenny was assigned to the Traffic Division in the Traffic Engineering section. However a year later, on June 12, 1967, he got his wish and was assigned to two wheel motorcycle patrol. Officer Cannavo remained on motorcycle duty right up to his retirement on February 23, 1984. Shortly after retirement Cannavo was hired by the US Marshall's Service on a security detail in the Federal Court House in Manhattan and White Plains where he worked for at least 20 years.

DET. ANDREW A. CAVALLO #676

APPOINTED: November 20, 1963
RETIRED: March 8, 1985

It was really no surprise when Andrew joined the Y.P.D. His older brother, Carmine, had done so years earlier. Andy was born in Yonkers on Aug. 21, 1940, attended local public schools and graduated from Commerce HS in 1958. He then went to work in the A&P store on Nepperhan Avenue as their Head Bookkeeper until the YPD called.

Andy was appointed to the Y.P.D. on Nov. 20, 1963 from 440 Marlborough Road and earned a starting salary of $5,200 a year. Following basic recruit training Andy was assigned to patrol in the 4th pct. Following the opening of the new 1st precinct on E. Grassy Sprain Rd, on Nov. 9, 1966 Andy was reassigned there. On Feb. 12, 1971 Cavallo was assigned to Detective Division, but as a "silver shield" detailed to the Youth Division as a Youth Investigator. However, the following year, on July 14, 1972, he was officially appointed a Detective in the DD. His low key but determined approach to investigations gained him a reputation as an asset to any squad he worked in.

During his career Det Cavallo was the recipient of the 1973 Yonkers Exchange Club Police Officer of The Year award for a number of investigations including, the arrest of a man wanted for 10 armed robberies, the arrest of a woman for Arson 1st, the arrest of two youths for gas station robberies, the arrest of two men for supermarket robberies, and preventing a suicide from a bridge. He also received numerous Macy awards. He was also one of the detectives that helped captured the Son Of Sam killer, David Berkowitz, in 1977.

First grade detective Andrew Cavallo retired on March 8, 1985 and went to work as a Real Estate agent. In September of 1988 Andy moved to Florida and continued to work in Real Estate for Atlantic Properties International where he was still employed in 2013.

Andy enjoys Florida living and is an usher at St Henry's Church in Pompano Beach and is also a member of The Knights of Columbus. He has one daughter, three stepchildren, and 6 grandchildren. One stepson, Brendan Rourke Casey is a NY State Police Captain.

PO RAYMOND V. LEINEN #144

APPOINTED: November 20, 1963
RETIRED: July 7, 1988

Ray Leinen was born on Aug. 31, 1938 in the City of Yonkers. Following his elementary schooling he graduated from Sacred Heart parochial H.S. During his high school years Ray was very active in sports. In 1954 he played baseball with the Yonkers Babe Ruth League on a team named the Yonkers Black Sox. Shortly after graduation Ray joined the Navy on August 30, 1957 and served on active duty up to Aug. 13, 1959. He was honorably discharged sometime later.

Ray made a living as a painter but, knowing his brother Peter was a Yonkers police officer, he decided to take the police test. Ray Leinen was appointed to the YPD on Nov. 20, 1963 while living at 123 Oliver Ave. When he completed basic training Ray was assigned to patrol duty in the 1st precinct earning a starting salary of $5,200 a year. In 1964 Ray was still active while off duty bowling in a Yonkers league. As part of a patrol personnel reorganization, on Nov. 9, 1966, Ray was reassigned to duty in the 4th precinct. Six years later on Jan. 29, 1973 he was transferred to H.Q. and assigned to the police repair shop working as an auto mechanic on the police vehicles.

Ray was returned to patrol duty in the North command on Aug. 20, 1974 and remained there until Oct. 10, 1977. It was then that he was reassigned to the warrant squad which had officially been organized as a centralized unit in 1973. Previous to that date warrants were executed by precinct personnel whenever the opportunity arose. In 1985 while assigned to Courts and Detention Services Div. in the Warrant Squad, Leinen and his partner, and childhood friend PO Ed Wissner, were honored as Police Officers of the year by the Yonkers Exchange Club. They received the award for several investigations, one being the arrest of a Florida fugitive for a double homicide and four attempted murders.

PO Leinen remained in that assignment right up to his retirement on July 7, 1988. He retired to his home in Fishkill, NY.

PO WILLIAM P. NEGRICH #185

APPOINTED: November 27, 1963
RETIRED: March 13, 1983

William Peter Negrich was born in the City of Yonkers on November 19, 1934. He attended local public schools and graduated from Saunders High School with a trade in carpentry. Not quite 18 years of age, Bill joined the Navy on September 16, 1952 during the Korean War serving aboard the USS Francis Robinson. He remained on active duty until September 8, 1954 and later received his honorable discharge. Bill worked for many years as a carpenter but on March 13, 1963 he was appointed to the Yonkers Fire Department. However, previously he had also taken to Yonkers police exam and was notified that he was to be appointed a police officer. As such, Bill resigned from the fire department on November 26, 1963 and was appointed to the police department the next day, November 27, 1963 while residing at 15 Belmont Terrace.

Following recruit training Bill's first assignment was to patrol duty in the 1st precinct earning a starting salary of $5,200 a year. After only two short years, on November 16, 1965, Negrich was fortunate enough to be reassigned to the plainclothes Juvenile Aid Bureau (JAB, later renamed the Youth Division) investigating crimes committed by juveniles. But, that only lasted one year and on December 1, 1966 he was returned to patrol in the 1st precinct. Nearly five years later, on April 14, 1971, Bill was again assigned to a plainclothes unit; this time in the Community Relations Division. But, after a short stay of four months, on August 24, 1971 he was transferred to patrol in the North Patrol Command and partnered up with PO Bob Sasko. Eight years later, on June 20, 1979, Negrich was moved to the N/E Patrol Division from which he would retire on March 13, 1983.

Bill enjoyed visiting with other veterans at the local VFW Post and playing pinochle cards. But on April 13, 2006, while walking on the street, he suffered a massive heart attack. Despite medical treatment Ret PO William Negrich died on April 14, 2006 in Lawrence Hospital. He was 71 years old.

PO JOSEPH P. SOKOLIK #127

APPOINTED: April 8, 1964
RETIRED: July 11, 1984

Joseph Sokolik was born in the City of Yonkers on December 3, 1941. He attended St. Casimir elementary school and then Sacred Heart high school, from which he did not graduate. However, he did receive his GED while in the service. After leaving school Joe joined the Naval reserve on December 8, 1958 and served two years on active duty. After completing his reserve obligation he was honorably discharged on December 7, 1964. Prior to the YPD Joe worked for the General Motors assembly plant in Tarrytown NY. Joe received his appointment to the police department on April 8, 1964 while living at 1159 Nepperhan Ave. Following recruit training Joe was assigned to the 1st precinct on June 1, 1964 earning a starting salary of $5,500 a year. On July 24, 1966 Sokolik was transferred to the Communications and Records Division detailed to the radio room dispatching radio cars. On March 6, 1967 Joe was reassigned to the 4th precinct on uniform patrol. On June 12, 1970 he was assigned to the DD, still as a police officer, but detailed to work in the Youth Division. He would later be permanently assigned there and remain in the Youth Division right up to his retirement on July 11, 1984.

PO JOHN E. RILLEY #122

APPOINTED: April 8, 1964
RETIRED: July 25, 1986

John "Jack" Rilley was born in Yonkers on June 6, 1940. He attended St. Joseph's Catholic school, Roosevelt H.S. and graduated from Saunders H.S. in 1959 with a trade in auto mechanics. Jack gained employment with the Western Electric Co. on Church Street in NYC as an installer. He received his appointment to the Y.P.D. on April 8, 1964 while residing at 45 Sunrise Terr. Following recruit training, on June 1, 1964 he was assigned to patrol in the 4th pct. earning $5,500 a year and on Nov. 9, 1966 he was reassigned to the new 1st pct located on East Grassy Sprain Road. Officer Rilley was assigned to the Special Operations Division on Oct. 19, 1971 and detailed to work in the Tactical Patrol Force. Eight months later, on June 23, 1972 Rilley was placed in the Traffic Division's two wheel motorcycle Unit where he remained for several years. PO "Jack" Rilley retired from the YPD on July 25, 1986 and within a short time he went to work as a field and laboratory technician for a consulting engineering firm in New York and New Jersey for approximately eighteen years. He is now fully retired.

PO THOMAS J. MILLEN #10

APPOINTED: April 8, 1964
RETIRED: April 16, 1999

Tom Millen was born in Yonkers NY on May 8, 1941. As a youth he attended PS# 12, Longfellow Jr. High School and Commerce High School. Prior to graduation Tom left school to join the Army on May 25, 1959. During his service Tom served as an MP and also served overseas in Korea. Tom also earned his high school GED in the military. He was honorably discharged on May 24, 1962 as a Specialist 4th class and over the next two years Tom worked for the Habirshaw Cable and Wire Corp. as utility man.

Thomas Millen was appointed to the Yonkers Police Department on April 8, 1964 while residing at 434 Walnut Street. He was following in the path of his uncle, PO Austin Millen. Following his recruit training, which ended on June 1, 1964, Millen was assigned to patrol duty in the 3rd precinct at 36 Radford Street earning $5,500 a year.

When rookie officer Millen reported for duty in the 3rd precinct he reported to then Capt. Edward Otis. The captain noticed that Millen was wearing shield number 10 and offered some stern advice. The captain said, "*That shield you're wearing is the same one my father, PO Michael Otis, wore and it's the same shield that I wore as a patrolman. Don't you ever let me find out that you dishonored it*." And the record is clear, he never did.

Officer Millen always preferred walking a foot post rather than riding in a radio car. He felt he could develop a closer relationship with the public walking amongst them. Throughout the 1960's Tom most often was assigned to the foot post along South Broadway and quickly gained a reputation as being available when needed but was tough and would not take any abuse. He "ran a clean post." Upon the implementation of a precinct centralization plan on January 1, 1971 PO Millen was reassigned to patrol in the South Command at 441 Central Park Avenue. During the 1970's PO Millen volunteered his off duty time serving as a counselor to those suffering from alcoholism and seeking confidential help.

After 24 years on patrol, on April 11, 1988, Millen was assigned to Courts and Detention Services on steady days serving as a City Court security officer. And later, on October 17, 1994, Tom was moved to the Property Clerk Unit in headquarters responsible for all stored evidence. Having made the decision to retire soon, and upon his own request, on September 29, 1997 Millen returned to patrol in the 2nd precinct and retired from there on April 16, 1999 after 35 years of honorable service.

PO THOMAS J. LINDER #264

APPOINTED: April 8, 1964
RESIGNED: June 30, 1967

Thomas John Linder was born in Yonkers NY on April 20, 1941. Tom attended St. Mary's Elementary School, Sacred Heart High School to the 11th grade and graduated from Lincoln High School. Shortly after school graduation Tom joined the Army serving from April 7, 1960 to May 7, 1962 and received an honorable discharge. Following the military Tom worked as an elevator "Wireman" for Otis Elevator Co in Yonkers for two years. It was then, on April 8, 1964, that he was appointed to the police department from 144 Seminary Avenue. Following recruit training Linder was assigned to radio car patrol duty in the 2nd precinct earning a starting salary of $5,500 a year. Having received Advanced First Aid training he often filled in working in the Emergency Unit. In February of 1967 his commanding officer recommended Linder for recognition for his ability to obtain critical information on the murder of an elderly woman. He did this while working on another unrelated assignment on June 1, 1966. Though it was some time later, his information resulted in the arrest of the murderers. For his part he was awarded a departmental Commendation on Feb 9, 1967. His wife was seriously injured in a MV accident and reportedly received a large financial settlement. And since she never liked Tom being a police officer he agreed to resign. When he submitted his letter of resignation for personal reasons, his C.O., Capt. Reid, described him as being conscientious, with a hard working attitude, performing commendable work and that he would be missed. His resignation became effective June 30, 1967. The Linder's moved to Falls Church, Virginia, and opened a Souvenir/Antique Shop in Washington DC. He later he moved to Atlanta, Ga. where he worked as a painting contractor. Former PO Thomas Linder died on June 14, 2002 at the age of 61 years.

SGT. JOHN D. BENCIVENGA #27

APPOINTED: April 8, 1964
RETIRED: June 28, 1984

John Bencivenga was born in NYC on Oct. 6, 1941. He attended St. Barnabas school and later graduated from DeWitt Clinton HS in NYC. John listed on his police application that he worked as a paper handler. John, or "JB" as he was known, received his appointment to the Y.P.D. on April 8, 1964 while he was living at 274 E. 240th St. in NYC. Following his recruit training his first assignment was patrol duty in the 1st pct earning $5,500 a year. On June 17, 1975, JB was reassigned to the South Command and on July 1, 1980 was transferred to HQ assigned to the Communications Div. working in the "Tele Serv Unit" accepting complaints over the telephone. The following year, on Dec 4, 1981, Bencivenga was returned to the South Command. John "JB" Bencivenga was promoted to the rank of Sergeant on Nov. 18, 1982 earning $28,313 a year and was transferred to the North Command serving as a patrol supervisor. Sgt Bencivenga retired from the police department on June 28, 1984.

PO SALVATORE A. CORRENTE #137

APPOINTED: April 8, 1964
RETIRED: May 12, 2000

The subject of the following profile is a very unique individual. He had a talent for music with a great singing voice, an easy going approach in dealing with police work, and a natural ability to be a boxing coach and role model for all the youths he came in contact with.

Salvatore A. Corrente was born on August 17, 1938 in Yonkers New York. He attended St. Mary's elementary School, Sacred Heart High School, and graduated from Saunders High School. Even at an early age Sal was interested in sports and body fitness. While in Saunders Sal played on the school football team and was a two time All City Halfback, and was designated the most valuable player (MVP) and highest scorer in the city in his senior year. It was no surprise when he was awarded a football scholarship to Northeastern Junior College in Sterling, Colorado. He graduated with a Liberal Arts/Physical Education degree. At the time he wanted to be a football coach.

Sal listed on his police application that he had been working as an owner/driver at Square Taxi at 35 South Broadway. Sal was appointed to the Yonkers Police Department on April 8, 1964 from 119 Beech Street and was assigned to the Communications & Records Division to receive his recruit training. Rookie Patrolman Sal Corrente's first assignment was patrol duty in the 1st precinct earning a starting salary of $5,500 a year. Just one year later, on July 8, 1965, officer Corrente and his partner pursued a robbery suspect and arrested him at gunpoint. For his action that day he was awarded a department Commendation. On November 9, 1966 Sal was reassigned to the 4th precinct where, after a while, he was assigned to a steady detail of working a foot post in Getty Square. He did that for many years and in doing so gained the trust and respect of the many store owners in that busy downtown area. And in 1968 he and then partner John Bonney received the Westchester Rockland newspaper Police Commendable Merit Award for a car chase and eventual capture of a male holdup suspect.

Sal was always very willing to help the young kids who seemed to have no direction and were at risk for getting into trouble. Often, while on patrol, youngsters would ask Sal if he could help them get into some boxing program and possibly the Golden Gloves. And his desire to help these kids led to his interest in boxing and forming a PAL boxing team. After nearly 20 years on patrol, on April 16, 1982, Sal was transferred to the Youth & Community Services Division officially as a youth crime investigator. However, his real purpose was to work in the PAL developing a boxing program for the youth of the city.

He began by working 4 hours in the schools and 4 hours in the PAL gym at 21 Alexander Street; the former home of the Naval Reserve. He trained perspective young wannabe boxers which often eventually led to Golden Glove champions, several National champions, and many Metro and Regional champions. Two of his PAL boxers went on to represent the USA in the Olympics, and several entered the pro ranks and fought for world titles. At one point he was invited, and did attend, an elite Coach's Certification course in Colorado Springs, Colorado along with other top trainers across the country, a course he would successfully complete.

Sal was not only a police officer, for the most part working a regular foot post in Getty Square, but in the early years, and all throughout his career, he led his own singing group called "Johnny Law and The Blue Coats." He was a three time winner on the Ted Mack Amateur Hour appearing in his police uniform and he went on to record with several vocal groups including "The Dials," "The Regents," and "The Trace's." Several years later Sal formed a wedding band with musicians and with him as lead singer they

PO Salvatore A. Corrente #137 (cont.)

would entertain at large receptions and parties, etc. He eventually changed the name of his group to "The Everyday People."

After many years working in Getty Square and then being assigned to work in the PAL, Sal became the foremost boxing coach in the metropolitan area. He worked with the poorest of the poor and went way beyond 8 hour days. He would often provide his own money to buy food for "his kids." Training hundreds and sending many on to success in the NY Daily News Golden Gloves, etc. And he kept singing as well. Even after he retired from the police department on May 12, 2000 he kept singing with his band and continued, as a volunteer, to be the PAL boxing coach. Sal had a very calm and quiet disposition which helped him deal with youths. In some ways he was a father figure to many boxers.

The following article was written about Sal by the local newspaper, Home News and Times.

"Sal Corrente of the Yonkers PAL became the 21st recipient of the Joseph Medill Patterson award for his contribution to amateur boxing and The Daily News Golden Gloves, on April 6, 2006. This award was given to Sal by the Daily News Charities, Inc. in the ring at the finals at Madison Square Garden.

"As a young man Sal, a Yonkers Patrolman, was more a singer and a Police Officer than a boxing instructor or coach. He knew little to nothing about the sport. Sal sang in a group back then called the Regents, the Dials, and also with the famous group called The Belmont's. He worked on stage with the dynamic Everly Brothers and Del-Vikings, and was a three time winner on the Ted Mack amateur hour. He was good but was still looking for his big break in music back in the late seventies. It was only because a young kid asked him for help to become a boxer that Sal obliged in the best way he could. He went to the library, read some books about boxing and the rest is history. The PAL had a boxing program (one man), and Sal became the trainer.

"Through the years the Yonkers P.A.L. has had hundreds of kids join the program and Sal has had his fair share of great fighters. Sal tells his P.A.L. kids that there is a whole world out there waiting for them. 'Go for it.' And his boxers have been listening. In 1975 a 112 lb. novice, Paul DeVorce, from the Yonkers PAL, won the first of thirty P.A.L. Daily News Golden Glove Championships, bringing great recognition to the City of Yonkers and the PAL. Sal trained 106 lb. David Villar who went on to win 6 Daily News Golden Glove awards; also lightweight Gabe Hernandez, welterweight Sean Knight, and lightweight Darling Jiminez. Former mayor Angelo Martinelli, President of the Yonkers PAL credited Sal with helping to make the PAL the home of one of the best boxing programs in the State. Sal also was credited for bringing the Golden Glove Awards Elimination Fights to the City of Yonkers and making the PAL a force to reckon with in boxing."

"Sal was a positive role model throughout his career and has brought much positive recognition to the Yonkers PAL, the City of Yonkers, and the Yonkers Police Department. While at the PAL, Sal has the sole distinction in the New York area of having trained 28 New York daily news Golden Glove champions. He has also been the head boxing coach of the Empire State games since its inception in 1978. On June 17, 2009 Sal was honored by the Yonkers PAL as "Man of the year" at a large fund raising luncheon. Sal summarized his experience with the PAL by saying: "My desire is that the young men who come through the Yonkers PAL become productive citizens; and that their PAL experiences interacting with, and being guided by, current and former police officers, has been a positive influence in their lives. Just one success story from former boxers at the PAL is worth more to me than the 28 Golden gloves titles. My hope is that I have been a positive influence and have at least turned one life around for the better."

I think that says it all.

PO JAMES W. MATTHEWS #226

APPOINTED: April 8, 1964
RETIRED: March 8, 1985

James W. Matthews was born in the City of Yonkers on June 1, 1937. Living in the "Hollow" section of Yonkers Jim attended Holy Trinity elementary school and graduated from Saunders High School. Shortly after high school Jim joined the Navy on November 30, 1954 and was honorably discharged as a Seaman 1st class on May 30, 1958. He then worked for several years for the General Motors assembly plant in Tarrytown working as a utility man.

Jim received his appointment to the YPD on April 8, 1964 while living at 367 Nepperhan Avenue. After recruit school was completed on June 1, 1964 Matthews was assigned to patrol duty in the 2nd precinct earning a starting salary of $5,500 a year. Two years later, on November 9, 1966, as part of a department wide reorganization, he was reassigned to patrol in the recently opened new 1st precinct. PO Matthews was selected to serve in the Emergency Service Unit (ESU) and was trained in various types of medical and rescue emergencies. Following this training he was officially assigned to the Emergency Unit on February 2, 1970. On January 1, 1971 he was moved to the South Command but remained in ESU.

Jim loved police work but he also loved to cook. In fact he started a catering business during off duty hours which kept him very busy. His brother-in-law was Det Charles Jankowski, who married Jim's sister Barbara. On March 28, 1980 Matthews was transferred into the plainclothes Youth Division investigating crimes committed by juveniles. Five years later, on March 8, 1985, officer Jim Matthews retired from the YPD.

Even though he was retired Jim was very active with the NY Police and Fire Retirees Association and was co-coordinator and chairman of the annual Metropolitan Police Conference gathering. Jim was a very likable guy, friendly and always available to help others. He was very active with the Yonkers PBA having served over the years as Vice President and Secretary. He was a founder of the Westchester County Police Pulaski Association and was past president of the New York Police and Fire Retirees Association. He was also past president of the Homefield Association and a member of the Westchester Police Golf Association. He loved to play golf and would always find time to play a round.

On March 13, 1993 retired police officer James Matthews died following a lengthy illness. He was only 55 years old.

DET. JOSEPH F. RASULO #626

APPOINTED: April 8, 1964
DIED: September 11, 1998

The subject of this profile is one of those individuals who seemed to always be in control of his emotions regardless of the situation. He was very soft spoken with a warm friendly personality. Joe Rasulo was born in Yonkers on March 21, 1940. His parents spoke Italian so quite naturally Italian became his second language. He attended PS# 18, Benjamin Franklyn Jr. High School, and graduated from Saunders High School with a trade in carpentry. But there was another side to Joe. He was a good singer. And in the late 1950's he was a back-up singer for a group known as "The Dials," led by Sal Corrente who would also join the YPD the same day as Joe.

Shortly after high school graduation Joe joined the Army on December 1, 1958 and served as a Specialist E-4 up to his military separation on November 30, 1960. He later received his honorable discharge and began working as a chauffeur.

Joe Rasulo was appointed to the YPD on April 8, 1964 while living at 1 Waverly Place. Following recruit training on June 1, 1964 his first assignment was patrol duty in the 3rd precinct earning a starting salary of $5,500 a year. On January 24, 1966 Rasulo was transferred to the Communications Division working as a dispatcher in the "radio room." That lasted for two years and, on April 26, 1968, he was reassigned to patrol in the 4th precinct. He was reassigned several times; on May 19, 1969 to the 1st precinct, on January 1, 1971 to the North Command, and on June 20, 1979 to the North East Patrol Command.

On October 21, 1983 Joe was honored when he was selected to be appointed a Detective in the Detective Division working in a general assignment squad, and later serving as an administrative aide to the division's commanding officer. While there he was proud to watch his son, Joseph Jr also appointed to the YPD in 1989.

Unfortunately, on September 11, 1998, while off duty at his home and without warning, Det Joseph Rasulo Sr. suffered a sudden heart attack while working in his yard and died. He was 58 years old.

PO JOHN N. MORRISSEY #292

APPOINTED: April 8, 1964
RETIRED: July 7, 2000

John N. Morrissey was born in NYC on July 29, 1938. Following his family's move to Westchester County John attended Dobbs Ferry elementary schools. His family then moved to Yonkers and John attended and graduated from Saunders HS with a trade in electric wiring.

Upon graduation John joined the Army's New York National Guard's 101st Signal Battalion located in the former Armory on North Broadway. He was designated a communications specialist. In September of 1957 John followed his trade and began working for Consolidated Edison located on Irving Place in NYC. John, along with his military unit, was activated for the Berlin Crisis of 1961- 1962 and was stationed at Fort Devens as a Radio Team Chief. When he was released from active duty he returned to work for Con Ed. Due to his in depth communications knowledge, in October of 1963 he was assigned as the Con Edison Representative to the World's Fair construction site regarding the installation of electrical sub stations.

On the evening of November 19, 1963 Patrolman Jim Waldron notified him to report to city hall at 9AM the following morning to be sworn in as a Yonkers police Patrolman. However, instead John went to work at the World's Fair Site on Nov 20th and then called the Public Safety Commissioners Office and spoke to his secretary and advised her I could not just leave Con Edison as I had a lot of important data re: my assignment at the World's Fair site. Commissioner Goldman picked up the phone and John advised him of the situation and PSC Goldman understood completely and told John his name would be put back on the list and I would get a week's notice the next time there would be new appointments. That would be five months later.

Morrissey was appointed to the Yonkers Police Department on April 8, 1964 while residing at 14 Rollins Street. Following his basic recruit training, on June 1, 1964 probationary police officer Morrissey was assigned to foot patrol in the 3rd precinct earning a starting salary of $5,500 a year. On April 6, 1968 Morrissey was transferred, on paper only, to the Detective Division and was detailed to work in the plainclothes Intelligence Unit to assist in sensitive investigations involving electronic eavesdropping devices, aka wiretaps. Two months later, on June 18, 1968, Morrissey was returned to patrol duty back in the 3rd precinct.

During this time period it became obvious to the Chief of Police that officer Morrissey had specialized knowledge in the communications field and his knowledge could be put to better use than simply performing uniform patrol duty. At that time the police communications system was not working as it should, police radio's had to be installed in newly purchased patrol cars, etc., and John was capable of assisting in all problems of this type. As such, a decision was made by the chief and on January 1, 1969, Morrissey was transferred to the Headquarters Command Division, assigned to the Communications Division. Meanwhile John was still in the military reserve and in 1970 Morrissey was designated the Battalion Signal Operations and Training NCO. He held that position for 16 years.

On January 1, 1971, the entire department was reorganized as part of a precinct centralization plan whereby the 1st and 3rd precincts were closed as operating precincts and the 2nd and 4th precincts were renamed the South and North Patrol Commands respectively. Among the substantial numbers of transfers

PO John N. Morrissey #292 (cont.)

was officer John Morrissey who was reassigned to patrol in the South Command located at 441 Central Park Avenue.

On June 17, 1974 Morrissey was one of many who volunteered to be assigned to the North Command and assigned as part of a federally funded specialized patrol unit named the Community Patrol Unit (CPU.) However the following year, on July 25, 1975, John was removed from the CPU at his own request and performed regular patrol duty in the North Command. In addition to routine patrol John was a Certified Emergency Technician (EMT) and was often utilized as a fill in on the Emergency Squad truck.

There seemed to be little doubt that the police department was still experiencing problems with their communications network because, on March 28, 1977, PO Morrissey was again reassigned back to the Headquarters Command Division, but this time to work from the Planning and Development Unit. It was here that John participated in preparing and submitting grants for upgrades in our communications system and any other communications related issues. On October 3, 1979 John's designated assignment was changed to the Communications Division where he remained up to his retirement.

John continued to provide the YPD with invaluable insight into anything that had to do with communications by personal effort or by working with hired professionals in this field. Throughout his police career John worked both as a police officer, communications expert and career soldier. He retired from the Army Reserve in 1998 as First Sergeant.

PO John Morrissey retired from the YPD on July 7, 2000 after 36 years of honorable and efficient service to the department. He would have stayed longer however the pension system required that he retire upon reaching the maximum age of 62 years. In his retirement order Commissioner Cola wrote in part, "*Police Officer Morrissey's knowledge and extensive background in electronics and communications has proven to be an invaluable asset to the Yonkers Police Department. Throughout his career, in times of high demand, commissioners and chiefs have relied upon John's technical expertise to quickly assemble police command posts and to successfully resolve numerous communication dilemmas*."

There's no doubt that the police department lost a valuable asset.

CAPTAIN RICHARD J. WILSON

APPOINTED: April 8, 1964
RETIRED: August 20, 1999

Richard Wilson was born in Yonkers on March 11, 1939. He attended PS# 81 on Riverdale Avenue in the Bronx, then Gorton High School. Shortly after school Richard joined the Marine Corps on April 10, 1956. Upon graduating from boot camp in Parris Island, S.C. Rich was assigned to the Montfort Point base in Jacksonville, North Carolina serving with the Floating Bridge's Platoon, one of only two in the Corps. These platoons were responsible for building Floating-Adjustable-Quick Assembly and Dis-assembly crossings over water or terrain. He completed his active duty on April 19, 1958 and after completing his inactive reserve obligation, received his honorable discharge as a PFC.

For several years Wilson earned his living working for Con Edison in New York City and also worked as a self-employed painter. There's no doubt that Richard looked up to his older brother Robert because Richard had joined the Marine Corps just as Robert had earlier. And then his brother Robert had been appointed a Yonkers police officer in 1957 and Richard had decided to join the department as well. Richard Wilson was appointed to the Yonkers Police Department on April 8, 1964 while residing at 60 Caryl Avenue in Yonkers. Upon completion of his police recruit training on June 1, 1964 rookie Patrolman Wilson was assigned to patrol duty in the 2nd precinct earning a starting salary of $5,500 a year.

Captain Richard J. Wilson (cont.)

While in the 2nd precinct and assigned to various radio car patrol sectors, Wilson was also a student of the martial arts and studied Karate. And at one point he also operated a tattoo shop during his off duty time. Rich remained on patrol for ten years and on May 15, 1974 was reassigned to the Youth Division as an investigator of juvenile crimes.

Richard Wilson received his first promotion on September 21, 1977 when he was elevated to the rank of Sergeant. Following his promotion he was transferred to the North Command as a patrol supervisor earning $18,712 a year. However, he remained there for just over a year and on January 19, 1979 he was returned to the Youth Division as a supervisor of a squad of youth investigators. While there, in addition to his other duties, Sgt Wilson instituted a Karate School as another PAL program. They ultimately held several charity tournaments raising money for the PAL. Wilson, who was the instructor, had studied Karate for 30 years as a hobby and held the black belt rank of 3rd degree Dan Kyokashi –Kai in Japanese Karate.

On May 24, 1983 Wilson continued his rise in the ranks when he was promoted to the rank of Lieutenant. At this time he was reassigned to the South Command as a patrol lieutenant and his salary rose to $35,364. As a lieutenant Wilson had a number of different assignments, i.e.; on December 21, 1983 to the Inspections Unit on patrol, on February 29, 1984 to the 3d precinct as a Watch Commander on patrol, and on May 29, 1987 to the 1st precinct as a Watch Commander.

Richard Wilson was promoted to the rank of police Captain on April 11, 1988, earning a salary of $56,429 and was assigned to the Field Services Bureau as a city wide patrol captain. Later that year, on November 15, 1988, Capt. Wilson was designated a Detective Captain and placed in command of the Special Investigations Unit. Two years later, on October 1, 1990, he was reassigned from detective status and transferred to the Courts and Detention Services Division which was located in the City Jail and was designated their commanding officer.

In October of 1997 Capt. Wilson was again returned to patrol duty for little more than a year when, on January 25, 1999, he was transferred to the 2nd precinct as their commanding officer. Seven months later, on August 20, 1999, Capt. Richard Wilson retired from the police department after more than 35 years service.

Richard Wilson's brother Robert was not the only relative in law enforcement. His uncle was former YPD PO Stephen McKee and his son Richard also was appointed to the YPD. Capt. Wilson had many interests. During his career he graduated from the Empire State College with a Bachelor's degree, he was a graduate OF POHS Institute of Insurance and held a Masters agent license in several locations, he was a member of the American College of Forensic Examiners Institute as a life member beginning in 2004, a member of the Certified Homeland Security Preparation & Response Team, a member of the Fraternal Order of Police, and was a NYS licensed private investigator.

Following his retirement Rich opened up and operated the Black Angus Steak House on Yonkers Avenue for several years, but sold it and then remained retired.

SGT. JOSEPH R. COMO #14

APPOINTED: August 12, 1964
RETIRED: January 4, 1986

Joseph R. Como, known by all his friends as "Skip," was born in the City of Yonkers on June 21, 1933. He attended PS #24 and graduated from Yonkers High School. Right after graduation "Skip" joined the Air Force during the Korean War on July 31, 1951. At one point he was commended for saving the life of a pilot during a blinding snowstorm in Rome, NY. Como received his honorable discharge on July 5, 1955 as a Staff Sergeant. On an employment application Como listed his previous employment as a Radio Operator.

"Skip" Como was appointed to the Yonkers Police Department on August 12, 1984 from 134 Beech St and, along with a group of other recruits earned a starting salary of $5,500 a year. The department was not ready to provide their basic recruit training so they were all sent to work patrol in the precincts for a month. When another recruit class was appointed a month later the two groups were merged. One group, which included Como, was trained at the NYPD police academy. This intensive physical and academic training ran from October 5, 1964 through February 5, 1965. Upon graduation Como was assigned to patrol in the 3rd precinct.

"Skip" stood just about 5' 8" and weighed about 150 Lbs. But what he lacked in size he made up for in energy, enthusiasm and hard work. On July 17, 1970 Joe Como was reassigned to the Communications Division dispatching. He received his promotion to Sergeant on Nov 24, 1973 earning $21,142 and was assigned as a patrol sergeant in the North Command. Still in the N/C, on May 28, 1981, he was detailed as temporary supervisor of the dept.'s Accident Investigation Emergency (AIE), which was later renamed the Emergency Service Unit. He was a good fit for this job as he was a natural when it came to resolving emergency situations and could handle just about any tool. He had even been trained as a hostage negotiator by the FBI in Quantico, Va.

Sgt Como was transferred to the Field Services Bureau on Sept 29, 1983 and utilized as a fill in sergeant throughout the city. Sgt Como retired from the police department on January 4, 1986 and moved with his wife to Preston Hollow, in upstate NY. Skip was a member of VFW Post 15033, the N.Y.S. Police & Firefighters Retiree Association, and the Northeast Wild Turkey Federation and he enjoyed hunting and fishing. Skip was a jack of all trades and seemed to be a master of all. He had endless energy and enjoyed helping people in any way he could.

Ret Sgt Joseph Como died suddenly at Albany Medical Center after a brief illness on March 31, 2011. He was 77 years old.

CAPTAIN ROBERT L. BLAIR

APPOINTED: August 12, 1964
RETIRED: August 28, 1997

Robert L. Blair was born in Yonkers NY on December 2, 1940. He attended local elementary school PS# 12, Longfellow Jr. High School, and Saunders High School. While in high school Bob was very athletic and played on the school football team. Following school Bob joined the Army on June 4, 1959 and was discharged with the rank of Sgt. E-4 on May 15, 1961. Following the military and prior to the YPD Blair worked as a driver for United Parcel Service.

Bob was appointed to the police department on August 12, 1964 along with 13 other men while living at 48 Gavin Street. Less than a month later, on Sept. 9, 1964, another group of men were appointed. Both groups were merged and half went for recruit training at Iona, and the second half, the group containing Bob, attended the NYPD Police Academy recruit school for basic recruit training. This intensive physical and academic training ran from October 5, 1964 to February 5, 1965.

Following graduation from the NYPD academy Bob was assigned to patrol duty in the 4th precinct earning a starting salary of $5,500 a year. Following a city wide reorganization of police personnel, on November 9, 1966 Bob was reassigned to the 3rd precinct on Radford Street. About eight months later, on June 12, 1967, PO Blair was transferred to the Traffic Division on two wheel motorcycle patrol. Bob really enjoyed traffic violation enforcement from the motorcycle but just short of two years

Captain Robert L. Blair (cont.)

later, on February 3, 1969, he was returned to routine patrol duty in the 3rd precinct.

On January 1, 1971, following the implementation of a precinct centralization plan, officer Blair was reassigned to the old 2nd precinct which had been renamed the South Patrol Command. Two months later, on April 15, 1971, Blair was returned to motorcycle duty working in the South Command as part of what was termed a Special Enforcement Squad. Later that year on October 19, 1971 he was assigned to the Special Operations Division/Traffic Unit, working in the Tactical Patrol Force. (TPF)

On February 22, 1973 it was announced that PO Robert Blair had been honored by the Yonkers Exchange Club as Policeman of the year. This honor was the result of officer Blair's actions when, while riding alone in his patrol car, he pursued and arrested three armed men responsible for having just held up the A&P store on Tuckahoe Road.

On October 26, 1973 Bob Blair was promoted to the rank of Sergeant earning a salary of $15,708 and was reassigned to the North Command as a patrol supervisor. With his promotion Bob's job changed from doing the work to supervising patrol operations. However, that didn't stop him from working closely with his officers and lending a hand when needed. It was on Tuesday July 31, 1974 that two men, who were overcome by an industrial cleaning fluid's noxious gas while they worked in a tank at the Phelps Dodge Cable and Wire Co. on Point' Street, were pulled to safety by Sgt Blair and PO Charles Colarusso. Thirty-four people, including Blair and Colarusso, were treated at Yonkers General Hospital for noxious fume inhalation. Two men had been cleaning the water tank and were overcome by Tri-Chlorethane III gas fumes as they climbed into the 15-foot high tank. They were discovered by their supervisor who saw the two men lying unconscious on the bottom. Police were called and Sgt Blair and PO Colarusso climbed down the ladder and pulled the men to safety before the gas forced them out of the tank. Both workers survived due to Sgt Blair's quick action and disregard for his own safety.

Sgt Blair received his promotion to the rank of police Lieutenant on November 18, 1982 earning $32,391 a year and was reassigned to the Field Services Bureau serving as a city wide patrol lieutenant.

On June 3, 1985 Lt Robert Blair was promoted to Captain and assigned to the Field Services Bureau serving as a citywide patrol duty captain overseeing the patrol operations throughout the city. But, the following year, on July 2, 1986, Capt. Blair had the opportunity to return to the Traffic Division as the commanding officer. He didn't hesitate and was back riding a motorcycle on special occasions. Capt. Blair had the pleasure of watching his son, Robert Blair Jr, be appointed a Yonkers police officer in 1991 and later be promoted to Sergeant.

The captain remained in the Traffic Division for nearly six years and was then transferred to the 2nd precinct on January 1, 1992 as the precinct commanding officer.

Five years later, Capt. Robert Blair retired from the Yonkers P.D. August 28, 1997 after serving over 33 years.

PO REYNOLD W. BAKER #651

APPOINTED: August 12, 1964
RETIRED: January 11, 1985

Reynold "Ray" Baker was born the son of Yonkers police officer George J. Baker Sr. and his wife Astrid on April 1, 1941 in Yonkers. He attended PS# 4, Lincoln H.S. and Saunders Trade School. Right after leaving school Ray joined the Navy in July of 1960 and during his enlistment he earned his high school equivalency diploma. Ray was honorably discharged on July 24, 1964. Having taken the police exam while on military leave, only one month after his discharge Ray was appointed to the YPD on August 12, 1964. Less than a month later, on Sept. 9, 1964, another group of men were appointed. Both groups were merged and half went for recruit training at Iona, and the second half, the group containing Ray, attended the NYPD Police Academy recruit school. The academy training ran from October 5, 1964 to February 5, 1965.

Following the police academy Ray was assigned to patrol duty in the 2nd precinct earning a starting salary of $5,500 a year. He remained in the 2nd precinct until July 16, 1971 at which time he was appointed a Detective. During this time Det Baker was detailed to work with a Joint Task Force in the Westchester County Sheriff's Office from December 22, 1971 through March 14, 1972. He also was detailed for a short time to the YPD Police Intelligence Unit.

Ray remained a Detective in the bureau until October 21, 1983 and was then returned to uniform patrol in the 4th precinct. He remained in the 4th right up to his retirement from the department on January 11, 1985 with just over 20 years of service.

Reynold Baker's family was a law enforcement family. Ray's father, as stated, was a Yonkers police officer, his brother George Jr was a Yonkers police officer, his brother Robert Baker was a Yonkers Captain, and his brother William Baker was a N.Y.S. Trooper.

In 1994 Ray moved his family to Connecticut where, on February 21, 2010, Ret PO Reynold W. Baker Sr died at the age of 68 years of age.

LT. DONALD B. TYNDAL

APPOINTED: August 12, 1964
RETIRED: April 14, 2000

Don Tyndal was born in NYC on June 11, 1942. He attended Traphagen Jr. HS in Mt. Vernon, Eastchester HS, and graduated from Roosevelt HS. Previous to the YPD Don was employed by the US Post Office as a clerk. He received his appointment to the Y.P.D. on Aug. 12, 1964 while living at 786 Bronx River Rd. Tyndal and his recruit class was sent to the NYC Police Academy for basic recruit training. This intensive physical and academic training ran from Oct. 5, 1964 through Feb. 5, 1965. Following graduation Tyndal was assigned to the 2nd pct earning a salary of $5,500 a year. PO Tyndal remained on patrol in the 2nd pct for 11 years when, on Feb. 11, 1976, he was promoted to Sergeant and reassigned as a patrol supervisor in the North Command. In 1979 he was assigned to the North East Command for a few years but on Sept. 16, 1982 he was returned to duty in the North Command. Sgt Tyndal received his promotion to Lieutenant on Feb. 17, 1984 earning $37,132 and was assigned as a patrol lieutenant in the 4th pct. On April 2, 1988, Lt Tyndal was assigned as the executive officer in the 4th pct. Lt Donald Tyndal, whose nephew is PO Anthony Tyndal, retired from the YPD on April 14, 2000 after nearly 36 years service.

DET. JOHN P. RAFFA #670

APPOINTED: August 12, 1964
RETIRED: August 12, 1984

John Raffa was born in Yonkers on July 29, 1941. He attended PS# 13, and Yonkers HS. On May 5, 1960 "Jack," as he was known, joined the Army and served up to May 17, 1962 receiving his GED and his honorable discharge. He also served in the 42nd Military Police Company of the NY National Guard Reserve. "Jack" was appointed to the YPD on Aug. 12, 1964 while living at 27 Fortfield Ave. He and his recruit class were sent to the NYC Police Academy for basic recruit training. This intensive physical and academic training ran from Oct. 5, 1964 through Feb. 5, 1965. Upon graduation PO Raffa was assigned to the 4th precinct earning $5,500 a year. Raffa was first transferred on Nov. 9, 1966 to the 3rd pct and, then two years later, on Mar. 6, 1968, he was reassigned to the Communications Div. On May 19, 1969 Raffa was designated a Detective in the DD. Det. Raffa had an unusual ability dealing with investigations of stolen vehicles and as a result he was assigned, full time, to an Auto Theft Unit. "Jack" Raffa also had the pleasure of watching his younger brother Dennis be appointed to the YPD. Det John Raffa retired from the YPD on Aug. 12, 1984 and moved onto a farm he had purchased prior to retirement. He moved to Ocala, Florida where he raised horses for 15 years as a business. He would later move to the Cooperstown, NY area in upstate N.Y. Jack Raffa died Oct. 5, 2013.

LT. GEORGE J. BELGER

APPOINTED: August 12, 1964
RETIRED: April 3, 1998

George Belger was born in the City of Yonkers on May 3, 1939. He attended PS# 19, Hawthorne Jr. High School and graduated from Yonkers High School. Shortly after graduation George joined the Navy on August 29, 1957 and was honorably discharged on August 28, 1961. At one point while serving aboard ship, and unknown to him at the time, also serving aboard that ship was Seaman Anthony Dellacamera who many years later would be appointed a Yonkers police officer on the same day as Belger. Following his military service Belger worked as a cable tester for Phelps Dodge Corp on Point Street, in Yonkers.

George was appointed to the Yonkers Police Department on August 12, 1964 while living at 227 Elm Street. George and the other members of his recruit class were sent to the NYC Police Academy for basic recruit training. This intensive physical and academic training ran from October 5, 1964 through February 5, 1965. Upon completion he was assigned to the 1st precinct on patrol duty earning a starting salary of $5,500 a year. Less than two years later, on November 7, 1966, he was reassigned to the 4th precinct. On September 4, 1970 Belger was appointed a Detective and assigned to work in the Narcotics Unit in plainclothes. This assignment lasted less than a year and on July 16, 1971 he was returned to uniform patrol in the North Command.

Belger was promoted to the rank of Sergeant on May 1, 1981 earning a salary of $35,574 and was reassigned to the South Command as a patrol supervisor. He was transferred to the Courts and Detention Services Bureau on March 4, 1984 serving as a booking officer in Central Booking located in the City Jail on Alexander Street. But after only four months he was returned to patrol duty in the 4th precinct. On March 5, 1987 Sgt Belger was transferred to the 1st precinct on paper, but was detailed to work plainclothes in the Youth Division.

Sgt Belger was promoted to the rank of Lieutenant on May 29, 1987 earning a salary of $43,357 and was reassigned to the 2nd precinct as a Watch Commander.

On December 25, 1987 he was moved to the 3rd precinct as a patrol watch commander. Four months later, on April 11, 1988, he was assigned to the Traffic Court as the YPD liaison officer.

On February 26, 1996 Lt. Belger was transferred to Central Booking once again and remained there up to his retirement from the police department on April 3, 1998 after nearly 34 years service.

PO ANTHONY F. DELLACAMERA #469

APPOINTED: August 12, 1964
RETIRED: August 12, 1984

Anthony Dellacamera was actually born Anthony LaCambra on January 19, 1939 in Yonkers NY, his father's actual surname. However, Tony related that at one point, after his father had died at a young age, for unknown reasons his mother officially changed the family name to Dellacamera. Tony attended PS# 8, Roosevelt High School and would later graduate from Saunders High School with a trade in auto mechanics.

Upon completing high school Anthony joined the Naval Reserve on Alexander Street on February 7, 1957. He served two years active duty serving as a Seaman aboard a Destroyer, the DD872 Forrest B. Royal and later the Destroyer Escort DE1030 Joseph K. Taussig, and was honorably discharged on February 7, 1959. Unknown to him at the time, also aboard that ship was Seaman George Belger who many years later would be appointed a Yonkers police officer on the same day as Dellacamera. Following his military service Dellacamera began working on the assembly line at the General Motors auto assembly plant in Tarrytown, NY.

Tony was appointed to the Yonkers Police Dept. on August 12, 1964 while living at 117 North Terrace Avenue in Mt. Vernon, NY as there were no residency requirements back then. Tony and the other members of his recruit class were sent to the NYC Police Academy for basic recruit training with intensive physical and academic training that ran from October 5, 1964 through February 5, 1965.

Following recruit school graduation PO Anthony Dellacamera was assigned to patrol duty in the 2nd precinct earning a starting salary of $5,500 a year. He recalls one occasion, while still in recruit gray uniform, when he was working a school crossing at Tuckahoe Road and Cross Street, when he noticed a male (known burglar) climbing out of a window of the corner building. Within a minute the man was in his custody. That was his first arrest in grays but it wasn't his most memorable incident.

It was April 27, 1966, and with just under two years on the job, and Tony was working overtime at the Raceway detail. It was about 8:00 p.m. while driving up McLean to Central Park Avenue and then headed north, passing the Thruway exit for Hall Street when he saw a large tractor trailer straddling the concrete divider separating the Thruway from Central Ave. The driver of the rig had apparently veered off the Thruway onto the divider, and knocked down the chain link fence in the process.

As he pulled up to the accident, Dellacamera noticed the ground was all wet with diesel fuel. He then noticed that the top length of fence pipe had separated from the chain link portion and had penetrated the front windshield. P.O. Dellacamera said, "*I climbed up on the driver's step of the cab and saw that the pipe that came through the windshield had also pierced the driver's stomach. He was impaled.*" Much to the officers surprise, he found that the man was still alive but semi-conscious, and was bleeding very little from the entrance wound.

He immediately called headquarters for an ambulance, the Emergency Unit, a priest, and the fire department to wash the diesel fuel. P.O. Dellacamera then took a closer look. He discovered that the nearly 2" diameter pipe had not just entered the drivers body, it had also passed, through the seat, through the metal cab enclosure, and straight back into the trailer portion for nearly 30 feet.

While waiting for help to arrive, Dellacamera wrapped a shirt he found in the truck around the exit

PO Anthony F. Dellacamera #469 (cont.)

wound in the man's back where bleeding was more profuse. ESU arrived and went to work. They administered oxygen and with the help of Dellacamera, began to saw the pipe in half, both in front of the man's stomach and just beyond his back. There were no power saws in the ESU inventory, so they had to work with hacksaws. The driver, a gypsy trucker from down south, was delicately removed from the cab to the ambulance, with the 2" pipe still protruding from both his stomach and back. He was transported to St Joseph's Hospital, lying on his side of course, where, following surgery and extensive medical treatment, he recovered fully. He left the hospital about six weeks later. Miraculously, the pipe had apparently passed through his body without severely damaging any vital organs.

If it hadn't been for Officer Dellacamera coming upon the accident, notifying HQ for medical assistance, and administering first aid, the outcome would have been much different. But it's still one he'll never forget.

It didn't take Tony long to continue to earn a good reputation. The May 1967 term of the Westchester Co. Grand Jury voted a special Commendation to officer Dellacamera for his "resourceful and courageous performance of duties in the capture of the person responsible for the armed robbery of a Service Station on April 19, 1967 and for the intelligent manner in which he testified."

On June 23, 1972 Dellacamera was transferred to the Special Operations Division, which incorporated the Traffic Unit, and was assigned to parking meter enforcement on a three wheel motorcycle. However, in 1979 the city hired civilian enforcement officers to perform that duty and as a result Dellacamera was returned to patrol in the South Command on April 4, 1979.

However, seven months later, on November 16, 1979, he was assigned to the Records Division in an administrative capacity. On October 10, 1983 Tony was returned to the 2nd precinct where he would retire the following year, after exactly 20 years, on August 12, 1984. Anthony was the son-in-law of Lt. Harold O'Neill and the cousin to YPD PO Christopher Dellacamera, former Mamaroneck, NY PO Frank Dellacamera, and an uncle to a police officer niece in Poughkeepsie, NY.

In retirement Anthony worked a number of different jobs in the security field; for Tiffany's Jeweler and later Pepsico Corp. in Harrison, NY. Several years later he moved to Florida with his entire family to enjoy the warm weather.

POLICE COMMISSIONER ALBERT R. McEVOY

APPOINTED: August 12, 1964
RETIRED: March 3, 2000

Albert Raymond McEvoy was born on Morningside Avenue, Yonkers, NY, on November 20, 1942. He attended St Joseph's Elementary School, and both Sacred Heart and Gorton High Schools. Al joined the Air Force on November 24, 1959 and served in Texas, Colorado, and the Middle East and remained in the military through 1963. From 1962 to 1963 he was stationed in Peshawar, Pakistan, attached to the 6937th Communications Group, United States Air Force Security Service. In 1961 he attended the Chemical, Biological and Radiological Instructor Development Course at Lowery Air Force Base in Denver, Colorado. After completion, he was assigned to teach the course to members of the CBR team at Sheppard Air Force Base, Texas; a wing of the Strategic Air Command. In 1965, the Yonkers Police Department would send him to a similar course at Cornell University in the event his knowledge in

Police Commissioner Albert R. McEvoy (cont.)

this area became necessary for public safety.

On September 6, 1963, Al was honorably discharged as an Airman first-class. Following his military service he worked for a very short time at Precision Valve Corp. on Nepperhan Avenue and was then hired by the NY Telephone Co. working from 555 Tuckahoe Road. It was while with the Telephone Company that he learned he had passed the Police Patrolman's examination and would soon be appointed.

While living at 157 Lake Avenue Albert R. McEvoy received his appointment to the police department on August 12, 1964 along with 12 other men. Probationary police officer McEvoy and his recruit class were sent to the New York City Police Academy for basic recruit training. This intensive physical and academic training ran from October 5, 1964 through February 5, 1965. Upon graduation, PO McEvoy was recognized as having achieved the highest academic scores throughout his training and for this honor he was awarded an off duty .38 cal. Smith & Wesson revolver.

Following recruit graduation PO McEvoy was assigned to foot patrol duty in the 4th precinct earning a starting salary of $5,500 a year. In just over a year's time Al had apparently distinguished himself on patrol because, on June 10, 1966, he was appointed a Detective in the Detective Division. Al later would recall that coincidentally, it was on that same day that the "Miranda" decision from the Supreme Court regarding constitutional rights upon arrest was announced as being law. During his tenure as a detective, McEvoy had proven himself to be an intelligent and effective investigator making many arrests for very serious crimes. An example is as follows;

In July of 1968 Det. McEvoy and his partner, Det. Charles Apadula, were just beginning the late tour on patrol when they observed a male driving a car on Central Park Avenue at Tuckahoe Road with blood on his arm. A closer look revealed the passenger car had commercial vehicle license plates. Following a high-speed chase and upon stopping the suspect's car, they questioned the man. Following a brief investigation the man admitted he had just murdered his girlfriend down in the Bronx. Upon notifying New York City police McEvoy and Apadula learned that the crime had not yet even been discovered until he notified them. They were awarded a departmental Commendation by the Public Safety Commissioner for their alertness and excellent detective work.

It is worthy of note that at this point in time politics had a great deal to do with who was appointed a detective, regardless of an officer's remarkable record. And so, on October 5, 1968, just over two years from being assigned as a detective, Al McEvoy was reassigned back to patrol duty in the 4th precinct. However, on February 7, 1969, he was again assigned as a Detective. But, at the end of that year, on December 20, 1969, he was once again returned to patrol, but this time in the 1st precinct. And fortunately, on December 11, 1970, Al was again returned to the Detective Division. During this time period, Public Safety Commissioner Frank Vescio was playing "musical chairs" with some of the detectives in an effort to secure council votes to keep his position. His efforts failed and he was replaced by William H. Sickley.

McEvoy remained in the DD for about a year and a half when, on May 5, 1972, he was promoted to the rank of Sergeant earning $13,685 a year and was reassigned as a patrol supervisor in the North Patrol Command. While there, in 1973, he was tasked by the commanding officer, Capt. John F. McMahon, to organize a command Tactical Patrol Force (TPF) to address special problem areas within

Police Commissioner Albert R. McEvoy (cont.)

the North Command. He did just that and supervised that squad of men for 18 months.

On August 13, 1976, Sgt. McEvoy was promoted to the rank of Lieutenant earning $20,642 a year and was transferred to the Communications Division as a tour supervisor. Following the retirement of Lt. Arthur Holsborg on January 7, 1977, Lt McEvoy was reassigned again and this time was designated commanding officer of the Planning and Development Unit. In this position he was responsible for the researching and preparation of applications for federal and state grants for the Yonkers Police Department for various projects including a new communications system.

Earlier, Al McEvoy had attended Westchester Community College earning his Associates Degree on a part time basis and had graduated in 1975 with honors by maintaining a perfect 4.0 average. For his effort he was awarded a full academic scholarship to Iona College. Al graduated from Iona College in 1977 with a B.S. degree while maintaining a straight "A" average for his four years. He also received the General Studies Award for academic distinction. Several years later Al would go on to obtain his Master's degree in Criminal Justice/Computer Applications from Iona graduate school in 1993. Al also attended the N.YU. Graduate School of Public Administration in 1978.

On October 2, 1981, during the tenure of PC Daniel Guido, a civilian named Tom Sweeney was hired and assigned to perform McEvoy's duties in the Planning Unit. As such, and at his own request, Lt. McEvoy requested and was returned to the Communications Division. After a short return to Communications, then Police Commissioner Charles Connolly reassigned him to the South Patrol Command as the Executive Officer where he was getting groomed to be promoted to Captain, as he was next on the list. A new Southwest Patrol Command, located on Riverdale Avenue, was opened on May 21, 1983. At that time Capt. Joseph V. Fernandes was the Commanding Officer of the South Command. However, that all changed when Fernandes was appointed Acting Police Commissioner. As a result, on May 24, 1983 Lt. Al McEvoy, Fernandes' second-in-command, was promoted to Captain and as such assumed command of the South Command and the new Southwest Command, both at the same time. The promotion brought Captain McEvoy's salary to $42,148 a year.

Following his promotion, Capt. McEvoy convinced Police Commissioner Fernandes to stop using the designation "North and South Command" and return to the traditional use of the designation "precincts." Fernandes agreed. McEvoy was then designated the commanding officer of the 2nd and 3rd precincts until Lt. Joseph Messina was promoted to Captain and assumed sole command of the 3rd, and McEvoy commanded the 2nd. While serving as the C.O. of the 2nd pct. Capt. McEvoy applied for, and was accepted as a candidate in the 139th session of the prestigious FBI National Academy in Quantico, Va. He attended the academy from September 10, 1984 up to graduation on December 14, 1984.

In February of 1985 Capt. McEvoy was honored by the Gannett Westchester Rockland Newspapers for an incident that occurred that previous May. At that time, while off duty and driving on Palmer Road near Kimball Avenue he observed a blue car with 3 men. He remembered that the car fit the description of one that had been seen leaving the scene of several armed robberies. At the time he was proceeding to Captain John Duffy's promotion party at Alex and Henry's in Eastchester where McEvoy was chairman of the event. He notified Yonkers headquarters on his unmarked police car radio of the situation and followed the vehicle into Bronxville. The car was pulled over by McEvoy and a Bronxville

Police Commissioner Albert R. McEvoy (cont.)

police officer that had been alerted by McEvoy's notification. That Bronxville police officer assisted McEvoy in subduing and taking into custody the three suspects, one of whom was armed. An investigation revealed that the three had heldup a dry cleaners store in Yonkers. They also were wanted for several armed robberies in White Plains, Elmsford, and Greenburgh.

On January 30, 1986 Capt. McEvoy was designated commanding officer of the Training Unit and in this position he was responsible for all police training. He determined the training curriculum to meet the needs of newly recruited police officers as well as all in-service training for existing personnel. A certified instructor himself, he also had to supervise and monitor the efficiency of the seven instructors who worked for him. The captain was required to conceptualize and supervise the development of various training aids to be utilized in training. He established testing for the evaluation of programs and personnel including physical training and firearms, as well as interacting with upper-level YPD management, FBI, County, State and Federal level training personnel. While assigned to training he attended a Secret Service Dignitary Protection Seminar, in Washington, D.C. which would prove invaluable in years to come.

On October 1, 1990 Capt. McEvoy was placed in charge of the Planning and Management Unit located in headquarters, by Commissioner Robert Olsen. This unit had the fundamental role of researching, drafting and revising the department's policy and procedure manual, developing the annual reports, the analysis of crime patterns, and in addition, publishing a monthly department newsletter. Just over a year later, on January 1, 1992, he was reassigned as the commanding officer of the 3rd precinct on Riverdale Avenue; but for just a short time. For on June 14, 1993 McEvoy was transferred back to command of the Training Unit.

Having been selected by then Mayor Terrence Zeleski to succeed outgoing PC Robert K. Olsen, on March 17, 1995, Capt. Albert R. McEvoy was sworn into office as the new Yonkers Police Commissioner at the age of 52 years. Although a police captain at the time, the mayor chose McEvoy over the current three deputy chiefs because he believed McEvoy was eminently qualified and the right man for the job. On hearing the news, one command level officer stated, "*Al certainly has a clear vision of what is right and what is wrong. He is an independent man and thinker. He sees himself as a professional police officer and is a 'back to the basic's' kind of leader*." Attending the heavily attended ceremony were many FBI officials, Westchester County Judges, members of the Secret Service, representatives from other local and county police departments as well as Yonkers command officers and even police retirees. Following his oath of office the new commissioner was given a standing ovation by the standing room only crowd.

While serving as police commissioner McEvoy had the honor of participating in the planning and security, working with the Secret Service, and overall supervision of the Yonkers department during the visit of His Holiness, Pope John Paul 2nd on his historic visit to St. Joseph's Seminary in Yonkers on October 6, 1995.

As has been mentioned earlier, Comm. McEvoy was a by the rules kind of guy. Do your job and do it right and there would be no problem. However, throughout his tenure, he and the PBA developed an adversarial relationship and the PBA wanted him replaced. Following the election of a new mayor in November of 1995 Comm. McEvoy was advised that Deputy Chief Christopher would be appointed

Police Commissioner Albert R. McEvoy (cont.)

commissioner to replace him and he, McEvoy, would be designated a Deputy Chief of Support Services Bureau working under PC Christopher. His reduction in rank was effective January 11, 1996.

Following his removal as police commissioner, on April 23, 1996, DC Al McEvoy filed a federal civil rights lawsuit naming Mayor John Spencer and the Yonkers PBA, alleging that his demotion amounted to a violation of his First Amendment rights. That the two had conspired to remove him as the city's “top cop” because of the PBA’s dislike of his management style. Two days later, on April 25, 1996, it was announced that McEvoy had been reduced in rank again, this time from Deputy Chief to his civil service rank of Police Captain and placed in command of the busy 3rd precinct on Riverdale Avenue. He remained there for four years and actually enjoyed every minute of it. And, only when he decided it was time to go, he would retire.

After nearly 36 years of dedicated service Albert McEvoy retired from the Yonkers Police Department effective March 3, 2000. It was then that he began devoting his full time as President and CEO of his private investigation agency named A.R.M. Associates. that he established in 1996.

Albert R. McEvoy was always interested in higher learning. His educational credentials are as follows;

He earned an Associate's degree from Westchester Community College in criminal justice in 1975; a Bachelor of Science degree from Iona College in criminal justice in 1977; attended the NYU graduate school of public administration, earning 16 credits in 1978; attended the prestigious FBI national Academy 139th session, from September to December of 1984; was trained by the US Secret Service in dignitary protection in 1986; and earned his Master's degree from Iona College in criminal justice/computer applications in 1993.

Regarding various honors and awards, Al McEvoy received four Citations of Commendable Merit and two Honorable Mention awards from the Westchester Rockland newspapers. He received two Certificates of Excellent Police Work and four Commendations from the Yonkers Police Department. He received a full tuition scholarship to Iona College based on 4.0 Index from Westchester Community College in 1975. He received a meritorious service award from the Second Precinct Community Council in 1985. He was selected as Policeman of the Year by VFW Post #1666 in 1985. He was awarded the Congressional Medal of Merit in 1985, and the Governor's Certificate of Merit also in 1985.

He was affiliated with, or a member of, the following organizations:

FBI National Academy Associates, American Academy for Professional Law Enforcement, American Society for Industrial Security, International Police Association, Yonkers Police Captains, Lieutenants, and Sergeants Association, the YPD Holy Name Society, the Police Emerald Society of Westchester, the Veterans of Foreign Wars- post-1666 American Legion, the Benevolent and Protective Order of Elks Lodge #707, and the Society of the Friendly Sons of Saint Patrick of Westchester County.

It is clear the Al McEvoy had always been very active throughout his career. And yet he still found time to enjoy boating, fishing, water sports, reading, and the theater. And after many years of part work and part retirement, Al moved to Florida to enjoy the sunshine. But he just couldn’t sit around without being productive. So, in December of 2008 he began working as a volunteer, on a part time basis, for the Daytona Beach, Florida Police Dept. working cold case homicide investigations with another retiree from a different department. Al McEvoy was back doing what he does best. And, in 2012 he married for the first time.

LT. JOHN J. HURLEY

APPOINTED: August 12, 1964
RETIRED: January 14, 2005

John Hurley was born in Yonkers NY on December 2, 1942. He attended PS# 6, Longfellow Jr High School, and graduated from Saunders High School. Right out of high school John joined the Air Force on January 29, 1960 and was honorably discharged on October 28, 1963. Prior to the police department John worked for a time for Precision Valve Corp.

He received his appointment to the YPD on August 12, 1964 while living at 142 Woodworth Avenue. John, along with the rest of his recruit class, was fortunate to attend the NYPD police academy for 4 months, from October 5, 1964 to February 5, 1965. Upon graduation Police Officer John Hurley was assigned to foot patrol duty in the 1st precinct at 10 St. Casimir Avenue earning a starting salary of $5,500 a year. He was not a probationary officer upon graduation because at the time the probation period ran for 90 days from appointment. He remained in the 1st precinct up to November 9, 1966 when he was reassigned to the 4th precinct. However, the following year, on June 14, 1967, he was transferred to patrol duty in the 3rd precinct at 36 Radford Street.

On April 27, 1970 John was assigned to the Detective Division, but not as a detective. He was assigned to work in the Youth Division as a patrolman investigating juvenile crime. However, on February 12, 1971 officer Hurley was appointed a Detective in the DD. John remained a detective for nearly two years and on September 15, 1972 he was returned to patrol duty in the then North Command at 53 Shonnard Place with his rookie partner Charles Gardner. John was very street wise and taught rookie Gardner a great deal on handling difficult and dangerous assignments. His hands on field training and guidance likely contributed, in part, to Gardner's approach to police work and many years later rising to be appointed police commissioner.

After nearly 25 years on patrol duty, Hurley received his first promotion to Sergeant on March 9, 1990 and was assigned as a booking officer in Central Booking. But, on December 10, 1990 he was transferred to the 4th precinct as a uniform patrol supervisor. Hurley's second promotion came on August 12, 1998 and he was reassigned to the Field Services Bureau as a city wide patrol lieutenant.

On January 1, 2000 Lt Hurley was moved to Central booking, a job he held earlier, but this time the position called for a lieutenant. His last assignment would be supervising the Communications Division from which he would retire on January 14, 2005.

Lt Hurley spent a great deal of his career on the street and his record of accomplishments reflects his work. Over his career he earned 3 Macy's Awards, 7 Commendations, 14 Certificates of Excellent Police Work, and the Yonkers Elks Policeman of the Year for 1984. John's wife Peggy's great grandfather, John Carey, was a Yonkers Police Hostler in the late 1800's.

John was enjoying his retirement when he became ill. After a yearlong fight Ret Lt John J. Hurley died on January 16, 2012.

PO JAMES J. LYNN Jr. #151

APPOINTED: August 12, 1964
RETIRED: May 19, 1987

James Joseph Lynn Jr. was born in Yonkers on January 31, 1936, the son of Yonkers police officer James Lynn Sr. As a youth he attended Holy Rosary elementary school and graduated from Cardinal Hayes High School in the Bronx, NY. Following graduation Jim, who was a big man standing over 6' 2" tall and weighing over 200 lbs., worked construction as a heavy equipment operator. In 1957 he was appointed to the NY State Police as a trooper and graduated from their training school in Troy NY on December 21, 1957. He remained a state trooper for five years working in the upstate area and was a member of their NY State Police Revolver Competition Team.

It was said that Jim decided to leave the State Police due to the requirement that he work far north of his home and family in Yonkers. Lynn worked a few miscellaneous jobs until he received his appointment to the YPD on August 12, 1964. Probationary police officer Lynn and his recruit class were sent to the NYC Police Academy for basic recruit training. This intensive physical and academic training ran from October 5, 1964 through February 5, 1965.

Following his class graduation Jim was assigned to patrol duty in the 3rd precinct earning $5,500 a year. Just over two years later, on August 25, 1967, Lynn was appointed a Detective in the DD. Det. Lynn, who spoke Spanish as a second language, earned an excellent reputation working as a squad detective. On November 25, 1968 he was awarded a Certificate of Commendable Merit by the Westchester Rockland newspaper Police Honor Awards Committee for his part in solving the murder of a Yonkers man. And in August of 1970 the Westchester Grand Jury voted Det. Lynn a special commendation for the arrest of persons who were rioting and assaulted him and others. However, following a citywide reorganization and centralization plan put in place effective January 1, 1971, Det. Lynn was transferred back to patrol duty in the North Command.

He remained there until September 15, 1972 when he was fortunate enough to be reassigned to the Special Operations Division assigned to general parking meter enforcement. In March of 1974 Lynn was commended by the Yonkers City Council for saving the lives of several residents by evacuating them from a building which had been on fire earlier that year on February 17, 1974. PO Lynn enforced meter violations for nearly seven years, always hoping for an opportunity to be assigned to two wheel motorcycle patrol. And that day came on April 6, 1979.

Jim Lynn was a very powerful man and also very athletic. One of his hobbies was that of an amateur scuba diver. He was also a member of the NYPD Emerald Society Pipe Band as a piper for many years. Not only was his father a Yonkers police officer but his sister Grace also joined the department in 1970.

Years earlier, on March 29, 1976, Lynn injured his back badly in a motorcycle accident. The injury never healed right and PO Lynn retired from the YPD on an accidental disability pension on May 19, 1987. Following retirement Jim lived in East Durham, NY.

Ret Det. James Lynn, the father of six children, died on July 2, 2004 in a nursing home in Norfolk, Va. after a long illness. He was 68 years old.

DET. RICHARD ISSER #689

APPOINTED: August 12, 1964
RETIRED: January 27, 1991

Richard Isser was born in the Bronx, NY on Oct. 26, 1941. He grew up in Manhattan, attended PS# 52 and PS# 98 and later graduated from the Bronx Vocational HS in the Bronx. On August 19, 1959 he joined the Navy serving aboard the USS Little Rock CLG- 4, a guided missile cruiser. He was honorably discharged on Nov. 29, 1962. Prior to the YPD Rich worked for the Manufacturers Hanover Trust Co. Located on Wall Street in NYC, and also for the Railway Express Agency in NYC.

Rich was appointed to the Y.P.D. on Aug. 12, 1964 while living at 71 Livingston Ave. Less than a month later, on Sept. 9, 1964, another group of men were appointed. Both groups were merged and half went for recruit training at Iona, and the second half, the group containing Isser, attended the NYPD Police Academy recruit school for basic recruit training. This intensive physical and academic training ran from October 5, 1964 through February 5, 1965. Following graduation Patrolman Isser was assigned to the 3rd pct on foot patrol earning a starting salary of $5,500 a year. On Nov. 9, 1966, as part of a large reorganization of personnel, Isser was transferred to duty in the newly opened 1st precinct at 730 East Grassy Sprain Road. However, this would only last four months when, on March 6, 1967, he was returned to the 3rd.

On Jan. 1, 1971 a precinct centralization plan was put in place where two precincts were closed as patrol precincts and the remaining two, the 2nd and the 4th, were renamed the South Command and the North Command. Many were transferred, including Isser, who was reassigned to the South Patrol Command. Isser remained working uniformed patrol there for several years and on occasion was detailed to work in plainclothes to patrol Bronx River Road to stop the numerous auto thefts that were occurring. In 1973 he was assigned to their auto theft detail, along with his partner, Vincent Patalano. They worked steady late tours along the Bronx River Road corridor of Yonkers in plainclothes to address the auto theft crime occurring in that area. On February 25, 1975 the YPD established a citywide Street Crime Unit (SCU), and among those assigned to that new unit was PO Isser. Though assigned to the SCU Isser continued to work the Bronx River Road detail on the late tour. He and Patalano did this while working closely with the other members of the SCU and did so with remarkable success.

Over the next eight years PO Isser earned an enviable reputation of getting the job done by making numerous arrests in the complaint areas he was assigned. It was because of his abilities that, on April 22, 1983, Richard Isser was appointed a Detective in the DD working in a general assignment squad. Five years later, on July 1, 1988, Det Isser was transferred to the Special Investigations Unit where very highly sensitive investigations were handled. The following year, on October 9, 1989, he was reassigned to work in the Internal Affairs Division where he remained up to his retirement from the YPD on January 27, 1991. During his police career Rich Isser recorded an outstanding arrest record and was awarded numerous departmental honors for his excellent police work.

Rich Isser was, throughout his entire career, very competitive. He was a bowler who played on several bowling leagues in addition to playing on the PBA softball team. But it was clear to all that he could not get enough of the game of golf. So it's no surprise that he and his wife moved to Florida to play golf in the sun, at every opportunity.

PO WILLIAM V. MANISCALCO #208

APPOINTED: August 12, 1964
RETIRED: January 13, 1995

William V. Maniscalco was born on Jan. 18, 1933 in Yonkers. He attended PS# 18, Benjamin Franklyn Jr. HS and graduated from Commerce HS having majored in Office Machines. Right after graduation Bill joined the Army on June 26, 1951 and served during the Korean War, serving as a Specialist 3rd class. He was honorably discharged four years later on Aug. 11, 1955. Utilizing his knowledge of various office and printing machines Bill gained employment with Manor Publications on Brookfield Street, in White Plains. He also worked for the Dade County Fl. Civil Service Commission for five years. Bill was appointed to the YPD on Aug. 12, 1964 while living at 132 Willow St. Following his recruit training at the Iona college campus Bill was assigned to patrol duty in the 1st pct earning $5,500 a year. On Nov. 9, 1966 he was transferred to the 4th pct but was detailed to work in the Planning and Training Unit. It was apparent that Bill was a skilled printer and on Feb. 14, 1968 he was officially assigned to Planning detailed to work exclusively in the YPD print shop preparing anything the department needed printed. PO Maniscalco remained working in the print shop for the remainder of his career, retiring on Jan. 13, 1995 after more than 40 years service.

PO RICHARD H. DENTON #421

APPOINTED: September 9, 1964
RETIRED: July 12, 1979

Richard was born in Yonkers on June 18, 1937. He attended St. Mary's catholic school and graduated from Halstead HS on North Broadway at Lamartine Avenue. Rich joined the Air Force on July 7, 1955 and was honorably discharged on July 7, 1958. During his school years Denton was always a very good ball player and pitcher. In fact, while in high school he was called by a scout to try out for the Detroit Tigers. Following his military service Denton worked for Con Edison in Rye, NY. And in early 1964 was a pitcher with the Baltimore Orioles Minor League organization. However, at one point he was in a serious motor vehicle accident suffering multiple injuries. As a result he never played ball again. Richard Denton was appointed to the YPD on Sept. 9, 1964 while living at 52 Mansion Ave. His first assignment was to the 2nd pct earning $5,500 a year. Nearly nine years later, on April 12, 1973, PO Denton was transferred to the Planning Unit in HQ. And a year later, on June 19, 1974, he was reassigned as a dispatcher in the Communications Div. Denton's last assignment took place on Jan. 9, 1976 when he was assigned to the North Command. However, during this time he was out on the sick list and remained as such right up to retirement on an ordinary disability on July 12, 1979.

PO ANTHONY J. BISACCIA #412

APPOINTED: September 9, 1964
RETIRED: April 27, 2001

Anthony J. Bisaccia was born in the City of Yonkers on August 26, 1940 and raised in the Park Hill section. Anthony attended PS# 24, Benjamin Franklin Junior High School, and graduated from Yonkers High School. Tony served in the 101st signal Battalion, Company D., of the New York National Guard as a Specialist 4th class from October of 1962 until his honorable discharge in 1968. He initially attended Westchester Community College for a time and then began working for Otis elevator Company. He remained there for about 2 years in the contractual engineering department as well as several other jobs during that period.

Anthony received his appointment to the police department on September 9, 1964 while living at 35 Cliff Street in Yonkers. He attended the Police Academy recruit school for basic recruit training located in Iona College. When the academy training was completed he was assigned to the 1st precinct on patrol duty earning a starting salary of $5,500 a year.

On November 9, 1966, following the opening of the new 1st precinct on E. Grassy Sprain Rd., Tony was transferred from the 1st to the 4th precinct. Three years later, on January 3, 1969, he was again transferred, this time to headquarters for administrative duties. Around 1970 he was assigned to the Police Print Shop and he remained there for four years. He remained in the print shop until June 1, 1973 when he was assigned to work in the Property Clerks office where he remained for about twenty two years.

Anthony Bisaccia served as the PBA trustee for headquarters command for 28 years, reportedly the longest running PBA board member in memory. In addition to the PBA Tony was a member of the police Holy Name Society and the Columbian Association.

About 1995 Bisaccia was reassigned to the Records Division performing administrative duties from which he later retired on April 27, 2001. Anthony's cousin was Sgt Mike D'Ambrosio.

DET. SGT. STEVEN E. KOGAN #82

APPOINTED: September 9, 1964
RETIRED: August 23, 1985

Steve Kogan was born in Brooklyn New York on April 25, 1943. After having been brought to Yonkers as a very young child Steve attended PS# 3, Hawthorne Jr high school, and graduated from Yonkers high school. At one point he also attended Bronx community college. Prior to the YPD Steve gained employment with St. John's Hospital as an ambulance driver where he became acquainted with many Yonkers police officers which led him to taking the police officer exam.

Steve was appointed to the Yonkers Police Department on September 9, 1964 while residing at 125 Elliott Ave. Probationary police officer Kogan and his recruit class were sent to the New York City Police Academy for basic recruit training. This intensive physical and academic training ran from October 5, 1964 through February 5, 1965. Upon graduation, PO Kogan was assigned to foot patrol duty in the 3rd precinct earning a starting salary of $5,500 a year.

The following year Kogan was involved in a dangerous disturbance call which he described as follows; "*The first shooting incident I was ever involved in was with PO Herb Engler and others in 1966 on Hawthorne Avenue near Hawthorne Jr. high school. It was at about 3 A.M. and a male who just got out of the Marine Corps. just had a fight with his wife and took it out on us as we left the radio car and attempted to walk up his front path to the house. He immediately began shooting at us from an upstairs window with a rifle and shotgun striking the patrol cars. After several backup cars arrived we were able to enter the building, without any of the protective equipment that is available today, and took the suspect into custody. Herb and I were fine, just shaken up.*"

The following year, on January 13, 1967, Kogan was appointed a Detective in the Detective Division. Two years later, in March of 1969, he was granted a one year unpaid leave of absence for personal reasons. When he returned he had hoped to resume his duties as a detective. He was wrong. When he returned to the YPD in March of 1970 he was returned to patrol duty in the 4th precinct walking a foot post. However, the following year, on May 14, 1971, Kogan was again appointed a detective and this time assigned to work in the department's Intelligence Unit.

On May 5, 1972 Detective Kogan was promoted to the rank of Sergeant earning a salary of $13,685 a year. Due to the sensitive nature of the work that Kogan had been performing and the experience he had gained in that position, he was not transferred, but was allowed to remain in the Intelligence Unit, and in addition was designated a Detective Sergeant.

The Intelligence Unit, later renamed the Special Investigations Unit, was a plainclothes, specialized unit which utilized covert photo and physical surveillance and court ordered wiretapping to monitor those individuals involved in organized crime, political corruption, and from time to time provided dignitary protection as well. This unit was the last to investigate, interview and sign off with recommendations for candidates for the position of police officer in the YPD. While performing their investigative duties the unit members worked very closely with other local, county, state and federal agencies such as the district attorney, state police, FBI, DEA, ATF, military intelligence, etc. Only the most trusted would be assigned.

Det Sgt. Steven E. Kogan #82 (cont.)

Det. Sgt. Kogan remained in this assignment right up to his retirement on August 23, 1985.

Upon retirement in 1985 Kogan went to work as a Special Investigator for the New York State Attorney General's Special Prosecutor's Office. While there he investigated Medicaid Fraud and patient abuse in hospitals and nursing homes. He was assigned to the New York City Office. In 1986 the agency sent him first to the FBI's Advanced Firearms Training and later to the FBI's Firearms Instructors Schools and he became the Principal Firearms Instructor for their agency statewide.

Steve then relocated to Boca Raton, Florida in 1993 and became an Agent with the State of Florida Office of the Attorney General. He held numerous supervisory positions leaving in 2003 as Chief of Investigations, a position he held for about seven years. In 2004 Kogan began employment with the State of Florida, Department of Business and Professional Regulation, Office of Para-Mutual Wagering. He was (2013) the Chief of Investigations with the agency and they are responsible for regulating Thoroughbred Racing, Greyhound Racing, Poker Rooms, Jai-Alai Games and Casinos throughout Florida. He loves working and has no plans to retire any time soon

---

PO ROBERT E. CANNON #411

APPOINTED: September 9, 1964
RETIRED: January 7, 2000

Robert E. Cannon was born in Yonkers on Jan. 16, 1938 where he attended PS# 13, Hawthorne Jr HS and left school early to join the US Coast Guard Reserve in Feb. of 1955 and was honorably discharged in March of 1963. While still in the reserves Bob was hired by Otis Elevator Co. where he remained right up to the YPD. Bob was appointed to the Y.P.D. on Sept. 9, 1964 while residing at 758 North Broadway. His brother Edward would be appointed the following year. Bob and his recruit class attended basic police training at the Iona campus in New Rochelle and upon graduation he was assigned to patrol duty in the 4th pct earning $5,500 a year. Bob was a friendly individual but at the same time very reserved and quiet in his demeanor. He was always very dependable and efficient in his assignments and was an absolute gentleman. He remained in the 4th pct. for 15 years until his transfer to the North East Command on June 20, 1979. On Sept. 13, 1982 Cannon was reassigned to the South Command on patrol. On May 21, 1983 a Southwest Patrol Command was opened on Riverdale Ave, later renamed the 3rd precinct, and PO Cannon was assigned there as the precinct desk officer and retired from there on January 7, 2000.

PO JOHN M. MEADE #417

APPOINTED: September 9, 1964
RETIRED: August 4, 1988

John Mitchell Meade was born in Yonkers on Dec. 1, 1938. He attended St. Joseph's School and graduated from Sacred Heart HS. On June 28, 1957 John joined the Air Force serving with the 43rd Field Maintenance Squadron as a mechanic with the rank of airmen 3rd class. He was honorably discharged on July 13, 1960. Following his military service and experience as a mechanic Mitch, as he was known, worked for the Lash Service Station located on Central Ave. He received his appointment to the Y.P.D. on Sept. 9, 1964 while living at 129 Cottage Ave. in Mt. Vernon and received his basic recruit training at the police academy which was then located in Iona College in New Rochelle. His first assignment was patrol duty in the 4th pct earning $5,500 a year. He remained on patrol in the 4th pct for 17 years until Dec. 4, 1981 when he was reassigned to the South Command. The following year on Sept. 13, 1982 he was reassigned to patrol duty in the Northeast Command on E. Grassy Sprain Rd. Four years later, on April 8, 1986, he was moved to the 1st pct assigned to their warrant squad. On June 24, 1987 he was transferred to the Courts and Detention Services Div. working in the city-wide warrant squad located in the city jail. Mitch remained in this assignment right up to his retirement on Aug. 4, 1988.

PO JOSEPH VERGALITTO #404

APPOINTED: September 9, 1964
RETIRED: November 1, 1985

Joe Vergalitto was born in Yonkers on June 9, 1938. He attended St. Peter's school, Hawthorne Jr. HS, and graduated from Saunders HS. Joe served in the NY National Guard from 1955 through 1958 and was honorably discharged. Prior to the YPD he had been employed by the Otis Elevator Co. working as a wireman. "Joe V," as he was known to friends, was appointed to the Y.P.D. on Sept. 9, 1964 while living at 102 Ash St. Joe and the other members of his recruit class were sent to the NYC Police Academy for basic recruit training which ran from October 5, 1964 through Feb. 5, 1965. Following graduation PO Vergalitto was assigned to the 1st pct earning $5,500 a year. On Nov. 9, 1966, following the opening of a new 1st pct on E. Grassy Sprain Rd, and the ensuing personnel reorganization, Joe was reassigned to the 4th pct on patrol duty. In early 1970 he was moved to the 1st pct and a year later to the Communications Div. as a dispatcher. In mid 1971 Joe returned to the old 4th pct., which in Jan. 1971 had been renamed the North Command, and was assigned a steady foot post in Getty Square. He remained in that assignment right up to his retirement on November 1, 1985.

PO LAWRENCE RICHARDSON #415

APPOINTED: September 9, 1964
RESIGNED: December 9, 1964

Lawrence Richardson was born in Toronto Canada on March 10, 1941. Available records indicate that he attended West Pembroke school, Hamilton, Bermuda, and later Roosevelt HS. Larry joined the Air Force on Mar 26, 1959 serving as an Airman 2nd class, and was honorably discharged on Dec. 10, 1962. Following his military service he worked at miscellaneous jobs including that of a laborer. Richardson was appointed to the Y.P.D. on Sept. 9, 1964 while residing at 2 Cottage Pl., Gardens. The starting salary at the time was $5,500 a year. Probationary PO Richardson and his recruit class were sent to the NYC Police Academy for basic recruit training scheduled to run from Oct. 5, 1964 through Feb. 5, 1965. However, prior to his appointment to the Y.P.D. he had also taken the police test for the NYPD. And much to his surprise, right in middle of his police academy training he was called for appointment to the NYPD. After only three months as a Yonkers recruit Lawrence Richardson resigned from the YPD on Dec. 9, 1964 to join the NYPD. It is said that he completed 23 years before he retired and then went on to be hired as the Assistant Director of Security for the National Basketball Association.

PO VITO PARISI #419

APPOINTED: September 9, 1964
RETIRED: October 3, 1980

Vito Parisi was born in New York City on March 1, 1941. Vito attended Annunciation boys school, St. Margaret's school at 259th St. in NYC, and graduated from DeWitt Clinton high school in New York City. Following his graduation from high school Vito joined the Air Force on August 27, 1958. He served as an airman 2nd class with the SAC 817th Medical Group, and later was trained at dental school while in the Air Force. Parisi received his honorable discharge on June 4, 1962. Following his military service Vito worked as a salesman for the Dugan Bakery Company.

Vito Parisi received his appointment to the police department on September 9, 1964 while living at 131 Scott Avenue in Yonkers. He attended the police academy recruit school for basic recruit training then located in Iona College. When the academy training was completed he was assigned to the 2nd precinct on patrol duty earning a starting salary of $5,500 a year. On January 1, 1971 the 2nd precinct was re-designated and renamed the South Patrol Command, and on April 15, 1971 PO Parisi was detailed to patrol duties in a special enforcement squad in that command. Later that year, on October 19, 1971, PO Parisi was transferred to the Special Operations Division assigned to the Tactical Patrol Force which was tasked to address special complaint areas throughout the city. On June 23, 1972 PO Parisi was transferred to the North command for precinct patrol duty. He remained in the North command on radio call patrol until July 9, 1979 when he was reassigned to the northeast patrol command and detailed to the Training Unit as an instructor for new recruits and to regular in-service training for police officers.

PO Vito Parisi retired on an accidental disability on October 3, 1980 and shortly thereafter began working as a driver on an 18 wheel truck for Grand Union. He drove for them for several years and then moved his family to Knoxville, Tennessee.

PO JOHN B. WEISE #402

APPOINTED: September 9, 1964
RETIRED: September 19, 1986

John Weise was born on October 2, 1942 in Phillipsburg NJ. Jackie, or Jack as he was known, moved to Yonkers while he was a young boy. He attended PS # 6, Longfellow Junior high school, and graduated from Saunders high school having learned a trade in auto mechanics. Following school Jack joined the Navy on August 29, 1960 serving as a seaman aboard the USS Boston, a guided missile cruiser. His duty was the ship's captain's aide and driver when in port and Jack called it the best duty he ever had. Weise served overseas in many different ports including Italy.

Jack developed a service related lung problem while in the Navy which ultimately resulted in an Honorable/Medical discharge and a military disability pension. He received his honorable discharge on October 2, 1962. Prior to the YPD, Jack worked for Hollow taxi service on Riverdale Avenue as a driver. And prior to his appointment to the police department the Yonkers Civil Service Commission initially denied his eligibility for appointment because of his disability discharge, even though he had passed all physical and agility tests. Weise had to contact the Navy Dept. to intercede, which they did, and he was hired.

Jack was appointed to the Yonkers Police Department on September 9, 1964 while living at 120 High Street. He attended the Police Academy recruit school for basic recruit training located in Iona College. When the academy training was completed he was assigned to the 1st precinct on foot patrol duty earning $5,500 a year. The following year, on January 24, 1966, Jack was transferred to the Traffic Division working in the motorcycle unit. On January 1, 1971, following the reorganization of various units within the police department, the traffic unit was decentralized and all officers were transferred to patrol commands. At that time PO Weise was reassigned to the North command but continued to perform his duty as a motorcycle officer as part of a special enforcement squad. Later that year, on October 19, 1971, Jack Weiss was transferred back to traffic duties in the Special Operations Division as part of the Tactical Patrol Force. But he was still riding his motorcycle.

When Jack started to plan his retirement he decided to spend his final years working in a patrol command. And so it was, on September 7, 1984 upon his own request, he was transferred from the Traffic Division to the north patrol command on routine patrol duties. PO John Weiss retired from Yonkers Police Dept. on September 19, 1986.

Throughout most of Jack's career he had been a member of the Teamsters local 456 and during his off-duty time often drove a tow truck to make extra money. Many years later Jack would obtain a job which he referred to as the best job he ever held. That job was working for a professional NASCAR racing driver driving the man's mobile house trailer throughout the country wherever races were taking place. His home was on the road and he loved it.

PO JAMES W. CURTIS #420

APPOINTED: September 9, 1964
RESIGNED: January 9, 1970

James Curtis was born in the City of Yonkers on November 4, 1940. As a youth he attended PS#16, Gorton high school, and graduated from Commerce high school. A short time after graduating from school James joined the Army on October 8, 1959 serving as a Specialist 4th class. He received his honorable discharge on February 2, 1962. Following his military service James gained employment working for Con Edison in Valhalla as a Lineman. But with his grandfather, Capt. William Crough, having been a part of the Yonkers Police Department, Jimmy took the civil service test for patrolman.

James was appointed to the Yonkers Police Department on September 9, 1964 while living at 26 Arthur St. Also appointed a police officer on that same day was his brother Gerald Curtis. Probationary police officer James Curtis and his recruit class were sent to the New York City Police Academy for basic recruit training. This intensive physical and academic training ran from October 5, 1964 through February 5, 1965. Upon graduation, PO Curtis was assigned to foot patrol duty in the 4th precinct earning a starting salary of $5,500 a year.

Four months later, on June 18, 1965, Curtis was reassigned to foot patrol in the 1st precinct located at 10 St. Casimir Avenue. However, the following year, on November 9, 1966 Curtis was reassigned back to the 4th precinct on patrol duties and for a few years was trained and assigned to work in the Emergency Services Unit.

In the late 1960s Curtis took the civil service exam for Yonkers Firefighter, passed, and was called for appointment to the fire department. As a result PO James Curtis resigned from the Yonkers Police Department on January 9, 1970 and was appointed a Yonkers firefighter.

Although he was now in the fire department, on May 25, 1970, James Curtis was awarded a Class 3 Commendation, retroactive to October 1969 when he was a police officer, for his first aid efforts to revive a man who later died from stab wounds on Oct. 7, 1969 at his home. At that time Curtis had quickly gathered preliminary information which several hours later led to the capture of two murder suspects in New Jersey.

Curtis worked "the line" in the YFD fighting fires for many years and rose to the rank of Lieutenant. Later in his career he served in the arson squad as an investigator and retired from that position. Curtis, who served several years as president of the Fire Departments Holy Name Society, was a well-liked man by everyone in both the police and fire departments. He had a very outgoing and friendly personality which led him to be the center of attraction when he walked into a room. He had great Irish wit and was always utilized as the master of ceremonies at various functions.

Though he was very successful working for the fire department Jim always wished he had remained a police officer.

PO MICHAEL P. LEONARD #409

APPOINTED: September 9, 1964
RESIGNED: November 18, 1965

Michael Leonard was born in the Bronx NY on Feb. 15, 1939. Young Michael attended St. Peter and Paul parochial school in the Bronx, and St. Brendan's also in the Bronx. He would later graduate from St. Anne's Academy in NYC in 1958. Mike joined the Marine Corps on July 1, 1958 and was honorably discharged as a Corporal on June 30, 1961. Following his discharge Mike worked for the Dept. of Corrections in the Bronx House of detention as a corrections officer. Michael Leonard, who stood 6' 3" tall, received his appointment to the Y.P.D. on Sept 9, 1964 while residing at 141 Lake Ave. in Yonkers. His brother Bill Leonard had been appointed a police officer the year before. Leonard and his recruit class were sent to the NYC Police Academy for basic recruit training. This intensive physical and academic training ran from Oct. 5, 1964 through Feb. 4, 1965. Upon graduation, PO Leonard was assigned to foot patrol duty in the 4th pct earning $5,500 a year. When Mike was appointed he was single and married shortly thereafter. Although it was apparent from the beginning that Mike Leonard was a good cop and well like by all, Michael Leonard resigned from the Yonkers Police Department on November 18, 1965 for personal reasons.

PO JOHN T. NEIDER #410

APPOINTED: September 9, 1964
RETIRED: March 7, 1986

John T. Neider was born in Yonkers on June 18, 1937. He attended St. Joseph's elementary school and graduated from Gorton HS. Following school John worked a variety of different jobs until Aug. 21, 1961 when he joined the Army and received special training and served both as an MP and with the Canine Corps. He was discharged as a Corporal on Aug. 20, 1963. Following his military John worked for Otis Elevator Co. as a time checker right up to the Y.P.D. Neider was appointed to the YPD on Sept. 9, 1964 while residing at 246 Woodworth Ave. He attended the Police Academy recruit school for basic recruit training in Iona College. Following graduation he was assigned to the 3rd precinct on foot patrol duty earning a starting salary of $5,500 a year. On January 1, 1971, following a major precinct centralization plan, PO John Neider was reassigned to the South Command working radio car patrol. However, for the last several years that he was on the job, John was assigned as a desk officer. He remained in that assignment right up to his retirement on March 7, 1986.

PO ANTHONY T. TROIA #413

APPOINTED: September 9, 1964
RESIGNED: June 16, 1972

Anthony Troia was born in the City of Yonkers on November 16, 1942. He attended St. Mary's elementary school, PS# 19, Hawthorne Jr. High school, and graduated from Saunders high school. Tony joined the Army National Guard on January 24, 1962 serving in a military police company in Mount Vernon. He completed his active duty service in July of 1962 and was honorably discharged from the reserves in 1967. While serving in the Army Reserve, and prior to the YPD, Troia worked as a mail carrier for the US Post Office.

Anthony was appointed to the Yonkers Police Department on September 9, 1964 while residing at 33 Highland Ave. Probationary police officer Troia and his recruit class were sent to the New York City Police Academy for basic recruit training. This intensive physical and academic training ran from October 5, 1964 through February 5, 1965. Upon graduation, PO Troia was assigned to foot patrol duty in the 3rd precinct earning a starting salary of $5,500 a year.

Very early in his career PO Troia was responsible for the arrest of a bank robbery suspect but never received any credit for it. It occurred in July of 1965 when the bank was held up in the Fleetwood section of Yonkers and a description of the vehicle along with the license plate number was obtained. The very next day Troia and his partner observed a vehicle fitting that description parked in front of the bank at Kimball Avenue and McLean Avenue. He knew he had the suspect vehicle and called for detectives and a sergeant. As the suspect exited the bank Troia pointed him out but the sergeant said, it's probably not him, let him go. But before he did he obtained the identification of the suspect and later turned that information over to the detectives. A week later the FBI thanked the detectives for the info that led to the arrest of that very same man for bank robbery. Officer Troia never received any credit for that arrest.

Troia was assigned to walking foot posts and patrolling in a radio car for several years. And on one occasion he was awarded a departmental Commendation on January 24, 1967 for a burglary arrest he made along with his partner Tom Ferguson. But in the late 1960s he was assigned to work in the 3rd precinct warrant squad locating wanted individuals and taking them into custody. On January 1, 1971, following the implementation of a precinct decentralization plan whereby two precincts were closed and the remaining two were renamed, Troia was reassigned to the former 2nd precinct, which had been renamed the South patrol command.

It was about this same time that he had taken the civil service examination for Yonkers Firefighter. He scored high on the exam and was called for appointment with the Yonkers Fire Department. And so, PO Anthony Troia resigned from the Yonkers Police Department on June 16, 1972 and was appointed a Yonkers Firefighter. Over the years Tony rose through the ranks in the Y.F.D. and achieved the rank of Assistant Chief. He was also very active in the Yonkers Fire Officers Association.

Assistant Chief Troia retired from the fire department in February of 2000 after 35 years of combined service to the police department and fire department. For several years after retirement Tony drove a school bus in the mornings but still enjoyed playing golf. In addition to his home in Fishkill New York he also has a winter home in South Carolina. His brother in law is Ret YFD Assistant Chief Paul Naef.

DET. LT. FRANCIS C. FERNANDES #40

APPOINTED: September 9, 1964
RETIRED: February 22, 1985

Francis Carl Fernandes was born on October 4, 1936 in Yonkers, New York while his family lived at 112 Ashburton Ave. He grew up as a youth living at 143 Nepperhan Ave. where he attended St. Casimir's Roman Catholic elementary school, Benjamin Franklin Junior high school, and later graduated from Saunders high school in 1954. Several years later he also graduated from John Jay College of Criminal Justice in New York City with an Associate's degree and a Bachelor's Degree, both in criminal justice. Many years later he would graduate from the American Military University (AMU) with a Master's degree in Military Science.

Prior to the YPD Frank had been employed as a car salesman for Curry Chevrolet on Central Park Avenue in Scarsdale. Having taken and passed the civil service test for Yonkers Patrolman, Frank received his appointment to the Yonkers Police Department on August 12, 1964 while residing at 80 Kimball Terrace. Probationary police officer Fernandes and his recruit class were sent to the New York City Police Academy for basic recruit training. This intensive physical and academic training ran from October 5, 1964 through February 5, 1965. Upon graduation, Patrolman Fernandes was assigned to patrol duty in the 2nd precinct earning a starting salary of $5,500 a year.

On January 24, 1966 police officer Fernandes was transferred to the Traffic Division assigned to two wheeled motorcycle patrol. He remained in this assignment for five years until December 1, 1970 when he was reassigned to serve as the Police Department's Traffic Safety Officer.

Frank was promoted to the rank of Sergeant on December 10, 1971 earning a salary of $13,685 a year and was allowed to remain assigned as a supervisor in the Traffic Division. He continued his duties as the Traffic Safety Officer with additional duties as liaison to the school crossing guards and to the Parking Enforcement Unit.

On February 18, 1977 Sgt. Fernandes was transferred to the Detective Division as a detective sergeant supervising a squad of detectives. During his time as a detective supervisor Sgt. Fernandes was involved in the investigations of many serious crimes. But none more serious than those committed by a man who was known as the "Son of Sam." Over a 13 month period, beginning in 1976 and into 1977, this self-proclaimed "Son of Sam" had been responsible for a string of handgun execution style shootings in NYC that left seven young people dead and seven others critically wounded. Following a lengthy and intense investigation by both the NYPD and the YPD the shooter, whose real name was David Berkowitz, was arrested at his home in Yonkers on August 10, 1977. During the arrest process Det Sgt Fernandes booked Berkowitz, read him his Miranda warning rights, and personally conducted the initial interview before turning him over to the NYPD personnel. Following the conclusion of this investigation Det Sgt Fernandes along with several other officers, was awarded a City of Yonkers citation commending them for their investigative work leading up to the arrest of David Berkowitz, aka, "The Son of Sam."

On July 7, 1980 Sgt. Fernandes was promoted to the rank of police Lieutenant earning $26,411 a year and was reassigned as a supervisor in the Communications Division. The following year, on

Det Lt. Francis C. Fernandes #40 (cont.)

February 17, 1981 Lt Fernandes was transferred to the North Patrol Command as a Zone Lieutenant on patrol.

On October 28, 1983 Lt. Fernandes was reassigned as the commanding officer of the Intelligence Unit, later renamed the Special Investigations Unit, as a detective lieutenant. This unit was considered an elite assignment which handled very sensitive and unusual investigations as well as dignitary protection. During his tenure in SIU, Det Lt Fernandes, along with others from the YPD Narcotics Unit, conducted an investigation that led to an arrest in South Yonkers for possession of 50 kilos of uncut cocaine along with the seizure of $165,000 in cash which was derived from drug sales. It was later determined that the cocaine had a street value of over $25 million. It was considered, at that time, one of the largest drug recoveries of its type in the New York metropolitan area.

Detective Lt Francis Fernandes retired from the Yonkers Police Department on February 22, 1985. Known to his friends as “Fran,” and whose brother Joseph had served as the Yonkers police Commissioner, Frank worked from 1986 to 1996 as a commercial pilot for Continental Express Airlines. His flying career started when he was in high school taking lessons at a seaplane facility in Dobbs Ferry, New York. He continued to fly private aircraft while in the military and while a member of the YPD. During this period he owned and operated several private airplanes. He was a member/instructor at the West Point Military Academy Aero Club located at Stewart Airport, Newburgh, NY. Frank retired from the airlines in October of 1996 with over 6000 of both private and commercial logged hours.

Running concurrently with his police career was his military career. Frank Fernandes’s military career spanned over a 40 year period. It began in 1955 and ended in 1996 when he retired. He completed tours in the U.S. Air Force, the U.S. Air Force Reserve and the New York Air National Guard. He enlisted as an Aircraft Mechanic, then upgraded to Flight Mechanic, then to Flight Engineer. He accrued over 7000 hours of global flight time while assigned to the above positions. During this period he flew missions supporting the European Airlift in 1960, the Cuban Missile Crisis in 1962, the Vietnam War in 1963 and the Gulf War in 1990.

While serving from 1955 to 1974 he attained the rank of E-7, Master Sergeant. On June 15, 1974 he was awarded a commission to the rank of Captain. Subsequently, he was promoted to Major, to Lt. Colonel, and ultimately retired as a full Colonel. His last military assignment prior to retirement was commanding officer of the 105th Logistics Squadron, NY Air National Guard, Stewart Air Base, in Newburgh, New York. His medals include but not limited to: the Meritorious Medal and the Vietnam Service Medal.

From 1996 to 2004 Frank was hired by the Northwest Florida State College as a part-time instructor teaching courses in the criminal justice department and also in the police academy. And from 2004 through 2008 he worked for a subcontractor of the Federal Bureau of Prisons as a director of a 96 bed halfway house facility in Tampa, Florida.

Ret Det Lt Francis C. Fernandes is now retired and currently resides in sunny Florida.

DET. VINCENT J. PATALANO #697

APPOINTED: September 9, 1964
RETIRED: May 28, 1987

Vincent Patalano was born in the N.Y.C. on May 20, 1933. He moved with his family to Westchester as a youth and attended St. Augustine's elementary school in Ossining N.Y., Ossining Junior HS, and graduated from Ossining HS. Vinnie was very athletic and loved to play softball and football throughout school. He would later continue to play softball on the PBA softball team. Shortly after graduation Vinnie joined the Air Force on July 27, 1952 and served as an airman 1st class in the Emergency Crash and Rescue Unit. He received his honorable discharge on July 19, 1956. Following his military service he worked for the Pleasantville Instrument Company.

Vincent J. Patalano received his appointment to the Yonkers Police Department on Sept. 9, 1964 while residing at 49 Aqueduct St. in Ossining NY. Probationary police officer Patalano and his recruit class were sent to the NYC Police Academy for basic recruit training where the intensive physical and academic training ran from Oct. 5, 1964 through Feb. 5, 1965. Upon graduation, PO Patalano was assigned to foot patrol duty in the 4th precinct earning a starting salary of $5,500 a year.

On November 9, 1966, following a department wide reorganization of personnel due to the opening of a new 1st precinct building on East Grassy Sprain Road, PO Patalano was transferred to patrol duty in the 3rd precinct located at 36 Radford Street working in a radio car with then PO James Bubbico. Four years later, on January 1, 1971, following the implementation of a precinct centralization plan whereby the first and the 3rd precincts were closed as precincts and the 2nd and 4th were renamed the South and North Patrol Commands, Patalano was reassigned to the South Command on Central Park Avenue.

On July 1, 1980 Vinnie was assigned to the auto theft detail in the South Command working a steady midnight tour in plainclothes with special attention to the Bronx River Road area to curtail auto thefts. During this time he rode with PO Richard Isser and they both worked closely with the citywide Street Crime Unit personnel.

Having developed an excellent reputation as an active, aggressive and productive police officer, on May 13, 1981 officer Patalano was appointed a Detective working in the Detective Division. While serving as a detective in the Detective Division Patalano investigated a multitude of crimes and arresting the responsible persons. But to him, nothing would compare to one particular murder investigation.

On February 24, 1985 Westchester County police officer Gary Stymilosky was brutally murdered execution style while sitting in his patrol car. The murder occurred in Yonkers and Vincent Patalano and his partner were assigned to investigate. During this very intense and difficult investigation it was learned that the person responsible not only had escaped, but had kidnaped a female, later killed her, and drove her car to upstate New York and across the border into Toronto, Canada. Det Patalano identified the subject as Alexander Mengel and following good police work traced him to Canada. Within a week's time, on March 2, 1985, Mengel was arrested. Being responsible for investigating the killing of a police officer is an awesome responsibility, matched only by the satisfaction when the person responsible is brought to justice. Which is exactly what Detective Patalano was able to accomplish.

Det. Patalano retired from the police department on May 28, 1987 and began working as a teamster driving a dump truck for three years. However, a few years later he moved to Ft. Lauderdale Florida enjoying retirement. He enjoyed softball, snorkeling and scuba diving for several years.

DEPUTY CHIEF GEORGE E. RUTLEDGE

APPOINTED: September 9, 1964
RETIRED: May 12, 2000

George Edward Rutledge was born July 25, 1941 in the northwest section of Yonkers N.Y. He attended PS# 6 and graduated from Saunders Trades and Technical H.S. with a trade in Electric Wiring. As a youth Rutledge was interested in sports and as a result for several years played on the basketball team for St John's Church in Getty Square. Prior to becoming a police officer Rutledge worked five years for the Otis Elevator Company as a "Wireman" installing the electric wiring circuitry for elevator controllers. It was around this same time period that he studied and practiced the art of Karate, competing in several semi-contact competitions where he earned a Brown Belt. It was during these matches that he received several injuries and decided to discontinue the sport. In 1961 he enlisted in the U.S. Marine Corps Reserve.

Deputy Chief George E. Rutledge (cont.)

Shortly after graduating from boot camp at Parris Island, South Carolina, he married his childhood sweetheart, Arline in 1962. He was appointed to the Yonkers police department in 1964. After completing his military enlistment he was honorably discharged with the rank of Lance Corporal.

Following his appointment to the police department on Sept 9, 1964 he and his recruit class were sent to the NYC Police Academy for basic recruit training. This intensive physical and academic training ran from October 5, 1964 through February 5, 1965. Police Officer Rutledge graduated #1 in his class with the highest overall class average. In recognition of this accomplishment he was presented with an off duty .38 cal. 2" barrel Colt "Agent" revolver by the Captains, Lieutenants & Sergeants Association president, Captain John Kennedy.

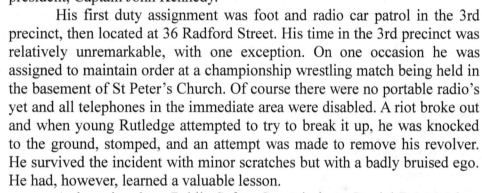

His first duty assignment was foot and radio car patrol in the 3rd precinct, then located at 36 Radford Street. His time in the 3rd precinct was relatively unremarkable, with one exception. On one occasion he was assigned to maintain order at a championship wrestling match being held in the basement of St Peter's Church. Of course there were no portable radio's yet and all telephones in the immediate area were disabled. A riot broke out and when young Rutledge attempted to try to break it up, he was knocked to the ground, stomped, and an attempt was made to remove his revolver. He survived the incident with minor scratches but with a badly bruised ego. He had, however, learned a valuable lesson.

A short time later Public Safety Commissioner Daniel F. McMahon formed the "Intelligence Unit" which was established with a primary purpose to monitor organized crime activities in Yonkers. Due to the need for a relatively unknown officer for undercover work, and because of his police academy record, Rutledge was chosen by then Public Safety Commissioner Daniel F. McMahon and assigned to this unit in 1965. Over the years officer Rutledge was trained in covert photographic surveillance, dark room negative processing and photo printing, was one of only a few trusted and trained in the installation of Electronic Telephonic Surveillance (Wire Taps) and distinguished himself as an expert in investigating and having detailed knowledge of Organized Crime and it's criminal activity in Yonkers. Having volunteered to work the Organized Crime section Rutledge ultimately became recognized as an expert in organized crime activities and their members in Westchester County.

In fact, in December of 1969, Rutledge observed a well-known organized crime figure known to many violate his probation while attending hearings by the NY State Investigation Commission in Yonkers City Hall. As a result of his reporting his observations he was subpoenaed to testify in the United States District Court, Southern

Deputy Chief George E. Rutledge (cont.)

District of New York, regarding the mans violation. This man was a well-known, dangerous and long-time organized crime figure who had many people with criminal records who worked for him. When called to testify as to what he observed in Yonkers, Rutledge did so, but also was able to point out to the court a number of organized crime associates sitting in the courtroom spread out in various locations. It was obvious to Rutledge that they were there to intimidate other witnesses who were scheduled to testify against the defendant. As a result of Rutledge's testimony the defendant was convicted and sentenced to a term of two years in federal prison.

Subsequent to the trial, on October 16, 1970, a letter was sent by the US Federal Probation Office to Rutledge's commanding officer which read in part; "*Investigator Rutledge was a splendid witness. He added immeasurable strength to our case against the defendant, Frank Sacco, by his ready ability to identify, by name, a number of the defendant's cohorts who had the temerity to attend the hearing. Their presence, we were very much aware, was to serve as a threatening force against a number of frightened witnesses the government had subpoenaed to testify. We particularly want to express our thanks for the splendid aid rendered by Investigator George Rutledge. He is a credit to a fine unit within a fine department.*" On July 1, 1971 Rutledge was appointed a detective.

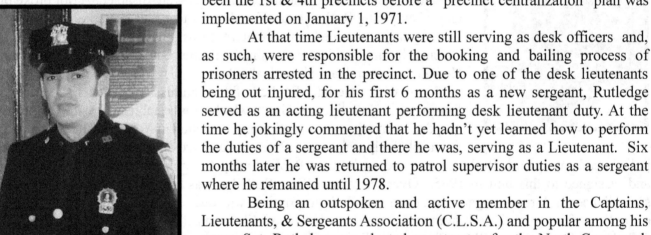

On October 27, 1972 Det. Rutledge was promoted to Sergeant and was reassigned to patrol duties in the "North Command." This command comprised the northern half of the city; that which had prior been the 1st & 4th precincts before a "precinct centralization" plan was implemented on January 1, 1971.

At that time Lieutenants were still serving as desk officers and, as such, were responsible for the booking and bailing process of prisoners arrested in the precinct. Due to one of the desk lieutenants being out injured, for his first 6 months as a new sergeant, Rutledge served as an acting lieutenant performing desk lieutenant duty. At the time he jokingly commented that he hadn't yet learned how to perform the duties of a sergeant and there he was, serving as a Lieutenant. Six months later he was returned to patrol supervisor duties as a sergeant where he remained until 1978.

Being an outspoken and active member in the Captains, Lieutenants, & Sergeants Association (C.L.S.A.) and popular among his peers, Sgt. Rutledge was elected as a trustee for the North Command, and sometime later was elected as Chairman of the Board of Trustees for the C.L.S.A. This latest position allowed him to serve on the executive board of the association. Of course all association business and activities were conducted during off duty hours so as not to interfere with his uniform patrol duties. After some convincing to run and a brief campaign, on January 1, 1978, Rutledge was elected to a one year term as president of the C.L.S.A. He was only the 2nd sergeant in the association's history to be honored in this way. The presidency was usually occupied by a captain or a lieutenant. The following year he was easily re-elected for a second term. During his first term in 1978 he co-founded the annual Old Timers Picnic, which for the first time brought retirees from all over the country back together in September each year to enjoy each other's company. It was also during 1978 that Sgt. Rutledge began his collection of Yonkers police memorabilia.

Deputy Chief George E. Rutledge (cont.)

Later, in 1979, this would lead him to establish the first Yonkers Police Museum in a small isolated room in police headquarters. The exhibit consisted almost entirely of his own collection and some donated items. He was allowed to use a room but there was absolutely no funding provided. For his efforts, Sgt. Rutledge was given the honorary title of Department Historian. In 1979 during his 2nd term as the C.L.S.A. president, and although considered a popular leader, Rutledge became dissatisfied conducting C.L.S.A. business and the requirement of dealing with politicians on a full time basis. In addition his father became terminally ill and he felt he could not devote all the time necessary to fulfill his responsibilities as president. He also missed the camaraderie he experienced while in uniform. As a result he voluntarily gave up his elected position mid-year to return to patrol duties in the North Command.

In February of 1981 Sgt. Rutledge and Lt. Martin Harding were both transferred to H.Q. and instructed to organized the first "Inspections Unit" which would monitor the efficiency of the operation of all units, commands, precincts and divisions within the department. In May of 1981, after organizing and making this unit operational, Sgt. Rutledge was selected by P.C. Charles P. Connolly to be the new Commanding Officer of the police plainclothes "Street Crime Unit." This highly respected and elite unit was charged with reducing street level crimes such as robberies, burglaries, muggings, larcenies, flim flams, prostitution, etc. After over two years of maintaining a high unit arrest record, on June 13, 1983 Sgt. Rutledge was reassigned to the Youth Division as an investigative supervisor.

On February 17, 1984 Sgt. Rutledge was promoted to the rank of Lieutenant and was assigned as a "watch commander" or supervising patrol lieutenant in the 2nd precinct.

He performed this duty working a rotating work schedule known then as the "clock" for one year and on April 1, 1985 he was reassigned back to the Youth Division, this time as the Executive Officer. In addition to his second in command administrative responsibilities and his supervision of all youth investigations, he also monitored and facilitated the implementation of all PAL programs that were provided for youths throughout the city.

Due to a vacancy created by the retirement of D.C. Anthony Tocco, on November 30, 1989 Lt. Rutledge was promoted to the rank of Captain and was again returned to patrol duties, this time as the citywide "Duty Captain." His working schedule was a combination of day and early tours. It was during this time that he instituted the after action critiquing of critical tactical incidents, having all personnel involved present, with officer safety and training being his primary concern.

As part of a reorganization of upper police management officers, nearly a year later, on October 1, 1990, Capt. Rutledge was

Deputy Chief George E. Rutledge (cont.)

reassigned by the new Police Commissioner Robert K. Olson to be placed in command of the Training Division. He had hoped to be put in command of the Detective Division but it was not to be. At least not yet. In addition to the regular training of new recruit classes and the continuous in- service training for the entire department, Rutledge instituted many new training programs within the department. They included; starting the changeover training of all personnel from the standard .38 caliber S&W revolver to the "Glock" semi-automatic pistol; forming and training a department wide Disorder Control Task Force; researched and made recommendations that laid the groundwork for the "DARE" program; etc.

However, again wanting to return closer to the patrol function, and after learning that the 1st precinct captain, George Pojer, was retiring, Rutledge requested, and was granted assignment as the commanding officer of the 1st precinct on April 26, 1991. It was during this time that the new "steady tour" working schedule was first instituted within the department. Due to the retirement of another captain, in addition to being the C.O. of the 1st Precinct, on March 20 1992 Capt. Rutledge was designated Acting C.O. of the Special Operations Division (SOD) as well. This Division consisted of the Traffic/Motorcycle Unit, the K-9 Unit, Truck Weight Enforcement Unit, Abandoned Auto Unit, and the Hack Inspection's Unit.

During this same time the departments Emergency Services Unit had been decentralized into working from the precincts, its personnel were demoralized, short of equipment and training, and in a state of disorganization. Capt. Rutledge persuasively argued to his deputy chief that if "ESU" were allowed to be "centralized" under his Special Operations Division, he was convinced he would return the units pride and effectiveness. His recommendation was acted upon and on July 1, 1992 ESU was merged with SOD. Sensing the challenge inherent in commanding such a diverse and specialized patrol unit, Rutledge requested to be assigned as full time commander of SOD. Less than a month later on July 22, 1992 Capt. Rutledge was transferred from being the CO of the 1st Pct, to commanding officer of this new, large, and complex Special Operations Division (SOD.)

After taking command of SOD, not only was the ESU ultimately brought back to a well-organized, trained, equipped, and highly motivated unit, but a renewed pride was also returned to the other units within SOD. Under Rutledge's command the Emergency Service Unit ordered and received new suburban and box style trucks with storage compartments configured for newly acquired equipment. Some of the equipment received were Ballistic rated Body Armor, Ballistic helmets, MP-5 sub-machine guns, new Body Bunker Shields, Sniper Rifles with training for designated snipers, French Barricades, updated repelling gear, cold water training and rescue suits, barricade and hostage rescue training, Concussion grenades, and Smoke grenades, and more. Through the captain's efforts, ESU received an armored vehicle known as the "Peace Keeper" from the military at no cost to the city, and tactical training for critical incidents such as barricade and hostage taking was given a high priority.

Deputy Chief George E. Rutledge (cont.)

Yonkers Police Emergency Services became recognized as the foremost experts in their field throughout all of Westchester County. In fact, due to their reputation, Rutledge received requests and approved training requests by other police departments in Westchester and NYC. ESU had become the elite unit he had promised it would be.

Captain Rutledge was always confident in what he felt was his ability to build morale and thereby, get the job done. He would often say, "*You lead from the front and by example.*" On most motorcycle details you would see the captain on his department issue Harley Davidson, leading the formation. While in command of SOD the division also received new motorcycles with ground breaking bright new color decal graphics, computer mobile data terminals in traffic enforcement vehicles, hand held laser radar units, and Portable DWI Breath Analyzers. Recognizing the need within the Detective Division he also instituted an Accident Investigation Unit with specialized training for motor vehicle accidents with near or actual fatalities to determine cause or culpability, if any.

The utilization of police motorcycles is a very effective, but dangerous tool. The captain knew it was of utmost importance to encourage safety. So, for the very first time, in 1993 the Yonkers Traffic Unit sponsored and hosted the annual "New York State Metro area Motorcycle Safety Rodeo Competition." Many local police departments as well as from out of state sent their riders to compete. It was a great success on many levels and became an annual event.

On March 17, 1995 Captain Albert McEvoy was sworn into office as the Yonkers Police Commissioner. On that same day, due to Capt. Rutledge's previous experience as a young detective in the criminal intelligence field, he was promoted to Detective Captain, transferred from Special Operations, and placed in command of the Special Investigation Division. This small but elite unit consisted of a group of detectives who were specially trained to conduct a variety of unique and highly sensitive investigations. Included in these were, organized crime activities and violations, European burglary gangs, street gangs and cults, official corruption by city employees, upper level employee background investigations, dignitary protection, etc.

On October 6, 1995 Pope John Paul the 2nd visited the City of Yonkers. Prior to his visit Det. Capt. Rutledge and his unit trained and worked very closely with the U.S. Secret Service in planning, coordinating and conducting "up close" security training during the Pope's visit. Virtually hundreds of uniformed and plainclothes officers were utilized to manage thousands of visitors and worshipers. The tight security measures put in place resulted in the discovery and arrest of a male entering the area with a unauthorized handgun. Because the police commissioner placed a great deal of importance on the security and autonomy necessary for this unit to operate effectively, Det. Capt. Rutledge reported on the activities of his unit directly to the police commissioner, and to no one else.

On May 8, 1997 Rutledge was again reassigned, this time to what some consider the jewel of police work. He was placed in command of the prestigious Detective Division. This high profile operation consisted of 70 of the department's best personnel, both sworn and civilian. The units under his direction were the General Assignment detective squads which investigated all felony crimes, the Burglary Squad, the Narcotics Squad, the Criminal Identification and Crime Scene Unit, and the Forensic Laboratory. During his first two years, under his close direction and supervision, his detectives investigated 15 to 20 homicides per year, averaging an 85 % clearance rate. Being a "hands on" type

Deputy Chief George E. Rutledge (cont.)

manager, Det. Capt. Rutledge directed his detective supervisors to keep him abreast of the progress of all major investigations. If a homicide occurred in the middle of the night, regardless of the hour, his orders were to notify him immediately and he would personally respond to the scene within minutes to oversee the preliminary stages of the investigation. He would also monitor investigative progress by holding frequent staff meetings with detective supervisors.

Over many years the captain had earned the respect of local, county, state, and federal law enforcement agencies. His reputation of integrity and his experience enabled him to work very closely with the District Attorney's office in the investigation and prosecution of major crimes. And as he was regularly designated the departments official spokesman he also enjoyed that same respect when dealing with the news media by his professional approach and honesty.

Captain Rutledge, had for some time, believed that the police department handled its ceremonial details in somewhat of a casual manner. He believed what was needed was an Honor Guard and a Color Guard with specially trained and chosen volunteers who could be counted on to present a professional appearance when the need arose. On February 12, 1998 Rutledge sent out a notice requesting volunteers to meet later that month on the 26th. Many turned out for the meeting and at that time the "new" Yonkers Police Honor Guard/Color Guard was officially established and Capt. Rutledge was unanimously voted as the unit's leader. During off duty hours the captain then organized this group of volunteers, and personally began training these officers in the manual of arms, military drill, and the proper protocols when handling funeral and parade details, etc. The unit spirit was very high and the results were worth the effort.

Following the retirement of Deputy Chief John Duffy, and a lengthy period of time where his position remained vacant, on October 15, 1999 Detective Captain George Rutledge was officially sworn in as a Deputy Chief by Police Commissioner Joseph Cassino. Rutledge had always felt very close to the men and women who wore the police uniform so it was no surprise that it was on his own request that the Chief was placed in command of the Field Services Bureau which was responsible for all patrol operations, nearly 450 uniformed and plainclothes personnel, and an annual patrol operations budget of nearly 25 million dollars.

In the early spring Commissioner Cassino announced he would retire on April 13, 2000. Speculation began as to who would be the new Police Commissioner. It was expected that of the three deputy chiefs one would certainly be selected to be the new police commissioner. Shortly after announcing his retirement plans Comm. Cassino called Chief Rutledge to his office and told him that during a pre-retirement meeting with the mayor, he was advised that the mayor had told him, "*George Rutledge is a good man. I like him. We'll go with him.*" Commissioner Cassino told Chief Rutledge, "*You're going to get a phone call from the mayor so be prepared to give an answer because he's going to ask you if you want the commissioners job*." Aside from the mayor's favorable opinion of Chief Rutledge becoming common knowledge, it was believed throughout the department by many that Rutledge was going to be the next Police Commissioner. They were all wrong.

On April 5, 2000, Mayor John Spencer really surprised the police department, in fact the entire

Deputy Chief George E. Rutledge (cont.)

community, by nominating his friend, PBA president Detective Charles A. Cola. The mayor never even considered or interviewed anyone else for the position. The mayor stated that Cola was "*the most qualified man for the job*." This was taken as an insult by the three deputy chiefs, including Rutledge, and all sixteen police captains who clearly had a much different opinion. Despite the turmoil, Charles Cola was confirmed by the city council and was sworn in as the new Police Commissioner on April 14, 2000. At the time, Deputy Chief Rutledge stated that he believed the selection process, actually the lack thereof, in which the choice was made, was likely an indication of the way many other issues would be addressed in the future. And that his nearly 36 years service and being a senior command level officer apparently meant little. After much deliberation he submitted his letter of intent to retire from the department effective the following month on May 12, 2000. The chief's request was granted by his new commissioner without an exit interview, a discussion, or even one question as to a reason for his abrupt decision.

On May 8th, four days before his retirement, Chief Rutledge requested and was granted permission to address all the members of the CLS Association at their monthly meeting. His intention was to thank all present for their cooperation over the years. The chief was stunned as he was escorted into the room whereupon he received a long standing ovation from the unusually large group of members. This was followed by individual congratulations and best wishes by almost every member who was present. When the room became quiet Chief Rutledge told the audience how grateful he was to receive such a warm welcome. He told them that he had mixed emotions about retiring, having served for nearly 36 years, but that he believed it was time. He reminded everyone that he had become a sergeant and member of the C.L.S.A. 28 years earlier in 1972; that he had been a Trustee, Chairman of the Board of Trustee's, and had the privilege of being the association's President. He thanked everyone for their cooperation, hard work, dedication, and especially their friendship. As he finished speaking the large group of captains, lieutenants, and sergeants again gave him a standing ovation.

On his last working day, Thursday May 11th, Chief Rutledge arrived for work, went directly to the Internal Affairs Division to pick up his new "Retired" identification card, and started toward the hallway leading down to his office. As he opened the door to the hall, he was greeted by an Honor Guard of captains and lieutenants, in full dress uniform, standing at attention on both sides of the corridor at "present arms." Beyond the honor guard was a large group of civilian employees and police officers cheering and clapping their hands. The chief was clearly taken by surprise. As he made his way through the group shaking hands, etc., he was so overwhelmed by such a tribute that he was unable to speak for several minutes. A reception followed in his now near empty office consisting of a variety of refreshments. He was then presented with a new Fax machine, as a parting gift, by his staff.

As the day came to a close Chief Rutledge was prepared to end his career with the police department. He was comfortable with the knowledge that he planned to continue to maintain the Police Museum and research the proud history of the department on a volunteer basis. He had also applied for, and received, a New York State Private Investigators License which he intended to use on a part time basis. It was late in the afternoon of this last day that he was summoned to Mayor John Spencer's office.

Deputy Chief George E. Rutledge (cont.)

It was there that the mayor congratulated him regarding his retirement and wished him well. It was at this time he was advised by the mayor that he, the mayor, also wanted the chief to continue his work with the Police Museum and researching the history of the police department, but he did not want him to do it on a volunteer basis any longer. Instead he wanted him to receive some type of compensation. It was then the chief was advised he had been approved to receive a "personal services contract" with the city for $17,000. a year, the maximum allowed by state law while still receiving a state pension, to continue this historical research. Rutledge graciously accepted the offer.

On June 16, 2000 a retirement party was held at the Manor House in Hastings N.Y. in honor of the retiring chief's commitment to his profession. A large crowd attended including the City Council President, several council members, a N.Y.S. Assemblyman, and a spokesman for the mayor who was out of town. Several city, county and state proclamations and resolutions honoring the retired chief's accomplishments were presented to him along with a letter of appreciation to the former chief from Governor George Pataki. A number of plaques were also presented. One in particular had all of the police shields the chief had earned; beginning with his silver police officer shield, right up to the gold and blue enameled Deputy Chief shield. Six shields in all mounted along with his police honor bars. Following the receipt of the many honorariums, the retired chief then addressed the audience. He said, ... *"What a fantastic night. Certainly one I'll never forget. But before I go any further, let me say thank you to all the members of tonight's committee and anyone else who has worked so hard to make this evening so special to me and my family. By the way, with me tonight is my wife Arline, my mother, my father in law, my brother Bill & his wife, my two daughters and their husbands, and several other members of my extended family. And, of course, my other family for nearly 36 years; all of you here tonight.*

"How do I find the words to describe what I'm feeling right now? Excitement, pride, humility, happiness; all these things and, at the same time, sadness. I believe I have been very fortunate to have had the opportunity to be a Yonkers police officer. From a "peg" post on Riverdale Avenue in 1965 right up to a few weeks ago as a chief. To quote a friend, over the years I have had a front row seat to the greatest show on earth. You name it, and you and I have seen it. And through it all we had a lot of laughs and made a lot of friends. And every minute I served as a police officer was with great pride in my profession. And now, nearly 36 years later, I truly don't know where the time went. And I'm not embarrassed to admit it; I love this job. If I had it to do over again I'd do it without hesitation. BUT, I can't. I had a good run, and I have only a few regrets. And now, for me, it's over. Knowing society's darkest secrets, the adrenaline rushes, the gun runs, lights and siren, the investigations, the ceremonies, pomp and circumstance, the snappy salutes in our dress uniform with honor bars and hash marks, ...all gone. I envy our new recruits because their career is just beginning and mine has just ended. Now I start a new phase in my life. But I'm not going anywhere. They can take my name off the roster but in my heart I'll always be a cop. I want to thank all of the men and women who worked with, and for me over the years, for making me look good. And I thank all of you for coming tonight. I'll always cherish my memories and your friendship. I would like to ask all my former colleagues for a favor. Despite your many frustrations with the job, always be proud of who you are and what you do. You ARE the finest. God Bless and Thank You !"

Deputy Chief George E. Rutledge (cont.)

Following his retirement Rutledge established his own private investigation and consulting business named, Personal Research Associates Inc. In addition to this new enterprise he also continued to research and write a reference book containing the names, photographs and police biographies of all who ever served with the YPD beginning in 1871.

Chief Rutledge always sought out new challenges and volunteered whenever there was a need. For several years throughout his career he willingly served as a fill in instructor for new police recruits at the departments police academy; for over ten years he served as the designated master of ceremonies at most official police functions; he volunteered and was utilized as the departments uniform formation coordinator where large numbers of police officers were gathered; served for several years as chairman of the awards committee; established and trained the Police Honor Guard, and also served on the uniform advisory committee. Everyone knew that if there was a question as to protocol, etc., just call Rutledge. In addition, for many years he served as the secretary of the Police Holy Name Society and was a long time member of the PAL Advisory Board. For many years Rutledge prepared an annual brochure entitled "Lest We Forget," which was distributed at the annual Holy Name Society Mass and Communion Breakfast, and which honored those police officers who had died during the previous 12 months. In 1990 Chief Rutledge also organized, established, and is president of the Yonkers Police Historical Society which was formed for those who wish to help research our department's history in an effort to ensure that all those who have served will never be forgotten. He still continues to do this research today. In researching the history of our department the chief identified 15 police officers who had died in the line of duty but who, over the years, had been completely forgotten by the department. Chief Rutledge worked with police memorial committees in Westchester County, New York State, and Washington D.C. and was successful in having the names of these 15 officers engraved on the Police Memorial Monuments that were erected in these three locations. He also served on the committee and assisted in the planning for the Yonkers Police and Fire Memorial which was ultimately constructed in Untermeyer Park. He was the first captain, not on patrol, to wear a uniform every day in the office; he recommended and was the first to wear light blue hash marks on the uniform sleeve; he was the first to wear the uniform name plate prior to official authorization. He was always looking for innovative ways to enhance the pride of the police officer.

Approximately 1992 Chief Rutledge began research to prepare a book which would include the name, photograph, and biography of every police officer who served with the Yonkers Police Department from its organization in 1871. His goal was, and still is, to ensure that all who had served our department would never be forgotten. Since that time he has made this book a reality by researching the information, locating photographs of the officers, and chronologically preparing each page with a personal biography of each officer up through the years. (This is that book.)

In April of 1996 Rutledge organized and chaired a police parade and department party celebrating the 125th anniversary of our department's organization. The event was a great success and generated a renewed feeling of pride among the rank and file. During the ceremony at H.Q. at which he was the Master of Ceremonies the Chief was surprised by being presented with framed proclamations and testimonials from the mayor, county and state representatives for his dedication to the police department.

Deputy Chief George E. Rutledge (cont.)

Police commissioner Donald Christopher then honored the Chief by authorizing the renaming of the Yonkers Police Museum, to the "George E. Rutledge Police Museum."

It is noteworthy that all of the special activities that Chief Rutledge had involved himself with was on a volunteer basis, on his own time, and in addition to his regular assigned police duties. Over his long and fascinating career, Chief Rutledge had accumulated several local and state proclamations and City Council resolutions of commendation, many engraved plaques from various organizations praising his commitment to the Yonkers Police Department, letters of commendation too numerous to count, a departmental Commendation for bravery, three Certificates of Excellent Police Work, two Unit Citations, the 1987 C.L.S.A. Police Commissioners Award of Excellence and Professionalism, the 1997 C.L.S.A. Presidents Award for leadership, and the Westchester County EMS Certificate of Merit along with their Unit Citation as well.

In 2007 Ret D.C. Rutledge bought a home in Florida where he found many other retired Yonkers police officers. While residing in his community he served several years on the Board of Directors of the community Home Owners Association (HOA). But he still continued to keep everyone, active and retired, in touch by emailing "The Call Box," a newsletter to all with miscellaneous police updates and historical information. Upon his retirement he said, you can remove my name from the roster, but I'm not going anywhere. He meant it. In 2019 he was still the YPD's historian, and still has a hand in operating the police museum. So, although everyone he worked with has also retired and been replaced by new police officers, in his heart it's still "his job."

DET. NICHOLAS A. DiMASE #636

APPOINTED: September 9, 1964
RETIRED: October 17, 1985

Nicholas Anthony DiMase was born in the City of Yonkers on August 8, 1943. He attended St. Peters parochial school, Sacred Heart H.S., and Saunders High School. Following high school Nick worked at his father's business, Glen Towing Co., located at 270 Nepperhan Ave. which some jokingly referred to as an unofficial mini precinct for the old H.Q. and 1st precinct on Wells Avenue and later located at 10 St. Casimir Avenue. This was said because so many police officers would regularly stop by and in doing so Nick became very interested in police work.

On September 9, 1964 Nick was appointed a police officer while residing at 55 Cliff Avenue. He attended the Police Academy recruit school for basic recruit training located in Iona College. When the academy training was completed he was assigned to the 3rd precinct on foot patrol duty earning a starting salary of $5,500 a year.

In April of 1965, only seven months after the unit was organized, DiMase was detailed to work undercover in the Narcotics Unit working with Det Charles Jackson, Charles Taylor and with then Sgt. Bill Sickley as the unit leader. It was quite evident that DiMase had proved himself as a motivated and effective investigator and as such, on January 28, 1966, he was appointed a Detective assigned to work in the Detective Division in General Assignment. At this point in the YPD history, politics played a very important role in who would be a detective, which resulted in unfortunate changes in assignments. And DiMase had his share. On July 10, 1970 he was reassigned from the DD out to patrol in the 2nd precinct; but on November 13, 1972 he returned to the DD as a detective. But, on July 2, 1973 he was again returned to patrol in the South Patrol Command.

While there Nick was detailed to work plainclothes in the South Command Auto Theft Unit with his partner, Joe Madden. They both worked a steady midnight shift and during their years together amassed an enviable record of arrests, and made a reputation as two of the best cops on the street.

On May 13, 1981 PO Nick DiMase was once again rewarded for his excellent police work when he was again appointed a Detective in the DD. The last few years as a Detective he was assigned to investigate "white collar" cases, i.e.; fraud crimes. During his career he was awarded at least ten Certificates of Excellent Police Work and four departmental Commendations. On November 25, 1968 he was awarded a Commendable Merit Citation by the Westchester Rockland newspaper police honor awards committee for his part in solving the murder of a Yonkers man in August of 1967. And, on November 11, 1971 he was again awarded a Citation of Commendable Merit by the Westchester Rockland newspaper police honor board.

Det Nick DiMase was one of those few men who was always full of energy and actually loved being a police officer. It was as if, it was not what he did, but actually who he was. Det Nicholas DiMase retired from the YPD on October 17, 1985 with that coveted reputation as being "a good cop."

In retirement Nick first worked for Chase Bank investigating credit card fraud until they began downsizing and he left and gained employment with the Westchester County Legal Aide Bureau as an investigator. And he was a licensed private investigator as well.

In what little free time he had, Nick loved to cook and be with his family; his wife Mary and sons Nick Jr. and Danny who was a Westchester County police officer and later joined the White Plains P.D.

Following a long illness Ret Det Nicholas DiMase died on December 15, 2015. He was 72.

DET. CAPTAIN GERALD T. CURTIS

APPOINTED: September 9, 1964
RETIRED: December 31, 2006

Gerald Curtis was born in the City of Yonkers on November 4, 1942. Actually he was born Gerald Crough, with his father's last name being Crough and his grandfather being Ret. YPD Capt. William Crough. Sometime later his mother remarried and his surname was changed to Curtis. As a youth Gerry attended PS# 16 and later graduated from Gorton High School. While there he was very athletic and was co-captain of the school football team. In fact he was named "All City" because of his athletic capabilities.

In early 1961 Curtis worked for Carvel Inc. as a warehouse manager. However on July 12, 1961 he joined the Army and at one point during his enlistment he served overseas in Korea. He was honorably discharged on June 26, 1963 as a Specialist 4th class. Following his discharge Curtis worked for Con

Det. Captain Gerald T. Curtis (cont.)

Edison in Eastview, NY. right up to being notified of his pending appointment to the YPD.

Gerald Curtis received his appointment to the police department on September 9, 1964 while living at 38 Annsville Trail in Yonkers. He attended the Police Academy recruit school for basic recruit training located in Iona College. When the academy training was completed he was assigned to the 4th precinct on foot patrol duty earning $5,500 a year. As a young officer PO Curtis was determined to be efficient in all his assignments and when enforcing parking violations he was very conscientious. In fact, it is said that in the early years he wrote so many summonses that he was teasingly nicknamed by his co-workers as "goldfinger."

On November 9, 1966 Curtis was transferred to the newly opened 1st precinct at 730 East Grassy Sprain Road. He remained there up to January 1, 1971 when a precinct centralization plan was implemented. At that time the old 4th precinct was renamed the North Patrol Command and Curtis was assigned there with many other officers.

PO Curtis received his first promotion to the position of police Sergeant on May 5, 1972 earning a new salary of $13,685 a year. With his promotion came a new assignment in the South Command as a patrol supervisor. Though recently promoted Curtis was determined to continue in his rise in the ranks and never stopped studying for the next promotional exam. And his efforts paid off because only two years later, on July 26, 1974, Curtis was promoted to the rank of Lieutenant, now earning $19,671 and was reassigned to the Field Operations Division as a patrol lieutenant. On January 1, 1979 Lt Curtis was assigned to the North Command on patrol and the following year, on January 1, 1980, he was moved to the same duty in the South Command.

On November 18, 1982 Lt Curtis achieved what his grandfather had achieved 56 years earlier. That being his promotion to the rank of police Captain. With this promotion came an increase in salary to $35,537. Following his promotion, Capt. Curtis was reassigned to the departments Inspections Unit as a city wide patrol duty captain overseeing the patrol operation first hand. Capt. Curtis received his first break from uniform patrol on December 21, 1982 when he was reassigned as the commanding officer of the Administrative Services Division in headquarters. He remained there for about six months and on July 1, 1983 he was transferred to the Youth Division as the commanding officer. The Youth Division, which was located at 21 Alexander Street, was responsible for the investigation of all crimes committed by juveniles and working closely with the family court. In addition, the captain was in command of the Police Athletic League (PAL) overseeing all the activities provided to the youth of the city in the hope of diverting them from crime to more positive activities.

Capt. Curtis remained in the Youth Division for nine years and on October 18, 1991 was reassigned back to patrol duties in the Field Services Bureau as a patrol captain. However, nine months later, on July 22, 1992, he was designated the commanding officer of the 1st precinct at 732 East Grassy Sprain Road. In 1995 following the appointment of Albert McEvoy as the new police commissioner, on March 17, 1995, McEvoy offered Curtis the position of Detective Captain as the commanding officer of the Internal Affairs Division. Curtis was not really interested in that assignment but the commissioner was convincing; and Curtis reluctantly accepted.

Det. Capt. Gerald Curtis, whose brother James had also been a Yonkers police officer who switched to the fire department, retired from the Yonkers Police Department, due to age limitations, on December 31, 2006 having served more than 42 years of honorable service.

PO HUGH P. KELLY #407

APPOINTED: September 9, 1964
RETIRED: February 2, 1985

Hugh Paul Kelly was born in the Bronx, NY on September 24, 1941. He moved to Yonkers with his family at a very young age and attended Yonkers schools at PS# 6, Longfellow Jr. High School, Gorton High School, and Saunders High School learning a trade as an auto mechanic. While in school, and even later, “Paul,” as he would be known throughout his entire adult life, loved swimming and at one point, because of his excellent swimming ability, he worked as a lifeguard at the local YMCA. Following school he worked many different jobs including that of an auto mechanic for Mahoney Motors in Yonkers from 1960 to 1962, a laborer, and then driving a taxi for Hollow Taxi. He was also a licensed electrician.

Paul was appointed to the police department on September 9, 1964 while living at 54 Fairview Street. He and the other members of his recruit class were sent to the NYC Police Academy for basic recruit training. This intensive physical and academic training ran from October 5, 1964 through February 5, 1965. Following recruit graduation PO Kelly was assigned to the 2nd precinct on patrol duty earning a starting salary of $5,500 a year.

On February 15, 1968 PO Kelly was granted his request to be assigned to the Traffic Division’s motorcycle unit. This was an assignment he really enjoyed. On January 1, 1971, following a precinct centralization plan, all motorcycle officers were dispersed among the two patrol commands and Kelly was assigned to the North Patrol Command, still on motorcycle duty which was designated “special enforcement.” Later that year on October 19, 1971 he and all other traffic men were returned to the Special Operations Division (Traffic) working in the Tactical Patrol Force (TPF).

After four years on motorcycle duty, on June 23, 1972, PO Kelly was reassigned to regular patrol in the South Command. Seven years later on June 20, 1979 Paul was transferred to the North East Command, and on March 18, 1981 back to the South Command. PO Hugh “Paul” Kelly, whose grandfather was PO Paul Both, retired from the YPD on February 2, 1985.

Today, Paul lives in Florida where he still swims laps every day and enjoys his boat on the water.

PO PHILIP F. MORRISSEY #470

APPOINTED: November 1, 1964
RETIRED: January 11, 1985

Philip Morrissey was born in Yonkers on Jan. 30, 1942. He attended local public school #7, Benjamin Franklyn Jr HS and Saunders HS learning a trade in Electric Wiring. On Aug. 17, 1960 Phil joined the Navy and served as an Electricians Mate 3rd class and was honorably discharged on July 17, 1962. Following the military Phil worked for the Geigy Chemical Corp in Yonkers. Morrissey was appointed to the Y.P.D. on Nov. 1, 1964 while residing at 31 Van Cortlandt Park Ave. He received his recruit training on the Iona college campus. Following graduation PO Morrissey was assigned to patrol in the 4th pct earning $5,500 a year. Throughout his early years Phil worked various assignments but in the early 1970's he was assigned a steady foot post in Getty Square. And in June of 1974 when a federally funded "Community Patrol Unit" was established Morrissey was made a part of those assigned but remained at his Getty Square post. He remained there up to Jan. 1, 1971 when he was assigned to the South Command. Phil Morrissey was a licensed electrician and worked his trade regularly while off duty. On Feb. 3, 1984 he was reassigned to the 3rd pct on Riverdale Ave. from which he retired on Jan. 11, 1985.

PO DENIS J. O'DONNELL #423

APPOINTED: November 4, 1964
RETIRED: June 2, 1995

Denis O'Donnell was born in NYC on Dec. 18, 1938. He attended St. Ann's school in the Bronx and graduated from Rice HS in Manhattan. O'Donnell joined the Army on July 21, 1958 and was honorably discharged on July 6, 1960. His early employment was listed as working for Pinkerton Detective Agency in NYC. From June 18, 1962 to May 2, 1963 he was a trooper with the NYS Police, from which he resigned. O'Donnell was appointed to the YPD on Nov. 4, 1964 while residing at 3505 Wayne Ave. in NYC. When first appointed he worked undercover narcotics and vice investigations as a Patrolman in the D.D. He did this from Nov. 4, 1964 through Mar 1, 1965. When O'Donnell attended recruit training he was awarded an off-duty revolver for attaining the highest grade in his class. O'Donnell's first patrol assignment was in the 3rd pct earning $5,500 a year. On Nov. 7, 1966 O'Donnell was transferred to the 1st pct. Then, on Jan. 1, 1971 he was assigned to the North command. On June 20, 1979, O'Donnell was again transferred, this time to the Northeast Patrol Command but on Dec. 4, 1981 O'Donnell was returned to duty in the North command. He retired on Oct. 13, 1985 and moved to Newark New Jersey where he gained employment as a police officer. However, in less than a year he was reinstated to the YPD. When O'Donnell finally retired on June 2, 1995 he moved to Greenwich Connecticut where both his sons, Dennis and Sean, were appointed to the Greenwich Police Department.

PO KENNETH A. VANTASSEL #141

APPOINTED: November 4, 1964
RETIRED: May 27, 1988

Kenneth VanTassel was born in the City of Yonkers on May 7, 1942 to Yonkers police officer Ambrose VanTassel. He attended PS# 16 on Palisade Avenue and Gorton high school. Ken joined the Army on July 26, 1961 serving in the 720th Military Police Battalion. He served his enlistment in the United States, but mostly in Fort Hood, Texas. He was honorably discharged as a Corporal on July 25, 1963. In April of 1964 Ken gained employment by working for the Yonkers Recreation Department. He remained there right up to his appointment to the YPD.

Kenneth VanTassel was appointed to the Yonkers Police Department on November 4, 1964 while residing at 593 Park Ave. Following his basic recruit training, which took place on the Iona College campus grounds, he was assigned to patrol duty in the 2nd precinct earning a starting salary of $5,500 a year.

On January 29, 1973 Ken was reassigned to work in the Criminal Identification Unit learning the skills involved in crime scene investigation. However that assignment was short-lived and on April 12, 1973 he was returned back to the 2nd precinct, which had been renamed the South Command. At one point while off duty he attended a school in NYC to learn how to be a butcher but decided not to pursue it.

On July 9, 1979 he was again reassigned, this time to the Northeast Patrol Command. VanTassel's brother Paul was a Yonkers police officer and his brother Roger a Yonkers firefighter.

VanTassel retired from the police department on May 27, 1988 and worked for a short time for an exterminator company and also worked private security for the Citi Group Corp.

PO JOEL F. PARISI #134

APPOINTED: January 1, 1965
RETIRED: February 9, 1986

Joel F. Parisi was born in the Bronx, NY on July 6, 1942. Following his formal education he made a living as a truck driver. He took the test for Yonkers police officer, passed, and on January 1, 1965 was appointed a Yonkers "Patrolman." His residence at that time was 2 Leewood Circle in Eastchester, NY. While waiting for recruit school to start and assigned to do miscellaneous assisting duties at headquarters, Parisi was approached by then Det Armando "Mandy" DeBlassis and told that because of his very slim build he could actually pass as a drug user or "junkie." It was then that he was offered to work as an undercover narcotics officer in the department's Narcotics Squad. Joel said he was really looking forward to wearing the uniform but, being a brand new rookie who had not even attended recruit school, and not wanting to say no to any job he was offered, he accepted.

The Narcotics Unit had just been organized a few months earlier on September 1, 1964 and Patrolman Parisi was directed to work with Det's Charles Taylor, Charles Jackson, Armando DeBlassis and Frank Skelton. Det DeBlassis would be his "handler" and give him direction and guidance. Their supervisor at the time was Sgt Joseph Huerstel. Parisi related that he worked the 6 PM to 2 AM shift undercover, in his own vehicle, making "buys" of illegal drugs using his own money and he carried no gun and had his shield pinned to his underwear.

When the recruit school began at Iona, he and others attended their recruit training classes during the day but, in addition, Parisi was instructed to work undercover at night. No overtime. No compensatory time. Eventually he was provided with money to make the drug "buys" but was never reimbursed for past expenses. Another officer, PO Leslie Feuer, hired in March of 1965 became his undercover partner. The two of them earned a reputation of being able to make dozens of arrests a month. In fact, Parisi was commended by the Westchester County Grand Jury not only for his many arrests but also for his

PO Joel F. Parisi #134 (cont.)

proficiency in testifying. During his years in the Narcotics Unit he was detailed to conduct investigations not only in Yonkers, but in various cities throughout Westchester County. He also worked jointly on many occasions with the Federal Bureau of Narcotics, later renamed the Drug Enforcement Agency (DEA).

All during the time Joel worked in the police department he said he always worked other jobs to make extra money. He operated a wholesale auto business buying trade-in cars and re-selling them to used car lots. He also purchased vending machines which he place throughout the area which sold candy and peanuts, etc. On January 28, 1966, after a major arrest consisting of 19 people, all the result of Parisi's work, he was rewarded by being appointed a Detective.

However, one year later, on January 13, 1967 he was reassigned to patrol duty in the 3rd pct, where he remained for 3 years. During those years it was said that narcotic arrests by the Narcotics Unit dropped dramatically and having a skill that the Detective Division needed during those years, Joel Parisi was once again appointed a detective on January 23, 1970. He worked for a short time in the Burglary Unit but was quickly moved back into Narcotics because of his past experience.

In July of 1971 Officer Parisi moved to Yonkers at 180 Underhill Street, which was followed shortly thereafter on September 15, 1972 by his being reassigned back to patrol duty in the then North Command (4th pct). Parisi worked patrol throughout the 1970's and early 1980's with a number of partners, but it is believed he rode in the sector car the longest with then PO Mike Fabrizio. They made quite a team and were affectionately given the nickname of "Freebie and the Bean." A name taken from a police movie of that era.

On June 4, 1985 PO Joel Parisi was transferred to the Communications Division serving as a dispatcher. Having completed 20 years PO Parisi retired from the YPD on February 9, 1986 and moved his family to Carlsbad, California. Years later, after a marital separation, he would move to Englewood, Florida where he bought a 20' boat which he loved to take trips with. In 2009 Joel Parisi was diagnosed with cancerous tumors in both his lungs, returned to Oceanside, California reuniting with his wife and children, and began treatment.

Ret. PO Joel F. Parisi died on February 3, 2011. He was 68 years old.

PO GERARD A. MURNAN #439

APPOINTED: February 15, 1965
RETIRED: September 2, 1983

Gerard Joseph Murnan was born in the City of Yonkers on March 1, 1935. He received his formal education at St. Dennis Elementary School and from Gorton H.S. Shortly after school Gerry reportedly joined the Marine Corps in November 1954 and received his honorable discharge in November of 1957. During his service he held the rank of Gunnery Sergeant. It is worth noting that his dates of service may not be accurate because his official obituary related that he served in the Korean War. (Which actually ended hostilities in July 1953.) It further related that he was reportedly one of the survivors of the Chosin Reservoir Battle, and was awarded the Silver Star, the Bronze Star and the Purple Heart.

The following story was told to me by retired Capt. Ron Martino. *"In one segment in a documentary movie clip about the battle at Chosin Reservoir, you see Marines walking alongside a truck as they fought their way out. This picture was also on the front of Life Magazine way back then. You can't see it too well in the movie but the young Marine with the mustache is our very own Jerry Murnan. When I say young I mean young; Jerry was wounded and as he lay in the hospital a major came in and said 'what the hell are you doing here.' That Major was his older brother. Jerry was soon discharged (administratively). But Jerry being Jerry, he joined up again as soon as he was able. He told me this story one day when I was on the desk at the South Command."*

Murnan gained employment as a bus driver but apparently became dissatisfied with his job and on May 1, 1962 he enlisted in the Army. Within a year, on February 18, 1963, he married and would ultimately raise five children. He would receive his second honorable discharge on February 1, 1964.

Upon his appointment to the YPD on February 15, 1965 and completing his recruit training at the NYC Police Academy, officer Murnan was assigned to the 3rd precinct and later worked patrol in the South Command. Gerry was an aggressive officer who distinguished himself many times. But on January 15, 1981 he was injured in the line of duty while responding to a call, slipped on a grassy incline, and severely damaged his knee. As a result Officer Murnan was retired on accidental disability on September 2, 1983 after serving for over 18 years.

After a while Gerry and his family moved to Port St. Joe, in Florida. It was there on November 27, 2009 that Ret PO Gerard Murnan died in his home at the age of 74 years.

PO PAUL H. NAEF #434

APPOINTED: February 15, 1965
RESIGNED: January 13, 1967

Paul Naef was born in New York City on Aug. 1, 1943. Paul attended Vale grade school in Morristown, NJ, spent the 6th and 7th grade in Switzerland, and graduated from Gorton HS. He spoke German as a second language. Following school Paul joined the Air Force on Aug. 8, 1962 serving as a Staff Sergeant in Japan with the Strategic Air Command, 310th Field Maintenance Squadron. He was honorably discharged on May 18, 1964. Prior to the YPD he was employed by the Robbins Pharmaceutical Co. in Yonkers. A few years later he joined the Air National Guard for 8 years and was discharged as a First Sergeant. Paul was appointed to the police department on Feb. 15, 1965 while living at 100 Convent Ave. Naef and his recruit class was sent to the NYC Police Academy for basic recruit training. This intensive physical and academic training ran from Feb. 15, 1965 until June 25, 1965. Following the Academy graduation his first assignment was to the 4th pct on foot patrol earning a starting salary of $5,880 a year. On Nov. 7, 1966 he was reassigned to the 1st pct on E. Grassy Sprain Road. Paul had taken the exam for Yonkers Firefighter and was called for appointment. He resigned from the YPD to join the Fire Dept. on Jan. 13, 1967. In the YFD Paul Naef rose to the rank of Assistant Chief and served several terms as president of the Uniformed Fire Officer Association.

PO MAURICE A. FOLEY #406

APPOINTED: February 15, 1965
RESIGNED: January 4, 1966

Maurice, or "Doc" Foley as he was known, was born in Yonkers on July 18, 1938. As a youth he attended St. Peter's School in Yonkers and graduated from Archbishop Stepinac High School in White Plains in June of 1956. Prior to the YPD "Doc" was employed by Otis Elevator Co. It is believed that Foley served in the Army Reserve from Aug. 16, 1959 to Feb. 15, 1961 which completed his six month active duty obligation. However, records indicate he served again from Oct. 1, 1961 to Aug. 5, 1962, and was honorably discharged. He was appointed a police officer on Feb. 15, 1965 while living at 106 Locust Hill Ave. and received his basic police recruit training at the NYPD police academy which ran from Feb. 15, 1965 through June 25, 1965. Following recruit graduation he was assigned to foot patrol in the 1st precinct earning a starting salary of $5,880 a year. Prior to his police appointment Foley had taken both the police and fire department exams. The YPD appointed him first. However, on Jan. 4, 1966, the Fire Dept. called him to be appointed as a Yonkers Firefighter, which he accepted and resigned from the YPD effective that date.

LT. LORENZO A. PAUL

APPOINTED: February 15, 1965
RETIRED: March 17, 2000

Lorenzo Alphonso Paul was born in New York City in the section known as Harlem on June 12, 1941. Larry, as he was known, moved with his family as a youth to Mount Vernon where he attended Sacred Heart school. He also attended and graduated from Mount St. Michael Academy in the Bronx. He would also attend Iona College from 1959 to 1962 majoring in Spanish. Larry was not tall but he was thick and strong as an ox. He played football while attending Mount Saint Michael high school in the Bronx which he attended even though he lived just across the line in Mount Vernon. As a teenager growing up in Mount Vernon Larry sang in a street acapella quartet, two white and two black youths and the group was named the "Plaids." Previous to the YPD Larry worked as a parking enforcement officer in Mt. Vernon.

Lorenzo Paul was appointed to the Yonkers Police Department on February 15, 1965 while he was living at 348 9th Ave., Mount Vernon. Following his appointment to the police department he and his recruit class were sent to the NYC Police Academy for basic recruit training. This intensive physical and academic training ran from Feb. 15, 1965 to June 25, 1965. Upon graduation from his basic police recruit training Larry was assigned to the 1st precinct on foot patrol earning a starting salary of $5,880 a year. During those early years when money was tight Larry worked off duty painting and hanging wallpaper.

Being only one of a few black police officers on the police department at the time, Larry was able to relate very well with the black community as well as the Hispanic community due to his ability to speak Spanish. To make use of this asset the chief of police transferred him to the Youth Division on January 24, 1966 to investigate crimes committed by juveniles as well as to work closely with the PAL in an effort to redirect the youth of the community to sports rather than crime.

PO Paul remained in the Youth Division for nearly two years when, on November 6, 1967, he was reassigned to the 4th precinct to uniformed patrol duties. Following the establishment of a Community

LT. Lorenzo A. Paul (cont.)

Relations Unit as part of the Detective Division, on March 7, 1969, police officer Paul was appointed a Detective and assigned as part of that unit. For a short time, beginning on January 1, 1971, Larry was directed to work right in the Detective Division. However on October 6, 1971 he was again reassigned, this time to the newly established Youth Services and Community Relations Division.

On April 12, 1973 officer Paul was again reassigned to patrol duties in the old 4th precinct which had since had its name changed on January 1, 1971 to the North Patrol Command. He continued to work uniform patrol for 10 years, up to June 17, 1983, when he was reassigned to the South West Patrol Command on Riverdale Avenue. But, only 4 months later, on November 5, 1983, Larry was again returned to the Youth and Community Services Division, but as an investigator, not a detective.

Police officer Paul was promoted to the rank of Sergeant on July 9, 1985 and assigned to the Field Services Bureau as a patrol supervisor designated to work in whichever command he might be needed. Two years later, on November 9, 1987, Sgt. Paul was returned to the Youth Services Division as a supervisor of the investigators. On July 1, 1988 Sgt. Paul was reassigned to the Community Affairs Division of the police department. He was instructed to work closely with the minority community in an effort to establish better relations between it and the police department. He was apparently very effective at this because on March 30, 1990 Sgt. Paul was elevated to Detective Sergeant and was allowed to remain in that same division.

On October 3, 1997 Lorenzo Paul was promoted to the rank of Police Lieutenant and, considering the excellent relationship he had built with the community, he remained in the Community Affairs Division and was designated as commanding officer. It was from this assignment that Lt. Paul retired on March 17, 2000.

Lorenzo Paul loved fishing and playing cards whenever he had the opportunity. He was also very active in many police and civic organizations such as, the PBA, the Police Holy Name Society, the Captains Lieutenants and Sergeants Association, Big Brothers, Knights of Columbus, Boy Scouts, and every year he would serve as a chef at the YMCA fund-raising cookout.

Retired Lt. Lorenzo Paul knew he was sick and his retirement would be short. He died on April 26, 2001 at the age of 59 years.

Lorenzo Paul was extremely well-liked and popular with everyone throughout the community and the Police Department. So it was no surprise that a City Council resolution, dated May 24, 2001, was passed recognizing the contributions of Lt. Paul to the Police Department and his community and authorized the honorary renaming of that portion of Radford St., between Saratoga Avenue and Bruce Avenue, "Ret Lt. Lorenzo Paul Lane." The sign hung on a pole in front of 36 Radford St., the site of the Community Affairs Division where Lt. Paul had worked. The official ceremony, when the sign was hung, took place on August 30, 2001 in front of the Community Affairs Division. The mayor, Council President, council members, Police Commissioner, many uniformed fellow officers, and an 8 officer motorcycle detail along with a color guard attended as an honor to the late Lt. Lorenzo Paul.

PO RAYMOND G. MANLEY #435

APPOINTED: February 15, 1965
RETIRED: May 29, 1986

Raymond Gerald Manley was born in Yonkers on July 6, 1941. He attended Our Lady of the Holy Rosary, and later graduating from Gorton HS. Ray joined the Army on Mar. 28, 1961 and served with the 503rd Engineering Company as a Specialist 4th class. He was honorably discharged on Mar. 16, 1964. Previous to the YPD Ray worked as a truck driver with the Stillwell Equipment Corp. in Elmsford. "Gerry," as he was known to close friends, was appointed to the Y.P.D. on Feb. 15, 1965 while living at 5 Mulford Gardens. Manley, along with the rest of his recruit class, attended the NYC Police Academy from Feb. 15, 1965 until June 25, 1965. Following graduation his first assignment was to the 1st pct. on patrol, earning a starting salary of $5,880 a year. On Nov. 9, 1966 he was reassigned to the 4th pct. on patrol. Four years later, on Feb. 2, 1970, he was transferred to headquarters, received emergency services training, and was assigned to the Emergency Services Unit. On Jan. 1, 1971 he was assigned to the North Command working in ESU. Ray worked in the Emergency Unit for several years and then rode in a routine sector car on patrol. In the last few years on the job he worked as a desk officer up to his retirement on May 29, 1986.

PO EDWARD J. CANNON #545

APPOINTED: February 15, 1965
RETIRED: February 16, 1995

PO Edward Cannon was born in Yonkers on June 26, 1940. He attended PS# 13 and graduated from Yonkers HS. Ed joined the US Coast Guard on Jan. 28, 1959 serving as a Seaman up to Jan. 24, 1961 when he was honorably discharged. Previous to the YPD Ed had worked for the Phelps Dodge Corp in Yonkers. Cannon received his appointment to the Y.P.D. on Feb. 15, 1965 while residing at 312 Jessamine Ave. and just five months following his brother Robert's appointment to the YPD. Ed's recruit class received their training at the NYPD police academy from Feb. 15, 1965 to June 25, 1965. Upon graduation PO Cannon was assigned to the 4th pct. on patrol earning $5,880 a year. On Nov. 9, 1966 Ed was transferred to patrol duty in the 1st pct. at 10 St. Casimir Ave. Two years later, on July 31, 1968, he was reassigned to work in the newly established Yonkers Police Marine unit. The establishment of this unit was not very successful and by the end of the summer it had been disbanded. On Oct. 1, 1968 Ed was returned to patrol duty in the 1st pct. On Nov. 6, 1970 he was moved to the 3rd pct. and on Jan. 1, 1971, to the North Command where he would remain, for 24 years, right up to his retirement on Feb.16, 1995. He died March 24, 2018.

DET. ANTHONY C. SOUZA #665

APPOINTED: February 15, 1965
RETIRED: March 8, 1985

Anthony Souza was born in Mt. Vernon NY on September 16, 1935 and attended local schools. He joined the Army on April 19, 1954, trained and served as a Military Police Officer in Korea, and was honorably discharged on April 18, 1957. Tony worked for many years both as a truck driver and as a public bus driver, in Mt Vernon.

Upon his appointment as a Yonkers police officer on February 15, 1965 at the salary of $5,800. per year, and upon completion of his recruit training at the NYPD police Academy, PO Tony Souza was assigned to the 3rd precinct on foot patrol. But only for a short time. He was subsequently detailed to the Narcotics Unit as a "silver shield," not a detective, working as an undercover officer assigned to gain the confidence of street drug dealers and when possible make "narcotic buys." Of course cases were built based on these "buys" which resulted in many indictments and arrests.

Due to his excellent record he was officially appointed a Detective on June 23, 1967 and remained in the Narcotics Unit partnered up with Det Nick Bianco. Tony and Nick not only worked drug cases but were often involved in homicide investigations that may have had some involvement with drugs and were usually organized crime connected.

When Yonkers PO Harry Woods was shot in a holdup, which resulted in his death on September 24, 1974, the entire Detective Division worked on the case along with the FBI and others. At one point, utilizing an FBI informant, Tony Souza while partnered with Det Tony Cerasi followed a car down into Manhattan and as Cerasi recalls, he and Souza, along with the FBI, stopped the car and at gun point arrested one of the two killers of officer Woods. They also recovered the weapon that was used.

Years later in 1973 while still a detective Tony decided to run for Yonkers City Council. He claimed the law allowed him to stay in the job and run, but if he won he must leave the job. Tony decided to take a leave of absence to campaign, not because he had too, but to spend more time campaigning. He lost the election by 36 votes.

Late in his career he was reassigned from Narcotics out to General Assignment in the D.D. from which he would retire on March 8, 1985 after having worked his entire career as a Detective in the Detective Division. Shortly thereafter Tony obtained his Private Investigators license doing business as "Anthony Souza Private Investigator," at which he continued up to his illness.

Tony Souza was always moving fast; walking and talking fast. He was a man who never seemed low on energy or drive. When asked, his former partner Ret Det Sgt Nick Bianco commented, "*Tony was a very tenacious detective and no one would want to be chased by him*."

Ret Det Anthony Souza suffered a massive stroke and on January 12, 2009 and died in White Plains Hospital. He was 73 years old.

SGT. LOUIS T. DEARSTYNE #57

APPOINTED: February 15, 1965
RETIRED: June 9, 2000

Born Louis Thomas Dearstyne on June 18, 1942 Lou attended Sacred Heart elementary as well as their high school, graduating from same in 1961. While in high school he was an excellent basketball player. Lou joined the Naval Reserve on September 27, 1961 and was honorably discharged on July 26, 1963. On his police application he listed his previous employment as an insurance claims agent and the NY Central Railroad in Croton, NY.

He was appointed to the Yonkers police department on February 15, 1965 while living at 41 Baldwin Lane, Mahopac, NY. His recruit class was only the second recruit group, in recent memory, to be invited to attend the NYPD Police Academy after many years of local training. They attended the police academy from February 15, 1965 through June 25, 1965 receiving intensive academic as well as physical training. Following graduation PO Dearstyne was assigned to the 2nd precinct earning a starting salary of $5,880 a year. While there, his partner for several years was Joseph Kilmurry. Lou was a very friendly and accommodating man who was ready to help anyone in need. He was very active in CLSA business and swam regularly to keep in shape. He was well liked by his peers and respected by the officers who worked with and for him.

Lou also graduated from Evidence Technician School held in Yonkers. As a trained designated Evidence Technician a uniformed patrol officer was responsible to accomplish basic photographing and gathering of evidence at minor crime scenes without the need to have CIU respond. On February 12, 1971 he was appointed a Detective in the Detective Division and six months later, on August 30, 1971, he was assigned to work in the Criminal Identification Unit maintaining criminal records and processing crime scenes for fingerprints or other evidence.

On August 13, 1976 he was promoted to the rank of Sergeant earning $18,043 and was transferred to the North Patrol Command as a patrol supervisor. On June 20, 1979 he was reassigned to the Northeast Patrol Division as a patrol sergeant. On December 19, 1983 he was reassigned to the Administrative Services Division in headquarters serving as the supervisor of the Criminal Identification Unit and those patrol officers who were serving as evidence technicians.

On April 5, 1991 he was offered the assignment of being the administrative aide to Deputy Chief Rudy DeDivitis, which he accepted and where he remained until the chief was appointed acting Police Commissioner on March 16, 1999. He then was assigned as the administrative aide to DC Donald Christopher until January of 1996 when Christopher was appointed police commissioner. He remained a Deputy Chief aide up to June 1, 1998 when he was reassigned to Community Affairs Division and remained there right up to his retirement on June 9, 2000.

All during this time, Sgt Dearstyne remained active in the Capt.'s, Lt's and Sgt's Association serving as its Secretary and later as Vice President. Sgt Dearstyne was one of those rare individuals who seemed to never lose his temper and was a pleasure to work with.

CAPTAIN EDWARD A. DALY

APPOINTED: February 15, 1965
RETIRED: April 12, 2002

Edward Albert Daly was born on November 30, 1942 in Augusta Georgia. After having moved to Yonkers with his family as a youth he attended St. Denis elementary school, Hawthorne Jr. high school, and graduated from Saunders high school. Shortly after high school Ed joined the US Army on May 7, 1962 and served as a Military Police Officer up to his honorable discharge on May 6, 1964. Following his discharge Ed worked as a salesman for the Sears & Roebuck Co. in Yonkers.

Having taken the Yonkers police test for Patrolman, Daly passed with a good score and received his appointment to the police department on February 15, 1965 while residing at 424 Park Hill Avenue. Probationary police officer Daly and his recruit class were sent to the NYC Police Academy for basic recruit training. This intensive physical and academic training ran from February 15, 1965 until June 25, 1965. Following the Academy graduation his first assignment was to the 3rd precinct on patrol, earning a starting salary of $5,880 a year.

Five years later, on November 6, 1970, he was reassigned to the first precinct and less than two months later, following a major reorganization and centralization of patrol precincts, on January 1, 1971 he was transferred to the North Command at 53 Shonnard Place. As part of this centralization move, of the four existing patrol precincts, the 1st and the 3rd precincts were closed as patrol precincts. The 4th

Captain Edward A. Daly (cont.)

precinct was renamed the North Command and patrolled the northern half of the city. The former 2nd precinct was designated the South Command and was responsible for patrolling the southern half of the city.

On May 5, 1972 PO Daly was promoted to the rank of Sergeant earning $13,685 a year and was reassigned from the North Command to the South Command as a patrol supervisor. Early on, Daly had decided he was going to work to achieve higher rank in the YPD. And after attending promotional schools regularly, on July 1, 1975 he was promoted to the rank of Lieutenant earning $20,642 and was transferred to the Field Operations Bureau as a citywide patrol lieutenant.

Throughout all this time Ed was continuing to attend college to further his education. On September 17, 1979 Lt Daly was transferred to the Communications Division as a tour supervisor. On September 26, 1980 he was reassigned to the North patrol division but detailed to headquarters to work on the Integrated Criminal Apprehension Program, (ICAP). As the project director of the Integrated Criminal Apprehension Program Lt. Daly managed and coordinated a federal grant directed towards the modernization and improved efficiency of all areas of departmental operations. He was also selected to coordinate and implement the department's Computer Assisted Dispatch System, (CADS). He was chosen to lead these programs due to his interest in difficult problems. Over the years he earned a Bachelor of Science degree in Criminal Justice from Mercy College in 1976 and a Master's degree in Social Science from Long Island University in 1982.

Ed scored high on the captain's examination and was waiting to be promoted. Prior to his appointment to the rank of captain he received a written evaluation from Capt. John F. McMahon which read in part, "*I have found him to be an efficient, sincere and dedicated officer. Lt Daly possesses a Master's degree in social science from Long Island University, was the director of our recent ICAP program and coordinated our computer assisted dispatch system installation. Department wise, he is the recipient of four commendations, four certificates of excellent police work, as well as three Westchester Rockland newspaper police awards. I recommend his promotion to the position of Captain without reservation.*"

There was no question that Ed Daly was intelligent and was willing to handle complicated administrative jobs, so it was no surprise when on August 16, 1984 Daly was promoted to the rank of police Captain earning $44,255 a year and was assigned to the Field Services Bureau as a citywide patrol duty Captain.

On April 16, 1986 Capt. Daly was transferred to the 3rd precinct, now located on Riverdale Avenue, and designated the commanding officer. The following year, on January 11, 1987, he was detailed from the 3rd precinct to the planning unit where his previous experience could be put to good use. And on July 1, 1988 this detail was ended and he was officially assigned as the commanding officer of the Planning Unit where his responsibilities ran from applying for state and federal grant monies for the YPD to the long term planning for the department as a whole.

Over the ensuing years Capt. Daly was reassigned to a number of units. On October 1, 1990 he was reassigned to the Administrative Services Division in HQ; July 1, 1991 he was assigned to the Inspectional Services Division to work on special projects; January 26, 1995 he was transferred from special projects to commanding officer of the Communications and Records Division; November 1, 1995

Captain Edward A. Daly (cont.)

from Communications Division back to special projects; September 9, 1995 to the 2nd precinct as commanding officer; September 1, 1998 from the 2nd precinct to commanding officer of the Records Division; May 29, 2004 from Records Division to commanding officer of the Special Operations Division; and his last assignment began on October 2, 2000 when he was moved from the Special Operations to the Courts and Detention Services Division as commanding officer.

As mentioned earlier, Ed Daly was a believer in education. During his career he earned an Associate's Degree from Westchester Community College, a Bachelor of Science Degree from Mercy College, and a Master's Degree from Long Island University. He was also privileged to have been selected to attend the prestigious FBI National Academy. He was a member of the Captains, Lieutenants, and Sergeants Association, the Police Benevolent Association, the Westchester Police Emerald Society, the Yonkers Elks club, the American Academy for Professional Law Enforcement and chairman of the International Police Association, region #3 of the United States section. And his fist cousin was former PO Dennis Alexa.

Capt. Edward Daly retired from the Yonkers Police Department after 37 years service on April 12, 2002 and years later moved to "The Villages" in central Florida.

PO DONALD N. GROSS #762

APPOINTED: February 15, 1965
RETIRED: July 11, 1975

Donald Gross was born in White Plains, NY on November 25, 1935. He attended Valhalla Jr High School and graduated from Valhalla High School. Don joined the U.S. Air Force December 14, 1952 serving up to December 1, 1956 and received an honorable discharge as an Airman 1st class. Prior to the YPD Donald earned his living as a painter and working for US Vitamin and Pharmaceutical. He was appointed to the police department on February 15, 1965 while living at 106 Valentine Lane. Gross, along with the rest of his recruit class, attended the New York City police Academy from February 15, 1965 until June 25, 1965. Following the Academy graduation his first assignment was to the 3rd precinct on patrol earning a starting salary of $5,880 a year. On January 1, 1971 he was reassigned to the South patrol command on Central Park Avenue. On October 12, 1973, while working a school crossing, PO Gross fell injuring his back. The injury required spinal fusion surgery and resulted in his being unable to perform his duties and being retired on an accidental disability pension effective July 11, 1975.

LT. ARTHUR A. BUTLER

APPOINTED: February 15, 1965
RETIRED: February 24, 1995

Arthur Butler was born in Yonkers on Jan. 2, 1939. He received his education attending St. Mary's parochial school and later graduated from Saunders HS. Arthur was a Navy veteran having served from Feb. 23, 1956 through Dec. 4, 1959 and was honorably discharged. While serving in the Navy he was in charge of one of their post offices and had the ability to operate a teletype. He was previously employed by the Anaconda Wire and Cable Co. in Hastings. Arthur Butler was appointed to the Y.P.D. on Feb. 15, 1965 while residing at 59 Maple St. Butler receives his basic police recruit training at the NYC Police Academy from Feb. 15, 1965 through June 25, 1965. Upon his graduation he was assigned to duty in the 1st pct. On Nov. 9, 1966, he was reassigned to foot patrol in the 4th pct. PO Butler was promoted to Sergeant on Mar 16, 1979 earning $21,142 a year and was assigned to the Communications Div. and then to the South Command as a patrol supervisor. On Nov. 1, 1987 Sgt Butler was transferred to the Field Services Bureau as a citywide patrol sergeant and on Dec. 25, 1987 he was assigned to the City Jail serving as a booking officer. On Oct. 18, 1991 Butler was promoted to Lieutenant and assigned to the Field Services Bureau as a patrol lieutenant but would later be reassigned to the Communications Div. as a tour supervisor from which he would retire on Feb. 24, 1995.

SGT. HERBERT P. ENGLER # 78

APPOINTED: February 15, 1965
RETIRED: January 3, 1986

Herbert Engler was born in the city of Yonkers on April 6, 1941 and grew up in the northwest section of that city. As a youth he attended PS #16, and later would graduate from Gorton high school. Herb joined the army on March 1, 1960 with a military specialty as a cryptographer. He served as a sergeant in the 2nd gunnery battalion, 38th artillery in Germany, and was honorably discharged on February 18, 1963. Not surprisingly he spoke German as a second language. Following his military service Herb worked as a dispatcher at Refined Syrup and Sugar's company.

Herb Engler was appointed to the Yonkers Police Department on February 15, 1965 while residing at 137 Morningside Place. Following his police recruit training at the NYC Police Academy Herb was assigned to patrol duty in the 3rd precinct earning a starting salary of $5,880 a year. Less than a year after he was appointed a police officer, on November 12, 1965, officer Engler and his partner were sent to break up a large disorder and fight at a dance hall named the "Upstairs Room" located on South Broadway. While Engler was taking a suspect into custody the violently resisting male kicked him in the face knocking out two front teeth, knocking him unconscious and leaving him with a concussion.

The following year, in 1966, PO Engler and others were sent to a house on Hawthorne Avenue near Hawthorne Jr. high school. It was at about 3 A.M. and a male who just got out of the Marine Corps. had a fight with his wife and took it out on Herb and his partner Steve Kogan as they attempted to walk up the front path to the house. The male immediately began shooting at the officers from an upstairs window with a rifle and shotgun striking the patrol cars. After several backup cars arrived Engler and his partner were able to enter the building, without any of the protective equipment that is available today, and took the suspect into custody without firing a shot. PO Engler would later be reassigned to the 2nd precinct on November 6, 1970.

Herb was promoted to the rank of sergeant on October 6, 1972 receiving an increase in salary to $14,399 and was reassigned as a patrol supervisor in the North command. While off-duty Engler earned an associate's degree from Westchester community college in 1975. In the mid-1970s the police repair shop was in need of supervision and since Engler was a good auto mechanic, on February 16, 1976 Sgt. Engler was assigned to headquarters command to be in charge of the police repair shop operation. However, the following year on July 8, 1977, Herb Engler was returned to patrol supervisory duties in the North command.

Herb had a good reputation for being dependable and efficient and it paid off. On October 3, 1979 Sgt. Engler was transferred to the Field services Bureau and assigned as an administrative aide to a deputy chief. This is a job that sounds very simple, but one that must be handled very delicately.

Sgt. Engler retired on January 3, 1986 and moved to Spring Hill, Florida where he began a new career as a contractor building new homes. And in his local church Herb was even a Eucharistic minister. On June 2, 2002, while sitting in his home at the breakfast table, retired Sgt. Herb Engler suffered a massive heart attack and died. He was 61 years old.

PO HAROLD M. PRICE #440

APPOINTED: February 15, 1965
RETIRED: August 24, 1985

Harold M. Price was born in Yonkers on Oct. 5, 1939. As a youth he attended school at PS# 6, Benjamin Franklyn Jr HS, and graduated from Saunders HS. Harry joined the Army on April 7, 1958 and was honorably discharged on April 7, 1960. Prior to the YPD he worked as a shipping clerk for the Crown Paper Co on Riverdale Ave. Harry was appointed to the Y.P.D. on Feb. 15, 1965 while living at 4 Locust Hill Ave. Following his recruit training at the NYC Police Academy from Feb. 15, 1965 to June 25, 1965, he was assigned to patrol in the 1st pct. earning $5,880 a year. On Nov. 9, 1966 Harry was reassigned to the 4th pct. Around 1973 Harry was assigned as the desk officer's administrative aide. At that time booking of prisoners was still being done in the commands by the desk officer and Harry was very efficient in assisting in the processing procedure. It should be known that, regardless of how efficient he was as a police officer, Harry worked even harder at his first love; golf. On June 17, 1975, Officer Price was transferred to the Communications Div. as a dispatcher right up to his retirement on August 24, 1985.

SGT. MICHAEL R. DiFATE #7

APPOINTED: February 15, 1965
RETIRED: September 1, 1998

Michael Rodney DiFate was born in Yonkers on Aug. 10, 1943. Following high school Michael worked as a licensed electrician for several years. He was appointed to the Y.P.D. on Feb. 15, 1965 while living at 2 Ivy Place in Hartsdale NY. PO DiFate and his recruit class were sent to the NYC Police Academy for basic recruit training which ran from Feb. 15, 1965 to June 25, 1965. Following graduation his first assignment was to the 2nd pct on patrol, earning $5,880 a year. The Vietnam War had been in progress but regardless of their draft classification, no Yonkers officer in the past had been subject to the draft. However, PO DiFate became the first Yonkers police officer to be drafted into the Army during the Vietnam War. He was drafted on Mar. 13, 1967 and served in the infantry for two years, and honorably discharged in early 1969. DiFate was reinstated to the Y.P.D. and on Feb. 20, 1969 was assigned to the 4th pct. on patrol. Over the next couple years he moved out to the 2nd pct, then to the North Command; in 1973 to headquarters, and on Feb. 13, 1976 back to the North Command. On June 20, 1979 he was assigned to the Northeast patrol command. On October 10, 1980 Mike DiFate was promoted to the rank of sergeant, earning $23,086 and was assigned as a patrol supervisor in the South Command. Sgt Mike DiFate was assigned to a number of units within the department, right up to his retirement on Sept. 1, 1998.

PO RICHARD P. McCONVILLE #444

APPOINTED: March 26, 1965
RETIRED: March 31, 1988

Richard McConville, or "Ducky" as he was known, was born in Yonkers on Nov. 26, 1937 and attended Holy Rosary School and Gorton HS. He joined the Army Reserve on Dec. 2, 1956 serving in the 68th Armored Div. He was honorably discharged on Dec. 2, 1962. Later Rich worked for Otis Elevator Co. Richard was appointed to the Y.P.D. on Mar 26, 1965 while living at 34 Point St. He received his recruit training at the Iona College campus which ran from April 5, 1965 to April 30, 1965. Upon graduation Rich was assigned to foot patrol in the 4th pct earning $5,880 a year. On July 26, 1965 while investigating a stalled motor vehicle, he was struck by a car severely injuring his back and hip. He returned to work but his injuries never healed right. On Nov. 9, 1966 McConville was reassigned to the 3rd pct. And, on Jan. 1, 1971 McConville was moved to the South Command. On July 1, 1980 PO McConville was transferred to the Communications Div. working in the Tele Serv Unit which accepted minor police reports over the telephone. In June of 1987 he began working as a police dispatcher. He would remain in Communications right up to his retirement on March 31, 1988 whereupon he moved to Roxbury, NY. Ret PO Richard McConville died on March 19, 2007 in Albany, NY. He was 69 years old.

PO ROBERT E. MARTIN #274

APPOINTED: March 26, 1965
RETIRED: June 28, 1985

Bob Martin was born in Yonkers on Mar 23, 1939 and as a youth he attended PS #14 and later graduated from Commerce HS. Following graduation Bob joined the Navy on Oct. 8, 1957 and served aboard the USS Howard Gilmore as a Seaman. He was honorably discharged on Sept. 7, 1959. On his police application he listed that he was employed by the NYC Railroad. Robert Martin was appointed to the Y.P.D. on Mar 26, 1965 while residing at 30 Crestmont Ave. He received his recruit training at the Iona College campus in New Rochelle whose curriculum ran from April 5th to the 30th of 1965. Upon graduation PO Martin was assigned to the 2nd pct at $5,880 a year. In the 1970's he was very active playing on the PBA basketball team as well as other sports. And on Aug. 13, 1971 he was assigned to the newly established Community Relations Unit and was appointed a Detective that date. Later, this unit was disbanded and merged with the Youth Division. Martin was returned to patrol and on Oct. 6, 1972 was assigned to the Police Athletic League. Bob spent the next 13 years working with troubled youths getting them involved in sporting activities instead of crime. Bob Martin retired on June 28, 1985 and moved to sunny Florida to enjoy golf.

LT. MARIO J. LOMBARDI

APPOINTED: March 26, 1965
RETIRED: June 22, 2001

Mario J. Lombardi was born in Oklahoma City, Oklahoma on January 23, 1944 while his father was serving in the Army. Later that year he and his mother moved to the Bronx to live with his maternal grandmother. His father joined them upon discharge in 1946. Young Mario and his family moved to Yonkers in 1955 and he attended PS# 15 and graduated from Roosevelt H.S. On his police application Mario listed his current employment as a Dugan Bros. Bakery salesman.

Mario, or "Butch" as he was known to all his friends, was appointed to the Yonkers Police Department on March 26, 1965 while living at 8 Wainwright Avenue. He and his group of ten new "rookies" received their basic police recruit training on the Campus of Iona College. This recruit training ran from April 5, 1965 to April 30, 1965. Upon graduation Probationary officer Lombardi was assigned to duty in the 2nd precinct earning a starting salary of $5,880 a year. Mario worked radio car patrol in the 2nd pct. for the next twelve years and during that time took and passed the civil service test for Sergeant. At one point the police department or City Hall, decided they wanted to promote a man to sergeant but there was no vacant position available. So, in their flawed wisdom, they created the position of Temporary Sergeant and promoted the man they wanted in that acting position. The plan was, when a vacancy occurred in the sergeant's rank they would then promote the temporary sergeant from the current valid sergeants list to a permanent position. Once they started doing this they continued the practice during the life of that Sergeants list.

On November 25, 1977 Mario Lombardi was now #1 on the sergeants list and as with others before him he was promoted to "Temporary Sergeant" on that date earning $18,712 and assigned as a patrol supervisor in the North Command. Unfortunately while he waited for the next permanent opening to occur, the Sergeants list he was on expired and the Civil Service Commission ruled that without a valid list to promote from, Acting Sgt Lombardi could not be promoted to permanent status and must be returned to the rank of police officer. After having served as a sergeant for nearly two years, on May 25, 1978, he was returned to police officer status and assigned to the Youth and Community Services Division on Alexander Street.

Needless to say, the practice of establishing an "Acting Sergeant" position was discontinued. As for Lombardi, he may have been down but not out. He renewed his studying, once again passed the next sergeants promotional exam, and was finally promoted to the "permanent" rank of Sergeant on November 13, 1981. His new assignment was as a patrol supervisor in the South West Patrol Command, later the 3rd precinct, on Riverdale Avenue. About 1983 he was reassigned out to the North East Command on East Grassy Sprain Road. And Lombardi didn't stop there.

On May 23, 1986 he was promoted to the rank of police Lieutenant and assigned to the Communications Division as a tour supervisor. Five months later, on October 17, 1986, Lt Lombardi was reassigned to the 1st precinct as a patrol Lieutenant. Over the next several years he was moved a number of times. On December 10, 1990 to the Courts and Detention Services Division as the Executive officer; April 27, 1998 to the Field Services Bureau; February 22, 1999 to the 4th precinct on patrol; January 1, 2000 to the 1st precinct on patrol; and lastly on April 17, 2000 to the Community Affairs Division designated as the commanding officer.

It was from this assignment that Lt Mario Lombardi retired on June 22, 2001.

PO JOHN F. KOMOSINSKI #264

APPOINTED: March 26, 1965
RETIRED: September 5, 1986

John was born in Yonkers on Nov. 28, 1941and attended Hawthorne Jr. HS and later graduated from Saunders HS with a trade in printing. Prior to the YPD, John earned his living as a chauffeur. He received his appointment to the Y.P.D. on Mar 26, 1965 while living at 129 Amackassin Terr. He and his group of "rookies" received their recruit training on the Campus of Iona College. This recruit training ran from April 5, 1965 to April 30, 1965. Upon his graduation PO Komosinski was assigned to patrol duty in the 1st precinct at 10 St. Casimir Ave. earning $5,880 a year. John was reassigned to the 4th precinct on Nov. 9, 1966 and remained there on patrol for the next 13 years until June 20, 1979 when he was transferred to the N.E. Command. He remained in that command up to his retirement on Sept. 5, 1986. Following his retirement Komosinski, whose brother in law was PO Bill Howell, moved upstate. He was always an avid hunter and started his own business on over 100 acres called the Mountain Spring Lodge in Bloomville, NY. His business specialized in stocking his fenced in land with all kind of animals and then, for a fee, provided guided trophy deer hunts, etc.

PO VICTOR CHIAMENTO #449

APPOINTED: March 26, 1965
RETIRED: March 7, 1986

Victor was born in NYC on Sept. 22, 1940. As a youth Victor attended Our Lady of Solace school, St John's School, and graduated from DeWitt Clinton HS, all of the Bronx, NY. Chiamento served in the Army beginning on Jan. 29, 1959 with the 513th Transportation Co. in Germany as an auto mechanic. He was honorably discharged in Dec. of 1961. Previous to the YPD Victor worked in NYC as an auto mechanic. On Mar. 26, 1965 Chiamento was appointed to the Y.P.D. Vic was living at 11 Garfield St. at the time. He received his recruit training at the Iona College campus which ran from April 5, 1965 to April 30, 1965. Upon graduation Vic was assigned to patrol in the 3rd pct earning $5,880 a year. On Nov. 9, 1966, he was reassigned to the newly opened 1st pct at 730 East Grassy Sprain Rd. He was later transferred to the Communications Div. on Mar 6, 1968 working as a dispatcher. In Dec. of 1975 he was returned to patrol in the South Command but five years later, on July 1, 1980, he was returned to Communications, this time working in the Tele Serv Unit which accepted minor police reports over the telephone. On his request Vic Chiamento was transferred to the 4th pct on June 4, 1985 and he retired the following year on March 7, 1986.

PO MICHAEL A. NICHOLAS #450

APPOINTED: March 26, 1965
RETIRED: August 31, 2000

The subject of the below profile was never promoted to any supervisory position, nor was he interested in doing so. And yet during his police career, and for many years even after his retirement and death, he achieved a persona and reputation that seems almost legendary to those who knew and worked with him.

Michael A. Nicholas was born in the City of Yonkers on July 11, 1938 of Portuguese ancestry. He often boasted that being born on 7-11 was his sign of good luck. As a youth he attended Hawthorne Jr. High School and later graduated from Saunders Trades School with a trade in Electric Wiring. He also attended the University of New York for one year earning 30 college credits but had to leave to start working and help his family. Even as a young man he was always an extremely high energy, outgoing and an athletic individual. In the early 1950's, after school, he played on the basketball team called the "Dumontiers" along with future Yonkers police officers Bob Martin, Bob Blair, Charles Crawford and Pat Faia. Their coach was Yonkers PO Nick Rossi. After school Mike worked construction with local #456 of the teamsters. He was taught to work hard, which he did, and respected other hard workers. But Mike had a dream. Being as flamboyant and high profile as he was, it's no surprise that he rode a motorcycle from a young age. And his dream was to be a motorcycle police officer. So, he took the police exam, passed it, and while waiting on the police Patrolman's list to be appointed to the YPD he would often stop his friend, motorcycle PO Jack Weise, and ask, *When I get on, how do I get on the Wheel?* To Mike there was nothing more important.

Mike Nicholas was ultimately appointed to the police department on March 26, 1965 while residing at 16 Regina Place. He and his recruit class of ten "rookies" received the basic police recruit training at the Iona College campus. Their training program ran from April 5th to the 30th of April 1965. Following graduation Probationary Patrolman Michael Nicholas was assigned to the 4th precinct on foot patrol, as well as occasionally assigned to a sector car, earning a starting salary of $5,880 a year. And while still new to "the job" he was a star player on the PBA softball team. But he always had his eye on the police motorcycle. I'm sure he often asked his brother-in-law, Vincent Castaldo, who was in Yonkers politics and would later be Yonkers City Manager, if he could get him assigned to the Traffic Division.

After over three years on patrol in the 4th precinct, on July 26, 1968, PO Nicholas achieved his goal by being assigned to the Special Operations Division's Tactical Unit on two wheel motorcycle patrol. This was the beginning of a storied career as a motorcycle police officer. As mentioned previously, Mike Nicholas was far from being a shrinking violet. He was loud, boisterous, pompous, short tempered and very opinionated. But at the same time very respectful to all his superior officers. While in uniform he was one of the best dressed officers in the unit. His uniforms were always new in appearance and tailored to fit; his leather equipment was maintained in 'like new' condition; he came in on his off duty time to wash and wax his motorcycle regularly which, regardless of its age, always looked brand new and had a little more chrome than anyone else's. Being a "wheel man" to Mike, put him on stage and he was the star performer. As far as Mike was concerned, riding a motorcycle was his life.

Lest one think he was all show it should be known that he was one of the best riders in the Traffic Unit. He was good, and he knew it. He often told a story that when he first went to traffic, whenever there was a new traffic cop assigned, you were required to pass what they called "Foody's Hill." What this meant was, you weren't really accepted as being a good rider in the unit unless you could ride up the

PO Michael A. Nicholas #450 (cont.)

steep Curtis Lane hill from Sprain Road and midway make a U-Turn back down; and Sgt Bob Foody would say, *Don't put your foot down and don't go on the ladies grass either."* This was very difficult on such a narrow street but could be done with the wheel base of a 1965 Harley; but much more difficult with newer models. Of course Mike could do this with no problem.

Mike was always outgoing and opinionated but beneath his bluster he had a heart of gold willing to help anyone. Although his way of offering help was typically Mike Nicholas. For example, he would offer to train new people in the unit how to ride, but only if, in his opinion, they really wanted to learn. When a new officer came into the unit Mike would offer to teach the new man. But his offer was typically very short, blunt and crudely to the point; Example; "*You want to learn, then listen to me and I'll teach you. If not, go f..k yourself.*" Profanity was very common and not even considered offensive by this group of tough, hard riding men. Another common refrain from Mike; "*You want to learn, then listen to the teacher*"! You never had any doubt what Mike meant when he spoke. You may not have liked it but there was no ambiguity in his message.

Mike Nicholas, sometimes referred to as "Broadway Mike," was a very unique personality and was very unique in his use of the English language. As he enjoyed putting on a show with his sharp wit and biting sarcasm he did so with his own use of English and his personal phrases to make a point. They were often humorous and on occasion hard to understand. His style of communicating to those he spoke to after pulling them over on a traffic stop or even to co-workers, was described by his friends as "Mikeanese." Very often when talking with a supervisor he respected he would refer to him as "Boss Man." Or when given a job by a supervisor he often would reply, "*10-4, You're the boss, I'm the horse. Consider it done 1, 2, 6.*" Or when instructing a tractor trailer driver to backup he would order, "*Back up the back Jack and don't break my back,*" which likely caused some confusion. Another was, "*It's in the hamper,*" or "*He's in the hamper*" which could mean, consider it done or someone is in trouble with him. His way of stating that someone was good at riding a motorcycle was to say, "*That man can really ride the fat lady's ass.*"

It should be clear that however unique and humorous his dialogue, Mike was serious about his work and determined to stand out. No problem there. In his early years in Traffic Nicholas liked to ride side by side with PO Robert Reynolds on the west side of the city. He and Reynolds, who was also all spit and polish, both seemed made to ride and were probably the toughest and surliest traffic officers to follow the old breed that were leaving through retirements. They each would get about 8 to 10 speed summonses each a day, which was double everyone else. Mike never left the motorcycle unit and later in his career, as he got a little older, Mike Nicholas was detailed to the Truck Weight Enforcement Unit within the Traffic Division. He was a certified Accident Investigator, and the in house motorcycle mechanic and maintenance officer for all the unit's motorcycles.

Unfortunately, even the toughest of men are still human. When diagnosed with malignant and terminal cancer and following major surgery, Mike told me during a hospital visit, in typical Nicholas bravado and in his own form of communicating, "*I know I'm on the thruway but I'm not at the toll booth yet.*"

Upon his retirement on August 31, 2000 he received a proclamation from the mayor's office

PO Michael A. Nicholas #450 (cont.)

commending him on his 35 years of dedicated service to the police department.

Two years later, on March 8, 2002, Ret PO Mike Nicholas died in St. John's hospital at 63 years of age. His funeral was provided with an Honor Guard and a motorcycle escort consisting of 34 motorcycles, including the entire Yonkers Motorcycle Unit (16), and motorcycles from departments throughout the county as well as from New Jersey and Connecticut. A fitting motorcycle send-off and tribute to "Broadway Mike."

PO ROBERT L. BLAIR #232

APPOINTED: March 26, 1965
RETIRED: December 25, 1992

Robert L Blair was born in the City of Yonkers on March 30, 1937. He attended PS# 14, Longfellow Jr High School, Mark Twain, and graduated from Roosevelt High School. A large powerful man Bob played on the school's baseball and football teams. He also played college football as well. On his application to the police department Bob listed his employment as working construction and for Carey's Bar & Grill in Yonkers.

Bob Blair received his appointment to the police department on March 26, 1965 while residing at 9 Orchard Street. He received his basic police recruit training at the Iona College campus from April 5th through April 30, 1965. Following recruit graduation Probationary Patrolman Robert Blair was assigned to the 1st precinct at 10 St. Casimir Avenue on foot patrol earning a starting salary of $5,880 a year. Officer Blair was one of those individuals with a great humorous personality which made him well liked by all. But when required he could be a very tough street cop. He was also very active in the Police Benevolent Association, (PBA) particularly their sporting activities, playing on their softball team for many years.

On November 9, 1966, the year following his appointment and part of a citywide reorganization, he was reassigned to patrol duty in the 4th precinct. And he remained there on January 1, 1971 when a large precinct centralization plan was implemented and resulted in the closing of two precincts. Bob received a break from the rotating work schedule when, on June 23, 1972, he was assigned to the Special Operations Division detailed to parking meter enforcement.

On January 29, 1973 Bob was transferred to his dream job when he was assigned to the Youth Division but was detailed to work in the Police Athletic League (PAL) organizing various sporting activities designated to distract and divert troubled juveniles from criminal activities to the physical outlet of sports. Blair, along with a few other officers assigned to PAL and serving as coaches, operated programs year round such as Basketball, softball, swimming, boxing, the martial arts, etc. The programs that PO Blair and others coached and supervised produced a number of semi pro sport figures and even some professionals. Their work saved a lot of children from involvement in crime.

PO Robert L. Blair, cousin to Capt. Robert Blair, retired on Christmas Day, December 25, 1992.

PO GEORGE HAZZARD #125

APPOINTED: March 26, 1965
RETIRED: April 5, 1985

George Hazzard was born George Hazarian of Armenian heritage in the Bronx, NY on June 28, 1942. He attended PS# 94, PS#80 Jr. HS, and later graduated from DeWitt Clinton HS, all of the Bronx. In addition to English George spoke Armenian as a second language. Following school George joined the Army on Oct. 18, 1961 and served up to Oct. 17, 1963 and was honorably discharged. He was previously employed by the Pinkerton Security Agency in 1965. Hazzard was appointed to the Y.P.D. on Mar. 26, 1965, the very first Armenian, while living at 272 East Gun Hill Road, in the Bx. He received his recruit training at the Iona College campus in New Rochelle from April 5th to the 30th of 1965. Upon graduation officer Hazzard was assigned to the 3rd pct on patrol earning a starting salary of $5,880 a year. When the South Command was established on Jan. 1, 1971 PO Hazzard was moved there and remained right up to his retirement on Apr. 5, 1985. As a second job, George had a private business selling jewelry throughout most of his career, and in retirement he worked part time in the NYC jewelry district as a jewelry auctioneer.

PO PETER DATTWYLER #452

APPOINTED: March 26, 1965
RETIRED: April 5, 1985

Born in Yonkers on Oct. 6, 1941 Pete Dattwyler attended the Immaculate Conception school in Tuckahoe NY and graduated from Roosevelt HS in 1959. Pete joined the Navy on Oct. 19, 1971 and served aboard the USS Lloyd Thomas as a barber. He was honorably discharged on Oct. 13, 1961. He previously worked for Western Electric in Yonkers. Pete was appointed to the Y.P.D. on Mar. 26, 1965 while living at 59 Grassy Sprain Rd. He received his recruit training at the Iona College campus in New Rochelle, NY which ran from April 5th to the 30th of 1965. Following graduation officer Peter Dattwyler was assigned to patrol duty in the 2nd pct and remained at that location until Oct. 19, 1971 when he was transferred to the Special Operations Division on two wheel motorcycle duty. On Jan. 1, 1980 Pete was detailed from Traffic duty to the Training Div. to serve as an instructor. Along with in-service training for working officers, the training staff was required to train new recruits as well. And Pete certainly served as an example of what a police officer should look like. PO Dattwyler was always meticulous in his appearance in uniform and was a fitness enthusiast. His physical trademark was his handle-bar mustache which he kept throughout his career. He even brought with him some boxing experience that he may have learned in the Navy. This made him a perfect fit for instructing Defensive Tactics to other officers. Although he remained in the Training Div. he was still assigned to the Traffic Unit right up to his retirement on April 5, 1985. After retiring Pete and his family moved to Florida.

PO LESLIE FEUER #563

APPOINTED: March 26, 1965
RETIRED: June 24, 1986

"Les" Feuer was born in the Bronx, NY on February 21, 1940. He attended PS #61 in the Bronx and graduated from Samuel Gompers Vocational High School also in the Bronx and was able to speak Hebrew as a second language. He joined the Marine Corps in January of 1957.

As a young man Les was an excellent auto mechanic by trade and operated a gas station in Yorktown. It was the early 1960's and just from kids talking, he knew where the kids were buying drugs and this knowledge led NYSP Investigator Charles Cassino to approach him and ask if he would be interested in working undercover for them making purchases of illegal drugs. At the time Les had taken both the NYPD and Yonkers Patrolman's exam, passed both, and was waiting to be called for appointment. He figured working for the State Police could only help with a future police appointment so he accepted the offer.

However, there was a problem. The State Police were unable to appoint him as a State Trooper without going through the usual testing process and Les needed police officer status to start his undercover work and have the protection of police officer status. But the State Police was able to have the Town of Greenburgh appoint Les as a police officer on a provisional basis. No exam was needed and he then had investigative and arrest powers. Les worked for about four years undercover as a paid undercover officer for the State Police and also the former Federal Bureau of Narcotics on undercover investigations throughout Westchester County and down in Harlem. His work was very dangerous as he worked alone making narcotic "buys" and documenting same for arrest and prosecution purposes. He did this until he was notified by Yonkers a position was available as a police officer.

Leslie Feuer was appointed to the Yonkers Police Department on March 26, 1965 while living at 765 Bronx River Road. Leslie and his recruit class received their basic recruit police training at the Iona College campus in New Rochelle, NY. This training curriculum ran from April 5th to the 30th of 1965. Following his graduation Probationary Patrolman Leslie Feuer was assigned to the 1st precinct earning a starting salary of $5,880 a year. Though he was assigned to the 1st precinct, and before he even graduated from recruit school, the Yonkers Police Narcotics Unit had plans for him.

As soon as probationary police officer Feuer completed the required recruit training he was immediately detailed to the Detective Division as a "silver shield," no detective status, and assigned to work undercover with the Narcotics Unit investigating and making purchases of illegal narcotics; but this time for the City of Yonkers. During the ensuing year he made a remarkable number of arrests and earned an enviable reputation. As a result he was appointed a Detective on January 28, 1966 and was partnered up with Det. Joel Parisi. Together they made a great team and made a tremendous impact on the illegal drug use and sales in Yonkers. In 1965 and 1966 the Westchester County Grand Jury voted a special commendation to Det's Feuer and Parisi for the resourceful and courageous performance of their duty in undercover work and the manner in which they testified. Det Feuer attended the Federal Bureau of Narcotics school from November through December of 1967 in Washington DC.

However, two years later, on October 1, 1968, Det Feuer was returned to police officer status and

PO Leslie Feuer #563 (cont.)

was reassigned from the Detective Division to uniform patrol duty in the 4th precinct. While in the 4th, which was later re-designated the North Command, Les partnered up with PO John "Mitch" Meade and worked the busiest patrol sector in the precinct. But that's just what PO Feuer wanted. He wanted to be where the action was. And Les was always a hard worker with two jobs. While assigned to patrol in the North Command, following his tour he would work in his own auto repair shop which he operated on Oak Street in Yonkers.

Les worked sector 8 until an opening occurred in the Emergency Services Unit, and in November of 1979 he attended the NYPD Emergency Service school in NYC. He would remain in ESU up to March 18, 1981 when he was reassigned to the South Command. PO Feuer retired from the YPD on June 24, 1986.

After retiring Les was hired as the night manager of the Top Brass Night Club on Yonkers Ave in Yonkers and sometime later he would gain employment in Spring Valley, NY as a court officer where he remained for 12 years. Years later Les moved with his wife to Florida's west coast where he worked for a number of years as security at the Sarasota airport and finally retired completely.

PO FRANCIS M. HORAN #466

APPOINTED: July 23, 1965
RETIRED: January 24, 1986

Francis Michael Horan was born in the City of Yonkers on February 17, 1943. However, as a young boy he and his family moved to the Bronx where he attended PS# 81 and the DeLasalle Institute, and later graduated from the DeWitt Clinton high school in the Bronx, New York.

Following high school Frank obtained employment working for a plumbing and heating company in Mount Vernon as a steam fitter. He also often worked as a security guard at the Yonkers Raceway. But Frank's family had a tradition in law enforcement that he was determined to follow. His grandfather, Michael Horan, was a Yonkers Police Sergeant and his father Frank, had been a police officer in the NYPD for 37 years. Now it was young Frank's turn to maintain the un-broken tradition.

And so, Francis M. Horan was appointed to the Yonkers Police Department on July 23, 1965 while he was living at 135 5th Avenue in North Pelham, NY. He and his recruit group received their basic police recruit training at the NYPD Police Academy and received both academic and physical training during a curriculum which ran from July 26, 1965 to November 28, 1965. Following recruit graduation Patrolman Horan was assigned to patrol duty in the 3rd precinct earning a starting salary of $5,880 a year.

On June 2, 1967 while investigating a report of a strange odor at 1 Post Street Horan and his partner discovered smoke coming from the building. While evacuating tenants they found the source being a locked 3rd floor apt. By body force they broke down the door finding the apartment filled with smoke and by crawling along the floor they found and rescued a 69 year old tenant. They again entered and found a 75 year old female unconscious on a couch with her clothing on fire. With a hall fire extinguisher they put out the fire on the couch and her clothing and carried her out to safety. For his actions officer Horan was recommended for a Commendation but received only a Certificate of Excellent Police Work.

On December 9, 1970 Frank Horan was reassigned from patrol duty to the Communications Division where he was assigned to various functions over the years. In fact, Frank would remain in the Communications Division right up to his retirement on January 24, 1986. Two years later, Frank would have the pleasure of watching his son, Francis Michael Horan Jr., be sworn in as a Yonkers police officer in 1988. From his grandfather's appointment in 1894, to his son's appointment in 1988, four generations of police officers had served the public.

DET. PATRICK J. FAIA #637

APPOINTED: July 23, 1965
RETIRED: February 25, 1997

Patrick Faia was born in the City of Yonkers on April 21, 1942 and after attending St. Mary's school, graduated from Commerce high school. On his application to the police department he listed his current employment as a delivery man for the Orza bakery.

Patrick was appointed to the Yonkers Police Department on July 23, 1965 while living at 268 New Main St. Probationary police officer Faia and his recruit class were sent to the New York City Police Academy for basic recruit training. This intensive physical and academic training ran from July 26, 1965 to November 28, 1965. Following graduation PO Faia was assigned to foot patrol duty in the 3rd precinct earning a starting salary of $5,880 a year. On August 8, 1969 Pat was transferred to the 4th precinct and in November reassigned to the 2nd precinct.

Officer Faia was appointed a Detective on April 17, 1970 and assigned to work in the Detective Division on general assignment investigations. Pat was very athletic and during the 1970s he was a very active member of the PBA basketball team. About a year after his appointment as a detective, on July 16, 1971, Det Faia was returned to police officer status and transferred to patrol duty in the South Command. At some point over the next 10 years Faia was detailed to headquarters to work in the Tele Serv Unit which took police reports over the telephone. This detail ended on May 22, 1981 and PO Faia was returned to patrol duty in the South Command. A little over four years later, on November 1, 1985, Patrick Faia was again appointed a Detective and was returned to the Detective Division.

Two years later, on April 22, 1987, Det Faia was detailed to the Special Operations Division working in the Hack Licensing Unit, and did so maintaining his position as a Detective. But once again he was returned to the Detective Division on October 31, 1988. Following an injury to his knee and the required surgery, he was out disabled throughout the last year that he worked on the job. Having served over 31 years, Det Patrick Faia retired from the police department on February 25, 1997.

DET. LT. WILLIAM J. DRAIN

APPOINTED: July 23, 1965
RETIRED: February 16, 2001

Bill Drain was born in the City of Yonkers on November 2, 1942. He attended St. Eugene's elementary school, Sacred Heart Junior high school, and later graduated from Roosevelt HS. He later worked for the People's Savings Bank as a teller until Oct. 24, 1962 when he joined the Army National Guard's 101st Signal Battalion. Following his release from active duty Bill returned to his job at the bank until he received a notice from the Yonkers Police Department.

Bill received his appointment to the Y.P.D. on July 23, 1965 while he was living at 279 N. Broadway. Officer Drain was sent to the New York City Police Academy for basic recruit training. This intensive physical and academic training ran from July 26, 1965 to November 28, 1965. Following graduation PO Drain was assigned to patrol duty in the 4th precinct earning $5,880 a year.

The following year, on June 12, 1967, he was transferred to work in the Youth Division which was located off the Columbus Place entrance of headquarters. He worked there for about a year, was returned to patrol in the 4th precinct in June of 1968 for two years, and then on April 27, 1970 he was returned to duty in the Youth Division. Apparently the investigative experience he gained investigating juvenile crime prove to be very valuable because on February 12, 1971 Bill was appointed a Detective in the Detective Division working in general assignment. Sometime later he was assigned to the gambling squad where he remained for several years.

Det Bill Drain was promoted to Sergeant on Sept. 30, 1983 and was reassigned to the 3rd precinct as a patrol supervisor. In 1985 he was returned to the D.D., this time as a Detective Sergeant supervising a squad of detectives. On May 23, 1986, Det Sgt Drain was promoted to the rank of Police Lieutenant and was transferred from the Detective Division out to the 2nd precinct as a patrol lieutenant.

On June 24, 1987 Lt Drain was again returned to the Detective Division and placed in charge of the burglary unit. In January of 1991 the division's major case lieutenant retired and Bill Drain was now designated the new Detective Division major case coordinator. And when necessary, Bill was also a trained hostage negotiator. On January 9, 1997 after the DD captain, Tom Kressman, retired he was not replaced right away and Lt Drain was designated acting commanding officer of the DD for several months. In June of 1997 a captain was assigned as the commanding officer. As a result Drain was reduced to second in command, and as a result on June 30, 1997 Lt Drain, upon his own request, was transferred and designated the C.O. of the Special Investigations Division.

Bill Drain was always an avid golfer; he was also a member of the Friendly Sons of St. Patrick, president of the Yonkers Police Holy Name Society, former financial secretary to the PBA, chairman of the welfare committee for the Captains, Lieutenants and Sergeants Association, Detective Division trustee, and in 1998 he was named Christ the King church, man of the year. Bill's father was a retired Yonkers Fire Dept. captain, his brother Eugene was a Yonkers Detective Sergeant, his brother Robert was a Yonkers firefighter, his nephew Sean was a Yonkers police officer, and his son-in-law was Det. Paul Rubeo.

Det Lt Bill Drain retired from the Yonkers Police Dept. on February 16, 2001 and following his retirement he was appointed Chairman of the Yonkers Municipal Housing Authority.

After a lengthy illness retired Lieut. Bill drain died on April 21, 2005. He was 62 years old.

PO RONALD W. CAMPANARO #469

APPOINTED: July 23, 1965
RESIGNED: January 13, 1967

Ronald William Campanaro was born April 12, 1940 in Yonkers, NY. He attended PS# 4 and later graduated from Saunders HS having majored in Electric Wiring. Ron joined the Air Force on Feb. 8, 1961 and served in the 525th F.I.S. He was honorable discharge on November 10, 1964. Prior to the YPD, Ron worked for the Reda TV Service in Scarsdale. He was appointed to the Yonkers Police Department on July 23, 1965 while residing at 15 Sumner Avenue. He and his recruit group received their basic police recruit training at the NYPD Police Academy and received both academic and physical training during a curriculum which ran from July 26, 1965 to November 28, 1965. Following recruit graduation Patrolman Campanaro was assigned to patrol duty in the 1st precinct earning a starting salary of $5,880 a year. On January 9, 1966 he was reassigned to the 4th precinct. He had earlier taken the Yonkers Fire Dept. test as well as the YPD test and was notified he could be appointed to the YFD. He decided to switch and resigned from the police department on January 13, 1967 to be appointed a Yonkers Firefighter.

PO FRANKLYN H. FARRELL #465

APPOINTED: July 23, 1965
RESIGNED: July 31, 1966

Born in Newmansville, PA. on November 14, 1943, Franklin Farrell attended the North Clarion School there from 1949 to 1961 from which he later graduated. "Frank" joined the Air Force on May 31, 1961 and served in the 539th F.I.S as a jet engine mechanic. He was honorably discharged on May 28, 1965 as an Airman 1st class. He listed his previous employment with the General Motors Corp, assembly line in Tarrytown. Frank was appointed to the YPD on July 23, 1965 while living at 154 Lockwood Avenue. He and his recruit group received their basic police recruit training at the NYPD Police Academy and received both academic and physical training during a curriculum which ran from July 26, 1965 to November 28, 1965. Following recruit graduation Patrolman Farrell was assigned to patrol duty in the 2nd precinct earning a starting salary of $5,880 a year. He had earlier taken the NYPD test as well as Yonkers and was notified he could be appointed in the city. On July 31, 1966 Frank resigned from the YPD and was appointed a police officer with the NYPD. Frank retired from the NYPD and moved to Putnam County where he worked as an exterminator.

LT. GILBERT G. BALEZENTIS

APPOINTED: July 23, 1965
RETIRED: July 12, 1993

The subject of the below profile could accurately be described as a very energetic, enthusiastic, good-humored, and gung ho personality. He had a great sense of humor but you never knew what was coming next.

Gilbert Balezentis was born in the City of Yonkers on August 1, 1941, attended PS #23 and later graduated from Saunders high school with a trade in carpentry. He also attended the University of Maryland taking a course in the German language from 1962 to 1963 and became very fluent in that language. Considering his outgoing personality it might be surprising to learn that he also attended Westchester Community College taking courses in accounting and typing.

Gil joined the Army on July 8, 1960 serving with the 507th Army Security Agency. He also reported that sometime during his enlistment he was a paratrooper and made several jumps. He received his honorable discharge on June 18, 1963 with the rank of Army specialist 5th class. On his application to the YPD he listed his current employment as a member of the Carpenters local #188.

Gilbert Balezentis was appointed to the Yonkers Police Department on July 23, 1965, while residing at 188 Cook Avenue. Probationary police officer Balezentis and his recruit class were sent to the New York City Police Academy for basic recruit training. This intensive physical and academic training ran from July 26, 1965 to November 28, 1965. Gil proved to be an excellent student and as a result was awarded an off-duty revolver for his excellent academic record. Following graduation PO Balezentis was assigned to foot patrol duty in the 3rd precinct earning a starting salary of $5,880 a year.

Following the opening of the new 1st precinct that was built at 730 E. Grassy Sprain Rd., on November 7, 1966 PO Balezentis was transferred to this new 1st precinct. On January 1, 1971, following the implementation of decentralization plan whereby two patrol precincts were closed, Gil was reassigned to the old 4th precinct which had been renamed the North command. Nearly two years later, on October 6, 1972, Gill received his first promotion to the rank of Sergeant earning a new salary of $14,399 and was

Lt. Gilbert G. Balezentis (cont.)

transferred to the South Command as a patrol supervisor.

Ever since the rank of police lieutenant was established in 1908 the officer holding that rank would serve as a precinct desk officer unless on special assignment. However that time honored tradition changed on March 12, 1973 when a reorganization plan was put into effect whereby former desk lieutenants were placed on patrol duty and a number of sergeants who were on patrol duty were now placed on desk duty. This move was not very popular with the rank and file but change would not come for some time, and when change did come the lieutenants would still not be returned to desk duty. In any event, the desk officer status which was now filled by a sergeant was designated as Station house Supervisor and Sgt. Gil Balezentis was assigned to this duty.

As Gil earned seniority younger sergeants replaced him on that desk duty and he was assigned to patrol supervision. He moved around over the next few years i.e., October 21, 1978 to the South command, and March 18, 1981 back to the North command. Balezentis was always very active as both a police officer and as a sergeant and as a result he was awarded the title of Police Officer of The Year by the Yonkers Exchange Club in April of 1986.

Gil received his second promotion on October 17, 1986 when he was promoted to the rank of Police Lieutenant and assigned as a supervisor of the Communications Division. But once again he was returned to patrol duty on May 29, 1987 in the 3rd precinct. And the following year, on December 2, 1988, he was reassigned to the newly formed Housing Unit as the supervising officer. The following year, on March 20, 1989, Gil was designated the commanding officer of the Housing Unit. His natural leadership abilities and his high esprit de corps motivated his police officers into one of the most efficient and effective units in the police department. All this, while patrolling some of the worst crime ridden housing units in the city.

Once again Gil moved around several times. On December 10, 1990 to the North command as an Operations Lieutenant, July 10, 1991 to the Field Services Bureau, and on July 22, 1992 to the Support Services Bureau assigned to the city jail in Central Booking.

Lt Balezentis had the pleasure of knowing that two of his sons, Thomas and Christopher, both followed him by being sworn in as members of the Yonkers Police Department. His son Thomas later left to be a Yonkers Parking Enforcement Officer.

Lt Gilbert Balezentis retired from the Yonkers Police Department effective July 12, 1993.

PO EDWARD J. OPACIUCH #462

APPOINTED: July 23, 1965
RETIRED: August 23, 1985

Ed Opaciuch was born in Poland on August 27, 1935. Both his parents were born in the U.S. so Ed was an American citizen at birth. After returning to America, as a youth Ed attended St. Casimir's school from 1947 to 1952, but left school to join the army on December 4, 1953. During his enlistment Ed served in the 4th Armored Division and was discharged as a Corporal on December 2, 1955. Upon his separation from the military Ed returned to school, entered Halstead High School on North Broadway in September of 1956 and earned his high school diploma. Sometime later Ed gained employment with the Otis elevator Company wiring elevator controllers. He did this right up until he was called by the YPD.

Ed Opaciuch was appointed to the police department on July 23, 1965, while residing at 170 Palisade Avenue. Probationary police officer Opaciuch and his recruit class were sent to the New York City Police Academy for basic recruit training. This intensive physical and academic training ran from July 26, 1965 to November 28, 1965. Following graduation PO Opaciuch was assigned to foot patrol duty in the 1st precinct earning a starting salary of $5,880 a year. Ed's brothers-in-law were Det. Joe Sokol, PO Joe Guglich and Deputy Chief Frank Sardo, three of whom married three sisters.

On November 9, 1966 Ed was transferred to the 4th precinct where he would remain on patrol duty for the next five years. It was on June 23, 1972 that he was transferred to the Special Operations Division for parking meter enforcement and after a short time was assigned to two wheel motorcycle duty as part of the Traffic Unit. Ed remained a member of the Traffic Unit's motorcycle squad right up to his retirement on August 23, 1985.

Following his retirement Ed served for many years as the vice president of the New York Police and Fire Retirees Association devoting countless hours to obtaining benefits to help police and fire department retirees. And whenever possible he would spend time trying to improve his golf game.

PO WALTER J. HLEWICKI #461

APPOINTED: July 23, 1965
RETIRED: January 12, 1995

Walter Hlewicki, who was born in the City of Yonkers on October 20, 1942, received his formal education by attending PS #12, PS# 27, and later graduatedfrom Yonkers high school. Walter also attended the Mondell Institute in New York City for Architectural Drafting from 1960 to 1961.

Walt joined the Army in July of 1962 and received military police training at Ft. Gordon, Georgia. He was then assigned to the 512th Military Police Company at Fort Hauchuca, Arizona. He would later serve with the 404th Military Police Company, 4th Armored Division, in Cooke Barracks, Goppingen Germany, and was later honorably discharged in January of 1965. Previous to the YPD Walter listed his employment with the Burroughs Welcome Co. in Tuckahoe as a shipping clerk.

Walter Hlewicki was appointed to the Yonkers Police Department on July 23, 1965. Probationary police officer Hlewicki and his recruit class were sent to the New York City Police Academy for basic recruit training whose intensive physical and academic training ran from July 26, 1965 to November 28, 1965. Following graduation PO Hlewicki was assigned to foot patrol duty in the 3rd precinct earning a starting salary of $5,880 a year. On January 1, 1971, following the closing of two precincts as part of a centralization plan, Walter was reassigned to the South Patrol Command, which had formerly been the 2nd precinct. Shortly thereafter PO Hlewicki's request to be assigned to the Emergency Services Unit was approved. He received all the necessary emergency training, and was assigned to the Emergency Service Unit in the South Command.

Ten years later, on December 4, 1981, Walter was transferred to the North Patrol Command but remained working in the Emergency Squad. In fact, he and his partner, PO Nick Iarriccio, were the first nationally registered Emergency Medical Technicians (EMT's) that received training that was paid for by the municipality instead of with their own money. After 16 years in the Emergency Squad, on June 24, 1987, Walt Hlewicki left the Emergency Squad and was transferred back to the 2nd precinct designated as their Crime Prevention Officer.

In 1991 Walter was assigned to the Community Affairs Division from which he would later retire on January 12, 1995. Known as "Wally" to his very close friends, Walter's great-uncle was Lt George Rusnack and his uncle was Yonkers City Jailer Joseph Budrock. Walt was always active in the PBA and other organizations and in retirement he served for many years as the recording secretary for the New York Police and Fire Retirees Association.

PO CHARLES M. STORMS #459

APPOINTED: July 23, 1965
RETIRED: February 21, 1986

Charlie Storms, or as he was known by everyone since he was a child, "Skippy" Storms, was born in the City of Yonkers on July 23, 1938. He attended PS# 12, Longfellow Jr. High School, and graduated from Commerce High School in June of 1956. The following year, on March 7, 1957, "Skip" joined the Army serving in the Artillery and was honorably discharged on March 6, 1960 as a Specialist E-5. He worked various jobs but the last job before the YPD was with the US Post Office in Yonkers.

Charles Storms was appointed to the police department on his birthday, July 23, 1965, while residing at 118 Mayfair Rd. Probationary police officer Storms and his recruit class were sent to the New York City Police Academy for basic recruit training. This intensive physical and academic training ran from July 26, 1965 to November 28, 1965. Following graduation PO Storms was assigned to foot patrol duty in the 2nd precinct earning a starting salary of $5,880 a year.

On April 27, 1970 Storms was assigned to the Detective Division, but not as a detective, and detailed to work in the Youth Division investigating crimes by juveniles. On January 1, 1971, following the closing of two precincts, Charlie was reassigned to the North Patrol Command patrolling then sector 10, a busy west side area. Around 1976, Skippy was transferred to the Youth Division. A former partner, PO Bill Vance was also assigned there and they worked as partners once again.

Early on in his career Skip was very active in sports. He played on the PBA softball and basketball team and later on the Over 40 League of the PBA. He was elected Treasurer of the PBA in 1975 and held that position right up to January of 1986, just before retiring. PO Charles "Skippy" Storms retired from the YPD on February 21, 1986 and began working as the office manager of HFS Electric Co. He retired from that position eight years later in March of 1994 and in 1996 he and his wife moved to Arizona where he enjoys playing golf in the sun.

DET. KENNETH M. ZAJAC #633

APPOINTED: July 23, 1965
RESIGNED: May 15, 1970

It is unlikely that anyone appointed a police officer would ever think that at some point in their career they would earn, and be the recipient of, the police department Medal of Honor, but that's exactly what occurred with the officer described below.

Kenneth Zajac was born in the City of Yonkers on May 4, 1941. As a youth he attended St. Casimir's elementary school, Longfellow Jr. High school, and Commerce High School.

Ken quit school in the 11th grade to join the Navy on August 5, 1959 and he served with the 6th fleet aboard the Flag Ship USS Moines, CA134, in the Mediterranean as a Boatswains Mate 3rd class. While in the Navy Ken earned his high school equivalency diploma. He received his honorable discharge on July 27, 1961. Following his military service Ken worked for short periods with a number of companies. There was Otis Elevator Co, and later as a NYS Ranger, and also as a "Special" officer with the Greenburgh PD. While with State Rangers or Park Police he was detailed to work undercover narcotics investigations for the NY State Police. He did not know it at the time but it was the beginning of an unimaginable journey.

Ken Zajac was appointed to the Yonkers Police Dept. on July 23, 1965 while residing at 32 Van Cortlandt Park Avenue. Probationary police officer Zajac and his recruit class were sent to the New York City Police Academy for basic recruit training. This intensive physical and academic training ran from July 26, 1965 to November 28, 1965. Following graduation PO Zajac was assigned to foot patrol duty in the 1st precinct earning a starting salary of $5,880 a year. The following year, on November 9, 1966, Zajac was transferred to the 4th precinct on patrol. Though Ken was clearly of Polish ancestry, it is likely that his mother may have been Irish because Ken was an original member of the Westchester County Police Emerald Society Pipe and Drum Band, as a piper.

Due to his previous experience with undercover narcotics work with the state police, on January 13, 1967 PO Ken Zajac was appointed a Detective and assigned to work undercover narcotics investigations in the Yonkers police Narcotics Unit. During this assignment Det Zajac worked very closely with various other jurisdictions including, the White Plains PD, the Greenburgh PD, the Peekskill PD, the Federal Bureau of Narcotics, and the Westchester County District Attorney's Office.

On June 23, 1967, following some personality "conflicts" with Det. Capt. Frank Vescio, Zajac found himself back on patrol in uniform in the 1st precinct. While there Zajac was assigned to a plainclothes robbery detail due to a number of motel armed robberies. It was nearing the holiday season and on the evening of December 7, 1967 he was supposed to have been with his partner P.O. Joe Abbondola, but Joe had taken the night off. So Ken went out alone in plainclothes armed with his S&W revolver and the precinct's trusty 12 ga. Ithaca pump shotgun, the heaviest weapon in the Y.P.D. inventory at that time. He began to make the rounds visiting the motels in the precinct.

On that night at about 4:20 a.m. he was a bit bored and had just stopped into the Tuckahoe Motel at 307 Tuckahoe Road. Leaving his shotgun standing behind the front desk, Ken told the female clerk he was going to use the lavatory in a room behind the desk. While in there, he later reported that he thought he heard from outside the door, *"This is a holdup."* Still not quite sure but with his revolver in his hand he

Det. Kenneth M. Zajac #633 (cont.)

opened the door and saw two males with guns only feet away. One of them held a .45 caliber semi-automatic pistol to the females head. For an instant both he and the suspects were startled, and the clerk dropped to the floor. At this point, as one of the men reportedly yelled *"Kill the %*&#,"* the second male opened fire point blank at Zajac who immediately ducked back into the bathroom.

As the two men fled, Zajac came out and returned fire with his revolver. Years later Zajac jokingly said he made direct hits on the front glass windows but nothing else. However, he then grabbed his shotgun loaded with 12 gauge double "0" buckshot and ran out into the lot after both men who had run westbound toward Tuckahoe Road. As Zajac ran behind them, they turned and again began firing at Zajac at which point he said that he dropped to the ground with the shotgun and fired at the fleeing gunmen while lying prone. His first shot hit one of the men and spun him around, but he kept on firing as he ran. To avoid the rounds fired at him, officer Zajac rolled to the side, aimed, and again fired. As Zajac described it to this writer, "*I struck one of them dead center as he ran and when he got hit, it actually lifted him off the ground and he flew over the hood of a nearby car like superman. I'll never forget it.*" That suspect remained motionless from that point on. Of the first officers responding to the scene were PO Joe Podeswa and rookie Patrolman Marty Schwartz who handcuffed the mortally wounded robber.

The second male escaped temporarily by running across the road and onto the Thruway. A passing motorist assisted Zajac by notifying headquarters of the incident. (Remember, there were no portable radios yet, or cell phones.) When more backup arrived the wounded gunman was taken to Lawrence Hospital where he died several days later. The second gunman was observed walking along the NYS Thruway, wounded by Zajac and bleeding from the arm. He was taken into custody by P.O. John Bocskay and his partner P.O. Bob Martin.

Two days later, on December 9, 1967, Zajac's 1st Precinct commander, Capt. John J. McCarthy submitted a recommendation to Public Safety Commissioner Daniel F. McMahon that P.O. Kenneth Zajac #464, be awarded the police department's Medal of Honor. The captain related the following; "*Officer Kenneth Zajac.............did perform intelligently in the line of police duty, at imminent personal hazard to life, with knowledge of the risk assumed.*" The captain's recommendation was unanimously approved.

On December 19, 1967 officer Zajac was officially awarded the Yonkers Police Medal of Honor and was promoted to the position of Detective, again, and returned to the Yonkers Narcotics Unit. A press release issued by then Chief Polsen read in part, "*Patrolman Zajac's actions in this police case serves to exemplify the highest standards of performance demanded of law enforcement bodies today. The commendable actions of this young officer will long be pointed out to others as an example of intelligence, courage and valor. Patrolman Zajac's name will be entered upon the rolls of those few men who have received the Bureau Medal of Honor while in the service of this city's police department over the years past. He joins an honored group of public servants, some of whom were awarded this medal posthumously, who lived up to their sworn responsibilities and beyond in accomplishing their duty.*"

When officer Zajac was awarded the Medal of Honor, he did not actually receive it. Although the department's first Medal of Honor was awarded back in 1931, no one had ever designed or authorized the making of such a medal. It wasn't until after the killing of P.O. Harold Woods, several years later in

Det. Kenneth M. Zajac #633 (cont.)

September of 1974, that Lt. Martin Harding designed a medal and approval was given for Wayne Silversmith on South Broadway to produce several of them. In fact, the first ribbons prepared for the presentation medals were made by Lt. Harding's wife. A ceremony was finally held in City Hall on May 6, 1975 and Ken Zajac, along with other subsequent recipients of the award, including Det. Thomas Brink, Det. Anthony Cerasi, and Dorothy Woods, the widow of P.O. Harold Woods were brought together and all received their Medals of Honor on the same day, nearly eight years after Zajac had earned his.

But while still in the Yonkers Narcotics Unit, for well over a year Det. Zajac was detailed to the Bureau of Narcotics and Dangerous Drugs (B.N.D.D.), whose name was later changed to the Drug Enforcement Agency (DEA), and continued his work detailed as a narcotics undercover operative for the federal government.

Following an employment offer, from what was then the Westchester County Sheriff's Office, to use his narcotic investigative skills throughout Westchester County, and after serious consideration, on May 15, 1970 Det. Zajac resigned from the YPD and accepted the job with the sheriff's office. Ken quickly rose through the ranks of that department where he remained until it later merged with the new Westchester County Department of Public Safety.

Besides being a senior investigator, Zajac was also one of the members of their department's first "SWAT" team. On one occasion when he was assisting in the court ordered destruction of 280 kilos of cocaine, the county blast furnace blew up, causing Zajac to suffer severe injuries to his neck and back. Though he returned to work after several surgeries, he later retired on a disability pension.

A heavy smoker most of his life, Kenny ended up living with the almost inevitable results. He spent his last few years on oxygen 24 hours a day alone at the Regency Extended Care Nursing Facility on Ashburton Avenue suffering from emphysema, and used a wheel chair to get around due to his injury in the explosion. When I visited him in 2003, although time had taken its toll, Ken's memory was still sharp, his wit and trademark loud laugh intact. I'm sure this Medal of Honor recipient wanted no one to feel sorry for him but, I bet he often thought to himself in those quiet moments, "You know, I remember when……"

Former Yonkers Detective and Ret Chief Investigator Kenneth Zajac died on February 2, 2004. He was 61 years old.

LT. TERRENCE M. McCUE

APPOINTED: July 23, 1965
RETIRED: August 22, 1985

When Terry McCue joined the Yonkers Police Department he was following in a proud family tradition. His two uncles were Capt. James McCue and Det Vincent McCue, and his great uncle was Yonkers PO Mike McCue.

Terry McCue was born in Ossining, NY on October 23, 1943 and following his birth his family moved 559 Palisade Avenue in Yonkers. As a youth Terry attended Sacred Heart, then PS #16, and later graduated from Gorton High School in 1961. The day after graduation, on June 29, 1961, Terry joined the Army and served in the Army Security Agency (a subsidiary of National Security Agency.) During his basic training at Ft. Dix, NJ, the Berlin Wall was built. Half of the training company went immediately to Germany, but he was sent to Ft. Devens, MA for school and went to Germany in February of 1962. He spent 28 months in Germany and was discharged from active duty on June 22 1964.

Upon his military discharge McCue drove a cab for Central Taxi in Scarsdale and took the Yonkers police test in March of 1965. Upon passing the exam Terry McCue was appointed to the Yonkers Police Department, along with 13 others, on July 23, 1965 while still living at 559 Palisade Avenue. Terry and his recruit group received their basic police recruit training at the NYPD Police Academy and received both academic and physical training during a curriculum which ran from July 26, 1965 to November 28, 1965.

Following recruit graduation Patrolman McCue was assigned to patrol duty in the 4th precinct earning a starting salary of $5,880 a year. On April 14, 1967 he was reassigned to the 1st precinct of 730 E. Grassy Sprain Rd, which had opened in November of 1966. On January 1, 1971, following the precinct centralization plan being implemented by closing two precincts, the 1st precincts was merged with the old 4th, then renamed the North Command and McCue was one of many transferred to that North Command.

PO McCue remained on patrol there until December 10, 1971 at which time he was promoted to the rank of Sergeant earning $13,685 a year. Following his promotion he was transferred to the South Command as a patrol supervisor and for a while he also led the Tactical Patrol Unit, and frequently worked desk sergeant duty.

In early 1975 McCue was a sergeant in the South Command and had organized and supervised the 2nd precinct task force and was aware of the existence of a plainclothes Street Crime Unit in the NYPD which was operating with remarkable success. This unit operated on a citywide basis. New York also had smaller precinct plainclothes units which were called “Anti-Crime Units.” Believing that a centralized Anti-Crime Unit in the Yonkers Police Department could make a significant impact in dealing with various crime problems within the City of Yonkers, Sgt McCue recommended to Chief William Polsen that our department establish an Anti-Crime Unit within the police department. After due consideration Chief William Polsen approved Sgt McCue’s recommendation and as a result McCue was directed to contact the NYPD Street Crime Unit (SCU.).

Sgt McCue was invited down to the NYPD and conducted an extensive study on the operation of their Street Crime Unit. He was even invited down to Randall's Island where the SCU had their HQ. Sgt McCue wrote up a lengthy evaluation on the concept of this style of policing, how to make use of it most

Lt. Terrence M. McCue (cont.)

effectively, the various scheduling of the personnel, and ideas on how to supply the personnel with the unique resources to accomplish the mission. McCue once said, "*I realized that the YPD needed a unit like the NYC Street Crime Unit because the Bronx was riddled with crime and a good deal of the Bronx crime and New York City problems were coming up to us*."

Once given the approval to organize such a unit by the chief, he had the preparations pretty much ready to go when something unexpected occurred. Although he had done all the research, Sgt McCue was not given command of the new unit ready to be established, but instead remained on desk duty in the 2nd precinct and another lieutenant was assigned to command this plainclothes unit.

He remained in the South Command until July 7, 1977 when Terry McCue was promoted to the rank of Lieutenant earning a salary of $21,407 a year. On January 1, 1979 Lt McCue was transferred back to the North Command as a patrol lieutenant. At that time the new police commissioner, Dan Guido, offered him the position of commanding officer of the Training Unit. McCue accepted and was immediately placed in command. In 1985 a captain was assigned as the C.O. of training and McCue became second in command. Lt McCue was not pleased with that turn of events and on March 11, 1985 McCue was transferred to the 3rd precinct as a patrol Watch Commander.

Lt. Terrence "Terry" McCue retired from the police department effective August 22, 1985. In retirement McCue worked as a private investigator and also taught a college course, but enjoyed neither. He then worked for the NYS Parks Police as a seasonal officer for a few years until he heard that the Greenwich, Ct. P.D. was holding a test for police officer. He took the test, ranked #1 on the appointment list, and was appointed a police officer with the Greenwich, CT. P.D. on October 10, 1989.

Terry McCue was very successful working with the Greenwich P.D. due to his Yonkers P.D. experience and in a short time was appointed a Detective. While still in the Army Reserve, Terry was activated with his unit in 1991 and served in the Persian Gulf War, designated Desert Storm. He returned to the Greenwich P.D. but was again activated with his unit for service in the Iraq War, designated Operation Iraqi Freedom. At one point he attained the rank of First Sergeant, or "First Shirt," earned a bronze star, and retired from the military after 24 years of combined reserve and active duty.

Ret Lt Terry McCue retired from the Greenwich P.D. as a Detective in February of 2007.

LT. JAMES D. BRADY

APPOINTED: July 23, 1965
RETIRED: September 19, 1986

James Brady was born in Yonkers NY on Dec. 3, 1942 and as a youth attended PS #4, and graduated from Lincoln HS as well as Iona College, in New Rochelle, NY where he earned his Bachelor's degree and Fordham University, Bronx, N.Y where he completed his Master's in business. Jim also attended the Frederick Military College in Chestertown, Maryland for one year. As a young man Brady worked a number of different jobs but, on May 13, 1965 he was hired as a Special police officer with the Westchester Co. Parkway P.D.

James Brady was appointed to the Yonkers Police Dept. on July 23, 1965 while residing at 315 Riverdale Avenue. Probationary police officer Brady and his recruit class were sent to the New York City Police Academy for basic recruit training. This intensive physical and academic training ran from July 26, 1965 to November 28, 1965. Following graduation PO Brady was assigned to foot patrol duty in the 1st precinct earning a starting salary of $5,880 a year. On November 9, 1966 he was reassigned to the newly opened 1st precinct at 730 E. Grassy Sprain Road. However, the following year, on April 14, 1967, he was transferred to the 4th precinct. On January 23, 1970 Jim achieved a personal goal when he was appointed a Detective in Detective Division. But apparently Jim Brady wanted more. He had earlier taken the test for LosAngeles, Cal. police officer, was contacted for appointment there, and on March 24, 1972 he was granted a one year leave of absence to be appointed a police officer with the LAPD. At one point Brady realized he had made a mistake. So, just short of a year, on Sept 8, 1972, he resigned from the LAPD and was re-appointed to the YPD.

On November 10, 1972 Brady was promoted to the rank of Sergeant earning $14,399 and sent to the South Command (2nd pct) as a patrol supervisor. On April 26, 1974 he was returned to the D.D. as a squad supervisor and designated a Detective Sergeant. On Jan. 1, 1979, Jim was transferred from D.D. to the Training Unit where he served as an instructor as well as a supervisor. Traditionally the Yonkers Training Unit conducted in-service training but sent new recruits to another agency for training. But that changed after Sgt Brady arrived. Along with the Training Unit C.O., Lt McCue, they began to operate their own police academy.

Jim Brady had a very flamboyant personality and as a result he was often given the nick name "Diamond Jim." He stood 6' 3" tall, and had a slim build, but hard as steel. Jim was very outgoing and could be the life of the party but he also had a short temper and had very little patience. On October 12, 1979 Sgt Brady left Training and was reassigned to patrol supervisory duties in the North Command.

On November 18, 1982 Sgt Brady was promoted to the rank of Lieutenant earning $32,391 and was subsequently reassigned to the Communications Division as a tour supervisor. Then, on March 7, 1984 Lt Brady was transferred to the 2nd precinct as a Watch Commander, and on May 23, 1984 was assigned as the Executive Officer in the 1st precinct.

Lt Jim Brady retired on September 19, 1986 and moved to Delray Beach, Florida where he was operating the Prudential Florida Realty in DelRay Beach. Jim's father had been a YFD Captain, his uncle was YPD PO Edward Keehan, and his great uncle was YPD PO James Keehan. For the last two years of his life Jim had been suffering with Pulmonary Fibrosis, a lung disease and on May 2, 2006 he received a lung transplant in Cleveland, Ohio. Following his surgery he had been having great difficulty recovering. Ret Lt James Brady died in the hospital in Ohio. He was 63 years old.

PO JOSEPH M. OCCHICONE #424

APPOINTED: July 23, 1965
RETIRED: August 9, 1985

Joe Occhicone was born in Yonkers on April 3, 1943 and attended PS# 77 in the Bronx, and later graduated from Lincoln HS in Yonkers. Joe joined the Army National Guard's 101st Signal Battalion on N. Broadway on Oct. 16, 1964. He served as a Lineman and completed his active duty reserve obligation on March 12, 1965. He was later honorably discharged. Joe listed his previous employment with the Joseph Salvatore Roofing Co. Occhicone was appointed to the Y.P.D. on July 23, 1965 while residing at 51 Hildreth Pl. PO Occhicone and his recruit class were sent to the NYC Police Academy for basic recruit training. This intensive physical and academic training ran from July 26, 1965 to Nov. 28, 1965. Following graduation he was assigned to duty in the 2nd pct. earning a starting salary of $5,880 a year. He remained on patrol in the 2nd pct for the next 17 years until Sept. 13, 1982 when he was transferred to patrol duty in the North Command. He was a very active uniformed officer during his career and retired from the Y.P.D. on Aug. 9, 1985 and was hired as a US Marshall working Security in the Federal Courthouse in Foley Square in NYC and later at the Federal Building in White Plains.

PO THOMAS V. KENWORTHY #467

APPOINTED: July 23, 1965
RETIRED: October 31, 1986

Thomas Kenworthy was born in Mount Vernon on Sept. 6, 1941. His family later moved to Dobbs Ferry where he attended St. Matthew's school and later graduated from Dobbs Ferry. Following school Tom joined the Navy on Sept. 22, 1958. He was honorably discharged on Sept. 21, 1964 with the rank of Seaman. Following his military he was employed as a truck driver with the Railway Express Agency in Ardsley NY. He also was an Ardsley police officer from Aug. of 1963 to June of 1964, and later resigned. Tom was appointed to the Y.P.D. on July 23, 1965 while living at 261 Ashford Ave. in Dobbs Ferry. PO Kenworthy and his recruit class were sent to the NYC Police Academy for recruit training ran from July 26, 1965 to Nov. 28, 1965. Following graduation PO Kenworthy was assigned to foot patrol duty in the 4th pct earning $5,880 a year. The following year Tom was assigned to the Communications Div. but on June 19, 1974 he was returned to patrol duty in the North Command. At one point Tom sustained a severe back injury while on duty and was out disabled for several years unable to return to work. On and off he came back in a light-duty capacity but never returned to full duty. PO Thomas Kenworthy retired on Oct. 31, 1986 on a performance of duty disability pension.

PO ALAN S. ZUKOWSKY #432

APPOINTED: September 24, 1965
RESIGNED: September 6, 1968

Alan Zukowsky was born on Aug. 15, 1942 in Yonkers, attended PS# 16 and later graduated from Gorton HS. He also attended Curry College in Milton, Mass. from Sept. of 1960 to May of 1964 where he obtained a Bachelor of Science degree in Business Administration. Alan joined the Marine Corps Reserve on Jan. 25, 1965 serving with the 2nd Battalion, 25th Marines, 4th Marine Division as a PFC. After completing his reserve obligation he was honorably discharged on Jan. 19, 1971. Al was appointed to the YPD on Sept. 24, 1965 and received his recruit training at the Iona College campus from Oct. 4th to the 25th of 1965. Following his recruit school he was assigned to the 1st pct on foot patrol earning a starting salary of $5,880 a year. On Nov. 9, 1966 he was reassigned to the 4th pct. Known as "Zeke" to his friends, Al was granted a leave of absence on Feb. 11, 1968 and while on leave resigned in order to be appointed to the Massachusetts State Police on Sept. 6, 1968.

PO HOWARD J. KEPPLER # 458

APPOINTED: September 24, 1965
RETIRED: November 1, 1985

Howard Keppler, known as "Buddy," was born in Yonkers on Dec. 1, 1942. He attended St. Mary's school and later graduated from Yonkers HS. He also attended the Western Carolina College in No.Carolina, and also the Westchester Community College from 1961 through 1965 working towards a liberal arts degree. Howard Keppler was appointed to the Y.P.D. on Sept. 24, 1965 while residing at 65 Elliott Ave. He received his recruit training at the Iona College campus in New Rochelle which ran from Oct. 4th to the 25th of 1965. Following graduation, Keppler was assigned to the 3rd pct earning $5,880 a year. On Nov. 7, 1966 he was moved to the 1st pct, and on Dec. 10, 1966 back to the 3rd. On January 1, 1971Keppler's new assignment was to the South Command. Buddy had severe back problems and sometime in 1971 required spinal fusion surgery. He recovered and returned to work. On July 1, 1982, he was transferred to the Communications Div. On July 24, 1984 Keppler received a permanent injury to his already damaged back while assigned to the Records Division. On Sept. 19, 1984 the police surgeon, Dr Goler, designated him totally disabled and incapable of any work at all. As a result PO Keppler retired from the police department on November 1, 1985 on disability pension. Ret PO Howard J. Keppler died on March 11, 2002. He was 59 years old.

COMMISSIONER OF POLICE JOSEPH P. CASSINO

Appointed: September 24,1965
Retired: April 14, 2000

Former Police Commissioner Joseph P. Cassino was born on Oak Street in the city of Yonkers on August 14, 1944. He was a typical youngster who grew up at 4 Van Cortlandt Park Avenue. A boy scout in his youth, he attended Holy Trinity elementary school and later would graduate from Sacred Heart High School. Commissioner Cassino admitted that he remembers always wanting to be a police officer and serve the public. He had excellent role models with his father being a Yonkers Fire Department Lieutenant, and his brother being a Lieutenant with the N.Y. State Police. In future years Joseph Cassino would go on to earn an Associate's degree from Westchester Community College in 1968, a Bachelor of Science degree in Social Science from Mercy College in 1971, and had done graduate work through the University of Virginia.

Prior to his police appointment he worked for the Gramatan National Bank Trust Co. and also

Police Commissioner Joseph Cassino (cont.)

made some extra money as a caddy on various golf courses. After taking the police test Cassino placed # 10 on the list and was eligible to be appointed with the class in February of 1965. However he was not yet 21 years of age and had to wait for his appointment until September of 1965.

Joe Cassino was appointed to the Yonkers Police Department on September 24 1965 from 4 Van Cortlandt Park Avenue. He received his basic police recruit training at the Iona College campus in New Rochelle with an academic curriculum running from October 4th though the 25th of 1965. Following his recruit graduation Cassino was assigned to walk a foot post in the 1st precinct then located at 10 St Casimir Avenue while earning a starting salary of $5,880 a year. In 1966, when the new 1st precinct building was constructed at 730 East Grassy Sprain Road, he was reassigned to the 4th precinct. In the spring of 1969 he was detailed "on paper" to the Intelligence Unit but was actually assigned to work for the Yonkers Narcotics Unit as an undercover narcotics officer and was placed on "loan" to the New Rochelle P.D. to make undercover narcotic "buys." Over a four month period he was very successful and as a result, multiple narcotic related arrests were made. It is quite likely that his ability to speak Spanish was an asset. On August 4, 1969 through August 15, 1969 Cassino attended the Federal Bureau of Narcotics Dangerous Drugs training school which was held in Washington, DC.

On December 16, 1969 PO Cassino was promoted to the rank of Detective and formally assigned to the Yonkers Narcotics Unit. In 1970 he and his partner, Det Kenneth Zajac, were sent to the Town of Mamaroneck as undercover officers and were just as successful as they were in New Rochelle.

On September 15, 1972 Det Cassino was promoted to Sergeant and reassigned to the North Command as a patrol supervisor. Approximately one year later Sgt Cassino was again reassigned, this time to the Traffic Division as a motorcycle squad supervisor. This was an easy transition for him because he had previous experience riding a motorcycle before joining the department.

Sgt Cassino remained in the Traffic Division until February 18, 1977 at which time he was promoted to the rank of Lieutenant and was transferred to Central Booking in the City Jail. In mid-1979 he was reassigned as a patrol or Zone Lieutenant in the 3rd precinct. However within months, from September to December 1979, Lt Cassino was detailed to attend the very prestigious FBI Academy in Quantico, Virginia. Upon his return from Virginia he returned to his duties as a patrol lieutenant in the 3rd precinct.

On July 1, 1983 Cassino was elevated to Detective Lieutenant and assigned as the Commanding Officer of the Narcotics Unit within the Detective Division, under the overall command of Det Captain Owen McClain. Cassino remained in the Narcotics Unit for just over two years and on December 18, 1985 was promoted to the rank of Captain. He worked as a patrol captain throughout 1986 but in January of 1987 was elected to the office of President of the Captains, Lieutenants, & Sergeants Association. Captain Cassino would hold that office for seven years, right up through December 1993. At that time he chose not to run for re-election and was transferred to command the Community Affairs Division on Radford Street.

Once again this would be short lived, for on March 17, 1995 Commissioner McEvoy promoted him to the rank of Deputy Chief of the Support Services Bureau. However, when Police Commissioner

Police Commissioner Joseph Cassino (cont.)

Christopher came into office, Deputy Chief Cassino was reassigned and placed in charge of the Investigational Services Division in January 1996.

Upon the retirement of Comm. Donald Christopher, Chief Cassino was chosen by Mayor John Spencer to be the new Police Commissioner effective May 13, 1998. Known as a man of few words, when he decided to retire, Commissioner Cassino stayed true to form when he drafted his own order regarding his retirement. It simply said,.....,

"*I, Joseph P. Cassino, Police Commissioner, am retiring from the Yonkers Police Department. I want to thank all of you for the cooperation and assistance you afforded me. May God bless all of you*".

His retirement was effective April 14, 2000. Though no longer a part of the Yonkers Police Department himself, former Commissioner Cassino is proud that his son, Police Officer Michael Cassino, has decided to follow in his footsteps; including wearing the same silver shield that his father wore decades ago and worked from the Narcotics Unit.

DET. SGT. NICHOLAS J. BIANCO #67

APPOINTED: September 24, 1965
RETIRED: January 10, 1986

Although Nick Bianco's family were residents of the Bronx, NY, Nick was born in a Mount Vernon Hospital on August 8, 1944. As a young boy Nick was raised in the Bronx and he graduated from Cardinal Hayes high school. Following his education Nick was employed for a while by the Robin Hood Archery Corp. in New York City.

Nick Bianco received his appointment to the Yonkers Police Department on August 24, 1965 while residing at 111 Urban Avenue in Mount Vernon. He received his basic police recruit training on the Iona College campus in New Rochelle. The academic curriculum for this training ran from October 4th to the 25th of 1965. Following his recruit graduation Nick was assigned to patrol duty in the 2nd precinct earning a starting salary of $5,880 a year.

Shortly after his appointment to the Yonkers Police Department it became clear that he was going to be a good police officer. On February 19, 1966 PO Edward Rubeo was struck and injured by shotgun pellets fired by some unknown assailant in a vehicle on Central Park Avenue. The officer was working an off-duty detail at the time. PO Bianco, during his off-duty time, uncovered information which proved vital in the apprehension of the two suspects responsible for the shooting of the police officer. Both suspects were charged with first-degree attempted murder and accessory to attempted murder first-degree. For his part in this investigation, while working on patrol and while off-duty, his commanding officer recommended him for a departmental commendation, which was disapproved.

On August 25, 1967, after nearly two years on patrol, Nick Bianco was assigned to the Detective Division as a detective working in the Narcotics Unit. His partner and good friend was Det Anthony Souza. Working together they developed an enviable reputation for themselves as outstanding narcotic investigators and detectives in general. On September 22, 1967 Detective Bianco graduated from the Federal Bureau of Narcotics advanced training school relating to narcotics enforcement. Bianco's ability to speak Italian and Spanish was, no doubt, a significant help during some investigations. And Nick continued his education in law enforcement by attending the New York State Police gambling and arson seminar in June of 1971.

Five years later, on May 5, 1972, Detective Bianco was promoted to the rank of Police Sergeant earning a new salary of $13,685, and was designated as a patrol supervisor in the North Command. Having been a sergeant for just over a year, on October 25, 1973 Sergeant Bianco was returned to the Detective Division's Narcotics Unit as a Detective Sergeant. During the ensuing 10 years that he served as head of the Narcotics Unit, Sgt. Bianco and his squad were responsible for an outstanding number of arrests, indictments, and convictions for illegal drug violations. On February 22, 1973 it was announced that Sgt Bianco had been honored by the Yonkers Exchange Club as Policeman of the year.

After 10 years as a Narcotics Unit supervisor, in 1983 Sergeant Bianco was reassigned from the Narcotics Unit to being a Detective squad supervisor for general assignment investigations.

However, during his career serving in the Narcotics Unit his record of arrests ranged from minor drug arrests to major dragnets culminating in the capture of several upper-level narcotics traffickers. But Bianco's major arrests were not limited to narcotics probes. In June of 1985 a well-known locksmith was

Det. Sgt. Nicholas J. Bianco #67 (cont.)

murdered in his 15 Riverdale Ave. shop. Initially there were no leads and apparently no witnesses. However, two months after the murder, Bianco's detective squad arrested the person responsible.

Ironically, one of the last homicide investigations Sgt. Bianco played a part in, was in 1985, also the first murder investigation he ever worked on; the 1968 gangland shooting death of Antonio Veniero near the Saw Mill River Road in Hastings near the Yonkers city line. Sgt Bianco had worked on the original case as a rookie detective with his partner Det Souza, but it went unsolved for many years. Although the investigative jurisdiction belong to the Westchester County Police Department, Bianco assisted county police and the district attorney's office with information which led to the suspects being arrested seventeen (17) years after the killing. At the time the county police commissioner wrote a letter to the Yonkers chief of police stating that, "*Sgt. Bianco's eagerness to become involved in the 17-year-old investigation, his recall concerning events as they took place 17 years earlier and the contributions he made to this investigation are admirable*."

During his twenty years in the police department Det. Sgt. Bianco received 13 commendations and one Honorable Mention award for burglary, narcotics, and murder investigations. He also won an award for bravery and police valor for disarming an armed drug suspect on a roof.

But, after nearly three years as a D.D. general assignment supervisor, Det. Sgt. Nicholas Bianco retired from the Yonkers Police Department on January 10, 1986 at the age of 41 years and immediately went to work as an investigator with the Westchester County Legal Aid Society. In 1996 Nick Bianco, a resident of Yorktown Heights, was elected to the Yorktown Town Board as a Councilman. He was reelected for 14 consecutive years to this position while continuing to work for the Westchester legal aid Society. Ret. Sgt Nick Bianco decided not to seek reelection to the Yorktown Town Board and retired from his employment with Legal Aid. Nick and his wife moved to Florida where they loved the warm weather.

PO RITA A. NELSON #302

APPOINTED: November 19, 1965
RETIRED: February 6, 1986

Born Rita Austin on June 2, 1937 in the Bronx, her family moved to Yonkers in June of 1946. As a youth she attended PS# 1, Longfellow Jr. High School, and later graduated from Roosevelt High School. Following her schooling Rita served in the United States Air National Guard beginning her active duty on May 21, 1950 and following the completion of her reserve obligation she was honorably discharged on July 30, 1957 as an Airman 3rd class.

Rita was first hired by the City of Yonkers as a Parking Enforcement officer on August 12, 1964. Her salary in that position was $4,536 a year. By then Rita had married and was now Rita Gross.

Prior to her official appointment to the Yonkers Police Department there had never been a permanent appointed policewoman in the Yonkers Police Department. In the 1940s there had been two female temporary war appointments, and in the early 1960s there were a number of provisional female appointments to the YPD. But, a decision had apparently been made that the Police Department would finally hire females. A special test for female candidates was scheduled. Rita took the test, passed it, and the stage was set for history to take place.

Rita A. Gross was appointed to the Yonkers Police Department, as a "Policewoman," on November 19, 1965 while residing at 55 School Street. It was not only groundbreaking to be one of the first female Yonkers police officers, but Rita was in fact the very first black female ever appointed to the department. Rita was hired on that date along with four other women earning a starting salary of $5,880 a year. There was no police recruit school scheduled until the following year, but on April 4th through May 6th of 1966, the five new policewomen joined with several new male recruits and attended their basic police recruit training at the Iona College campus in New Rochelle.

When first appointed, Rita was not provided with uniforms and the police department wasn't sure what policewomen should wear, so she wore business attire. The police department, either willingly or under pressure, had made the commitment to appoint female policewomen to the department but they weren't sure just how to utilize them.

Although it is believed that Policewoman Gross never actually wore them on patrol, initially the YPD decided that policewomen should wear a uniform different from male officers. Rita and the others were provided with black walking shoes, navy blue skirt and uniform style jacket/blouse and a white blouse to wear beneath the jacket. She was provided with a black leather pocketbook with strap to hang to the waist and which had sewn inside two pockets; one for handcuffs and one for their issued .32 caliber, 2" barrel, Smith and Wesson revolver.

Following her recruit graduation Policewoman Rita Gross was assigned to duty in the Detective Division, not as a detective, but working in the Juvenile Aid Bureau (JAB) in plainclothes. Later she would be assigned to the Community Affairs Unit with the goal to foster better relations with the community. She was widely known and respected in the community and known to most as "Miss Rita." While in this assignment, on August 13, 1971 she was appointed a Detective, but when the unit was

PO Rita A. Nelson #302 (cont.)

closed down on October 6, 1972, she was returned to the rank of Policewoman and was transferred to the Youth Division investigating crimes by juveniles.

Up until this time no policewoman was ever required to wear a uniform and go out on patrol. But, on January 29, 1974, a number of female officers, including Rita Nelson, were assigned to the patrol commands. On that date Rita was assigned to patrol duty in the North Command performing the same duties as her male counterparts. It was also ordered that all female officers would wear the exact same uniform as male officers. Of the several that were reassigned to patrol duty at that time, most only remained for a few weeks and then returned to their plainclothes details. PO Nelson remained on patrol in the North command. And, by now the title “Policewoman” had been abandoned and all male and female officers were referred to as police officers.

Two years later, on August 24, 1976, PO Nelson was returned to plainclothes duty in the Youth Services and Community Relations Division.

A long time member and Past Matron of the "Terrace City Chapter # 26, PHOES," PO Rita Gross Nelson retired from the Yonkers Police Department on February 6, 1986. At one point during her time in retirement she worked as the Chief of Security for the Hudson River Museum and in 2012 she was the Executive Director of the Yonkers YMCA.

PO FRANCES E. McLAUGHLIN #304

APPOINTED: November 19, 1965
RETIRED: February 21, 1986

Frances E. McLaughlin was born in the City of New York on February 1, 1935. She attended St Anthony of Padua and St John Chrysostom schools in the Bronx, New York and ultimately graduated from Cathedral High School in New York City. On her application for appointment to the Yonkers Police Dept. she listed her current employment as an Infant Care Technician at St. Joseph's Hospital.

Prior to her official appointment to the Yonkers Police Department there had never been a permanent appointed policewoman in the YPD. In the 1940s there had been two female temporary war appointments, and in the early 1960s there were a number of provisional female appointments to the YPD. But, a decision had apparently been made that the Police Department would finally hire females. A special test for female candidates was scheduled, Fran took the test and passed it, and the stage was set for history to take place.

Frances E. McLaughlin was appointed to the Yonkers Police Department as a "Policewoman" on November 19, 1965 while residing at 273 Hawthorne Ave. Fran was hired on that date along with four other women earning a starting salary of $5,880 a year. There was no police recruit school scheduled until the following year, but on April 4th through May 6th of 1966, the five new policewomen joined with several new male recruits and attended their basic police recruit training at the Iona College campus in New Rochelle.

When first appointed, Fran was not provided with uniforms and the police department wasn't sure what policewomen should wear, so she wore business attire. The police department, either willingly or

PO Frances E. McLaughlin #304 (cont.)

under pressure, had made the commitment to appoint female policewomen to the department but they weren't sure just how to utilize them.

Although it is believed that Fran never wore them on patrol, initially the YPD decided that policewomen should wear a uniform different from male officers. Fran and the others were provided with black walking shoes, navy blue skirt and uniform style jacket and a white blouse to wear beneath the jacket. She was provided with a black pocketbook with strap to hang to the waist and which had sewn inside two pockets; one for handcuffs and one for their issued .32 caliber, 2" barrel, Smith and Wesson revolver.

Following her recruit graduation Policewoman Fran McLaughlin was assigned to duty in the Juvenile Aid Division (later renamed Youth Division). On June 14, 1968 a "paper transfer" took place whereby Policewoman McLaughlin was assigned to the Detective Division, not as a detective, and continued to work in the Juvenile Aid Division. Six years after her initial assignment to the J.A.D., on March 6, 1972 she was transferred to the Communications Division in headquarters. However, she was returned to the J.A.D. once again on October 25, 1973.

Up until this time no policewoman was ever required to wear a uniform and go out on patrol. But, on June 19, 1974 a number of female officers, including McLaughlin, were assigned to the precincts. On that date Fran was assigned to patrol duty in the North Command performing the same duties as her male counterparts. It was also ordered that all female officers would wear the exact same uniform as male officers. Of the several that were reassigned to patrol duty at that time, most only remained for a few weeks and then returned to their plainclothes details. And, by now the title "Policewoman" had been abandoned and all male and female officers were referred to as police officers. PO McLaughlin, who had married and whose name was now Fran Miller by marrying PO Ted Miller, remained on patrol in the North command.

Two years later, on February 13, 1976, PO McLaughlin/Miller was returned to plainclothes duty in the Youth Services and Community Relations Division. Once again Fran Miller returned to patrol duties on January 1, 1979 in the North command. The following month in February of 1979 Fran divorced her husband Ted and returned to using her maiden name Frances McLaughlin. On June 20, 1979 Fran was reassigned from the North Command to patrol duty in the Northeast Patrol Command located at 730 E. Grassy Sprain Rd.

PO Frances McLaughlin, who was able to speak French as a second language, retired from patrol duty on February 21, 1986. Unfortunately, in 2005 Fran became ill with a number of medical problems and following a lengthy battle, died on April 30, 2005. She was 70 years old.

SGT. DIANE E. KATZ #60

APPOINTED: November 19, 1965
RETIRED: May 4, 1987

Born Diane E. Canepi on June 21, 1936 in the City of Yonkers, she attended PS# 27, Hawthorne Jr High School and later Gorton High School, but did not graduate. However she would later obtain her equivalency diploma. As a young child and into early adulthood Diane was an avid horse lover, as her father, Dolph Canepi, owned the riding academy in Van Cortlandt Park in the Bronx. Prior to the YPD she worked as a receptionist at an animal hospital in the Bronx and later attended Wilfred Academy of Beauty.

By 1965 she was married and her name changed to Diane Condon. She took the newly established civil service exam for "Policewoman" and placed # 1 on the list with a rating of 95.33. Of course that was no surprise because she had a very high IQ and was a registered member of the Mensa Society. And so it was that history was made when, on November 19, 1965, Diane Katz, then known as Diane Condon, was appointed one of the very first official permanent Policewomen to be sworn into the Yonkers Police Department from 260 Valentine Lane. She was one of five policewomen sworn in that same day. The other four women of the "First Five," as they would become known, were Frances Miller (McLaughlin), Sharon Rohan (McMahon), Rita Gross (Nelson), and Jane Grenyo (Colgan).

The five women joined with a group of male recruits hired on March 4, 1966 and all received their basic police recruit training at the Iona College campus in New Rochelle. The academic curriculum ran from April 4 th to May 6, 1966. When first appointed, and earning a starting salary of $5,880 a year, Katz was not provided with uniforms and the police department wasn't sure what policewomen should wear, so she wore business attire. The police department, either willingly or under pressure, had made the commitment to appoint female policewomen to the department but they weren't sure just how to utilize them.

Although it is believed that Diane never wore them, initially the YPD decided that policewomen should wear a uniform different from male officers. Diane and the others were provided with black walking shoes, navy blue skirt and uniform style jacket and a white blouse to wear beneath the jacket. She was provided with a black pocketbook with strap to hang to the waist and which had sewn inside two pockets; one for handcuffs and one for their issued .32 caliber, 2" barrel, Smith and Wesson revolver.

Following her recruit graduation policewoman Diane was assigned to duty in the Juvenile Aid Division (Later renamed Youth Division). On February 14, 1968 she was assigned to the Detective Division, not as a detective, and was detailed to work in the Public Safety Commissioners office in City Hall as an assistant/secretary.

In 1970 Diane took the test for the position of Sergeant, an accomplishment she was determined to achieve. On May 5, 1972, by then remarried and known as Diane Katz, she achieved her goal and was promoted to the rank of Sergeant earning $13,685, and issued shield #60. To become not only the first woman Sergeant in the history of the Yonkers Police Department, but also the first woman Sergeant in all of Westchester County, was quite an accomplishment at that time. She remained in her assignment as a Sergeant until July 2, 1973 when she was assigned to the Youth Division, a plainclothes unit.

A big change occurred on October 3, 1977 when it was decided that Sgt Katz would be transferred

Sgt. Diane E. Katz #60 (cont.)

to the North Patrol Command in uniform as a patrol supervisor in the Community Patrol Unit. It was ordered that she would wear the same uniform as male police officers. Initially there was concern as to how the men would react having to take orders, for the first time ever, from a female superior officer. But Sgt Katz was up to the challenge and there were no problems at all. Her friendly disposition and good natured personality allowed her to be assertive when required, but well liked.

Six years later, on July 1, 1983, Sgt Katz was transferred from patrol to headquarters serving as the administrative assistant to the Deputy Chief of Support Services. Then, on September 25, 1985 she was moved to the Records Division but detailed to the Medical Control Unit.

Diane retired on Accidental Disability on May 4, 1987 after 27 years of service, 15 of those as a Sergeant. The plaque that was presented to her by her colleagues upon her retirement has her first shield, #300 and her gold shield #60 set side by side, and the plaque named her, "The First Lady of the Yonkers Police Department."

Diane made many of her dreams come true; she overcame many obstacles in her way, including surviving brain surgery for a brain aneurysm in July of 1974 and spinal surgery to remove and inch from her spine. She loved to read, was an avid scrabble player, and enjoyed spending time at the beach. She also became a member of the International Association of Women Police and held an office in that association. And she became active in the church, serving as lector for several years in the Cathedral of St. John in Savannah, GA. Following her last divorce Diane returned to her maiden name, Diane Canepi.

Ret Sgt Diane Katz Canepi passed away on November 29, 2002 in Savannah, GA. However, her funeral mass was held at the Church of St. Denis in Yonkers. She was 66 years old.

PO SHARON McMAHON #303

APPOINTED: November 19, 1965
RETIRED: January 12, 1995

Born Sharon Rohan on September 6, 1944 to Yonkers police officer Robert Rohan, she would attend Sacred Heart elementary school and graduate from Sacred Heart High School. She also spent one year attending Westchester Community College with a major of Medical Assistant.

Having a father who was a Yonkers police officer, she was well aware that there had never been a permanently appointed female officer in the history of the police department. But when it was announced there would be a test for "Policewoman," she jumped at the chance. She was only 20 years old but in 1965 Sharon took the newly established civil service exam for "Policewoman" and passed.

And so it was that history was made when, on November 19, 1965, Sharon Rohan was appointed one of the very first official permanent Policewomen to be sworn into the Yonkers Police Department from 129 Convent Avenue. She was one of five policewomen sworn in that same day. The other four women of the "First Five," as they would become known, were Diane Canepi (Katz), Frances Miller (McLaughlin), Rita Gross (Nelson), and Jane Grenyo (Colgan).

The five women joined with a group of male recruits hired on March 4, 1966 and all received their basic police recruit training at the Iona College campus in New Rochelle. The academic curriculum ran from April 4th to May 6, 1966. When first appointed, and earning a starting salary of $5,880 a year, Rohan was not provided with uniforms and the police department wasn't sure what policewomen should wear, so she wore business attire. The police department, either willingly or under pressure, had made the commitment to appoint female policewomen to the department but apparently they weren't sure just how to utilize them. Although it is believed that Sharon never wore them, initially the police department

PO Sharon McMahon #303 (cont.)

determined that policewomen should wear a uniform different from male officers. Sharon and the others were provided with black walking shoes, navy blue skirt and uniform style jacket and a white blouse to wear beneath the jacket. She was provided with a black pocketbook with strap to hang to the waist and which had sewn inside two pockets; one for handcuffs and one for their issued .32 caliber, 2" barrel, Smith and Wesson revolver.

Following her recruit graduation, Probationary Policewoman Rohan, as were the other women, was assigned to the Juvenile Aid Division (JAB) to investigate crimes committed by juveniles. Though assigned there Rohan was detailed directly to the Detective Division in the Narcotics Unit. Approximately 18 months later, on February 14, 1968, Policewoman Rohan was officially assigned to the Detective Division, not as a detective, but still working plainclothes in the Narcotics Unit. She was very young looking and it was thought that she could be effective in an undercover capacity. Her assignments in that division consisted mainly of illegal narcotic investigations and sometimes working undercover at times conducting investigations concerning gambling. While assigned to the D.D. she also assisted in a variety of investigations such as homicides where women were involved as well as providing numerous lectures to various community groups relating to illegal narcotics, illegal gambling and how women could better protect themselves etc.

For a short time in the late 1960's Plwn. Rohan was detailed from the Detective Division to the Intelligence Unit assisting in organized crime investigations and was very helpful in that capacity. However, after a time she was returned to the D.D. to continue her duties there. It was now the mid 1970's and the title Policewoman had been abandoned and all females were now referred to as police officers, the same for male officers. PO Rohan remained working undercover in Narcotics in the Detective Division for about seven years. At one point she said, while in the D.D. she would always receive excellent evaluations but they would not appoint her a Detective. As a result, Rohan, and a few other females in the D.D. Narcotics Unit filed a class-action lawsuit with the Human Rights Commission. PO Rohan won their suit and shortly thereafter PO's Frances DeBlassis and Walter Moray, both in Narcotics, were appointed detectives. Officer Rohan was not.

It was about this time that one of several female officers assigned to uniform patrol was having severe anxiety and, still being uncomfortable in the Narcotics Unit not as a detective, Rohan volunteered to switch places with that female patrol officer. And so, on February 13, 1976 PO Rohan was transferred from the Detective Division out to uniform patrol duty in the North Command.

Being the first females to ever be appointed police officers and required to ride on patrol with a male counterpart regularly, did result in friction whereby male officers initially refused to ride with females until given a direct order. The job of those first female officers was ground breaking and difficult.

On April 24, 1978 McMahon was reassigned to the Special Operations Division as the department's Traffic Safety Officer. That same year she married Capt. John F. McMahon. However, within a year, on January 1, 1979, PO McMahon was returned to patrol duty back in the North Command. Seven years later, on December 4, 1985 she was transferred to the 3rd precinct assigned as the precinct captain's aide. In 1994 PO Sharon McMahon was working in the Community Affairs Division where she remained right up to her retirement on January 12, 1995.

DET. JANE F. COLGAN

APPOINTED: November 19, 1965
DIED: August 14, 1978

Jane Frances Colgan was born on August 4, 1931, her father's birthday, to Yonkers police officer James Colgan. She attended PS# 4, Mark Twain Jr. High School and graduated from Commerce HS. For a time Jane was employed in the Alexander Smith Carpet Factory as a secretary. Jane was skilled at secretarial work but she also had an analytical mind and was interested in law enforcement, like her dad. As a young woman she worked as an investigator for the Retailers Commercial Agency and later was a licensed private investigator working for the Westchester County Detective Agency.

Although there were no women in the Yonkers Police Dept. at the time, she always hoped that might change some day. On August 15, 1958 Jane was hired by the police department as a Parking Meter Enforcement officer; or as they were nicknamed, a Meter Maid. Her salary in that position was $3,465 a year. She started to get closer to her goal when it looked like the police department was going to hire women. Unfortunately there was no civil service test for such a position so, on July 29, 1964, she was appointed a "Provisional Policewoman" earning a salary of $5,500 a year. Note the title, Policewoman, not police officer. Upon her provisional appointment she was assigned to the Juvenile Aid Bureau (JAB) where she would assist in the investigations of crimes committed by juveniles.

For reasons unknown, but likely political, Jane's provisional position was terminated six months later, on December 16, 1964, and she was returned to working as a Parking Enforcement Officer, the salary of which had risen to $4,936 a year. It is believed that about this time the city made plans for a test for Policewoman and in anticipation of Jane Colgan passing, they again appointed her as a Provisional Policewoman on January 15, 1965. On February 6, 1965 Jane and several other women took the very first Civil Service test for Policewoman and Jane placed # 2 on the list which was established on September 13, 1965.

Following the official test and placing high on the list, history was made on November 19, 1965 when Jane Colgan was appointed one of the very first official permanent Policewomen to be sworn into the Yonkers Police Department. She was one of five policewomen sworn in that same day. The other four women of the so called "First Five," as they would become known, were Frances Miller (McLaughlin), Sharon Rohan (McMahon), Rita Gross (Nelson), and Diane Canepi (Katz).

The five women joined with a group of male recruits hired on March 4, 1966 and all received their basic police recruit training at the Iona College campus in New Rochelle. The academic curriculum ran from April 4th to May 6, 1966. When first appointed, and earning a starting salary of $5,880 a year, Colgan was not provided with uniforms and the police department wasn't sure what policewomen should wear, so she wore business attire. The police department, either willingly or under pressure, had made the commitment to appoint female policewomen to the department but they weren't sure just how to utilize them.

Although it is believed that Jane never wore them, initially the police department decided that policewomen should wear a uniform different from male officers. Jane and the others were provided with black walking shoes, navy blue skirt and uniform style jacket and a white blouse to wear beneath the jacket. She was provided with a black pocketbook with strap to hang to the waist and which had sewn

Det. Jane F. Colgan (Cont.)

inside two pockets; one for handcuffs and one for their issued .32 caliber, 2" barrel, Smith and Wesson revolver.

Following her recruit graduation policewoman Jane Colgan was assigned to duty in the Juvenile Aid Bureau (JAB), the forerunner of the Youth Division, investigating crimes committed by juveniles and prosecuted in family court. Two years later, on February 14, 1968 Plwn. Colgan was reassigned to the Detective Division in a plainclothes unit. On June 9, 1972 Jane was transferred to the Intelligence Unit in an administrative capacity and appointed a Detective.

On June 19, 1974 an order was issued by the public safety commissioner that all female officers, all of whom had never been on uniformed patrol, were to be assigned to patrol precincts on patrol duty. By this time the title "policewoman" had been abandoned and male and female officers were designated "police officers." Jane had married a Yonkers Firefighter and was now PO Jane Grenyo and was transferred out of the Intelligence Unit to patrol in the North Command. Jane reported for duty without a word of complaint and did her job well. But it only lasted a few weeks and she was returned to the I.U.

After a divorce she returned to her maiden name, Colgan. Jane was a tall attractive lady with red hair with a warm and friendly personality. She was an amateur artist and was a charter member of the Westchester County Police Emerald Society and was their associations first Recording Secretary.

A proud Irish lady, Jane always dreamed of visiting Ireland, but never would. Det Jane Colgan was diagnosed with cancer and died on August 14, 1978. She was only 47 years old.

DET. COLE L. SCOTT #639

APPOINTED: March 4, 1966
RETIRED: March 21, 1986

Cole Livingston Scott Jr. was born in Charleston, South Carolina on November 10, 1943. Following his family moving to Yonkers he attended PS# 19, Ben Franklin Jr. High School, and graduated from Saunders High School. As a child he grew up living at 36 Riverdale Avenue. While in school Cole was very active in the Civil Air Patrol "CAP" and was on their drill team. His previous occupation was with Crown Carpet Shops on Central Avenue in Yonkers.

Cole was appointed to the Yonkers Police Department on March 4, 1966, while residing at 55 School St. He received his basic recruit training at the NYPD police Academy, whose academic and physical curriculum ran from March 28, 1966 through July 13, 1966. Upon his graduation from the academy his first patrol assignment was to the 4th precinct earning a starting salary of $6,000 a year.

Only two years later, on July 26, 1968, PO Scott would be appointed a Detective and would remain working in the Detective Division right up to his retirement. On November 11, 1971 Det Scott, known to friends as "Scottie," was awarded a Citation of Commendable Merit by the Westchester Rockland Newspaper Police Honor Board.

Det Scott was a big man. He stood over 6' tall and weighed over 200 lbs. Although he had a very dry sense of humor and was well liked, he took no nonsense from the criminal element. In the 1970's Det Scott was also very active playing on the PBA basketball team. Det Cole Scott retired from the police department on March 21, 1986 and began working as the city's Director of Community Outreach Program, where he remained for nine years. He also worked for the Office of Fair Housing in Yonkers. In November of 2004 Cole Scott moved to Delaware and began working for Delaware State Police in their Telecommunication Section. Ret Det Cole Scott died on January 26, 2016.

DET. ROBERT C. DEE #687

APPOINTED: March 4, 1966
RETIRED: March 21, 1986

Bob Dee was born in Yonkers NY on Sept. 20, 1944, attended St. Joseph's Elementary School and graduated from Saunders HS. Prior to the YPD Bob was employed by the Post Office in Scarsdale, NY. Bob was appointed to the Y.P.D. on Mar. 4, 1966 while living at 140 Ravine Ave. He received his recruit training at the NYPD Police Academy, with an academic and physical curriculum that ran from Mar. 28, to July 13, 1966. PO Robert Dee was assigned to patrol in the 4th pct earning $6,000 a year. On April 16, 1971 he was assigned to the Communications Div., but the following year, on Nov. 10, 1972, he was transferred to the Traffic Div. on two wheel motorcycle duty. Nearly 7 years later, on April 11, 1980, Bob was appointed a Detective in the D.D. He had a very outgoing personality with a fast talking sense of humor. His quick talking and questioning of suspects often led them to get confused and get caught lying, which made him very effective. Det Dee retired from the police D.D. on Mar. 21, 1986 and moved to Florida. In the late 1990's he moved back to Peekskill, NY and in 2000 was Director of Security for the Westchester Mall in White Plains. He later changed jobs to work for the Metropolitan Transportation Authority Police in lower Manhattan in risk management. Bob's brother Eddie Dee is a retired NYPD Detective and published author, and Bob's son was an FBI agent.

PO CHRISTOPHER N. COYNE #475

APPOINTED: March 4, 1966
RETIRED: June 13, 1986

Chris Neal Coyne was born on July 5, 1944 in the City of Yonkers. He attended PS# 23, Benjamin Franklin Jr HS and graduated from Yonkers HS in 1962. Prior to the Y.P.D. Chris was employed by Con Edison, and worked as a helper on a line truck out of their Worth Street yard in Yonkers. Coyne was appointed to the Yonkers Police Department on March 4, 1966, while residing at 15 Virginia Street. He received his basic recruit training at the NYPD Police Academy, whose academic and physical curriculum ran from March 28, 1966 through July 13, 1966. Upon his graduation from the academy his first patrol assignment was to the 1st precinct at 736 East Grassy Sprain Rd. earning a starting salary of $6,000 a year. On January 1, 1971, as part of a department centralization plan, Chris was reassigned to patrol in the North Command. On June 20, 1979 he would be transferred to the North East Command. PO Christopher N. Coyne, whose brother was Sgt Paul Coyne and whose son, Christopher E. Coyne was a Yonkers police officer for 12 years, retired from the police department on June 13, 1986.

LT. JOSEPH A. BEAIRSTO

APPOINTED: March 4, 1966
RETIRED: March 21, 1986

Joseph A. Beairsto was born in the City of Yonkers on August 17, 1940. He attended St. Denis elementary school, but completed his formal education in public schools. As a young man he was a bit of a sportsman, loved hunting, and as a result was an excellent shot with a rifle. On his application to the police department Joe listed his employment with the Coca-Cola Company in Tuckahoe, New York.

Joe was appointed to the Yonkers Police Department on March 4, 1966 while living on Lawrence Street. He received his basic police recruit training at the NYPD Police Academy, with an academic and physical curriculum that ran from March 28, 1966 through July 13, 1966. Following his recruit graduation PO Joseph Beairsto was first assigned to patrol duty in the 3rd precinct earning a starting salary of $6,000 a year. Following the centralization of the patrol precincts on January 1, 1971 Joe was reassigned to patrol duty in the South Command, formerly the 2nd precinct.

On November 17, 1975 Beairsto was promoted to the rank of Sergeant and remained working in the South Command as a patrol supervisor. But two years later, on October 3, 1977, he was reassigned to patrol supervision in the North Command. But, he was moved again; on March 18, 1981, he was again returned back to patrol duty in the South Patrol Command.

On September 30, 1983, Sgt. Beairsto was promoted to the rank of police Lieutenant earning a salary of $35,364 a year and was subsequently assigned to the citywide Inspections Unit, again on patrol. Joe finally got an inside job when, on December 21, 1983, he was reassigned to work as a tour supervisor in the Communications Division. On February 29, 1984 Lt. Beairsto was transferred to the 3rd precinct and designated a Watch Commander, on patrol.

Two years later, on March 21, 1986, Lt Joseph Beairsto, whose great uncle was PO Thomas Beairsto, retired from the Yonkers Police Department. And being a man who loved to play cards it was no surprise when he moved to Las Vegas.

PO ALFRED P. CHIAVERINI #489

APPOINTED: March 4, 1966
RETIRED: March 7, 1986

Alfred P. Chiaverini was born in the City of Yonkers on September 11, 1937. He attended Benjamin Franklin Jr High School and later graduated from Yonkers High School. While in high school Al received "letters" for his skill at playing Varsity Football. After high school Al worked as a photographer for Rizzolli"s Photo Shop, Giorgi Studios, Bissesi Studio, and the Macy Chain of Newspapers which included The Yonkers Herald Statesman. Prior to taking the Yonkers Police exam he was the official photographer for the Tom Carvel Ice Cream Co.

After having passed the exam Al was appointed to the Yonkers Police Department on March 4, 1966 while living at 63 Park Hill Avenue. He received his basic police recruit training at the NYPD Police Academy, with an academic and physical curriculum that ran from March 28, 1966 through July 13, 1966. His training at the academy was actually shortened somewhat due to occurring NYC riots and the need for additional uniforms on the street. Following his recruit graduation PO Alfred Chiaverini was first assigned to foot patrol duty in the 1st precinct at 10 St. Casimir Avenue earning a starting salary of $6,000 a year. In November of 1966, following the opening of the new 1st precinct at 730 East Grassy Sprain Road, Al was reassigned to the 4th precinct at 53 Shonnard Place.

On one evening while on foot patrol working the early tour Al noticed an elderly man about 200 yards away being pushed into a hallway. Al observed a suspect viciously beating the elderly male who was lying on his back against the stairs. PO Chiaverini arrested the assailant but the victim lost his hearing as a result.

On another occasion Al was assigned to investigate an abduction of a young male. A search was conducted and while passing the aqueduct PO Chiaverini searched a small wooded area and noticed fresh blood on some fallen leaves and followed the trail of blood drops. It was then that Al observed a young male setting fire to the abducted youngster. Al yelled out to the suspect to stop and fired a warning shot in the ground, but the suspect ran off. Chiaverini then ran to the victim and ripped off the shirt which was on fire. Based on PO Chiaverini's description the suspect was later arrested.

Al and his partner also received a department Commendation for the arrest of a robbery suspect on the roof of a Schroeder Street building.

Not long after a major reorganization of the patrol force, on July 16, 1971, Al was appointed a Detective in the Detective Division. On June 2, 1978 Det Chiaverini and Sgt Anthony Ragazzo were honored at the annual Columbian Association Dinner and recognized for the Excellent Police Work in the apprehension of a mother and son wanted for torture and murder of another male in April of 1978.

Al was assigned to investigate the murder of an active Yonkers police officers son. With some difficulty Det. Chiaverini worked through the night, questioning many persons of interest, and an arrest was made of the individual responsible for the senseless murder. A conviction of the suspect was obtained and still today, in retirement, when the inmate comes up for parole, Al writes to the parole board opposing his release.

PO Alfred P. Chiaverini #489 (cont.)

While serving with the department Al owned a few jewelry stores in both Yonkers and Mt Vernon. He also became interested in magic in 1970 watching a magic show with magician Doug Henning. As a result he bought some basic magic tricks, practiced, bought more elaborate ones and started doing shows and party's for a small fee. At one point he was even elected the president of the local chapter of the Society of American Magicians. He performed under the name, "The Amazing Chiaverini." Al then revised the Yonkers P.B.A.'s Children's Christmas Party, of course, by performing magic and having Santa Clause, played by P.O. Nick Iarriccio, appear in a Magic Trick prepared by Al.

While being active with the Yonkers P.B.A., Al was elected a trustee for the Detective Division and later elected Chairman of the Board of Trustees. Det. Chiaverini also served as chairman of the Yonkers P.B.A. annual dinner dance. He was also on the PBA negotiations committee. He was also elected the President of The Columbian Police Association.

Al remained a Detective for twelve years until May 10, 1983 when he was reassigned to patrol duty in the North Command. Three years later, on March 7, 1986, PO Alfred Chiaverini retired from the police department. Al moved to Florida in 1997 and continues to perform his feats of prestidigitation for various organizations on the Treasure Coast as the Amazing Chiaverini. Although he performs professionally and receives fees for his performances, he performs free shows for many charitable organizations. He was named the president of the local Port St. Lucie Magicians Association.

Al gets together with many retired Yonkers Police Officers in Florida quite frequently for lunch and dinner.

PO FRED A. BASLI #437

APPOINTED: March 4, 1966
RETIRED: March 7, 1986

Fred Basli was born in the City of Yonkers on November 25, 1932. He attended and graduated from Holy Trinity parochial school in 1947, and would later graduate from Saunders High School. As a young teenager in school Fred was very strong and athletic. In fact he was a star half back on the Roosevelt football team throughout his high school years and was always gaining sports notoriety in the local newspaper. He also became very interested and active in bowling, playing on various local leagues during the early 1960's.

Fred was always a tough kid so it was no surprise when he joined the US Marine Corps on February 16, 1950, just prior to the beginning of the Korean War. During his four year hitch he served with a Marine "Recon" Reconnaissance Company in the 2nd Marine Division and was shipped to Korea in a combat zone. He served until his honorable discharge on February 16, 1954, just shortly after the war ended. Fred was a house painter and wall paper hanger by trade but in 1958 was working for Phelps Dodge Corp.

Fred A. Basli was appointed to the Yonkers Police Dept. on March 4, 1966, at the age of 33 years, while residing at 180 Lockwood Avenue. He was allowed to exceed the age limit of 29 years by deducting his military time from his age. Probationary police officer Basli and his recruit class were sent to the New York City Police Academy for basic police recruit training. This intensive physical and academic training ran for about four months but the 1960's were a turbulent time for police. As a result their class was graduated about three weeks early due to major rioting taking place throughout NYC and the need for more uniforms on the city streets. Upon his recruit graduation, PO Basli was assigned to foot patrol duty in the 4th precinct earning a starting salary of $6,000 a year.

At one point Fred had also worked in the 3rd precinct. He worked desk aide duty on occasion as well as riding radio car patrol. Though he was older than most when appointed, he still had a unique sense of humor. PO John Hodio, who remembers Fred from the early years stated that, "*Freddy moved around in the 3rd pct in a radio car and also as a desk aide. He was also elected the trustee for the PBA for a while.*" John went on to say that in those early years, "I only remember Fred being a lot of laughs and he would make remarks about a rookie like *'That kid's pants ain't even shiney yet.' But he was someone who always had your back.*"

When the precinct centralization plan went into effect closing two precincts on January 1, 1971, among many moves, PO Basli was reassigned to the North Command. During the 1970's Fred seldom rode in a radio car. He preferred to walk a foot post, generally in Getty Square, by himself. For those who knew him, fear of anyone or anything was never a consideration. He was a very strong and tough cop and yet in his later years developed a very carefree indifferent attitude toward "the job." He preferred not to get involved; a desire which was often unsuccessful.

Fred Basli retired from the YPD on March 7, 1986 and the years that followed were extremely difficult ones for him. And then, on May 7, 2012, following a head injury, Ret PO Fred Basli died. He was 79 years old.

PO LAWRENCE E. KUNZE #474

APPOINTED: March 4, 1966
RETIRED: March 23, 1995

Larry Kunze was born in the City of Yonkers on December 31, 1943. He attended PS # 7, Ben Franklin Jr. High School, and graduated from Yonkers High School. On August 13, 1964 Larry joined the New York National Guard's 101st Signal Battalion. He was released from active duty on December 15, 1964, and after completing his reserve obligation was honorably discharged. Previous to the YPD Larry had worked for the Anaconda Wire and Cable Co. in Hastings, New York.

He was appointed to the Yonkers Police Department on March 4, 1966, while living at 66 Chestnut St. He received his basic police recruit training at the NYPD Police Academy, with an academic and physical curriculum that ran from March 28, 1966 through July 13, 1966. Following his recruit graduation PO Lawrence Kunze was assigned to foot patrol duty in the 4th precinct earning a starting salary of $6,000 a year. On May 4, 1967 it was reported that officer Kunze and his partner, Don Grono, were commended by the department for their work in the apprehension of two persons responsible for an armed robbery at 550 Saw Mill River Road at 9:54 a.m. on March 20, 1967.

On July 17, 1970 Larry was assigned to work in the Emergency Services Unit (ESU), which at the time was based in headquarters, and he received all the appropriate medical and rescue training. But, six months later, on January 1, 1971, following the centralization of the patrol precincts, he was transferred back to the North Command, but continued to work in ESU. His partner for many years was PO Nick Iarriccio. Larry was very athletic and during the 1970's was very active playing on the PBA basketball team.

Larry worked in the Emergency Unit for 16 years, up until March 10, 1986, when he requested and was reassigned to regular uniform patrol in the North command. On June 2, 1986 he was transferred to the 1st precinct on routine precinct patrol.

PO Lawrence Kunze retired from the police department on March 23, 1995 after 29 years of honorable service. Larry's cousin was former PO Anton Steblak and in 2002 Larry's son Stephen was appointed a police officer in the Town of Carmel.

SGT. ROBERT L. THOMPSON #62

APPOINTED: March 4, 1966
DISMISSED: August 10, 1978

Robert Leroy Thompson was born in NYC on Feb. 24, 1944. He attended Henry B. Endicott school in Endicott, NY, and Rogers HS in Newport Rhode Island from which he graduated in 1962. Thompson served in the United States Navy aboard the USS Abbott from Sept. 21, 1962 through Sept. 11, 1964 and was honorably discharged. Prior to the YPD Thompson worked at Otis elevator Co. Robert Thompson was appointed to the Y.P.D. on Mar. 4, 1966, while living at 764 Warburton Ave. He received his recruit training at the NYPD police Academy, which ran from March 28, through July 13, 1966. Upon graduation he was awarded an off duty revolver for attaining the highest academic grade in his recruit class. He was obviously intelligent, and his future looked bright. His first patrol assignment was to the 4th pct, earning $6,000 a year. He remained in that command until Oct. 26, 1973 when he was promoted to the rank of sergeant earning $15,708 and was reassigned to the South Command as a patrol supervisor. In 1978, Sgt. Thompson found himself charged with violations of departmental rules and regulations, and after having been found guilty, was reduced in rank from sergeant to police officer and was dismissed from the department effective Aug. 10, 1978.

PO JOHN G. MORAN #487

APPOINTED: March 4, 1966
RETIRED: October 2, 1987

John "Jack" Moran was born in Yonkers on Dec. 19, 1944. He attended St. Mary's elementary, and Sacred Heart HS, graduating in 1962. Prior to the YPD Moran worked for the US Health Club at 25 N. Broadway in Yonkers. Jack was appointed to the Police Department on Mar. 4, 1966. He received his recruit training with the NYPD police Academy, whose academic curriculum ran from March 28, through July 13, 1966. Following Moran's recruit graduation, his first patrol assignment was in the 3rd precinct. Four years later, on Nov. 6, 1970, Moran was transferred to patrol in the 4th precinct. Jack was an early member of the Westchester County Police Emerald Society Pipes and Drums Band as a piper. PO Moran had his request granted when, on Oct. 19, 1971, he was transferred to the Special Operations Division, assigned to the Tactical Patrol Force (TPF). And on June 23, 1972, he was assigned to the Traffic Unit on two wheel motorcycle patrol. PO John Moran retired from the police department on Oct. 2, 1987. His son Brian was a YPD sergeant and his son Darren is a YPD police officer. His son Sean, formerly a YPD police officer, is a YFD Fire lieutenant.

DET. EDWARD R. OAKLEY #678

APPOINTED: March 4, 1966
RETIRED: March 16, 2001

Ed Oakley was born in Yonkers on July 7, 1939. He attended St. Joseph's school, Longfellow Jr. HS, and left high school to join the Marine Corps on July 13, 1956. He served with the 8th Engineer Battalion at Camp Lejeune, North Carolina, earned his high school equivalency diploma, and was honorably discharged on July 12, 1959. Prior to the YPD Ed had been employed by the Yonkers Post Office. Oakley was appointed to the Y.P.D. on Mar. 4, 1966, while living at 77 Saratoga Ave. He received his recruit training at the NYPD Police Academy, whose academic and physical curriculum ran from Mar. 28, through July 13, 1966. Following graduation he was assigned to the 3rd pct earning $6,000 a year. On Mar. 6, 1972 he was assigned to the Detective Division, not as a detective, but working in the Youth Division investigating juvenile crime. But, on May 15, 1972, he was appointed a Detective in the D.D. On October 21, 1983, due to a personnel shakeup, he and 8 others were transferred out. Ed went to the South Command but on Mar. 6, 1987, he was again appointed a Detective. Det Oakley worked general assignment in the D.D. until his last few years when he was assigned as the division's desk officer. Two of his sons were Lt. John Oakley and Det. Marvin Oakley. Det Edward Oakley retired from the YPD on March 16, 2001.

PO ANTON L. STEBLAK

APPOINTED: March 4, 1966
RESIGNED: June 16, 1972

Anton "Buddy" Steblak was born in Yonkers on Feb. 7, 1941. He attended St. Casimir's school and graduated from Sacred Heart HS in 1959. He also attended the University of Maryland. Anton joined the Air Force as a medic on Feb. 24, 1960 and was honorably discharged on Nov. 8, 1964. Prior to the YPD he worked for Fisher Body Co. in North Tarrytown. Anton was appointed to the Y.P.D. on Mar. 4, 1966 while living at 132 Caryl Ave. He received his recruit training at the NYPD police Academy, which ran from March 28, to July 13, 1966. Following his recruit graduation he was assigned to the 3rd pct earning $6,000 a year. On Jan. 1, 1971 he was transferred to the South Command and on Oct. 19, 1971 he was moved to the Special Operations Div. in the Tactical Patrol Force. " Buddy " was a gentlemen and a good cop who was one of those guys who would have been a success in any thing he did. He also had taken the Fire Dept. test before his police appointment and they offered him the job. A cousin to PO Larry Kunze, "Buddy" resigned from the YPD on June 16, 1972 to join the YFD where he would rise to lieutenant. Unfortunately Anton Steblak died suddenly on Sept. 3, 1984. He was only 43 years old.

PO GEORGE COSSIFOS #488

APPOINTED: March 4, 1966
DIED: October 27, 1970

George Cossifos was born in Yonkers on April 30, 1940. He attended PS# 18 and graduated from Yonkers HS. He also attended the RCA Institute in NYC. George joined the Navy on Dec. 12, 1957 and was honorably discharged. Prior to the YPD he was employed as an Electronics Technician. George Cossifos was appointed to the Y.P.D. Mar. 4, 1966 while living at 50 Leighton Ave. He received his recruit training at the NYPD Police Academy, whose academic and physical curriculum ran from March 28, to July 13, 1966. Following his graduation he was assigned to the 3rd pct. earning $6,000 a year. George was appointed a Detective on June 14, 1968 and was assigned to the Burglary and Narcotics Units. However, on February 20, 1970, he was reassigned back to uniform patrol in the 4th pct. George was very popular among his peers and earned 2 departmental Commendations, 4 Certificates of Excellent Police Work, and a Westchester Rockland Newspaper Award. PO Cossifos always complained of stomach problems and decided to undergo surgery for an ulcer. Unfortunately, following complications during stomach ulcer surgery in Doctors Hospital in NYC, PO George Cossifos died on Oct. 27, 1970. He was only 30 years old and had served only four years as a police officer.

PO PAUL C. KAISER #490

APPOINTED: March 4, 1966
RESIGNED: December 17, 1971

Paul Conrad Kaiser was born in Dobbs Ferry on Sept. 5, 1938 and attended Dobbs Ferry Elementary school and Dobbs Ferry HS. Paul joined the Marine Corps Reserve on Oct. 4, 1957 and following six months active duty, completed his reserve obligation and was honorably discharged in 1961. A racing enthusiast, Paul owned his own race car and prior to the YPD he had been serving as a police officer with the Pelham Manor P.D. beginning on Jan. 15, 1964. Paul was appointed to the Y.P.D. on Mar. 4, 1966 while living at 679 Warburton Ave. Because he was already a trained police officer very little recruit training was necessary. Upon graduation, his first patrol assignment was to the 4th pct earning $6,000 a year. At an award ceremony held on May 10, 1969 he was awarded the departments Honorable Mention for acts of bravery involving personal risk to life. On Mar. 30, 1970 Paul was reassigned to work in the Communications Div. in HQ. But the next year, on April 16, 1971, he was reassigned to patrol duty in the South Command. Paul resigned from the YPD on Dec. 17, 1971 reportedly due to his wife's ill health. It was said that he moved to Florida and for short time worked for the Ft. Myers Sheriff's Office. It was also said that for about 30 years he was a dealer in firearms with a F.F.L. license. In 2005 Paul Kaiser was living in Tennessee.

PO ABDI I. H. ALI #420

APPOINTED: March 4, 1966
RETIRED: April 29, 1995

Abdi Ismail Hipha Ali was born in the City of Yonkers on December 28, 1935. He attended PS # 1, Longfellow Jr. High School, and Commerce High School. Sonny joined the Marine Corps on March 8, 1954 and served in the 2nd Marine Division and was honorably discharged as a Corporal on March 8, 1958. Prior to the Yonkers P.D. he worked for the Phelps Dodge Corp.

Ali was appointed to the Yonkers Police Department March 4, 1966 while living at 55 Ravine Ave. He received his basic police recruit training at the NYPD Police Academy, whose academic and physical curriculum ran from March 28, 1966 through July 13, 1966. Following his graduation his first patrol assignment was in the 3rd precinct earning a starting salary of $6,000 a year. On January 1, 1971 following the implementation of a city-wide patrol precinct centralization plan, "Sonny," as he was known by friends, was reassigned to the South Command.

"Sonny" spent 13 years there on patrol and at his own request was assigned to a foot post in the high crime area of Elm Street. The community had a large diverse ethnic population, had a high crime rate and was considered a dangerous area by its residents and police alike. For whatever reason that challenge was what he wanted. PO Ali was not a large and muscular man but he was wiry and like iron in his determination to control crime on his post; Elm Street. After all, he was a former Marine who never quit, who always proudly displayed his USMC belt buckle while in uniform, and he had no doubts about his capabilities. Also often visible was a small pearl handle revolver tucked into his waistband. There was even an unsubstantiated story that, on occasion, he brought a bull whip on post while on patrol. Probably just a tale told by those who actually feared officer Ali.

To accomplish his objectives he was friendly and kind to the good people and harsh and gave no breaks to the bad. He was a good tough cop who was not appreciated by some but admired by others. On one occasion he was even shot by a rifle while on his foot post. It only deepened his determination.

Following some health issues "Sonny" was reassigned to the 4th precinct on September 3, 1984 on light duty and on June 24, 1987 was transferred to headquarters as court security.

Abdi Ali retired from the police department on a disability pension after 29 years on April 29, 1995. Unfortunately, only four months later, on August 14, 1995 he would succumb to cancer. PO "Sonny" Ali was so respected that a portion of his old foot post was honorarily renamed "Abdi Ali Way." He was 69 years old.

DET. DENNIS M. RAFFA #671

APPOINTED: March 4, 1966
RETIRED: March 23, 1993

Dennis M. Raffa was born in the City of Yonkers on September 14, 1942. He attended PS# 13, Benjamin Franklin Jr High School, Gorton High School, and later graduated from Saunders High School with a trade in printing. Dennis was a big man standing 6' 3" and well over 200 lbs. so it was only natural that while in Saunders he played football on the Saunders football team. As big as Dennis was he was very fast and played tight end or defensive end on the team. And due to his skill on the field he was offered a full football scholarship to Tarkio College in Tarkio, MO. However, he only attended and played for 6 months and then returned to Yonkers. Upon his return he played football on the "Blackhawks" semi pro football team in a league, but was employed by the Dobbs Ferry Register newspaper as a Printer. During this same time he did some boxing and began a 40 year study in the martial art of Karate.

Following in his brother John and cousin Nick Rossi's footsteps, Dennis was appointed to the Yonkers Police Department March 4, 1966 while living at 231 W. 246th St. NYC. He received his basic police recruit training at the NYPD Police Academy, whose academic and physical curriculum ran from March 28, 1966 through July 13, 1966. Following his graduation PO Dennis Raffa's first patrol assignment was in the 4th precinct earning a starting salary of $6,000 a year.

On December 26, 1969 PO Raffa was appointed a Detective in the Detective Division. In 1971 he was returned to patrol in the 4th precinct and in June of 1972 he went to the Special Operations Division. But a few months later, on September 15, 1972, Raffa was again appointed a Detective. In the 1970's he was still very active playing on the PBA softball and basketball team. In 1982, during the Federal investigation of the Yonkers Tylenol poisoning murders, Raffa was detailed to the FBI for two years to assist in their investigation. He was also interested and very knowledgeable on organized crime activities in Yonkers.

Det Dennis Raffa retired from the police department on March 23, 1993. Following retirement he worked as a security director for the Pergament store in Yonkers for a few years.

DET. SGT. MICHAEL P. SLATTERY #44

APPOINTED: March 4, 1966
RETIRED: May 23, 2003

Born Michael Patrick Slattery in the Bronx NY on June 9, 1941, Mike attended PS# 201 in the Bronx up to the 3rd grade and after his family moved to Yonkers he continued his education by attending St. Barnabas elementary school, Mark Twain Jr. high school, and graduated from Commerce High School on Palisade Avenue. Just a month following graduation, on July 30, 1959, he joined the Marine Corps for a two year enlistment serving as a cook. While in the Marine Corps Mike gained experience with a rifle, shotgun, pistol and later was a certified instructor for the NRA. He received his honorable discharge on October 18, 1961. Following his discharge he worked as a Local # 3 electrician apprentice.

Mike worked as an electrician right up to his appointment to the Yonkers Police Dept. on March 4, 1966 while living at 1 Jervis Road. He received his basic police recruit training at the NYPD Police Academy, with an academic and physical curriculum that ran from March 28, 1966 through July 13, 1966. Following his recruit graduation PO Michael Slattery was first assigned to foot patrol duty in the 4th precinct earning a starting salary of $6,000 a year.

On February 2, 1970 he was assigned to the Emergency Services Unit in the 1st precinct on St Casimir Avenue until the precinct was closed on January 1, 1971, at which time he was reassigned to the North Command still in the Emergency Unit. He worked in the Emergency Unit for a few years and later was assigned to the North Command's Warrant Squad. When the precinct warrant squad became a city wide operation on April 12, 1973, Mike worked executing warrants from the Central Booking Warrant Squad in headquarters at 10 St Casimir Ave.

On June 17, 1975 PO Slattery, known as “Sluggo” to everyone, was transferred to the Criminal Investigation Unit (CIU) as a crime scene photographer and evidence technician. On October 6, 1978 Mike Slattery was promoted to the rank of sergeant, earning a salary of $21,142 a year and was reassigned as a patrol supervisor in the South Command.

Always having an interest in the Captains, Lieutenants, & Sergeants Association (CLSA) it was about this time that he was elected Secretary of the "association." In the years to come he would work as a sergeant in Central Booking and supervise the Records Division, the Criminal Identification Unit (CIU) operation, and later the "Tele-Serv" program in the Communications Division. It was in this assignment that he was appointed Trustee at Large for the CLSA.

On December 21, 1982 Sgt. Slattery was transferred to the Administrative Services Division as the executive officer, and January 1, 1983 he was reassigned to the Communications Division. In 1984, 1985, and again in 1986 Sgt Slattery was elected President of the Captains, Lieutenants, & Sergeants Association and was again assigned to the Administrative Services Division on paper, but detailed to work full-time on the superior officers associations business. On February 24, 1987 he was returned to the Criminal Investigation Unit, as part of the Detective Division, as its supervisor. In addition to the duties overseeing the processing and evidence collecting at crime scenes he was also placed in charge of the Police Forensic Laboratory and on March 1, 2002 was elevated to "Detective Sergeant."

He retired from the Yonkers Police Department on May 23, 2003 after serving the department for over 37 years. Ret Det Sgt Michael Slattery moved to Ireland where he lives with his wife.

LT. ALPHONSE V. FONTANA

APPOINTED: March 4, 1966
RETIRED: March 30, 2001

Alphonso Vincent Fontana, known by all as "Vinnie," was born in the City of Yonkers on August 27, 1947. He attended St. Casimir's elementary school and graduated from Tuckahoe High School in 1961. He joined the Army Reserve on May 14, 1963 serving with the 42nd Military Police Company, in Mount Vernon, New York, and served on active duty until November 13, 1963. Following completion of his reserve obligation he was honorably discharged. Previous to the YPD "Vinnie" worked for the Singer Sewing Machine Company in Yonkers.

Alphonso Fontana was appointed to the Yonkers Police Department on March 4, 1966 while living at 42 Yonkers Ave. in Tuckahoe New York. He received his basic recruit training at the NYPD Police Academy, whose academic and physical curriculum ran from March 28, to July 13, 1966. Following recruit graduation, his first assignment was patrol duty in the 1st precinct earning a starting salary of $6,000 a year. However, on November 12, 1966 he was reassigned to the 4th precinct. On February 7, 1969 Fontana was moved back to the 1st precinct and on September 7, 1972, to the Traffic Division on two wheeled motorcycle patrol. He would later return to patrol duty in the North East Patrol Command on April 11, 1980.

On November 18, 1982 PO Fontana was promoted to the rank of Sergeant earning a salary of $28,313 a year and was reassigned to the North Command as a patrol supervisor. On May 30, 1986, Sgt Fontana was assigned to the Special Operations Division (SOD) in the Traffic Unit.

On October 13, 1989 Sgt. Fontana was promoted to the rank of police Lieutenant earning $53,931 a year and designated the Executive Officer for SOD. Beginning in 1991 he was reassigned to the Field Services Bureau, then on July 22, 1992 moved to the Communications Division. Three years later, on November 1, 1995, he was moved to his last assignment, in Central Booking in the City Jail.

Alphonso Vincent Fontana retired from the police department on March 30, 2001 after 35 years of honorable service.

DET. LT. THOMAS E. REESE

APPOINTED: March 4, 1966
RETIRED: March 10, 1994

Tom Reese was born on April 9, 1942 in Yonkers, NY, attended St. Mary's elementary school and later graduated from Saunders High School. Shortly after graduation Tom joined the Navy on January 16, 1961 and was honorably discharged on January 15, 1965. Prior to the YPD Reese was employed by the Yonkers Post Office.

Tom was appointed to the Yonkers Police Department on March 4, 1966 while living at 4 Undercliff Street. He received his basic police recruit training at the NYPD Police Academy, with an academic and physical curriculum that ran from March 28, 1966 through July 13, 1966. Following his recruit graduation PO Thomas Reese was first assigned to foot patrol duty in the 3rd precinct earning a starting salary of $6,000 a year. Following the implementation of a precinct centralization plan, on January 1, 1971 PO Reese was transferred to the South Patrol Command.

On March 6, 1972 Tom was reassigned to the Detective Division, but not as a Detective, and was detailed to work juvenile crime investigations in the Youth Division. But 2 months later, on May 15, 1972, Reese was appointed a Detective in the DD. On November 17, 1975 Tom was promoted to Sergeant earning $37,351 and was transferred to the South Command as a patrol supervisor. During some of his years in the South Command Sgt Reese was in charge of a precinct Task Force organized to address special crime problems. It took a while but, on October 28, 1983, Sgt Reese was again returned to the D.D. now as a Detective squad Sergeant. On August 16, 1984 he was promoted to Lieutenant and moved to the Communications Division for a few months but on February 22, 1985 he was returned to the Detective Division as the Executive Officer.

Det Lt. Thomas Reese remained there right up to his retirement from the YPD on March 10, 1994. Ret. Det. Lt. Tom Reese died July 25, 2014.

PO RALPH J. PALLETT #481

APPOINTED: March 4, 1966
RETIRED: June 27, 1986

Ralph Pallett was born in New Rochelle, NY on November 14, 1939. He attended Hutchinson and Daniel Webster Elementary school and A.B. Davis High School in Mt. Vernon, NY. Right after graduation Ralph joined the Marine Corps. on November 29, 1956 and was honorably discharged as a Corporal on September 28, 1959. As a young man Ralph earned a living as an auto mechanic.

Ralph was appointed to the Yonkers Police Department on March 4, 1966 while living at 322 5th Avenue in New Rochelle. He received his basic police recruit training at the NYPD Police Academy, with an academic and physical curriculum that ran from March 28, 1966 through July 13, 1966. Following his recruit graduation PO Ralph Pallett was first assigned to foot patrol duty in the 1st precinct earning a starting salary of $6,000 a year. On November 9, 1966 PO Pallett was reassigned to patrol in the 4th precinct. Ralph was recommended for a Commendation for a fire rescue on December 6, 1969 when he and his partner rescued an elderly man trapped in his apartment at 160 Palisade Ave. Pallett remained in the 4th on January 1, 1971 when it was renamed the North Command.

At one point due to the poor condition of the fleet of police cars, additional auto mechanics were needed. And because of his skill as an auto mechanic, on January 29, 1973 Pallett was transferred to Headquarters Command detailed to work as a mechanic in the police repair shop. With the exception of a few short assignments PO Pallett remained working as a police mechanic up to March 22, 1984 when, upon his request, he was transferred to patrol duty in the 3rd precinct.

PO Ralph Pallett retired from the police department on June 27, 1986.

PO EDWARD REIGER #485

APPOINTED: March 11, 1966
RETIRED: May 16, 1986

It is relatively uncommon that police officers are put in a position to actually physically fight for their life. But at one point, when he was not expecting it, the below officer was forced to do just that.

Edward Reiger was born in the Town of Mt. Kisco, NY on March 1, 1941. As a child his family moved to Yonkers and he attended St. Mary's elementary school and he graduated from Lincoln High School. Not long after graduation Ed joined the Air Force on July 15, 1960, during the very early stages of what would be the Viet Nam War, and was honorably discharged as an Airman 4th class on January 7, 1964. Previous to the YPD Ed was employed by the U.S. Health Club in Yonkers. Ed was not unusually tall but was built like a tank and could clearly handle himself.

Ed followed his father, who was a sergeant with the NY State Police, by going into law enforcement when Ed was appointed to the Yonkers Police Department on March 11, 1966 while living at 23 Huber Place. He received his basic police recruit training at the NYPD Police Academy, whose academic and physical curriculum ran from March 28, 1966 through July 13, 1966. Following his graduation PO Edward Reiger's first patrol assignment was in the 4th precinct earning a starting salary of $6,000 a year.

Following the implementation of a precinct centralization plan on January 1, 1971 PO Reiger was transferred to the North Patrol Command. Ed was of stocky build with a mostly bald head whose mouth almost always had a cigar sticking out of it. He played on the PBA softball team for many years and was known as a power hitter. Ed was a very dependable and efficient officer but always complained; even if there was nothing to complain about. But if you had a problem on the street, Ed would be among the very first to respond as your backup.

On Oct 21, 1977, while off duty and at the 300 Yonkers Avenue motel at about midnight, officer Reiger walked into the motel office right into a robbery in progress. He observed a male pointing a gun in the face of the night clerk and demanding money. Being only feet apart, officer Reiger drew his off duty revolver, announced he was a police officer and told the suspect to drop the gun. Instead, the male turned and pointed the gun at Reiger who then grabbed the man's gun hand. Reiger's gun hand was held off as well and a virtual life and death struggle ensued. During the violent struggle both weapons were fired at each other, fortunately with no one hit. As they fought, exhaustion setting in, both men fell to the floor and as Reiger's revolver struck the floor the cylinder opened. The suspect took this opportunity and ran from the motel. However, due to Reiger's quick decisive action, disregard for his own safety and placing himself in imminent danger, as well as providing information to responding officers, the suspect was subsequently arrested. For his actions that night officer Edward Reiger was awarded the police departments second highest award at that time; the Honorable Mention award.

On September 7, 1984 Reiger was reassigned to patrol duty in the 1st precinct from which he would retire on May 16, 1986. Unfortunately, following a long illness Ret PO Edward Reiger died on January 26, 2002. He was 60 years old.

DET. ROBERT P. REYNOLDS #646

APPOINTED: March 11, 1966
RETIRED: July 15, 1989

Generally speaking, when one thinks of a police officer, some of the traits would be self-confidence, assertiveness and having an outgoing personality. The subject of this profile was all of these and many more.

Robert P. Reynolds was born in the City of Yonkers on September 5, 1940. He attended St Mary's elementary school and later graduated from Saunders Trade & Technical High School. And even while in school he displayed such outgoing and gregarious qualities that people wanted to be around him. Bob joined the Army on October 22, 1957 and served in the Army's 82nd Airborne Division as a paratrooper. He was honorably discharged on October 17, 1960.

Following his military service Bob worked as a welder with the Saw Mill Iron Works in Yonkers. He also was an amateur "finish" carpenter and enjoyed working with his hands building small furniture. And strong hands they were as Bob was always working out in the Gym, building up the size of his multi tattooed arms.

Robert Reynolds was appointed to the Yonkers Police Department March 11, 1966 while living at 5 Van Cortlandt Park Avenue. He received his basic police recruit training at the NYPD Police Academy, whose academic and physical curriculum ran from March 28, 1966 through July 13, 1966. Following his graduation PO Bob Reynolds' first patrol assignment was in the 4th precinct earning a starting salary of $6,000 a year.

Bob had an opportunity to be assigned to the two wheel motorcycle unit which fit his personality of attracting attention. And so, on February 20, 1970, Reynolds was assigned to the Traffic Division's

Det. Robert P. Reynolds #646 (cont.)

motorcycle unit. It would not be an exaggeration to say that PO Reynolds' personal appearance in uniform was as near perfection as one could get. Though not tall in height his well-built physique fit into his tailor fit uniforms like a glove. He was, at all times, spit and polish. Bob was very strict with traffic law violators but always professional. Among all who knew him he was the life of any party, knew the best jokes, and had the loudest laugh. And yet, as self-assured as he was, some might even say cocky, Bob was always respectful to ranking officers.

At one point while riding his motorcycle along East Grassy Sprain Road a car cut in front of him. Bob's motorcycle crashed straight into a vehicle causing him to be thrown off his "wheel" and into, and partly through, the car windshield. He had multiple injuries but most severe was to his arm which the doctors said they could not repair and should be amputated. Bob refused to sign permission and instructed the doctors to operate and do what they could. Bob's determination led him through a long healing and physical therapy routine which ultimately resulted in him regaining strength in his arm and he actually returned to weight lifting and his police motorcycle duties.

A member of the Police Emerald Society Bob Reynolds loved being Irish. And it showed. So it was only natural that he would join the Pipes & Drums of the Police Emerald Society of Westchester Band. He couldn't play any instrument but said he would learn; and he did. He would ultimately take the position of Bass Drummer and even served as Band Master.

After 11 years on motorcycle duty, on May 13, 1981, PO Reynolds was assigned to the Taxi & Bus (Hack) Licensing Unit, which was still a part of the Traffic Division. While still in the "Hack" Unit, on November 1, 1985, Reynolds was appointed a Detective and remained in the Hack Unit. On November 21, 1988 Det Reynolds was reassigned to the Detective Division working general assignment investigations. Bob remained in the D.D. right up to his accidental disability retirement on July 15, 1989.

Following his retirement Reynolds moved to Vermont and was employed as a Federal Marshall for the US Immigration Service up to 1997 when he became ill with Leukemia. He fought long and hard and never once felt sorry for himself. He knew his fate and accepted it with dignity and even a little dark humor. During a telephone conversation toward the end he told a friend, "I'll be coming to Yonkers soon. In case you don't recognize me, I'll be the guy in the urn."

Ret Det Robert Reynolds died on February 4, 2005. He was 64 years old.

PO JAMES J. DeMAIO #505

APPOINTED: March 25, 1966
RETIRED: March 27, 1986

James Joseph DeMaio was born in NYC on May 13, 1936. Jim attended St. Mary's school, PS# 113 and 118 all in the Bronx. He graduated from Evander Childs HS in the Bronx in 1954. Jim entered the Army on Jan. 11, 1955 and was later honorably discharged .on Jan. 3, 1958. Prior to the Y.P.D. Jim was employed by the Katonah Private Rental Car Co. in the Bronx. James DeMaio was appointed to the Y.P.D. on Mar. 25, 1966 while living at 3307 Hull Ave., Bronx, NY. He received his recruit training at the Iona College campus in New Rochelle whose academic curriculum ran from April 4, to May 6, 1966. Following his graduation he was assigned to the 2nd pct earning a starting salary of $6,000 a year. On Nov. 9, 1966 he was reassigned to patrol duty and the 3rd pct and on Jan. 1, 1971 he was transferred to the newly designated South Command. Jim believed what one man's junk was another's treasure and quickly earned the nickname, "Jimmy Junk." In 1983 he was transferred to patrol in the 3rd pct where he would retire on March 27, 1986. James DeMaio moved to Denver, Colorado and following a lengthy illness died on July 4, 2008. He was 72 years old.

PO JOHN SHEEHAN #497

APPOINTED: March 25, 1966
RETIRED: April 4, 1986

John's Sheehan was born in NYC on April 13, 1939. He attended Sacred Heart elementary school, Power Memorial Academy Jr. HS, and graduated from St. Simon Stock HS in the Bronx, NY in 1958. John joined the Army on Aug. 19, 1958 serving as a Cryptographer and was honorably discharged as a Specialist 4th class on Aug. 2, 1960. Prior to joining the YPD John was employed by the Pan American Airways at Kennedy Airport in NYC. John Sheehan was appointed to the Y.P.D. on Mar. 25, 1966 while living at 75 St. Andrews Pl. He received his recruit training at the Iona College campus in New Rochelle whose academic curriculum ran from April 4, to May 6, 1966. Following graduation Sheehan's first assignment was in the 3rd pct earning $6,000 a year. On Jan. 1, 1971, following the centralization of the four patrol precincts, officer Sheehan was transferred to the South Patrol Command. John was a great street cop who was respected by his peers. He also had a good sense of humor and was a proud Irishman. There is no doubt that his Irish ancestry resulted in his good friends nicknaming him, "Harpo." John Sheehan remained in the South Command for the remainder of his career retiring on April 4, 1986.

PO RAYOT A. DiFATE #491

APPOINTED: March 25, 1966
RETIRED: April 1, 1981

Rayot DiFate was born in the City of Yonkers on July 31, 1941. He attended PS# 12, Longfellow Jr. High School, and graduated from Commerce High School in 1959. Ray entered the Army on October 24, 1960 and was later honorably discharged holding the rank of Specialist 4th class, on October 23, 1963. During his enlistment he had served in C Battery, 1st Battalion, 29th Artillery. Prior to the YPD he was employed by the Fisher Body Co. in Tarrytown, New York.

Rayot DiFate was appointed to the Yonkers Police Department on March 25, 1966 while residing at 2 Ivy Pl. in Yonkers. He received his recruit training on the campus of Iona College in New Rochelle whose academic curriculum ran from April 4, 1966 to May 6, 1966. Following his recruit graduation Patrolman DiFate's first assignment was patrol duty in the 2nd precinct earning a salary of $6,000 a year.

On November 7, 1966, following a department wide reorganization, he was transferred to the newly opened 1st precinct at 730 E. Grassy Sprain Rd. Three years later, on December 27, 1969, he was reassigned to patrol in the original 3rd precinct located at 36 Radford Street. Once again, following the implementation of a precinct wide centralization plan on January 1, 1971, DiFate was transferred to patrol duty in the South Patrol Command. "Ray," as he was known, and whose brother was Sgt Mike DiFate, was a very active and effective street cop. He also had studied the martial arts for several years and was an expert in karate and judo. In fact, on a few occasions he was even allowed to teach precinct personnel and members of various other police departments in the effective use of a nightstick for defensive and offensive purposes.

Ray served several years in the Anti-Crime Unit right from its inception on February 25, 1975. While in Anti-Crime he was seriously injured while involved in a motor vehicle accident. He had been parked at the curb staking out the area on St. Johns Avenue when his parked vehicle was struck hard, pushing it at least 20 feet from its location. Rayot DiFate remained out injured for some time, but retired on an Accidental Disability Pension effective April 1, 1981.

DET. RICHARD W. MILLER #674

APPOINTED: March 25, 1966
RETIRED: March 30, 2001

Richard W. Miller was born in Yonkers on September 30, 1941. He attended holy Trinity school and Saunders HS. Rich entered in the U.S. Navy on March 15, 1960 and was honorably discharged on January 13, 1964. Previous to the YPD Miller was employed by the Romar Specialties, Inc. in Yonkers.

Richard Miller was appointed to the Yonkers police department on March 25, 1966 while residing at 28 Cedar St. He received his basic police recruit training on the campus of Iona College in New Rochelle from April 4, 1966 to May 6, 1966. Following the recruit graduation his first assignment was patrol duty in the first precinct. Following a department wide patrol reorganization, on November 9, 1966, he was transferred to the 4th precinct. Sixteen years later, on September 13, 1982, Rich was reassigned to the South Patrol Command. While there, for several years Miller worked a steady night shift from 10 PM to 6 AM in plain clothes in the 2nd precincts Auto Theft Squad with his partner, PO Joseph Tchorzyk. PO Miller and his partner were very successful in their number of arrests and in doing so developed a reputation for being an outstanding team who were respected by all.

At one point PO Miller was detailed to the D.D. as a silver shield, no detective status, and assigned to work in their auto theft squad. But, on March 30, 1990 Miller was appointed a Detective and continued to work in their auto theft squad for several years. He would later be reassigned to the Burglary Squad. Det. Miller was a highly respected police officer and Detective who, during his career with the police department earned 10 Certificates of Excellent Police Work; The 1986 2nd precinct Community Council Award; the 1988 Elks Lodge 707 Uniform Appreciation Award; the 1988 Exchange Club Police Officer of the Year Award; the 1989 VFW Post 1666 Recognition Award, and numerous letters of appreciation. He also served many years as the Sergeant at Arms for the PBA. His nephew, David Miller, would later also join the YPD.

Det Richard Miller retired from the police department on March 30, 2001 five days shy of 35 years of dedicated service. In retirement he continued his love of fishing.

PO MATTHEW J. WALSH #492

APPOINTED: March 25, 1966
DIED: May 23, 1993

Born in Yonkers on June 23, 1941 Matthew Walsh attended Our Saviour's Elementary school in the Bronx from 1947 to 1955. He then attended Mount St. Michael's Academy High School in the Bronx from 1955 to 1959 when he graduated. Previous to the YPD Matthew earned a living working as an auto mechanic.

Matthew Walsh was appointed to the Yonkers Police Department on March 25, 1966 while residing in Yonkers. He received his basic police recruit training on the campus of Iona College in New Rochelle whose academic curriculum ran from April 4, 1966 to May 6, 1966. Following his recruit graduation Patrolman Walsh's first assignment was patrol duty in the 1st precinct. However, on November 9, 1966, he was reassigned to patrol duty in the 4th precinct.

Matty was a well like guy but he had a very strong sense of what was right and wrong and often walked his own path, as opposed to that of the rest of the department. He was a very dedicated and aggressive officer who gave 100% all the time, no breaks, no stories, and was not at all flexible. As a result, Matty frequently found himself at odds with superiors and was, not surprisingly, transferred often. On August 14, 1968 Walsh was reassigned to the Headquarters Command Division. On November 15, 1969 he was transferred to the 3rd precinct.

It was about this time that Matty was assigned to the Tactical Patrol Unit and on one evening PO Walsh fired his revolver and struck a 17 year old male, fortunately with only a crazing wound to his head. Walsh said it was self-defense. There was an intense investigation as to whether the force was necessary but nothing came of it. Matty was never charged, however Deputy Chief Frank Sardo never trusted Matty again and wanted him off street patrol and had him transferred on January 1, 1971, to the South Command on desk duty. Not to be allowed on patrol. The chief's purpose was to contain Walsh to only administrative duty. It didn't work all the time. Even on desk duty PO Walsh found cause, on occasion, to arrest a "walk in" civilian off the street.

Finally, twelve years later, on April 20, 1983, Matty was reassigned back to patrol duty in the 1st precinct. On March 6, 1992 while investigating a bank alarm ringing (a 10-18) at the Hudson Valley Bank, Matty accidentally shot himself in the foot with his shotgun. He recovered and after extensive rehabilitation he returned to full duty. A year later, in March of 1993 Matty was assigned to the Special Operations Division to write Summonses.

On May 23, 1993 Matthew Walsh suffered a heart attack while driving to work, and died. He was 51 years old.

PO LOUIS W. PULICE #465

APPOINTED: March 25, 1966
RETIRED: January 9, 1998

Lou Pulice was born on September 21, 1938 in NYC and attended PS# 6 in the Bronx and graduated from the Machine and Metal Trades HS in Mineola, NY. Prior to the YPD Lou worked at a number of different jobs but when he applied to the YPD he was unemployed and needed this job. Louis Pulice was appointed to the Yonkers Police Department on March 25, 1966 while living at 3400 Bronxwood Ave. in the Bx. He received his recruit training at the Iona College campus in New Rochelle whose curriculum ran from April 4, to May 6, 1966. Following his graduation Patrolman Louis Pulice's first patrol assignment was in the 3rd precinct earning a starting salary of $6,000 a year. On January 1, 1971 Lou was transferred to the South Patrol Command and 10 years later, March 18, 1981, he was reassigned to the North Patrol Command. On May 16, 1988 Pulice was detailed from the 4th pct. to the Warrant Squad. Two years later, on November 12, 1990, he was officially transferred to the Courts and Detention Services Division working in the Warrant Squad located in the City Jail on Alexander Street. Louis Pulice retired from the YPD on January 9, 1998 after nearly 36 years service.

PO JAMES P. CLARKIN #493

APPOINTED: March 25, 1966
RETIRED: October 18, 1974

James Clarkin was born in the Bronx, NY on Mar. 25, 1943. He attended St Barnabas school in the Bronx and graduated from Cardinal Hayes HS in 1960. On his police application Clarkin listed his employment with the Paper Handlers Union. Jim Clarkin was appointed to the Y.P.D. Mar. 25, 1966 while living at 23 Huber Pl. He received his recruit training at the NYPD Police Academy, whose academic and physical curriculum ran from March 28, to July 13, 1966. Upon graduating Clarkin was awarded an off duty revolver for attaining the highest academic average in his recruit class. PO James Clarkin's first patrol assignment was in the 2nd pct earning $6,000 a year. Jim was an early member of the Westchester County Emerald Society Pipes and Drums Band as a piper. On Nov. 24, 1971 officer Clarkin, who had been assigned to patrol on a police scooter, was involved in an accident while on the scooter and severely broke his leg. He was forced to go out disabled until Sept. 4, 1973. During that time he had several major operations to repair the damage to his leg. On Oct. 25, 1973 he returned to light duty status in S.O.D. on desk duty and subsequently was awarded a disability retirement pension on Oct. 18, 1974.

PO RICHARD L. TOCCI #103

APPOINTED: March 25, 1966
RETIRED: August 24, 1990

Being one of 20 children, Richard L. Tocci was born on November 18, 1936 in Yonkers, NY. Richie attended Sacred Heart elementary school and Sacred Heart HS but did not graduate. He left school and Joined Navy on September 16, 1954 at the age of 17 years and served as a Boiler Attendant with rank of Petty Officer 3rd class. He served 4 years, during which he obtained his equivalency diploma, and then re-enlisted for two more years serving aboard the USS Francis Robinson and was honorably discharged. Following his military service Rich joined the Carpenters Union local #188 and prior to, and throughout his police service, he worked as a carpenter as a second job for 17 years.

Richard Tocci was appointed to the Yonkers Police Department on March 25, 1966 while living at 30 College Pl. in Yonkers. He received his recruit training at the Iona College campus in New Rochelle whose curriculum ran from April 4, to May 6, 1966. Following his graduation Patrolman Richard Tocci's first patrol assignment was in the 1st precinct earning a starting salary of $6,000 a year.

On November 9, 1966 Patrolman Tocci began a series of assignments; on that date he was assigned to duty in the 4th precinct, on May 19, 1969 to the 2nd precinct, on September 15, 1972 to the North Command, and on June 20, 1979 to the N.E. Patrol Command. Throughout the 1970's Tocci was very athletic and active playing on the PBA softball team. On December 30, 1985 Tocci was transferred to the Youth Division and detailed to work in the Police Athletic League (PAL). Tocci always worked out in the gym and was an amateur body builder so it was no surprise that he instituted a weight lifting program for the youths in the PAL.

Richard Tocci, whose nephews were PO's Joe Abbondola and Stanley Galuska, retired on August 24, 1990 while still serving in the PAL as their Weight Lifting Program coach.

Rich Tocci and his wife moved to Palm Coast, Fla. where he remained up to the death of his wife. He then returned to live with his daughter in Yorktown Heights where he died on July 14, 2013.

PO LOUIS C. DeANGELO #495

APPOINTED: March 25, 1966
RESIGNED: June 16, 1966

Born in Yonkers Louis DeAngelo attended PS# 18 and Saunders HS. He entered the Army on Jan. 4, 1960 and was honorably discharged March 1, 1962. Upon his discharge from the Army he received a letter of appreciation from his commanding officer. *"Your mature judgment, reliability, and initiative were material in increasing the efficiency of the motor pool operations and in releasing the motor sergeant from administrative duties to spend more time with his mechanics. It is with much regret that we lose you from this unit but an end must come to all good things. The very best of luck to you in the future and thanks again for a job well done."* Previous to the YPD he was employed by the Yonkers water department. Louis was appointed to the Yonkers Police Department on March 25, 1966 while living at 125 Linden St. He attended the Iona recruit training school from April 4, to May 6, 1966. Following his graduation he was assigned to the 1st pct on foot patrol earning $6,000 a year. In addition to English he also spoke Italian fluently. After only three months, on June 16, 1966 Louis DeAngelo resigned and returned to the Water Dept. (DPW.)

PO FIORILLO VALENTI #117

APPOINTED: March 25, 1966
RESIGNED: September 8, 1967

Fiorillo Valenti was born in the city of White Plains on April 19, 1940. He attended local elementary schools and graduated from White Plains high school. Shortly after graduating Fiorillo joined the Marine Corps on July 11, 1958 and was honorably discharged on July 10, 1961. On his Police Department application Valenti listed his employment as the Pleasantville N. Y. Post Office. Fiorillo Valente was appointed to the Yonkers Police Department on March 25, 1966 while living at 298 Jessamine Avenue. He received his basic police recruit training at the Iona College campus in New Rochelle whose curriculum ran from April 4, 1966 through May 6, 1966. Following his graduation PO Fiorillo Valenti's first patrol assignment was in the 4th precinct earning a starting salary of $6,000 a year. On May 29, 1967 Valenti was transferred to the Communications Division. In addition to taking the police department exam, Valenti also took the fire department examination and was on their list for appointment. Valenti was notified that he could be appointed a firefighter and, he submitted his resignation to the Yonkers Police Dept. effective September 8, 1967 in order to join the Yonkers Fire Department.

DET. ANTHONY M. CERASI #681

APPOINTED: March 25, 1966
RETIRED: January 17, 2003

The subject of the below profile is a member of a very small group of Yonkers police officers who, due to actions taken by them in the performance of duty, were awarded the Yonkers Police Department's Medal Of Honor.

Anthony M. Cerasi was born in the Town of New Rochelle on January 3, 1943. He attended Immaculate Conception elementary school in Tuckahoe and later graduated from Eastchester High School. When Tony applied to the Yonkers Police Department for appointment he listed his employment as a Patrolman with the NYC Railroad.

Anthony Cerasi was appointed to the Yonkers Police Department on March 25, 1966 while living at 17 Beaumont Circle. He received his basic police recruit training at the Iona College campus in New Rochelle whose curriculum ran from April 4, 1966 through May 6, 1966. Following his graduation Probationary Patrolman Anthony Cerasi's first patrol assignment was in the 1st precinct earning a starting salary of $6,000 a year. Several months later, on November 9, 1966, Cerasi was reassigned to patrol in the 4th precinct.

On April 9, 1970 the First National Bank at 370 Warburton Avenue was held up at gunpoint. The entire incident began shortly before noon when a man walked into the bank and stuck a gun in the back of the bank security guard. He told the 68-year-old guard to walk with him quietly or he would kill him. The two walked past long lines of customers directly to a bank teller. It was then that the robber demanded that money be placed in a bag that he shoved over to the teller.

Det. Anthony M. Cerasi #681 (cont.)

At that point the security guard jammed his elbow into the robber's stomach and pulled out his own gun. That's when the shooting began. Reportedly, shots bounced off the ceiling and floor of the bank as the two men battled for each other's gun. The suspect was clearly desperate and dangerous. The fight ended when the security guard received a gunshot wound to his upper arm. It was then that the bank robber grabbed the bag filled with money and ran out into the street.

At that time Patrolman Cerasi was sitting in a radio car at a school crossing not far from the bank, while his partner guided children to safety crossing the street, when he heard the bank alarm ringing. Officer Cerasi exited his radio car to investigate and observed the suspect running down the street, gun in hand, right in his direction. Within seconds they came face to face. It was reported that they both looked at each other for a second and then the suspect pointed his gun right at the officer. Although he had the legal authority to shoot the male, Cerasi pointed his revolver at the man and told him to drop his gun. For several brief moments it was a stand-off but the suspect surrendered without Cerasi firing a shot and the bank money was recovered.

For his actions on that day, for disregarding his own safety and while in imminent personal danger to himself and others, Patrolman Anthony Cerasi was awarded the Yonkers Police Department's highest award, the Police Department Medal Of Honor.

Having captured the bank robber at gun point Patrolman Cerasi was rewarded by being appointed a Detective on April 17, 1970 and assigned to the Detective Division's Narcotics Unit in an undercover capacity.

In September of 1974 Yonkers PO Harold Woods was shot and killed in an armed robbery. Every available police officer and detective worked on and off duty to locate the two shooters. But, although assigned to Narcotics, it was Det Anthony Cerasi and his partner Det Tony Souza who apprehended one of the shooters in New York City and also recovered the handgun used to kill officer Woods.

In 1990 Det Cerasi served a short time in the prestigious Special Investigations Unit where extremely sensitive investigations were conducted, but returned to the Narcotics Unit where he served out the remainder of his career. Det. Cerasi was the recipient of the Medal of Honor, one Commendation, 2 Certificates of Excellent Police Work, a Unit Citation, a NYC Mayors Citation of Merit, the Journal News Macy Award, and a Westchester County Shields Association Award.

A charter member of the Yonkers Police Honor Guard and whose son is an Eastchester police officer, Det Anthony Cerasi retired from the YPD on January 17, 2003.

In retirement Tony could not sit and do nothing so he began working as a security supervisor at the Empire City Racetrack & Casino in Yonkers NY.

PO ROBERT J. ROFRANO #499

APPOINTED: March 25, 1966
RETIRED: April 18, 1986

Robert Rofrano was born in NYC on August 9, 1941, attended PS# 17, Jr. High School #123, and graduated from James Monroe High School, all located in the Bronx, NY. Following high school Bob listed his employment with the Continental Bank in NYC.

Robert Rofrano was appointed to the Yonkers Police Department on March 25, 1966 while living at 2924 E. 194th Street in Bronx. He received his basic police recruit training at the Iona College campus in New Rochelle whose curriculum ran from April 4, 1966 through May 6, 1966. Following his graduation Patrolman Robert Rofrano's first patrol assignment was in the 2nd precinct earning a starting salary of $6,000 a year. In 1969 Bob, better known to his friends as "Peppers," was awarded Policeman of the Year by the Yonkers Exchange Club along with his partner Thomas Hargraves, for the arrest and recovery of a stolen flatbed trailer full of stolen copper. Bob remained on patrol in the 2nd precinct, which was later renamed the South Command, up to February 6, 1976 when he was selected to be assigned to the newly organized Anti-Crime Unit of the YPD. Bob was a very active street cop in the precinct and when he joined the Anti-Crime Unit, which was all plainclothes/undercover work, he was able to be even more productive. The Westchester Co. Police Emerald Society Pipe and drum Band needed a tenor drummer but the band was all Irish. However, Bob could really play the drum well so he became the only non-Irish member of the band. They nicknamed him, "Bob O'Rofrano." During his career Rofrano earned 4 Commendations, and 5 Certificates of Excellent Police Work and remained in the Anti-Crime Unit, later renamed the Street Crime Unit, right up to his retirement on April 18, 1986. He worked for the New York State Park Police after he retired and also as security for Foxwoods Casino in Connecticut. Ret. PO Robert Rofrano died August 14, 2014.

PO CHARLES A. COLARUSSO #501

APPOINTED: March 25, 1966
RETIRED: June 27, 1986

Charles Colarusso was born in Mount Vernon New York on April 3, 1941. He attended Columbus 5th Avenue elementary school, and graduated from Edison High School in Mount Vernon. He joined the Navy on June 23, 1958 and was honorably discharged as a Seaman on June 1, 1964. Previous to the YPD he was employed by the Gramatan Farms company, in Mount Vernon as a milkman. Charlie's father, Anthony, was a Detective Sergeant with the Mount Vernon Police Dept., having served from 1947 to 1971, so it was no surprise when his son decided to follow in his footsteps in law enforcement.

Charles Colarusso was appointed to the Yonkers Police Department on March 25, 1966 while living at 353 North High Street in Mount Vernon, NY. He received his basic police recruit training at the Iona College campus in New Rochelle whose academic curriculum ran from April 4, 1966 through May 6, 1966. Following his graduation Probationary Patrolman Charles Colarusso's first patrol assignment was in the 1st precinct earning a starting salary of $6,000 a year.

On November 9, 1966, as part of a department wide patrol reorganization, Charlie was transferred to the 4th precinct. He remained there on January 1, 1971 when the precinct was renamed the North Patrol Command. At one point Colarusso's request to be assigned to the Emergency Services Unit was approved and he received the necessary medical and rescue training as well as certification as an Emergency Medical Technician (EMT). Charlie had a very friendly personality and was well liked by his fellow officers. More important, he was respected by them because he was a good street cop who could be counted on if someone needed backup. And his supervisors knew when given a job, they knew it would be handled correctly.

PO Charles A. Colarusso #501 (cont.)

On July 31, 1974 PO Colarusso, along with other officers, pulled two men to safety that were overcome by an industrial cleaning fluid's noxious gas while they worked inside a tank at the Phelps Dodge Cable and Wire Co. on Point Street. Being unable to reach the men trapped inside the tank, PO Charles Colarusso and his partner, PO John Drosdowich, climbed part way down the ladder and pulled them to the top before the gas forced the officers out of the tank. Thirty-four people, including police and firemen, were treated at Yonkers General Hospital for noxious fume inhalation.

Another memorable assignment occurred in the dead of winter. PO Colarusso and his partner Bob Webb received a call about a boy on the ice in the Hudson River off shore near the Greystone train station. When they arrived they observed a boy out on the ice approximately a couple of hundred yards from shore. They agreed to tie a rope around Colarusso's waist and he would go out on the ice to get the boy. Everything worked well until he got near the boy and Charlie fell through the ice into the freezing water. Still, he was able to rescue the boy by putting him over his shoulder while PO Webb pulled him and the boy ashore. PO Colarusso and the boy were both treated at the hospital for exposure. Charlie received a nice letter from the boy's parents but absolutely no recognition from the department.

And Charlie still remembers his first delivery of a baby. The address was 26 Caryl Ave. and the woman was in active labor on the living room rug. Everything went well and the baby was premature at 3 lbs. 8 oz. and Colarusso was happy to hear the baby cry when he cleaned out its mouth and laid it on the mom's stomach. The ambulance came and took them to St. John's Hospital. The ironic part was, approximately ten years later, while on Tuckahoe Road on another assignment, Colarusso met a 10 year old girl who, it turned out, was the baby he delivered on Caryl Ave. He never forgot that.

PO Colarusso served in the Emergency Unit until June 20, 1979 when he was reassigned to the Northeast Patrol Command on routine radio car patrol. During his last three years with the YPD Charlie served as a desk officer until he retired from the YPD on June 27, 1986.

In 2006 Charlie stated he was a Security Manager for Citigroup, in Armonk, NY. and always made it a point to offer employment to retired Yonkers police officers.

PO JOHN C. BOCSKAY #496

APPOINTED: March 25, 1966
RESIGNED: June 16, 1972

Born John Cornelius Bocskay in NYC on July 21, 1944, after moving to Yonkers John attended Mark Twain Jr High School and graduated from Lincoln High School. Soon after high school John joined the Navy on July 19, 1962 serving as a Radio Operator and Cryptographer with top secret clearance aboard the USS Monrovia APA31 and the USS Keith DD775. He received and decoded messages from the fleet to his ship. Bocskay also did Cryptography work in the Saigon, Viet Nam US Embassy. John was a Viet Nam veteran having served there during his last enlistment year. He received his honorary discharge as an E-5 on July 19, 1965. Following his military service John was employed as a mechanic with Con Edison.

No doubt influenced by the fact that his father, John, was an NYPD 1st grade Detective, John Bocskay applied for and was appointed to the Yonkers Police Department March 25, 1966 while living at 93 Hart Avenue. He received his basic police recruit training at the Iona College campus in New Rochelle and whose curriculum ran from April 4, 1966 through May 6, 1966. Following his graduation PO John Bocskay's first patrol assignment was in the 2nd precinct earning a starting salary of $6,000 a year.

On December 7, 1967 at about 4 AM a holdup occurred at a motel on Tuckahoe Rd. The suspects fired on the off duty officer detailed there and a gun battle ensued. One suspect was mortally wounded by the off duty officer and the second was captured on the NY Thruway by PO's Bocskay and his partner Bob Martin, both of whom had responded as backup. Both men were commended for their quick response and action and were awarded an Honorable Mention by the Macy's newspaper chain.

On July 31, 1968 PO Bocskay was transferred to the Service and Maintenance Division and was

PO John C. Bocskay #496 (cont.)

detailed to the newly established Marine Unit. A number of police officers and firefighters were assigned to this unit to patrol the waterfront for safety violation and potential rescues. Bocskay was a certified diver and held a Coast Guard certificate in boat handling 20' and over. The boat that was acquired for this purpose was old, obsolete and basically unserviceable. And so, once the summer months were over, on October 1, 1968, the Marine Unit was disbanded and Bocskay was returned to patrol in the 2nd precinct.

Officer Bocskay still held a 2nd class FCC license in radio communications from his time in the Navy and had experience in the Navy working with computers, something that was not yet utilized a lot by the public. As a result of these credentials Bocskay was selected to assist in putting in place a new communications system named Computer Oriented Program System (COPS) which was in fact the YPD's first initiative toward computerization in the police department. To do this Bocskay was transferred to headquarters on March 7, 1969 to work in the Communications Division assisting in the implementation of "COPS."

Though knowledgeable in this field, it was not the work PO Bocskay wanted. Following his request for transfer back to patrol, on September 10, 1971 he was reassigned to patrol in the South Command. Due to his specialized training in the Navy, the following year the DA's office asked him to assist them in the use of a sophisticated piece of equipment to filter out sound pattern frequencies on a tape recording that had voice overrides, (background voices). PO Bocskay was detailed to the DA's office on temporary assignment with the approval of Chief Polsen. John worked with the DA's investigators for about a week filtering out the background frequencies using this equipment that they had obtained. At trial he was sworn in and after questioning by the Defense, he was accepted as an Electronics expert by the 9th Division NY State Supreme Court. His testimony resulted in a murder conviction.

As a result John was offered an opportunity to work with the Westchester County District Attorney's Office as a Criminal Investigator. It sounded very challenging so John requested and was granted an unpaid leave of absence from the YPD on April 23, 1972 to work with the D.A.'s office to see if it was something he might want. After careful consideration PO John Bocskay submitted his resignation to the Yonkers Police Department effective June 16, 1972 and accepted the appointment as a District Attorney Criminal Investigator. During most of his time there John worked in an undercover capacity, with full beard, etc.

John Bocskay remained there right up to his retirement in 1989. In 1995 he and his wife Christine moved to Vero Beach, Fla. where, for many years, he operated his own ceramic tile maintenance business.

Unfortunately John became ill and in less than a year he died on November 1, 2013. He was 69.

PO ANTHONY J. BORASSI #494

APPOINTED: March 25, 1966
RETIRED: April 4, 1986

Tony Borassi was born in Yonkers on Nov. 13, 1937. He attended PS# 23 and later graduated from Yonkers HS in 1956. Tony entered the Army on May 15, 1957 and was honorably discharged on April 3, 1963 holding the rank of Specialist 4th class. Previous to the YPD Anthony was employed by the Mt. Vernon Construction Co. in Mt. Vernon, NY. Anthony Borassi was appointed to the Y.P.D. on March 25, 1966 while residing at 118 Locust Hill Ave. in Yonkers. He received his recruit training on the campus of Iona College in New Rochelle whose academic curriculum ran from April 4, to May 6, 1966. Following graduation Patrolman Borassi's first assignment was patrol duty in the 4th precinct earning $6,000 a year. Following a citywide reorganization of patrol precinct personnel on Nov. 9, 1966, PO Borassi was transferred to patrol duty in the 1st precinct. On Jan. 1, 1971, when a precinct centralization plan was implemented and two precincts were closed, Anthony was transferred to patrol duty in the North Command. PO Anthony Borassi, who was a friendly easy-going guy with a ready smile, remained on patrol in the North Command right up to his retirement on April 4, 1986.

PO SAMUEL C. MAROTTA #758

APPOINTED: May 20, 1966
RETIRED: July 9, 1987

Sam Marotta was born in Yonkers on Aug. 30, 1942. He attended PS# 5 and later graduated from Roosevelt HS in 1960. In 1964 he joined the N.Y. National Guard's 101st signal Battalion on North Broadway and was honorably discharged in Dec. of 1968. Having a trade in plumbing, previous to the YPD Sam worked for a Plumbing Contracting Co. of Yonkers. Sam Marotta was appointed to the Y.P.D. on May 20, 1966 while residing at 62 Clarendon Ave. He received his recruit training at the Iona College campus in New Rochelle, NY where the academic curriculum lasted for several weeks. Following his recruit graduation his first assignment was patrol duty in the 4th pct earning $6,000 a year. On Feb. 12, 1971 Sam was reassigned to the Detective Div., but still only as a patrolman, and was assigned to work in the Youth Div. investigating juvenile crime. Throughout his entire career Sam continued to work off-duty as a plumber to make extra money. He remained working in the Youth Div. as an investigator for the remainder of his career retiring on July 9, 1987. In 2005 Sam had the pleasure of watching his son Gregg be appointed a Yonkers police officer

PO MADELINE R. O'TOOLE #503

APPOINTED: May 20, 1966
RETIRED: April 18, 1992

Madeline O'Toole was born on September 5, 1934 in Yonkers NY, the daughter of Yonkers Patrolman Stephen Dankovic. She was born into a Yonkers Police family not only because of her father, but her two uncles, Peter and John Dankovic were also Yonkers police officers.

"Matty," as she was known to all, began working for the Yonkers Police Department as a Police Parking Enforcement Officer (Meter Maid) on September 9, 1957. At one point, no doubt following long debate, the City of Yonkers had decided it was time to appoint women to the police department. However, haven taken no test and therefore having no civil service list to draw from, Matty was appointed a Provisional "Policewoman" on July 29, 1964 earning a starting salary of $5,500 a year. Her first assignment was in the Juvenile Aid Bureau, later renamed the Youth Division.

When a test was held O'Toole took it, passed, but did not score high enough for the first appointments so she returned to being a Parking Enforcement Officer on November 19, 1965. When vacancies allowed, Madeline O'Toole was appointed to the permanent position of "Policewoman" on May 20, 1966 while residing at 219 Nepperhan Avenue and earning a starting salary of $6,000 a year. (The titles "Policewoman" and "Patrolman" would not change to "Police Officer" until the mid-1970's) In those early years of hiring women in police positions there was neither policy for the wearing of a uniform nor one for going out on routine patrol in uniform. She spent the next several years working in the Juvenile Aid Bureau. While there she served as the desk officer and gained a great deal of knowledge about Family Court law and was very familiar with all the local troubled youths. She was a great asset to the division.

Women were not yet allowed to perform patrol duty so following a department centralization plan on January 21, 1971, and the resulting transfers, she was assigned to the DD as a silver shield, not a detective, performing clerical duty. On October 6, 1972 she went back to Youth Division until January 22, 1979 when she was reassigned to the Records Division.

In late 1979 the new police commissioner, Dan Guido, decided that female police officers should be treated the same as males and transferred a number of female officers to patrol duty in the various patrol commands. None of the policewomen transferred had ever worn a uniform on duty or been on patrol in a precinct. PO O'Toole was one of those transferred and assigned to the North Command at the age of 42 years. It was an extremely difficult adjustment for her and in a short time she was returned to the Records Division.

It was about this time that she was detailed from Records to the Forensic Lab then located at 87 Nepperhan Ave. doing clerical and statistical analysis work. On July 1, 1991 she was reassigned to the Medical Control Unit.

She began to experience a variety of illnesses and as such, PO Madeline O'Toole retired from the police department on April 18, 1992 on Accidental Disability after a long time out sick. Matty was also affectionately nicknamed "Gramma" by her close friends in the department.

Ret PO Madeline O'Toole died on August 10, 2005. She was 70 years old.

PO BARBARA J. GONSALVES #507

APPOINTED: May 20, 1966
RESIGNED: April 7, 1970

Barbara Jean's Gonsalves was born in San Francisco, California on December 8, 1938. She attended Our Saviors Elementary school in the Bronx, and graduated from Theodore Roosevelt High School also in the Bronx. In addition to English Barbara was fluent in both Italian and Spanish. On her application to the Yonkers Police Department Barbara listed her previous employment as an Occupation Department Manager.

At one point, no doubt following long debate, the City of Yonkers had decided it was time to appoint women to the police department. However, haven taken no test and therefore having no civil service list to draw from, Barbara was appointed a Provisional "Policewoman" on July 29, 1964 earning a starting salary of $5,500 a year while living at 16 Agawam Road South. Her first assignment was in the Juvenile Aid Bureau, later renamed the Youth Division. Then, two weeks later, on August 11, 1964, Barbara was terminated from her provisional position because she failed to meet the minimum height requirement that had been set for men. However, on August 26, 1964, following a change in the female height requirement, she again received an emergency provisional appointment as "Policewoman."

In 1965 the first Civil Service test for permanent Policewoman was taken, a list was established, but she did not place high enough on the list to be appointed permanently. Consequently, one day before permanent hiring took place, on November 18, 1965 her provisional appointment was officially terminated.

When vacancies allowed, Barbara Gonsalves was appointed to the permanent position of Policewoman on May 20, 1966 earning a starting salary of $6,000 a year. In those early years of hiring women in police positions there was no policy for women for the wearing of a uniform nor one for going out on routine patrol in uniform. As such, she spent the first few years working in the Juvenile Aid Bureau. But, on February 14, 1968 Barbara was transferred to the Detective Division working in plainclothes in the Narcotics Unit in an undercover capacity.

In 1969 officer Gonsalves was recruited by the Westchester County Sheriff's office to work with them as a criminal investigator working undercover on narcotic investigations. To do this she requested a leave of absence from the YPD to run from April 7, 1969 through April 6 of 1970. When that year was about to expire and she was due to return to Yonkers, she stated that she was involved in major narcotic investigations and requested a one-year leave of absence extension. This request was denied and she was ordered back to work with the Yonkers Police Department. It was at this point that Barbara decided to remain with the sheriff's office and subsequently resigned from the Yonkers Police Department effective April 7, 1970.

PO SAMUEL BELTON #146

APPOINTED: November 15, 1966
RETIRED: October 1, 1995

Samuel Belton was born in Hopkins, South Carolina on September 8, 1940. After having moved with his family to Yonkers as a youth, Sam attended PS # 18, Benjamin Franklin Jr. High School, and graduated from Commerce High School in 1959 with honors. Following his graduation he also attended Elizabeth Seton State Teachers College from 1959 through 1962 on a scholarship.

In September 1965, while awaiting his appointment to the Yonkers Police Department, he accepted a provisional appointment as a corrections officer at the Sing Sing Prison in Ossining New York. Though he had been found guilty of only minor violations, since he was only provisional, he was dismissed by the prison system. On his police department application Sam listed his employment as a recreation leader for the Yonkers Parks Department.

Sam Belton was appointed to the Yonkers Police Department on November 15, 1966 while living at 34 point street. Prior to the beginning of his police training, on February 3, 1967 he was assigned to the 4th precinct earning a starting salary of $6,000 a year. He received his basic police recruit training at the Iona College campus in New Rochelle where the academic curriculum ran from April 3, 1967 to May 5, 1967.

On July 17, 1970 PO Belton was appointed a Detective working out of the Detective Division. However, that only lasted one year, and on July 16, 1971 he was transferred to patrol duty in the North Command. Sam had proved his academic skills but in addition he was also an excellent basketball player before, and while serving as a police officer. He was very active playing on the PBA basketball team.

On May 8, 1972 Sam was returned to duty in the Detective Division, but on October 6, 1972 he was reassigned to the Youth Division. At one point it was thought it would be beneficial to establish a Community Relations Unit within the department where its members could work closely with the minority community. And so, on August 13, 1973 a Community Relations Unit was organized within the YPD with the above stated goals. However, the following year, on May 15, 1974, the unit was abolished and Sam Belton was returned to patrol duty in the North Command.

At one point Belton reported himself sick and while out on full paid sick leave he was actually working his second job as security in Yonkers General Hospital. Belton was brought up on departmental charges, was found guilty and on May 23, 1980 was dismissed from the Yonkers Police Department.

Officer Belton believed that the punishment of dismissal was for too extreme for his wrongdoing and appealed in the courts. His appeal was successful and Belton was reinstated to the Police Department. He later retired from the YPD on October 1, 1995.

Retired PO Sam Belton died on February 2, 2003. He was 62 years old.

DET. CHARLES A. APADULA #664

APPOINTED: November 18, 1966
RETIRED: February 19, 1987

Charles A. Apadula was born in the City of Yonkers on January 8, 1941. He attended PS #23, PS #4, Mark Twain Jr. High School, and graduated from Commerce High School in 1958. He also attended New York University from September 1958 to May of 1962 majoring in business administration. It is believed that Charles served in the Army Reserve from 1960 through 1962 when he was honorably discharged. Previous to the YPD he was employed by the Tom McCann shoe company in Yonkers.

Charles Apadula was appointed to the Yonkers Police Department on November 18, 1966 while residing at 150 Edgewood Ave. He received his basic police recruit training at the Iona College campus in New Rochelle where the academic curriculum ran from April 3, 1967 to May 5, 1967. Following his recruit graduation his first assignment was patrol duty in the 4th precinct earning a starting salary of $6,000 a year.

Just over a year later, on July 26, 1968, he was appointed a Detective in the Detective Division working in the burglary and narcotics squads. In July of 1968 Detective Apadula and his partner were just beginning the late tour on patrol when they observed a male driving a car at Central Park Avenue at Tuckahoe Road with blood on his arm. A closer look revealed the passenger car had commercial vehicle license plates. Following a high-speed chase and upon stopping the suspect's car, they questioned the man. Following a brief investigation the man admitted he had just murdered his girlfriend down in the Bronx. Upon notifying New York City police Det Apadula learned the crime had not even been discovered until they had made the call. Detective Apadula was awarded a Commendation by the Public Safety Commissioner for his alertness and excellent detective work.

On September 4, 1970 he was reassigned, still as a detective and still with his ever present pipe, to working in the Bureau of Criminal Identification (BCI). He remained in this assignment up to October 22, 1971 when he was assigned to the Intelligence Division, as a 1st grade Detective.

Throughout most of his career Charlie, whose uncle was PO Carmine Apadula, worked a second job to make ends meet. Det Charles Apadula retired from the Yonkers Police Department on February 19, 1987. As a member of the Police and Fire Retirees Association, Charlie served as their treasurer for many years. In 2001 Charlie was working as the Director of Security for the Galleria Mall in White Plains, and in 2003 was associated with Allied Security, also in White Plains.

PO DOMINICK T. BORELLI #511

APPOINTED: November 18, 1966
RETIRED: March 5, 1987

Dominic Borelli was born in Yonkers on Jan. 4, 1938. He attended PS#24 and later graduated from Yonkers HS in 1957. Dom entered the Army's National Guard 101st Signal Battalion Reserve on Dec. 1, 1959 and was honorably discharged on Nov. 30, 1965 holding a rank of Specialist 4th class. Previous to the YPD Dominic had worked for the Bellino Brothers Contracting Corp. He was appointed to the Y.P.D. on Nov. 18, 1966 while residing at 29 Truman Ave. He received his basic recruit training at the Iona College campus in New Rochelle where the academic curriculum ran from April 3, 1967 to May 5, 1967. Following graduation his first assignment was patrol duty in the 4th precinct earning $6,000 a year. Dominick, who was nicknamed "Bo," was very active in PBA activities. In fact his cousin was PBA President Alfred Portanova. He remained on patrol in what had become the North Command until Dec. 4, 1981 when he was reassigned to patrol in the South Command. Dom retired on March 5, 1987 and worked many years for St. John's Hospital Security. In 1999 he was proud to watch his son Dennis be appointed to the YPD.

PO RALPH FORELLA # 509

APPOINTED: November 18, 1966
RETIRED: January 8, 1987

Ralph was born in the Bronx Sept. 28, 1941. He attended PS # 16, PS # 103, and the Evander Childs HS in NYC. Ralph joined the Air Force on Sept. 29, 1960 and was honorably discharged on Feb. 28, 1964 holding the rank of E-3. Previous to the YPD Ralph was employed by the Mt. Vernon Diecasting Corporation in Stamford Connecticut. He was appointed to the Y.P.D. on Nov. 18, 1966 while residing at 3824 Bronx Blvd in the Bx. He received his recruit training at the Iona College campus in New Rochelle where the curriculum ran from April 3, to May 5, 1967. Following graduation he was assigned to duty in the 4th pct earning $6,000 a year. On July 26, 1968, Ralph was transferred to the 2nd pct. On Dec. 12, 1974 it was announced that Ralph Forella and Frank Hollywood had received 1st place honor awards from the Westchester Rockland newspapers for their work in capturing an armed robbery suspect. The officers tackled one of two suspects, disarmed and arrested him. Ralph Forella would remain assigned to the 2nd pct for the remainder of his career, the last several years of which he served as the precinct desk officer, right up to his retirement on Jan. 8, 1987. Ret. PO Ralph Forella died on October 18, 2013. He was 72.

PO ROLAND W. PETRUZZI #513

APPOINTED: November 18, 1966
RESIGNED: September 8, 1967

Roland Petruzzi was born in New York City on October 11, 1942. He attended St. Thomas Aquinas Elementary school in the Bronx, Bedford Park school in the Bronx, and graduated from Lincoln high school in Yonkers in 1960. Prior to the police department he was employed by the Feurer Bros. Co. in White Plains New York. Roland took the Yonkers police and fire department exams and was first called by the YPD. He was appointed to the Yonkers Police Department on November 18, 1966 while living at 801 Bronx River Road. He received his basic police recruit training at the Iona College campus in New Rochelle where the academic curriculum ran from April 3, 1967 to May 5, 1967. Following his recruit graduation his first assignment was patrol duty in the 4th precinct earning a starting salary of $6,000 a year. However his tenure as a police officer did not last very long because he was offered appointment to the Yonkers Fire Department and accepted. He resigned from the YPD effective September 8, 1967 to be a firefighter.

PO RALPH A. FREDDOLINO #521

APPOINTED: May 19, 1967
RESIGNED: August 7, 1970

Ralph Freddolino was born in Yonkers on Jan. 27, 1944, attended St. John's elementary school, Sacred Heart HS and graduated from Lincoln HS. He also attended Long Island University in Brooklyn, NY in 1963 majoring in business administration. Ralph listed his previous employment as a Salesman in Scarsdale, NY. Ralph Freddolino was appointed to the Y.P.D. on May 19, 1967 while living at 200 Seminary Ave. As required, he attended the Municipal Police Recruit Training School held at the Iona College campus in New Rochelle where the academic curriculum ran from Sept 5th to October 16, 1967. Following his recruit graduation Probationary Patrolman Ralph Freddolino was assigned to the 4th precinct earning a starting salary of $6,000 a year. On July 26, 1968 he was assigned to work in the Youth Division investigating juvenile crime but the following year, on March 7, 1969, he was transferred to the Communications Division working as a dispatcher. On July 17, 1970 Ralph was reassigned to patrol in the 3rd precinct and the following month, on August 7, 1970, he resigned from the YPD. In his letter of resignation he stated that he wanted to start his own business in contracting. Several years later both his sisters, Linda Powers and Gail London would be appointed police officers with the YPD.

SGT. JOHN PRATO #82

APPOINTED: May 19, 1967
RETIRED: January 17, 2003

John Prato was born in Yonkers on Sept. 6, 1941, attended Longfellow junior HS, and graduated from Saunders HS with a trade in order mechanics. John entered the Army on July 18, 1960 and was honorably discharged on July 18, 1963 with the rank of specialist 4th class. Prior to the YPD John worked for Frank Chevrolet Co. in Tarrytown. John Prato was appointed to the Y.P.D. on May 19, 1967 while living at 149 Buena Vista Ave. As required, he attended the Municipal Police Recruit Training School held at the Iona College campus in New Rochelle where the academic curriculum ran from Sept 5th to October 16, 1967. Following his recruit graduation Probationary Patrolman John Prato was assigned to the 4th precinct earning a starting salary of $6,000 a year. John had a very quiet demeanor about him and usually only spoke when necessary. It was no surprise when he was nicked named "Quiet John." After 16 years on patrol duty Prato was appointed to the rank of Sergeant on May 21, 1993 earning a salary of $52,754 and was reassigned to the 3rd precinct as a patrol supervisor. He returned to the 4th precinct in August of 1996 but in August of 1998 he was transferred to the 1st precinct where he remained right up to his retirement on January 17, 2003.

PO JOSEPH KILMURRAY #522

APPOINTED: May 19, 1967
RETIRED: May 28, 1987

Joe Kilmurry was born in Yonkers on June 8, 1945, attended St. Peters school, Hawthorne Jr. HS, and graduated from Sacred Heart HS. On Sept. 30, 1963 Joe joined the NY National Guard and served up to Sept. 29, 1964. He received his honorable discharge on May 6, 1967. Joe listed his employment as the US Post office. Joe Kilmurray was appointed to the Y.P.D. on May 19, 1967 while living at 106 Morris St. As required, he attended the Municipal Police Recruit Training School held at the Iona College campus in New Rochelle where the academic curriculum ran from Sept. 5th to Oct. 16, 1967. Following his recruit graduation Probationary Patrolman Joseph Kilmurray was assigned to the 3rd precinct earning a starting salary of $6,000 a year. On January 1, 1971 Joe was assigned to work out of the South Command, formerly the old 2nd precinct, but on February 12, 1972 was reassigned to work in the Youth Division. That lasted only a few months and he was first assigned to the North Command and then the South Command. Kilmurry was very happy when, on July 18, 1973, he was assigned to the Special Operations Division in the motorcycle section of the Traffic Unit. PO Joseph Kilmurray retired from the YPD's Traffic Division on May 28, 1987.

LT. JOSEPH T. MERRIGAN

APPOINTED: May 19, 1967
RETIRED: January 5, 2001

Joseph Thomas Merrigan was born in Yonkers on Sept. 15, 1939. Joe attended St. Joseph's elementary school, Gorton HS, and would later graduate from Saunders HS. He served in the Navy from July 8, 1958 until his honorable discharge on Nov. 12, 1962. On his application to the Y.P.D. Joe listed his employment as a private security officer for the Chevrolet Motors Corp. in Tarrytown.

Joe Merrigan was appointed to the Y.P.D. on May 19, 1967 while living at 153 Parkhill Ave. Before the start of recruit school, on June 12, 1967 Joe was assigned to the 4th pct as a rookie always working with a senior officer to start patrol training. As required, he attended the Municipal Police Recruit Training School held at the Iona College campus in New Rochelle where the curriculum ran from Sept 5th to Oct. 16, 1967. Following graduation PO Joseph Merrigan remained assigned to the 4th pct earning a starting salary of $6,000 a year. On Nov. 28, 1969 PO Merrigan was transferred to patrol duty in the 2nd precinct.

Within a short time he was partnered up with PO Robert Jones working the precincts Auto Theft Detail from 10 PM until 6 AM. Their primary patrol area, in plainclothes and in an unmarked car, was the Bronx River Road area. At that time it became a common occurrence for thieves from NYC to come to that area, steal a car and escape by jumping on the Bronx River Parkway and drive into the city. Merrigan, as part of this detail, made substantial numbers of arrests, often after having to pursue the suspects into NYC. And often they did not submit to arrest quietly. In fact, for a time, it became a fairly common occurrence to hear gunshots being fired in the middle of the night. It was a dangerous assignment but Joe loved the challenge and adrenaline rush required to be effective. As a result PO Merrigan received multiple awards for his work as well as a reputation as a "good street cop." In fact, during the course of his career he would earn the departments Honorable Mention, a departmental Commendation, 10 Certificates of Excellent Police Work, and in 1972 he was named Police Officer of The Year by the Yonkers Exchange Club.

On May 19, 1972 PO Merrigan was promoted to Sergeant and was reassigned as a patrol supervisor in the North Command. While there he was detailed to work in the federally funded Community Patrol Unit (CPU), which was part of what was known as Community Oriented Policing with a goal toward working closely with the community. He also served as the street supervisor for the Emergency Services Unit. He remained there for four years when, on April 12, 1976 he was transferred to the South Command. Joe was very witty with a good sense of humor but could be a very tough task master with a sharp tongue. Because of his presence and attitude he was nicknamed "The Duke" for the tough talking movie actor John Wayne. And Joe was an early member of the Westchester County Emerald Society Pipes and Drums Band as a bagpiper.

Sgt. Merrigan was promoted to Lieutenant on Feb. 17, 1984 earning $37,132 a year and remained working in the South Command as their executive officer. On April 23, 1990, Joe was reassigned as the executive officer for the Courts and Detention Services Division (City Jail). A number of transfers followed; February 9, 1991 to the Communications Div.; July 10, 1991 to the 4th precinct on patrol; and on October 20, 1991 Joe was designated a Detective Lieutenant assigned to the Internal Affairs Division.

On November 1, 1995 Joe Merrigan, whose grandfather was PO Joseph Hart, was reassigned to the Communications Div. as a tour supervisor and would remain there up to his retirement on January 5, 2001.

DET. SGT. ROBERT P. TAUBER #18

APPOINTED: May 19, 1967
RETIRED: June 21, 1991

Robert Tauber was born in the City of Yonkers on February 22, 1945. Bob attended Hawthorne Jr. High School and graduated from Yonkers High School in 1963. On July 10, 1963 Bob was inducted into the Army and served until being honorably discharged in June of 1965. In June of 1966 Bob was appointed to the White Plains Police Department where he attended the Municipal Police Recruit Training School held at the Iona College campus in New Rochelle.

Robert Tauber was appointed to the Yonkers Police Department on May 19, 1967 at which time he was living at 167 Radford Street with his wife Marie (D'Apice) Tauber earning a starting salary of $6,000 per year. Because Bob had previously attended the required recruit training, he was immediately assigned to patrol duty in the 3rd Precinct.

On January 1, 1971, those assigned to the 3rd Precinct, were re-assigned to the newly established South Patrol Command, previously the old 2nd Precinct, at 441 Central Park Avenue. Three months later, on March 31, 1971, Bob was transferred to the Special Operations Division assigned to two wheel motorcycle patrol.

On July 16, 1979, Bob was promoted to the rank of Sergeant with a salary of $23,086 and was assigned to the North Command as a patrol supervisor. In February of 1984, he was transferred to the 1st precinct and on May 7, 1984, he was assigned to the Traffic Division as a motorcycle patrol supervisor. The following year, on March 14, 1985, Bob was transferred to the Detective Division with a designation of Detective Sergeant.

Detective Sergeant Tauber retired on June 21, 1991 after serving twenty-five years of service and re-located to Boca Raton, Florida with his wife where he began a career in the shopping center industry as a Director of Security. Within a year, he was advanced to the position of Director of Operations and is still employed in that capacity in 2014 at Town Center at Boca Raton.

LT. FRANCIS V. MOZDZIAK

APPOINTED: May 19, 1967
RETIRED: January 4, 2002

Frank Mozdziak was born in the City of Yonkers on January 21, 1943. He attended St. Casimir elementary school, Gorton High School, and graduated from Saunders High School. Frank also attended Westchester Community College where he earned an Associate's Degree in Applied Science. He joined the Army National Guard in March of 1964 and was released from active duty in February of 1965. He would receive his honorable discharge in 1970. On his police application Frank listed his employment with the Western Electric Co. as an installer.

Francis Mozdziak was appointed to the Police Department on May 19, 1967 while living at 69 Morningside Ave. Prior to the scheduling of recruit school, on June 12, 1967 Frank was assigned to the 4th precinct as a rookie always working with a senior officer to start patrol training. As required, he attended the Municipal Police Recruit Training School held at the Iona College campus in New Rochelle where the academic curriculum ran from Sept 5th to October 16, 1967. Following his recruit graduation Probationary Patrolman Francis Mozdziak remained assigned to the 4th precinct earning $6,000 a year.

Frank received his first promotion to the rank of Sergeant on August 13, 1976 earning $24,471 and was transferred to the South Patrol Command as a patrol supervisor. On March 2, 1984 Sgt Mozdziak was reassigned to Central Booking where he processed prisoners as they were brought to the city jail.

He received his next promotion, to the rank of Lieutenant, on April 11, 1988 then earning $51,609 and was transferred to the Communications Division as a tour supervisor. On August 1, 1991 he returned to patrol but, two months later, on October 28, 1991 he was assigned as the commanding officer of the Property Clerk Office. He would later be reassigned back to the Communications Division where he remained up to his retirement on January 4, 2002.

LT. THOMAS F. HARNEY

APPOINTED: May 19, 1967
RETIRED: February 1, 2002

Thomas Francis Harney was born in the City of Yonkers on January 26, 1940. As a youth his family had moved to Florida for a time but returned to Yonkers. As such, he attended elementary school in Florida and later graduated from Saunders High School. After graduation Tom worked as a Wire Lather by trade for a few years and on April 24, 1962 he joined the Navy. He completed his enlistment on May 20, 1964 and was later honorably discharged. On his police application Tom listed his employment as working for the National Acoustics Co. in NYC.

Thomas Harney was appointed to the Yonkers Police Department on May 19, 1967 while living at 27 Pelton Street in Yonkers. Prior to the scheduling of recruit school, on June 12, 1967 Tom was assigned to the 3rd precinct as a rookie always working with a senior officer to start patrol training. As required, he attended the Municipal Police Recruit Training School held at the Iona College campus in New Rochelle where the academic curriculum ran from Sept 5th to October 16, 1967. Following his recruit graduation Probationary Patrolman Thomas Harney remained assigned to the 3rd precinct earning a starting salary of $6,000 a year.

Over the next few years he had a number of different assignments on patrol. On February 20, 1970 he was moved to the 4th precinct; then on March 23, 1970 back to the 3rd pct.; and on January 1, 1971, following the implementation of a precinct wide centralization plan, Tom Harney was assigned to the old 2nd pct., which had been renamed the South Command.

Tom received his first promotion to the rank of Sergeant on May 19, 1972, the same day and month he was appointed, and was reassigned to the North Patrol Command as a patrol supervisor. About that time a federal grant was secured establishing a community based mini precinct which was named the Community Patrol Unit (CPU) and Sgt Harney was assigned to that sub unit of the North Command.

Sgt Harney was again promoted on March 16, 1979 to the rank of Police Lieutenant earning a new salary of $24,187 and he was transferred to the Communications Division as a tour supervisor. Five years later, on March 2, 1984, Lt Harney was designated a Watch Commander on patrol in the 1st precinct. Seven years later, on April 20, 1991 when the opening occurred, he moved inside as the Executive Officer in the 1st pct.

A proud Irishman with red hair Tom loved boxing. As a youth he fought in the Golden Gloves and throughout his police career he continued to work out regularly in the gym on the heavy bag. And he had a handshake like a vise. Being a member of the Police Emerald Society Tom taught himself how to play a drum and was accepted as a member of the Westchester County Police Pipes and Drums band as a tenor drummer.

Following the reorganization of the Special Operations Division which combined Traffic, Emergency Services, K-9, Taxi & Bus Inspection (Hack) and Abandoned Auto, on July 22, 1992 Lt Harney agreed to accept the challenge of being the Executive Officer of such a large specialized division. Seven years later, on February 22, 1999 Lt Harney was transferred to the Communications Division and on January 29, 2001 was designated their executive officer.

The very next year Lt Thomas Harney retired from the police department on February 1, 2002.

LT. ROBERT R. JONES

APPOINTED: May 19, 1967
RETIRED: May 28, 1987

Bob Jones was born in Yonkers on March 2, 1937, attended Dobbs Ferry elementary school and graduated from Hastings High School. Not long after school Bob joined the Army on July 10, 1956, served in the Military Police, and was honorably discharged on June 23, 1959. On Bob's application to the YPD he listed his employment with the Chevrolet Motor Co. in Tarrytown, NY.

Robert Jones was appointed to the Yonkers Police Department on May 19, 1967 while living at 55 Griffith Avenue. He had actually exceeded the age limit of 29 years for hiring eligibility, but was able to apply his military time in order to be eligible. Prior to the scheduling of recruit school Bob was assigned to the 2nd precinct as a rookie and was always with a senior officer to start patrol training. As required, he attended the Municipal Police Recruit Training School held at the Iona College campus in New Rochelle where the academic curriculum ran from Sept 5th to October 16, 1967. Following his recruit graduation Probationary Patrolman Robert Jones remained assigned to the 2nd precinct earning a starting salary of $6,000 a year.

Within a short time he was partnered up with PO Joe Merrigan working the precincts Auto Theft Detail from 10 PM until 6 AM. Their primary patrol area in plainclothes and in an unmarked car, was the Bronx River Road area. At that time it became a common occurrence for thieves from NYC to come to that area, steal a car and escape by jumping on the Bronx River Parkway and drive into the city. Jones, as part of this detail, made substantial numbers of arrests, often after having to pursue the suspects into NYC. And often they did not submit to arrest quietly. In fact, for a time, it became a fairly common occurrence to hear gunshots being fired in the middle of the night. It was a dangerous assignment but Bob loved the challenge and adrenaline rush required to be effective. As a result PO Jones received multiple awards for his work as well as a reputation as a "good street cop."

No doubt a result of his excellent work, on May 15, 1972, officer Jones was appointed a Detective in the Detective Division. He worked as a detective up to October 26, 1973 when he was promoted to the rank of Sergeant and reassigned to the North Command as a patrol supervisor. On January 20, 1979 Sgt Jones was returned to the D.D. and designated a Detective Sergeant in charge of a squad of detectives. He remained there for 5 years and on October 18, 1983 he was transferred back to uniform patrol in the South Command.

"Bobby" Jones was promoted to the rank of Lieutenant on December 18, 1985 and assigned to the Communications Division as a tour supervisor. Lt Jones wanted to spend his last year on patrol so, on October 17, 1986 he was assigned as a Watch Commander in the 3rd precinct. He retired from the YPD on May 28, 1987.

Ret Lt Robert Jones died on April 21, 1995. He was 58 years old.

PO MARTIN W. SCHWARTZ #465

APPOINTED: May 19, 1967
RESIGNED: September 15, 1969

The subject of this profile began his career as a police officer but I believe he knew at the time that he had plans to achieve much loftier goals in law enforcement. However, learning the job of a police officer would be an excellent foundation.

Martin W. Schwartz was born in NYC on September 30, 1944. He attended PS# 77, PS# 96, and Jr. High School, all in the Bronx, NY. Marty graduated from Christopher Columbus High School in the Bronx. From 1961 to 1965 he attended New York University where he earned his BA degree and then entered Brooklyn Law School. Prior to his appointment to the YPD he was already a 2nd year law student.

After placing #1 on the civil service list for Yonkers Patrolman, Martin W. Schwartz was appointed to the Yonkers Police Department on May 19, 1967 while residing at 480 Riverdale Avenue. Though appointed in 1967 his recruit training did not begin until October 7, 1968 as he was given an exemption by civil service to delay his training in order to continue his studies in law school. Prior to his recruit training he was initially assigned to the 3rd precinct then located at 36 Radford Street. However, in March of 1968 he was reassigned to the 1st precinct at 730 East Grassy Sprain Road. He completed his Municipal Police Recruit Training School held at the Iona College campus in New Rochelle and graduated on Nov 9, 1968.

Following his recruit graduation Probationary Patrolman Martin W. Schwartz remained assigned to the 1st precinct earning a starting salary of $6,000 a year. While he was a police officer he was attending law school full time and worked mostly early tours (4 - 12 midnight).

On September 15, 1969 PO Martin W. Schwartz resigned from the Yonkers Police Department. In his letter of resignation, Marty stated that, since he now had a law degree he was going to pursue a career working as an attorney. In early 1970 he was appointed as a Special Agent, U.S. Treasury Dept., U.S. Customs Service, in NYC. He remained there until 1971 when he took a leave of absence and was hired as an Assistant District Attorney in Bronx County, NY working for the District Attorney, Burton Roberts. In 1973, following the appointment of DA Roberts as a judge, ADA Schwartz decided to return to Customs as a Special Agent. As an agent with the U.S. Customs Service, Schwartz was said to have been one of the first federal law enforcement officers to fly as a temporary sky marshal during the hijacking scares of that era.

Martin W. Schwartz retired from the US Customs Service in 1990 with a line-of-duty injury and went into private law practice, business, and free-lance writing. One could say that the Yonkers Police Departments loss was definitely the federal governments gain

LT. ROBERT W. PUFAHL

APPOINTED: May 19, 1967
RETIRED: January 11, 2007

Robert Pufahl was born in the Bronx, NY on December 6, 1942. As a youth his family moved to Yonkers and he attended PS# 29, and graduated from Roosevelt High School. Bob attended Iona College from 1962 to 1964 and earned a degree in accounting. Prior to the YPD Bob worked for Klein's Department Store.

Robert Pufahl was appointed to the Yonkers Police Department on May 19, 1967 while living at 9 Shoreview Drive in Yonkers. Prior to the scheduling of recruit school, on June 12, 1967 Bob was assigned to the 2nd precinct as a rookie always working with a senior officer to start patrol training. As required, he attended the Municipal Police Recruit Training School held at the Iona College campus in New Rochelle where the academic curriculum ran from Sept 5th to October 16, 1967. Following his recruit graduation Patrolman Robert Pufahl remained assigned to the 4th precinct earning a starting salary of $6,000 a year.

On April 20, 1973 Pufahl was promoted to the rank of Sergeant earning $15,232 a year and he was reassigned to the North Command as a patrol supervisor. On September 1, 1975 he was reassigned to the South command but the following year, on April 12, 1976, he was returned back to the North command and detailed to work as a supervisor in the Community Patrol Unit (CPU). When the CPU lost its grant funding it was shut down and Bob returned to the North Command as a patrol supervisor. Bob was very active as a member of the Captain's, Lieutenants, and Sergeants Association, and in January of 1978 he was elected Sergeant At Arms of that organization, a position he would continue to be elected to for 29 years right up to his retirement. Bob had a very outgoing personality and was well-liked by all of his peers. He was a hunter and an amateur bodybuilder and was very strong. He was also very industrious. Throughout his career he continued to work construction jobs while off duty to make extra money.

By October 17, 1986 Sgt Pufahl was still in the 4th precinct and was designated a task force supervisor. On January 16, 1989 Bob was detailed to the Street Crime Unit to serve as a plainclothes supervisor. One year later, on January 12, 1990, Sgt Pufahl was transferred to the Street Crime Unit and designated its commanding officer. On November 13 1990 the entire Street Crime Unit, which was located on Alexander Street at the time, was decentralized and divided up into each of the precincts. On this date Sgt Pufahl and about four police officers were reassigned to plainclothes duty in the 1st precinct.

On January 23, 1995 Bob was transferred from the 1st precinct to the Detective Division, without detective status, and detailed to work in the Narcotics and Street Crime Units. At that time both units were merged together to operate in plainclothes. On October 6, 1997 Sgt Pufahl was designated a Detective Sergeant in the Narcotics Unit.

On August 12, 1998 Sgt Pufahl was promoted to the rank of Lieutenant and transferred from the Narcotics Unit to the Detention Services Bureau working in Central Booking. Two weeks later, on August 27, 1998, Bob was reassigned to the Field Services Bureau working in the Inspections Unit. In 1999 he was assigned to patrol duty in the 1st precinct and in 2000 assigned to patrol in the 4th precinct. However, once again he was assigned to plainclothes duty when he was assigned as commanding officer of the now re-named Anti-Crime Unit on February 1, 2001.

Sgt Robert Pufahl would remain in this assignment right up to his retirement on January 11, 2007.

SGT. PAUL T. COYNE #22

APPOINTED: May 19, 1967
RETIRED: May 28, 1987

Born in Yonkers on Aug. 25, 1942, Paul T. Coyne attended PS# 23, Benjamin Franklin Jr. HS and graduated from Yonkers HS. Paul joined the Air Force on Sept. 1, 1960 and was later honorably discharged on Aug. 31, 1964. He listed his current employment with the General Electric Co. Coyne was appointed to the Y.P.D. on May 19, 1967 while living at 126 Van Cortlandt Park Ave. He attended the Recruit Training School held at the Iona College campus in New Rochelle where the academic curriculum ran from Sept 5th to Oct. 16, 1967. Following graduation Patrolman Paul was assigned to patrol duty in the 3rd pct at 36 Radford St. earning $6,000 a year. On Jan. 1, 1971, following a precinct centralization plan, Paul was transferred to the South Command at 441 Central Park Ave. On Jan. 1, 1979, Coyne was reassigned to H.Q. working in the Criminal Identification Unit (CIU). Paul Coyne was promoted to the rank of Sergeant on May 1, 1981 earning $23,086 and was transferred to the North Command as a patrol supervisor. On March 11, 1985 he was assigned to the Field Serviced Bureau on city wide patrol and two years later retired on May 28, 1987. Paul's brother was PO Chris Coyne and his nephew was PO Christopher E. Coyne.

PO WALTER J. HAYDEN #528

APPOINTED: May 19, 1967
RETIRED: May 28, 1987

Walter Hayden was born in Yonkers on June 22, 1945. He attended St. Peters school and our Lady of the Rosary elementary school and then graduated from Commerce HS in 1963. Previous to the police department Walter was employed by the National Vacuum Molding Company in Yonkers. Walter was appointed to the Y.P.D. on May 19, 1967 while residing at 650 Warburton Ave. He attended the recruit training school held at the Iona College campus in New Rochelle. The academic curriculum for the school ran from Sept. 5th to Oct. 16, 1967. Following his recruit graduation Patrolman Walter Hayden was assigned to patrol duty in the 4th pct earning $6,000 a year. He worked radio car patrol initially but later spent several years assigned to City Hall on a security detail. "Benny," as he was known to his friends, remained in this assignment until Jan. of 1976 when he was transferred to the H.Q. Command Div. and worked in the Warrant Squad executing outstanding warrants. On Feb. 13, 1984 he was reassigned to the 1st pct on patrol duty. A cousin to PO Harold Woods, "Benny" Hayden retired from the YPD on May 28, 1987. Ret PO Walter Hayden, who never married, died on September 16, 2005. He was 60 years old.

PO JOHN J. DEVLIN #238

APPOINTED: May 19, 1967
RETIRED: January 4, 1995

"Jack" Devlin was born in the City of Yonkers on July 5, 1944, attended St. Peters Elementary School, Sacred Heart High School and Yonkers High School. Right out of school Jack joined the Navy on July 31, 1961, served as a Seaman, and was honorably discharged on June 16, 1965. Prior to the YPD Devlin listed his employment with the Tennis Service and Supply in Yonkers.

John Devlin was appointed to the Yonkers Police Department on May 19, 1967 while living at 1 Post Street. Prior to the beginning of recruit training Jack was assigned as a rookie in the 4th precinct on June 12, 1967. As required, he attended the Municipal Police Recruit Training School held at the Iona College campus in New Rochelle. The academic curriculum ran from Sept 5th to October 16, 1967. Following his recruit graduation Probationary Patrolman John Devlin continued his assignment in the 4th precinct.

On September 15, 1972 Jack was transferred to the Detective Division, but not as a detective, and assigned to work in the Youth Division investigating crimes committed by juveniles. However, the following year on July 2, 1973+ Devlin was returned to the old 4th precinct, now renamed the North command.

For reasons unknown, in late 1974 Jack resigned from the YPD but after only 3 months, on January 24, 1975, he was reinstated back to duty in the North Command. He remained there until November 18, 1982 when he was transferred out to the Northeast Command. By mid-1985 PO Devlin was designated the now 1st precinct Crime Prevention Officer. Toward the end of his career he was transferred to patrol duty in the 3rd precinct. In the 1970s and 1980s Jack was very active playing on the PBA basketball team and for a number of years, including 1992, he played on the YPD hockey team in various competitions. In addition, in 1987 he served as the PBA first vice president.

PO John Devlin retired from the Yonkers Police Department on January 4, 1995.

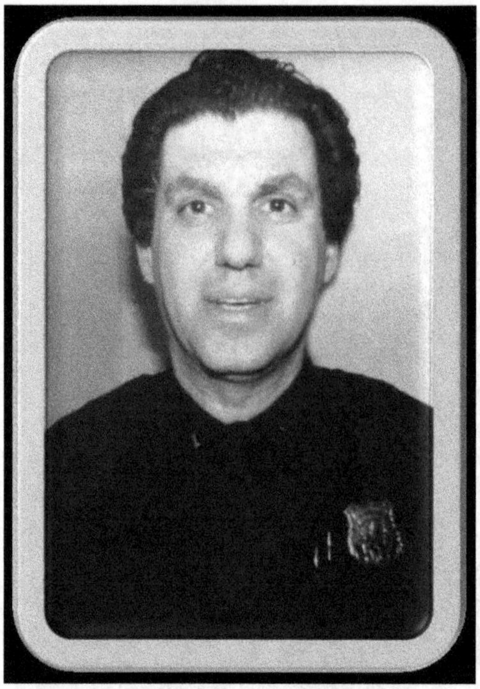

PO EDWARD M. DiNAPOLI #517

APPOINTED: May 19, 1967
RETIRED: April 28, 1988

Edward DiNapoli was born in the Bronx, NY on January 12, 1942. He attended St. Mary's elementary school in the Bronx and later graduated from Evander Childs high school, also in the Bronx. Ed entered the Navy on May 4, 1961 and served as a Seaman up to his honorable discharge on May 3, 1965. Prior to the YPD Ed listed his employment with the County Uniform Co. in Mount Vernon as a driver.

Edward DiNapoli was appointed to the Yonkers Police Department on May 19, 1967 while living at 1051 Mile Square Road in Yonkers. Prior to the scheduling of recruit school, on June 12, 1967 Ed was assigned to the 4th precinct as a rookie always working with a senior officer to start patrol training. As required, he attended the Municipal Police Recruit Training School held at the Iona College campus in New Rochelle where the academic curriculum ran from Sept 5th to October 16, 1967. Following his recruit graduation Probationary Patrolman Edward DiNapoli remained assigned to the 4th precinct earning a starting salary of $6,000 a year.

On March 23, 1970 Ed was transferred to the 1st precinct but, on January 1, 1971, he was returned to duty in the former 4th precinct, renamed the North Command. Ed had an easy-going personality. In fact it was very laid back. He even spoke slowly which resulted in him sarcastically being given the nickname "Fast Eddie." But he was a hustler and while off-duty he worked as a painter and bricklayer. On March 24, 1981 DiNapoli graduated from Evidence Technician School held in Yonkers. As a trained designated Evidence Technician a uniformed patrol officer was responsible to accomplish basic photographing and gathering of evidence at minor crime scenes without the need to have the crime scene unit respond. On September 13, 1982 PO DiNapoli was transferred to the Northeast Patrol Command where he remained up to his retirement on April 28, 1988.

PO DENNIS DURNIAK #520

APPOINTED: May 19, 1967
RESIGNED: November 19, 1971

Dennis Durniak was one of many police officers who began his professional career in public safety with the Yonkers Police Department but would later change his mind.

Dennis was born in the City of Yonkers on December 3, 1943, attended PS# 8 and later graduated from Roosevelt High School. As a young man Dennis was employed by the Westchester County Dept. of Public Works. He joined the Air Force on January 28, 1963, served as an F-101 Jet mechanic with ADC (Air Defense Command) stationed at Oxnard AFB California. He was honorably discharged and resumed working for the County of Westchester.

Dennis Durniak was appointed to the Y.P.D. on May 19, 1967 while living at 78 Grassy Lane in Yonkers. Prior to the scheduling of recruit school, on June 12, 1967 Dennis was assigned to the 4th pct working with a senior officer to start patrol training. As required, he attended the Municipal Police Recruit Training School held at the Iona College campus in New Rochelle where the academic curriculum ran from Sept 5th to October 16, 1967. Following his recruit graduation Probationary Patrolman Dennis Durniak remained assigned to the 4th precinct earning a starting salary of $6,000 a year.

While in the 4th pct. Dennis worked a few years in the precinct Warrant Squad with his partner, and later police captain, Ed Foley. After continual coaxing by his YFD uncle, touting better working hours for raising a family and closer camaraderie, Dennis took the Yonkers Fire Dept. examination. He placed 6th on the list and was offered appointment to the Yonkers Fire Department. After a great deal of indecision and much deliberation, PO Dennis Durniak resigned from the police department on November 19, 1971 and was appointed a Yonkers Firefighter on the same date. Dennis Durniak retired from Yonkers Fire Dept. as a Lieutenant on May 24, 2002 after 35 years of combined service.

PO JOHN A. CASERTA #525

APPOINTED: May 19, 1967
RETIRED: May 28, 1987

John Caserta was born in NYC on Aug. 20, 1941. He attended our Lady of Mt. Carmel School and Mount St. Michael's Academy, both in the Bronx and from which he graduated in 1959. He also attended Iona College in New Rochelle from 1959 to 1962 majoring in marketing, business, and law. John joined the USMC reserve on July 6, 1962 and was separated from service on Jan. 24, 1963, and was honorably discharged. Previous to the YPD John was employed as a night manager at the Hartsdale Esso service center. John was appointed to the Y.P.D. on May 19, 1967 while living at 2421 Raton Ave. in the Bx. He attended recruit training held at the Iona College campus in New Rochelle. The academic curriculum ran from Sept 5th to Oct. 16, 1967. Following graduation PO John Caserta was assigned to the 3rd precinct at 36 Radford St. On Jan. 1, 1971, following the implementation of a pct centralization plan, John was reassigned to the newly renamed South Command. He remained there on patrol for 10 years until May 22, 1981 when he was transferred to the Communications Div. working in the Tele Serv Unit. John "Johnny Red" Caserta, with his red hair, retired from the department on May 28, 1987. Unfortunately, it wasn't long before he became ill and after a long fight Ret PO John Caserta died on Aug. 31, 1990. He was 49 years old.

PO GEORGE A. BAKER #534

APPOINTED: August 11, 1967
RETIRED: August 20, 1987

George A. Baker was born in NYC on April 26, 1943. He attended PS# 11 in NYC and, after his family moved to Yonkers, PS# 8 and graduated from Roosevelt HS. George worked at Western Electric Co on Tuckahoe Rd even though he was an accomplished carpenter. George A. Baker was appointed to the Y.P.D. on Aug. 11, 1967. He attended recruit training at the Iona College campus in New Rochelle which ran from Sept. 5th to Oct. 16, 1967. Following graduation PO Baker was assigned to the 1st pct earning $6,000 a year. On Jan. 1, 1971 he was transferred to the North Command and on Oct. 25, 1973, he was selected to be assigned to the Criminal Identification Unit (CIU). His job was crime scene investigation. But, on June 17, 1975 he was returned to patrol. On one occasion in the 1970's PO Baker dove into the Grassy Sprain Reservoir while off-duty and swam about 40 feet and rescued a motorist who was trapped in a sinking car which had plunged through a guard rail. The motorist could not swim and could not open the door or the electrically controlled windows. For his actions he was awarded the Westchester newspaper chain Macy Award. While in the North Command, George walked a foot post in Getty Square right up to his retirement on Aug. 20, 1987.

PO NICHOLAS J. IARRICCIO #36

APPOINTED: August 11, 1967
RETIRED: August 20, 1987

Nicholas Iarriccio was born in the city of Yonkers on April 3, 1942. Nick attended PS # 23, Benjamin Franklin Jr. high school, and later graduated from Yonkers High School. Right after his high school graduation he joined the Marine Corps on June 30, 1960 and served for one year on board a ship as part of a Marine Guard Detail. Nick was honorably discharged four years later on June 29, 1964. Prior to his interest in the Y.P.D. Nick was employed at the United Parcel Service in New York City.

Nicholas Iarriccio was appointed to the Yonkers Police Department on August 11, 1967 while living at 121 Beech Street, Yonkers. As required, he attended the Municipal Police Recruit Training School held at the Iona College campus in New Rochelle where the academic curriculum ran from September 5th to October 16, 1967. Following his recruit graduation Probationary Patrolman Nicholas Iarriccio was assigned to the 1st precinct on patrol earning a starting salary of $6,000 a year.

On January 19, 1970 Nick was transferred to the 4th precinct and, following an opening occurring, was trained by the NYPD Emergency Service Unit in emergency accident and rescue work, and assigned to the Yonkers Police Emergency Service Unit (ESU). He and his partner at the time, PO Walter Hlewicki, were the first Nationally Registered Emergency Medical Technicians (EMT's) and all training was paid for by the City of Yonkers. He remained in ESU for over 12 years dealing with tragedy and death on a regular basis. And yet, during his service in ESU he had the good fortune of delivering 14 babies before an ambulance could respond. He remained in ESU until October 21, 1983 when he was reassigned to the Support Services Bureau working in the Criminal Court Case Review Unit.

Nick was very active in PBA sponsored events and often served as Santa Claus during Christmas parties for children. He also served as a trustee for the PBA for many years. Nick retired on August 20, 1987 while working in the Courts and Detention Services Bureau and he and his wife Gloria moved to Florida to enjoy their retirement.

PO ANTHONY G. MAZZELLA #532

APPOINTED: August 11, 1967
RETIRED: March 18, 1993

Anthony G. Mazzella was born in NYC on October 5, 1942, attended PS# 96 and graduated from Morris High School, both in the Bronx. Tony served in the Army from May 9, 1960 as a Specialist 4th class up to his honorable discharge on August 27, 1964. Prior to the YPD Mazzella was a construction Mason Tender in Whitestone, NY. Anthony Mazzella was appointed to the Yonkers Police Department on August 11, 1967 while living at 3604 Willet Avenue in the Bronx. As required, he attended the Municipal Police Recruit Training School held at the Iona College campus in New Rochelle where the academic curriculum ran from September 5th to October 16, 1967. Following his recruit graduation Probationary Patrolman Anthony Mazzella was assigned to the 1st precinct earning a starting salary of $6,000 a year. On Jan. 1, 1971 he was reassigned to the North Command, on June 20, 1979 to the North East Command, and on March 18, 1981 back to the North Command. In 1982 Mazzella found himself in trouble and upon conviction of departmental charges he was dismissed from the YPD effective Feb. 11, 1982. Mazzella appealed his punishment and was re-instated to the 3rd precinct on October 2, 1984. He retired from the YPD on March 18, 1993 and died September 17, 2017.

PO PHILIP S. PIZZOLA #533

APPOINTED: August 11, 1967
RETIRED: July 28, 1983

Philip Pizzola was born in the Bronx on March 31, 1942. He attended PS# 89 in the Bronx, and after moving to Yonkers attended St. Paul's school, and graduated from Lincoln HS. Phil served in the Navy from Oct. 6, 1962 and was honorably discharged on Oct. 5, 1964. Prior to the YPD Philip Pizzola worked for Con. Ed. in NYC. Philip Pizzola was appointed to the Y.P.D. on Aug. 11, 1967 living at 11 Central Park Ave., Yonkers. He attended recruit training held at the Iona College campus in New Rochelle which ran from Sept. 5th to Oct. 16, 1967. Following graduation Patrolman Philip Pizzola was assigned to the 2nd pct on patrol earning $6,000 a year. Phil had a reputation of being a very tough and aggressive police officer which enabled him to make many arrests and receive many departmental awards. It was likely because of his ability to make good arrests that led him to be selected and assigned as a member of the newly organized plainclothes Street Crime Unit on Feb. 25, 1975. Phil Pizzola, whose brother was Det Lt Peter Pizzola, was injured while on duty and which resulted in his being retired on an accidental disability pension effective July 28, 1983. During retirement Pizzola developed a heart condition and died on July 24, 2003 at the age of 61 years.

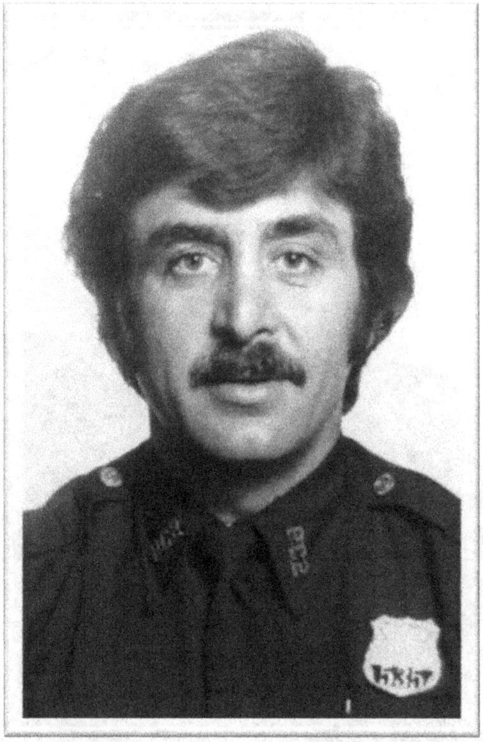

PO REED A. CROSBY #535

APPOINTED: August 11, 1967
RETIRED: September 19, 1986

Reed Crosby was born in the City of New York on August 13, 1939. He attended Rita's Elementary School in the Bronx, and graduated from Cardinal Hayes high school also in the Bronx. Reed joined the Navy on September 28, 1956 and received his honorable discharge on September 27, 1962. He was previously employed as a delivery supervisor for the United Parcel Service in New York City.

Reed Crosby was appointed to the Yonkers Police Department on August 11, 1967 while living at 15 Radford Street, Yonkers. As required, he attended the Municipal Police Recruit Training School held at the Iona College campus in New Rochelle where the academic curriculum ran from September 5th to October 16, 1967. Following his recruit graduation Probationary Patrolman Reed Crosby was assigned to the 1st precinct earning a starting salary of $6,000 a year.

In 1968, the Yonkers Police Department established for the first time, a Yonkers Police Marine Unit for use on the Hudson River. On July 31, 1968 PO Reed Crosby, along with several other officers, were assigned to work in the Marine unit. Unfortunately, by the end of the summer the Marine Patrol program was disbanded, and on October 1, 1968 Crosby was reassigned to the 1st precinct on patrol.

On November 6, 1978 Reed was transferred to the 3rd precinct on patrol; on January 1, 1971 he was sent to the South Command; and on December 4, 1981 he was moved to the North Command. He was assigned to the Administrative Services Division on December 1, 1983 working clerical duty in the Records Division. On January 9, 1984 he was assigned to the Youth and Community Services Division on desk duty.

PO Reed Crosby retired from the Yonkers Police Department on September 19, 1986 and moved to Florida.

PO PAUL D. VanTASSEL #141

APPOINTED: September 5, 1967
RETIRED: January 13, 1995

Paul VanTassell was born in the City of Yonkers on August 18, 1943. He attended PS# 16, and would later graduate from Gorton high school. As young man Paul worked in Otis Elevator Co. at the Saw Mill River Road facility working on parts for Bowling Pin Setter machines. Paul entered the army on April 21, 1965 serving in the 1st Headquarters Battalion, 79th Artillery while serving in Korea. He was honorably discharged as a Specialist 4th class on April 22, 1967. Prior to thinking about law enforcement Paul worked for the Yonkers Recreation Department for several years.

But it was no surprise when Paul VanTassell decided to take the civil service test for Yonkers police patrolmen. After all, his father Ambrose VanTassell was a veteran Yonkers police officer, and his brother Kenneth was also a Yonkers police officer. Paul passed all the civil service requirements and was appointed a Yonkers police officer on September 5, 1967 while living at 593 Park Ave. As required, he attended the Municipal Police Recruit Training School held at the Iona College campus in New Rochelle where the academic curriculum ran from September 5th to October 16, 1967. Following his recruit graduation Probationary Patrolman Paul VanTassell was assigned to the 3rd precinct on patrol earning a starting salary of $6,000 a year.

On January 1, 1971, following the implementation of a precinct centralization plan, VanTassell was reassigned to patrol in the South command located at 441 Central Park Ave. While assigned to patrol duty in the South command Paul developed a reputation as being a good street cop who had a natural ability to identify a suspect in a crime and make the arrest. It seems no doubt that due to these natural police instincts, in 1979 Paul was selected by then Commissioner Guido to be assigned to the citywide

PO Paul D. VanTassel #141 (cont.)

plainclothes Anti Crime Unit. This unit, which would later be renamed the Street Crime Unit, was a centralized unit where Paul and his fellow plainclothes officers would work for the next 11 years earning for themselves an outstanding record of making arrests throughout the city.

However, on November 13, 1990, the police commissioner decided it would be better to have the Street Crime Unit decentralized, and as a result all the members of the unit were sent to various patrol precincts to work as teams in plainclothes. At that time Paul VanTassell was sent to the 1st precinct. Up to this point, starting from when he was first hired as a young police officer, Paul had always worked on the west side of the city where the crime rate was higher and he was always busy. And then having been reassigned to the 1st precinct VanTassell was not very happy because in his words, it was too quiet. He much preferred the west side of the city where there was a lot more action.

Paul had a dry sense of humor, which could sometimes be mistaken for being grumpy. But he was very serious and conscientious about his profession and always gave 100%. And his amazing arrest record speaks for itself. During his career he had earned 8 Commendations, 28 Certificates of Excellent Police Work, 2 Unit Citations, 2 Gannet newspaper (Macy) awards for second place 1980 & 1993. The first was for an armed robbery arrest of two males, while off duty, at a jewelry store at So. Broadway and Radford Street, and the second one with his partner, Lou DeLango, for the arrests of three armed robbery suspects at the Dunkin Donut on Tuckahoe road;

He was also awarded the PBA off duty PO Harold Woods award, the Yonkers Elks Club Award, with his partner PO Bill Cave for, during a working fire at 4:00 AM, they ran into the burning hotel to help an elderly man trapped on one of the floors of the Hotel. Both officers also became trapped for several minutes and as VanTassell put it, "*I learned the true meaning of fear*." Police Officer VanTassell also was awarded the American Red Cross Life Saving Award for applying CPR, while off duty, on an elderly man on Yonkers Avenue who had collapsed from a heart attack and stopped breathing. VanTassell later recalled that he was asked to come to the home of the man he had revived because his wife and daughter wanted to personally thank him for saving their loved ones life. He was also invited by the New York Mets baseball team to attend a game and join in pre-game ceremonies in his honor, along with other "life savers" from that year. There were also many letters of appreciation from the public that are too numerous to even begin to list.

PO Paul VanTassell, whose father Ambrose, brother Kenneth and son-in-law PO Kevin Campanaro were also Yonkers police officers, retired from the police department on January 13, 1995, after nearly 28 years of honorable service, and having earned a reputation throughout the police department as being one of the best police officers working the streets.

PLWM. DIANE E. SULLIVAN #539

APPOINTED: April 5, 1968
RESIGNED: August 1, 1968

Diane Sullivan was born in the City of Yonkers on June 13, 1942 and received her formal education in the public school system. She attended PS# 19, Hawthorne Jr. high school and graduated from Commerce high school. Prior to the YPD she worked at the Yonkers General Hospital. Diane was appointed a Parking Enforcement Officer (Meter Maid) in November of 1965 earning $4,000 a year. However, two years later, on August 24, 1967, she resigned from that position. She was subsequently appointed a Yonkers Policewoman, along with several other women, on April 5, 1968 while living at 10 Lamartine Avenue and earning a salary of $6,500 a year. Following her basic police recruit training which took place on the Iona College campus in New Rochelle, Elaine was assigned to the Youth Division investigating youth crimes and liquor law violations. At the time she had just recently married then Lt Bill Kamp and decided to become a full time housewife and resigned from the YPD on August 1, 1968, only four months after she was hired.

PO ELAINE M. WESTERVELT #540

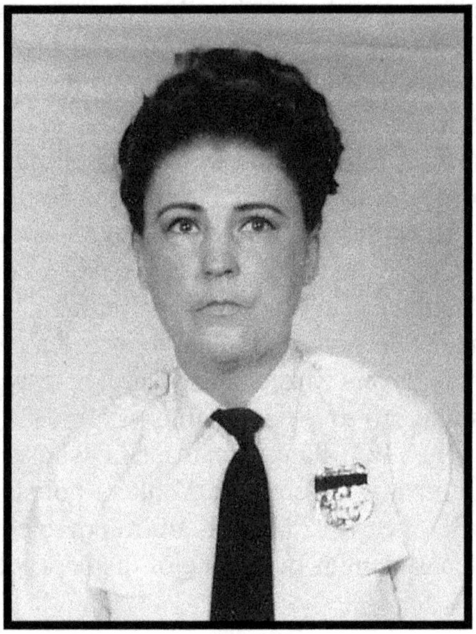

APPOINTED: April 5, 1968
RETIRED: December 8, 1978

Elaine Westervelt was born in Yonkers on April 22, 1935. As a youth she attended St. Mary's school and later graduated from Commerce HS. Prior to her employment with the YPD she worked as a waitress for the Mayflower Restaurant in Dobbs Ferry NY. Elaine's husband, Ted, was already a Yonkers police officer so she decided to take the examination for Yonkers Policewoman. Elaine passed the civil service examination and was appointed to the Yonkers Police Dept. on April 5, 1968 while living at 607 Bellevue Ave. In those early years of hiring women in police positions there was no policy in place for the wearing of a uniform, nor one for going out on routine patrol in uniform. As a result, following her basic police recruit training, which was received at the Iona College campus in New Rochelle, on June 14, 1968 she was assigned to the Detective Division, but actually worked out of the Youth Division investigating juvenile crime and earning $6,500 a year. At one point Elaine Westervelt was injured while on duty rendering her disabled. She applied for, and was granted, accidental disability retirement effective December 8, 1978.

DET. FRANCES M. DeBLASSIS #694

APPOINTED: April 5, 1968
RETIRED: February 25, 1994

Frances DeBlassis was born in the City of Yonkers on January 16, 1930. As a youth she attended PS# 4, Mark Twain Jr. High School and graduated from Commerce High School. Fran spoke Italian as a second language and prior to the YPD worked for the Metropolitan Life Insurance Co. in NYC. On August 12, 1964 Fran was sworn in as a Parking Meter Enforcement Officer but later resigned on November 18, 1965. Fran's husband, Armando, was already a Yonkers police officer so it was no surprise when Fran decided to take the examination for Yonkers Policewoman.

Frances DeBlassis was appointed a Yonkers Policewoman on April 5, 1968 while living at 125 Hillside Avenue and earning $6,500 a year. Following her basic police recruit training, which took place on the Iona College campus in New Rochelle, on June 14, 1968 she was assigned to the Detective Division, but working at the Youth Division investigating crimes by juveniles. On April 17, 1970 Fran was now working in the Detective Division detailed to the Narcotics Unit, but not as a detective. In the early 1970s the title of Policewoman was officially changed to that of "Police Officer," the same to apply to all formerly designated patrolman as well as policewomen. While in the Narcotics Unit she was very effective contributing to several major narcotic arrests. On March 10, 1977 it was announced that she was the very first recipient of the Westchester County Committee, American Legion Auxiliary's "Law & Order Award."

On March 21, 1975 Fran was appointed a Detective and was assigned to continue to work in the Narcotics Unit. In fact, she had the distinction of being the very first Yonkers female police officer to be appointed a detective in the department's history.

Det Fran DeBlassis retired from the Yonkers Police Department effective February 25, 1994. Unfortunately, she died only two years later on July 8, 1996. She was 66 years old.

PO BONITA J. FARANDA #542

APPOINTED: April 5, 1968
DIED: October 2, 2000

The below police officer fell victim to a bureaucratic nightmare which left her unable to work and unable to retire. Bonita J. Faranda was born in Yonkers on June 16, 1942. She attended PS# 5, graduated from Blessed Sacrament Academy in 1960 and from Merchant and Bankers Business College, NYC in 1964 where she received a certificate as a Court Stenographer. She enlisted in the Marine Corps. during the early 1960's in a HQ and Service Battalion working in a military legal office. Following her honorable discharge Faranda worked for the West. Co. Probation Dept. for a short time. Being very interested in the youth of Yonkers "Bunny," as she was known, organized a drill team at both Sacred Heart and St. John's grade schools. She was also a CCD instructor at St. Bartholomew's church.

At one point the city decided it was time to hire policewomen. However, there was no written examination available for females. As a result, on July 29, 1964 Bonita Faranda was "provisionally" hired from 90 Briggs Ave. to the emergency position of Policewoman, with a salary of $5,500 a year, pending a future written test and assigned to the Juvenile Aid Bureau. A civil service test was held for Policewomen in 1965 and not placing high enough on the list she was discharged, and on Jan. 28, 1966 was hired as a police telephone operator earning $4,000. When vacancies allowed, Bonita Faranda was appointed to the permanent position of Policewoman April 5, 1968, earning $6,500 a year. In those early years of hiring women in police positions there wasn't a policy for the wearing of a uniform, nor one for going out on routine patrol in uniform. As such, "Bunny" was assigned to the Juvenile Aid Bureau. "Bunny" Faranda was a tough lady. She had been determined to be a Policewoman and with her Marine Corps discipline she was aggressive and very effective. In fact, she was awarded an Honorable Mention from Westchester Rockland newspapers for the 1st quarter of 1965.

While on duty on Aug. 31, 1968 and during an altercation while making an arrest, Faranda was thrown against the frame of a car door causing severe injuries to her lower back for which she was hospitalized with multiple serious back injuries. Following an injury to a police officer the police department is required to forthwith notify the state pension system of each and every injury. In this case, someone forgot to make that notification. PO Faranda's injuries required several spinal surgeries and she was designated by the police surgeon as totally disabled. However, when the city applied to the pension system for disability retirement, the state replied they have no information about any such injury and the request was denied.

Faranda was severely injured and required to wear a back brace to move but yet still wanted to return to work. On April 17, 1972 she was assigned to work, in a light duty capacity, in the Youth Div. Over the years application was made many times to have Faranda retired but each time the request was denied due to the original failure to notify the state pension system. Over the years, throughout the 1980's and 1990's, Faranda's condition worsened but she still attempted to come to work for short periods of time and still unable to retire. Her only option was to resign with no pension at all, which she refused.

PO Faranda died on October 2, 2000. In the police commissioner's general order to the department announcing her death he wrote in part, "*....although an on duty car accident deprived many of us from knowing officer Faranda. I can personally assure you that no one loved being a cop more than she. By all accounts, Bunny, a former Marine, was a good one.*"

PO DOROTHY M. YASINSKI #94

APPOINTED: April 5, 1968
RETIRED: April 28, 1988

Dorothy Yasinski was born in the City of Yonkers on January 9, 1935. She attended Holy Trinity elementary school and later graduated from Commerce high school. Previous to any thoughts about law enforcement "Dottie" worked as a waitress and typist, and was proficient in sign language as well. She was appointed a Yonkers Parking Enforcement Officer on Nov. 19, 1965, working out of the police Traffic Div. and earned a salary of $4,020 a year.

Dorothy Yasinski resigned from that position to accept appointment to the position of Yonkers Policewoman on April 5, 1968 and her new salary was $6,500 a year. In those early years of hiring women in police positions there wasn't a policy for the wearing of a uniform, nor one for going out on routine patrol in uniform. As a result, following her basic police recruit training, which was received at the Iona College campus in New Rochelle, on June 14, 1968 she was assigned to the Detective Division, but actually worked out of the Youth Division investigating juvenile crime and on occasion working in the Narcotics Unit.

On March 6, 1972 Yasinski was reassigned to the Communications Division to work as a dispatcher. However, on October 6, 1972 she was returned to duty in the Youth Division. Up to this time all sworn policewomen had only worked in plainclothes in various units and had never been assigned to precincts performing routine patrol duties in uniform. That changed on June 19, 1974 when several females throughout the department were reassigned to various patrol commands in uniform and wearing the exact same uniform as their male counterparts. It was on this date that PO Dorothy Yasinski was assigned to patrol duties in uniform in the North Patrol Command.

"Dottie" was a very active member of the Yonkers PBA and very outspoken on matters that she felt were important. During the 1970s she was even elected vice president of the PBA and at one point ran, unsuccessfully, for president of the PBA. On June 20, 1979 she was transferred to the Northeast Patrol Command until December of 1985 when she was assigned to the Training Division serving as the department's safety officer giving lectures to various organizations throughout the city on the subject of safety. She was known as "officer Dottie" to all the school children that she interacted with.

Dorothy retired from the Yonkers Police Department on April 28, 1988 and moved to Arizona. But she had made quite a mark while on the YPD. While still in the department she was the founder and the 1st vice president of the Westchester County Police Pulaski Association. When Dottie joined the YPD she was part of a tradition in law enforcement. Her brother was PO John Karasinski, her son Joe Jr. was a Deputy Commissioner for the Westchester County Dept. Of Public Safety, her daughter Deborah was a police officer in the Daytona Beach Police Department in Florida, her daughter-in-law was Yonkers Detective Patricia Yasinski, and her sister Alice's brother-in-law was Capt. John Potanovic.

Dorothy had an irrepressible and outgoing friendly personality and although being one of the early policewomen in the department she was tough and could hold her own with any male officer.

In early 2000 Dorothy became ill and despite a long hard fight, Ret PO Dorothy Yasinski died in Arizona on February 17, 2005. She was 70 years old.

CAPTAIN EDWARD J. FOLEY

APPOINTED: May 3, 1968
RETIRED: November 3, 1995

Ed Foley was born in the City of Yonkers on November 20, 1944. He attended St. Casimir's elementary school and graduated from Yonkers High School. Ed entered the Army on January 18, 1966 serving up to December 10, 1967 and later received his honorable discharge. Prior to the police department Foley worked as a "storeman" for the N.Y. Telephone Co. in Yonkers.

Edward Foley was appointed to the Yonkers Police Department on May 3, 1968 while residing at 156 Nepperhan Avenue. Ed received his basic police recruit training on the Iona College campus in New Rochelle. The training curriculum ran for about a month and following recruit graduation Probationary Patrolman Edward Foley was assigned to the 4th precinct on June 10, 1968 earning a starting salary of $6,500 a year. The 4th precinct was renamed the North Command on January 1, 1971, as part of a precinct centralization plan, and though many personnel transfers occurred, Ed remained in the North Command. However, the following year on September 15, 1972 Foley was transferred from the North Command to working steady day tours in the Records and Service Maintenance Division, detailed to administrative duties in the Records Unit.

On May 14, 1979 PO Foley was reassigned to work in the Planning and Development Unit in

Captain Edward J. Foley (cont.)

headquarters. A part of his responsibilities in this assignment was to assist in the research and preparation of the police department budget, recommending and preparing of new policies and procedures, and the preparation of application for various county, state, and federal financial grants for the police department.

On November 18, 1982 Ed Foley received his first promotion, that being to the rank of Sergeant earning a salary of $28,313 a year. With his promotion came the transfer to the South Patrol Command as a patrol supervisor. However, his knowledge of the operation of the Planning Unit resulted in his being returned to that unit on May 30, 1983, this time designated as its commanding officer.

Four years later, on April 26, 1987, Sgt Ed Foley was transferred from the Planning Unit to the City Jail as a Central Booking officer. However, by the end of that year, on December 24, 1987, Christmas Eve, Sgt. Foley received an unexpected call from the police commissioner and told to report to his office immediately as he was being promoted to the rank of Lieutenant. Though surprised, it was a wonderful Christmas gift and Lt Ed Foley was reassigned to the Communications Division as a tour supervisor.

As time passed Lt Foley did not stop studying because the examination for Police Captain was on the horizon. He took the examination for police captain and placed #4 on the promotion list. On October 12, 1990 Lt. Ed Foley was promoted to the rank of police Captain earning $61,622 and was reassigned to the Field Services Bureau as a citywide patrol captain.

Captain Edward Foley retired from the police department on November 3, 1995 and initially moved to South Carolina. He now resides in Arizona.

DET. JOSEPH F. McDONALD #685

APPOINTED: May 3, 1968
RETIRED: June 7, 1991

Joe was born in the City of Yonkers on December 10, 1941. As a youth he attended St. Barnabas elementary school, Mark Twain Jr High School, and graduated from Saunders High School. Joe entered the Army in December of 1958, serving up to March 27, 1962 when he was honorably discharged. Prior to the YPD Joe worked as a switchman for the NY Telephone Co. Joseph McDonald, whose brother Gary was also a Yonkers police officer for a short time, was appointed to the Y.P.D. on May 3, 1968 while living at 4331 Katonah Avenue, in the Bronx. He received his recruit training at the Iona College campus in New Rochelle, NY. The academic curriculum lasted about a month and on June 10, 1968, following recruit graduation, Probationary Patrolman Joseph McDonald was assigned to the 3rd precinct earning a starting salary of $6,500 a year. He was reassigned to patrol in the 2nd precinct on June 12, 1970 but two years later, on March 6, 1972, he was transferred to the Detective Division, not as a detective, and was detailed to work in the Youth Division. He must have impressed someone because, two months later on May 15, 1972 Joe was appointed a Detective working in a detective squad. He was returned to patrol in 1983 for a short time but on October 28, 1985 he was re-appointed a Detective and remained in that assignment right up to his retirement on June 7, 1991.

PO THOMAS F. ROBINSON #552

APPOINTED: May 3, 1968
DISMISSED: May 6, 1983

Thomas F. Robinson was born in New York City on November 5, 1944. After moving to Yonkers he attended PS# 12 and graduated from Yonkers High School. Robinson served in the Army from August 24, 1965 through August 17, 1967 and was honorably discharged. He previously worked as a Westchester County Deputy Sheriff in the Westchester County Jail. Robinson was appointed to the YPD on May 3, 1968 while living at 39 Riverview Place. On June 10, 1968, following his basic police recruit training at the Iona college campus in New Rochelle, he was assigned to the 4th precinct, earning a starting salary of $6,500 a year. On June 20, 1979 he was assigned to the northeast patrol division and on December 4, 1981 he was transferred to the South command. On January 27, 1982 he was suspended from the police department, pending a criminal investigation. He was dismissed from the Yonkers Police Department on May 6, 1983.

PO LOUIS TALIA #554

APPOINTED: May 3, 1968
RETIRED: May 13, 1988

Louis was born in the City of White Plains on August 25, 1937. He attended the Halstead Avenue school in Harrison, NY and graduated from Harrison HS. Louie served in the U.S. Air Force from 1957 to 1961 and was honorably discharged. Prior to the YPD he worked for the Dairy Corp. of America in NYC as a driver. Louis Talia was appointed to the Y.P.D. on May 3, 1968, while living at 83 Cook Ave. On June 10, 1968, following his basic police recruit training, which was held at the Iona College campus in New Rochelle, NY, he was assigned to patrol duty in the 3rd precinct earning a starting salary of $6,500 a year. On January 1, 1971, following the centralization of the four patrol precincts, Talia was assigned to the South Patrol Command at 441 Central Park Avenue. He would later return to patrol duty in the 3rd pct, but in 1985 was transferred to the patrol in the 1st precinct on E. Grassy Sprain Rd. Following an entire career on patrol, and as he had planned early on, Louis Talia retired from the police department after 20 years on May 13, 1988.

PO JOHN F. McCABE #556

APPOINTED: May 3, 1968
RETIRED: May 13, 1988

John McCabe was born in Yonkers on Sept. 14, 1945. As a youth he attended St. Mary's school, Sacred Heart Jr. HS and Saunders HS. As a young man John worked as a machine operator for Phelps Dodge Corp. and also worked as a laborer. McCabe was appointed to the Y.P.D. on May 3, 1968. He received his recruit training at the Iona College campus in New Rochelle which lasted for about a month and following graduation, on June 10, 1968, Prob. Ptlm. John McCabe was assigned to the 4th pct earning $6,500 a year. John was a very slim built man but he had a reputation as being a tough street cop. His work apparently caught some ones eye because in late 1969 John was detailed to the D.D., not as a detective, and assigned to youth crime investigations. He later worked in plainclothes trying to clean up the prostitution in the Larkin Plaza area. Because of his work, on Jan. 23, 1970, he was appointed a Detective assigned to undercover work in the Detective Divisions Narcotics Unit. He spent several years there and later working as a squad detective. Around 1977 McCabe was returned to patrol duty in the North Command. About 1980 he was transferred to the South Command and was married, for several years, to PO Carol Chomicki. His last assignment was patrol in the 3rd precinct and would retire on May 13, 1988. In October of 2012 John McCabe moved to Tarpon Springs, Florida to enjoy the warm weather.

DET. VINCENT J. MONTEMURRO #646

APPOINTED: May 3, 1968
RETIRED: October 26, 1990

Vincent Montemurro was born in the city of Yonkers on July 1, 1943. He attended PS# 23, PS# 5, and later graduated from Roosevelt HS. Vinnie, who spoke Italian as a second language, also attended Fordham University in 1961 taking a course in pharmacology. Previous to the YPD Vincent made his living working for the Phelps Dodge Corp. He joined the NY Air National Guard on May 2, 1962 and upon completing his reserve obligation was honorably discharged on May 2, 1968.

Vincent Montemurro was appointed to the Police Department on May 3, 1968 while living at 10 Hildreth Pl. On June 10, 1968, following his basic police recruit training, which was received at the Iona College campus in New Rochelle, he was assigned to patrol duty in the 2nd precinct earning a starting salary of $6,500 a year. On January 1, 1971, following the centralization of the patrol precincts into patrol commands, he was assigned to the North Patrol Command. However, on May 21, 1971, he was returned to the former 2nd precinct, then renamed the South Command.

On May 15, 1972 Montemurro was assigned to the Detective Division, not as a detective, and actually worked in the Youth Division investigating crimes committed by juveniles. However, two months later, on July 14, 1972, Vincent was appointed a Detective working in the Detective Division. While serving as a detective he was very effective in identifying persons responsible for crimes. As just a few examples, following an investigation he arrested 2 males for attempted murder on December 1, 1972 after they had stabbed another male in the neck in the early morning hours. On another occasion he arrested a male and charged him for a murder which took place on July 9, 1973 by stabbing a 19-year-old female. To make this arrest he secured an arrest warrant and had the suspect returned from Puerto Rico to face those charges. And on December 19, 1973 Det. Montemurro prevented a deranged man from committing suicide by jumping off the Saw Mill Parkway Bridge over Lockwood Avenue. Just as the man jumped, Vinnie grabbed him and pulled him to safety.

Det Montemurro was awarded the Yonkers Exchange Club 1973 Police Officer of the Year award for a number of incidents including, the arrest of a man wanted for 10 armed robberies, the arrest of a woman wanted for arson first-degree, the arrest of 2 youths for gas station robberies, the arrest of 2 men for supermarket robberies, and for preventing that bridge suicide. On June 2, 1978 Det. Montemurro, along with his partner and squad sergeant, were honored at the annual Colombian Association dinner and recognized for the excellent police work utilized in the apprehension of a male and female wanted for torture and murder of another male in April of 1978. Eleven years later, on October 21, 1983, Vinny was reassigned back to patrol duty in uniform in the Northeast Patrol Command. But, on April 25, 1986 Montemurro was again designated a Detective and assigned to the Special Operations Division working in the taxi licensing unit.

Det. Montemurro was transferred on June 24, 1988 to the prestigious Special Investigations Unit. The group of detectives assigned here were responsible for very sensitive and confidential investigations along with monitoring the activities of those individuals involved in organized crime. He remained there until September 20, 1991 when he was returned to the Detective Division in a general assignment squad.

The following month, on October 26, 1990, Det. Vincent Montemurro retired from the Yonkers Police Department. Upon retiring from DD started his own printing business, "Hart Press Inc." which he operated for many years out of his home

PO WILLIAM BERKMAN #557

APPOINTED: May 3, 1968
RETIRED: August 19, 1988

Hubert Berkman was born in Germany on Feb. 14, 1942, and came to the USA with his parents as a youth. He was naturalized as a citizen in NYC on Nov. 30, 1959 and at which time his name was changed from Hubert to William Berkman. Bill attended PS# 27 in Staten Island and PS# 14 in Yonkers. He graduated from Lincoln HS and spoke German as a second language. Bill was a tall well-built muscular man who, as a young man, worked as a laborer in New Rochelle, NY. Berkman was appointed to the Y.P.D. on May 3, 1968 while living at 68 Tibbetts Rd. He received his recruit training at the Iona College campus in New Rochelle, NY which lasted for about a month and following graduation, on June 10, 1968 Prob. Ptlm. Berkman was assigned to the 3rd pct earning $6,500 a year. Considering his size and being a very imposing figure, Bill was actually a soft spoken easy going officer who rarely lost his temper and was well liked by his fellow officers. On Jan. 1, 1971 PO Berkman was transferred out to the South Command. He remained on patrol in the 2nd pct for the next 16 years and on June 1, 1987 was reassigned to patrol the 1st pct from which he would retire on Aug. 19, 1988.

PO ROBERT E. WEBB #555

APPOINTED: May 3, 1968
RETIRED: May 4, 1988

Bob Webb was born in NYC on October 19, 1945. He attended St. Casimir's elementary school and graduated from Sacred Heart High School. Bob's previous employment was listed as a warehouse man with Western Electric Co. Robert Webb was appointed to the Yonkers Police Department on May 3, 1968 while living at 185 Lockwood Avenue. He received his basic police recruit training at the Iona College campus in New Rochelle, NY. The academic curriculum lasted for about a month and following the recruit graduation, on June 10, 1968 he was assigned to the 4th precinct earning $6,500. Webb was an easy going officer who was well liked by his fellow officers and would serve his entire career in the 4th precinct, retiring on May 4, 1988. Bob moved to Melbourne, Fla and worked as a police officer in the Cocoa Beach P.D. Because of his experience he was quickly appointed a detective. He was even named rookie of the year by the department and advanced to 1st line supervisor. However, due to budgetary issues, after 4 years, Webb resigned rather than be laid off. He was fortunate to see his son Robert join the Y.P.D. in 1994.

DET. LT. MICHAEL S. NOVOTNY

APPOINTED: June 28, 1968
RETIRED: April 3, 1995

Mike Novotny was born in Yonkers the son of Yonkers police officer Michael Novotny Sr. on July 30, 1946. As a youth he attended St Paul the Apostle elementary school and graduated from Sacred Heart High School. He also attended St John's University from 1964 to 1966. After school, and being an excellent swimmer, Mike was employed by Westchester Co. as a life guard at Tibbetts Brook Park Pool. At the age of 20 years and residing at 55 Putnam Avenue, Mike submitted his application for appointment as a Yonkers Police Cadet which had just been recently established. Mike received his appointment as a Yonkers police cadet, along with several other young men on September 9, 1966 earning $2,000 a year. The terms of the police cadet appointment required four hours a day of schooling at Westchester Community College, and the second four hours assigned to working in various positions within the YPD. The agreement was that upon completion of two years of this school/work combination, and when a position became available, that he would be appointed a full time police officer.

At this point in time the military draft was still in effect and an increasing number of soldiers were being sent to Vietnam to fight. Deferments from the draft had earlier been secured but during this particular time the public safety commissioner sent written requests to the Yonkers Draft Board to continue all the Cadet draft deferments due to urgent manpower needs. It was approved but was not a request that was made by the cadets.

Upon completion of the cadet program Mike was appointed a police officer on June 28, 1968 while residing at 55 Putnam Avenue. His basic police recruit training took place on the Iona College campus in New Rochelle whose curriculum ran from October 7, 1968 through November 19, 1968.

Following recruit graduation Probationary Patrolman Michael Novotny was assigned to patrol

Det. Lt. Michael S. Novotny (cont.)

duty in the 3rd precinct, like his father before him, earning a starting salary of $6,800 a year. On July 12, 1968, following his recruit schooling, Novotny was assigned to the Service and Maintenance Division, detailed to the newly established Marine Unit to patrol the Hudson River and enforce those laws applying to boating.

Following the end of summer that year, the Marine Unit was disbanded and on October 1, 1968 Novotny was assigned to patrol duty in the 3rd precinct. On May 19, 1969 he was moved to the Communications Division and on July 17, 1970 to the 4th precinct back to patrol. On August 30, 1971 Novotny was assigned to the Criminal Identification Unit as a crime scene investigator gathering all available evidence left at a crime scene. Mike was a graduate of Mercy College in 1971 when they first started their Criminal Justice Program where he earned an Associates and BA degree.

Mike Novotny was promoted to the rank of Sergeant on July 6, 1973 earning $15,708 and was reassigned to the North Command as a patrol supervisor. As a member of the Capt.'s, Lt's, & Sgt's Association (CLSA) Mike ran for, and was elected to, vice president of that association effective January 1, 1978. Nonetheless, he remained on patrol. He was re-elected to that position again in 1979. Also effective Jan. 1, 1979 Sgt Novotny was transferred to the Internal Affairs Division (IAD) of the YPD. While still in IAD, on December 14, 1982, Novotny was elevated to Detective Sergeant.

Det Sgt Novotny was promoted to the rank of Lieutenant on June 3, 1985 and because of his experience in IAD investigations and the complete trust the commissioner had in him, Lt Novotny was allowed to remain assigned to IAD as a Det. Lt. He was also privileged to have attended and graduated from prestigious FBI National Academy on September 12, 1985. Among his many awards, his most prized was the "Bart Hose Memorial Award for Excellence in Police Work," presented by the FBI.

Mike had a family tradition in law enforcement. His father, Michael, was a Yonkers police officer, his brother Robert was a former Westchester County Parkway Police Officer, and his cousin Jerry Novotny was a New York State Trooper. Mike was also a long time member of the Yonkers Elks Club and held the position of Exalted Ruler in 1975 and 1976.

After 15 years in the Internal Affairs Division, on April 14, 1994 Det Lt Novotny was designated the commanding officer of the Intelligence Division with the responsibility to investigate very sensitive areas such as organized criminal activity as well as dignitary protection. In 1995 a new police commissioner took office and with him came several reassignments. Lt Mike Novotny was transferred to the Communications Division on March 17, 1995 but never returned to work. After remaining out sick for a month he retired from the YPD on April 3, 1995.

Following his retirement Mike obtained a private investigators license and started his own investigative business under his own name. He later obtained a contract with the Yonkers Municipal Housing Authority to conduct internal investigations.

DET. THOMAS T. WHALEN #654

APPOINTED: September 6, 1968
RETIRED: January 10, 1997

Thomas Whalen was born in the City of Yonkers on August 18, 1947. He attended Sacred Heart elementary school, Sacred Heart High School, and graduated from Gorton High School. Fresh out of school he worked for the First National Stores in Yonkers. In early September of 1966 at the age of 19 years and residing at 198 Park Avenue, Tom submitted his application for appointment as a Yonkers Police Cadet, a position which had just been established.

Tom Whalen received his appointment as a Yonkers Police Cadet, along with several other young men, on September 9, 1966 earning $2,000 a year. The terms of the police cadet program required four hours a day of schooling at Westchester Community College, and the second four hours assigned to working in various positions within the YPD. The agreement was that upon completion of two years of this school/work combination, and when a position became available, that he would be appointed a full time police officer.

At this point in time the military draft was still in effect and an increasing number of soldiers were being sent to Vietnam to fight. Deferments from the draft had earlier been secured but during this particular time the public safety commissioner sent written requests to the Yonkers Draft Board to continue all the Cadet draft deferments due to urgent manpower needs. It was approved but was not a request that was made by the cadets.

Upon completion of the cadet program Tom was appointed a police officer on September 6, 1968 while residing at 198 Park Avenue. His basic police recruit training took place on the Iona College campus in New Rochelle whose curriculum ran from October 7, 1968 through November 19, 1968. Following recruit graduation Probationary Patrolman Thomas Whalen was assigned to patrol duty in the 4th precinct earning a starting salary of $6,800 a year.

On January 1, 1971, when the 4th was renamed the North Command, Tom remained there and on April 24, 1978 he was detailed to patrol in the federally funded Community Patrol Unit (CPU) which was established to improve relations between the police and the minority community. On September 13, 1982 PO Whalen was transferred to the South Command and then to the 1st precinct on December 16, 1983. (In mid-1983, the two Command configuration which had replaced the precincts in 1971, was discontinued and the four precincts were identified by number once again.)

On October 30, 1985 Tom was offered, and he accepted, an assignment to the Training Unit of the YPD where, as a certified instructor, he would train in-service member of the department as well as new recruits in various topics as well as periodic firearms training. Almost four years later, on April 4, 1989, Whalen was detailed to the Narcotics Unit to work undercover. His work was so remarkable that, on October 7, 1994, Tom Whalen was appointed a Detective and immediately detailed to work with the Federal Drug Enforcement Agency Task Force on major investigations.

Det. Thomas Whalen retired from the police department while still detailed to the DEA on January 10, 1997. Several years following his retirement, Tom moved to Arizona in 2011.

PO WILLIAM R. SCAPPLEHORN #568

APPOINTED: October 4, 1968
RETIRED: August 31, 2000

Bill Scapplehorn was born in NYC on February 9, 1948. He attended PS# 80 Jr. High school in NYC, Evander Childs High School in the Bronx and, after having moved to Yonkers, graduated from Yonkers High School in June of 1966.

On Sept 9, 1966 Bill, along with several others, were hired by the Yonkers Police Dept. as civilians to be part of a new program in the YPD as a Police Cadet. After being hired from 111 East Mosholu Parkway in the Bronx, Bill attended Westchester Community College, paid by the city, 4 hours a day in class and the other four working in the police department and his salary was $2,000 a year. Upon completion of the two years Bill had earned an Associate's degree and was hired as a police officer on October 4, 1968 with the annual salary of $6,500. Scapplehorn and the other former cadets attended their Municipal Police Recruit Training School at the Iona College campus in New Rochelle from October 7, through November 19, 1968.

Following recruit graduation Probationary Patrolman William Scapplehorn was assigned to patrol duty in the 3rd precinct. Known as "Scappy" to all his friends, on January 1, 1971 he was reassigned to the South Command where he remained on patrol until July 1, 1991 when he was transferred to the Records Division in HQ. Two years later, on November 4, 1993, Bill was transferred to the plainclothes Youth Division as a youth crime investigator. Bill was a big man with a matching big heart. For a number of years he served on the Annual Old Timers Picnic Committee and played on the YPD Hockey Team in various competitions.

On November 22, 1999 he returned to patrol in the 2nd precinct and retired the next year on August 31, 2000.

PO STUART KING #569

APPOINTED: October 4, 1968
RETIRED: January 5, 1989

Stuart "Stu" King was born January 21, 1948 in Glasgow, Scotland. It is believed that he came to America as a young child because he had no noticeable Scottish accent whatever. He would later become a naturalized citizen in Aug. of 1968. Stu attended PS# 9 and graduated from Gorton HS in 1966. That same year, on Sept 9, 1966 King, along with several others, was hired by the Yonkers Police Dept. as a civilian to be part of a new program in the YPD as a Police Cadet. King and others attended Westchester Community College, paid by the city, 4 hours a day in class and the other four working in the police dept. and their salary was $2,000 a year.

Upon completion of the two years he had earned an Associate's degree and was hired as a police officers on October 4, 1968 with the annual salary of $6,500. He and the other former cadets attended their Municipal Police Recruit Training School at the Iona College campus in New Rochelle from October 7, 1968 through November 19, 1968.

Following graduation, on Nov. 19, 1968, Patrolman Stuart King was assigned to uniform patrol in the 4th precinct. At one point, being an excellent auto mechanic, Stu was detailed to work in the police vehicle repair shop for a while before returning to the 4th precinct. He remained in the 4th until April 14, 1980 when his wish came true. He was assigned to the Traffic Divisions motorcycle unit. Stu loved riding his own motorcycle but 7 years later on March 6, 1987, for reasons unknown, Stu left his dream job and was transferred to the Youth Div. where he remained up to his retirement on Jan. 5, 1989.

Being a big man Stu could be an intimidating physical presence and was good to have around when things got touchy. The truth was, there was nothing intimidating about him at all. He was a gentle giant rarely resorting to physical force when patience and words would suffice.

Following his retirement and for the next 15 years, he worked for P&E Property in NYC. Formerly of New Rochelle, King moved to Pt. Pleasant, NJ. Unfortunately Stu developed some major medical issues and as a result, on July 28, 2008, he died at the age of 60 years.

DET. JAMES F. KIRKWOOD #638

APPOINTED: October 4, 1968
RETIRED: January 3, 2003

Jim Kirkwood was born in the Village of Bronxville New York on September 16, 1947. He attended Annunciation Elementary school, Walt Whitman Jr. high school, and graduated from Roosevelt high school in 1965. In September of 1966 at the age of 18 years and residing at 318 Read Ave., Jim submitted his application for appointment as a Yonkers Police Cadet. At the time he was working for Suburban Pet Supply in the Town of Tuckahoe.

Jim received his appointment as a Yonkers police cadet, along with several other young men, on September 9, 1966 earning $2,000 a year. The terms of the police cadet appointment required four hours a day of schooling at Westchester community college, and the second four hours assigned to working in the Communications and Records Division with the YPD. The agreement was that upon completion of two years of this school/work combination, and when a position became available, that he would be appointed a certified police officer. At this point in time the military draft was still in effect and an increasing number of soldiers were being sent to Vietnam. Deferments from the draft had earlier been secured but during this particular time the public safety Commissioner sent written requests to the Yonkers Draft Board to continue all the cadet draft deferments due to urgent manpower needs. It was not a request that was made by the cadets.

Upon completion of the cadet program Jim was appointed a police officer on Oct. 4, 1968 while residing at 188 Voss Ave. Following his recruit training, on Nov. 15, 1968 officer Jim Kirkwood was assigned to patrol duty in the 4th precinct earning a starting salary of $6,800 a year. During the 1970s for many years his partner was PO Mike Beddows. After 11 years on patrol duty in the 4th precinct Jim was reassigned to the N/E Patrol Command on June 20, 1979. Jim was an even tempered man who was liked and respected by all who knew him. He did his job efficiently and effectively and so it was no surprise that on October 21, 1983 he was appointed a detective in the Detective Division. As a detective he continued to display his intelligent approach to investigations which gained him an enviable reputation.

On Sept. 20, 1994 Det. Kirkwood was assigned to the Inspectional Services Div. But it was on March 3, 1995 that Jim was assigned to the prestigious Special Investigations Div. This unit was responsible for such sensitive investigations as monitoring the activities of organized crime members living and operating in Yonkers, dignitary protection, and working closely with county, state and federal law enforcement agencies. They reported directly to the police commissioner.

Det. Kirkwood retired from the police department on January 3, 2003 after a total of more than 36 years service. Despite his 6' 4" stature, Jim was not an intimidating type person. He was soft-spoken, easy-going, and the term gentleman fit perfectly. During his career he was the recipient of two police commendations, five certificates of excellent police work, as well as numerous letters of appreciation from citizens who appreciated the way he conducted himself.

Before retiring, Jim had moved to Mohegan Lake with his wife where he remained during his police retirement. Not long after retiring Jim began working for the Yonkers Municipal Housing Authority as an investigator into Medicaid fraud and other violations by housing residents.

Suddenly and without warning retired Detective Jim Kirkwood suffered a heart attack while off duty in his back yard on May 31, 2011. Unfortunately he was not discovered for some time and suffered severe brain damage. Ret. Det. James Kirkwood died on June 11, 2011 at the age of 63 years.

CAPTAIN FRANCIS J. MESSAR

APPOINTED: October 4, 1968
RETIRED: June 2, 2006

Francis Messer was born in the City of Yonkers on October 5, 1947. He attended St. Joseph's school on Ashburton Avenue and graduated from Sacred Heart high school. For a short period of time he worked for the Western Electric Co. on Tuckahoe Road. Frank applied for, and was appointed to, the first Police Cadet class on September 9, 1966 and which earned him a salary of $2,000 a year.

The Cadet program consisted of a combination of 2 years in class at Iona College and working as an intern with the Yonkers Police Department. Four hours each day were spent in class at Iona, and four hours with the YPD learning various aspects of the department. Upon completion all cadets had earned an associate's degree. Coincidently, while at Iona College in October of 1968 there was an anti-Vietnam War rally on campus and the entire Cadet class was told that they had to leave. The demonstrators were very

Capt. Francis J. Messar (cont.)

violent and while leaving on a police bus their vehicle was struck by fists, bottles and verbal abuse.

Following the Cadet program Frank was appointed a police officer on October 4, 1968 while living at 10 Bailey Ave. in Yonkers and started earning a salary of $6,500 a year. He received his basic recruit training at the old Iona Prep high school located on the Iona College campus in New Rochelle. Upon graduation on November 15, 1968 probationary police officer Francis Messar was assigned to patrol duty in the 3rd precinct. On January 1, 1971, following the implementation of a precinct centralization plan, Frank was assigned to the newly established South Command.

Frank was promoted to the rank of Sergeant on October 18, 1973 and was assigned as a desk officer / patrol supervisor in the North command. In May of 1977 Messar was recommended for the Fire Department's Medal of Honor along with a firefighter for their actions as a general alarm fire at 377 N. Broadway. However the chief of police would not allow him to accept a fire department award and instead awarded him a certificate of excellent police work. Messar had developed an excellent reputation for making high quality and multiple arrests. As a result, on September 17, 1979 he was selected to be the new commanding officer of the Street Crime Unit. Up to this point the YPD had only utilized black-and-white photographs for their identification photo arrays. Sgt. Messar is credited with being the first to recommend and actually implement the first color photograph photo array which was later implemented department-wide. He remained the C.O. of that unit until May 1, 1981 when he was promoted to the rank of police Lieutenant earning a salary of $26,411. He remained in the Street Crime Unit for one month until June 22, 1981 when he was transferred to the Communications Division as a tour supervisor. On November 18, 1982 he was reassigned to the South Command as a zone commander and in October of 1986 he returned to the Communications Division.

On December 1, 1989 Lt. Messar was reassigned and designated the executive officer in the Youth Division where he worked with the gang unit and other authorities in Westchester County to bring to light the emergence of gangs and gang violence in Westchester County. Frank was promoted to the rank of Captain on December 18, 1993 earning $70,393 and was designated the early tour patrol captain. On March 17, 1995 he was reassigned to the Field Services Inspection Unit for a short time and later was designated as lead officer, or incident commander, for the October 7, 1995 visit of Pope John Paul II.

On May 22, 2000 Capt. Messar was reassigned as the CO of the Special Operations Division which consisted of traffic, hack inspectors, abandoned auto unit, K-9 Unit, Emergency Services Unit, and the Street Crime Unit. It was during this time he was detailed to a number of terrorist awareness courses and it became evident that SOD, as constructed at that time, needed to be reorganized. Working closely with his Street Crime Unit he began a relationship with the FBI Joint Terrorism Task Force which also led to a number of raids and a great deal of intelligence about local activities in support of terrorism financing. Due to the success of their work one of his officers was permanently assigned to this task force. Also, at the same time, the captain was assigned to the NYPD Command and Control at One Police Plaza as the liaison for Westchester County in preparation for Y2K, so named for the turning of a new century, from June of 1999 until January 1, 2000. Upon returning to the City of Yonkers the captain was designated the commanding officer of the Emergency Services Unit and K-9 unit, both of which had been separated from SOD, as well as the Street Crime Unit which became a stand-alone unit led by a lieutenant.

While serving as the CO of the ESU they procured a grant through the Generoso Pope foundation

Capt. Francis J. Messar (cont.)

and established a Marine Unit for River Patrol as part of ESU. Following the terrorist attack on September 11, 2001 the department and the captain in particular were able to write grants and establish funding for new vehicles, training, equipment and the establishment of department-wide training in courses such as terrorism awareness, weapons of mass instruction and hazmat training for ESU officers. Capt. Messar applied for, and was accepted as, one of the first 50 police officers nationwide to attend and advanced terrorism training course in Washington DC. He also began to train with and train for the New York State Office of Emergency Management.

Following Capt. Messar's retirement on June 2, 2006 after nearly 40 years service, he accepted an offer from the New York State Office of Emergency Management now called the Division of Homeland Security New York and settled in as both an instructor and member of the state incident management team. Since that time he has responded to nationwide events of national significance such as forest fires, hurricanes, flooding, storms, etc. He is also a graduate and certified national instructor for the Emergency Management Institute in Emmitsburg Maryland.

Some of captain Messar's accomplishments and various involvements with the Police Department are as follows; in 1978 he was a co-founder of the annual Old-Timers Retirees Picnic; he was elected the Secretary of the Capt.'s, Lt's, and Sgt's Association serving in 1978 and 1979; he was very active in athletics and coached police softball teams for many years; he was a charter member of the Westchester County Police Emerald Society Pipe and Drum Band; In May of 2005 Capt. Messar was presented with the Police Commissioner's Award based on his significant personal contributions to the Department. In the course of his thirty-nine plus years of service, some other contributions to the department have included the following: - He was the previous chairman of the Honor Board of Review, a position he held for more than 12 years. He has also served for many years as the master of ceremonies for all departmental ceremonies. He has dedicated many years of his career to organizing and coaching sports and recreation teams for the benefit of the members of the department in their off-duty hours, - He has served the Police Holy Name Society as its Secretary, Vice-President, and President, and has organized and run the department's Annual Communion Breakfast. - He has been a mainstay of the Annual Handicapped Children's Picnic, an event that reflects favorably upon the department and is a source of much goodwill between the department and the community. - He was also instrumental in the 1980's in coordinating department members' participation in the NYS Community Mayors' Handicapped Children's Christmas Party. He was recognized as the departments anti-terrorism expert and he was designated the departments coordinator between the department and other local, county, state and federal agencies.

At the time of his retirement Deputy Chief Tom Sullivan commented, "*Frank has always been a consummate professional. He has dedicated his life to the Yonkers Police Dept. In the last several years he has become an expert in homeland security issues, and he was our front man with state and federal agencies on that issue. He is a recognized expert in the field. He will be a very hard person to replace*."

During his career Capt. Messar was the recipient of the following awards;
1 Meritorious Service Bar, 5 Commendations, 7 Certificates of Excellent Police Work, 9 Unit Citations, 2 Police Commissioners Awards, 1 Papal Visitation bar, 1 Lifesaving Award, 2 CLSA Presidents Awards, 1 PBA Off-Duty award, 1 Pulaski Society award, 1 Emerald Society award, 1 Elks Club Uniform Services award, 3 Exchange Club Uniform Services awards, 1 VFW Uniform Service award, a Commendation from the FBI, a Commendation from the Motion Picture Association of America, a N.Y.S. Senate Award,

Capt. Francis J. Messar (cont.)

and numerous citations from the Yonkers Mayor and City Council.

In 2013 Frank served as a NIMS-ICS instructor for the Division of Homeland Security New York and at the Westchester County police Academy. He also served as a Deputy Operation Section Chief on the New York State I.M.T. He served as a designated incident commander and operations section chief for the City of Yonkers Police Department. He was certified as a general topics instructor, counterterrorism instructor, law enforcement response to terrorism both awareness and operations level instructor. He participated in the Empire 2009 radiological dispersion drill in Albany with the Department of Energy and New York State office of Emergency Management as a drill facilitator and during a hurricane drill of 2008 served as deputy operations section chief.

Capt. Messar, whose son Michael is a Yonkers Sergeant, created a significant void in expertise when he retired.

PO JAMES M. WEISSE #567

APPOINTED: October 4, 1968
RETIRED: January 5, 1989

Jim Weisse was born in NYC on Jan. 14, 1948 he moved to Yonkers as a young boy and attended St. Barnabas school, and graduated from Lincoln HS. On Sept. 9, 1966 Weisse, at age 18, along with several others, was hired by the YPD as civilians to be part of a new program in the YPD as a Police Cadet. Those hired would attend Westchester Community College, paid by the city, four hours a day in class and the other four working in the police department and earning $2,000 a year. Upon completion of the two years they had earned an Associate's degree and Jim was hired as a police officer on Oct. 4, 1968 from 35 Bainton St, with the salary of $6,500. He attended recruit training at the Iona College campus in New Rochelle from Oct. 7, through Nov. 19, 1968. Upon completion of recruit school Patrolman Weisse was assigned to the 4th pct. On Aug. 16, 1976 he was assigned to work in the Criminal Investigation Unit (CIU) as a crime scene investigator photographing and processing fingerprints and other evidence. Throughout his career Jim had a Federal Firearms license to sell firearms and did so off duty. James Weisse retired from the YPD on Jan. 5, 1989 and died suddenly and unexpectedly on Jan. 17, 1991. He was only 43 years old.

PO WILLIAM A. LEAVY #574

APPOINTED: March 7, 1969
RETIRED: June 16, 1995

Bill Leavy was born in Yonkers on August 22, 1945. He attended PS# 7, Longfellow Jr. High School and graduated from Commerce High School. Prior to the YPD, Bill earned his living working for the Nestles Co. in White Plains. William Leavy was appointed to the police department on March 7, 1969 from 30 Thurman Street. He received his basic police recruit training at the Iona College campus in New Rochelle for approximately one month. Following graduation Probationary Patrolman William Leavy was assigned to patrol duty in the 4th precinct earning a starting salary of $7,000. On January 29, 1973 he was transferred to the Traffic Division however, he advised the captain he didn't like writing summonses all day and was returned back to patrol duty. Bill was a friendly easy going person who maintained a low profile. As a result he was nicknamed by his friends as, "Billy Who?" He was assigned to the Youth Division on January 1, 1992 but returned to the 4th precinct on patrol the following year on November 1, 1993. Bill Leavy retired from the YPD on June 16, 1995.

PO DONALD F. HAGGERTY #107

APPOINTED: March 7, 1969
RETIRED: May 4, 1995

Don was born in Brooklyn, NY on Aug. 6, 1946, attended St. Patrick's elementary school and after his family moved to Yonkers attended St. Eugene's, Iona Grammar School, Iona Prep school in New Rochelle, and graduated from Roosevelt H. S. Don also attended Curry College from 1966 to 1968 majoring in Business Administration. Prior to the YPD Don was employed by the Circle Line ships in NYC.

Haggerty was appointed to the Y.P.D. on Mar 7, 1969 residing at 145 Winnebago Road. He received his police recruit training at the Iona College campus in New Rochelle. On April 25, 1969, following recruit graduation, Prob. Ptl. Don Haggerty was assigned to patrol duty in the 2nd pct. earning a starting salary of $7,000. On Jan. 1, 1971, following the implementation of a precinct centralization plan where two precincts were closed and two were re-named, PO Haggerty was transferred to patrol in the North Patrol Command at 53 Shonnard Place. The following year, on June 23, 1972, Don's request was approved and he was reassigned to two wheel motorcycle duty in the Traffic Division. Don was the epitome of a spit and polish traffic cop. He was physically a well-built officer with large arms, the result of long hours in the gym. And his uniform was always tailored to perfection.

On Jan. 1, 1979, PO Haggerty, along with many in Traffic, was detailed to the patrol commands but continued with traffic duties. Six months later Haggerty was detailed to the Street Crime Unit for special duty. Exactly one year following his detail to the North Command, on Jan. 1, 1980, Don was returned to Traffic. However, due to the untimely death of Training officer Ron O'Rourke, Haggerty was transferred to the Training Division as O'Rourke's replacement. Following training he was designated a state certified instructor and was, with others, responsible for the in-service training for all members of the YPD, as well as the recruit training for new police recruits.

Having a strong interest in how to keep the human body physically fit, and feeling there was more he could do, Don attended Lehman College in the Bronx, while off duty, studying anatomy and physiology. It was about this time he noticed a large unused room in the basement of the 1st pct and his plan to establish a Gymnasium for police officers began. With the help of many, especially Det. Joe Surlak, the police gym was established.

While still in the Training Davison Don was himself trained and then certified as a DCJS/FBI certified firearms instructor. He graduated from the S & W Academy in Mass. and in time gained "Judicial Notice" as a firearms identification and operations expert for NYS. Don also served as the YPD range master and armorer. And, for 5 years he was the defensive tactics instructor for the zone 3 police academy for police recruits throughout the county. Keep in mind all this was at the same time that Don had been serving as the YPD physical fitness instructor and establishing our very first police gym. Don often trained family members of officers as well as helping officers with cardiac rehab programs.

At one point Don was reassigned to the PAL where he established a co-ed physical fitness program for the underprivileged children of Yonkers ages 12 to 14 years. PO Haggerty retired from the YPD PAL on May 4, 1995. His reflective thoughts years after retiring? .... *I' loved the job and the men and women I worked with. I'm proud to have created something that will live on after I'm gone: that being the YPD Gym."*

DEPUTY CHIEF WILLIAM W. McBRIDE

APPOINTED: March 7, 1969
RETIRED: March 15, 2007

Bill McBride was born in Yonkers NY on March 15, 1946. As a youth Bill attended St. Casimir's and PS# 12 elementary schools, Longfellow Jr. High School, and graduated from Saunders Trade & Technical High School on South Broadway. Previous to any interest in the YPD Bill worked for Rosner's Hardware Store on New Main Street.

William McBride was appointed to the Yonkers Police Department on March 7, 1969 while residing at 73 Page Avenue. He received his basic police recruit training at the Iona College campus in New Rochelle with an academic curriculum that ran for approximately one month. On April 25, 1969, following recruit graduation, Probationary Patrolman William McBride was assigned to patrol duty in the 4th precinct earning a starting salary of $7,000. On January 1, 1971, following the implementation of a precinct centralization plan whereby two precincts were closed and two were renamed, PO McBride remained assigned to the renamed North Command.

The following year, on May 15, 1972, McBride was assigned to the Detective Division, but not as a detective, and remained what was termed a "silver shield." (Patrolman) While there, he was detailed to work in the Youth Division investigating crimes committed by juveniles. But only four months later, on

Deputy Chief William W. McBride (cont.)

September 15, 1972, McBride was appointed a Detective and assigned as an undercover officer working from the D.D. Narcotics Unit.

On February 17, 1973, while Det McBride and his partner Det Ed Courtney were delivering a prisoner to the city jail on Alexander Street, they observed through the windows of the jail that prisoners were roaming around the hallways inside the jail and breaking windows. They had even armed themselves with revolvers from a storage cabinet. McBride had come upon a jail break attempt in progress where a jailer and jail matron had been overpowered, assaulted and locked in a cell. McBride notified headquarters and backup units quickly arrived maintaining an exterior perimeter. Once the prisoners realized they were surrounded they laid down their weapons and returned to their cells. Det McBride had prevented a near jailbreak.

But Bill was about to really be put to the test. In 1978 Det McBride found himself in a life or death shootout while on duty.

The date was May 21, 1978. Bill McBride, who at the time had nine years in the job, was working as a Detective in the Detective Division assigned to the Narcotics Unit. Like most of us in the early years, he worked a second job to make a little extra. He and a few other officers were authorized by the department to work as night clerks at the Holiday Inn at 125 Tuckahoe Rd. On this night Bill McBride was on a day off and was working the 6 PM to 7 AM shift at the motel along with another clerk, a young student. Both sat at a desk in the front lobby area. Directly behind them were two rooms, each connected to the other by a doorway and both with entrances to them from the lobby. The room immediately behind them was the counting room, the wall of which had a door leading into it with a wall honeycombed with mail slots or openings. Alongside that room was the Innkeeper's office.

Though assigned to narcotics, McBride was aware of a stickup team operating that had recently hit twice in Elmsford and again in Port Chester with the only description being 2 males, one white and one black. On this night, as usual, evening started out quiet but things were about to change, dramatically! At about 10 PM two men, one white and one black, entered the lobby and approached the desk. They wore long trench coats and large floppy hats. McBride said, even though at that point they had done nothing wrong, he knew in his heart that this was going to be a robbery. He said he couldn't have been more sure if they wore signs. McBride stated that he immediately got up and started for the counting room right behind him to call for backup and take a position of cover.

As he did, he thought he heard what sounded like the slide action on a weapon. At that point one male yelled, "Hey buddy, hey buddy," and just as McBride dove into the room the white male opened fire at McBride with a revolver right through the wall with the open mail slots. McBride yelled, "police officer, police officer," in the hope that they would turn and leave. It was a waste of breath. The young clerk started to rise from his chair but fell back where he remained frozen with a bird's eye view of the suspect who began firing at McBride right over the clerks head.

Detective McBride had his revolver out and in an effort to dodge the rounds entering the room he was in, attempted to move through the doorway into the Innkeeper's office to his left. But as he did, the black male stuck a shotgun through the door from the lobby into the innkeeper's room and fired it at

Deputy Chief William W. McBride (cont.)

McBride. This, along with .38 caliber rounds coming into the room at him, made changing position an absolute necessity. But at best he could only enter the room alongside him, which is where the 2nd male was not completely visible, but was sticking a shotgun through the open door and a jabbing motion and quickly firing at the detective.

McBride returned fire at the male with his shotgun but with no luck because of the cautious method of the suspect sticking the shotgun through the door, firing, and quickly retrieving it. Taking fire from two directions and being trapped, there were few options. After watching the shotgun jammed through the doorway and fire separately three times, McBride waited, slowly taking aim at the position where the 2nd shooter kept sticking the shotgun through and firing. As the shotgun came in for a 4th time and fired, so did McBride who's round this time struck the suspect in the wrist. (It was later learned that although the round entered the suspect wrist it had exited from his elbow.) When the man was hit he let out a yell and he and his accomplice turned and fled the scene.

As they ran out of the lobby door, McBride ran out of the rear room firing at them but unfortunately missing them, but shattering all the glass in the entrance way; no doubt much to the displeasure of the motel management. The suspects made good their escape but fortunately neither McBride nor the desk clerk were injured. Detective McBride, who would later rise to be Deputy Chief, told me the entire shootout probably lasted for a minute or two but it seemed a whole lot longer. He said, "*it seemed like everything was in slow motion and, after they left, a distinctive quiet and calm came over the room. I remember it so well that I can still smell the burnt gunpowder that filled the rooms.*"

During the investigation a wallet belonging to one of the suspects was found on the ground outside the motel providing the identity of one of the men. Both men were later identified as predicate felons. The white male with the .38 caliber revolver had only been released 3 weeks earlier on parole after serving 7 years of a 25 to life sentence for the murder of a bartender during a robbery in Buffalo. The black male with the shotgun had convictions for previous home robberies.

Two days later, during another attempted holdup in Elmsford, the police received a tip and the suspects were both arrested and were both subsequently convicted for the attempted murder of Detective McBride in the Yonkers shootout.

During meetings of the awards committee, it was suggested by some that Detective McBride be awarded the Medal of Honor. However someone suggested that the NYPD had a medal named the Combat Cross, and that the Yonkers Police Dept. should adopt such an award. Further, that this award should be presented to Detective McBride. Consequently Detective William McBride became the first Yonkers police officer to be awarded the Police Combat Cross; and well-earned!

After 11 years as a Detective working in the Narcotics Unit, on October 21, 1983 McBride was reassigned back to uniform patrol in the North Command. He received his first promotion to the rank of Sergeant on October 13, 1989 earning $47,401 and was transferred to the 2nd precinct as a patrol supervisor. His second promotion came on May 3, 1996 when he was promoted to the rank of Lieutenant. Upon this promotion McBride had been working as an Acting Lieutenant in the Communications Division. After the promotion he remained assigned to Communications as a tour supervisor. But, this only lasted for 5 months because on October 2, 1996 Lt McBride was reassigned to the Field Services

Deputy Chief William W. McBride (cont.)

Bureau as a city-wide patrol lieutenant. On February 22, 1999 Lt McBride was transferred to duty in the 4th precinct.

Bill's continuing efforts toward studying for promotional exams was well worth the time. On July 3, 2002 Lt McBride was promoted to the rank of police Captain and was assigned to the Support Services Bureau to obtain New York State Accreditation for the Yonkers Police Department. He was also placed in charge of updating the Department's Policy and Procedures manual.

Later, after a year working from the Field Services Bureau, on September 24, 2004 Commissioner R. Taggart selected and promoted Capt. McBride to the position of Deputy Chief. As Deputy Chief McBride was in charge of the Inspectional Services Bureau which incorporates Internal Affairs, Fleet Services, Fiscal Services, Records Division and the Planning Unit.

Chief McBride is the recipient of several Department awards including a Combat Cross, 3 Commendations, and 6 Certificates of Excellent Police Work. He also was awarded 2nd Place Journal News Award (Macy Award). His daughter Kim Hettwer is an investigator with the New York State Police.

Deputy Chief William W. McBride, whose hobby was collecting photographs of trains from across the country and actually wrote and had published a book about trains, retired from the police department on his 61st birthday, March 15, 2007.

CAPTAIN JOHN H. MacDOUGALL

APPOINTED: March 7, 1969
RETIRED: March 7, 2003

John H. MacDougall was born in Utica, NY on October 16, 1945. John was of Scottish ancestry due to his grandfather having been born in Scotland. John spent his childhood in Utica attending Kemble elementary school and later graduating from Notre Dame High School. As a young man John's family had moved to Yonkers and John began working for the Dept. of Public Works Water Bureau.

John MacDougall was appointed to the Yonkers Police Department on March 7, 1969 while residing at 1 Vincent Road. He received his basic police recruit training at the Iona College campus in New Rochelle with an academic curriculum that ran for approximately one month. On April 25, 1969, following recruit graduation, Probationary Patrolman John MacDougall was assigned to patrol duty in the 3rd precinct earning a starting salary of $7,000.

Having a desire to earn a college degree, during his off duty hours John earned a BA degree in Criminal Justice from John Jay College in NYC. On January 1, 1971, following the implementation of a precinct centralization plan where two precincts were closed and two were re-named, PO MacDougall was transferred to patrol in the South Patrol Command at 441 Central Park Ave. On June 17, 1974 MacDougall was transferred to the North Command and was assigned to work from the newly established

Captain John H. MacDougall (cont.)

and federally funded Community Patrol Unit (CPU). Its purpose was to foster closer and more trusting relations with the minority community.

It was about that time that MacDougall became a charter member of the newly organized Westchester County Emerald Society Pipes and Drums Band as a piper.

On September 30, 1983 MacDougall was promoted to the rank of Sergeant earning a salary of $31,082 and was transferred to the Support Services Bureau working in the Planning Unit and Management Information Services (MIS). A part of his responsibilities in this assignment was to assist in the research and preparation of the police department budget, recommending and preparation of new policies and procedures, and the preparation of applications for various local, county, state, and federal financial grants for the police department.

Four years later, on April 26, 1987, Sgt John MacDougall was transferred from the Planning Unit to the City Jail as a Central Booking officer. However, by the end of that year, on December 24, 1987, Christmas Eve, Sgt. MacDougall received an unexpected call from the police commissioner and told to report to his office immediately as he was being promoted to the rank of Lieutenant. Though surprised, it was a wonderful Christmas gift and Sgt MacDougall was promoted to the rank of police Lieutenant earning a salary of $49,386 and was assigned to the Communications Division as a tour supervisor.

Lt MacDougall was determined to again be promoted and spent a great deal of time studying for the anticipated Police Captain's examination. His hard work paid off when he placed #1 on the civil service list and received his promotion to Captain on September 15, 1989 earning $58,969. Once again due to promotion John MacDougall was reassigned, this time to the Field Services Bureau as a city-wide patrol duty captain. However, within six months, on March 30, 1990, Capt. MacDougall was transferred to the 3rd precinct as commanding officer.

Having a background of working in the Planning Unit earlier in his career, on January 1, 1992 Capt. MacDougall was selected to be the new commanding officer of the Planning Unit. But, once again he was transferred back to city-wide patrol duty responsibilities on January 26, 1995. But only two months later, on March 20, 1995, the new police commissioner designated him the commanding officer of the 1st precinct.

Capt. MacDougall, whose son Michael was a NYPD Detective, received his last assignment on October 2, 2000 when he was reassigned to the Special Operations Division as its commanding officer. Capt. John MacDougall retired from the Yonkers Police Department on March 7, 2003, with exactly 34 years of honorable service. But it wasn't very long before John and his wife decided to move to Florida and join many other Yonkers police retirees.

PO PETER R. EISELMAN #203

APPOINTED: March 7, 1969
RETIRED: June 23, 1988

Peter Roy Eiselman was born on Staten Island in NYC on June 17, 1942. As a youngster he attended Willow Road School in Valley Stream, LI, and after his family moved to Yonkers he attended and graduated from Lincoln High School. Prior to the YPD Eiselman worked for the Anchor Motor Co in Tarrytown NY.

Peter Eiselman was appointed to the Yonkers Police Department on March 7, 1969 while residing at 76 DeHaven Drive. He received his basic police recruit training at the Iona College campus in New Rochelle with an academic curriculum that ran for approximately one month. On April 25, 1969, following recruit graduation, Patrolman Eiselman was assigned to patrol duty in the 3rd precinct earning a starting salary of $7,000. On July 10, 1970 Peter Roy, as he was always known, was transferred to the 1st precinct, and on April 15, 1971 he was reassigned to the North Command where he would remain for the rest of his career. Pete always claimed to have made more DWI arrests than anyone due to a tragedy from a DWI occurring to a friend of his.

On October 10, 1987 PO Eiselman, along with other officers, was attempting to arrest a violent male. During the struggle several shots were fired by the suspect and Eiselman was shot in the stomach and his trigger finger was also hit. During award ceremonies held on May 19, 1988 Peter was awarded the departmental Combat Cross for his actions on the day he was shot. He also received the Exchange Club of America Blue and Gold Wounded in Service Award.

Following an examination by the police surgeon PO Peter R. Eiselman was determined to be physically disabled and was retired on an accidental disability pension effective June 23, 1988. Following his retirement Pete worked as the Assistant Director of Security in the Westchester Mall in White Plains for a while and then in January of 2000 moved to Marco Island, Florida. In 2010 he was working as a Realtor in Marco Island, Fla.

PO ROBERT W. COLLINS #573

APPOINTED: March 7, 1969
RETIRED: May 4, 1995

Bob Collins was born in Yonkers NY on January 21, 1943. As a youth he attended PS# 4 elementary school and graduated from Sacred Heart HS. Bob entered the Army in June of 1966 and received his honorable discharge in May of 1968. Prior to the YPD Bob was employed by Morley's Supermarket on Yonkers Ave.

Robert Collins was appointed to the Yonkers Police Department on March 7, 1969 while residing at 68 Bruce Avenue. He received his basic police recruit training at the Iona College campus in New Rochelle with an academic curriculum that ran for approximately one month. On April 25, 1969, following recruit graduation, Probationary Patrolman Robert Collins was assigned to patrol duty in the 2nd precinct earning a starting salary of $7,000.

On January 1, 1971, following the implementation of a precinct centralization plan where two precincts were closed and two were renamed, PO Collins was transferred to patrol in the North Patrol Command at 53 Shonnard Place. About 1974 Collins was assigned to work from the newly established and federally funded Community Patrol Unit (CPU) located at 250 Warburton Ave. Its purpose was to foster closer and more trusting relations with the minority community. "BC," as he was commonly known, responded to a bank robbery in progress on South Broadway on May 15, 1978 along with his partner. A gun battle took place in front of the bank and another officer was shot in the leg. When one of the suspects attempted to flee, Collins and his partner located him and took him into custody. For his actions that day, PO Robert Collins was awarded the police departments Medal of Honor.

On November 18, 1982 Collins was reassigned to the North East Patrol Command where he remained right up to his retirement on May 4, 1995.

LT. EDWARD J. COURTNEY

APPOINTED: March 7, 1969
RETIRED: January 7, 1987

Ed Courtney was born in Yonkers on December 21, 1941. As a youth he attended St. Joseph's elementary school, PS# 81 in the Bronx, Longfellow Jr. High School, and graduated from Yonkers High School. Prior to the YPD Courtney attended Westchester Community College from 1961 to 1963 majoring in business marketing. Following college Ed entered the Army in February of 1964 and was honorably discharged in February of 1966. On his application to the YPD Ed listed his current employment as a police officer with the White Plains P.D. since 1967.

Edward Courtney was appointed to the Yonkers Police Department on March 7, 1969 while residing at 2 Lewis Avenue. He received his basic police recruit training at the Iona College campus in New Rochelle with an academic curriculum that ran for approximately one month. On April 25, 1969, following recruit graduation, Probationary Patrolman Edward Courtney was assigned to patrol duty in the 3rd precinct earning a starting salary of $7,000. On January 1, 1971, following the implementation of a precinct centralization plan whereby two precincts were closed and two were renamed, Courtney was reassigned to the South Patrol Command.

On July 16, 1971 Ed was transferred to the Detective Division, but not as a detective, and was assigned to work in the Youth Division investigating crimes committed by juveniles. However, on February 12, 1972 Ed was officially appointed a Detective in the D.D. On February 17, 1973 while Det. Courtney and his partner were delivering a prisoner to the city jail for booking, they observed through the jail windows that prisoners were roaming around the hallways inside the jail and breaking windows. The prisoners had even armed themselves with revolvers from a storage cabinet. They had come upon a jail break attempt in progress where a jailer and jail matron had been overpowered, assaulted and locked in a cell. Det Courtney and his partner notified headquarters and backup units quickly arrived maintaining an exterior perimeter. Once the prisoners realized they were surrounded they laid down their weapons and returned to their cells. Det Courtney and his partner had prevented a jailbreak.

On August 9, 1974 Det. Courtney was promoted to the rank of Sergeant and was reassigned to the South Command as a uniform patrol supervisor. Sgt Courtney was transferred to the North Command on September 5, 1975 and detailed to work in the Community Patrol Unit (CPU). In November of 1975 he was moved to the South Command for three years until January 1, 1979 when he was transferred to the Planning and Development Unit. Three months later, on March 16, 1979, Sgt. Courtney was designated the commanding officer of this unit. A part of his responsibilities in this assignment was the research and preparation of the police department budget, recommending and preparing of new policies and procedures, and the preparation of application for various local, county, state, and federal financial grants for the police department.

Sgt. Courtney was promoted to the rank of Lieutenant on November 18, 1982 earning $32,391 and was transferred to the North Command to serve as a Zone Lieutenant. In February of 1984 he was moved to the 3rd pct. as a Watch Commander and on July 26, 1985 he was returned to the Planning Unit as their C.O. Lt Courtney was then designated the Acting Director of Civil Defense on Oct. 7, 1985.

Lt Edward Courtney retired from the YPD on January 7, 1987 and would eventually be appointed the Yonkers Deputy Public Works Commissioner.

PO IAN D. COYLE #550

APPOINTED: March 7, 1969
RESIGNED: June 16, 1972

Ian Coyle was born in Warrington, England on May 25, 1945. He was born an American citizen due to his father's citizenship. Upon returning to the USA, young Ian attended St. Joseph's elementary school and graduated from Commerce High School in 1963. Ian joined the Air Force in August of 1963 and was honorably discharged in December of 1966. Prior to the YPD Ian was serving as a White Plains police officer. Ian Coyle was appointed to the YPD on March 7, 1969 while living at 168 Webster Avenue. He received his basic police recruit training at the Iona College campus in New Rochelle with an academic curriculum that ran for approximately one month. On April 25, 1969, following recruit graduation, Patrolman Ian Coyle was assigned to patrol duty in the 3rd precinct earning a starting salary of $7,000. On January 1, 1971, following the implementation of a precinct centralization plan whereby two precincts were closed and two were renamed, Coyle was reassigned to the North Patrol Command. On April 5, 1971 "Ernie, as he was known, was reassigned to the South Command. Ian Coyle, whose father George was a police Garage Attendant and his daughter Dana a police dispatcher, resigned from the YPD on June 16, 1972 to be appointed to the Yonkers Fire Department.

LT. RICHARD P. DOHENY

APPOINTED: July 4, 1969
RETIRED: January 11, 2007

Richard Doheny was born in Yonkers on September 17, 1948. The year before his birth his father had been a Yonkers officer for a short time but returned to his previous employer. Rick attended Sacred Heart school and graduated from Gorton high school in 1966. Prior to the YPD he was employed by Otis Elevator Company as an inventory clerk. Richard Doheny was appointed a "Police Cadet" on September 6, 1967 earning a salary of $2,000 a year. Following completion of the cadet program Richard Doheny was appointed a Police Officer on July 4, 1969 from 133 Shonnard Place with the annual salary of $7,000 per year. The basic police recruit training lasted about a month, and was held on the Iona College campus in New Rochelle. Following his recruit training, on November 24, 1969 PO Doheny was assigned to patrol in the 1st precinct. On September 4, 1972 he was moved to the North Command. He was promoted to Sergeant on March 11, 1985 and was reassigned as a booking officer in Central Booking. On April 24, 1998 Sgt Doheny was promoted to Lieutenant earning $78,602 and was reassigned to the 2nd precinct on patrol. During his last several years in the department "Rick" served as the 2nd precinct executive officer and retired on January 11, 2007. In retirement Rick enjoys his free time playing music with his band.

POLICE COMMISSIONER ROBERT P. TAGGART

APPOINTED: July 4, 1969
RETIRED: November 3, 2006

Bob Taggart was born on March 17, 1949, St. Patrick's Day, in the Bronx, NY. He and his family actually lived on Oak Street in Yonkers but his mother had been spending a great deal of time in the Bronx caring for his grandmother. It was during this time that Bob decided to make his proud entrance. Fortunately his father, Robert, was able to be present that day, considering he was a career Army National Guard soldier and was on active duty very often. Prior to Bob's birth his father had served on active duty during WW 2 and later would also be called to active duty again to serve in Korea during that "war." He would even be called up to active duty during the Berlin Crisis in the Fall of 1961. After a brief time with the family living in Georgia while his dad fought in Korea, the Taggart family returned to Yonkers.

Young Bob received his formal education in several parochial and local schools including, St.

Police Commissioner Robert Taggart (cont.)

Joseph's Elementary School, Longfellow Jr. H.S., Emerson, Saunders, and Yonkers High Schools. While many of his classmates would find interest in various sporting activities, Bob Taggart was more interested in cars and motorcycles. He became aware early that he was mechanically inclined and used that talent to build, repair, and race various vehicles in area competitions. For a time he actually worked as a motorcycle mechanic while still in school. Around this same time he also worked as an ambulance attendant for Yonkers General Hospital. It is believed that early on it became apparent Bob Taggart was not interested in some quiet mundane job; but rather in a job providing some degree of excitement and challenge.

While in his senior year of high school Bob took, and passed, the civil service test for "Yonkers Police Cadet." This was an experimental program that had been created to increase the recruitment of personnel who would earn a college degree and ultimately join the Yonkers Police Department. Young men, 17 or older, were offered the opportunity to take the civil service police officer test. The top candidates were put on a special list for police cadet. Those selected for the cadet position would be appointed as cadets and were guaranteed a police officer position after completion of a two year degree program at Westchester Community College. While residing at 120 Ashburton Avenue Bob was appointed as "Police Cadet" on September 6, 1967 along with eleven other men earning a salary of $2,000. a year. His group was only the second class of cadets ever appointed. For the next two years he and his fellow cadets would work five days a week; four hours a day taking academic courses at Westchester Community College, courtesy of the City of Yonkers, which would lead to an associate's degree, and the second four hours of each day assigned to work at various police commands learning various operations within the police department.

Following his successful completion of the cadet program and graduation from Westchester Community College, and without being required to take additional civil service tests for Police Officer, Bob was appointed a Police Officer on July 4, 1969 with the annual salary of $7,000. per year. He was then presented with the long coveted "silver shield" containing number 581.

Since the state mandated MPTC "recruit school" would not begin until October, Probationary PO Taggart and 5 other recruits were chosen to spend those first few months on patrol as part of a special plainclothes unit called "the mugging" detail working either 10 PM to 6 AM or 6 PM to 2 AM. He hadn't even attended recruit school and yet he was already out on the street on special patrol assignments.

At that time basic recruit training lasted about a month, and was held in Iona College and at Camp Smith. Following his basic recruit training, on November 24, 1969 PO Taggart was assigned to the 2nd precinct on routine patrol under the command of Capt. Michael Ostrowski. However, his stay would be relatively short. After only 10 months, on September 4, 1970, he was reassigned to patrol duties in the 4th precinct at 53 Shonnard Place. Bob was still in the 4th pct when, on January 1, 1971, as part of a major centralization concept, the 1st and the 4th precincts were combined into one. These two combined precincts were referred to as the "North Command' and its boundaries dramatically reconfigured.

The late 1960's and early 1970's were a very tumultuous time for law enforcement. The highly unpopular Viet Nam War was raging and often riotous demonstrators were causing great problems for police agencies across the country. To help deal with these growing disturbances, units such as the uniformed "TPF," Tactical Patrol Force, were organized, trained in riot control, and utilized as a sort of "conditions" car. Whenever an unusual condition arose, TPF was sure to be used to bring the situation

Police Commissioner Robert Taggart (cont.)

under control. The TPF unit was organized under the Special Operations Division. On January 29, 1973 officer Taggart was transferred to the Special Operations Division and afforded the opportunity to be part of this newly organized "Tactical Patrol Force" (TPF). Although he was busy with his duties in the TPF, officer Taggart was not only willing to be involved in those activities sponsored by the PBA and the Westchester County Police Emerald Society, but he was also eager to try something brand new. Such was the case in 1974 when he and a few other officers formed what would later become known the world over as the, "Pipes and Drums of the Police Emerald Society of Westchester County." Though in 1974 this was all still just a dream, Taggart was determined to learn to be the best bagpipe player he could be. He did just that and throughout his career he remained a band member, continuing to play the pipes.

Although the value of the Tactical Patrol Unit, which was part of the Special Operations Division located at 730 East Grassy Sprain Road, was never in question, nonetheless, after about a year in operation the TPF unit was disbanded and PO Taggart was allowed to remain in SOD as a traffic duty officer.

In January of 1976 the Traffic Division was notified that due to personnel shortages one officer would have to be transferred out of the division. On the 17th of that month Bob Taggart was notified that he would be that officer. His next assignment would be to Headquarters Command Division working in the Warrant Squad located within the City Jail on Alexander Street, and his partner was (then) PO Edward Powers. However this assignment would only last 6 months.

On July 1, 1976 officer Taggart was assigned to the plainclothes Anti-Crime Unit. This unit had only been in operation for a relatively short period of time, but it had established itself as an "elite" sought after police unit where those officers looking for the excitement and activity of such a unit, would find it. PO Taggart, who had grown a beard to be more effective on surveillance's, along with the other officers, was responsible for the suppression of street level crimes such as, armed robberies, muggings, burglaries, etc. Being an excellent and active street cop, the high volume of arrests made by this unit was just what Taggart was looking for. He really enjoyed the work. In the Street Crime Unit you were not expected to respond after a crime had occurred. You were expected to search the city using all your skills to detect and stop a crime before or as it occurred. An example of Taggart's innate ability to sense a crime about to happen, occurred on one routine day tour. While patrolling on Bronx River Road Taggart noticed a male exit from a car and approach the entrance to a bank. He also had noted that the male had apparently left the engine of his car running while he walked into the bank. He and his partner PO John Mullins set up surveillance. Within minutes HQ advised that the alarm at the bank, where Taggart and Mullins were watching the suspect, had been triggered. The suspect then exited the bank, jumped into his vehicle and left the area. PO Taggart and his partner followed the male and after a short distance he was stopped and taken into custody. Investigation revealed that the male had been wanted for several bank robberies in the metropolitan area and was attempting to enter and rob this last one without success. That's exactly how a good street crime cop worked.

On January 19, 1979 Bob Taggart achieved a special goal he had set for himself. This came about when he was promoted to the rank of Sergeant at the annual salary of $21,142. He was assigned shield #22 and was reassigned from the Anti-Crime Unit to the North Patrol Command as a patrol supervisor.

Police Commissioner Robert Taggart (cont.)

Although the North Command was large in both the size of its patrol boundaries, it's residential and business population and, there were large numbers of officers to be supervised and train, Sgt Taggart needed more. It was about this time that he became active on his off duty time in the affairs of the Captains, Lieutenants, & Sergeants Association (CLSA) and was elected to the post of Vice President. And yet, with all this, Sergeant Taggart was determined to advance even further in rank. His determination to advance was soon to pay dividends.

On May 1, 1981, having placed #1 on the civil service promotional list for Lieutenant, Sgt. Taggart was promoted to the rank of Lieutenant after serving only 18 months as a sergeant. He received an increase in salary to $23.086. There was no need to familiarize himself with a new work place as he was allowed to remain in the North Command and was designated a Zone Commander. Throughout all this, Lt. Taggart never lost interest in his off duty involvement with the CLSA. In fact, as a lieutenant he was very concerned about the conditions in which police superior officers were required to work and the need for improvement. It was this genuine concern and his natural drive to be involved as much as possible that led him to campaign to be elected as the president of the CLSA. In the fall of 1981 elections were held by the CLSA and Lt. Robert Taggart was elected the 19th president of the Captains Lieutenants & Sergeants Assoc. His term of office began January 1, 1982 and he was detailed to the CLSA on a full time basis so that he could work full time on working to negotiate better wages and working conditions for the association membership. It was here that Lt. Taggart gained a great deal of experience dealing with negotiations, grievance procedures, arbitration, etc., and afforded him access to the mayor, the council members, and the always enlightening political world of Yonkers politics. It was clear to all who knew him that Lt. Taggart was an officer who displayed that type of leadership that was needed in the Yonkers Police Dept. Because of his reputation and after being re-elected in 1983, in March of that year Taggart was selected by Police Commissioner Charles P. Connolly to attend the prestigious National FBI Academy training school for police executives for three months in Quantico, Va. Following the acceptance of his application by the FBI, Lt. Taggart attended and graduated with the 133rd class of the FBI National Academy in June 1983 having greatly enhanced his knowledge in the field of law enforcement. Upon his return to Yonkers he resumed his duties as president of the CLSA. After serving two terms as president he made a decision not to run for re-election and as a result, at the start of 1984, he was reassigned back to uniform patrol to serve as a Zone Commander in the 3rd precinct at 435 Riverdale Avenue.

Taggart resumed his patrol lieutenant duties with his usual enthusiasm, but had also continued his studies for further promotion. To the surprise of very few, and for the second time, he placed # 1 on the promotion list and was promoted to the rank of Captain on February 8, 1985 with an annual salary of $44,255. Having received this promotion at the young age of 35 years, it is believed that Captain Taggart is the youngest man to achieve that rank in the history of the department. As was tradition, regardless of rank or capability, Captain Taggart was assigned to the Field Services Bureau as the patrol Duty Captain with city wide responsibilities. The following year in January of 1986 Capt. Taggart was designated commanding officer of the 4th precinct at 53 Shonnard Place. Though the assignment was a challenging one due to the complexities of the problems that existed within the precinct boundaries, the captain

Police Commissioner Robert Taggart (cont.)

operated his command very efficiently with the respect and cooperation of his officers and the confidence of the public his police officers served.

When Capt. Taggart took command of the 4th precinct, the departments Emergency Service Unit (ESU) and its personnel were operating from both the 4th precinct and the 2nd precinct. The captain quickly realized that administration and management of the ESU from two locations caused unnecessary difficulties in command and control. He recommended that all ESU personnel and equipment be centrally located in the rear of the 4th precinct and operate from that command. His recommendation was approved and implemented. In addition to his command responsibilities the captain felt very strongly that all his personnel should be provided with the very best equipment available to do their very difficult job.

It was with this in mind that he served on the committee to identify resources in order to provide new bullet resistant vests for all members of the police department. He also served as the chairman of the committee that was charged with researching the value of the department switching from the S&W .38 caliber revolver to a semi-automatic pistol, capable of much greater firepower with the reduced need to reload. The major concern, in addition to funding, was a question of the semi-automatic pistols reliability. However, as a result of Capt. Taggart's in depth research and convincing proposals, the police department ultimately did change from the revolver to the Glock semi-automatic pistol and received additional new body armor as well.

Around that same time the Police department had been targeted for a study by an outside consulting firm that ultimately criticized police operations. Though there was room for improvement, the report was considered inaccurate in many respects. For those who held leadership positions within the department they knew that the department did need reform. As a result an internal committee was formed consisting of people within the department to study police operations and were charged with the responsibility of making long-term plans to increase the efficiency of the entire police department. When the committee was named, it was no surprise when Capt. Taggart was one of those chosen to serve. This committee recommended better training programs, an expanded system for receiving civilian complaints, suggested areas where we might be able to apply for grants, and recommended revitalization of precinct community councils. They also recommended that precinct Captains be given greater discretion in setting up patrol strategies and that the department work harder to achieve better relations with the community. And, in what was seen as a key element to success, Capt. Taggart and his fellow committee members strongly recommended that the leadership of the Police department should make the decisions effecting the police department and that they not be made by politicians. Making these recommendations was relatively easy. Effective implementation was quite another thing. However, after some time they were quite successful.

Capt. Taggart continued to serve as the C.O. of the 4th precinct for nearly five years when, following the retirement of Deputy Chief John F. McMahon, PC Joseph V. Fernandes appointed Taggart

Police Commissioner Robert Taggart (cont.)

to the position of Deputy Chief on December 1, 1989 with a salary of $78,250. a year. During the ceremony, which was held in the City Hall Council chambers, Mayor Nicholas Wasicsko commented, "*I think that Deputy Chief Taggart will stand up as a great role model.*"

In referring to DC Taggart's earlier unsuccessful run for election as the Putnam County Sheriff that same year, the mayor said, "*Putnam County's loss is our gain.*" And City Manager Neil DeLuca was quoted as saying, "*Bob Taggart is one of the most key people in the police department.........*" When fellow officers were interviewed regarding the new chief they described Taggart as being "*....a quintessential professional whose integrity has garnered respect during his career.*" When a reporter asked the new deputy chief what changes he had planned, his answer was to the point: "*What I'd like to be is somebody who can give strong direction to the officers into the 1990's.*"

At that time there still remained one vacancy for a third Deputy Chief and Chief Taggart was placed in command of both the Support Services Bureau and the Field Services Bureau until such time as another deputy was designated. The thought of being placed in charge of two bureaus at once might seem daunting to some, but Chief Taggart managed them both very efficiently and without a problem. When the vacant chief's position was filled by the appointment of Donald Christopher, Chief Taggart was then assigned the Field Services Bureau.

In August of 1990 Robert K. Olson was appointed Police Commissioner and at that time a new police headquarters and court facility, which was named the Cacace Center, was being constructed at 104 South Broadway. Nearly half of this former Saunders HS structure would house a new police headquarters to replace the extremely unsuitable headquarters at 10 St.Casimir Avenue. The difficult task of planning for all the needs of the police department in the new building and formulating a plan to move the entire headquarters operation and all of its units and divisions into the new building had earlier been assigned to a committee chaired by Chief Taggart. Despite the many challenges that arose, Chief Taggart's recommendations to Comm. Olson resulted in a relatively smooth transition into the new facility.

In early 1991 DC Taggart was successful in obtaining approval to change the police issue .38 S&W 4" service revolver to a Glock semi-automatic pistol. He allocated money in the budget for the department wide transition from revolver to semi-automatic pistol and the necessary training required for every sworn member to qualify with the new Glock. It was not easy to convince everyone that it was the smart thing to do. Many held on to the traditional idea that *"there's nothing wrong with what we have."* In the end it proved to be a change needed to improve officer safety and capability.

In late 1991 another innovative and historic change occurred when PC Olson directed that the police department change from a rotating work schedule to "Steady Tours." For over one hundred years the YPD had been working on a rotating work schedule and to devise a plan to make this change was certainly challenging. And as such, as nearly all expected, Chief Taggart was the chief assigned the responsibility of proposing a plan that would not only work but, in the interest of cooperation, one that the PBA and CLSA would agree to. Once again he researched, recommended, and implemented his plan to almost everyone's satisfaction. It was clear that Chief Robert Taggart had established a reputation as being the "go to guy" if you wanted something done, and done right. That being said, in the police department there are no guarantees.

On March 17, 1995 a new police commissioner was appointed and with him came many dramatic changes. For the new commissioner's own personal reasons several high ranking officers and many other

Police Commissioner Robert Taggart (cont.)

officers in sensitive positions were transferred the very same day the new commissioner took office. Chief Taggart was among those wide sweeping changes and was reassigned as a captain in command of the Special Operations Division.

Taggart accepted his new assignment without complaint and, in one way, actually enjoyed the opportunity to be back among the officers of SOD which now included the Emergency Unit, K-9 Unit, Hack Unit, Abandoned Auto Unit, and the Traffic Motorcycle Unit. Being a motorcycle enthusiast he quickly became police motorcycle certified and commanded street operations from the seat of his police motorcycle.

In 1997 following a citywide election for mayor Deputy Chief Donald Christopher was appointed by the new mayor to be the new police commissioner and following the retirement of Deputy Chief John Duffy, PC Christopher corrected a clear injustice. On October 3, 1997 he re-appointed Bob Taggart to the rank of Deputy Chief in command of the Support Services Bureau. The annual salary at that time was $103,000.

On April 14, 2000, following the retirement of Comm. Joseph Cassino, PBA president Det. Charles Cola was appointed by Mayor John Spencer as the new police commissioner. Following council confirmation, two of his early orders were to designate Chief Taggart as First Deputy Chief of the department and to move him from command of Support Services Bureau to the Field Services Bureau. At the time there was a vacancy for a third deputy and as a result Chief Taggart was designated not only Chief of Field Services, but also Chief of Investigative Services, i.e.; Chief of Detectives. Command of either of these commands is an awesome responsibility; being in command of both could be overwhelming to a lesser man. However, Chief Taggart managed the daily needs of each bureau efficiently and effectively, working twice as hard of course, but experiencing little difficulty.

On April 14, 2000, following the retirement of Comm. Joseph Cassino, PBA president Det. Charles Cola was appointed by Mayor John Spencer as the new police commissioner. Following council confirmation, two of his early orders were to designate Chief Taggart as First Deputy Chief of the department and to move him from command of Support Services Bureau to the Field Services Bureau. The establishment of this new title occurred on May 12, 2000. At the time there was a vacancy for a third deputy and as a result Chief Taggart was designated not only Chief of Field Services, but also Chief of Investigative Services, i.e.; Chief of Detectives. Command of either of these commands is an awesome responsibility; being in command of both could be overwhelming to a lesser man. However, Chief Taggart managed the daily needs of each bureau efficiently and effectively, working twice as hard of course, but experiencing little difficulty.

On April 1, 1999 the title Deputy Chief was officially changed in the city budget to the new designation of, Deputy Commissioner. Despite the change, all chiefs were still universally referred to by everyone as Deputy Chiefs or simply "Chief."

Upon the retirement of Comm. Charles Cola on Sept 19, 2003, Cola recommended to Mayor Spencer that D.C. Robert Taggart be his replacement. Cola reportedly stated, "*There is no one more knowledgeable than Chief Taggart in regards to the Yonkers Police Dept.*" Taggart was contacted by the mayor that same day and offered the position of police commissioner, and he accepted. Of course officially the appointment still needed confirmation by the city council.

Police Commissioner Robert Taggart (cont.)

Mayor Spencer appointed Bob Taggart to the position of Police Commissioner effective 1600 hours Sept 19, 2003. When asked for a comment by the news media Comm Taggart was quoted as saying, "*I was very pleased to find out that the mayor has selected me to run the police department. I intend to take the reins of the police department and run it the way I think it should be run now, and for the future*." On this same date Commissioner Taggart issued this, his first, memo to the entire police department;

"All personnel are hereby notified and advised that this day, September 19, 2003, the Honorable John D. Spencer, Mayor of the City of Yonkers has appointed me to the position of Police Commissioner. I have assumed command of the department as of 1600 hours. All orders, commands, directives, policies and procedures established by Commissioner Charles A. Cola, shall remain in effect unless otherwise directed through this office. I would like to take this opportunity to thank Commissioner Cola for the excellent service that he has rendered to the department and wish him well in his retirement. I would also like to thank the many men and women of the department for the spirit of cooperation that has been afforded during his tenure. I am confident that we can continue to build upon his legacy to maintain the high standards of service to our community and I look forward to leading this fine department."

On Sept 26, 2003 the ceremonial swearing in of Commissioner Taggart took place in the River Front Library. It was attended by all YPD commanding officers, police department personnel, city, county, state and federal dignitaries, local political officials and civic leaders. Following his ceremonial swearing in Commissioner Taggart gave the following address to the audience:

"Before I start, I have to tell everybody that today is September 26th; it is a most important day in my life. And no Mr. Mayor, it's not because today is the day I was made Police Commissioner. Thirty-three years ago, on this very day, that beautiful lady and I got married; (pointing to his wife) today is our 33rd wedding anniversary. And I want to thank her for all her support that I have received over those 33 years.

"I also want to thank all the law enforcement ethnic societies that came out and responded to my invitation to be here this morning. I want you to know that I recognize that your participation in those societies is a reflection of your commitment and your pride in being a police officer - and I know that it's also a reflection of your commitment to community because those societies do good work in the communities where they operate, and I want to thank you for joining me here today - and more importantly, - I want to thank you for the commitment to your profession and to your communities. Thank you for coming.

"I am extremely grateful to all the law enforcement executives who came out to be here with me this morning. I thank you for coming. I am so proud that you people came out here to show the world - in essence - that law enforcement is combined, to working together to make good things happen, I am grateful for your attendance here this morning. And of course, Mr. Mayor, I want to thank you for your decision to make me Police Commissioner today and allow me to lead this fine department.

"You see, decisions are what it's all about, that's what's important; making decisions. I recently listened to a speech by President Clinton and in that speech he said something to the effect of this:

Police Commissioner Robert Taggart (cont.)

'Leaders of government do not cause economic decline, they do not cause markets to fall or the quality of life to deteriorate any more than they can cause prosperity or peace. All they can do is make decisions and all we can ask them to do is to make good decisions. To make the kinds of decisions that will be good for the greatest number of people. It is the long-term effect of those decisions that determine our destiny.'

"Many years ago, here in the City of Yonkers, its people and its Police Department were in dire straits. The city was at the verge of bankruptcy. People were suffering from high crime; the department was in trouble. The Police department was under funded, undermanned, poorly trained, ill equipped and seriously at odds with the community that we were trying to serve. This city was regarded as a high crime area and Police Officers, frustrated by the lack of community support, had to do whatever they could to suppress crime. Despite our lack of resources our Police Officers were, well, let us say resourceful.

"To some extent we got the job done, we did the best we could in bad times. But along the way we built barriers between ourselves and the community that we were trying to serve. It was not easy for us to get our jobs done without the support of the people that we desperately needed. We desperately needed our leaders to make the right kinds of decisions. But instead of receiving righteous decisions we got political interference. The Police department was targeted for a study by an outside consulting firm that criticized our operations. That report was inaccurate in many respects. But those of us that held leadership positions within the department knew that the department needed reform.

"That was about 14 years ago. A committee was formed from people within the department to study issues for the department. An internal committee was formed, we were charged with the responsibility of making long-term plans to make this a better department. The committee included myself and former Commissioner Cassino, former Commissioner Don Christopher and others. We put together a list of recommendations. We recommended better training programs, expanded system for receiving civilian complaints, we suggested areas where we might be able to apply for grants, we recommended revitalization of the community councils, and I want to mention too that the community councils are here today and they have been revitalized and are doing vital work for this city. They are keeping the Police Department in touch with our citizens.

"We recommended that precinct Captains be given greater discretion in setting up patrol strategies. And we recommended that we work hard to get better relations with our community. Most of all we recommended that the leadership of the Police department should make the decisions in the department. Police decisions should be left to police professionals; let us do our job.

"One of our strong recommendations was to work to build better community relations. To that end another committee was formed and this was the committee to improve relations for the department. Persons representing minority groups, women, the clergy, homeowners, were selected to serve with us and to make these recommendations. The committee included:

"Burt Wallace of NAACP, Pat Sadler from the YWCA, Mr. Crawford from the Human Rights Commission, my good friend Wilda Mejias from the Spanish Progress Foundation, Gene Capella, the Reverend Evans, police personnel and community residents. And again a list of recommendations were made, these included the drafting of a mission statement, a recommendation for civilian review of the internal affairs process and a recommendation that we set standards for this department that would be high enough that to allow us to receive accreditation from the Department of Criminal Justice Services. Shortly

Police Commissioner Robert Taggart (cont.)

after those submissions were made they were submitted. Nearly thirteen years ago, I was approached and asked to become the Deputy Chief of the Police Department to make the things that were contained in those recommendations a reality.

"I knew that it would be a daunting task, you know it's very easy to make recommendations, it's quite something else to make them happen. It's very difficult to make things happen at times. I thought that the risk of failure would be very high and that in the final analysis I would be made to look bad. But I love my Police department and wanted to do what I could.

"I thought of the words of Abraham Lincoln, he said that, the probability that we might fail in the struggle ought not to deter us from the support of a cause we know is just.'That is why I accepted the assignment and began a long and difficult task of working towards improving this department. Early on we made some progress but it was very slow. Then about 7 ½ years ago we had a new Mayor elected, Mayor John Spencer and he had to make decisions, because what happens in the world is determined by the decisions. He had to make the decisions, about who would run the Police Department and he decided to allow the Police professionals within the department to run the department. What a novel idea! Let the police leaders lead the department. Although we've had succession of police commissioners his decision to allow those Police Commissioner's to run the department really drove us to be a better department today. And I am pleased to tell you that, that succession of Police Commissioners allowed me to serve as second as command all during that 7-½ years. I am very proud that I have been allowed to serve with such great men as Joe Cassino, Don Christopher, and Charlie Cola because together we just tried to make the right decisions.

"In a little over 7 years we saw our relationship with the community improve. We saw our department grow from a department of fewer than 500 officers to a department of more than 600 officers. Today we have better training, better equipment, newer equipment, we saw a communications system that was stalled in developed, finally come on line. We just tried to do our job better with the professionals leading us. I think we did do the job better.

"Economic development in the city improved. If you have about 2 ½ hours to listen to me I'll tell you a story about how a good police department can drive the economy of a city, but I'll spare you that for now.

"The goals that I thought would be so elusive just became so much easier with the professionals that were running the job. One by one each one of those recommendations has been implemented. Even the very difficult task of attaining DCJS accreditation was achieved just earlier this month and I have to tell you that we've been certified as an 'Accredited Agency" and fewer than 20% of the Police departments in this state can make that claim. And I am very proud of the work that our officers did to make that happen.

"Now the Mayor has made another decision. He has decided to allow me to run this fine department and I can only hope that the decisions that I make will serve to improve the quality of life for the citizens of Yonkers. As your new leader, to our Police Officers I will say this; from O'Dell to Radford from the Hudson to the Bronx River, we are here to protect our people, the good people of the City of Yonkers, and we will do our job just that way; we will protect our people. From East Side to West side all around town there are good people and good people that deserve our protection, deserve our service and we will deliver it to them. All we need to do to get the support of the community is decide, decide that

Police Commissioner Robert Taggart (cont.)

you want their support and work with the community that you serve. And to get that support all you need to do is to decide that you're going to act professionally. That you're going to perform your job in a righteous manner. You will exercise your duties without favor or prejudice.

"Our community support is very high. I'll tell my police officers our community support is high! It is high in communities where you may not think it so! We're doing a good job all over this city and all over the city people just want to be safe, that's all they want. The good people of our community support us. If it were not so we could not have achieved all that we have. What we need to do is build more bridges, better bridges to the community that we serve. In your daily work as a police officer you have to decide, who are good people? And who are the doers of evil. That is not an easy task. To make that determination you have to rely upon your training. You cannot decide that on the basis of the color of their skin, their economic status, or the neighborhood in which they live. You need to understand the content of their character and that's not easy. I don't expect it to be easy; you'll make mistakes. I'll make mistakes. But if we're well trained and rightly motivated, good things will happen to this Police department and will continue to happen to this city. This Police department has gotten better and the city has gotten better.

"Years ago it was a city where bad decisions were made and bad things happened in the city economically, development wise. And in the long run bad things happened to the Police department. Take a look around now at what's happened in the City.

"Over the last 7 years we've seen incredible revitalization. I'd invite the people in this audience today that think they know Yonkers or think that they know what the West side of Yonkers is like, when you leave here take a walk around and see what's going on in this city. The development is fabulous, this city is going places, and you can be part of it. And I'm so proud to be the Police Commissioner at a time then good things are going to happen. They are going to happen for this city and they're going to happen for our police officers.

"Our police officers need to know that the destiny of this city and the quality of our community is directly tied to their own destiny. If the city prospers then department will prosper. And that is what we need to work for making this a better and safer city. We have portions of our city where the economic conditions are already somewhat better than they are here but I have to tell you something, if we don't diligently patrol those neighborhoods, if we don't develop strategies for our better communities, we'll simply trade one bad neighborhood for another. We need to redouble our efforts in those communities to make sure that the quality of life doesn't decline in neighborhoods where the quality of life today is pretty good and I think we can do that. At this juncture if we fail to make good decisions bad things will happen. To prevent crime, to win friends for the department, to discourage rowdies seriously, discouraging rowdies doing away with disorder will all serve to make our community better and make our department more well liked.

"To those in the department who might scoff at the idea that we can be professional, let me tell you this, 99% of our police officers hit these streets every day and they risk their lives, they put their lives on the line, they do their job right, they do it professionally and when you don't act professionally you cast dispersions upon those good officers. I will tell you this; If you besmirch the name of this Yonkers Police Department, I will have little forgiveness for that. I expect you to do your job.

Police Commissioner Robert Taggart (cont.)

"To our newly appointed detectives, I will tell you that you were selected to be Detectives because you have proved yourselves by virtue of your work and your service not only to your department but to your fellow police officers, don't forget where you come from. The uniform officers on this job deserve your support and your respect. They're out there every day doing a difficult job and you are the persons that will have the skills to assist them, that's what it's all about backing up the uniform people, that's why you've been made detectives. God bless you that's what I want you to do. Remember where you came from.

"To our newly appointed supervisors, you now have to make decisions. You will have to make decisions that will affect the safety of our city, the careers of your subordinates and the reputation of this department. In making those decisions use your leadership skills, remember our officers are dedicated to each other and dedicated to the task at hand. They don't need to be pushed, they need to lead and you need to lead them by your example. If you lead by example, they will follow. Know your job and do it well. That is all we can ask.

"To the law enforcement officials that are here I will tell you that we will cooperate in every way possible to create and protect a better greater community. We will protect the greater community and we'll work together to protect our nation. We'll enhance our intelligence unit and we will gather information and share that information with surrounding communities to the extent that we can. We will continue to support our joint operation task forces and will do our part to protect homeland security.

"To the people of the City of Yonkers I will say this, I have decided that I will do the best to give you the best police department that you can possibly have; I think you already have the best department in the state. We'll make it better I promise you that. We will develop plans to suppress disorderly persons, we'll enhance our domestic violence unit, expand their training. We'll work towards the goal of putting more officers on the street and we'll work very closely with those civic groups and communities groups to keep our city safe.

"And to the criminal element that is here in the city of Yonkers ------I am going to tell you what a criminal once told me, 'Yonkers cops don't play.'We will hunt you down, we will lock you up, we will bring you before the bar of justice, we'll put you away, we don't play.

"And to the Mayor I vow that this day will be the day that you remember as the day you made a good police commissioner. Thank you. People that know me know that I am fond of quoting the great philosophers scientists, and presidents. And so I will leave you with the favorite closing of President George Bush. Thank you, God bless you and God bless America."

During the time that Commissioner Taggart led the Yonkers Police Department he already had put in place those changes that were necessary to move our department forward. While PC Taggart was the Deputy Chief, and upon PC Cola being appointed the YPD commissioner, Cola utilized Taggart and his vision for the department because of the wealth of experience and knowledge Taggart had acquired over the years. So when Bob Taggart was appointed police commissioner many changes were already made based on Taggart's recommendations and most of the department was operating very efficiently.

Although there were many things that Comm. Taggart felt were important, one in particular was to endeavor to try to keep any undue and inappropriate influence being brought to bear from city hall. It seems fair to say he was successful for a few years but toward the end of his third year PC Taggart found himself struggling to hold his ground against outside pressure. Of course in the world of politics this is a

Police Commissioner Robert Taggart (cont.)

prescription for serious problems and which ultimately led to PC Taggart retiring rather than compromise on that which he felt a matter of principle.

And so, after much deliberation but still determined not to compromise on his leadership principals, Police Commissioner Robert Taggart retired from the Yonkers Police Department on November 3, 2006 having completed more than 37 years of honorable service.

It may be of interest to note that after his initial schooling at Westchester Community College, he also attended Mercy College, John Jay College of Criminal Justice, Empire State College, and a University of Virginia Criminal Justice course. He received his Bachelor's degree from the State University of New York.

Some of the police training courses he took were, Sniper team training, NYC Auto Theft School, Motorcycle instructor training, certified Breathalyzer operator, NYS MPTC Crime Prevention Officer's School, FBI Crime Scene Search and Fingerprint Development School, NYS MPTC School for Police Executive Development, NYS MPTC Instructor's Development School, The American Management Association Training Center in NYC, Senior Management Institute for Police at Harvard University and the F.B.I National Academy in Quantico Virginia.

PO WILLIAM J. O'BRIEN #580

APPOINTED: July 4, 1969
RETIRED: January 11, 1997

William John O'Brien was born in the City of Yonkers in a leap year on February 29, 1948. He attended St. Joseph's elementary School and graduated from Sacred Heart High School. Right out of school Bill worked nights operating the elevator in City Hall. He then joined the Yonkers Police Cadet program in September of 1967 and graduated from Westchester Community College with an Associate's degree in Police Science.

Following completion of the Cadet program Bill was appointed a Yonkers police officer on July 4, 1969 while living at 21 Mulford Gardens. He was following a career in law enforcement similar to his father John "Jack" O'Brien who, at that time, was the Undersheriff of Westchester Co. working for then Sheriff Daniel F. McMahon. His younger brother, Ronan, was appointed a police officer in the Westchester Co. P.D. His older brother Jack (deceased) chose to be involved in politics in the City of Yonkers working in City Hall.

Following his basic recruit training Probationary Patrolman O'Brien was assigned to the 3rd precinct earning a starting salary of $7,000 a year, but for only a month. On December 27, 1969 he was reassigned to patrol duty in the 1st precinct at 10 St Casimir Ave. Records indicate he remained there until a precinct centralization plan was implemented on January 1, 1971, and he was reassigned to the North Command.

On May 15, 1974 "OB," as he was frequently nicknamed, was transferred to the plainclothes Youth Division as an investigator investigating crimes by juveniles. At one point while partnered with Carmine Cavallo, it is said that they came across a holdup in progress on Main Street which necessitated the shooting of the suspect by O'Brien. Although the shooting was completely justified, the stress from the incident took its toll on Bill's health for some time.

Having no construction training, but with a can do attitude, Bill served as the contractor and built his own house at 410 Bellevue Avenue, during off duty hours. A house for him and his wife Carol and three girls, Kelly, Kim, and Kerry.

PO O'Brien's knowledge about juvenile law and the family court system made him an asset to the Youth Division, and as such he would remain in the Youth Division right up to his retirement on January 11, 1997 after nearly 28 years; 30 if you count his Cadet time..

At one point during his career Bill lived at 188 Voss Avenue and was well known in the Lake Avenue area. He was a member of the Shamrocks A.C. and the Lakers Club. He was also an active member of the Catholic Slovak Club, in Yonkers and the Habirshaw Club. Bill was a dedicated family man who had one of those infectious smiles and a very outgoing and friendly personality to go with it. Following his retirement Bill and his wife owned and operated O'B's Bar on Morningside Ave. and later on Yonkers Ave. by Trenchard Street, across from the Yonkers Raceway.

Unfortunately Bill became ill and following a serious infection he died on February 21, 2012 at the age of 63 years.

DET. ROBERT J. MOLINARO #643

APPOINTED: July 4, 1969
RETIRED: March 23, 1995

Robert Molinaro was born in Yonkers on May 5, 1940. He attended PS#18, Benjamin Franklin junior HS, and graduated from Yonkers HS. Following school Bob was employed by the US Post Office. He was appointed a police cadet on Sept. 6, 1967 and worked part time with the YPD while attending Westchester Community college. Bob Molinaro was appointed to the Y.P.D. on July 4, 1969 while living at 237 Willow St. He received his recruit training at the Iona College campus in New Rochelle which lasted about a month. Following graduation Bob was assigned to duty in the 4th pct earning $7,000 a year. He worked patrol duty up to the early 1980s when he was transferred to the Crime Analysis Unit. He was very effective in his job and as a result, on July 10, 1987, he was appointed a Detective and remained in Crime Analysis. In the early 1990s PO Molinaro was reassigned to work in the Community Affairs unit where he remained until Jan. 4, 1993 when he was moved into the Detective Division and a general assignment squad. Known as "Molly," Bob Molinaro retired from the YPD on March 23, 1995. Shortly after retiring Bob began working as the Dean of Students in a Catholic high school

---

LT. MICHAEL D. STERN

APPOINTED: July 4, 1969
RETIRED: February 14, 2003

Michael Stern was born in the Bronx on March 4, 1948. Years later he would attend PS# 21 and graduated from Lincoln HS in 1966. Mike took the test for Police Cadet and was appointed a Cadet on Sept. 6, 1967. He was appointed a police Patrolman on July 4, 1969 while living at 10 Jost Place. He attended his recruit training at the Iona College campus and upon graduation was assigned to the 4th pct earning $7,000 a year. Having lost most of his hair early in life, when he was a police officer he was affectionately known as "stymie" from the old "Our Gang" comedies. On Aug. 3, 1973 he was moved to the South Command for 8 years and on February 6, 1981 was selected to work in the Street Crime Unit (SCU). After having to fight to make an arrest, Mike picked up the nickname “Mad Dog.” On Dec. 24, 1987 Stern was promoted to Sergeant and assigned to the Field Services Bureau as a patrol supervisor. On April 25, 1988, Sgt Stern was assigned as the aide to a deputy chief. On March 9, 1990 he was promoted to Lieutenant and assigned to the Records Division as Executive Officer. A series of assignments followed including: the 3rd precinct, to Central Booking, to citywide patrol, and to the Communications Div. where he would eventually serve as their Executive officer. On Jan. 29, 2001 Lt Stern was transferred to the Fleet services Bureau, where he remained right up to his retirement on Feb. 14, 2003.

CAPTAIN JOSEPH S. KOSTIK

APPOINTED: July 4, 1969
RETIRED: February 24, 2006

As you will see, the below Medal of Honor recipient is only one in a family tradition in Yonkers law enforcement. Joseph S. Kostik was born in the City of Yonkers on October 12, 1946. As a youth Joe attended PS# 19, Benjamin Franklin Jr. High School and graduated from Yonkers High School. Following his schooling Joe worked as a Tools and Appliance Parts Advisor for Sears and Roebuck Co.

At one point Kostik took, and passed, the civil service test for "Yonkers Police Cadet." This was an experimental program that had been created to increase the recruitment of personnel who would earn a college degree and ultimately join the Yonkers Police Department. Young men, 17 or older, were offered the opportunity to take the civil service police officer test. The top candidates were put on a special list for police cadet. Those selected for the cadet position would be appointed as cadets and were guaranteed a police officer position after completion of a two year degree program at Westchester Community College. Joe Kostik was appointed as a "Police Cadet" on September 6, 1967 earning a salary of $2,000 a year. For the next two years he and his fellow cadets would work five days a week; four hours a day taking academic courses at Westchester Community College, courtesy of the City of Yonkers, which would lead to an associate's degree, and the second four hours of each day assigned to work at various police

Captain Joseph S. Kostik (cont.)

commands learning various operations within the police department.

Following his successful completion of the cadet program, graduation from Westchester Community College, and without being required to take an additional civil service test, he was appointed a Police Officer on July 4, 1969 while living at 180 Hawthorne Avenue with the annual starting salary of $7,000. per year. Since the state mandated MPTC "recruit school" would not begin until October, Probationary PO Kostik was assigned to various units within the department pending the beginning of recruit school.

At that time basic recruit training lasted about a month, and was held at the Iona College campus in New Rochelle. Following recruit graduation, on November 24, 1969, Patrolman Joseph Kostik was assigned to patrol duty in the 4th precinct. On July 16, 1971 Kostik was appointed a Detective and he was assigned to a squad in the Detective Division. However, on May 15, 1972 Kostik was returned to patrol in the North command. While there he was detailed to be part of the Community Patrol Unit (CPU) which was located at 250 Warburton Ave. This unit was established in the early 1970's with the use of a federal grant and having the objective of improving community relations between the police and the minority community. Kostik and his partner, Robert Collins, continued their usual police work but were required to remain patrolling in CPU designated areas.

PO Kostik and his partner responded to a bank robbery in progress at the Hudson Valley Bank on South Broadway on May 15, 1978. As the robbers tried to make good their escape a gun battle took place with other officers in front of the bank and one of the officers was shot in the leg. As the suspects attempted to escape they split up. After a search Kostik quickly apprehended one and his partner arrested the other. As PO Kostik approached the suspect he located, the male tried to fire his weapon at Kostik but it misfired. He was quickly subdued and placed under arrest. For his actions that day, PO Joseph Kostik was awarded the police departments Medal of Honor. Along with this honor came the designation of "Detective" for the remainder of his career, no matter his assignment.

Joe was a very active police officer who not only did what he was told to do, but often actively initiated police work that resulted in numerous arrests. Kostik was a man with a very outgoing personality, well-liked and respected by his peers and always ready with a joke or prank of some kind. This boundless energy carried over to his athletic abilities. He was not only active on the PBA softball and basketball teams, but was in addition a certified basketball referee.

On May 19, 1978 Joe Kostik was promoted to the rank of sergeant earning a salary of $21,142 a year and was reassigned as a patrol supervisor in the South Patrol Command. Five years later, on October 28, 1983, Sgt. Kostik was transferred back into the Detective Division as a Detective Sergeant and was placed in charge of a squad of detectives. However, his stay there was very brief because on February 17, 1984 he was promoted to the rank of Lieutenant earning a salary of $37,132 a year and was transferred to the 4th precinct to serve as a patrol lieutenant. Again, only 2 weeks later on February 29, 1984, Lt. Kostik was transferred to the 2nd precinct to serve as a watch commander.

Lt. Kostik was very effective as a patrol lieutenant but the Detective Division was shorthanded. As a result, on December 19, 1985, Kostik was returned to the Detective Division as a Detective Lieutenant and again designated the commanding officer of the Narcotics Unit. In March of 1990

Captain Joseph S. Kostik (cont.)

circumstances developed whereby there was no longer a captain in command of the Detective Division. The previous captain, Don Christopher, had been promoted to Deputy Chief and had not been replaced. It was at that time that acting Police Commissioner DeDivitis decided temporarily not to fill that captain's position and instead, on March 16, 1990, he designated Det. Lt. Joe Kostik as the acting commanding officer of the entire Detective Division. Joe held that position for a little over a year, and on July 15, 1991 he was reassigned to serve as the acting commanding officer of the Training Division.

Joe Kostik received his promotion to the rank of police Captain on August 2, 1991 and was officially designated the commanding officer of the Training Division. Two years later, on June 14, 1992, Capt. Kostik was reassigned from Training to the 3rd precinct on Riverdale Avenue as their commanding officer.

On February 17, 1995, following the appointment of a new police commissioner, Capt. Kostik was offered and accepted the position of Deputy Chief and placed in command of all those assigned to the Field Services Bureau. Basically the entire patrol operation. And because the police commissioner trusted Chief Kostik implicitly, on June 5, 1998, he designated Kostik as First Deputy Chief, which was basically the right hand of the commissioner. Kostik was busy at work but also enjoyed his off duty time. Chief Kostik held a Commercial Pilots License and could fly for hire on small charter lines. He was also a CFI, Certificated Flight Instructor.

Following the election of a new city mayor and the retirement of then Comm. Cassino on April 14, 2000, it was expected by some that First Deputy Kostik would be appointed the new police commissioner. That did not happen. Instead the mayor appointed the PBA president to be the new commissioner. The following month, on May 12, 2000, Chief Kostik voluntarily decided to leave his duties as a deputy chief and returned to the rank of captain in command of the Training Division. On January 22, 2004 now Capt. Kostik was placed in command of the Special Operations Division, his last assignment before retiring.

Joe's family tradition in the Yonkers Police Dept. began when his grandfather Joseph Kostik was appointed in 1923 and was later killed in the line of duty, Kostik himself appointed in 1969, his brother Sgt. Richard Kostik in 1971, and his son, Joseph M. Kostik in 2002. During his career he had earned the Medal of Honor, two Commendations, nine Certificates of Excellent Police Work, and a Unit Citation.

Capt. Joseph Kostik retired from the Yonkers Police Department on February 24, 2006. Although Joe loved golf he didn't completely retire. Within a short time he had been hired by the Yonkers Raceway to be the new Director of Security for the Empire City Casino located at the same location. He worked there for a few years before completely retiring.

CAPTAIN FRANCIS J. HOWE

APPOINTED: July 4, 1969
RETIRED: July 12, 1996

Francis Howe was born in Yonkers on February 1, 1948. As a youth Frank attended Holy Trinity parochial elementary school and graduated from Gorton High School in 1966. Prior to applying for a position as a police cadet, Frank worked for the United States Post Office.

At one point Frank took, and passed, the civil service test for "Yonkers Police Cadet." This was an experimental program that had been created to increase the recruitment of personnel who would earn a college degree and ultimately join the Yonkers Police Department. Young men, 17 or older, were offered the opportunity to take the civil service police officer test. The top candidates were put on a special list for police cadet. Those selected for the cadet position would be appointed as cadets and were guaranteed a police officer position after completion of a two year degree program at Westchester Community College. Frank Howe was appointed as a "Police Cadet" on September 6, 1967 earning a salary of $2,000 a year. For the next two years he and his fellow cadets would work five days a week; four hours a day taking academic courses at Westchester Community College, courtesy of the City of Yonkers, which would lead to an Associate's degree, and the second four hours of each day assigned to work at various police commands learning various operations within the police department.

Captain Francis J. Howe (cont.)

Following his successful completion of the cadet program, graduation from Westchester Community College, and without being required to take an additional civil service test for Police Officer, Frank Howe was appointed a Police Officer on July 4, 1969 while living at 63 Vineyard Avenue with the annual starting salary of $7,000. per year. Since the state mandated MPTC "recruit school" would not begin until October, Probationary Patrolman Howe was assigned to various units within the department pending the beginning of recruit school.

At that time basic recruit training lasted about a month, and was held at the Iona College campus in New Rochelle. Following recruit graduation, on November 24, 1969, Patrolman Francis Howe was assigned to patrol duty in the 1st precinct. On February 20, 1972 Frank was moved to the 4th precinct and remained there on patrol until June 20, 1979 when he was reassigned to the North East Command.

Frank Howe was promoted to the rank of Sergeant on September 30, 1983 earning a salary of $31,082 and was reassigned as a patrol supervisor in the North Command. Six months later, on March 2, 1984, Howe was transferred to the Traffic Division on two wheel motorcycle as a traffic unit supervisor.

Less than three years later, on May 23, 1986, Sgt Howe was promoted to the rank of police Lieutenant and assigned to the 3rd precinct. He was later returned to the Special Operations Division/Traffic Division on October 17, 1989 and designated their executive officer. Two years later, on February 9, 1991, Lt Howe was transferred to patrol duty in the citywide Inspectional Services Division.

Lt. Francis Howe was promoted to the rank of Captain on October 18, 1991 and was reassigned as the commanding officer of the Youth Services Division. In this assignment he was responsible for overseeing the investigation of crimes by juveniles, as well as maintaining an active PAL program.

Capt. Francis J. Howe retired from the police dept. on July 12, 1996 and moved to Florida.

DET. SGT. JOSEPH B. RODRIGUEZ #13

APPOINTED: September 12, 1969
RETIRED: July 12, 1996

Joseph Rodriguez was born on June 4, 1948 in the city of Yonkers. As a young boy, Joe attended St. Joseph's elementary school, Sacred Heart High School, and would later graduate from Gorton High School. Prior to his appointment as a Yonkers Police Cadet, Joe was employed by a jewelry store as a watchmaker's apprentice.

Joe took the test for Yonkers Police Cadet and was appointed a cadet on September 9, 1967. As part of the program Cadets were required to attend Westchester Community College four hours a day and work in the YPD for the other four hours assisting and learning about various unit functions. Joe worked in the Bureau of Criminal Identification, Property Clerk, Records Division, Narcotics Unit, and the Intelligence Unit. Upon completing the two-year cadet program he graduated and received an Associate's Degree in Police Science.

Rodriguez was appointed a police Patrolman on September 12, 1969. He attended his basic police recruit training at the Iona College campus in New Rochelle which lasted about a month and upon graduation was assigned to patrol duty in the 3rd precinct earning a starting salary of $7,000 a year. On January 1, 1971, following the implementation of a precinct centralization plan, Rodriguez was reassigned to patrolling the South command. However, he only did that for two weeks because, on July 16, 1972, Joe was appointed a Detective working in the Detective Division. As a detective Rodriguez attended John J. College for Criminal Investigation courses, F.B.I. training courses for Homicide and Sex Crime investigations, and the H. Arrons School for Forensic Hypnosis. He remained a detective for 12 years until October 21, 1983 when, as part of a reorganization of the D.D., he and several other detectives were transferred and Joe returned to patrol duty in the South Command.

PO Joseph Rodriguez was promoted to the rank of Sergeant on April 11, 1988 and was assigned to the Field Services Bureau as a patrol supervisor. In November of that year he was reassigned to patrol in the 1st precinct. The following year, on January 20, 1989, Sgt. Rodriguez was designated a Detective Sergeant and was assigned to the highly prestigious Special Investigations Unit, where some of the most confidential and sensitive investigations were conducted. Later that year, on August 21, 1989, Joe was reassigned to work from the Internal Affairs Division. However, three years later, on November 19, 1992, Sgt. Rodriguez was returned to patrol duty in the Inspectional Services Division. But, it was only two years later, on May 11, 1994, that he was reassigned back to the Detective Division, working as a supervisor in the burglary squad.

Known to his friends as "Joe Rod," throughout his career during his off-duty hours he operated a sign making business out of his basement. Sgt. Rodriguez was well-respected by those who worked for him, and with his easy-going disposition he was well liked as a man and very effective as a supervisor. During his career he earned three departmental Commendations, three Certificates of Excellent Police Work, two Westchester Gannett Macy Awards, and one Police Officer of The Year from the American Legion.

Detective Sgt. Joseph Rodriguez retired from the Yonkers Police Department on July 12, 1996. Unfortunately Joe became ill and after a long hard fight died on November 18, 2014.

PO ROBERT E. WILLIAMS #584

APPOINTED: September 12, 1969
RETIRED: January 4, 1990

Robert Williams was born in the City of Yonkers on July 22, 1948. As a youth Bob attended PS# 24, and later graduated from Gorton high school. Prior to him applying to be a Yonkers Police Cadet, Bob was employed by the P&H service station on the Nepperhan Avenue. Bob took the test for Yonkers Police Cadet and was appointed on September 9, 1967. Upon completing the two-year cadet program he was appointed a police Patrolman on September 12, 1969 while living at 243 Woodland Avenue. He attended his basic police recruit training at the Iona College campus which lasted about a month and upon graduation was assigned to patrol duty in the 4th precinct earning a starting salary of $7,000 a year. On March 23, 1977 Bob Williams injured his knee while on-duty but continued to work. However, he had been suffering with back pain for some time and on October 21, 1982 he had spinal surgery to correct the condition. Following his rehabilitation, on February 28, 1983 he was reassigned from the North Command to the Crime Analysis Unit where he was allowed to work steady days. PO Williams was returned to patrol duty in the 4th precinct on July 1, 1986 and four years later, on July 4, 1990, he retired from the YPD on a disability pension.

PO RONALD J. BLOSE #175

APPOINTED: January 9, 1970
RETIRED: January 17, 1992

Ronald Blose was born in the City of Yonkers on October 22, 1943. He attended St. Joseph's elementary school, Longfellow Jr. HS, and graduated from Saunders HS in 1961. Ron entered the Army in March of 1963 and was honorably discharged in March of 1966. Prior to the YPD Ron was employed as an Offset Pressman in Irvington NY. Ronald Blose was appointed to the Y.P.D. on Jan. 9, 1970 while living at 1285 Saw Mill River Rd, in Yonkers. He attended his recruit training at the Iona College campus in New Rochelle, whose academic curriculum ran from March 30 through May 12, 1970. On May 14, 1970, following his graduation, PO Blose was assigned to patrol duty in the 4th pct. Over the years, Ron was transferred a number of times; on Nov. 6, 1970 he was transferred to the 3rd pct, on Jan. 1, 1971, to patrol in the South Command, on Jan. 1, 1979 to the Special Operations Division, on May 18, 1979 back to the South Command, on Mar. 18, 1981, to patrol in the North Command, on July 1, 1991 to the 1st precinct, but detailed to the Medical Control Unit. PO Ronald Blose retired from the Yonkers Police Department on Jan. 17, 1992.

PO GRACE E. McARDLE #151

APPOINTED: January 9, 1970
RETIRED: December 31, 1981

The daughter of Yonkers PO James Lynn, Grace Lynn McArdle was born in Yonkers on Aug. 12, 1937 and attended local schools. Grace was appointed to the YPD on Jan. 9, 1970, living at 112 Oliver Ave. and was issued her father's police shield #151. She received her recruit training at the Iona College campus in New Rochelle, which ran from March 30 to May 12 of 1970. Following her graduation Policewoman Lynn (she was not yet married) was assigned to the 2nd pct on May 14, 1970 but actually worked out of the Youth Div. Two years later, on Feb. 10, 1972, she was assigned to work in the Planning and Research Unit. On Jan. 29, 1974, her official title had already been changed from Policewoman to Police Officer, and she was transferred to the North Command. A good part of the time assigned to the North Command was spent working on patrol in the Community Patrol Unit (CPU). On June 20, 1979 Grace was reassigned to work in the N/E Patrol Command. Five days later, on June 25, 1979, she sustained a serious back injury while on duty and was placed on the disabled list and never returned back to work. PO Grace McArdle was granted a disability pension, effective December 31, 1981. Officer McArdle's father was PO James Lynn Sr., and her brother was PO James Lynn Jr. Upon her retirement, she worked as the secretary to the director of housing at St. Christopher's Inn at Graymoore in Garrison, NY. She then moved to Zephyrhills, Florida to enjoy her retirement and then moved to Universal City, Texas in 2013. Ret PO Grace McArdle died on January 31, 2016

PO ERNEST V. BIERMAN #716

APPOINTED: January 9, 1970
RETIRED: January 9, 1990

Ernest Bierman was born in Yonkers on Jan. 19, 1944. His family must have moved to the Bronx because he attended St. Jerome's elementary school and St. Michael's Academy and after returning to Yonkers, graduated from Lincoln HS. Ernie entered the Navy in July of 1964 and was honorably discharged in July of 1967. Prior to his interest in the YPD Ernie had worked for the NY Telephone Co. in the Bronx. Ernest Bierman was appointed to the Y.P.D. on Jan. 9, 1970, while living at 20 Yale Ave. in Ossining, N. Y. Bierman received his recruit training at the Iona College campus in New Rochelle. Upon graduation, on May 14, 1970 Prob. Ptlmn. Bierman was assigned to patrol duty in the 3rd pct earning $8,000 a year. On Jan. 29, 1974 he was transferred to the Communications Division serving as a dispatcher. Ernest Bierman, who was well-liked by his coworkers and had a very easy-going personality, was transferred back to patrol duty in the 1st precinct on September 25, 1987. Bierman retired from the Yonkers Police Department on January 9, 1990, exactly 20 years from the day of his appointment. It was said that at one point during his retirement he lived in Nevada and worked as a US Marshal and Federal Court Officer in their federal court system.

PO GARY T. McDONALD #589

APPOINTED: January 9, 1970
RESIGNED: December 15, 1970

Gary McDonald was born in the City of Yonkers on July 8, 1946. He attended St. Barnabas elementary school in the Bronx and graduated from Lincoln high school in Yonkers. Gary entered the Army in July of 1963 and was honorably discharged in July of 1966. He was previously employed by the New York Telephone Company in the Town of Greenburgh. Gary was appointed to the Yonkers Police Department on January 9, 1970, attended his basic police recruit training at the Iona College campus in New Rochelle with an academic curriculum that ran from March 30 through May 12, 1970. On May 14, 1970, following his recruit graduation, he was assigned to the 4th precinct on patrol duty, earning a starting salary of $8,000 a year. His brother was Yonkers Detective Joseph McDonald. PO Gary McDonald resigned from the Yonkers Police Dept. on December 15, 1970 in order to be appointed a police officer in the town of Clarkstown, New York.

PO EUGENE J. KOVALSKY #594

APPOINTED: January 9, 1970
RETIRED: June 11, 1990

"Gene" Kovalsky was born in Yonkers NY on January 26, 1947. He attended Holy Trinity elementary school and graduated from Sacred Heart High School. Prior to the Y.P.D. Eugene worked as an auto mechanic on Tuckahoe Rd. Kovalsky was appointed to the Yonkers Police Dept. on January 9, 1970 while residing at 78 Mansion Ave. Kovalsky received his basic police recruit training at the Iona College campus in New Rochelle where the academic curriculum ran from March 30 to May 12, 1970. Following graduation on May 14, 1970 PO Kovalsky was assigned to patrol in the 3rd precinct earning a starting salary of $8,000 a year. On October 19, 1971 Gene was transferred to the Special Operations Division Traffic motorcycle unit. Gene was a good rider but was an even better motorcycle repairman. As such he was soon assigned to the Truck, Weight, & Scales unit. While in this unit he also spent time on miscellaneous repairs and service to motorcycles as needed. Eugene Kovalsky retired from the Y.P.D. on June 11, 1990. He moved to Tennessee and drove tractor trailers and for a time opened a motorcycle repair business. Following a lengthy illness Ret PO Eugene Kovalsky died on July 11, 2007. He was 60 years old.

DET. THOMAS M. CHAMBERLAIN #691

APPOINTED: January 9, 1970
RETIRED: January 9, 2003

Tom Chamberlain was born in Yonkers on April 8, 1946. He attended St. Joseph's school and graduated from Saunders HS in 1964. Tom entered the Army in Nov. of 1965 and was honorably discharged in Nov. of 1967. Prior to the YPD Tom was employed by the U-Vend Co. Inc. on Yonkers Ave. Tom was appointed to the Y.P.D. on Jan. 9, 1970 from 50 Coolidge Ave. He attended his recruit training at the Iona College campus, located in New Rochelle. The recruit academic curriculum ran from March 30 to May 12, 1970. Following graduation, on May 14, 1970, PO Thomas Chamberlain was assigned to the 3rd pct, earning $8,000 a year. On Jan. 1, 1971 Tom was reassigned to the North Patrol Command. Throughout 1977, a series of murders and shootings were being perpetrated by a suspect known only as, The Son of Sam, later identified as David Berkowitz. PO Chamberlain and his partner were instrumental in identifying the suspect by name, and that he lived in Yonkers. This information later led to the arrest of the infamous killer. On September 2, 1977, following the arrest of David Berkowitz, Tom was appointed a Detective in the D.D. He remained there throughout the remainder of his career working the last few years as the Detective Division desk officer. Tom retired on January 9, 2003.

PO WALTER R. BRESNAHAN #585

APPOINTED: January 9, 1970
RESIGNED: October 22, 1970

Walter Bresnahan was born in the City of Yonkers on November 7, 1944. As a youth he attended St. Peter's elementary school and later graduated from Yonkers high school. Walter entered the Army on August 10, 1964 and was honorably discharged on July 21, 1966. Previous to the YPD he was employed by the Con Edison Company in Eastview New York. Walter was appointed to the Yonkers Police Department on January 9, 1970 while residing at 504 Warburton Ave. He received his basic police recruit training on the Iona College campus in New Rochelle whose academic curriculum ran from March 30, through May 12, 1970. Following his recruit graduation Patrolman Bresnahan was assigned to patrol duty in the 3rd precinct on May 14, 1970 earning a starting salary of $8,000 a year. Five months later, and for unknown reasons, Police Officer Walter Bresnahan resigned from the Yonkers Police Department, effective October 22, 1970.

DET. WALTER P. MORAY #691

APPOINTED: January 9, 1970
RETIRED: January 27, 2006

Walter Moray Jr, known to everyone as "Butch," was born in the City of Yonkers on July 14, 1947. Butch attended St. Mary's elementary school and graduated from Yonkers High School. Prior to the police department Moray was employed by the Westchester Paint & Dry Wall Co. in Yonkers.

Walter Moray was appointed to the Yonkers Police Department on January 9, 1970 while residing at 141 Oak Street. He attended his basic police recruit training at the Iona College campus in New Rochelle with a curriculum that ran from March 30th to May 12, 1970. Following graduation Probationary Patrolman Walter Moray was first assigned to patrol duty in the 4th precinct on May 14, 1970 earning a starting salary of $8,000 a year.

Only two years later PO Butch Moray received a big break when he was assigned to the Detective Division on May 15, 1972. However, he was not assigned as a detective and actually worked in plainclothes as an investigator of juvenile crime in the Youth Division. At one point he was utilized as an undercover officer purchasing illegal drugs and developing cases to be brought before a grand jury for indictments. Moray must have made a positive impression because, two years later on March 21, 1975, he was officially appointed a Detective in the Detective Division but assigned to the Narcotics Unit.

Det Moray worked undercover investigations along with his partner, Tony Cerasi, for 15 years making some of the largest illegal narcotic seizures on record along with arresting those involved. In the early years the drug arrests were for relatively small amounts and by local dealers. As time went by Moray and others conducted joint investigations with multiple agencies shutting down illegal international drug operations run by major drug cartels.

On July 13, 1990 Det. Moray was reassigned, as a detective, to the very prestigious Special Investigations Unit which was responsible for the most sensitive investigations, ie; dignitary protection, and organized crime activities. However, this only lasted two months. On September 20, 1990 the unit was disbanded and Moray was returned to the Narcotics Unit.

As new young detectives came and went, some moving into the Detective Division's general assignment squad, Det Moray preferred to remain in Narcotics. There was very little "Butch" Moray didn't know about the illegal use, sale, and distribution of all forms of drugs. He was a wealth of knowledge. And it was this knowledge, not connections that allowed him to spend nearly his entire career in the Narcotics Unit.

After 31 years with the police department, 29 years of which serving as a narcotics Detective, Det. Walter Moray retired from the police department on January 27, 2006.

PO DENNIS P. ALEXA #488

APPOINTED: January 9, 1970
RESIGNED: August 20, 1976

Dennis was born in the City of Yonkers on August 7, 1945, attended St. Mary's elementary school as a youth and graduated from Sacred Heart High School. Shortly after graduating Dennis entered the Navy in September of 1963 and was honorably discharged in September of 1967. Prior to applying to the Y.P.D. Alexa was employed by the Pan American World Airways at JFK airport. Dennis Alexa was appointed to the Yonkers Police Dept. on January 9, 1970 while residing at 59 Radford Street. He received his basic police recruit training at the Iona College campus in New Rochelle where the academic curriculum ran from March 30 to May 12, 1970. Following his graduation his first assignment on May 14, 1970 was patrol duty in the 4th precinct earning a starting salary of $8,000 a year. Two years later, on June 23, 1972, PO Alexa was transferred to the Traffic Division on two wheel motorcycle patrol. A first cousin to Capt. Edward Daly, Dennis married the daughter of the owner of D'Agostino Garden Center in Mahopac and decided to work for his father-in-law full time. Dennis Alexa resigned from the Y.P.D. on August 20, 1976. He is said to have later been working for PC Richards store in Danbury, Ct. as a salesman.

PO THOMAS F. BONANNO #586

APPOINTED: January 9, 1970
RESIGNED: August 4, 1972

Thomas Bonanno was born in Yonkers on May 15, 1943. Tom attended parochial schools by attending Sacred Heart elementary school and graduating from Sacred Heart HS. Tom entered the Marine Corps on Feb. 3, 1963, served as a helicopter gunner in Viet Nam for 2 years, and was honorably discharged on Feb. 6, 1967. Prior to the YPD Tom was employed by the Molloy and Murray Co. in Yonkers. Bonanno was appointed to the YPD on Jan. 9, 1970 while living at 106 Lake Ave. He received his recruit training at the Iona College campus in New Rochelle which ran from March 30th to May 12, 1970. Following his graduation, on May 14, 1970 PO Thomas Bonanno, whose cousin was Capt. Joe Barca, was assigned to patrol in the 3rd precinct earning a starting salary of $8,000 a year. On January 1, 1971 he was moved to the South Command until April 30, 1971 when he was assigned to the Special Enforcement Squad. On October 19, 1971 Tom was detailed to the Tactical Patrol Force (TPF) in the Special Operations Division until his request for Traffic duty was granted. On June 23, 1972 Tom was assigned to motorcycle duty in the Traffic Division. However, having previously taken and passed the test for the Yonkers Fire Dept., Tom resigned from the YPD on August 4, 1972 for appointment as a Yonkers firefighter. He retired in May of 2002 as a YFD Lieutenant. Two of his four sons were YFD captains.

PO CHRISTOPHER G. PALANDRA #587

APPOINTED: January 9, 1970
RETIRED: October 23, 1996

Christopher Palandra was born in Plymouth, Pa. on August 25, 1939 but moved with his family to Yonkers when he was very young. He attended St. Mary's elementary school, Benjamin Franklin Jr. high school, and graduated from Yonkers high school as a three sport athlete excelling in baseball, football, and basketball. Chris also attended Northeastern College on a football scholarship. Upon graduation, Chris joined the Navy in June of 1957 serving on the Destroyer USS Purdy. Having always had an interest in sports and being very athletic, while aboard ship Chris was in charge of ship sports activities. Chris was honorably discharged in June of 1960. Prior to even taking the examination for police patrolmen Chris worked for the Pecora Construction Co. of Yonkers.

Chris was appointed to the Yonkers Police Department on January 9, 1970 while living at 138 Mansion Ave. He attended the Iona College basic police recruit training school which ran from March 30, 1970 through May 12, 1970. Following his basic recruit graduation Chris was assigned to patrol duty in the 4th precinct on May 14, 1970. On January 1, 1971, following the implementation of a precinct centralization plan, which resulted in the closing of two precincts and the renaming of the other two, PO Palandra remained in the old 4th precinct which had now been renamed the North Patrol Command.

On May 15, 1975 Chris was reassigned to the Youth Services and Community Relations Division, detailed to work exclusively in the PAL. At this time the PAL was almost non-existent, having no building, funds, nor personnel to run it. Chris saw the urgency of getting the PAL operating again and with the help of Youth Division co-workers Bob Blair, Bob Martin, Sal Corrente, and Richard Wilson,

PO Christopher G. Palandra #587 (cont.)

began to restructure the PAL. Chris, with his insistent drive and natural ingenuity found out that the Naval Reserve building at 21 Alexander St. was being vacated and convinced City Administrators that this would be an ideal location for the PAL. In 1975 the PAL took possession of the building and started implementing the many programs offered to Yonkers kids.

Officer Palandra was a founder and organizer of many programs which include "Don't Talk to Strangers." This program included the fingerprinting of more than seven thousand children. Chris also designed an auto replica that was used in the schools to demonstrate the program. He made more than seventy trips to Rahway State Prison, taking hundreds of kids to view the life of the prisoners under the "Scared Straight" program. He was also made an honorary member of their "Lifer's Group." Palandra also helped bring the National PAL League and American Legion Baseball to Yonkers. This also brought to Yonkers the Tokyo All Star Games which was a huge accomplishment. Chris has also supervised and coached PAL Pony League baseball, softball and basketball.

One of Chris's greatest satisfactions was when some of the young teenagers who played for him on PAL teams became Yonkers police officers. Officers Gary Reilly, Lou Venturino, Charles Baker, Debbie Kopfensteiner, Lou-Ann Cloit, and Vincent Tilson were all once members of PAL teams. Chris was also a PAL member playing ball as a youth, never realizing that the day would come when he would be a PAL supervisor.

As a Yonkers police officer, Palandra had been a PBA trustee for 17 years and had served on numerous committees for the PBA Dinner Dance, Golf Outing, Christmas Party, Old Timers Picnic, Holy Name Breakfast, and programs for the handicapped. In the PAL he worked with children in many capacities; basketball, softball, swimming, coordinating the PAL handicapped children's Christmas party, and Easter Egg Hunt where he dressed as the Easter Bunny.

Chris was also proud having his son Chris, Jr. following in his career path as a YPD officer in the 3rd precinct. Chris, Jr. also worked with the PAL Handicapped team that played for the state championship in Cooperstown, NY.

Chris remained in the PAL assignment for the next 21 years and retired on October 23, 1996. He retired on a disability pension due to a leg injury but continued to do extensive volunteer work with the PAL with programs and building maintenance. He also remained a member of the PAL Advisory Board as Sgt at Arms.

On June 15, 2005 Ret PO Christopher Palandra was honored at the annual PAL Luncheon at the Polish Community Center as the 2005 PAL "Man of The Year" which was attended by nearly 400 people.

SGT. LAWRENCE J. WILLIAMS #46

APPOINTED: January 9, 1970
RETIRED: January 19, 1990

Lawrence Williams was born in the City of Yonkers on September 16, 1943. He attended PS #4 and later graduated from Lincoln High School. Shortly after graduation Larry joined the Air Force in 1962 and found himself involved in the Viet Nam War in the early years. His military occupational specialty (MOS) was Radio Operator and Loadmaster on a C-140 transport aircraft. He served landing in various locations in Viet Nam bringing in cargo and leaving, often with wounded personnel. He was also stationed in Japan for a time. Larry served his four years, was extended for an additional 6 months, and was honorably discharged in 1966.

Following the military Larry worked as an insurance underwriter for the CIT Insurance Company on South Broadway. He then owned and operated a Mobile gas station in Bronxville and while there, took the police test.

Larry was appointed to the Yonkers Police Department on January 9, 1970 while residing at 270 North Broadway. Following his basic police recruit training, which was held at the Iona College campus in New Rochelle, on May 14, 1970 he was assigned to the 2nd precinct earning a starting salary of $8,000 a year. He was transferred to the 3rd precinct on November 6, 1970 for two months and following the centralization of the precincts to commands on January 1, 1971 Larry was assigned to the South Command (formerly 2nd precinct).

On May 1, 1981 Larry was promoted to the rank of Sergeant earning $23,086 and was assigned to the North Command as a patrol supervisor. Two years later, on June 13, 1983, he was designated commanding officer of the Street Crime Unit (SCU), located off Columbus Place in the 10 St Casimir Avenue HQ building. He remained in the SCU right up to his retirement on January 19, 1990.

Following retirement Larry owned and operated the Holiday Travel Agency on Central Park Avenue near Mile Square Rd. He sold the business around 1999 and was then hired as Director of Security at the Osborn Retirement Home in Rye, NY, from which he again retired in 2005. In 2002 he had moved his family to Bethel, Ct. where he remained. He did have a winter home in Palm City, Florida where he often gathered for lunch with other YPD retirees. And he was very pleased when his nephew, PO Ronald R. Williams, was appointed to the YPD.

Larry often said he loved "our job" and would take great pleasure in reflecting back on old times and old friends. But, over the last several years Larry had become ill, and yet never lost his positive, upbeat attitude on life, insisting with his favorite saying, don't worry, "it's a piece of cake." Despite a long tough fight Ret Sgt Lawrence Williams died on July 17, 2011. He was 67 years old.

SGT. ROBERT R. LINDNER #12

APPOINTED: July 10, 1970
RETIRED: January 16, 2004

Robert Lindner was born in the City of Yonkers on October 16, 1949. He attended Sty. Joseph's elementary school, Gorton High School, and graduated from Saunders High School. Prior to the Y.P.D. Bob was employed by the Tiros Plastics Corp in Tarrytown, NY. He then joined the Yonkers Police Cadet program on September 16, 1968 and graduated from Westchester Community College with an Associate's degree in Police Science.

Following completion of the Cadet program Bob Lindner was appointed a Yonkers police officer on July 10, 1970 while residing at 358 Riverdale Ave. He received his basic police recruit training at the Iona College campus in New Rochelle and upon graduation was assigned to patrol duty in the 4th precinct. On December 4, 1981 Lindner was transferred to the South Patrol Command for about 6 months and then on June 18, 1982 he was trained and certified as a police K-9 handler and provided with a trained dog as his partner.

PO Lindner was promoted to the rank of Sergeant on April 11, 1988, was no longer designated a K-9 handler but allowed to keep his dog, and was reassigned to the Jail in Central Booking. By the end of the year, on December 2, 1988, Sgt Lindner was assigned to the 3rd precinct as a patrol supervisor.

Sgt Lindner was detailed to work as a supervisor in the plainclothes Street Crime Unit on April 27, 1990, but for only a short time. On November 13, 1990 he was reassigned to patrol duty in the 2nd precinct. He remained in the 2nd for nearly 7 years and on June 23, 1997 was transferred to the Special Operations Division's Traffic Division as their sergeant. Two years later, on May 31, 1999, Sgt Lindner was reassigned to the Y.P.D. Training Division where he not only supervised the training of new recruits and all in-service training, but he was also a certified instructor. Bob always had an interest in hunting and firearms of all types. As such he was an asset to training with his knowledge about firearms.

Sgt Robert Lindner retired from the police department on January 16, 2004.

DET. JOHN C. ZYGMUNT #680

APPOINTED: July 10, 1970
RETIRED: January 4, 2002

John C. Zygmunt was born in the City of Yonkers on September 18, 1949. As a youth he attended Longfellow junior high school, and later graduated from Saunders HS. While he was attending high school he was reported to be one of the best gymnasts they had on the exercise horse, parallel bars, rope and rings, etc. Previous to his employment with the Police Department, John listed his employment as a clerk for Beck Chevrolet.

At one point Zygmunt took, and passed, the civil service examination for "Yonkers Police Cadet." This was an experimental program that had been created to increase the recruitment of personnel who would earn a college degree and ultimately join the Yonkers Police Department. Young men, 17 or older, were offered the opportunity to take the civil service police officer test. The top candidates were put on a special list for police cadet. Those selected for the cadet position would be appointed as cadets and were guaranteed a police officer position after completion of a two year degree program at Westchester Community College.

John Zygmunt was appointed as a "Police Cadet" on September 16, 1968 earning a salary of $2,000 a year. For the next two years he and his fellow cadets would work five days a week; four hours a day taking academic courses at Westchester Community College, courtesy of the City of Yonkers, which would lead to an associate's degree, and the second four hours of each day assigned to work at various police commands learning various operations within the police department.

Following his successful completion of the cadet program, graduation from Westchester Community College, and without being required to take additional civil service tests for Police Officer, Zygmunt was appointed a Police Officer on July 10, 1970 while living at 127 Morningside Avenue. (Later he went to Mercy College and obtained his Bachelor of Science degree during his off-duty time.) John received his basic police recruit training at the Iona College campus in New Rochelle. Following his recruit graduation, which lasted a little more than a month, Probationary Patrolman John Zygmunt's first assignment was patrol duty in the 4th precinct earning a starting salary of $8,000 a year.

On April 15, 1971 John was one of many officers detailed to a special enforcement squad to address special needs throughout the city. Two years later, on January 29, 1973, Zygmunt was transferred to the Planning and Development Unit in headquarters working steady days. But by the end of the year he would be transferred to an assignment where he would remain for almost the remainder of his career. It was on October 25, 1973 that John was reassigned to work in the Criminal Identification Unit (C.I.U.). This unit, previously known as the Bureau of Criminal Identification (B.C.I.), was responsible for the investigating and processing of crime scenes by gathering any available evidence, including fingerprints, blood, and any other evidence left behind and which could be turned over to detectives to assist them in solving the crime. But John was not a Detective; he still held the rank of police officer.

Over the years John became recognized as a fingerprint expert, a trained polygraph operator, attended the FBI photography school, was a skilled crime scene photographer, and dark room film processing prior to the department using digital photography. After 27 years working as an expert in his field and only holding the rank of police officer, John Zygmunt was finally appointed a Detective on August 3, 2000. He was reassigned to the Detective Division as a squad detective and retired from that assignment on January 4, 2002.

PO WILLIAM HAVRISH #597

APPOINTED: July 10, 1970
RETIRED: July 9, 1990

William Havrish was born in the City of Yonkers on May 23, 1949. He attended public school #12 and later would graduate from Gorton high school in 1967. With a strong interest in music bill attended the Berkley School of Music from 1967 to 1968. Prior to his employment with the police department Bill worked for a short time for the Otis Elevator Company as a stock clerk. He then joined the Yonkers Police Cadet program on September 16, 1968 and graduated from Westchester Community College with an Associate's degree in Police Science.

Following completion of the Cadet program William Havrish was appointed a Yonkers police officer on July 10, 1970 while residing at 107 Van Cortlandt Park Avenue. He received his basic police recruit training at the Iona College campus in New Rochelle and upon graduation was assigned to patrol duty in the 4th precinct. While assigned to the 4th precinct Bill worked patrol duty in a radio car for a while and for several years he also was assigned to the Emergency Services Unit (E.S.U.). On June 2, 1986 Bill Havrish was transferred to the 1st precinct at 730 E. Grassy Sprain Rd. The following year on April 21, 1987, PO William Havrish, the nephew of former Sgt John Havrish, was assigned to motorcycle duty in the Special Operations Division's Traffic Unit. Because of his uncle, Bill was commonly referred to as "The Nephew." Bill Havrish's last assignment was to the "Hack Unit" on October 31, 1988 and from which he would later retire on July 9, 1990.

DEPUTY CHIEF WILLIAM J. CAVE

APPOINTED: July 2, 1971
RETIRED: May 8, 2015

William Cave was born in Augusta Georgia on December 9, 1950. Actually, both he and his twin brother Warren were born to an active duty Army Lieutenant on an Army base named Camp Gordon, in Augusta, Ga. His father had also served in the Marine Corps during World War 2. While still a young boy William and his family returned to Yonkers and he attended St. Paul's elementary school and later graduated from Sacred Heart high school.

At one point Cave took, and passed, the civil service test for "Yonkers Police Cadet." This was an experimental program that had been created to increase the recruitment of personnel who would earn a college degree and ultimately join the Yonkers Police Department. Young men, 17 or older, were offered the opportunity to take the civil service police officer test. The top candidates were put on a special list for Police Cadet. Those selected for the cadet position would be appointed as cadets and were guaranteed a police officer position after completion of a two year degree program at Westchester Community College. William Cave was appointed a "Police Cadet" on September 22, 1969 earning a salary of $2,000 a year. For the next two years he and his fellow cadets would work five days a week; four hours a day taking

Deputy Chief William J. Cave (cont.)

academic courses at Westchester Community College, courtesy of the City of Yonkers, which would lead to an associate's degree, and the second four hours of each day assigned to work at various police commands learning various operations within the police department.

Following his successful completion of the cadet program, graduation from Westchester Community College, and without being required to take additional civil service tests for Police Officer, William Cave was appointed a Police Officer on July 2, 1971 while living at 78 Sedgewick Avenue. Immediately following his appointment he was ordered out on patrol in plain clothes with his shield pinned to a casual shirt, and wearing a gun belt with a revolver. He did this while working alongside a senior officer up until recruit school could be scheduled.

Bill received his MPTC basic police recruit training in the basement of a firehouse located on North Avenue in New Rochelle, by instructors from throughout the county, and whose curriculum ran from Oct. 26, 1971 to Dec. 16, 1971. Following his recruit graduation, which lasted a little more than a month, on December 20, 1971 Probationary Patrolman William Cave's first assignment was patrol duty in the North Command earning a starting salary of $8,000 a year. On June 17, 1974 PO Cave was reassigned to patrol in the South Command. During the next 9 years Bill Cave rode in a sector car and on occasion filled in working in the Emergency Service Unit.

Officer Cave would be promoted to the rank of Sergeant on January 1, 1983 earning $31,082 and was assigned to the North Command as a patrol supervisor. PO Cave, whose brother was also a police officer at the time, was an energetic and efficient sergeant but he never stopped studying and going to promotional schools. As a result of that effort Sgt. Cave was promoted to the rank of police Lieutenant on May 29, 1987, was reassigned to the 3rd precinct on Riverdale Avenue, and was designated a tour Watch Commander (Pct. Patrol lieutenant). On November 13th of that same year Lt. Cave was selected to serve as the 3rd precinct captain's executive officer.

Once again his hard work paid off when, on October 13, 1989, Bill Cave was promoted to Captain and reassigned as the commanding officer of the 4th precinct. As Capt. Cave moved up the ranks he had developed an excellent reputation for getting the job done. And so, it was no surprise that when a new police commissioner, Robert K. Olson was appointed in August of 1990, a short time later, on October 1, 1990, he chose Capt. Cave to command the Detective Division as a Detective Captain. Two years later, on October 12, 1992, Cave was assigned as the C.O. of the highly sensitive Internal Affairs Division.

After nearly three years leading the detectives in Internal Affairs, on March 20, 1995 Capt. Cave was transferred to the Training Unit to oversee the training of all new recruits as well as all in-service training for members of the entire police department. The captain was a very "hands on" boss who was also a certified instructor. However, circumstances changed and there became a need for a new detective captain. Aware of Capt. Cave's experience and capability, on October 21, 1999 Comm. Joseph Cassino selected Bill Cave to once again command the Detective Division as a Detective Captain.

Once again Det Capt. Cave excelled in leading his detectives in investigating and solving a variety of major cases including murders. On one occasion Det Capt. Cave and his detectives were awarded a Unit Citation for their work on what was named "Operation Blood Out," an initiative against gang members, some of whom were suspected of influencing the drug trade between Yonkers and White Plains.

Deputy Chief William J. Cave (cont.)

On October 7, 2004 this operation resulted in the arrest of 26 gang members on Federal Arrest Warrants for narcotics and weapons charges. A total of 19 guns were removed from the streets, along with large amounts of cocaine. The FBI/Westchester County Violent Crime Task Force was also of invaluable assistance in this operation, and was presented with the Yonkers Police Commissioner's Award for their contribution.

On March 1, 2010 Capt. Cave was chosen to be a Deputy Chief and due to his experience he was put in command of the Investigational Services Division. Following the appointment of a new police commissioner, Charles Gardner, Chief Cave was selected by the commissioner to be "1st Deputy Chief," basically the commissioner's right hand who would act on his behalf whenever the P.C. was unavailable. It was a wonderful compliment and tremendous responsibility.

Throughout his career Bill Cave was proud that his brother Warren was a Detective Sergeant, his son William is a police officer, his brother-in-law was Capt. Frank Messar, and his nephew is Sgt. Michael Messar. Chief Cave also has a daughter, Jennifer, who is a teacher and married to Nicholas Bottone and lives in Yonkers. Even his mother, Theresa was a retired member of our Communications Division. It is believed Chief Cave learned his sense of duty from his father, William who served in World War II with the Fourth Marine Division, made four landings, including the Battle of Iwo Jima, and later switched over to the Army and also served in the Korean War. His Dad retired from the US Army Reserve as a Brigadier General.

Chief Cave later earned a Bachelor of Science Degree from Manhattan College, where he graduated magna cum laude with a Major in Sociology and Psychology and a Minor in Religious Studies, and even made the Dean's List. His specialized Police Training courses are myriad, highlighted by his completion of the Senior Management Institute for Police. He is a certified Police Instructor, and has also attended training courses in Child Abuse Investigations, DNA Analysis, Intelligence Awareness, FBI Hostage Negotiations, Managing Major Crime Scenes, Investigating Police Involved Shootings, Basic and Intermediate Incident Command Structure, NYPD HIDTA, numerous Anti-Terrorism Symposia, and the always valuable FAA course in Flying While Armed. He has earned 2 Commendations, 7 Certificates of Excellent Police Work, 2 Unit Citations, the PBA Harold Woods Award, 2 Papal Visit Awards, a Certificate of Recognition from the Mayor's Office, and the VFW Police Officer of the Year Award. He is a member of Lodge 9 of the Fraternal Order of Police and the Police Emerald Society of Westchester.

Chief Cave and his wife Nancy reside in Yonkers.

CAPTAIN JOSEPH BARCA

APPOINTED: July 2, 1971
RETIRED: April 24, 2015

As you will see, the subject of this profile was one of the most well-liked and respected officers in the YPD and one of the most decorated for his service to the community.

Joseph Barca was born in the City of Yonkers on December 8, 1950. He attended PS# 25 Warburton Ave., Our Lady of the Rosary - Lamartine Ave., and graduated from Salesian High School - New Rochelle. He also attended and graduated from Westchester Community College having earned an A.A.S. degree in Police Science His family owned a grocery store, "Barca's Grocery," on Warburton Avenue at Wells Avenue and young Joe worked there after his high school graduation. Young Joe was always a high energy person who wanted to help his community when necessary so he became very active in the Yonkers Civil Defense organization.

At one point Barca took, and passed, the civil service test for "Yonkers Police Cadet." This was an experimental program that had been created to increase the recruitment of personnel who would earn a college degree and ultimately join the Yonkers Police Department. Young men, 17 or older, were offered the opportunity to take the civil service police officer test. The top candidates were put on a special list for police cadet. Those selected for the cadet position would be appointed as cadets and were guaranteed a

Captain Joseph Barca (cont.)

police officer position after completion of a two year degree program at Westchester Community College. Joe Barca was appointed as a "Police Cadet" on September 22, 1969 earning a salary of $2,000 a year. For the next two years he and his fellow cadets would work five days a week; four hours a day taking academic courses at Westchester Community College, courtesy of the City of Yonkers, which would lead to an associate's degree, and the second four hours of each day assigned to work at various police commands learning various operations within the police department.

Following his successful completion of the cadet program, graduation from Westchester Community College, and without being required to take additional civil service tests for Police Officer, Barca was appointed a Police Officer on July 2, 1971 while living at 429 Warburton Avenue. Joe received his MPTC basic police recruit training in the basement of a firehouse located in New Rochelle whose curriculum ran from Oct. 26, 1971 to Dec. 16, 1971.

Following his recruit graduation, on December 20, 1971 Probationary Patrolman Joseph Barca's first assignment was patrol duty in the South Command earning a starting salary of $8,000 a year. Joe married his wife Helen in 1973 and moved to 41 Caryl Ave. where they raised their children. PO Barca first became a member of the Emergency Services Unit (E.S.U.) in 1974 when PO Andy Roza had to leave E.S.U. due to injuries. There was no General Order issued because Barca was already in the South Command at the time and just took Roza's place on the work chart. He rode in "the truck" with Patsy Bruno at that time.

On October 10, 1985 PO Barca and PO Warren Cave revived a man in his home who was near death. For their skill and action that day they were awarded the American Red Cross' highest award which was signed by President Ronald Reagan.

Joe remained in the South Command E.S.U. until September 19, 1988. At that time the E.S.U. was centralized and its members were all assigned to all work from the rear garage of the 4th precinct. At that time PO Barca was reassigned to the 4th precinct, assigned to work in the Emergency Service Unit from that location.

Two years later, on December 1, 1990, PO Barca was transferred into the Training Unit, as a certified instructor, to assist in the training of new recruits and routine in-service training. He remained there for only a short time because on August 2, 1991 Barca was promoted to the rank of Sergeant earning $52,754 and was reassigned to the 3rd precinct as a patrol supervisor.

On July 22, 1992 Sgt Barca was then transferred to work in the Special Operations Division (SOD) as a supervisor of multiple units including, Traffic Unit, K-9 unit, Abandoned Auto Unit, Taxi & Bus Inspection Unit (Hack), and the ESU. Although a supervisor of all, Sgt Barca put extra emphasis on reorganizing ESU into a better equipped and trained Unit. On October 2, 1993 while assigned to ESU Sgt. Barca disarmed a barricaded man who was wielding a machete. Two months later, on December 29, 1993 Sgt. Barca was credited with breathing life back into a two-month-old child after she had stopped breathing in an apartment at 77 Linden St.

Sgt Barca was promoted to the rank of Lieutenant on October 3, 1997 earning $73,866 and was moved from ESU to the Field Services Bureau as a city-wide patrol lieutenant. However, everyone was aware of the extensive experience and knowledge in the field of emergency service so, on October 22, 1999, Lt Barca was returned to SOD overseeing the ESU operation. Following the deadly terrorist air attacks on Sept 11, 2001, which destroyed and collapsed the 110 story World Trade Center buildings in

Captain Joseph Barca (cont.)

NYC and killed nearly 3000 people, Lt Barca led a detail to the collapse site as part of a YPD-ESU rescue team. For a week the team worked nearly nonstop digging with their hands to remove debris in hopes of locating survivors.

On May 6, 2003 Lt Barca was awarded a departmental Commendation for his actions off duty on Nov. 12, 2002 when he personally pursued, and arrested a male wanted for stabbing another. In addition, on May 12, 2003, Lt Barca was awarded the Journal News Police Award in Category 1, 1st place.

Lt Barca remained in SOD-ESU up to June 30, 2006 when he received his promotion to the rank of police Captain and was then assigned to the Inspectional Services Bureau (ISB). His new assignment was to work as a city-wide patrol captain overseeing the entire patrol operation and to make recommendation in those areas that needed attention. But there was an interesting back story to Capt. Barca's promotion. The following was written for the Home News & Times newspaper in July of 2006.

"After waiting 35 years to be promoted to the rank of Yonkers Police Captain, conspicuously absent from the promotional ceremonies June 30th, at the River Front Library, was Lt. Joseph Barca. His love and devotion to his job and to achieve the rank of Captain was more than enough to guarantee that he would be there – but Capt. Barca's love and devotion to special children and special adults won out. He knew the difference and that's what makes Capt. Barca a special police officer; to the Mayor, to the Police Commissioner, to his peers and to his City.

"One police officer from each State was chosen by the National Committee of the Special Olympics to represent his State and Captain Joe, New York States choice, was in Iowa at the Law Enforcement Torch Run for Special children and adults. When the Captain was asked why him? His modest answer was, 'My appointment was basically due to my involvement and awareness of the Special Olympics and I'm so proud of that.' Police Commissioner Robert Taggart agreed and told us, "I was proud of the selection made by the National Committee in choosing Capt. Barca and given the importance of the situation I excused him from the promotional ceremonies. It's a great honor for him, his family, and the City of Yonkers. Accepting his Captains shield at the ceremony was his wife Helen and his three sons; PO Christopher, PO David, and teacher Matthew Barca. Capt. Barca has been involved with the P.B.A. handicapped children's parties for 20 years along with the P.A.L. children's programs and has been a Cub Master for 15 years."

Effective January 1, 2007 Capt. Barca was transferred from the Inspection Service Bureau to the Field Services Bureau, designated Duty Captain on patrol working the steady midnight tour.

Over the course of Captain Joseph Barca's incredible career he was awarded many citations, some of which are listed below;

3 Hon Mention, 8 Commendation, 10 Unit Citations, 4 Certificates of Excellent Police Work, 2 Papal visit awards, 2 - 1st place Macy Awards, PBA Harold Woods Award, 3 CLSA Awards for Outstanding Police Work, 2 CLSA Life Saving Awards, 1 American Heart Assoc Life Saving Award, 2 American Red Cross Life Saving Awards, 3 Elks Police officer of the year in 1984, 1988, and 1994, 1 American Legion Law & Order Award 1987, 1 VFW Heroism award 1986, 1 Exchange Club Police Officer of the Year 1987, 2 Westchester Co. EMS Council Meritorious Service Awards, 1 - 2nd Precinct Police officer of the Year - 1987, and 1 Journal News Award.

It would be hard to find another officer more dedicated to his faith, his family and his career. Capt. Joseph Barca retired from the YPD on April 24, 2015 with 45 years of honorable service.

DET. SGT. WARREN J. CAVE #16

APPOINTED: July 2, 1971
RETIRED: July 4, 1997

Warren Cave was born in the city of Augusta, Georgia on December 9, 1950. He and his twin brother William were born to a career military officer who was on active duty at the time. While still a child Warren and his family returned to Yonkers and he attended St. Paul's elementary school and later graduated from Sacred Heart high school.

Warren learned of a new Yonkers police program to prepare young people for a future as a Yonkers police officer. Having passed the examination Warren Cave was appointed a Yonkers Police Cadet on September 22, 1969 earning $2,000 a year.

After completing a two year training program which earned him an Associate's degree from Westchester Community College, Warren Cave was appointed a Yonkers police officer on July 2, 1971 while residing at 78 Sedgewick Ave. Cave received his mandatory MPTC basic police recruit training in the basement of a firehouse located in New Rochelle whose curriculum ran from Oct. 26, 1971 to Dec. 16, 1971. Upon graduation Probationary Patrolman Cave was assigned to patrol in the North Command on Dec. 20, 1971 earning a starting salary of $8,000 a year. PO Cave quickly became one of the most popular men in the department because of his outgoing and friendly personality and his ability to see humor in nearly everything.

In 1975, upon his own request, PO Cave received emergency medical technician training in preparation for assignment in the Emergency Services Unit (ESU). The specialized training consisted of medical, rescue and special weapons and tactics training. Upon completion of this training police officer Cave was assigned to work in ESU. On September 29, 1983 PO Cave was transferred to patrol duty in the 2nd precinct but remained working in ESU. On October 10, 1985 PO Warren Cave and PO Barca revived a man in his home who was near death. For their skill and action that day they were awarded the American Red Cross' highest award which was signed by President Ronald Reagan.

Warren Cave received his promotion to the rank of Sergeant on July 24, 1987 earning a salary of $42,212 a year and was reassigned to the field services Bureau as a patrol supervisor. However, only 3 months later, on November 1, 1987, Cave was returned to the 2nd precinct as a patrol supervisor. The following year, on November 1, 1988, Sgt. Cave was reassigned to duty in the medical control unit located in headquarters. He remained there for a year and on October 13, 1989 he was assigned to work in the Internal Affairs Division (I.A.D.), where only the most trusted personnel would be assigned. His supervisors must have been pleased with his work performance because on August 2, 1991 he was appointed a Detective Sergeant and remained in I.A.D.

Det. Sgt. Warren Cave, whose brother William was a Deputy Chief, remained in this assignment right up to his retirement from the YPD on July 4, 1997.

SGT. HOWARD J. HORTON #79

APPOINTED: July 2, 1971
RETIRED: September 1, 2006

Howard Horton was born in the City of Yonkers on July 14, 1950, and attended and graduated from local public schools. He learned of a new police program to prepare young people for a future as a police officer. Having passed the examination "Howie" was appointed a Yonkers Police Cadet on September 22, 1969 earning $2,000 a year.

After completing a two year training program which earned him an Associate's degree from Westchester Community College, Howard Horton was appointed a Yonkers police officer on July 2, 1971 while residing at 161 Palisade Ave. Horton received his MPTC basic police recruit training in the basement of a firehouse located in New Rochelle whose curriculum ran from Oct. 26, 1971 to Dec. 16, 1971. Upon graduation Patrolman Horton was assigned to patrol in the South Command on Dec. 20, 1971 earning a starting salary of $8,000 a year.

While in his home and off duty in April of 1985 he saw a tan van parked in front of 50 Valentine Avenue, near his home. It was an area that had been plagued by recent burglaries. The vehicle, with a man sitting behind the wheel, fit the description of a van seen in the neighborhood following earlier burglaries. Horton also saw a male ringing the doorbell at 50 Valentine Ave. Horton went into his home nearby, phoned HQ and requested backup, grabbed his revolver and then went out and confronted the suspects. One suspect fled in the van. The second male attacked Horton, trying to grab the officers off duty gun but Horton was able to subdue and arrest the suspect following a violent struggle. The second suspect was arrested a short while later and it was learned that more than $30,000 in jewelry had been stolen from 50 Valentine Ave.

Over the next 16 years PO "Howie" Horton developed a reputation of being an aggressive and hardworking street cop. He was always meticulously dressed, uniforms tailored and was often teased about how well groomed he kept his hair, rarely wearing his uniform hat. His neat appearance belied just how tough he could be and in fact he was nicknamed "The Hammer" by fellow officers. On May 20, 1987 PO Horton was reassigned to the Special Operation Division's Traffic Unit on two wheel motorcycle but detailed to the Taxi & Bus Inspection Unit (Hack Unit).

PO Horton was promoted to the rank of Sergeant on October 12, 1990 earning $49,534 and was transferred to the 4th precinct as a patrol supervisor. Five years later, on July 14, 1995, Horton was moved to the 3rd precinct for a year and on August 24, 1996 he was assigned to the Field Services Bureau to patrol duty in whatever precinct was shorthanded. But less than two months later, on October 5, 1996 Sgt Horton was assigned to the Housing Unit whose responsibility was to specifically patrol the large housing complexes, from the roof to the basement, to target the heavy volume of crime.

Sgt Horton, whose great uncle was PO Joseph Nolan and whose cousin was Lt Tom Kivel, was the recipient of 4 police Commendations, and 4 Certificates Excellent Police Work.

He seriously injured his leg, on duty, on January 8, 2003, the healing of which became complicated due to diabetes. Infection set in and was almost impossible to control and caused further damage. Following several surgeries Sgt Howard Horton was granted an accidental performance of duty disability retirement pension effective September 1, 2006.

PO ROBERT KELLY #561

APPOINTED: July 2, 1971
RETIRED: August 3, 1990

Bobby Kelly was born in the Bronx, NY on April 8, 1951 but received his formal education in Yonkers, graduating from Roosevelt H.S. While at Roosevelt, Bob played on their school football team in the position of Defensive Lineman. He was an avid Giant football fan. Following graduation Bob was hired on Sept. 22, 1969 by the Y.P.D. as a Police Cadet. He spent the next two years with 4 hours at Westchester Community College, and the other 4 learning various tasks throughout the Y.P.D. Following this two year program Bob was appointed a full time police officer on July 2, 1971 earning $8,000 a year. Bob received his MP TC basic police recruit training in the basement of a firehouse in New Rochelle with an academic curriculum which lasted about six weeks. Following graduation PO Kelly was assigned to the South Patrol Command. During his total 21 years with the YPD Bob always served on uniform patrol. Robert Kelly retired on a disability pension on August 3, 1990. He worked various jobs in retirement including operating a pet store, and a gas station in Carmel, NY. Retired PO Robert Kelly died suddenly on Sept. 27, 2009. He was 58 years old.

PO KENNETH KRENTSA #296

APPOINTED: July 2, 1971
RESIGNED: March 17, 1981

Kenneth Krentsa was born in Yonkers on Feb. 10, 1950. He attended PS# 22, Longfellow junior HS, Emerson junior HS, and later graduated from Roosevelt HS in 1968. Ken took the exam for police cadet program which was the same exam as for police officer, and was appointed a Yonkers police cadet on Sept. 22, 1969. Following the completion of his two-year cadet program Kenneth Krentsa was appointed a Yonkers police officer on July 2, 1971 from 77 Delaware Ave. He received his recruit training in the basement of a firehouse located in New Rochelle which ran from Oct. 26, 1971 to Dec. 16, 1971. Following graduation his first assignment was patrol duty in the South command. PO Krentsa developed an excellent reputation as being a good cop, and as a result, on October 27, 1978, Ken was assigned to the anti-crime unit, later renamed the Street Crime Unit. All during this time police officer Krentsa had a pilot's license and enjoyed flying. He eventually obtained a commercial pilot's license and really wanted to fly commercial airlines. PO Ken Krentsa, also known to his friends as "Nails," loved the police department and the excitement that he found there. But his desire to fly commercial airlines won the day. PO Kenneth Krentsa resigned from the Yonkers Police Department on March 17, 1981 and was last known to be flying as a captain with United Airlines.

PO JAMES MURRAY #598

APPOINTED: July 2, 1971
RETIRED: February 14, 1992

James "Jimmy" Murray was born in Yonkers on Aug. 10, 1950 and attended local public schools. Having passed the examination for a new position entitled "Police Cadet" Murray was appointed a Yonkers Police Cadet on Sept. 22, 1969 earning $2,000 a year. After completing a two year training program which earned him an Associate's degree from Westchester Community College, Jim Murray was appointed a police officer on July 2, 1971 while residing at 84 Tibbetts Rd. He received his MPTC recruit training in the basement of a firehouse located in New Rochelle whose curriculum ran from Oct. 26, to Dec. 16, 1971. Upon graduation Patrolman Murray was assigned to patrol in the North Command on Dec. 20, 1971. After a time he served as an ESU fill in officer beginning in 1976 and a few years later was assigned there as a trained paramedic. PO Murray requested out of ESU on Jan. 19, 1987 and was assigned to the 2nd pct as the desk officer. He retired from there on Feb. 14, 1992. Following his retirement Jim Murray operated his own trophy manufacturing business known as Crown Trophy.

DET. JOHN PERKINS #646

APPOINTED: July 2, 1971
RETIRED: January 23, 1991

John Perkins was born in Yonkers on Mar. 31, 1951 and graduated from local public schools. Having passed the examination for a new program entitled "Police Cadet," Perkins was appointed a Yonkers Police Cadet on Sept. 22, 1969 earning $2,000 a year. After completing a two year training program which earned him an Associate's degree from Westchester Community College, Perkins was appointed to the YPD on July 2, 1971 while residing at 1 Lawrence St. He received his MPTC recruit training in the basement of a firehouse located in New Rochelle whose curriculum ran from Oct. 26, to Dec. 16, 1971. Upon graduation PO Perkins was assigned to the South Command on Dec. 20, 1971. On Mar 24, 1978, off duty PO Perkins was credited with saving the life of a woman choking on food in a restaurant. On January 1, 1979 PO Perkins was transferred into the Police Forensic Laboratory as a lab assistant. Due to the knowledge and experience gained there, on June 19, 1989, John was appointed a Detective in the Lab. It was from there that he retired on Jan. 23, 1991. Since age of five years he had been very interested in the martial arts, Karate and Judo. By Feb. of 2001 he was an 8th degree black belt. He taught martial arts one day a week free at the PAL Youth Center and was hired to teach a class a week in Yonkers, Hastings, and Manhattan. In addition he is an opera singer who also performs for a fee.

DET. LT. PETER PIZZOLA

APPOINTED: July 2, 1971
RETIRED: February 28, 2002

Peter Pizzola was born in the city of Yonkers on December 10, 1950. Peter attended local public schools and later graduated from Lincoln high school. At one point Pizzola took, and passed, the civil service examination for "Yonkers Police Cadet." This was an experimental program that had been created to increase the recruitment of personnel who would earn a college degree and ultimately join the Yonkers Police Department. Young men, 17 or older, were offered the opportunity to take the civil service police officer test. The top candidates were put on a special list for police cadet. Those selected for the cadet position would be appointed as cadets and were guaranteed a police officer position after completion of a two year degree program at Westchester Community College.

Pete Pizzola was appointed as a "Police Cadet" on September 22, 1969 earning a salary of $2,000 a year. For the next two years he and his fellow cadets would work five days a week; four hours a day taking academic courses at Westchester Community College, courtesy of the City of Yonkers, which would lead to an associate's degree, and the second four hours of each day assigned to work at various police commands learning various operations within the police department. His police duty was to work in the Forensic Science Laboratory and while there he discovered that he loved that type of work.

Following his successful completion of the cadet program, graduation from Westchester Community College, and without being required to take additional civil service tests for Police Officer, Pizzola was appointed a Police Officer on July 2, 1971 while living at 11 Central Park Avenue. Peter received his MPTC basic police recruit training in the basement of a firehouse located in New Rochelle whose curriculum ran from Oct. 26, 1971 to Dec. 16, 1971. Following his recruit graduation, which lasted a little more than a month, on December 20, 1971 Probationary Patrolman Peter Pizzola's first assignment was patrol duty in the North Command earning a starting salary of $8,000 a year.

One year later, on January 29, 1973, PO Pizzola was transferred back to the Forensic Lab designated as the laboratory director. Having been returned to the Forensic Lab, his dream assignment, Pete embarked on a career of education in forensic science. Over the years during his off duty hours PO Pizzola obtained a Bachelor of Science (Cum Laud) and a Master's degree in forensic science from John

Det. Lieutenant Peter Pizzola (cont.)

Jay College of Criminal Justice. In later years he received his PhD and was noted for his thesis on blood splattering interpretation and had lectured to various police organizations on the subject of blood trajectory. He has also published several articles on forensic subjects.

PO Peter Pizzola was promoted to the rank of Sergeant on June 3, 1985 and although fairly unusual, because of his expertise in forensics, he was allowed to remain assigned to the Forensic Lab. And, three months later Sgt Pizzola was designated a Detective Sergeant on Sept. 6, 1985 and remained in the Lab.

Det Sgt Pizzola was promoted to the rank of police Lieutenant on August 2, 1991 earning a salary of $60,021 and was assigned to the Detective Division and placed in command of the Criminal Identification Unit (C.I.U.) as well as the Forensic Lab. Being placed in command of C.I.U. was a logical move as their responsibility was the collection of evidence at crime scenes and which could leave behind that which only a forensic scientist could recognize, gather, and process. One year following his promotion to lieutenant he was advanced to Detective Lieutenant.

In 1996 Lt Pizzola received his Master of Philosophy degree; in 1998 he received his Doctor of Philosophy (PHD) degree; in 2000 he was assigned to the Detective Division as their Major Case supervisor and later that year as the C.O. of C.I.U., and in 2001 as interim Director of the Forensic Laboratory.

Det Lt Pizzola, whose brother was PO Philip Pizzola, was widely recognized as an expert in the field of Crime Scene Reconstruction. He has also published several articles on forensic subjects. Det Lt Pizzola enjoyed constructing order out of disorder. He loved to tackle a crime scene and collect all the important pieces of evidence, spending an average of 4 to 5 hours combing through a homicide scene. He improved the Forensic Laboratory from a simple two-man chemical lab to a modern five person unit with three scientists and state-of-the-art equipment.

He was the recipient of the Arthur Niederhoffer Memorial Fellowship Award for Academic Performance and Contributions to Criminal Justice, the General section Regional Award for his work in Blood Droplet Dynamics, the Jerome Metzner Science Award for his Graduate Research, and the Claude E. Hawley Memorial award for Superior Academic Performance. His professional memberships include the American Academy of Forensic Scientists, the Northeastern Assoc: of Forensic scientists, the American Assoc: of Crime Laboratory Directors, and the NYS Crime Laboratory Advisory Committee, and Lt. Pizzola holds a board position of President Elect on the Northeastern Association of forensic scientists.

While he was Director, the Forensic Laboratory was recognized by the Yonkers Exchange Club, and in conjunction with the CIU received Departmental recognition for their work. It was because of Doctor Pizzola's foresight, commitment, direction, and hard work that the police department was able to achieve laboratory accreditation in 1996, and the CIU became accredited for the first time in 2002.

On February 28, 2002, Det. Lt. Peter Pizzola retired from the Yonkers Police Department. Two years later, in 2004, Pete was hired by the NYPD as their Deputy Director of the Crime Lab, and 6 months later their director. In 2011 Lt Peter A. Pizzola, PhD, D-ABC, SCSA-IAI, was serving as the Deputy Director, Special Investigations Unit, NYC Office of Chief Medical Examiner.

PO LAWRENCE VELLUCCI #251

APPOINTED: July 2, 1971
RESIGNED: May 28, 1976

Lawrence Vellucci was born in the City of Yonkers on October 12, 1949 and attended and graduated from local public schools. Larry applied for and was appointed to the Yonkers Police Cadet Program on September 22, 1969. Following a two-year police preparatory program by which he obtained an Associates Degree from Westchester Community College, Larry was appointed a Yonkers Police Officer on July 2, 1971 while residing at 257 Mary Lou Ave. He received his MPTC basic police recruit training in the basement of a firehouse located in New Rochelle whose curriculum ran from Oct. 26, 1971 to Dec. 16, 1971. Following the recruit graduation his first assignment was patrol duty in the South Patrol Command earning a starting salary of $8,000 a year. PO Lawrence Vellucci was a good police officer, but had an opportunity to work in a family run business. He took that opportunity and resigned from the police department on May 28, 1976.

PO FRANCIS BERLETIC #556

APPOINTED: July 2, 1971
RETIRED: October 3, 1986

Francis Berletic was born in the City of Yonkers on July 14, 1949 and attended and graduated from local public schools. Frank learned of a new Yonkers police program to prepare young men for a future as a Yonkers police officer. Having passed the examination Frank was appointed a Yonkers Police Cadet on September 22, 1969 earning $2,000 a year. After completing a two year training program which earned him an Associate's degree from Westchester Community College, Francis Berletic was appointed a Yonkers police officer on July 2, 1971 while residing at 52 Ashburton Ave. Frank received his MPTC basic police recruit training in the basement of a firehouse located in New Rochelle whose curriculum ran from Oct. 26, 1971 to Dec. 16, 1971. Upon graduation Probationary Patrolman Berletic was assigned to patrol in the North Command on Dec. 20, 1971 earning a starting salary of $8,000 a year. In March of 1979 PO Berletic was named Police Officer of the year by the Yonkers Exchange Club. After several years riding with PO Frank Thuman, PO Berletic ultimately was given a steady foot post, at his request, on Lake Avenue where he remained right up to his early retirement on an accidental disability pension on October 3, 1986. Years later his former partner, PO Thuman, would say this about Berletic. *"During the time I rode with Frank Berletic he was top notch, excellent, compassionate and decent police officer. I broke him in as a rookie right from the start and all he wanted was to be was a good cop....."*

DET. SGT. RICHARD KOSTIK #61

APPOINTED: July 2, 1971
RETIRED: August 12, 2005

Richard Kostik was born in the city of Yonkers on May 31, 1950 and attended and graduated from local public schools. Kostik's grandfather PO Joseph Kostik, who was killed in the line of duty, and his brother then PO Joseph Kostik, had just about set the stage as to what career path Richard would be taking. Richard learned of a new Yonkers police program to prepare young men for a future as a Yonkers police officer. Having passed the examination Richard Kostik was appointed a Yonkers Police Cadet on September 22, 1969 earning $2,000 a year.

After completing a two year training program which earned him an Associate's degree from Westchester Community College, Rich Kostik was appointed a Yonkers police officer on July 2, 1971 while residing at 180 Hawthorne Ave. Kostik received his MPTC basic police recruit training in the basement of a firehouse located in New Rochelle whose curriculum ran from Oct. 26, 1971 to Dec. 16, 1971. Upon graduation Probationary Patrolman Kostik was assigned to patrol in the North Command on Dec. 20, 1971. In June of 1974, officer Kostik was assigned to the newly organized Community Patrol Unit which was federally funded and designed to work closely with the minority community. Like his brother Joe, Richard was very athletic and was very active with the P.B.A. playing on their softball and basketball teams.

In September of 1982 Richard was assigned to the Northeast command for a year and on October 21, 1983 he was appointed a Detective assigned to the Detective Division. Two years later, on March 11, 1985, Richard Kostik was promoted to the rank of Sergeant, earning $20,593 a year, was designated a Detective Sergeant, and remained in the Detective Division as a squad supervisor. Four years later, on January 20, 1989, Det. Sgt. Richard Kostik was reassigned to work in the Internal Affairs Division.

Nearly 9 years later, on October 6, 1997, Det. Sgt. Richard Kostik was returned to the Detective Division, this time working in the burglary unit. Det Sgt. Kostik really enjoyed working as a supervisor in the burglary squad. So much so that, on March 1, 2002, when he was notified that he would be promoted to the rank of police Lieutenant, he declined the promotion in order to stay working in the burglary unit.

Det Sgt. Richard Kostik, whose father-in-law was Deputy Chief Owen McClain, retired from the Yonkers Police Department on August 12, 2005.

DET. RONALD J. NEGRO #637

APPOINTED: December 17, 1971
RETIRED: January 4, 2002

Ron Negro was born in Brooklyn on March 9, 1948 and would later move with his family to Yonkers. He attended PS# 14 and graduated from Lincoln High School in 1966. Following graduation from High School Ron served in the Army from July 1968 to July 1970 at which time he received his Honorable Discharge. On his application to the YPD Ron listed his occupation as a Truck Driver.

Ronald Negro was appointed to the Yonkers Police Department on December 17, 1971 while residing at 279 North Broadway. Probationary Patrolman Negro's recruit school was held at Pepsico Headquarters, Anderson Hill Road in Purchase, NY. The curriculum ran from February 7th through March 17th, 1972. Following graduation from recruit School Ron was assigned to the South Command on uniform patrol with a starting salary of $8,000 a year. Ronnie was a high energy person, and very aggressive in performing his duties. Though, while in a uniform sector car he would always be there to back up the 2nd precinct plainclothes officers when they were in need. And in doing so he picked up the style of patrol required to work plainclothes, which he was often assigned to while still in the 2nd precinct.

On November 21, 1988 Ron was selected to be assigned to the Street Crime Unit (SCU) where he became a definite asset. On January 23, 1995 the SCU, as plainclothes officers, were merged with the Narcotics Unit in the Detective Division, but not as detectives. Around that time, at the age of 47, Negro had a heart attack, resulting in heart by-pass surgery. Following his recovery he did not retire, or take a desk job. He went right back to full duty and on December 22, 1997 Ron got his wish. He was appointed a Detective in the Detective Division. He remained working as a detective in the Narcotics Unit from which he retired on January 4, 2002.

Ron had earned four (4) Departmental Commendations, 19 Certificates of Excellent Police Work, the 1985 Colombian Association Exceptional Police Duty Award, the 1998 Gannett Newspaper 2nd place award, the 1999 Journal News 2nd place award, and a Unit Citation. But he was not only known for being an excellent police officer; he also had a great sense of humor. Among just about everyone in the department he was nicknamed, "Ronnie Rumor." Ron was the consummate prankster and purveyor of false information. He would love to start a ridiculously untrue rumor, with a straight face, and then watch as it swirled throughout the entire department, even though there was not a shred of fact to it.

Following retirement Ronnie and his wife Mary bought a winter home down in Florida which he really loved and where he spent a lot of time. His hobby was collecting valuable baseball memorabilia.

On November 29, 2008 Ron Negro was in Georgia visiting relatives when, without any warning, he had a heart attack and died. He was 60 years old.

LT. CHRISTOPHER J. RICH

APPOINTED: December 17, 1971
RETIRED: July 8, 1995

Christopher Rich was born in the Bronx, NY on June 29, 1950. His family moved to Yonkers and he graduated from local public schools. Following graduation Chris learned of a new Yonkers police program to prepare young men for a future as a Yonkers police officer. Having passed the examination Chris Rich was appointed a Yonkers Police Cadet on November 3, 1969 earning $2,000 a year.

After completing a two year training program which earned him an Associate's degree from Westchester Community College, Chris was appointed a Yonkers police officer on December 17, 1971 while residing at 487 McLean Avenue. Rich's recruit school was held at Pepsico Headquarters, Anderson Hill Road in Purchase, NY. The curriculum ran from Feb. 7th through Mar. 17th, 1972. Upon graduation Patrolman Christopher Rich was assigned to patrol duty in the North Command. On June 20, 1979 PO Rich was reassigned to patrol in the North East Command on East Grassy Sprain Rd. At the time the YPD had only one police dog and k-9 handler and Chris became interested in becoming the second. He was able to convince the police commissioner and he attended and graduated from the Philadelphia, P.D. Canine Training School on April 11, 1980 along with his new partner, a German Shepard dog named "Champ."

For the next four years, while assigned to the Special Operations Division (SOD), PO Rich and Champ became a very successful team in assisting the patrol force in capturing suspects in hiding. PO Chris Rich was promoted to the rank of Sergeant on August 10, 1984 earning $35,574 and was returned to the 1st precinct as a patrol supervisor. He was allowed to keep his ex-partner, Champ, at his home as a pet. Sgt Rich was promoted to Lieutenant on October 12, 1990 and was assigned to the Field Services Bureau as a city-wide patrol lieutenant.

Lt Rich was returned to the SOD on July 15, 1991 working as the executive officer. The following year, on July 22, 1992, Lt Rich was reassigned to the Support Services Bureau. Lt Christopher Rich retired from the YPD on an accidental disability pension effective July 8, 1995.

PO FRANK A. NAPPI #21

APPOINTED: December 17, 1971
RETIRED: January 8, 2010

Frank Nappi was born in the City of Yonkers on September 24, 1950. Frank attended St. Joseph's elementary school and graduated from Gorton High School. Young Frank learned of a new Yonkers police program to prepare young men for a future as a Yonkers police officer. Having passed the examination Nappi was appointed a Yonkers Police Cadet on November 3, 1969 earning $2,000 a year.

After completing a two year training program which earned him an Associate's degree from Westchester Community College, Frank Nappi was appointed a Yonkers police officer on December 17, 1971 while residing at 51 Mulford Gardens. Frank Nappi's recruit school was held at Pepsico Headquarters, Anderson Hill Road in Purchase, NY. The curriculum ran from February 7th through March 17th, 1972.

Upon graduation Probationary Patrolman Nappi was assigned to patrol in the South Command. Frank was a big man, standing well over 6' and of husky build. However, in the 1970's he was still very active playing on the PBA baseball and basketball team. In December of 1974 while on duty in uniform PO Nappi was in a bank when a man entered and attempted to rob the bank using a note. The bank teller signaled Nappi who then quickly arrested the male for attempted bank robbery.

On May 10, 1976 PO Nappi was reassigned to the Communications Division dispatching radio cars, but on July 19, 1978 he was returned to patrol duty in the South Command. Frank remained on patrol for the next 8 years with his partner Bob Kelly. The two made quite a visual impression. Frank was a bear of a man while Kelly was a foot shorter and more than 50 lbs. lighter. But they were a good team. Nappi remained on patrol until November 12, 1986 when he was returned to the Communications Division working in the Tele Serv Unit. Toward the end of June 1987 PO Nappi was offered a job in headquarters serving as the departments Validations Officer; a job requiring the determination as to whether a reported theft, etc., was still active or resolved. Later he was also designated Tape Reproducer assigned to privately review police audio recordings for court and prosecution purposes.

In July of 2009 Nappi was issued shield #21, at his request, as his son Frank Jr had just been appointed to the YPD and he wanted his son to be able to wear his original shield #210.

PO Frank Nappi retired from the police department on January 8, 2010.

DET. SGT. MICHAEL P. FABRIZIO #18

APPOINTED: December 17, 1971
RETIRED: January 22, 2010

Mike Fabrizio was born in Yonkers on Sept. 11, 1950, and attended and graduated from local public schools. Mike learned of a new police program to prepare young men for a future as a police officer. Having passed the examination Fabrizio was appointed a Yonkers Police Cadet on Nov. 3, 1969 earning $2,000 a year. After completing a two year training program which earned him an Associate's degree from Westchester Community College, Mike was appointed to the YPD on Dec. 17, 1971 while residing at 42 Oak St. Fabrizio's recruit school was held at Pepsico Headquarters, Anderson Hill Rd. in Purchase, NY. The curriculum ran from Feb. 7th to Mar. 17th, 1972. Upon graduation PO Fabrizio was assigned to patrol duty in the North Command. Throughout the 1970's Mike's partner and friend was PO Joel Parisi. On June 20, 1979 Fabrizio was reassigned to the N/E Patrol Command. Mike was promoted to the rank of Sergeant on Oct. 3, 1997 earning $64,503 and was assigned to the 3rd pct as a patrol supervisor. The following year, on May 4, 1998, he was sent to work in the now 1st pct. On Oct. 24, 2005 Sgt Fabrizio was assigned to the D.D. as a detective sergeant. Mike Fabrizio, known as a friendly, soft spoken "boss," retired from the YPD after more than 38 years on Jan. 22, 2010.

DET. ROBERT J. RYAN #682

APPOINTED: December 17, 1971
RETIRED: January 13, 2006

Bob Ryan was born in Binghamton, NY on Aug. 31, 1948. His family moved to Yonkers and Bob attended St. Mary's elementary school and graduated from Gorton HS in 1966. Prior to his YPD employment Ryan worked for the William Wrigley Jr Co. in Saddlebrook, NJ. Bob was appointed to the YPD on Dec. 17, 1971 while living at 203 Woodland Ave. His recruit class received their Municipal Police Training Council (MPTC) school at Pepsico Headquarters, Anderson Hill Rd. in Purchase, NY. The curriculum ran from Feb. 7th to Mar. 17th, 1972. Upon graduation PO Ryan was assigned to patrol in the South Command. Five years later, on July 15, 1977, PO Ryan was transferred to the Youth Div. investigating crimes by juveniles. As a result he was appointed a Detective on Mar. 28, 1980 working as a squad detective in the D.D. Det. Ryan was detailed to the FBI Academy from July 9 to the 11th in 2002 to attend a Homicide Profiling Seminar. Bob proved himself to be an excellent detective and outstanding homicide investigator. A soft spoken and well liked man, Bob Ryan remained in the DD right up to his retirement on January 13, 2006. During his career he earned 2 Commendations, 7 Certificates of Excellent Police Work, 2 Unit Citations, and 3 Journal New Category 2 awards.

DET. CHARLES J. JANKOWSKI #655

APPOINTED: December 17, 1971
RETIRED: January 4, 2002

Charles Jankowski was born on May 25, 1941 in Yonkers. He attended St. Casimir's school and graduated from Saunders HS. Charlie entered the Army in Dec. of 1963 and was honorably discharged in Nov. of 1965. Prior to the YPD Jankowski was employed by the US Post Office in Scarsdale, NY. With an age limit of 29 years to be hired, Charlie used his military time as credit and, at the age of 30 years, was appointed to the YPD on Dec. 17, 1971 while residing at 223 Nepperhan Ave. His recruit school was held at Pepsico HQ, Anderson Hill Road in Purchase, NY. The curriculum ran from Feb. 7th to Mar. 17th, 1972. Upon graduation PO Jankowski was assigned to the South Command. On Mar 24, 1981 he graduated from Evidence Technician School held in Yonkers. As a trained designated Evidence Technician a uniformed patrol officer was responsible to accomplish basic photographing and gathering of evidence at minor crime scenes without the need to have CIU respond. PO Jankowski was transferred on March 22, 1984, on his own request, to the Youth Division investigating crimes by juveniles. On Dec. 25, 1987 all Youth Officers titles changed from police officer to Youth Investigator. Charlie Jankowski, whose son-in-law was PO Christopher Kowatch and brother-in-law was PO James Matthews, was appointed a Detective on Oct. 7, 1994 working in a squad and retired from the police department on Jan. 4, 2002

PO RICHARD J. CLARK #297

APPOINTED: December 17, 1971
RETIRED: January 28, 1993

Richard Clark was born in the Bronx, NY on Oct. 13, 1946. As a youth he attended Holy Rosary school and graduated from Mt. St. Michael's Academy HS, both in the Bronx. A few years later Rich entered the Navy in Dec. of 1966 and honorably discharged in Nov. of 1968. Prior to the YPD Clark was employed as a driver for the Fort Hill Private Car Service. Clark was appointed to the YPD on Dec. 17, 1971 while residing at 40 Morrow Ave. PO Clark's recruit school was held at Pepsico HQ, Anderson Hill Road in Purchase, NY. The curriculum ran from Feb. 7th to March 17th, 1972. Upon graduation Clark was assigned to the South Patrol Command until January 14, 1980 when he was transferred into the Training Unit. Rich was a very friendly person with excellent communications skills. These traits were helpful when he was designated a certified instructor and later the YPD firearms instructor and armorer. PO Clark played a major role in 1991 in the police department's transition from the Smith & Wesson revolver to the semi-automatic Glock pistol. PO Richard Clark retired from the YPD on January 28, 1993.

DET. WILLIAM R. KORWATCH #686

APPOINTED: December 17, 1971
RETIRED: January 17, 1992

Bill Korwatch was born in the City of Yonkers on January 17, 1947. He attended PS# 19, Hawthorne Jr. High School, and graduated from Saunders High School. Almost immediately following graduation in 1965 Bill joined the Marine Corps. After a few years in the Corps as a Lance Corporal, in 1967 he was sent to Viet Nam serving in the 2nd Battalion, 4th Marine Regiment, 3rd Marine Division known as the "Magnificent Bastards." He was an Infantry combat Marine in Vietnam in 1967 and saw heavy combat in the bloody battle of Con Tien where his platoon went in with nearly 30 men and came out with only 14. He received two battlefield promotions, two Purple Hearts and the Vietnamese Cross of Gallantry. Following his service he was separated from service in June of 1968 as a Platoon Staff Sergeant and honorably discharged on May 20, 1971.

Prior to applying for appointment to the Yonkers Police Dept. Bill worked for the Polychrome Corp. in Yonkers. William Korwatch was appointed to the police department on December 17, 1971 while residing at 78 St. Andrews Place. Probationary Patrolman Korwatch's mandatory Municipal Police Training Council (MPTC) recruit school was held at Pepsico Headquarters, Anderson Hill Road in Purchase, NY. The curriculum ran from February 7th through March 17th, 1972. Since they were in a corporate setting as guests, all recruits wore business suits instead of uniforms. The schools director was Sheriff Daniel F. McMahon, former Yonkers Public Safety Commissioner.

Upon graduation Probationary Patrolman Korwatch was assigned to patrol in the North Command. Having had his military experience, it was no surprise that Bill Korwatch was going to do the job and do it well. And during his off duty time he would earn an Associate's degree from Westchester Community College in 1977 and a Bachelor's degree from Iona College in 1979.

In 1975 plans were formulated to establish a city-wide plainclothes Anti-Crime Unit and when made operational PO Bill Korwatch was one of the original officers chosen due to his excellent record as a street cop. In this new assignment PO Korwatch was able to be more flexible and innovative which only enhanced his ability to be more effective. It was because of his skills and effectiveness that on November 23, 1979 that Bill Korwatch was appointed a Detective assigned to work in the Detective Division. After more than 12 years as a Detective, Det. Bill Korwatch retired from the YPD on January 17, 1992.

After retiring Bill worked as investigator for the Westchester Co. Legal Aid Society for just short of 15 years but learned he was a diabetic and then had a pancreas transplant, a problem which he attributes to exposure to Agent Orange in Viet Nam. As a result he was awarded a 90 % disability pension from the military.

Bill moved with his wife to Alabama and is enjoying the good life.

PO EDWIN J. ZABONIK #250

APPOINTED: December 17, 1971
RETIRED: January 18, 1991

Ed Zabonik was born in the City of Yonkers on August 15, 1950. He received his education in local public schools. Following graduation Ed learned of a new Yonkers police program to prepare young men for a future as a Yonkers police officer. Having passed the examination Edwin Zabonik was appointed a Yonkers Police Cadet on November 3, 1969 earning $2,000 a year.

After completing a two year training program which earned him an Associate's degree from Westchester Community College, Ed Zabonik was appointed a Yonkers police officer on December 17, 1971 while residing at 207 Farquar Avenue. Zabonik's recruit school was held at Pepsico Headquarters, Anderson Hill Road in Purchase, NY. The curriculum ran from February 7th through March 17th, 1972. Upon graduation Probationary Patrolman Edwin Zabonik was assigned to patrol duty in the South Command. As a young man Ed learned the trade of Roofing and he continued his roofing work while off duty. On March 22, 1984 Edwin Zabonik was transferred to patrol in the 3rd precinct where, after spending his entire career on uniform patrol, he would retire from the Yonkers Police Department on January 18, 1991.

PO MICHAEL E. BEDDOWS #583

APPOINTED: December 17, 1971
RETIRED: February 14, 1992

Mike Beddows was born in Mt. Vernon, NY on Feb. 14, 1945. His family moved to Yonkers and Mike attended PS# 14, and later graduated from Lincoln HS in 1963. He entered the Army on Sept. 20, 1965 and served with the 383rd Airborne as a Specialist 4th class and received his honorable discharge on Sept. 19, 1967. On Mike's police employment application he listed he was working for the Dellwood Dairy Co. on Saw Mill River Rd. in Yonkers. Michael Beddows was appointed to the YPD on Dec. 17, 1971 while residing at 57 Cross Hill Ave. PO Beddows' recruit school was held at Pepsico HQ, Anderson Hill Road in Purchase, NY. The curriculum ran from February 7th to Mar. 17th, 1972. Upon graduation PO Beddows was assigned to the North Patrol Command. Mike was assigned a sector in the most easterly portion of the North Command, bordering the Bronx River. On June 20, 1979 Mike was transferred out to the North East Command, later to be the 1st precinct, and remained on patrol for several years. Toward the end of his career PO Beddows was detailed to steady days working as the precinct captain's aide. He retired from the YPD on Feb. 14, 1992.

PO WILLIAM D. WUCHTER #268

APPOINTED: December 17, 1971
RETIRED: January 5, 2001

William Wuchter was born in Yonkers NY on March 12, 1943. As a youth he attended PS# 21 and graduated from Lincoln High School in 1961. Bill was employed by the Westchester County Police Dept. from 1966 to 1968. Wuchter entered the Army in June of 1968, served as an M.P. in Vietnam for a year, and was honorably discharged a sergeant in June of 1971. Bill Wuchter was appointed to the Yonkers Police Dept. on December 17, 1971 while residing at 11 Crotty Avenue. Probationary Patrolman Wuchter's recruit school was held at Pepsico Headquarters, Anderson Hill Road in Purchase, NY. The curriculum ran from February 7th through March 17th, 1972. Following recruit School Wuchter was assigned to the North Command on uniform patrol with a starting salary of $8,000 a year. On June 20, 1979 PO Wuchter was reassigned to patrol in the North East Patrol Command. In early 1982, following departmental charges, Wuchter was dismissed from the department, but following his appeal, he was re-instated to duty in the 3rd precinct on November 2, 1984. During his last years he worked as the desk officer in the 3rd before retiring on January 5, 2001.

100 YEARS OF CHANGE
THEN - NOW

POLICE OFFICER

I was that which others did not want to be.

I went where others feared to go,

and did what others feared to do.

I asked nothing from those who offered nothing,

and willingly accepted the possibility of failure and even death…should I not succeed.

I have looked in the face of mortal danger; felt the stinging chill of fear, and occasionally enjoyed the rare sense of appreciation received.

I've felt sympathy, pain, sadness; have cried over a child, and yet still responded to the next call for help; ……but most of all, I have experienced, first hand, the ugly face of life that most others would say were best forgotten.

But, at least someday I will be able to say that,

I was proud of what I was……….A POLICE OFFICER.

Author unknown

CPSIA information can be obtained
at www.ICGtesting.com
Printed in the USA
LVHW020023130220
646774LV00002B/3

9 781644 261552